*Less managing. More teaching. Greater learning.*

 **INSTRUCTORS...**

Would you like your **students** to show up for class **more prepared**?
*(Let's face it, class is much more fun if everyone is engaged and prepared...)*

Want ready-made application-level **interactive assignments,** student progress reporting, and auto-assignment grading? *(Less time grading means more time teaching...)*

Want an **instant view of student or class performance** relative to learning objectives? *(No more wondering if students understand...)*

Need to **collect data and generate reports** required for administration or accreditation? *(Say goodbye to manually tracking student learning outcomes...)*

Want to **record and post your lectures** for students to view online?

 **With McGraw-Hill's *Connect® Business Law,***

**INSTRUCTORS GET:**

- Interactive Applications – **book-specific interactive assignments** that require students to APPLY what they've learned.

- Simple **assignment management**, allowing you to spend more time teaching.

- **Auto-graded** assignments, quizzes, and tests.

- **Detailed Visual Reporting** where student and section results can be viewed and analyzed.

- Sophisticated **online testing** capability.

- A **filtering and reporting** function that allows you to easily assign and report on materials that are correlated to accreditation standards, learning outcomes, and Bloom's taxonomy.

- An easy-to-use **lecture capture** tool.

# STUDENTS...

Want an online, **searchable version** of your textbook?

Wish your textbook could be **available online** while you're doing your assignments?

### Connect® Plus Business Law eBook

If you choose to use *Connect® Plus Business Law*, you have an affordable and searchable online version of your book integrated with your other online tools.

### Connect® Plus Business Law eBook offers features like:

- Topic search
- Direct links from assignments
- Adjustable text size
- Jump to page number
- Print by section

# STUDENTS...

Want to get more **value** from your textbook purchase?

Think learning Business Law should be a bit more **interesting**?

### Check out the STUDENT RESOURCES section under the *Connect®* Library tab.

Here you'll find a wealth of resources designed to help you achieve your goals in the course. You'll find things like **quizzes, PowerPoints, and Internet activities** to help you study. Every student has different needs, so explore the STUDENT RESOURCES to find the materials best suited to you.

# Business Law

## With UCC Applications

### Gordon W. Brown

PROFESSOR EMERITUS

NORTH SHORE COMMUNITY COLLEGE | DANVERS, MASSACHUSETTS

### Paul A. Sukys

PROFESSOR OF LAW AND APPLIED PHILOSOPHY

NORTH CENTRAL STATE COLLEGE | MANSFIELD, OHIO

13e

BUSINESS LAW WITH UCC APPLICATIONS

Published by McGraw-Hill/Irwin, a business unit of The McGraw-Hill Companies, Inc., 1221 Avenue of the Americas, New York, NY, 10020. Copyright © 2013, 2009, 2006, 2001, 1997, 1993, 1989, 1983, 1978, 1972, 1966, 1961, 1953 by The McGraw-Hill Companies, Inc. All rights reserved. Printed in the United States of America. No part of this publication may be reproduced or distributed in any form or by any means, or stored in a database or retrieval system, without the prior written consent of The McGraw-Hill Companies, Inc., including, but not limited to, in any network or other electronic storage or transmission, or broadcast for distance learning.

Some ancillaries, including electronic and print components, may not be available to customers outside the United States.

This book is printed on acid-free paper.

1 2 3 4 5 6 7 8 9 0 DOW/DOW 1 0 9 8 7 6 5 4 3 2

ISBN        978-0-07-352495-5
MHID       0-07-352495-6

Vice president and editor-in-chief:   *Brent Gordon*
Editorial director:   *Paul Ducham*
Executive editor:   *John Weimeister*
Executive director of development:   *Ann Torbert*
Development editor II:   *Megan Shultz*
Editorial coordinator:   *Jonathan Thornton*
Vice president and director of marketing:   *Robin J. Zwettler*
Marketing director:   *Amee Mosley*
Executive marketing manager:   *Sarah Schuessler*
Vice president of editing, design, and production:   *Sesha Bolisetty*
Lead project manager:   *Pat Frederickson*
Buyer II:   *Debra R. Sylvester*
Interior designer:   *Cara Hawthorne, cara david DESIGN*
Senior photo research coordinator:   *Keri Johnson*
Photo researcher:   *Ira C. Roberts*
Lead media project manager:   *Brian Nacik*
Cover design: *cara david DESIGN*
Typeface:   *10/12 Times Roman*
Compositor:   *Aptara®, Inc.*
Printer:   *R.R. Donnelley*

**Library of Congress Cataloging-in-Publication Data**

Brown, Gordon W.
    Business law with UCC applications / Gordon W. Brown, Paul A. Sukys. — 13th ed.
        p. cm.
    Includes index.
    ISBN-13: 978-0-07-352495-5 (alk. paper)
    ISBN-10: 0-07-352495-6 (alk. paper)
    1. Commercial law—United States. I. Sukys, Paul A. II. Title.
KF889.85.B76 2013
346.7307—dc23

                                                            2011044046

This book is dedicated with much love and many thanks to my wife, Susan. As I've learned during our life together—as a team—the possibilities are limitless.

Also to Jennifer, Ashley, and Megan, all three of whom have grown up to be excellent educators in their own right. They have made me very proud.

Paul Sukys

# About the Authors

 **Gordon W. Brown,** Professor Emeritus, North Shore Community College, Danvers, Massachusetts, where he has taught for 30 years, is the author of *Legal Terminology* and *Administration of Wills, Trusts, and Estates* and the co-author, with Dr. Paul A. Sukys, of *Understanding Business and Personal Law.* Mr. Brown received his law degree from Suffolk University and practiced law in Beverly, Massachusetts, while teaching full time at North Shore Community College. He is a member of the Massachusetts and federal Bars.

 **Paul A. Sukys** is a professor of law and applied philosophy at North Central State College in Mansfield, Ohio. He is coauthor of *Business and Personal Law* and *Civil Litigation,* a textbook for paralegals. He is also the author of *Lifting the Scientific Veil: Science Appreciation for the Nonscientist,* which explores the relationships among science and other disciplines, focusing on the interaction of science and the law. He has a Ph.D. in applied philosophy from The Union Institute and University in Cincinnati. Dr. Sukys received his law degree from Cleveland State University. He is a member of the Ohio Bar.

# Preface

The thirteenth edition of *Business Law with UCC Applications* updates many key areas of the law. As in previous editions, a great deal of care has been taken to present business law concepts in the most coherent and accessible way and to provide up-to-date coverage of business law topics that are essential to today's students. All of the chapters for this edition have been updated, and we have continued to enhance our coverage of the important topics of cyber-commerce, international law, identity theft, trade secrets, abandoned property, eminent domain, mortgages, bankruptcy, limited liability companies (LLC), ethics, the Dodd-Frank Act, the revised Uniform Partnership Act, the Health Insurance Portability and Accountability Act, the Genetic Information Nondiscrimination Act, the War Powers Act, changes in state law regarding collective bargaining, the Troubled Asset Relief Program, the Home Affordable Modification Program, the Patient Protection and Affordable Care Act, proposed changes in the court system, the War Powers Act, and alternative dispute resolution.

The popular format of the twelfth edition has been enhanced, with learning objectives identified in the margin where that material appears in the text. Each chapter begins with an outline followed by The Opening Case, with numbered questions and Chapter Objectives. Titles have been given to every example. Major headings and chapter summaries continue to be numbered, following the chapter outline. The popular case illustrations, presenting either hypothetical or actual situations based on well-founded court decisions, have been retained and updated. Our Quick Quiz feature appears in each chapter and allows students to test their knowledge of the chapter topics while they actively study the text. A new Self-Evident Truths feature has been included in many chapters in this edition, giving both the instructor and the students an opportunity to discuss stimulating, provocative, and controversial topics suggested by the content in each chapter.

We also have retained case studies pertaining to each of the nine parts of the book, which summarize an actual litigated case, present a lengthy extract from the judge's decision, and provide follow-up questions that are pertinent to the cases and are appropriate as a review of the legal concepts involved. Activities at the end of each chapter, including Key Terms, Questions for Review and Discussion, and Cases for Analysis, help students self-check their understanding of the terms and concepts presented in the chapter. We also have included the Question of Ethics element throughout the text. The U.S. Constitution appears in Appendix A. Included in Appendix B are four articles of the Uniform Commercial Code. Marginal references within the chapters tie these specific documents to the content. The thirteenth edition of *Business Law with UCC Applications* thus offers a comprehensive package of materials to meet both instructors' and students' needs.

# Acknowledgments

We are grateful to the following individuals for their review feedback. We appreciate their ideas and suggestions.

Joan Alexander
Nassau Community College

Bonnie S. Bolinger
Ivy Tech Community College

Dennis Bromley
Salt Lake Community College

Myra Bruegger
Southeastern Community College

H. Stanley Carson
Eastern Maine Community College

Gregory L. Dalton
Genesee Community College

Nancy K. Dempsey
Cape Cod Community College

Pamela S. Evers
University of North Carolina Wilmington

Warren C. Hodges
Forsyth Technical Community College

Norman Hollingsworth
Langston University

Walter E. Lippincott
Naugatuck Valley Community College

Benjamin Neil
Towson University

Beth Snodgrass
Mountain Empire Community College

Deborah Vinecour
SUNY Rockland Community College

John M. Golden
Slippery Rock University

We also extend special thanks to Jane A. Brown for her excellent photograph of Dr. Sukys on the About the Authors page.

Special thanks are also extended to the Business Law classes for Fall Quarter 2003 and Winter Quarter 2004 at North Central State College for pilot testing the Mock Hearing Process found in the ancillary materials for *Business Law with UCC Applications, 13e*. An extra special thank you also goes out to the Business Law class for Spring Quarter 2011 at North Central State College for pilot testing the new configuration of contract law material in this book.

# A Guided Tour

*Business Law with UCC Applications,* 13/e, is full of useful chapter features to make studying productive and hassle-free. The following pages show the kind of engaging, helpful pedagogical features that complement the accessible, easy-to-understand approach to teaching business law.

## Chapter Outline

Each chapter features an outline that allows students to recognize the organization of the chapter at a glance. For reinforcement, the outline's numbering system is used throughout the body of the chapter and is repeated in the end-of-chapter Summary.

### Chapter 3 — The Judicial Process and Cyber-procedure

**3-1 The Court System**
The Federal Court System • Court Jurisdiction • State Court Systems

**3-2 Civil Procedure**
Commencement of the Action • Service of Process • The Pre-Answer Stage • The Answer • The Pretrial Stage • The Civil Trial • The Appeal • Execution of the Judgment

**3-3 Cyber-procedure**
Cyber-jurisdiction • Cyber-filing • Cyber-discovery

**3-4 Criminal Procedure**
The Arrest and Initial Appearance • The Preliminary Hearing • The Formal Charges • The Arraignment • The Criminal Trial

---

**THE OPENING CASE** When Is a Citizen Not a Citizen?

One of the most perplexing problems that litigators often face is where to bring a lawsuit. In the federal courts jurisdiction can be established either by demonstrating the case involves an issue directly related to federal law (federal question) or by demonstrating diversity jurisdiction. In most cases of diversity, the parties, the plaintiff and the defendant, must be citizens of different states. Again the problem is not difficult when dealing with flesh and blood people. However, when one of the parties is a corporation, the problems begin. This is because federal law defines the corporate citizenship as a duality. A corporation is a citizen (1) in the state in which it is incorporated and (2) where it has its principal place of business. Unfortunately, the concept of "principal place of business" is vague at best. In the case of *Hertz Corporation v. Friend* the United States Supreme Court directly addressed the issue of corporate duality. Of course, whether the court improved or aggravated the situation is still open to debate. In that case the Hertz Corporation was sued by a group of California citizens in a state court. Hertz, sensing the probable hostility of a California jury, asked that the case be removed to federal court, arguing that the proper forum would be in New Jersey where its corporate headquarters was located. The plaintiffs disagreed. In the alternative, they maintained that Hertz's "principal place of business" was really located in California because it was in California that Hertz did

the vast majority of its business. The trial court agreed, ruling that California was the corporation's principal place of business. The appeals court followed suit, but the U.S. Supreme Court did not. The Supreme Court ruled that a corporation has its "principal place of business" where its nerve center is located, that is, the state in which the activities of the corporation are controlled by corporate management. New Jersey, then, was the proper forum for Hertz, not California. Ironically, although in this case Hertz, the corporate defendant, won the battle, their victory may prove to be a mixed blessing. It is a victory because it will help corporations get into federal court by making diversity a more straightforward proposition. However, the decision will also increase the number plaintiffs that can sue the corporation in federal court, especially in class action cases. Why does limiting a corporation's principal place of business increase the number of potential plaintiffs? Think about that question when diversity jurisdiction is covered later in the chapter. [See *Hertz Corporation v. Friend*, No. 08-1107, slip. op. (February 23, 2010); and Michael McNamara and Christine Henge, "'Hertz' Expands Companies Access to Federal Court," *The National Law Journal*, April 12, 2010, pp. 16–17.]

**Opening Case Questions**

1. Is this case a civil lawsuit or a criminal action? Explain.

---

## The Opening Case

A brief case opens each chapter and introduces the chapter concepts, followed by numbered questions addressing legal issues in the case. Every Opening Case is re-examined throughout the chapter in The Opening Case Revisited features. Those scenarios that become Opening Cases are chosen carefully to bring a broad spectrum of illustrations to the text. Some of these are hypotheticals, created specifically for the material in the chapters. Others are drawn from today's headlines and are not yet in the courts. Still others are classic cases that have been used in law courses for decades and thus represent the best illustrations of key points in the law.

## Learning Objectives

Succinct, crisply written learning objectives follow The Opening Case at the beginning of each chapter. The numbered objectives describe what the students can expect to learn as a result of completing the chapter. Each objective is identified by a unique symbol in the margin where the material appears in the text.

### LO Learning Objectives

1. Explain the fundamental nature of the American courts.
2. Determine when a case can be brought in federal court.
3. Recognize those cases that can be heard by the U.S. Supreme Court.
4. Identify the structure of most state court systems.
5. Define civil litigation.
6. List the most common discovery techniques.
7. Detail the nature of an appeal.
8. Determine the extent of cyber-jurisdiction.
9. Explain the nature of electronically stored information (ESI).
10. Describe the steps in a criminal prosecution.

## New! Self-Evident Truths

A new Self-Evident Truths feature has been included in many chapters in this edition, giving both the instructor and the students an opportunity to discuss stimulating, provocative, and controversial topics suggested by the content in each chapter.

### Self-Evident Truths

Read the following quotation on the nature of morality. As you read the quotation and reflect on the ideas that the author presents, ask yourself if the position represents your own point of view. Then answer the following questions based on the reading. Make sure that you are prepared to defend each response in a thoughtful manner.

From the American founding until World War II, there was a widespread belief in this country that there is a moral order in the universe that makes claims on us. This belief was not unique to Americans. It was shared by Europeans since the very beginning of Western civilization, and it is held even today by all the traditional cultures of the world. The basic notion is that morality is external to us and is binding on us. In the past, Americans and Europeans, being for the most part Christian, might disagree with Hindus and Muslims about the exact source of this moral order, its precise content, or how a society would convert its moral beliefs into legal and social practice. But there was little doubt across the civilizations of the world about the existence of such an order. Moreover, the laws and social norms typically reflected this moral consensus. During the first half of the twentieth century, the moral order generated some clear American social norms. . . . The point is not that everyone lived up to the dictates of the moral code, but that it supplied a standard, accepted virtually throughout society, for how one should act.
—Dinesh D'Souza, *The Enemy at Home* (New York: Doubleday, 2007), 19.

### Self-Evident Questions

1. The author observes that before World War II people believed in an external morality that binds us all. What sociological, political, and economic events might have worked together to destroy that belief in an external morality? Explain.

---

### A QUESTION OF ETHICS

**Federal Supremacy, Discrimination, and a Lesson in Ethics**

A quick review of the Opening Case at the beginning of this chapter will remind us that Arizona passed a statute that empowered the local police to demand identification papers from anyone suspected of being in the country illegally. In response, the federal government sued the state of Arizona in an attempt to block the administration of the law arguing that federal law trumped state law in this situation because the Constitution gave the power to control immigration to the national government alone. Recall that the federal government could have argued that the law was discriminatory because it had a disparate impact on people of a particular color and a certain national origin. The question we pose here is not the relatively easy one of whether the Arizona statute is unethical. Rather, the question we ask is whether it is ethical for the Justice Department to use the relatively safe argument of federal supremacy while ignoring the far greater legal and moral transgression of deliberate, unapologetic, legislative discrimination?

**A Question of Ethics** boxes challenge students' understanding of previously discussed chapter examples by asking questions specifically relating to ethical dilemmas.

---

### About the Law

The American Arbitration Association publishes a booklet entitled *National Rules for the Resolution of Employment Disputes*. The booklet includes rules on both mediation and arbitration.

An arbitration hearing can be planned and executed by the parties themselves. Generally, this step means that the parties set the ground rules for choosing the arbitrator or arbitrators, for conducting discovery, for presenting evidence, for determining the outcome, and for enforcing the reward. In addition, details such as setting the time and the place of the hearing, filling vacancies on the arbitration panel, recording the proceedings, handling objections, granting time extensions, and so on, must also be agreed upon. Because of the intricacies of such a process, many individuals who select arbitration prefer to use professional arbitration organizations such as the American Arbitration Association to handle the details of their arbitration proceeding.

Like most forms of ADR, arbitration is not without its difficulties. One shortcoming is that an arbitration hearing is run like a trial but without the safeguards that come with the rules of civil procedure, discovery, and motion practice. This characteristic may actually extend the time involved in arbitration because attorneys and negotiators must prepare a wide variety of legal arguments, some of which might have been eliminated during motion practice. Discovery also sometimes reveals facts that lead the parties into settlement negotiations that might not otherwise take place. Moreover, the wide discretion that is usually

**About the Law** boxes provide additional clarification of chapter concepts.

---

laws, and treaties as the supreme law of the land. Finally, Article VII outlines how the original 13 states would go about ratifying the new Constitution. Table 2-1 outlines the content of each article in the Constitution.

**The Amendments** The amendments to the Constitution establish the rights that belong to the people, change some of the provisions in the original articles, and add ideas that the Framers did not include in those articles. Thus, the amendments are attempts to fine-tune the Constitution and update its provisions to meet the demands of a changing socioeconomic structure. The first 10 amendments of the Constitution compose the Bill of Rights. They were added soon after the ratification of the Constitution by the original 13 states. Other amendments that secure the rights of the people include the Thirteenth, which prohibits slavery; the Fourteenth, which guarantees equal protection of the law and due process; the Fifteenth, which guarantees voting rights; the Nineteenth, which extends voting rights to women; the Twenty-

### Did You Know?

Roman law was first codified into The Law of the Twelve Tables in 450 BC. The Twelve Tables declared that all free citizens had certain fundamental rights.

**Did You Know?** boxes are interesting factoids directly linked to the chapter concept being discussed.

---

### EXAMPLE 2-1: Attempting a Fair and Equitable Tax

Sometimes lawmakers must apply an abstract principle, such as the idea that the government should be fair when it taxes the people, to a concrete piece of legislation. This is exactly what happened at the end of President Obama's first two years in office when Republicans and Democrats negotiated a tax plan that addressed the concerns of taxpayers, businesses, and unemployed workers. In brief, here is what resulted when the *abstract* met the *concrete*. Every taxpayer saw a two-year continuation of the tax rates that were in place under the old law. Lower income workers received an increase in the child tax credit of $1000. Upper income taxpayers saw a favorable alteration in the estate tax rate and middle

**Examples** are titled and numbered throughout each chapter and use short vignettes to explain how concepts can be applied in real-life situations.

people act in unpredictable ways on a regular basis, while others react to what their neighbors have done. What is true in economics is equally true in the law. (See Richard Posner, *A Failure of Capitalism* (Cambridge; Harvard UP, 2009), pp. 83–84.)

### quick quiz 2-1

1. The law consists of rules of conduct established by the government to maintain harmony, stability, and justice within a society.   true | false

2. Often justice must be sacrificed for harmony and stability, but the opposite is never true.   true | false

3. Legislators and judges bring their own personal prejudices and biases into the process.   true | false

## 2-2 Constitutional Law

The law has been defined as rules of conduct created by the government to maintain harmony, stability, and justice within a society. This definition is adequate, but it is also somewhat limited. It does not explain where the government comes from or who gives it the power to make those rules.

**Quick Quiz** boxes follow each numbered section and give students the chance to test themselves with three true/false questions. Answers are provided at the end of each chapter.

**Questions for Review and Discussion** provide a means for students and the instructor to reexamine and discuss the key points of law. All objectives listed at the beginning of each chapter are also reviewed.

### Questions for Review and Discussion

1. What is the fundamental nature of the American court system?
2. Under what circumstances might a federal court have jurisdiction to hear a case?
3. Under what circumstances might the U.S. Supreme Court hear a case?
4. What is the structure of a typical state court systems?
5. What is civil litigation?
6. What are the most common discovery techniques?
7. What is involved in an appeal?
8. How is cyber-jurisdiction determined?
9. What is electronically stored information?
10. What are the steps in a criminal prosecution?

### Summary

2.1 The law consists of rules of conduct established by the government to maintain harmony, stability, and justice within a society. Ideally, the primary objectives of the law are to promote harmony, stability, and justice. In everyday life, the balance is not easy to maintain. The law or, more properly, the entire legal framework consists of a series of dualities that must be resolved somehow.

2.2 A constitution is the basic law of a nation or state. The United States Constitution provides the organization of the national government. Each state also has a constitution that determines the state's governmental structure. The body of law that forms a constitution and its interpretation is known as constit

2.3 The laws passed by a legisla statutes. At the federal level, these by Congress and signed by the pre level, statutes are enacted by state le must be arranged, cataloged, and in erence by compiling state and fede many different statutes are passed 50 state legislatures, there are impo

The National Conference of Commissioners on Uniform State Laws (NCCUSL) was founded to write these uniform laws.

2.4 Courts make law through common law, the interpretation of statutes, and judicial review. Common law is the body of previously recorded legal decisions made by the courts in specific cases. Statutory interpretation is the process by which the courts analyze those aspects of a statute that are unclear or ambiguous or that were not anticipated at the time that the legislature passed the statute, and judicial review is the process by which the courts determine the constitutionality of various legislative stat

### Key Terms

| | | |
|---|---|---|
| administrative law, ••• | constitutional law, ••• | tat- |
| Articles of Confederation, ••• | cyber-commerce, ••• | m- |
| binding precedent, ••• | devolution, ••• | ig- |
| code, ••• | Federal Register, ••• | ese |
| Code of Federal Regulations (CFR), ••• | judicial review, ••• | der |
| | law, ••• | hat |
| common law, ••• | persuasive precedent, ••• | on- |
| constitution, ••• | precedent, ••• | |

**Summary** Numbered to match the outline at the beginning of the chapter and the main heads within each chapter, the Summary provides an encapsulated review of the chapter's content.

**Key Terms** Each key term is printed in boldface and defined when introduced in the text. A list of key terms and the page number of first usage appears at the end of each chapter. A glossary of the key terms is provided at the back of the text.

**Cases for Analysis** have been updated extensively for the thirteenth edition and chosen for their relevance, ease of understanding, and interesting fact patterns. Many are abridgements of actual court decisions; some are taken from current news stories; and still others are hypothetical situations written to emphasize legal issues and concepts presented in the text.

### Cases for Analysis

1. On the very day that President Obama signed the 2010 Health Care bill into law, the attorney general of Virginia filed a lawsuit in federal district court arguing that parts of the statute were unconstitutional. Specifically, the attorney general argued that the new statute was unconstitutional because it required people to buy health insurance, which amounts to an unconstitutional extension of the Commerce Clause of the U.S. Constitution. The federal government argued that the Supreme Court has upheld federal laws regulating commercial activity even when that activity takes place solely within a single state, if the activity has an effect on interstate commerce. Clearly

the Kerr-McGee power plant. Under state tort law, Silkwood's estate was awarded actual damages of $505,000 ($500,000 for personal injuries, and $5,000 for property loss), and $10 million in punitive damages, that is, damages designed to punish the defendant for its wanton misbehavior. The power plant argued that when Congress passed the Atomic Energy Act, it intended to completely outlaw any state regulation of nuclear power plants. Permitting the plaintiff to receive punitive damages in this case would destroy that intent. Silkwood's father, as the plaintiff in the case, argued that there was no intent expressed by Congress to preempt tort law in the

The Case Study at the end of each of
the nine parts begins with a summary of the
facts of the case, is followed by an excerpt
from the court's opinion, and concludes
with a series of questions.

## Part 1 Case Study

**United Citizens v. Federal Election Commission**
United States Supreme Court
130 S. Ct. 876 (2010)

### Summary

During the 2004 presidential campaign, Michael Moore promoted the film, *Fahrenheit 9/11,* which was critical of the Bush presidency and which expressly urged the removal of Bush from the presidency. The film was released, promoted, distributed, and shown using funds supplied by Moore and other entities, all of which had made contributions to a series of political candidates of a clearly identifiable political persuasion. A conservative nonprofit political group named Citizens United, also with a clearly identifiable political agenda, filed a complaint with the Federal Election Commission asking that the film be censored under provisions of the Bipartisan Campaign Reform Act of 2002. The federal reform law, which is popularly known as the McCain-Feingold Act, forbids all "electioneering communications" by all unions, and by all profit and nonprofit corporations, 60 days before an election and 30 days before a primary. The McCain-Feingold law did allow some political advertisements during that same period of time, just as long as those advertisements were funded by the candidate's campaign. For clarity, McCain-Feingold defined "electioneering communications" as speech that is intended to promote a candidate's election or, in the alternative, the defeat of a candidate. In response to the complaint, the Federal Election Commission ruled that the activities of Moore and his associates in the release, promotion, distribution, and showing of the film had not in any way violated the law. The commission decided that the money spent on the promotion and release of the film including the film's website and trailers were, in fact, simply commercial activities and not political speech as defined within the act. As a result, the complaint was dismissed. (It is interesting to note that at this point neither Citizens United nor the Federal Election Commission had presented any arguments regarding the law's constitutionality. That was about to change.)

Taking its cue from this decision, in the 2008 election campaign, Citizens United fought back by producing its own film entitled *Hillary: The Movie.* The

## Appendix A  The Constitution of the U~~nited States~~

### Preamble

We the People of the United States, in Order to form a
more perfect Union, establish Justice, insure domestic
Tranquility, provide for the common defence, promote the
general Welfare, and secure the Blessings of Liberty to
ourselves and our Posterity, do ordain and establish this
Constitution for the United States of America.

### Arti~~cle~~

Section ~~1.~~
vested i~~n~~
consist ~~of~~
Sec~~tion~~
compos~~ed~~

[2] Immediately after they sha~~ll~~
quence of the first Election, the~~y~~
as may be into three Classes. Th~~e~~
first Class shall be vacated at t~~he~~
Year, of the second Class at the ~~Ex~~
and of the third Class at the Ex~~
that one third may be chosen e~~
cancies happen by Resignation, ~~
cess of the Legislature of any ~~
~~p~~ointm~~ent~~
shall th~~e~~
Sena~~te~~
ty Ye~~ars~~
states, ~~
of th~~

## Appendix B  Uniform Commercia~~l~~
(Articles 1, 2, 2a, and~~

### Article 1: General Provisions

Part 1: Short Title, Construction,
Application and Subject Matter of the Act

§1-101. ~~
be cited as~~

§1-102. ~~
Variatio~~n~~

§1-105. Te~~
Parties' Po~~

~~c~~ept as ~~
~~tr~~ansactio~~n~~
~~also~~
~~the tha~~t
~~or m~~

to be implied~~
construction~~

## Appendix C  United ~~Nations~~
on Cont~~ract~~
Sale of ~~Goods~~

THE STATES PARTIES TO THIS CONVENTION,
BEARING IN MIND the broad objectives in the resolu-
tions adopted by the sixth special session of the General
~~Assembly of the United Nations on the establishment of a~~

Three appendices provide critical
material for the students: The
Constitution of the United States
(Appendix A), Articles 1, 2, 2a, and
3 of the Uniform Commercial Code
(Appendix B), and the United Nations Convention for the International Sale of Goods (Appendix C).
Marginal references throughout the
text refer students to the page of the
appendix where the original source
of the law being discussed can be
found.

# Supplements

## Online Learning Center (OLC)

**www.mhhe.com/brown13e**

The Online Learning Center (OLC) is a Web site that follows the text chapter by chapter. The 13th edition OLC contains resources for both Instructors and Students:

- *Instructor's Manual.* Updated by Vonda Laughlin of Carson-Newman College, the 13th edition Instructors Manual provides insights into the major topics introduced in each chapter, provides background information for key concepts, and has a "Teaching Tips and Additional Resources" section that poses ideas for stimulating classroom dialogue and activities.

- *PowerPoint Slides.* PowerPoint slide sets for every chapter, updated by Brad Cox at Midlands Technical College, are for use in the classroom or for studying. These slides refer back to figures and concept summaries from the text as well as introduce original material not found anywhere else.

- *Test Bank.* The Test Bank consists of true-false, multiple choice, and short essay questions for each chapter. We've aligned our Test Bank with new AACSB guide-lines, tagging each question according to its learning objective, knowledge and skill areas.

- *You Be the Judge Online (www.mhhe.com/ybtj).* You Be the Judge Online video segments include 18 hypothetical business law cases. All of the cases are based on real cases from our Business Law texts. Each case allows you to watch interviews of the plaintiff and defendant before the courtroom argument, see the courtroom pro-ceedings, view relevant evidence, read other actual cases relating to the issues in the case, and then create your own ruling. After your verdict is generated, view what an actual judge ruled (unscripted) in the case and then get the chance to defend or change your ruling.

- *The Business Law Newsletter, Proceedings.* We have developed this resource to help keep your classes interesting and current. One electronic newsletter is emailed to you per month. Instructors across the country have told us they are looking for ways to include current examples and cases, and we hope this newsletter provides you with just that. It is meant to be an easy and effective place to turn for some new discussion topics for your business law courses. Each edition includes:
  - Article abstracts with critical thinking questions,
  - Video links with discussion questions and answers,
  - Case hypotheticals and ethical dilemmas (with answers),
  - Teaching tips to help you incorporate this newsletter into your class, and
  - A chapter key that integrates all of the above with each of our McGraw-Hill Business Law texts.

# McGraw-Hill Connect® Business Law

## Less Managing. More Teaching. Greater Learning.

McGraw-Hill *Connect Business Law* is an online assignment and assessment solution that connects students with the tools and resources they'll need to achieve success.

McGraw-Hill *Connect Business Law* helps prepare students for their future by enabling faster learning, more efficient studying, and higher retention of knowledge.

## McGraw-Hill Connect Business Law features

*Connect Business Law* offers a number of powerful tools and features to make managing assignments easier, so faculty can spend more time teaching. With *Connect Business Law*, students can engage with their coursework anytime and anywhere, making the learning process more accessible and efficient. *Connect Business Law* offers you the features described below.

**Simple assignment management**   With *Connect Business Law*, creating assignments is easier than ever, so you can spend more time teaching and less time managing. The assignment management function enables you to:

- Create and deliver assignments easily with selectable end-of-chapter questions and test bank items.
- Streamline lesson planning, student progress reporting, and assignment grading to make classroom management more efficient than ever.
- Go paperless with the eBook and online submission and grading of student assignments.

**Smart grading**   When it comes to studying, time is precious. *Connect Business Law* helps students learn more efficiently by providing feedback and practice material when they need it, where they need it. When it comes to teaching, your time also is precious. The grading function enables you to:

- Have assignments scored automatically, giving students immediate feedback on their work and side-by-side comparisons with correct answers.
- Access and review each response; manually change grades or leave comments for students to review.
- Reinforce classroom concepts with practice tests and instant quizzes.

**Instructor library**   The *Connect Business Law* Instructor Library is your repository for additional resources to improve student engagement in and out of class. You can select and use any asset that enhances your lecture. The *Connect Business Law* Instructor Library includes:

- *eBook*
- *Instructors Manual*

2. **Deep integration of content and tools.** Not only do you get single sign-on with Connect and Create, you also get deep integration of McGraw-Hill content and content engines right in Blackboard. Whether you're choosing a book for your course or building Connect assignments, all the tools you need are right where you want them—inside of Blackboard.

3. **Seamless Gradebooks.** Are you tired of keeping multiple gradebooks and manually synchronizing grades into Blackboard? We thought so. When a student completes an integrated Connect assignment, the grade for that assignment automatically (and instantly) feeds your Blackboard grade center.

4. **A solution for everyone.** Whether your institution is already using Blackboard or you just want to try Blackboard on your own, we have a solution for you. McGraw-Hill and Blackboard can now offer you easy access to industry leading technology and content, whether your campus hosts it, or we do. Be sure to ask your local McGraw-Hill representative for details.

## AACSB Statement

The McGraw-Hill Companies is a proud corporate member of AACSB International. Understanding the importance and value of AACSB accreditation, *Business Law with UCC Applications,* 13th edition recognizes the curricula guidelines detailed in the AACSB standards for business accreditation by connecting selected questions in the test bank to the six general knowledge and skill guidelines in the AACSB standards.

The statements contained in *Business Law with UCC Applications,* 13th edition are provided only as a guide for the users of this textbook. The AACSB leaves content coverage and assessment within the purview of individual schools, the mission of the school, and the faculty. While *Business Law with UCC Applications,* 13th edition and the teaching package make no claim of any specific AACSB qualification or evaluation, we have within *Business Law with UCC Applications,* 13th edition labeled selected questions according to the six general knowledge and skills areas.

## McGraw-Hill Customer Care Contact Information

At McGraw-Hill, we understand that getting the most from new technology can be challenging. That's why our services don't stop after you purchase our products. You can e-mail our Product Specialists 24 hours a day to get product-training online. Or you can search our knowledge bank of Frequently Asked Questions on our support website. For Customer Support, call **800-331-5094,** e-mail **hmsupport@mcgraw-hill.com,** or visit **www.mhhe.com/support.** One of our Technical Support Analysts will be able to assist you in a timely fashion.

# Contents in Brief

# Contents

## Part Three

Sales and Consumer Protection  275

## Part Four

Negotiable Instruments and Banking  341

# Part Five

Insurance, Secured Transactions, and
Bankruptcy  401

# Part Six

Agency and Employment  469

# Part Seven

Business Organization and Regulation  541

## Part Eight
Property Law  633

## Part Nine
The Legal Environment  703

# Part One

## Ethics, Law, and the Judicial System

# Chapter 1

# Ethics, Social Responsibility, and the Law

## THE OPENING CASE  WikiLeaks, Secret Documents, and Deception

One of the essential weapons in the diplomatic arsenal is the guarantee of secrecy. If diplomats cannot be certain that their cables, letters, and dispatches will be kept secret, they will not be able to communicate candidly with the decision makers back home. So what happens when a group like WikiLeaks reveals such secrets? Is it ethical for such online groups to reveal the contents of secret dispatches that were obtained illegally in the first place? What happens to the trust that is inherent within the diplomatic process when secrets can be accessed so easily? Does bringing diplomatic activity out into the open help or hinder the public's ability to evaluate the ethical behavior of our diplomats? A case in point can be found among documents disclosed by WikiLeaks that revealed that American diplomats in the former Soviet nation of Georgia may have relied too heavily on the inside reports given to them by Georgian leaders and less on more objective intelligence from outside sources. The secret cables released by WikiLeaks also indicate that the Georgian leaders, with their own agenda aimed at getting United States support for their plan to resist Russian dominance, may have deliberately distorted the information passed onto the Americans. Even more serious, the secret cables reveal that the Georgians probably provoked an encounter with South Ossetia, an enclave that had broken away from Georgia and, in

the process, had sought Russian protection. In fact, it now appears that the Georgians launched a first strike against South Ossetia and then told the Americans that the Ossetians had attacked them. The documents released by WikiLeaks indicate that the Americans relied on the one-sided accounts manufactured by the Georgian government and did not seek any outside verification of the reports. It is clear that the American diplomats made several tactical errors in the management of this incident. However, were they not ethically correct in supporting the democratic Georgian state against the autocratic Russian Federation? Is it not a morally superior position to defend democracy even at the expense of the truth? Or does "truth" occupy a morally superior position in the hierarchy of ethical values? Should the Georgian officials have been more candid with the Americans or did they have a higher responsibility to protect their own people and territory that justified their distortion of the truth? Keep these issues in mind as we explore the nature of ethics in this chapter. (See C. J. Chivers, "Embracing Georgia, U.S. Misread Signs of Region's Rifts, Cables Show," *The New York Times,* December 2, 2010, p. A-15.)

**Opening Case Questions**

1. Was WikiLeaks justified in obtaining the leaked cables illegally? Explain.

2. Does gaining American support (the end), justify the Georgian first strike against South Ossetia (the means)? Explain.

3. Were the Georgian officials justified in distorting the truth to protect their own citizens and territory? Explain.

4. Does the duty to protect a democracy "trump" the telling of the truth? Explain.

5. Does the morality of a nation-state differ from the morality of an individual? Why or why not?

 Learning Objectives

1. Define law and morality.
2. Distinguish among natural law, positive law, negative rights theories.
3. Explain ethical relativism.
4. Describe social contract theory.
5. Outline the steps in applying utilitarianism.
6. Define rational ethics.
7. Explain the dual nature of ethics in government
8. Outline the arguments supporting social responsibility.
9. Explore the need for law in our society.
10. Clarify how the law and ethics are usually in harmony with each other.

# 1-1 Defining the Law, Morality, and Ethics

In a perfect world, everyone would know what the law is and why the law is an important aspect of our lives. Similarly, in an ideal situation, everyone would know what the term "ethics" means and how it is different from the concept of morality. Of course, a quick glance at any daily newspaper or a brief look at the evening news will reveal that people hold widely diverse views on the difference between right and wrong. If this were not the case, if everyone thought exactly the same about right and wrong, there would have been no conflict over the posting of secret documents by WikiLeaks, no dispute over North Korea's bombing of a South Korean island, no need for the assassination attempts on Iranian nuclear scientists, and no disagreement about the Pope's fluctuating position on birth control. In fact, in a perfect world in which everyone held similar, if not identical, ethical values, there would be no need for secret dispatches, nuclear weapons, or lectures on birth control. Yet in each of these cases, and others like them, many people's opinions clash not only on how to handle each situation but also on the ethical or moral nature of the actions themselves.

It is therefore no surprise that most legal textbooks and many treatises on ethics begin by defining these disciplines. This tradition stands in marked contrast to most other studies. Few physics textbooks pause to tell the reader what physics is. Fewer history books devote space to explaining the term *history,* and almost no math texts begin by defining *math.* However, that is as it should be. These disciplines and others like them are fixed in our minds as implacable fields of study. In history, for example, the fact that Barrack Obama was sworn in as the first African-American president of the United States in 2009 is not open to debate. Nor is our understanding that such an event is historical fact. The same is true of the second law of thermodynamics in physics and the multiplication tables in mathematics. These facts are not debatable, except in the most esoteric way. [See Jeffrie G Murphy and Jules L. Coleman, *The*

*Philosophy of Law* (Boulder, CO: Westview Press, 1990), p. 6; and John C. Calhoun, "A Disquisition on Government," in *Philosophy in America,* eds. Paul Russell Anderson and Max Harold Fisch (New York: Appleton-Century Crofts, Inc, 1939), pp. 356–357.]

## The Law and Morality

This is not the case with morality and the law. People *will* argue about whether the law is a form of civil management or a way to dictate individual behavior, whether it ought to be created by a national government or a regional state system, and whether it should change regularly or stay the same indefinitely. They will even argue about whether the rules made by the government demand absolute, unquestioned obedience or simply ask for occasional recognition as optional guiding principles. People will also argue about moral issues. They will argue about whether schools should censor student newspapers, whether capital punishment should be permitted, and whether waging a preventative war is morally correct. This is why we pause at the beginning of *Business Law with UCC Applications* to define the law and morality and to distinguish between ethics and morals, concepts that many of us usually do not think about on a daily basis.

The law consists of rules of conduct established by the government of a society to maintain harmony, stability, and justice. It accomplishes these objectives by defining the legal rights and duties of the people. The law also provides a way to protect the people by enforcing these rights and duties through the courts, the executive branch, and the legislature. The law is therefore a means of civil management. Certainly, the law usually cannot stop a person from doing wrong. However, the law can punish an individual who chooses to do that wrong, whatever it might be. The law then draws the line between conduct that is permissible and that which is not allowed, so people, at the very least, know that they can be punished if they choose to disobey the law.

In contrast, morals are values that govern a society's attitude toward right and wrong and toward good and evil. As a result, we should see morality as more fundamental than law. Therefore, morality ought to serve as a guide for those bodies within our society, such as the courts, the executive branch, the legislature, and the administrative agencies, that make, interpret, and enforce the law. Most of the time, these law-making, law-interpreting, and law-enforcing bodies will follow the belief that morality and legality ought to match up with each other. Indeed, there are even those philosophers of law who argue that morality is a necessary element of the law. They would say that you cannot have a philosophically valid law that is not grounded in morality.

## Values and Ethics

So far we have defined **law** as a set of rules created by the government to establish a means of civil management that directs people to do what is right and avoid what is wrong. The purpose served by the law includes the creation of order, stability, and justice. The assumption is that if these purposes are met, right will be served and wrong defeated. Moreover, we have also defined **morals** as those fundamental values that tell us the difference between right and wrong in the first place. What we have not explained, however, is where those values come from. This is the job of ethics. Ethics is the attempt to develop a means of determining what these values ought to be and for formulating and applying rules that enforce those values.

## Natural Law Theory

According to one system of legal thought, morality and the law are united in a common bond based on their intrinsic nature. This system of thought, which is generally known as **natural law**, sees law as originating from some objective, superior force that stands outside the everyday experience of most people. That superior force might be God, human nature, rational thought, or some other source of universal truth. Thus, according to natural law, there exists an unbreakable link joining morality to the law in a fundamental way. This link exists because a law must, in its most basic form, be moral. Otherwise, it is not lawful. A law with an immoral purpose is not a law at all. Instead it is an anomaly that does not fit into our concept of either law or the legal process. It is, of course, one thing to say that laws must be firmly grounded in morality and quite another to argue that legality and morality are always the same thing. There are, in fact, some laws that have no moral content whatsoever. Thus, a statute that requires a driver to have an operator's license has no intrinsic moral substance, though such a law is not immoral on its face either. The natural law theorist would say that a law must, at the very least, be morally neutral to have any integrity as a law. In a larger sense, a law that says people must be licensed to drive, while not intrinsically moral, contributes to the orderly and stable functioning of society and is therefore moral because of its purpose and effect.

## Positive Law Theory

Natural law is sometimes confused with positive law because both depend on an outside force for their understanding of law, morality, and human rights. The difference is that positive law says that the law comes from social institutions rather than from God, from human nature, or from human rationality. Positive law, then, is a legal theory that says that the law originates from an outside source that has emerged from within society. The process works something like this: The people of a society discover their rights as they live and work together. This discovery leads to commonly held rights that are described in a series of documents, such as the Magna Carta and the U.S. Constitution. Exactly why people discover rather than invent universal rights is not clear. One argument says that rights are intuitively understood to exist within the human character. So, when people write documents such as the Constitution, they include certain human rights such as the right to be treated fairly under the law. (See Alan Dershowitz, *Rights from Wrongs: A Secular Theory of the Origin of Rights,* New York: Perseus Books Group, 2004, 39–42.)

Some people say that human decency will ultimately triumph over human cruelty, giving rise to a just and moral society that will eventually abolish the worst sins of humanity. This brand of positive law is sometimes called the *Law of Peoples.* Not everyone agrees with this position, but such agreement is not necessary, so long as principles of decency and social justice can be found in certain universal documents such as the Bill of Rights in the United States Constitution or the United Nations Universal Declaration of Human Rights. Despite the differences between positive law and natural law, they hold one idea in common, namely, the belief that human values apply to all people at all times. Neither theory, however, tells us how to make ethical decisions. For that reason, we now turn to the next topic, ethical decision making. [See John Rawls, *The Law of Peoples* (Cambridge, MA: Harvard University Press, 1999), pp. 6–7.]

## Negative Rights Theory

Before moving on to ethical decision making, there is a minority position on human rights that deserves some attention. That opinion argues that "rights" are a human invention designed to help people escape moral law. Thus, the right to privacy is actually a way to hide the truth from the public at large; the right to bear arms is the right to harm, perhaps even kill; the right to free speech is the right to lie and get away with it, and the right to private property is the right to exploit, plunder, and pollute that property. This theory of "negative-rights," as it is sometimes called, admits that the rights themselves do not create the escape from responsibility that they permit. Rather, these so-called rights give people an escape clause when they are caught doing something shameful. Thus, when people are caught with stolen goods or other contraband, they often claim that their privacy was invaded.

## THE OPENING CASE *Revisited, Part I*
## WikiLeaks, Secret Documents, and Deception, Round 2

A quick review of the opening case at the beginning of this chapter will demonstrate the problems highlighted by the negative rights theory. For example, should the WikiLeaks people be apprehended by the authorities, they will likely defend their posting of the secret papers by arguing that they were merely defending the people's right to know. Moreover, from a more personal perspective, they will also probably argue that they were simply exercising their own right to free speech. On the other hand, the diplomats whose papers were revealed will contend that WikiLeaks invaded their right to privacy by posting the secret papers. Similarly, the governments involved will insist that their property rights were violated when the papers were stolen in the first place. Finally, newspapers like *The New York Times* that published news stories about the secret papers will argue that they had the right to do so based on the First Amendment's guarantee of a right to a free press. A negative rights

theorist would argue that every single one of the parties, from the WikiLeaks people to *The New York Times,* has done something wrong and is now trying to escape responsibility by claiming that one of the other parties violated their rights.

Similarly, when media people are sued for libel, they frequently defend their actions by claiming the protection of a free press. Finally, when slumlords fail to repair dilapidated apartment buildings, they claim the right to private property. [See Slavoj Zizek, *The Fragile Absolute* (London and New York: Verso, 2000), pp. 101–102.]

## Ethical Decision Making

People make ethical decisions every day. However, how they make those decisions is not always clear. Some people say that they do not think about ethics but instead act instinctively when faced with a moral problem. Others say that they just do what they "believe" is right. Still others say that they follow the rules they learned in school, in their place of worship, or in their family setting. Some professions, businesses, and organizations develop guidelines, usually called rules of conduct or canons of professional responsibility. Such rules generally describe certain levels of behavior. Some behaviors are encouraged; others are discouraged. Punishments are often included in these guidelines.

While such rules are admirable, they are often so long and complex that they end up covering pages of text that require an in-depth study just to understand the basics. A case in point involves the Ohio Rules of Professional Conduct for attorneys. The code consists of eight different subsections, each of which includes from four to eighteen rules. Each rule is then followed by a series of official comments that review, explain, and clarify each of the rules and any amendments that have been made to those rules. In all, the Ohio Rules cover 74 pages of text. Moreover, and more to the point, such rules are aimed at professional conduct alone and often do not even address general moral conduct. Sometimes such codes even go so far as to excuse or ignore immoral conduct. For instance, Official Comment 2 following Rule 8.4 of the Ohio Rules covering the misconduct of an attorney, states that "matters of personal moral fitness, such as adultery and comparable offenses . . . have no specific connection to fitness for the practice of law." Perhaps, most telling, is the fact that these rules frequently supply "loopholes" that permit people to escape culpability even when such culpability is obvious. Again, Official Comment 4 following Ohio Rule 8.4 states that "(a) lawyer may refuse to comply with an obligation imposed by law upon a good faith belief that no valid obligation exists." We can legitimately question the effectiveness of an obligation that can be avoided simply by manufacturing a "good faith belief that no valid obligation exists."

## quick quiz 1-1

1. Natural law theory holds that there is no link between morality and law.   true | **false**

2. Law has nothing to do with civil management.   true | **false**

3. Ethical decisions are made in a variety of ways.   **true** | false

# 1-2 Ethical Theories

Throughout the history of philosophy, many scholars have offered techniques for determining those values that ought to guide all ethical decisions. Although these theories differ in their particulars, they all have one thing in common: Each theory is based on the assumption that people want to live ethical lives. If this were not the case, there would be no need to fashion these theories in the first place. Nevertheless, despite this common assumption, the theories differ greatly in their individual approaches to the problem of determining the nature of the values that underline ethical decision making.

## Ethical Relativism

**Ethical relativism** says that there are no objective or absolute standards of right and wrong. Rather, the standards used to distinguish between right and wrong change from circumstance to circumstance and from person to person. Thus, ethical rules are relative; that is, the rules vary depending upon the actor, the circumstances, and countless other factors that may affect a person's ethical judgments. Because relativism emphasizes the highly individualized nature of ethical decision making, it is also called subjective ethics.

Ethical relativism is a very common position among Americans because the United States is a country of immigrants from a wide variety of cultures, many of which have different social values. Because many Americans want to respect these different cultures and their value systems, they often conclude that each culture is right within its own world, even when the values of those cultures clash with one another. Moreover, the United States was founded on a tradition that allows and even encourages a free exchange of ideas, feelings, and opinions on all subjects, including ethics.

### Shortcomings of Ethical Relativism
It should be instantly clear that ethical relativism cannot be reconciled with either natural law or positive law, because both of these two fundamental theories assume the existence of a universal standard of behavior. Natural law says that this universal standard originates on a superior plane of existence, perhaps with God or with human nature, while positive law says that it emerges from within certain documents such as the United Nations Universal Declaration of Human Rights or the Bill of Rights of the United States Constitution. In contrast, ethical relativism denies the existence of any universal standard of behavior. Thus, according to ethical relativism, no one can ever do, say, or think anything wrong. Moreover, no one can disagree

with anyone just because another person holds a different view on the morality of an action. In fact, if we pursue ethical relativism to its logical end, neither natural law nor positive law can exist.

These results are not unlike those that flow from an application of negative rights theory. In both cases the primary objective of the moral actor is to absolve himself or herself of moral responsibility and to shift that moral responsibility to some other moral (or perhaps immoral) actor. Similarly, as noted previously, professional codes of conduct sometimes provide such loopholes. Of course, since everyone else is in the process of using one or more of these strategies for denying moral responsibility, the net result is that no one admits to any moral responsibility at all.

**Situational Ethics**   Still, certain aspects of relativism are appealing, including the notion that the ethical decisions of other individuals ought not to be judged without taking into consideration the special situation in which those individuals find themselves. This is why some people favor a variation of relativism that takes different situations into consideration but does not necessarily use those different situations to exonerate the actor completely. This theory, which is known as situational ethics, argues that each of us can judge a person's ethical decisions only by initially placing ourselves in the other person's situation. This technique allows us to be aware of the various factors that led to the other person's situation. Such an approach encourages people to look at others with tolerance and patience, an outlook that all of us would like to see practiced by those who might be inclined to judge our ethical decisions. However, it would be more satisfying if we agreed on a single ethical standard for making such moral judgments. Consequently, we must look elsewhere for a more consistent set of ethical values.

## Social Contract Theory

**LO4**

**Social contract theory** holds that right and wrong are measured by the obligations imposed on each individual by an implied agreement among all individuals within a particular social system. At the most fundamental level, the social contract says that for people to live together harmoniously, they must give up certain freedoms to receive certain protections in return. Thus, all individuals give up the freedom to do as they please and in return receive a guarantee that other individuals will curb their behavior, thus protecting everyone else in that society from random and indiscriminate actions. The existence of the implied social contract permits us to live together in peace and harmony. For example, one rule that emerges from the social contract is that people should never make unsupported judgments about one another but should instead always investigate the facts in an effort to uncover the truth about the character of a person or the nature of a situation. Such a rule prevents people from avoiding one another, cheating one another, or, even worse, attacking one another simply because of the way another person looks, speaks, or acts.

Naturally, for the social contract to work, most people must adhere to its rules, and those who do not must be punished. If this were not the case, then the social contract would disintegrate, and the society would return to a "state of nature" in which people must fend for themselves. As is true of ethical relativism, there are problems with social contract theory. One problem is that social contract theory is descriptive rather than prescriptive. A **descriptive theory** simply describes the values at work within a social system, rather than explaining how the values originated in the first place. In contrast, a **prescriptive theory** explains how to come up with the values that permit a society to run smoothly. Of course, not everyone believes that social contract theory is descriptive only. Some ethical theorists argue that social contract ethics is a prescriptive theory because it places a value on the obligation itself. Thus, the benefits that people receive by knowing others will not judge them creates the obligation not to judge anyone else. Social contract ethics therefore

## THE OPENING CASE *Revisited, Part II*
## WikiLeaks, Secret Documents, and Deception, Round 3

If we apply the principles of social contract ethics to the WikiLeaks case, we can see that the decision by the WikiLeak people to post the secret documents on the Web violates the social contract. There is a time-honored principle within the diplomatic social contact that states that the content of diplomatic messages is to remain secret. The principle is designed to assure diplomats that they will be able to communicate openly with the decision makers back home. This process helps government officials make informed decisions based on the assessment of diplomats who have first-hand knowledge of events and personalities in foreign countries. Without the assurance of secrecy, those involved in foreign affairs will be tempted to present a less than candid picture of the conditions present in their assigned areas, thus crippling the decision-making process. The tradition of secrecy works because of the perceived mutual benefit that is gained from the frank nature of diplomatic communication. There is, however, no foolproof way to protect secrecy especially with the Internet, texting, e-mail, and so on. Thus, it is not difficult for the WikiLeaks people or others like them to gain access to and then post secret dispatches. Certainly, there are legal ways to deal with those who violate the principle after the fact. This, however, does not solve the problem once sensitive information has been released and the damage has been done. If the social contract is consistently and regularly violated in this way, the entire social system can unravel.

concentrates on each individual's obligation to everyone else and on the belief that, as long as these obligations are met, social stability will be preserved.

## Utilitarianism

**Utilitarianism** is an ethical theory that says that the morality of an action is determined by its ultimate effects. The more good that results, the more ethical is the action. Conversely, the more bad that results, the less ethical is the action. Unlike ethical relativism, which is constantly shifting, utilitarianism seeks only one stable goal: the greatest good for the greatest number. Determining the greatest good for the greatest number, however, is not as simple as it sounds. For one thing, we must resist the temptation to transform the greatest good for the greatest number principle into the "greatest good for me" principle. One way to avoid mistakes that can result from an improper application of utilitarianism is to follow these steps:

*Good or Bad all the way*

1. The action to be evaluated should be stated in unemotional, general terms. For example, "stealing another person's property" is emotional language; "confiscating property for one's own use" is somewhat less emotional.

2. Every person or class of people that will be affected by the action must be identified.

3. Good and bad consequences in the relation to those people affected must be considered.

4. All alternatives to the action stated in step 1 must be considered.

5. Once step 4 has been carried out, a conclusion must be reached. Whichever alternative creates the greatest good for the greatest number of people affected by the action is the one that ought to be taken.

Despite the systematic approach of the utilitarian theory, many people are uncomfortable with it. One questionable aspect of utilitarianism is that, in business at least, it can be confused with utility thinking. **Utility thinking**, which is also referred to as **cost-benefit thinking**, looks only at corporate benefits and problems rather than the benefits and problems that will result for others outside the boardroom.

## EXAMPLE 1-1: The Secret America of the Post 9/11 Age

In the aftermath of 9/11 and in a good faith attempt to create an information network among law enforcement agencies across the United States, the Department of Homeland Security, the FBI, and the Department of Defense have enlisted the aid of local law enforcement agencies in a plan designed to create an enormous database that includes information about American citizens on all aspects of their lives. Part of this project, which has poured billions of dollars into state and local law enforcement agencies, is the Nationwide Suspicious Activity Reporting Initiatve, or SAR. Under the SAR strategy, law enforcement agencies are empowered to gather information on American citizens who are suspected of engaging in suspicious activities. The ultimate goal is to create an enormous database of information that can be accessed and shared across the nation at all levels. To aid in this goal, the term *suspicious activity* has been defined by the government as "observed behavior reasonably indicative of pre-operational planning related to terrorism or other criminal activity." The plan and its objectives appear good on paper. However, a closer look might raise some doubts. For example, the definition of suspicious activity seems unduly vague and exceptionally open-ended. What if a tourist, for example, is spotted taking photographs of a town square? So far so good. But what if the local police station or sheriff's office is also located on the square? Could that be grounds for labeling the photographer's activity as "pre-operational planning related to terrorism"? Probably. As a result, the identity of an innocent tourist becomes imbedded within a national database listing suspected terrorists. Now, the utility thinker would argue that the overall security of the United States is worth the cost of the invasion of privacy suffered by one innocent citizen. This might be good utility thinking, but is it pure utilitarian thinking? The utilitarian must always balance the greatest good produced by an action against the effect that the action has on the greatest number of people. (See Dana Priest and William M. Arkin of *The Washington Post,* "Fallout of 9/11: A Secret America," *The Columbus Dispatch,* December 21, 2010, pp. A-1 and A-6.)

## Self-Evident Truths

Read the following quotation on the nature of morality. As you read the quotation and reflect on the ideas that the author presents, ask yourself if the position represents your own point of view. Then answer the following questions based on the reading. Make sure that you are prepared to defend each response in a thoughtful manner.

> From the American founding until World War II, there was a widespread belief in this country that there is a moral order in the universe that makes claims on us. This belief was not unique to Americans. It was shared by Europeans since the very beginning of Western civilization, and it is held even today by all the traditional cultures of the world. The basic notion is that morality is external to us and is binding on us. In the past, Americans and Europeans, being for the most part Christian, might disagree with Hindus and Muslims about the exact source of this moral order, its precise content, or how a society should convert its moral beliefs into legal and social practice. But there was little doubt across the civilizations of the world about the existence of such an order. Moreover, the laws and social norms typically reflected this moral consensus. During the first half of the twentieth century, the moral order generated some clear American social norms. . . . The point is not that everyone lived up to the dictates of the moral code, but that it supplied a standard, accepted virtually throughout society, for how one should act.
>
> —Dinesh D'Souza, *The Enemy at Home* (New York: Doubleday, 2007), p. 19.

## Self-Evident Questions

1.  The author observes that before World War II people believed in an external morality that binds us all. What sociological, political, and economic events might have worked together to destroy that belief in an external morality? Explain.

2. Do you agree that Christians, Hindus, and Muslims, all shared in the consent of that universal moral code? Why or why not?

3. If many people saw fit to completely ignore this common code of conduct, then what was the point of having such a code in the first place? Explain.

4. What "clear American norms" might have been generated by this universal moral order? Explain.

5. Given the cosmopolitan world in which we live today, does a universal moral code make any sense at all? Explain.

Thus, in the Secret America-9/11 case, the goals and the techniques of the Nationwide Suspicious Activity Reporting Initiative, seem to benefit a great number of people at a cost that affects only a few innocent citizens. Yet, a closer examination reveals that these activities may actually undermine the long-term stability of the entire American system. If the practice continues, it will inevitably extend to more and more people. Eventually, what appears to be a harmless violation of the rights of one or two people begins to affect us all. Before we know it, children are reporting the "suspicious" activities of their parents; police officers are detaining innocent citizens; business people and politicians are naming names in front of Congressional committees, and the entire social fabric has begun to unravel. Certainly, this is not the intent of utilitarianism nor would well-meaning utilitarian thinkers endorse this kind of social collapse. Nevertheless, because utilitarian thinkers can sometimes be led astray by utility thinking, it is wise for us to look at an additional ethical theory.

## Rational Ethics

Rational ethics replaces the shifting standards of relativism, the prescriptive approach of social contract theory, and the result-oriented standard of utilitarianism with a system that is objective, logical, and relatively consistent. **Rational ethics** is a philosophical theory that says ethical values can be determined by a proper application of human reason. The theory assumes that, because all human beings are rational, all human beings will have the same ethical values. Therefore, rational ethics ought to establish universal rules of behavior that apply to all people at all times. For this reason, rational ethics is often referred to as *objective ethics*. Rational ethics begins with the premise that only human beings are morally responsible for their actions. Animals, plants, and inanimate objects may cause injury or harm, but they are never held morally responsible because they are incapable of making rational decisions. Therefore, we say that they are *amoral*. The only thing that separates moral beings from those that are amoral is the rationality of the moral beings.

LO6

Ethic value
By
human
reaso

Amoral - cant make
Reasonable
decisions

### The Golden Rule and Rational Ethics
As rational beings, people think for themselves and, in doing so, recognize their own self-worth as individuals. Along with self-worth comes a belief in certain rights. These rights include the right to life, the right to be free from injury, the right to be treated fairly, the right to self-determination, and so on. Rational beings recognize that they do not want to be killed or cheated. They do not want their freedom taken away without just cause and due process. Because they believe in their own rights, they also recognize that all people share these same rights. Thus, each individual has a duty to refrain from violating the rights of all other human beings.

### The Logical Premise of Rational Ethics
As rational beings, people also realize that it is logical to establish rules that support the continued existence of society. A rule that destroys a society that tries to follow it would be an illogical rule. Consider the following rule: "False promises are morally correct as long as they are made to gain some

advantage." A person who adheres to rational ethics would instantly recognize that such a rule is both illogical and immoral. If everyone in a society were to adopt such a rule, no one could make a promise, and no one would accept a promise, even if it were made. A society without promises would be a society without commerce, diplomacy, credit cards, religion, pizza deliveries, marriage, airline schedules, democracy, and baseball, all of which require promises in one way or another. Such a society would be illogical and therefore immoral.

**EXAMPLE 1-2:** The Secret America of the Post 9/11 Age Reconsidered

Let's return to the Secret America Case in Example 1-1. Recall that, under the Nationwide Suspicious Activity Reporting Initiative [SAR], law enforcement agencies are empowered to gather information on American citizens who are suspected of engaging in suspicious activities. Recall also that the term *suspicious activity* has been defined by the government as "behavior reasonably indicative of pre-operational planning related to terrorism or other criminal activity." In Example 1-1 we speculated that, under this initiative, an innocent tourist caught taking photographs of a local police station or sheriff's office might be tagged as engaging in "pre-operational planning related to terrorism." The utility thinker argued that the overall security of the United States is worth the cost of invading the privacy of one innocent person. Rational ethics leads to a different conclusion. The Golden Rule of rational ethics states, "Act so that you treat others as you believe you would want to be treated. Be sure to respect others as ends in themselves and not as a means to an end." In this case, any law enforcement officer tempted to tag our tourist as a suspicious person should ask, "Would I want to be tagged as 'suspicious' simply because I stopped to take a photograph in a strange town?" Most of us, including our law enforcement agent, would hopefully answer, "no," to this question. The other question required of rational ethics asks, "Can a society that follows such a rule survive?" In other words in this case, "Can a society that tags an innocent activity such as taking a photograph as a suspicious act survive?" As we saw above, when we endorse this type of conduct (the "tagging," not the picture taking) as the norm, then people become suspicious of even the most innocuous acts and everyone becomes a target of suspicion. Eventually, the concept of trust evaporates, and our orderly society along with it.

## quick quiz 1-2

1. Utilitarianism focuses on the consequences of an action.   true   false
2. Rational ethics is a form of ethical relativism.   true   false
3. Utilitarianism and rational ethics always reach the same moral conclusion.   true   false

# 1-3 Ethics and the Government

So far our study of ethics has focused on individuals. This is natural because ultimately all ethical decisions, even those that drive governmental regulations and corporate policies, are made by individuals. However, the decisions made by individuals affect the policies and procedures carried out by institutions that have the power to affect many parts of our social structure. Probably the most powerful institution that we deal with on a regular basis is the government. Governments run nation-states and, on the international scene, nation-states run the world. This is because nation-states possess territory, raise money through taxation, police their borders, protect their people, and if necessary, use force in a legitimate and responsible way. The government of a nation-state has two objectives that simultaneously justify its power and enable the proper exercise of that power. Those two objectives are (1) to protect its own existence and (2) to protect the lives, health, and well-being of its own citizens.

## The Ethic of Ultimate Ends

Many of the misunderstandings about moral decisions within the world today exist because people do not understand the dual nature of international morality. The 20th century philosopher Max Weber explains the problem in his essay, "Politics as a Vocation." In that essay, Weber argues that, often people make the error of assuming that political morality and personal morality are identical. Instead, Weber proposes a dual system of morality represented by the "ethic of ultimate ends" and the "ethic of responsibility." The "ethic of ultimate ends" must be practiced by individuals while the "ethic of responsibility" must be practiced by national leaders. The ethic of ultimate ends must be practiced by individuals because individuals can never completely foresee "the ultimate ends" of their actions. Therefore, individuals must obey absolute moral precepts, such as "turn the other cheek" and "love thy neighbor as thyself" despite the fact that the ultimate consequences of those actions are unclear or uncomfortable.

To express it in even more absolute terms, the ethic of ultimate ends asserts that the action itself is right or wrong in and of itself, regardless of the consequences of the action. From this perspective, we can see why the ethic of ultimate ends is also often referred to as the ethic of benevolence. Under the ethic of benevolence the immediate ends can never justify the means because, even if the immediate ends are foreseeable, the ultimate ends are not. Thus, it does no good to consider those ends. In fact, considering those ends often has the opposite effect. Rather than prompting a moral actor to do the right thing, it gives that actor an excuse for bending or breaking the rules in order to effectuate a "greater good." Under the ethic of ultimate ends, an individual must do the right thing because it is right in and of itself.

## The Ethic of Responsibility

On the other hand, the ethic of responsibility demands that the moral actor, in this case a national leader, consider his or her responsibilities to those people who depend on that leader for protection, safety, and sometimes even for their very lives. The ethic of responsibility is the morality of the nation-state and it is not the same as individual morality. The nation-state has a duty that outweighs all other duties and that duty is to promote the civil peace of the nation-state and the value that is rooted in the lives its own people. What this means from the practical perspective of world leaders is that, if a neighboring nation-state is belligerent, aggressive, or determined to fight ancient cultural, religious, and ethnic wars, the leaders of the first nation cannot ignore that threat, as much as they might want to. In short, they are not permitted to "turn the other cheek" because to do so would endanger the innocent people they have the duty to protect.

The threat discussed in the Opening Case Revisited, Part III involves an imminent threat to an individual nation-state that is doing what it needs to do to survive. This justifies its twisting of the truth as reported above. The principle of responsibility might even be stretched to include a regional or a global threat that would indirectly threaten a distant nation-state such as the United States. If a threat is global, as with rogue nations such as Iran or North Korea, a fragmented state such as the Sudan or Somalia, or an autocratic, closed state, such as Cuba or the Russian Federation, then it is unwise for the leaders of the threatened nation-states to act benevolently toward the nation that has initiated the global threat. Moreover, it may also be necessary for a nation that has the power to protect other

## THE OPENING CASE *Revisited, Part III*
## WikiLeaks, Secret Documents, and Deception, Round 5

Recall in the Opening Case at the beginning of the chapter that some of the secret cables released by WikiLeaks revealed that Georgian leaders had provoked an encounter with the breakaway province of South Ossetia, in order to garner American support against the Russians who the Georgians believed were planning to reassert control over their newly independent nation. In fact, it now appears that the Georgians actually launched a first strike against South Ossetia and then told the Americans that the Ossetians had attacked them. Under the ethic of responsibility, the Georgian leaders can argue convincingly that they had a duty to protect their people and to preserve their national sovereignty against the threat of a military attack by Russia which had openly declared that it did not recognize Georgia's right to secede from the former Soviet Union. Georgia's responsibility to its own people and territory would take precedence over its duty to tell the truth, even to allies like the United States. (See C. J. Chivers, "Embracing Georgia, U.S. Misread Signs of Region's Rifts, Cables Show," *The New York Times,* December 2, 2010, p. A-15.)

nations to act insofar as it is able, insofar as is necessary to protect innocent people, and insofar as it puts its own people in harm's away no more than necessary. [See Max Weber, "Politics as a Vocation (from Wirtschaft und Gesellschaft)," in *The Great Political Theories: From the French Revolution to Modern Times,* eds. Michael Curtis (New York: Harper, 2008), 426–436; See also: Helene Cooper and Martin Fackler, "U.S. Asking China to Help Rein in North Koreans," *The New York Times,* November 25, 2001, p. A-1.]

## EXAMPLE 1-3: The Secret America of the Post 9/11 Age Reconsidered Once Again

At this point it might be a good idea to return once more to the Secret America Case in Example 1-1. Remember, under the Nationwide Suspicious Activity Reporting Initiative [SAR], law enforcement agencies are empowered to gather information about people who are engaged in suspicious activities in order to build a database to help the government fight the threat of terrorism. Utilitarianism suggested that the actions, while basically inoffensive to all but a few in the short run, would, nevertheless, be harmful to the overall security of the social structure. Similarly, the principles of rational ethics would reject SAR as a clear violation of the Golden Rule and the rule of social preservation. However, under the ethics of responsibility, a national leader would endorse the SAR initiative, because that national leader has a duty to ensure the health, safety, well-being, and lives of the nation's citizens.

## quick quiz 1-3

1. Political and personal morality are not the same thing.    true | false

2. The ethic of ultimate ends says that the action itself is right or wrong.    true | false

3. The ethic of responsibility is the ethic of the nation-state.    true | false

# 1-4 Social Responsibility in the Business Sector

Up until now, our examination of ethics has involved only individuals and the government. This is not surprising since many ethics dilemmas entangle politics and the individual. Individuals make the actual day-to-day decisions, and the bureaucracy of the government, often in the form of the courts or law enforcement officers, carry out those decisions. Nevertheless, to make our study complete, we need to add a third element into the equation, the corporation. Corporations carry a great deal of influence over the economy, the community, and the people. There are those who say that a corporation has no social responsibility beyond making a profit for its shareholders. This is, in fact, the traditional view of corporate responsibility. It is a view that has remained so ingrained in our system that, until recently, it was the only view built into statutory and common law. Recently, however, voices have been raised arguing that corporations have a high degree of social responsibility to those people affected by their decisions.

## The Traditional Corporate Culture

Although all businesses affect the economy and the community, the greatest force in the American industrial state is the corporation, in general, and the multinational corporation, in particular. The reality of corporate power is revealed by the fact that philosophers on both ends of the political spectrum can point to the corporation as a guiding force in modern civilization. For instance, in his treatise, *Individualism Old and New,* the *pragmatic* American philosopher, John Dewey, notes, "The United States has steadily moved from an earlier pioneer individualism to a condition of corporate dominance." Similarly, the *theoretical* philosopher, Herbert Marcuse, once remarked that no one, not even the former enemies of capitalism, can escape the influence of corporate power. In fact, Marcuse goes so far as to say that in the modern global marketplace, "the socialist and communist systems are linked with capitalism." (See John Dewey, *Individualism: Old and New*. New York: Capricorn Books, 1962; Herbert Marcuse, *Five Lectures: Psychoanalysis, Politics, and Utopia,* trans. Jeremy J. Shapiro and Shierry M. Weber, Boston: Beacon Press, 1970.)

One reason that corporations have such power is that they are legal persons, created under the authority of federal and state statutes. This status as a "legal person" gives the corporation certain rights and abilities that other business entities do not always have. For instance, as legal persons they are accorded certain constitutional rights, such as the right not to be deprived of property without due process of law. They can also own property in their own name and have lawsuits filed to protect them or vindicate their rights. There are, of course, many types of corporations. Our focus will be on those corporations that are privately run to make a profit for their owners, who are referred to as shareholders. The traditional view says that privately owned corporations are created solely to make a profit for their shareholders. Consequently, the foremost job of any manager is to maximize those profits. In fact, under the traditional rule of shareholder dominance, the managers of a corporation could be held liable in a court of law for making decisions that do not guarantee that the shareholders would receive a maximum return on their investment.

As defined previously, the type of thinking promoted by the court in Example 1-4 is referred to as utility thinking or cost-benefit thinking. Using utility thinking, a corporate manager simply looks at the action he or she is about to take and asks whether the benefit to the shareholders will outweigh the cost to the corporation. If the shareholders' benefits offset corporate costs, then the action is taken. If not, the action is abandoned. Proponents of this position justify cost-benefit thinking in three ways. First, the profits to the shareholders must always come first. Second, it would be unfair to divert funds that belong

## EXAMPLE 1-4: Corporate Culture and Utility Thinking

When Lynn Cummings discovered that the managers of a corporation in which she owned stock had made a decision that had caused shareholders to lose money in a merger plan, she sued, seeking a reversal of the merger or a suitable payment from the managers that would make up for her losses. Basically, Cummings second-guessed the way that the managers had made their decision, arguing that they had not properly researched the merger and had not placed the shareholders' profits first. The managers argued that they had made their decision based on the long-term benefits of the merger to everyone involved, including the local community and the economy of the nation and state. The court sided with Cummings, noting that the job of the managers was to look out for the shareholders' profits, not the long-term benefits to the community or the economy.

to the shareholders to activities that do not directly benefit the shareholders. Third, a corporation's managers are accountable to the shareholders and to no one else. The problem with utility thinking is that it often results in actions that are clearly unethical and potentially illegal.

## EXAMPLE 1-5: Maximum Corporate Irresponsibility

The managers of Taylor-Beechaum Pharmaceuticals, Inc., received a report that the corporation's latest weight loss drug, biomiocin, was having unpredicted side effects that caused problems for several people. The managers of Taylor-Beechaum ordered the accounting department to determine how much it would cost to recall all the biomiocin now on the market, suspend manufacturing, and conduct more tests on the drug's safety. The accountants reported that it would be more cost effective to simply leave the drug on the market and pay off anyone who might be injured and who might bring a lawsuit against Taylor-Beechaum. Keeping the drug on the shelves will allow the corporation to continue to pay dividends to the shareholders. In contrast, if the drug were taken off of the market, the payment of dividends would be suspended pending the outcome of the new testing program. Consequently, the corporate managers decided to leave biomiocin on the shelves. This decision not only violated virtually every ethical standard that we've studied thus far (except ethical relativism) but also evaded the corporation's social responsibility to consumers, to the government, to the shareholders, and to the public at large.

## Reasons for Social Responsibility

The fact that corporate officers and directors have made such irresponsible decisions should not be surprising. Nor should it be surprising that, until recently, the law supported such decisions. The idea that a corporation is a legal person did not spring full grown into the law when the first corporations were formed. In fact, it took jurists quite some time to see that corporations were neither partnerships nor miniature democratic states but instead vehicles for making a profit. Once jurists recognized the unique position that corporations hold within the hierarchy of business associations, however, they easily granted certain privileges to corporate entities. Despite this, as the jurists entered the modern age, they began to see that there were a number of reasons that corporations, like Taylor-Beechaum in Example 1-5, should accept social responsibility for their actions. Some of these reasons are built on the legal advantages granted to corporations. Others are based on the idea that many corporations are powerful forces in their communities. Still others focus on the self-interest of the corporation. Whatever the case, these arguments are being voiced more loudly and with more conviction with each passing fiscal year.

**Legal Advantages Granted to the Corporation** The first argument supporting corporate social responsibility is based on the premise that corporations are granted certain rights as a result of the incorporation process. For example, the corporate form offers limited liability to those who share in its ownership. This means that the personal assets of the corporate owners cannot be taken if the corporation defaults on a contract or commits a tort or a crime. In addition, under provisions of most incorporation statutes, a corporation is considered an artificially created person. This means that, under provisions of the U.S. Constitution and those of most state constitutions, a corporation, like a natural person, cannot be deprived of life, liberty, or property without due process of law. This also means that a corporation can own property in its own name and bring a lawsuit to vindicate its rights. Because corporations have all these rights, they owe an obligation to the public and to the community at large to act responsibly. In practical terms, this means that the decisions of corporate managers must not be narrowly focused on the profits of the shareholders.

**EXAMPLE 1-6:** The Andrean-Harrison Donation

As part of a downsizing campaign, the Andrean-Harrison Corporation was about to close down operations in Tulsa. The company owned an office building and a small laboratory on the outskirts of Tulsa that are adjacent to 30 acres of undeveloped land. The corporation had a chance to sell the land at a price that would have made a profit for the shareholders of the company. Rather than take advantage of this offer, Andrean-Harrison decided to donate the land to the city. The fact that the corporation was a legal person meant that it owned the land and could donate it to the city. Corporate officials acted responsibly in this case, taking advantage of the corporation's right to own land in its own name.

**The Impact of Corporate Decision Making** A second reason for demanding social responsibility from corporations is that corporate decision making clearly has an impact on more people than just the shareholders and the managers. Those who support corporate social responsibility often argue that many corporate decisions, such as the decision to open or close a factory, will affect everyone in the local community. Those affected by such decisions include suppliers, consumers, employees, support businesses, and community members. Consequently, the argument goes, all of these groups should be taken into consideration when corporate managers make decisions. Some individuals who support this form of extreme corporate social responsibility would like to see representatives from the employees' union, from consumer protection groups, from environmental protection groups, and from the local chamber of commerce on every corporation's board of directors. Others, however, argue that because corporate decisions affect more individuals and groups than just the shareholders and managers, those decisions should be made by an impartial group of corporate outsiders. Often the corporate outsiders named are governmental officials.

## EXAMPLE 1-7: Corporate Cooperation and Compromise

When the directors of Igar International Corporation were working on plans to diversify their operation, they considered opening a chemical plant in Santa Ana. Before making the decision, they sent a team of experts to Santa Ana to investigate the possibility of establishing an operation just within the city limits. Although the city officials promised Igar a tax abatement plan and agreed to donate several acres of land to the corporation, citizens' groups were against the plant because of environmental and health concerns. The corporation could have simply found a more receptive or, perhaps, a less vocal city in which to locate. However, instead of simply discarding their consideration of Santa Ana, they worked with the citizens' groups to meet their concerns. Ultimately the two sides agreed on modifications to the project and moved forward. The willingness of the company to discuss the proposed changes in its operation reflected an understanding of the corporation's social responsibility based on the fact that corporate decisions have a far-ranging impact.

**Enlightened Corporate Self-Interest** Finally, there are those who argue, rather convincingly, that accepting social responsibility is actually in the long-term best interests of the corporation. This argument, which is generally referred to as enlightened self-interest, is based on the notion that socially responsible corporations benefit by creating goodwill for themselves, thus motivating consumers to purchase their products, investors to buy their stock, and lawmakers to grant them further legal advantages. In addition, the corporation benefits because the community at large gains from such decisions. If the community at large is healthy, the argument goes, then the corporation that relies on that community will be healthy also.

## EXAMPLE 1-8: Failed Negotiations Lead to Problems

The president of Pilder and Wesselkamper International, Inc., decided to suspend negotiations with union representatives when he learned that they were about to demand a salary increase that he believed was untenable given the corporation's financial health, or lack thereof. The union threatened to file a complaint with the National Labor Relations Board, charging that the president and his staff were not cooperating with the collective bargaining process. The union also indicated that it was considering publishing an advertisement in *The New York Times* denouncing the president's decision and eventually would authorize a strike. The president continued to resist further negotiations and simply shut down operations. Eventually, the company filed for bankruptcy and dissolved its operation. Neither of the parties involved in this case opted to pursue a course of enlightened self-interest, which resulted in the worst possible conclusion for all those involved.

## Efforts to Promote Social Responsibility

As noted previously, the traditional view of a corporation says that its primary role is to make a profit for its shareholders. This means that corporate managers are obligated to make decisions that maximize those profits. Moreover, under the traditional role of corporate managers, those managers could be sued for making a decision that hurt the corporation's profits and thereby reduced or eliminated dividends. However, recent amendments to many corporate statutes have been designed to encourage corporate managers to make broader-based decisions. Thus, some statutes now permit managers to consider factors beyond profit in making corporate decisions. These factors include the economic well-being of the nation, the state, and the local community; the interests of employees, consumers, and suppliers; and the betterment of the environment, the economy, and the overall social structure. These statutes generally hold managers immune from shareholder lawsuits, which claim that the managers did not put the shareholders' profits first.

---

**EXAMPLE 1-9:** Corporate Trade-Offs Mean Corporate Survival

The directors of Chindi-Mowry Enterprises, Inc., were under fire because of a takeover bid against Chindi-Mowry engineered by an alien corporation known as Rixensart Industries. To stave off the assault, the directors invited a friendly bid from Sandoff, Inc., a firm that promised not to dismantle Chindi-Mowry after the deal was entered. The final amount of the offer from Sandoff was less than that offered by Rixensart, and so those shareholders who sold their stock received less on the sale to Sandoff than they would have received had the directors endorsed the Rixensart plan. However, in making their decision, the directors were persuaded that the deal offered by Sandoff would save jobs, help the community, boost the national and state economy, and eventually result in a long-term gain for the corporation and for those shareholders who remained with the company.

---

## quick quiz 1-4

1. Cost-benefit thinking will always result in ethical decisions.          true | false

2. Corporations are not allowed to own property.          true | false

3. Some statutes allow corporate managers to consider factors          true | false
   beyond shareholder profits in making business decisions.

# 1-5 The Relationship between Law and Ethics

Thus far, we have seen that ethics and morals can be distinguished from one another. We have defined values, examined the causes of unethical conduct, and determined how to develop an ethical lifestyle. Some people determine an ethical lifestyle as simply doing what is legal. Such a course of action may often result in ethical conduct. However, that is not always the case. Even when most people know that a particular type of conduct is illegal, that does not prevent some people from engaging in that conduct. For example, everyone knows that killing is illegal. Yet that knowledge does not stop the national murder rate from remaining disturbingly high. Similarly, everyone knows that child abuse, spousal abuse, and elder abuse are immoral, but that consensus has not eliminated the problem of abuse from our society.

## The Need for Law in Our Society

The law is needed because, though people know better, they do not always follow ethical principles. As noted previously, the law consists of rules of conduct established by the government of a society to maintain harmony, stability, and justice in that society. It does so by defining the legal rights and duties of the people. It also provides a way to protect the people by enforcing these rights and duties through the courts and the legislature. Ethical principles can tell us what is right, but they cannot stop us from doing that which is wrong. The law also cannot stop us from doing wrong. However, the law can punish us if we choose to do wrong. The law draws the line between permissible and impermissible conduct, so that people, at the very least, are punished if they hurt or cheat one another or threaten society as a whole.

Of course the law also has other functions. For instance, the law serves as the ultimate rule maker, providing a sense of stability and harmony when order breaks down in any other area of society, from our schools and universities to the family itself. This is why each state has established a system of juvenile courts and a network of domestic relations courts to handle such disputes when they arise. The law also promotes economic growth by granting tax abatements, by rezoning certain urban areas for the establishment of stores and businesses, and by exercising the power of *eminent domain* to confiscate privately owned land for community purposes. In addition, the law guards property rights by enforcing contracts and other similar agreements and providing a forum for tort victims and their families. The law also protects the environment by regulating those industries that might overdevelop the land and those that dump waste materials and other pollutants on to the land and into the waterways. Finally, as noted, the law is responsible for advancing social justice and guaranteeing personal freedom by granting all people due process and equal protection and providing a system by which legitimate grievances can be resolved in an orderly and timely fashion.

Is the law perfect? Does the law always succeed in its goals and objectives? Certainly not. As is true of all institutions, the law is flawed. It is filled with loopholes, foolishness, red tape, and, at times, absolute idiocy, much of which is unintentional and most of which could be avoided if people just take the time to think coolly and rationally. For example, it makes very little sense for Congress to pass legislation to punish flag burners when it is quite clear that the Supreme Court will declare that legislation unconstitutional. Or, in a similar vein, it makes no sense for Congress to pass unfunded mandates that force the state governments to raise money to perform tasks that the federal government should have taken care of in the first place. Yet this type of thing happens all of the time. Nevertheless, having an imperfect but functioning legal system is always preferable to the alternative— anarchy and all the unpleasantness that would surround a descent into chaos.

## Ethical and Legal Harmony

In a utopian society, ethics and the law would always coincide. Our society is not perfect however, and it is not likely to become perfect in the foreseeable future. Therefore, our society needs the law and the legal system to give it structure, harmony, predictability, and justice. However, ethical considerations should always form the foundation of law and the legal system. If the law is not founded on ethics, it will rarely succeed in reaching its objectives. Ethics can lead the way in difficult situations or in areas of the social structure into which the law has yet to venture.

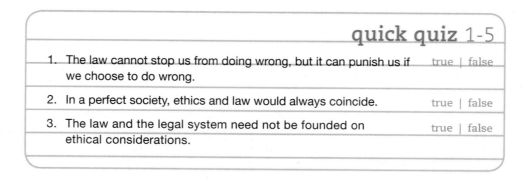

## quick quiz 1-5

1. The law cannot stop us from doing wrong, but it can punish us if we choose to do wrong.                    true | false

2. In a perfect society, ethics and law would always coincide.                    true | false

3. The law and the legal system need not be founded on ethical considerations.                    true | false

# Summary

**1.1**   The law consists of rules of conduct established by the government of a society to maintain harmony, stability, and justice. Morals involve the values that govern a society's attitude toward right and wrong. Ethics, in contrast, attempt to develop a means for determining what those values ought to be and for formulating and applying rules in line with those values.

**1.2**   Ethical relativism holds that there are no fixed or stable standards of right and wrong. Social contract theory holds that right and wrong are measured by the obligations imposed on each individual by an implied social agreement. Utilitarianism determines right and wrong by looking at the consequences of a person's actions. According to rational ethics, actions are either right or wrong, regardless of the circumstances and regardless of the consequences.

**1.3**   The government of a nation-state has two objectives that simultaneously justify its power and enable the proper exercise of that power. Those two objectives are (1) to protect its own existence and (2) to protect the lives, health, safety, and well-being of its own citizens. In order to meet those two objectives, national leaders must recognize the conflict that emerges from (a) the exercise of individual morality, represented by the ethic of ultimate ends, and (b) the exercise of national morality, represented by the ethic of responsibility.

**1.4**   Corporations owe society a level of responsibility because the government has granted certain legal advantages to corporations. Another reason for expecting socially responsible decisions from corporate executives is that corporations have a great deal of power in the economic structure, and with power comes responsibility. Finally, corporations should act responsibly because it is in their own best interest to do so.

**1.5**   In a perfect society, ethics and the law would always coincide. Our society is not perfect and is not likely to become so in the foreseeable future. Therefore, our society needs the law and the legal system to give it structure, harmony, predictability, and justice.

# Key Terms

cost-benefit thinking, 9
descriptive theory, 8
ethic of responsibility, 13
ethic of ultimate ends, 13
ethical relativism, 7
law, 4

morals, 4
natural law, 4
negative rights theory, 6
positive law theory, 5
prescriptive theory, 8

rational ethics, 11
situational ethics, 8
social contract theory, 8
utilitarianism, 9
utility thinking, 9

# Questions for Review and Discussion

1. What is the difference between law and morality?
2. What are the differences among positive law, natural law, and negative rights?
3. What is ethical relativism?
4. What is social contract theory?
5. What are the steps in applying utilitarianism?
6. What is rational ethics?
7. What is the dual nature of ethics in government?
8. What are the arguments supporting social responsibility?
9. Why is law needed in our society?
10. How is harmony established between the law and ethics?

# Cases for Analysis

1. The Oklahoma state constitution was amended by a vote of the people to prohibit judges in the state courts from considering any law other than state or federal law in their cases. The new constitutional amendment read, "Courts shall not look to the legal precepts of other nations or cultures. Specifically, the Court shall not consider International law or Sharia law." A federal judge issued an injunction nullifying the vote because, according to the judge, the amendment is an unconstitutional violation of the Supremacy Clause and of the First Amendment of the U.S. Constitution. The main target of the amendment appears to be the Islamic legal tradition of Sharia. The Islamic legal tradition is an interesting one because it requires Islamic judges to use a specific methodology that helps them to examine and interpret religious texts in an attempt to determine the will of God. Which of the three major ethical theories that we have examined in this chapter would support the action of the federal judge? Explain. Which of these ethical theories would support the position of the Oklahoma voters? Explain. (See Abed Awad, "Oklahoma Amendment Is Unconstitutional: Barring Courts form Considering Sharia Law violates the Supremacy Clause and the First Amendment," *The National Law Journal,* November 15, 2010, p. 39.)

2. When former Illinois Governor Rod Blagojevich was on trial, the judge was asked to keep the identities of the jurors hidden from the community. The request was unusual because it violates the legal practice of permitting the public to have access to information about jurors in order to build public faith in the objectivity of the legal system. Despite this principle, the judge ordered that the identities of the jury members be kept secret to prevent the jurors from being influenced by e-mail, blogging, texting, Facebook, tweats, and other electronic media. The appeals court urged the judge to reconsider the ban, arguing that denying the public access to the identity of the jury flies in the face of the long-standing legal tradition of accessibility and candor. Using utilitarianism, construct an argument that supports the appeals court. Now use rational ethics to construct an argument that upholds the judges' original ruling. Explain each argument and determine which of the two positions you prefer. Explain that preference. (See David J. Bird and Jeffrey M. Weimer, "Keep Jurors' Identities Public," *The National Law Journal,* August 23, 2010, p. 50.)

3. Under provisions of the Alien Tort Statute, the federal courts are permitted to hear civil cases involving international law. Following the dictates of that statute, a group of Somali citizens brought a lawsuit against a former government official of the Somali government alleging that defense forces under his command illegally detained, tortured, and murdered their family members. The trial court dismissed the case under the Federal Sovereign Immunity Act which prevents foreign governments from being sued in U.S. Courts unless the foreign government agrees to the action. The U.S. Court of Appeals for the Fourth Circuit and the U.S. Supreme Court both overturned the decision of the trial court. The two higher courts ruled that the immunity act protected foreign governments but not foreign individuals. Using the ethic of responsibility and the ethic of ultimate ends, defend the ruling that was made by the two higher courts in this case. Explain your defense. (See John B. Bellinger III, "Ruling Burdens State Department," *The National Law Journal,* June 28, 2010, p. 47.)

4. Some political commentators have argued convincingly that in recent years the United States Supreme Court has shifted from a liberal to a conservative interpretation of the United States Constitution. These commentators have characterized the court as a battleground between two ways of interpreting the rights guaranteed under the Constitution: the conservative position represented by Chief Justice John Roberts, Justice Clarence Thomas, Justice Samuel Alito, and Justice Antonin Scalia; and the liberal position represented by Justice William Brennan and Justice Ruth Bader Ginsburg. Some decisions made by the court have limited the ability of plaintiffs to bring civil rights actions, while others have limited the right to privacy and the rights of criminal defendants. Using the negative rights theory, defend the court's limitation of such rights. Now using rational ethics show how such limitation might be considered unethical. (See Erwin Chemerinsky, "Constitutional Protections Under Attack," *The National Law Journal,* September 13, 2010, p. 43.)

5. Ethical codes of conduct are helpful standards that develop general guidelines for the conduct of professionals. However, they are frequently limited in their application because of their length, their complexity, and their ambiguity. A case in point is Rule 8.5 of the Ohio Rules of Professional Conduct for Attorneys. This rule dictates that the rules themselves will apply in multijurisdictional cases to the jurisdiction in which the lawyer "*reasonably believes* the predominant effect of the lawyer's conduct will occur." Of course, the complexity of multijurisdictional transactions and the ambiguity of the phrase "reasonably believes" leave the rule open to a wide variety of interpretations. Consequently, the jurisdiction with the "predominant effect" may not be immediately self-evident. Explain how the theory of utilitarianism might help clear up the ambiguity inherent in this situation. Now explain how utilitarian principles might deteriorate into utility thinking in this situation. (See "Ohio Professional Conduct Rule 8.5 Discipline Authority; Choice of Law." See also: Deborah L. Rhode, "Legal Ethics on a Global Scale," *The National Law Journal,* September 20, 2010, p. 38.)

6. William Yurchak, vice president of production for Dragonfly Enterprises, was passed over for what he believed was a much deserved promotion to the presidency. Instead of promoting Yurchak, the board of directors of Dragonfly, a firm that specializes in the development and production of recreational aircraft, decided to hire an outsider. Clyde Kellor, the chair of the board of Vostok Incorporated, one of Dragonfly's chief competitors, offers Yurchak the presidency of Vostok. Although Yurchak still has three years to run on his contract with Dragonfly, he is tempted to take Kellor's offer because he feels that he has been badly treated by Dragonfly and because he could use the 50 percent raise that Kellor has offered him. Kellor has added one stipulation: He wants Yurchak to bring with him the plans for Dragonfly Six, the corporation's latest revolutionary aircraft. Was it ethical for the board of Dragonfly to hire an outsider as president? Is Kellor's offer to Yurchak ethical? Would the offer be ethical if Kellor had not added the request for the Dragonfly Six plans? What is the ethical course of action for Yurchak? Explain all of your answers.

7. Barbara McMahon is a reporter for *The Lake County Press.* McMahon is approached by Julie Bryant, a research scientist for the International Chemical Corporation. Bryant, who asks for and receives a promise of confidentiality from McMahon, informs the reporter that International Chemical has been disposing of its chemical waste product by illegally dumping it in the Lake County River. On the strength of Bryant's word alone, *The Lake County Press* runs a series of articles on the illegal dumping. The district attorney of Lake County elects to prosecute the president and board members of International. At the trial, McMahon is called as a witness and asked to reveal her confidential news source. The state in which Lake County is located does not recognize any journalist–news source privilege. The judge tells McMahon that if she does not reveal her source, she will be placed in jail until she does so. Was it ethical for Bryant to go to McMahon with her confidential story in the first place? Was it ethical for McMahon to print the news stories on the basis of Bryant's word alone? Would it be ethical for the judge to place McMahon in jail? What is the ethical course of action for McMahon? What is the ethical course of action for Bryant? Defend all of your responses.

## quick quiz Answers

| 1-1 | 1-2 | 1-3 | 1-4 | 1-5 |
|-----|-----|-----|-----|-----|
| 1. F | 1. T | 1. T | 1. F | 1. T |
| 2. F | 2. F | 2. T | 2. F | 2. T |
| 3. T | 3. T | 3. T | 3. T | 3. F |

# Chapter 2 — Sources of the Law

## THE OPENING CASE  When the States Challenge Federal Authority

In an attempt to deal with the problems associated with illegal immigration, the state of Arizona passed a new statute that empowered local law enforcement officials to inspect the identification papers of anyone who might be in the country illegally. The law caused a wave of protests across the nation, mostly from people who saw the statute as racially biased. Arizona state officials argued that they had been forced to act because the federal government had done a terrible job of policing the borders and that, as a result of this neglect, there had been an unprecedented rise in violence associated with illegal border crossings. Many American citizens supported the Arizona law and encouraged their state governments to pass similar legislation. Despite the support for the state immigration statute, the federal government sued the State of Arizona in an attempt to block the administration of the law. The Justice Department, under the control of Attorney General Eric Holder, argued that federal law trumped state law in this case because the Constitution gave the power to control immigration to the national government. The Supremacy Clause of the U.S. Constitution does in fact state that, "(t)his Constitution and the Laws of the United States . . . shall be the supreme Law of the Land." Thus, it would seem that the federal government had a solid argument. Still it

is strange that the government avoided the discrimination claim and chose, instead, to rely on the technical argument of federal supremacy. In essence, the Justice Department chose to challenge the law based on a minor "technicality," rather than on a more substantive civil rights claim. As you read the chapter, see if you can determine if the federal government is right in its claim. Also, see if you can offer a few counter arguments to support Arizona's position. Finally, try to determine why the Justice Department decided to fight the law based on a technicality, rather than something more substantial. (See "Immigration: Why Did Obama Sue Arizona?" *The Week*, July 23, 2010, p. 6.)

**Opening Case Questions**

1. What powers regarding citizenship were given to the federal government in the U.S. Constitution? Explain.

2. What powers regarding citizenship were given to the state governments in the U.S. Constitution? Explain.

3. In what article and section is the Supremacy Clause of the U.S. Constitution located and why did the Framers include such a clause? Explain.

4. What clause in the U.S. Constitution gives the executive branch of the federal government the power to make certain that the laws of the United States are faithfully executed? Explain.

5. If Arizona (or any other state for that matter) wanted to shift the power to regulate immigration to the states, what would it have to do and how can that be accomplished? Explain.

 Learning Objectives

1. List the objectives of the law.
2. Clarify the duality of the law.
3. Outline the content of the U.S. Constitution.
4. Explain several central constitutional principles and powers.
5. Explain the role of statutory law in the legal system.
6. Defend the need to set up a system of uniform laws.
7. State the role of common law in the legal system.
8. Describe how the principle of *stare decisis* provides stability within the law.
9. Differentiate between statutory interpretation and judicial review.
10. Account for the legislature's need to establish administrative agencies.

# 2-1 The Purpose and Operation of the Law

As explained in Chapter 1, the **law** consists of rules of conduct established by the government to maintain harmony, stability, and justice within a society. Ideally, the primary objectives of the law should be balanced equally at all times. Unfortunately, in "real life," this balance is not easy to maintain. Often justice must be sacrificed for harmony and stability. Sometimes the opposite is true.

## The Law as a Balancing Act

The law should be viewed as a delicate balancing act. One person's rights are enforced while another's are not. One group is allowed to act while another group is limited in what it is permitted to do. One person is allowed to go free while another is imprisoned, fined, and forced to forfeit his property. One corporation's contracts are upheld while another's are struck down. Trade-offs like this occur within the law on a regular basis. Generally, the objectives of order, stability, and justice are kept in mind when such decisions are made. Because the law is made by people, however, it is not perfect. Legislators, judges, and administrators bring their own limitations into the process. Still, most of them do their best to be as objective and fair as possible. The law is made even more complex because it involves a series of competing dualities.

## The Dualities within the Law

What is often *not* clear is that the need to balance rights and duties within the law is not unusual. Rather, this balancing act is part of the law's fundamental nature. As Anthony Chase explains in his study, *Law and History,* the legal system is shaped by several dualities, each of which is essential to the law's success. These dualities include the balance between the spirit and the letter of the law, between legal words and their interpretation, and between abstract principles and concrete situations. This balancing act also comes into play in the application of the Uncertainty Principle to the law. [See Anthony Chase,

"Historical Jurisprudence: I. Inside/Outside," *Law and History: The Evolution of the American Legal System* (New York: The New Press, 1997), pp. 12–19.]

### The Spirit and the Letter of the Law

According to Chase, one of the most obvious dualities in the law is the balance between the **spirit** and the **letter of the law.** Generally, a person who follows the spirit of the law has found its actual intent, while one who is tied to the letter of the law has missed its true meaning. However, this is not always the case. Sometimes, following the letter of the law to avoid the spirit of the law can be a good thing. Thus, a shop owner who is discouraged by the complexity and intrusiveness of the law might avoid a prohibition against the sale of alcohol on Sunday by "giving away" bottles of wine to his customers who come in the next day and "give" the shop owner cash which just happens to be equivalent to the cost of their Sunday "gift." The shop owner has met the letter of the law by not "selling" alcohol on Sunday, but he and his customers have clearly violated the spirit of the law. Is this a good thing? We'll leave that to your imagination. (See Chase, pp. 12–14.)

### Words versus Interpretation

Chase explains that much of the confusion over the spirit of the law emerges when the law is written down. Because words are often ambiguous, the language of the law can become a hindrance rather than a help in the execution of the law. This is why it is sometimes necessary to manipulate the language in order to uncover the actual intent of the lawmakers and to apply that intent in a consistent and fair fashion. Certainly, this oddity opens the law to adjustments that are sometimes good and sometimes bad. However, to view this particular brand of duality, **words** versus **interpretation**, as either a strength or a weakness would be an error because it is neither. Instead, it is merely how the law works. (See Chase, pp. 14–15.)

### The Abstract and the Concrete

According to Chase, duality in the law is also seen in the work of judges, legislators, and administrators. In one way or another, all three are involved in the law-making process, and as a result, all three must tackle a third type of duality, that which exists between *abstract* principles and *concrete* situations (Chase, p. 15.) Thus, at times, legislators must take a principle, such as the idea that the government should be fair and equitable whenever it enacts a new tax bill, and apply that abstraction to a concrete piece of legislation. Similarly, a judge must take an abstract principle, such as the notion that all physicians must act with due care in performing their duties, and apply that principle in a case in which Dr. Jones's fails to properly diagnose Mr. Smith's ailment. In all such cases, it is not possible to eliminate the tension that exists between the duality of the abstract and the concrete. The only thing that can be done is for lawmakers to deal with the concrete incident without violating the abstract principle. This is not the end to the duality issue, however. In another study of the law, Gerald Turkel points out that this duality (Turkel calls is bipolarity) exists in the very nature of a lawsuit when the plaintiff and the defendant face off against one another. This bipolarity, is the essence of the adversarial system. [See Gerald Turkel, *Law and Society: Critical Approaches* (Boston: Allyn and Bacon, 1996), p. 13.]

### EXAMPLE 2-1: Attempting a Fair and Equitable Tax

Sometimes lawmakers must apply an abstract principle, such as the idea that the government should be fair when it taxes the people, to a concrete piece of legislation. This is exactly what happened at the end of President Obama's first two years in office when Republicans and Democrats negotiated a tax plan that addressed the concerns of taxpayers, businesses, and unemployed workers. In brief, here is what resulted when the *abstract* met the *concrete*. Every taxpayer saw a two-year continuation of the tax rates that were in place under the old law. Lower income workers received an increase in the child tax credit of $1000. Upper income taxpayers saw a favorable alteration in the estate tax rate and middle income workers received an extension of a tax credit for students. Businesses received a continuation of research and development tax credits and unemployed workers continued to receive the same benefits in place under the old law. Was the bill completely fair? Probably not. Was everyone satisfied? Certainly not. Did the system and everyone in it survive? Of course. Why? Simple. The legislature took an abstract principle ("let's be fair to everyone when we develop a new tax law") and applied that abstract principle to the concrete reality of competing constituencies (taxpayers, businesses, and the unemployed). In the ultimate mix everybody gets something and everybody loses something, and in the final analysis, that is the way a well-balanced legal system works. (See Jonathan Weisman, John D. McKinnon, and Janet Hook, "Deal Struck on Tax Package: Grand Bargain Includes One-Year Drop in Wage Levy, Estate Tax of 35%" *The Wall Street Journal,* December 7, 2010, pp. A-1-A-2).

**The Uncertainty Principle**   Duality also exists in the way a decision is intended and the way it is actually executed. The two, intent and result, almost never coincide, and when they do it is generally a matter of luck, nothing more. This principle, which is generally referred to as the *uncertainty principle,* exists in physics, in politics, and in economics. John Maynard Keynes recognized the uncertainty principle in economics and made it one of the lynch pins of his economic theory. Uncertainty between intentions and results in the law is very common. It occurs when legislators pass statutes that are vetoed by the chief executive; when a trial judge rules on a case that gets overturned by an appellate court; and when the chief executive makes an appointment that is nullified by the legislature. (See Chase, p. 19; See also Robert Skidelsky, "Keynes's Economics: Uncertainty," *Keynes: The Return of the Master* (New York: Public Affairs, 2010), pp. 83–85.) Moreover, the legal scholar Richard Posner tells us that this inclination toward  uncertainty, especially as it relates to economics, is exacerbated by the fact that some

## THE OPENING CASE *Revisited, Part I*
When the States Challenge Federal Authority, Round 2

In the Opening Case at the beginning of this chapter, we learned that Arizona passed a statute that enabled the police to inspect the identification papers of anyone who might be in the country illegally. The intended goal of the new law was to solve the problems associated with illegal immigration. However, instead of solving those problems, the new law unexpectedly ignited a series of unintended consequences. First, the new law sparked a wave of protests across the nation, mostly from people who saw it as a racially biased statute that victimized minorities. Second, the federal government, which the Arizona state officials argued was doing a terrible job of policing the borders, did not address the border problem but instead sued the state of Arizona in an attempt to block the administration of the new law. Third, the federal government's suit did nothing to address the issue of immigration or the problems associated with illegal immigration. Instead, the Attorney General and his entourage simply used

the much safer technical argument of federal supremacy. Thus, nothing intended by the state came to pass, and much that was unintended emerged, demonstrating the unavoidable operation of the uncertainty principle. (See "Immigration: Why Did Obama Sue Arizona?" *The Week,* July 23, 2010, p. 6.)

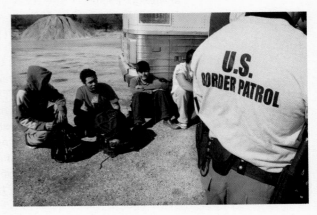

people act in unpredictable ways on a regular basis, while others react to what their neighbors have done. What is true in economics is equally true in the law. (See Richard Posner, *A Failure of Capitalism* (Cambridge; Harvard UP, 2009), pp. 83–84).

---

### quick quiz 2-1

| | | |
|---|---|---|
| 1. The law consists of rules of conduct established by the government to maintain harmony, stability, and justice within a society. | true \| false | |
| 2. Often justice must be sacrificed for harmony and stability, but the opposite is never true. | true \| false | |
| 3. Legislators and judges bring their own personal prejudices and biases into the process. | true \| false | |

---

# 2-2 Constitutional Law

The law has been defined as rules of conduct created by the government to maintain harmony, stability, and justice within a society. This definition is adequate, but it is also somewhat limited. It does not explain where the government comes from or who gives it the power to make those rules.

In some societies, the government is represented by a hereditary monarchy. In others, the establishment of a government depends on which political faction can muster the necessary power to take control of that nation's resources. In the United States, the government was established by a constitution.

A **constitution** is the basic law of a nation or state. The United States Constitution provides the organization of the national government. Each state also has a constitution that establishes the state's governmental structure. The body of law that makes up a constitution and its interpretation is known as **constitutional law**.

---

## EXAMPLE 2-2: Constitutional Law in the UK

Unlike the United States Constitution, the British Constitution has never been reduced to a single document. However, contrary to popular opinion, including the views offered by Jon Stewart on *The Daily Show,* this does not mean that the British government has no constitution. On the contrary, the principles that make up the British Constitution are found in many documents including the *Magna Carta,* an endless series of court cases, and a complex mix of statutory law. There are of course problems with this fragmented approach. First, the amalgam of legal precedents that makes up the British constitution plays right into the problems associated with the uncertainty principle. This occurs because it is difficult to know what precedent will be called upon to support or to attack a particular legal position. Second, the absence of a written failsafe system like that found in the American Constitution opens the door to power abuse in the British system. Third, while the British constitutional method avoids the ambiguities associated with the need to determine the difference between the words and the interpretation of those words, the British must still deal with this duality whenever statutes and cases are interpreted by the courts. Finally, when interpreting the British constitution, there is no need to distinguish between the letter of the law and the spirit of the law since, at least in relation to constitutional law, in the British system, there simply is no letter of the law. (See Sarah Lyall, "As a New Government Goes to Work, the Constitution Offers Britain Few Guides," *The New York Times,* May 25, 2010, p. A6.)

# The Articles of Confederation

The Constitution of the United States, as it exists today, is not the nation's first constitution. The first constitution was known as the **Articles of Confederation**. The Articles of Confederation were created to hold together a fragile coalition of states, each of which was determined to maintain its own independent existence. Although the Articles of Confederation fulfilled a much needed function during the first years in the life of the United States, they contained certain weaknesses.

One of the primary weaknesses was the fact that the United States in Congress, as the national legislature was known under the Articles, could not impose taxes or tariffs. Although a common treasury was supposed to be supplied by the states in proportion to the value of the land within each state, the states retained the power to levy and collect taxes. In essence, this rule meant that the United States in Congress had to rely on the goodwill of the states to obtain money. Such revenues were rarely forthcoming. Some states paid nothing at all; others turned over a portion of what they owed but rarely by the date the payments were due. Part of this problem was caused by the fact that the states were not about to trade one dictatorial central government for another and, therefore, simply ignored the national government.

Moreover, the desire to prevent the type of tyranny that the colonies had experienced under the rule of King George and the British Parliament led the framers of the Articles to include other limitations on the national government. For instance, all delegates to the Congress were appointed by the state legislatures and served at their pleasure. Several times, the national government found itself powerless to act, because some of the legislatures did not even bother to send delegates to Congress. In addition, whereas the United States in Congress had the authority to regulate the value of any money created under its own authority or under the authority of a state, the states retained the power to issue their own currency.

This is not to say that the Articles did not have some strong points. The Articles did, in fact, establish a few principles that became part of the U.S Constitution and a few others that we arguably should have kept. For example, under both the Articles and the U.S. Constitution, members of Congress are guaranteed that they will not be arrested while on the way to or returning from a session of Congress, except for treason, a felony, or breach of the peace. Both documents also contain a full faith and credit clause under which each state is required to honor the public acts, records, and judicial proceedings of all the other states. The Articles also contain a clause that limits the terms of congressional delegates and one that limits the term of the president, something that should have been retained from the outset under the U.S. Constitution.

Despite these strong points, the weaknesses of the Articles far outweighed its strengths and so, in the summer of 1787, 12 of the 13 states sent delegates to a Constitutional Convention in Philadelphia. The purpose of the convention was to revise the Articles. However, the Articles were so weak and the nation was in such disarray that the delegates decided to write a new constitution, the result of which is the present U.S. Constitution. In writing this new constitution, the delegates must have done something right because their document has lasted for more than two centuries. Still, some legal scholars and several historians argue that the action taken by the delegates at the convention was illegal. Moreover, there is some merit to this position. Article XIII of the original Articles states that the only way to amend the Articles is by a vote taken by "a Congress of the United States." Did the Constitutional Convention act as "a Congress of the United States" or were the delegates acting on their own and outside the authority of the Articles? It is an interesting question, one that might merit further attention at some time in the future. For now, however, we turn to an examination of the U.S. Constitution.

# The Principles of the United States Constitution

The Constitution of the United States is based on two fundamental principles that were supported by many of the delegates to the convention in Philadelphia. Those two principles promote, first, a separation of national powers among three distinct branches of government

## THE OPENING CASE *Revisited, Part II*
### When the States Challenge Federal Authority, Round 3

In the Opening Case, Arizona passed a statute that enabled the police to demand identification papers from anyone suspected of being an illegal alien. Also recall that, in reaction to this law, the federal government sued Arizona in an attempt to block the administration of that law. In its brief, the Justice Department argued that federal law trumps state law in this case because, under Article I, section 8, clause 4, of the U.S. Constitution, Congress alone has power to control the naturalization of citizens. To further cement their position the Justice Department also called upon the Supremacy Clause which says that, "(t)his Constitution and the Laws of the United States . . . shall be the supreme Law of the Land." Thus, it would seem that the Justice Department has a solid argument in this case. Interestingly enough, under the Articles of Confederation, the results would have been different. When we examine the Articles we would find that, under Article II, "(e)ach state retains its sovereignty, freedom, and independence, and right, which is not by this Confederation expressly delegated to the United States, in Congress assembled." Moreover, a lengthy and detailed search of the Articles reveals that the naturalization of citizens is not mentioned anywhere. The Articles do explain that, in most situations, only Congress can negotiate treaties, send and receive

ambassadors, and declare war, but the Articles make no mention of immigration or naturalization, indicating that, under Article II, such matters are left to the states. Now remember that there are reputable legal scholars and historians who believe that the Articles of Confederation were violated when the delegates to the Philadelphia convention created a new constitution. Consequently, if Arizona wanted to play hard ball with the feds, it could argue (1) that the Articles of Confederation could only be amended by a "Congress of the United States"; (2) that the Constitutional Convention held in Philadelphia did not qualify as "a Congress of the United States" and could not, therefore, amend the Articles; (3) that, even if the Convention was "a Congress of the United States," it did not have the power to simply "tear up the original Articles" and "start from scratch"; (4) that, in either case, the Articles of Confederation are still in effect and that, under those Articles, the states retain the power to control the naturalization process, which means that the Arizona statute cannot be subject to a nonexistent supremacy clause and, therefore, is constitutionally sound under Article II of the Articles of Confederation. This argument would not work, of course, because it would require any federal court that so rules to recognize that it also has no right to exist, something that is unlikely to happen ever.

and, second, a system of checks and balances that allows each branch to oversee the operation of the other two branches. The principle of the separation of powers set up the now familiar three branches of the national government: the executive branch, the legislative branch, and the judicial branch. The principle of checks and balances allows each branch to share in the power of the other two branches.

## The Structure of the United States Constitution

The U.S. Constitution is divided into two parts: the articles and the amendments. The articles establish the organization of the national government. The amendments change provisions in the original articles and add ideas that the framers did not include in those articles.

U.S. Const. Articles I–VII (see pages 807–811)

**The Articles**   The first three of the seven articles distribute the power of the government among the legislative, executive, and judicial branches. Article I establishes Congress as the legislative (statute-making) branch of the government. Article II gives executive power to the president, and Article III gives judicial power to the Supreme Court and other courts established by Congress. Article IV explains the relationships among the states and the relationship between the federal government and the states, while Article V outlines the methods for amending the Constitution. Article VI establishes the U.S. Constitution, federal

## Table 2-1   Articles of the U.S. Constitution

| Articles | Content |
|----------|---------|
| Article I | Establishes the legislative branch of the federal government (the Congress) <br> Defines the duties and powers of each house <br> Outlines how Congress must conduct its business <br> Lists legislative powers granted to Congress <br> Lists powers denied to Congress <br> Lists powers denied to the states |
| Article II | Gives executive power and responsibilities to the president <br> Outlines the president's term of office, qualifications, and manner of election <br> Identifies the president as commander in chief <br> Gives the president power to make treaties |
| Article III | Establishes the Supreme Court and authorizes the establishment of other federal courts <br> Provides for trial by jury for crimes <br> Defines treason against the United States |
| Article IV | Defines interstate relations <br> Sets up the full faith and credit clause obligating each state to recognize the public acts and proceedings of other states <br> Provides for extradition of those accused of crimes in other states |
| Article V | Outlines the method of amending the Constitution |
| Article VI | Establishes the Constitution, federal laws, and federal treaties as the supreme law of the land |
| Article VII | Provides for the original ratification of the Constitution |

laws, and treaties as the supreme law of the land. Finally, Article VII outlines how the original 13 states would go about ratifying the new Constitution. Table 2-1 outlines the content of each article in the Constitution.

**The Amendments**   The amendments to the Constitution establish the rights that belong to the people, change some of the provisions in the original articles, and add ideas that the Framers did not include in those articles. Thus, the amendments are attempts to fine-tune the Constitution and update its provisions to meet the demands of a changing socioeconomic structure. The first 10 amendments of the Constitution compose the Bill of Rights. They were added soon after the ratification of the Constitution by the original 13 states. Other amendments that secure the rights of the people include the Thirteenth, which prohibits slavery; the Fourteenth, which guarantees equal protection of the law and due process; the Fifteenth, which guarantees voting rights; the Nineteenth, which extends voting rights to women; the Twenty-Fourth, which prohibits poll taxes; and the Twenty-Sixth, which extends the right to vote to eighteen-year-old citizens. Table 2-2 provides a more detailed look at the amendments.

## States Rights, Democracy, and the Amendment Process

The Articles of Confederation did not set up a democracy. From the very first statement to the very last sentence, the Articles expressly support state supremacy. Article II, for instance, explicitly establishes that each state retains its sovereignty, while Article V requires each state to keep a well-armed militia and empowers those states to launch a preemptive strike in the event

**Did You Know?**

Roman law was first codified into The Law of the Twelve Tables in 450 BC. The Twelve Tables declared that all free citizens had certain fundamental rights.

U.S. Const. Amendments I–XXVII (see pages 811–815)

## Table 2-2 Amendments to the U.S. Constitution

| The Bill of Rights | Pre–Civil War Amendments | Civil War Amendments | Progressive Amendments | Depression-Era Amendments | Modern Amendments |
|---|---|---|---|---|---|
| *Amendment I* Freedom of religion, speech, press, assembly | *Amendment XI* Lawsuits against the states | *Amendment XIII* Slavery is abolished | *Amendment XVI* The income tax is established | *Amendment XX* Terms of president, vice president, senators and representatives altered | *Amendment XXII* President's terms limited to two |
| *Amendment II* The right to bear arms and set up a militia | *Amendment XII\** President and vice president elected together | *Amendment XIV* Equal protection of the law, due process, citizenship | *Amendment XVII* Senators elected by direct election | *Amendment XXI* Prohibition repealed | *Amendment XXIII* Washington, DC gets electors |
| *Amendment III* The quartering of soldiers in homes is prohibited | | *Amendment XV†* Voting rights guaranteed | *Amendment XVIII‡* Prohibition established | | *Amendment XXIV* Poll taxes outlawed |
| *Amendment IV* Search and seizure by probable cause | | | *Amendment XIX* Women given right to vote | | *Amendment XXV* Disability of the president; vacancies in the vice presidency |
| *Amendment V* Grand juries, double jeopardy, self-incrimination, due process, and eminent domain | | | | | *Amendment XXVI* Vote extended to 18-year-olds |
| *Amendment VI* Procedures allowed in criminal cases | | | | | *Amendment XXVII* Congress prevented from voting itself instant pay raises |
| *Amendment VII* Jury trials in common law cases guaranteed | | | | | |
| *Amendment VIII* Bill of Rights guaranteed, cruel and unusual punishment prohibited | | | | | |
| *Amendment IX* People retain other rights | | | | | |
| *Amendment X* Powers reserved to states | | | | | |

\*Altered somewhat by the Twentieth Amendment. †Voting age changed by Twenty-sixth Amendment. ‡Repealed by Twenty-first Amendment.

of an imminent attack. Moreover, under the Articles, each state had only one vote in Congress and all Congressional delegates were chosen by the state legislatures and served at their pleasure. When the U.S. Constitution was written, many but not all of these provisions were lost. States no longer have the right to launch preemptive military strikes on their own, for example, and the members of the House of Representatives are now chosen by a vote of the people. Under the original Constitution, however, Senators were still chosen by the state legislatures, much as the delegates to Congress were chosen under the original Articles. This changed with the Seventeenth Amendment when the people were empowered to vote directly for senators.

There are some people who would like to see the Seventeenth Amendment repealed, or replaced with a new amendment that returns the process of electing senators back to the state legislatures. At first blush this idea may seem strange. After all, we have always been taught that the power of the government originates in the hands of the people. So why should the people not vote for senators in the same way that they vote for representatives. Those commentators who support the repeal of the Seventeenth Amendment are not anti-democracy as much as they are pro-states' rights. Like the delegates who wrote the original Articles, they believe that the states should have a voice in national politics. The federal government, or so the argument goes, would not be as powerful, as intrusive, as debt ridden, or as willing to spend tax dollars on pointless projects if the senators had to periodically answer to their state legislatures.

In fact, these commentators argue that the Seventeenth Amendment (along with the Sixteenth Amendment which led to our present income tax system) opened the way to a powerful central government which, despite the direct voting power of the people, is extremely undemocratic, at least in the way it responds to (or perhaps does not respond to) the will of the people. In contrast, those commentators who favor keeping the Seventeenth Amendment intact, argue, rather convincingly, that the amendment was part of a progressive trend that gave the vote to women (the Nineteenth Amendment), provided electors for the District of Columbia (the Twenty-Third Amendment), eliminated the poll tax (the Twenty-Fourth Amendment), and gave the right to vote to 18-year-olds (the Twenty-Sixth Amendment). Therefore, repealing the amendment would be a step backward, at least in terms of individual political rights. Moreover, one of the main purposes of the Seventeenth Amendment is to insulate the election of senators from the influence of corporations which, before the amendment, often provided monetary incentives for state legislatures to elect senators who favored big business. (See Tony Mauro, "The 17th Amendment Under Fire," *The National Law Journal,* November 22, 2010, pp. 1 and 8.)

## State Constitutions

Each state in the union adopts its own constitution. A state constitution establishes the state's government. It also sets down principles to guide the state government in making state laws and conducting state business. Most state constitutions are patterned after the U.S. Constitution. However, state constitutions tend to be longer and more detailed than the U.S. Constitution, because they must deal with local as well as statewide matters.

## The Principle of Supremacy

A basic principle of constitutional law is that the U.S. Constitution is the supreme law of the land. This principle of constitutional supremacy means that all other laws must be in line with constitutional principles. If a law somehow conflicts with the Constitution, that law is said to be unconstitutional. If it does not conflict, it will be upheld by the court as constitutional.

U.S. Const. Article VI
(see page 811)

## The Principle of Preemption

The Constitution also says that all federal laws that are made in line with constitutional principles are to be considered the supreme law of the land. Cases that involve such conflicts, however, are not always as clear cut as those that involve state statutes that conflict with the Constitution. **Preemption** is the process by which the courts decide that a federal statute must take precedence over a state statute. The preemption of a state statute can occur in three situations. First, Congress can be very clear about its intent and explicitly state that the federal statute preempts any state statute that covers the same issues. If that is the case, then all that remains for the courts is to determine which statutes are covered by the preemption clause. Second, state statutes can be preempted by federal statutes when they conflict with the objectives of federal legislation. Third, the courts will preempt a state statute that has entered an area of the law that is traditionally an area that the federal government handles, such as foreign affairs or banking.

## The Doctrine of Devolution

**Devolution** occurs when the courts redefine a right and shift the obligation to enforce a right from an upper level authority to a lower one. For instance, a court may decide that a state agency, rather than a federal one, can control what governmental employees, in the course of performing their duties, are permitted to talk or write about in relation to official policies, procedures, and programs. Such a prohibition might appear to violate the employee's Constitutional right of free speech as a U.S. citizen. However, in such cases, the court has decided that the duty and the power to define and enforce that right belongs to the state rather than to the federal government. It is important to note that the devolution of a right does not destroy that right. Rather, devolution simply redistributes the authority to define the nature of that right in certain situations. (See Isidore Silver, "Recent Supreme Court Opinions: A Devolving Constitution," *The National Law Journal*, March 12, 2007, p. 22; Robert Tannenwald, "Devolution: The New Federalism—An Overview," *New England Economic Review*, May/June 1998, 1–7.)

## A QUESTION OF ETHICS

### Federal Supremacy, Discrimination, and a Lesson in Ethics

A quick review of the Opening Case at the beginning of this chapter will remind us that Arizona passed a statute that empowered the local police to demand identification papers from anyone suspected of being in the country illegally. In response, the federal government sued the state of Arizona in an attempt to block the administration of the law arguing that federal law trumped state law in this situation because the Constitution gave the power to control immigration to the national government alone. Recall that the federal government could have argued that the law was discriminatory because it had a disparate impact on people of a particular color and a certain national origin. The question we pose here is not the relatively easy one of whether the Arizona statute is unethical. Rather, the question we ask is whether it is ethical for the Justice Department to use the relatively safe argument of federal supremacy while ignoring the far greater legal and moral transgression of deliberate, unapologetic, legislative discrimination?

## The Commerce Clause

The states have the power to regulate business under their inherent police power, a power that the federal government does not have. In contrast, the federal government's power to regulate business has emerged over the years out of the Commerce Clause of the U.S. Constitution. The Commerce Clause is found in Article I, Section 8, Clause 3. The wording of the clause is a study in simplicity; the interpretation is not. In fact, the clause and its long history clearly demonstrate the duality that exists in the law at all three levels: spirit versus letter, words versus interpretation, and abstract principle versus concrete situation. The clause reads, "Congress shall have Power To . . . regulate Commerce with foreign Nations and among the several states." The U.S. Supreme Court has held that the phrase "commerce power" means "the power to . . . prescribe the rules by which commerce is to be governed." This ruling sounds reasonable enough and, had the Court stopped at that point, many future problems might have been avoided.

The Court, however, did not stop. Nor was it obliged to. Over the years, as case piled upon case, the Supreme Court further refined its position, gradually broadening the federal government's power to regulate business. The power to regulate is so broad today that the federal government can regulate any business activity that affects interstate commerce, even if that activity takes place solely within the borders of a single state. Just about the only thing that the U.S. Supreme Court has not yet allowed the government to do is to force citizens, or anyone else for that matter, to participate in an activity whether they want to or not. In contrast, the states do sometimes order their citizens to engage in some forms of commerce, as when they require automobile owners to buy insurance. Such legislation, however, is permitted under the state's police power. On the other hand, even that power is limited. The state can require insurance, but only if a citizen actually wants to own a car. It is unlikely that a state can order a person to engage in a business activity merely because that person exists. Moreover, it is even more unlikely that the federal government has that power.

## The First Amendment

The First Amendment of the U.S. Constitution has been the source of much power over the last two centuries. However, it has also been the source of much controversy. This is to be expected because the First Amendment contains some of the most important rights in the Bill of Rights. These include freedom of the press, freedom of speech, freedom of assembly, and freedom of religion. Freedom of speech has always been a source of controversy because, by its very nature, speech has a political dimension that must be balanced with the actions that might be sparked by that speech. The limits that are placed on speech are easy to articulate but difficult to implement. One of these limits states that one person's freedom of speech is limited by next person's rights. Thus, if a person lies about someone and that lie hurts the other person's reputation, the speaker may find himself or herself liable for the tort of defamation. Similarly, people have the right to free speech including the right to criticize political candidates, but they do not have the right to incite violence.

**quick quiz** 2-2

1. The present U.S. Constitution is the only constitution that the United States has ever had.   true | false

2. The principle of separation of powers was never adopted by the framers of the U.S. Constitution.   true | false

3. A basic principle of constitutional law is that state law is the supreme law of the land.   true | false

# 2-3 Statutory Law

Laws passed by a legislature are known as statutes. At the federal level, statutes are the laws made by Congress and signed by the president. At the state level, statutes are enacted by state legislatures, such as the Ohio General Assembly or the Oregon Legislative Assembly. Many statutes prohibit certain activities. Most criminal statutes are prohibitive statutes. For instance, Ohio criminal law prohibits hazing, which is defined as coercing someone into doing an act of initiation that has a substantial risk of causing mental or physical harm. Other statutes demand the performance of some action. For instance, Ohio statutory law requires all motor vehicle drivers and passengers to wear safety belts. Some statutes, such as those that create governmental holidays or name state flowers, simply declare something.

## Codes and Titles

Statutes must be arranged, cataloged, and indexed for easy reference. This is done by compiling state and federal codes. A **code** is a compilation of all the statutes of a particular state or the federal government. All federal statutes, for instance, are gathered in the United States Code (USC), while all Ohio statutory law is collected in the Ohio Revised Code (ORC). In general, codes are subdivided into **titles**, which are groupings of statutes that deal with a particular area of the law. Title 17 of the Ohio Revised Code, for example, covers corporations and partnerships. Often titles are subdivided into chapters, and chapters subdivided into sections. Thus, ORC 1701.03, *Purposes of a Corporation,* can be read from right to left as the third section of the first chapter of Title 17 of the ORC.

## Uniform Laws

Because many different statutes are passed each year by the 50 state legislatures, statutory law differs from state to state. This lack of consistency can cause problems when legal matters cross state boundaries. One solution to the problem of inconsistent statutory law is for all the state legislatures to adopt the same statutes. The National Conference of Commissioners on Uniform State Laws (NCCUSL) was founded to write these uniform laws. The NCCUSL is composed of commissioners that come from every state, the District of Columbia, Puerto Rico, and the Virgin Islands. These commissioners are usually selected by the governor. Most of the commissioners serve for a term of years set by the state. Some however have no set term and therefore can be replaced by the governor at any time. The number of commissioners from each jurisdiction is established by that jurisdiction. Some jurisdictions decide to have a lot of commissioners, while others decide to send only a few. California, for example, appoints 14, while New Hampshire limits its number to 3. The states are also responsible for sending money to the NCCUSL to support its activities. The more populated states generally pay more than the smaller states.

Just about anybody can submit a suggestion for a uniform law. However, most often, such suggestions come from the states, the American Bar Association, and those people in a particular profession or activity who have a specific interest in that area of the law. Recent topics that have been considered for uniform laws include genetic engineering, organ donation procedures, and the electronic discovery of evidence during lawsuits. Once a suggestion has been made, the NCCUSL's Committee on Scope and Program will appoint a committee to study the advisability of working on that uniform law. If the committee decides that such a law would be useful and appropriate, the committee members send the proposal back to the Scope and Program Committee, which then transmits the proposal to the executive committee and, eventually, to all of the commissioners. If everyone approves the proposal, they set up a drafting committee. As the name suggests, the job of the drafting committee is to write the actual uniform law, point by point. After the draft is written, it must be reviewed and voted upon. This can be a long and involved process that includes input from the states, legal experts, and those people, businesses, organizations, and institutions directly affected by a newly proposed law. Once the entire group of commissioners has voted to endorse a law, the state delegations must then vote to confirm it also. After a proposed uniform law is accepted by the state delegations within the NCCUSL, it is recommended to the state legislatures for adoption. Some states may adopt it, others may not. Remember that a uniform law does not become a binding statute until it has been officially passed by a state legislature.

## A QUESTION OF ETHICS

### The NCCUSL and a Lesson in Ethics

Very few people, even those commentators who are concerned with the injustice associated with the Arizona immigration law, the inequities within the new tax law, or the attack on states' rights symbolized by the Seventeenth Amendment, care, discuss, or even notice the vast power that has been placed in the hands of a group of unelected legal experts who write uniform laws and then pass those laws onto state legislators, many of whom simply enact those uniform codes into law, sometimes without changing a single word. The NCCUSL manufactures literally dozens of these uniform codes covering such diverse topics as tort law, corporate law, family law, and surrogate parenting law, just to name a few. Is it ethical for legislators to abdicate their responsibility for the state's legislative agenda by turning it over to these unelected, private "experts"?

## The Uniform Commercial Code

The most significant development in uniform state legislation has been the Uniform Commerical Code. The **Uniform Commercial Code (UCC)** is a unified set of statutes designed to govern almost all commercial transactions. The basic principles of commercial law were not changed by the UCC provisions. By defining and clarifying often misunderstood business and legal terms, the UCC helps parties involved in commercial transactions prepare their contracts. Even the famed UCC, however, has been adjusted by various states, and not all states decide to the accept suggested amendments that come from the NCCUSL from time to time. Some states have even decided to eliminate some of the chapters and articles in the UCC that they have found obsolete or irrelevant or that do not fit within their established legal traditions. Louisiana, for example, which still uses the Napoleonic Code, has adopted only four of the nine articles. Nevertheless, the UCC remains one of the most successful achievements of the NCCUSL. The National Conference of Commissioners on Uniform State Laws maintains a Web site that includes the final drafts of all uniform acts that have been approved and recommended for adoption by the state legislatures.

## Cyber-Law Statutes

The advent of the Information Age has sparked the need for specific cyber-law statutes that address the problems associated with cyber-commerce. **Cyber-commerce** is the term applied to all cyber-transactions. The NCCUSL has responded to this challenge by creating several new uniform laws. For example, the Uniform Computer Information Transactions Act (UCITA) is designed to deal directly with cyber-contracts that involve the sale or licensing of digital information. Another uniform cyber-law approved by the commissioners for enactment by state legislatures is the Uniform Electronic Transactions Act (UETA). This uniform cyber-law points out those principles that should be used in every state to make certain that cyber-contracts are enforceable.

### quick quiz 2-3

| | |
|---|---|
| 1. Laws passed by a legislature are known as amendments. | true \| false |
| 2. Once the NCCUSL adopts a uniform law, it becomes binding in all states. | true \| false |
| 3. Cyber-commerce is the term that is applied to all cyber-transactions. | true \| false |

# 2-4 Court Decisions

When most people think of the law, they think of the Constitution or of statutes passed by Congress and the state legislatures. Although these two sources are important, they are not the only two sources of law in this country. The courts also make law in the following ways:

- Common law
- Interpretation of statutes
- Judicial review

## Common Law

The term *common law* comes from the attempts of early English kings to establish a body of law that all the courts in the kingdom would hold in common. At that time, judges in towns and villages had instructions to settle all disputes in as consistent a manner as possible. The judges maintained this consistency by relying on previous legal decisions whenever they faced a similar set of circumstances. In this way, they established a body of common law. As the process continued, judges began to record their decisions and share them with other judges. **Common law** is the body of previously recorded legal decisions made by the courts in specific cases. The process of relying on these previously recorded legal decisions is called *stare decisis* (let the decision stand). The previously recorded legal decisions themselves are referred to as precedents.

The legal system of the United States, except Louisiana, is rooted in the common law of England. These roots derive from the early American colonists who came from England and were governed by the English monarchy. Over time, English common law has been eroded in the United States by the passing of state statutes and court decisions that better meet the needs of today's society. Nevertheless, parts of the common law as practiced in England still exist in the laws of the United States today. Courts still apply the common law when there are no modern court decisions or statutes dealing with an issue in dispute.

Today's judges make decisions in the same way as their counterparts from the Middle Ages. They rely on precedent according to the principle of *stare decisis*. A **precedent** is a model case that a court can follow when facing a similar situation.

There are two types of precedent: binding and persuasive. **Binding precedent** is precedent that a court must follow. **Persuasive precedent** is precedent that a court is free to follow or ignore. Generally, whether a precedent is binding or persuasive is determined by the court's location. For instance, decisions made by the Florida Supreme Court would be binding in all Florida state courts but persuasive in all other states' courts.

Precedents, past decisions, form the basis of common law.

The U.S. Supreme Court has frequently emphasized the crucial role that precedent plays in the American legal system. In emphasizing the importance of precedent, the Court has outlined a series of questions that judges should ask as they contemplate whether to overturn a rule of law established in an earlier case. These questions include the following:

- Is the established rule still practical?
- Have so many people relied upon the rule that overturning it would cause difficulty and injustice?
- Is the rule still legally viable, or has it become merely a relic of an outdated and deserted legal doctrine?
- Is the rule still up to date, or has it become obsolete because of changes in society?

Only if judges can answer these questions satisfactorily should they consider overturning an established precedent.

## Statutory Interpretation

A second way that court decisions make law is in the interpretation of statutes. **Statutory interpretation** is the process by which the courts analyze those aspects of a statute that are unclear or ambiguous or that were not anticipated at the time the legislature passed the statute. When legislators enact a new statute, they cannot predict how people will react to the new law. Nor can they foresee all of its future ramifications and implications. Thus, when two or more parties have a dispute that challenges the statute, they may differ as to what the legislature had in mind when it wrote the statute. Also, legislators may have purposely made the language of a statute general. The job of reacting to unforeseen circumstances and making generalities fit specific circumstances falls to the courts. As a result, a judge may be called upon to determine how a certain statute should be interpreted.

Courts are not, however, free to interpret a statute at random. A court cannot interpret a statute unless it is faced with a case involving that statute. In interpreting a statute, a court looks to a variety of sources, including the legislative history of the statute and the old statute that the new statute replaced, if any. Naturally, the court also must review any binding precedent that interprets that statute. This requirement exists because the court must still rely upon previous cases when engaged in statutory interpretation, just as it does when deciding questions of common law.

## Judicial Review

A third way that courts make law is through **judicial review**, which is the process of determining the constitutionality of various legislative statutes, administrative regulations, or executive actions. In exercising the power of judicial review, a court will look at the statute, regulation, or action and compare it with the Constitution. If the two are compatible, no problem exists. However, if they are contradictory, one of the two must be declared void. Because the Constitution is the supreme law of the land, the Constitution always rules, and the statute, regulation, or action is ruled unconstitutional.

Naturally, in exercising the power of judicial review, the court also must review any binding precedent involved in the constitutional issue, because the court still must rely upon previous cases in judicial review, just as it does in common law and statutory interpretation. The lower courts in this country have the capacity to review issues of constitutionality and interpret the meaning of provisions within the U.S. Constitution. However, the ultimate authority, and therefore the final word, on such issues rests with the United States Supreme Court.

### quick quiz 2-4

| | |
|---|---|
| 1.  The process of relying on previous decisions is called *stare decisis*. | true \| false |
| 2.  Common law originated in France. | true \| false |
| 3.  Judicial review is another name for statutory interpretation. | true \| false |

# 2-5 Administrative Regulations

Neither legislators nor judges can administer to all aspects of today's society. Moreover, legislators are generalists; they are rarely experts in all areas over which they have power. Because legislators are generalists and today's problems are so complex, statutory law, created by legislators, is very limited in what it can do. To broaden the power of statutory law, legislators delegate their power to others. They do this when they create administrative agencies.

## Administrative Agencies

Federal administrative agencies administer statutes enacted by Congress in specific areas, such as communication, aviation, labor relations, working conditions, and so on. Similarly, agencies have been designated by the states to supervise intrastate activities. These agencies create rules, regulate and supervise, and render decisions that have the force of law. Their decrees and decisions are known as **administrative law**.

## Administrative Procedures Act

Problems sometimes occur because administrative agencies have the power to make the rules, enforce the rules, and interpret the rules. To help prevent any conflict of interest that could arise from these overlapping responsibilities, Congress passed the federal Administrative Procedures Act. Similarly, most states have adopted a uniform law known as the Model State Administrative Procedures Act. Under these two acts, an administrative agency planning new regulations must notify the affected parties and hold hearings to allow those parties to express their views. These acts also allow the courts to review agency decisions and rulings.

Fuel economy standards are rising, increasing the need for more fuel efficient vehicles to be produced.

## The Federal Register and the Code of Federal Regulations

The **Federal Register** is a publication that produces a daily compilation of new regulations issued by federal administrative agencies. The Federal Register operates within the National Archives and Records Administration under the authority of the Office of the Federal Register. The Government Printing Office is reponsible for actually printing the document, though today it is also available online. Most of the documents included within the Federal Register are directly related to the agencies. Those subdivisions devoted to the agencies include a section on rules and regulations, one on proposed rules, and one on notices of hearings, meetings, application deadlines, and administrative orders. There is also a section devoted to presidential orders and proclamations. Once a rule is finalized, it is included in the **Code of Federal Regulations (CFR)**, which is updated each year.

## quick quiz 2-5

| | |
|---|---|
| 1. Together, legislators and judges can administer all aspects of today's society. | true \| false |
| 2. Most legislators are specialists. | true \| false |
| 3. The decrees and decisions made by administrative agencies are known as administrative law. | true \| false |

# Summary

**2.1**  The law consists of rules of conduct established by the government to maintain harmony, stability, and justice within a society. Ideally, the primary objectives of the law are to promote harmony, stability, and justice. In everyday life, the balance is not easy to maintain. The law or, more properly, the entire legal framework consists of a series of dualities that must be resolved somehow.

**2.2**  A constitution is the basic law of a nation or state. The United States Constitution provides the organization of the national government. Each state also has a constitution that determines the state's governmental structure. The body of law that forms a constitution and its interpretation is known as constitutional law.

**2.3**  The laws passed by a legislature are known as statutes. At the federal level, these are the laws made by Congress and signed by the president. At the state level, statutes are enacted by state legislatures. Statutes must be arranged, cataloged, and indexed for easy reference by compiling state and federal codes. Because many different statutes are passed each year by the 50 state legislatures, there are important differences in state statutory law throughout the nation. One solution to the problem of inconsistent statutory law is for the legislatures of all the states to adopt the same statutes.

The National Conference of Commissioners on Uniform State Laws (NCCUSL) was founded to write these uniform laws.

**2.4**  Courts make law through common law, the interpretation of statutes, and judicial review. Common law is the body of previously recorded legal decisions made by the courts in specific cases. Statutory interpretation is the process by which the courts analyze those aspects of a statute that are unclear or ambiguous or that were not anticipated at the time that the legislature passed the statute, and judicial review is the process by which the courts determine the constitutionality of various legislative statutes, administrative regulations, or executive actions.

**2.5**  Federal administrative agencies administer statutes enacted by Congress in specific areas, such as commerce, communication, aviation, labor relations, and working conditions. Similar agencies have been designated by the states to supervise intrastate activities. These agencies create rules, regulate and supervise, and render decisions. To help prevent any conflict of interest that could arise from these overlapping responsibilities, Congress passed the federal Administrative Procedures Act. Similarly, most states have adopted a uniform law known as the Model State Administrative Procedures Act.

# Key Terms

administrative law, 40

Articles of Confederation, 29

binding precedent, 38

code, 36

Code of Federal Regulations (CFR), 40

common law, 38

constitution, 28

constitutional law, 28

cyber-commerce, 37

devolution, 34

Federal Register, 40

judicial review, 39

law, 25

persuasive precedent, 38

precedent, 38

preemption, 34

statutes, 35

statutory interpretation, 39

titles, 36

Uniform Commercial Code (UCC), 37

# Questions for Review and Discussion

1. What are the objectives of the law?
2. How does the law reflect a series of complex dualities?
3. What are the functions of the articles and the amendments of the U.S. Constitution?
4. What is the difference between the principle of preemption and the doctrine of devolution?
5. What is the role of statutory law in the legal system?

6. Why does this country need to set up a system of uniform state laws?

7. What is the role of common law in the legal system?

8. How does the principle of *stare decisis* provide stability to our legal system?

9. What is the difference between statutory interpretation and judicial review?

10. Why does the legislature need to establish administrative agencies?

## Cases for Analysis

1. On the very day that President Obama signed the 2010 Health Care bill into law, the attorney general of Virginia filed a lawsuit in federal district court arguing that parts of the statute were unconstitutional. Specifically, the attorney general argued that the new statute was unconstitutional because it required people to buy health insurance, which amounts to an unconstitutional extension of the Commerce Clause of the U.S. Constitution. The federal government argued that the Supreme Court has upheld federal laws regulating commercial activity even when that activity takes place solely within a single state, if the activity has an effect on interstate commerce. Clearly the failure to purchase health insualrance affects interstate commerce because, when one person does not purchase health insurance, the cost of treating that person will fall on the rest of society in one way or another. The Virginia attorney general disagreed, arguing that the cases that have upheld this principle have always involved commercial activities already taking place. They have never approved a mandate that forces someone to begin an activity that they would not have entered (in this case buying health insurance) absent the federal mandate. Therefore, the attorney general concluded, the health care law is unconstitutional. Should the statute be upheld or overturned given these arguments? Explain. (See Kevin Sacks, "Lying Ahead for Health Law, Years of Constitutional Wrangling," *The New York Times,* December 14, 2010, p. A22; See also: Kevin Sack, "Core of Health Care Law," *The New York Times,* December 14, 2010, pp. A1 and A22.)

2. Karen Silkwood was an employee at the Kerr—McGee Nuclear Power Plant in Oklahoma. During her employment there, she was apparently contaminated by exposure to plutonium. The contamination was so severe that she had to be sent to a special facility for an examination, and her personal belongings at her home had to be destroyed. After Silkwood died in an unrelated car accident, her father, as administrator of her estate, brought a lawsuit against the Kerr-McGee power plant. Under state tort law, Silkwood's estate was awarded actual damages of $505,000 ($500,000 for personal injuries, and $5,000 for property loss), and $10 million in punitive damages, that is, damages designed to punish the defendant for its wanton misbehavior. The power plant argued that when Congress passed the Atomic Energy Act, it intended to completely outlaw any state regulation of nuclear power plants. Permitting the plaintiff to receive punitive damages in this case would destroy that intent. Silkwood's father, as the plaintiff in the case, argued that there was no intent expressed by Congress to preempt tort law in the area of nuclear regulation. In fact, when the plaintiff searched the Congressional Record, he could find no evidence that Congress intended to replace state tort law by passing the Atomic Energy Act. He also found that whenever Congress passed statutes similar to the Atomic Energy Act, there was never any intention to replace state tort law. Therefore, the plaintiff concluded, Congress did not intend to preempt state tort law in this case either. Is the plaintiff correct? Explain. *Silkwood v. Kerr-McGee Corporation,* 464 U.S. 238 (U.S. Supreme Court).

3. Richard Ceballos worked as a deputy district attorney for the city of Los Angeles. Ceballos wrote a memo in which he criticized the accuracy of an affidavit in a case that he had been assigned to handle. In the memo, he expressed doubt about the truthfulness of another employee in the department. Ceballos also testified in court about his doubts in relation to the affidavit. Afterward, Ceballos was victimized by reassignments, transfers, and the loss of a promotion. He argued that the actions of his superiors violated his right to speak freely about this problem in his department. The district attorney's office argued that a public employee's right to free speech could be limited by a state agency when that speech was made in the exercise of his or her official duties. Ceballos argued that his free speech rights, as guaranteed by the First Amendment to the U.S.

Constitution, trumped any state action. The district attorney argued that the power to control the right of free speech in relation to public employees had devolved to the states. Is the district attorney correct? Explain. *Garcetti, et al. v. Ceballos,* 126 S. Ct. 1951 (U.S. Supreme Court).

4.  Barbara Rome entered Flower Memorial Hospital to undergo a series of X-rays. When she was ready for the X-rays, she was assisted by a student radiological intern. The intern placed Rome on the X-ray table and strapped her onto the table correctly. However, the intern did not properly fasten the footboard, which was located at the foot of the table. As a result of this error, Rome fell and was hurt when the table was raised. As a consequence, Rome brought a lawsuit against Flower Memorial Hospital alleging that the ordinary negligence of the intern had caused her injury. In contrast, the hospital argued that the lawsuit involved a medical claim, as defined under the state's medical malpractice statute. Whether a case involves ordinary negligence or a medical claim would determine whether the state's two-year statute of limitations for negligence or the state's one-year statute of limitations for medical claims would apply. This case clearly involves a difference of opinion on the interpretation of a statute. What sources might the court consider when interpreting the statute in question? *Rome v. Flower Memorial Hospital,* 635 N.E.2d 1239 (OH).

5.  The Heart of Atlanta Hotel brought an action against the United States seeking a judgment that would declare Title II of the Civil Rights Act of 1964 unconstitutional. Congress's power to enact the Civil Rights Act is based upon Article I, Section 8, Clause 3, which gives Congress the power to regulate commerce among the states. The Heart of Atlanta Hotel argued that the statute was an unconstitutional extension of congressional power. The hotel also contended that the unconstitutional nature of the act especially applied to establishments like itself, which are incorporated and do business in only one state. However, because at any given time, three-fourths of the hotel's registered guests came from other states, the hotel clearly had an impact on interstate commerce. Do the lower federal courts have the authority to determine the constitutionality of Title II of the Civil Rights Act? What court has the ultimate authority to determine the constitutionality of the Civil Rights Act? Speculate on the outcome of this case. Do you think that the court should uphold the act? Explain. *Heart of Atlanta Hotel v. United States,* 370 U.S. 241 (U.S. Sup. Ct.).

## quick quiz Answers

| 2-1 | 2-2 | 2-3 | 2-4 | 2-5 |
|-----|-----|-----|-----|-----|
| 1. T | 1. F | 1. F | 1. T | 1. F |
| 2. F | 2. F | 2. F | 2. F | 2. F |
| 3. T | 3. F | 3. T | 3. F | 3. T |

# The Judicial Process and Cyber-procedure

## THE OPENING CASE   When Is a Citizen Not a Citizen?

One of the most perplexing problems that litigators often face is where to bring a lawsuit. In the federal courts jurisdiction can be established either by demonstrating the case involves an issue directly related to federal law (federal question) or by demonstrating diversity jurisdiction. In most cases of diversity, the parties, the plaintiff and the defendant, must be citizens of different states. Again the problem is not difficult when dealing with flesh and blood people. However, when one of the parties is a corporation, the problems begin. This is because federal law defines the corporate citizenship as a duality. A corporation is a citizen (1) in the state in which it is incorporated and (2) where it has its principal place of business. Unfortunately, the concept of "principal place of business" is vague at best. In the case of *Hertz Corporation v. Friend* the United States Supreme Court directly addressed the issue of corporate duality. Of course, whether the court improved or aggravated the situation is still open to debate. In that case the Hertz Corporation was sued by a group of California citizens in a state court. Hertz, sensing the probable hostility of a California jury, asked that the case be removed to federal court, arguing that the proper forum would be in New Jersey where its corporate headquarters was located. The plaintiffs disagreed. In the alternative, they maintained that Hertz's "principal place of business" was really located in California because it was in California that Hertz did

the vast majority of its business. The trial court agreed, ruling that California was the corporation's principal place of business. The appeals court followed suit, but the U.S. Supreme Court did not. The Supreme Court ruled that a corporation has its "principal place of business" where its nerve center is located, that is, the state in which the activities of the corporation are controlled by corporate management. New Jersey, then, was the proper forum for Hertz, not California. Ironically, although in this case Hertz, the corporate defendant, won the battle, their victory may prove to be a mixed blessing. It is a victory because it will help corporations get into federal court by making diversity a more straightforward proposition. However, the decision will also increase the number plaintiffs that can sue the corporation in federal court, especially in class action cases. Why does limiting a corporation's principal place of business increase the number of potential plaintiffs? Think about that question when diversity jurisdiction is covered later in the chapter. [See *Hertz Corporation v. Friend,* No. 08-1107, slip. op. (February 23, 2010); and Michael McNamara and Christine Henge, "'Hertz' Expands Companies Access to Federal Court," *The National Law Journal,* April 12, 2010, pp. 16–17.]

**Opening Case Questions**

1. Is this case a civil lawsuit or a criminal action? Explain.

2. Why does this case begin in the state court? Explain.

3. Why would the defendant corporation want to move the case into the federal court system? Explain.

4. Under what circumstances can a case be held in the federal court system? Explain.

5. What Article in the U.S. Constitution established the federal court system and what branch actually establishes the courts? Explain.

## **LO** Learning Objectives

1. Explain the fundamental nature of the American courts.
2. Determine when a case can be brought in federal court.
3. Recognize those cases that can be heard by the U.S. Supreme Court.
4. Identify the structure of most state court systems.
5. Define civil litigation.
6. List the most common discovery techniques.
7. Detail the nature of an appeal.
8. Determine the extent of cyber-jurisdiction.
9. Explain the nature of electronically stored information (ESI).
10. Describe the steps in a criminal prosecution.

# 3-1 The Court System

The laws of the American government are interpreted and implemented by a system of courts authorized by either the federal or state constitutions and generally established by legislative authority. **Courts** are judicial tribunals that meet in a regular place and apply the law in an attempt to settle disputes by weighing the arguments presented by advocates for each party. Each of these official bodies is a forum for the party who presents a complaint, the party who responds to the complaint, and the jury and/or judge who settles the dispute. As noted in the previous chapter, the law involves a set of competing dualities including the spirit of the law versus the letter of the law, the words of the law versus the interpretation of those words, and the abstract principles of the law versus the concrete situations to which those principles are applied. Nowhere in the law are these dualities more obvious on a daily basis than in the court system. The same is true of the uncertainly principle which is played out every time a plaintiff and defendant place their case in the hands of a judge and jury.

## The Federal Court System

The federal court system is authorized by Article III of the U.S. Constitution, which states, "The Judicial Power of the United States shall be vested in one supreme court, and in such inferior courts as Congress may from time to time ordain and establish." The present federal court system includes the Supreme Court, courts of appeals, and federal district courts.

U.S. Const. Article III
(see page 810)

## Court Jurisdiction

The authority of a court to hear and decide cases is called the court's **jurisdiction**. It is set by law and limited as to territory and type of case. A court of **original jurisdiction** has the authority to hear a case when it is first brought to court. Those courts that have the power to review a case for errors are courts of **appellate jurisdiction**. Most of the time courts with appellate jurisdiction will be empowered to determine whether the lower courts have made errors of law. This process is referred to as plenary review. Sometimes an appellate court will review the factual decisions made by the judge or the jury in lower courts. Such a review, however, only occurs when the appeals court determines that the decision made in the lower court was undeniably wrong, given the facts and evidence in the case. This determination relies on the clearly erroneous standard. Appellate courts also have the ability to determine whether the judge in the lower court has in some way misused his or her authority. This type of review is referred to as abuse of discretion.

Courts with the power to hear any type of case are said to exercise general jurisdiction. Those with the power to hear only certain types of cases have special jurisdiction. Examples of courts with special jurisdiction are probate courts and courts of claims. Courts also exercise subject matter jurisdiction and personal jurisdiction. Subject matter jurisdiction is the court's power to hear a particular type of case. Personal jurisdiction is the court's authority over the parties to a lawsuit.

## Federal District Courts

Each state and territory in the United States has at least one federal district court. These courts are also known as *U.S. district courts*. The district courts are the courts of general jurisdiction in the federal system. Most federal cases begin in the federal district court. Not all cases belong there, however. The federal courts have subject matter jurisdiction over two types of cases: those involving federal law and those involving diversity.

Federal district courts have subject matter jurisdiction over cases that pertain to a federal question. A federal question could involve the U.S. Constitution, a federal statute or statutes, or a treaty. A state law issue can be included in a suit involving a federal question if the state claim is part of the same situation that created the federal question. If the federal claim is thrown out by the federal court, the state law issue usually cannot stand by itself. The people bringing the lawsuit would have to take their case to a state court.

Subject matter jurisdiction in federal court also arises in cases of diversity, even when no federal law is involved. Diversity cases include lawsuits that are (1) between citizens of different states, (2) between citizens of a state or different states and citizens of a foreign nation, and (3) between citizens of a state and a foreign government as the plaintiff. This last method of establishing jurisdiction usually applies only when a foreign government sues a citizen of a state. Congress has, however, provided an exception to this rule: Federal law now permits lawsuits in the federal courts against a foreign state when that state supports terrorism. The lawsuit must involve a request for damages arising from terrorist acts related to that support and as those acts are defined by law.

In diversity cases, and for other legal purposes, corporations are considered citizens of the state in which they are incorporated and the state where they have their principal place of business. In federal court, if even one defendant is a citizen of the same state as one of the plaintiffs, diversity cannot be established. In such a case, the law says that "diversity is not complete." Diversity cases also must involve an amount over $75,000.

Sometimes a case that begins in a state court can be transferred to the federal court. The process of moving a case from a state court to a U.S. District Court is called removal. Such requests are not granted on a whim. A defendant who wants to move a case from state court to federal court must have proper grounds for that removal. To convince the court to remove a case, a defendant must show that the case actually belonged in the federal court in the first case. This requirement means that the defendant will have to show that diversity exists or that a federal question was involved from the start. The defendant must file a motion to remove the case within 30 days of being served. It is also possible to remove a case to federal court even after the case has started, if circumstances change in the middle of a case, creating grounds for the removal. The statute of limitations on this type of move, however, is one year from the time that the case began, with the filing of the complaint.

## THE OPENING CASE *Revisited, Part I*
## When Is a Citizen Not a Citizen? Round 2

Recall that in the Opening Case, that the Hertz Corporation was sued by a group of California citizens who brought the case in a state court. Recall also that Hertz filed a motion asking that the case be removed from the California state court to the federal district court in New Jersey, where its corporate headquarters was located. In order to succeed in such a motion, Hertz would have to demonstrate that it had proper grounds for that removal. In this case, proper grounds would involve establishing diversity. That was the point of dispute in the case. The defendant argued that New Jersey was the proper pace for the case because New Jersey was where its "principal place of business" was located. On the other side, the plaintiffs contended that Hertz's "principal place of business" was California because Hertz did the vast majority of its business in that state. The trial court agreed with plaintiffs and dismissed the motion. The appeals court agreed and upheld the dismissal. The U.S. Supreme Court, however, disagreed and ruled that a corporation has its "principal place of business" where the activities of the corporation are controlled by corporate management. In this case that turned out to be New Jersey. Ironically, although in this case Hertz, the corporate defendant, won the battle, the victory may be a mixed blessing. It is a victory because it will help corporations get into federal court by making diversity a more straightforward proposition. However, the decision will also increase the number plaintiffs that can sue the corporation in federal court, especially in class action cases. Limiting a corporation's principal place of business increases the number of potential plaintiffs because it extends diversity jurisdiction to at least one additional state. Thus, before the *Hertz* case, if California actually were the corporation's principal place of business and if New Jersey were the state of incorporation, both the federal courts in California and those in New Jersey would have jurisdiction over the corporation. However, that also means that citizens of California and citizens of New Jersey cannot sue the corporation in federal court in their home states because there would be no diversity. After the *Hertz* case, with California eliminated as a "citizenship state," the citizens of California could sue the corporation in federal court in California under diversity. Of course, the citizens of California would also have to invoke the California "long arm" statute and either the doctrine of "minimum contacts" or the newer "stream of commerce" test, but at least they would have an initial forum for their case (See Example 3-1).

Establishing subject matter jurisdiction will not be enough to get a case into federal court if the federal court does not have personal jurisdiction over a party. To establish personal jurisdiction, the court must look at the long-arm statute in the state in which the federal court is physically located. The court must then look to see if an appropriate level of contact has been made with the home state. A long-arm statute lists circumstances in which a court can exercise personal jurisdiction over an out-of-state defendant. Typically, these circumstances include the following:

- Owning real property in the state.
- Soliciting business in the state.
- Having an office or a store in the state.
- Committing a tort within the state.
- Transacting business in the state.

Some of the circumstances listed in the long-arm statute are relatively clear. Committing a tort in a state, for instance, leaves little room for misunderstanding. Other circumstances, however, such as "transacting business in the state," are not as precise. Therefore, personal jurisdiction under a state long-arm statute also requires meeting the required minimum contacts with the state. The concept of **minimum contacts** identifies the fewest number of contacts needed to allow the court to exercise jurisdiction over the out-of-state defendant. For example, let's say that a state allows the court to establish personal jurisdiction over any person who transacts business in the state. Now suppose a person buys a newspaper at an airport during a layover in the state. Does the purchase of that single newspaper constitute "transacting business" in the state?

The question turns on whether the purchase establishes a minimum contact with the state. In this case, the answer is probably "no." In general, the courts exclude contacts that are passive or that do not rise to a level that would permit the person transacting the business to reasonably foresee that he or she would come under the court's jurisdiction as a result of that transaction. It is difficult to conclude that the casual purchase of a newspaper at an airport kiosk would lead a person to foresee that he or she has voluntarily submitted to the jurisdictional power of a state. Something more would have to be involved. For instance, if the person in question specifically targeted the airport layover time to conduct negotiations with a client, and if a contract resulted from those negotiations, then the minimum contacts requirement would have been met and jurisdiction established.

Most of the time a court will determine subject matter jurisdiction before turning to the question of personal jurisdiction. Determining subject matter jurisdiction first, however, is not absolutely necessary. If the issue of personal jurisdiction is very obvious to the court, the court is free to dismiss the case before considering the question of subject matter jurisdiction. For example, this dismissal might happen if the defendant meets none of the categories in the long-arm statute or clearly does not meet the minimum contacts required by the case law of a state. In fact, if determining subject matter jurisdiction is especially difficult, the court is free to look at personal jurisdiction first, without even considering the question of subject matter jurisdiction.

## EXAMPLE 3-1: The Stream of Commerce Theory

When attempting to establish personal jurisdiction over an out-of-state defendant, the plaintiff must convince the judge that the defendant had a set of "minimum contacts" with the state. Generally, the establishment of "minimum contacts" requires some kind of proactive strategy on the part of the defendant. This proactive strategy might involve opening a store, an office, a manufacturing plant, or a service center in the state. However, in some jurisdictions this is not always true. In the case of *Nicastro v. McIntyre,* for example, the Supreme Court of New Jersey established a standard called the *stream of commerce theory.* In this case, the plaintiff was injured by a product made by a British manufacturer. The plaintiff sued the manufacturer for failing to warn the ultimate user of a danger involved in the operation of the product, a metal press, and for a manufacturing defect related to the absence of an appropriate safety guard. The trial court dismissed the case because the plaintiff had failed to demonstrate the needed minimum contacts. The Supreme Court of New Jersey agreed that the plaintiff had not met the minimum contact test. Oddly, this did not stop the court from establishing personal jurisdiction over the manufacturer. To establish personal jurisdiction, the New Jersey court embraced a new theory of jurisdiction, the stream of commerce test. Under the stream of commerce test, the plaintiff must demonstrate that the defendant, in this case a foreign manufacturer, sent one of its products into "the stream of commerce" using a plan of national distribution that the manufacturer knew or at least reasonably should have known would in some way impact New Jersey. The New Jersey Supreme Court was satisfied that this was what had happened in the *Nicastro v. McIntyre* case. However, the New Jersey court *did limit* the stream of commerce standard to *product liability cases,* that is, cases in which the plaintiff claims to have been injured by a product manufactured or sold by the defendant. [See *Nicastro v. McIntyre,* 2010 N.J. Lexis 19 (N.J. Feb. 2, 2010); and J. Russell Jackson "Buy Globally, Sue Locally for Products Liability," *The National Law Journal,* March 22, 2010, p. 10.]

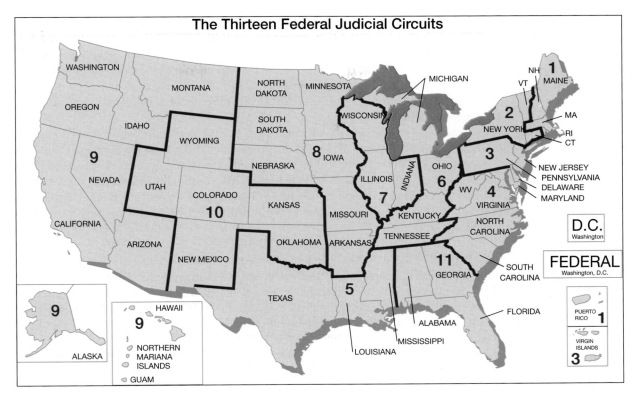

**Figure 3-1**   The U.S. federal court system is divided into 13 circuits, including the Washington, D.C., and federal circuits. Each circuit has several district courts.

## U.S. Courts of Appeals

The judges at the appellate level must be guided by the standard of review that is appropriate to each case. The standard of review tells the appellate-level judges the degree to which they must remain faithful to the decision of the lower court judge. As noted previously, the three standards of review are *plenary, clearly erroneous,* and *abuse of discretion.* Although they do not hear as many cases each year as the district courts, there are fewer U.S. courts of appeals and therefore fewer judges to hear those cases. The U.S. Courts of Appeals hear appeals from the district courts, the U.S. Tax Court, and from many of the administrative agencies. At present, there are 13 U.S. courts of appeals within the federal court system (see Figure 3-1). Eleven of these appellate courts cover geographical groupings of states. For example, the Sixth Circuit Court of Appeals includes Michigan, Ohio, Kentucky, and Tennessee. The Fifth Circuit includes Texas, Louisiana, and Mississippi. There is also a special appellate court for the District of Columbia called the U.S. Court of Appeals for the District of Columbia.

In addition to 12 appellate courts, organized on a geographical basis, there is a thirteenth appellate court that has special jurisdiction over certain types of cases. This court is known as the U.S. Court of Appeals for the Federal Circuit. The Federal Circuit was established by Congress primarily to streamline and unify patent law. However, the Federal Circuit was also given the power to hear appeals in cases that entail government contracts, trademark disputes, federal workers, veterans' benefits, and international trade, among others. Still, more than one-third of the appeals that end up in the Federal Circuit are patent cases that come either from the U.S. district courts or the U.S. Patent and Trademark Office. Critics of the Federal Circuit have argued that the court's approach to patent law has become too narrow and too formalistic. (See Marcia Cole, "Critics Target Federal Circuit," *The National Law Journal,* October 16, 2006, pp. 1, 20–21.)

### The United States Supreme Court

Established by the Constitution, the U.S. Supreme Court is the court of final jurisdiction in all cases appealed from the lower federal courts and in cases coming from state supreme courts. It has original jurisdiction in cases affecting ambassadors or other public ministers and consuls and in cases in which a state is a party. The Supreme Court is composed of a chief justice and eight associate justices. They are appointed by the president with the consent of the Senate and hold office during good behavior.

U.S. Const. Article III
(see page 810)

In many situations, a case will reach the U.S. Supreme Court only if the court agrees to issue a writ of certiorari. A **writ of certiorari** is an order from the Supreme Court to a lower court to deliver its records to the U.S. Supreme Court for review. The Court will issue a writ of certiorari if several lower courts have dealt with an issue but cannot agree on how it should be handled. If the case involves an issue that affects a large segment of society, the Court is likely to grant a writ. Finally, the Court may also hear a case if it involves a constitutional issue.

### Applicable Law

When a federal court hears a case involving only federal law or the U.S. Constitution, it must follow that federal law, the Constitution, and/or any line of federal precedent that can be used to interpret the situation. Circumstances are different in diversity cases or federal law cases that also concern issues of state law. For instance, if a federal judge in Minnesota hears a diversity case between a Minnesota citizen and an Iowa citizen, would that judge use federal law, Minnesota law, or Iowa law? As a general rule, a federal court hearing a diversity case will apply the law of the state in which it is physically located.

---

### EXAMPLE 3-2: The "Foreign-Cubed" Theory

Often, the question of what law to apply in a case is crucial to the management of a lawsuit. The law of one jurisdiction may favor the plaintiff while another may support the defendant. Often whoever wins the battle of jurisdictions also wins the battle of the law and, ultimately, the war itself. Such was the situation in the case of *Morrison v. Australian National Bank.* In that case, Morrison, the plaintiff, and the Australian National Bank, the defendant, were foreign citizens and the alleged fraud was carried out in a foreign country. Despite all of this, the case ended up in the United States District Court and eventually in the United States Supreme Court. The class action lawsuit was filed by the investors who argued that the bank had defrauded them by overvaluing the bank's mortgage portfolio. The suit was filed in federal court in the United States because much of the original data used to create the overvalued portfolio was compiled in the United States. When a foreign plaintiff files a case against a foreign defendant alleging fraud committed in a foreign country, that plaintiff has filed a "foreign-cubed" lawsuit. What makes a foreign-cubed case so complicated, besides the obvious jurisdictional problems, is the fact that often the alien plaintiffs file in the United States because their own home jurisdictions do not consider the behavior of the bank to be fraudulent. Thus, the questions of jurisdiction and choice of law become more than simply legal issues. They become ethical issues as well. Should the United States become the "world police" guarding against investment fraud anywhere on the planet, or should the American courts stay out of the dispute, thus respecting foreign traditions? (See Tony Mauro, "A Border Battle Over Lawsuits: High Court Challenges the Use of American Courts by Foreign Plaintiffs," *The National Law Journal,* March 29, 2010, pp. 1 and 26.)

---

### State Court Systems

The courts of each state are organized according to the provisions of the state constitution. Despite differences from state to state, such as the names for similar types of courts, there are basic similarities. For example, each state has an arrangement of inferior, or lower-level,

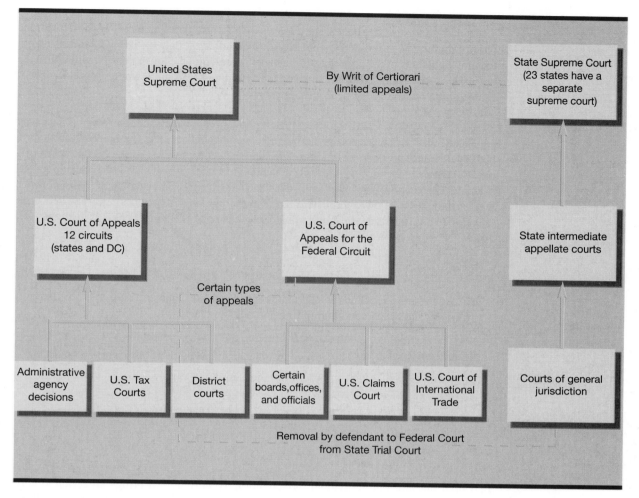

Figure 3-2  Federal and state court systems.

courts that serve as limited jurisdiction trial courts. Higher-level trial courts with broader jurisdiction are also provided. In addition, each state has appellate courts to which questions of law (not questions of fact) may be appealed. Figure 3-2 provides a general outline of the federal and the state court systems.

## State Trial Courts

The state trial courts, also known as general jurisdiction courts, have the power to hear any type of case. They are often called superior courts, circuit courts, or courts of common pleas. Some states, notably New York, refer to them as supreme courts. These courts are usually organized around the counties of the state, so that each county has its own trial court of general jurisdiction. Most states also have other trial courts that are lower than the general jurisdiction courts. These limited jurisdiction courts usually hear only certain types of cases. For instance, a municipal court may be empowered to hear only those cases that involve municipal ordinances, criminal cases involving crimes within the city limits, and other cases that involve monetary claims of less than $10,000. Many localities have small-claims courts that hear civil cases involving small dollar amounts, ranging from $500 to $5,000, depending on state law.

## State Intermediate Appellate Courts

State court systems provide for a variety of appellate court structures. Still, the purpose of the appellate courts remains the same, that is, to hear appeals on questions of law from the lower courts. Usually, appeals are heard by a three-judge panel. The panel examines the records of the lower court, reads the written arguments submitted by the attorneys, studies the law on its own, and listens to the oral arguments of the attorneys. If the panel agrees with the lower court, it will affirm the decision of that court. However, if the panel disagrees with the lower court's decision, it can set aside or modify the decision of that court.

**State Supreme Courts**   Twenty-seven states rely on their supreme court as their only appellate court. These states have no intermediate appellate courts. The other 23 states have both intermediate appellate courts and state supreme courts. Most supreme courts consist of a panel of three to nine judges. As is true at the intermediate appellate level, the panel of judges examines the records of the lower court, reads the written arguments submitted by the attorneys, studies the law on its own, and listens to the oral arguments of the attorneys. The decisions of state supreme courts are final unless a federal issue or a constitutional right is involved.

---

### quick quiz 3-1

| | | |
|---|---|---|
| 1. Courts are judicial tribunals that meet in a regular place and apply the laws in an attempt to settle disputes fairly. | true | false |
| 2. The authority of a court to hear and decide cases is called the court's jurisdiction. | true | false |
| 3. A writ of certiorari is an order from the Supreme Court to a lower court to deliver its records to the U.S Supreme Court for review. | true | false |

---

# 3-2 Civil Procedure

In a civil lawsuit, one individual, organization, or corporation brings an action against another individual, organization, or corporation. The objective of a civil suit is usually to obtain money to compensate the victim. **Civil litigation** is another name for the process of bringing a case to court to enforce a right.

## Commencement of the Action

The principal parties to a lawsuit are the plaintiff and the defendant. The **plaintiff** is the person who begins the lawsuit by filing a complaint in the appropriate trial court of general jurisdiction. The **defendant** is the person against whom the lawsuit has been brought and from whom a recovery is sought.

**Filing the Complaint**   The **complaint** sets forth the names of the parties to the lawsuit, identifying them as plaintiffs or defendants. Generally, the complaint includes the addresses of all parties. The complaint also sets forth the following:

- The facts in the case from the plaintiff's perspective.
- The alleged legal violations by the defendant.
- The injuries that the plaintiff suffered.
- The plaintiff's request for relief.

If the plaintiff wants a jury trial, this information must also be specified in the complaint. In federal court, the complaint must also include a statement of jurisdiction, which will tell the court whether the case has been brought in federal court because of a federal question or because of diversity among the plaintiffs and the defendants.

**Class Action Lawsuits**  At times filing a complaint is pointless because the amount of recovery for one plaintiff would be so low that it would not be worth the effort, energy, and expense a lawsuit. Sometimes, however, the extent of the harmful conduct is so pervasive and the number of plaintiffs so high that the cost of conducting the lawsuit is justified. This was the motivation that led to the creation of the class action lawsuit. A **class action** is a lawsuit in which one (or a small number) of the potential plaintiffs file a lawsuit on behalf of the entire class. The courts will permit a class action lawsuit provided that (1) it is not feasible for the members of the group to bring the action on their own; (2) the members of the group share common questions of law that can be tried together; and (3) the class action approach is far better than forcing the plaintiffs to file separate actions.

Unfortunately, class action lawsuits are easy to abuse. One of the most common abuses is forum shopping. **Forum shopping** occurs when a plaintiff searches for a jurisdiction with law that is favorable to its case, and then files the case in that jurisdiction. The defendant can do something similar by filing a motion to remove a case filed in state court to federal court. When a case features multiple plaintiffs, as in a class action lawsuit, forum shopping becomes easier because the number of possible jurisdictions increases as the number of plaintiffs from different states increases. In order to counteract abuses, Congress enacted the Class Action Fairness Act (CAFA). The act included a number of innovations designed to limit forum shopping and to counteract some of the other abuses associated with class actions.

For example, CAFA requires that the amount in controversy for a class action in federal court exceed $5 million. Second, CAFA also requires that the class bringing the actual class action lawsuit number at least 100 plaintiffs. Third, CAFA offers what is called the "home state exception" to personal jurisdiction. The exception limits federal jurisdiction by declaring that if two-thirds of the class action plaintiffs and the corporate defendants are from the same state there will be no federal jurisdiction. The net effect of all three of these provisions is to limit the tactic of filing in federal court, thus effectively limiting the forum shopping option. (See Archis Parasharami and Kevin Ranlett, "The Class Action Fairness Act, Five Years Later," *The National Law Journal*, April 12, 2010, pp. 14 and 18; and Michael McNamara and Christine Henge, "'Hertz' Expands Companies Access to Federal Court," *The National Law Journal*, April 12, 2010, pp. 16–17.)

## THE OPENING CASE *Revisited, Part II*
### When Is a Citizen Not a Citizen? Round 3

Recall that in the Opening Case of *Hertz Corporation v. Friend* the Hertz Corporation was sued by a group of California citizens who brought the case in a state court. Hertz, knowing that it would find little sympathy in a California court, filed a motion to remove the case to the federal court in New Jersey, arguing that the proper forum would be the site of its corporate headquarters. The plaintiffs disagreed, claiming that Hertz's "principal place of business" was California because it did most of its business there. The Supreme Court decided that a corporation has its "principal place of business" where its decision-making body is headquartered. For Hertz that would be New Jersey, not California. The Supreme Court's ruling is going to have an effect on class action cases. In essence what the court has done is limit the citizenship of corporate defendants to fewer, perhaps even, in some situations, to a single state. Explain why this decision will probably increase the number of class action cases that end up in federal court.

## Service of Process

The complaint is presented to the appropriate court officer, usually the clerk of courts. The clerk will then see that the defendant is served with a copy of the complaint and a summons. The *summons* names the court of jurisdiction, describes the nature of the action, and demands that the defendant answer the complaint within a specified period of time, usually between 20 and 30 days, depending on the state rules of civil procedure. Giving the summons and the complaint to the defendant is called service of process.

## The Pre-Answer Stage

As noted, once the defendant has been served, he or she has 20 to 30 days to file an answer. Usually, however, the defendant will ask for and receive an extension of that time period. The time between service and the answer is termed the *pre-answer stage*. During this stage, the defendant will take some time to examine the nature of the claim that has been filed by the plaintiff. The defendant may, as a result of this initial examination, decide to file one or more pre-answer motions. A *motion* is a request for the court to rule on a particular issue. One possible motion is a motion for dismissal of the case for failure to state a claim for which relief can be granted. Some states call this a demurrer. Other motions to dismiss may be based on the grounds that the court lacks subject matter jurisdiction, that the court lacks personal jurisdiction, or that the court cannot hear the case because the statute of limitations has passed.

### EXAMPLE 3-3: To Demurrer or Not to Demurrer

Lauren Jensen agreed to purchase a desk for $295 from the Stephens Sisters Furniture Store. During a management change at Stephens, Jensen's order was lost, and the furniture was never delivered. Jensen never contacted Stephens but instead purchased a similar desk for $495 at another store. Five years later, Jensen decided to bring suit against Stephens for breach of contract. She wants to recover the extra $200 that she paid to the second store. Stephens' attorney realizes that the state statute of limitations for such contracts is four years. As a result, she files a motion to dismiss for failure to state a claim for which relief can be granted. Some states call this motion a demurrer. If Stephens's attorney is correct, the suit will be dismissed.

## The Answer

The answer is the defendant's official response to the complaint. In the answer, the defendant admits or denies the allegations in the complaint. The defendant's answer can also include affirmative defenses. An affirmative defense is a set of circumstances that indicate that the defendant should not be held liable, even if the plaintiff proves all of the facts in the complaint. One affirmative defense is *assumption of the risk*.

### EXAMPLE 3-4: Assessing the Risk of a Risky Business

Carol Jennings took a cruise of the Mediterranean on the Underwood Cruise Line, a firm incorporated and doing business in the United States. While the cruise ship *Principia* was docked at a Greek island, Jennings joined a tour group. She was cautioned numerous times to remain with the tour group and not to wander off by herself because of the danger of being attacked and robbed. Nevertheless, Jennings ignored the warnings and left the tour group. While on her own, she wandered into a particularly dangerous part of the city where she was beaten and robbed. She later brought a lawsuit against the Underwood Cruise Line. In its answer to Jennings' complaint, the cruise line may wish to use the defense of assumption of the risk. Such a defense would argue that Jennings was aware of danger when she chose to abandon the tour group and wander off by herself. As a result, the cruise line might argue, she assumed the risk of being attacked and robbed.

The defendant's answer may also contain counterclaims and cross-claims. A *counter-claim* is a claim that a defendant has against a plaintiff. A *cross-claim* is a claim filed by a defendant against another defendant in the same case. At this time, a defendant may also wish to file a *third-party complaint,* which is a complaint filed by the defendant against a third party not yet named in the lawsuit.

## The Pretrial Stage

After the answer has been filed, the parties must await trial. During this waiting period, cleverly dubbed the pretrial stage, several activities can be carried out, including the pretrial conference, discovery, and the filing of pretrial motions.

### Pretrial Conference
Some courts require cases to go to a pretrial conference after the complaint and the answer have been filed. A pretrial conference usually has two purposes. One is to discuss the possibility of settling the case without the need for a trial. Another is to decide on the details involved in bringing the case to trial. Such a conference is generally called a *case management conference.* Issues that might be discussed at a case management conference include the way that the parties will conduct discovery or the need to place a limit on the number of expert witnesses that will be called at trial.

### Pretrial Motions
Several motions may be filed during the pretrial stage. One motion available at this time is a motion for summary judgment. A **summary judgment motion** is a motion that asks the court for an immediate judgment for the party filing the motion. This motion is filed when there is no genuine issue as to any material fact, and the party filing the motion is entitled by law to a favorable judgment. The motion cannot be filed without supporting legal arguments written out in a brief and accompanied by applicable supporting evidence.

### Discovery
**Discovery** is the process by which the parties to a civil action search for information that is relevant to the case. The objective is to simplify the issues and avoid unnecessary arguments and surprises in the subsequent trial. Discovery techniques and tools include the following:

**Depositions** are oral statements made out of court under oath by witnesses or parties to the action in response to questions from the opposing attorneys. The answers are recorded by a court stenographer and can be used for later reference.

**Interrogatories** are written questions that must be answered in writing under oath by the opposite party. Interrogatories cannot be given to witnesses. Only plaintiffs and defendants can be required to answer interrogatories.

**Requests for real evidence** ask a party to produce documents, records, accounts, correspondence, photographs, or other tangible evidence. The request may also seek permission to inspect land.

LO6

**Requests for physical or mental examination** ask a party to undergo a physical or a mental examination. Such requests can be made only if the physical or the mental condition of the party is in controversy; it must be a central concern to the lawsuit.

**Requests for admissions** are made to secure a statement from a party that a particular fact is true or that a document or set of documents is genuine. An admission eliminates the need to demonstrate the truthfulness of the fact or the genuineness of the documents at trial.

The discovery process cannot be taken lightly by the litigants. The rules of court provide severe penalties for those who fail to cooperate with discovery. Should a litigant withhold his or her cooperation, the other litigant can ask the court to compel the uncooperative party to respond to the discovery request. If the uncooperative party has a reason for not complying, then he or she may try to persuade the court of the validity of the refusal. If, for instance, the discovery request seeks information protected by the attorney–client privilege, the judge may refuse to compel the litigant to comply with the request.

If, however, the litigant cannot persuade the judge that the refusal is legally justified, the judge may impose severe penalties on the litigant. For example, the judge may elect to dismiss the lawsuit completely. The judge may also decide to render a default judgment against the uncooperative party. Reasonable expenses caused by the refusal to comply with discovery may also be assessed against the uncooperative party. These expenses may include attorney's fees. In many states, the rules allow the expenses to be assessed against either the attorney or the litigant.

## The Civil Trial

Upon completion of discovery, the pretrial conference, and any hearings held on pretrial motions, the case is ready for trial. A trial by jury is an adversarial proceeding in which the judge's role is secondary to that of the jury's. Competition between attorneys permits the jury to sort out the truth and arrive at a just solution to the dispute.

### Jury Selection
Once it is decided that the case will involve a jury, the process of *voir dire* (to speak the truth) begins. In this process, the lawyers for both parties question prospective jurors to determine whether they will be allowed to sit on the jury. Prospective jurors may be rejected if they are unable to render an impartial judgment. One reason for rejecting a prospective juror is if he or she had a personal relationship with the litigant or with a witness.

Prospective jurors may also be rejected if they have a financial interest in the outcome of the trial. However, the financial interest must be a direct, substantial interest. Remote financial interests in a trial will not disqualify a juror. Thus, the fact that the outcome of a trial may result in higher insurance rates would not disqualify a juror who has an insurance policy.

Another reason might be if the prospective juror has had past experience that would prevent him or her from being impartial in the present case. Thus, a juror who has had a bad experience with a psychologist, for instance, might be unable to judge impartially the actions of a psychologist who has been sued for malpractice.

In most lawsuits, *voir dire* is conducted in the open, which means that the process is generally accessible to the press and the mass media. However, in cases that have attracted a lot of public attention, the judge may order that the media's access to the *voir dire* process be limited. Often news reporters will be limited to reading abridged copies of the transcript of the *voir dire* process after the process has been completed. The

Prospective jurors may be selected or rejected based on their ability to render an impartial judgment.

names of the jurors may also be censored, along with personal data about those jurors. This limit on the access to *voir dire* usually occurs in notorious criminal trials, but it could also happen in high-profile civil lawsuits.

**Opening Statements**  At the beginning of the trial, both attorneys have the opportunity to make an opening statement. In the *opening statement,* an attorney presents the facts in the case and explains what he or she intends to show during the trial. Attorneys are not permitted to argue their case in the opening statement. There is widespread disagreement, however, as to what constitutes "arguing the case" during the opening statement. Consequently, the degree of argument permitted during the opening statement often depends on what the judge will allow.

**The Plaintiff's Case in Chief**  The plaintiff's case in chief is the plaintiff's opportunity to present evidence that will prove his or her version of the case to the jury. The plaintiff's attorney calls witnesses and immediately subjects those witnesses to direct examination. Direct examination is designed to present the facts that will support the plaintiff's version of those facts. Opposing attorneys then have the chance to challenge the truthfulness of each piece of evidence presented. In this process of cross-examination, the witnesses answer questions of the defense attorney.

**The Defendant's Case in Chief**  After the plaintiff has ended the presentation of his or her case in chief, the defendant has the opportunity to present his or her case in chief. The defendant's attorney calls witnesses for direct examination, and the plaintiff's attorney has an opportunity to cross-examine the defendant's witnesses.

**The Rebuttal and the Surrebuttal**  Once the plaintiff and the defendant have presented their cases in chief, each attorney may present evidence to discredit the evidence presented by the opposition and reestablish the credibility of his or her own evidence. This step is called the rebuttal. The term surrebuttal is used in some states when referring to the defendant's rebuttal.

**Closing Statements**  After the rebuttals are completed, each attorney makes a closing statement. In this statement, the attorneys emphasize aspects of the testimony and other evidence they believe will best persuade the judge or jury.

**Jury Instructions**  Because juries comprise many people who are not familiar with particular aspects of the law, someone must explain the law to the jury. This is one of the duties of the judge. Although the attorneys may suggest to the judge what instructions ought to be used, the judge makes the decision. The judge's instructions explain the rules of law that the jurors are to apply to the facts in reaching their decision.

**Verdict and Judgment**  After receiving the judge's instructions, the members of the jury retire to a private room, where they apply the rules stated by the judge to the evidence presented by the witnesses. The jury eventually reaches a verdict. A verdict is a finding of fact. The verdict may be limited to the question of liability, or it can be extended to include the issue of damages. Liability means that the defendant is held legally responsible for his or her actions. The term damages refers to the money recovered by the plaintiff for the injury or loss caused by the defendant. The verdict is entered by the judge in the court records, and the case is said to be decided. According to the terms of the judgment, the defeated party either is required to pay the amount specified or do a specific thing, such as perform the terms of the contract. Court costs are usually paid by the losing party.

In some cases, money will not be adequate to satisfy the plaintiff. In such cases, the plaintiff may seek an equitable remedy. An equitable remedy requires a party to do something or to refrain from doing something beyond the payment of money. One equitable remedy is specific performance, which would require a party to a contract to go through with the terms of the contract. Usually, specific performance is permitted only in cases involving real estate or unique, one-of-a-kind goods such as art objects or rare antiques. Another equitable remedy is an injunction. An injunction stops a party from doing something. For instance, an employer may seek an injunction against a former employee to prevent that employee from using a trade secret on his or her new job if that trade secret is the property of the original employer.

## A QUESTION OF ETHICS

### Televised Trials: Threat or Transformation

In California, Proposition 8 was placed on the ballot in order to outlaw same sex marriages. The legality of the proposition was challenged in the federal trial court in the Northern District of California. Noting the great interest in the case and recognizing its social and political significance, the presiding judge suggested televising the trial at least within the courthouse in San Francisco where the trial was located. Later the judge, in consultation with the Chief Judge of the 9th Circuit, suggested widening the broadcast field to include all courthouses in the 9th Circuit. Those who supported the proposition opposed the plan to televise the trial and attempted to get a *writ of mandamus* to prevent the broadcast. The 9th Circuit denied the *writ*, but the United States Supreme Court reversed the decision and stopped the broadcast indefinitely. The Supreme Court stated that it suspended the broadcast to protect witnesses who might otherwise be threatened or harassed. The ethical issue here is not the morality of Proposition 8. Rather the question is whether a trial of this transformative significance should be broadcast, or "gagged" as the Supreme Court ruled. Using both utilitarianism and rational ethics (See Chapter 1-Ethics, Social Responsibility, and the Law), analyze the decision made by the U.S. Supreme Court and decide whether the Supreme Court's decision can be defended using either theory. Explain your rationale using each theory. (See David R. Fine, "Television Trials," *The National Law Journal*, January 25, 2010, p. 38.)

## The Appeal

An **appeal** is the referral of a case to a higher court for review. For an appeal to be successful, it must be shown that some legal error occurred. For example, a party could argue that some of the evidence that was admitted should have been excluded or that evidence that was not allowed should have been allowed. A party could also argue that the judge's instructions were erroneous or were stated in an inappropriate manner. Generally, an appeal is filed by the party that lost the case in the trial court. However, it is also possible that the party that prevailed at trial may wish to file an appeal. This step is referred to as a **cross-appeal**. For instance, if the trial court upheld most of the claims made by the plaintiff but denied one or two key claims, the plaintiff may wish to file a cross-appeal. It may also be advisable to file a cross-appeal if the trial court did not award the appropriate amount in damages, if it refused to grant attorney's fees, or if it allowed money damages but refused to permit equitable relief. (See Aaron S. Bayer, "Appellate Law: The Cross-Appeal," *The National Law Journal*, February 9, 2004, p. 13.)

## Execution of the Judgment

In civil cases, if the judgment is not paid, the court will order the loser's property to be sold by the sheriff to satisfy the judgment. This order by the court is known as a **writ of execution**. Any excess from the sale must be returned to the loser. Execution of the judgment also may be issued against any income due to the loser, such as wages, salaries, or dividends. This process is known as execution against income, or garnishment, and the proceedings are known as garnishee proceedings. Checking accounts are also subject to garnishment.

## quick quiz 3-2

1. In state court, a complaint must include a statement of jurisdiction.    true | false

2. The defendants' answer must not include either counterclaims    true | false
   or cross-claims.

3. *Voir dire* must always be open to the press.    true | false

# 3-3 Cyber-procedure

The world of litigation has changed dramatically because of the electronic revolution. Gone are the days when litigators could wait until the last minute to conduct discovery prior to trial because they could see the limited number of paper documents sitting in a neat pile on their desks. Also gone are the days when attorney-client privilege could be protected by simply closing the office door. Electronically stored data comes in so many different formats (e-mail, texting, Facebook, Linked-In, voice mail, spreadsheets, instant messages, databases, and so on) and is stored in so many different electronic devises (laptops, mobile phones, iPods, Kindles, GPS units, PDAs, desktop PCs, fax machines, scanners, smartphones, and so on) that litigators have to get the jump on the process from the first moment that a lawsuit is threatened. Add to that the fact that many courts now expect and some even require the electronic filing of documents, and it becomes obvious that lawyers, paralegals, and business people cannot ignore the electronic age even if they want to.

## Cyber-jurisdiction

Whether courts have jurisdiction over out-of-state defendants has been complicated by the electronic age. Previously, back in the age of face-to-face, U.S. Mail, and over-the-phone transactions, it was fairly obvious where a corporation or an institution had its principal place of business. Of course, exactly what was meant by "principal place of business" might be at issue, but at least everyone knew the alternative sites available. Doing business on the Internet complicates all of this. Using the Internet, sellers can solicit business on their Web site, negotiate and enter a contract using "the point and click method," receive payment using PayPal, and deliver goods via FedEx or UPS without leaving the comfort of their home office and without revealing where they, the sellers, are located, how the goods were obtained, where they were stored, and how they were transported and delivered to the seller before being loaded on a FedEx or UPS truck.

LO8

Does the type of activity described above reach the level of minimum contacts needed to establish personal jurisdiction? Should the minimum contacts standard be replaced by the New Jersey stream of commerce standard for electronic buying and selling? **Cyber-jurisdiction**, (AKA **electronic jurisdiction** and **e-jurisdiction**) is the power of the court to hear a case based on Internet-related transactions. While this area of the law is still in its adolescence, we can, nevertheless, extract at least one general principle:

Cyber-transactions must be handled on a case-by-case basis.

because of its complex nature, cyber-jurisdiction is a moving target. To help attorneys, paralegals, and business people, hit this moving target, the courts have established a sliding scale on which several types of jurisdiction can be measured.

On one side of the scale are business transactions that are carried out from beginning to end using the Internet. These would include operations that are run like those engineered by Amazon.com and e-Bay. Transactions that involve solicitation, negotiation, finalization, payment, and shipping arrangements exclusively on the Internet, establish the minimum contacts needed for the state of the buyer. Moreover, if a case involves product liability, the type of transaction described above would satisfy New Jersey's stream of commerce standard. Of course, it is possible for the seller to specify the state that will serve as the forum for settling any dispute that arises from the contract. Still, such stipulations can always be challenged if the matter actually gets to court.

On the other side of the sliding scale, are those cases in which the defendant simply placed an inactive advertisement on the Internet. Such inactive advertisements will not usually establish jurisdiction under the minimum contacts test or the New Jersey stream of commerce test. The final type of transaction falls in between the two extremes. These cases include cyber-transactions that involve more than simply placing an advertisement on the Internet. The courts have not established any single normative approach to such transactions and so the matter must be handled on a case-by-case basis.

## Cyber-filing

The federal court system officially joined the 21st century when it added a provision to the Federal Rules of Civil Procedure that permits lawyers to file court documents electronically. Moreover, under Rule 5 (3) the courts can even go so far as to require that documents be filed electronically, as long as the court also accepts reasonable exceptions from those unable to comply with the new provision. Those federal courts that have adopted the new procedure have found that cyber-filing (electronic filing or e-filing) is more cost effective and efficient than paper filing. Because some of the electronic systems used to keep track of court documents are accessible on the Internet, papers are no longer lost or misplaced as often as they once were. The Internet filing network also permits people to access the papers at their own convenience. This is an important feature of the electronic system because, once a party has been served properly, that party is sent a notice whenever a new document is filed electronically with the court. This eliminates the old-fashioned and time-consuming process of filing a formal notice with each party.

Still, cyber-filing does have its disadvantages. Not every law firm is properly equipped for cyber-filing and so the courts must maintain a dual filing system to accommodate "cyber-challenged" firms. Moreover, just because a firm is electronically up to date does not guarantee that its attorneys are cyber-savvy. Consequently, many courts have been forced to provide training and ongoing assistance to these attorneys at the court's expense. Also, from the attorney's perspective, since cyber-filing process is controlled by local rules, learning one set of electronic rules is rarely enough. Instead, the attorney must learn the rules for every court in which he or she does regular business. Fortunately, however, there are consistent features in these rules from one court to the next and so a diligent and conscientious attorney can survive as long as he or she is willing to be flexible.

# Cyber-discovery

That part of the litigation process that has been affected the most by the cyber-revolution is the discovery process. Part of this is due to the actual changes caused by the cyber-revolution itself and part of it has been caused by extensive changes made in the rules of discovery by the federal courts to accommodate the revolution. There was a time when the federal courts were satisfied to look at electronic evidence as if it were just another way to produce paper documents. To deal with data stored in or produced by computers, they simply used the catchphrase *data compilations* to cover all such evidence, whether produced by hand or by the computer. Unfortunately, this shortcut no longer works. The Federal Rules now refer to cyber-evidence as **electronically stored information (ESI)**. Moreover, the rule makers have officially recognized that ESI can cause many difficulties that cannot be solved by the old rules. For example, as noted above, computers produce and store so much ESI in so many different formats that it is difficult for the average lawyer to keep current. This complexity makes coming up with an effective discovery a difficult challenge. Another problem is caused by the unavoidable fact that electronic devices delete some material automatically and hold on to material that the user believes has been deleted months earlier.

The courts have made several changes in the federal rules to deal with these difficulties. These changes were designed to alter the behavior of attorneys so that they adjust to the peculiar characteristics of ESI. First, the rules now force attorneys to get an early start on all discovery plans or they will be unable to comply with the time limits built into the rules. Second, attorneys must now deal with the question of which electronic format will be used to request and deliver data. Third, attorneys can rest assured that the rules provide several ways to deal with those problems that arise with ESI and privilege. Fourth, attorneys can use the rules to help in the recovery of ESI that might otherwise be difficult to find. Fifth, to deal with the expenses that are involved in the identification and collection of ESI, attorneys can now refer to provisions in the rules that guarantee a fair apportionment of these expenses. Finally, attorneys can also be certain that everyone will cooperate with the new electronic discovery process, because the rules have provided severe penalties for those who ignore or disobey the new ESI discovery rules.

---

## quick quiz 3-3

1. Cyber-jurisdiction is the power of the court to hear a case based on Internet-related transactions.    true | false

2. The Federal Rules of Civil Procedure do not permit lawyers to file court documents electronically.    true | false

3. The Federal Rules now refer to cyber-evidence as data compilations.    true | false

---

# 3-4 Criminal Procedure

The objectives of a criminal prosecution are to protect society and to punish the wrongdoer by a fine or imprisonment. The steps in a criminal prosecution include the following:

- Arrest and initial appearance.
- Preliminary hearing.
- Formal charges.
- Arraignment.
- Trial.

# The Arrest and Initial Appearance

A crime is an offense against the people. Once a law enforcement agency learns that a crime has been committed, the agency begins a criminal prosecution. The first step in a criminal prosecution is to gather evidence of the crime and identify all possible suspects. When the law enforcement agency is convinced that it has ample evidence of both the crime and the identity of the suspect, an arrest warrant is issued, and the suspect is arrested. At the time of arrest, the defendant must be informed of his or her rights. One of the principal rights of the accused is the right to be represented by counsel. This right is guaranteed by the Sixth Amendment to the Constitution. Another important right is the right to remain silent, which is protected under the Fifth Amendment, which states that a criminal defendant cannot be compelled to be a witness against him- or herself. The U.S. Supreme Court has ruled that the Fourteenth Amendment to the Constitution requires that both the right to remain silent and the right to representation by counsel must also be protected by state governments. The defendant is then brought before a judge or a magistrate for an initial appearance, where once again the defendant is reminded of his or her rights. At this time, a preliminary hearing is also scheduled.

Defendants must be informed of their rights at the time of arrest. Two important rights are the right to representation by counsel and the right to remain silent.

# The Preliminary Hearing

A **preliminary hearing** is a court procedure during which the judge decides whether probable cause exists to continue holding the defendant for the crime. The government is represented by an attorney called the **prosecutor**. In some states, this government official is called the district attorney. During the preliminary hearing, the prosecution and the defendant are permitted to make arguments and call witnesses. The case will move on to the next step if there is probable cause to hold the defendant. If not, the defendant is set free.

# The Formal Charges

In the United States, formal charges against the defendant may be brought either by indictment or by information. Some states do not have a grand jury system and therefore can bring formal charges only by an information. In those states that use both, the indictment is usually used to bring formal charges for serious crimes.

## A QUESTION OF ETHICS

### Reading Rights: What is Right and What Is Wrong?

Edward McDonough, assistant district attorney for the city of Middletown, has just left a session with Harold Harrison, a criminal defendant accused of armed robbery. During the session, acting under the advice of Jennifer Miller, his attorney, Harrison confessed to the crime and entered a plea bargain agreement that will place him in prison for 10 years. On his way back across the city square to his office, ADA McDonough is stopped by Sgt. Anne Wade, who confesses to him that neither she nor her partner, Sgt. Sam Newton, read Harrison his rights. McDonough knows that this admission means that the confession he just obtained is tainted and would be thrown out of court if it were challenged by Miller on behalf of Harrison. From an ethical point of view, what action should McDonough take now?

**An Indictment** The federal courts and many state courts bring formal charges against the defendant by issuing an indictment. An **indictment** is a set of formal charges against a defendant issued by a grand jury. A *grand jury* consists of citizens who serve as jurors for a specified period of time to review a variety of criminal cases. The objective of a grand jury review is to determine whether probable cause exists to believe that a crime has been committed and that this particular defendant may have committed the crime. Grand jury proceedings are held in secret and are directed by the prosecutor or district attorney. If the grand jury finds probable cause exists, an indictment is issued.

**An Information** An **information** is a set of formal charges against a defendant drawn up and issued by the prosecutor or district attorney. No grand jury is involved in this process. Nevertheless, an information does the same thing that an indictment does. If the prosecutor has found that probable cause exists to indicate that a crime has been committed and that this particular defendant committed the crime, an information is issued.

## The Arraignment

The **arraignment** is a formal court proceeding, during which the defendant, after hearing the indictment or information read, pleads either guilty or not guilty. Should the defendant enter a guilty plea, a sentence may be imposed immediately. If the defendant enters a plea of not guilty, the case moves on to the trial.

## The Criminal Trial

If the defendant has requested a jury trial, a jury is selected. After the jury has been seated, each side makes its opening statement. Opening statements are followed by the production of evidence by both the prosecution and the defendant. One very significant difference between a criminal trial and a civil trial is the burden of proof. In a civil trial, the plaintiff must prove his or her case by a preponderance of evidence. In contrast, in a criminal case, the prosecution must prove the defendant's guilt beyond a reasonable doubt. As is the case with civil procedure, the criminal trial is completed by the attorneys' closing statements and the judge's instructions to the jury. The jury members are then allowed to retire to deliberate and decide on a verdict. In most states, a defendant can be found guilty only by the unanimous agreement of all of the jurors. A defendant who is found not guilty is released. One who has been found guilty is sentenced by the judge.

## quick quiz 3-4

| | |
|---|---|
| 1. The objectives of a criminal prosecution are to protect society and to punish the wrongdoer by a fine or imprisonment. | true \| false |
| 2. The steps in a criminal prosecution include the arrest and initial appearance, the preliminary hearing, the formal charges, the arraignment, and the trial. | true \| false |
| 3. A crime is an offense against a single individual. | true \| false |

# Summary

**3.1** Courts are judicial tribunals that meet in a regular place and apply the laws in an attempt to settle disputes fairly. The federal court system is divided into three levels: the district courts, the courts of appeals, and the U.S. Supreme Court. State systems vary in structure but often consist of several levels, including lower-level limited jurisdiction trial courts, higher-level trial courts, intermediate appellate courts, and state supreme courts.

**3.2** Litigation begins when the plaintiff files a complaint with the appropriate trial court. The defendant must then be given a copy of the complaint and a summons. During the pre-answer stage, the defendant may attempt to dismiss the lawsuit by filing certain pre-answer motions. In the answer stage, the defendant will file an answer, which may contain affirmative defenses, counterclaims, and/or cross-claims. The defendant at this time may also file third-party complaints. During the pretrial stage, conferences may be held, motions may be made, and discovery conducted. The trial includes the opening statement, each side's case in chief, the opportunity for rebuttal and surrebuttal, the closing arguments, and the jury instructions. The jury then renders a verdict. Either party may appeal the case if that party believes that a legal error was made during the trial that influenced the verdict unfavorably. If a judgment is not paid, the court may issue a writ of execution.

**3.3** Cyber-jurisdiction (AKA electronic jurisdiction and e-jurisdiction) is the power of the court to hear a case based on Internet-related transactions. The Federal Rules of Civil Procedure now permit federal courts to allow, and at times even require, lawyers to file court documents electronically. The Federal Rules now refer to cyber-evidence as electronically stored information (ESI). The rules also now deal with special situations involving ESI and discovery.

**3.4** The steps in a criminal prosecution include the arrest and initial appearance, the preliminary hearing, the formal charges, the arraignment, and the trial. At the time of the arrest, the defendant must be informed of his or her rights. Immediately following the arrest, the defendant is brought before a judge or a magistrate for an initial appearance, at which time the defendant is again reminded of his or her rights. A preliminary hearing is also scheduled. A preliminary hearing is a court procedure during which the judge will decide whether probable cause exists to continue to hold the defendant pending formal charges. Formal charges against the defendant may be brought either by indictment or by information. The arraignment is a formal court proceeding, during which the defendant pleads guilty or not guilty. The trial includes the opening statement, each side's case, the closing arguments, and the jury instructions. The jury then renders a verdict.

# Key Terms

abuse of discretion, 46

affirmative defense, 54

answer, 54

appeal, 58

appellate jurisdiction, 45

arraignment, 63

case in chief, 57

civil litigation, 52

class action, 53

clearly erroneous standard, 46

complaint, 52

courts, 45

cross-appeal, 58

cross-examination, 57

cyber-jurisdiction, 59

damages, 57

defendant, 52

demurrer, 54

deposition, 55

direct examination, 57

discovery, 55

diversity cases, 46

electronic/e-jurisdiction, 59

electronically stored information (ESI), 61

equitable remedy, 57

federal question, 46

forum shopping, 53

general jurisdiction, 46

indictment, 63

information, 63

injunction, 58

interrogatories, 55

jurisdiction, 45

liability, 57

minimum contacts, 47

original jurisdiction, 45

personal jurisdiction, 46

plaintiff, 52

## Questions for Review and Discussion

1. What is the fundamental nature of the American court system?
2. Under what circumstances might a federal court have jurisdiction to hear a case?
3. Under what circumstances might the U.S. Supreme Court hear a case?
4. What is the structure of a typical state court systems?
5. What is civil litigation?
6. What are the most common discovery techniques?
7. What is involved in an appeal?
8. How is cyber-jurisdiction determined?
9. What is electronically stored information?
10. What are the steps in a criminal prosecution?

## Cases for Analysis

1. William Stevenson offered to help Rayford Le-Blanc remove his truck from the mud. At first, LeBlanc refused. However, later, when the towing company that LeBlanc had called proved to be unavailable, he accepted Stevenson's offer of assistance. LeBlanc then bought a towing strap from a nearby store to help in the removal of his truck from the mud. The first two attempts at removing the truck failed. On the third attempt, while LeBlanc was still in the process of connecting the straps to his truck, Stevenson, apparently without warning, pulled his vehicle forward. This movement caught LeBlanc by surprise. His hand was still wrapped up in the strap, and therefore, as Stevenson's vehicle moved forward, LeBlanc's hand was severely injured. LeBlanc sued Stevenson for damages related to the injuries to his hand. The jury decided that Stevenson was not at fault, and LeBlanc found himself on the losing end of the lawsuit. Accordingly, he appealed the case. The appellate court threw out the jury's factual finding and awarded LeBlanc over $190,000 in damages. Stevenson hollered "foul" and asked the Supreme Court of Louisiana to hear his request to have the decision reversed. The high court accepted the case. One of the central issues involved the question of whether, and under what circumstances, an appellate court can overturn decisions of fact made by a jury. Should the supreme court uphold the appellate court's decision? What standard of review should be involved here? Explain. *LeBlanc v. Stevenson,* 770 So.2d 766 (Sup. Ct. LA).

2. On October 12, 2000, an American naval vessel, the U.S.S. *Cole,* was bombed while it was berthed in Aden Harbor in Yemen in the Middle East. The bombing, which killed 17 American sailors, was planned and executed by Al-Qaeda. Relatives of those 17 sailors brought a lawsuit in U.S. District Court against the foreign state of the Republic of Sudan, alleging that Sudan was responsible for the bombing because that government supported al-Qaeda in general and the terrorists who carried off this assault in particular. The government of the Republic of Sudan moved to dismiss the case, arguing that the court lacked subject matter jurisdiction. The argument was based on the fact that the case involved citizens of states of the United States in an attempt to sue a foreign government, something not permitted under federal law. Is the government of Sudan correct in this case? Explain. *Rux v. Republic of Sudan,* 461 F.3d. 461 (4th Cir. 2006).

3. The state of Alabama was required under the provisions of its own constitution to reapportion its electoral districts every 10 years. However, the state had failed to reapportion districts for more than half a century. Since then, the population of Alabama had grown to such an extent that severe inequalities existed among the electoral districts. The inequalities were so great in some cases that the votes of citizens in some parts of the state carried as much as 10 times the weight of the votes of citizens in other parts of the state. A suit was brought in federal court on the grounds that the inequalities in voting power violated certain guarantees found in the U.S. Constitution. The defendants argued that the federal court should not interfere in what is essentially a state matter and that by doing so, it would upset the delicate balance between the states and the federal government. Nevertheless, the federal district court struck down the apportionment scheme as unconstitutional. Does this case belong in the U.S. Supreme Court? Explain the reasons for your response. Should the Supreme Court uphold or overturn the federal district court's decision? Explain. *Reynolds v. Sims,* 377 U.S. 533 (U.S. Sup. Ct.).

4. Speculate on which of the following cases the U.S. Supreme Court might decide to review: a case involving a dispute over whether computer software can be copyrighted; a case involving an appeal of a zoning board's decision to limit the number of adult book stores on any single city block; a case involving the constitutionality of an abortion statute; a case involving an antitrust suit based on a violation of a federal antitrust statute between the National Football League and a former seller of NFL sports gear; a libel case against a small town newspaper involving allegations of the mayor's dishonesty; a case involving the placement of a religious scene on city property; a case brought by a steel company to enjoin employees from going on strike; a case involving the distribution of antiwar flyers at a private shopping mall; and a case involving the search of a high school student's locker without her permission. In each case, give reasons for your answer.

5. Eight limited partners filed a lawsuit in the Lucas County Court of Common Pleas, alleging that the general partners in 10 different limited partnerships had engaged in an extensive pattern of self-dealing that had involved converting partnership property for their own personal use. Also named in the lawsuit was the accounting firm of Donald J. Goldstein, CPA, a resident of Florida, and Goldstein, Lewis, and Company, a professional corporation located in Florida. The plaintiffs claimed that the accountant and the accounting firm had known of the general partners' misconduct and were therefore liable to the plaintiff for that malpractice. The accountant and the accounting firm decided to end the suit as quickly as possible. Consequently, they filed a motion for dismissal. The motion stated that the courts of Ohio lacked personal jurisdiction over them because they were from Florida. They further stated that they did not solicit business in Ohio, maintained no place of business in Ohio, had no license to act as accountants in Ohio, owned no property in Ohio, provided all services from Florida, and filed no documents with the state of Ohio. Thus, they concluded that they fell outside the power of Ohio's long-arm statute. Conversely, the plaintiffs argued that the defendants transacted business in the state of Ohio on a continuing and ongoing basis by regularly submitting financial statements to the limited partners in Ohio and by being actively involved in the decisions of the general partnership. Did the activities of the accountant and the accounting firm place them under the jurisdiction of the Ohio court, according to the state "long-arm" statute? Explain. *Goldstein v. Christiansen,* 638 N.E.2d 541 (OH).

6. The criminal defendant in this case, a man named Gideon, broke into a pool room in Florida with the objective of committing a minor crime. Because Gideon was without any means of financial support, he could not afford an attorney. He asked for but was denied representation by a court-appointed attorney. Consequently, he represented himself at trial. Ultimately, he was found guilty and sentenced to five years in prison. Gideon later challenged his conviction on the grounds that he had been deprived of his constitutional right to representation by an attorney. In opposition, Florida argued that, though all fundamental rights guaranteed by the federal government through the Bill of Rights should also be guaranteed by state governments, the right to legal representation was not such a fundamental right. In fact, the right to a court-appointed attorney arose only when the criminal defendant had been accused of a very

serious crime. The U.S. Supreme Court agreed to hear the case. How should the Supreme Court rule in this case? Is the right to an attorney a fundamental right that should be guaranteed to criminal defendants by the states, regardless of the seriousness of the crime? Explain. Examine the Constitution and find the Amendment that guarantees the right to representation by an attorney. Examine the Constitution and find the Amendment that extends that right to defendants in state criminal actions. *Gideon v. Wainwright,* 372 U.S. 355 (U.S. Sup. Ct.).

7. Ernesto Miranda was arrested in his own home for a serious crime and held in an interrogation room. He was not informed of his right to remain silent, nor was he informed that he could be represented by an attorney. Eventually, after a two-hour interrogation conducted by two police officers, Miranda signed a statement that indicated he had voluntarily confessed to the crime of which he was accused. On the basis of the confession, Miranda was found guilty. He appealed to the Arizona Supreme Court, which affirmed the guilty verdict. Miranda asked the U.S. Supreme Court to hear his appeal. Is this the type of case that belongs in the U.S. Supreme Court? Explain the reasons for your response. Should the Supreme Court uphold or overturn the state court's conviction of Miranda? Explain the Constitution and find the Amendment that guarantees the right to remain silent when arrested for a criminal action. Examine the Constitution and find the Amendment that extends that right to defendants in state criminal actions. *Miranda v. Arizona,* 384 U.S. 436 (U.S. Sup. Ct.).

## quick quiz Answers

| 3-1 | 3-2 | 3-3 | 3-4 |
|-----|-----|-----|-----|
| 1. T | 1. F | 1. T | 1. T |
| 2. T | 2. F | 2. F | 2. T |
| 3. T | 3. F | 3. F | 3. F |

# Chapter 4

# Alternative Dispute Resolution

## THE OPENING CASE   Mediation, Arbitration, and the Science Court

One of the most difficult questions that faces anyone who has initiated a lawsuit is whether to continue down the rigorous and expensive route of litigation or to take a detour down the road of alternative dispute resolution (ADR). ADR is not the same as negotiation. Every lawsuit involves some negotiation, no matter how brief or pointless that process might seem at the time. The decision to enter ADR is different. That decision involves taking an uncommon route, the road less traveled as it were. Sometimes ADR is the best path to take and sometimes it does not work. Consider the following case. Two power co-ops, the Cooperative Power Association and the United Power Association, announced their intention to construct high-voltage power lines across Minnesota farmland. The owners of the farms involved in the plan challenged the project, arguing that the planned route of the lines would destroy their ability to use their own farmland appropriately. The governor of Minnesota called for the creation of a science court to resolve the issue. The science court would be made up of scientists, engineers, and other experts educated in the discipline and the industry involved in the dispute, thus allowing them to use their expertise in deciding the case. The science court would also permit the parties to avoid the long and involved process of litigation. Other ways of solving this problem might

be to submit the dispute to mediation or arbitration. In mediation, the parties to the dispute invite an impartial third party, the mediator, to assist them in solving the problem. In arbitration, the parties invite a third party, the arbitrator, to actually settle the dispute. In the Minnesota Powerline Case any one of these processes might have been used to develop a compromise that would have satisfied everyone involved, at least to some extent. As you read the chapter, ask yourself which of these methods would have been used most effectively in this case. [See Barry Casper and Paul Wellstone, *Powerline: The First Battle of America's Energy War* (Amherst: University of Massachusetts Press, 1981); and Barry Casper and Paul Wellstone, "Science Court on Trial in Minnesota," *Science in Context: Readings in the Sociology of Science,* ed. Barry Barnes and David Edge (Cambridge, MA: MIT Press, 1982).]

**Opening Case Questions**

1. Is this case a civil lawsuit or a criminal action? Explain.

2. Why would the parties want to avoid a trial in this case? Explain.

3. What advantages and disadvantages might arise in the establishment of a science court? Explain.

4. Under what circumstances would mediation be a proper route to take in the settlement of a dispute? Explain.

5. Under what circumstances would arbitration be a proper route to take in the settlement of a dispute? Explain.

 **Learning Objectives**

1. Examine the shortcomings of litigation.
2. List the advantages and the disadvantages of ADR.
3. Identify the advantages of mediation.
4. Explain the nature of an arbitration hearing.
5. Outline the med-arb process.
6. Relate the role of the early neutral evaluator.
7. Describe the process of running a summary judgment trial.
8. Clarify the private options available under proactive ADR.
9. Specify the governmental options available under proactive ADR.
10. Discuss the advantages and disadvantages of the science court proposal.

# 4-1 A Primer on ADR

As we have seen at various points throughout the text, the law is often reflected in a series of dualities. These dualities include the symmetry sought between the spirit and the letter of the law, between legal words and their interpretation, and between abstract principles and concrete situations. This synchronization is also involved in the application of the uncertainty principle to legal disputes. Thus far we have focused on the dispute-solving process known as litigation. Litigation has always been part of the American legal system. Lately, however, things have begun to change. The complexity, the expense, and the time involved in litigation have discouraged many potential litigants who have decided to sidestep the regular court system in favor of pursuing more efficient, effective, and economical methods of settling their disputes. These unconventional methods are referred to as the alternative dispute resolution process, or simply as ADR. **Alternative dispute resolution (ADR)** occurs whenever people move outside the traditional adversarial system and try to solve their legal dispute by using creative settlement techniques many of which have fact finding and truth as their goals rather than simply achieving a final victory. Thus, we have a fourth duality in the law: the duality that exists between the traditional litigation system and the unorthodox ADR process.

## Problems with Litigation

Many people choose a dispute resolution process that sidesteps the adversarial approach of civil litigation because they believe that it is the best way to achieve justice. Part of this belief is based on the suspicion that, with an adversarial approach, victory often depends not on who is in the right but on which advocate is the better tactician. Watching assistant district attorney Jack McCoy outwit hapless defense attorneys in a decade's worth of *Law and Order* reruns has probably contributed to this image. Unfortunately, the best tactician is often one of the most expensive advocates available, which can mean that justice often goes to those who can afford it. For this reason, many people seek an alternative that is less costly to both sides.

Litigation can also be expensive because of the initial steps that lead to the filing of a lawsuit. For instance, before an attorney can file a medical malpractice lawsuit, he or she must obtain the client's medical records, which means paying an initial copying fee that can amount to hundreds or even thousands of dollars. The attorney must then hire an expert to evaluate the records to determine whether the information in the records indicates that the client has a viable claim. Again this expense can run into hundreds or thousands of dollars. All these expenses are encountered before the attorney even knows that a claim actually exists.

In addition to being expensive, litigation can be time consuming. The initial steps after the filing of a complaint can delay progress on a lawsuit for many months. For instance, should the defendant's motion for dismissal be granted by the court, a lengthy and time-consuming appeal process may ensue. In some cases, the appeal could even find its way to the highest court in the jurisdiction. In such a case, if the highest court reverses the lower court's dismissal of the action, the case quite literally returns to the starting line. Another time-consuming step in litigation is the process of discovery. Taking depositions, answering interrogatories, filing, and responding to requests for real evidence and handling requests for mental or physical examinations can tie up a lawsuit for months.

Moreover, some jurisdictions require litigants to submit to case management hearings and settlement hearings before they can secure a trial date. Even when a court date is secured, many court dockets, especially those in large urban areas, are backed up for months, or even years, which often means that the parties to a lawsuit must wait for long periods of time before having their day in court. Even once a trial has occurred and a decision rendered, recovery can be delayed as the parties enter a second phase of the lawsuit, the execution of the judgment phase. This process involves its own complex set of procedures which, like the actual lawsuit, can cause expensive and time-consuming delays.

## The ADR Option

However, ADR can provide an economical and efficient alternative to litigation. Depending on the ADR technique employed, the time involved in settling a dispute can be shortened considerably and the expenses lowered significantly. Arbitration and mediation, for example, can be scheduled quickly, even before a lawsuit is filed. When scheduling either a mediation or an arbitration session, the parties need not consult the court's dockets or worry about any preliminary requirements, such as a case management conference. Moreover, even if the arbitration or mediation session does not end the dispute, it can save time by narrowing the issues or providing an evaluation of the strength of each side's case. The arbitration or mediation session may also, in some cases, provide a shortcut to discovery, thus saving time and lowering expenses.

ADR options provide a timely, cost-efficient method for resolving legal issues.

Other ADR approaches, such as early neutral evaluation (ENE), can save money and time by providing an assessment of the issues at stake and the range of damages available, should the outcome of the case demand a remedy of some sort. Summary jury trials, private trials, and minitrials can all be inexpensive and quick because they can be scheduled without regard to the court's docket and can be held without the expenses involved in hiring expert witnesses and providing travel and hotel accommodations for those witnesses. The cost and time involved in lengthy discovery processes can also be avoided by selecting any one of these ADR techniques.

Private proactive ADR techniques such as drafting contract clauses and entering partnering agreements can help to make litigation unnecessary from the outset. The idea behind the proactive ADR approach is to anticipate and deal with disputes before they occur. By providing a solution to problems before those problems arise, proactive ADR eliminates the uncertainty and risk inherent within the litigation process.

## Shortcomings of ADR

Yet ADR is not without problems. On the contrary, some critics of the alternative dispute resolution process have pointed out that the private administration of justice hampers the development of the law. Because many ADR techniques completely sidestep the courts, many critical social issues may never reach the judicial system, causing gaps in the evolution of case law and the progression of legislation. Another criticism of ADR involves its limited scope. Some legal conflicts, notably employment, contract, and tort cases, are especially well suited for ADR. However, other legal problems, primarily those involving constitutional law, civil rights, and criminal law, could never be brought before an ADR panel.

### EXAMPLE 4-1: Contract, Property, or Civil Rights?

Some cases are perfectly well suited for easy transfer from the regular court system to the ADR forum. Others are not. Still others may appear to be a good fit for ADR, but on further examination, turn out to be ill suited for any of the alternative approaches to the law. Such is the case of *State v. Bontrager.* The facts in the case are simple. Adam Bontrager, the defendant, purchased a piece of land. Before the sale, the previous owner had been notified by the Department of Health that the current septic system on the property was not up to specs. Consequently, the Health Department ordered a systems upgrade. Once Bontrager bought the property the obligation to upgrade the system passed to him.

Bontrager began the process of upgrading the system and then stopped. Without the system upgrade, untreated sewage was flowing into a local stream causing a health hazard. As a result, the defendant was cited for a violation of the administrative code and fined accordingly. Nevertheless, he still refused to build the upgrade that had been ordered by the Health Department, which then brought the current suit. Now on the surface this does not appear to be a complicated case. Nor does it appear to involve any significant matter of law. After all, we're talking about septic tanks and sewage here, not issues of constitutional law. Or are we? Just what is the issue at stake here?

If the case had turned out to be a contract dispute, perhaps between Bontrager and the original owner, then ADR might have been pursued before the Health Department, was forced to bring this action. Or if Bontrager had disputed the need for a new system because he had found another way to deal with the sewage problem, then arbitration or mediation might have been appropriate. That was not the case, however. Instead, Bontrager argued that, since he was Amish and since his religion forbid him to use electricity, which the upgrade required, the Health Department order was a violation of his religious rights under the U.S. Constitution. Unlike contract disagreements or property utilization disputes, a civil right action like this one is not appropriate for ADR. (See *State v. Bontrager,* 149 Ohio Misc.2d 33 (Newton Falls Municipal Court).)

Other difficulties associated with ADR have also appeared in recent years. One problem is that ADR does not always save time and money the way it is supposed to. Typically, two of the advantages that supporters of ADR promote are the ideas that ADR is less expensive and less time consuming because such procedures do not get tangled up in the red tape of the court system. Unfortunately, this is not always the case. Sometimes even cases that are decided by arbitration end up in the court system. Most often this happens when one or more of the parties decide to challenge the decision of the arbitrator. When such challenges occur, there is only one place for the parties to go: to court.

Two additional advantages of ADR are that little discovery and very few motions are involved in the process, thus saving the litigants a lot of money. Although this argument sounds good in theory, it does not always play out in reality. Unfortunately, sometimes a case may actually take longer to resolve because there is no discovery or motion practice involved. Part of the delay is due to the fact that discovery and motion practice often help attorneys focus on the most crucial issues in a case. Also, discovery will sometimes reveal that it is necessary to settle a case rather than proceeding to trial. When there is no discovery or motion practice, the issues remain wide open. This gap means that attorneys must anticipate all the possible moves that their opponents might make. The lack of discovery also means that the small flaws in an argument may not be revealed, and a case that would have been settled during a conventional lawsuit might drag on in arbitration.

Admittedly, ADR is not intended as a replacement for the legal system. Rather, it is intended to provide potential litigants with a wider variety of choices when they are facing a legal dispute. As noted previously, because of the delays and the expense involved in litigation, many people would like to avoid that route altogether. Others would like to find a way to streamline the litigation process, so that, should the need for a trial finally present itself, the preliminary steps can be administered as painlessly as possible. With these facts in mind, we will proceed with an examination of ADR techniques.

## quick quiz 4-1

1. Adversarial litigation has only recently become a part of the American legal system.    true | false

2. Two of the advantages that supporters of ADR promote are the ideas that ADR is less expensive and less time consuming than litigation.    true | false

3. ADR is not intended as a replacement for the legal system.    true | false

**Did You Know?**

When mediation is used to settle cases of sexual harassment in the workplace, 85 percent of those cases are resolved successfully without having to go to court.

# 4-2 ADR Techniques

There are numerous ADR techniques that can be invoked once a dispute has arisen between parties. These include but are not limited to mediation, arbitration, med-arb, early neutral evaluation, summary jury trials, and private civil trials.

## Mediation

According to the American Arbitration Association, **mediation** is "a non-binding process where a neutral third party works with the parties to reach a mutually agreeable settlement." The neutral third party is referred to as a **mediator.** Some people erroneously confuse mediation with negotiation. Negotiation is the usual way that attorneys handle disputes before they end up in litigation. Such negotiation is part, or at least should be a part, of every dispute that might possibly lead to litigation. In fact, negotiation is something that can take place before a lawsuit is filed, after it has been filed, before trial, and even during trial. There is no specially designated neutral third party "negotiator" during negotiation as there is during mediation. The job of the mediator is to convince parties to adjust or settle their dispute. The mediator will try to persuade the parties to reach some sort of compromise but cannot decide what the parties will do. (See American Arbitration Association, FAQ's. Retrieved on June 28, 2010, from http://www.aamediation.com/FAQ.)

Like the timing of a negotiation conference, the timing of a mediation session can vary. Sometimes mediation follows the filing of a lawsuit but sometimes it occurs to prevent a lawsuit from being filed. Mediation can occur before a conflict, during a conflict, after a conflict, or when a settlement following a conflict is not being followed properly. (See The JAMS Foundation, retrieved on July 28, 2010 from http://ww.jamsdr.com.) Mediation is often more successful than litigation, because in mediation the parties remain involved in the settlement of the dispute. Unlike litigation, which is decided by a judge or jury, a mediation session is in the hands of the parties. The mediator does not decide the disagreement. Rather, he or she serves as an intermediary who attempts to understand what brought the parties into disagreement and what issues lay at the heart of the disagreement. The mediator does not act as a therapist, a judge, or an advocate. Rather, he or she acts as an impartial outsider who can suggest solutions that will please all the parties involved in the dispute. Often the mediator can cut to the center of a dispute in objective ways that are unavailable to the parties themselves.

## EXAMPLE 4-2: Mediation: Practical Solutions to Practical Problems

Bruce Langton brought suit against David Winchester in small claims court after Winchester's daughter, Jackie, backed her car into Langton's truck, causing extensive damage to the front end of the vehicle. Langton wanted damages in the amount of $4,000. Langton's sister-in-law, Wendy Miller, suggested that the parties hire a mediator to try to reach a settlement. During the mediation session, the mediator saw that the real issue was the fact that Langton's truck was still damaged. Winchester's brother, who owned and operated an auto body shop, agreed to fix Langton's truck at no cost. This solution satisfied both parties. Langton had his truck fixed, and Winchester suffered no out-of-pocket expenses.

## Arbitration

**Arbitration** is the process by which the parties invite a third party, called an **arbitrator**, to settle their dispute. The procedures involved in arbitration are generally more flexible than those followed in a lawsuit. The rules are either set by law or agreed to by an arbitration agreement. The hearing may be relaxed, with the arbitrator or arbitrators receiving informal testimony from the parties, or it may be rigidly controlled, with the arbitrator or arbitrators following strict rules of evidence and requiring lengthy explanations. The parties may agree in advance to be bound by the arbitrator's decision. If they do not so agree, the arbitrator's decision can be appealed in court. There is a common misconception that arbitration, and mediation for that matter, are carried out exclusively by non-lawyers. Sometimes arbitrators are lawyers and sometimes they are not. This is made clear by the American Arbitration Association which states that arbitrators must have, "senior level experience in law, business, industry or another profession." (See American Arbitration Association, FAQ's. Retrieved on June 28, 2010, from http://www.aamediation.com/FAQ.)

Some states require arbitration prior to trial in certain cases. Required arbitration is called *mandatory arbitration*. Some litigants have challenged government-imposed mandatory arbitration as an unconstitutional deprivation of their right to a trial by jury and equal protection under the law. Most states faced with this question have disagreed with these arguments as long as the arbitration requirement does not replace the jury trial and as long as the motives for requiring arbitration are reasonable.

An arbitration hearing can be planned and executed by the parties themselves. Generally, this step means that the parties set the ground rules for choosing the arbitrator or arbitrators, for conducting discovery, for presenting evidence, for determining the outcome, and for enforcing the reward. In addition, details such as setting the time and the place of the hearing, filling vacancies on the arbitration panel, recording the proceedings, handling objections, granting time extensions, and so on, must also be agreed upon. Because of the intricacies of such a process, many individuals who select arbitration prefer to use professional arbitration organizations such as the American Arbitration Association to handle the details of their arbitration proceeding.

Like most forms of ADR, arbitration is not without its difficulties. One shortcoming is that an arbitration hearing is run like a trial but without the safeguards that come with the rules of civil procedure, discovery, and motion practice. This characteristic may actually extend the time involved in arbitration because attorneys and negotiators must prepare a wide variety of legal arguments, some of which might have been eliminated during motion practice. Discovery also sometimes reveals facts that lead the parties into settlement negotiations that might not otherwise take place. Moreover, the wide discretion that is usually granted to arbitrators has, in some cases, led to unreasonable decisions and unjustifiable awards. Sometimes the decision made by an arbitrator comes under the review of the courts, which may result in a reversal of the arbitration order and thus frustrate the whole object of entering arbitration in the first place. Some of these difficulties can be overcome by stipulating that an arbitration award cannot be reversed by the courts except to correct a violation of the arbitration agreement itself.

## EXAMPLE 4-3: Is Arbitration Worth the Effort?

In the case of *Natare v. D.S.I. Duraplastec Systems, Inc.,* the arbitrator agreed that D.S.I. had violated the non-disparagement contract that had been negotiated between the two companies. Consequently, he ordered D.S.I. to pay Natare $5,000. However, the arbitrator did not order D.S.I. to pay Natare attorney's fees, something that the managers of Natare felt was due to them under the agreement. Natare then brought a claim in state court asking the court to overturn the decision of the arbitrator. The case went to the trial court, then to the appellate court, and finally to the Supreme Court of Indiana. The Indiana Supreme Court found no abuse of discretion on the part of the arbitrator, and the ruling stood. This ruling meant that Natare, which had hoped to use the arbitration clause to avoid the delays and the expense of the state court system, may have actually spent more time and money than it would have had the case started in the court system in the first place.

The difficulties associated with discovery can be solved by streamlining the discovery process in arbitration, without going to the extremes represented by the way that discovery is conducted in litigation. Other problems can be solved by making sure that arbitrators follow the same rules in all hearings and insisting that they write down the reasons behind their decisions.

## Med-Arb

**Med-arb** is an ADR process that combines mediation with arbitration. Under med-arb procedures, the parties first submit their dispute to a mediation session. If the dispute is settled via mediation, then all of the parties can leave satisfied. If, however, some matters are left undecided, the parties can move on to an arbitration hearing. During the hearing, the undecided issues would be placed before an arbitrator for final deliberation.

# Early Neutral Evaluation

**Early neutral evaluation (ENE)** is an ADR process in which the parties permit a referee to assess their case on the basis of the facts and legal arguments alone. At the outset of an ENE process, an independent, objective referee is provided with an overview of the facts involved in the dispute and a summary of the legal arguments on which each side has built his or her case. The evaluator, after examining the facts and the law, renders an impartial assessment of the legal rights of each party and a determination of the amount of the award that should be rendered, if any. The parties can use this impartial evaluation to either settle the case or proceed to trial. Even if the ENE does not result in a final decision, it can be used to shape the issues, plan discovery, and guide any research that the attorneys must conduct as the case proceeds to trial.

# Summary Jury Trials

A **summary jury trial** is a shortened version of a trial conducted in less than a day before an actual jury that then renders an advisory verdict in the case. The summary jury process offers litigants a chance to see how a jury would react to the facts of the case, as well as to the legal arguments that will be made by both sides at trial. On the day of the summary jury trial, lawyers from both sides present an abbreviated version of the case to an actual jury. The presentations are simplified, focusing on the essential facts and law. In this way, the summary jury trial eliminates much of the redundancy that occurs during a "real" trial and allows the judge and jury to focus on the essentials of the case.

As noted previously, the ultimate objective of a summary jury trial is to help both sides evaluate the effectiveness of their arguments in front of a judge and jury. This effort in turn helps the attorneys shape the issues and select the positions that are most advantageous to their case. This knowledge is enhanced by the fact that, after the trial, each side has the chance to interview the jurors to see why they reacted as they did.

The success or failure of a summary jury trial depends on several factors. First, only those cases that involve a *bona fide* dispute as to the facts or authentic questions of law should be considered for a summary jury trial. Second, advanced planning is necessary to ensure a successful summary jury trial. The judge must be consulted, issues should be settled, the facts should be composed properly, the jury instructions should be determined, and a date and time established before the trial begins.

Third, during the process, strict controls and ironclad time limits must be imposed on the parties. For instance, opening statements should last no more than 20 minutes. Both sides should have no more than one hour for the presentation of their case in chief and 30 minutes for their rebuttal. The closing arguments should also be limited to no more than 20 minutes. Finally, a conference should be held after the trial, during which the parties have the opportunity to discuss an immediate settlement. Such a conference should be held after the jury has been polled so that their input can be factored into the settlement discussion.

## EXAMPLE 4-4: Summary Jury Trials: A Posttrial, Pretrial Settlement

When Ashley Utalizar was discharged from her job with Solarpower Industries Inc., she was certain that the dismissal had been in direct violation of an implied contract that had been created by Solarpower's employee policy manual. When she brought a lawsuit against Solarpower, both parties decided to hold a summary jury trial. After the trial was held, both sides participated in a posttrial settlement conference. The results of the jury poll indicated that, though the jury had decided in favor of Utalizar, they were unable to agree on the amount of damages that should be awarded to her. As a result, both Solarpower and Utalizar decided that it would be in their best interests to settle the case immediately. The attorneys for Solarpower agreed to the settlement because they saw that the jury was sympathetic to Utalizar, while Utalizar's attorneys agreed that they could not be certain that Utalizar would receive an adequate award if the jury were permitted to decide the amount of damages.

Because one reason for holding a summary jury trial is to determine how the judge and jury will react to the facts and the arguments, it is helpful to have observers gauge how the judge and the jurors react to the points made by both sides. The observers, who are often students recruited from local law schools and paralegal institutes, will record the reactions of the judge and the jurors during the trial. As an alternative, the entire process can be recorded, so that reactions can be observed later.

## Private Civil Trials

A **private civil trial** is an ADR technique by which the parties hire a retired judge or magistrate to hear their dispute, following the same rules used in an official trial. Many states now permit the parties to a lawsuit to have their cases tried in a private civil trial rather than an official court. One advantage of a private trial is that the parties can hold the trial at a time and a place of their own choosing. In addition, the parties have the opportunity to choose their own judge. Decisions rendered by a judge in a private civil trial are just as binding as those made by judges on the official court docket. Moreover, private trial decisions can be appealed in the same way that public decisions are appealed.

Private civil trials are not postponed nor are they interrupted because the court has more pressing duties to perform. In addition, a private trial receives the undivided attention of the judge, who is not sidetracked by the need to attend to other matters such as the sentencing of criminal defendants. Intricate, lengthy civil cases are ideally suited for private civil trials because, in such cases, time is money. Consequently, the shorter the trial, the less expensive the final bill facing the client.

In recent years, some private firms have appeared that specialize in setting up private civil trials. Such firms will make most of the arrangements for the litigants. These arrangements include securing a judge, providing the place for the trial, and providing all necessary administrative support. These firms can also provide a jury for the trial. Jurors for private trials are generally selected from a pool of individuals who have recently served on a jury in an official trial. Therefore, the jurors at the private civil trial are well acquainted with the trial procedures.

## quick quiz 4-2

| | | |
|---|---|---|
| 1. The job of a mediator is to convince the contending parties to adjust or settle their dispute. | true | false |
| 2. Some states require arbitration prior to trial in certain cases. | true | false |
| 3. The early neutral evaluator process is similar to that of a settlement hearing. | true | false |

# 4-3 Proactive ADR

All of the ADR techniques discussed thus far are invoked after a dispute has arisen. Since ADR has become so popular in recent years, some business people are taking a proactive approach to the situation by agreeing in advance to submit to one of the alternative dispute resolution tools should a disagreement between the parties arise at a later date. These proactive ADR techniques include, but are not limited to, partnering, ADR contract clauses, settlement week, negotiated rule making, post-appellate procedures, international arbitration agreements, and the science court proposal.

## Partnering

**Partnering** is a process that establishes supportive relationships among the parties to a contract to head off disputes before they occur. Generally, partnering is best used when a contract involves complex interrelationships among a wide variety of different parties. Construction agreements are ideally suited to partnering arrangements, because construction contracts involve contractors and subcontractors, all of whom must perform in a cooperative manner to fulfill a contract that often takes a long period of time to complete.

Partnering attempts to deter the disorder that can arise during a dispute by drawing up certain ground rules that all the parties agree to observe. The entire process begins with a meeting held after the contract has been finalized but before the project has begun. The meeting is held at a location that is unrelated to the business of any party to the contract. In this way, the process can procede in an uninterrupted fashion.

Moreover, the meeting should be directed by an objective third party, whose job it is to help create an atmosphere of trust among the parties to the contract. The parties attempt to anticipate problems that may arise during the project as well as potential solutions to those problems. The parties agree to address all problems when they arise and to look for solutions that will mutually benefit all those involved in the project. Ultimately, the goal is to improve efficiency, ensure safety, and maximize profit by minimizing expenses, especially those that arise from cost overruns.

The parties agree to handle problems according to some ADR technique rather than by litigation. Finally, they agree to deal with one another in a fair manner within the confines of their legal relationships.

## A QUESTION OF ETHICS

### When Breaking Your Word is Easy to Do

Andrew Zapior, the president and CEO of Zapior Industries, and Oliver McMurray, the president of Georgetown Construction, have just finalized a contract for the construction of Zapior's new research facility in Cincinnati, Ohio. To minimize the problems that may arise, they agree to enter a partnering arrangement. At the end of a three-day meeting, the parties draw up an agreement, one clause of which states that they will submit any claim to mediation. In the third month of the contract, one of Georgetown's suppliers goes on strike, delaying an important shipment of material to the construction site. Zapior demands that McMurray and Georgetown find a different supplier. McMurray, who has done business with this supplier for 20 years, resists the suggestion and calls for a mediation session. Zapior refuses to comply, stating that there is no need to delay the project to maintain a contractual relationship with a supplier that can easily be replaced. Analyze the ethical stand taken by McMurray. Now do the same for Zapior. Which stand do you find easier to support? Explain.

## ADR Contract Clauses

An **ADR contract clause** will specify that the parties to the agreement have promised to use an alternative dispute resolution technique when a disagreement arises rather than litigating the issue. Like partnering, the drafting of ADR contract clauses is a proactive attempt to ensure that litigation will be avoided should a dispute arise. Unlike partnering, which is best suited to long-term construction contracts, ADR clauses can be included in just about any contract.

These ADR clauses can take many shapes and forms. It is possible, for instance, to insert a clause that states merely that the parties have the option of using an ADR technique. Such a clause is weak, at best, serving only to remind the parties that they do not have to sue one another to gain satisfaction. One step beyond the optional clause is a compulsory clause. This clause states that the parties are required to submit all claims that arise under the contract to an ADR technique, most often mediation or arbitration, before filing a lawsuit. The final type of clause would require the parties to submit any claim to binding arbitration. This strictest type ADR clause forces the parties to abide by the decision of the arbitrator.

Regardless of the type of clause used by the parties, the language should include certain standard provisions. For instance, the clause should specify the types of disagreements that will be submitted to ADR, the ADR technique or techniques that can be used, the scope of discovery allowed, the substantive law and the procedural rules that will be followed in the proceeding, the remedies that will be authorized, the grounds for and the procedure to follow in an appeal, and the methods of enforcing an award. The failure to follow provisions specified in an ADR clause may be grounds for the court to revoke a ruling made by an arbitrator.

Such ADR clauses have several advantages. They are especially helpful when two or more parties have embarked on an extended affiliation that may involve numerous contracts, because ADR clauses clearly establish a reliable and predictable method of dealing with the disputes that will inevitably arise whenever two parties are involved in a lengthy association with each other. In addition, ADR clauses are very beneficial to those parties with the weakest position within a contractual relationship. Often, when a dispute does arise, the more powerful party will threaten litigation, secure in the knowledge that he or she can afford a lawsuit more easily than the weaker party. An ADR clause eliminates this leverage point.

---

### EXAMPLE 4-5:   ADR Clause: Power to the Powerless

Audrey Kemmelman, a freelance photographer, entered a work-for-hire agreement with The Daily Montgomery Central Times Corporation. During the negotiation stages, Kemmelman asked that an ADR clause be added to the contract that would compel the signatories to submit any claim to ADR. The clause stated that, in the event of any dispute, the signatories to the contract would first discuss the points of conflict informally. If after 30 days, no satisfactory solution had been reached, the signatories agreed to submit the problem to the American Arbitration Association, which would assist in selecting an objective moderator who would help the signatories decide on an appropriate ADR method. This ADR clause would benefit Kemmelman because, as the weaker party, she might not have the resources to finance a lengthy and expensive lawsuit.

---

Because the parties to an ADR clause are agreeing, at least initially, to forgo the right to litigate any claims that arise among them, the courts prefer that such clauses be clear and precise. Clauses that are drafted in imprecise and ambiguous language may be invalidated by the court. If the parties intend to submit all the claims arising out of their contractual relationship to ADR, they should spell that out as precisely and completely as possible. Otherwise a party that, at a later date, wishes to invoke the clause, may find that the court is reluctant to support that position. When writing an ADR contract clause, it is best to use standard expressions that the court will recognize. Clauses that say that the parties agree to use ADR for "any controversy or claim arising out of or relating to the agreement" will convince the court to enforce the clause for most disputes between the parties. Anything less may meet with judicial resistance.

## Settlement Week

**Settlement week** is a five-day period during which a court's docket is cleared of all business, except for settlement hearings. Prior to the opening of settlement week, all attorneys with cases pending before the court are asked to choose which of those cases might be best handled by a mediator. Judges are also permitted to nominate cases for mediation during settlement week. Also before the opening of settlement week, a list of volunteer mediators is compiled. Cases are then matched with mediators, and a schedule is established. Attorneys are required to be present for the mediation session.

A mediation session is then held for each case. Following each session, the mediator is required to file a report with the court, stipulating the results of the session and asking for the judge's approval. Occasionally, some cases, chiefly those that do not involve determining liability, are submitted to an arbitration panel rather than to a single mediator. In such a situation, the plaintiff chooses one of the arbitrators, the defendant chooses one, and the court names the final one. Not all cases scheduled for settlement week are actually resolved during that time. However, the technique is an effective way to lighten the court's docket and is becoming more and more popular.

## Negotiated Rule Making

**Negotiated rule making (reg-neg)** is a process by which an agency invites the people and the organizations to be affected by a new rule to have input into the writing of that rule. A working team is established that consists of representatives of the affected groups, including the agency issuing the rule. One member of the team is an objective outsider trained in the art of facilitating such discussions. The objective of negotiated rule making, of course, is to avoid disputes before they have a chance to blossom.

All representatives have the opportunity to present their point of view in relation to the proposed rule. Discussions follow, during which all of these issues are examined. Eventually, the team is expected to formulate a rule that reflects a consensus of the representatives. This consensus does not necessarily mean that all parts of the rule are enthusiastically embraced by all of the representatives. Rather, it means that all of the parties agree that they have fashioned a rule that everyone on the rule-making team can live with. The text of the proposed rule is then submitted to the rule-making agency. The success of the process depends on the willingness of the members of the team to work in a cooperative fashion and the willingness of the agency to accept the results of the team's deliberations.

Despite its advantages, negotiated rule making cannot be used in all situations. Certain subject areas are more fitting than others. A suitable subject area for reg-neg would be one that will ultimately affect a wide range of individuals and institutions, is both complicated and controversial, and would meet with resistance if those individuals and institutions affected did not have a hand in shaping the rule. Reg-neg is also a wise course of action when the subject area affected involves nuances that fall outside the expertise of the agency representatives.

## EXAMPLE 4-6:  Reg-Neg: The Great Lakes Initiative

The Ohio Environmental Protection Agency (OEPA) was charged with the task of drafting a series of rules to implement the Great Lakes Initiative. Rather than simply writing the rules and placing them before the affected parties, the OEPA decided to take a negotiated rule-making approach. Consequently, it created the Great Lakes Initiative External Advisory Group (EAG). The EAG was composed of representatives from the agency itself, from the regulated industry, and from environmental groups. The team engaged in eight months of intense negotiations. These negotiations followed a precisely planned series of steps carried out under the watchful eyes of professional facilitators. The EAG reached a firm consensus on most of the issues that arose during the negotiations. Consequently, the Joint Committee on Agency Rule Review of the Ohio General Assembly adopted a set of rules to implement the Great Lakes Initiative in a relatively harmonious atmosphere and with almost no conflict. This is an extremely successful example of reg-neg in action.

## Post-Appellate Procedures

**Post-appellate procedures** involve taking a case that has been rejected or dismissed by a domestic court to an international organization such as the Inter-American Commission on Human Rights of the Organization of American States. In such a situation, a party that has exhausted all domestic remedies available, up to and including the United States Supreme Court, might ask such a **non-governmental organization (NGO)** to hear its case. The post-appellate case is brought against the government of the aggrieved party for allegedly failing to provide an appropriate legal remedy to redress the grievances of the victim. The claim generally involves the violation of some fundamental right, generally a due process or an equal protection right that is guaranteed by an international document such as the American Declaration of the Rights and Duties of Man or the United Nations Universal Declaration of Human Rights. The NGO then hears the case, considers the evidence, and determines whether the party's claim is justified. The NGO may demand that the government of the aggrieved party provide compensation for the injuries visited upon the victim. The NGO may also suggest actions beyond that compensation, including needed reforms in the governmental and/or judicial system to prevent such problems from occurring in the future. Whether the NGOs actually have jurisdiction over such claims is open to debate. Moreover, even if they have jurisdiction, whether their findings are actually enforceable against the government in question is problematic.

## International Arbitration Agreements

An **international arbitration agreement** involves a pledge to use arbitration should the parties find themselves in disagreement as to the enforcement rights under the original contract. Generally, the agreement permits the parties to agree on a forum in which the arbitration will be held that is different from the home forum of either party. The parties also can agree to use the rules and procedures promulgated by an independent institution, such as the International Bar Association's Rules of International Commercial Arbitration.

There are several clear advantages to entering an international arbitration agreement. First, because the parties to the agreement are incorporated in different nation-states, they are free to specify whatever forum they can agree upon as the place to hold an arbitration hearing, should that become necessary. This agreement is in contrast to a litigation clause that might specify that the law of one or the other nation would apply to any legal dispute between the parties. Ultimately, such a clause can become very restrictive. The law of a particular nation-state might, for instance, specify that a dispute that arises within the borders of that nation-state would have to be tried within that nation-state. This rule can put one of the two corporations at a distinct disadvantage that may not become evident until the lawsuit has begun. Arbitration agreements can avoid this problem because the arbitration hearing can be held on neutral ground.

Second, when negotiating an arbitration agreement, the parties are also free to specify the identity of the arbitrators or leave open the option to choose the arbitrators at the time of the dispute from a large pool of potential experts. The arbitrators can thus reside in any location that satisfies all of the parties. Third, the same option is open to the parties in relation to their choice of legal representation. Rather than being limited to the forum in which the dispute is to be heard, the parties can bring in representation from any point on the globe. Fourth, using an international arbitration agreement avoids one of the most troublesome problems linked to international litigation: enforcement. Often a party that has won a favorable decree in one nation will find it challenging to execute that decree in any other nation. International arbitration eliminates this problem because the original arbitration contract will include the terms of enforcement.

Of course, as is often the case, the best laid plans of mice and CEOs often go astray. Thus, sometimes a corporation will find that the jurisdiction that it has chosen for an arbitration hearing has different ideas about whether certain arbitrators and/or attorneys will be permitted to practice within its borders. If a country decides that certain legal representatives and certain arbitrators are not welcome in its jurisdiction, then the parties may find themselves using local attorneys and/or arbitrators, something that not only defeats the objective of the international arbitration agreement but also places the validity and acceptability of the entire arbitration process at risk. This possibility also delays the process further because when an arbitrator is dismissed, the entire action usually must begin again.

Nor are these risks trivial. The danger is especially acute in Latin America, where some nation-states still apply a nineteenth century legal principle that says that foreign corporations doing business in a Latin American country or involved in an international legal dispute within the borders of such a country must apply the law of that country, regardless of any agreement made by the parties to the contrary. Sometimes this agreement means simply securing local legal assistance, but it can also mean that the foreign attorneys operating within that jurisdiction are subject to local law, which sometimes includes criminal penalties for not following the procedural rules of that jurisdiction. (Note: For a more detailed look at the problems associated with international arbitration agreements see Lawrence W. Newman and David Zaslowsky, "International Litigation/International Arbitration—Pitfalls for Participants," *International Litigation and Arbitration Newsletter* November 2006, pp. 3–7 retrieved from http://www.bakernet.com. The article first appeared in *The New York Law Journal,* September 29, 2006).

## The Science Court Proposal

A **science court** acts as a forum for disputes involving scientific and technological controversies. Individuals and institutions with concerns about certain scientific activities, such as genetic engineering, nuclear energy research, and so on, might ask the court to act as an impartial arbitrator in the evaluation of those concerns. The judges on the science court would be scientists educated in the areas under investigation, thus allowing them to use their expertise in deciding cases.

LO10

Supporters of the establishment of a science court argue that a panel of objective judges with scientific backgrounds provides a neutral body capable of making unbiased, well-informed decisions. Moreover, the science court would not necessarily provide the last word in any case held under its jurisdiction. An appeal stage would be a part of the process. Finally, the decision-making process involved in science-related controversies would be centralized by the science court, thus providing a forum that many individuals could use to their advantage.

Critics of the science court proposal argue that a panel made up of objective judges with scientific backgrounds would be almost impossible to convene. Moreover, critics point out that

## THE OPENING CASE *Revisited, Part I*
## Mediation, Arbitration, and the Science Court, Round 2

Recall that in the Opening Case at the beginning of the chapter, two power co-ops, the Cooperative Power Association and the United Power Association, planned to construct a system of high-voltage power lines across farmland located in Minnesota. The farm owners objected to the way in which their land was appropriated for the project by the government and the co-ops. The farmers also objected to the planned location of the power lines because they would interfere with their ability to farm the land properly. The governor of Minnesota called for the creation of a science court to resolve the dispute. Unfortunately, the situation rapidly became politicized. The co-ops, which had received a green light for the project from conventional authorities, refused to cooperate with the science court

unless they were allowed to continue building the power lines during the science court's deliberations. The farmers argued that the purpose for calling the science court in the first place would be undermined if the construction of the power lines was allowed to continue. Moreover, the farmers wanted an extended set of issues placed before the court, including the possible rerouting of the lines and the consideration of alternative power sources. The co-ops, in contrast, wanted the issues narrowed to an examination of any health problems associated with the power lines. Ultimately, the governor was compelled to withdraw his science court proposal because it caused more political problems than it had solved.

the science court would represent an additional level of bureaucratic red tape. In addition, such a forum could rapidly become buried under an avalanche of claims, many of which would be a frivolous waste of the court's time. Finally, some critics argue that because the issues placed before a science court would be highly controversial, the entire process could be plagued with political considerations that would threaten the legitimacy of the entire process.

The Minnesota experience taught certain valuable lessons about the establishment of a science court. First, a science court will not succeed unless it has the power to compel the parties to submit to its authority. In the Minnesota case, for instance, the co-ops saw no reason to cooperate with a voluntary court because their project had already been approved by conventional authorities. Second, a successful science court must have the power to halt work done on any project that is the focus of the court's investigation. Otherwise, the court's entire process becomes an exercise in futility. Third, a successful science court will ensure that all sides have the opportunity to present their views on all issues facing the court. Permitting certain parties to speak on certain issues while denying the same right to others can destroy the credibility of the court and of those involved in its creation and operation.

# Summary

**4.1** Litigation has always been a part of the American legal system. Lately, however, things have begun to change. The extensive backlog in many court systems and the perceived injustice of many verdicts have led many people to seek other methods to redress their grievances. These other methods are often grouped under the heading of alternative dispute resolutions (ADR). Alternative dispute resolution occurs whenever individuals attempt to resolve a disagreement by stepping outside the usual adversarial system and applying certain creative settlement techniques, many of which have fact finding and the discovery of truth as their goal.

**4.2** There are many different ADR techniques that can be invoked once a dispute has arisen between parties. These include but are not limited to mediation, arbitration, med-arb, early neutral evaluation, summary jury trials, and private civil trials.

**4.3** Since ADR has become so popular in recent years, some business people are taking a proactive approach to the situation by agreeing in advance to submit to one of the alternative dispute resolution tools should a disagreement between the parties arise at a later date. These proactive ADR techniques include, but are not limited to, partnering, ADR contract clauses, settlement week, negotiated rule making, international arbitration agreements, the post-appellate option, and the science court proposal.

# Key Terms

ADR contract clause, 77

alternative dispute resolution (ADR), 69

arbitration, 73

arbitrator, 73

early neutral evaluation (ENE), 75

international arbitration agreement, 80

med-arb, 74

mediation, 72

mediator, 72

negotiated rule making (reg-neg), 79

non-governmental organization (NGO), 80

partnering, 77

post-appellate procedures, 80

private civil trial, 76

science court, 81

settlement week, 79

summary jury trial, 75

# Questions for Review and Discussion

1. What are the shortcomings of litigation?
2. What are the advantages and disadvantages of ADR?
3. What are the advantages of mediation?
4. What is the nature of an arbitration hearing?
5. What happens during the med-arb process?
6. What is the role of an early neutral evaluator?
7. What happens in the running of a summary judgment trial?
8. What are the private options available under proactive ADR?
9. What are the governmental options available under proactive ADR?
10. What are the advantages and disadvantages of the science court proposal?

# Cases for Analysis

1. Turner Pte. Ltd. was the main contractor in the building of *Gateway*, a long-term project to be constructed in the heart of Singapore. One of Turner's subcontractors was a company called Builders Federal Ltd. (BFL). As part of the overall contract, the two companies signed an arbitration

agreement, which was designated as Clause 22 in the main contract. When the two parties found themselves in the middle of several serious disputes, they invoked Clause 22 and began arbitration. Turner asked that Mr. David Gardam be appointed as the arbitrator, and BFL asked for Mr. Douglas Smith. The court appointed Smith. From the outset there was bad blood between Turner and Smith, which was revealed in a series of letters that went back and forth between the parties and Smith. At one point in the process, Turner realized that Clause 22 actually had no legal effect until each party activated it by giving their permission to proceed with arbitration. Smith denied that this was the case and ordered the arbitration process to continue. Turner objected, and Smith, who admitted that Turner had made a fairly convincing case, agreed to submit that argument to the High Court of Singapore. Nevertheless, Smith pushed the arbitration process forward. BFL was delighted, but Turner objected. Still the action went forward despite the precarious nature of Smith's position as arbitrator. Can the high court of Singapore dismiss Smith even though BFL is quite satisfied with his work as arbitrator? What grounds might be used to dismiss Smith? If Smith is dismissed, will the arbitration process continue or start over? *Turner (East Asia) Pte. Ltd. v. Builders Federal (Hong Kong) Ltd.* SLR 532 SGHC 47 (Singapore High Court).

2. Jessica Gonzales obtained an official restraining order from a Colorado court that prevented her estranged husband from approaching either her or her children any closer than 100 yards. The order, however, did not stop her husband, who kidnapped their three children. Mrs. Gonzales went to the police and asked for their help. The police did very little to help her, despite the restraining order. Early the next morning, Mr. Gonzales arrived at the police station and began shooting at police officers, who shot back and eventually killed him. After the shooting was over, the police found the bodies of the three young daughters in Mr. Gonzales' truck. Mrs. Gonzales brought suit against the police department, arguing that her due process rights had been violated when the police did not enforce the restraining order. The case went from trial court to the appellate court to the United States Supreme Court, with no result other than a dismissal of the suit. Mrs. Gonzales, with the assistance of the American Civil Liberties Union, filed a post-appellate complaint against the United States with the Inter-American Commission on Human Rights. In her complaint, Mrs. Gonzales argued that she had been deprived of due process and equal protection under the American Declaration of the Rights and Duties of Man, an agreement that the United States was legally bound to follow. Mrs. Gonzales and her attorneys hoped that the commission would issue a judgment in her favor and against the United States. What two initial questions must be answered first before this post-appellate case can begin? Explain. *Jessica Ruth Gonzales v. The United States of America,* Petition No. P-1490-05, The Inter-American Commission on Human Rights of the Organization of American States.

3. In a case involving an ADR clause, the parties to a contract disagreed as to whether the clause required them to submit a dispute over a trade secret problem to arbitration. The clause required the parties to submit "any controversy or claim arising out of the agreement" to arbitration. Strictly speaking, the trade secret controversy did not arise "out of" the agreement. However, it was clear that the trade secret dispute was related to the agreement. The trial court held that the language of the ADR clause was too narrow and that because the trade secret dispute did not arise out of the controversy, the parties were not required to send it to arbitration. Should the appellate court overrule the trial court's decision rejecting the requirement that the parties arbitrate the trade secret dispute? Explain your response. *Tracer Research Corp. v. National Environmental Services, Co.,* 42 F.3d 1292 (9th Cir.).

4. In the early 1990s, serious concerns about the dangers associated with genetic engineering arose after an incident pertaining to the use of certain genetically altered mice in experiments involving a highly infectious disease. In the wake of these concerns, the National Institute of Allergy and Infectious Diseases held a conference to discuss the level of safety that should be followed in laboratories involved in such research. Those involved in the conference included the researchers themselves, certain biosafety experts, representatives from organizations involved in or planning to be involved in similar research, and governmental representatives from the Centers for Disease

Control, the National Institutes of Health, and the Food and Drug Administration. Would this type of situation be appropriate for a reg-neg approach? Explain. Might a science court handle this type of situation even better than an agency's reg-neg procedure? Explain.

5. Andrei Kerensky, CEO of the Malenkov Electronic Surveillance Corporation, entered negotiations with Thomas John King, president and chair of the board for Beckett Industries, Inc., the purpose of which was to develop a new security system for Beckett. The system would use a newly designed security system based on a new laser electronic coding system developed by engineers at Malenkov. King and Kerensky finalized the deal, and the security system was installed at Beckett. After Malenkov's engineers installed the system, security personnel and engineering technicians at Beckett made some subtle alterations in the system's computerized control system. Shortly thereafter, the entire system crashed. When Malenkov's bill was not paid, Kerensky went to see King at Beckett's corporate headquarters. During a short encounter, King informed Kerensky that Beckett was not going to pay Kerensky and Malenkov because the system had crashed. King argued that Malenkov's engineers were responsible for the breakdown, while Kerensky insisted that the modifications made by the engineers at Beckett were at fault because of their unauthorized and incompetently rendered modifications to the system. Kerensky wants to sue King and Beckett but is hesitant to do so because the primary factual issues in the case focus on the engineering modifications. Consequently, he is apprehensive that a judge and jury will be lost by the technical jargon that may be used at trial. What alternatives are available to Kerensky?

## quick quiz Answers

| 4-1 | 4-2 | 4-3 |
|-----|-----|-----|
| 1. F | 1. T | 1. T |
| 2. T | 2. T | 2. F |
| 3. T | 3. T | 3. T |

## THE OPENING CASE   The Gulf Spill Vendetta and Corporate Criminal Liability

Judges and legislators are often faced with making decisions that make no sense or, rather, that make sense only after the fact. A case in point involves the explosion of the Deepwater Horizon drilling rig that led to a massive oil spill in the Gulf of Mexico. The destruction that followed the explosion of the rig left many people demanding that someone be punished for what happened to the workers on the rig, to the wildlife in the Gulf, and to the lives of the people living in the area.

Such action is not as easy as it sounds. Had the rig been destroyed by a terror attack or by a criminal cartel, everyone would know what to do. The FBI and local law enforcement departments would investigate the crime scene, collect the evidence, hunt down the perpetrators, and make their arrests. The Justice Department would then prosecute the defendants to the fullest extent of the law. That, however, is not what happened. Instead of career criminals or radical fundamentalists, the Justice Department had to deal with business people and with corporations. Is it possible to prosecute the people involved in the incident? Certainly. What is more, there are specific laws under which such action can be taken. Laws such as the Clean Water Act, the Refuse Act, and the Migratory Bird Treaty Act could be used to prosecute the offenders. But what about the corporations themselves?

What about British Petroleum, and Halliburton, and Transocean? How do we hold a corporation liable?

As you will learn in this chapter, criminal liability requires that the prosecutor prove that the defendant possessed a particular mental state when the criminal act was committed. Corporations, however, do not have mental states let alone mental states that can demonstrate criminal liability, so how do we prove corporate criminal liability? What about punishment? How is a corporation punished and just who is actually punished when a corporation is fined? Is it the board of directors and the officers? One would hope so, but often that punishment is shared by the stockholders, the employees, the customers, the community, pensioners, and the public-at-large, most of whom had nothing to do with the actual wrongs committed. Keep all this in mind as you read this chapter. The results of your reading may surprise you. (See David M. Uhlmann, "Prosecuting Crimes Against the Earth," *The New York Times*, June 4, 2010, p. A-23.)

**Opening Case Questions**

1. Would the case against British Petroleum be a civil lawsuit or a criminal action? Explain.

2. Would a case against British Petroleum be brought in state or federal court or could it be brought in both? Explain.

3. What legal theory or theories might be used to hold a corporation liable for the torts of an employee? Explain.

4. How is a corporation punished in a case like this? Explain.

5. Since shareholders, employees, and customers end up paying for the corporation's wrongdoing, does it really make any sense to pursue such prosecutions? Explain.

 **Learning Objectives**

1. Explain the purpose of criminal law.
2. Enumeate the various categories and classes of crimes.
3. Describe the nature of an act within the concept of criminal liabiliy.
4. Identify the four mental states to be found in the criminal code.
5. Explain the nature of corporate criminal liability.
6. Explain the various theories of punishment within criminal law.
7. Enumerate and explain the elements of several key crimes.
8. Define and explain the nature of cybercrimes.
9. Explain the three standards for the insanity defense in criminal law.
10. Outline the requirements of entrapment as a defense in criminal law.

# 5-1 Definition and Classes of Crimes

Perhaps one of the most discussed and least understood areas of the law is criminal law. Most people think they know a lot about criminal law, because they read about it frequently in the newspaper and view programs about it on television. In fact, there is a lot of misinformation spread in the media about criminal law and procedure. This section of the chapter attempts to rectify some of these misconceptions by defining crime and explaining the various classes of crimes.

## Definition of a Crime

A **crime** is an offense against the public at large. As such, a crime threatens the peace, safety, and well-being of the entire community. For this reason, crimes are punishable by the official governing body of a nation or state. Also for this reason, the state or federal government, representing the public at large, is the prosecution, that is, the one who brings the criminal action. The person accused of the crime is called the defendant. No act can be considered criminal unless it is prohibited by the law of the place where it is committed, and the law provides for the punishment of the offenders. These laws are created by the federal government and the governments of the 50 states.

**LO1**

### The Objectives of Criminal Law
The primary objectives of criminal law are to protect the public at large, to preserve order and stability within society, to punish those who commit criminal acts, and to discourage future criminal activity. In contrast, as we shall see, tort law is concerned with private wrongs that have caused injury to an individual's physical well-being, property, business, or reputation. Because tort law involves private wrongs rather than public ones, it focuses on the victim. Because criminal law protects the public, it seeks to eliminate crime by punishing wrongdoers and removing them from

society. When a tort is committed, the victim has a cause of action against the person who has committed the tort, which may permit the victim to recover money as compensation for any injuries that he or she has suffered. In contrast, when a crime is committed the government may prosecute the accused.

### Prosecutions and Lawsuits

A single act can be both a crime and a tort. Thus, when a criminal battery is committed against a victim, the criminal defendant will be prosecuted for that battery in a criminal case, the results of which can include imprisonment, a fine, or both. However, the defendant can also be sued by the victim in tort law. The victim will seek damages from the defendant which can include money for hospital bills, lost wages, pain and suffering, and so on. The standard of proof required in a criminal case differs from that required in a tort case. In a criminal case the prosecutor or district attorney is required to prove that the criminal defendant is guilty of the crime *beyond a reasonable doubt*. In a tort case the plaintiff's attorney must prove that the defendant is liable for the tort *by a preponderance of the evidence*. Because criminal defendants can lose their freedom, be fined, and sometimes, in capital cases, even lose their lives, the level of proof needed for a conviction is higher than what is needed to demonstrate liability in a tort case.

### Double Jeopardy

The United States Constitution protects people from being tried twice for the same crime. This principle is called the rule of double jeopardy. Double jeopardy, however, does not protect a defendant from being tried for a criminal offense and then being sued under tort law for that same wrongful act. This is what happened in the case of O.J. Simpson. After being found not guilty for the crime of murder, he was sued by his children for the wrongful death of their mother. This did not violate the rule of double jeopardy. Note that the Simpson case also illustrates the difference between the standard of proof in a criminal case and the standard in a tort case. Thus, although the prosecutors failed to prove Simpson guilty *beyond a reasonable doubt,* he was found liable for wrongful death *by a preponderance of the evidence*. It is also interesting to note that a single offense may trigger two prosecutions if the offense can be designated as two different crimes and can be tried in two different courts. Thus, it is possible, for example, for a police officer to be tried in a state court for assaulting a suspect and be tried in federal court for depriving that same suspect of his civil rights.

### Victim's Rights

Under common law, criminal law did not focus on the victim. The theory was that, if the victim needed some sort of compensation for the actions of the defendant, it was up to the victim to pursue that case in tort law. This has been altered somewhat by the legislatures that have enacted statutes that create a series of victim's rights. These rights often include notice to the victim that an offender has been arrested, the name of the criminal defendant, the defendant's eligibility for pretrial release, the telephone number of the law enforcement agency responsible for the defendant, and the date, time, and place of the defendant's release, if that occurs. Later in the legal process the victim is also generally notified of the defendant's acquittal or conviction, the defendant's incarceration, the defendant's appeal, and the defendant's release date. Victims are also permitted to provide the prosecutor with a written description of his or her injuries. In addition, in many states the victim is permitted to be present at the defendant's trial, is entitled to the return of his or her property, is empowered to give the court a victim's impact statement before sentencing and another statement when the defendant's possible release is pending. In most cases, it is the prosecutor or the district attorney who is charged by law with enforcing the rights of victims.

# Criminal Law in the American System

The American legal structure consists of the federal and the state systems. Both make and enforce criminal law. However, because there are 50 states and the District of Columbia, it is actually more accurate to say that the American system is made up of 52 systems. Nevertheless, it is helpful to limit any discussion of the law to an examination of federal and state systems. We simply must remember that each state has its own code and its own procedures, which, though similar in most respects to all other states, may have its own peculiarities.

**Federal Criminal Law**   Another peculiarity about the American system is that the federal government has no express power in the Constitution that allows it to enact criminal law statutes or establish a national police force. Yet the federal government does enact criminal law and has set up the Federal Bureau of Investigation (FBI) as a national police force. The federal government also has a cabinet-level criminal law enforcement official called the attorney general who has the power to conduct federal criminal investigations. The existence of the federal criminal law system and the various national law enforcement agencies is made possible by the adaptive processes at work within the legal system itself.

**Criminal Law as Adaptation**   The way Congress has assumed powers never granted to it by the Framers of the Constitution demonstrates how the law is a balancing act. The process works something like this: The Framers of the Constitution intended that Congress have only those powers enumerated in Article I, Section 8, of the Constitution. Because the term "police power" is not mentioned anywhere in the Constitution, the Framers did not give that power to the federal government but instead expected the states to exercise all police power. Consequently, Congress can create criminal law statutes only in those areas over which it has jurisdiction. For instance, Congress has the power to coin money, so it can set up laws against counterfeiting. Yet, as we've seen, Congress has created criminal law statutes in areas beyond counterfeiting. If there has been no constitutional amendment explicitly handing Congress police power, how did Congress get the power to create a set of criminal law statutes and a national police force?

The answer is that Congress balanced the actual *words* of the Constitution against the need to *interpret* those words to protect the people from criminal activity. The balance occurred when Congress extended its power through a generous interpretation of the Commerce Clause. The Commerce Clause, found in Article I, Section 8, Clause 3, permits Congress to pass laws that regulate commerce "among the several States." Congress used this clause to regulate interstate criminal activities, which impact "commerce." Although the ultimate results were a long time coming, eventually the courts, through a series of cases, culminating in the case of *Wickard v. Filburn* (63 S.Ct. 82), gave their "stamp of approval" to the legislature's creative balancing act. In a sense then, Congress and the courts cooperated to give the federal governmnent police power, a power it did not have under the Constitution. That power includes the authority to create federal criminal law.

# Classes of Crimes

**LO2**

Under common law, crimes were dealt with in the order of their seriousness: treason, felonies, and misdemeanors. Most states now divide offenses into felonies and misdemeanors. A **felony** is a crime punishable by death or imprisonment in a federal or a state prison for a term exceeding one year. Some felonies are also punishable by fines. Some states define a felony as a crime subject to "punishment by hard labor," as an "infamous crime," or as a "crime subject to infamous punishment." Manslaughter, armed robbery, and arson are examples of felonies.

Some states also have separate categories for their most serious crimes. For instance, a state might classify premeditated murder and murder as *special felonies* or *capital felonies* if these are the only two offenses that might result in a death sentence or life imprisonment. States may also have a separate category for violent offenses. Sometimes these violent offenses are termed *aggravated felonies*. Assault with a deadly weapon might be an example of an aggravated felony.

A **misdemeanor** is a less serious crime, generally punishable by a prison sentence of not more than one year. Included in this category are offenses such as disorderly conduct. Some states also have a separate category for their least serious offenses. The label for these least serious offenses varies, but two of the most common are *petty offenses* and *minor misdemeanors*. Traffic violations and building code violations are usually within this classification.

Following her arrest for driving under the influence, Lindsay Lohan was charged with a misdemeanor and sentenced to 23 days in jail.

## quick quiz 5-1

| | |
|---|---|
| 1. A misdemeanor is a crime punishable by death or imprisonment in a federal or a state prison for a term exceeding one year. | true \| false |
| 2. The primary objective of criminal law is to protect victims. | true \| false |
| 3. It is impossible for a single act to be both a tort and a crime. | true \| false |

# 5-2 Elements of a Crime

The two elements necessary to create criminal liability are a criminal act and the required state of mind. Although it is difficult to generalize about both of these concepts, certain characteristics are common to each, regardless of jurisdiction. Nevertheless, keep in mind that criminal law is largely statutory in nature. Consequently, specific statutory definitions may vary from state to state.

## A Criminal Act

Under American law, a crime cannot be committed unless some act has occurred. An individual cannot be accused of a crime for merely thinking of a criminal act. However, even a small act that appears by itself to be innocent can, in the proper context, become an illegal act. For example, even something as simple as inserting a key into the ignition of a vehicle can constitute an act under the law, if the driver is intoxicated at the time. The act is such an important element to criminal liability that convictions may be avoided or overturned if defendants can show that the statute under which they were prosecuted is ambiguous in its description of the act. Often, such ambiguity will occur when the legislature passes a statute that creates a new offense, when the statute outlaws an activity that may be protected by the U.S. Constitution, or when the statute seeks to outlaw statutes or behavior that cause no imminent negative effect but may eventually lead to great public harm. For instance, the courts have frequently held statutes that outlaw a status, such as drug addiction or vagrancy, to be void for vagueness. The courts have also struck down statutes that are overbroad. The language of a criminal statute is overbroad if the courts cannot determine what specific activity the legislature intended to outlaw.

**Omissions and Refusals to Act**  At times, the failure to act, an omission, or the outright refusal to act may be considered criminal. Generally, however, an omission must be coupled with a legally imposed duty. An air traffic controller who sees two planes on a collision course, yet fails to warn the pilots, would be held criminally liable for this omission. This liability exists even though the controller did not act but instead failed to act.

**Involuntary Movement or Behavior**  Many states specifically exclude involuntary movement and behavior from their general definition of a criminal act. Convulsions, reflexes, movements during sleep or unconsciousness, or behavior during a seizure are all considered involuntary movement or behavior falling outside the limits of criminal liability. However, the mere fact that someone is unconscious during a seizure may not absolve that individual of criminal liability if that person knew that he or she might suffer the seizure, yet took no precautions to avoid harming people or property. A person who decides to drive an automobile knowing that she or he is subject to sudden, unpredictable epileptic seizures may be criminally liable if a seizure causes that person to lose control of the vehicle and kill or injure someone.

## The Required State of Mind

In general, a crime cannot be committed unless the criminal act named in the statute is performed with the required state of mind. Many state criminal codes include the following four states of mind:

- Purpose
- Knowledge
- Recklessness
- Negligence

**Purpose**  Individuals act with **purpose** when they intend to cause the result that in fact occurs. For example, if a person were to point a loaded gun at another person with the intention of shooting that second person, and if shots are actually fired, the person with the gun would have acted with purpose. Some states choose to call this mental state *intent*. Intent or purpose should not be confused with *premeditation,* which is often an added condition in the case of aggravated or first-degree murder. Some states specifically define premeditation as an action that results from the criminal defendant's "prior calculation and design." If, in the previous example, the person with the gun had also planned to shoot the victim, and then actually carried out this plan, the shooting would have been premeditated.

**Knowledge**  When people act with an awareness that a particular result will probably occur, they act with **knowledge**. For instance, if the person with the gun in the preceding example took that loaded gun to a crowded shopping mall and began to fire at random, not aiming at anyone in particular, that person would be acting with the knowledge that a lot of people would be either wounded or killed. This awareness would be true even if the person with the gun were to yell, "I really don't want to shoot anyone. I hope I don't hit anybody!"

**Recklessnes**  Recklessness involves a perverse disregard of a known risk of negative consequences. People act recklessly when they are indifferent to a serious risk they know to exist. Two drivers who challenge each other to an illegal drag race on a public highway are acting recklessly. In other words, they have disregarded the possible serious consequences of their decision to engage in an illegal drag race.

**Negligence**  People act with negligence when they fail to see the possible negative consequences of their actions. A person who cleans a hunting rifle without checking to see if it is loaded is acting with negligence, because that person has not bothered to look for any possible negative consequences that could result from those actions. Criminal negligence should not be confused with negligence in tort law. Negligence in tort law is concerned with the compensation of accident victims (see Chapter 6). In contrast, negligence in criminal law is concerned with punishing the wrongdoer and protecting the public at large.

## The Matter of Motive

*Motive* in criminal law is the wrongdoer's reason for committing the crime. One common misconception about criminal law, which is perpetuated by countless television programs and films, is that motive is an element of criminal liability. Such is not the case. Establishing motive may help the prosecution persuade the jury that the accused is guilty, but proving an evil motive is not necessary for a criminal conviction.

## The Matter of Corporate Liability

Criminal liability requires that the prosecutor prove that the defendant possessed a particular mental state when the criminal act was committed. Such mental states are generally stated quite clearly in the statute that creates the criminal offense. In fact, since criminal liability requires only two elements, the act and the mental state, legislators are very careful in drafting criminal law statutes to make certain that they explain both elements stating booth with great specificity. It is not always easy for a prosecutor to prove that a defendant possessed the required mental state. Still, when the criminal defendant is an individual, at least the prosecutor knows how to proceed. The prosecutor must produce evidence, generally consisting of actions and words, that demonstrate what was in the mind of the defendant at the time that the criminal act was committed. This is hard enough with a flesh and blood defendant. Corporations, on the other hand, do not have mental states, let alone mental states that can demonstrate criminal liability. Nor do they act or speak, except through their corporate officers and employees. How, then, does a prosecutor go about proving criminal liability when the criminal defendant is a corporation?

**Corporate Personality**  The law provides a fairly complete picture of a corporate identity. The law has established that corporations are "legal people." As a corporate person, a corporation possesses an identity, a corporate self, if you will, that maintains an existence that is separate from those who formed it in the first place. The upside to this is that the corporation will exist long after its founders. The downside is that corporations are taxed directly for what they earn as part of the marketplace. The courts have also decided that corporations have just enough "personhood" to qualify for constitutional protections. Thus, under the Fourteenth Amendment, a corporation has the right to life, liberty, and property, rights that cannot be violated by the government either at the state or the federal levels. In addition, as a legal person, a corporation can institute a lawsuit or can be the target of a lawsuit.

**Corporate Liability Theories** Despite popular opinion, corporations are not modern inventions developed in the 19th century. In fact, we know that corporate-like organizations existed in the Middle Ages. At that time, however, common law judges could not conceive of corporate liability because corporations did not possess a mind with which to form a mental state. The modern age changed all of that. Once the courts decided that a corporation was person enough to sue or be sued, it was not a huge leap for them to conclude that a corporation could be held criminally liable as well. One of the earliest theories on corporate criminal liability emerged from within the doctrine of *strict liability*. Strict liability was an appropriate theory at the time, because it did not require intent, something that was difficult to prove in the case of a corporation. By the beginning of the 20th century, however, the courts began to hold corporations liable for the criminal acts of their employees using the doctrine of vicarious liability, a theory which is also called *respondeat superior*. Under this approach, the courts decided that a corporation could be declared criminally responsible if one of its employees committed a crime while on the job, working for the benefit of the corporation. The doctrine has been liberalized to such an extent that today, even if a worker is expressly prohibited from doing anything outside the law, the corporation might still be declared liable for a crime committed by that worker.

## THE OPENING CASE *Revisited, Part I*
## The Gulf Spill Vendetta and Corporate Criminal Liability, Round 2

Recall that, in the Opening Case at the beginning of this chapter, many people called for the prosecution of British Petroleum, Halliburton, and Transocean because they were believed to be responsible for the explosion of the Deepwater Horizon drilling rig and the massive oil spill in the Gulf of Mexico. In response, the federal government set up a special panel to investigate the incident. More than six months after the accident, the panel reported that the problems aboard the drilling rig resulted from a substandard level performance *common throughout the entire oil industry.*

   This finding could be a problem for prosecutors who, under the *respondeat superior* test, must demonstrate, first and foremost, that a corporate agent committed a crime. This may not sound difficult at first blush, but the more we consider the situation, the darker it becomes. The problem plays out like this: If a crime requires intent or knowledge, then the prosecutor will have to prove, beyond a reasonable doubt, that the corporate agent purposely or knowingly performed the wrongful act outlined in the statute. So, for example, suppose the prosecutor wants to target one of the corporations by using an aggravated arson statute to prosecute a rig operator, who was acting as a corporate agent at the time of the

explosion. Aggravated arson would require the prosecutor to demonstrate that the defendant, by fire or explosion, knowingly created a risk of serious physical harm to another person or to an occupied structure. So far, this sounds like an open and shut case. But remember the explosion was not set off by the rig operator throwing a bomb. It resulted from the day-to-day operation of the rig. If the day-to-day operation of the rig was well within industry standards (okay, substandards, but standards, nonetheless), then how can the prosecutor show that the defendant "knowingly" created a "substantial risk"? How do I knowingly create a substantial risk if I am just doing what everyone in the entire industry does as a matter of day-to-day operational conduct? The answer is that I can't and if I can't be held responsible, neither can the corporation. Of course, the prosecutor may have a case against the agent and, therefore, the corporation, for a lesser offense, perhaps one like criminal damaging, which requires only recklessness or negligence as the appropriate state of mind. However, convictions under these lesser offenses may not satisfy those victims of the oil spill who want the prosecutor to "throw the book" at the defendants, especially the defendant corporations.

## THE OPENING CASE *Revisited, Part II*
## The Gulf Spill Vendetta and Corporate Criminal Liability, Round 3

As noted above, many people were outraged by the oil spill that resulted in the Gulf of Mexico from the explosion of British Petroleum's Deepwater Horizon drilling rig. Much of this anger was directed, in general, at British Petroleum and, in particular, at BP's CEO, Tony Hayward. In hearings held in Washington, D.C., the CEO testified that he did not directly participate in any of the decisions made in relation to that particular rig. Under the Model Penal Code, corporate criminal liability requires the authorization, the approval, or the reckless toleration of criminal activity by the board of directors or by a managing officer who is clearly responsible for establishing corporate policy, especially in relation to the incident under investigation. If, in fact,

the CEO did not know what was going on at the Deepwater Horizon drilling rug then, under the Model Penal Code, neither he nor the corporation can be held liable. By distancing himself from the decision-making process, the CEO had clearly adopted a defense of plausible deniability. In engineering this defense, he was undeniably acting in the corporation's best interests, as well as his own. However, he was not acting in the best interests of the shareholders, other employees, the community, and so on. Still, under the Model Penal Code, there was nothing wrong with his conduct. In fact, his conduct was perfectly understandable and eminently reasonable. What does that tell us about the Model Penal Code?

**The Model Penal Code**    The Model Penal Code offers a third theory of corporate liability. Under this theory, a corporation might be held criminally liable if the directors or officers of a corporation authorize, approve, or recklessly tolerate the criminal actions of their employees. Like the doctrine of *respondeat superior,* the directors or the officers must be acting on the job when the crimes occur. On the surface, this policy looks like an effective tool for stopping corporate criminal activity. However, in practice, the Model Penal Code may simply encourage directors and officers to remain ignorant of the actions of their employees in order to develop a defense of "plausible deniability." The defense of plausible deniability allows corporate managers to "honestly" testify that they knew nothing about the criminal activity of which they, their employees, and the corporation are accused.

## The Matter of Punishment

The ultimate purpose of criminal law is to protect the public. This purpose means that criminal law must outline not only the offenses that are prohibited but also the negative consequences that result when an individual has committed one of those offenses. Many legal experts disagree however about what that punishment ought to be. Still, these experts have narrowed the debate to two approaches to the sentencing of convicted criminals: (1) consequences that are designed to protect the public at large and (2) those that are tailored to fit the individual offense or the individual offender.

### Protecting the Public at Large
Consequences that have been created to protect the public send a message not just to the convicted felon but also to all potential offenders. These techniques include deterrance, education, and retribution. Those experts who believe in *deterrence* advocate long and difficult prison sentences so that other people in society are dissuaded from committing similar offenses and thus suffering the same fate. Those who support the theory of *education* say that the criminal process should be presented in a public way so that the public will learn the difference between acceptable and unacceptable behavior. Finally, those who believe in *retribution* are convinced that it does society good to seek revenge against those who have disrupted the smooth running of the social system.

This theory probably has the fewest supporters today. Still, some experts argue that obtaining retribution against those who seek to gratify themselves at the expense of others will prevent many potential offenders from committing similar misdeeds in the future.

## Individual Offenses and Punishment

Consequences that have been created to fit a particular offense or to punish a specific offender are designed to make certain that the individual offender will no longer engage in criminal activity in the future. The techniques for promoting this approach are prevention, restraint, and rehabilitation. Those experts who believe in *prevention* support long sentences in unpleasant prisons so that criminal defendants will abandon their criminal careers. Those who support *restraint* believe that criminal defendants should be incarcerated or even executed for capital offenses to prevent them from ever committing that crime—or any crime, for that matter—ever again. Finally, those who support the theory of *rehabilitation* say that convicted defendants ought to be given the opportunity to reform their conduct, restructure their lives, and start over.

## The Death Penalty

The use of the death penalty in criminal cases has been subject to a series of controls designed to limit the imposition of this punishment to those cases in which the criminal defendant truly deserves to be put to death. Generally, these limits are built into the criminal code and are applied by the court which is responsible for sentencing the convicted criminal defendant. The safeguards come in the form of aggravating and mitigating circumstances, which must be taken into consideration by the court at the time of sentencing.

Aggravating circumstances are those that involve offenses so appalling that the death penalty is clearly warranted. In most jurisdictions the list of aggravating circumstances looks like this: (a) the assassination of the president, the vice president, the governor, or the lieutenant governor of the state; (b) a murder for hire; (c) a murder committed to escape detection, apprehension, trial, or punishment; (d) a murder committed while the offender was in detention; (e) a murder by a convicted murderer; (f) a murder of a law enforcement officer; (g) a murder of a witness against the offender; (h) a murder of a child under 13 years of age; or (i) a murder during the commission of a felony. Usually, the death penalty cannot be imposed without the presence of at least one of these aggravating circumstances.

Moreover, even if aggravating circumstances are present, the death penalty might still be avoided, if the mitigating circumstances outweigh the aggravating circumstances. Mitigating circumstances include: (a) the victim somehow induced the offense; (b) the offender was coerced or provoked; (c) the offender was suffering from a mental impairment of some sort; (d) the offender is very young; (e) the offender has no past criminal record; (f) the offender was not the principal actor in the offense; (g) or the offense was subject to other factors that might be relevant to a reduced sentence. It is also extremely important for the judge who administers the death penalty to be fair and impartial and to be free from undue pressure, conflict of interest, and any other external influence. Generally, the appellate court that reviews the application of the death penalty is required by the rules to evaluate the conduct of the sentencing judge for any hint of partiality, impropriety, or outside pressure.

### quick quiz 5-2

| | | |
|---|---|---|
| 1. The two elements needed to create criminal liability are a criminal act and the requisite state of mind. | true | false |
| 2. Individuals act with negligence when they act with the intention to cause the result that does in fact occur. | true | false |
| 3. Motive is an element of criminal liability. | true | false |

# 5-3 Specific Crimes

Statutory definitions and classifications of crimes vary from jurisdiction to jurisdiction. Nevertheless, several generalities can be drawn to simplify an examination of specific crimes. Crimes can be classified as crimes against people, crimes against property, crimes involving business, and crimes against justice.

## Crimes against People

Crimes against people include, but are certainly not limited to, first-degree murder, second-degree murder, manslaughter, battery, and assault. A more recent addition to this list involves hate speech.

**First-Degree Murder**  Any killing of one human being by another is labeled as a homicide. Criminal homicide is either murder or manslaughter. When the unlawful killing is done with premeditation and deliberate intent, it is labeled first-degree murder, aggravated murder, or premeditated murder, depending on the jurisdiction. The definition of first-degree murder differs from state to state. However, some of the elements are consistent. In general, most states define first-degree murder to include one of the following circumstances: killing someone with premeditation (thinking about it and planning the homicide in advance with "prior calculation and design") and/or killing someone while committing a major crime, such as rape, robbery, or kidnapping. Moreover, several jurisdictions have added other circumstances to the definition of first-degree murder, including causing the death of a victim under 13 years of age; causing the death of a law enforcement officer, when the offender knows or has reasonable cause to know that the victim is a police officer; causing the death of another while the offender is escaping detention for a felony; and killing someone in a cruel way such as with torture. Some states have added most or all of these to their statutory definition of first-degree murder, while others have added a combination of these new factors. It should also be obvious that these states have included some of the aggravating circumstances related to the death sentence within the definition of first-degree murder. The inclusion of these circumstance within the core definition of first-degree murder makes the application of the death penalty more likely.

**Second-Degree Murder and Manslaughter**  If none of the conditions for first-degree murder apply, the crime is known as second-degree murder or, in some states, murder. In many jurisdictions, the difference between first- and second-degree murder is important because first-degree murder usually carries the death penalty, whereas second-degree murder does not. In contrast to murder, manslaughter is an unlawful killing of a person without the intent to kill. A killing that results when a person is in a state of extreme fright, terror, anger, or blind rage that destroys the ability to reason is known as voluntary manslaughter. When the killing results from negligence, it is usually called involuntary manslaughter.

**Did You Know?**

In 1999, SabreTech, Inc., was indicted by a grand jury in Miami for the 110 deaths that resulted from the crash of ValuJet Flight 592. In the case, the corporation faced 110 counts of murder.

## EXAMPLE 5-1: First Degree Murder and Voluntary Manslaughter

Brent Haywood entered a convenience store and robbed the clerk at gunpoint. As he was leaving the store, the clerk pulled a revolver from under the counter and ordered Haywood to stop. In response, Haywood fired his weapon at the clerk, who returned fire. In the exchange of gunshots, an innocent bystander, nine-year-old Teddy Newman, was shot and killed. Haywood was convicted of first-degree murder and sentenced to death by lethal injection. However, the judge, who opposed the death penalty, gave Haywood a life sentence. Teddy's father was in the courtroom when this sentence was announced. In a state of extreme rage, Teddy's father attacked and killed Haywood. Even though Teddy's father's actions were clearly intentional, they were performed in a state of extreme rage as a result of a reasonable provocation. Consequently, he was charged with voluntary manslaughter.

**Battery and Assault**  Throughout most of English and American history, the term **battery** has been used to describe a crime in which the offender causes actual physical harm to the victim. In contrast, **assault** has generally been taken to include the threat of harm to the victim. Today, however, this simple distinction is no longer applicable because many states have created a wide variety of levels and degrees of battery and assault. Some states have even altered the actual language of the law. Ohio, for example, has completely eliminated the term battery and replaced it with the word assault. In Ohio, then, the term assault is used to describe various crimes involving the infliction of physical harm on the victim. To describe offenses that should be identified with the word assault, Ohio uses the terms *aggravated menacing* and *menacing*. Moreover, Ohio has added a few new offenses to the criminal code that are related to, but are not exactly the same as, assault and battery. These include stalking, hazing, and abuse. Given these subtle distinctions, it is always best to check the criminal code in your own jurisdiction before discussing assault and battery.

**Hate Speech**  In recent years, many legislative bodies have attempted to criminalize the use of certain symbols, writings, and speech intended to provoke outrage or fear on the basis of race, religion, color, or gender. These statutes and ordinances are frequently referred to as laws against *hate speech*. Such statutes are constitutional only if they are not content specific. Therefore, though it may be acceptable to draft a statute that outlaws any speech designed to rouse fear or outrage, regardless of the content of that speech, it would be impermissible to outlaw speech aimed at inciting outrage or fear based solely on race, religion, color, gender, or any similar category.

Has 9/11 increased hate speech focused on Muslim women?

## Crimes against Property

Crimes against property include but are not limited to: burglary; breaking and entering; trespass; aggravated arson; arson; aggravated robbery; robbery; theft; fraud, and related offenses.

**Burglary, Breaking and Entering, and Trespass**  The crime of burglary has evolved since the Middle Ages. It was once limited to the unlawful entry into a dwelling place at night. Modern legislatures have extended the definition of **burglary** to include using force, deceit, or cunning to trespass into an occupied structure with the intent to commit a crime. A more serious form of burglary is generally referred to as **aggravated burglary**. Aggravated burglary includes everything that burglary includes but adds the use of a deadly weapon, the infliction of harm, the threat of harm, or the attempt to harm another person. A third related offense is **breaking and entering**, which generally includes using force, deceit, or cunning to trespass into an unoccupied structure with the intent to commit any theft or any felony. Breaking and entering can also involve trespassing on land with the intent to commit a felony. The last offense that is related to these three offenses is **trespass**, which involves knowingly entering land without permission to do so. Some, but not all, forms of trespass include entry onto the land with the intent to commit a misdemeanor.

### Aggravated Arson and Arson

Under common law rules, arson involved the burning of another person's home. Legislatures have expanded this definition so that arson now includes more than one offense. **Aggravated arson** includes using fire or explosives to create a substantial risk of physical harm to an individual or to an occupied building. Often also included in this offense is the hiring of another person to carry out the burning or the use of the explosives. A lesser offense is ordinary **arson**, which involves using fire or explosives to harm or cause a substantial risk of harm to the property of another or to do the same to another's property or to the offender's own property in order to carry out fraud. Again also included in this is the hiring another to actually burn the property or use the explosives. Some states have expanded the arson statutes even further to specifically include the burning or use of explosives against government owned buildings, government parklands, government wildlife preserves, and so on.

### Aggravated Robbery and Robbery

Like many of the criminal offenses already discussed in this chapter, robbery involves more than one offense. Unlike many of the others, however, the definition of robbery has not changed much over the years. The more serious offense is generally known as aggravated robbery. **Aggravated robbery** involves attempting to commit or actually committing a theft using a deadly weapon or a dangerous ordnance or doing the same by inflicting physical harm on the victim. **Robbery** involves essentially the same elements as aggravated robbery. However, in ordinary robbery the offender possesses a deadly weapon but neither uses nor shows the weapon. Robbery can also involve attempting to commit or actually committing a theft by inflicting or attempting to inflict physical harm on another person.

### Theft, Fraud, and Related Offenses

Today many jurisdictions will place theft, fraud, and a series of related offenses, such as receiving stolen goods or passing bad checks, together under a single heading. What each of these offenses has in common is the attempt to separate the rightful owner of property from that property or to somehow profit from that separation once it has taken place. **Theft**, the simplest, and arguably the oldest of these offenses is defined in many jurisdictions as knowingly taking or obtaining control over the property of another individual without that individual's consent using deceit, threats, or coercion. **Fraud** covers a wide variety of crimes today including such diverse activities as identity fraud, Medicaid fraud, worker's compensation fraud, telecommunications fraud, insurance fraud, defrauding a rental agency, and defrauding creditors. What each type of fraud has in common, however, is a deliberately engineered deception that the offender uses to obtain property or services that belong to another. The offenses that are related to theft and fraud cover a wide variety of situations including motion picture piracy, misuse of credit cards, trademark counterfeiting, receiving stolen property, and tampering with records.

## Crimes Involving Business

Nonviolent in nature, business crimes are those carried out by a business or individual in the course of doing business to obtain a business related advantage. Covering a wide range of illegal business practices, business crimes are directed against individuals, other businesses, the government, or the public. The business crimes discussed here include embezzlement, forgery, criminal simulation, passing bad checks, and defrauding creditors.

### Embezzlement

In many jurisdictions, **embezzlement** is defined as wrongfully taking property or funds that have been entrusted to the care of the offender. Unlike similar offenses such as theft, robbery, and burglary, a fundamental element of embezzlement is that the embezzler had control over the property or the funds that were wrongfully taken. Thus, embezzlement often occurs in a business setting and frequently involves the employees of the victim.

### Forgery, Criminal Simulation, and Passing Bad Checks

The crime of **forgery** involves the false making or changing of a writing (without proper authorization) with the intent to defraud. It is also forgery to possess or sell an altered or false writing with the intent to defraud. Some states have expressly added identity cards to their forgery statutes to emphasize the criminal nature of forged IDs. These states generally make it a crime to create, sell, use, or possess a false ID. **Criminal simulation** is analogous to forgery because it also involves the alteration or falsification of an object or a document with intent to defraud. However, criminal simulation involves altering or falsifying art objects, antiques, photographs, films, tapes, recordings, and/or antiquities with the intent to defraud. **Passing bad checks** includes issuing or transferring a check or other negotiable instrument knowing it will be dishonored and with the intent to defraud.

### Defrauding Creditors

Many jurisdictions have statutes that are specifically designed to protect the rights of creditors. The statute against **defrauding creditors** is the crime of removing, hiding, destroying, giving away, or transferring any person's property with the intent to defraud creditors. Under these statutes it is also criminal to hide, misrepresent, or refuse to disclose information about the existence, amount, or location of a person's property to a fiduciary who has been appointed to administer that person's affairs or estate. The crime of defrauding creditors can be either a felony or a misdemeanor depending on the amount of the property involved in the fraud.

### Racketeer Influenced and Corrupt Organizations Act

To prevent a criminal invasion of legitimate businesses, Congress enacted the Racketeer Influenced and Corrupt Organizations (RICO) Act. Under provisions of this statute, conducting a legitimate business with the funds acquired from a "pattern of racketeering activities" can give rise to criminal liability. Many of the offenses that fall within the scope of "racketeering activity"—such as arson and robbery—are serious crimes. Others, however, are less sinister. For example, both mail fraud and wire fraud fall within the definition of racketeering activities. The provisions of RICO can give rise not only to criminal charges but also to civil liability. Thus, it is not uncommon for individuals to seek damages in lawsuits filed against corporations that have violated RICO.

## Crimes against Justice

Crimes against justice involve offenses committed by or with the cooperation of a public servant or a public official. Such crimes include bribery, theft in office, and dereliction of duty. Others, such as intimidation, are committed against a public official or public servant. Still others, such as obstruction of justice, resisting arrest, perjury, and tampering with evidence are committed against the justice system itself.

### Bribery and Theft in Office

In most states, **bribery** involves offering, promising, or actually giving something of value to a public official with the goal of influencing that official in the discharge of his or her public duties. It is also bribery when the public official solicits or accepts a thing of value in exchange for that public official's influence in whatever capacity. Many states have further expanded the crime of bribery to include witnesses who are offered or given something of value in exchange for their testimony. The bribery can be committed by the person who offers the bribe and by the witness who solicits or accepts the bribe. Another offense that involves public servants is theft in office. Most jurisdictions define theft in office to include any theft offense in the criminal code that is committed by a public official or a party official. The theft must involve the use of that official's governmental or party power to obtain unlawful control over governmental or party property or services.

### Dereliction of Duty

In most states the crime of dereliction of duty can involve law enforcement officers and public servants. In relation to *law enforcement officers,* dereliction of duty is any activity that involves the officer's failure to carry out his or her lawful duties. These duties include, but are not limited to, serving lawful warrants; preventing the commission of a crime; controlling unruly prisoners; preventing the escape of prisoners; carrying out criminal proceedings; providing persons confined in a detention facility with food, shelter, and medical assistance; preserving sanitary conditions in detention facilities, and, in general, properly managing those detention facilities. *Public servants* are charged with carrying out those duties that are specifically related to the proper operation of their governmental office. In addition, many dereliction of duty statutes also expressly state that public servants have an affirmative duty to keep their department or agency within the budget set for it by the state legislature.

### Intimidation

The crime of intimidation involves threats of harm to the person or property of a public servant, party official, or witness with the intention of coercing that individual into some violation of his or her public duty. Some jurisdictions have expanded the definition of intimidation to include threats of harm to the public servant's reputation by the publication of false information. This would seem to include not only the publication of false statements in newspapers and magazines and on television, but also the posting of such false information on the Internet via the various social media outlets, such as Facebook, Linked-In, and so on.

### Obstruction of Justice and Resisting Arrest

Most jurisdictions define obstruction of justice as any activity designed to prevent the discovery, apprehension, arrest, prosecution, conviction, or punishment of a criminal defendant. Each jurisdiction also specifies those activities that qualify as obstruction of justice. These activities include but are not necessarily limited to: hiding a criminal defendant; providing that defendant with money, transportation, weapons, disguises, and so on; warning that person of possible discovery or arrest; destroying or concealing evidence; and communicating false information to law enforcement officials about the defendant. Resisting arrest is defined as interfering in the lawful arrest of a criminal defendant. Most statutes defining this offense also penalize the resister for any harm that comes to a law enforcement officer involved in the arrest.

### Perjury and Tampering with Evidence

Under the laws of most states, perjury is defined as making a false statement under oath. However, many jurisdictions also add that the false statement must be material to the proceeding. A statement is material if it can have an impact on the final disposition of the case. Interestingly enough, in most cases, the fact that the perjured testimony is inadmissible as evidence makes no difference; the false statement is still perjury. However, a person cannot be convicted of perjury by a single witness. Tampering with evidence means altering, destroying, or removing any piece of evidence with the intent to somehow lessen the probative value of that evidence. In addition, tampering with evidence includes presenting false evidence to a public official in order to somehow destroy the effectiveness of an official investigation.

## quick quiz 5-3

1. In most states, the distinction between first- and second-degree    true | false
   murder is important because first-degree murder usually carries
   the death penalty while second-degree murder does not.

2. It is acceptable to draft a statute that outlaws speech aimed at    true | false
   inciting outrage or fear based solely on race, religion, color, gender, or any similar category.

3. Passing bad checks includes issuing or transferring a check or    true | false
   other negotiable instrument knowing it will be dishonored and
   with the intent to defraud.

# 5-4 Cybercrimes

As is true of most other crimes, statutory definitions and classifications of cybercrimes (electronic crimes and e-crimes) vary from state to state. Moreover, in the case of cybercrimes, the
definitions are even more varied because there is no agreement on what constitutes a cybercrime. One approach is to state that cybercrimes involve any criminal act that includes
a computer. This strategy, which is often referred to as cyber-trespass, computer trespass, or
e-trespass, can solve many of the problems associated with cybercrime, if only by an indirect
treatment of such crimes. Another way to classify cybercrimes is to distinguish between
crimes committed with a computer and crimes committed against a computer.

## Cyber-trespass

A problem arises when crimes that are already on the books are committed with a
computer. As noted previously, one way to deal with this situation is to create a single
generic offense called cyber-trespass, electronic trespass, or e-trespass. **Cyber-trespass**
is the process of gaining access to a computer with the intent to commit a crime. In effect, in one single stroke, this strategy incorporates the rest of the criminal code into this
one crime, making it an offense to use a computer to commit any other crime in the
code. In a state that takes this approach, all criminal statutes, especially those pertaining
to fraud, embezzlement, blackmail, and theft, become part of this one crime known as
cyber-trespass.

## Crimes Committed with a Computer

Another approach to dealing with cybercrime is to distinguish between using a computer to
commit a crime and committing an offense against a computer. Naturally some of these
crimes will overlap. Nevertheless, enough of a distinction exists between the two to make
this a viable approach to the subject. Cybercrimes that focus on the use of a computer include cyber-extortion, cyber-stalking, cyber-harassment, cyber-assault, cyber-bullying,
cyber-spoofing, phishing, smishing, and vishing.

**Cyber-extortion**   *Cyber-extortion, electronic extortion,* or *e-extortion* can occur when
an experienced hacker gains access to the computer records of a corporation or other institution and discovers some sort of illegal, negligent, unethical, or embarrassing conduct that
might damage the reputation of the target organization. Using the computer, the hacker can
then contact the organization to threaten exposure unless he or she is rewarded financially.

**Cyber-stalking** *Cyber-stalking, e-stalking,* or *electronic stalking* involves targeting individuals for exploitation using computer connections. Cyber-stalkers usually target vulnerable individuals who may be searching for a genuine connection on the Internet. Minors are often targeted by cyber-stalkers. After gaining the trust of the minor or other innocent victim, the cyber-stalker arranges a meeting so that he or she can take advantage of the innocent party.

**Cyber-harassment** *Cyber-harassment, electronic harassment* or *e-harassment* involves using computer connections, often via e-mail or some other social media, to blanket the target with offensive sexual, racial, religious, or political comments, photographs, videos, and so on aimed at disrupting the victim's peace of mind. The psychological impact of cyber-harassment is severe, but often difficult to prove, thus making cyber-harassment an especially vicious crime.

**Cyber-assault** *Cyber-assault, electronic assault,* or *e-assault* has several definitions depending on the jurisdiction. Cyber-assault can involve using social media to threaten to inflict immediate and severe bodily harm on the target victim. In this sense of the term, it is simply an extension of common law assault. However, cyber-assault can also mean a direct attack on a computer system with the intent to disrupt that system.

**Cyber-bullying** *Cyber-bullying, electronic bullying,* or *e-bullying* involves intentional, aggressive, upsetting activities by a single individual or a group of individuals aimed at destroying the mental well-being of a peer. Generally, cyber-bullies use a variety of cyber-social media, including chatrooms, discussion groups, blogs, Web pages, texting, instant messaging, and so on to disrupt the life of the target. The term cyber-bullying is generally used to describe the cyber-activities of students against one another. In most jurisdictions it is not yet a crime.

**Cyber-spoofing** To commit *cyber-spoofing, electronic spoofing,* or *e-spoofing,* a cyber-criminal must falsely adopt the identity of another computer user or create a false identity on a Web site to commit fraud. A simple form of cyber-spoofing involves adopting the identity of an e-mailer to defraud the recipients of the original e-mail. Another type of cyber-spoofing involves creating phony Web sites or diverting users from legitimate Web sites to obtain credit card numbers, debit card numbers, PINs, passwords, or other confidential information to commit a wide variety of fraudulent activities.

**Phishing and Spear Phishing** Phishing and spear phishing are two forms of cyber-spoofing. *Phishing* involves sending out phony e-mails that solicit buyers and, in the process, obtain credit card information, account numbers, PINs, account balances, and so on. When the e-mail has been customized to such an extent that the recipient believes the e-mail comes from a co-worker, a friend, or a relative, the offense is called *spear phishing.* (See "Briefing Cyberwar: War in the Fifth Domain," *The Economist,* July 3, 2010, p. 26.)

**Smishing and Vishing** *Smishing* links SMS (short message service) texting with phishing. *Vishing* connects phishing to voice messaging. In both situations, cyber-criminals send out messages at random, sometimes targeting a particular city, profession, or exchange number, and sometimes using a particular phone list purchased or obtained illegally from an institution like a savings and loan, a credit card company, or a department store. The messages will warn the recipients that their credit card information needs to be updated, or that their account is overdrawn, prompting the victims to contact a number or to access an Internet site. The victims then provide private information such as account numbers, PINs, passwords, and so on. These confidential numbers and passwords are used to infiltrate the victim's financial records, credit card accounts, debit card records, and so on. (See "Smishing and Vishing and Other Cyber Scams to Watch Out for this Holiday," *The FBI-Federal Bureau of Investigation,* November 2010, http:www.fbi.gov/news/stories/2010/ november/cyber_112410/cyber_112410.)

## Crimes that Target Computers

Cybercrimes that target computers attempt tp disable the computer itself, to disable the system that it operates, or to confiscate and use the information stored in the computer, sometimes after erasing the original data. Crimes that target computers include cyber-terrorism, identity theft, cyber-vandalism, and cyber-germ warfare.

### Cyber-terrorism
*Cyber-terrorism, electronic terrorism,* or *e-terrorism* involve using a computer to disrupt or destroy one of the critical elements of the nation's cyber-infrastructure, such as the power grid, the air traffic control system, water and sanitation plants, the ground transportation system, a harbor traffic-control network, a cell tower network, the nation's stock exchange, the banking system, hospital back-up generator systems, or the national defense system.

### Identity Theft
Another cybercrime that targets computers and computer information is identity theft. In identity theft, a perpetrator uses one of the techniques noted previously to steal credit card information, PINs, financial data, access codes, passwords, or debit card information. The perpetrator then passes himself or herself off as the victim. Using this technique, the identity thief can clean out bank accounts, run up credit card debt, divert cash transfers, buy and sell stocks, enter electronic auction networks, approve or cancel shipments, make or revoke hotel and travel reservations, and disrupt the financial and the personal life of the victim.

### Cyber-vandalism
Sometimes expert vandals can attack a computer system so that a Web site is completely destroyed or paralyzed to the extent that legitimate business can no longer be conducted on that site. This type of attack is known as *cyber-vandalism, electronic vandalism,* or *e-vandalism.* Often cyber-vandalism is used to cripple a business as a form of revenge for real or imagined wrongs, to exercise power over a business, or to hurt the owner of a business just for "fun."

## A QUESTION OF ETHICS

Ronald King, who was recently elected mayor of a fairly large Midwestern city, has learned that an underground organization, named the Kesselmen Group, has infected the city's computer system with a virus that threatens to disrupt the city's safety forces' communication system and the city's water supply. If the virus is activated, it will prevent the police and the fire department from receiving emergency calls. The virus will also cause the city's sewer system to contaminate the city's main reservoir. The Kesselmen Group makes one demand: that Mayor King resign so that the deputy mayor, Diane Robertson, can become mayor. As the mayor's chief of staff, what would you advise him to do? Explain the reason for your response using one of the ethical theories identified in Chapter 1 of this textbook.

### Cyber-germ Warfare
When cyber-criminals use viruses to attack a computer system, they are engaged in cyber-warfare, cyber-germ warfare, electronic germ warfare. Clearly, viruses can be used to enter computer systems for many of the crimes listed previously. Thus, a cyber-extortionist can threaten to unleash a virus into a computer system unless

he or she is paid a certain amount of money. In effect, the cyber-extortionist is using the virus to extract ransom money from the business. Similarly, the cyber-terrorist or cyber-vandal can use a virus to disrupt a computer system for political or psychological reasons.

## Federal Cybercrimes

Many states have enacted legislation to combat these cybercrimes and other cyber-offenses. The federal government has also attempted to deal with the issue by passing a number of anti-cybercrime statutes. The statutes of primary importance as determined by the Computer Crime and Intellectual Property Section of the United States Department of Justice include the Computer Fraud and Abuse Act (CFAA), the Electronic Communications Privacy Act (ECPA), the Communications Assistance for Law Enforcement Act (CALEA), the Economic Espionage Act (EEA), the National Stolen Property Act (NSPA), the Identity Theft and Assumption Deterrence Act (ITADA).

**The Computer Fraud and Abuse Act (CFAA)**   Congress first specifically addressed the subject of cybercrime over two decades ago when, as a part of a comprehensive crime control statute, it passed the Computer Fraud and Abuse Act (CFAA). Currently, this act outlaws the following activities: obtaining national security information, compromising the confidentiality of a computer, trespassing in a government computer, accessing a computer to defraud, damaging a computer, damaging computer information, trafficking in passwords, and threatening to damage a computer.

**The Electronic Communications Privacy Act (ECPA)**   Originally the Federal Wiretap Act was designed to cover only wire and oral communications. The Electronic Communications Privacy Act (ECPA) amended the original wiretap act to cover communication by computer. The purpose of the amendment was to protect the privacy of electronic communication in the same way that wire and oral communication are protected. To do this, the act prohibits the intentional interception of electronic communication.

**The Communications Assistance for Law Enforcement Act (CALEA)**   The ECPA was later amended to help law enforcement officials keep pace with modern advances in electronic communication. The Communications Assistance for Law Enforcement Act (CALEA) amended the earlier law by requiring communication companies to update their electronic equipment in order to make certain that such law enforcement officers could carry out their surveillance duties properly.

**The Economic Espionage Act (EEA)**   The Economic Espionage Act (EEA) is designed to protect trade secrets. A trade secret is a plan, process, or device that is used in a business and is known only to those employees who need to know the secret to carry out their work. Examples of trade secrets include customer lists, chemical formulas, manufacturing processes, marketing techniques, pricing methods, and food or beverage recipes (think *Coca-Cola*). The EEA outlaws the downloading of trade secrets.

**The National Stolen Property Act (NSPA)**   Under the National Stolen Property Act (NSPA), it is a federal crime to use interstate or foreign commerce to transport personal property, currency, or securities that an individual is aware were stolen, were secured by fraud, or were taken by some other illegal method including an unauthorized electronic transfer.

**The Identity Theft and Assumption Deterrence Act (ITADA)**   The Identity Theft and Assumption Deterrence Act (ITADA), which was amended by the Identity Theft Penalty Enhancement Act, outlaws the unauthorized transfer, possession, or use of a means of identifying another person to violate federal law. The amendment adds a new crime, called *aggravated identity theft* to the original statute. The section on aggravated identity theft makes it clear that identity theft is much worse when it involves certain very serious felonies, including terrorism.

**The CAN SPAM Act**   Spam is the nickname for all of those pop-up advertisements that appear on computer screens while users are tapped into the Internet. The CAN SPAM Act is designed to deal with this problem, as well as the problem of unsolicited commercial e-mail.

## The Global Cyber-crisis

The U.S. government, U.S. corporations, and the U.S. military have become increasingly aware of both the power and the vulnerability of the Internet. National and global computer networks tie together a wide variety of systems that are used to make the global infrastructure more manageable, more efficient, and more affordable than ever before. Moreover, given the chance, very few of us would return to the days of manually controlled banking, line-of-sight air traffic control, in-person stock market trading, three-channel television, land-line rotary phones, and manually operated passenger rail service. Nevertheless, with efficiency and convenience comes a tradeoff. That tradeoff is vulnerability. The computer network is susceptible to collapse. A solar storm, a shift in the earth's magnetic field, a volcanic eruption, poorly written software, an incorrect file number, or inadequately maintained hardware can disrupt even the best computer system. Human operators can enter an outdated password, an inaccurate code, or the wrong person's PIN. Most of these errors are predictable and can be handled with a minimal amount of inconvenience. Other problems, those that are deliberate and knowingly target a computer system, are less easily solved.

For example, an enemy nation, a drug cartel, a crime syndicate, a gang of cyber-pirates, or a team of terrorists can, with a minimal amount of effort, send an e-mail with an attached PDF file that, when opened, will install a deadly software program in a computer system. The software might command the system to shut down, delete data, or, perhaps worse, transfer control of the system to the attacker. Generally, when this type of terror attack occurs, no one knows what happened until the damage is done. Thus, without warning, the nation's air traffic control system might be shut down, a city's water supply might be contaminated, a hospital's blood bank could lose refrigeration, or a banking system might be wiped clean of all transactions. Constructing a plan for dealing with a deliberate computer attack is difficult at best. Nevertheless, steps must be taken to deal with such attacks. (See "Briefing Cyberwar: War in the Fifth Domain," *The Economist,* July 3, 2010, p. 25.)

**Cyber-Strategies and Cyber-Solutions**   One step might be to split up data and send it along a series of different routes so that, if one data stream is compromised, the others continue on their way unimpeded. This strategy is effective most of the time. However, even this tactic does not always work. One weakness in the submerged fiber-optic cable system, along which many data streams travel, is a network of bottlenecks, sites at which these streams intersect and fall under the control of a limited number of domain-name servers, making them tempting targets for cyber-criminals and cyber-terrorists. These bottlenecks appear in the Middle East, in South East Asia, and along the Eastern seaboard of the United States, any one of which is a tempting target. (See "Briefing Cyberwar: War in the Fifth Domain," p. 25.)

**Cyber-Command (Cybercom)**   The federal government has responded to these threats in a number of ways. First, the Pentagon has established a new cyber-command center which is charged with the job of protecting the military's computer command system. This new agency, which is officially referred to as Cyber Command or Cybercom, is under the control of the National Security Agency. It has been charged not only with protecting the American cyber-system from attack, but also with developing plans to undermine the computer systems of enemy nations. One of its goals might be to protect the "chokepoints" in the submerged fiber-optic system, but also to uncover effective ways to use the system in a way that benefits the American military (See "Briefing Cyberwar: War in the Fifth Domain," p. 25.)

**Internet Crime Complaint Center (IC3)**  On the homefront, the federal government has taken steps to combat domestic cybercrime by establishing the Internet Crime Complaint Center (AKA IC3). The IC3 operates as a joint venture between the National White Collar Crime Center (NW3C) and the Federal Bureau of Investigation (FBI). The IC3 handles complaints involving cybercrimes such as hacking, trade secret infringement, identity theft, cyber-extortion, and internet fraud. Individuals and businesses can file complaints with the IC3 by accessing their Web site online. The IC3 also works closely with administrative agencies as well as with local, state, and federal law enforcement agencies. (See *Internet Crime Complaint Center,* http://www.ic3.gov)

**Domestic Strategies**  The battle against cyber-abuse can now be fought in the home. Using a variety of computer software programs, parents can filter e-mails, text messages, and social site contacts on the Internet to prevent their children from receiving messages that are symptomatic of cyber-bullying and similar unwanted cyber-contacts. One popular weapon in this battle is the MouseMail software package developed by Safe Communications. The MouseMail stystem permits a parents to have e-mails, text messages, and other cyber-contacts heading to their children to be intercepted and filtered by a rapid comparison between the content of the message and a list of improper words. Unfamiliar senders are also tagged. The tagged messages are sent to the parents first who handle them from that point on. Other similar software packages include Cyber/Bully/Alert.com and Social Shield.com. (See Mike Snyder, "MouseMail Traps Kids' Cyberbullies," *USA Today,* January 5, 2011), 1A; see also *Welcome to Mouse Mail,* http://mousemail.com.)

---

## quick quiz 5-4

| | | |
|---|---|---|
| 1. Statutory definitions and classifications of cybercrimes have become uniform within all jurisdictions in the United States. | true \| false |
| 2. Cyber-trespass is defined as gaining access to a computer with the intent to commit a crime. | true \| false |
| 3. The federal government has passed several cybercrime statutes. | true \| false |

---

# 5-5 Defenses to Criminal Liability

Because criminal liability lies within the elements of an act and the required mental state, a logical defense would be aimed at eliminating one or both of those elements. Most defenses attempt to do just that. The most common defenses are insanity, entrapment, justifiable force, and mistake. (See Table 5-1.)

## The Insanity Defense

Although the insanity defense has been around for a long time, many people do not understand the nature of the defense. One of the key points of confusion is the difference between *competency to stand trial* and the *insanity defense* itself.

| **Table 5-1**  Criminal Liability and Defenses | |
| --- | --- |
| **Criminal Liability** | **Criminal Defenses** |
| The act:<br>  Criminal behavior specifically<br>    outlined by statute | Defenses to the act:<br>  Act as defined is "status" only<br>  Act as defined is ambiguous<br>  Act as defined is overbroad |
| The mental state:<br>  Mental state specifically<br>    outlined by statute<br>  Purpose<br>  Knowledge<br>  Recklessness<br>  Negligence | Defenses to the mental state:<br>  Insanity<br>  Entrapment<br>  Justifiable force<br>  Mistake |

**Competency to Stand Trial**  Criminal defendants are generally presumed to be mentally competent to stand trial. However, the issue of competency to stand trial can be raised if the court, the defense attorney, or the prosecutor suspects that the defendant is not competent. If the issue of competency is raised, the defendant will undergo psychiatric examinations to determine his or her level of competency. Generally, defendants are considered competent to stand trial if they understand the nature and the purpose of the charges against them, and if they are capable of aiding their attorneys in their defense. When defendants are found to be incompetent, they are usually given treatment to improve their competency level so that they can understand what is going on and can assist in their case.

## EXAMPLE 5-2:  Competency and the Ability to Assist

The question of competency to stand trial was a key factor in a case in which Harold Gunther was prosecuted for the murder of one person and the attempted murder of two others. Listening at the door of an apartment, Gunther believed he heard three co-workers plotting against him. Convinced that he was about to be attacked, Gunther entered the apartment and assaulted his three co-workers, killing one and severely injuring the other two. Gunther consistently maintained that he was the intended target of a plot to destroy him. No evidence was ever presented that such a plot existed. In contrast, expert testimony indicated that Gunther was paranoid and delusional. Consequently, his defense attorney moved for a competency hearing. Despite the expert testimony, the judge in the case found Gunther competent to stand trial. The competency ruling was based on the fact that, despite Gunther's mental problems, he was capable of understanding the charges against him and was able to assist in his defense. Under state law, these were the only qualifications needed for a competency finding by the court. Gunther met these qualifications and was found competent to stand trial.

**Not Guilty by Reason of Insanity (NGRI)**  American law recognizes that individuals cannot be held responsible for their actions if they do not know what they are doing. In addition, it serves no practical purpose to imprison someone who needs the care of mental health professionals. For these reasons, insanity is recognized as a valid defense to criminal conduct.

The oldest test of insanity is the **M'Naughten Rule**. Under this rule, a defendant can be found NGRI if, at the time the criminal act was committed, he or she was suffering from a mental disease that was so serious that the defendant did not know the nature of the act or did not know that act was wrong. Another test of insanity is the **irresistible impulse test**. This test holds that criminal defendants can be found NGRI if, at the time of the offense, they were stricken with a mental disease that prevented them from knowing right from wrong or that compelled them to commit the crime.

Under the **American Law Institute (ALI) test**, a person is not responsible if "as a result of mental disease or defect he lacks substantial capacity either to appreciate the criminality of his conduct or to conform his conduct to the requirements of law." The ALI test is plainly a relaxation of the usual insanity standard, as expressed in M'Naughten and the irresistible impulse test, because both of the older tests require "total" rather than "substantial" impairment. M'Naughten requires an inability to appreciate the wrongfulness of an action, and the irresistible impulse test requires a thorough loss of self-control.

It is important to understand that people found not guilty by reason of insanity do not automatically go free. Instead, they are committed to institutions and must undergo periodic psychiatric examinations. Once they are found to be sane, they may be released. Many people object to the fact that these individuals can look forward to release without serving any time in prison.

## Entrapment

If a law enforcement officer induces a law-abiding citizen to commit a crime, **entrapment** may be used as a defense. The person using the defense must show that the crime would not have been committed had it not been for the inducement of the officer. The defense of entrapment is not available to a defendant who would have committed the crime even without the involvement of the officer. This factor is referred to as the propensity to commit the crime. The entrapment defense can be used in many different types of criminal cases. However, it occurs most often when the police have engineered a sting operation designed to tempt individuals who already have the propensity to commit the crime in question. Often in a sting operation, the main players are undercover law enforcement officers. However, sometimes they can be informants or reformed crminals who are used by the police to tempt individuals who are known by the police to be presently involved in a pattern of criminal activity. The fact that the police have used informants rather than undercover agents will not negate the entrapment defense, as long as all of the other elements are present.

## Justifiable Force

In general, the law will not condone the use of force to solve problems. Still, special circumstances may arise that justify the use of force. Three of these situations lead to the following defenses: self-defense, defense of others, and battered spouse syndrome.

### Self-Defense   When individuals have good reason to believe that they are in danger of death or serious injury, they can use force to protect themselves. This action is known as **self-defense**. In some states, the person claiming self-defense must retreat, if possible, before resorting to force. However, a person does not have a duty to retreat before using force if the attack occurs in his or her own home. When self-defense is used in a criminal case, the defendant must show that he or she was not the one who started the altercation in the

first place. Moreover, in all cases, the person claiming self-defense must not have used more force than necessary to stop the unprovoked attack.

### Defense of Others

If a person uses force to rescue another person who is the victim of an apparent attack, most states will allow the rescuer to escape criminal liability. This exception is known as the **defense of others**. As in the case of self-defense, the rescuer must have good reason to believe that the victim was in danger of severe bodily injury or even death.

### Battered Spouse Syndrome

The law also protects a married individual from being abused by his or her spouse. In most cases of spouse abuse, the wife is victimized by the violent outbursts of her husband. Many communities have established shelters where abused and battered wives can seek safety and receive counseling and legal services for themselves and their children. Wives who wish to protect themselves from the continual abuse caused by their husbands may seek legal help from the courts.

One such remedy is a *protective order*. Protective orders bar the abusing spouse from maintaining any contact with the victim. Such orders are enforced by the local police. Unfortunately, protective orders are not always effective. In some very severe cases, the victimized spouse has taken the law into her own hands and killed her tormentor. The set of circumstances that leads a woman to believe that the only way that she can escape death or severe bodily injury is to use force against her tormentor is called **battered spouse syndrome**. These circumstances are also known as *battered woman* or *battered wife syndrome*. Because the spouse had good reason to believe that she was in danger of death or severe bodily injury, battered spouse syndrome is considered a form of self-defense in some courts.

## Mistake

Mistake is a defense to charges of criminal liability, as long as the mistake destroys one of the elements necessary to that crime. If the mistake does not destroy an element, it is not a valid defense. To be a successful defense, the mistake must be based on a reasonable belief. It would be no defense for a defendant to say that he shot his wife because he believed she was an invader from Mars. Note also that it is not a defense for an accused to say that she did not know that this particular conduct was prohibited by law. Nor is it a defense to a gambling charge for the defendant to argue that she did not know that the gambling law applied to her. Finally, the mistake must destroy the criminal nature of the act in the mind of the accused. It would be no defense, for example, if a defendant argued that he injured an individual by mistake when he was actually trying to injure someone else.

### quick quiz 5-5

1. Most defendants who are found NGRI are released immediately.    true | false
2. A person does not have to retreat to his or her own home before resorting to force to repel an attack.    true | false
3. Mistake is never a defense to a charge of criminal liability.    true | false

# Summary

**5.1** A crime is an offense against the public at large. As such, a crime threatens the peace, safety, and well-being of the entire community. For this reason, crimes are punishable by the official governing body of a nation or state. A felony is a crime punishable by death or imprisonment in a federal or a state prison for a term exceeding one year. Some felonies are also punishable by fines. A misdemeanor is a less serious crime that is generally punishable by a prison sentence of not more than one year.

**5.2** The two elements necessary to create criminal liability are (a) an act and (b) the requisite state of mind. Generally speaking, a crime cannot be committed unless the criminal act named in the statute is performed with the requisite state of mind. Many state criminal codes include four possible states of mind: (a) purpose, (b) knowledge, (c) recklessness, and (d) negligence. Establishing motive may help investigators pinpoint the guilty party, but proving an evil motive is not necessary for a criminal conviction. Conversely, establishing the existence of a good motive will rarely absolve a defendant of criminal liability.

**5.3** Crimes against people include but are certainly not limited to first-degree murder, second-degree murder, manslaughter, battery, and assault. A more recent addition to this list involves hate speech. Crimes against property include but are not limited to burglary; breaking and entering; trespass; aggravated arson; arson; aggravated robbery; robbery; theft; fraud, and related offenses. Crimes involving business include embezzlement, forgery, criminal simulation, passing bad checks, and defrauding creditors. RICO offenses also involve business crime. Crimes against justice include bribery, theft in office, and dereliction of duty. Others, such as intimidation, are committed against a public official or public servant. Still others, such as obstruction of justice, resisting arrest, perjury, and tampering with evidence are committed against the justice system itself.

**5.4** Cybercrimes include cyber-trespass, which involves any conventional crime committed with a computer. Cybercrimes that focus on the use of a computer include cyber-extortion, cyber-stalking, cyber-harassment, cyber-assault, cyber-bullying, cyber-spoofing, phishing, smishing, and vishing. Crimes that target computers include cyber-terrorism, identity theft, cyber-vandalism, and cyber-germ warfare. Federal cybercrimes include Computer Fraud and Abuse Act (CFAA), the Electronic Communications Privacy Act (ECPA), the Communications Assistance for Law Enforcement Act (CALEA), the Economic Espionage Act (EEA), the National Stolen Property Act (NSPA), the Identity Theft and Assumption Deterrence Act ((ITADA).

**5.5** Because criminal liability relies on the two essential elements of act and requisite mental state, a logical defense aims at eliminating one or both of those elements. Most defenses attempt to do just that. The most common defenses are insanity, entrapment, justifiable force, and mistake.

# Key Terms

aggravated arson, 98

aggravated burglary, 97

aggravated murder, 96

aggravated robbery, 98

American Law Institute (ALI) test, 108

arson, 98

assault, 97

battered spouse syndrome, 109

battery, 97

breaking and entering, 97

bribery, 99

burglary, 97

crime, 87

criminal simulation, 99

cyber-trespass, 101

cyber-extortion, 101

defense of others, 109

defrauding creditors, 99

dereliction of duty, 100

double jeopardy, 88

embezzlement, 98

entrapment, 100

felony, 89

first-degree murder, 96

forgery, 99

fraud, 98

homicide, 96

intimidation, 100

involuntary manslaughter, 96

## Questions for Review and Discussion

1. What is the purpose of criminal law?
2. What are the various categories and classes of crimes?
3. What is the nature of an act according to the meaning of criminal liability?
4. What are the four mental states that can be found in the criminal code?
5. What is motive, and how does it differ from the elements of criminal liability?
6. What are the various crimes against people?
7. What are the various theories involved in criminal punishment?
8. What are the various ways that the federal government has dealt with cybercrime?
9. What are the three standards for the insanity defense found in criminal law?
10. What are the requirements of entrapment as a defense against criminal liability?

## Cases for Analysis

1. Fred Pomeroy was an assistant traffic manager for the New York Central and Hudson River Railroad Company. In that capacity, he handed out "rebates" to the American Sugar Refining Company in New York and New Jersey and to W. H. Edgar & Son in Detroit. The goal of the rebates was to convince the sugar refiner and the sugar dealer, to use the railroad for their shipments rather than some other method. The problem with this arrangement was that the shipping rates were fixed by federal law and, thus, the rebates amounted to a bribe. Pomeroy and New York Central were prosecuted under the Elkins Act and were found guilty. On an appeal that went all the way to the U.S. Supreme Court, New York Central argued that, while Pomeroy could be prosecuted under the criminal statute, the corporation could not. Can the corporation be prosecuted? What theory would you advise the court to use in this case? Explain. What will the outcome be? (See *New York Central & Hudson River Railroad v. United States,* 212 U.S. 481 (U.S. Supreme Court).)

2. The hospitality industry in Portland, Oregon, instituted an organization that was designed to bring convention business to the city. Association members made fixed contributions to the organization and companies in the supply business were expected to donate funds based on a percentage of their sales. Supply companies that did not contribute were boycotted by the membership. This boycott was a clear violation of the federal Sherman Antitrust Act. Both the president of Hilton Hotels Corporation and the manager of the Portland Hilton ordered the purchasing agent of the Portland Hotel to ignore the boycott entirely and to make purchases based only on the quality of the products and service from suppliers. The purchasing agent for the Portland Hilton, however, out of personal resentment toward the sales rep of a particular supplier, enforced the boycott. After being found guilty of violating federal law, Hilton appealed, arguing that the trial court misinterpreted the law because the corporation could only be held liable if the purchasing agent committed a crime within the scope of employment with the intention that the corporation gain some benefit from that crime. In this case, it was clear that the agent had committed a crime but the acts were not within the scope of

employment because he had been expressly forbidden to continue the boycott. What was the result on appeal? Explain. *United States v. Hilton Hotels Corporation,* 467 F. 2d 1000 (9th Circuit).

3. After Charles Hood was convicted of murder, he was sentenced to death in accordance with Texas law. It was later revealed, however, that the judge who presided at Hood's trial had been involved in a lengthy affair with the prosecutor in the case. Neither the judge nor the prosecutor had revealed this relationship during the trial. Moreover, after the trial, they denied the relationship until they were compelled to tell the truth under oath. The Texas Court of Criminal Appeals later agreed to a new sentencing hearing for Hood. However, the hearing was limited to questions concerning the jury instructions and, therefore, did not involve the conflict of interest problem caused by the affair. Hood filed a petition for certiorari with the United States Supreme Court. Should the U.S. Supreme Court hear the case? Explain. See Mark White, "Death Penalty Must Be Fair," *The National Law Journal,* March 29, 2010, p. 43.)

4. Antonio Martinez, also known as Muhammad Hussain, discussed the killing of American soldiers with an unnamed individual who, unknown to Martinez, was actually an FBI informant. The informant passed that information to FBI agents who arranged a sting operation during which Martinez helped build a phony car bomb. Martinez was arrested as he attempted to set off the phony car bomb in front of a recruiting center in suburban Baltimore. Martinez claimed that he was entrapped by the federal agents. Martinez's attorney argued that the defendant was not capable of developing the plan to make the bomb on his own. The federal attorney also argued that Martinez had clearly been making plans to attack U.S. soldiers before the informant contacted him. The federal attorney also argued that whether Martinez was capable of actually building a bomb on his own did not matter since, he not only believed that he could do it, but also actually tried to do it, and would have done it had the bomb not been a fake. The prosecuting attorney also had a tape of Martinez arming the bomb. The video shows that Martinez enjoyed the prospect of killing the soldiers. Was Martinez entrapped? Explain by outlining the elements of entrapment. "Lawyer

Argues Entrapment in Bomb Plot," *The New York Times,* December 14, 2010, p. 18.)

5. Katie Roberts was wasting away from the effects of an incurable disease. She asked her husband Frank to help her commit suicide. In response to her request, Mr. Roberts mixed poison and water and placed the mixture on a chair within her reach. She took the poison and died several hours later. Mr. Roberts admitted placing the poison within her reach but denied having the required mental state for first-degree murder because he was responding to his wife's request and was motivated by love and mercy. Will he prevail? Explain. *People v. Roberts,* 178 N.W.690 (MI).

6. Several teenagers taped the broken legs of a chair together to create a cross, which they then ignited and placed on the lawn of an African-American family in the neighborhood. One of the teenagers, a minor, was charged with a misdemeanor under the St. Paul Bias-Motivated Crime Ordinance. The St. Paul ordinance criminalized the placing on private property of any "symbol, object, appellation, characterization or graffiti . . . which one knows or has reasonable grounds to know arouses anger, alarm, or resentment in others on the basis of race, color, creed, religion or gender." The defendant argued that the ordinance was an unconstitutional violation of the First Amendment. The city contended that the statute was constitutional because it was necessary for the preservation of a compelling state interest, namely, the right of group members who have been discriminated against in the past "to live in peace where they wish." Is the St. Paul ordinance constitutional? Explain. *R.A.V. v. St. Paul,* 505 U.S. 1992 (U.S. Sup. Ct.).

7. Tomas Reese entered a fast-food restaurant before the restaurant had opened for business through an unlocked rear entrance. The door had been left unlocked by an accomplice who was an employee of the restaurant. After entering the restaurant, Reese pushed one employee against a soda machine and, while holding a gun to the neck of the manager, forced her to open the safe. Reese then locked the employees in a cooler and fled the scene with over $5,000. Has Reese committed burglary, robbery, or larceny? Explain. *State v. Reese,* 113 Ohio App. 3d. 642 (OH).

8. Cuttiford and Banks lived in the same duplex; Banks lived upstairs and Cuttiford lived down-

stairs. The two apartments shared a common internal stairway at the back of the duplex. A confrontation began between Banks and Cuttiford in the rear stairway of the duplex. Banks became rather violent and threatened Cuttiford and Cuttiford's wife. Cuttiford went to his apartment on the bottom floor and retrieved two guns from his bedroom. When he returned to the back door near the stairway, Banks told him, "You don't have the guts to use that, because you're going to have to use it because I'm going to kill you!" Banks then came at Cuttiford, lunging from the common stairway into the kitchen of the Cuttiford's apartment. Cuttiford then shot and killed Banks. At trial, Cuttiford argued that he shot Banks in self-defense. The trial court refused to instruct the jury that Cuttiford did not have to retreat into his own home before acting to repel an attacker. The court apparently believed the prosecution, which had argued that because Banks and Cuttiford occupied the same duplex, Cuttiford had the duty to retreat before repelling Banks's attack. Was the trial court judge correct in his instruction to the jury regarding self-defense? Explain. *State v. Cuttiford,* 639 N.E.2d 472 (OH).

9. Cowen had on many occasions operated as a paid drug informant for the FBI and the Ventura Police Department. The Ventura police asked Cowen to keep in touch with them, should he become involved in any deals. Subsequently, Cowen asked Busby to introduce him to any drug dealers he knew. Busby introduced Cowen to Mandell, who sold Cowen several samples of cocaine in anticipation of a $41,500 deal. Cowen then contacted the Ventura police. A police officer posed as Cowen's buyer, and both Busby and Mandell were arrested and eventually turned over to the federal authorities. Busby was convicted of possession of cocaine with the intent to distribute it. He appealed this conviction, claiming that he had been entrapped by Cowen. Will Busby's entrapment defense succeed on appeal? Explain. *United States v. Busby,* 780 F.2d 804 (9th Cir.).

## quick quiz Answers

| 5-1 | 5-2 | 5-3 | 5-4 | 5-5 |
|-----|-----|-----|-----|-----|
| 1. F | 1. T | 1. T | 1. F | 1. F |
| 2. F | 2. F | 2. F | 2. T | 2. T |
| 3. F | 3. F | 3. T | 3. T | 3. F |

# Chapter 6 — Tort Law and Cybertorts

## THE OPENING CASE  Juriscience and Tort Law: *Daubert v. Merrell Dow Pharmaceuticals, Inc.*

The law is a balancing act that struggles to assimilate new ideas while maintaining useful and effective traditions. Sometimes this balancing act works well; and sometimes it just falls apart. A case in point is *Daubert v. Merrell Dow Pharmaceuticals, Inc.,* a United States Supreme Court case in which the frontiers of science and the cultural paradigms of the law collide. The case involves a lawsuit filed by the Dauberts against Merrell Dow in which the plaintiffs argue that Bendectin, a drug produced by Merrell Dow, and taken by Mrs. Daubert for nausea during her pregnancy, had caused birth defects in their children. The case depends on the issue of causation, a traditional tort law principle that says that, to succeed in a negligence lawsuit, a plaintiff must prove that the defendant's action caused the plaintiff's injury. However, because of the scientific nature of the case, the court needed expert testimony to determine causation. This point in the case, the point at which science and the law intersect, is referred to as *jusriscience.*

The judges at each level, from the trial court, through the appellate court, up to the Supreme Court, and then back down to the appellate court, had to weigh the scientific evidence on causation leading from the development of the drug Bendectin to the birth defects. The judges were faced with two competing lines of evidence, one presented by the plaintiffs, the other by the defendants. The defendants' evidence included peer-reviewed articles published in scientific journals and studies issued by the Federal Drug Administration (FDA). None of these reports or articles could find a link between Bendectin and birth defects. In response, the plaintiff's scientific experts offered a reanalysis of the accepted data. This reanalysis demonstrated that the original data had been badly misinterpreted by previous scientists.

To determine which line of evidence should be followed, the court had to interpret Rule 702 of the Federal Rules of Evidence and *Frye v. United States,* a case that predated Rule 702, but that had, nevertheless, set up a standard that the federal courts had used for decades to evaluate expert testimony. Ultimately, the Supreme Court decided that expert evidence did not have to be "generally accepted" as *Frye* had suggested, because some scientific discoveries may be "too particular, too new, or of too limited interest to be published." The court thus emphasized that the Rules had to be interpreted liberally rather than narrowly in determining the use of expert testimony. Still, the Supreme Court concluded that such testimony did have to "rest on a reliable foundation and (be) relevant to the task at hand." Since the lower courts had used only the *Frye* standard, the case was sent back to the appeals court, which still supported Merrell Dow because the evidence produced by the plaintiffs did not demonstrate a definite causation link between Bendictin and birth defects. [See *Daubert v. Merrell Dow Pharmaceuticals, Inc.,* (509 U.S. 579) (U.S.S.Ct.); see also *Daubert v. Merrell Dow Pharmaceuticals, Inc.,* 43 F.3d 1311 (Ninth Circuit)]

**Opening Case Questions**

1. Would *Daubert v. Merrell Dow Pharmaceuticals, Inc.* be a civil lawsuit or a criminal action? Explain.

2. Was *Daubert v. Merrell Dow Pharmaceuticals, Inc.,* heard in state or federal court? Explain.

3. What legal theory or theories might be used to hold a corporation liable for the torts of an employee? Explain.

4. How does causation fit into a case like this? Explain.

5. Could a case be constructed based on strict liability in the *Daubert* case? Why or why not?

 Learning Objectives

1. Differentiate between the objectives of tort law and those of criminal law.
2. Outline the nature of *respondeat superior.*
3. Describe the element of duty.
4. Identify the principal intentional torts and outline the elements of each.
5. Explain the four elements of negligence.
6. Contrast contributory negligence, comparative negligence, and assumption of the risk.
7. Judge when the doctrine of strict liability applies.
8. Discuss the emerging trends in cybertort law.
9. Outline the various remedies available in tort law.
10. Point out some developments in tort reform.

# 6-1 Tort Law Defined

A **tort** is a private wrong that injures another person's physical well-being, emotional health, business, property, or reputation. The English word "tort" comes from the Latin word *tortus,* which can be translated as "twisted." A person who commits a tort and has thus engaged in "twisted" behavior is called a **tortfeasor**. The other party is alternately referred to as the injured party, the innocent party, the victim, or the plaintiff if a lawsuit has been filed. In the case of a lawsuit, the tortfeasor would be called a defendant.

## Tort Law versus Criminal Law

One purpose of tort law is to compensate the injured party for his or her loss. Another objective is to protect potential victims by deterring future tortious behavior. In contrast as noted in the previous chapter, criminal law involves a public wrong, that is, a wrong that affects the entire society. When a crime is committed, the government authorities begin a legal procedure that is designed to remove the offender from society, and to punish that offender to the fullest extent allowed by the law. As noted in the last chapter, however, it is possible for a single act to be both a crime and a tort. As noted in the chapter on criminal law, the U.S. Constitution protects people from being tried twice for the same crime. This rule is known as the principle of *double jeopardy*. Double jeopardy does not protect a defendant from being sued under tort law for the consequences of an action, even if that defendant has already been tried for the same wrongdoing in a criminal court using criminal law.

## Respondeat Superior

**About the Law**

The doctrine of *respondeat superior* is also known as vicarious liability.

In criminal law the courts will hold a corporation liable when an employee commits a crime on the job to benefit the corporation. In like fashion, in tort law the courts use *respondeat superior* to hold a business or organization liable for the torts of an employee whenever an employee commits a tort while working for that business or organization. Later in the book, when we reach the chapter on agency law, this concept will be examined in depth and the proper legal terms of *master* and *servant* will be explained at length. For now it is enough to remember that employers are at risk in tort law when their employees commit torts, and for that reason alone, both employers and employees must have some working knowledge of tort law.

## The Element of Duty

One approach to the law is to think of legal liability in terms of elements. This approach emphasizes that no liability can be imposed against an individual unless all the elements are present. In tort law, the first element is duty. A **duty** is an obligation placed on individuals because of the law. The second element is a violation of that duty. A duty can be violated intentionally, through negligence, or under the theory of strict liability.

## Causation and Juriscience

A negligence case requires the plaintiffs to prove that the defendants caused their injuries. In negligence cases there are two kinds of causation, actual cause and proximate cause. These two types of causation will be examined at length later in the chapter. However, for now it is enough to point out that actual cause is cause "in fact" or "real" cause. Real cause exists in the physical universe and is thus subject to experiments, tests, measurements, and other forms of proof. This means that the plaintiff will often have to use scientific evidence to demonstrate how action "A" led to effect "B." Moreover, because of the scientific nature of a case, the court generally needs to hear the testimony of an expert to determine causation. This stage in a case, where science and the law intersect, is referred to as **juriscience**.

## THE OPENING CASE *Revisited, Part I*
### Juriscience and Tort Law: *Daubert v. Merrell Dow Pharmaceuticals, Inc.* Round 2

In the *Daubert v. Merrell Dow Pharmaceuticals, Inc.*, the Dauberts sued Merrill Dow in tort law. The Dauberts argued that Merrell Dow had produced and marketed a dangerous drug named Bendectin. Mrs. Daubert took that drug for nausea during her pregnancy which caused birth defects in her children, or so the argument goes. The case is grounded in negligence which requires the plaintiff to prove the existence of four elements: (a) duty, (b) breach of duty, (c) proximate cause, and (d) actual harm or injury. Duty exists when one party has a responsibility not to harm another party. Since the idea of duty is at the center of tort law it is rarely, if ever, at issue. In the *Daubert* case, it would be nothing short of ludicrous for Merrell Dow to argue that it has no duty to the people who take their drugs.

## THE OPENING CASE *Revisited, Part II*
## Juriscience and Tort Law: *Daubert v. Merrell Dow Pharmaceuticals, Inc.* Round 3

In *Daubert v. Merrell Dow Pharmaceuticals, Inc.*, the Dauberts sued Merrell Dow because Bendectin, a drug produced by Merrell Dow, caused birth defects in their children. The case revolved around the issue of causation. In a negligence case, the plaintiff must prove that the defendant's action caused the plaintiff's injury. The corporation, however, cannot act on its own. It can only act through its employees. This is why, in a case like *Daubert v. Merrell Dow Pharmaceuticals,* the plaintiffs must be aware of the doctrine of *respondeat superior*. The doctrine of *respondeat superior* requires that (a) the defendants (those who committed the tort) were actually employed by Merrell Dow and (b) those employees were on the job when they developed Bendectin. None of this seems to have been at issue in this case. The real issue was the alleged negligence of Merrell Dow in placing a dangerous drug on the market. As we will see later, this is why expert testimony was required in the case.

Judges at all levels, but especially those in the trial courts, must determine the validity of scientific evidence. Unfortunately, because the law is an adversarial process, judges will frequently be forced to choose between two or more competing lines of scientific proof. Judges, however, are educated in the law not science, and so they need help unraveling the intricacies of scientific evidence beyond simply listening to the experts, many of whom may have hidden agendas.

The Federal Rules of Evidence provide some help. After *Daubert v. Merrell Dow,* the federal rule on expert testimony was amended to help judges make this determination. The rule states that an expert may testify on a scientific matter as long as, "(1) testimony is based upon sufficient facts or data, (2) the testimony is the product of reliable scientific principles and methods, and (3) the witness has applied the principles and methods reliably to the facts in the case." Still, even this standard is somewhat vague and ambiguous. Many questions remain unanswered. Who is to determine when testimony has reached a level of "sufficient facts or data"? What makes a scientific principle or method "reliable"? How will the judge know when a witness has applied a principle in a reliable way? Some states have tried to be more specific in the formulation of this rule. Ohio, for example, as gone so far as to say that, if an expert witness bases an opinion on a test or an experiment, that test or experiment is reliable *only* if *all* of the following apply: "(1) the theory upon which the procedure, test, or experiment is based is objectively verifiable or validly derived from widely accepted knowledge, facts, or principles; (2) the design of the procedure, test, experiment reliably implements the theory; and (3) the particular procedure, test, or experiment was conducted in a way that will yield an accurate result."

## quick quiz 6-1

1. A person who commits a tort is engaged in "twisted" behavior.    true | false

2. The purpose of tort law is to protect the public at large.    true | false

3. Employers are never liable for the torts of their employees    true | false
   because such a move would violate the constitutional prohibition
   against double jeopardy.

# 6-2 Intentional Torts

Intentional violations of duty include a vast variety of intentional torts, all of which have their own individual elements. Table 6-1 summarizes the primary intentional torts.

## Assault and Battery

Under U.S. tort law, assault and battery, though often closely associated with each other, are separate torts. An **assault** occurs when the victim is placed in fear or apprehension of immediate bodily harm by a tortfeasor who has the present apparent ability to inflict that harm. No actual physical contact is needed for an assault. The essence of the tort lies in the fear or apprehension that is created in the victim.

### EXAMPLE 6-1: Assault with a Deadly Dart

Terry Kline and Patrick Fisher were playing a friendly game of darts at the Wood Street Tavern one evening when they invited Fred Feeney and David Ballentine to join them. Unknown to either Kline or Feeney, Ballentine was intoxicated. After losing several games, Ballentine became enraged and tried to hit Kline by throwing several darts at him. In his intoxicated state, Ballentine's aim was poor, and he did not hit Kline. Nevertheless, Ballentine has committed an assault.

| Table 6-1 | Intentional Torts |
| --- | --- |
| **Tort** | **Definition** |
| Assault | An assault occurs when the victim is placed in fear or apprehension of immediate bodily harm by tortfeasor who has the present apparent ability to inflict that harm. |
| Battery | A battery involves an offensive or harmful, unprivileged touching. |
| False imprisonment | When one party prevents another party from moving about freely, the first party has committed the intentional tort of false imprisonment. |
| Defamation | Any false statement communicated to others that harms a person's good name or reputation may constitute the tort of defamation. |
| Invasion of privacy | Invasion of privacy occurs when one person unreasonably denies another person the right to be left alone. |
| Misuse of legal procedure | Misuse of legal procedure occurs when one person brings a legal procedure action with malice and without probable cause. |
| Intentional infliction of emotional distress | Intentional or reckless infliction of emotional distress occurs when an individual causes another to undergo emotional or mental suffering, even without an accompanying physical injury. |
| Disparagement | Disparagement involves any false statement communicated to others that somehow questions the quality of an item of property or that raises uncertainty as to who actually has legal ownership rights to the property in question. |
| Fraud | Fraud involves false statements or actions, or a combination thereof, that misrepresent facts so that an innocent party relies on those misrepresentations and suffers an injury or loss as a result. |

A **battery** involves an offensive or harmful, unprivileged touching. Naturally, if in Example 6-1, Ballentine had actually managed to hit Kline, he would have committed a battery. However, as the definition points out, a touching need not be harmful to be a battery. Moreover, a battery does not always require the touching of the actual person of the victim, if the tortfeasor touches something closely associated with that victim. So, if a prankster pulls a chair out from under someone before that person sits down, and the person falls to the floor, the joker has committed a battery. Or if he or she knocks a cafeteria tray out of a diner's hands, again he or she has committed a battery, despite the fact that the actual person or the victim has not been contacted.

## EXAMPLE 6-2: Battery by Antibody

Lucy Pickett works as a nurse at Garner County Hospital. Because she knows that her patient, Jim Luger, is afraid of needles, she sneaked up behind him and injected him with an antibiotic that had been ordered by his primary physician. Despite her desire to help Luger, and her wish to save him from feeling unnecessary fear, Pickett has committed a battery.

## False Imprisonment

When one party prevents another party from moving about freely, the first party has committed the intentional tort of **false imprisonment**. This tort is called false arrest in some states. The victim of false imprisonment need not be locked in a prison or a jail cell. All that is required is that the person's freedom of movement be restricted. For example, a physician who refuses to return a patient's clothing until a partial payment is received for a long overdue bill has committed false imprisonment.

Store owners must be very careful about detaining suspected shoplifters, because such a detention could result in a false imprisonment lawsuit if not handled properly. Still, because of the growing problem of shoplifting in society today, most states have laws that allow storekeepers to detain a suspected shoplifter if they have reasonable grounds to suspect that a shoplifting incident has occurred. However, the storekeeper must detain the suspect in a reasonable manner and for no longer than a reasonable length of time.

## Defamation and Disparagement

Intentional torts such as battery, assault, and false imprisonment involve direct physical and psychological injury to an individual. These injuries are not the only type of harm, however, that can be imposed on individuals in tort law. Sometimes the injury results from words that damage a reputation and lead to monetary loss. Two of these word-oriented torts are defamation and disparagement.

### Defamation
Any false statement communicated to others that harms a person's good name or reputation may constitute the tort of **defamation**. To be defamatory, the statement must hold the victim up to ridicule, contempt, or hatred. Defamation in a temporary form, such as speech, is **slander**; in a permanent form, such as writing, movies, videocassettes, or DVDs, it is **libel**.

People can usually bring a libel suit whenever the permanent statement is damaging to their reputation, is false, and is communicated to a third party. However, under common law, individuals can bring slander lawsuits even if they have suffered no actual loss if the false statements fall into one of the following categories:

1.  An accusation that the victim of the slanderous statements has committed a very serious crime, such as murder or rape.

2.  An accusation that the victim has a communicable disease, such as venereal disease.

3.  An accusation that the victim has engaged in improprieties in a business, trade, or profession.

4.  An accusation that an unmarried female victim has been unchaste.

Individuals may speak the truth without being sued successfully for defamation as long as it is done without spite or ill will. In addition, statements made by senators and representatives on the floor of Congress and statements made in a court of law are privileged. Privileged statements are not the proper subject of a defamation lawsuit. The idea behind creating these privileges is to promote the open debate of legislative and judicial matters.

The U.S. Supreme Court has given journalists the extra protection of the actual malice test when they write about public officials. Under the **actual malice test**, a public official must prove not only that the statement made or printed was false but also that it was made with actual malice. **Actual malice** means that the statement was made or printed either with the knowledge that it was false or with a reckless disregard for its truth or falsity. Later decisions expanded the actual malice test to cover public figures. Public figures are people like television actors, sports figures, and rock stars who seek out public fame and are readily recognizable by the public at large.

**Temporary public figures** are people who are placed against their will into the public view by some event beyond their control. Disaster victims, hostages, and rescuers are examples of temporary public figures. Generally, such people are held to the actual malice test as long as their notoriety lasts.

## Disparagement    **Disparagement** involves any false statement communicated to others that somehow questions the quality of property or raises uncertainty as to who has legal ownership of that property. Generally, to recover for disparagement, the plaintiff must show monetary loss. Such losses may include the loss of sales, money spent to correct the public's image of a product, or expenses spent on litigation due to the disparagement. The difference between defamation and disparagement is that in defamation, the false charge is made about the victim's reputation, whereas with disparagement, the falsehood is made about a person's property or product. The falsehood usually casts doubt on the value of the product or on the property rights of the owner.

### EXAMPLE 6-3: Toys, Tots, and Tall Tales

Warren Barrington owned and operated Toys and Tots—From Two to Twelve, a toy store that specialized in educational toys for children between two and twelve years of age. Barrington and his wife, who operated the store as a partnership, did their best to market only original toys made of natural materials. Electronic toys, computers, and toys made of plastic were never sold in the store. During the National Toy and Model Association of America convention, Raymond Matthews, who owned a competitive shop, started several rumors, most of which suggested that many of the toys that were being shown by the Barringtons at the convention were not made of natural materials as advertised. He also suggested that those toys that were made of natural materials involved ideas stolen from him and that the Barringtons did not have the right to market them as they were doing at the convention. Matthews has clearly committed disparagement here. He has planted false reports about both the value of the Barrington's products and about the Barrington's property rights to the toys.

## Fraudulent Misrepresentation

Another word-oriented tort is fraudulent misrepresentation. **Fraudulent misrepresentation**, or **fraud** as it is known in some states, occurs when false statements or actions, or a combination thereof, are made by one party in a way that causes another party to rely on those misrepresentations and then to suffer an injury or loss as a result. Frequently, fraud involves a business relationship and works to destroy the mutual assent that ought to exist between the parties that are involved in a contract. For that reason, it is discussed at length in Chapter 9. However, fraud is also a tort and need not involve a contract.

## Invasion of Privacy

The courts in the United States have consistently held that people have a right to privacy. Consequently, a violation of that right would involve the tort of **invasion of privacy**. The right to privacy can be violated in several ways:

1. Revelation of confidential records
2. Intrusion
3. Creating a false light
4. Exploitation

**Revelation of Confidential Records**   Individuals who, because of their jobs, work with confidential records containing private information must ensure that those records remain private. A failure to protect such confidential matters could result in an invasion of privacy lawsuit. Although it is not a violation of privacy for individuals to discuss confidential matters for professional reasons, it could be an invasion of privacy to discuss those same records for non-professional reasons. The motive of the person who releases the information does not matter. Moreover, whether there has been an invasion of privacy depends on the level of privacy expected by that person in that situation. For instance, an employee would expect privacy involving his or her employment record but not concerning the information that is printed on his or her identification badge.

**Intrusion**   An individual's privacy can also be violated if there is an unwarranted intrusion into the person's expectation of privacy. Such an intrusion might occur if a person's photograph is taken and then published on the front page of a local newspaper. The issue at the heart of such case is the question of whether the plaintiff had a high expectation of privacy. Recall that the expectation of privacy depends on the situation. A person walking across a college campus has a very low expectation of privacy, whereas a person who is in his or

Public officials and public figures, such as the President of the United States and his family, have little or no expectation of privacy when they are on stage at a political event. Therefore, they can not claim intrusion, when their photos end up on the front page of most every newspaper in the country.

her own home has a very high expectation of privacy. Thus, the publication of a photo of a person walking across campus would *not* be actionable as an invasion of privacy, but taking a similar photo while that person was in his or her home would be.

### Creating a False Light

Creating a false light is closely akin to defamation because it involves the publication of information about a person that paints him or her in a way that the majority of the population would see as unfavorable. A fashion model who poses for photographs for a bathing suit catalog and finds her image printed in a sexually explicit magazine would have a cause of action for being placed in a false light.

### Exploitation

The courts have held that an individual holds the rights to his or her own likeness to make money. An invasion of privacy can occur when one party uses an individual's photo, likeness, or name without permission for advertising, marketing, or publicity. Some courts treat the misappropriation of a person's likeness as a separate tort, calling it an invasion of the right to publicity.

## Intentional Infliction of Emotional Distress

In recent years, the courts have recognized a tort called the **intentional or reckless infliction of emotional distress**. Before these more enlightened court decisions were handed down, victims who were injured emotionally by the wrongful acts of others could not recover damages without proving some sort of bodily injury. Today, in many states, someone who intentionally or recklessly causes another individual to undergo emotional or mental suffering will be responsible, even without an accompanying physical injury. The actions complained of must be extreme and outrageous and cause severe emotional suffering.

### EXAMPLE 6-4: Extreme and Outrageous Silence

Marc Christian, who gained notoriety as the live-in boyfriend of Rock Hudson, sued the estate of the late actor for the intentional infliction of emotional distress. Christian argued that he had been induced to continue having "high-risk" sexual relations with the late screen star because Hudson had remained silent and failed to inform him that he had contracted AIDS. As a result of Hudson's misrepresentations, Christian contended that he suffered extreme emotional distress when he learned that Hudson was ill. This was true, Christian argued, despite the fact that he was not HIV positive himself. Although Hudson did not attempt deliberately to transfer the virus to Christian and did not plan to cause Christian emotional distress, the inherent harmfulness of Hudson's actions could easily amount to extreme and outrageous conduct.

## Misuse of Legal Procedure

The intentional tort known as the **misuse of legal procedure** occurs when one person brings a legal action with malice and without probable cause. When the misuse of the legal procedure involves the filing of a false civil lawsuit, it is called **wrongful civil proceedings**. In contrast, when the misuse involves bringing false criminal charges, it is labeled **malicious prosecution**. Some states use only the term "malicious prosecution" to refer to both forms of the tort. All of the following conditions must be present for a lawsuit based on misuse of legal procedure to succeed:

1. The defendant (the person against whom the misuse of legal procedure suit has been filed) must have brought civil or criminal charges against the plaintiff at an earlier time.

2. The earlier case must have been resolved favorably for the plaintiff.

3. The plaintiff must prove that the earlier case was brought by the defendant with malice and without probable cause.

When these conditions are present, an individual may be able to recover damages from the defendant for making the innocent party the target of a legal action without a good cause.

A related cause of action, which can easily be confused with malicious prosecution, is abuse of process. **Abuse of process** occurs when a legal procedure is used for a purpose other than that for which it is intended. It differs from malicious prosecution in that there is no requirement that the earlier case be brought without probable cause or be resolved favorably for the plaintiff. The tort can involve either a criminal or a civil case. Typically, abuse of process happens when a perfectly legal process is used as a pressure tactic to convince someone to do something he or she would not be inclined to do under ordinary circumstances.

## EXAMPLE 6-5: Misuse and Abuse: Crossing the Legal Line

Janice Franklin and Karen Yalta were involved in a very difficult dissolution of their partnership. As a result of this problematic dissolution, as well as many other factors, the two young women did not like each other. Accordingly, Franklin filed a lawsuit against Yalta for defamation. The lawsuit was resolved in Yalta's favor. Yalta then sued Franklin for wrongful civil proceedings. Yalta won the case because she was able to prove that the original defamation suit against her was fabricated by Franklin, who was motivated by hatred and ill will. This suit is an example of the misuse of legal proceedings. If Franklin had filed a defamation suit to force Yalta to agree to Franklin's terms in the dissolution, she would be involved in abuse of process. This involvement would be true even if Franklin had legitimate reasons for filing the defamation suit.

### quick quiz 6-2

1. Assault and battery never exist simultaneously.                                    true | false

2. To be defamatory, a statement need not be communicated to a                         true | false
   third party.

3. The intentional infliction of emotional distress has yet to be                      true | false
   recognized as a tort in any state jurisdiction.

# 6-3 Negligence

People and property are sometimes injured even when no one intends that the injury occur. Such an occurrence is usually labeled an accident. Although no one acted with intent, someone was injured. The victim has experienced pain and suffering, lost wages, or incurred medical or repair bills. Justice demands that the injured party be compensated. The part of tort law that is concerned with the compensation of accident victims is called **negligence**.

## Elements of Negligence

The issue before the court in a negligence action is as follows: Under what circumstances can the actions of an alleged tortfeasor be labeled negligent so that the victim can be compensated? Four elements must be present to establish negligence: legal duty, breach of duty, proximate cause, and actual harm. Table 6-2 gives an overview of these four elements.

### Legal Duty

A determination that a legal duty exists between the parties must be made to establish liability through negligence. This issue is solely a question of whether the tortfeasor should have reasonably foreseen a risk of harm to the injured party. Often today, the element of duty is not at issue in a lawsuit. However, there are some instances, often when a novel case comes before a court, that the legal duty of the defendant may be placed at issue. The phrase "at issue" refers to a legal question that must be answered for the case to be decided.

### Breach of Duty

The judge or the jury must determine whether the person accused of negligence has breached the duty owed to the victim. A breach of duty occurs if the alleged tortfeasor has not met the appropriate standard of care. To determine if the alleged tortfeasor has met the appropriate standard of care, the court uses the reasonable person test. This test compares the actions of the tortfeasor with those of a reasonable person in a similar situation. If a reasonable person would not have done what the tortfeasor actually did, then the tortfeasor is liable. The reasonable person standard is an objective test. Circumstances may change, but the standard of care applied by a reasonable person does not. How a reasonable person would behave in one set of circumstances may not be the same in another set of circumstances.

| **Table 6-2**   The Elements of Negligence | |
|---|---|
| **Element** | **Definition** |
| Legal duty | A determination that a legal duty exists between the parties must be made to establish liability through negligence. This is solely a question of whether the tortfeasor should have reasonably foreseen a risk of harm to the injured party. |
| Breach of duty | The judge or the jury must determine whether the person accused of negligence has breached the duty owed to the victim. To determine if the alleged tortfeasor has met the appropriate standard of care, the court uses the reasonable person test. |
| Proximate cause | For the tortfeasor to be held liable, the unreasonable conduct must be the proximate cause of the victim's injuries. Proximate cause is the legal connection between the unreasonable conduct and the resulting harm. |
| Actual harm | The injured party in a lawsuit for negligence must show that actual harm was suffered. |

## EXAMPLE 6-6: The Case of the Unreasonable Limo Service

Luigi Tarentino hired a limousine from Highland Limo Service so that he and his wife, Maybeth, could attend their high school reunion in style. When the limousine arrived, Tarentino told the driver to take them to the Regency Hotel. Once they were on the freeway, it became clear that the driver did not know how to reach the hotel. Every time the driver took a wrong turn, Tarentino attempted to correct him. The driver continued to ignore Tarentino's instructions. Eventually, the driver, who later said he was aggravated by Tarentino's frequent interruptions, stopped the limousine and told Tarentino and his wife to walk to their reunion. He then drove off and left his passengers several miles from the hotel in the middle of an ice storm. While walking to the hotel, Tarentino slipped on a patch of ice and fell and broke his arm. Later the Tarentinos learned that the driver had a long history of similar conduct and that the limousine company had not done a proper search into the driver's work history before hiring him. The question to the jury was, "Would a reasonable person hire an employee who will be responsible for the safety of paying passengers without checking the work history of that potential employee?" The jury said no, and Highland was held liable for the injuries that befell Tarentino from this breach of duty to protect paying passengers from harm.

If the defendant in a particular case is a professional, such as a physician or an engineer, the circumstances—not the test—change. To determine whether the defendant acted reasonably, the jury would have to know how the reasonable professional would act under similar circumstances. Determining this point may require the use of expert witnesses to testify as to a reasonable professional's conduct under the circumstances.

### Actual and Proximate Cause

It is not enough to simply show that the tort-feasor's actions were unreasonable. For the tortfeasor to be held liable, the unreasonable conduct must be tied to actual and proximate cause. **Actual cause**, or **cause in fact**, demonstrates that the cause (the unreasonable conduct) led to the effect (the injury to the plaintiff). The question can be viewed like a problem in physics. We look at the plaintiff's injury (the effect) and deconstruct the events that preceded it, ending with the original unreasonable behavior (the cause). Imagine a set of dominoes falling one after the other and you'll have an accurate image of this process. So, let's say that a driver is texting while driving and that inattentiveness causes him to run a red light and collide with another vehicle, injuring the other driver and totaling the other car. To find actual cause we deconstruct events from the crash and, working backwards, see that, if the driver had not been texting, then the second vehicle would not have been hit. This is called the "but for" test. Using the "but for" test, the judge tells the jury to ask themselves, "Would there have been no accident, 'but for' the unreasonable conduct of the defendant?" In this case, it is clear that the accident would not have happened "but for" the unreasonable conduct (texting while driving). This gives us actual cause.

The problem with actual cause is that there is no end to the consequences that flow from the defendant's unreasonable conduct. Thus, in the car accident mentioned above, negative effects can flow from the accident for days and weeks afterwards, events that would not have occurred "but for" the original unreasonable conduct (the texting while driving). Thus, our innocent victim may lose work, may have to pay medical bills, may have to buy new clothing, may have to cancel a dinner date, may lose the services of a baby sitter, may miss her favorite television show, might be unable to attend a Rotary luncheon, may be fined for an overdue library book because she has no car, may fail to defrost her refrigerator because she is distraught or has a broken arm, and so on. The law must place a limit on these effects. This policy is referred to as **proximate cause** or **legal cause**. The law

Recall in the Opening Case, *Daubert v. Merrell Dow Pharmaceuticals, Inc.,* the Dauberts brought a lawsuit against Merrell Dow in which the plaintiffs argued that Bendectin, a drug produced by Merrell Dow and taken by Mrs. Daubert during her pregnancy, had caused birth defects in their children. The case is grounded in negligence which requires the plaintiff to prove the existence of four elements: (a) duty, (b) breach of duty, (c) proximate cause, and (d) actual harm or injury. The case turned on the issue of causation, which means that the plaintiffs had to prove that the defendant's action caused the plaintiff's injury. Recall, however, that causation involves two parts, actual cause, which is also known as cause in fact, and proximate cause, which is also referred to as legal cause. In this case the initial issue was the existence of actual cause. The issue before the court was the question of whether the Bendectin actually led to the birth defects. Because of the scientific nature of the case, the court needed expert testimony to determine causation. The judges at each level, from the trial court to the Supreme Court, had to weigh the scientific evidence on causation leading from the development of the drug Bendectin to the

birth defects. After the standard was reformulated by the Supreme Court, the case was handed back to the appellate court which had to make a judgment as to whether actual cause existed in the case. The court, after considering the scientific evidence from both sides, concluded that the Dauberts had not proven actual cause. The court formulated its conclusion in the following way: "But what the plaintiffs would have to prove is not that Bendectin causes some defects but that it caused *their* defects. To show this, the plaintiffs' experts would have to testify either that Bendectin actually caused plaintiff's injuries (which they could not say) or that Bendectin doubled the likelihood of limb reduction birth defects (which they did not say). As the district court properly found below, 'the strongest inference to be drawn for the plaintiffs based on the epidemiological evidence is that Bendectin could *possibly* have caused the plaintiff's injuries.'" 727 F. Supp. At 576. Since the plaintiffs had not proven the existence of actual cause there was no need to go on the issue of proximate cause. *Daubert v. Merrell Dow Pharmaceuticals, Inc.,* 43 F.3d 1311 (Ninth Circuit).

says there must be a final effect for which we will hold the defendant liable. The test used to determine this "last effect" is referred to as the **foreseeability test**. In determining proximate cause, the court asks whether the harm that resulted from the original unreasonable conduct was foreseeable at the time of the original action. If the effect was foreseeable at the time of the unreasonable conduct, the defendant is liable for the damages that flow from that effect. If the effect was not foreseeable, the defendant cannot be held liable for it. In this case the driver's injuries, the damage to the car, the medical bills, and the lost wages were all foreseeable. The overdue library fines, the undefrosted refrigerator, the lost babysitter, and so on, were not.

**Actual Harm**   The injured party in a lawsuit for negligence must show that actual harm was suffered. In most cases, the harm suffered is a physical injury and is therefore visible. Harm suffered due to fright or humiliation is difficult to demonstrate. Courts often deny damages in actions for negligence unless they can see an actual physical injury. Actual harm can also come in the form of property damage.

## Defenses to Negligence

**LO6**   Several defenses can be used by the defendant in a negligence case. These defenses include contributory negligence, comparative negligence, and assumption of the risk.

**Contributory Negligence**   The defense of contributory negligence involves the failure of the injured party to be careful enough to ensure his or her personal safety. Contributory negligence completely prevents the injured party from recovering damages. In other words, if the injured party's negligence contributed to personal injury, the tortfeasor wins. Last clear chance is the injured party's defense to a charge of contributory negligence. Under this doctrine, a tortfeasor may be held liable if the injured party can show that the tortfeasor had the last clear chance to avoid injury.

**Comparative Negligence**   To soften the harsh effects of contributory negligence, many states have adopted comparative negligence statutes that require courts to assign damages according to the degree of fault of each party. Rather than deny all recovery, the court weighs the relative degree of wrongdoing in awarding damages. If the tortfeasor was 80 percent negligent, the injured party may be allowed to recover 80 percent of the losses suffered. Some states have adopted the "50 percent rule." Under this rule, an injured party who was found to be more than 50 percent negligent cannot recover any damages from the tortfeasor.

**Assumption of the Risk**   Another defense to negligence is assumption of the risk, which involves the voluntary exposure of the victim to a known risk. If the injured party was aware of the danger involved in a situation, and by his or her actions indicated a willingness to be exposed to the danger, then he or she has assumed that risk. An awareness of the extent of the danger is the court's primary consideration in awarding or denying damages. It is important that the victim's decision to enter the risky situation be voluntary. If he or she is forced to enter the risky situation because no other choice is available, it is not an assumption of the risk.

> **Did You Know?**
>
> Assumption of the risk can be raised as a defense in a case in which the plaintiff has been injured in a voluntary sports activity such as touch football. For a player in a touch football game to be found liable for injuries to another player, the first player would have to have caused the injuries intentionally or with a degree of recklessness beyond the usual action within such a sport.

---

## quick quiz 6-3

1. Legal duty is never at issue in any lawsuit today.                                          true | false

2. Proximate cause is sometimes referred to as legal cause.                                     true | false

3. Under the defense of comparative negligence, the plaintiff                                    true | false
   always loses all the damages that he or she might have been
   awarded, absent the defense.

---

# 6-4 Strict Liability

Under certain circumstances, the courts may judge a person liable for harm even though that person was not negligent and did not commit an intentional tort. This doctrine is known as strict liability or absolute liability. In recent years, strict liability has also been applied to product liability cases.

## Grounds for Strict Liability

Under strict liability, the court will hold a tortfeasor liable for injuries to a victim even though the tortfeasor did not intend the harm and was not in any way negligent. Strict liability is generally applied when the harm results from an ultrahazardous or very dangerous activity. Such activities include using explosives and keeping wild animals. A number of dangerous activities, such as flying an airplane, operating X-ray equipment, and laying public gas lines, are not subject to liability without fault. These activities are recognized as essential to the economic health and welfare of the public.

Counterfeit Colgate toothpaste was recently imported from China and sold in dollar stores across the United States How does this affect Colgate's reputation?

# Product Liability

Product liability is a legal theory that imposes liability on the manufacturer and seller of a product produced and sold in a defective condition. A product in **defective condition** is unreasonably dangerous to the user, to the consumer, or to property. Anyone who produces or sells a product in defective condition is subject to liability for the physical or emotional injury to the ultimate consumer and for any physical harm to the user's property. The courts have regularly held that liability for a defective product extends to the producer of the product, the wholesaler, and the retailer. The seller or producer must be engaged in the business of selling such products. In addition, the product manufactured or sold must be expected to reach the ultimate consumer without substantial change in the conditions under which it was originally manufactured or sold.

Product liability is not without its limits. In most states, product liability also is not available as a cause of action if the only property damaged is the defective property itself. In such a situation, the product owner must seek a remedy in sales law for breach of warranty. (Note: People who are injured by faulty products might also be able to bring a product liability lawsuit in sales law. This issue is discussed at length in Chapter 15.)

---

## quick quiz 6-4

1. Keeping wild animals is an ultrahazardous activity.                                  true | false

2. Strict liability is also known as absolute liability.                                 true | false

3. Product liability is completely unrelated to strict liability, and the           true | false
   two torts should never be confused with each other.

---

# 6-5 Cybertorts

Computers have provided unscrupulous individuals with new ways to commit crimes and torts. In the previous chapter, we examined several cybercrimes. In this chapter, we focus on another group of legal problems, cybertorts. We look first at the nature of cybertorts and then at the problems associated with defining, describing, and preventing cybertorts.

## The Nature of Cybertorts

A **cybertort** involves the invasion, distortion, theft, falsification, misuse, destruction, or exploitation of information stored in or related to electronic devices, including but not limited to desktop PCs, laptops, mobile phones, mainframe computers, phonecams, PDAs, mobile phones, and home computers that stand alone or are part of a computer network. Cybertorts rarely, if ever, involve any physical harm to a victim. Instead, the victim's reputation has been hurt because a false statement has been posted on FaceBook; the victim's emotional state has been disturbed because a his or her privacy has been invaded by a photograph passed from cell phone to cell phone; the victim has suffered extensive financial loss due to identity theft; or the victim has been terrified by repeated threats from cyberbullies sending text messages in a relentless, ruthless fashion.

# Cyber-defamation

**Cyber-defamation** is the communication of false and destructive information about an individual through the use of electronic devices. Most legal moves in cyber-defamation have been designed to limit, rather than extend liability for defamatory comments disseminated electronically. For example, when the courts were first involved in cyber-defamation, they easily extended liability for defamation from the party who posted the defamation on the Internet to the Internet Service Provider (ISP), such as America Online, that provided the vehicle for the posting. Thus, for example, it was not difficult in one case for a court in New York to decide that the Prodigy Service Company was responsible when an investment banking firm sued for defamation after false statements were posted on a **cyber-bulletin board** that was under Prodigy's control.

After the Prodigy case, however, the Communications Decency Act was enacted by Congress to protect ISPs from future defamation lawsuits for false statements posted by other individuals on the net. Despite the passage of the law, many cases have been filed attempting to hold ISPs liable for defamatory postings. Few have succeeded, but they remain a nuisance to the providers. Still, the greater nuisance, that to the innocent victims, has not been handled adequately. In one case, AOL was found not liable for defamation even though the provider had been informed of the defamatory content of a posting and still delayed its removal. Moreover, the protection granted to ISPs has gone far beyond protection for defamatory postings. The courts have found that ISPs are not liable when hackers place a virus into a system, when piracy is involved on the Net, or when an invasion of privacy takes place via a provider's link.

# Cyber-disparagement

Disparagement involves false statements communicated to others that in some way casts doubt upon the ownership or the quality of an item of property or a product offered for sale. **Cyber-disparagement** involves the same activity on the Internet. The FaceBook phenomenon has opened an avenue for the relatively new tort of cyber-disparagement. Businesses now solicit videos from their consumers for postings on their own Web sites. These businesses often go so far as to run games and contests in which clients and customers can submit homemade advertisements or videos that will be added to the Web site of the business. Unfortunately, this process is filled with legal risks, not the least of which is the possibility of a cyber-disparagement lawsuit. Such homemade videos typically target the product of a company's competitor. Thus, a company that posts such videos must make certain that the competitor's product is not subject to false statements and descriptions. This assurance requires an enormous effort aimed at monitoring the content of such submissions. Legal activity in this area has not been heavy as of yet, but that is because the tort is so new. As time goes on and competitors find themselves injured by such postings the activity will increase and more cyber-disparagement lawsuits will be filed.

# Cyber-invasion of Privacy

A **cyber-invasion of privacy** is the unwelcome intrusion into private matters initiated or maintained by an electronic device. Because the development of computer technology is in a constant state of flux, it is not surprising that the law is still uncertain about just what constitutes a cyber-invasion of privacy. One area that has been expanded recently involves computer-related privacy in the workplace. As the result of at least one federal case, workers employed by businesses that keep a close eye on their workers' time on the Internet have no expectation of privacy, at least in relation to their Fourth Amendment rights, provided that the employer has openly informed the workers of the surveillance.

When employees know that their employer monitors their Internet use, those employees have no expectation of privacy.

### Privacy and Employees

The low expectation of privacy has long been a part of the law in relation to governmental employees. Thus, it has been clear that the Fourth Amendment Right against unreasonable searches and seizures does not protect a governmental employee who knows that the government regularly monitors its employees' Internet use. The same standard now extends to employees within the private sector. How this ruling relates to the tortious invasion of privacy is problematic. However, because the standard for the invasion of privacy is based on the level of privacy expected, the fact that a worker knows that the company monitors computer use means that the expectation is low. The moral of the story is twofold: (1) Employers should routinely remind their workers that all computer use is monitored by the information technology department, and (2) workers should use computers for work-related tasks only.

### Privacy and Clients

Businesses and other organizations, such as educational institutions, health care facilities, and financial institutions must also deal with the privacy of their customers, students, patients, and clients. Most invasions of privacy affect private records that pertain to employees who, because of their jobs, work closely with confidential files, such as educational, medical, and financial records. The failure to protect such records, whether they are on paper or in a computer, can result in an invasion of privacy lawsuit. Nevertheless, some courts have held that records that are stored in a computer require a degree of protection that is greater than the protection given to paper records because paper records can be kept hidden away or locked in a filing cabinet or a safe, whereas computer records are easy to retrieve, compile, and disseminate. Still, not every claim of a computer-related invasion of privacy automatically translates into a successful lawsuit. The laws is still unsettled in several key areas, not the least of which is the question of whether ISPs are permitted to protect the privacy rights of their subscribers.

### Private Privacy and Public Privacy

Most of the time, private information, or private private information, as it is sometimes called, includes reports on personal matters, family relationships, sexual habits, employment records, medical data, and financial records. However, the law also recognizes a fundamental difference between *private privacy* and *public privacy*. The law is familiar with private privacy concerns about matters such as health concerns, sexual preferences, family matters, and so on. However, the computer age has given rise to another privacy issue, that is, the concern over the publication of what is essentially public information, or what has been termed public-privacy matters. As noted above, many people believe that computer records deserve a higher degree of protection because, unlike paper documents, they are more readily vulnerable to hacking from remote sites.

### Data Mining of Public Private Data

The process of data mining takes place when a hacker links multiple strings of data together and develops a data package that the target considers a compilation of private information, despite the public sources from which the hacker composed the package. The issue here is whether the hacker's mining of public databases to construct a private data portrait violates the target's privacy. Some commentators argue that an individual's right to privacy is invaded if, in the process of gathering the data, the hacker ignores or bypasses the target's consent to produce a data portrait that embarrasses, disturbs, ridicules, bullies, exploits, or financially harms the innocent target. To the extent that the victim is harmed, he or she ought to have a cause of action against the hacker.

## EXAMPLE 6-7: ATMs, Digital Cameras, and Data Mining

Frank Vilnius, a dedicated health enthusiast and avid cyclist, rode his recumbent bike into town each week to do his errands. One of the errands involved a stop at the ATM at the local branch of Superior Savings. Unknown to Vilnius, the ATM contained a digital camera that photographed the bank's customers when they used the machine. Vilnius suddenly found himself the target of spam, telemarketing calls, text messages, and snail mail ads, selling products for cyclists. After some investigative work of his own, Vilnius discovered that one of Superior's subsidiaries, "B-A-Cyclist" was a sports equipment chain with an active Internet presence. "B-A" regularly tapped into Superior's data bank and used the photos and other customer data to target potential customers. Vilnius was not financially hurt by the intrusion, but he was annoyed enough to remove his savings from Superior Savings and move his business to the St. Georges Savings across town.

In the Vilnius case in Example 6-7, the various pieces of data that Superior Savings mined included Vilnius's address, phone number, e-mail address, mobile phone number, bank account balance, and his hobby as a cyclist. Arguably, all this data is public when looked at in isolation. Nevertheless, privacy rights emerge because the public pieces of data have been mined to produce a valuable public private data portrait that was exploited by Superior and its subsidiary, "B-A," without Vilnius's consent and in a manner that annoyed him enough to lead him to move his business to St. Georges. Unfortunately, there is still little case law on the issue of public private data portraits. Moreover, the law that does exist militates against the firm establishment of a public privacy right, despite the convincing case that can be made for its acceptance.

### quick quiz 6-5

1. Cybertorts always involve information that has been invaded, distorted, stolen, falsified, or destroyed by an electronic device.    true | false

2. Most legal moves in cyber-defamation have been designed to extend liability.    true | false

3. Government employees have a high expectation of privacy in the workplace.    true | false

# 6-6 Remedies for Torts

When a wrongdoer has injured another person by committing a tort, the victim can usually be compensated with monetary damages. However, at times, the equitable remedy of an injunction is more appropriate.

## The Right to Damages

The compensation paid to the victims of a tort is known as **damages**. Damages can come in several forms. **Economic compensatory damages** are those that are directly quantifiable. These include damages awarded for lost wages, medical expenses, and expenses incurred in the repair or replacement of property. **Noneconomic compensatory damages** are those that result from injuries that are intangible and therefore not directly quantifiable. For example, damages resulting from pain and suffering, mental anguish, and loss of companionship are considered noneconomic. If the tortfeasor's acts are notoriously willful and malicious, a court may also impose punitive damages. These are damages above and beyond those needed to compensate the injured party. **Punitive damages** are designed to punish the tortfeasor so that similar malicious actions are avoided by others. For this reason, they are also referred to as exemplary damages. Some courts say that another purpose of punitive damages is to comfort the victim.

## The Right to an Injunction

If a tort involves a continuing problem, such as the dumping of chemical waste into a river, the injured party may ask the court for an injunction. An **injunction** is a court order preventing someone from performing a particular act. If a tort involves some permanent fixture that harms the interests of the injured party, the court may order the wrongdoer to take positive steps to alleviate the problem. Thus, the court might order a company to clean up a landfill that has become a nuisance to neighborhood homes. If the company failed to complete the cleanup, it would be in contempt of court. Contempt of court is a deliberate violation of the order of a judge that can result in a fine or in jail time for the wrongdoer.

**quick quiz** 6-6

| | |
|---|---|
| 1. Economic and noneconomic compensatory damages are essentially the same thing. | true \| false |
| 2. Punitive damages are designed to compensate the victim of a tort. | true \| false |
| 3. An injunction is never granted by the court in any kind of tort case. | true \| false |

# 6-7 Developments in Tort Law

Tort law is in an unsettled stage of development. Much of tort law is still common law, but public dissatisfaction with the high number of tort-based lawsuits has caused some legislatures to pass statutes aimed at tort reform. Some of these moves make sense, as with the passage of wrongful death and survival statutes. The advisability of others is not quite as clear. Nevertheless, this evolutionary surge in tort law is part of the legal culture's ongoing attempt to create a balanced system. The balance this time is between the rights that victims have to be compensated for injuries caused by tortious conduct and the right that society has to be spared the heavy cost of unjustified and expensive litigation.

## Survival Statutes and Wrongful Death

Under common law, if someone died from another's wrongful act, then the right to bring a lawsuit also died. This rule originated because the king would execute the wrongdoer and then take his or her property. As a result, there was no property left for the next of kin to recover in a tort suit. In the modern world, this practice makes no sense, and so the state legislatures have nullified the rule with legislation. The two statutes that deal with this problem are survival statutes and statutes that deal with wrongful death.

**Survival Statutes**   Many state legislatures have revised common law by passing survival statues. Survival statutes allow a lawsuit to be brought even if the plaintiff, or the defendant, or both are deceased. Many states also have survival statutes that preserve the right to bring a lawsuit no matter what caused the death or deaths. Most states also allow such suits if the tort involves damage to real or personal property. However, there are some limitations placed on survival statutes. For example, suits cannot be brought for libel or slander after the death of a defamed person, because such a suit is for injury to a live person's reputation. Survival suits are brought or defended by the lawful representative of the estate of the deceased.

**Wrongful Death Statutes**   Unlike survival statutes, **wrongful death statutes** preserve the right to bring a lawsuit only if the death is caused by the negligence or the intentional conduct of the person who caused the death. Generally, only those family members who have lost the support of the deceased have the right to bring a wrongful death suit. The definition of family members generally includes husbands, wives, children, and parents. Under wrongful death statutes, creditors, business partners, and the like have no right to bring lawsuit.

## The Tort Reform Movement

Other suggestions for tort reform include the introduction of statutes of repose in product liability and medical malpractice cases, the use of comparative negligence in product liability cases, and alterations in the availability of wrongful death lawsuits

**Statutes of Repose**   One suggested tort reform would introduce a statute of repose into product liability lawsuits. **Statutes of repose** establish a limit in years, usually but not necessarily 15 years, beyond which an injured party could not bring a lawsuit for an injury caused by a product. The limitation would be placed on end users. An *end user* is a purchaser or a user who is not involved in the production or the assembly of the product. A statute of respose differs from a statute of limitations in that the statute of limitations begins to run when the injury occurs, while the statute of repose begins to run when the product is sold. Often such statutes carry limitations and exceptions. Thus, if the manufacturer fraudulently represented the condition of the product and that fraud led to the harm caused by the product, the statute of repose would not apply. Extremely dangerous products might also fall outside the protective zone of the statute of repose.

Statutes of respose have been suggested also as tort reform measure in medical malpractice lawsuits. Time limits for such statutes vary from four to six years and usually begin to run when the professional services have been rendered. As is the case with statutes of repose for product liability lawsuits, the statute of respose for medical malpractice would include exceptions under which the statute would not apply. For instance, the statute would not apply if the defendant in such a lawsuit engaged in fraud in relation to the relevant facts pertaining to the professional services that form the basis of the suit.

**Comparative Negligence and Product Liability**   Another reform that has been suggested in some states is the application of comparative negligence as an affirmative defense in some product liability cases. Under this standard, the responsibility of the manufacturer in a product liability case can be lessened by the degree to which the plaintiff's own negligence contributed to his or her injury. Some statutes even say that the manufacturer can escape liability altogether if the plaintiff's share in the responsibility exceeds 50 percent.

**Wrongful Death Reform**    Some states have introduced a reform measure aimed at eliminating any chance of a double recovery under wrongful death statutes. Such reform provisions generally maintain that a wrongful death action cannot be instituted by family members if the deceased recovered damages from the defendant in a prior lawsuit. Thus, if during his or her lifetime, the deceased recovered damages from the defendant in a negligence action, the family cannot bring a subsequent wrongful death action based on the same facts that gave rise to the original negligence lawsuit. In essence, under such a provision, the deceased is said to have waived all rights to bring the wrongful death action when he or she recovered under the original negligence action.

## Cultural Paradigms and Balance in Tort Law

There is a great deal of opposition to tort reform within the legal community, especially among attorneys who represent plaintiffs. The most fundamental complaint is that tort reform threatens the very paradigm upon which tort law is based. Fundamental to this argument is the belief that the tort law paradigm establishes a delicately balanced legal system that is threatened by the well-intentioned, but essentially clueless, supporters of tort reform.

### Cultural Paradigms
A paradigm is an unchallenged world view that establishes the rules by which everyone in a particular culture thinks, speaks, and acts. This is true whether we are dealing with a national cultural, a religious culture, a political culture, or a professional culture. The problem with tort reform is that it challenges the assumptions of the legal paradigm without offering an alternative paradigm. Instead, it offers a piecemeal, patchwork approach that borrows concepts and principles from other areas of the law and applies them in ways that are inappropriate at best. This approach to reform reveals a fundamental misunderstanding of the tort law paradigm.

### Balance in Tort Law
As noted above, the delicately balanced system of tort law is threatened by legislators and reformers who mean well, but who seem unable or unwilling to understand and appreciate the intricacies and the complexities of the tort law paradigm. In his treatise, *Law's Empire,* the legal philosopher Ronald Dworkin, argues that two very strong reasons exist for preserving the current tort law paradigm. Dworkin explains it this way: "Our law as a whole recognizes two principles as pertinent to the loss people should be permitted to suffer through accidents. The first is the principle of collective sympathy. It holds that the state should try to protect people from being ruined by accidents even when the accident is their own fault. The principle is most apparent in regulative safety programs of different sorts, in workmen's compensation statutes and in state-subsidized schemes of insurance for risks to property and person not adequately covered in the private insurance market. The second is the principle of apportioning the costs of an accident among the private actors in the drama that produced it. It holds that accidental loss should be bourne by the person at fault, not the innocent victim. This principle is most evidently at work in negligence law, including legislative amendments or supplements to common law of negligence." The second principle is the one that concerns us the most here. In a succinct and direct way, Dworkin has restated the fundamental rule of the tort law paradigm: people have a duty not to harm one another and when they do cause harm, whether intentionally, through carelessness, or by engaging in a dangerous activity, they pay. The principle is both logical and fair because it rehabilitates the innocent victim at the expense of the wrongdoer. It's just that simple. (See Ronald Dworkin, *Law's Empire,* Cambridge: The Belknap Press of Harvard University, 1986, p. 269.)

## quick quiz 6-7

1. Survival statutes allow a lawsuit to be brought even if both the plaintiff and the defendant are deceased.          true | false

2. Statutes of repose establish a limit in years beyond which an injured party could not bring a lawsuit for an injury caused by a product.          true | false

3. A paradigm is an unchallenged world view that establishes the rules by which everyone in a particular culture thinks, speaks, and acts.          true | false

## Summary

**6.1**   A tort is a private wrong that injures another person's physical well-being, emotional health, property, or reputation. A person who commits a tort is called a tortfeasor. The other party is alternatively referred to as the injured party, the innocent party, or the victim. The primary purpose of tort law is to compensate the innocent party by making up for any loss suffered by that victim. The doctrine of *respondeat superior* may impose legal liability on employers and make them pay for the torts committed by their employees within the scope of the employer's business.

**6.2**   The principal intentional torts include assault, battery, false imprisonment, defamation, disparagement, fraudulent misrepresentation, invasion of privacy, intentional infliction of emotional distress, and malicious prosecution.

**6.3**   Negligence is the failure to exercise the degree of care that a reasonable person would have exercised in the same circumstances. Negligence includes four elements: duty of care, breach of duty through a failure to exercise the appropriate standard of care, proximate cause, and actual harm. Three defenses to negligence are contributory negligence, comparative negligence, and assumption of risk.

**6.4**   Under the doctrine of strict liability, when people engage in ultrahazardous activities, they will be liable for any harm that occurs because of that activity, regardless of intent and regardless of care.

**6.5**   Cybertorts involve computer data that has been invaded, distorted, falsified, misused, destroyed, or exploited financially by an electronic devise. Therefore, cybertorts rarely involve any harm to a party's physical well-being. Instead, the victim's reputation has been hurt because a false statement has been placed on the Internet, the victim's emotional state has been disturbed, because his or her privacy has been invaded by a posting on Facebook, or the victim has suffered monetary harm because of identity theft.

**6.6**   Tort remedies include monetary damages and injunctions.

**6.7**   Survival statutes allow a lawsuit to be brought even if both the plaintiff and the defendant are deceased. Wrongful death statutes preserve the rights of third parties affected by the death of the deceased to bring a lawsuit. Statutes of repose establish a limit in years beyond which an injured party could not bring a lawsuit for an injury caused by a product or by medical malpractice. Another reform that has been suggested in some states is the application of comparative negligence as an affirmative defense in some product liability cases.

## Key Terms

abuse of process, 123

actual cause, 125

actual malice, 120

actual malice test, 120

assault, 118

assumption of the risk, 127

## Questions for Review and Discussion

1. What is the difference between a tort and a crime?
2. What is *respondeat superior?*
3. What is meant by the legal term "duty"?
4. What are the principal intentional torts?
5. What are the elements of negligence?
6. What are the differences among contributory negligence, comparative negligence, and assumption of the risk?
7. When does strict liability apply?
8. What is a cybertort?
9. What remedies are available in tort law?
10. What innovations have been suggested for contemporary state tort reform?

## Cases for Analysis

1. Patrick Clawson was described by reporter Karen Branch-Brioso in a newspaper story as a "1970s era St. Louis journalist turned private eye turned FBI informant." The story was published in the *St. Louis Post-Dispatch*. The fact that he had been characterized as an "informant" bothered Clawson, who saw it as damaging to his reputation. Accordingly, he brought a libel case against the *Post-Dispatch*. Recall that to be libelous, a statement must be false and "hold the victim up to ridicule, contempt, or hatred." Clawson would have preferred the term "whistleblower" rather than "informant," because that term commands more respect. Why is the use of the term "informant" to describe Clawson not libelous? Explain. *Clawson v. St. Louis Post-Dispatch,* No. 04-CV-486; see also "Media Law: Label of 'Informer' Is Found Not Defamatory," *The National Law Journal,* September 11, 2006.

2. Curtis Ellison was riding as a passenger in his own vehicle when it was pulled over by the police for a parking violation. The vehicle had actually been targeted because the police had routinely checked the license plate through the department's database. This routine check had revealed that the owner of the vehicle had an outstanding warrant pending against him. When the police searched the van, they found two firearms hidden in the vehicle. As a result, Ellison was charged with felonious possession of a firearm. He argued that the search had violated his Fourth Amendment rights and that his right to privacy had been infringed. The trial

court agreed and dismissed the case. The case went to the appellate court. The issue before the appellate court was whether Ellison had a high expectation of privacy about the number on his license plate. Although this is a criminal case, it is still interesting to speculate on how the court would rule on the expectation of privacy in relation to a license plate. Why should the appeals court reverse the ruling by the trial court that there is a high expectation of privacy in relation to a license plate? Explain. *United States v. Ellison*, No. 04-1925; see also "Criminal Practice: No Privacy Expectation on License Plate Numbers," *The National Law Journal*, September 18, 2006, p. 16.

3.  A St. Louis police officer was speeding the wrong way down a one-way street when he collided with a vehicle being driven by Ann Martin. Martin was seriously injured in the crash and brought a lawsuit against the police officer, the City of St. Louis, and the board of police commissioners. The board of commissioners is an agency of the state of Missouri. Martin passed away, and her daughter, Kimberly Hodges, took over as the plaintiff in the case. The case was settled in relation to the board and the officer but not the city. The City of St Louis argued that the officer could not be employed by both the board and the city at the same time. The city further argued that the officer's real employer was the board, so it, the city, could not be held liable under the doctrine of vicarious liability. Why should the city be held liable under the doctirne of vicarious liability? Explain. *Hodges v. City of St. Louis*, No. SC87513; see also "Torts: Officer Is City Agent Even if Working for State Board," *The National Law Journal*, March 12, 2007, p. 15.

4.  At the height of the modern civil rights movement, *The New York Times* ran a full-page advertisement entitled "Heed Their Rising Voices." The advertisement detailed police efforts in Montgomery, Ala., to suppress the nonviolent civil rights demonstrations being carried on there by thousands of college students. The police commissioner of Montgomery, L.B. Sullivan, filed a lawsuit against *The New York Times*, alleging that he had been libeled by information carried in the advertisement, even though he was never mentioned by name. Should the Court use the actual malice test in this case to determine whether the newspaper libeled the commissioner? Explain. *New York Times Co. v. Sullivan*, 376 U.S. 254 (U.S. Sup. Ct.).

5.  Five Commerce City police officers were summoned to break up a disturbance at a local party of teenagers. At the party, Ralph Crowe, who had consumed eight cups of beer and three cups of alcoholic punch, became rowdy and had to be detained by the officers. The police released Ralph after receiving the assurances of his brother Eddie that he would drive Ralph home. After leaving the party, Eddie Crowe allowed Ralph to take the wheel. Instead of going home, Ralph drove to the site of another party, where he lost control of the car and ran down six people. The police officers were sued for negligence in releasing Ralph. Did the five officers owe a duty to the six victims of Ralph's drunk-driving accident? Explain. *Leake v. Cain*, 720 P.2d 152 (CO).

6.  Seventy-four years of age at the time, Ramona Booker entered a drugstore by pushing her way through one door and then through a second. Both doors were extremely heavy, so Booker was compelled to use both hands, causing her cane to drag on the ground. As she entered the second door, the tip of her cane caught on the exposed coil of a security device, causing her to fall and injure herself. Booker brought a lawsuit against Revco DS, Inc., to recover for her injuries. Did the drugstore owe a duty to Booker and other customers to maintain a safe environment? Explain. Is Booker's lawsuit based on allegations that the store owners committed an intentional tort or that they were negligent? Explain. What test would be used to judge whether the drugstore owners should be held liable for Booker's injuries? Explain. *Booker v. Revco DS, Inc*. 681 N.E.2d 499 (OH).

7.  Queenway Tankers, Inc., Kingsway Tankers, Inc., the East River Steamship Corporation, and Richmond Tankers, Inc., all chartered supertankers designed by Transamerican Delaval, Inc. Under the terms of the charters, each shipping company was financially responsible for many repairs to the tankers. From the start, there were problems with the tankers' turbines, which needed extensive and costly repairs. The plaintiffs brought a product liability suit against Delaval. The suit alleged that the manufacturing defects caused the damage. Should the shipping companies have prevailed in product liability against the manufacturer? Explain. *East River Steamship Corporation v. Transamerican Delaval, Inc.*, 106 S. Ct. 2305 (U.S. Sup. Ct.).

8. Myers was injured when she slipped and fell on an ice patch on the front walkway of the Canton Centre Mall. The mall is owned and operated by Forest City Enterprises. Forest City had employees who were responsible for clearing the ice off of the mall walkways every morning. On this particular morning, they had cleared the ice from the walkway a short time before Myers took her tumble. Nevertheless, an ice patch had formed, and Myers did fall, sustaining injuries. Cooper, one of the employees charged with the ice-removal task, theorized that water may have been splashed up onto the sidewalk by passing cars where it froze sometime after their initial cleaning of the day. According to Cooper, "the vehicles could have splashed this back up on there . . . we're constantly moving around the building at all times, so anything can be going on in this half of the building while you're over here doing this half coming around." Was Forest City negligent in failing to keep the sidewalk clear of ice at all times that winter? What test would be used to judge Forest City's conduct? Explain. *Myers v. Forest City Enterprises, Inc.* 635 N.E.2d 1268 (OH).

9. Michelle Wightman was driving toward a railroad crossing at which the gates were down and the lights flashing. Wightman noted a stopped train a short distance from the gate. Believing the stopped train to be the cause of the closed gate, she drove around the gate and was struck and killed by a train that suddenly appeared from behind the stopped train. The stopped train had blocked her view of the oncoming train. Both trains were owned and operated by Consolidated Rail Corporation (CRC). Wightman's mother brought a wrongful death lawsuit and a survivorship action against CRC. In response, CRC claimed that Wightman's action of driving around the gates, in violation of both state and city law regarding the operation of a motor vehicle at a railroad crossing, constituted negligence on her part. Furthermore, CRC argued that if Wightman had not crossed the tracks, she would not have been struck by the train. Therefore, her actions were the sole cause of the accident, and the railroad corporation should not be held liable for her death. The attorney for the plaintiff argued that the placement of the first train, blocking the view of the other track, contributed to the accident and that CRC should be held liable for Wightman's death. Should Wightman's own negligence be a complete bar to the plaintiff's recovery of damages in this case? Explain. *Wightman v. Consolidated Railroad Corporation,* 640 N.E.2d 1160 (OH).

## quick quiz Answers

| 6-1 | 6-2 | 6-3 | 6-4 | 6-5 | 6-6 | 6-7 |
|-----|-----|-----|-----|-----|-----|-----|
| 1. T | 1. F | 1. F | 1. T | 1. T | 1. F | 1. T |
| 2. F | 2. F | 2. T | 2. T | 2. F | 2. F | 2. T |
| 3. F | 3. F | 3. F | 3. F | 3. F | 3. F | 3. T |

# Part 1 Case Study

**United Citizens v. Federal Election Commission**
United States Supreme Court
130 S. Ct. 876 (2010)

## Summary

During the 2004 presidential campaign, Michael Moore promoted the film, *Fahrenheit 9/11,* which was critical of the Bush presidency and which expressly urged the removal of Bush from the presidency. The film was released, promoted, distributed, and shown using funds supplied by Moore and other entities, all of which had made contributions to a series of political candidates of a clearly identifiable political persuasion. A conservative nonprofit political group named Citizens United, also with a clearly identifiable political agenda, filed a complaint with the Federal Election Commission asking that the film be censored under provisions of the Bipartisan Campaign Reform Act of 2002. The federal reform law, which is popularly known as the McCain-Feingold Act, forbids all "electioneering communications" by all unions, and by all profit and nonprofit corporations, 60 days before an election and 30 days before a primary. The McCain-Feingold law did allow some political advertisements during that same period of time, just as long as those advertisements were funded by the candidate's campaign. For clarity, McCain-Feingold defined "electioneering communications" as speech that is intended to promote a candidate's election or, in the alternative, the defeat of a candidate. In response to the complaint, the Federal Election Commission ruled that the activities of Moore and his associates in the release, promotion, distribution, and showing of the film had not in any way violated the law. The commission decided that the money spent on the promotion and release of the film including the film's Web site and trailers were, in fact, simply commercial activities and not political speech as defined within the act. As a result, the complaint was dismissed. (It is interesting to note that at this point neither Citizens United nor the Federal Election Commission had presented any arguments regarding the law's constitutionality. That was about to change.)

Taking its cue from this decision, in the 2008 election campaign, Citizens United fought back by producing its own film entitled *Hillary: The Movie.* The film, which was admittedly critical of Senator Hillary Clinton, was scheduled to be promoted in television commercials and ultimately broadcast on Direct TV. As a preemptive strike, Citizens United brought an action in Federal District Court, arguing that McCain-Feingold, at least to the extent that it might be applied to *Hillary: The Movie,* was unconstitutional and asking for an injunction to prevent the Federal Election Commission from using the law to interfere with the promotion and presentation of the film. The Federal Election Commission argued that both the film and the commercials advertising the film violated both the spirit and the letter of the McCain-Feingold Act. Therefore, the commission was entitled to a summary judgment in the case. Citizens United opposed the summary judgment motion, arguing that the film was a documentary that was plainly nonpartisan, that the film was not "publically distributed," and that, as a result, the film was not "electioneering communication." Therefore, they concluded that none of their activities violated McCain-Feingold. Moreover, Citizens United also contended that, even on the remote chance that their actions did violate McCain-Feingold, the law itself was unconstitutional. Specifically, Citizens United believed that the section of McCain-Feingold that censored political films like *Hillary: The Movie* and the section that mandated certain disclosure and reporting requirements were both unconstitutional. The court did not agree with Citizens United and ruled that the film, which had been financed by Citizens United, was a deliberate, unapologetic attempt to malign the reputation of Senator Clinton and, as such, violated the statute's prohibition against "independent expenditures" for "electioneering communications" within 30 days of a primary. Also, following a previous case, *Austin v. Michigan Chamber of Commerce,* in which the U.S. Supreme Court ruled that corporate political speech could be censored by law without violating the First Amendment, the district court in the Citizens United case ruled McCain-Feingold to be constitutional. As a result, two interesting and obviously contradictory rulings were now caught within the legal system: the *Fahrenheit 9/11* ruling, permitting the promotion and release of a corporately financed, obviously political film, and the ruling in *Hillary: The Movie,* outlawing what was essentially the same thing. As you would expect, the case ended up in the United States Supreme Court.

The Supreme Court was actually faced with a dispute that consisted of two levels of inquiry. The first level is the issue of whether the activities of Citizens United in relation to the distribution, promotion, and presentation of *Hillary: the Movie* violated the provisions of the McCain-Feingold Act. Generally, if a court can decide a case on the narrower issue of strict legality rather than the broader issue of constitutionality, the court will do so. Such a decision has a much more limited and, therefore, much less disruptive effect on the legal system outside of the current case, thus promoting two of the three purposes of the law, order and stability. Deciding a case in this way is also part of the balancing function of the law. One of the most obvious dualities in the law is the balance between the spirit and the letter of the law. Generally, a person who follows the "spirit" of the law has found its actual intent, while one who is tied to the letter of the law has missed its true meaning. In this case, the Court could have followed the letter of the law and ruled that the activities of Citizen's United violated McCain-Feingold. This would have ended the case right then and there. However, such a decision on the part of the Court would have violated the spirit of the law, represented by the U.S. Constitution, in general, and the First Amendment, in particular. For these reasons it makes sense to defend the Supreme Court's decision to move on to the issue of McCain-Feingold's constitutionality. This means that the Court elected to immerse itself within the process of *judicial review,* that is, it decided to determine the constitutionality of a portion of McCain-Feingold. The Citizens United case revolved around the First Amendment's guarantee of free speech, especially as it relates to politics and corporations.

Whenever rights become the focus of a legal discussion, it is informative to look first at the *theory of negative rights*. The theory of negative rights argues that "rights" are a human invention designed to help people escape moral law. Thus, under this theory, the right to free speech is actually the right to lie and get away with it or, stated another way, it is the right to say what one wants, without legal consequences. The courts rarely follow this line of reasoning. Nevertheless, judges sometimes limit the right of free speech perhaps because, intuitively or subconsciously, they perceive the truth of the negative rights theory. Thus, it is not impossible for the law to impose some limits on free speech. The law can limit free speech, for example, to protect individuals from slander and libel, to protect an author's copyright and, thus, to preserve his nor her right to receive royalties, or to limit what a governmental agent might say in carrying out his or her duties as a representative of the government. Despite these limitations, in most instances, speech is protected from prior restraint (read "censorship" here) by the Federal government under the First Amendment, and by the states under the First and the Fourteenth Amendments.

The Court then goes on to explain that there are two clearly delineated situations in which the government cannot limit free speech. First, the government is not permitted to prohibit or punish speech simply based on the content of that speech. Second, the government is not permitted to prohibit or punish speech based on the identity of a speaker. Thus the government cannot let one speaker speak while prohibiting another speaker from taking the same podium. The only exception to this rule involves government employees. Here the courts says that the government, in exercising its duty to see that the government itself runs smoothly and fairly, may prohibit what its own employees may say in a governmental capacity. Applying these standards to the present case, the Supreme Court could not condone the censorship of corporations and unions under the provisions of the McCain-Feingold Act based on the content of the speech and on the identity of the speaker. Thus, the Court declared unconstitutional that part of the McCain-Feingold Act that prohibited the release, promotion, and airing of *Hillary: The Movie.* The Court concluded that Congress could not censor political speech simply because it was supported by the "independent expenditures" of a nonprofit corporation. Such censorship was clearly aimed at prohibiting the political content spoken by a particular speaker, a nonprofit corporation, and as such was a violation of free speech as guaranteed by the First Amendment. In making this decision, the Court was also compelled to overturn the line of precedent that followed and supported the case of *Austin v. Michigan Chamber of Commerce.*

## Justice Kennedy delivered the opinion of the Court.

Federal law prohibits corporations and unions from using their general treasury funds to make independent expenditures for speech defined as "electioneering communication" or for speech expressly advocating the election or the defeat of a candidate . . . limits on electioneering communications were upheld in *McConnell v. Federal Election Comm'n,* 540 U.S. 93, 203–209 (2003). The holding in McConnell rested to a large extent on an earlier case, *Austin v. Michigan Chamber of Commerce,* 494 U.S. 652 (1990). *Austin* held that political speech may be banned based on the speaker's corporate identity.

In this case we are asked to reconsider *Austin* and, in effect, *McConnell.* It has been noted that "*Austin* was a significant departure from ancient First Amendment principles" . . . We agree with that conclusion and hold that *stare decisis* does not compel the continued acceptance of *Austin.* The Government may regulate corporate political speech through disclaimer and disclosure requirements, but it may not suppress that speech altogether. We turn to the case now before us.

### I

Citizens United is a nonprofit corporation. It brought this action in the United States District Court for the District of Columbia. A three-judge court later convened to hear the cause. The resulting judgment gives rise to this appeal.

Citizens United has an annual budget of about $12 million. Most of its funds are from donations by individuals; but in addition, it accepts a small portion of its funds from for-profit corporations.

In January 2008, Citizens United released a film entitled *Hillary: The Movie.* We refer to the film as *Hillary.* It is a 90-minute documentary about then-Senator Hillary Clinton, who was a candidate in the Democratic Party's 2008 Presidential primary elections. *Hillary* mentions Senator Clinton by name and depicts interviews with political commentators and other persons, most of them quite critical of Senator Clinton. *Hillary* was released in theaters and on DVD, but Citizens United wanted to increase distribution by making it available through video-on-demand.

Video-on-demand allows digital cable subscribers to select programming from various menus, including movies, television shows, sports, news, and music. The viewer can watch the program at any time and can elect to rewind or pause the program. In December 2007, a cable company offered, for payment of $1,2 million, to make *Hillary* available on video-on-demand channel called "Election'08.". . . . Some video-on-demand services require viewers to pay a small fee to view a selected program, but here the proposal was to make *Hillary* available to viewers free of charge.

To implement the proposal, Citizens United was prepared to pay for the video-on-demand; and to promote the film, it produced two 10-second ads and one 30-second ad for *Hillary.* Each ad includes a short (and, in our view, pejorative) statement about Senator Clinton, followed by the name of the movie and the movie's Web site address . . . Citizens United desired to promote the video-on-demand offering by running advertisements on broadcast and cable television.

Before the Bipartisan Campaign Reform Act of 2002 (BCRA), federal law prohibited—and still does prohibit—corporations and unions from using general treasury funds to make direct contributions to candidates or independent expenditures that expressly advocate the election or defeat of a candidate, through any form of media, in connection with certain qualified federal elections . . . An electioneering communication is defined as "any broadcast, cable or satellite communication" that refers to a clearly identified candidate for Federal office" and is made within 30 days of a primary or 60 days of a general election . . . The Federal Election Commission's (FEC) regulations further define an electioneering communication as a communication that is "publicly distributed. . . .Corporations and unions are barred from using general treasury funds for express advocacy of electioneering communications . . .

### II

Before considering whether *Austin* should be overruled, we first address whether Citizen's United's claim that section 441b cannot be applied to *Hillary* may be resolved on other narrower grounds. (Note: After an extensive, in-depth examination of this issue covering fifteen pages, the court decided that the case could not be decided by using the statute alone and moves on to the constitutional issue of First Amendment free speech guarantees.)

## III

The First Amendment provides that "Congress shall make no law . . . abridging the freedom of speech." Laws enacted to control or suppress speech may operate at different points in the speech process. The following are just a few examples of restrictions that have been attempted at different stages of the speech process—all laws found to be invalid: restrictions requiring a permit at the outset . . . imposing a burden by impounding proceeds on receipts or royalties . . . seeking to exact accost after the speech occurs . . . and subjecting the speaker to criminal penalties.

The law before us is an outright ban, backed by criminal sanctions. Section 441b makes it a felony for all corporations—including nonprofit advocacy corporations—either to expressly advocate the election or defeat of candidates or to broadcast electioneering communications within 30 days of a primary election and 60 days of a general election. Thus, the following acts would be felonies under 441b: The Sierra Club runs an ad, within the crucial phase of 60 days before the general election, that exhorts the public to disapprove of a Congressman who favors logging in national forest; the National Rifle Association publishes a book urging the public to vote for the challenger because an incumbent U.S. Senator supports a handgun ban; and the American Civil Liberties Union creates a Web site telling the public to vote for a presidential candidate in light of that candidate's defense of free speech. These prohibitions are classic examples of censorship. . . .

Premised on a distrust of governmental power, the First Amendment stands against attempts to disfavor certain subjects or viewpoints. . . . Prohibited too are restrictions distinguishing among different speakers, allowing speech by some but not others . . . As instruments to censor, these categories are interrelated: Speech restrictions based on the identity of the speaker are too often simply a means to control content.

Quite apart from the purpose or effect of regulating content, moreover, the Government may commit a constitutional wrong when by law it identifies certain preferred speakers. By taking the right to speak from some and giving it to others, the Government deprives the disadvantaged person or class of the right to use speech to strive to establish worth, standing, and respect for the speaker's voice. The Government may not by these means deprive the public of the right and privilege to determine for itself what speech and speakers are worthy of consideration. The First Amendment protects speech and speaker, and the ideas that flow from each . . .

The Court has recognized that First Amendment protection extends to corporations . . . This protection has been extended by explicit holdings to the context of political speech . . . Corporations and other associations, like individuals, contribute to the discussion, debate, and the dissemination of information and ideas that the First Amendment seeks to foster . . . The Court has thus rejected the argument that political speech of corporations or other associations should be treated differently under the First Amendment simply because such associations are not "natural persons." . . .

Less than two years after *Buckley*, *Bellotti*, 435 U.S. 765, reaffirmed the First Amendment principle that the Government cannot restrict political speech based on the speaker's corporate identity. *Bellotti* could not have ben clearer when it struck down a state-law prohibition on corporate independent expenditures related to referenda issues . . .

Thus, the law stood until *Austin*. *Austin* upheld a direct restriction on the independent expenditure of funds for political speech for the first time . . . There, the Michigan Chamber of Commerce sought to use general treasury funds to run a newspaper ad supporting a specific candidate. Michigan law, however, prohibited corporate independent expenditures that supported or opposed any candidate for stew office. A violation of the law was punishable as a felony. The Court sustained the speech prohibition. . . .

Our precedent is to be respected unless the most convincing of reasons demonstrates that adherence to it puts us on a course that is sure error. "Beyond workability, the relevant factors in deciding whether to adhere to the principle of *stare decisis* include the antiquity of the precedent, the reliance of interests at stake, and of course whether the decision was well reasoned. . . . We have also examined whether "experience has pointed up the precedent's shortcomings . . . These considerations counsel in favor of rejecting *Austin,* which itself contravened this court's earlier precedent in *Buckley* and *Bellotti*. "This Court has not hesitated to overrule decisions offensive to the First Amendment." . . . *Stare decisis* is a principle of policy not a mechanical formula of adherence to the latest decision." For the reasons above, it must be concluded that *Austin* was not well reasoned. . . .

Some members of the public might consider Hillary to be insightful and instructive; some might find it to be neither high art nor a fair discussion on how to set the Nation's course; still others simply might suspend judgment on the points but decide to think more about issues and candidates. These choices and assessments, however, are not the Government's to make. "The First Amendment underwrites the freedom to experiment and to create in the realm of thought and speech. Citizens must be free to use new forums, for expression of ideas. The civic discourse belongs to the people, and the Government may not prescribe the means used to conduct it . . .

The judgment of the District Court is reversed with respect to the constitutionality of 2 U.S.C. 441b's restrictions on corporate independent expenditures . . .

*It is so ordered.*

# Questions for Analysis

1. The Federal Elections Commission filed a summary judgment motion with the District Court to have the case brought by Citizens United dismissed. What is a summary judgment motion and why is it appropriate in this case? Explain.

2. Citizens United filed a request for an injunction in the same case. What is an injunction and why is it appropriate in this case? Explain.

3. What is at stake in the balancing act generally involved in the law-making process in a case like this? Explain.

4. What is the negative rights theory of ethics and just how does it impact this case? Explain.

5. The court stipulates that there are some very specific situations in which the government is permitted to censor free speech. What are they?

6. The court explains that there are two situations in which the government cannot limit free speech. What are they?

7. Which of these two situations would explain why the courts have outlawed hate speech crimes? Explain.

8. In this case, the Supreme Court must engage in both statutory interpretation and in judicial review. Explain the difference between the two.

9. Explain how *stare decisis* is at the heart of this case. What case is overturned and why is it overturned? Explain.

10. In the Supreme Court's opinion, Justice Kennedy outlines three situations that will permit a case to be overturned. List those three situations.

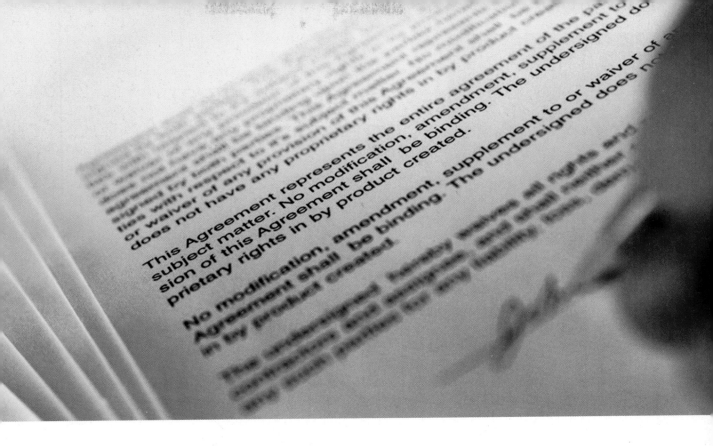

# Part Two

## Contract Law

# Chapter 7

# The Essentials of Contract Law

## THE OPENING CASE Multidimensional Contract Law: *Tubelite Co., Inc. v. Original Sign Studio*

In the balancing act that is the law, judges and attorneys must often weave their way through a series of overlapping and inconsistent legal dimensions before arriving at a solution to their problems. Unfortunately, even that does not always work. Such was the case in a multidimensional lawsuit entitled *Tubelite Co., Inc. v. Original Sign Studio.* The lawsuit concerns two agreements between Tubelite, the seller, and Original Sign Studio, the buyer. The first agreement was an application for credit, in which Original Sign agreed to pay for all materials shipped by Tubelite and to remit an 18 percent finance charge for overdue payments. In the second agreement, Tubelite agreed to be Original Sign's exclusive supplier. The terms of the contract were reduced to writing in a letter written by an agent of Original Sign but never signed by anyone from Tubelite. The agreement stated that Tubelite would supply Original Sign with all the material that it requested but that it would bill Original Sign only for the materials that the sign company actually used and then, in exchange for being Original Sign's exclusive supplier, it would charge a discounted rate of somewhere between 10 and 25 percent. Tubelite also agreed to install shelving at Original Sign's warehouse for proper storing of the materials. Tubelite shipped the materials that Original requested and installed the shelving as per the agreement. So far so good. Then the trouble started.

Tubelite billed Original for all the material it shipped, not just the material used. Moreover, the bill that Tubelite sent to Original ignored the discounts promised under agreement number two. Original ignored the bill as written by Tubelite and, instead, paid only for the materials it had used at a 25 percent discount rate. Tubelite insisted that, under agreement one, Original still owed money for the unused portion of the material. In addition, since that payment was now late, Tubelite tacked on its 18 percent penalty (remember the "finance charge"). Original argued that agreement two, the discount agreement, superseded, agreement one, the credit agreement. Tubelite argued that agreement one, the credit application, was still in effect because agreement two, was never signed by anyone from Tubelite. Therefore, the agreement failed to meet Statute of Frauds requirements (the statute that tells us what contracts must be written), and was unenforceable. Besides, Tubelite added, agreement number two was too vague to be enforced, even if the writing were okay. It should be clear that, if any dispute is multidimensional, this one is. Look at all the questions in these two contacts that remain. What law applies here? Common law or the Uniform Commercial Code (UCC)? Which contract rules? Did Original err in not getting a Tubelite agent to sign the agreement? Is the writing really too vague or is Tubelite pulling a fast one? These and other similar questions will be addressed in the Unit called Contract Law. [See *Tubelite Co., Inc. v. Original Sign Studio,* 176 Ohio App.3d 241 (Tenth District).]

**Opening Case Questions**

1. Would *Tubelite Co., Inc. v. Original Sign Studio* be a civil lawsuit or a criminal action? Explain.

2. What law will the court apply in this case to answer the questions noted above? Will the court use common law or the Uniform Commercial Code (UCC)? Explain.

3. What is the legal status of a contract that is supposed to be in writing under the law, but is never reduced to writing? Explain. *Valid, unenforceable*

4. What legal exceptions exist to the rule that says that certain contracts must be in writing? Explain.

5. When an agent fails to perform one of the many duties imposed on agents by law, what are the legal consequences for that agent? Explain.

## LO Learning Objectives

1. Define contract.
2. Explain the origin of the law merchant.
3. Discuss the relationship between common law and the law merchant.
4. Identify the four elements of a contract.
5. Explain the objectives of contract law.
6. Explain the place of the UCC in contract law.
7. Distinguish contracts from other agreements.
8. Explain the role of privity and agency in contract law.
9. List the contracts that must be in writing to be enfoceable.
10. List the characteristics of a contract.

# 7-1 The History of Contract Law

A **contract** is an agreement between two or more competent parties based on mutual promises and an exchange of things of value, to do or refrain from doing some particular thing that is neither illegal nor impossible. The agreement results in an obligation or a duty that can be enforced in a court of law. Most people understand the basic nature of a contract as a process of give and take. There are rules, however, that govern how those agreements are made, how they are carried out, how they end, and how disputes are resolved when someone yells, "foul." Before delving into these basic principles, however, we will pause for a moment to consider how these rules originated.

## Mercantile Law, Ancient Rome, Capitalism, and the Church

The history of contract law is intertwined with the parallel development of Western mercantile law, often referred to alternately as the **law merchant** and *lex mercatoria.* The law merchant outlines the laws and the procedures followed by merchants in commercial transactions. As Harold J. Berman explains in his landmark study, *Law and Revolution: The Formation of the Western Legal Tradition,* mercantile law originated among the merchants themselves who needed a formalized way to deal with one another when disputes arose. According to Berman, the law merchant saw a sudden and unprecedented burst of development between the 11th and the 13th centuries in Western Europe, both on the continent and across the channel in England. This is not to say that there was no commercial law before the 11th century. Between the fall of Rome and the rise of the mercantile city states of the late Middle Ages, which is to say during the second half of the first millennium, commercial transactions were limited to seasonal festivals, small town marketplaces, and coastal cities. The law that governed these transactions emerged from rules within the ancient traditions of the Justinian Code of the old Roman Empire. All of this began to change with a series of agricultural innovations and a sudden European population explosion. [See Harold J. Berman, *Law and Revolution: The Formation of the Western Legal Tradition,* (Cambridge: Harvard UP, 1983), pp. 333–341.]

### Agriculture, Technology, and Population

Ancient Roman law was adequate at the time because commerce itself was limited during that era. The population of Europe barely topped 20 million at the end of the first millennium and most people lived out their lives in the small villages and manors that dotted the countryside. Several irresistible driving forces changed all of that in the 11th century. Technological developments in agriculture (including a number of important inventions such as a new type of horse collar, a heavy plow, horse shoes, fish farming, three-field crop rotation, the overshot waterwheel, and the wind powered post mill) led to crop surpluses that could be sold for a profit; changes in manor law freed many peasants who turned to selling as a livelihood; and Europe saw an unprecedented population explosion. This all led to a new group of professional sellers who developed their own system of laws over a relatively short time. That system came to be called *mercantile law* or the *law merchant.* [See Berman, 333–341; see also Rodney Stark, *The Victory of Reason: How Christianity Led to Freedom, Capitalism, and Western Science* (New York: Random House, 2005), pp. 38–44.] In his book, *The Victory of Reason,* Rodney Stark notes that, despite popular views to the contrary, an enormous amount of progress occurred during the Muddle Ages, including the inventions listed above. [See Stark, pp. 38–44.]

### The Development of the Law Merchant

Mercantile law is also closely associated with the development of capitalism. Capitalism is an economic system that operates on the basis of competition and a free market that responds to the movement of supply and demand. Contrary to the thesis proposed by Max Weber in *The Protestant Ethic: The Spirit of Capitalism,* European capitalism did not begin with the Protestant Reformation in the 16th century, but in the 11th and 12th centuries, some 400 years before Martin Luther nailed his famous 95 theses on the cathedral door in Wittenberg. Moreover, one of the driving forces behind the growth of capitalism was the Roman Catholic Church which helped provide a rational and moral foundation for the principles and procedures that guided the activities of merchants in their communities, their courts, and in the making of their contracts. The Church refused to condemn commercial activity. Instead, the Church monitored how those activities were carried out. In short, the Church encouraged this new class of sellers to establish guilds that followed the law of the Church, a legal tradition that is generally referred to as canon law. The Church also insisted that these emerging businessmen never engage in deceit or dishonesty and always follow a good faith approach to contract development. As long as they followed these basic precepts, the Church reassured the members of the new and expanding class of professional sellers that there was nothing inherently wrong with their chosen profession. [See Berman, pp. 336–341; and Stark, xi. See also Henri Sée, *Modern Capitalism: Its Origin and Evolutions,* trans. Homer B. Vanderblue and Georges F. Doriot (New York: Adelphi Co. 1928), pp. 7–13.]

## A QUESTION OF ETHICS

Of course, the Roman Catholic Church was not always as supportive of capitalism as it eventually became. In fact, both Henri Sée in a study entitled *Modern Capitalism* and Harold Berman in his book *Law and Revolution* refer to the work of the French historian, Henri Pirenne, who wrote extensively about the development of capitalism in Europe in the Middle Ages. According to Berman, Pirenne points out that the Church often took a decidedly anti-capitalist position, especially in relation to such things as moneylending and placing an unfair value on goods. On the other hand, Sée points out that, when circumstances were right, in certain areas of Europe, notably the Low Countries of Holland and Zeeland, the Church was willing to support those emerging businessmen who worked diligently to create an authentic form of modern capitalism that included moneylending. Even Max Weber does not deny that certain theologians in the Medieval Church managed to support the growth of capitalism. (Specifically, he refers to Anthony of Florence and Bernhard of Siena, although, to be fair, Weber does hide this reference in a lengthy footnote at the back of his book.) The question before us is this: What religious values would operate to oppose capitalism? What is it about the very nature of religious doctrine that places it in opposition to making a profit? On the other hand, what arguments can overcome this religious opposition to making a profit? Explain all your answers. (See Berman, pp. 336–337; Sée, pp.12–13; and Max Weber, *The Protestant Ethic: The Spirit of Capitalism* (Mineola, NY: Dover, 2003), p. 197.)

# The Characteristics of the Law Merchant

With the Roman Catholic Church supplying political and social support, with canon law providing a moral framework, and with practicality guiding their activities over a 300-year period, the this new class of businessmen developed a body of effective commercial law. Berman tells us that this legal system was distinguished by six characteristics: neutrality, universality, mutuality, involvement, integration, and evolution.

### Neutrality of the Law Merchant
The law merchant was made up of fairly neutral system of laws and procedures. *Neutrality* characterizes any system of laws that is consistently applied in the same evenhanded way, no matter who the antagonists might be. The law developed in the festivals, marketplaces, and coastal cities of Europe by practical men who saw the value of recording their procedures and principles in writing so that commercial activities, financial transactions, and dispute settlements could be carried out in a customary, predictable, and even-handed way. The legal treatises and codebooks that resulted covered the making of negotiable instruments, the execution of contracts, and the procedures used in the mercantile courts. The actual process of writing these things down was authorized and supported by the ruling classes, especially those in the merchant cities of Genoa, Milan, and Pisa, and by the birth of a class of professional notaries, whose job it was to write down contracts and draft negotiable instruments which, by virtue of this process, were lawful, valid, and enforceable. (See Berman, pp. 341 and 355.)

### Universality and the Law Merchant
*Universal* laws are those that apply to everyone regardless of their social status or their place of origin. The universal applicability of the law merchant was made necessary by the global nature of trade in the late Middle Ages. The city-states of Europe hosted international fairs and the coastal cities became permanent centers for international trade. Towns and coastal cities began to adhere to the law merchant rather than their local laws which tended to be prejudiced against foreigners. In *Law and Revolution,* Berman tells us that, as the influence of the central government began to grow, some

rulers agreed to incorporate the law merchant into their national documents, such as the *Magna Carta* in 1215 which contains a clause that specifically grants safe passage to foreign merchants in England. Other rulers, notably those in Italy, entered formal agreements that guaranteed that the law merchant would be used in settling any contract disagreements that might involve their people. (See Berman, pp. 342–344.). Weber agrees with Berman that a successful capitalist system depends upon the establishment of a legal system with formal rules that emerge from a rational process (Weber, p. 25). Moreover, Henri Sée concurs that the international character of trade gave birth to modern capitalism (Sée Henri See, pp. 25, 29–30).

**Mutuality and the Law Merchant** The concept of *mutuality* or *reciprocity* in the law merchant is the notion that commercial arrangements always involve a process of evenhanded cooperation between the parties. Mutuality in the law merchant emerged organically from within the commercial culture which had at its foundation a belief in reciprocity. Moreover, Berman tells us that the principle of reciprocity insisted on mutuality at two levels. First, parties to any commercial transaction were expressly forbidden to cheat, lie, or trick one another. Second, all commercial transactions had to be fair to each party. This principle outlawed contracts that involved outrageous prices and those that took advantage of a party's weakened position (See Berman, pp. 344–346). Of course, Weber reminds us that there is a practical foundation for the principle of reciprocity as there are for all such virtues. Honesty, he reports, has its value, if only because it will earn good credit for trustworthy merchants. (Weber, p. 52). Does the utilitarian nature of reciprocity make it wrong? No. However, it does make the pursuit of reciprocity a bit less romantic.

**Involvement and Law Merchant** *Involvement* requires that those affected by the law participate in its making and its execution. According to Berman, from the outset merchants were involved in the establishment and the operation of the courts that adjudicated disputes involving contracts and other commercial disagreements such as those that might question the authenticity of negotiable instruments. Specifically, the courts held in European markets and fairs were run by businessmen who were elected to act as judges. The courts established by the guilds were run by the elected guild leaders who often hand picked guild members to assist in deciding certain disputes. Some territories also developed staple courts that dealt with cases involving the primary product or "staple" of a certain town or village. The courts in the Italian city-states such as Milan also elected merchants to hear disputes involving contract and other commercial transactions. Many of the coastal cities created their own local courts, sometimes referred to as admiralty courts, to handle commercial disputes involving goods carried as cargo by the ships that docked at those ports. (See Berman, pp. 346–348.) Berman, however, is careful to remind us that this exclusive control of the courts by the business class also had its down side. Berman argues that when people have the power to control their own legal system they can use that power to protect themselves, which is exactly what happened to the new business class in Europe during the Middle Ages (See Berman, p. 348). Another legal scholar, Gerald Turkel, agrees with Berman arguing that it is generally best for the legal system to stand on its own, free from the outside influences of other institutions within the social structure. This permits the legal system to develop its own cultural identity, something that can help legal practitioners to resist outside pressure. (See Gerald Turkel, *Law and Society: Critical Approaches* (Boston: Allyn and Bacon, 1996), p. 133).

## The Law Merchant and the Common Law

The integration of mercantile law into the diverse legal traditions in Europe was especially difficult in England where a strong common law tradition had developed during the late Middle Ages. As noted in Chapter 2, The Sources of the Law, common law was established in England as a way to bring all English law together into a single, consistent, comprehensive system. This program put the law merchant and the merchants who administered that law on a collision course with common law and with common law lawyers and judges. Such collisions did occur from time to time, but ultimately the law merchant evolved and was integrated into common law.

**Fair Courts and Staples Courts**  The first merchant courts in England were established in the 11th century as part of every royal charter that legalized a local fair. These **fair courts** (also known as **pie powder courts** because of the dusty feet ["pie poudre"] of the merchants who took part in the proceedings) were empowered to hear cases involving commercial disputes, and since the juries were inevitably made up of merchants, the law merchant was used to adjudicate the cases. The fair courts lost their power with the creation of staple courts under the Ordinance of the Staple of 1353. **Staple courts** heard cases that involved certain set commodities. They were run by mayors who were forced to learn and apply mercantile law. This worked well for about two centuries. Then in the 16th century the staples courts were taken over by the judges of the King's Court and common law dominated that court [See E. Allan Farnsworth and John Honnold, *Commercial Law: Cases and Materials* (Mineola, NY: The Foundation Press, 1976), pp. 3–4; Berman pp. 348–350.]

**Admiralty Courts, Arbitration, and Statutory Law**  **Admiralty courts** were tribunals set up in seaport towns to handle disputes involving maritime law, shipping contracts, contests over docking rights, collisions at sea, and the like. When the common law judges took over the staples courts, the merchants took their cases to the admiralty courts to ensure that the law merchant would be used to settle their disputes. This tactic became ineffective when the common law courts were given jurisdiction over most commercial cases throughout England, including those that had been handled by the admiralty courts. The merchants fought back by establishing their own arbitration groups to avoid common law altogether. The common law courts finally began to see the wisdom of integrating common law with the law merchant and this integration practice became more accepted by the beginning of the 18th century. When Lord Mansfield became the Chief Justice, the program kicked into high gear and for more than three decades the Chief Justice worked to integrate the law merchant into common law. His work continued for the next century. Then late in the 19th century, Parliament passed the Bills of Exchange Act and the Sale of Goods Act both of which codified common law principles which by that time had successfully absorbed most law merchant principles. When the National Conference of Commissioners was established in 1895 in the United States, they developed two model laws, the Uniform Negotiable Instruments Act which followed the Bills of Exchange Act

| quick quiz 7-1 | | |
|---|---|---|
| 1. A valid contract results in an obligation that can be enforced in a court of law. | true | false |
| 2. Mercantile law, the law merchant, and *lex mercatoria* are all different names for the same area of law. | true | false |
| 3. The six characteristics of the law merchant are neutrality, universality, mutuality, involvement, integration, and evolution. | true | false |

## Table 7-1  Law Merchant Principles in Modern Law

### CONTRACT LAW

The division between a law that focuses only on goods and one that centers on real property

The development of the rights of a good faith purchaser in goods

The transfer of ownership of goods based on the transfer of documents.

The development of the concept of warranties of fitness and warranties of merchantability.

### NEGOTIABLE INSTRUMENTS

The development of negotiable bills of exchange and promissory notes.

### BUSINESS ORGANIZATIONS

The invention of limited joint stock companies and the "company under a collective name"—forefathers of the modern corporation

Development of joint property ownership in partnerships

The development of survivorship rights among partners in a partnership

### SECURED TRANSACTIONS

The invention of the chattel mortgage

### CREDIT AND BANKING

Development of credit institutions at the great monasteries in Europe

The banking and lending operations of the Teutonic Knights and the Templars lead to modern banking procedures

### INSURANCE CONTRACTS

The development of maritime insurance

The appearance of "private" insurance in the Middle Ages

The development of insurance companies in the 17th century

### INTERNATIONAL LAW

Increased international trade leads to the need to develop international agreements

### INTELLECTUAL PROPERTY

The creation of patents and trademarks

*Sources:* Table adapted from information in Harold J. Berman, *Law and Revolution: The Formation of the Western Legal Tradition,* (Cambridge: Harvard UP, 1983), 349–350 and Henri Sée, *Modern Capitalism: Its Origin and Evolution* (New York: Adelphi Company, 1928), 20–24.

and the Uniform Sales Act which was patterned after the Sale of Goods Act. (See Farnsworth and Honnold, pp. 4–5) Despite this tangled power struggle between common law and the law merchant, the two traditions were merged, with the principles of the law merchant dominating the law governing commercial transactions. Some of these principles are charted in Table 7-1. (See Berman, pp. 348–350 and Henri Sée, pp. 20–24.)

# 7-2 The Multidimensional Nature of Contract Law

Contract law forms the basis of all other law in the corporate capitalist setting. Without contract law there could be no buying and selling, no transfer of property rights, no properly planned and executed deliveries, no hiring of agents, no partnership agreements, no stock transfers, and so on. Like many other areas of the law, contract law is based on safeguarding people's rights. We saw this in criminal law and in tort law, and we see it now in contract law. The difference is that in criminal law and tort law, most of the time, human rights are inherent within the social setting. In other words, people have rights just because they are a part of our social structure. In contract law, people adopt new rights and duties as part of their contractual relationships which are entered voluntarily. For this reason among a few others, contract law is a multidimensional area of the law, laying out not only what our rights and duties are, but also whether we have actually undertaken those duties and been given those rights. To explore this in more detail, we will first look at the elements of a contract and then at several additional multidimensional aspects of contract law, including the objectives of contract law, remedies in contract law, contracts and the UCC, contracts and other agreements, contracts and agency law, and contracts that must be written.

## The Elements of a Contract

In order for a contract to be legally binding on all parties, each element must be present. There are four elements that make up a contract. If even one of these elements is missing, there is no contract. This does not mean that there is no agreement. It simply means that there is no contract and no contractual relationship that can be vindicated in a court of law. The four elements are mutual assent, consideration, capacity, and legality. (Note: Before reading about these elements you might want to study Table 7-2 on page 155.)

**Mutual Assent**  A valid *offer* requires that the *offeror* make a definite expression of the desire to enter a contract in terms that are clear and unambiguous and that are communicated to the *offeree*. An *acceptance* occurs when, without changing the essential terms of the offer, the offeree communicates an acceptance to the offeror. Once the offer has been properly made by the offeror and accepted properly by the offeree, then *mutual assent* exists between them. Often the courts will say that mutual assent exists when there has been a *meeting of the minds* among the parties to the agreement. If mutual assent has been destroyed, the relationship that results is said to be defective. Those situations that might destroy assent include: *fraud* (both active and passive*), misrepresentation, mistake, duress,* and *undue influence.*

Contracts create binding legal obligations that each party may enforce against the other.

**Consideration**  *Consideration* is the thing of value promised to the other party in exchange for something else of value promised by the other party. Each side in a contract must give up something, their legal detriment, and must gain something, their legal benefit. The courts are generally not concerned with the adequacy of consideration. This means that the courts avoid determining "how much" consideration is enough consideration. That determination is up to the parties to the contract. However, if the consideration

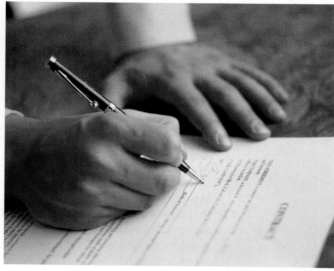

is *unconscionable* (ridiculously out of line with the nature of the contract), the court might intervene. The parties can settle value-related disputes on their own through a process of *accord and satisfaction*. Some things that might at first appear to be consideration are not consideration. These things include: *past consideration, pre-existing duties, illusory promises,* and *future gifts*. On the other hand, those situations involving *promissory estoppel* will not eliminate a party's responsibility to compensate an innocent party, even in the absence of real consideration.

## Capacity

The third contractual element is *capacity,* that is, the legal ability to make a contract. All the parties to a contract are legally permitted to assume that the other parties possess capacity. This assumption, however, is a *rebuttable presumption* which means that any one of the parties to the contract can attack or rebut that presumption. Many, perhaps most, capacity questions involve minors. The law permits a minor to rescind his or her contracts. This means that minors actually have "extra-capacity," that is, the capacity to enter and the capacity to leave a contract. There are limits to this privilege, however. Minors must provide the reasonable value for *necessaries,* that is, materials that are needed for the minor's health, safety, and welfare that are not provided by a parent or a guardian. Minors must also abide by certain contracts required by law, such as insurance contracts, contracts for educational loans, agency contracts, valid marriage contracts, enlistment contracts, contracts concerning child support, and those for pregnancy care, among others. Capacity also appears as a question in cases involving a party with a mental impairment. Some mental impairments result from physical injuries; others are genetic; some are health-related illnesses; and others are psychological in nature. Whatever the source of the difficulty, a person's mental impairment may also eliminate contractual capacity, but only if the party claiming the impairment can demonstrate that the impairment was so severe at the time the contract was made that he or she could not understand the nature, the purpose, or the effect of the agreement. If that is the case, then the contract will be voidable by the party lacking capacity. In contrast, if a person has been declared incompetent by a court, then that person's contracts are absolutely void.

## Legality

The final element of a binding contract is *legality*. Parties cannot be permitted to enforce a contract that involves something that the law says cannot be done. Clearly, any contract to commit a crime or a tort would be illegal and, therefore, void. Some contracts are also made illegal by statutory law. These include usurious contracts, gambling contracts, unlicensed agreements, unconscionable agreements, and some Sunday agreements. There are also some contracts that have been made illegal by the courts based on the doctrine of *public policy*. These include agreements to obstruct justice, agreements interfering with public safety, agreements to defraud creditors, agreements to escape liability (AKA exculpatory clauses), agreements in restraint of trade, and agreements to suppress competition. In some states, several of these contracts, agreements to obstruct justice, for instance, are also made illegal by statutory law.

## The Objectives of Contract Law

In general the law is designed to promote order, stability, and justice. All the subdivisions within the law are charged with these same goals. Criminal law does this by defining criminal behavior with great specificity and then by providing a set of procedures that are followed fairly and consistently in order to make certain that those who threaten order, stability, and justice no longer walk among us. Tort law does the same thing by providing a system of compensation for the innocent victims of deliberate and accidental torts. Contract law is much more complicated and multidimensional than other areas

| Table 7-2 | The Four Elements of a Contract |
|-----------|--------------------------------|

| Element | Explanation |
|---------|-------------|
| **Mutual Assent** | Once the offer has been properly made by the offeror and accepted properly by the offeree, then mutual assent exists between them. Often the courts will say that mutual assent exists when there has been a meeting of the minds among the parties to the agreement Those situations that might destroy assent include: fraud (both active and passive), misrepresentation, mistake, duress, and undue influence. |
| **Consideration** | Consideration is the thing of value promised to the other party in exchange for something else of value promised by the other party. Each side in a contract must give up something, their legal detriment, and must gain something, their legal benefit. The courts are generally not concerned with the adequacy of consideration. |
| **Capacity** | The third contractual element is capacity, that is, the legal ability to make a contract. All the parties to a contract are legally permitted to assume that the other parties possess capacity. This assumption, however, is a rebuttable presumption which means that any of the parties can attack or rebut that presumption. Many, perhaps most, capacity questions involve minors. Capacity also appears as a question in cases involving some sort of mental impairment. |
| **Legality** | The final element of a binding contract is legality. Clearly, any contract to commit a crime or a tort would be illegal and, therefore, void. Some contracts are also made illegal by statutory law. These include usurious contracts, gambling contracts, unlicensed agreements, unconscionable agreements, and some Sunday agreements. There are also some contracts that have been made illegal by the courts based on the doctrine of public policy. |

of the law because it must not only provide the mechanism for punishment or compensation but also explain why that mechanism is used and not some other simpler and more effective method.

**Rehabilitation in Contract Law**   The underlying objective of contract law is to determine whether the parties to the contract entered the agreement freely. If the court determines that the parties willingly entered the agreement, then the contract is valid. Then, if the court finds that one of the parties breached the contract, that party will have to rehabilitate the innocent party by compensating that party for any loss that results from the breach. Usually the courts will not force a party to go through with the terms of a contract, even when a breach has been proven. This is especially true of service contracts. However, the courts will compel the breaching party to rehabilitate the innocent party for any loss that resulted from the breach. The courts say that the objective of this rehabilitation is to place the innocent party in as good a position as he or she would have been had the contract been performed.

**The Payment of Damages**   In contract law the victims are compensated by the payment of money damages to make up for their losses. Generally, these damages are equal to the real financial loss suffered by the innocent victim. These damages are called *actual* or *compensatory damages*. Sometimes victims are entitled to damages for indirect losses. *Incidental damages* are those that are paid by the breaching party to make up for any expenses paid by the victim to prevent any additional loss. *Consequential damages* are indirect damages that result because of special circumstances that exist with a particular contract. **Punitive damages** are designed to punish the wrongdoer for his or her outrageous conduct. As a general rule, the courts do not award punitive damages in contract cases. Such damages are generally more appropriate in tort law cases. Nevertheless, there are exceptions to this rule. For instance, in cases of fraud, a court may approve punitive damages, because a party who commits fraud has attempted to undermine the entire contract system, something the court will not abide.

### Recovery Limits and Equitable Relief

There are built-in limits to the measure of the damages awarded in a contract case. For example, the innocent party cannot take advantage of the breach by deliberately raising the amount of damages that the other party must pay. This principle is called the duty to mitigate the damages or just the *duty to mitigate*. Also, there is an exception to the rule that says that the courts cannot force a party to go through with a contract. The court may force a party to perform the terms of an agreement if the contract involves land or some other unique item, such as an original work of art or a family heirloom. This is an equitable remedy called *specific performance*. *Equitable remedies* are those that are imposed by the courts when the payment of money would not compensate for the loss suffered by the innocent party. Another equitable remedy is injunction. In contract law, an *injunction* is a court order issued by a court directing a party to refrain from some activity that represents a breach of contract. Injunctions can be temporary or permanent. A temporary injunction is issued as a way to delay further activity until the court can decide whether to make the injunction permanent. A party who disobeys an injunction does so under threat of a contempt of court.

## Multidimensional Principles of Contract Law

Stacked on top of the elements of a contract, the objectives of contract law, and the remedies offered in contract law are a series of additional aspects that must be examined to set the stage before entering a more detailed study of contract law. We have referred to these additional areas of the law as the multidimensional principles of contract law. These multidimensional principles include contracts and the Uniform Commercial Code, contracts and other agreements, contracts and privity, contracts and agency law, and contracts and the Statute of Frauds.

### Contracts and the Uniform Commercial Code

The Uniform Commercial Code (UCC) is a model set of laws designed to govern almost all commercial transactions. The UCC is organized in the following way: sale of goods contracts (Article 2); commercial paper (Article 3); bank deposits and collections (Article 4); letters of credit (Article 5); bulk transfers (Article 6); warehouse receipts, bills of lading, and other documents of title (Article 7); investment securities (Article 8); secured transactions, sales of accounts, contract rights and chattel paper (Article 9); effective date and repealer (Article 10); and transition provisions (Article 11). All other types of contracts, such as employment contracts and real property (land) contracts, are covered by common law and by special statutes dedicated to some aspect of those contracts. Thus, employment contracts will be affected by labor law and minimum wage statutes; real property contracts will be covered by zoning laws and property tax laws; while both employment and real property contracts will be affected by civil rights legislation.

### Contracts and Other Agreements

All contracts are agreements, but not all agreements are contracts. An agreement may or may not be legally enforceable. To be enforceable, an agreement must conform to the law of contracts. This means at the very least that to be a legally recognized contract, an agreement must possess the four elements

## THE OPENING CASE *Revisited, Part I*
Multidimensional Contract Law: *Tubelite Co., Inc. v. Original Sign Studio*, Round 2

Recall that the Opening Case at the beginning of this chapter involved a dispute over two agreements between the Tubelite Co., the seller, and Original Sign Studio, the buyer. The first agreement was an application for credit, in which Original Sign agreed to pay for all materials shipped by Tubelite and to remit an 18 percent finance charge for overdue payments. In the second agreement, Tubelite agreed to be Original Sign's exclusive supplier. The terms of the agreement were written in a letter by an agent of Original Sign but never signed by anyone from Tubelite. The agreement stated that Tubelite would supply Original Sign with all the material that it requested but that it would bill Original Sign only for the materials that the sign company actually used and then, in exchange for being Original Sign's exclusive supplier, it would charge a discounted rate of somewhere between 10 and 25 percent.

Tubelite also agreed to install shelving at Original Sign's warehouse for proper storing of the materials. Both agreements, the one for credit and the one for the actual shipment of construction materials concern goods and, therefore, fall within Article 2 of the Uniform Commercial Code. Although this might seem obvious, the appellate court felt compelled to make certain that both parties understood this. Thus, the court writes, "Goods are 'all things (including specially manufactured goods) which are movable at the time of identification to the contract for sale other than the money in which the price is to be paid, investment securities, and things in action.' R.C. 1302.01(A)(8). Here Tubelite seeks to recover payment for signage materials that it sold to Sign Studio. As these materials are 'movable' the Ohio Uniform Commercial Code applies to the transactions at issue."

of a contract: mutual assent, consideration, capacity, and legality. The courts have never been inclined to enforce social agreements such as dates, dinner engagements and so on. Many states have extended this concept to agreements to marry and agreements to live together without the benefit of a marriage contract.

**Contracts and Privity** The general rule of contract law is that the parties must stand in privity to one another. **Privity** means that all parties must have a legally recognized interest in the subject of the contract if they are to be bound by it. Parties who do not have such an interest in the subject matter of the contract may not be bound by it. Their right to bring a lawsuit in the event of a breach of contract would also be in question. Despite the privity rule, it is possible for two or more parties to provide benefits to a third party under the terms of a contract. However, the law still makes a distinction between third parties who are *intended beneficiaries* and third parties who are *incidental beneficiaries*. For example, in a life insurance contract, the parties who are named as those who will receive payment on the death of the insured would be intended beneficiaries. Given a breach of that contract, those intended beneficiaries would have a cause of action against the defaulting life insurance company. Moreover, an exception to the general rule of privity exists in cases involving warranties and product liability.

UCC 1-201(11) and (21) (see pages 817 and 818)

**Contracts and Agency Law** An *agent* is a party who has been hired or appointed by a *principal* to perform some sort of work, usually of a business nature, for the principal. Agents owe several levels of duty to the principal. For example, the agent must obey the instructions of the principal, must be loyal to the principal, must exercise due care in doing work for the principal, must perform the work for the principal personally, must account for all money and property that is entrusted to his or her care by the principal, and must communicate all relevant agency information to the principal. The agent has all of these duties because, in effect, when the agent acts the principal acts. Agents can, therefore, bind the principal to a contract, even if the principal is not present. If the agent creates a contract for the principal and there is a breach of contract suit filed by the third party, the principal will be the initial target of that lawsuit. If the principal loses the lawsuit, and the fault lies with the agent, the agent will be liable to the principal for the losses he or she incurred because of that lawsuit.

### Contracts and the Statute of Frauds

The *Statute of Frauds* is a law that outlines those contracts that must be in writing to be enforceable in court. The original Statute of Frauds was passed by Parliament in 1677 and was officially named the Act for the Prevention of Frauds and Perjuries. The statute was part of colonial law in New England and was, thus, assimilated into American law by the states after the Revolution. It is still part of the statutory law covering contracts in every state and in the District of Columbia. Six types of contracts must be in writing to be enforceable. These six include (1) contracts that cannot be completed within one year; (2) contracts involving land; (3) contracts in consideration of marriage; (4) contracts made by executors to pay a debt of the estate out of his or her own finances; (5) a promise to pay the debt of another; and (6) contracts for the sale of goods valued at $500 or more. If the statute of frauds demands a written contract

## THE OPENING CASE *Revisited, Part II*
## Multidimensional Contract Law: *Tubelite Co., Inc. v. Original Sign Studio*, Round 3

Recall that the lawsuit entitled *Tubelite Co., Inc. v. Original Sign Studio* involved two agreements. The first agreement was an application for credit, in which Original Sign agreed to pay for all materials shipped by Tubelite and to remit an 18 percent finance charge for overdue payments. In the second agreement, Tubelite agreed to be Original Sign's exclusive supplier. The terms of the agreement were in a letter written by an agent of Original Sign and presented to an agent of Tubelite. The letter read in part, "The purpose of this document reflects the agreements reached between the parties . . . The parties agreed to a full consignment program, as described by the participants from, Tubelite Co., Inc., to the participants representing, The Original Sign Studio, Inc." This letter, however, was never signed by anyone from Tubelite.

In an effort to jettison the second agreement, Tubelite argues that the second agreement was never placed in writing, as the Statute of Frauds demands, and should, therefore, be disregarded in favor of the first agreement. The people from Tubelite are correct when they argue that the contract was not in writing as it should be under the Statute of Frauds. However, one of the exceptions provided under the UCC applies in this case, removing the need for a writing. The exception tracks this way. First, the contract was presented to agents of Tubelite. Second, those agents had 10 days to reject that version of the contract. Third, Tubelite agents never took advantage of that grace period and did not reject the writing. This means that, under the Statute of Frauds, the letter created by the Original Sign agent becomes a writing that satisfies the statute's rules. This is, in fact, how the appellate court ruled in the lawsuit.

Another issue emerges in this case. The Tubelite agent who did not reject the letter from Original Sign within the 10-day period will be liable to Tubelite should it lose the case. The agent breached his duty of due care when he did not reject the letter. It is that failure to act that makes the second contract enforceable and opens the door to a likely loss for Tubelite. If Tubelite does lose the case, it would have the right to bring a separate cause of action against that agent. Such a move is unlikely, however. Companies like Tubelite rarely bring such lawsuits. As you can imagine, they are very bad for corporate morale.

and, for some reason, the parties never reduce that contract to writing, the contract remains valid but is unenforceable, which means that the court will probably dismiss the action.

### Exceptions to the Statutory Rule

Several interesting exceptions apply to the rules imposed by the Statute of Frauds in relation to sale of goods contracts. The statute says that a contract for the sale of goods valued at $500 or more must be in writing unless the contract is for specially manufactured goods. The writing also becomes unnecessary with a sale of goods contract if the goods have already been shipped and accepted or a payment has been received and accepted. Also, if one of the parties reduces the contract to writing and sends that writing to the other party, that unsigned paper will be sufficient as a writing under the statute unless the receiving party objects in writing within 10 days. Finally, in a court action if the party that has invoked the Statute of Frauds to escape enforcement has also admitted under oath that the contract exists, no writing is needed.

### Rules of Interpretation

Despite the careful precision with which the Statute of Frauds was written, whenever contracts are reduced to writing, someone is going to disagree on what was meant by the written terms. To deal with this problem, the courts have developed rules of construction to guide judges as they interpret the written word. The first rule is the *standard construction rule* which tells judges that their primary objective in the interpretation of a written contract is to uncover the goals that the parties had when they entered the contract in the first place. As a corollary of that rule, the courts must also interpret any ambiguous clause against the party who actually wrote the contract. The goal of this rule is to encourage those parties who actually put pen to paper (or fingers to keyboard) to be as clear

## THE OPENING CASE *Revisited, Part III*
## Multidimensional Contract Law: *Tubelite Co., Inc. v. Original Sign Studio*, Round 4

As noted above, *Tubelite Co., Inc. v. Original Sign Studio* involved two agreements. The first agreement was an application for credit, in which Original Sign agreed to pay for all materials shipped by Tubelite and to remit an 18 percent finance charge for overdue payments. In the second agreement, Tubelite agreed to be Original Sign's exclusive supplier. The terms of the agreement were reduced to writing in a letter written by an agent of Original Sign and presented to an agent of Tubelite. Although the letter was never signed by anyone at Tubelite, under the Uniform Commercial Code, inaction by Tubelite transformed the letter into a written version of a consignment agreement between the two companies. It is important to understand that, while the court ruled that the letter satisfies the Statute of Frauds requirements for a writing, it did not say that the letter is a contract. So the court has decided that the case can be heard in court, but it has not decided who will

win. This requires determining which agreement, the credit application or the consignment letter, was valid. To determine this the court must look at two things, the words themselves and the conduct of the parties. The words of the credit application are by themselves too incomplete to create a valid contract. There is no way to identify subject matter, quantity, or price. In contrast, the second agreement, the consignment letter, describes the goods ordered, sets out the quantity that Original Sign has requisitioned, establishes the price of the items, and outlines a payment plan. Thus, between the two agreements, the odds-on favorite to be declared the actual contract between the parties is the consignment letter. Of course the court is free to also consider the conduct between the parties to establish which of these documents is the actual contract and so the final resolution is still up in the air. (See UCC 2-204 (1).)

and straightforward as humanly possible. Otherwise, if a question of interpretation comes up later, they risk having the judge rule against them. A different problem arises when some of the terms are not just vague or ambiguous, but are actually missing from the contract. Terms such as the subject matter, the quantity, and the price to be paid are essential to a binding contractual relationship. On the other hand, at least under the UCC, it is not always necessary to have all of the terms just as long as the judge has enough information to determine a "reasonably certain basis for giving an appropriate remedy." (See UCC 2-204 (3).

## quick quiz 7-2

| | |
|---|---|
| 1. The four elements are mutual assent, consideration, capacity, and legality. | true \| false |
| 2. The courts says that the objective of rehabilitation is to place the innocent party in as good a position as he or she would have been had the contract been performed. | true \| false |
| 3. All contracts must be in writing to be enforced in a court of law. | true \| false |

# 7-3 Contractual Characteristics

Contractual characteristics fall into five different categories: valid, void, voidable, and unenforceable; unilateral and bilateral; express and implied; informal and formal; and executory and executed. Any given contract can be classifiable in all five ways. Thus, for example, a single contract could be said to be valid, bilateral, express, formal, and executed, or any other acceptable combination of characteristics.

## Valid, Void, Voidable, and Unenforceable Contracts

A **valid contract** is one that is legally binding and fully enforceable by the court. In contrast, a **void contract** is one that has no legal effect whatsoever. For example, a contract to perform an illegal act would be void. A **voidable contract** is one that may be avoided or canceled by one of the parties. Contracts made by minors or induced by fraud or misrepresentation are examples of voidable contracts. An **unenforceable contract** is one that, because of some rule of law, cannot be upheld by a court of law. An unenforceable contract may have all the elements of a complete contract and still be unenforceable.

## Unilateral and Bilateral Contracts

A **unilateral contract** is an agreement in which one party makes a promise to do something in return for an act of some sort. The classic example of a unilateral contract is a reward contract. A person who promises to pay $5 to the finder of a lost driver's license does not expect a promise in return. Rather, the person expects the return of the lost license. When the license is returned, the contract arises and the promisor owes the finder $5.

In contrast, a **bilateral contract** is one in which both parties make promises. Bilateral contracts come into existence at the moment the two promises are made. A **breach of contract** occurs when one of the two parties fails to keep the promise. When there is a breach of contract, the injured party has the right to ask a court of law to somehow remedy the situation. (Breach of contract and remedies are discussed in detail in Chapter 12.)

# Express and Implied Contracts

A contract can be either express or implied. An **express contract** requires some sort of written or spoken expression indicating a desire to enter the contractual relationship. An **implied contract** is created by the actions or gestures of the parties involved in the transaction.

## Express Contracts
When contracting parties accept mutual obligations, either through oral discussion or written communication, they have created an express contract. Oral negotiations in many cases will be reduced to writing, but this is not always necessary.

A written contract does not have to be a long, formal preprinted agreement. Although such lengthy, preprinted forms are common in some businesses, other, less formal written documents are frequently used to show that a contract exists. For example, a written contract may take the form of a letter, sales slip and receipt, notation, or memorandum. A written contract may be typed, printed, keystroked, scrawled, or written in beautiful penmanship. In some situations, state laws require certain types of contracts to be in writing. (See Chapter 11.)

## A QUESTION OF ETHICS

Suppose you posted a reward notice that read, "Reward: $50 for the return of my lost college class ring." Suppose further that someone who did not know of the reward offer found your ring and returned it. Legally you would not have to pay the reward money to the person who found your ring because he or she did not know about your offer. However, would it be ethical not to pay the reward to the finder? Explain.

When a contract is placed in writing, it is essential that the content be as clear and unambiguous as possible. When faced with a dispute over an ambiguous clause, the court may be compelled to look at factual evidence to determine the actual intent of the parties. This review may mean that a case that could have been dismissed early will have to go to trial so that the court can make a factual determination of intent by looking at evidence beyond the terms in the writing.

When the law does not require a written agreement, an *oral contract* resulting from the spoken words of the parties will be enough. Parties to such an agreement, however, should anticipate the difficulty of proving the contractual relationship, should disputes arise later. Nevertheless, expressing every agreement in writing, in anticipation of a future need of proof, is impractical in the fast-paced modern world of business.

## Implied Contracts
One who knowingly accepts benefits from another person may be obligated for their payment, even though no express agreement has been made. An agreement of this type can be either implied-in-fact or implied-in-law. A contract implied by the direct or indirect acts of the parties is known as an **implied-in-fact contract**. Pumping gas into a car at a self-service gas station is an example of an implied-in-fact contract. Because the parties to a contract enter that contract by an exercise of free will, the court follows the **objective concept rule** in interpreting the acts and gestures of a party. Under this rule, the meaning of one's actions is determined by the impression those actions would make upon any reasonable person who might have witnessed them, not by a party's self-serving claim of what was meant or intended by the actions.

## About the Law

The law that declares which contracts must be in writing is called the Statute of Frauds. In its original form when it was passed by Parliament in 1677, it was known as the Act for the Prevention of Fraud and Perjuries.

### EXAMPLE 7-1: Implied-in-Fact Deals: Can Inaction Create a Contract?

Herbert Ward watched workers employed by the Rice Lawn and Garden Greenhouse as they chemically treated his front lawn. In fact, Ward had no contract with Rice and had not ordered any chemical treatments of his property. The treatment should have been performed on another house at 750 Maple Street, instead of at Ward's, which had an address of 570 Maple St. Ward never stopped the work crew, even though he knew that a mistake had been made. Rice would be within its rights to believe that the work was being done with Ward's consent. In assessing damages for the cost of the improvement, the court would apply the objective concept rule. A reasonable person who might have watched Rice treat the front lawn would conclude that Ward had freely consented to the work.

An **implied-in-law contract** is imposed by a court when someone is unjustly enriched. It is used when a contract cannot be enforced or there is no actual written, oral, or implied-in-fact agreement. Applying reasons of justice and fairness, a court may obligate one who has unfairly benefited at the innocent expense of another. An implied-in-law contract is also called a **quasi-contract**.

### EXAMPLE 7-2: Implied-in-Law Deals: Can Injustice Be Prevented?

Karl Rapp was found unconscious in his hotel room by Jan Stevens, the third-floor maid. She immediately called 911 and then notified Ken Kramer, the hotel manager. Kramer arranged to have Rapp placed in a hospital for emergency treatment. When Rapp regained consciousness, he refused to pay for the treatment, claiming that he was not aware of what was going on and had not agreed to what had been done to him. The case illustrates a quasi-contractual situation, wherein it would be unfair to allow the injured person to benefit at the expense of the hospital. In any suit that might arise over this expense, a court would require Rapp to pay the fair value of the services rendered.

The quasi-contract concept cannot apply, however, to obtain payment for an act that a party simply feels should be done. The concept also cannot be applied when one party bestows a benefit on another unnecessarily or through misconduct or negligence. A quasi-contract is not a contract in the true sense of the word, because it is created by the court. It does not result from the mutual assent of the parties, as do express or implied-in-fact contracts.

## Informal and Formal Contracts

The law sometimes requires that contracts follow formalities prescribed by statute or common law. These are called formal contracts. All others are classified as informal.

### Informal Contracts
Any oral or written contract that is not under seal or is not a contract of record is considered an **informal contract**. An informal contract is also known as a *simple contract*. An informal contract generally has no requirements as to language, form, or construction. It comprises obligations entered into by parties whose promises are expressed in the simplest and usually most ordinary, nonlegal language.

UCC 2-203 (see page 823)

### Formal Contracts
Under common law principles, a **formal contract** differs from other types of contracts in that it has to be (1) written; (2) signed, witnessed, and placed

under the seal of the parties; and (3) delivered. A *seal* is a mark or an impression placed on a written contract indicating that the instrument was executed and accepted in a formal manner. The UCC removed the requirement for a seal in sale-of-goods contracts. Some states, however, still require the use of the seal in agreements related to the sale and transfer of real property.

Today, a person's seal may be any mark or sign placed after the signature intended to be the signer's seal. In states still requiring the seal or formal contract, it is sufficient to write the word *seal* after the signature.

## EXAMPLE 7-3: Formal Contracts: Is a Seal Still Needed?

Audrey Kimmel signed an agreement with Corey Baumberger to buy seven acres of farmland owned by Baumberger just outside Bellville. Later that day, Baumberger found another interested buyer who was willing to pay seven times as much as Kimmel had offered for the land. Kimmel had signed the sales agreement without including any representation of the seal. In any state that required such formality in all real property contracts, Kimmel would now be helpless in attempting to enforce the original contract that she had made with Baumberger.

**Contracts of Record**  A special type of formal contract is known as a **contract of record**. Often, such a contract is confirmed by the court with an accompanying judgment issued in favor of one of the parties. The judgment is recorded, giving the successful litigant the right to demand satisfaction of the judgment. A contract of record is not a contract in the true sense of the word, because it is court created. Although it does not have all of the elements of a valid contract, it is enforced for public policy reasons.

## EXAMPLE 7-4: Contracts of Record: When Can Litigants Demand Their Money?

Mortimer Byrne installed a new roof on Alexander Harper's house in Lakeside for the agreed-upon price of $7,500. Harper paid Byrne $4,000 so that he could secure materials. After the job was completed, Byrne sent Harper a bill for $3,500. Harper sent Byrne a check for $2,500, on which was written "in full payment of all money owed." These words were in very fine print and not seen by Byrne. Byrne sued Harper in the small claims division of the Ottawa County Court of Common Pleas for the amount still owed. The court ruled in favor of Byrne and entered a judgment against Harper for the money owed. Entry of the judgment created a contract of record, which was enforceable against Harper.

## Executory and Executed Contracts

A contract that has not yet been fully performed by the parties is called an **executory contract**. Such a contract may be completely executory, in which case nothing has been done, or it may be partly executory, in which case the contract is partially complete. When a contract's terms have been completely and satisfactorily carried out by both parties, it is an **executed contract**. Such contracts are no longer active agreements and are valuable only if a dispute about the agreement occurs.

## quick quiz 7-3

1. A void contract is one that can be avoided by one or more of the parties.    true | false
2. A formal contract is also known as a simple contract.    true | false
3. A contract that has not yet been fully performed by the parties is called an executory contract.    true | false

## Summary

**7.1**  With the Roman law providing a model, with the Roman Catholic Church supplying political and social support, with canon law supplying a moral framework, and with practicality guiding their activities over a 300-year period, the merchants of the late Middle Ages developed a body of active law that was characterized by neutrality, universality, mutuality, involvement, integration, and evolution. The law merchant was developed by the merchants themselves. The law merchant also successfully integrated itself into other legal tradition such English common law. Many of its provisions still exist in today's court decisions and statutes.

**7.2**  Contract law is a multidimensional area of the law, laying out not only what our rights and duties are, but also whether we have actually undertaken those duties and been given those rights. To explore this in more detail, we looked at the elements of a contract and at several additional multidimensional aspects of contract law including the objectives of contract law, remedies in contract law, contracts and the UCC, contracts and other agreements, contracts and agency law, and contracts that must be written.

**7.3**  Contractual characteristics fall into five different categories. These categories are valid, void, voidable, or unenforceable; unilateral or bilateral; express or implied; informal or formal; and executory or executed.

## Key Terms

admiralty court, 151
bilateral contract, 160
breach of contract, 160
canon law, 148
capitalism, 148
contract, 147
contract of record, 163
executed contract, 163
executory contract, 163
express contract, 161
fair court, 151
formal contract, 162
implied contract, 161
implied-in-fact contract, 161
implied-in-law contract, 162
informal contract, 162
law merchant, 147
objective concept rule, 161
pie powder court, 151
privity, 157
punitive damages, 156
quasi-contract, 162
rehabilitate, 155
staple court, 151
unenforceable contract, 160
unilateral contract, 160
valid contract, 160
void contract, 160
voidable contract, 160

## Questions for Review and Discussion

1. What is a contract?
2. How did the law merchant develop?
3. How did the law merchant merge with common law?
4. What are the four elements of a contract?

5. What is the objective of contract law?
6. What is the role of the UCC in contract law?
7. How do contracts differ from other agreements?
8. What are the roles of privity and agency in contract law?
9. What contracts must be in writing to be enfocrceable?
10. What are the characteristics of a contract?

## Cases for Analysis

1. Several businesspeople secured a contract with the state of Massachusetts that permitted them to construct a bridge spanning the Charles River. The businesspeople intended to charge a toll for passage over the bridge to recover the expense of building the bridge and make a sizable profit off its operation. Later, another group of businesspeople made a similar contract. They too were permitted to build a bridge and charge a toll. There was, however, a six-year limit on the tolls that would be charged on the second bridge, transforming it into a free bridge after the end of the six-year period. The first group of businesspeople realized that the existence of a free bridge would make their bridge worthless. Accordingly, they sued to prevent the second bridge from being constructed. They argued that the original contract that they had negotiated with the state implied that no other bridge would be built. The second group argued that because there was no explicit agreement in the first contract preventing a second bridge from being built, the court, under the Contracts Clause of the Constitution, could not impair the rights they had freely negotiated under the new contract to build a second bridge. The case ended up in the United States Supreme Court. How did the Supreme Court decide the case? Explain. *Proprietors of the Charles River Bridge v. Proprietors of the Warren Bridge,* 11 Pet. 420 (USSCt. 1837). See also L. Friedman, "Economy and Law in the Nineteenth Century," *Law in America* (New York: The Modern Library, 2002), pp. 49–54.

2. The Borg-Warner Protective Services Corporation and Burns International Security Services contracted to provide security for the Cleveland Institute of Art (CIA). Robert Adelman was struck by an object thrown by a CIA student from the roof of one of the Institute's buildings. Adelman sued both the CIA and the security corporations. The security corporations moved for summary judgment, arguing that they had contracted with CIA to protect the faculty and the students and that they therefore had no duty to protect pedestrians outside the buildings. Adelman argued that the contract specifically obligated the security corporations to control the activities of CIA students within the Institute's buildings. The disputed clause read that the security corporations agreed "to control the movement and activities of students within the buildings at all hours." The trial court granted the summary judgment motion, and Adelman appealed. Should the appellate court reverse the decision of the lower court? Explain. If the case goes to trial, how will the court determine the meaning of the ambiguous clause? Explain. *Adelman v. Timman,* 690 N.E.2d 1332 (OH).

3. One of Stewart's clients gave him a check for $185.48. The check had been drawn up by the client's corporate employer and properly endorsed by the client. Nevertheless, the bank refused to cash the check for Stewart, even though there was enough money in the account to cover the $185.48. Could Stewart sue the bank for not cashing the check as he requested? Explain. *J.E.B. Stewart v. Citizens and Southern National Bank,* 225 S.E.2d 761 (GA).

4. Vokes was told that she would become a professional dancer if she took a very expensive dancing course offered by Arthur Murray, Inc. She was also continually told that she had great talent. The contract called for payments amounting to a total of $31,000. As it turned out, she never became a professional dancer and, in fact, had little or no talent. She sued Arthur Murray, claiming that the Arthur Murray people misrepresented the facts to entice her to enter the contract. The court agreed and found in her favor. Would Vokes have the right to void the contract? Explain. *Vokes v. Arthur Murray, Inc.,* 212 So.2d 906 (FL).

5. Anderson, a farmer, orally agreed to buy a used tractor from the Copeland Equipment Company for $475. Copeland delivered the tractor to Anderson, who used it for 11 days. During this period, Anderson could not borrow enough funds to cover

the purchase price. Anderson therefore returned the tractor to Copeland. Both parties agreed that their sales contract was canceled when the tractor was returned. However, Copeland later claimed that under the doctrine of quasi-contract, Anderson was required to pay for the 11-days' use of the tractor. Do you agree with Copeland? Explain your answer. *Anderson v. Copeland,* 378 P.2d 1006 (OK).

6. B.L. Nelson & Associates, Inc., entered into a contract with the city of Argyle to design and construct a sanitary sewer collection and treatment facility for the city. The city attempted to get out of the contract by citing certain provisions of the state constitution. These provisions made it illegal for the city to enter a contract for services if it did not have the money to pay for these services. Because the city did not have the funds to pay Nelson, it argued that the contract was illegal and therefore void. Was the city correct? Explain. *B.L. Nelson & Associates, Inc. v. City of Argyle,* 535 S.W.2d 906 (TX).

7. Peters entered into a contract to purchase Dowling's business. The following terms were agreed to: (a) Peters would take over all of Dowling's executory contracts, (b) Peters would purchase Dowling's tools at an agreed-to price, (c) Peters would accept full responsibility for all warranties made by Dowling on previous contracts, and (d) Dowling would remain as a consultant to the new firm for a period of five years. Analyze each part of this contract and classify each term according to whether it is executed or executory. *Wagstaff v. Peters,* 453 P.2d 120 (KS).

## quick quiz Answers

| 7-1 | 7-2 | 7-3 |
|-----|-----|-----|
| 1. T | 1. T | 1. F |
| 2. T | 2. T | 2. F |
| 3. T | 3. F | 3. T |

# Chapter 8 — Offer, Acceptance, and Mutual Assent

## THE OPENING CASE  Mutual Assent and Its Destruction: *Urbanek v. All State Home Mortgage Company*

The success or the failure of a contractual relationship is frequently a matter of faith. The buyers trust the sellers (or their agents) to play fair with them by providing a full and accurate account of the condition and the value of the subject matter of the contract. Does it always work out that way? Certainly not. Sometimes the seller makes a mistake. Sometimes the buyer fails to hear or to understand what is said. Often there are things that interfere with the arrangement that no one notices until it is too late to undo the contract. It is at that point that the courts must get involved. A situation on point is the case of *Urbanek v. All state Home Mortgage Company*. The plaintiff in the case, Edward Urbanek, was a landscaper who, at the urging of an agent of All State Mortgage, decided to get into the housing market as a way to compile an investment portfolio and improve his credit. At the prompting of two All State agents, Urbanek purchase three houses in Cleveland. The houses had been appraised, but there was no evidence that Urbanek ever received, read, or considered the appraisal, which was made some time before Urbanek visited or made an offer for the three houses. Evidently Urbanek trusted the All State agents implicitly because, once he was told the asking prices of the three houses, he made his offer to purchase without challenging those figures.

It was at this point that Urbanek's problems began in earnest. Urbanek had been told that the houses were being rented. Yet, after the sale, he found he could not collect any rent. In fact, he began to suspect that the renters were fictitious. Later, he was asked for and, without hesitation, turned over $14,186.34 for repairs on one of the houses. As it turned out the house was never repaired and he never received a refund of that money. Perhaps even more telling, he never received keys for any of the houses at the closing.

Without the rental income, Urbanek could not keep up the payments and he tried to sell the houses. It was at that time that he learned from local realtors that the value of each property was overinflated. As a result, the houses sold in foreclosure, for prices that were appreciably under the original prices. The plaintiff sued All state and its agents along with Ace Home Loans, Inc., and its agents, and the appraiser. Who was the offeror in this case? Who was the offeree? At what point did the acceptance go into effect? Did the actions of the agents disrupt the assent? Was fraud or mistake an issue here? What about undue influence? Any hint of that or duress? See if you can answer these questions as you read through this chapter on offer, acceptance, and mutual assent. (See *Urbanek v. All State Home Mortgage Company,* 178 Ohio App.3d 493 (2008-Ohio-4871)).

**Opening Case Questions**

1. Would *Urbanek v. All State Home Mortgage Company* be a civil lawsuit or a criminal action? Explain

2. What law will the court apply in this case to answer the questions noted above? Will the court use common law or the Uniform Commercial Code (UCC)? Explain.

3. Who is the offeror in the sale of the houses and who is the offeree? Explain.

4. At what point is there a "meeting of the minds" in this case, if at all? Explain.

5. Does Urbanek have a case based on fraud in this situation? Explain.

## LO Learning Objectives

1. Define mutual assent.
2. Identify the elements of an offer.
3. Explain the UCC's concept of offer in contract law.
4. Explain the nature of acceptance.
5. Define the mirror image rule
6. Explain the process of revocation.
7. Identify those statutes that affect mutual assent in cyberspace.
8. Explain the elements of fraud and misrepresention.
9. Identify the effects of mistake on mutual assent.
10. Describe duress and undue influence.

# 8-1 Mutual Assent and the Offer

Contractual relationships are, to a large extent, unique relationships that people enter voluntarily. Nevertheless, once a party has agreed to the terms of a contract, he or she has assumed a set of duties that are just as binding as those that are imposed automatically by law. This is why the courts and the legislatures have been very careful about spelling out the details involved in forming a contract. Many of these rules have evolved as part of the law merchant and common law. Others have been adopted by the legislature in response to social and economic changes such as the cyberspace revolution. Whatever the case, the objective of the law is to provide a proper balance between the duties of each party and their rights, both of which emerge in the contract-making process. To understand how this works we will first examine the nature of mutual assent and the method for creating that assent through the process of offer and acceptance.

## The Nature of Mutual Assent

A **contract** is an agreement between two or more competent parties based on mutual promises and an exchange of things of value, to do or refrain from doing some particular thing that is neither illegal nor impossible. The agreement results in a set of duties that can be enforced in a court of law. The power of the courts to enforce these duties comes from the fact that both parties have agreed to accept those duties. This is **mutual assent**. It is the first of the four elements of a valid contract. The courts are fond of saying that mutual assent emerges when the parties to the contract have a "meeting of the minds." In other words, both parties know what the terms of the agreement are and both willingly agree to be bound by those terms. Mutual assent can be reached quickly as in buying a Kindle on Amazon.com, or it may result from a long and involved series of negotiations as in the purchase of a house. Whatever

| Table 8-1   Requirements of an Offer | |
| --- | --- |
| **Requirement** | **Explanation** |
| Serious intent | The offeror's words must give the offeree assurance that a binding agreement is intended. |
| Clarity and reasonably definite terms | The terms of an offer must be sufficiently clear to remove any doubt about the contractual intentions of the offeror. Most courts require reasonable rather than absolute definiteness. |
| Communication to the offeree | The proposed offer must be communicated to the offeree by whatever means are convenient and desirable. The communication of the offer can be express or implied. Public offers are made through the media but are intended for one party whose identity or address is unknown. Invitations to trade are not offers. |

the case, the assent that emerges comes from a communication of an open offer by an offeror that is authentically accepted by the offeree. The twin keys to mutual assent then are an "open offer" and "authentically accepted." Remember those key terms.

## Requirements of an Offer

An **offer** is a proposal freely made by one party to another indicating a willingness to enter a contract. The person who makes the offer is the **offeror** and the person to whom it is made is the **offeree**. If certain requirements are met, the court concludes that the parties intended to make and accept an offer. In the case of an open offer, the courts have established three elements that must exist: (1) serious intent; (2) clear and reasonably definite terms; and (3) communication to the offeree. We now turn to a discussion of these requirements.

**Serious Intent**   An offeror's offer is invalid if that offeror makes the alleged offer as a joke, during an emotional outburst of rage or anger, or under circumstances that convey a lack of seriousness. The offeror's words and actions must give the offeree assurance that a binding agreement is intended. This is what makes an offer an open offer, that is, it is open to acceptance by the offeree. Serious intent will be present within the actions and the words of the offeror. (see Table 8-1)

**Clear and Reasonably Definite Terms**   The communicated terms of an offer must be sufficiently clear to remove all doubt about the contractual intentions of the offeror. No valid offer will exist when terms are indefinite, inadequate, vague, contradictory, or confusing. To determine whether the terms in the alleged offer are clear and definite enough ask whether the terms are so clear that, if there were a breach, the court would know how to assess a remedy. If the answer is yes, the terms are probably definite enough. If the answer is no, then some critical term in the alleged offer is missing or too obscure to create a contract.

## EXAMPLE 8-1:  When Is it Possible to Assess a Remedy?

The Lindbergh-Sikorsky Aircraft Corporation e-mailed an offer to Kenneth Hiebel, the owner of the Triple R-Bar Ranch in Idaho. The e-mail stated, "Please consider this our offer to purchase 20,000 acres of your 61,200-acre ranch land near Harrington, Idaho. Our offering price is between $60,000 and $65,000 per acre. Please respond soon." If we apply the suggested test, we can easily see that this e-mail is not a legally effective offer. The terms are much too indefinite. The e-mail does not specify which of Triple R-Bar's acres Lindbergh-Sikorsky wants to purchase. Nor does it specify a set price per acre. If there were a breach of contract, the court would not know how to set damages. Would it use the $60,000 figure, the $65,000 figure, or something in between? If Lindbergh-Sikorsky asked for specific performance of the contract, the court would not know which acres to transfer to the aircraft company. All in all, the terms lack an appropriate level of clarity and definiteness to constitute an offer.

## Degree of Definiteness

In general, an offer should include points similar to those covered in a newspaper story—who, what, when, where, and how much—if it is to be clear, definite, and certain. This requirement means that the offer should identify (1) the parties involved in the contract, (2) the goods or services that will be the subject matter of the contract, (3) the price the offeror is willing to pay or receive, and (4) the time required for the performance of the contract. Most courts require reasonable rather than absolute definiteness. Offers will be upheld as long as the language is reasonably definite enough to enable the court to establish what the parties intended the terms to be so that, should there be a breach, a remedy can be set.

## Offers and the UCC

The UCC permits offers to omit certain information. It states that "even though one or more terms are left open, a contract for sale does not fail for indefiniteness if the parties have intended to make a contract and there is a reasonably certain basis for giving an appropriate remedy." Under this section of the UCC, cost-plus contracts, output contracts, requirement contracts, and current market price contracts are enforceable even though they are not complete in certain matters. A **cost-plus contract** does not include a final price; rather, the contract price is determined by the cost of labor and materials, plus an agreed-to percentage or dollar markup. A **requirements contract** is an agreement in which one party agrees to buy all of the goods it needs from the second party. The terms of a requirements contract must be carefully worded. If the agreement allows the buyer to purchase only those goods that the buyer desires or wishes, the agreement is unenforceable, because it is illusory in that the buyer is not really obligated to do anything. An **output contract** is an agreement in which one party consents to sell to a second party all of the goods that party makes in a given period of time. Finally, a **current market price contract** is one in which prices are determined by reference to the market price of the goods as of a specified date.

UCC 2-204 (3) (see page 823)

## Communication to the Offeree

To be valid an offer must be freely communicated to the offeree. The offeror's intent may be communicated by whatever means are convenient and desirable. For example, the offer may be communicated orally, by mail, by fax, by e-mail, by text, or by any other capable means. It may be implied. The proposing party's acts and conduct in many cases are successful in communicating he intention to make an offer to another party that witnesses them. When acts and conduct are sufficient to convey an offeror's intentions, an implied offer results.

*Public Offers*   At times, an offer must be communicated to a party whose name, identity, or address is unknown. In such cases, the public offer is made. A **public offer** is one that is made through the public media but is intended for only one person whose identity or address is unknown to the offeror. A classic example of a public offer is an advertisement in a lost-and-found notice on an electronic bulletin board. Although it is a public offer, it is legally no different from other types of offers.

*Invitations to Trade*   By contrast, invitations to trade are not offers. An **invitation to trade** is an announcement published to reach many persons for the purpose of creating

Recall that in the Opening Case at the beginning of this chapter, the plaintiff in the case, Edward Urbanek, decided to get into the housing market as a way to compile an investment portfolio and improve his credit. At the prompting of two All State agents, Urbanek purchased three houses in Cleveland. The houses had been appraised but there was no evidence that Urbanek ever received, read, or considered the appraisal, which was made some time before Urbanek visited or made an offer for the three houses. Apparently, Urbanek trusted the All State agents completely because, once he was told the list price, he agreed to purchase them at that price. In the housing market such a move is highly unusual. The price named by the seller is almost never intended as an offer, but as an invitation to trade or an invitation to which Urbanek would make his own offer. When Urbanek agreed to purchase the houses at the list price, he actually made an offer that the owner then accepted, creating the contract. Generally, however, it would have been expected for him to make an offer at a lower price, which the seller would have responded to with a counteroffer.

interest and attracting responses. Newspaper and magazine advertisements, radio and television commercials, store window displays, price tags on merchandise, for rent signs, and prices in catalogs fall within this definition. In the case of an invitation to trade, no binding agreement develops until a responding party makes an offer that the advertiser accepts. Probably one of the most common invitations to trade is the listing price for real property. A **list price** for real property is the price that the seller asks initially when the property is placed on the market. The price is an invitation to the buyer to make an offer. Traditionally, there is little expectation that the buyer will actually make an offer based on that price. The expectation is that the buyer will make an offer at a price under the list price which the seller will then respond to with a counteroffer. Counteroffers are discussed below.

In very rare circumstances, advertisements may be held to be offers. However, such advertisements would have to contain very particular promises, use phrases like "first-come, first-served," or limit the number of items to be sold. Because the number of people who can buy the product is very limited, the advertisement becomes an offer.

*Auctions*   An **auction** is a sale that is open to the public, during which potential buyers compete for the right to purchase certain items by placing higher and higher bids until the highest bid is reached and the auctioneer accepts on behalf of the seller. Many people have the mistaken belief that in an auction the original property owner, that is, the seller, is the offeror and that the bidder is the offeree. These roles are true only if the auction has been expressly labeled as an **auction without reserve**. If the auction has not been so designated, it is considered an **auction with reserve**, which means that the bidders are the offerors and the seller is the offeree. Consequently, the seller can stop the bidding at any time that he or she wants, up to the time that the auctioneer declares a winner, generally by striking the podium with the gavel. A seller can also control the bidding somewhat if he or she establishes the lowest acceptable bid. In such a case, should the auctioneer *not* hear a bid that meets the least possible bid, he or she can reject all of those bids, and the seller retains the property.

*Bait-and-Switch Confidence Games*   The **bait-and-switch confidence game** is a deliberately deceptive practice that entices buyers into a place of business when the seller actually has no intention of selling the item at the price stated in the advertisement. The practice has been outlawed by the Federal Trade Commission. In addition, many, and perhaps most, states have similar laws prohibiting bait-and-switch confidence games.

## quick quiz 8-1

1. The person who freely makes an offer is called an offeree.    true | false

2. An offer is valid only if it has (a) serious intent, (b) clear and    true | false
   reasonably definite terms, and (c) communication to the offeree.

3. No valid offer will exist when terms are indefinite, inadequate,    true | false
   vague, or confusing.

# 8-2 Acceptance of an Offer

The second major element in a binding contract is acceptance of the offer. As previously stated, **acceptance** means that the offeree agrees to be bound by the terms set up by the offeror. Only the offeree, the one to whom the offer is made, has the right to accept the offer. If another party attempts to accept, that attempt would actually be a new and independent offer.

Unilateral contracts do not usually require oral or written communication of an acceptance. When the offeror makes a promise in a unilateral contract, the offeror expects an action, not another promise in return. Performance of the action requested within the time allowed by the offeror and with the offeror's knowledge creates the contract.

---

**EXAMPLE 8-2:**   When Is a Unilateral Offer Accepted?

Patrick Barnes and George Layton were employed by the Sailors' Maritime Service. When they expressed dissatisfaction with their jobs, their employer offered them a new contract whereby they would receive a 10 percent bonus on company profits if they remained with the firm. Several times they discussed the terms of the new agreement with an official of Sailors' Maritime. Eventually, they decided that the offer was a good one, and they continued on the job as usual. Sailors' Maritime later refused to pay the 10 percent bonus, claiming that its offer had never been accepted. The court ruled this scenario to be a unilateral agreement and that their performance in remaining with Sailors' Maritime constituted acceptance.

---

In bilateral contracts, unlike unilateral ones, the offeree must communicate acceptance to the offeror. Bilateral contracts consist of a promise by one party in return for a promise by the other. Until the offeree communicates a willingness to be bound by a promise, there is no valid acceptance.

---

**EXAMPLE 8-3:**   When Does a Bilateral Agreement Go into Effect?

Suppose in the previous example, Sailors' Maritime had said to Barnes and Layton, "We will consider your written acceptance of this new proposal as binding us to the payment of the 10 percent bonus." This statement would indicate the intent to create a bilateral contract, supported by mutual promises by both Sailors' Maritime on the one hand and Barnes and Layton on the other.

## Communication of Acceptance

The communication of the acceptance of an offer may be either express or implied. In an express acceptance, the offeree chooses any method of acceptance, unless the offer states that the acceptance must be made in a particular manner. A stipulation such as "reply by fax" or "reply by e-mail" included in the offer must be carried out to achieve acceptance.

The offer can dictate the form of acceptance required. If using an e-mail or text message to accept an offer, always follow up with a written and signed correspondence to create a permanent record.

**Face-to-Face and Telephone Communication**  No special problem as to the timing of acceptance usually arises if the parties are dealing face-to-face. The acceptance becomes complete and effective as soon as the offeror hears the words of acceptance spoken by the offeree. In a similar vein, if the parties are negotiating over the telephone, the acceptance becomes effective when the offeree speaks the words of acceptance into the telephone receiver (see Table 8-2). When the parties negotiate by mail, telegram, private courier, e-mail, or fax, problems may arise, and the law provides certain rules as to when acceptance occurs.

**Long-Distance Communication**  Under traditional common law principles, if a long-distance acceptance is made by an authorized method of communication, the acceptance is effective when it is sent. An authorized means of communication is one that has been endorsed by the offeror. The endorsement can be made either expressly or by implication. An acceptance is expressly endorsed by the offeror if he or she specifies the means of acceptance to be used by the offeror. Under traditional common law rules, an authorization of an acceptance is implied when the offeree accepts by the same means or by a means that is faster than that used to make the offer. Thus, an offer made through the mail is accepted when the acceptance is mailed or sent by a faster means such as a private courier (DHL, FedEx, or UPS), a fax, a phone call, an e-mail, or an in-person visit.

**Text Messages**  Text-messages have become an integral, accepted method of communicating in many people's daily routine. It is quite common for people to "text" one another about informal, personal matters. However, texting business colleagues is another matter entirely. While text messages are efficient and fast, they are also, by nature and

### Table 8-2  Communication of Acceptance

| Method Used | Legal Effect |
| --- | --- |
| Face-to-face communication | Acceptance is complete and effective when offeror hears the words of acceptance. |
| Telephone communication | Acceptance is complete and effective when offeror hears the words of acceptance. |
| Text messages | Acceptance is complete when text message is sent, if offeror has asked for a text response. If not, the acceptance is complete when sent, only if a text message is faster than the requested method. |
| Authorized means of communication | Acceptance is complete and effective when given by that same medium (e.g., mailed offer is accepted when acceptance is dropped in the mail). |
| Acceptance improperly dispatched | Acceptance is complete and effective when it actually reaches offeror. |

design, without detailed content. These shortcomings probably explain why texting is still not the usual way to communicate in the business world. Nevertheless, should an offeror ask for a text message acceptance, the offeree should not hesitate to respond as requested. An acceptance will be valid when sent if the offeree uses a technique requested or endorsed by the offeror. However, it is also good practice to follow up such an acceptance with something more detailed and more permanent, such as a confirmation letter.

### The Uniform Commercial Code
The Uniform Commercial Code asserts that a contract comes into existence if any reasonable means is used to communicate the acceptance. The UCC is quite explicit in noting that to establish a contract for the sale of goods, unless otherwise indicated by the offeror or by the circumstances, the offeree may accept the offer in any manner and by any medium that is reasonable. A contract for the sale of goods then comes into existence when the acceptance is sent, as long as the method used to send is reasonable. The actual text of this rule is found in UCC 2-206 (1) (a).

## Unequivocal Acceptance

To be effective, an acceptance must be *unequivocal,* which means that the acceptance must not change any of the terms stated in the offer. Under common law, this requirement is known as the mirror image rule.

### The Mirror Image Rule
Under the **mirror image rule**, the terms as stated in the acceptance must exactly "mirror" the terms in the offer. If the acceptance changes or qualifies the terms in the offer, it is not an acceptance. A qualified acceptance is actually a counteroffer. A **counteroffer** is a response to an offer in which the terms of the original offer are changed. No agreement is reached unless the counteroffer is accepted by the original offeror.

### Counteroffers under the UCC
The UCC has changed the mirror image rule for sale-of-goods contracts. Under the UCC, as long as there is a definite expression of

UCC 2-207 (see page 823)

## THE OPENING CASE *Revisited, Part II*
### Mutual Assent and Its Destruction: *Urbanek v. All State Home Mortgage,* Round 3

Take another look at the Opening Case at the beginning of this chapter. In that case, the plaintiff, Urbanek, had entered the housing market to compile an investment portfolio and improve his credit. At the prompting of two All State agents, Urbanek purchase three houses in Cleveland. Recall that the All State agents introduced Urbanek to three houses and told him the list price. Once Urbanek knew the list price of the three houses, he agreed to purchase them at that price. In the real estate game this type of a move is very unusual. The price named by the seller is never (rarely?) intended as an offer. Instead, that price is considered as an invitation to trade or an invitation to make an offer to which Urbanek would respond with his own offer.

When Urbanek agreed to purchase the houses at the list price, he actually made an offer that the owner then accepted, creating the contract. Generally, however, it would have been expected for him to make an offer at a lower price, which the seller would have responded to with a counteroffer. The next move would then belong to the buyer who would make his own counteroffer (a counter-counteroffer, if you will). The exchanging of counteroffers would continue until both the buyer and the seller agree on a final price, or in the poetic words of the courts, "the battle of the counteroffers continues until the acceptance *mirrors* the offer." Of course, it is always possible that one of the two parties will pull out of the battle. This happens if the price goes too low for the seller or stays too high for the buyer.

acceptance, a contract will come into existence, even if an acceptance has different or additional terms. If the parties are not both merchants, the different or additional terms are treated as proposals for additions to the contract. If both parties are merchants however, the different or additional terms become part of the contract unless (1) they make an important difference to the contract, (2) the offeror objects, or (3) the offer limits acceptance to its terms. This exception is discussed further in Chapter 13.

Unordered merchandise delivered by mail can be treated as a gift by the recipient. If a package is delivered by an agency other than the post office, the disposition of the merchandise is determined by state law.

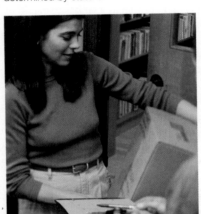

## Implied Acceptance

Acceptance may result from the conduct of the offeree. Actions and gestures may indicate the offeree's willingness to enter into a binding agreement.

**Unordered Merchandise**  According to the Postal Reorganization Act, the recipient of unordered merchandise through the mail may treat such goods as a gift. The receiver has no obligation to pay for or return the goods or to communicate with the sender in any way. When unordered merchandise is delivered by agencies other than the post office, the common law rule is usually followed. Under the common law rule, the receiver is not obligated to contact the sender or to pay for the goods. There is, however, an implied obligation to retain the good and give them reasonable care over a reasonable period of time. After that time, the receiver may consider that the sender no longer claims the goods and may use or dispose of them as desired. Some states, however, have laws similar to the postal law that allows recipients of unordered goods to consider them as gifts no matter who delivers them.

## Silence as Acceptance

As a general rule, in most situations, the offeror cannot bind the offeree just by declaring that the offeree's silence will signal an acceptance. However, should both parties agree that silence on the part of the offeree will be regarded as an acceptance, then the offeree's silence would operate as a valid acceptance.

### EXAMPLE 8-4:  When Will Silence Be Acceptance?

Sarah Jameson read an advertisement in *The Independent* inviting her to become a member of the New Era DVD Club. Jameson chose several DVDs that were listed in the advertisement. She paid only $1 for those DVDs and became a member of the DVD club. In doing so, she also agreed to purchase four more DVDs in a year's time. Under terms clearly specified in the advertisement, Jameson knew she would receive a brochure 12 times a year listing selections. The brochure would also identify the main selections, which would be sent to her automatically unless she sent a reply form to stop the shipment. In effect, Jameson agreed that whenever she did not return the reply card, her silence would amount to acceptance of the main selections.

## A QUESTION OF ETHICS

Suppose, after conducting a survey that revealed most people did not know about their rights under the Postal Reorganization Act, a company began a mailing campaign that sent unordered merchandise to certain targeted groups. Would such a move be ethical? Explain.

Another exception to the general rule occurs when the offeree has allowed silence to act as an acceptance. The offeror cannot force the offeree into a contract by saying silence will mean acceptance. The offeree, however, can force the offeror into a contract if the offeror set up the silence condition.

## EXAMPLE 8-5: Who Can Make Silence Acceptance?

Jason Riley wanted to sell his 1962 Volkswagen. He wrote a letter to Rita Tenpenny offering to sell the Volkswagen to Tenpenny for $25,000. Riley ended the letter by stating, "If I don't hear from you by December 3 of this year, I will take your silence to mean you accept my offer." Tenpenny received the letter and did not reply. Although Riley could not bind Tenpenny to this contract, Tenpenny could hold Riley to his offer because Riley set up the silence condition himself.

## Rejection and Revocation

A **rejection** comes about when an offeree expresses or implies a refusal to accept an offer. Rejection terminates an offer and all negotiations associated with it. Further negotiations could commence with a new offer by either party or a renewal of the original offer by the offeror. Rejection is usually achieved when communicated by the offeree. A **revocation** is the calling back of the offer by the offeror. With the exception of an option contract and a firm offer, an offer may be revoked any time before it is accepted. The offeror has this right, despite what might appear to be a strong moral obligation to continue the offer. An offer may be revoked by the following methods and circumstances: communication, death or insanity of the offeror, automatic revocation, destruction of the subject matter, passage of time, and the subsequent illegality of the contract.

## Option Contracts

An **option contract** is an agreement that binds an offeror to a promise to hold open an offer for a predetermined or a reasonable length of time. In return for this agreement, the offeror receives money or something else of value from the offeree. Parties to an option contract often agree that the consideration may be credited toward any indebtedness incurred by the offeree in the event that the offer is accepted. Should the offeree fail to take up the option, however, the offeror is under no legal obligation to return the consideration. An option contract removes the possibility of revocation through death or insanity of the offeror. The offeree who holds the option contract may demand acceptance by giving written notice of acceptance to the executor or administrator of the deceased offeror's estate or to the offeror's legally appointed guardian.

**About the Law**

Although the Ch'ing Dynasty, which ruled China from 1644 to 1911, codified the law of criminal offenses, it left civil law, for the most part, in the hands of the family and clan.

## EXAMPLE 8-6: Who Controls an Option Agreement?

Takashi Osaka offered to sell Andras Galai a collection of rare Japanese prints for $755,000. Galai requested time to consider the offer, and Osaka agreed to hold the collection for Galai for one week in return for Galai's payment of $755. Osaka died several days later. When Galai tendered the $755,000, the executor refused to deliver the collection, claiming that death had revoked the offer. The court ruled otherwise, with judgment given to the offeree based on the option agreement between Galai and the deceased.

### Firm Offers and Sale of Goods Contracts

A special rule that involves the creation of a firm offer has been developed under the Uniform Commercial Code. A **firm offer** is created when a merchant agrees in writing to hold an offer open. Under this condition, no consideration is needed to hold the offer open. A firm offer may be made for a specified period of time. If no time limit is specified, then the offer may remain open for a reasonable amount of time. However, the upper limit for a firm offer is three months. Remember that a firm offer under the UCC involves only sale-of-goods contracts.

UCC 2-205 (see page 823)

### Lease Options and Real Property

A **lease option** is a contract that permits a party to lease real property while at the same time holding an option to purchase that property. Generally, to hold open the option to purchase the leased property, the person leasing the property will make an additional deposit beyond the amount that an ordinary renter would make, so that he or she retains the opportunity to purchase that property at a later time. Because a lease option involves two separate contracts, the lease contract and the option contract, it is often divided into two documents. The lease contract will detail the terms of the lease, whereas the option contract will outline the terms under which the renter can exercise the option to purchase the property.

---

## quick quiz 8-2

| | |
|---|---|
| 1. An acceptance means that the offeree agrees to be bound by the terms set up by the offeror. | true \| false |
| 2. According to the Postal Reorganization Act, the recipient of unordered merchandise through the mail may treat such goods as a gift. | true \| false |
| 3. A rejection comes about when an offeree expresses or implies a refusal to accept an offer. | true \| false |

---

# 8-3 Mutual Assent in Cyberspace

As is true of most areas of the law, contract law, in general, and the law of offer and acceptance, in particular, have been affected by the use of computers in commercial settings. In many situations, the courts have taken orthodox laws that govern contracts and applied them to **cyber-contracts**, **electronic contracts** or **e-contracts**, that is, to contracts that are made using computers either via e-mail or the Internet or contracts that involve computer-related products such as databases and software. This application is true of the law as represented in the Uniform Commercial Code and the Restatement (Second) of Contracts. In addition, the courts must also be aware of several new approaches to cyber-contract law as represented by federal law and by the model codes written by the National Conference of Commissioners on Uniform State Laws. The new rules are found in the federal Electronic Signatures in Global and National Commerce Act (E-Sign Act), the Uniform Electronic Transactions Act, and the Uniform Computer Information Transactions Act.

## The E-Sign Act

The E-Sign Act was passed by Congress several years ago and represents an effort by the national legislature to make certain that commercial cyber-documents are given the same credence as their paper counterparts. Simply stated, the act provides that cyber-contracts that are entered into over the Internet or via e-mail will be valid, provided that the parties to the e-contract have agreed that electronic signatures will be used. As long as the cyber-contract can be duplicated and stored, it will have the same validity as a paper contract. The act expressly applies to Article 2 (Sale of Goods Contracts) and Article 2A (Leases) of the UCC.

## The Uniform Electronic Transactions Act

The Uniform Electronic Transactions Act (UETA) was written by the NCCUSL to ensure that cyber-contracts are given the same legal effect as their paper equivalents. The act does not create any new rules applying to mutual assent, consideration, capacity, and legality but instead makes certain that the laws that govern these elements apply to cyber-contracts just as they apply to paper contracts. There are three basic elements under the UETA. First, the participants must concur on the use of an electronic medium to create their contractual relationship. This agreement is usually not a problem, because the parties to an cyber-contract are generally aware of the nature of their relationship when they sit down at a computer. Second, once the first requirement is met, the act says that the electronic record generated by the computerized transaction will have the same weight that a paper document would have in a traditional transaction. Third, once the first requirement is met, the act acknowledges that an cyber-signature is just as effective as a written signature on a paper document.

## The Uniform Computer Information Transactions Act

The Uniform Computer Information Transactions Act (UCITA) arose when the NCCUSL and the ALI attempted to revise Article 2 (Sale of Goods Contracts) and Article 2A (Leases) of the UCC. Revising these articles to meet the demands of cyber-commerce and cyber-contractual relationships proved very difficult. In fact, the attempt was so difficult that the ALI dropped out of the process altogether, leaving the NCCUSL on its own. The NCCUSL then elected to write an entirely new act that came to be known as UCITA. One of the problems encountered by the NCCUSL in the writing of the new act was that many of the contracts that are entered into in cyberspace are more akin to licensing agreements than sale-of-goods contracts. The UCITA therefore covers such diverse areas as database contracts, software licensing agreements, customized software formulation, and the rights to multimedia commodities.

Many of the legal questions associated with Internet-made cyber-contracts are answered by the new act. For example, Section 102 of UCITA makes it clear that a license is to be considered "a contract that authorizes access to, or use, distribution, performance, modification, or reproduction of, information or information rights, but expressly limits the access or uses authorized or expressly grants fewer than all rights in the information, whether or not the transferee has title to a licensed copy." The UCITA has unified, streamlined, and refined the legal principles regarding such diverse areas as reverse engineering, consumer protection, shrinkwrap licenses, fair use, and consumer warranties. Despite all of this effort, the UCITA has been an extremely controversial act because many groups see it as increasing the rights and protections of software manufacturers rather than those of consumers.

## Offer and Acceptance in Cyberspace

In addition to the terms included in most other offers, an cyber-offeror should insert the following terms in his or her offer: (1) payment criteria, (2) remedies that can be used by the offeree, (3) refund policies, (4) return procedures, (5) dispute settlement instructions, (6) the applicability of cyber-signatures, (7) liability disclaimers if needed, and (8) provisions relating to the offeree's manner of acceptance. In general, the offeree's acceptance in an cyber-contract is referred to as a "click-on" acceptance or a "click-on" agreement. A **click-on acceptance** or a **click-on agreement** is one that is created by having a party click on a box on the computer screen that states he or she agrees to be bound by the terms of the contract. Otherwise, it is important to recall that, as explained previously, when the agreement deals with goods, the provisions of Article 2 of the UCC will apply.

## quick quiz 8-3

1. The Uniform Electronic Transactions Act (UETA) was passed by Congress as a federal law.    true | false

2. The Electronic Signatures in Global and National Commerce Act was written by the National Conference of Commissioners on Uniform State Laws.    true | false

3. The process of accepting an online offer is often referred to as a "click-on" agreement.    true | false

# 8-4 The Destruction of Mutual Assent

As is true of most other parts of the legal system, contract law seeks to balance the rights and the duties of two or more parties. In contract law those two parties are the offeror and the offeree and the rights and the duties are assumed voluntarily. The balance emerges from a dialectic that pairs the offer with the acceptance and sets the stage for the development of a synthesis between the two. That synthesis is referred to as mutual assent. As the first element of a contract, mutual assent must stand on its own, without being propped up by artificial supports. Mutual assent, however, can be elusive. Unfortunately, some emergent agreements that appear to be correctly constructed at first glance are, in fact, substantively false, despite the pretty picture that they might create. Those forces that destroy assent come in five flavors: fraud, misrepresentation, mistake, duress, and undue influence.

## Fraud and Misrepresentation

Both fraud and misrepresentation disrupt mutual assent. They do so by sabotaging the essential component of trust upon which all agreements, but especially contracts, are based. This is what makes both fraud and misrepresentation so insidious. They are based on deceitful practice that makes a mockery of the entire commercial process. Of the two, fraud is the more serious and the more despicable because it is deliberate. It is also the more difficult of the two to prove. This may be why many cases that should be litigated as fraud, end up in court as misrepresentation lawsuits.

**Fraud**  To destroy mutual assent through a claim of **fraud**, the complaining or innocent party must prove the existence of five elements.

1. The complaining party will have to prove that the other party made a false representation about some **material fact** (i.e., an important fact, a fact of substance) involved in the contract. A material fact is one that is very crucial to the terms of the contract.

2. The plaintiff must demonstrate convincingly that the other party made the representation knowing that it was false.

3. The plaintiff must show that the false representations were made with the intent that they be relied upon by the innocent party.

## THE OPENING CASE *Revisited, Part III*
### Mutual Assent and Its Destruction: *Urbanek v. All State Home Mortgage*, Round 4

A situation that appears to involve several levels of fraud can be found in the Opening Case at the beginning of this chapter. Recall that in the case, the plaintiff, at the prompting of two All State agents, purchased three houses. Now with fraud in mind, consider the following allegations. According to the judge's opinion in the case, the houses had been appraised but there was no evidence that Urbanek ever received, read, or considered the appraisal, which was made some time before Urbanek visited or made an offer for the three houses. Nevertheless, as it turned out when the plaintiff tried to sell the houses he discovered that the value of each property was overinflated. The plaintiff argued that he had been defrauded by the overinflated appraisal of the houses.

If we look at the elements of fraud, we should be able to unravel this claim. First, in any fraud claim, the plaintiff must prove that the other party made a false representation about some material fact involved in the contract. The appraisal of the property would clearly involve a series of material facts. No one could argue that the value of the property was

not material. Second, the plaintiff must prove that the other party made the representation knowing that it was false. This is more difficult to prove but, given the fact that the houses were, in fact, overinflated, added to the other alleged deceptions involved in the case, the plaintiff might be able to pass that hurdle successfully. Third, the plaintiff must show that the false representations were made with the intent that they be relied upon by the innocent party. This should not be difficult, since the point of an appraisal is to provide the buyer with evidence of value so that the buyer . . . buys. Fourth and fifth, the plaintiff must establish that he actually relied on the false representations and suffered a loss as a result. These last two points are the ones the judge found difficult to believe. She stated that the plaintiff offered "no evidence that he relied on the appraisal when making his decision to purchase the property. Therefore, she concluded that the plaintiff "failed as a matter of law to establish the reliance element of fraud." (See *Urbanek v. All State Home Mortgage Company,* 178 Ohio App.3d 493, at 499 (2008-Ohio-4871)).

4. The complaining party must establish that there was a reasonable reliance on the false representations.

5. The plaintiff must verify that he or she actually suffered some loss by relying on the false representation after entering the contract.

A case involving either active or passive fraud must be based on these five elements.

**Types of Fraud**   There is more than one way to commit fraud. The law distinguishes between fraud in the inception and fraud in the inducement. **Fraud in the inception** occurs when one party tricks another party into a contract by lying to the innocent party about the actual nature of the contract. In effect, because of false representations made by one party, the innocent party believes that he or she is doing "A" when he or she is actually doing "B." For example, if an insurance agent were to tell an accident victim that the paper she was signing was a privacy waiver, when it was actually an agreement releasing the insurance company from all liability, it would be fraud in the inception. **Fraud in the inducement** occurs when one party tricks another into a contract by lying about the terms of the agreement to get the innocent party to enter the contract under false pretenses. In this case, because of the false representations made by one party, the innocent party believes that he or she is doing "A," but "A" turns out to be actually "A−" or "A+" or "a" rather than simply "A." If, for instance, a loan officer at a bank were to tell a borrower that the interest rate on the loan would be 8 percent when it was actually 18 percent, that officer would have committed fraud in the inducement.

LO8

## EXAMPLE 8-7: *Rhodes v. Hayden*

Gabriel Hayden owned a motorboat that was docked at the Butler Reservoir. Hayden, however, was about to move to the city and so was anxious to get rid of a boat for which he would have no use in the city. Kelly Rhodes, who was new in town, wanted to purchase a motorboat quickly so that she would have several weeks of summer weather left to enjoy the boat. Sensing that he could make a real killing on the deal, Hayden told Rhodes about the boat. Rhodes was impressed by Hayden's sales pitch, but she wanted to see the boat first and take it for a test run on the reservoir. Hayden agreed. Before Rhodes arrived the next day for the test run, Hayden patched up several obvious holes in the bottom of the boat with putty and poster board. Hayden knew the repairs would not make the boat seaworthy for longer than 15 minutes, but he figured that would be enough time to fool Rhodes into thinking that the boat was in good condition. Deceived by the apparently good condition of the boat, Rhodes purchased it. The next time she took it out on the reservoir, the boat quickly sank. Even though Hayden never actually told any verbal lies to Rhodes, he would still have committed fraud.

To be fraudulent, statements must involve facts. Opinions and sales puffery consist of the persuasive words and exaggerated claims made by salespeople to induce a customer to buy their product. As long as the comments are reserved to opinion and do not misstate facts, they cannot be considered fraud in a lawsuit, even if they turn out to be grossly wrong.

## EXAMPLE 8-8: *Oldacker v. Kellog Formal Wear Shoppe*

Fran Holiday, a sales clerk representing the Kellog Formal Wear Shoppe, was trying to sell a tuxedo to Ken Oldacker. During the sales discussion, Holiday told Oldacker that the tux (1) came with two pairs of pants, (2) was made of 100 percent wool, (3) had a very rich texture, (4) looked very good on Oldacker, and (5) would make him look like James Bond. The first two statements are statements of material fact and could be the basis of a lawsuit for fraud if they are proven false. The others are either opinions expressed by the seller or the persuasive puffery that might induce Oldacker to buy the tux and therefore could not be used as the basis of a lawsuit for fraud.

Fraud can occur in many ways. A consumer's best defense is to be knowledgeable, listen, and ask questions

**Active and Passive Fraud** As noted previously, active fraud occurs when one party actually makes a false statement intended to deceive the other party in a contract. In contrast, passive fraud, which is generally called concealment or nondisclosure, occurs when one party does not say something about certain facts that he or she is under an obligation to reveal. If this passive conduct is intended to deceive and does in fact deceive the other party, fraud results. In general, a party is not required to reveal every known fact related to the subject matter of a contract. Certain facts may be confidential and personal. However, if the problem or defect is hidden and the other party cannot reasonably be expected to discover the defect, provided the problem involves some material fact, the offeror may be obliged to reveal it. Some states have held that sellers are legally bound to reveal only problems so hidden that even an expert would not be able to uncover them. In these states, problems such as insect or rodent infestation would not be hidden problems because an expert could easily uncover them.

## EXAMPLE 8-9: *Bernstein v. Crowley*

Franklin Bernstein had decided to purchase an apartment building in lower Manhattan near the World Financial Center, which he intended to convert into condominiums. Before finalizing the deal, he visited the building several times with the real estate agent representing the seller, Keyfitz Management, Inc. Each time, Bernstein examined a different aspect of the building, concentrating first on the plumbing, then on the electrical system, then on the heating and air conditioning system, and so on. He also hired Guftanson Contractors Ltd. to make a thorough inspection of the entire building. What Bernstein did not know and could not reasonably be expected to discover was that the foundation had been damaged when the World Trade Center collapsed in 2001. Max Crowley, the actual owner, knew of the damage. However, he did not reveal the problem to Bernstein. Crowley had committed passive fraud or concealment because he did not reveal a serious hidden problem that Bernstein could not reasonably be expected to discover on his own.

A **fiduciary relationship** is a relationship based on trust. Such relationships exist, for example, between attorneys and clients, guardians and wards, trustees and beneficiaries, and boards of directors and corporations. If one party is in a fiduciary relationship with another party, then an obligation arises to reveal what otherwise might be withheld when the two parties enter an agreement.

## A QUESTION OF ETHICS

Suppose that you are showing your car to Tim Jorgenson, a potential buyer. You know that if Jorgenson takes your car out for a ride, he will notice that the front end rattles at speeds in excess of 35 miles per hour and that the brakes grind badly. Jorgenson, however, does not take the car on a test drive and therefore fails to detect any defects. Would you have an ethical duty to tell Jorgenson about the car's problems? Explain.

### Table 8-3  Agreements Made Defective by Falsehood

| Falsehood | Definition | Remedy |
| --- | --- | --- |
| Active fraud | Active fraud occurs when one party to a contract makes a false statement intended to deceive the other party and thus leads that party into a deceptively based agreement. | Damages Rescission |
| Passive fraud | Passive fraud occurs when one party says or does not say something about certain facts that he or she is obligated to reveal. Obligations arise in situations involving hidden problems and fiduciary relationships. | Damages Rescission |
| Misrepresentation | Misrepresentation occurs when a false statement is innocently made. | Rescission |

## EXAMPLE 8-10: *San Rafael Motor Corporation v. Groza*

Otto Groza was vice president of business and finance for the San Rafael Motor Corporation when he learned that Toth Properties Ltd. wanted to buy 12,000 acres of ranch land owned by San Rafael. Groza was the only one at San Rafael who knew that a new extension of the interstate was going to be located on the acreage owned by the company. Moreover, Groza knew that Toth wanted the land for an outlet mall and an adjoining hotel and was willing to pay $19,000 per acre. Groza made a deal with Toth agreeing to sell the land at that price. He then went to the CEO and the board of San Rafael and offered to buy the farmland without revealing anything about the Toth deal. As a result, he purchased the acreage for $1,000 per acre and made an $18,000 profit on each acre he resold to Toth. Groza will be liable to San Rafael because he concealed a material fact that he was obligated to reveal because of his fiduciary relationship with the company.

**Misrepresentation**   A false statement made innocently with no intent to deceive is **misrepresentation**. Innocent misrepresentation makes an existing agreement voidable, and the complaining party may demand rescission. **Rescission** means that both parties are returned to their original positions, before they entered into the contract. Unlike cases based on fraud, which allow rescission and damages, cases based on innocent misrepresentation allow only rescission, not monetary damages. If a party to an agreement makes an innocent misrepresentation and then later discovers that it is false, that party must reveal the truth. If the party does not reveal the truth, the innocent misrepresentation becomes fraud.

## EXAMPLE 8-11: *Sanderson v. Straus*

Anthony Sanderson was browsing on eBay when he located what was labeled as a 1932 edition of *Brave New World* by Aldous Huxley, produced by Chatto and Windus, the London publisher that had printed the first edition of that landmark novel. The book was advertised as coming along with a companion book by Julian Huxley, entitled *If I Were Dictator,* published in 1934 by the London publishing house of Methuen. The seller was Juliette Straus, who set the minimum bid for the two volumes at GBP 8,700. Sanderson, who quickly bid on the two books, eventually won the auction with a successful bid of GBP 9,800. Later, after receiving the two books, Sanderson discovered that the copy of *If I Were Dictator* was actually a 1948 reprint of the original work. Without any indication of wrongdoing, Straus would be liable for nothing more than an innocent misrepresentation. In cases of this kind, the parties often renegotiate the purchase price if the agreement is affirmed.

## Mistake, Duress, and Undue Influence

When there has been no real meeting of the minds because of a mistake, mutual assent was never achieved, and the agreement may be rescinded. As in misrepresentation, mistake permits rescission. Both duress and undue influence rob a person of the ability to make an independent, well-reasoned decision to enter a contractual relationship freely. Both of these conditions therefore strike at the heart of contract law.

**The Nature of Mistake**   A mistake made by only one of the contracting parties is a **unilateral mistake** and does not offer sufficient grounds for rescission or renegotiation.

**Table 8-4**  Agreements Made Defective by Mutual Mistake

| Mistake | Legal Effect |
| --- | --- |
| Mistake as to description | Rescission will be granted. |
| Mistake as to existence | Proof that subject matter was destroyed *before* the agreement was made gives grounds for rescission. |
| Mistake as to value | Rescission will not be granted since value is a matter of opinion, not fact. |

When both parties are mistaken, it is a **bilateral mistake**. A bilateral mistake, which is also called a **mutual mistake**, may permit a rescission by either the offeror or the offeree. Mutual mistakes are of several kinds. Some are universally accepted as grounds for rescission. Others are not grounds for rescission. Still others can give rise to lawsuits, but not in all courts or in all states. When both parties are mistaken in the identification and description of subject matter, there is a real mutual mistake, and rescission will be granted.

Proof that the subject matter had been destroyed before the agreement was made gives grounds for rescission. Thus, if one party accepted an offer to purchase a boat that both parties mistakenly believed to be berthed at a specified marina, the agreement would be voidable if it were proved that moments before acceptance, the boat had been destroyed. Had the boat been destroyed after final acceptance, there would have been no mutual mistake, and an enforceable contract would have resulted. When two parties agree on the value of the subject matter and later find they were both mistaken, it is a mutual mistake of opinion, not of fact. Mutual mistakes of opinion are not grounds for rescinding a contract.

### The Nature of Duress

In general, **duress** may be viewed as an action by one party that forces another party to do what need not otherwise be done. Duress forces a person into a contract through the use of physical, emotional, or economic threats. In contrast, undue influence merely involves the use of excessive pressure. Moreover, undue influence requires the existence of a special relationship, generally of a confidential or fiduciary nature. **Physical duress** involves either violence or the threat of violence against an individual or against that person's family, household, or property. If only threats are used, they must be so intense and serious that a person of ordinary prudence would be forced into the contract without any real consent. Threats of physical duress are relatively rare today. Perhaps more common are threats that create emotional duress. **Emotional duress** arises from acts or threats that would create emotional distress in the one on whom they are inflicted. It is generally necessary that the action threatened be either illegal or illicit.

**Economic duress**, also known as **business compulsion**, consists of threats of a business nature that force another party without real consent to enter a commercial agreement. To establish economic duress, the complaining party must demonstrate the existence of three elements:

1.  The plaintiff must prove that the other party wrongfully placed the plaintiff in a precarious economic situation.
2.  The plaintiff must show that he or she had no alternative other than to submit to the contractual demands of the wrongful party.
3.  The plaintiff must demonstrate that he or she acted reasonably in entering the contract.

If the plaintiff can prove the existence of these three elements, the court will rule the contract voidable on grounds of economic duress.

**LO10**

## EXAMPLE 8-12: *National Air Races Inc. v. Macon City Airport*

The owners and operators of National Air Races negotiated a seven-year lease with the city of Macon for use of the Macon City Airport. Each summer, during the Fourth of July weekend celebration, the National Air Races were held at the Macon City Airport. One week before the first race of the fourth year under the contract, Macon City officials informed the owners and operators of the National Air Races that they would no longer be able to use the Macon City Airport for the Fourth of July races unless they paid a substantial rent increase. The owners and operators of the Air Races, who had already sold at least 5,000 tickets per race, accepted entry fees from 95 pilots, and had contracts with 20 concessionaires, could not find any other suitable airport within 120 miles of Macon. As a result, they agreed to the terms. Later, the owners of the Air Races sued Macon to have the rent increase rescinded. The court ruled that the rent increase was voidable due to economic duress.

### Did You Know?

It is possible for a party to ratify a contract made under duress if, after the duress has ended, the party makes a new promise to abide by the terms of the original agreement. In such a situation, the party ratifying the contract need not supply any new consideration.

**The Nature of Undue Influence**  The problem of **undue influence** occurs when the dominant party in a special relationship uses excessive pressure to convince the weaker party to enter a contract that greatly benefits the dominant party. A plaintiff who wants to demonstrate that he or she was enticed into a contract by undue influence must prove the existence of two elements.

1. The plaintiff must show that a special relationship existed between the parties. A special relationship can generally be characterized as one that is fiduciary in nature or one that involves domination. Examples of fiduciary relationships include the relationships of parent to child, guardian to ward, attorney to client, physician to patient, pastor to parishioner, and so forth. Relationships that involve dominance frequently occur when the stronger of the two parties is acting as a caretaker of the weaker party.

2. Second, the plaintiff must show that the other party used excessive pressure to take advantage of him or her to enter a contract that greatly benefits the party applying the pressure.

In most cases involving undue influence, one party in the special relationship has enough strength and leadership to dominate the other party, who is obviously weaker and dependent.

### Table 8-5    Agreements Made Defective by Force or Pressure

| Type of Force or Pressure | Explanation |
| --- | --- |
| Physical duress | Violence or threat of violence to person, family, household, or property. |
| Emotional duress | Acts or threats that create emotional distress in the one on whom they are inflicted. |
| Economic duress | Threats of a business nature that force another party without real consent to enter a commercial agreement. |
| Undue influence | Dominant party in a special relationship uses excessive pressure to convince the weaker party to enter a contract. |

## quick quiz 8-4

1. Misrepresentation is a false statement made with no intent to deceive.    true | false

2. Mutual mistake is grounds for rescinding a contract.    true | false

3. Economic duress is also known as business compulsion.    true | false

## Summary

8.1   If certain requirements are met, the court will conclude that the parties intended to make and accept an offer. Mutual assent is created when an offer is made by one party and accepted by the other party. An offer is valid if it is made with serious intent, displays clear and definite terms, and is communicated to the offeree.

8.2   The second major part of mutual assent is the acceptance of the offer. Communication of the acceptance may be either express or implied. Under the mirror image rule, an acceptance must not change any of the terms of the offer. The UCC has altered the mirror image rule. At any time prior to acceptance, the offeror can withdraw the offer. Still, some types of offers cannot be revoked by the offeror. These involve option contracts, firm offers, and lease option contracts.

8.3   The principal rules concerning the interpretation of the enforcement of cyber-contracts are found in the E-Sign Act, the Uniform Electronic Transactions Act (UETA), and the Uniform Computer Information Transactions Act (UCITA).

8.4   Fraud involves deliberate deception about some material fact that leads a party into an agreement that is damaging to that party. Misrepresentation is a false statement innocently made with no intent to deceive. A mutual mistake may allow for rescission by either party. Duress and undue influence rob a person of the ability to make an independent, well-reasoned decision to enter freely into a contract.

## Key Terms

acceptance, 173

active fraud, 182

auction, 172

auction with reserve, 172

auction without reserve, 172

bait-and-switch confidence game, 172

bilateral mistake, 185

business compulsion, 185

click-on acceptance or agreement, 179

concealment, 182

contract, 169

cost-plus contract, 171

counteroffer, 175

current market price contract, 171

cyber-contract, 178

duress, 185

economic duress, 185

electronic contracts or e-contracts, 178

emotional duress, 185

fiduciary relationship, 183

firm offer, 178

fraud, 180

fraud in the inception, 181

fraud in the inducement, 181

invitation to trade, 171

lease option, 178

list price, 172

material fact, 180

mirror image rule, 175

misrepresentation, 184

mutual assent, 169

mutual mistake, 185

nondisclosure, 182

offer, 170

offeree, 170

offeror, 170

option contract, 177

output contract, 171

## Questions for Review and Discussion

1. What is mutual assent?
2. What are the elements of an offer?
3. What is the UCC's concept of an offer?
4. How does an acceptance come about?
5. What is the mirror image rule?
6. What is revocation?
7. What statutes affect mutual assent in cyberspace?
8. What are the elements of fraud and misrepresention?
9. What are the effects of mistake on mutual assent?
10. What are duress and undue influence?

## Cases for Analysis

1. An advertisement appeared in the *Chicago Sun-Times* for the sale of a Volvo station wagon at Lee Calan Imports, Inc., for $1,095. The advertisement had been misprinted by the *Sun-Times*. The actual price of the automobile was $1,795. O'Keefe showed up at Lee Calan and said he would buy the Volvo for $1,095. Lee Calan refused to sell the car for $1,095. O'Keefe sued, claiming that the advertisement was an offer that he accepted, creating a binding agreement. Was O'Keefe correct? Explain. *O'Keefe v. Lee Calan Imports,* 262 N.E.2d 758 (IL).

2. The Great Minneapolis Surplus Store published the following advertisement in a Minneapolis newspaper: "Saturday 9 A.M. 2 Brand New Pastel Mink 3-Skin Scarfs selling for $89.50—Out they go Saturday. Each . . . $1.00. 1 Black Lapin Stole. Beautiful, Worth $139.50 . . . $1.00. First Come, First Served." Leftkowitz, the first customer admitted to the store on Saturday, tried to buy the Lapin stole. The store refused to sell, stating that the offer was for women only. Leftkowitz sued. Was the offer definite enough to allow Leftkowitz to tender a valid acceptance? Explain. *Leftkowitz v. Great Minneapolis Surplus Store,* 86 N.W.2d 689 (MN).

3. Morrison wanted to sell a certain parcel of land to Thoelke. He decided to make an offer by sending Thoelke a letter. When Thoelke received the letter, he decided to accept. He wrote a letter to Morrison saying that he would buy the land at the price quoted in the letter. Thoelke then mailed the letter. Before he received the letter from Thoelke, Morrison changed his mind and withdrew the offer to Thoelke. When Thoelke found out Morrison would not sell the land to him, he sued. Was Thoelke's letter a valid acceptance, binding Morrison to the sale? Explain. *Morrison v. Thoelke,* 155 So.2d 889 (FL).

4. Wholesale Coal Company ordered 25 carloads of coal from Guyan Coal and Coke Company. Guyan could not come up with 25 carloads. However, it did have 7 carloads available. Before shipping the coal, Guyan wrote back to Wholesale stating, "You can be sure that if it is possible to ship the entire twenty-five carloads, we will do so. But under the circumstances, this is the best we can promise you." When Guyan heard nothing from Wholesale, it shipped the 7 carloads. When Wholesale did not pay for the 7 carloads, Guyan brought suit to compel payment. Wholesale countersued, claiming Guyan had not yet delivered the remaining 18 carloads. Was Wholesale correct? Explain. *Guyan Coal and Coke Company v. Wholesale Coal Company,* 201 N.W. 194 (MI).

5. Tockstein wrote an offer to purchase a house owned by Rothenbeucher. Tockstein signed the offer and personally delivered it to Rothenbeucher. The offer included a condition that acceptance must be made within 24 hours. At the end of that 24-hour period, the offer would be automatically revoked if Rothenbeucher had not accepted. Rothenbeucher signed the agreement within the 24-hour period. However, he did not deliver the acceptance to Tockstein personally, as Tockstein had done with the offer. Instead, Rothenbeucher delivered the acceptance to his own real estate agent, who delivered it to Tockstein after the

automatic revocation time. Tockstein claimed that the offer was automatically revoked when Rothenbeucher did not deliver it within the specified time period. Was Tockstein correct? Explain. *Rothenbeucher v. Tockstein*, 411 N.E.2d 92 (IL).

6. Walker and Cousineau were both in the gravel business. Walker placed an advertisement for a tract of land, claiming that he had an engineer's report that indicated the land held at least 80,000 cubic yards of gravel. In fact, Walker knew the land\contained much less gravel. Cousineau purchased the land and began to excavate it. After 6,000 cubic yards of gravel had been removed, the supply ran out. Cousineau sued Walker, asking the court to rescind the contract. Did Cousineau win the case? Explain. *Cousineau v. Walker,* 613 P.2d 608 (AL).

7. Young sold a residential lot to Sorrell without revealing that the lot had been filled. The landfill was not obvious, and Sorrell could not have been reasonably expected to detect it. When Sorrell discovered the landfill, he sued Young and asked the court to rescind the agreement. Young claimed he was under no obligation to reveal the fill to Sorrell. Was Young correct? Explain. *Sorrell v. Young,* 491 P.2d 1312 (WA).

8. Boskett offered to sell a 1916 dime to Beachcomber Coins, Inc. Beachcomber examined the coin carefully and agreed to pay Boskett $500 for it. Later, Beachcomber asked a representative from the American Numismatic Society to examine the coin. The coin turned out to be counterfeit. No evidence existed to indicate fraud on Boskett's part. Beachcomber sued Boskett for rescission and a return of the $500. Beachcomber claimed this bilateral mistake of fact created grounds for a rescission. Was Beachcomber correct? Explain. *Beachcomber Coins, Inc. v. Boskett,* 400 A.2d 78 (NJ).

9. Prisoners rioted at the Iowa State Penitentiary and held prison staff members as hostages. The warden agreed in writing that no reprisals would be levied against the rioting inmates. In exchange, the prisoners released the hostages. After the hostages were released, several of the prisoners were punished for the riot. One prisoner, Wagner, was placed in solitary confinement for 30 days. He also received 180 days of administrative segregation and the loss of 1,283 days of goodtime earned. On what legal grounds could the warden refuse to keep his promise to the inmates? Explain. *Wagner v. State,* 364 N.W.2d 246 (IA).

10. Loral Corporation had a contract with the U.S. government to manufacture radar sets. Loral subcontracted with Austin Instrument for the production of precision parts to be used in the radar sets. In the middle of production, Austin told Loral that it would deliver no more parts unless Loral agreed to pay Austin a good deal more than originally agreed upon. Loral could not obtain the same parts in time from any other company. As a result, Loral agreed to the price increase. After delivering the radar sets, Loral sued Austin and asked the court to rescind the price increase. Did the court grant Loral's request? Explain. *Austin Instrument, Inc. v. Loral Corporation,* 272 N.E.2d 533 (NY).

## quick quiz Answers

| 8-1 | 8-2 | 8-3 | 8-4 |
|------|------|------|------|
| 1. F | 1. T | 1. F | 1. T |
| 2. T | 2. T | 2. F | 2. T |
| 3. T | 3. T | 3. T | 3. T |

# Chapter 9

# Consideration and Cyber-payments

## THE OPENING CASE  Benefits and Detriments: *Hamer v. Sidway*

Literature instructors are fond of saying that a poem, a play, a novel, or a short story is considered good, sometimes even great, if it has stood the "test of time." The same is true of many legal cases. Such is the situation with the long-standing case of *Hamer v. Sidway*, a lawsuit that most law students and paralegals encounter at some time in their academic careers. *Hamer and Sidway* begins at a golden wedding anniversary celebration. At the party, Uncle William promised his nephew and namesake, William, that if he, the nephew, would give up a long list of vices that included smoking and swearing, until his 21st birthday, he, the uncle, would pay his nephew, William, $5,000. The challenge was made in front of a room full of family members and close friends, and so, William agreed to the arrangement. Following this and in compliance with the agreement, William embarked on an extensive period of abstinence that lasted several years. Soon after his 21st birthday, William wrote to his Uncle telling him of his accomplishments and asking for the $5,000 due to him under the contract. Uncle William wrote a lengthy letter back to young William in which he praised his nephew for his perseverance. He also promised to pay the money that was due. Unfortunately, Uncle William passed away before sending the money to his nephew. Undeterred, the nephew petitioned the executor of Uncle William's estate for payment.

The executor refused to pay and William brought this lawsuit. William argued that he had performed as promised and was, therefore, entitled to the money. The executor recognized that William had, indeed, refrained from smoking and swearing, but argued that, in contract law, both sides must suffer a detriment for consideration to be valid and for a contract to exist. In this case, the executor said, young William had not suffered a detriment. In fact, the opposite was true. He was much healthier than he would have been, absent the promise, and he had, therefore, benefited greatly from giving up his bad habits for such an extended period of time. In the absence of consideration, no contract ever existed and, as a result, the estate did not owe young William a single cent. The court in the case referred to a standard treatise on contract law and noted that, consideration "means not so much that one party is profiting as that the other abandons some legal right in the present, or limits his legal freedom of action in the future, as an inducement for the promise of the first." How would you predict the court will rule in this case? Did the nephew give up enough under the law, or is his promise to Uncle William a cleverly constructed illusion? See if you can answer these questions as you read through this chapter on consideration. [See *Hamer v. Sidway,* 124 N.Y. 538, 27 N.E. 256 (Court of Appeals of New York).]

**Opening Case Questions**

1. Would *Hamer v. Sidway* be a civil lawsuit or a criminal action? Explain

2. What law will the court apply in this case to answer the questions noted above? Will the court use common law or the Uniform Commercial Code (UCC)? Explain.

3. What is the nature of the consideration that passed from the nephew to the uncle? Explain.

4. What is the nature of the consideration that passed from the uncle to the nephew? Explain.

5. Can the court determine the value of the nephew's detriment in this case? Explain.

## LO Learning Objectives

1. Define the term *consideration*.
2. Identify the different types of detriment.
3. Explain the characteristics necessary for valid consideration.
4. Define the term *unconscionable*.
5. Explain whether a promise not to sue can be consideration.
6. Explain whether a charitable pledge can be consideration.
7. Define accord and satisfaction.
8. Identify those enforceable contracts that lack consideration.
9. Explain *promissory estoppel*.
10. Describe the issues involved in cyber-payments.

# 9-1 Requirements of Consideration

In Chapter 8, we explored the nature of mutual assent, the first of the four elements of a contract. The second element is the mutual promise to exchange benefits and sacrifices among the parties. This exchange of things of value is called **consideration**. If an agreement has no consideration, it is not a binding contract. For example, a promise to give someone a ride to the campus in the morning is not a contract. Instead, it is simply a social arrangement because the rider has given nothing in exchange for the ride. In contrast, if the rider decides to take the bus, call a cab, or rent a vehicle to get to campus then a contract will exist. This is because, in the second case, the rider will have to transfer consideration in the form of a fare or a rental price in exchange for the ride to class.

## The Nature of Consideration

Consideration consists of a mutual exchange of gains and losses between contracting parties. In the exchange, a gain by the offeree is at the same time a loss to the offeror. Likewise, the gain bargained for by the offeror will result in a loss or sacrifice by the offeree. The legal term used to designate the gain that each party experiences is that party's legal benefit. Similarly, the legal term used to describe the sacrifice that each party must experience is that party's **legal detriment**. A legal detriment can be any of the following: (1) doing something (or promising to do something) that one has a legal right not to do; (2) giving up something (or promising to give up something) that one has a legal right to keep; and (3) refraining from doing something (or promising not

## THE OPENING CASE *Revisited, Part I*
### Benefits and Detriments: *Hamer v. Sidway*, Round 2

Recall that in the Opening Case at the beginning of this chapter, Uncle William promised his nephew and namesake, William, that if he, the nephew, would give up a long list of vices that included smoking and swearing, until his 21st birthday, he, the uncle, would pay his nephew, William, $5,000. Young William agreed and embarked on an extended period of abstinence that lasted several years. Soon after his 21st birthday, William wrote to his Uncle telling him of his accomplishments and asking for the $5,000 due to him under their contract. Unfortunately, Uncle William passed away before sending the money to his nephew. Undeterred, the nephew petitioned the executor of Uncle

William's estate for payment. The executor refused to pay and William sued. In court, the executor argued, rather convincingly, that consideration requires that both parties suffer a detriment and reap a benefit. In this case, young William had not suffered a detriment. In fact, the executor said, the opposite was true. William was actually much healthier than he would have been, absent the contract. The court disagreed with this analysis. The court noted that, when William gave up something that he had a legal right to do, he had suffered a detriment sufficient to provide the consideration needed to make the agreement into a *bona fide* contract. End of story—period.

### Did You Know?

When the Roman Emperor Justinian (527–565 CE) began a program of extensive legal reform, he made certain that transferring property became a relatively simple process.

to do something) that one has a legal right to do. This last type of detriment is known as **forbearance**.

It is likely that William improved his health by giving up smoking. However, the fact that William gained a medical benefit does not eliminate his sacrifice. The simple reality here is that he stopped doing something that he had the legal right to do. This "non-act" by itself is consideration. William has suffered what the courts call a legal detriment, so giving up smoking has legal value, and the contract is valid.

## The Characteristics of Consideration

Consideration has three characteristics: (1) The agreement must involve a bargained-for exchange; (2) the contract must involve adequate consideration; and (3) the benefits and detriments promised must themselves be legal.

**LO3**

**Bargained-for Exchange**  The law will not enforce an agreement that has not been bargained for. An agreement involves a **bargained-for exchange** when (1) a promise is made in exchange for another promise, (2) a promise is made in exchange for an act, or (3) a promise is made for forbearance of an act. The concept of bargaining means that each party will be hurt in some way if the other party fails to keep a promise. Conversely, each party gains something when the promises are kept and the exchange is made.

### EXAMPLE 9-1:  When Is a Contract not a Contract?

David Sable agreed to loan Carla Laszlo his car so that Laszlo could drive across country to attend a literary workshop on Ralph Waldo Emerson and the Transcendentalists planned for a week in June in Concord, Massachusetts. There was no understanding that Laszlo would pay for the use of the vehicle. Sable then refused to allow Laszlo to drive his car. Although Sable might have an ethical duty to lend Laszlo the car, their agreement was not an enforceable one, because it contained no bargained-for promise.

## Adequacy of Consideration

The fact that a contract has legal value is not the same as saying that it has adequate consideration. However, there are no specific requirements, other than being legal, regarding what one party may promise the other party in return for a pledge to deliver goods and services. The promise itself is adequate consideration when it represents something of value. Thus, the promise to assist another to repair an automobile would be something of value promised. The value placed on goods and services need not be street or market value. It is important only that the parties freely agreed on the value and the price. In general, the courts do not look into the adequacy of consideration; that is, they do not look to see whether the value of the consideration was fair to both parties. Ever since industrial capitalism became the primary economic system in the West, the courts no longer looked to see if the things exchanged in a contract are of equal value. Such a move would violate the profit-making principle of capitalism. Therefore, the courts let people make their own agreements, placing their own values on the goods or services exchanged. The court then enforces those agreements.

The price and value of the goods exchanged need not be equal as long as the agreement is voluntary.

There are, however, exceptions to this general rule. In one exception, the courts give a party relief when the consideration is so outrageous that it shocks the conscience of the court. A court may refuse to enforce a contract or any clause of a contract if it considers the contract or clause **unconscionable**, that is, the consideration is so ridiculously inadequate that it shocks the court's conscience. This designation usually happens when there is a great inequality in bargaining power between the two parties. In very specific matters, usually related to taxes, some states have adopted statutes dealing with adequacy. In general though, courts remain reluctant to disturb the promises made by parties to an enforceable contract.

## THE OPENING CASE *Revisited, Part II*
## Benefits and Detriments: *Hamer v. Sidway*, Round 3

In the Opening Case at the beginning of the chapter, Uncle William promised his nephew, William, $5,000 if the nephew would give up smoking, until he turned 21. Young William agreed and did so. Sadly, Uncle William passed away before sending the money to his nephew. Undaunted, the nephew asked the executor of the estate for the money. The executor refused, arguing that consideration requires that both parties suffer a detriment and reap a benefit, and William had suffered no detriment. The court disagreed and said that, when William gave up something that he had a legal right to do, he had suffered a detriment sufficient to provide consideration. But what about *Uncle* William? Certainly he suffered a detriment in parting with his $5,000. However, what benefit did he receive in the contract? Can the court place a value on a healthy nephew? The court did not set a value on what Uncle William received. However, it did not have to set any value on it, as long as it was clear to the court that the uncle did, in fact, value the actions and the results that he had requested. The adequacy of the consideration is of no concern to the court. To demonstrate this point, the courts said, "we see nothing in this record that would permit a determination that the uncle was not benefited in a legal way." And that, as they say in the law, was that.

## Self-Evident Truths

Although he does not necessarily endorse the position himself, in his book, *Public Goods, Private Goods,* Raymond Geuss of Cambridge University notes that some people have suggested that there ought to be two ways to determine the value of consideration, one for contracts made with private individuals and another for contracts made with the government. Geuss explains it this way: "What is judged to be 'good,' 'right,' 'valuable' (and alternatively, 'bad,' 'wrong,' 'nuisance') in the public sphere is to be evaluated by different standards from what is 'good' in the private sphere. The standards and procedures for justifying a particular course of action or choice, and the audience in whose eyes the justification must be convincing, are often thought to differ depending on whether what is at issue is a 'private' act (e.g., individual purchase of food for one's own consumption) or a public one (procurement of new trains for the municipal underground or new submarines for the navy)." This position sounds remarkably similar to the ethic of responsibility which we discussed in Chapter 1. Recall that the ethic of responsibility demands that the moral actor, in this case a national leader, consider his or her responsibilities to those people who depend on that leader for protection, safety, and sometimes even for their very lives. The ethic of responsibility is the morality of the nation-state and it is not the same as individual morality. The nation-state has a duty that outweighs all other duties and that duty is to promote the civil peace of the nation-state so that the lives its own people remain undisturbed. What this means from the practical perspective of governmental leaders is that, if the military needs a new weapons system to protect its people from a belligerent, aggressive, or suicidal rogue state, then the cost of that weapons system must be evaluated by a process that is divorced from the methods used to determine value in the private sector. In short, national leaders are not permitted to turn down a contract for this weapons system simply because it would "cost too much" in terms of money because doing so would endanger the innocent people they are duty-bound to protect.

## Self-Evident Questions

1. Do you agree or disagree with the premise that two different rules should apply to consideration, based on whether the transaction is private or public? Explain,

2. Regardless of your answer to the first question, which of the two realms, private or public, should be valued higher? Explain.

3. How should this differentiation be determined? Is it up to governmental officials or should private citizens be consulted? Explain.

4. Should there be a different standard for military procurements, such as a weapons system, than for an administrative project, such as a new bridge, dam, highway, or hospital? Explain.

5. What if the cost of doing business includes an illegal action such as bribing the military personnel of a foreign nation to obtain permission for our bombers and fighters to fly through their airspace? Should such illegal payments be sanctioned under the ethic of responsibility? Explain.

See Raymond Geuss, *Public Goods, Private Goods* (Princeton: Princeton University Press, 2001), p. 5. See also Max Weber, "Politics as a Vocation (from Wirtschaft und Gesellschaft)," in *The Great Political Theories: From the French Revolution to Modern Times,* eds. Michael Curtis (New York: Harper, 2008), pp. 426–433.

**Legality of Consideration** Consideration requires that the benefits and sacrifices promised between the parties be legal. Absence of legality renders the consideration invalid. Thus, a party cannot agree to do something that he or she does not have the legal right to do. Similarly, a party cannot promise not to do something that he or she has no legal right to do. Also, a party cannot make valid consideration out of a promise to stop doing something that was illegal to do in the first place.

**quick quiz** 9-1

| | |
|---|---|
| 1. The fact that each party has received a benefit and suffered a detriment means that the consideration has legal value. | true \| false |
| 2. The legal term used to designate the gain that each party experiences is the party's legal benefit. | true \| false |
| 3. Consideration does not require that the benefits and sacrifices promised between the parties be legal. | true \| false |

# 9-2 Types of Consideration

Generally, consideration takes the form of money, property, or services. In certain special kinds of agreements and promises, however, the benefits and sacrifices are in some manner unique and not immediately obvious to the casual observer. Significant among these agreements are promises not to sue and charitable pledges.

## Money as Consideration

Money is so closely connected with global commerce that we forget that it was not always part of the marketplace. The shift from a barter to a cash economy occurred when transporting goods to the market became difficult and hazardous. By the ninth century, the use of cash as a medium of exchange had become prevalent in medieval Europe. This shift to a cash economy was also accelerated by the need for credit. Because goods are perishable and the quality of goods can vary from transaction to transaction, contracts that required future payments were more attractive to merchants when coins rather than goods were involved. Thus, agreements based on credit backed up by coins had become commonplace throughout Europe by the eleventh century, as had the practice of lending coins in exchange for interest. By the thirteenth century, the use of mortgage agreements based on transferring the right to receive all of the cash income from a tract of land had become routine. Today, we are once again in an era of change as we move from a cash/credit economy to one based almost totally on electronic transfers. Nevertheless, when electronic transfers are involved, people still tend to think in terms of cash, even those who have not actually handled coins or currency for some time. For this reason, it is best to always remember that hidden at the foundation of all contracts is the idea of cash equivalency. (See Rodney Stark, *The Victory of Reason: How Christianity Led to Freedom, Capitalism, and Western Success,* New York: Random House, 2005, pp. 60–61.)

## Property and Services as Consideration

Before money in the form of cash was accepted as a medium of exchange, consideration consisted of property and services. Sometimes, even today during recessionary or inflationary cycles, parties find it more beneficial to enter into barter agreements than to base their promises on cash payments. The courts have held that barter agreements contain valid consideration. For example, the exchange of services in return for the use of another's car or a promise to trade a DVD player for a cell phone represent benefits and sacrifices that constitute valid consideration to support a legally binding contract.

**Did You Know?**

Common law judges would rarely entertain arguments regarding the adequacy of consideration, even in unconscionable situations. One exception involved the promise to repay immediately a greater sum of money than that originally transferred. This is what happened in the case of *Schnell v. Nell,* an 1861 case, in which a man promised to pay $600 in return for the loan of one penny.

## Promises Not to Sue

A promise not to sue, when there is the right, or at least the apparent right, to sue, is enforceable when it is supported by consideration. Promising not to sue is a forbearance. A promise not to sue in exchange for an amount of money is a customary way to settle or prevent a pending lawsuit. Settlements of this type often are preferred to expensive and time-consuming litigation. Such settlements are also better than submitting a claim to alternate dispute resolution procedures, such as arbitration or mediation.

### EXAMPLE 9-2: Releases and Promises Not to Sue

Danny Hollinger was injured when a delivery van ran a red light and collided with his vehicle. Hollinger discussed his legal rights with an attorney, who suggested that he might receive compensation from the delivery company if he brought suit against the driver and the company. When faced with the suit, the delivery company's insurance company elected to offer Hollinger $250,000 if he would agree not to bring suit against the company. Hollinger agreed to these terms and signed a release in exchange for the money. The "thing of value" that Hollinger transferred to the insurance company was his right to bring a lawsuit. A court would uphold this agreement on the basis of the promise between the parties.

Acceptance of an agreement not to sue, supported by consideration, terminates one's right to continue any lawsuit, presently or in the future, on grounds described in the agreement. A promise not to sue is commonly called a **release**. Agreements of this kind are usually negotiated and agreed upon before a suit is even filed. However, occasionally they are negotiated between attorneys after a lawsuit has been filed and sometimes even after a trial has begun. In such an event, the settlement is arranged in cooperation with the court and presiding judge. Interestingly enough, some states will uphold a promise not to sue exchanged for consideration, even if circumstances later indicate that the party granting the release did not have the right to sue in the first place, as long as at the time of the agreement, the exchange was made in good faith and fraud was not involved.

## Charitable Pledges

Courts today enforce charitable pledges by applying promissory estoppel and public policy.

Under traditional rules, charitable pledges are not enforceable as contractual obligations because they are not supported by consideration. The dependence of charitable institutions and nonprofit organizations on the solicitation of contributions has encouraged the courts to enforce charitable pledges as though they were contractual obligations. Basically, there are three ways that the courts can seek to uphold charitable pledges. The first way involves actual consideration, which occurs when charitable contributions are made on the condition that the promisor be remembered for the gift by having his or her name inscribed in some way on a memorial associated with the project. Some courts see this promise to install a memorial to the pledgor as consideration.

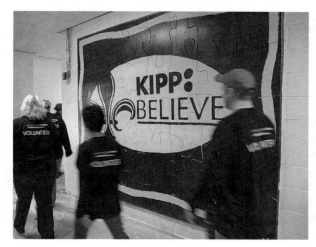

A more contemporary approach is to use either promissory estoppel or public policy to support the claim. Promissory estoppel involves the detrimental reliance on a promise made by another party. If in reliance on a pledge or a series of pledges, a charity goes forward with a project, such as building an addition to the church hall or adding a wing to the synagogue, the courts will see the commencement of the project as evidence that the charity relied on the promises and will stop the promisors from denying the effects of the promise. At times pledges are used for the general operation and maintenance of a charitable or nonprofit organization rather than for a specific project.

When there is no promise to carry out a specific project, the courts have held that each pledge made is supported by the pledges of all others who have made similar pledges. This concept of consideration is used in support of all promises of money for undefined causes. The ultimate argument in this situation is that it would violate public policy to allow one pledgor to get away with denying his or her pledge when the other promisors relied on one another in making their individual pledges.

---

## quick quiz 9-2

1. Today contractual parties never find it beneficial to enter barter agreements.                                                                    true | false

2. If a party promises not to sue another party, and it is later discovered that the first party never really had the right to sue, the original promise not to sue is invalid in every state, and the consideration must be returned.                                    true | false

3. Even though charities depend on the solicitation of contributions, the courts have refused to enforce charitable pledges.                         true | false

---

# 9-3 Problems with Consideration

Problems sometimes arise when the consideration involved in a contract is money and the parties disagree as to the amount of money that the debtor owes the creditor. How such problems are resolved depends on whether the transaction involves a genuine dispute as to the amount owed. One way such disputes can be settled is by an agreement known as accord and satisfaction.

## Disputed Amounts

A **disputed amount** is one on which the parties never reached mutual agreement. It may be difficult at first to see how the amount due under a contract can end up as the focal point of a dispute, until we recall that the law permits a certain degree of incompleteness in the final terms of an agreement, provided there is a way to settle on the eventual amount owed. For instance, when a contractor is hired to do work on a home or an accountant is retained to figure out a client's taxes, the final amount owed is never laid out in absolute terms. Instead, the custom is to settle on an amount per hour, estimate the number of hours that will be spent on the job, and then settle on the final amount once the job is finished.

If a creditor accepts as full payment an amount that is less than the amount due, the dispute has been settled by an **accord and satisfaction**. **Accord** is the implied or expressed acceptance of less than what has been billed the debtor. **Satisfaction** is the agreed-to settlement contained in the accord. Only if the dispute is honest, and the offer to settle made in good faith, and not superficial or trivial will the courts entertain arguments based on accord and satisfaction.

## EXAMPLE 9-3: Accord and Satisfaction in Action

Jon Delaware, a freelance writer of magazine articles and short stories, hired Monica Mather to figure out his income tax for last year. During the initial consultation with Delaware, Mather told him that her rate was $250 per hour. Mather estimated that the job would take 10 to 20 hours of intensive work. (The fact that Delaware turned all of her records over to Mather in a paper bag may have had something to do with this relatively high estimate, even though Mather used a software package to do all her clients' returns.) When Mather completed the work, he sent a bill to Delaware for 20 hours of work at $250 per hour for a total of $5,000. The number of hours included a five-hour seminar that Mather took at the local college. When questioned about this, Mather said that she had attended the seminar to learn how to deal with a problem that had cropped up in Delaware's return in relation to Delaware's royalties. Delaware balked at the added expense for Mather's seminar and subtracted $1,250 from the bill and sent Mather a check for $3,750. Delaware wrote the following notation on the check: "In full payment for all services involved in making out my tax return for last year." Mather cashed the check and later sued Delaware in small claims court for the balance. Mather is doomed. She will lose the suit because she had already accepted a lesser amount, which had been offered by Delaware in good faith, in full payment of the amount in dispute. As an accountant, Mather should have known better.

## Undisputed Amounts

An **undisputed amount** is one on which the parties have mutually agreed. Although a party may have second thoughts about the amount promised for goods or services rendered, the amount that was agreed to by the parties when they made their contract remains an undisputed amount. A part payment in lieu of full payment when accepted by a creditor will not cancel an undisputed debt.

## EXAMPLE 9-4: An Undisguised Undisputed Amount

Bonnie Findley had new shingles placed on the roof of her summer home, agreeing to pay the Rollins Roofing Company $2,625 for parts and labor. A week later, before paying the $2,625, Findley saw the same shingles at the Sandusky Home and Garden Show. She talked to the representative at the show, who told her that he would have been able to sell her the shingles and have them installed for only $2,125. Findley sent a check to Rollins for $2,125 with the notation "In full payment for the shingles applied to the roof of my house at 765 Pine Street in Lakeside." Rollins deposited the check and demanded payment of the balance of $500. Findley would still be obligated to pay that balance. In this situation, there was no good faith dispute over what Findley owed to Rollins.

### quick quiz 9-3

| | | |
|---|---|---|
| 1. A disputed amount is one on which the parties never reached mutual agreement. | true \| false |
| 2. If a creditor accepts as full payment an amount that is less than the amount due, the dispute has been settled by promissory estoppel. | true \| false |
| 3. An undisputed amount is one on which the parties have mutually agreed. | true \| false |

# 9-4 Agreements without Consideration

As a general rule, an agreement without consideration will not be an enforceable contract, because consideration is so important as the binding element within a contractual relationship. Nevertheless, some states eliminate the requirement of consideration in specific types of agreements. In contrast, there are certain promises that the courts always refuse to enforce because they lack even the rudimentary qualities of valid consideration, even though on the surface they may appear to offer that much-needed element.

## Enforceable Agreements

As noted previously, some states have chosen to eliminate the element of consideration in a few specifically named contracts. Unfortunately, as is frequently the case in such matters, there is no uniformity among jurisdictions as to the types of agreements subject to such laws. Still, some typical agreements falling into this category include promises under seal, promises after discharge in bankruptcy, debts barred by the statute of limitations, promises enforced by promissory estoppel, and options governed by the UCC (see Table 9-1).

**Promises under Seal**   A **seal** is a mark or an impression placed on a written contract indicating that the instrument was executed and accepted in a formal manner. Today a seal is usually indicated by the addition of the word "seal" or the letters "L.S." (*locus sigilli*, meaning "place of the seal") following a party's signature. Years ago, contracts under seal required no consideration. Some states still honor a promise under seal, but most have abolished this concept especially in relation to sale of goods contracts. In fact, the UCC has eliminated the use of the seal in all sale of goods contracts. However, a few states still require the use of the seal in real property and certain other types of transactions. Because there is no uniformity in this regard, it is advisable to research and consult the specific requirements in your jurisdiction.

UCC 2-203 (see page 823)

## Table 9-1   Agreements without Consideration

| Agreement | Legal Status |
| --- | --- |
| Promises under seal | Enforceable in some states for contracts not involving goods; unenforceable under the UCC for contracts involving goods |
| Promises after discharge in bankruptcy | Enforceable in most states |
| Promise to pay debts barred by statute of limitations | Enforceable |
| Promises enforced by promissory estoppel | Enforceable only if offeror knew that offeree would rely on the promise and offeree places himself or herself in a different and difficult position as a result of that promise |
| Option | Enforceable under the UCC if made by a merchant, in writing, stating the time period over which the offer will remain open |
| Illusory promises | Unenforceable |
| Promise of a gift | Unenforceable |
| Past considerations | Unenforceable |
| Preexisting duties | Unenforceable as a consideration in a new contract |

**Promises after Discharge in Bankruptcy** Persons discharged from indebtedness through bankruptcy may reaffirm their obligations, prompted perhaps by moral compulsion. In the past, reaffirmation has been the subject of abuse by creditors who used pressure against those whose debts have been excused. In response, Congress passed a bankruptcy reform act that makes it more difficult for creditors to extract such promises. The bankruptcy court must now hold a hearing when a reaffirmation is intended, informing the debtor that reaffirmation is optional, not required, and of the legal consequences of reactivating a debt. It is also up to the court to approve such reaffirmations. State laws, in most cases, provide that no new consideration need be provided in support of reaffirmation. Most states require that a reaffirmation be supported by contractual intent. Some states require the new promise to be in writing. However, when there is no such provision, an oral promise or reaffirmation is usually sufficient.

**Debts Barred by Statutes of Limitations** State laws known as **statutes of limitations** limit the time within which a party is allowed to bring suit. The time allowed for the collection of a debt varies from state to state, usually from three to ten years. Some states allow more time for collection when the document of indebtedness is under seal, as in the case of a promissory note containing the seal of the maker. Debtors may revive and reaffirm debts barred by the statutes of limitations without the necessity of new consideration. Affirmation will result from the part payment of the debt. When a debt is revived, the creditor again is permitted the full term, provided by the statute of limitations, to make collection. Some states require a written reaffirmation when a debt made unenforceable by the statute of limitations is reactivated. Consequently, it would be best to check the rule in your jurisdiction.

**LO9**

**Promises Enforced by Promissory Estoppel** The doctrine of **estoppel** denies rights to complaining parties that are shown to be the cause of their own injury. **Promissory estoppel** is a legal doctrine that restricts a party from denying that a promise was made under certain conditions, even though consideration has not been exchanged to bind an agreement. To be effective, promissory estoppel requires that the party making the promise know, or be presumed to know, that the other party might otherwise make a definite and decided change of position in contemplation of those promises. In reaching this doctrine, courts have accepted the principles of justice and fairness in protecting the party receiving the promise from otherwise unrecoverable losses.

---

## EXAMPLE 9-5: Raymond and Remington and Promissory Estoppel

Rachel Raymond was arrested for a crime she did not commit. Rick Remington, her supervisor at Anwar Enterprises, told her that he had to suspend her. However, he also told her that if she were later found not guilty and released, she would have her old job back with the same seniority and pay grade that she had when she left. Two months later, the charges were dropped, when another person confessed to the crime, and Raymond tried to get her job back. Remington refused to let her return to work. It took Remington six months to secure suitable employment. In a suit brought by Raymond against Anwar to recover the pay she lost during those four months, the court ruled in her favor. Remington and Anwar were stopped from denying the promise they'd made to Raymond despite the absence of consideration from her because she had relied on that promise and had not looked for other work while suspended.

**Option** An **option** is the giving of consideration to support an offeror's promise to hold open an offer for a stated or a reasonable length of time. The UCC has made an exception to the rule requiring consideration when the offer is made by a merchant. In such cases, an offer in writing by a merchant, stating the time period during which the offer will remain open, is enforceable without consideration. The offer, which is called a **firm offer** or an **irrevocable offer**, must be signed by the offeror, and the time allowed for acceptance may not exceed three months. When the time allowed is more than three months, firm offers by merchants must be supported by consideration to be enforceable.

UCC 2-205 (see page 823)

## Unenforceable Agreements

The promises just described are exceptions to the general rule that consideration must support a valid contract. The exceptions are allowed by state statute or because the courts, in the interest of fairness or justice, find it inappropriate to require consideration. There are certain promises, however, that the courts will not enforce because they lack even the rudimentary qualities of valid consideration. Included in this category are promises based on preexisting duties, promises based on past consideration, illusory promises, and promises of future gifts and legacies.

**Preexisting Duties** A promise to do something that one is already obligated to do by law or by some other promise or agreement cannot be made consideration in a new contract. Such obligations are called **preexisting duties**. The same rule of consideration applies to police officers, firefighters, and other public servants and officials who may pledge what appears to be some special service in exchange for a monetary reward, when all they have actually promised is to execute the duties they are already obligated to perform. Suppose, for instance, that the local fire chief, in exchange for a monetary reward, promises an apartment owner that he or she will provide protection should a fire break out in the owner's building. Neither the fire chief nor the apartment owner could enforce such an agreement in court. The promise is based on the chief's empty guarantee to do what is already his or her job.

**Past Consideration** A promise to give another something of value in return for goods or services rendered and delivered in the past, without expectation or reward, is **past consideration**. Only when goods or services are provided as the result of bargained-for present or future promises is an agreement enforceable.

## EXAMPLE 9-6: Past Consideration Is No Consideration

Gale Hansen wanted to have her hair dyed before her college graduation party but could not afford to pay the $120 fee that was expected by the local hairdresser. Without any mention of payment, her friend Marianne Everett helped Hansen dye her hair. After seeing what a good job Everett did on her hair, Hansen told Everett that she'd give her $35 for helping. Hansen's promise to Everett is not enforceable because Everett has already completed the work. Her consideration is therefore in the past.

## A QUESTION OF ETHICS

In Example 9-6, legally Hansen does not have to pay Everett a single penny, despite her promise to do so. However, is she ethically bound to keep her pledge and deliver to Everett the $35 that she promised to give her? Explain.

**Illusory Promises**  An **illusory promise** is one that seems genuine but that on close examination actually fails to obligate the promissor to do anything. A party who makes an illusory promise is the only one with any right to determine whether the other party will benefit in any way. Illusory promises fail to provide the mutuality of promises required in establishing consideration.

**EXAMPLE 9-7:** As Many Illusory Promises as You Might Desire

Pemberton Grocery agreed to buy such fruits and vegetables as it "might desire" for one summer season from Enchanted Farms, Inc. In return for this promise, Enchanted negotiated terms whereby it would give Pemberton a special schedule of discounts for the fruits and vegetables. The promise to buy as much as it "might desire" had actually obligated Pemberton to do nothing. Its promise was illusory because Pemberton might desire absolutely no fruits and vegetables and still keep its promise. The benefits that Pemberton were to derive from the schedule of discounts were not supported by a real or enforceable promise on Pemberton's part. A suit brought by either party to enforce this agreement would fail for want of consideration.

**Future Gifts and Legacies**  The promise of a gift to be given at some future time or in a will is not enforceable if no consideration is given for the promise. Included here are promises to provide gratuitous services or to lend one's property without expectation of any benefits in return.

### quick quiz 9-4

1. An option is the giving of consideration to support an offeror's promise to hold an offer open for a stated length of time.    true | false

2. Although illusory promises provide the mutuality of promises required in establishing consideration, the courts will not enforce them due to the doctrine of unconscionability.    true | false

3. The promise of a gift to be given at some future time or in a will is completely enforceable even if no consideration is given for the promise.    true | false

# 9-5 Cyber-Payment Tactics and Concerns

Cyber-buying and cyber-selling has become second nature to most American consumers. Part of this process involves setting prices that are attractive to the buyer and profitable for the seller. Since the price involved in a contract is a major part of the consideration equation, and since the online marketplace has affected the pricing process, it is appropriate that we pause at this point to consider the legal ramifications of this new approach to the making of a contract. We will examine two aspects of the online pricing process (1) cyber-price and competition and (2) cyber-payments. As these ideas develop, we will also cover several pieces of cyber-legislation.

# Cyber-Price and Competition

Businesses that buy products, supplies, and services from one another have always held an advantage over the average consumer. In the commercial network of market competition, businesses could frequently negotiate with one another over the value of the consideration involved in their contracts. The same was not true of consumers who were generally paralyzed by the price set by the other party. Oddly, this was true whether the offeror was the buyer or the seller. Certainly, there have always been consumers who would comparison shop as they sought the best prices available to them. Most consumers, however, were not that ambitious. The Internet has helped improve the pricing process. Consumers can now use the Internet to seek out competitive prices, thus improving their ability to set the consideration at a level with which they are comfortable.

### Cyber-Price Shopping
Consumers have a wide variety of ways to comparison shop when it comes to establishing consideration in online contracts. Some online cyber-consumers now make regular use of electronic agents, referred to as a *bot* (*robot, shopping bot, cyber-bot or e-bot*) to comb the vast reaches of cyberspace to find the lowest price available on an item or a service. Cyber-consumers must be aware of the legal ramifications of this process. Two model acts that cover this process are the Uniform Computer Information Transactions Act (UCITA) and the Uniform Electronic Transactions Act (UETA).

### Cyber-Shopping Costs
Cyber-shopping is not without its drawbacks. One such drawback involves the danger of hidden costs. One hidden cost is the Internet access fee. Most of the time, however, Internet users can track the number of minutes, or more often the number of megabytes, that they have utilized under the contract so that they can pace their time on the net, and either cut back or renegotiate a new contract with their internet service provider (ISP). Another "hidden" cost comes in the form of shipping and handling fees. Most sellers provide shipping and handling data at the outset or at least as the contract is finalized so that the consumer enters the contract knowing the full value of the consideration paid for the goods purchased on line. Some shippers, however, will over estimate the shipping costs just to make certain that they are not caught paying more for shipping than they are prepared to spend. Buyers should be aware of this unavoidable and often untraceable hidden cost, and be ready to absorb the extra cost if they really want the merchandise.

### Cyber-Shopping and the Law
Cyber-shopping is not without its legal entanglements and its illegal practices. Cyber-buyers and cyber-sellers must both be attuned to the difficulties lying in wait when when the enter the online cyber-commerce arena. Some traditional and reccuring illegal practices, such as discriminatory price-setting and credit card fraud, are still prevalent in cyberspace. Others, such as the bait-and-switch schemes that we discussed in the previous chapter, are almost impossible to detect online until the damage is done. While both buyers and sellers can be targeted, it is the sellers who are especially vulnerable to credit card fraud and identity fraud. This is because it is much easier for buyers to use stolen credit cards and identity information online. To protect consumers, Congress passed the Identity Theft and Assumption Deterrence Act (ITADA). Later, ITADA was amended by the Identity Theft Penalty Enhancement Act (ITPEA), which outlaws the unauthorized transfer, possession, or use of a means of identifying another person to violate federal law. The amendment adds a new crime, called *aggravated identity theft,* to the original statute.

# Cyber-Payments and Cyber-Contracts

Shopping online has many advantages that make it one of the fastest-growing market places on record. Most people shop online because it is quick and efficient. In addition, as noted above, shopping online also permits consumers to compare prices and to settle on the amount of consideration that they can afford. Additionally, some products that are not available in stores, are accessible online. Hard-to-get products available online include out-of-print books, antiques, vintage clothing, rare works of art, hi-fi speaker systems, Polaroid cameras, obsolete auto parts, black and white TV's, rotary dial phones, turntables and vinyl records, out-dated appliances, old license plates, carbon paper, old-fashioned audio tapes, vacuum tubes, pulp magazines, out-of date VHS and Beta cassettes, Golden and Silver Age comics, and other vintage products. Still, despite these advantages online shopping still has many difficulties, not the least of which is selecting a payment method.

### Cyber-Payment Options
Online consumers can choose from several payment methods. One of the most popular methods is by credit card or debit card. It would be very rare today for an online seller to refuse to accept credit or debit card payments. Most online sellers will accept the major credit cards such as Visa, Master Card, Discover, and so on. Many online cyber-sellers also moving toward the use of direct on-line payment systems such as PayPay. This type of system protects both the buyer and the seller. The system is so effective that at some time in the future this may be the only way permissible to buy and sell in cyberspace. This process may become the most acceptable process because most of the time when people buy and sell in cyberspace they are they are dealing with strangers. The issue is especially acute in the cyber-auction industry, involving firms such as eBay. The on-line payment process elimnates (well, almost nearly eliminates) the identity verification problem. This is important because one of the biggest concerns about online shopping is security. Once a buyer and a seller have agreed on consideration, they both want to make certain that the contract is fulfilled as promised.

### Cyber-Payment Security Issues
Consumers who shop online must provide the seller with a means of payment. As we have seen, the most popular method of making payment online is through the use of credit and debit cards. Unfortunately, the ease and efficiency of using such cards is frequently offset by the security concerns associated with their use. Oddly, the United States is not as up-to-date as the European Union in providing data and privacy protection to its consumers. The **EU Data Protection Directive** along with the **EU E-Privacy Directive** guarantee the rights of European citizens while, at the same time, ensuring the smooth exchange of data among those nation-states that honor the privacy and data protection standards themselves. U.S. corporations that are involved with EU corporations must demonstrate that, despite the lack of legislation in the United States, the companies themselves will promise to honor the same degree of protection to data and to privacy as guaranteed by the EU. These guarantees have been labeled the **Safe Harbor Principles**. They are enforced by the U.S. Department of Commerce. Ironically, this means that U.S. consumers who deal with European companies or with U.S. companies that follow the EU standards will have more security protection than those who deal with purely U.S. companies. Unfortunately not all companies who claim to follow the safe harbor provisions actually do so. It is best for a consumer to check directly with the United States Department of Commerce to determine the true status of a company rather than just relying on the company's blanket assertion that they follow the safe harbor standards. Exactly when the United States will officially adopt more protective privacy rights is anybody's guess at the present time.

## quick quiz 9-5

1. The Internet has helped to improve the transparency of the pricing process.                                    true | false

2. Bait and switch are almost impossible to detect online until the damage is done.                                true | false

3. The European Union has provided greater protection for cyber-shoppers than the United States.                   true | false

# Summary

**9.1**  The fifth element necessary to any valid contract is consideration. Consideration is the mutual exchange or promise to exchange benefits and sacrifices between contracting parties. Consideration has three requirements: (1) promises made during bargaining depend on the consideration to be received, (2) the consideration must involve something of value, and (3) the benefits and detriments promised must be legal.

**9.2**  Generally, consideration takes the form of money, property, or services. There are certain special kinds of agreements and promises to which the benefits and sacrifices are unique. Among these are promises not to sue and charitable pledges.

**9.3**  Problems sometimes arise when the consideration involved in a contract is money and the parties do not agree on the amount of money owed. If there is a genuine dispute, a creditor can accept an amount as full payment even though it is less than the amount claimed. Once the creditor has accepted the lesser amount, the dispute is settled by an act of accord and satisfaction. If the dispute is not genuine, accord and satisfaction do not apply.

**9.4**  As a general rule, contracts are not enforceable without consideration. However, some states eliminate the need for consideration in some agreements. These agreements include promises bearing a seal, promises after discharge in bankruptcy, debts barred by the statute of limitations, promises enforced by promissory estoppel, and options governed by the UCC. There are other agreements that seem to involve consideration but that the courts will not enforce. These agreements involve preexisting duties, past consideration, illusory promises, and gifts.

**9.5**  The measurement of consideration has become an issue when consumers buy and sell online. Consumers can comparison shop online using shopping search engines, patronizing user-friendly industries, and shopping with companies that provide price comparison rates on their Web sites. Cyber-shopping hidden costs include Internet access fees and shipping and handling costs. Some illegal practices involved in online shopping include: discriminatory price-setting, credit card fraud, and bait-and-switch schemes. Online consumers can choose from several payment methods including credit cards, debit cards, smart cards, and alternative cyber-payment systems such as PayPal. Privacy protection and security, however, are limited.

# Key Terms

accord, 197

accord and satisfaction, 197

bargained-for exchange, 192

consideration, 191

disputed amount, 197

estoppel, 200

EU Data Protection Directive, 204

EU E-Privacy Directive, 204

firm offer, 201

## Questions for Review and Discussion

1. What is consideration?
2. What are the different types of detriment?
3. What characteristics are necessary for consideration to be valid?
4. What is meant by the term "unconscionable"?
5. Can a promise not to sue be consideration?
6. How can a charitable pledge be consideration?
7. What is the procedure that a debtor and creditor may use to settle a claim by means of accord and satisfaction?
8. What agreements may be enforceable by a court of law even though they lack consideration?
9. What is the doctrine of promissory estoppel?
10. What issues are involved in the cyber-payment process?

## Cases for Analysis

1. Twenty-two congressional representatives proposed a bill that would permit corporate shareholders to review the consideration packages that had been granted to key corporate executives of public corporations. The bill, which was named the Shareholder Vote on Executive Compensation Act, would empower the shareholders of public corporations to evaluate and vote on the appropriateness of the compensation packages that had been granted to the corporation's top five officers. The vote, however, would not obligate the corporation to change the compensation package if the shareholders disapproved of its terms. Would such a bill, if enacted into law, conflict with established contract law principles that permit parties to negotiate their own level of consideration? Explain. See Donna Block, "Proposal Seeks Shareholder OK on Executive Pay," *The National Law Journal,* March 12, 2007, p. 9.

2. Consideration can serve as a strong motivator. At least this is what a newly founded shareholder forum believes. The forum was formed to monitor the salaries of top corporate executives, especially CEOs, by matching those salaries with the executive's incentive package, which includes the corporation's latest list of objectives and the number or the percentage of those objectives that the executive must meet to receive incentive pay. The goal of incentive pay is to motivate top executives to do more than sit in the CEO's office from 9:00 to 5:00 each day. Is incentive pay a violation of the principle that says that preexisting duties cannot be used as consideration in a new contract? Explain. See Gretchen Morgenson, "Hear Ye, Hear Ye: Coralling Executive Pay," *The New York Times,* June 17, 2007, sec 3, pp. 1 and 8.

3. General Motors decided to move a car producing operation to Arlington, Texas, from a plant located in Ypsilanti, Michigan. As a result, the township of Ypsilanti brought a lawsuit to stop General Motors from making the move. Ypsilanti argued that GM had promised to keep the plant in Ypsilanti in exchange for certain tax privileges. The township argued further that it had relied on those promises when it granted that tax abatement to the corporation. Therefore, GM should be forced to keep its promise to maintain the Ypsilanti plant. Should the court stop this move based on the doctrine of promissory estoppel? Explain. *Charter Township of Ypsilanti v.*

*General Motors,* 508 N.W.2d 556 (Michigan Court of Appeals).

4. Aviation Electronics entered a contract with Sky Train Institute of Montana in which Aviation agreed to supply the institute with 17,000 component parts for the development of the institute's remote control bomber. The bomber had to be operational by December 3; otherwise, the institute would lose a research grant from the Department of Defense. After delivering 5,000 parts, Aviation told Sky Train that it wanted an additional $4 million beyond the original price agreed upon to deliver the remaining parts. Sky Train attempted to obtain the parts from other firms, none of which could fill the order in the time limit required by the DOD contract specifications. To make the deadline stipulated in the government contract, Sky Train reluctantly agreed to the new price demanded by Aviation. What "thing of value," if any, has Aviation transferred to the institute that it did not already owe the institute under the original contract? Explain.

5. Savaretti offered to pay his niece, Wilma, $2,000 if she would agree to give up eating meat and pastries and drinking caffeinated beverages for six months. Wilma agreed and gave up these activities for six months. At the end of those six months, Savaretti refused to give Wilma the $2,000, arguing that because giving up caffeine, meat, and pastries was beneficial to her health, she suffered no detriment and was owed nothing. Wilma took Savaretti to small claims court and demanded payment of the $2,000. She argued that because she had the legal right to consume the caffeine, meat, and pastries, she suffered a legal detriment and was entitled to her money. How should the referee rule in this case? Explain.

6. Daniel Davidson told Velma Evans that he would hire her to work on an architectural job. He gave her a date to show up for work and told her to leave her present job. Relying on Davidson's statements, Evans left her job. Davidson never let Evans begin work, and as a result, she was out of work for six months. Evans sued Davidson for the wages she lost during those six months. Davidson argued that because they'd never decided on the final terms of employment, no contract ever existed between the two of

them. Evans argued that the principle of promissory estoppel should apply here. Is Evans correct? Explain.

7. Mers was arrested and charged with a felony. Dispatch Printing, his employer, told him that he had to be suspended. However, Mers was also told that he could return to work if the case against him was resolved in his favor. Relying on this promise, Mers did not seek other employment. The case ended in a hung jury, and Mers reported back to work. Dispatch Printing, however, refused to let him work or pay him any back pay. In a suit against Dispatch Printing, what legal argument might Mers use to compel Dispatch Printing to pay him for any losses due to his reliance on the promise to let him return to work when the case ended in his favor? Explain. *Mers v. Dispatch Printing,* 483 N.E.2d 150 (OH).

8. The Mighty Fine Food Emporium agreed to buy such fruits and vegetables as it "might desire" for one summer season from Kennelsworth Farms and Vineyards. In return for this promise, Kennelsworth negotiated terms whereby it would give Mighty Fine a special schedule of discounts for the fruits and vegetables. Did the promise to buy as much as it "might desire" obligate Kennelsworth in any way? Are the benefits that Kennelsworth was to derive from the schedule of discounts supported by an enforceable promise on Kennelsworth's part? Would a suit brought by either party to enforce this agreement succeed? Explain each answer.

9. Graham O'Hanlon, without any mention of payment, helped his friend, Patricia Tippon, move from Westerville to Pepper Pike. The entire move took 48 hours to complete. At the end of the day, after she was in her new house, Tippon told O'Hanlon that she'd give him $200 for helping her move. Is Tippon's promise to O'Hanlon enforceable? Why or why not?

10. Vanoni Biological Supplies, Inc., contracted with the Hayden Institute to supply the Institute with 24,000 biological specimens for a series of experiments that the Institute has agreed to perform for the Maritime University of Columbia. The Institute must have the specimens by September 9 to meet the University's schedule. After delivering 12,000 of the specimens,

Vanoni told the Institute that it wanted an additional $1,600 to deliver the remaining 12,000 specimens. Can Vanoni make the delivery of the remaining 12,000 specimens consideration in a new agreement with the Institute? Explain.

11. Seier agreed to pay $10,000 to Peek in exchange for all the stock in a corporation. The agreement was placed in writing. Nevertheless, when the time came for payment, Seier refused to live up to his end of the deal. His argument was that the stock was not worth the $10,000 that he had agreed to pay for it. Did the court listen to Seier's argument and attempt to determine the value of the consideration? Explain. *Seier v. Peek*, 456 So.2d 1079 (AL).

12. N.B. West Contracting Co., Inc., agreed to repave Koedding's parking lot. When the repaving work was done, Koedding was unsatisfied with the quality of the work. Consequently, he informed West of his intention to bring suit. West told Koedding that the lot would be resealed and that the job would be guaranteed for two years if Koedding agreed not to pursue the lawsuit, which had already commenced. Koedding agreed. After the repaving was completed a second time, Koedding was still not satisfied. Would the agreement not to sue stop Koedding's lawsuit? Explain. *Koedding v. N.B. West Contracting Co., Inc.*, 596 S.W.2d 744 (MO).

13. Evans used his credit card to run up a $98.75 bill with the Rosen Department Store. When Rosen tried to collect, Evans wrote a check for $79.00. He wrote on the check that he meant it to be "full payment of all accounts to date." Rosen cashed the check. When Rosen sued Evans for $19.75 balance, Evans argued that under accord and satisfaction, the fact that Rosen cashed the $79.00 check meant that it had accepted that amount as full payment. Was Evans correct? Explain.

14. Jill Anderson agreed to purchase William and Teresa Dawson's flower shop for $75,000. Anderson paid the Dawsons $20,000 when the contract was signed. She also agreed to pay the balance of $55,000 at an interest rate of 8.5 percent per year for five years. This agreement meant that she would be making monthly installments of $1,128.41 to the Dawsons. During the negotiation stages of the contract, Anderson was told that all of the equipment in the store was in perfect condition. Moreover, the Dawsons told Anderson that she could expect a profit of $75,000 per year. Anderson discovered that the equipment needed extensive repairs and that the financial condition of the business had been misrepresented so that she made considerably less than the $75,000 that the Dawsons had cited. Accordingly, Anderson sent a check to the Dawsons for $6,560.21. On the reverse side of the check she wrote, "Payment in full for University Flower Shop." This final check would mean that after making installment payments for more than a year and a half, she had paid a total of $50,000 for the flower shop. In a letter that accompanied the check, Anderson indicated that because she had been misled by the Dawsons about the condition of the equipment and the financial state of the business, the store had actually been worth only $50,000 at the time she purchased it. The Dawsons disagreed but deposited the check and then brought suit against Anderson for breach of contract. Anderson argued that when the Dawsons negotiated her check, the debt was discharged under accord and satisfaction. Is Anderson correct here? Explain. *Dawson v. Anderson*, 698 N.E.2d 1014 (OH).

15. Tim W. Koerner and Associates, Inc., was a distributor for electrosurgical products for Aspen Labs, Inc. Zimmer U.S.A., Inc., purchased Aspen and replaced Aspen's distribution system with its own. Aspen remained in business as a subsidiary. Koerner sued Aspen and Zimmer, joined as defendants, trying to force them to honor a contract that Aspen and Zimmer had made compensating former Aspen dealers for their past efforts. Zimmer refused to honor the agreement. For whom did the court find and why? *Tim W. Koerner & Assocs., Inc. v. Aspen Labs, Inc.*, 492 F. Supp. 294 (S.W. TX).

16. Trisko purchased a loveseat from the Vignola Furniture Company. The loveseat arrived at Trisko's home in a damaged condition. Vignola agreed to repair the loveseat if Trisko agreed not to sue. Trisko agreed but then later brought suit. Vignola argued that Trisko could not bring suit because he had promised not to sue them in exchange for the repair of the loveseat. Trisko

argued that Vignola had a preexisting duty to deliver an undamaged love-seat. This preexisting duty could not therefore be consideration in a new agreement. Was Trisko correct? Explain. *Trisko v. Vignola Furniture Company,* 299 N.E.2d 421 (IL).

**quick quiz** Answers

| 9-1 | 9-2 | 9-3 | 9-4 |
|-----|-----|-----|-----|
| 1. F | 1. F | 1. T | 1. T |
| 2. T | 2. F | 2. F | 2. F |
| 3. T | 3. F | 3. T | 3. F |

# Chapter 10

# Capacity and Legality: The Final Elements

## THE OPENING CASE — Public Policy, Statutory Law, and Contract Validity: *R.R. v. M.H. & Another*

New England Surrogate Parenting Advisors (NESPA) is a nonprofit organization the purpose of which is to match potential surrogate mothers with couples who are unable to have children of their own. In this case, a surrogate mother candidate was matched up with a couple who wanted to have a baby but could not do so on their own. The couple and the surrogate mother entered an agreement that stipulated that the father would pay for all pregnancy expenses plus a $10,000 fee to the mother for "conceiving, carrying and giving birth to the child." The fee was to be transferred to the surrogate mother in installments based on a structured payment plan. The final $3,500 was to be paid to the surrogate mother when the child was born. All three parties to the agreement—the surrogate mother, the father, and the father's wife—underwent psychological screening by a psychologist. The psychologist reported that the surrogate mother was a stable, considerate, and knowledgeable woman who was aware of what she was doing and would be emotionally and psychologically capable of transferring custody to the child's biological father. For a while everything went according to the contract. The surrogate mother conceived a child by the father. The first two payments were sent and accepted by the mother. However, at the end of the sixth month, after receiving the third payment, the

mother changed her mind, returned that third payment, and told the father's attorney that the contract was ended. That was the only money returned. She kept the first two payments and the expense money she had received under the agreement. The father sued for custody, arguing that the surrogate mother had breached the contract. The judge agreed and transferred custody to the father based on the contract and because she believed such a move would ultimately be in the child's best interests. The surrogate mother appealed. The state supreme judicial court noted that, since the state had no statute covering this type of agreement, it would apply an adoption statute that was roughly analogous to the situation. Under that statute, a mother could not give up her child for adoption until four days after the child's birth. The statute also outlawed the payment of money to the mother for an adoption, although she could be paid pregnancy expenses. If the court applies this statute to this case, the contract is illegal and, therefore, void. Can the court apply an adoption statute to a contract claim? If so, should the court apply that statute in this case? Moreover, if it does apply the statute, what is the net effect of that application in this case? In other words, who wins? (See *R.R. v. M.H. and Another,* 426 N.E.2d 790 (Supreme Court of Massachusetts).)

**Opening Case Questions**

1. Can the judge apply adoption law to a contract case or should she confine her ruling to contract law? Explain

2. Sometimes a judge will apply the public policy doctrine in this type of a case. What is public policy? Explain.

3. Does public policy apply here? Explain. If public policy applies, what would the result be? Explain.

4. Could the surrogate mother argue that the contract is void because she was suffering from a mental impairment when she entered the agreement? If so, would she win? Why or why not?

5. Should the court consider the best interests of the child in a contract case like this? Explain.

## LO Learning Objectives

1. Identify the age of minority and the age of majority.
2. Explain the legal status of a contract made by a minor.
3. Differentiate between ratification and disaffirmance.
4. Identify the effects of mental impairment on a contract.
5. Discuss the contractual capacity of a drugged or intoxicated person.
6. Explain the legality of agreements to commit torts and crimes.
7. Identify those agreements made illegal under statutory law.
8. Enumerate those agreements contrary to public policy.
9. Explain what happens under the doctrine of *in pari delicto*.
10. Explain the effects of illegality.

# 10-1 The Final Elements

The final two elements of a contract are capacity and legality. A contract can have a valid offer, an effective acceptance, mutual assent, valid consideration, and still be void if it involves doing something illegal. An **illegal agreement** is one that violates criminal law or tort law, a statute, and/or public policy as established by the court. In general, the law will aid neither party involved in an illegal agreement. **Capacity** is the legal ability to enter a valid contract. Generally, a person has the ability to enter a contract if he or she possesses free will, displays a certain degree of self-knowledge and is informed about the nature, purpose, and effect of the agreement. The chapter here is designed to first explore the various factors that affect capacity and then the take a look at what makes a contract illegal and what happens as a result of that illegality.

Minors are able to rescind most contracts. However, adults that contract with minors generally cannot.

## The Nature of Capacity and Minority

Capacity is considered to be a **rebuttable presumption**; that is, a defending party has the right to attack that presumption to rescind the contract. Under the current state of the law, for instance, contracts entered by minors are voidable by the minor. The law allows minors the privilege to **disaffirm** (negate) a contract to protect them from unscrupulous adults (or unscrupulous minors for that matter) who might take advantage of the young people who might not fully comprehend the responsibilities that they are assuming. When a minor indicates by a statement or act an intent not to live up to a contract, that minor is entitled to a return of everything given to the other party. This right exists even when the property transferred to the minor under the contract has been damaged or destroyed. A few states will deduct something from the amount due back to the minor if the goods are damaged. Most states, however, deduct nothing.

**Definition of Minority**   Under common law, minority, was a term that described persons who had not yet reached the age of 21 years. Upon reaching that age, a person was said to have reached majority. Ratification and adoption of the Twenty-Sixth Amendment to the U.S. Constitution in 1971 lowered the voting age in federal elections from 21 to 18 years. To avoid the confusion that would result from having two voting ages, the states started to enact new laws that enabled 18-year-olds to vote in state and local elections. Then states began to lower the age of majority to 18 years for certain types of contracts. Still, there are other age requirements that differ from state to state in relation to matters such as the legal ability to purchase alcoholic beverages, enter a marriage, buy tobacco products, purchase firearms, and operate motor vehicles. Recently, for instance, in response to outside influences from a variety of social organizations and governmental institutions, many states have raised the legal age for purchasing and consuming alcohol to 21 years.

U.S. Const. Amendment 26 (see page 953).

**Emancipation and Abandonment**   In some jurisdictions, minors who become emancipated, that is, no longer under the control of their parents, are responsible for their contracts. This responsibility means that they cannot void a contract, despite their apparent minority. Emancipated minors include those who are married, those in the armed forces, and those who leave home and, in the process, give up all right to parental support. In certain states, minors are even allowed to ask the court for a legally sanctioned emancipation. In all these cases, emancipated minor are said to have abandoned the usual protective shield given them. Although minors in these categories are no longer protected from liability on their contracts, merchants are still reluctant to deal with them on a credit basis, fearing that they may still attempt to disaffirm, or repudiate, their contracted debts. Again, for practical, not legal, reasons, merchants often require that minors get the signature of a responsible adult who will agree to guarantee payment of money owed.

Moreover, the hesitancy felt by some merchants in relation to emancipated minors is justified because a few states still hold to the opposite rule, that is, that emancipated minors do not give up the legal advantages associated with minority simply because they leave home or become married. To support this position, the courts in these jurisdictions note that the rule that allows minors to rescind contracts is based on the idea that minors are less experienced and less knowledgeable than adults about the consequences of their actions. It is therefore difficult to see why getting married or leaving home somehow bestows more common sense on a minor who does so. In fact, one court remarked that getting married and leaving home may actually indicate that a minor has less good sense than another minor who does neither. Because this rule differs from state to state, it would be a good idea to check on the rule of law in your jurisdiction.

**Misrepresentation of Age**   Minors sometimes lie about their age when making a contract. Despite this misrepresentation of age, most states will allow the minor to disaffirm or get out of the contract. Some jurisdictions, however, do not permit the minor to get away with the lie. Some states require the minor to place the adult party to the contract in the same situation that he or she was in before the contract. Others allow the adult to use tort law, rather than contract law, to sue the minor for fraud. Some states have also enacted statutes that allow recovery against a minor who is engaged in business and who misrepresents his or her age in a commercial contract. A number of states, for example, have statutes that deny disaffirmance if the minor has signed a written statement falsely asserting adult status. Without such a statute, the minor would be allowed to get out of the primary contract despite her or his signature on that primary contract or the contract asserting adult status.

## Contractual Capacity of Minors

Executory contracts, those that have not been fully performed by both parties, may be repudiated by a minor at any time. A promise to deliver goods or render services at some future time need not be carried out by the minor who decides not to do so. This privilege is not available to an adult who contracts with a minor. If goods delivered to a repudiating minor are still in the minor's possession, it is the minor's duty to return them to the other party.

### EXAMPLE 10-1: Cancellation of an Executory Contract

Gina Scott, who was 16 years old, purchased a new flat screen TV from the Planetary Electronics Supply Store. Scott paid $50 down and agreed to pay the balance in six monthly installments. Two weeks later, after she had used the TV, Scott decided she didn't want it any longer. When Planetary refused to take back the computer, Scott sued the company in small claims court for the return of her down payment and the cancellation of the balance she still owed. In most states, Planetary would be required to make the refund and cancel the debt. Scott would have to return the computer.

**Contracts for Necessaries** Goods and services that are essential to a minor's health and welfare are called **necessaries**. Thus, necessaries can include clothing, food, shelter, medical and dental services, tools and equipment needed for the minor to carry out his or her business, and even, in some cases, educational expenses. If a minor makes a contract for necessaries, he or she will be liable for the fair value of those necessaries. Despite the general tenor of this principle, if the necessaries have already been provided to the minor by parents or others, the rule does not apply. In addition, not everything that a party claims as a necessary will actually be a necessary. To determine whether goods and services qualify as genuine necessaries, the court will inquire into the minor's family status, financial strength, and social standing or station in life. Necessaries, then, are not the same to all persons.

**Did You Know?**

Despite being designated as "necessaries," such things are not always needed to preserve or protect life. In fact, in one case the court held that funeral expenses were necessaries.

### EXAMPLE 10-2: Necessaries as an Exception to the Rule

Rachel Kennedy had lived in Hawaii her entire life. Because she had "skipped" third and fifth grades, she was 16 when she entered college. The college she attended was in Buffalo, New York. She had never owned a winter coat, so she purchased one in October from the Jacob Brothers Department Store, while she was still 16. This coat would be a necessary, and any attempt to repudiate the purchase would probably fail.

Technically, a minor's contract covering necessaries is not enforceable against the minor in the truest sense of the term. Instead, the minor is required to pay the fair value of the necessaries that have been provided by the adult. The fair value is determined by the court.

This approach to the law is an extension of the concept of quasi-contract. Remember that when applying the concept of quasi-contract, the court will require the parties to act as if there were a contract, even though a true contract does not exist. The point of requiring the minor to pay the fair value of the item is to play it straight with adults who carry the risk of dealing with minors in relation to necessaries. Allowing the minor to get away with completely rescinding such contracts would amount to unfair enrichment of the minor. The concept of quasi-contract is aimed at preventing this type of unjust enrichment.

There is an interesting corollary related to the concept of necessaries that many people, including minors and the adults who deal with them, overlook. This corollary is the standard that states that the rules related to necessaries apply only to executed contracts. An executed contract is one whose terms have been completely and satisfactorily carried out by both parties. In contrast, an executory contract is one that has not yet been fully performed by the parties. Wholly executory contracts calling for a future delivery or rendering of services may be repudiated by the minor. Thus, in the foregoing example, had Kennedy's coat been ordered but not delivered or paid for, she could have repudiated her agreement with no damages or monetary loss being assessed against her.

Technically, parents are liable for a contract executed by a minor, even a contract for necessaries, *only* when they cosign the agreements. When a parent, or anyone else for that matter, cosigns for a loan or for a contract involving installment payments, the cosigner becomes a guarantor. A guarantor promises to pay the other party's debts if that party does not settle those debts personally. This promise is known as a guaranty of payment. In contrast, if parents do not cosign a contract, they are *not liable* for that contract, even though the contract was made by their minor child. As might be expected, there is an exception to this general rule. If a parent has neglected or deserted the minor, the parent may be held liable to a third person for the fair value of the necessaries supplied by the third party to the minor.

**Other Contracts not Voidable**   By statute and court decision, certain other types of contracts have been excepted from the general rule that the contracts of minors are voidable at the minor's option. For public policy reasons, minors may not at their option disaffirm a valid marriage or repudiate an enlistment contract in the armed forces based on a claim of incapacity to contract. Neither may a minor repudiate a contract for goods and services required by law; for example, minors may not repudiate payments for inoculations and vaccinations required for attendance at a university or college or required in securing a visa for travel in certain foreign lands. They may also be prevented from terminating contracts with banks and other financial institutions for educational loans. Some states bar minors from repudiating agency contracts and insurance contracts. Others prevent them from voiding contracts for psychological care, pregnancy care, the transfer of stocks and bonds, and contracts involving child support. These exceptions are state-by-state issues, so it is wise to check your own state statutes to determine which of these contracts are not voidable by minors in your jurisdiction.

### About the Law

Under the Napoleonic Code, people under 30 years of age could not marry without their father's permission. In addition, a father could have his child incarcerated for as long as six months on his word alone.

**Shield or Sword Doctrine**   If tempted to see the rescission rights of minors as unfair, we must keep in mind the original intent of the court in granting this power. As noted previously, the right to rescind contracts was given to minors as a protective device or "shield" against those unscrupulous adults who might try to take unfair advantage of the immaturity and inexperience of minors. This type of situation is precisely what the law envisioned when it granted minors the "shield" that allows them to rescind contracts.

The problem with this protective device is that it can be exploited by minors who use it to rescind legitimate contracts. In effect, an unprincipled minor can take this safeguard, which is meant as a protective shield, and transform it into a sword that violates the rights of the other party. Fortunately, the courts are not oblivious to this type of abuse. Because the doctrine was never meant to allow minors to take advantage of innocent people, the courts have no difficulty denying rescission rights to minors when they use it as a weapon against another contracting party.

---

### EXAMPLE 10-3: The Shield and Sword Doctrine

Amber Sampson, who was 16 years of age, purchased a round-trip ticket on New England Airlines for a trip from Portland, Maine, to San Diego, California, for spring break. When spring break was over, Sampson returned to Portland and, on arrival, demanded the return of all the money that she had paid for the round-trip ticket. Her demands were based on her rescission rights as a minor. Clearly, Sampson was using her right to rescind to take advantage of New England Airlines. She was not using her rights as a minor as a protective shield, as the law intended. It is doubtful that Sampson will be permitted to recover money for her ticket.

---

**Voidable Contracts and Innocent Third Parties**   Another curb on a minor's right to rescind contracts appears in the provisions of the UCC. These provisions protect the rights of an innocent third party who purchases goods from an individual who originally purchased those same goods from a minor. Although individuals who buy goods from minors have voidable ownership rights, under the UCC, those same individuals can transfer valid ownership rights to an innocent third-party purchaser of those goods. Thus, rescission by a minor will not require the innocent purchaser to return the goods.

---

### EXAMPLE 10-4: Protecting the Innocent

David Wittmer, age 17 years, sold his laptop to Lustbader Electronics, LLC. Lustbader refurbished the ancient laptop and then sold it to Alex Myers, an innocent third-party buyer. Before Wittmer became an adult, he decided to get back his laptop from Myers by disaffirming his contract with Lustbader. Wittmer is out of luck here. He will not be able to recover the laptop by disaffirming his contract with Lustbader. Myers is an innocent third party and is thus protected by the UCC.

---

The UCC rule refers to the sale of personal property. In cases in which a minor has sold real estate to one who subsequently sells it to an innocent third party, the minor, on reaching adulthood, may disaffirm the sale and recover the real property.

**Ratification and Disaffirmance**   People may ratify their contracts made during minority only after reaching their majority or within a reasonable time thereafter. Ratification or affirmance is the willingness to abide by contractual obligations. It may be implied by using the item purchased, making an installment payment, paying off the balance of money owed on a previously voidable contract, continuing to accept goods and services being provided under a contract, or just doing nothing about the contract after reaching majority. Affirmation may also result from the person's oral or written declaration to abide by the contract. These acts, as well as others, ratify an existing agreement and elevate it to the status of one that is enforceable against an adult.

An individual may disaffirm an agreement made during minority before or within a reasonable time after reaching adulthood. The exact period of time will vary depending on the nature of the contract and on applicable state and local laws. Failure to disaffirm within a reasonable period of time would imply that the contract had been ratified. The method of disaffirmance is fundamentally the same as the method of ratification. Disaffirmance may be implied by the acts of the individual after achieving majority, such as by a failure to make an installment payment. Similarly, an oral or written declaration of disaffirmance would achieve the same end. In general, there are no particular protocols attached to the act of disaffirmance by a minor. However, it is generally a good idea to make the disaffirmance in writing so that there is a record of the transaction should questions arise at a later time. This recommendation is especially true if the contract is disaffirmed after the minor has reached the age of majority.

## quick quiz 10-1

1. Executory contracts, those which have not been fully performed by both parties, may be repudiated by a minor at any time.   true | false

2. Ratification is the willingness to abide by contractual obligations.   true | false

3. Necessaries are the same for all persons.   true | false

# 10-2 Other Capacity Problems

Persons deprived of the mental ability to comprehend contractual obligations have the right to disaffirm their contracts. Their rights are, in many respects, the same as the rights of minors. Agreements of mentally impaired persons are valid, voidable, or void, depending on the seriousness of their disability and whether they have been declared insane.

## Persons Mentally Impaired

Under the orthodox rule of competency in contract law, a contract made by a person who is mentally infirm, has brain damage, is suffering from a physical illness such as Alzheimer's disease, or suffers from a psychological disorder may be voidable if the person's impairment is severe enough to rob that person of the ability to understand the nature, purpose, and effect of that contract. The question will be whether the mental problem existed at the time the contract was made and was so serious that the person did not understand the nature of the contract. If that is the case, the mentally impaired person may disaffirm any contract made under the influence of that mental impairment. The incompetent person must return all consideration received. This rule is true especially when the other party had no knowledge of the person's mental impairment. If, however, the other party knew about the person's mental impairment and took advantage of that knowledge, there is no requirement to return the other party to the identical place that he or she was in before the original agreement was established.

A second rule is also recognized by the Restatement of Contracts and by some states. That rule says that a person's contractual obligations may be voidable if that person suffers from a mental impairment that prevents him or her from acting in a reasonable manner. Under this version of the rule, a person may understand the nature of the contract but, because of his or her impairment, be unable to stop himself or herself from entering the contract. In such a situation, as long as the contract has yet to be executed or, if executed,

## THE OPENING CASE *Revisited, Part I*
### Public Policy, Statutory Law, and Contract Validity: *R.R. v. M.H. & Another,* Round 2

Recall that in the Opening Case at the beginning of this chapter a married couple and a surrogate mother entered an agreement that stipulated that the father would pay for all pregnancy expenses plus a $10,000 fee to the mother for "conceiving, carrying and giving birth to the child." The fee was to be transferred to the surrogate mother in installments based on a structured payment plan. As part of the screening process, the surrogate mother, the father and the father's wife each underwent a psychological session orchestrated by a psychologist. The psychologist reported that the surrogate mother was a stable, reasonable, and knowledgeable woman who was aware of what she was doing and would be emotionally and psychologically capable of transferring custody to the child's biological father.

For a while everything went according to the contract. However, at the end of the sixth month, after receiving the third payment, the mother changed her mind, returned that third payment, and told the father's attorney that the contract was ended. That was the only money returned. She kept the first two payments and the expense money she had received under the agreement.

If the surrogate mother defended her decision to rescind the contract by saying that she lacked capacity due to a mental impairment, she would have difficulty making her case. The first standard would require her to demonstrate that the mental impairment prevented her from truly appreciating the nature the purpose and the effect of the agreement. This would be unlikely to happen given the psychologist's report. If the state adhered to the second standard her chances would be a bit better. That standard would require her to demonstrate that the mental impairment prevented her from acting in a reasonable manner. Still, even using this standard, she would have to counteract the psychologist's report that stated she was a stable, considerate, and knowledgeable woman. In either case, she would be required to return all of the money that she received from the couple.

can be shown to be very unjust, the impaired person may void the contract. If the contract is executed or fair, the impaired party may still void the contract but also must return the other party to the place he or she was in before the contract was entered. If returning the other party to his or her precontract condition cannot be done, the court will decide on a fair alternative.

A person declared to be insane by competent legal authority is denied the right to enter contracts. Such persons will be under the care of a guardian who acts on behalf of the impaired person, who has in effect become a ward of the court. Any contractual relationship with others results is nothing more than a void agreement. In most states, persons who knowingly take advantage of one declared insane are subject to criminal indictment and prosecution.

## Persons Drugged or Intoxicated

A contract agreed to by someone under the influence of alcohol or drugs may be voidable. Incompetence related to either alcohol or drugs must be of such a degree that a contracting party would have lost the ability to comprehend or be aware of obligations being accepted under the contract. A person who enters into a contract while in this condition may either affirm or disaffirm the agreement at a later time. Disaffirmance in such cases requires the return to the other party of all consideration that had been received. However, such a return may be refused when evidence indicates that the other party took advantage of the person's drunken or otherwise weakened condition.

## EXAMPLE 10-5: Involuntary Intoxication Invalidates a Contract

Samuel K. Richardson III attended a reception at the Yakuza Gallery on Madison Avenue at 75th Street in Manhattan. Unknown to Richardson, the punch at the reception had been laced with alcohol. After drinking several glasses, Richardson became highly intoxicated. While intoxicated, he agreed to sell the original manuscript of the novel, *The Bay Tree,* to an antiquarian book dealer named Maynard Posner, who was also at the reception and who was quite sure that Richardson was "tipsy" at the time of the sale. When Richardson recovered, he sought to disaffirm the contract. Because his involuntary state of intoxication had robbed Richardson of his ability to comprehend the contract he was making with Posner, he would be allowed to get out of the agreement.

### quick quiz 10-2

1. For a contract to be voidable by a person with a mental impairment, the mental problem must exist at the time the contract was made.    true | false

2. A person declared to be insane by competent legal authority cannot be denied the right to enter contracts.    true | false

3. A contract made by a person who is intoxicated is completely void.    true | false

# 10-3 Agreements to Engage in Unlawful Activity

The final element of a valid contract is legality. Ordinarily, the court will leave the parties to an illegal agreement where they placed themselves. If an illegal agreement is still executory, the court will not order it performed or award damages for breach of contract. If the illegal agreement has been executed, the court will not award damages or assist in having it annulled. The most obvious type of illegal contract is one in which parties agree to perform some sort of unlawful activity. This activity could be a crime or a tort, depending on the circumstances. However, when we use the term "unlawful activity" in this context, we are referring to activities that are clearly wrong in and of themselves. These unlawful activities include crimes and torts that most people would recognize as wrong, even if there were no statute, regulation, or court decision to tell them it was wrong.

## Agreements to Commit Torts and Crimes

The law will not uphold any contract that obligates one of the parties to commit a tort. For example, a network television reporter who agrees to defame several politicians in return for a position as their opponent's press secretary would find no remedy in the law should her benefactor fail to follow through after the libelous story was printed. The agreement to commit a tort would be void in the eyes of the law. This approach only makes good sense. The law cannot lend its approval to a contract that breaks the law, no matter how complete it is in relation to the other five elements.

In like manner, the law cannot honor any agreement if the purpose of the agreement is to commit a crime. If, for example, a storekeeper would pay a known criminal to vandalize the shop of a competitor, that storekeeper would not be able to sue the criminal for breach of contract should the criminal take the money and run. As strange as it may seem, the nature of criminality is not always as clear as might be imagined. Because criminal law involves serious offenses that can result in the loss of a person's freedom or, more seriously, the loss of a person's life, all criminal statutes must be drawn as precisely and as clearly as possible. A statute that is obscure or outlines conduct that is ambiguous may be struck down by the court as void for vagueness. This ruling would mean that a contract that involves the conduct that is allegedly outlawed by a vague statute might not be void.

## Agreements Illegal under Statutory Law

Most people of good faith would know, even in the absence of any statute, regulation, ordinance, rule, or court decision, that the behavior outlined in the previous examples would be wrong. It is difficult to imagine, for instance, that the shopkeeper would be surprised to discover that it is wrong to hire someone to destroy his competitor's property. Similarly, it is not easy to believe that the television reporter who agreed to lie in a television broadcast thought that her behavior was in any way admirable. In contrast, some activities that do not seem wrong on the surface may have been made wrong by specific statutory enactments. Therefore, the fact that some of these activities are illegal may catch us by surprise. For example, the shopkeeper knows vandalism is illegal but may be confused to learn that he cannot hold a garage sale without a license. Or the reporter who knows that libel is wrong may be amazed to learn that her Wednesday evening poker game is not legal. For this reason, we will examine those activities that are wrong because a statute says they are wrong. These activities include usurious agreements, wagering agreements, unlicensed agreements, unconscionable agreements, and Sunday (Sabbath) agreements.

**Usurious Agreements**  The illegal practice of charging more than the amount of interest allowed by law is called **usury**. To protect borrowers from excessive interest charges, each state has passed laws that specify the rate of interest that may be charged in lending money. These interest rates vary from state to state. Agreements to charge more than is allowed by law are illegal. Special statutes, however, allow small loan companies, pawn shops, and other lending agencies that accept high-risk applicants for credit to charge a higher rate of interest.

**Wagering Agreements**  Any agreement or promise concerning a wager or some other form of gambling is invalid and may not be enforced. States make exceptions when bets are placed in accordance with laws that permit horse racing, state lotteries, church related or charitable games of bingo, and gambling casinos regulated by state authority. However, even in states in which gambling is legal, borrowing money to gamble it is frequently still illegal.

**Unlicensed Agreements**  Certain businesses and professions must be licensed before they are allowed to operate legally. One reason for requiring a license is to provide a source of revenue, part of which is used to supervise the business or profession being licensed. A city ordinance requiring all residents to obtain a license before holding a yard or garage sale would fall into this category. Another purpose that the government has in licensing individuals is to provide supervision and regulation of businesses and professions that might inflict harm on the public if they were allowed to operate without such controls. Physicians, nurses, dentists, attorneys, engineers, architects, public school teachers, and others in public service must be supervised for the protection of the public. The law distinguishes between licenses purely for revenue and licenses for protection of the public. If a license is required simply to raise revenue, the lack of a license will not necessarily make a contract void; if a licensing requirement is designed to protect the public, unlicensed persons will not be able to enforce their contracts.

### Unconscionable Agreements

A court will not enforce a contract or any part of a contract that it regards as unconscionable. An agreement is considered unconscionable if its terms are so grossly unfair that they shock the court's conscience. When the court so desires, it will limit how the unconscionable clause in an agreement is carried out, provided it can do so without causing any unfair consequences.

### Sunday Agreements

State statutes and local ordinances that regulate the making and performing of contracts on Sunday are called **blue laws** because one of the first laws banning Sunday or Sabbath contracts was written on blue paper. Today, the enforcement of restrictive blue laws varies in different geographical areas. Certain states have eliminated uniform statewide laws regulating Sunday activities but permit counties and incorporated cities, towns, and villages to adopt their own ordinances under a concept known as **local option**. Other states have rolled back these laws almost entirely, permitting most contracts while prohibiting or limiting only a few select Sunday contracts, such as those involving the sale of alcohol. Where laws do restrict Sunday business, two rules are usually observed. First, agreements made on Sunday or any other day requiring performance on Sunday may be ruled invalid. Exceptions to this rule are those agreements necessary to the health, welfare, and safety of the community and its residents. Second, agreements made on Sunday for work to be done or goods to be delivered on a business day are valid and enforceable. However, some states still require that there be an affirmation of such agreements on a day other than Sunday if such agreements are to be enforceable. The enforcement of blue laws varies widely from state to state, county to county, and village to village.

## Agreements Contrary to Public Policy

The general legal principle of **public policy** says no one should be allowed to do anything that injures the public at large. Agreements most commonly invalidated as contrary to public policy are those to obstruct justice, interfere with public service, defraud creditors, escape liability, and restrain trade. Some of these agreements are prohibited by statute, such as those that suppress competition and those that interfere with public service. Consequently, they could have been listed and explained in the last section. Instead, these contracts are listed here with the other public policy–related contracts, because they share one thing in common, though such contracts are made between private individuals, they would hurt the entire social structure if the law enforced them in any way.

### Agreements to Obstruct Justice

Agreements to obstruct justice include agreements to protect someone from arrest, to suppress evidence, to encourage lawsuits, to give false testimony, and to bribe a juror. The category also includes a promise not to prosecute someone or not to serve as a witness in a trial. Any agreement promising to perform any of these activities would be void.

### Agreements Interfering with Public Service

Agreements interfering with public service are illegal and void. Contracts in this group include agreements to bribe or interfere with public officials, to obtain political preference in appointments to office, to pay an officer for signing a pardon, or to illegally influence a legislature for personal gain.

## THE OPENING CASE *Revisited, Part II*
## Public Policy, Statutory Law, and Contract Validity:
## *R.R. v. M.H. & Another, Round 3*

In the Opening Case at the beginning of this chapter we learned that a married couple and a surrogate mother entered an agreement that stipulated that, in exchange for expenses and a $10,000 fee, the mother agreed to conceive, carry, and give birth to a child for the infertile couple. The fee was to be transferred to the surrogate mother in installments based on a structured payment plan. The contract went forward as planned until the sixth month when the mother changed her mind, returned that third payment, and told the father's attorney that the contract was ended. The father sued for custody of the baby, arguing that the surrogate mother had breached the contract. The judge agreed with the father and awarded him custody. The judge also believed such a move would ultimately be in the child's best interests. The surrogate mother appealed. The state supreme court decided that, since the state had no statute covering this type of agreement, it would apply an adoption statute that covered situations that were roughly analogous to the surrogacy situation. Under the adoption statute, a mother could not give up her child for adoption until four days after the child's birth. The statute also outlawed the payment of money to the mother for an adoption, although she could be paid pregnancy expenses. The state supreme court recognized that the legislature had a good reason for requiring a four-day waiting period before a mother could give up her child for adoption. The court took judicial notice of the fact that a mother comprehends the power of the connection between mother and child after the fourth day and is, therefore, in a better position to be fully aware what she is surrendering in an adoption. Using public policy, the court applied those same principles to the surrogate mother contract. In doing so, it concluded that, since the surrogate mother contract did not include a four-day waiting period, it was an illegal contract and was, therefore, void as a matter of law.

## A QUESTION OF ETHICS

In February 2011, the Egyptian people displayed their dissatisfaction with the government of Hosni Mubarak by demonstrating in Tahrir Square in Cairo and in the port city of Alexandria. The demonstrations led to Mubarak's abdication and to a military takeover of the government. The military leaders pledged to develop a new constitution and to turn the government over to civilian control as soon as possible. Nevertheless, despite the movement's victory over Mubarak and his government, many protestors continued to disrupt the peaceful transition to domestic peace. Chief among these demonstrators were members of the labor movement who had created a tightly knit network of agreements under which striking textile employees, airport workers, ambulance drivers, electrical engineers, and journalists continued to cause economic disruption. All of this continued to occur despite warnings by the military government that such actions should cease. Clearly the strikers believe that their cause is moral and their actions ethical despite their dubious legality. Under American law, agreements to strike illegally would violate public policy. Should the ethical motivation of the strikers trump the illegality of their actions? Defend your response using one of the ethical theories discussed in Chapter One of the text.

**Agreements to Defraud Creditors** An agreement that tends to remove or weaken the rights of creditors is referred to as an agreement to defraud creditors. Such agreements are void as contrary to public policy. Thus a debtor's agreement to sell and transfer personal and real property to a friend or relative for far less than actual value would be void if done for the purpose of hiding the debtor's assets from creditors with a legal claim to them.

### Agreements to Escape Liability

A basic policy of the law is that all parties should be liable for their own wrongdoing. Consequently, the law looks with disfavor on any agreement that allows a party to escape this responsibility. One device frequently used in the attempt to escape legal responsibility is the **exculpatory agreement**. Such an agreement is usually found as a clause in a longer, more complex contract or on the back of tickets and parking stubs. The exculpatory clause will state that one of the parties, generally the one who wrote the contract, will not be liable for any economic loss of physical injury even if that party caused the loss or injury.

### EXAMPLE 10-6: *Newsome v. Tibbs*

Pat Newsome, who worked for Van Sloane, Wentworth, and Michelson, was the chief architect on a project that involved building a new community center on the west side of Baltimore. Before the center could be built, a set of four high-rise apartment buildings, the Towers, had to come down. That job went to Tibbs TNT, LLC, an expert in razing ancient buildings. When Newsome arrived at the job, he was told by Elizabeth Tibbs, the owner of Tibbs TNT that he had to sign an additional contract with Tibbs. One of the clauses in the additional contract included an exculpatory clause that stated that Newsome would hold Tibbs blameless should Newsome be injured during the tear down of the Towers. The actual implosion of the Towers went without incident. However, afterwards, Newsome was injured when the brakes on a Tibbs-owned truck failed and ran over Newsome. Newsome sued Tibbs. Tibbs pointed to the exculpatory clause and said she was not liable. The court disagreed, saying that the exculpatory clause could not protect Tibbs from liability for injuries that result from negligence on the part of Tibbs or her employees.

This exculpatory clause is an example of the type that the courts have found to be a violation of public policy. Such exculpatory clauses are not favored by the law because they permit behavior to fall below acceptable standards, which was what happened in the Newsome case. A clause simply disclaiming liability in general terms is often insufficient to release a party from his or her own negligence. Still, some courts will enforce exculpatory clauses if they do not offend public policy and there is no inequality of bargaining power between the parties. However, whenever an exculpatory provision is ambiguous, confusing, vague, incomplete, or can be interpreted in different ways, the court will construe the clause against the party it was designed to protect.

### Sale of Business

When a business is sold, it is common practice for the agreement to contain covenants that restrict the seller from entering the same type of business. Such **restrictive covenants** in a contract for the sale of a business will be upheld by the court if they are reasonable in time and geographical area. What is reasonable is determined by a careful examination of the business being sold. For example, an agreement by the seller of a barbershop not to open a similar shop in the same community for the next year would seem to be reasonable. In contrast, the opening of a different business, over a wider geographical area, or for a longer period of time might not be allowed by the court.

### Restrictive Employment Covenants

A **restrictive employment covenant**, or **noncompete agreement** as it is often called, limits a worker's employment options after leaving his or her present job. The idea is to protect the present employer from an employee who might take trade secrets, customer lists, or other confidential material to a competitor. In a typical restrictive employment covenant, an employee promises not to work for a competitor in the same field for a specified time period and within a specified geographical area after leaving the current job. Restrictive employment covenants must be reasonable in the type of work they prohibit, the length of time involved in the prohibition, and the geographical area covered by the prohibition.

## Nondisclosure Agreements

A nondisclosure agreement requires employees to promise that, should they leave their present place of employment, they will not reveal any confidential trade secrets that they might learn while on their current job. Because the limitation is placed on the use of confidential information rather than actual employment of the worker, such agreements do not deprive people of their employment and therefore do not constitute an extensive limit on competition. Although helpful, nondisclosure agreements are often not needed to protect trade secrets. The court will generally issue an injunction to prevent the revelation or the utilization of trade secrets if the employer can convince the court that (1) the information revealed by the former employee was actually a trade secret, (2) the secret information was crucial to the running of the employer's business, (3) the employer had the right to use the trade secret, and (4) the former employee came into possession of the trade secret while in a position of trust and confidence and in such a way that it would be unfair for the former employee to disclose that trade secret in a way that would hurt his or her former employer.

---

### quick quiz 10-3

1. The illegal practice of charging more than the amount of interest allowed by law is called usury.   true | false

2. If a license is required simply to raise revenue, the lack of a license will make a contract void.   true | false

3. A restrictive employment covenant limits a worker's employment options after leaving his or her present job.   true | false

---

# 10-4 Consequences of Illegality

Illegality of contract, as in promises to commit criminal acts, not only serves to void existing agreements but may also lead to indictment and prosecution when sufficient evidence warrants such an action. Persons who agree to commit criminal acts for a promised consideration are involved in what criminal law defines as a conspiracy. Agreements that do not violate criminal laws may still be invalid. Thus, many agreements considered contrary to public policy have been declared invalid as against the public good but not illegal in terms of criminal liability. Both types of agreements fail to have the characteristics that permit legal enforcement.

## In Pari Delicto Contracts

When both parties to an illegal agreement are equally wrong in the knowledge of the operation and effect of their contract, they are said to be *in pari delicto* (in equal fault). In such cases, the court will give no aid to either party in an action against the other and will award no damages to either. When the parties are not *in pari delicto,* relief will often be allowed if sought by the more innocent of the two. Although this rule is not applicable when one may be less guilty of premeditation (plotting or planning an illegal act) and intent to achieve a gain through known illegal acts, it may be applied when one party is not aware that a law is being broken and there is no intent to do a wrong.

## Partial Illegality in an Agreement

**LO10**

Sometimes an agreement will be partly legal and partly illegal. If the legal part of a contract can be removed from the illegal part, without changing the essential nature of the contract, then the agreement is said to be divisible. The court will enforce the legal part but not the illegal part. As long as the main purpose of the agreement can be reached without enforcing the illegal part, the courts are likely to uphold the agreement.

---

### quick quiz 10-4

1. Persons who agree to commit criminal acts for a promised consideration are involved in a conspiracy.    true | false

2. When both parties to an illegal agreement are equally wrong in the knowledge of the operation and effect of their contract, they are said to be *in pari delicto*.    true | false

3. If the legal part of a contract can be removed from the illegal part, without changing the essential nature of the contract, the court will enforce both parts.    true | false

---

## Summary

**10.1** The third element essential to a legally effective contract is the legal ability to enter into a contractual relationship. This legal ability is known as capacity. Under the law, there is a rebuttable presumption that anyone entering a contract has the legal capacity to do so. Because the presumption is rebuttable, a party can attack it. Minors are allowed this privilege. Minority means that an individual has not yet attained the age of majority. An exception to the rule about minors and contracts involves necessaries. By statute and court decision, certain other types of contracts have been excepted from the general rule that the contracts of minors are voidable at the minor's option.

**10.2** Contracts of persons who are mentally infirm or mentally ill, but not legally declared insane, may be valid or voidable, depending on the seriousness of the mental problem. Persons declared to be insane by competent legal authority are denied the right to enter into contracts, and contracts entered into may be declared void. Incompetence related to alcohol or drugs must be of such a degree that the contracting party has lost the ability to comprehend or be aware of the obligations being accepted under the contract.

**10.3** An agreement might have offer, acceptance, mutual assent, competent parties, and consideration and still be invalid if the objective of the agreement is to do something that is illegal. These contracts include those to commit crimes, to commit torts, or to violate statutory law. Public policy is a general legal principle that says no one should be allowed to do anything that tends to hurt the public at large. Agreements found void for a violation of public policy include agreements to obstruct justice, agreements interfering with public service, agreements to defraud creditors, exculpatory agreements, and agreements in restraint of trade.

**10.4** Contracts that involve illegal agreements are invalid. Moreover, promises to commit illegal acts may lead to indictment and prosecution. If an entire agreement is illegal, no binding contract results. If only part of an agreement is illegal, the court may rescind only those parts found to be illegal. When both parties are equally at fault in creating an illegal agreement, the court will award no damages to either. When the parties are not in equal fault, relief will often be granted if sought by the innocent party.

## Key Terms

| | | |
|---|---|---|
| abandoned, 212 | illegal agreement, 211 | public policy, 220 |
| affirmance, 215 | in pari delicto, 223 | ratification, 215 |
| blue laws, 220 | local option, 220 | rebuttable presumption, 211 |
| capacity, 211 | majority, 212 | restrictive covenants, 222 |
| conspiracy, 223 | minority, 212 | restrictive employment |
| disaffirm, 211 | necessaries, 213 | covenant, 222 |
| emancipated, 212 | noncompete agreement, 222 | usury, 219 |
| exculpatory clause, 222 | nondisclosure agreement, 223 | |

## Questions for Review and Discussion

1. What is the age of minority and what is the age of majority?
2. What is the legal status of a contract made by a minor?
3. What is the difference between ratification and disaffirmance?
4. What are the effects of mental impairment on a contract?
5. What is the contractual capacity of a drugged or intoxicated person?
6. What is the legal status of an agreement to commit a tort or a crime?
7. What agreements are illegal under statutory law?
8. What agreements are contrary to public policy?
9. What happens under the doctrine of *in pari delicto?*
10. What are the effects of illegality?

## Cases for Analysis

1. After she was married, Sherri Mitchell, a young woman of 17 years of age, was in an automobile accident in which she was hurt enough to require medical treatment. She was later approached by an insurance agent who offered her $2,500 as a settlement. All she had to do was sign a release that would absolve the insurance company of any complaint that she might have against it in regard to the accident. She agreed to accept the $2,500 and signed a release to that effect. However, she then changed her mind and decided to void the agreement. She argued that since she was 17 at the time she signed the release, she was a minor and could therefore void the contract. Is Mrs. Mitchell correct? Explain. *Mitchell v. State Farm Mutual Automobile Insurance Co.,* 963 S.W.2d (Ky. Ct. App.).

2. Sperry Ford sold a car to Bowling when Bowling was only 16 years old. Once Bowling had paid the full purchase price in cash, Sperry turned over the car and the certificate of title. After driving the car for only a week, Bowling discovered that the main bearing was burned out. When Bowling found out that repair costs would almost equal the price he'd paid for the car, he left the car on Sperry's lot and asked for his money back. Sperry Ford refused to give Bowling his money. Was Sperry justified in this refusal? Explain. *Bowling vs. Sperry,* 184 N.E.2d 901 (IN).

3. Quality Motors, Inc., refused to sell a car to Hays because he was only 16 years old. However, Quality told Hays that they would sell the car to an adult and then show Hays how to transfer the title to his name. Hays agreed with the scheme and came back with a friend who was 23. Quality sold the car to Hays's friend. Quality then gave Hays the name of a notary public who would transfer

the title to Hays. After the transfer was accomplished, Hays's father found out about the deal and tried to get Quality Motors to take the car back. Quality replied that the car had been sold to an adult, so Hays could not disaffirm the contract. Is Quality correct? Explain. *Quality Motors v. Hays,* 225 S.W.2d 326 (AR).

4. Lonchyna enlisted in the U.S. Air Force while he was still a minor. Three times he applied for and received educational delays that put off the beginning of his tour of duty. The last time, he claimed he could void the contract, because he'd entered into it when he was a minor. Was Lonchyna correct? Explain. *Lonchyna v. Brown, Secretary of Defense,* 491 F. Supp. 1352 (N.D. IL).

5. Darwin Kruse was a construction worker. He was injured while working for the Coos Head Timber Company. Subsequent to the accident, Kruse signed an agreement with his employer that granted Kruse compensation in exchange for his promise not to sue. Kruse is now trying to have the agreement voided. Evidence introduced proved that Kruse had an IQ of 83 and that he dropped out of school at age 18. When he dropped out of school, he was in the eighth grade but was doing less than sixth grade–level work. Will Kruse's "slowness" necessarily invalidate the contract? Explain. *Kruse v. Coos Head Timber Co.,* 432 P.2d 1009 (OR).

6. Clear Channel Broadcasting, Inc., required Diane Ignazio to sign a new contract that included an arbitration clause under which she agreed that all grievances that she might have with Clear Channel would be settled by arbitration. As part of the agreement, Ignazio gave up any right to bring a lawsuit against Clear Channel. When Ignazio was discharged, instead of moving to arbitration, she sued Clear Channel for discrimination and wrongful discharge. Clear Channel filed a motion to dismiss the case, arguing that Ignazio was bound by the arbitration agreement. Ignazio pointed to a clause in the agreement that rendered the entire agreement illegal. The clause allowed the arbitration award to be reviewed by a court based on the same broad standards used by an appeals court in reviewing a trial court's decision. This provision contradicts state law, which states that if an appeals court reviews an arbitration decision, it can only use a very limited approach to the appeal, including only such things as clerical

error or misconduct. Clear Channel argued that even if the clause was illegal, it could be severed from the agreement, and the rest of the agreement could be enforced. In fact, the contract even included a clause that stated that any clause found illegal ought to be removed from the contract, so that the rest of the contract could be upheld. The question before the court was whether the illegal clause could be removed from the agreement without changing the essential nature of the contract. Is it legally permissible to remove the illegal part of a contract so that the court can uphold the legal part? Should the court sever the illegal clause in this case? Explain. *Ignazio v. Clear Channel,* 113 Ohio St.3d 276 (Ohio Supreme Court).

7. Cyberian Enterprises and BrandAid Marketing Corporation entered a deal under which Cyberian was supposed to purchase $21 million in Brand-Aid's stock. Cyberian, however, did not have the funds available to make the actual purchase, a fact that was concealed by Cyberian representatives. When BrandAid discovered the lie, it filed a lawsuit against Cyberian for fraud, breach of contract, and breaking federal securities law. Cyberian brought a countersuit against BrandAid for fraud because BrandAid had apparently failed to tell Cyberian about its own financial difficulties. However, BrandAid's financial problems were on file with the Securities and Exchange Commission (SEC). When the case went to District Court, the judge dismissed the case because, citing the doctrine of *in pari delicto,* he stated that both parties were at equal fault in concealing their financial difficulties. The case then went to the Second Circuit Court of Appeals, which decided that the trial court had made a mistake in dismissing the case. Why did the appeals court overturn the decision of the trial court? Explain. *BrandAid Marketing Corp. v. Biss,* 05-5243-cv (2d U.S. Cir. Ct. of App.). (See also Beth Bar, "Civil Practice: Finding of Equal Fault Is Overturned," *The National Law Journal,* September 11, 2006, p. 13.)

8. Shannon Audley, a professional model, signed an agreement before starting work on a photo shoot at Bill Melton's studio. The agreement stated: "I, Shannon Audley, realize that working with wild and potentially dangerous animals (i.e., lion, white tiger, hawk) can create a hazardous situation resulting in loss of life or limb. I take all responsibility upon myself for any event as described above that may

take place. I hold Bill Melton and T.I.G.E.R.S. or any of their agents free of any or all liability. I am signing this of my own free will." During the photo shoot, Audley was bitten on the head by the adult male lion with which she had been posing. Audley brought suit against Melton. Would the exculpatory clause be upheld by the courts? Explain. *Audley v. Melton*, 640 A.2d 777 NH).

9. Judy Myers and the Terminix International Company entered a contract in which Terminix agreed to inspect Myers's home and eliminate any termite problem found there. The service cost Myers an initial payment of $1,300 plus annual renewal fees

of $85. Terminix failed to eradicate the termite infestation, causing more than $41,000 in damage to Myers's home. The contract contained a clause that required the parties to submit any disputes to arbitration under the American Arbitration Association (AAA). What the contract did not disclose was that Myers would be required to pay a filing fee to submit a claim to AAA. In this case, the filing fee amounted to $7,000. In a lawsuit filed for breach of contract, Myers asserted that the undisclosed filing fee requirement was unconscionable. Is Myers correct? Explain. *Myers v. Terminix*, 697 N.E.2d 277 (OH).

## quick quiz Answers

| 10-1 | 10-2 | 10-3 | 10-4 |
|------|------|------|------|
| 1. T | 1. T | 1. T | 1. T |
| 2. T | 2. F | 2. F | 2. T |
| 3. F | 3. F | 3. T | 3. F |

# Chapter 11

# Written Contracts and Cyber-Commerce

## THE OPENING CASE  Written Contracts and The New Frontier: *Wilcox v. Trautz*

The Statute of Frauds was first introduced into the legal system in 1677 when Parliament created the Act for the Prevention of Frauds and Perjuries. The act outlined those contracts that had to be in writing to be enforced by the courts. One of those contracts was an agreement made in consideration of marriage. This did not include the marriage contract itself, but only those ancillary agreements to distribute property if the marriage broke up. Today, we call such contracts prenuptial agreements. The members of Parliament were quite progressive in adding "pre-nups" to the statute. However, even with the benefit of their combined wisdom, they never foresaw the strange case of *Wilcox v. Trautz*. Carol Wilcox and John Trautz lived together as an unmarried couple for 25 years, beginning when they were both youngsters in their twenties. During those two and a half decades, Wilcox managed to contribute only $25 each week for household expenses. However, she also performed all the household duties, and she used her own money to buy food and clothing. Unfortunately, all good things must come to an end, and so, when Trautz discovered that Wilcox had become involved in another relationship, he sought legal advice regarding his rights with respect to the assets acquired during their relationship. At that point, the two parties negotiated, wrote, and signed an agreement providing, among other things that "each party's earnings and

property is his or hers alone, and the other party shall have no interest in the property of the other." The assets, all in Trautz's name, included a house, valued at $180,000; an amphibious airplane, valued at $55,000; various bank accounts totaling $1,300; individual retirement accounts; and a one-half share in some real estate in Maine, valued at $15,000. Wilcox had no assets other than a small bank account, the other one-half share of the Maine real estate, household furniture, clothing, and jewelry. Had the written contract been a genuine prenuptial agreement, it would have been fine. It did exactly what a "pre-nup" is supposed to do, that is, it explained the terms of the agreement in specific, understandable language. However, it was not really a pre-nup, and that single fact gave the court pause. As a result, after due deliberation, the judge ruled that the agreement could not be enforced. In addition, the judge also decided that, to prevent unjust enrichment, Trautz would have to pay Wilcox damages amounting to approximately $30,000. Trautz appealed the decision. Read on to see what happened. (See *Wilcox v. Trautz*, 693 N.E.2d 141 (Supreme Judicial Court of Massachusetts).)

**Opening Case Questions**

1. Can the court use the Statute of Frauds to decide this case? Explain.

2. Does the actual written agreement satisfy all the requirements of the Statute of Frauds? Explain.

3. Does public policy apply here? Explain. If public policy applies, what should the result be? Explain.

4. If the court follows a strict interpretation of the law here, it will have to dismiss the contract as unenforceable, not because it does not meet the Statute of Frauds, but because it encourages the cohabitation of unmarried couples. Does this principle make sense in the modern world or is it simply an outdated, old-fashioned notion that should not influence the court today? Explain.

5. Should the courts try to reshape social norms this way or should that job be left to the legislature? Explain.

## LO  Learning Objectives

**1.** Identify the goals of the Statute of Frauds.
**2.** Identify those contracts that must be in writing.
**3.** List the information that must be in the writing.
**4.** Explain the Standard Construction Rule.
**5.** Discuss the Parol Evidence Rule.
**6.** Explain the exceptions to the Parol Evidence Rule.
**7.** Explain the Best Evidence Rule.
**8.** Discuss the Equal Dignities Rule.
**9.** Explain the problems associated with cyber-commerce.
**10.** Outline the latest cyber-commerce statutes.

# 11-1 The Statute of Frauds

Often when people hear the word *contract,* they immediately think of a piece of paper. Instead, they should think of an agreement, which may or may not be in writing. Many contracts do not have to be in writing to be enforceable. Most oral contracts are valid and upheld by the court. Although it may be desirable to put a contract in writing so that its terms are clear, only certain kinds of contracts are required to be in writing. This chapter discusses the **Statute of Frauds**, which is the law that requires certain contracts to be in writing to be enforceable.

## Contracts that Must Be in Writing

According to the Statute of Frauds, applicable in most states, six types of contracts must be in writing to be enforceable:

1.   Contracts that cannot be completed within one year.
2.   Contracts transferring real property rights.
3.   Contracts for the sale of goods of $500 or more.
4.   Certain contracts entered into by executors and administrators.
5.   Contracts by one party to pay a debt of another party.
6.   Contracts in consideration of marriage.

The third contract on the list, contracts for the sale of goods of $500 or more, is actually included in the Uniform Commercial Code rather than the Statute of Frauds. This point is covered in depth in Chapter 13.

**Contracts that Cannot Be Completed Within One Year**    If the terms of a contract make it impossible to complete the agreement within one year, the contract must be in writing.

## EXAMPLE 11-1: *Strachan v. Wright Weber Construction*

Frank Strachan entered a contract with Wright Weber Construction for the building of an addition to his new home in Lakeside. The construction firm was to begin building the addition on April 2. Wright Weber agreed that the addition might be finished by March 1 of the following year, but also stipulated that May 1 of the following year was a more reasonable estimate. The details of the agreement were never reduced to writing. When Wright Weber ran into labor problems in August, it had to put the construction of the addition on hold. One month later, unable to resolve the labor dispute, Wright Weber shut the company down and abandoned the Strachan work site. As a result, Strachan had to negotiate a new contract with a new construction firm. The new contract cost $12,900 more than it would have had Weber completed the job as promised. In addition, because the Lakeside house could not be used during construction, Strachan incurred storage costs for his furniture because he had to move out of the home he was living in to accommodate the new owners. He also had to live in a hotel for four months while the Lakeside addition was completed. Strachan sued Wright Weber. Wright Weber moved for a dismissal because the contract was not in writing. Strachan argued that the contract could have been completed within one year and was therefore outside of the statute. As a result, he correctly concluded that the writing was not needed.

### About the Law

In addition to those mentioned here, states have enacted various statutes requiring other types of contracts to be in writing, such as promises to leave something to someone in a will, promises to pay debts that have been discharged in bankruptcy, and certain types of assignments.

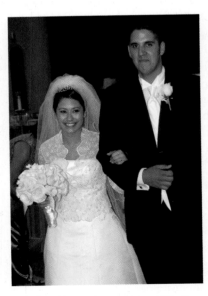

Although the marriage agreement itself does not have to be written, some contracts associated with marriage do.

### Contracts Transferring Real Property Rights

Under the Statute of Frauds, conveyances of real property must be in writing to be enforceable. This provision covers the sale of land; however, it also covers trusts that are created by one party, the trustor, that permit a second party, the trustee, to possess and control the land for the advantage of a third party, the beneficiary. Whether the provision includes leases is problematic, because some jurisdictions permit short leases, generally those that last less than a year, to be oral. Most states, however, are relatively clear that leases that are designed to last longer than one year must be in writing to be enforceable. Moreover, it is not enough that the lease actually be in writing; the writing must also be presented to the court for it to be enforceable.

When a party owns land, he or she owns a bundle of rights that can be distributed among various other parties. Thus, it is possible, for example, for

### EXAMPLE 11-2: *Nicklesworth v. Marblehead Properties*

Walt Nicklesworth entered a lease agreement with Marblehead Properties, under which Nicklesworth used the property located at 5293 Lake Shore Boulevard as a used bookstore. The terms of the lease included a right of first refusal, such that Nicklesworth could purchase the property if Marblehead ever decided to sell. Two years into the five-year lease, Marblehead sold the property to Daniel O'Donnell. Nicklesworth brought suit for breach of contract. At trial, no one could produce a written copy of the lease for the judge. The judge dismissed the case because the Statute of Frauds required a writing, and none could be produced at court.

the owner of a parcel of land to divide the rights to that land among several different parties. One party might hold a lease to a house on the land allowing her to live there, a second could have an easement that permits him to cross the land, a third might own the right to mine the land, and so on. The Statute of Frauds requires a writing for each of these different transactions. The object of this requirement is to make certain that there is a way to follow the trail of each of these rights to determine who owns them, should a dispute arise concerning them.

### EXAMPLE 11-3: *Xavier v. Brookhaven*

In 1919, Pasha Patel owned several acres of land in the Upper Peninsula of the state of Michigan. Half a pond was located on Patel's land. The other half of the pond was located on land owned by Brooke Brookhaven. For a small consideration, Patel transferred the right to cut ice on her side of the pond each winter to Fred Xavier. The contract was oral and supposed to last for the next five winters. Each day from early October to late March, Xavier would cut the ice and remove it. He would carefully carve the ice into large cubes that fit perfectly into the ice boxes located in the rental cabins dotting the upper peninsula. (This was 1919, remember.) He then sold the ice to the cabin renters. One summer Brookhaven drained her part of the pond. In October, this action meant that ice was sparse, and what was available was sunk into the mud at the bottom of the lake and thus unusable for carving and sale. Xavier brought suit against Brookhaven, arguing that her action in draining the lake made his interest in the property worthless. The court asked for a copy of the written contract transferring the right to cut the ice to Xavier. When Xavier could not produce one, the judge dismissed the case.

An exception to the rule that contracts for the sale of land must be in writing is called **part performance** or **equitable estoppel**. The exception applies when a person relies on an owner's oral promise to sell real property and then makes improvements on the property or changes his or her position in an important way. The plaintiff in such a case must prove three elements to succeed in a lawsuit. First, the plaintiff must show that he or she made the improvement relying on the original promise and without suspecting that the other party intended to renege on the agreement. Second, the plaintiff must show that any other remedy, such as restitution for the amount spent, is not enough to satisfy his or her effort or outlay of funds. Third, the plaintiff must show that the part performance itself is evidence of the existence of the contract.

## EXAMPLE 11-4: *Zuer v. Iafigliola*

Jake Iafigliola agreed in an oral contract to sell Dwight Zuer a run-down parcel of storefront property for $50,000. The storefront was located across the street from the site of a new Target that was about to be established in the neighborhood. Relying on Iafigliola's agreement, Zuer spent $20,000 improving the premises so that he could move his DVD rental business into the storefront. Iafigliola then backed out of the deal. Zuer sued, asking the court to order Iafigliola to go through with the contract. Iafigliola argued this was a real property contract and it had to be in writing to be enforceable. Zuer asked the court to apply the part performance doctrine. Zuer made the following case: First, he had made the improvements relying on the original promise. Second, he pointed out that any other remedy, such as restitution for the amount spent, would not be enough, because he clearly wanted the storefront in the lot across from the new Target. Third, Zuer argued that the fact that he spent $20,000 to improve the storefront could not be explained in any other way other than his reliance on the contract. The court agreed and allowed the lawsuit even without the writing.

The courts do not require a writing for a contract in which the owner of land agrees to improve the land for the use of another party who has already received a partial interest in the land. In such a situation, the courts believe that once the real interest in the land has been transferred, the contract to improve the land does not create a new interest. Instead, the new contract is solely a promise to provide labor and make changes in the land. It therefore falls outside the statute, and no writing is required.

## EXAMPLE 11-5: *Dewey v. Collins*

Rene Collins owned a piece of land in rural Pennsylvania, just outside Streetsboro. Frederick Dewey received an easement across Collins's land. The easement, which was supposed to last for five years, was executed in a written document. After the first year, Dewey asked Collins to lay gravel on the small road that constituted the easement. Collins said that she would not lay the gravel herself but would permit Dewey to do so and reimburse him for the expense. Dewey laid the gravel and presented Collins with the bill. Collins refused to reimburse Dewey as agreed. Collins argued that because there was no writing, the contract, which involved land, was unenforceable. The referee disagreed, concluding that the agreement to lay gravel did not create a new interest. Instead, it simply involved a commitment to pay for improvements to land in which Dewey already owned an interest.

UCC 2-201 (see pages 822–823)

**Contracts for the Sale of Goods of $500 or More**    Under the UCC, contracts for the sale of goods (moveable items) for $500 or more must be in writing to be enforceable. However, there are four exceptions to this rule. Oral contracts for the sale of goods of $500 or more will be enforced in situations involving the following:

1. Oral contracts between merchants when a written confirmation has been received by one party and not objected to by the other party.
2. Specially manufactured goods that cannot be resold easily.
3. Admissions in court.
4. Executed agreements.

## Certain Contracts Entered by Executors and Administrators

An *executor* is a person who is named in a will to oversee the distribution of the estate of a deceased according to the provisions outlined in the will. An *administrator* is a person named by the court to do the work of an executor if none is named in the will or if the executor cannot or will not perform those duties. As a general principle of law, neither an executor nor an administrator is personally liable for the debts of the decedent's estate. Executors and administrators must pay the debts of the estate, to be sure, but out of the assets of the estate, not out of their own pockets. Thus, any promise to pay the debts of the estate using the executor's or the administrator's own funds is unenforceable without a writing.

## EXAMPLE 11-6: *Trautman v. Quinn*

Max Quinn was named the executor of his sister's estate. One of his sister's creditors, Nancy Trautman, demanded immediate payment of a debt of $6,600 owed by the deceased. To protect his sister's good name, Quinn promised Trautman that he would pay her the amount owed out of his own funds if the estate could not cover that amount. Trautman refused to agree unless Quinn placed the agreement in writing. Quinn agreed. After things calmed down, Trautman tried to collect the debt. Quinn refused to pay. Trautman was able to enforce the promise because she had written evidence of Quinn's agreement to pay the debt.

**Contracts by One Party to Pay a Debt Incurred by Another Party** A promise made by one party to pay another person's debts, if that person fails to pay the debt, falls within the statute and must be in writing to be enforceable. Several terms have been used to describe these types of transactions. They are alternately referred to as a **guaranty of payment**, a **guaranty contract**, or a **collateral contract**. The promisor is usually called a **guarantor**. Often in a commercial setting, the guarantor is referred to as a **cosigner**. The person to whom the promise is made is the **obligee**, and the person who owes the original debt is referred to as the **obligor**. It is crucial to distinguish between guaranty contracts and original contracts.

An exception to this rule is known as the primary objective test. Under the **primary objective test** (also referred to as the **leading objective test** and the **main purpose test**), if the promise to pay another party's debt is actually made to obtain a gain for the guarantor, there is no need for a writing to enforce the promise. Suppose, for instance, that Hans McKnight, the owner of Scottish Inn, depends on the Hometown Bakery for the inn's sub buns for its lunch trade. Suppose further that McKnight knows that the Hometown Bakery has had some financial trouble and may have to shut down its operations if it cannot pay Jakub's Supply for its regular flour shipment. If McKnight promises Jakub's that, if it continues to supply Hometown with flour, he will pay the bill, that promise falls under the primary objective test and need not be in writing to be enforceable.

**Contracts in Consideration of Marriage** Agreements made in consideration of marriage must be in writing to be enforceable. This part of the statute does not refer to the marriage contract itself or to engagement promises to marry, which are almost always oral. Rather, it refers to promises made by parties before marriage, in which they accept additional obligations not usually covered in the marriage vows. A **prenuptial agreement** (also referred to as a **premarriage agreement** and an **antenuptial agreement**) involves two people who are planning marriage and who agree to change the property

## THE OPENING CASE *Revisited, Part I*
## Written Contracts and The New Frontier:
## *Wilcox v. Trautz*, Round 2

The Statute of Frauds was first introduced into the legal system in 1677 when Parliament enacted a bill entitled the Act for the Prevention of Frauds and Perjuries. The members of Parliament were quite forward looking in adding prenuptial agreements to the statute. Still, even with the benefit of their foresight, they never imagined that the rules would be applied to a contract like the one that existed between Carol Wilcox and John Trautz. Recall that Wilcox and John Trautz lived together as an unmarried couple for 25 years, until Trautz discovered that Wilcox had become involved in another relationship. At that point, after Trautz consulted his lawyer, the two parties negotiated, wrote, and signed an agreement providing, among other things that "each party's earnings and property is his

or hers alone, and the other party shall have no interest in the property of the other." The assets, all in Trautz's name, included a house, valued at $180,000; an amphibious airplane, valued at $55,000; various bank accounts totaling $1,300; individual retirement accounts; and a one-half share of real estate in Maine, valued at $15,000. Wilcox had no assets other than a small bank account, the other one-half share of the Maine real estate, household furniture, clothing, and jewelry. Had the written contract been a genuine prenuptial agreement, it would have been an exemplary model. After all, it did exactly what a pre-nup is supposed to do. It proved the parties had made an agreement and it outlined the terms of that agreement in specific, understandable language.

rights they possess by law in a marriage. Such promises are enforceable only if they are in writing and agreed upon prior to the marriage. Many state legislatures, as well as the District of Columbia, have enacted the Uniform Premarital Ageement Act (UPAA). The UPAA supports the use of prenuptial agreements and provides for their enforcement.

**Other Contracts**   Each state has enacted special statutes outlining other agreements that must be in writing. Other contracts that are usually required by special statutes to be in writing include the release of a party from debt (general release) and the resumption of obligations after bankruptcy. In addition, some states require real estate listing contracts and insurance binders to be in writing. Other contracts that require a writing under the UCC are contracts for the sale of securities (stocks and bonds) and agreements creating security interests.

## The Contents of a Writing

The Statute of Frauds requires that the agreement be in writing—nothing more. The purpose of the writing is twofold. First, it proves that the parties entered an agreement. Second, it provides detailed information about the terms of that agreement. To accomplish these goals, the writing must be intelligible, but it need not follow any preset format. It can be found in letters, memos, documents, invoices, packing slips, and purchase orders that have been mailed, privately delivered, faxed, or sent electronically between the parties. It may be written on any surface suitable for the purpose of recording the intention of the parties, as long as all the required elements are present. A writing can even be placed in an e-mail, in a text message, or on a Web site, as long as it is possible to store and reproduce the electronic record of the agreement, and as long as the cyber-record includes an electronic signature as defined by the appropriate cyber-commerce statute.

**THE OPENING CASE** *Revisited, Part II*
Written Contracts and The New Frontier:
*Wilcox v. Trautz*, Round 3

The written agreement between Wilcox and Trautz does what all written agreements are supposed to do. First, it provides evidence of the agreement itself. Second, it identifies the terms of the agreement. These terms include the subject matter (the house, the airplane, the bank accounts, the IRAs, the Maine real estate, the furniture, the clothing, and the jewelry), the consideration that passed from one to the other (a release from any future obligations in exchange for the property outlined in the agreement), and the names and signatures of both parties. As such, we have a perfectly enforceable written agreement that satisfies the Statute of Frauds. It was made by competent parties, who had the capacity to contract, who understood the terms, who had an opportunity to seek legal advice, and who entered the agreement with full mutual assent. This, by the way, is exactly how the appeals court ruled when it overturned the decision of the lower court.

**Elements of a Writing**   To be absolutely complete, a written agreement, or **memorandum**, as it is often called, should contain the following elements:

- Terms of the agreement.
- Identification of the subject matter.
- Statement of the consideration promised.
- Names and identities of the persons to be obligated.
- Signature of the party sought to be bound to the agreement.

**LO3**

### quick quiz 11-1

1. A contract is said to be outside the statute if it must be in writing to show that the two objectives of the Statute of Frauds have been met.   true | false

2. An administrator is a person who is named in a will to oversee the distribution of the estate of a deceased person according to the provisions outlined in the will.   true | false

3. Agreements made in consideration of marriage must be in writing to be enforceable.   true | false

# 11-2 Legal Rules for Written Contracts

The legal system has developed certain basic criteria that make the construction and interpretation of written contracts as flawless as possible. These criteria act very much the way basic axioms or rules work in mathematics. Therefore, we could characterize these rules as unquestioned assumptions about the text of a writing that must be followed when an attorney, a magistrate, or a judge interprets a writing that claims to contain the terms of a contract. These four rules are: (1) the standard construction rule, (2) the parol evidence rule, (3) the best evidence rule, and (4) the equal dignities rule. The first two rules cover the interpretation of contracts, whereas the latter two govern their enforcement.

## The Standard Construction Rule

Appropriately, the first of the interpretation rules is the most critical and the most fundamental of the four. The **standard construction rule** guides the entire interpretation process by directing the interpreter of a contract to determine the principal objective of the parties in the making of the contract. The *principal objective* is the primary or main goal that the parties hoped to accomplish by entering the agreement in the first place. Once this principal objective is stated, everything else must be interpreted to promote that principal objective. In line with this rule, the law also says that common words used in the contract are given their expected, everyday definition, and technical terms or professional slang will be given their technical or professional definitions. The standard construction rule also says that any standard operating procedures that are used in the parties' professions or trades should be followed whenever there is any doubt about what procedure should be used in the contract.

Because the standard construction rule is the most fundamental guideline involved in the interpretation of written contracts, it also guides the interpreter on matters of ambiguity and misinterpretation. The rule says that whenever an ambiguous term, clause, or line is found in a prewritten or preprinted contract, that ambiguity is interpreted against the party who wrote the contract. This approach should encourage those people who draft contracts to do so in clear and unambiguous terms, because if they draft a clause that is ambiguous, it will be interpreted against them. Thus, there is no profit in making things difficult to understand in any written contract.

## The Parol Evidence Rule

Under the **parol evidence rule**, evidence of oral statements made before signing a written agreement is usually not admissible in court to change or contradict the terms of a written agreement. Following oral discussion and negotiation, parties may reduce their agreements to some written form. When this is done, only the terms, conditions, and promises included in the writing will be allowed as evidence in court. This provision is enforced because the court presumes that the parties will have put everything they agreed to in the writing.

### EXAMPLE 11-7: *Twaine v. Krell, Inc.*

Emily Twaine purchased a $1,250 desktop computer from Krell, Inc. Before all of the documents of sale were signed, the salesperson promised that she would get round-the-clock tech support from Krell technicians whenever she had a problem with her computer or any of the software associated with the computer. Krell subsequently refused to take care of any problems that Twaine had with the computer. The court ruled that the salesperson's oral warranty statements were not admissible in court because they were not contained with the other conditions in the written sales agreement.

**Exceptions to the Parol Evidence Rule**  The parol evidence rule will not apply when unfair and unjust decisions might result from its application. In cases in which a written agreement is incomplete, oral evidence may be used to supply the missing terms. Similarly, when a written contract is obscure or indistinct in certain of its terms, oral evidence may be used to clarify those terms. Also, if a written agreement contains a typographical or clerical error of some sort, the court will allow oral evidence as to the true intent of the parties.

## EXAMPLE 11-8: *Bulwark v. Greene*

Edgar Bulwark was hired as an independent contractor to produce a series of magazine and journal articles that would appear under the name of a famous, and very busy, newspaper columnist named Arnold Greene. The written agreement had an error that indicated that Bulwark would receive $500 per article. The actual amount of consideration was supposed to be $5,000. The court would likely allow oral evidence to correct this obvious error.

In general, the courts allow a party to a written agreement to introduce oral testimony to show that the contract is void or voidable due to a lack of mutual assent or contractual capacity. The courts are willing to allow such testimony because it does not affect the terms of the agreement. Rather, it seeks to discredit the entire transaction. Thus, it is permissible to introduce oral evidence as to fraud, duress, misrepresentation, mistake, and undue influence. Similarly, it is appropriate to offer oral testimony as to a party's minority or mental incompetence.

## EXAMPLE 11-9: *Staniland v. Morris*

James Staniland contracted with Richard Morris to purchase an original painting by Henrietta Stein, an artist who was part of the Dadaist movement in Paris during the 1920s. After signing the written contract, Staniland took the painting and had it placed in the lobby of his business office. After one week, a customer spotted the painting and told Staniland that it was a forgery and that he had been defrauded by Morris. When Staniland took the witness stand during the trial, he was permitted to introduce evidence of the oral statements made by Morris that led him to the fraudulent conclusion that the painting was a genuine work by Stein. The court allowed the testimony because it did not affect the terms of the agreement. Rather, it sought to discredit the entire transaction.

If a written agreement depends on some event before it becomes enforceable, oral evidence may be offered regarding that condition precedent. A **condition precedent** is an act or promise that must take place or be fulfilled before the other party is obligated to perform his or her part of the agreement. The courts allow this type of oral evidence because, like the oral evidence involving assent and capacity, it does not have an impact on the terms of the agreement, but it does affect the enforceability of the entire contract.

## EXAMPLE 11-10: *Lauretig v. Pierce*

Asa Pierce agreed to lease Jay Lauretig's warehouse. The terms of the lease were laid out in a lengthy, detailed written agreement. However, as a condition precedent, a credit history and background check by Lauretig on Pierce would have to come back flawless; otherwise, the deal would be canceled. When the Search and Discover Detective Agency reported that Pierce had both a bad credit rating and two criminal convictions on drug charges, Lauretig refused to go through with the contract. At court, the judge permitted oral testimony about the credit check and the criminal background search because they were precedent conditions that had to be met before the contract went into effect.

Oral evidence may be used to prove that the parties orally agreed to rescind or modify the terms of a written contract after entering into it. Subsequent negotiations to change or rescind the agreement are permitted, and evidence to that effect does not undermine the spirit of the parol evidence rule. However, if the change in the contract involves an agreement that would have to be in writing under the Statute of Frauds, then a writing would be required. Similarly, if the original written contract requires later modifications to be in writing, then that written requirement will rule.

## EXAMPLE 11-11: *George Laurie Construction v. Popson*

George Laurie Construction entered into a contract with Terry and Sherrie Popson, the terms of which indicated that Laurie Construction was to place aluminum siding, downspouts, and gutters on the Popson vacation house on Kelley's Island. The agreement was written out in a long, preprinted contract with blanks for the pertinent individual information. All of the appropriate blanks were filled in, the contract was signed by all the parties, and the job began on schedule. Once Laurie was on the job for three days, Sherrie Popson decided that she wanted a window placed on the house. She discussed the cost of the additional work with George Laurie, who agreed to make the change indicated. The additional terms were not put in writing. After the job was completed, the Popsons paid the original amount but did not pay the added cost of the new window. The small claims court allowed testimony as to the terms involving the window because those terms represented negotiations subsequent to the original agreement to change the original terms.

UCC 1-205, 2-202, 2-208 (see pages 820 and 823)

As a final exception to the parol evidence rule, the UCC allows oral testimony about how the parties have done business together over a long time period. The UCC makes allowance for this type of testimony because, from a practical point of view, parties often get so used to dealing with each other in a particular way that they neglect to include certain terms in their written agreements. Similarly, some practices are so universal in a particular trade, business, or industry that the parties feel no need to include such universal practices in their written contracts. Accordingly, the UCC allows oral testimony to supplement a written agreement as to these practices.

## EXAMPLE 11-12: *Commonwealth Chemical Company v. St. Clair Printing, Inc.*

St. Clair Printing, Inc., and the Commonwealth Chemical Company have been doing business for 20 years. St. Clair prints all labels, business cards, letterheads, invoices, and purchase orders for Commonwealth. During their long time working together, St. Clair has always delivered orders to Commonwealth. When a new foreman took over the bindery and delivery operation for St. Clair, he decided that there would be no deliveries to any customers outside a five-mile radius of the print shop. As a result, Commonwealth did not receive an important order of labels and lost several big orders. When Commonwealth sued St. Clair for breach of contract, St. Clair pointed out that there was nothing mentioned in the written contract about delivery responsibilities falling to St. Clair. However, because of their 20-year history of consistently dealing with each other, the court allowed oral testimony about past practices to supplement the written contract.

## The Best Evidence Rule

Under the **best evidence rule**, the courts generally accept into evidence only the original of a writing, not a copy. Under this rule, a written instrument is regarded as the primary or best possible evidence. Thus, the best evidence rule concurs with and supports the parol evidence rule.

## The Equal Dignities Rule

The **equal dignities rule**, which is followed in some states, provides that when a party appoints an agent to negotiate an agreement that must be in writing, the appointment of the agent must also be in writing. In contrast, the appointment of an agent to negotiate an agreement that the law does not require to be in writing may be accomplished through an oral agreement.

---

### quick quiz 11-2

1. Whenever an ambiguous term is found in a preprinted contract, that ambiguity is interpreted in favor of the party who wrote the contract.  true | false

2. The principal objective is the main goal that the parties hope to accomplish by entering an agreement.  true | false

3. Parol evidence is another term for written evidence.  true | false

---

# 11-3 Formalities of Construction

Certain formalities are usually followed in the formation of anything other than the simplest kinds of written agreements. Although the Statute of Frauds may necessitate nothing more than the briefest written disclosure of promises, conditions, and terms, plus the signature(s) of the obligated party or parties, usually contracts in general commercial and consumer use are carefully written, researched for legal compliance, and signed. Furthermore, leases and contracts for the sale of real property may have additional requirements of content and formality that extend beyond these demands.

## Signature Requirements

Written agreements should be, but need not be, signed by both parties. If signed by only one party, any obligation in the agreement would be limited to that party alone. Parties should use their usual signatures, that is, the signatures used in other matters in the regular course of business. However, any mark that the signer intends to be a signature will be the legal signature of that person. Although it is unusual, a party may adopt any name desired in creating a contractual obligation, as long as the party intends to be bound by that signature.

**Facsimile Signatures** With the increased use of facsimile (fax) machines, methods have been adopted to bypass the best evidence rule by giving authentication to signatures sent by way of facsimile machines. A facsimile signature will be acceptable on a contract if the contract states that facsimile signatures are valid. More commonly, however, people fax copies of signed documents to other parties, and follow it up by sending the original signed documents by overnight mail or express delivery. Some states have enacted statutes allowing certain facsimile signatures.

### EXAMPLE 11-13: Massachusetts General Laws Chapter 92

Massachusetts has enacted the following statute relative to residence insurance agents: "A facsimile of a signature of any such resident agent imprinted on any property or casualty insurance policy issued by mail, computer modem or facsimile machine, so-called, shall have the same validity as a written signature." (Mass. Gen. Laws Chapter 92, s. 43.)

In addition, some states have adopted the **Uniform Facsimile Signatures of Public Officials Act**. This law allows the use of facsimile signatures of public officials when certain requirements are followed.

In cases in which a party cannot sign the written agreement due to illness, physical disability, or some other physical reason, another person may sign for that person. The signature should be followed by a statement indicating that the contracting party was physically unable to sign the document and that a signature was placed on the document by another person in the contracting party's presence and at the request of the contracting party. The person who has signed for the contracting party then signs the document (see Figure 11-1). Persons who lack the ability to read or write are often obliged to sign contracts. In such situations, the law accepts the person's mark, usually an X, properly witnessed, as a valid signature (see Figure 11-2).

## Witnesses and Acknowledgments

Witnesses are required in the signing of a will and sometimes a deed, but in most other documents, their signatures are at the option of the contracting parties. To ensure that no misunderstanding will arise as to the acceptance and signing of a written agreement, the use of witnesses is advised. Certain official documents, such as a certificate of title to a motor vehicle and a deed to real property, require the owner's signature and an acknowledgment by a notary public that the signature was the person's free act and deed. The notary

Figure 11-1  The signature for an incapacitated person bears a witness's name.

Her

Samantha X Cunningham

Mark

WITNESS:   I hereby attest that Samantha Cunningham made her
mark as her signature and that, at her request, I
added her name to her mark.

*Lindsay Quartermain*

**Figure 11-2**   The signature (*X*) of a person who does not know how to write has
been witnessed.

witnesses the signing of the document and then acknowledges this act by signing the document and adding the official seal to it. A notary is not authorized to read the document being signed and may be prevented from doing so.

## quick quiz 11-3

| | |
|---|---|
| 1. Written agreements must always be signed by both parties to the contract. | true \| false |
| 2. Facsimile signatures are not acceptable in any state. | true \| false |
| 3. A notary is required by law to read and understand all documents that he or she has witnessed. | true \| false |

# 11-4 Cyber-Commerce and the Law

Cyber-commerce (computer commerce, electronic commerce, or e-commerce) involves transacting business by computer. One of the most common cyber-commerce techniques involves buying and selling directly on the Internet by accessing a company's Web site. Some companies, such as Amazon.com, have made a name for themselves by perfecting this e-commerce technique. Other enterprises, such as eBay, have made a business of providing a marketplace for putting buyers and sellers together in an electronic auction setting. Others, such as Orbitz and Priceline, have found a niche in the marketplace by providing bargain prices for airlines and hotels. There are, of course, problems associated with buying and selling on the Internet, one of which involves the difficulty of verifying the identity of the party on the other side of an Internet connection. Another problem involves how to make up for the lack of paper documents in cyber-commerce. In both cases, the law has provided a solution. We will look at the problems associated with verification first.

Online shopping is fast, easy, and convenient. Utilizing digital signatures is an effective method used by businesses to verify the legitimacy of the transaction.

# Verification Problems

Verification problems can be solved in a number of ways. In fact, the parties can avoid the problem altogether by adding a term that delays the creation of the contract until the identities of the parties can be verified by some means other than computers. Or a business might elect to use its Web site only as an advertisement site. These solutions are unsatisfactory to most businesspeople, however, because they eliminate the advantages of doing business on the Internet. Another technique is for the parties to an Internet transaction to customize the verification process for each contract individually. However, in the interests of efficiency and cost, it would be preferable to have a process that applies to all contracts. A possible solution to this problem is the use of digital signatures. As we shall see, the Uniform Electronics Transactions Act defines a **digital signature** as "an electronic sound, symbol, or process attached to or logically associated with a record and executed or adopted by a person with the intent to sign the record." A digital signature is also referred to as a cyber-signature, an *electronic signature,* and an *e-signature.* Those businesses and legal practitioners who promote the use of digital signatures hope that the courts and/or the legislatures will institute a principle that states the use of a digital signature creates a rebuttable presumption that the signature is authentic and that the terms of the transaction have not been altered in transmission.

## Offer and Acceptance Online

An electronic party should always ensure that a copy of the contract is available on a hyperlink that will display the actual language of the agreement. The following terms should appear in any online agreement package: (1) payment procedures; (2) a limitation on the remedies that can be used by the parties; (3) refund policies; (4) the return process; (5) dispute settlement, forum selection, and choice-of-law provisions; (6) the applicability of cyber-signatures; (7) liability disclaimers; and (8) provisions relating to the offeree's manner of acceptance. In general, the other party accepts by clicking on a box on the computer screen that states that the party agrees to be bound by the terms of the contract. Sometimes this process is referred to as a *click-on acceptance* or *click-on agreement*. In a sense then, the *click* amounts to the party's signature. It is also critical to remember that when a cyber-agreement deals with goods, the provisions of Article 2 of the Uniform Commercial Code apply.

## Online Advertisement "Click" Fraud

One problem that arises in this area is verifying the identity of the "clicker." When companies are actually creating contracts, they police the process of verification rather closely. However, the click-on process functions not only in online contracts but also for online advertisements. Companies that advertise on the Internet often make contracts with search engines like Bing, Google, Yahoo, or America Online. The terms of these contracts generally include a provision that states that the company that places the advertisement online will pay the search engine on the basis of the number of clicks detected on that advertisement. The clicks are supposed to be a foolproof way to gauge interest in the advertiser's service or product. However, policing the exact nature of each click has proven difficult. Thus, hundreds of thousands of phony clicks have occurred in advertisements, inflating the bills of the advertisers which pay per click. The problem arises because the search engines often farm out the actual posting of the ads to intermediary companies, called *domain parkers,* that get paid on the basis of the number of clicks on the ads for which they are responsible. The domain parkers then transfer the ads to subsidiary Web sites. Some of these Web sites display advertisements and nothing more. This scenario provides a fertile ground in which the phony click campaigns grow. Some owners of these subsidiary Web sites pay fraudulent clickers a small amount to click on the ads, thus driving up the cost for the advertisers and increasing the Web site owner's split of the proceeds. Some even use "clickbot" software, capable of mechanically clicking on certain advertisements at programmed intervals. All of the major search engines have found themselves in litigation because of this new *cyber-confidence game*. (See Brian Grow and Ben Elgin, "Click Fraud: The Dark Side of Online Advertising," *BusinessWeek*, October 2, 2006, pp. 46–57.)

## Cyber-Commerce Legislation

Cyber-commerce legislation has taken many forms over the past decade. However, the three most influential acts have been the E-Sign Act, the Uniform Electronic Transactions Act (UETA), and the Uniform Computer Information Transactions Act (UCITA). A fourth new law that deals with a slightly different but no less serious problem, that of credit cards and identity theft, is the Fair and Accurate Credit Transactions Act (FACT).

### Self-Evident Truths

The cyber-revolution cannot be ignored by anyone who wants to succeed in business today. Manufacturers and sellers regularly use the Internet to advertise, to negotiate, and to send payments across the globe. Business people, however, are not the only ones who have discovered the power of the net. Political activists have also learned how to use the Internet to make governments pay attention to their demands. In his book *The Lexus and the Olive Tree,* Thomas L. Friedman predicted this revolution years ago when wrote, "In such a world, activists (will) learn how to use globalization to their advantage. They (will) learn how to compel companies to behave better by mobilizing global consumers through the Internet. I call this the 'network solution for human rights,' and it's the future of social advocacy. It is bottom up regulation, or side by side regulation—not top down regulation. You empower the bottom, instead of waiting for the top, by shaping a coalition that produces better governance without global government." What Friedman predicted in 2005 has come to pass. Populist movements have used the net to topple governments in Tunisia and Egypt and they threaten other governments the world over. So far this strategy seems to have worked fairly well for the protestors, but can you spot any dangers that might be hidden within the cyber-politics revolution? Think about that as you answer the following questions.

### Self-Evident Questions

1.  Do you agree with Friedman's premise that the electronic "network solution for human rights" is beneficial? Explain.

2.  Regardless of your answer to the first question, do you see the growth of populist movements, such as the Muslim Brotherhood and the Kefaya, as a good thing? Explain.

3.  Play devil's advocate for a moment. How might an autocrat like Qaddafi in Libya use the World Wide Web to keep himself in power? Explain.

4.  Are electronic populist movements the wave of the future or just a temporary tactic that the autocrats will soon learn to suppress? Explain.

5.  What if the net is used to coordinate violent populist movements? Is violence avoidable or does it always result from political advocacy? Explain

(*Source:* Thomas L. Friedman, *The Lexus and The Olive Tree,*  Random House, 2000, p. 207.)

## THE OPENING CASE *Revisited, Part III*
Written Contracts and The New Frontier:
*Wilcox v. Trautz*, Round 4

Recall that in the Opening Case at the beginning of this chapter, when Carol Wilcox and John Trautz broke up, they negotiated, wrote, and signed an agreement providing, among other things, that "each party's earnings and property is his or hers alone, and the other party shall have no interest in the property of the other." The written agreement did what all written agreements are supposed to do. It provided evidence of the agreement itself, along with evidence of the terms to which the parties agreed. As such, it was a perfectly enforceable written agreement that satisfied the Statute of Frauds. Nevertheless, if the parties had negotiated the contract today and had used an electronic method to record the agreement, it would still have to be reduced to a paper format and duplicate originals of that paper format would have to be distributed to both parties. This limitation results because the E-Sign Act excludes prenuptial agreements from those that can be produced electronically. While the Trautz-Wilcox agreement is not, strictly speaking a "pre-nup," it is close enough to that kind of an agreement to demand that the parties follow the E-Sign rules, just in case it becomes an issue later. After all, as they say, it is better to be safe than sorry.

**The E-Sign Act** The E-Sign Act is a federal act designed to deal with problems associated with cyber-commerce, especially those related to the recognition of electronic contracts and electronic signatures. Basically the act states that if the parties to a contract have voluntarily agreed to transact business electronically, the cyber-contract that results will be just as legally acceptable as a paper contract. The act also notes that the parties must be able to store and reproduce the cyber-record of the contract; otherwise, the cyber-record will not be legally sufficient under the act. The final word here is that under the provisions of the E-Sign Act, cyber-contracts and cyber-signatures are just as legitimate as their ink counterparts. There are a few documents that are not covered by this statute, including court records, eviction notices, health insurance cancellations, wills, foreclosure notices, prenuptial contracts, and divorce papers. However, sale and lease of goods contracts as covered by the Uniform Commercial Code are included in the E-Sign Act.

**The Uniform Electronic Transactions Act (UETA)** The Uniform Electronic Transactions Act establishes the same type of legal parity between electronic records and paper records as does the E-Sign Act. It does not establish any new guidelines governing contracts just because they are entered electronically. The approach therefore is not to establish the differences between electronic contracts and paper agreements but instead to focus on the similarities. As a result, once the parties to a contract have voluntarily agreed to enter a transaction using an electronic medium, the agreement that results in electronic form, including the cyber-signatures, will be just as valid as a paper agreement. The UETA applies only to transactions that involve some sort of commercial, business, or governmental matter. The law also states that if an act, such as the Statute of Frauds, requires a writing and a signature, then a cyber-record and a cyber-signature will fulfill that requirement. Also, under provisions of the E-Sign Act, the UETA will trump the E-Sign Act provided that the state that has adopted the UETA has not altered its content. Most states, 48 at last count, have adopted the UETA. However, some states have altered provisions in the act and so it is best to check the version that has been enacted by your state. This is also why it would be smart to check the forum selection clause in any cyber-contract that you are about to enter. (See The E-Sign Act, 15 USC Section 7002 9 (2) (A) (I))

## The Uniform Computer Information Transactions Act (UCITA)

The Uniform Computer Information Transactions Act (UCITA) focuses on contracts that involve the sale or lease of computer software, computer databases, interactive products, multimedia products, and any other type of computer information. The UCITA is in line with the basic provisions of the E-Sign Act and the UETA, in that it also declares that any transaction entered into using an electronic medium is just as valid as a paper agreement. Not all states have adopted the UCITA, so it is important to check on the applicability of the statute in your jurisdiction.

## The Fair and Accurate Credit Transactions Act (The FACT Act)

The Fair and Accurate Credit Transactions Act (The FACT Act) is Congress's antidote to one manifestation of the identity theft epidemic. The new law, which is actually an amendment to the Fair Credit Reporting Act (FCRA), is designed to cut down on identity theft related to the use of credit cards. The act prohibits merchants from using credit card receipts that show anything other than the last five credit card numbers. Receipts also cannot display credit card expiration dates. In effect, because the act outlaws such numerical displays, identity thieves will no longer be able to assume the identity of a consumer by obtaining a copy of a credit card receipt and using the credit card number and expiration date on the receipt to "verify their identity" over the phone or online.

### quick quiz 11-4

1. The E-Sign Act is a model act designed to deal with problems associated with cyber-commerce.    true | false

2. The Uniform Electronic Transactions Act was passed by Congress to deal with the legality of electronic transactions.    true | false

3. The UCITA is not in line with any of the provisions of the E-Sign Act or the UETA.    true | false

## Summary

**11.1**   The Statutes of Frauds outlines six types of contracts that must be in writing to be enforceable. These include contracts that cannot be completed within one year; contracts transferring real property rights; contracts for the sale of goods of $500 or more; certain contracts entered by executors and administrators; contracts by one party to pay a debt incurred by another party; and contracts in consideration of marriage.

**11.2**   The legal system has developed certain basic criteria that make the construction and interpretation of written contracts consistent. These four criteria are (1) the standard construction rule, (2) the parol evidence rule, (3) the best evidence rule, and (4) the equal dignities rule.

**11.3**   Certain formalities are followed in the formation of contracts. Written agreements need not be signed

by both parties. However, any agreement signed by only one party would obligate only that party. Facsimile signatures are allowed on a contract if the contract states that such signatures are valid. Some states have statutes allowing facsimile signatures. Persons who are illiterate usually sign written contracts with an X. Such signatures should be witnessed. Witnesses are not required when parties enter written agreements. However, to avoid misunderstandings, the use of witnesses is advisable. The law provides that some documents must be recorded in a public office for inspection by the public.

**11.4**   There are problems associated with buying and selling on the Internet. One of these problems involves the difficulty of verifying the identity of the person on the other side of an Internet connection. Another involves the question of how to deal with the fact that electronic transactions do not produce paper documents. In both cases, the law has provided some solutions to these difficulties. Three laws that address these problems include the E-Sign Act, the Uniform Electronic Transactions Act (UETA), and the Uniform Computer Information Transactions Act (UCITA). A fourth act that deals with the problem of identity theft is the Fair and Accurate Credit Transactions Act (FACT).

## Key Terms

acknowledgment, 240
antenuptial agreement, 233
best evidence rule, 239
collateral contract, 233
condition precedent, 237
cosigner, 233
cyber-signature, 242
equal dignities rule, 239
equitable estoppel, 231

guarantor, 233
guaranty contract, 233
guaranty of payment, 233
leading objective test, 233
main purpose test, 233
memorandum, 235
obligee, 233
obligor, 233
parol evidence rule, 236

part performance, 231
premarriage agreement, 233
prenuptial agreement, 233
primary objective test, 233
standard construction rule, 236
Statute of Frauds, 229
Uniform Facsimile Signatures of Public Officials Act, 240

## Questions for Review and Discussion

1. What are the goals of the Statute of Frauds?
2. What contracts must be in writing under the Statute of Frauds?
3. What information must be in a writing under the Statute of Frauds?
4. What is the standard construction rule?
5. What is the parol evidence rule?
6. What are the exceptions to the parol evidence rule?
7. What is the best evidence rule?
8. What is the equal dignities rule?
9. What are the problems associated with cyber-commerce?
10. What are the latest cyber-commerce statutes?

## Cases for Analysis

1. Several identity theft victims filed a series of class action lawsuits against firms that had not made the changes required by the Fair and Accurate Credit Transactions Act (FACT) by the statutory deadline. One of the issues before the court was whether the victims had to demonstrate that the offending company deliberately refused to comply or did so with reckless disregard for the new requirements. Which standard would be the appropriate one in this situation? Explain. Amanda Bronstad, "Suits Multiply over Credit Card Exposure: Cash Registers Displaying Too Many Digits Spark Dozens of Class Actions," *The National Law Journal,* February 19, 2007, p. 4.

2. Harold Perdue entered an individually negotiated employment contract with Nicholas Paynter. Under terms of the contract, Perdue was to work for Paynter as a private investigator in Paynter's newly established firm, known as Eye-Spy Investigations. The employment contract was on a trial basis and was to last for nine months. That nine-month period was set to begin one month after Paynter had set up shop. However, Paynter could not begin his operation until the contractors finished remodeling his office. Johnson Contractors, Ltd., had promised to have the office completed within one to three months. One month after the contract had been finalized, Paynter notified Perdue that he had hired someone else and that his services were no longer needed. Perdue, who had relied on the contract, had turned down several other lucrative offers that had since been filled by other operatives. Moreover, Perdue was now having trouble getting a similar job. Perdue threatened to bring suit against Paynter. Paynter told

Perdue to go ahead and sue. Privately, Paynter believes that he is immune to a lawsuit because, since Johnson Construction had three months to finish remodeling the office, the contract could not have been performed within one year. Perdue argued that, because Johnson could have finished in less than one month, the contract could be performed within a year, and it did not have to be in writing to be enforceable. Who is correct here? Explain.

3. Meng, a vice-president at Boston University, resigned his position to protest what he regarded as the unethical and unprofessional behavior of the university's president, John Silber, in terminating a recently renewed contract with Linkage Corporation. Silber orally promised Meng, as a severance package when he resigned, 14 months of salary and benefits and free tuition for two of his children if either should attend the university. Was the oral promise enforceable? Explain. *Meng v. Trustees of Boston University*, 96-9776 Appeals Court (MA).

4. As part of an employment agreement, Bazzy orally promised to give Hall an option to buy 1,000 shares of company stock at $20 per share. Hall brought suit against the company when it refused to sell the stock to him. What legal argument may Bazzy's company use to refuse to sell the stock to Hall as agreed? *Hall v. Horizon House Microwave, Inc.*, 506 N.E.2d 178 (MA).

5. Anna Wilson was assistant manager of a Montgomery Ward store. When Montgomery Ward announced that it would be closing the store, the manager quit, leaving Wilson in charge. A district manager orally promised Wilson that if she stayed on and assisted in the closing of the store, she would receive a sum of money calculated according to a certain formula. Wilson stayed on and managed the closing of the store (which took two months) in addition to her regular duties. Montgomery Ward refused to pay her the money, claiming that the oral promise was unenforceable. Was the store correct? Why or why not? *Wilson v. Montgomery Ward*, 610 F. Supp. 1035 (DC IN).

6. Curtis Hendrix orally agreed to compensate Beverly Spertell for services rendered in connection with their living together out of wedlock. Later, when suit was brought to collect the money, Hendrix argued that the oral contract was unenforceable under the Statute of Frauds. Do you agree with Hendrix? Explain. *Spertell v. Hendrix*, 461 N.Y.S.2d 823 (NY).

7. Lawson hired Konves to conduct extensive audits of her 87 boutiques, located throughout the United States. As part of the agreement, Lawson required Konves to spend one week at each boutique. Konves demanded a written agreement before she would agree to Lawson's terms. Why was Konves correct in making this demand?

8. Butler leased a certain piece of property from Wheeler with an option to purchase it at a later date. The agreement was handwritten and consisted of two separate documents, each listing part of the transaction. Butler later attempted to purchase the property but Wheeler refused to sell, claiming that the agreement was unenforceable because it was contained in two documents. Was Wheeler correct? Explain. *Butler v. Lovoll*, 620 P.2d 1251 (NV).

9. Ray's Motor Sales sold a mobile home to Hathaway. Before the written contract was signed, the salesperson told Hathaway that Ray's would take care of any problems that Hathaway might have with the mobile home. This promise was not included in the written document. When Hathaway had problems with the mobile home, he asked Ray's to take care of them. Ray's refused to be of any assistance. Could Hathaway enforce Ray's promise? Explain. *Hathaway v. Ray's Motor Sales*, 247 A.2d 512 (VT).

## quick quiz Answers

| 11-1 | 11-2 | 11-3 | 11-4 |
|------|------|------|------|
| 1. F | 1. F | 1. F | 1. F |
| 2. F | 2. T | 2. F | 2. F |
| 3. T | 3. F | 3. F | 3. F |

# Chapter 12

# Third Parties, Discharge, and Remedies

## THE OPENING CASE  Punitive Damages and the Limits of the Law: *State Farm Mutual v. Campbell*

When one party breaks the terms of a contract, and the other party sues, the court will do its best to place the parties in as good a position as they would have been had the contract been performed as promised in the first place. In this way contract law differs from other areas of the law, such as criminal law, which generally seeks to punish the wrongdoer and deter the criminal conduct in the future. Contract law also differs from tort law which is designed to compensate the victim, punish the wrongdoer, and deter tortious behavior in the future. One reason for this policy is that people voluntarily assume responsibilities when they make a contract and those responsibilities affect only the parties and not the general public as is the case with criminal law and, at times, tort law.

All of this is fine as far as it goes, but what happens when the breaching party has deliberately undermined the basic intent of contract law by committing fraud not just in the contract at issue, but as a pattern of conduct, perhaps even an official policy, affecting hundreds and thousands of other contracts? This is precisely what happened in *State Farm Mutual v. Campbell*. In that case, the

Campbells had been involved in an automobile accident. They filed their case with State Farm, which refused to settle out of court, despite the desires of the Campbells and the advice of State Farm's own investigators. The original case went to trial and the Campbells lost.

When State Farm refused to pay the full amount of the award, the Campbells sued the insurer for bad faith, fraud, and intentional infliction of emotional distress. The Campbells offered evidence that the refusal to settle was not just fraudulent in relation to their contract, but was, instead, part of a larger pattern of conduct planned and executed by State Farm over a 20-year period against hundreds of policy holders. The conduct involved a national campaign referred to as the Performance, Planning, and Review (PP&R) Policy. Once the jury heard evidence about the systematic execution of the PP&R policy, they awarded the Campbells $145 million in punitive damages. The judge then reduced the punitive damages to $25 million. On appeal the Campbells stressed the fraudulent nature of the PP&R policy and State Farm argued that their conduct in relation to the other contracts should not be used to punish them for their conduct in relation to the contract that they had with the Campbells. The supreme court of Utah agreed with the Campbells and reinstated the $145 million in punitive damages. The case made its way to the United States Supreme Court. As you read the chapter consider the facts in the Campbell case, remember the general principles of contract law, and see if you can predict the Supreme Court's ultimate decision in the case. [See *State Farm Mutual Automobile Ins. Co. v. Campbell,* 538 U.S. 408 (United States Supreme Court).]

**Opening Case Questions**

1. In what way does the Campbell case against State Farm Mutual appear to be both a contract case and a tort case? Explain

2. Should the evidence brought by the Campbells in relation to State Farm's conduct outside of the contract be considered to determine the measure of damages? Explain.

3. Should the reprehensible conduct of the company be considered in measuring the extent of the damages? Explain.

4. What if the conduct that the Campbell's complained of was perfectly legal in the other states? Should the court punish conduct that is illegal in its home state but is perfectly legal in another state? Why or why not?

5. Should the courts be allowed to punish a corporation that makes a contract in bad faith? Explain.

 Learning Objectives

1. Explain the legal rights given to all beneficiaries.
2. Identify the legal rights given to incidental beneficiaries.
3. Explain the assignment of rights and the delegation of duties.
4. Explain the nature of a novation.
5. Relate what constitutes satisfactory performance of a contract.
6. Outline the difference between complete and substantial performance.
7. List the ways that a contract can be discharged by nonperformance.
8. Clarify the concept of anticipatory repudiation.
9. Enumerate the types of damages available in the event of a breach of contract.
10. Contrast specific performance with injunctive relief.

# 12-1 Contracts and Third Parties

A **third party** is a person who may in some way be affected by a contract but who is not one of the contracting parties. A third party, also known as an **outside party**, is at times given benefits from a contract made between two or more other parties. A third party receiving benefits from a contract made by others is known as a **third party beneficiary** or sometimes simply as a **beneficiary** to the contract. Although not obligated by the agreement made between those in privity, third parties may have the legal right to enforce the benefits given them by such agreements.

## Intended Beneficiaries

A beneficiary in whose favor a contract is made is an **intended beneficiary**. With exceptions in some states, an intended beneficiary can enforce the contract made by those in privity of contract. Those who are most frequently recognized to be intended beneficiaries and have the right to demand and enforce the benefits promised are creditor beneficiaries, donee beneficiaries, and insurance beneficiaries.

**Creditor Beneficiaries** A **creditor beneficiary** is an outside third party to whom one or both contracting parties owe a continuing debt of obligation arising from a contract. Frequently, the obligation results from the failure of the contracting party or parties to pay for goods delivered or services rendered by the third party at some time in the past.

**Donee Beneficiaries** A third party who provides no consideration for the benefits received and who owes the contracting parties no legal duty is known as a **donee beneficiary**. However, the contracting parties owe the donee beneficiary the act promised; if it is not forthcoming, the donee beneficiary may bring suit. The consideration that supports this type of agreement is the consideration exchanged by the parties in privity of contract.

**Insurance Beneficiaries** An individual named as the beneficiary of an insurance policy is usually considered a donee beneficiary. The beneficiary does not have to furnish the insured with consideration to enforce payment of the policy. In some cases, an insurance beneficiary may also be a creditor beneficiary. This situation occurs in consumer or mortgage loans when the creditor requires the debtor to furnish a life-term insurance policy naming the creditor as the beneficiary. The policy will pay the debt if the debtor dies before the loan has been repaid.

## Incidental Beneficiaries

An **incidental beneficiary** is an outside party for whose benefit a contract was not made but who would substantially benefit if the agreement were performed according to its terms and conditions. An incidental beneficiary, in contrast to an intended beneficiary, has no legal grounds for enforcing the contract made by those in privity of contract.

### EXAMPLE 12-1: *Faber v. The Brotherhood of Aerospace Workers*

Mark Faber owned a hotel and restaurant in downtown Indianapolis. The Brotherhood of Aerospace Workers (BAW) had a contract with the city for the use of the municipal auditorium for the union's annual convention. One week before the convention, the union announced that it was canceling the meeting. The move was a clear violation of BAW's contract with the city. Faber brought suit against the BAW for damages due to lost business caused by the breach. The court dismissed the case on a motion for summary judgment. The court ruled that Faber was an incidental beneficiary and therefore had no grounds on which to bring the suit against the union.

### quick quiz 12-1

1. A third party who provides no consideration and owes no legal duty to the contracting parties is a donee beneficiary.  true | false

2. The principle of privity stopped many judges from establishing third party rights.  true | false

3. Incidental and intended beneficiaries have the same rights.  true | false

# 12-2 The Law of Assignment

When people enter contracts, they receive certain rights and incur particular duties. It is completely accepted today that, with some exceptions noted subsequently and unless the contract itself provides otherwise, these rights and duties can be transferred to others. An **assignment** is a transfer of a contract right, and a **delegation** is a transfer of a contract duty.

## Assignment and Delegation

In general, rights are *assigned,* and duties are *delegated.* In most cases, both are governed by the same rules. If A is owed money by B, A may assign to C the right to collect the money. However, if A has agreed to pay B to harvest 200 acres of wheat for a price, B may delegate the duty of harvesting to C. Restrictions against the delegation of duties are presented later in this chapter.

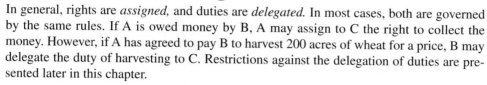

EXAMPLE **12-2:** *Wesley, et al. v. Lerro*

Lee Wesley agreed to lay cement on the driveway leading up to Walter Lerro's house for $24,000. Plans and specifications were provided by Lerro. Wesley delegated the duties involved in laying the asphalt to Hanover Construction, Inc., another contractor. Hanover then assigned the right to collect the $24,000 from Lerro to Olsen Construction Supplies, Ltd. Lerro, who did not like the way his job and his money were being bounced all over the tri-county area, refused to pay Olsen. Lerro then called Wesley and ordered him to tear out the driveway because he was insulted by the fact that Wesley thought so little of his job that he had assigned it to Hanover. In hindsight, this choice was probably a poorly thought out decision, because everyone involved in the situation, from Wesley to Hanover to Olsen, sued Lerro, who still ended up paying the original $24,000—and then some.

## Parties to Assignment

Three parties are associated with any assignment. Two of the parties are the ones who entered the original agreement. The party who assigns rights or delegates duties is the **assignor**. The outside third party to whom the assignment is made is the **assignee**. The remaining party to the original agreement is the **obligor**.

EXAMPLE **12-3:** *From King to Gomez to Walker*

Lisa Gomez owed Roger King $500 for some photography work that King had done for her. At the same time, King owed Ted Walker $500 back rent. King assigned Walker the right to receive the money from Gomez. In this situation, King was the assignor, Walker the assignee, and Gomez the obligor. The following flowchart clearly illustrates these points.

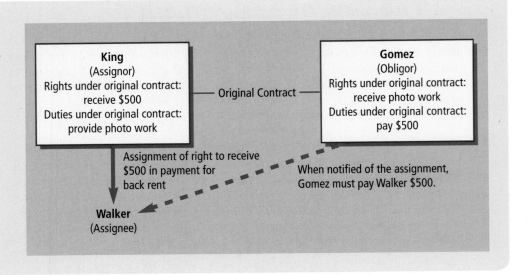

## Consideration in Assignment

Consideration is not required in the assignment of a contract. When there is no supporting consideration, however, the assignor may repudiate the assignment at any time prior to its execution. In the previous example, the consideration supporting King's assignment is found in the rental agreement between King and Walker.

In addition, when no consideration is given for an assignment, creditors of the assignor may have the assignment rescinded on the grounds that it is a fraudulent conveyance. A **fraudulent conveyance** is a transfer of property with the intent to defraud creditors. If the $500 assignment to Walker in Example 12-3 had been a gift instead of payment for back rent, King's creditors could have had the assignment rescinded, because they could rightfully anticipate the money coming from Gomez.

## Assignment Methods

To be valid, an assignment must follow certain accepted procedures designed to protect all of the parties. Form of assignment, notice of assignment, and the rights of parties in successive or subsequent assignments must conform to practices established by case law and state statutes.

**Form of Assignment** Assignment may be accomplished through written, oral, or implied agreements between the assignor and the assignee. Parties to an assignment must observe the requirement provided by the equal dignities rule discussed in Chapter 11. Under that rule, the law requires that if the agreement by the original parties must be in writing, the assignment also must be in writing.

**Notice of Assignment** An assignment is valid at the time it is made. As a measure of protection against subsequent assignments, the assignee should give notice of the assignment to the obligor. Although this obligation falls to the assignee, either party may give notice. Once notice is received, the obligor should deal with the assignee. If notice is not given, it would be normal practice for the obligor to render performance to the original contracting party, the assignor. If due notice has been given and the obligor makes payment to the assignor, the obligor is not excused from making payment to the assignee.

**Bryant, Inc.**

**6225 St. Clair Avenue**
**Cleveland, OH 44103**

June 15, 20 - -

Mr. Carl Newfield
750 Maple Street, Apt. 4-C
Lakewood, Ohio 44117

Dear Mr. Newfield:

You are hereby notified that Pendleton Architects Limited of Euclid, Ohio, has assigned to Bryant, Inc., all rights to its claim against you in the amount of $750.

You are further notified to direct all payments to Bryant, Inc., at the above address to ensure credit for payment.

Sincerely yours,

*Norbert Bryant*

Norbert Bryant
Vice-President

**Figure 12-1** The format used by Bryant, Inc., in the case described in Example 12-4, to notify Newfield of the assignment from Pendleton.

**EXAMPLE 12-4:** *Bryant, Inc. v. Newfield*

Carl Newfield owed Pendleton Architects Limited $750 as a final payment for architectural work. Pendleton in turn owed Bryant, Inc., a substantial sum. As partial payment of that amount, Pendleton assigned Newfield's debt to Bryant. As the assignee in this case, Bryant sent a letter to Newfield indicating that the debt that Newfield owed to Pendleton should now be paid to Bryant, Inc. Figure 12-1 presents a copy of the letter that Bryant sent to Newfield informing him of the assignment. Newfield would now be legally required to adhere to the assignment. When Newfield refused to honor the assignment, Bryant could bring suit against him.

**Subsequent Assignments** Should the assignor make a subsequent assignment of the same right, the courts must decide which of the two assignees has a superior right and claim against the obligor. A majority of the states hold that the first assignee has a superior right, even if a later assignee was the first to give notice of the assignment to the obligor. A minority of courts hold that whichever assignee was first to give notice of assignment has a superior right and claim to any assigned benefits.

### quick quiz 12-2

| | |
|---|---|
| 1. A delegation is the transfer of a contractual right. | true \| false |
| 2. The equal dignities axiom has no application in the law of assignment. | true \| false |
| 3. It is the responsibility of the assignor to give notice of the assignment to the obligor. | true \| false |

**About the Law**

An assignment, rather than a negotiation, occurs when a check is transferred to a third party without a required endorsement.

## 12-3 Assignment Rights, Duties, and Restrictions

Rights can be assigned, and duties can be delegated. Although this rule seems simple enough, disputes still arise regarding both assignment and delegation. What is generally in dispute is whether a particular right or duty can be transferred and, if so, what legal effects arise from that transfer.

### Rights and Duties of the Assignee

The rights and duties of the assignee are the same as those previously held by the assignor under the original contract. It is fair to say that the assignee "steps into the shoes" of the assignor. Claims the assignor may have had against the obligor now belong to the assignee. Also, defenses the obligor may have had against the assignor's claims may now be used against the assignee.

The assignee's duty in an assignment is to give notice of the assignment to the obligor. The obligor is allowed a reasonable time to seek assurance that an assignment has been truly made. Making the assignment in writing reduces the possibility of fraudulent representation as an assignee.

### EXAMPLE 12-5: The Quitter–Stalker Assignment, Part I

Quitter appeared at the payroll department of the Meadville Delivery Company and told the paymaster that one of Meadville's drivers, Stalker, had made an assignment of part of his paycheck to her. Under terms of the assignment, Quitter was to receive $150 of the money that Meadville owed Stalker. Meadville, the obligor, would not have to pay Quitter the $150 until the paymaster had a reasonable amount of time to verify the assignment.

# Liabilities and Warranties of the Assignor

The assignor is obligated to any express and implied warranties that serve to protect either the assignee or the obligor. A **warranty** is a promise, statement, or other representation that a thing has certain qualities.

## Warranties to the Assignee

The assignor is bound by an implied warranty that the obligor will respect the assignment and make the performance, as required by the original agreement between the assignor and the obligor.

---

### EXAMPLE 12-6: The Quitter–Stalker Assignment, Part II

Suppose, in the Quitter–Stalker assignment, that the Meadville Trucking Company had been either unwilling or unable to pay Quitter the $150. Stalker would be bound by an implied warranty to Quitter that the $150 would be paid. If the assignment were a gift to Quitter, there would be no enforceable warranty in the absence of consideration between the assignor and the assignee.

---

## Warranties to the Obligor

If the assignor delegates to an assignee duties owed the obligor, there is an implied warranty that the duties delegated will be carried out in a complete and satisfactory manner.

# Restrictions on Assignments

Although most contracts may be assigned, those for personal and professional services may not. The right of assignment may also be restricted by agreement of the original parties to the contract and, in certain cases, by law.

## Restrictions on Personal and Professional Service Contracts

A party may not delegate duties that are of a personal or professional nature. *Personal,* in this context, means "other than routine." Musicians or artists, for example, could not delegate their services to someone else. They are chosen for their ability or artistic talent. Professional services are those rendered by physicians, lawyers, certified public accountants, ministers, and others. People in these occupations are selected because of their special abilities, and their services could not be delegated to someone else. In contrast, routine services may usually be delegated. These are services performed by electricians, mechanics, woodworkers, plumbers, waitstaff, bankers, publishers, and others whose skills and abilities are judged according to the usual customs and standards of the marketplace.

Professionals, like dentists, are chosen based on their particular skills and abilities and may not delegate their professional duties to another.

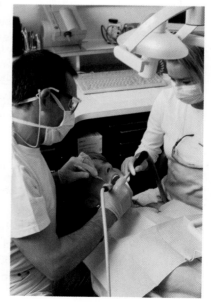

## Restrictions Imposed by Original Contract

Parties to a contract may include a condition that will not allow its assignment. Some courts have held that a restriction against the assignment of a debt owed by the obligor robs the assignor of a property right guaranteed by law and would be contrary to public policy. Other courts have permitted this restrictive condition.

## Restrictions Imposed by Law

Assignment, in special situations, may be restricted by law or declared void because it is contrary to public policy. Thus, members of the armed services may not assign any part of their pay except to a spouse or family member. Police officers, persons elected or appointed to public office, and others are likewise restricted from making assignment of their pay or of duties that they have been especially chosen to perform.

## Novation and Assignment

Sometimes a party to a contract will assign all rights and delegate all duties to a third party (the assignee). Once this happens, the assignee will work directly with the obligor, performing the duties and receiving the benefits. Nevertheless, the assignor will remain in privity of contract with the obligor and be liable to the obligor if the assignee does not perform or performs improperly.

**EXAMPLE 12-7:** *Superfine Market v. Allgood Canning Company*

Allgood Canning Company entered into a contract to sell 1,000 cases of baked beans to Superfine Market for a specific price. Shortly thereafter, Allgood delegated its duty to ship the beans and assigned its rights to receive the money to Fastway Canning Company. The beans Fastway shipped turned out to be bad. If Superfine were to bring suit for damages, it would have to be brought against Allgood, because that was the company with which it had contracted. There was no privity between Superfine and Fastway.

In contrast, if all three parties agree, the assignor can be released from liability at the time of the assignment, and privity of contract can exist between the assignee and the obligor. Such an arrangement is called a **novation**, which is a substitution, by mutual agreement, of a new party for one of the original parties to a contract. If, in Example 12-7, Superfine and Fastway had agreed to release Allgood from responsibility under the original contract, a novation would have occurred. Privity of contract then would have been between Superfine and Fastway. Superfine's only recourse upon receiving the bad beans would have been to bring suit against Fastway because, by mutual consent, Allgood had been discharged.

### quick quiz 12-3

| | | |
|---|---|---|
| 1. The phrase "assignment of a contract" means the same thing as the phrase "assignment of rights." | true | false |
| 2. Personal and professional duties are just as transferable as all other duties. | true | false |
| 3. Novations have been outlawed under the Restatement of Contracts. | true | false |

## 12-4 Discharge by Performance

Most contracts are discharged by **performance**, which means that the parties do what they agreed to do under the terms of the contract. When performance occurs, the obligations of the parties end. Sometimes, however, the parties do not perform in a timely or satisfactory manner. At other times, they perform partially but not completely. At still other times, they do not perform at all.

# Time for Performance

When the time for performance is not stated in the contract, the contract must be performed within a reasonable time. A **reasonable time** is the time that may fairly, properly, and conveniently be required to do the task that is to be done, considering attending circumstances. Whether a task is performed within a reasonable time is a question of fact to be decided by the jury in a jury trial or the judge in a nonjury trial.

## EXAMPLE 12-8: *Rostow Aviation, Ltd. v. Futuregraphics, Inc.*

Rostow Aviation, Ltd., entered a contract with Futuregraphics, Inc., for the design and implementation of a new Web site for Rostow. The Web site was supposed to be up and operational within 60 days of the making of the contract. Futuregraphics was one week late in the completion of the Web site. Rostow attempted to rescind the agreement, claiming that time was of special importance. The court ruled that it had not been clearly established that time was essential for the completion of the Web site. Because time was not essential to the satisfactory performance of the agreement, Rostow was held to the contract.

## A QUESTION OF ETHICS

The court held Rostow to the contract in Example 12-8 even though Futuregraphics was one week late in fulfilling its part of the agreement. Because time really was not essential to the agreement, and because Rostow presumably knew that, was it ethical for Rostow to raise the issue of Futuregraphics' lateness in the first place? If time had been important to the completion of the Web site, did Rostow have a responsibility to raise the issue of time before the contract was finalized? If Futuregraphics knew it was running behind schedule, did it have a duty to notify Rostow and offer some sort of compensation for the breach? Explain your answers.

When the time for performance is stated in the contract but there is nothing to indicate that time is of particular importance, the court will usually allow additional time to perform. When the time for performance is stated in the contract and there is something special about the contract that indicates time is essential, the time for performance will be strictly enforced.

## EXAMPLE 12-9: *Carter City School System v. Spectrum Images, Inc.*

Spectrum Images, Inc. entered a contract with the entire Carter City school system for the design, production, and distribution of the yearbooks for each of the system's three high schools. A very strict schedule was developed for each high school yearbook staff, specifying when the manuscript, art, and photos had to be delivered to Spectrum; when the material had to be read and returned; and when the page proofs had to be read, corrected, and returned to Spectrum. The yearbooks were to be delivered to each high school 90 days after Spectrum had received all page proofs so that they would be ready for distribution on the graduation day for each of the high schools. In such a situation, it is clear that time is an important factor in this agreement. Unfortunately, the students at two of the three schools did not return the proofs on time, and the yearbooks were late. This missed deadline caused an extra expense for the city school system, which had to send the yearbooks to students by FedEx because they were no longer on campus to pick up their books personally. When Carter City sued Spectrum, the court ruled that because the students knew that time was of the essence and had not made the scheduled deadline, the city could not complain when Spectrum failed to meet the delivery date.

Similarly, when the phrase "time is of the essence" is included among the terms of a written contract, the time period will be enforced. The phrase makes it clear that the time element is of the utmost importance to the parties. Some contracts use a "best efforts" clause to avoid committing parties to a date but instead committing them to do their best to perform by a certain date.

## Satisfactory, Complete, and Substantial Performance

**Satisfactory performance** exists when either personal taste or objective standards have determined that the contracting parties have performed their contractual duties according to the agreement. Satisfactory performance is either an express or implied condition of every contract. Sales agreements for consumer goods often note this condition by including the words: "money back if not entirely satisfied." In other contracts, satisfaction may be carefully defined according to the expectations of the parties. When there is no express agreement, the law implies that work will be done in a skillful manner and the materials or goods will be free of defects. Ordinarily, the parties may be discharged from a contract only if there has been satisfactory performance. Sometimes, one person will agree to do something to another person's satisfaction. Services rendered in a beauty salon or barbershop, photographs taken at a studio, and portraits painted by an artist fall within this classification. Regardless of the skill and application of the person doing the work, dissatisfied customers may, on the basis of their personal judgment and satisfaction, refuse to make payment.

**Complete performance** occurs when all the parties fully accomplish every term, condition, and promise to which they agreed. **Substantial performance** occurs when a party, in good faith, executes all promised terms and conditions with the exception of minor details that do not affect the real intent of their agreement. Complete performance terminates an agreement, freeing the parties of any further obligation. Ordinarily, substantial performance also serves to discharge the agreement but with one difference: A party who correctly complains that the other party's performance has been substantial but not complete has the right to demand reimbursement from the offending party to correct those details that were not performed.

EXAMPLE **12-10:** *South Central State College v. McLaughlin Construction, Inc.*

McLaughlin Construction, Inc., was the primary contractor for the construction of a new engineering center for South Central State College. The construction of the center was supposed to be completed within one year, and the doors were to open in time for the fall term. The building was completed by fall, but the architect for McLaughlin had committed an error. Apparently he had failed to take into consideration the stress that would be placed on the floor-to-ceiling windows in the building's lobby.

As a result, several of those floor-to-ceiling windows developed cracks. An inspection by the state engineers demonstrated that the cracks posed no danger to anyone in or near the building. Nevertheless, the cracked windows were quite unsightly, and they leaked heavily when it rained, flooding the lobby. Consequently, the college demanded that the construction company make repairs at its own expense. The company refused, and the college threatened to rescind the entire contract. Instead, cooler heads prevailed, and the college hired another construction firm to make adjustments to the stress so that the floor-to-ceiling windows would be the showpieces they were supposed to be. When the college asked for and was refused reimbursement for the additional expense, it sued McLaughlin. The court held that there had been substantial performance of the original contract. However, because the cracked windows were caused by an error on the part of the McLaughlin architect, the court awarded reimbursement costs to the college.

## Conditions and Tender of Performance

Some contracts have conditions or terms that determine the rights and duties of the parties prior to performance, during performance, and following performance. These conditions may be classified as conditions precedent, conditions concurrent, or conditions subsequent. Also, in most situations it is necessary for a nonbreaching party to continue to offer to perform as promised. This is referred to as a tender of performance. It is discussed below at length.

**Conditions of Performance**   A **condition precedent** is a condition that requires the performance of certain acts or promises before the other party is obligated to pay money or provide any other agreed to consideration. In a *unilateral contract,* the performance of a condition precedent serves as the offeree's acceptance of the offer. In a *bilateral contract,* it is a promise that if not performed leads to either rescission or termination of the entire agreement.

### EXAMPLE 12-11:  The Pressler Case

Pressler, a third-year law student, signed an agreement to accept a position with a law firm. The members of the firm agreed to hire Pressler on the condition that she receive her law degree and pass the bar examination in their state. Earning the law degree and passing the bar examination are conditions precedent to the performance of the obligation of the law firm in giving Pressler the position.

A condition that requires both parties to perform at the same time is a **condition concurrent**. A promise to deliver goods supported by the buyer's promise to pay on delivery is a very common condition concurrent. Real estate sales agreements, by custom, usually state that the owner–seller will deliver a good and complete deed to the real property on the buyer's presentation of either cash or a certified check for the amount of the purchase price. Failure of either to do as promised concurrently would be a breach of the express contract condition. A **condition subsequent** is one in which the parties agree that the contract will be terminated when a prescribed event occurs or does not occur. An agreement between a builder and a client stating that contract performance would terminate if a required building permit were not obtained from the issuing public authority within 60 days after the contract is signed is a condition subsequent. Some warranties included in contracts also illustrate these conditions.

## EXAMPLE 12-12: *Graham v. Metcalf*

Luben Metcalf agreed to remodel Trisha Graham's back porch for $15,000. Both parties signed a written agreement. One clause in the agreement stated that Metcalf guaranteed the improvements would be free of defects for 12 months after the work was completed. Graham agreed to pay for the improvements upon completion. Metcalf's guarantee constituted a condition subsequent, that is, a condition that applies after both parties have performed their primary obligations under the contract. When, after only one month, the roof of the porch roof leaked, Graham demanded that Metcalf return and fix the problem. Metcalf repeatedly refused to do anything about the leaky roof. Graham was forced to hire another contractor to correct Metcalf's errors. Graham then successfully sued Metcalf and recovered the cost of the repairs.

**Tender of Performance**  In contract law, **tender of performance** means to offer to do what one has agreed to do under the terms of the contract. If someone has agreed to sell a parcel of land for $40,000, for example, tender of performance would be offering to give a signed deed to the buyer at the agreed time. Similarly, **tender of payment** would be presenting the $40,000 to the seller at the agreed time. It is important to make tender even if one knows that the other party is not going to perform the contract. This provision is necessary in some states to test the other party's willingness and ability to perform. If neither party has made tender, the court would hold that a breach of contract has not been established. Thus, neither party would be in a position to bring suit against the other. People who must perform acts (e.g., selling goods, performing services) are excused from performing if they make proper tender and it is rejected. However, people who must pay money are not excused from paying if their tender of payment is rejected. They are merely excused from paying further interest.

### quick quiz 12-4

1. Very few contracts are discharged by performance.                                                  true | false

2. A condition precedent is a condition that requires the                                             true | false
   performance of certain actions before the other party to the
   contract is obligated.

3. Tender of performance means to offer to do what one has                                            true | false
   agreed to do under the terms of the contract.

## 12-5 Discharge by Nonperformance

Nonperformance may be defined as failing to fulfill or accomplish a promise, contract, or obligation according to its terms. Sometimes the failure to perform makes a party vulnerable to legal action. However, not every instance of nonperformance results in a legal action. Sometimes, nonperformance results from mutual agreement between the parties. At other times, nonperformance is excused because of conditions that make performance impossible or by operation of law. Nevertheless, under certain circumstances, nonperformance will result in a breach of contract. Discharge by nonperformance often comes about in the following ways:

- Discharge by agreement.
- Discharge by impossibility and by operation of law.
- Discharge by breach of contract.

# Discharge by Agreement

Parties to a contract may stipulate the time and conditions for termination and discharge as part of their agreement. They also may subsequently agree not to do what they had originally promised. The latter is the case when there is a mutual rescission of the contract, a waiver of performance by one or more of the parties, a novation, or an accord and satisfaction to liquidate an outstanding debt or obligation.

### Termination by Terms of the Contract
During contract negotiations, parties may agree to certain terms that provide for automatic termination of the contract. For example, a professional athlete may contract with management that the agreement will be terminated if for any reason the player becomes either physically or mentally incapable of rendering full performance.

### Mutual Rescission
Contracting parties may, either before or after performance commences, rescind their contract as a result of further negotiation and by their mutual assent. **Mutual rescission**, in the majority of cases, requires both parties to return to the other any consideration already received or pay for any services or materials already rendered.

### Termination by Waiver
When a party with the right to complain of the other party's unsatisfactory performance or nonperformance fails to complain, **termination by waiver** occurs. It is a voluntary relinquishing (waiver) of one's rights to demand performance. A waiver differs from a discharge by mutual rescission in that a waiver entails no obligation by the parties to return any consideration that may have been exchanged up to the moment of rescission. Discharge by waiver, when made, is complete in itself.

### Novation
By novation, the parties to a contract mutually agree to replace one of the parties with a new party. The former, original party is released from liability under the contract. Novation is discussed in detail earlier in the chapter.

### Accord and Satisfaction
An accord and satisfaction is a new agreement resulting from a bona fide dispute between the parties as to the terms of their original agreement. The mutual agreement to the new terms is the accord; performance of the accord is the satisfaction—thus, accord and satisfaction. The accord, though agreed to, is not a binding agreement until the satisfaction has been made. The original agreement therefore is not discharged until the performance or satisfaction has been provided as promised.

### General Release
A **general release** is a document expressing the intent of a creditor to release a debtor from obligations on an existing and valid debt. A general release terminates a debt and excuses the debtor of any future payment, without the usual requirement that consideration be given in return.

# Discharge by Impossibility and by Law

Occasionally, it becomes impossible to perform a contract. For example, when the subject matter of a contract, without the knowledge of the parties, had been destroyed before the contract was entered into, the contract would be discharged. Sometimes a contract that is legal when it is originally entered into by the parties becomes illegal before it is performed. This leads to a discharge by operation of law.

### Types and Conditions of Impossibility

Conditions that arise subsequent to the making of a contract may either void the agreement or make it voidable by one of the parties. Discharge through impossibility of performance may, in some situations, be allowed only if the specific and anticipated impossibility has been made a condition to the agreement. When the exact subject matter of an executory contract has been selected by the parties and later is destroyed, the performance obligation is discharged. In contrast, when the contract is not specific in the description or the location of the subject matter, a promisor is not discharged if the subject matter intended for delivery is destroyed. In this case, the promisor is obligated to locate and deliver subject matter of the same kind and quantity that could be secured elsewhere. Any financial losses due to the misfortune must be borne by the promisor.

When the performance of a contract requires actions declared illegal because of existing common law, statute, or public policy, the contract is void from its inception. When the performance of a contract is made illegal through the passing of laws subsequent to the formation of the contract, the contract is likewise declared void, and the parties are discharged. The death, insanity, or disability of a party obligated to perform an act that requires a special talent or skill terminates and discharges an agreement, including promises to perform by musicians, artists, writers, skilled craftspeople, and certain professionals. When promised services are to be performed for the personal benefit of a promisee, the death of the promisee will also terminate the agreement. When the contract relates to services that may be performed by others and do not demand the personal services of the contracting party, performance is not excused through death, insanity, or disability. The guardian of the party involved or the estate of the deceased may be held liable for performance.

### Frustration-of-Purpose Doctrine

The **frustration-of-purpose doctrine** releases a party from a contractual obligation when performing the obligations would be thoroughly impractical and senseless. The doctrine is applied only in those cases in which a party recognizes and understands possible risks and accepts them in contemplation of performance.

---

### EXAMPLE 12-13: *Stewart v. Gaverick*

George Gaverick rented a 50th-floor apartment from Thomas Stewart for the night of December 31. The apartment had a balcony overlooking Times Square in midtown Manhattan. The rental period was for only 24 hours, and the landlord knew that the purpose of the contract was to allow Gaverick an unrestricted view of Times Square for the city's New Year's Eve celebration. Unfortunately, a terrorist alert canceled the entire Times Square celebration that year. Stewart still demanded payment from Gaverick and brought a suit in small claims court to recover the amount due. The referee refused to force Gaverick to pay for the apartment. The referee concluded that, because the apartment was of no use to Gaverick, the purpose of the agreement was frustrated, and Gaverick would not have to pay the rent.

---

### Commercial Impracticability

Although not identical to the frustration-of-purpose doctrine, a related concept is known as **commercial impracticability**. Under this doctrine, the courts may excuse the nonperformance of one party to a contract because an unforeseen and very severe hardship has arisen that would place an enormous hardship on that party. Commercial impracticability is not the same as impossibility, because the party still can perform the contract. It is just that the performance itself would cause a great deal of adversity. Also with commercial impracticability, the purpose of the contract is not undermined by the unforeseen event, so the frustration-of-purpose doctrine does not apply. Nevertheless, under this relatively modern doctrine, some parties may escape performance if the unforeseen event was truly unforeseen and not in any way the fault of the party seeking an escape from performance.

## Operation of Law

The performance of a promised act may be discharged by operation of law. Some law that causes the parties to be discharged from their obligations, such as bankruptcy or the statute of limitations, comes into play in this case. Through the provisions of the Bankruptcy Reform Act, a discharge in bankruptcy from a court will be allowed as a defense against the collection of most, but not all, debts of the bankrupt. Therefore, most contractual obligations to pay money come to an end when a party files for bankruptcy. State statutes providing time limits within which suits may be brought are known as statutes of limitations. Each state sets its own time limits. In general, actions for collection of open accounts (charge accounts) must be brought within 3 to 5 years, written agreements within 10 years, and judgments from 10 to 20 years. Those states requiring a seal on certain contracts have still other limitations and requirements that are much broader than those applied to simple contracts. The time limit for bringing suit for breach of a sales contract is four years under the Uniform Commercial Code. The statute of limitations does not technically void the debt, but it gives the debtor a defense against any demand for collection.

## Discharge by Breach of Contract

When there is a breach of contract, the injured party has the right to remedy in court. There are several ways in which a breach may occur.

### Deliberate Breach of Contract
A breach of contract results when one of the parties fails to do what was agreed to under the terms of the contract. When time is of the essence, there is a breach if performance is not completed within the time limits agreed to by the parties. A breach also results if the performance has been negligent or unskillful. The services rendered must adhere to the standards of skill, as determined by the custom of the marketplace. Wrongful performance or nonperformance discharges the other party from further obligation and permits that party to bring suit to rescind the contract or recover money to compensate it for any loss sustained. Such compensation is known as *damages*.

### Repudiation and Anticipatory Breach
An anticipatory breach occurs when a party to a contract either expresses or clearly implies an intention not to perform the contract, even before being required to act. The repudiation must indicate a deliberate refusal to perform according to the terms of the contract. Breaches of this kind are also called *constructive breaches*. The injured party may either commence suit at the time of the anticipatory breach or await the date agreed to for performance, thus giving the breaching party time to reconsider and begin performance. To succeed in a case based on anticipatory repudiation, the injured party must demonstrate that he or she was ready, willing, and able to comply with the contract but could not do so because of the other party's material breach. Anticipatory breach cannot be used if the only action repudiated was the promise to pay money to another party.

**Abandonment of Contractual Obligations** Stopping performance once it has begun is called **abandonment of contractual obligations**. Leaving or deserting a party's obligations discharges the other party from any promises made and permits a suit for damages. A temporary, or short-lived, interruption of performance is not deemed abandonment. To constitute abandonment, the promisor must have inexcusably interrupted performance with the obvious intention of not returning to complete the obligations promised.

---

### quick quiz 12-5

1. A general release is a document expressing the intent of a creditor to release a debtor from the obligations of an existing and valid debt.  true | false

2. With commercial impracticability, the purpose of a contract is undermined by an unforeseen event.  true | false

3. Stopping a performance once it has begun is called abandonment of contractual obligations.  true | false

---

# 12-6 Damages and Equitable Remedies

A breach of contract releases the injured party from any obligations under the contract and gives that party the right to ask a court of law for a remedy. The usual remedy for breach of contract is the payment of damages in the form of money. At times, however, the payment of monetary damages is not enough to satisfy the injured party. In such situations, the injured party will ask the court for rescission, specific performance, or an injunction.

## Damages in Contract Law

Damages describe money awarded to parties who have been victimized or suffered injury to their legal rights by others. Damages are of different kinds, and the nature of a claim usually determines what type of damages will apply. In some states, by statute or judicial rule, juries are charged with two decisions: They must decide which party is to be given favorable judgment and determine how much is to be awarded in damages. Appeals to a higher court are allowed when the amount of damages awarded appears to be unreasonably low or excessively high.

**Actual or Compensatory Damages** **Actual damages** are the sum of money equal to the real financial loss suffered by the injured party. Because they are intended to compensate the injured party, actual damages are also called **compensatory damages**. Thus, damages awarded for nondelivery of promised goods or services would be an amount equal to the difference between the price stated in the contract and what the promisee would have to pay elsewhere. Should the same goods or services be conveniently available elsewhere at the same or at a lower price, no actual loss could be claimed.

**Incidental and Consequential Damages** Incidental damages and consequential damages are awarded for losses indirectly but closely attributable to a breach. **Incidental damages** cover any expenses paid out by the innocent party to prevent further loss. **Consequential damages** result indirectly from the breach because of special circumstances that exist with a particular contract. To recover consequential damages, the injured party must show that such losses were foreseeable when the contract was made.

## Punitive or Exemplary Damages

Damages in excess of actual losses suffered by the plaintiff awarded as a measure of punishment for the defendant's wrongful acts are **punitive damages**, also called *exemplary damages*. They are a court-ordered punishment rather than compensation for a known loss. Punitive damages are awarded when a defendant is responsible for abusive and dishonest practices in consumer transactions that are unconscionable and contrary to the public good. Often such abusive and dishonest practices are associated with certain business-related torts, including fraudulent misrepresentation, disparagement, the violation of an implied covenant of fairness and honesty, and intentional interference with an existing contract.

### Fraudulent Misrepresentation
As noted previously, **fraud**, or **fraudulent misrepresentation**, occurs when one party makes false statements or commits some sort of false action that causes another party to rely on those falsehoods then experience and an injury or loss as a result. Because fraud is a deliberate attempt to subvert proper business relationships, the court views it as especially reprehensible, and those that commit fraud will find themselves paying not only compensatory damages, if applicable, but also punitive damages. The idea of punitive damages is to punish the defrauding party to such an extent that he or she will be dissuaded from any future fraudulent conduct. Punitive

## THE OPENING CASE *Revisited, Part I*
Punitive Damages and the Limits of the Law:
*State Farm Mutual v. Campbell*, Round 2

As we learned in the Opening Case at the beginning of this chapter, when one party breaks the terms of a contract and the other party sues, the court will do its best to place the parties in as good a position as they would have been had the contract been performed as promised in the first place. One reason for this policy is that people voluntarily assume responsibilities when they make a contract and those responsibilities affect only the parties and not the general public as is the case with criminal law and, at times, tort law.

As we saw, all of this is fine in most cases, but what happens when the breaching party has deliberately undermined the basic intent of contract law by committing fraud not just in the contract at issue in the case, but as a pattern of conduct, perhaps even an official policy, affecting hundreds and thousands of other contracts? This is exactly what happened in *State Farm Mutual v. Campbell*, the Opening Case at the beginning of Chapter 12. In that case, the Campbells offered evidence that State Farm's refusal to settle their case was not just fraudulent in relation to their contract but was,

instead, part of a larger pattern of conduct planned and executed by State Farm over a 20-year period against hundreds of policyholders. After the jury heard this evidence, they awarded the Campbell's $145 million in punitive damages. The judge then reduced the punitive damages to $25 million.

On appeal the Campbells stressed the fraudulent nature of State Farm's conduct and State Farm, in turn, argued that their conduct in relation to the other contracts should not be used to punish them for their conduct in relation to the contract that they had with Campbells. The Utah Supreme Court agreed with the Campbells and reinstated the $145 million in punitive damages. The case made its way to the United States Supreme Court. The U.S. Supreme Court struck down that portion of the punitive damages that involved conduct unrelated to the Campbell's claim. The Court concluded that awarding punitive damage for conduct unrelated to the claim before the court in the present case violated the basic principles of due process.

damages are also supposed to serve as a deterrent so that other people do not even think about committing fraud. For this reason, punitive damages are also called *exemplary damages*. Exemplary damages are used as an example for other "would-be con artists" who ought to know better than to subvert the law through fraud.

**Nominal Damages** Token damages awarded to parties who have experienced an injury to their legal rights but no actual loss are nominal damages. Common law usually awarded six cents to the successful plaintiff when no actual losses were shown. In today's practice, the award is usually one dollar.

**Present and Future Damages** Damages may be awarded for present injuries and for others that might reasonably be anticipated in the future. Thus, a party charged with fraud in the sale of a building infested with termites may be held liable for all damages revealed at the time of the suit and for damages that would reasonably be forthcoming as a result of the undisclosed and concealed infestation of the property.

**Liquidated Damages** Parties may stipulate (agree) as a condition of their contract to the amount of damages that might be assessed if there is a breach. Damages agreed to in the initial contract are called liquidated damages. Liquidated damages must be realistic and in proportion to the losses that might be reasonably anticipated should there be a breach. When liquidated damages are found to be excessive or unreasonable, a court will disregard them and leave the matter of setting damages to the discretion of a jury.

**Damages under *Quantum Meruit*** The doctrine of *quantum meruit* (i.e., as much as one had earned) is important in assessing damages in cases founded on contracts implied in law, or quasi-contracts. Thus, when there has been no express or implied mutual agreement, a court will at times impose an obligation against a party who has been unjustly rewarded at the innocent expense of another. Damages awarded are in an amount considered reasonable in return for the benefits the one party derived through the quasi-contract relationship.

**Speculative Damages** Courts do not allow speculative damages. These damages are computed on losses that have not actually been suffered and that cannot be proved; they are damages based entirely on an expectation of losses that might be suffered from a breach. They differ from future damages in that speculative damages are not founded on fact but only on hope or expectation. Their basis is nothing more than a calculated guess as to the gains a party might have received had there not been a breach.

**Mitigation of Damages** The injured party has an obligation to do what is reasonably possible to mitigate the damages, that is, to keep damages to a minimum. A party who has been wronged by another's breach must exercise reasonable precautions to prevent the damages from becoming unfairly and unreasonably burdensome to the other party.

## Equitable Remedies

When money in the form of damages is not enough to provide a fair and just award to the injured party, the court may grant an equitable remedy. Rather than simply order the breaching party to pay damages, a court issuing an equitable remedy compels the breaching party to perform an act or refrain from performing an act. The two most common equitable remedies are specific performance and injunctive relief.

**Specific Performance** A decree of specific performance is a court order calling for the breaching party to do what he or she promised to do under the original contract. The courts order specific performance only when the subject matter of a contract is unique or rare. The classic example of unique subject matter calling for specific performance is a contract for the sale and transfer of title to land, because each piece of land is unique. However, unique or rare subject matter could also include such items as antiques, family heirlooms, original works of art, and special animals, such as a particular race horse. Obviously, an award of monetary damages would not provide the injured party satisfaction in any of these situations. Contracts for personal services are rarely enforced through specific performance. Demanding that an unwilling party perform promised personal services would be contrary to Amendment 13 of the U.S. Constitution, which prohibits human servitude. A remedy in cases of this kind, however, may be found through injunctive relief.

**Injunctive Relief** An **injunction** is an order issued by a court directing that a party do or refrain from doing something. An injunction may be either temporary or permanent. A temporary injunction is issued as a means of delaying further activity in any contested matter until the court determines whether a permanent injunction should be entered or the injunction should be removed entirely. One who disobeys an injunction does so under threat of penalty of contempt of court.

## quick quiz 12-6

1. Actual damages are also called compensatory damages.                                  true | false
2. Punitive damages cover any expenses paid out by the innocent party to prevent further loss.                                  true | false
3. The courts order specific performance only when the subject matter of a contract is unique or rare.                                  true | false

## Summary

**12.1**  Third parties are at times given benefits through a contract made between two other parties. Some contracts are made specifically to benefit a third party. Such a third party is known as a third party beneficiary. Three types of intended beneficiaries include creditor beneficiaries, donee beneficiaries, and insurance beneficiaries. Some third parties benefit from a contract even though the contract was not made for their benefit. These parties are known as incidental beneficiaries.

**12.2**  The transfer of contract rights to a third party outside of the original agreement is an assignment. In general, rights are assigned, and duties are delegated. However, the rules apply to both transfers in the same way. The party who assigns rights or delegates duties is the assignor. The outside third party to whom the assignment is made is the assignee. The remaining party

to the original agreement is the obligor. The assignee must give notice of assignment to the obligor.

**12.3**  The rights and duties of the assignee are the same as those held by the assignor under the original agreement. Contracts for personal or professional services cannot be assigned. Assignments also can be limited by agreement. A novation occurs when two contracting parties agree to replace one of the parties with a new party.

**12.4**  Most contracts are discharged by performance, which means that the parties do what they agreed to do. Unless the parties agree otherwise, satisfactory performance will be determined by objective standards. Substantial performance will discharge the agreement with the right to reimbursement for correcting details that were not completed. Conditions may determine the rights and duties of the parties prior to performance, during performance, and following performance. If neither party makes tender, a breach of contract is not established.

**12.5** Nonperformance can discharge contractual obligations. Not every instance of nonperformance results in a breach of contract. Parties can agree to discharge a contractual obligation by terms in the contract, mutual rescission, waiver, novation, accord and satisfaction, or general release. Contractual obligations can also be discharged when it becomes impossible to perform a contract or under the frustration-of-purpose

doctrine. These obligations can also be discharged by operation of law under principles of bankruptcy and the statute of limitations.

**12.6** An injured party is released from any obligations under the contract following the other party's breach. In addition, the injured party has the right to ask a court of law for a remedy. The usual remedy is the payment of damages in the form of money. When the payment of monetary damages is not enough, the injured party will ask the court for rescission, specific performance, or an injunction.

## Key Terms

abandonment of contractual obligations, 264

actual damages, 264

anticipatory breach, 263

assignee, 251

assignment, 251

assignor, 251

beneficiary, 249

commercial impracticability, 262

compensatory damages, 264

complete performance, 260

condition concurrent, 259

condition precedent, 259

condition subsequent, 259

consequential damages, 264

creditor beneficiary, 250

delegation, 251

donee beneficiary, 250

fraud (or fraudulent misrepresentation), 265

fraudulent conveyance, 252

frustration-of-purpose doctrine, 262

general release, 261

incidental beneficiary, 250

incidental damages, 264

injunction, 267

intended beneficiary, 249

liquidated damages, 266

mutual rescission, 261

nominal damages, 266

novation, 256

obligor, 251

outside party, 249

performance, 256

punitive damages, 265

reasonable time, 257

satisfactory performance, 258

specific performance, 266

speculative damages, 266

substantial performance, 258

tender of payment, 260

tender of performance, 260

termination by waiver, 261

third party, 249

third party beneficiary, 249

warranty, 255

## Questions for Review and Discussion

1. What are the legal rights given to all beneficiaries?
2. What are the legal rights given to incidental beneficiaries?
3. What is involved in an assignment of rights and a delegation of duties?
4. What is a novation?
5. What constitutes the satisfactory performance of a contract?
6. What is the difference between complete and substantial performance?
7. How can a contract be discharged by nonperformance?
8. What is anticipatory repudiation?
9. What types of damages are available in the event of a breach of contract?
10. What is the difference between specific performance and injunctive relief?

# Cases for Analysis

1. Under a divorce decree, Blackston was ordered to pay $600 a month in child support to his former wife. The decree provided that the payments were to be paid to the clerk of the court's office. The clerk of the court assigned the right to receive the payments to the Department of Human Resources. Who was obligated to notify Blackston of the assignment? *Blackston v. State Ex Rel. Blackston,* 585 So.2d 58 (AL).

2. Gary Jones retained the law firm of Irace and Lowry after being injured in a motorcycle accident. Later, Jones required surgery after dislocating his shoulder in an unrelated incident. Having no money to pay the surgeon, Jones signed a letter requesting that the money from the accident settlement be assigned to Dr. Herzog for treatment of a shoulder injury that occurred at a different time. The law firm was notified of the assignment. When the settlement was received by the law firm, Jones instructed the firm to pay the money to him rather than to the surgeon. It did, and the surgeon was never paid. Could Dr. Herzog recover the money owed him from the law firm? Why or why not? *Herzog v. Irace,* 594 A.2d 1106 (ME).

3. Copeland contracted with McDonald's Systems, Inc., for a franchise. Copeland was granted the fast-food outlet franchise for Omaha. McDonald's also gave Copeland first refusal rights for any plans to open other franchise outlets in Omaha. Copeland exercised the right several times, opening several additional outlets. He then sold the franchise to Schupack and assigned to Schupack the right to open new McDonald's outlets in Omaha. When Schupack tried to exercise the first refusal right, McDonald's objected, claiming its relationship with Copeland developed through a special confidence in Copeland's ability to manage and promote its new franchise outlets. Was McDonald's correct? Explain. *Schupack v. McDonald's Systems, Inc.,* 264 N.W.2d 827 (NE).

4. Timbercrest built a house for the Murphys. After occupying the house for a while, the Murphys complained of several problems. Timbercrest fixed the problems, and the Murphys had no further complaints. The Litwins bought the house from the Murphys three years later. When the house was sold, neither the Litwins nor the Murphys were aware of any problems. After living in the house for two years, the Litwins became aware of several problems. The Litwins then contacted the Murphys and had the Murphys assign them their rights under the original construction agreement with Timbercrest. The Litwins then sued Timbercrest, claiming Timbercrest had breached its contract with the Murphys by not providing them with a house free of defects. Were the Litwins correct? *Litwins v. Timbercrest Estates, Inc.,* 347 N.E.2d 378 (IL).

5. Nolan wrote the song "Tumbling Tumbleweeds" and, in an agreement with Sam Fox Publishing Company, transferred all rights to the song to the company. In return, Nolan was to receive royalties according to terms laid out in the agreement. Sam Fox later assigned all rights and interests in "Tumbling Tumbleweeds" to Williamson Music, Inc. Was it necessary for Sam Fox to obtain Nolan's consent before making the assignment to Williamson? Explain. *Nolan v. Williamson Music, Inc.,* 300 F. Supp. 1311 (S.D. NY).

6. When Kent contracted to have his new house constructed, he specifically noted that the plumbing must be made by Reading manufacturers. After the house had been completed, Kent did an inspection tour during which he discovered that, though much of the plumbing had come from Reading, there were some parts that did not. After making his discovery, Kent demanded that the non-Reading plumbing fixtures be ripped out and replaced with the supplies he had specified in the contract. In addition, Kent refused to pay the contractor until the proper plumbing supplies were added to the house. The contractor brought suit against Kent, arguing that though there were minor deviations from certain specified parts of the contract concerning the plumbing fixtures, he had nevertheless substantially performed his end of the deal. Kent stuck to his strict construction of the contract and labeled the contractor's performance unsatisfactory. He thus claimed to be released from the agreement unless the contractor lived up to every term in the original agreement. Who should prevail in this case? Explain. *Jacob and Young v. Kent,* 129 N.E. 889.

7. Sai Grafio agreed to paint Gerald Weaver's and Katherine Brewer's house for $5,650. Weaver and Brewer paid for the paint job in installments but

stopped payment on the final $1,845 check, claiming that Grafio had breached the contract by doing a poor job. The lower court judge found that the only defect in the paint job was a footprint left on the roof that would cost $50 to repair. How much money, if any, and under what legal theory, did the court allow Grafio to recover for the paint job? *Weaver v. Grafio*, 595 A.2d 983 (DC).

8. Arthur Murray, Inc., and Parker entered a series of contracts under which Arthur Murray agreed to teach Parker how to dance. Under the terms of each agreement, refunds were impossible, and the lessons could not be canceled. After the contracts were entered, Parker suffered a permanent disability that made it physically impossible for him to dance. When Arthur Murray refused to refund any part of Parker's money, he sued to rescind the contracts on grounds of impossibility. Arthur Murray claimed that the non-refund clause must be upheld by the court. Was Arthur Murray correct? Explain. *Parker v. Arthur Murray, Inc.*, 295 N.E.2d 487 (IL).

9. Bob Pagan Ford, Inc., hired Smith to work as a car salesperson in Galveston County. As part of his contract, Smith agreed not to work as an auto salesperson in Galveston County for three years after leaving his employment with Bob Pagan Ford. Smith worked for Bob Pagan for only a few months. He then left and took a sales job with another dealership in Galveston County. Was injunctive relief an appropriate remedy in this case? Explain. *Bob Pagan Ford, Inc., v. Smith*, 638 S.W.2d 176 (TX).

10. Kucha sold a house to Pilder for $75,293. The agreement was in writing, as required by the Statute of Frauds. As part of the contract, Kucha agreed to pay for the remodeling of the sun porch. However, when Kucha found out that it would cost $12,728 to do the remodeling, he refused to sell the property. Pilder sued to compel Kucha to go through with the deal. Kucha argued that under the circumstances the court could not force him to sell under any equitable remedy. Was Kucha correct? Why or why not?

## quick quiz Answers

| 12-1 | 12-2 | 12-3 | 12-4 | 12-5 | 12-6 |
|------|------|------|------|------|------|
| 1. T | 1. F | 1. F | 1. F | 1. T | 1. T |
| 2. T | 2. F | 2. F | 2. T | 2. F | 2. F |
| 3. F | 3. F | 3. F | 3. T | 3. T | 3. T |

# Part 2 Case Study

## Murray v. Accounting Center & Tax Services, Inc., et al.
Court of Appeals of Ohio, Sixth District
178 Ohio App. 3d 432 (2008)

## Summary

Julie Ray Murray had worked as an accountant for Accounting Center and Tax Services for eight years when her boss, Phillip Roberts, asked her to sign a noncompete agreement. Under the agreement, Murray would be unable to work for any of her former clients for two years after leaving the Accounting Center, unless she got written permission from the firm to do so. Moreover, if she chose to work for such clients without written permission, she would be obligated to pay the Accounting Center an amount set out by the terms of the agreement. The agreement also contained an assignment clause that permitted Accounting Services to transfer the noncompete agreement, should the firm be sold. That is exactly what happened. The firm was sold to Timothy Pinkelman and Murray's noncompete agreement was assigned to him as part of that sale. Despite this, Pinkelman tried to persuade Murray to sign a new noncompete agreement that included a change in her compensation. Under the old system, she was an hourly employee. Under the new system, she would be paid on commission. Murray refused to sign the new non-compete agreement and Pinkelman fired her. Two days later Pinkelman sent a letter to Murray reminding her of the original noncompete agreement and warning her that, should she violate the agreement, she would be subjected to a wide variety of legal consequences, none of them pleasant. Undaunted, Murray worked for the prohibited clients and, as a preemptive strike, brought a lawsuit against the Accounting Center seeking a declaratory judgment that would strike down the noncompete agreement as unfair. The trial court agreed with Murray and the Accounting Center appealed that decision.

## The Court's Opinion

Skow, Judge

This is an appeal from a judgment by the Lucas County Court of Common Pleas, granting summary judgment in favor of appellee, Julie Ray Murray, and against appellants, Accounting Center & Tax Services, Inc. and TPAC, Inc. For the reasons that follow, we reverse the judgment of the trial court.

(Note: TPAC, Inc. and Accounting Center &Tax Services, Inc. are one and the same entity, TPAC, Inc. having changed its name to Accounting Center & Tax Services sometime after February 27, 2004. Thus, although the complaint in this case names both TPAC, Inc. and Accounting Center & Tax Services, Inc. as defendants, there is, in fact, just one defendant corporation.) . . .

On January 16, 2007, Murray filed a complaint in this action seeking declaratory judgment. Appellant responded with an answer and counterclaim. The parties subsequently filed cross-motions for summary judgment, and on December 12, 2007, the trial court issued an opinion and judgment entry granting Murray's motion for summary judgment that appellant currently appeals, raising the following assignment of error:

I. "The trial court erred as a matter of law when it found that the non-compete agreement entered into between the plaintiff-appellee and her former employer was not enforceable by defendant-appellant."

An appellate court reviewing a trial court's granting of a summary judgment does so de novo, applying the same standard used by the trial court. *Grafton v. Ohio Edison Co.* (1996), 77 Ohio St. 3d 102, 105, 671 N.E. 2d 241. Civ, R, 56 (C) provides:

"Summary judgment shall be rendered forthwith if the pleadings, depositions, answers to interrogatories, written admissions, affidavits, transcripts of evidence, and written stipulations of fact, if any, timely filed in the action, show that there is no genuine issue as to any material fact and that the moving party is entitled to judgment as a matter of law. No evidence or stipulation may be considered except as stated in this rule. ***."

Summary judgment is proper where (1) no genuine issue as to any material fact remains to be litigated and (2) the moving party is entitled to judgment as a matter of law, and (3) when the evidence is viewed most strongly in favor of the nonmoving party, reasonable minds can come to but one conclusion, a conclusion adverse to the nonmoving party. *Ryberg v. Allstate Ins. Co.* (July 12, 2001), 10th Dist. No. 00AP-1243, 2001 WL 777121, citing *Tokles & Son, Inc. v. Midwestern Indemn. Co.* (1992), 65 Ohio St. 3d 621, 629, 605 N.E. 2d 939.

The moving party bears the initial burden of informing the trial court of the basis for the motion and identifying those portions of the record that demonstrate the absence of a genuine issue of fact as to an essential element of one or more of the nonmoving party's claims. *Dresher v. Burt* (1996), 75 Ohio St. 3d 280, 292, 662 N.E. 2d 264. Once the burden has been satisfied, the nonmoving party has the burden as set forth at Civ. R. 56 (E), to offer specific facts showing a genuine issue for trial Id.

The instant case requires us to determine: (1) whether the 1999 employment-and-noncompete agreement was properly assigned to appellant when it acquired Roberts's business; and if so, (2) whether, and to what extent, the 1999 employment-and-noncompete agreement is enforceable against Murray.

Here, the assignment clause contained within the 1999 employment-and-noncompete agreement expressly provides that the agreement and its provisions are transferable upon the merger or sale of the firm. The agreement (although clearly not the product of any meaningful negotiation) was signed, and apparently assented to, by Murray. In 2004, in conjunction with Roberts's sale of the firm to appellant, the employment-and-noncompete was properly assigned to appellant by way of the assignment-and-assumption agreement executed by Roberts and Pinkelman.

Arguing that there was no valid assignment, Murray points out that she was not notified of the assignment at the time of the 2004 transfer of the business. In making this argument, Murray fails to cite (and this court's research fails to reveal) any authority to support her position that notification to her was required for a valid assignment.

Having found that the 1999 employment-and-noncompete agreement was validly assigned, we must next determine whether, and to what extent, it may be enforced against Murray. In Ohio, reasonable noncompete agreements are enforced, and unreasonable noncompete agreements are enforced to the extent necessary to protect an employer's legitimate interest. *Procter & Gamble Co. v. Stoneham* (2000), 140 Ohio App. 3d 260, 270, 747 N.E. 2d 268. "A covenant restraining an employee from competing with his former employer upon termination of employment is reasonable if the restraint is no greater than is required for the protection of the employer, does not impose undue hardship on the employee, and is not injurious to the public." *Raimonde v. Van Vlerah* (1975), 42 Ohio St. 2d 21, 71 O.O. 2d 12, 235 N.E. 2d 544, paragraph two of the syllabus.

If a covenant not to compete is unreasonable, courts are empowered to modify the terms to create a reasonable covenant between the parties. *Rogers v. Runfola & Assoc., Inc.* (1991), 57 Ohio St. 3d 5, 8, 565 N.E. 2d 540. In so doing the courts should consider the following factors:

"'[T]he absence or presence as to time and space, * * * whether the employee represents the sole contact with the customer; whether the employee is possessed with confidential information or trade secrets; whether the covenant seeks to eliminate competition which would be unfair to the employer or merely seeks to eliminate ordinary competition; whether the covenant seeks to stifle the inherent skill and experience of the employee; whether the benefit to the employer is disproportional to the detriment to the employer; whether the covenant operates as a bar to the employee's sole means of support; whether the employee's talent which the employer seeks to suppress was actually developed during the period of employment; and whether the forbidden employment is merely incidental to the main employment.' ***." Id., quoting *Raimonde,* 42 Ohio St. 2d at 25, 72 O.O. 2d 12, 325 N.E.2d 544.

With these facts in mind, we conclude that the restraints and resulting hardships on Murray do, in fact, exceed that which is reasonable to protect appellant's legitimate business interests. Temporally, Murray is prohibited from working for customers of appellant for a period of 24 months. For 16 years, Murray has supported herself, in whole or in part, by doing tax-preparation work. She has done so by working for employers, such as appellant, and by working on her own. We find that imposing a two-year time restriction is unreasonable and will create an undue hardship on her.

Our inquiry does not end here, however. We must next determine whether some restrictions prohibiting Murray from competing are necessary to protect appellant's business interests. The record reveals that appellant and his predecessor in interest developed a clientele with which Murray had direct contact, on a regular and ongoing basis. Certainly, appellant has a legitimate commercial interest to protect. For this reason, we find appellant's assignment of error well taken.

Balancing the restraints and projected hardships on Murray with appellant's interests, and upon the authority of *Raimonde,* 42 Ohio St. 2d 21, 71, O.O. 2d 12, 325 N.E. 2d 544 and App. R. 12 (B), we modify the 24-month restriction as follows:

Sixty days from the date of this order, Murray shall be prohibited for a period of one year from servicing appellant's clients.

For all of the foregoing reasons, the judgment of the Lucas County Court of Common Pleas is reversed. Appellee is ordered to pay the costs of this appeal pursuant to App. R. 24. Judgment for the clerk's expense incurred in preparation of the record, fees allowed by law, and the fee for filing the appeal is awarded to Lucas County.

Judgment reversed

Handwork and Osowik, J., concur.

# Questions for Analysis

1. What is a summary judgment motion? What must be proven for a successful summary judgment motion? Who has the initial burden? What is that burden? What happens when the burden shifts to the other party? What is that party's responsibility at that point? Explain everything here.

2. Who is the assignor in this assignment? Who is the assignee? Who is the obligor? Explain.

3. The court labels the transfer of Murray's employment-and-noncompete agreement from Roberts to Pinkelman as an assignment. Is the court correct or are is the transfer actually a novation? Explain.

4. The court concludes that Roberts had no duty to give notice of the assignment (if it was an assignment) to Murray? Is the court correct here? Explain.

5. As we learned in Chapter 12, the law states that "a party may not delegate duties that are of a personal or professional nature." Is that what happened in this case? Why or why not?

6. Has the assignor transferred any warranties to the assignee in this case? If not, why not? If so, what are they?

7. What are the limits that are placed on Murray in the noncompete agreement?

8. How does the court evaluate these limits? Are they fair or unfair? Do you agree or disagree with the court? Explain.

9. What consideration did Roberts transfer to Murray for her signature on the noncompete agreement? Is this consideration adequate? Explain. What consideration did Pinkelman promise to transfer to Murray for her signature on the noncompete agreement? Would that consideration have been adequate? Why or why not?

10. In general, noncompete agreements like the one in this case are not favored by the law. Why is this so?

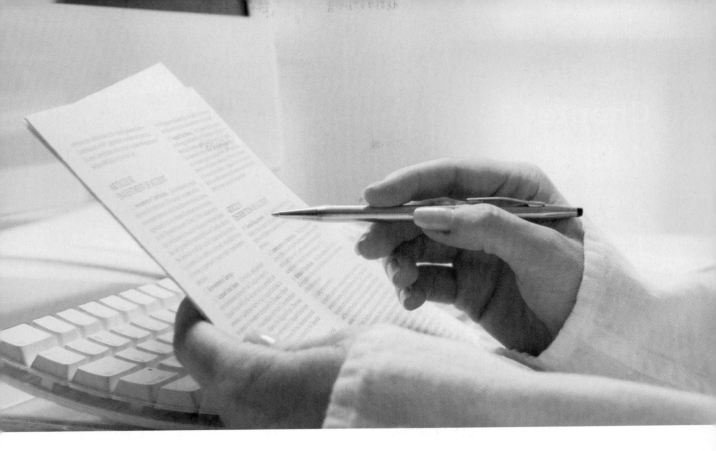

# Part Three

## Sales and Consumer Protection

# Chapter 13

## Sales Contracts: Formation, Title, and Risk of Loss

## THE OPENING CASE  Purchase Orders and the UCC: XCEL Mold & Machine v. DeVault Indus.

The Uniform Commercial Code (UCC) governs contracts that are made for the sale or the lease of goods. Goods, as we have seen, are movable tangible objects such as vehicles, electronic devices, and clothing. Many of the rules that are found in the UCC are straightforward, unambiguous expressions of legal principles that have been imbedded in the law for centuries. This simple fact makes the case of *XCEL v. DeVault* relatively easy for the court to solve. The facts in the case play out like this. DeVault Industries manufactures custom built shotguns. XCEL has perfected a wire-cutting process that is ideally suited for the trigger assemblies in the DeVault shotguns. After an initial trial run, during which XCEL successfully produced six trigger assemblies, DeVault sent a purchase order (No. 27) to XCEL for 20 additional units (although there was enough material to produce 60 units), at a total cost of $1,080. XCEL received and accepted purchase order No. 27. Within a few days, however, Mr. Cain, the president of XCEL, phoned Mr. DeVault, the president of DeVault, and told him that XCEL could not manufacture the parts at that price. DeVault remembers the phone call differently, arguing that the two men did not talk price but, instead, discussed the quantity of the

order, which was set at 20. However, DeVault did admit that Cain said he needed to produce more than 20 units to cover the set-up costs for that initial 20 units. DeVault told him not to worry because they would later figure out what a fair price would be. XCEL did, in fact, manufacture the units and sent them to DeVault. Once DeVault received the units, they sent a check to XCEL for $1,080. The check included a notation that read, "pymt in full PO#27 60 pcs@18.00 ea." Someone at XCEL cashed the check and deposited the proceeds in an XCEL bank account. Nevertheless, Cain continued to claim that DeVault had not paid the full amount owed under the contract. Later XCEL sent its own check for $1,080 back to DeVault. By this time it was too late. DeVault would no longer listen to Cain and Cain refused to hear DeVault. That was when the lawsuit erupted. So what do you think? Did DeVault and XCEL enter a contract here? If so, when was the offer made? When did the acceptance occur? Did the parties need to put all of this in writing? Consider these questions as you read this chapter on selling and leasing goods. (See *XCEL Mold & Machine v. DeVault Indus.*, 146 Ohio Misc. 2d 32, 2008-Ohio-269.)

**Opening Case Questions**

1. Is the case of *XCEL v. DeVault* governed by common law or by the Uniform Commercial Code? Explain.

2. Does the contract involved in this case have to be in writing to be enforceable? Explain.

3. When was the offer made here? When was it accepted? When did mutual assent emerge during the flow of events? Explain.

4. Will the court listen to and consider evidence based on the content of the phone conversations? Why or why not?

5. Is the cashed check significant in this case? Why or why not?

## LO Learning Objectives

**1.** Define the term goods and explain the nature of a sale.
**2.** Explain how Article 2 of the UCC applies to contractual relationships.
**3.** Explain the UCC rules that relate to written contracts.
**4.** Explain the two laws related to cyber-sales contracts.
**5.** Contrast an auction with reserve with an auction without reserve.
**6.** Explain title, void title, and voidable title.
**7.** Determine when title of goods passes from seller to buyer.
**8.** Decide when the buyer or seller must bear the risk of loss.
**9.** Compare a sale on approval with a sale or return.
**10.** Define an insurable interest.

# 13-1 The Sale and Lease of Goods

In the previous unit we discussed the general principles of contract law as they relate to common law principles regardless of what is being purchased or sold. Now we shift our focus to contracts that involve the sale or the lease of goods. Recall that goods are movable, tangible pieces of property such as vehicles, clothing, and electronic devices. As we saw in Chapter 7, much of the law regarding the sale of goods evolved from the law merchant on the European continent. With the Roman Catholic Church supplying political and social support, with Canon Law providing a moral framework, and with practicality guiding their activities over a 300-year period, the merchants developed a body of active law that was characterized by neutrality, universality, mutuality, involvement, integration, and evolution. The law of sales has gone through many changes over the years. However, throughout all these changes, even those that have integrated advanced cyber-technology into the sales contract, the people responsible for the Uniform Commercial Code (UCC) have attempted to preserve those six basic principles. The UCC, which has been adopted either in whole or in part by every state in the United States, will, therefore, be the focal point of our study of sales law.

## Sales of Goods

Some medieval version of the 21st century Madison Avenue advertising executive knew exactly what he was doing when he branded the subject matter of every sales contracts as "goods." It would hardly have attracted sales to call them "bads" or to settle on some other mundane label. Nevertheless, as we all know by the time we are old enough to read a

UCC 2-105(1) (see pages 959–960)

UCC 2-105(2) (see
page 960)

UCC 2-106(2) (see
page 960)

Christmas catalogue, **goods** are things (other than money, stocks, and bonds) that are tangible, movable, and valuable (to someone). They include toys, candy, growing crops, timber, and minerals if they are to be sold separately from the real property. Office furniture, mobile homes, milk, wedding pictures, electricity, vehicles, computers, waste paper, kerosene, books, clothing, jewelry, horses, soybeans, PDAs, DVDs, and baseball caps are all considered goods. Goods that are not yet in existence or under the control of people are called **future goods**. They include fish in the sea, minerals in the ground, goods not yet manufactured, and commodities futures. Whenever anyone buys food in a supermarket, gasoline at a gas station, clothing at a shopping mall, a meal at a restaurant, or even a daily newspaper, a sale of goods occurs. In fact, several sales contracts usually occur for a particular item before the item reaches the consumer and sometimes even after it reaches the consumer.

## EXAMPLE 13-1: Sales Contracts at Different Levels

The Steven Andrew Corporation manufactures lawn mowers. The company enters into sales contracts with its suppliers every time it purchases parts and materials to make the mowers. In addition, the company enters into sales contracts with wholesalers when it sells the mowers. Similarly, wholesalers enter into sales contracts when they sell the mowers to retailers. In the same manner, retailers enter into sales contracts when they sell the mowers to consumers. Going even further, consumers enter into sales contracts when they sell their second-hand lawn mowers to other private parties. All of these contracts are governed by the UCC.

A gift is not considered a sale because, though title passes, it is not given for a price. Similarly, a bailment (e.g., when an item is left at a store to be sold on consignment) does not meet the definition of a sale because title does not pass between the parties. Article 2 of the UCC applies whenever people buy or sell goods, whether in person, online, over the telephone, or in any other manner. This law applies to sales of goods between private parties and sales of goods by businesspeople or merchants. To determine whether the UCC applies, ask if the contract is a contract for the sale of goods. If the answer is yes, apply the law under the UCC. If the answer is no, apply the common law of contracts. (See Table 13-1).

UCC Article 2 (see
pages 821–842)

## Leases of Goods

UCC 2A-101-532 (see
pages 842–862)

The leasing of goods is governed by Article 2A of the Uniform Commercial Code. This article includes leasing of such things as automobiles, trucks, machinery, computers, furniture, electronic equipment, and all types of tools. Many of the rules that are found in the UCC relating to the sale of goods (discussed in the following chapters) also apply to the leasing of goods under Article 2A of the UCC.

## Goods and Services

When a contract includes both goods and services, the dominant element of the contract determines whether it is a contract for goods or a contract for services. If the sale of goods is dominant, as when someone purchases a furnace and has it installed, the law under the UCC applies. In contrast, if the performance of services is dominant, as when someone has a furnace repaired and a few new parts are installed, the common law of contracts applies instead.

**Table 13-1**  Different Laws Apply to Different Transactions

| Transaction | Applicable Law |
| --- | --- |
| Contract for the sale of real estate | General contract law (sometimes referred to as common law) and real property law |
| Contract for employment | General contract law and employment law |
| Sale of goods between two private parties | UCC (Article 2) |
| Sale of goods by a merchant to a consumer | UCC (Article 2) and state consumer protection laws |
| Sale of goods between two merchants | UCC (Article 2) |
| Contract for a mixture of goods and services—consisting mostly of goods | UCC (Article 2) |
| Contract for a mixture of goods and services—consisting mostly of services | General contract law |
| Sale of goods over the Internet | UCC (Article 2) |
| Sale of goods at an auction | UCC (Article 2) |
| The leasing of goods | UCC (Article 2A) |
| International sales of goods | United Nations convention on Contracts for the International Sale of Goods (CISG) |
| Sale of stock on the stock market | UCC (Article 8) |
| The writing of a check, promissory note, or draft | UCC (Article 3) |

## quick quiz 13-1

1. A gift is considered a sale.                                          true | false
2. Money, stocks, and bonds are movable items that are        true | false
   not goods.
3. The dominant element of a contract determines whether it is a    true | false
   sales contract or a services contract.

# 13-2 Rules for Sales Contracts

The fundamental rules of contract law, discussed in the Contract Law Unit, serve as a foundation for the principles found in the UCC, but the UCC is often more flexible. This flexibility is built into the UCC in order to accommodate the day-to-day reality of the world of sales. The daily operation of the commercial world requires a rapid response to the demands of customers and the needs of suppliers. Unlike real property contracts, which sometimes seem to be moving in slow motion, sales contracts for goods often occur at a moment's notice with little or no preparation. Unlike collective bargaining contracts that require that all the parties agree to each word in each clause of each part of the agreement, purchase orders

UCC 1-203 (see page 820)

UCC 1-205 (see page 820)

UCC 2-204(1)(2) (see page 823)

and invoices often have different terms hidden in the fine print, terms that might contradict one another, but which really do not matter to the actual completion of the contract. Unlike employment contracts, that will not begin until the parties know exactly what is expected of them, a shipment of goods might have to get started before all of the details of a deal are finalized. As we shall see, the UCC handles these realities in an effective and responsible way. In a very real sense, it is the almost universal adherence to the UCC that makes our commercial world work as well as it does. Some of these special rules for sales contracts are covered below.

## Good Faith, Course of Dealings, and Usage of Trade

Under the UCC, every contract or duty imposes an obligation of good faith. In other words, the parties to a sales contract must act and deal fairly with each other. When the parties have dealt with each other before, their prior dealings give special meaning to sales contracts. Similarly, **usage of trade**, that is, any method of dealing that is commonly used in the particular field, is given special meaning. Unless the parties express otherwise, a course of dealings or usage of trade may be used to supplement or qualify the terms of a sales contract.

## Formation of a Sales Contract

UCC 2-206(1)(a) (see page 823)

UCC 2-206(1)(b) (see page 823)

UCC 2-106(2) (see page 822)

Contracts may be formed either orally or in writing; however, a writing may be required by the Statute of Frauds for the contract to be enforceable.

A contract may be made in any manner that shows that the parties reached an agreement. It may be oral (with some exceptions) or in writing, or it may be established by the conduct of the parties. An enforceable sales contract may come about even if the exact moment of its making cannot be determined and even though some terms are not completely agreed upon.

**Offer and Acceptance**  To establish a contract for the sale of goods, unless otherwise indicated by the offeror or the circumstances, the offeree may accept the offer in any manner and by any medium that is reasonable. A contract for the sale of goods comes into existence when the acceptance is sent, as long as the method used to send it is reasonable. Unless the buyer indicates otherwise, an order or other offer to buy goods for prompt shipment may be accepted by either a prompt shipment or a prompt promise to ship. Under this rule, the goods that are shipped may be either conforming or nonconforming goods. **Conforming goods** are those that are in accordance with the obligations under the contract. **Nonconforming goods** are those that are not the same as those called for under the contract or that are in some way defective.

**Firm Offer**  The UCC holds merchants to a higher standard than nonmerchants. A **merchant** is a person who deals in goods of the kind sold in the ordinary course of business or who otherwise claims to have knowledge or skills peculiar to those goods. Although most rules under the UCC apply to both merchants and nonmerchants alike, some rules apply only to merchants. One such rule involves a firm offer.

No consideration is necessary when a merchant promises in writing to hold an offer

## THE OPENING CASE *Revisited, Part 1*

Purchase Orders and the UCC: *XCEL Mold & Machine v. DeVault Indus.,* Round 2

In the Opening Case at the beginning of this chapter we learned that DeVault, a shotgun manufacturer, sent a purchase order (No. 27) to XCEL for 20 trigger-assembly units (although there was enough material to produce 60 units and although XCEL did manufacture 60 units), at a total cost of $1,080. XCEL received and accepted purchase order No. 27. Within a few days, however, Mr. Cain, the president of XCEL, phoned Mr. DeVault, the president of DeVault, and told him that XCEL could not manufacture the parts at that price. DeVault remembers the phone call differently, arguing that the two men did not talk price but, instead, discussed the quantity of the order, which was set at 20. However, DeVault did admit that Cain said he needed to produce more than 20 units to cover the set-up costs for that initial 20 units. DeVault told him not to worry because they would later figure out what a fair price would be. XCEL did, in fact, manufacture all 60 units and sent them to DeVault. Once DeVault received the units, they sent a check to XCEL for $1,080. The check included a notation that

read, "pymt in full PO#27 60 pcs@18.00 ea." Someone at XCEL cashed the check and deposited the proceeds in an XCEL bank account. Nevertheless, Cain continued to claim that DeVault had not paid the full amount owed under the contract. He argued that the purchase order was not a valid offer and that the alterations made by phone actually provided the terms for a new contract under which DeVault had agreed to pay $9,000 for the trigger assembly units. The court, using the UCC, had no trouble determining that a contract existed under the terms of the purchase order. As noted above, unless the buyer indicates otherwise, an order or other *offer to buy goods* for *prompt shipment* may be accepted by either a prompt shipment or a prompt promise to ship. The court identified DeVault's purchase order as the *offer to buy goods* and the XCEL's *prompt shipment* of the trigger assemblies as the acceptance. Moreover, since there was no indication that the goods were nonconforming, there could be no successful challenge to the existence of the contract.

open for the sale or lease of goods. Known as a **firm offer**, the writing must be signed by the merchant, and the time period for holding the offer open may not exceed three months. This rule differs from the general rule of contract law which requires consideration in an option contract.

## Open-Price Terms

Another change that the UCC has made is that a contract for the sale of goods may be established even though the price is not settled. Such **open-price terms** may occur when the parties intend to be bound by a contract but fail to mention the price or decide to set the price later. Under non-UCC law, no contract would come about because the terms are not definite. The UCC allows such a contract to come into existence. If the parties cannot agree on the price at the later date, the UCC requires that the price will be reasonable at the time the goods are delivered.

UCC 2-104(1) (see page 821)

UCC 2-205 (see page 823)

UCC 2-305(1) (see page 825)

## Output and Requirements Terms

Sometimes, a seller will agree to sell "all the goods we manufacture" or "all the crops we produce" to a particular buyer. This agreement is known as an **output contract**. At other times, a buyer will agree to buy "all the oil we need to heat our building" (or some similar requirement) from a particular seller. This agreement is called a **requirements contract**. Such contracts often were not allowed under common law because the quantity of the goods to be bought or sold was not definite. The UCC allows output and requirements contracts for the sale of goods, as long as the parties deal in good faith and according to *reasonable expectations.*

UCC 2-306 (see page 825)

## EXAMPLE 13-2: Unreasonable Expectations

Spencer Oil Co. agreed to sell to Lopaz Manufacturing Co. all the heating oil Lopaz would need during the next year. Spencer knew that Lopaz used about 5,000 gallons of oil each year. During the summer, Lopaz enlarged its building to an extent that it would require 25,000 gallons of heating oil during the next year. Spencer would not be bound to supply that amount of oil to Lopaz because it was far beyond the amount it expected to supply.

UCC 2-207 (see page 823)

**Additional Terms in Acceptance** Under the general rules of contract law, an acceptance of an offer must be an absolute, unqualified, unconditional assent to the offer. If the acceptance differs in the slightest from the offer, it is considered a rejection. The UCC changes this rule somewhat. A contract for the sale of goods occurs even though the acceptance states terms that are additional to or different from those offered or agreed upon (unless acceptance is made conditional on assent to the additional terms). The additional terms are treated as proposals for additions to the contract if the parties are not both merchants. If both parties are merchants, the additional terms become part of the contract unless they materially alter it, the other party objects within a reasonable time, or the offer limits acceptance to its terms. This rule is intended to deal with two typical situations. The first is when an agreement has been reached either orally or by informal correspondence between the parties and is followed by one or both of the parties sending formal acknowledgments or memos that contain additional terms not discussed earlier. The second situation in which this rule applies is one in which a fax or letter intended to be the closing or confirmation of an agreement adds further minor suggestions or proposals, such as "ship by Thursday" or "rush."

## EXAMPLE 13-3: Additional Terms in Acceptance

Cobb and Sons, Inc., reached an oral agreement with Valley Theatres, Inc., for the sale of an air conditioning system. Later, Cobb put the agreement in writing, signed it, and sent it to Valley for its signature. Valley signed the writing but added additional terms relative to the date of completion of the contract. Because both parties were merchants, the additional terms would become part of the contract unless Cobb objected to them within a reasonable time. Had one of them not been a merchant, the contract would have to come into existence without the additional terms, and the added terms would have been treated as proposals for additions to the contract.

## EXAMPLE 13-4: Different Terms in Acceptance

Cal-Cut Pipe and Supply, Inc., offered in writing to sell used pipe to Southern Idaho Pipe and Steel Co., specifying a delivery date. Southern Idaho accepted by sending a check but changed the delivery date. Cal-Cut mailed a confirmation containing the original delivery date with the postscript, "We will work it out." The court held that there was a binding contract between them despite the conflicting delivery terms.

**Modification** Under the general rules of contract law, if the parties have already entered into a binding contract, a later agreement to change that contract needs consideration to be binding. The UCC has done away with this rule in contracts for the sale of goods. An agreement modifying a contract for the sale of goods needs no consideration to be binding. Any such modification may be oral unless the original agreement is in writing and provides that it may not be modified except by a signed writing. Any such clause in a form supplied by a merchant to a nonmerchant, however, must be separately signed (such as in the margin) by the nonmerchant to be effective.

UCC 2-209(1) (see page 823)

UCC 2-209(2) (see page 824)

---

## quick quiz 13-2

1. Under the UCC, a contract comes into existence when the acceptance is sent if the method used is reasonable.   true | false

2. No consideration is necessary to establish a firm offer when a consumer promises in writing to hold an offer open for the sale or lease of goods.   true | false

3. Under the UCC, a contract for the sale of goods may be established even though the price is not settled.   true | false

---

# 13-3 The Form of a Sales Contract

The Uniform Commercial Code also outlines the rules that must be followed in relation to written sales contracts. This is critical because many contracts in the commercial world are written. Today many sales contracts are also made online which has required some fine tuning of the law. As we shall see, however, there are not quite as many changes in the law as one might expect because of the cyber-revolution in sales. This is a testimony to the law of sales which has adopted a set of rules so well adjusted to its subject matter that it can adapt to even the most radical upheavals in the economic world without missing a beat. Some of this flexibility is made possible by the members of the National Conference of Commissioners on Uniform State Laws who have been willing to accommodate the needs of those involved with the new technology

UCC 2-201(1) (see page 822)

## The Written Sales Contract

As long as the value of the goods involved in a sales contract do not exceed $500, the contract can oral and still be enforceable. Once the price is $500 or more, however, the contract must be in writing to be enforceable. Also under the UCC, a lease of goods must be in writing if the total payments to be made under the lease are $1,000 or more.

**LO3**

UCC 2A-201(1) (see page 845)

UCC 2-201(2) (see page 822)

**Exceptions to the General Rule** There are four exceptions to the requirement that contracts for the sale of goods for $500 or more and the lease of goods for $1,000 or more must be in writing to be enforceable. These exceptions involve the following:

1. Oral contracts between merchants in which a confirmation has been received by one party and not objected to by the other party.

2. Specially manufactured goods.

3. Admissions in court.

4. Executed contracts.

## THE OPENING CASE *Revisited, Part II*
## Purchase Orders and the UCC: *XCEL Mold & Machine v. DeVault Indus.*, Round 3

In the Opening Case at the beginning of this chapter, you will recall that Mr. DeVault, the president of DeVault Industries, sent a purchase order to XCEL Industries for 20 (later changed to 60) trigger assembly units for DeVault's shotguns at a total cost of $1,080. Within a few days, however, Mr. Cain, the president of XCEL, phoned DeVault and told him that XCEL could not manufacture the parts at that price. At some point in the conversation, DeVault told Cain not to worry because they would later figure out a "fair price" for the units. It seems that Cain believed that this "fair price" would be $9,000. XCEL manufactured the units and sent them to DeVault. Once DeVault received the units, someone in his office sent a check to XCEL for $1,080. The check included a notation that read, "pymt in full PO#27 60 pcs@18.00 ea." In the lawsuit that followed, Cain argued that the oral modification of the written purchase order for the "fair price" of $9,000 should be upheld by the court. In contrast, DeVault argued that the real agreement was embodied in the purchase order that included the $1,080 price. The court had little problem coming to a conclusion. The court saw the purchase order as a written confirmation of the initial agreement. Under the UCC, after this written confirmation was sent by DeVault and received by XCEL, the only way to countermand that confirmation was to send a written objection. Cain sent no written objection. Instead, he called DeVault to complain about the price. Unfortunately for Cain, that phone conversation changed nothing and the contents of the original purchase order, including the $1,080 price, was seen as the real contract.

**Oral Contracts between Merchants** An exception to the general rule occurs when there is an oral agreement made between two merchants. If either merchant receives a written confirmation of the oral agreement from the other merchant within a reasonable time and does not object to it in writing within 10 days, the writing is sufficient under the UCC even though it has not been signed by the other party. It is important to understand that this exception applies only to merchants, not to ordinary consumers. The UCC defines a merchant as "a person who deals in goods of the kind" that are the subject matter of the contract at hand. It is also crucial to note that any objection to the original written confirmation must be in writing. If that is not the case then the court will honor the original written confirmation, no matter how loudly and how persuasively the other party objected to the agreement.

**Specially Manufactured Goods** Another exception occurs when goods are to be specially manufactured for the buyer and are not suitable for sale to others in the ordinary course of the seller's business. If the seller has made either a substantial beginning in manufacturing the goods or commitments to buy them, the oral agreement will be enforceable.

UCC 2-201(3) (see page 822)

## EXAMPLE 13-5: Specially Manufactured Goods

Lifetime Windows, Inc., entered into an oral agreement to manufacture 15 oversized windows for Harold Cohen for the price of $6,000. The windows were such an odd shape that no one else would have a need for them. When the windows were manufactured, Cohen refused to take them on the ground that the oral contract was unenforceable. The court held against Cohen, however, and enforced the oral agreement. The windows were specially manufactured and were not suitable for sale to others.

**Admissions in Court** If the party against whom enforcement is sought admits in court that an oral contract for the sale of goods was made, the contract will be enforceable. The contract is not enforceable under this exception, however, beyond the quantity of goods admitted.

UCC 2-201(3)(b) (see page 823)

**Executed Contracts** When the parties carry out their agreement in a satisfactory manner, the law will not render the transaction unenforceable for want of an agreement in writing. Executed contracts (those that have been carried out) need not be in writing; the writing requirements apply only to contracts that are executory, that is, not yet performed. This provision means that contracts for goods that have been received and accepted need not be in writing. If there has been a part payment or a part delivery, the court will enforce only that portion of the agreement that has been performed.

UCC 2-201(3)(c) (see page 823)

**Requirements of Writing** The writing that is required to satisfy the UCC must indicate that a contract for sale has been made between the parties and mention the quantity of goods being sold. It must also be signed by the party against whom enforcement is sought (the defendant). A writing is acceptable even though it omits or incorrectly states an agreed-upon term. However, a contract will not be enforceable beyond the quantity of goods shown in such writing. For that reason, it is necessary to put the quantity of goods to be bought and sold in the written agreement. Although a paper similar to the one shown in Figure 13-1 may be used, an informal note, memorandum, fax, or sales slip will satisfy the writing requirements.

UCC 2-201(1) (see page 822)

**Signature Requirements** Under the UCC, a signature includes any symbol made with the intent to authenticate a writing. Thus, in addition to a handwritten signature, the courts have held various kinds of marks, including an X and a typewritten name, qualify as a signature as long as they were written with the intent to be signatures.

UCC 1-201(39) (see page 819)

## Cyber-Sales Contracts

Statutes covering the problems associated with cyber-sales contracts have taken many forms over the past decade. One of the problems that required a solution was how to treat an online contract that required a written form. Two acts that have dealt with that problem are the E-Sign Act and the Uniform Electronic Transactions Act (UETA).

**The E-Sign Act** Congress passed the E-Sign Act to address some of the difficulties associated with cyber-commerce, especially those that involve the recognition of electronic contracts and electronic signatures. In short, the statute declares that, as long as the parties to a cyber-contract have freely decided to conduct business electronically, the cyber-contract that results will have the same legal effect as a paper contract. The statute makes it clear that the parties to the contract must have some way to store and duplicate a cyber-record of the contract; otherwise, the cyber-record will not be legally sufficient under the act. It is also important to understand that some critical documents are not covered by the act. These include court records, eviction notices, health insurance cancellations, foreclosure notices, prenuptial contracts, and divorce papers. On the other hand, UCC contracts for the sale and lease of goods are included in the E-Sign Act.

**The Uniform Electronic Transactions Act (UETA)** The Uniform Electronic Transactions Act (UETA), which was produced by the NCCUSL, is very similar to the E-Sign Act. The UETA promises the same legal parity between electronic records and paper records that is guaranteed by the E-Sign Act. However, the UETA applies only to

CONTRACT FOR SALE OF GOODS

AGREEMENT made by and between Ozzie Caldwell (Seller) and Geordi Hasenzahl (Buyer).

It has been agreed between the two parties that:

1. Seller agrees to sell, and Buyer agrees to buy, the following described property: one regulation-size pool table now located at the residence of Ozzie Caldwell, RD #1, Box 118, Ashberry, Kentucky.

2. Buyer agrees to pay Seller the total price of $850.00;

   payable as follows:

   $600.00 deposit herewith

   $250.00 balance by cash or certified check at time of transfer

3. Seller warrants he has full legal title to said property, authority to sell said property, and that said property shall be sold free and clear of all claims by other parties.

4. Said property is sold in "as is" condition. SELLER HEREBY EXCLUDES THE WARRANTY OF MERCHANTABILITY AND FITNESS FOR A PARTICULAR PURPOSE.

5. Parties agree to transfer title on February 7, 20 - -, at RD #1, Box 118, Ashberry, Kentucky, the address of the Seller.

6. This agreement shall be binding on the parties, their successors, assigns, and personal representatives.

7. This writing is intended to represent the entire agreement between the parties.

Signed under seal this nineteenth day of January, 20 - -.

_Geordi Hasenzahl_
Buyer

_Ozzie Caldwell_
Seller

**Figure 13-1**  With four exceptions, contracts for the sale of goods of $500 or more must be in writing to be enforceable. A formal writing such as this is not necessary to satisfy the writing requirements of the UCC, however.

transactions that involve a business, governmental, or commercial situation. Still, the statute does ensure that, whenever a writing is required under the Statute of Frauds, any electronic signature that results from a cyber-transaction will fulfill that requirement. Under the UETA an electronic signature is defined as "an electronic sound, symbol, or process attached to or logically associated with a record and executed or adopted by a person with the intent to sign the record."

## International Law

Interestingly, the trend in other countries is to eliminate the requirement that a sales contract be in writing. Great Britain, for example, after having such a requirement for 277 years, did away with it in 1954. International sales law also has no writing requirements for a sales contract; instead, a sales contract may be proved by any means.

International sales law, called the United Nations **Convention on Contracts for the International Sale of Goods (CISG)**, applies only to sales between businesses whose places of business are in different countries that have adopted the law. It does not apply to sales of goods that are bought for personal, family, or household purposes. Also, the international law does not apply to auction sales; sales of stock, securities, negotiable instruments, or money; sales of ships or aircraft; or sales of electricity. The United States adopted the international sales law in 1988, and by 2007, 70 countries had made it part of their law.

CISG Articles 1 and 2 (page 883)

CISG Articles 4 and 5 (page 883)

The CISG is similar in many ways to the UCC. It also contains some differences. The CISG governs only the formation of a sales contract and the rights and duties of the parties that arise from it. The CISG is not concerned with the validity of a contract regarding, for example, the sale of illegal drugs, which would be governed by other laws. In addition, the CISG does not apply to the liability of the seller for death or personal injury caused by the goods to any person. In such a case, people would have to look to other laws for a remedy.

UCC 2-328(2) (see page 829)

UCC 2-328(3) (see page 830)

## Auction Sales and Cyber-Auction Fraud

In an auction sale, the auctioneer presents goods for sale and invites the audience to make offers, which are known as bids. This process is similar to an invitation to trade. Bidders in the crowd respond with their offers. The highest bid (offer) is accepted by the auctioneer, usually by the drop of the gavel, together with the auctioneer's calling out the word *sold.* If, while the gavel is falling, a higher bid comes from those in the crowd, the auctioneer has two options: declare the goods sold or reopen the bidding.

UCC 2-328(4) (see page 830)

An auction sale is "with reserve" unless the goods are expressly put up without reserve. In an **auction with reserve**, the auctioneer may withdraw the goods at any time before announcing completion of the sale if the highest bid is not high enough. In an **auction without reserve**, after the auctioneer calls for bids on an article or lot, that article or lot cannot be withdrawn unless no bid is made within a reasonable time. In either case, a bidder may retract a bid until the auctioneer's announcement of completion of the sale. A bidder's retraction does not revive any previous bid.

Auctions are frequently used to dispose of unwanted property, satisfy judgments, and to liquidate foreclosed property.

The practice of planting persons in the crowd for the purpose of raising bids by innocent purchasers is not allowed. Except in a forced sale, such as by a sheriff, if a seller (or the seller's agent) makes a bid at an auction without notifying other bidders, a buyer has two options. Under the UCC, a buyer may either avoid the sale or take the goods at the price of the last good-faith bid prior to the completion of the sale. In a forced sale, as when a sheriff auctions property on foreclosure or to satisfy a lien creditor, the owner is allowed to bid on the property being sold.

Auctions on the Internet provide the opportunity to buy and sell goods worldwide as well as locally. An Internet auction (AKA a cyber-auction and an e-auction) can be either person-to person or business-to-person. In person-to-person auctions, sellers offer items directly to consumers. The highest bidder must deal directly with the seller to arrange for payment and delivery. In contrast, operators of business-to-person auctions have control of the items being offered and take charge of payment and delivery of goods bought and sold.

Cyber-auction fraud is alarming. Sometimes sellers don't deliver the goods or deliver something less valuable than they advertised. At other times, sellers don't disclose everything about a product or fail to deliver it when they say they will. The Federal Trade Commission (FTC) provides helpful information about cyber-auctions in its free brochures and on its Web site.

## quick quiz 13-3

1. A lease of goods must be in writing if the total payments to be made under the lease are $500 or more.    true | false

2. The E-Sign Act was developed, written, and passed by the U.S. Congress.    true | false

3. The practice of planting persons in the crowd for the purpose of raising bids by innocent purchasers is not allowed.    true | false

# 13-4 Title, Passage of Title, and Risk of Loss

It is good for us to remember that the law of sales was born within the context of the law merchant and that the law merchant was closely associated with the development of capitalism. Moreover, it is also critical to recall that one of the driving forces behind the growth of capitalism was the Roman Catholic Church which helped provide a rational and moral foundation for the principles and procedures that guided the activities of merchants in the making of their contracts. One of the things that the church insisted upon was that merchants never engage in fraud and always follow a good faith approach to contract development. The problem of determining title to goods, especially determining just when title legitimately passes from one party to another, is a problem that must be solved to ensure the basic fairness of the law of sales. After all, it is not only ownership that passes with title, but also the risk associated with that ownership. [See Harold J. Berman, *Law and Revolution: The Formation of the Western Legal Tradition,* (Cambridge: Harvard UP, 1983), pp. 336–341; and Rodney Stark, *The Victory of Reason: How Christianity Led to Freedom, Capitalism, and Western Science* (New York: Random House, 2005), p. xi. See also Henri Sée, *Modern Capitalism: Its Origin and Evolutions*, trans. Homer B. Vanderblue and Georges F. Doriot (New York: Adelphi Co. 1928), pp. 7–13.]

## Valid Title, Void Title, and Voidable Title

**Title**, or **valid title**, is the right of ownership to goods. People who own goods have title to them. Sellers sometimes give a bill of sale to a buyer as evidence that the sale took place. A **bill of sale** is a written statement that provides evidence of the transfer of personal property from one person to another. It does not prove, however, that the seller had perfect title to the goods. The goods may have been stolen, obtained by fraud, purchased from a minor or an incompetent person, or entrusted with the seller by the true owner and sold by mistake. The question that arises in such cases is whether an innocent purchaser for value receives good title to the goods. The answer to this question depends on whether the seller's title to the goods was void or voidable and whether the goods had been entrusted to a merchant.

With the exception of voidable title, buyers of goods acquire whatever title their sellers had to the property. If a seller has **void title** (no title at all), a buyer of the goods obtains no title to them. The continued sale of the stolen property through several innocent buyers would not in any way defeat the real owner's right to the property. The rights of possession and title of successive buyers of stolen property can never be any better than the rights of the thief, who had no title at all. Of course, innocent purchasers may bring suit against the person from whom stolen goods were purchased for breach of warranty of title.

Anyone who obtains property as a result of another's fraud, misrepresentation, mutual mistake, undue influence, or duress holds only voidable title to the goods. **Voidable title** means title that may be voided if the injured party elects to do so. This kind of title is also received when goods are bought from a minor or a person who is mentally impaired. Some people refer to voidable title as title that is valid until voided. Anyone with voidable title to goods is able to transfer good title to others. According to the UCC, "A person with voidable title has power to transfer a good title to a good faith purchaser for value."

### Entrusting Goods to a Merchant

People often entrust goods that belong to them to merchants. For example, they leave their watches with jewelers and their vehicles with the body shop to be repaired. When this occurs, if the merchant sells the goods in the ordinary course of business to a third party who has no knowledge of the real owner's rights, the third party receives good title to them. The original owner who entrusted them to the merchant loses title to the goods altogether but may bring an action against the merchant for money damages caused by the loss. The reason for this rule of law is to give confidence to people who buy in the marketplace. People can be assured that they will receive good title to property (except stolen property) that they buy from a merchant who deals in goods of that kind in the ordinary course of business.

## Passage of Title and Risk of Loss

It is not unusual for goods to be stolen, damaged, or destroyed while they are awaiting shipment, are being shipped, or are awaiting pickup after a sales contract has been entered. When something happens to the goods, it becomes necessary to determine who must suffer the loss: the seller or the buyer. The rules for determining the risk of loss are contained in the UCC. Except when goods are to be picked up by the buyer and in a few other cases, whoever has title to the goods bears the risk of loss. Goods must be identified in the contract before title can be transferred to the buyer. **Identified goods** are specific goods that have been selected as the subject matter of the contract. Once goods are identified, title passes to the buyer when the seller does whatever is required under the contract to deliver the goods. Contracts calling for the seller to deliver the goods are either *shipment contracts* or *destination contracts*.

### Shipment Contracts

A **shipment contract** is one in which the seller turns the goods over to a carrier for delivery to the buyer. The seller has no responsibility for seeing that the goods reach their destination. In a shipment contract, both title and risk of loss pass to the buyer when the goods are given to the carrier. Shipment contracts are often designated by the term *f.o.b. [the place of shipment]* (such as f.o.b. Chicago). The abbreviation **f.o.b.** means "free on board." When goods are sent **f.o.b. the place of shipment**, they will be delivered free to the place of shipment. The buyer must pay all shipping charges from there to the place of destination. The terms indicate that title to the goods and the risk of loss pass at the point of origin. Delivery to the carrier by the seller and acceptance by the

| Table 13-2 | Abbreviations |
|---|---|
| **Abbreviation** | **Meaning** |
| f.o.b. New York | Free on bard to New York<br>(This would be a *shipment contract* if shipped from New York.) |
| f.o.b. Los Angeles | Free on board to Los Angeles<br>(This would be a *destination contract* if shipped from New York.) |
| c.o.d. | Collect on delivery |
| c.i.f. | Cost of goods shipped, insurance, and freight |
| c.f. | Cost of goods shipped and freight |
| f.a.s. | Free alongside vessel or at a dock |

carrier complete the transfer of both title and risk of loss. Thus, the buyer accepts full responsibility during the transit of the goods. (See Table 13-2.)

**Destination Contracts** If the contract requires the seller to deliver goods to a destination, it is called a **destination contract**. Both title and risk of loss pass to the buyer when the seller tenders the goods at the place of destination. **Tender** means to offer to turn the goods over to the buyer. Destination contracts are often designated by **f.o.b. the place of destination** (such as f.o.b. Tampa); goods shipped under such terms belong to the seller until they have been delivered to the destination shown on the contract. Similarly, the risk of loss remains with the seller until the goods are tendered at destination. Tender at destination requires that the goods arrive at the place named in the contract, the buyer is given notice of their arrival, and a reasonable time is allowed for the buyer to pick up the goods from the carrier.

When terms of shipment do not specify shipping point or destination, it is assumed to be a shipment contract. Adding the term **c.o.d.** (collect on delivery) instructs the carrier to

## THE OPENING CASE *Revisited, Part III*
## Purchase Orders and the UCC: *XCEL Mold & Machine v. DeVault Indus.*, Round 4

In the Opening Case at the beginning of this chapter we learned that DeVault, a shotgun manufacturer, sent a purchase order to XCEL for trigger-assembly units, at a total cost of $1,080. XCEL received and accepted purchase order No. 27. Within a few days, however, Mr. Cain, the president of XCEL, phoned Mr. DeVault, the president of DeVault, and told him that XCEL could not manufacture the parts at that price. DeVault told him not to worry because they would later figure out what a fair price would be. XCEL did, in fact, manufacture all 60 units and sent them to DeVault. If the order had been a shipment contract, the seller, XCEL, would have turned the trigger-assembly units over to a carrier for delivery to DeVault. The seller, XCEL, would then have no responsibility for seeing that the trigger-assemblies reached DeVault. In a shipment contract, both title and risk of loss pass to the buyer when the goods are given to the carrier. In contrast, if the order had been a destinations contract, then both title and risk of loss would have passed to the buyer, DeVault, when XCEL delivered the trigger-assemblies to DeVault's place of business, which was, of course, the final destination of the shipment.

**Table 13-3** Passage of Title and Risk of Loss

| Terms of Contract | Title Passes | Risk of Loss Passes |
| --- | --- | --- |
| Shipment contract | When goods are delivered to carrier | When goods are delivered to carrier |
| Destination contract | When goods are tendered at destination | When goods are tendered at destination |
| No delivery required | When contract is made | *Merchant seller:* When buyer receives goods; *Nonmerchant seller:* When seller tenders goods to buyer |
| Document of title | When document of title is given to buyer | When document of title is given to buyer |
| Agreement of the parties | At time and place agreed upon | At time and place agreed upon |

retain possession until the carrier has collected the cost of the goods. The term **c.i.f.** (cost, insurance, and freight) instructs the carrier to collect all charges and fees in one lump sum. This sum includes the cost of goods shipped, insurance, and freight charges to the point of destination. The term **c.f.** means that insurance is not included in the sum. The term **f.a.s. vessel** (free alongside vessel) at a named port requires sellers to deliver the goods, at their own risk, alongside the vessel or at a dock designated by the buyer.

**No Delivery Required** When the contract calls for the buyer to pick up the goods, title passes to the buyer when the contract is made. Risk of loss, however, passes at different times depending on whether the seller is a merchant. If the seller is a merchant, the risk of loss passes when the buyer receives the goods. If the seller is not a merchant, the risk of loss passes to the buyer when the seller tenders the goods to the buyer (See Table 13-3).

**Fungible Goods** The UCC defines **fungible goods** as "goods of which any unit is, by nature or usage of trade, the equivalent of any like unit." Wheat, flour, sugar, and liquids of various kinds are examples of fungible goods. They have no important characteristics that identify them as coming from a particular supplier, and they are usually sold by weight or measure. Title to fungible goods may pass without the necessity of separating goods sold from the bulk. Under the UCC, "an undivided share of an identified bulk of fungible goods is sufficiently identified to be sold although the quantity of the bulk is not determined."

## EXAMPLE 13-6: Fungible Goods

Logan Trucking Co. owned a large fuel storage tank that was partially filled with diesel fuel. The exact quantity of fuel in the tank was not known. The company was going out of business. Interstate Trucking Co. contracted to buy half of the fuel in the tank, and Union Trucking Co. contracted to buy the other half. Both buyers agreed to send their own trucks to pick up the fuel. Title passed to the buyers when the contract was made even though the exact quantity of each sale was unknown and neither buyer had taken a share of the fuel from the entire lot.

**Documents of Title** Sometimes, when people buy goods, they receive a document of title to the goods rather than the goods themselves. They then give the document of title to the warehouse or carrier that is holding the goods and receive possession of them. A

**document of title** is a paper giving the person who possesses it the right to receive the goods named in the document. Bills of lading and warehouse receipts are examples of documents of title. However, an automobile title certificate has not been given the legal status of a document of title, as the term is used in the UCC. When a document of title is used in a sales transaction, both title and risk of loss pass to the buyer when the document is delivered to the buyer.

**Agreement of the Parties** The parties may, if they wish, enter into an agreement setting forth the time that title and risk of loss pass from the seller to the buyer. With one exception, title and risk of loss will pass at the time and place agreed upon. If the agreement allows the seller to retain title after the goods are shipped, title will pass to the buyer at the time of shipment, regardless of the agreement, and the seller will have a security interest in the goods rather than title. A security interest gives the seller a right to have the property sold in the event that the buyer fails to pay money owed to the seller.

## EXAMPLE 13-7: Security Interest

Raymond agreed to sell Glover her John Deere tractor for $12,000. The agreement called for Glover to pay $3,000 down and the balance in monthly installments for two years. Under the terms of the agreement, title to the tractor would not pass to Glover until the $12,000 was paid in full. Because Raymond delivered the tractor to Glover on the day that the agreement was signed, title passed to Glover at that time, regardless of the terms in the contract. The effect of those terms was to give Raymond a security interest in the tractor for the balance of the money owed to her.

**Revesting of Title in Seller** Buyers, after entering into sales contracts, sometimes refuse to accept the goods that are delivered or are otherwise made available to them. In all such cases, title to the goods returns to the seller. This reversion is true whether or not the buyer's rejection of the goods is justified. Similarly, title to goods returns to the seller when the buyer accepts the goods and then for a justifiable reason decides to revoke the acceptance. A justifiable reason for revoking an acceptance would be the discovery of a defect in the goods after having inspected them. When the seller sends goods to the buyer that do not meet the contract requirements and are therefore unacceptable, the risk of loss remains with the seller. For situations in which the buyer accepts the goods but later discovers some defect and rightfully revokes the acceptance, the passage of risk of loss depends on whether the buyer is insured. If the buyer has insurance, that insurance will cover the loss. If there is no insurance, the risk of loss remains with the seller from the beginning. When the buyer breaches the contract with regard to goods that have been the contract, the seller may, to the extent of having no insurance coverage, treat the risk of loss as resting with the buyer.

**International Sales** The rules governing international sales are given in the United Nations Convention on Contracts for the International Sale of Goods (CISG). The international law does not address questions dealing with the passage of title because the laws of each country vary considerably. Instead, it leaves such questions to be decided by domestic law. This determination exists because third parties are usually involved in claiming title for themselves, and the laws of each country vary considerably. In contrast, the rules governing the passage of risk of loss are addressed in international law and are quite similar to those found in the UCC. The risk of loss passes to the buyer when the goods are handed over to the first carrier for transmission to the buyer unless the seller agrees to hand them over at a particular place. In that case, the risk of loss passes to the buyer at that time. Sometimes, goods are sold when they are in transit. When this kind of sale occurs (with some exceptions), the risk of loss passes to the buyer when the contract is made. In all other situations, the risk of loss, in general, passes when the buyer takes over the goods. The CISG has several exceptions in the contracts that it covers. It does not apply to goods bought for personal, household, or family use, or to contracts that mainly supply services. Nor does it cover the liability of the seller for death or injury caused by the goods sold.

---

## quick quiz 13-4

| | | |
|---|---|---|
| 1. *Void title* means title that may be voided if the injured party elects to do so. | true | false |
| 2. *Voidable title* means no title at all. | true | false |
| 3. Fungible goods must be separated from the bulk before title to them can pass to a buyer. | true | false |

---

# 13-5 Sales, Returns, and Insurable Interest

Because of competition and a desire to give satisfaction, goods are sometimes sold with the understanding that they may be returned even though they conform to the contract. Determination of ownership and risk of loss while such goods are in the buyer's possession is sometimes necessary. Sales with the right of return are of two kinds: sale on approval and sale or return.

## Sale on Approval

A sale that allows goods to be returned even though they conform to the contract is called a **sale on approval** when the goods are primarily for the buyer's use. When goods are sold on approval, they remain the property of the seller until the buyer's approval has been expressed. The approval may be indicated by the oral or written consent of the buyer or by the buyer's act of retaining the goods for more than a reasonable time. Using the goods in a reasonable and expected manner on a trial basis does not imply an acceptance. Grossly careless use and a failure to inform the seller of the buyer's intent to return, however, could constitute an acceptance. Goods held by the buyer on approval are not subject to the claims of the buyer's creditors until the buyer decides to accept them. In addition, the risk of loss remains with the seller until the buyer has accepted the goods.

## Sale or Return

A sale that allows goods to be returned even though they conform to the contract is called a **sale or return** when the goods are delivered primarily for resale. When such a sale occurs, the buyer takes title to the goods with the right to revest (reinstate) title in the seller after a specified period or reasonable time. In such cases, the buyer must accept all of the obligations of ownership while retaining possession of the goods. Goods held on sale or return are subject to the claims of the buyer's creditors. While in the buyer's possession, the goods must be cared for and used in a reasonable manner, anticipating their possible return in the same condition as when received, after making allowance for ordinary wear and tear. Also, the goods must be returned at the buyer's risk and expense.

## EXAMPLE 13-8: Consignment Contract

Butcher owned a gift shop in which she sold other people's goods on consignment. Hanson delivered a dozen handmade braided rugs to Butcher with the understanding that she would be paid for any that were sold. Any rugs that did not sell after three months would be returned to Hanson. This agreement was a sale or return because the rugs were delivered primarily for resale. Butcher would be required to pay Hanson for any rugs that were damaged, lost, or stolen while in Butcher's possession.

## Insurable Interest

People must have an insurable interest in property to be able to place insurance on it. An insurable interest is the financial interest that an insured party has in the insured property. Buyers may place insurance on goods the moment a contract is made and the goods are identified to the contract. At this point, buyers receive an insurable interest in the goods they buy. They obtain an insurable interest even though they might later reject or return the goods to the seller. Notwithstanding the buyer's right to insure the goods, sellers retain an insurable interest in the goods as long as they have title to them.

## EXAMPLE 13-9: Dual Insurable Interests

While shopping on vacation in an antique store in Connecticut, Maniff, who lived in Nevada, came upon a Native American totem pole she liked. She decided to buy the totem pole on the condition that the antique dealer would ship it f.o.b. Winnemucca, Nevada. The dealer agreed. Maniff received an insurable interest in the totem pole when it was identified to the contract. At the same time, the dealer retained an insurable interest in it until it was tendered at its destination in Winnemucca. Both Maniff and the antique dealer could insure the totem pole.

| | **quick quiz** 13-5 | |
|---|---|---|
| 1. | Goods that are sold on approval are subject to the claims of the buyer's creditors until the buyer decides to accept them. | true \| false |
| 2. | Goods that are sold on approval remain the property of the seller until the buyer's approval has been expressed. | true \| false |
| 3. | Goods that are sold on sale or return are not subject to the claims of the buyer's creditors. | true \| false |

# Summary

**13.1**   The Uniform Commercial Code (UCC), which contains the law of sales, has been adopted, either in whole or in part, by every state in the United States. Article 2 of the UCC applies whenever people buy or sell goods. It applies to transactions between private parties as well as transactions by businesspeople or merchants. Article 2A applies to leases of goods.

**13.2**   The following rules that are different from general contract law apply to sales contracts:

- A sales contract may be made in any manner that shows that the parties reached an agreement.
- Unless otherwise specified, an offeree may accept an offer in any way that is reasonable, including a prompt shipment of the goods.
- A written promise by a merchant to hold an offer open needs no consideration to be binding.
- A sales contract may be made even though the price is not settled.
- Output and requirements contracts are allowed in sales contracts as long as the parties deal in good faith and according to reasonable expectations.
- A sales contract may result even when an offeree adds different or additional terms from those offered or agreed upon.
- No consideration is necessary to modify a contract for the sale of goods.

**13.3**   With four exceptions, a contract for the sale of goods for $500 or more and the lease of goods for $1,000 or more must be in writing. The exceptions are oral contracts between merchants in which a confirma-tion has been received by one party and not objected to by the other party, specially manufactured goods, ad-missions in court, and executed contracts. The United Nations Convention on Contracts for the International Sale of Goods (CISG) applies to sales between U.S. businesses and foreign businesses.

In an auction sale, offers are made by the people in the audience. The acceptance takes place when the auctioneer bangs the gavel.

**13.4**   Title to goods can be either valid, void, or voidable. When a merchant sells goods without authority, the purchaser obtains good title. With few exceptions, such as when goods are to be picked up by the buyer, whoever has title to the goods bears the risk of loss. Once goods are identified, title passes to the buyer when the seller does whatever is required under the contract to deliver the goods. Title to fungible goods may pass without the need to separate goods sold from bulk. With a document of title, title and risk of loss pass to the buyer when the document is delivered. Title returns to the seller when the buyer refuses the goods. The risk of loss remains with the seller when the goods do not meet the requirements.

**13.5**   Goods sold on approval remain the property of the seller until the buyer approves. The seller retains the risk of loss. In a sale or return, the buyer takes title to the goods but is given the right to return the goods to the seller at a later time. The buyer must care for the goods in a reasonable manner and suffer the risk. Buyers have an insurable interest in goods the moment a contract is made and the goods are identified to the contract.

# Key Terms

## Questions for Review and Discussion

1. What are goods and what is a sale?
2. When does Article 2 of the UCC apply to contractual relationship?
3. What are the UCC rules that relate to written contracts?
4. What are the two laws that relate to cyber-sales contracts and what do they accomplish?
5. What is the difference between an auction with reserve with an auction without reserve?
6. What are valid title, void title, and voidable title?
7. When does the title to goods pass from seller to buyer?
8. When must the buyer and when must the seller bear the risk of loss?
9. What is the difference between a sale on approval and a sale or return?
10. What is an insurable interest?

## Cases for Analysis

1. Brenda Brandt had a medical device implanted as part of her treatment for a serious medical condition. A charge for the device was included in the hospital bill. Later, the device was recalled by its manufacturer as substandard. Brandt had suffered serious complications, and the device was removed. She brought suit against the hospital for, among other things, breach of warranty under the Uniform Commercial Code. Was the purchase of the medical device from the hospital covered under the Uniform Commercial Code? Explain. *Brandt v. Boston Scientific Corporation,* Docket No. 93982, Illinois Supreme Court (IL).

2. Alberto Parreira, a lobsterman, contracted in writing to sell Sam Adams 1,000 pounds of fresh lobsters at a particular price during the following season. A few months later, when lobsters became plentiful and the price went down, Adams tried to get out of the contract. He argued that the contract was not enforceable because the lobsters had not yet been caught when the contract was made. Do you agree with Adams? Why or why not?

3. Harnois entered into an oral contract with Neverson to lease a compact computer and a printer for three months for $600. In an attempt to rescind the contract, Harnois claimed that the contract was unenforceable because it was not in writing. Do you agree with Harnois? Why or why not?

4. Carolina Transformer Co., Inc., brought suit against Anderson for several thousand dollars owed it for the purchase of transformers. Anderson testified in court that he had orally negotiated the contract and reached a final agreement with Carolina for the purchase of the transformers. Anderson argued, however, that he was not responsible because under the UCC, a contract for the sale of goods of $500 or more is not enforceable unless it is in writing. Do you agree with Anderson? *Carolina Transformer Co. v. Anderson,* 341 So.2d 1327 (MS).

5. Representatives of a fish marketing association (AIFMA) and a fish company (NEFCO) met at Bristol Bay, Alaska, to negotiate a marketing agreement for the forthcoming fishing season. At this meeting, NEFCO's agent, Gage, signed an agreement that contained the price that was to be paid for the fish and other details about the transaction. It omitted the quantity of fish to be purchased. Later, when suit was brought on the agreement, NEFCO argued that it was unenforceable because the written agreement failed to mention the quantity. Do you agree with NEFCO? Explain. *Alaska Indus Fish Mktg. Assoc. v. New England Fish Co.,* 548 P.2d 348 (WA).

6. Wheel Sports Center entered into a sales contract agreeing to deliver a motorcycle to Ramos for the price of $893. Ramos paid the full price for the motorcycle and immediately had it insured and

registered in his name. However, before it was de-livered to Ramos, the motorcycle was stolen from Wheel Sports Center. Who must suffer the loss, Wheel Sports Center or Ramos? Why? *Ramos v. Wheel Sports Center,* 409 N.Y.S.2d 505 (NY).

7. Fanning, who was 17 years old, sold her bicycle to Gerard, an adult, for $75. The next day, Gerard ad-vertised the bicycle for sale in the classified sec-tion of a local newspaper and sold it for $150. The person who bought the bicycle was unaware that it had belonged to Fanning. When Fanning discov-ered what Gerard had done, she attempted to get the bicycle back from the person who bought it, claiming that Gerard had voidable title to the bicy-cle. Does Fanning have the legal right to the return of the bicycle? Why or why not?

8. Harold Marcus entered into a contract with Corri-gan's Yacht Yard & Marine Sales, Inc., to trade in his 34-foot Silverton power boat toward a later model Mainship boat. He delivered his Silverton boat to the yacht yard at the time of the contract in November. The new boat was not to be delivered until the following April. The yacht yard sold the Silverton boat to William Heiselman soon after re-ceiving it. When the yacht yard was unable to de-liver the Mainship boat to Marcus in April, Marcus took back his Silverton boat. Who had title to the boat, Marcus or Heiselman? Explain. *Heiselman v. Marcus,* 488 N.Y.S.2d 571 (NY).

9. Eberhard Manufacturing Company sold goods to Brown Industrial Sales Company without agreeing on who would bear the risk of loss. The contract contained no f.o.b. terms. Eberhard placed the goods on board a common carrier with instructions to deliver them to Brown. The goods were lost in transit. Who suffered the loss, Eberhard or Brown? Why? *Eberhard Mfg. Co. v. Brown,* 232 N.W.2d 378 (MI).

10. Henry Heide, Inc., received a warehouse receipt for 3,200 100-pound bags of sugar that it bought from Olavarria. The corporation withdrew 800 bags of the sugar from the warehouse (where thousands of pounds were stored), but when it returned for the balance, it discovered that the warehouse was pad-locked and empty. Some 200,000 pounds of sugar had mysteriously disappeared from it. Henry Heide, Inc., carried insurance for such a loss, but its insurance company refused to pay, claiming that the corporation had no insurable interest in the sugar. Do you agree with the insurance company? Why or why not? *Henry Heide, Inc., v. Atlantic Mut. Ins. Co.,* 363 N.Y.S.2d 515 (NY).

## quick quiz Answers

| 13.1 | 13.2 | 13.3 | 13.4 | 13.5 |
|------|------|------|------|------|
| 1. F | 1. T | 1. F | 1. F | 1. F |
| 2. T | 2. F | 2. T | 2. F | 2. T |
| 3. T | 3. T | 3. T | 3. F | 3. F |

# Chapter 14

# Sales Contracts Rights, Duties, Breach, and Warranties

## THE OPENING CASE    The Case of the Disappearing Delivery: *Ninth Street East, Ltd. v. Harrison*

Any contract that involves clothing, even avant-garde clothing, is covered by the Uniform Commercial Code (UCC). Keep in mind, as you read this case that the commissioners who wrote the UCC did their best to protect all the parties involved in a contract, even those who might not deserve that protection. In this case, the plaintiff is a Los Angeles clothing manufacturer and the defendant is a retailer doing business in Westport, Connecticut, as a clothing store named The Rage. The manufacturer received an order from The Rage for a shipment of clothing that amounted to $2,216.00. The clothing was packaged carefully and then turned over to a reputable and dependable shipper named the Denver-Chicago Shipping Company (Denver). Denver gave a bill of lading to the manufacturer and the manufacturer sent along four separate invoices to The Rage. The invoices stated explicitly that the shipment was "F.O.B. Los Angeles," that the shipper was Denver-Chicago, and that the buyer bore the risk of loss. Moreover, the bill of lading stated quite clearly that all shipping charges would be paid by The Rage. At some point along the way between LA and Westport, exactly where is never made clear, Denver handed the shipment off to another trucking firm, this one named the Old Colony Transportation Company of South Dartmouth, Massachusetts. When

the Old Colony truck arrived at The Rage, the driver refused to deliver the goods inside of the store, preferring, instead, to deliver them outside the premises. When the store manager refused to accept the eight cartons of clothing unless they ended up inside the store, the trucker drove off, still in possession of the shipment. The clothing was never seen again. The owner of The Rage sent an immediate letter of protest to the manufacturer, which filed a claim against Denver, which Denver refused to honor. Meanwhile, back in Connecticut, the owner of The Rage continued to demand that the missing shipment be delivered inside the store. Yet, whenever the manufacturer tried to contact the owner, he was unavailable. When the manufacturer finally sued, the owner of The Rage argued that he could not possibly be liable for goods he never received. Instead, he claims that the manufacturer is responsible for the loss of the shipment because he chose an unreliable shipper who apparently ran off with the goods. In turn, the manufacturer argues that, since the risk of loss passed to the retailer when the shipment was delivered to the trucker, and since the retailer refused to accept a shipment that was quite literally on his doorstep, he must pay for the eight cartons of clothing whether he actually received them or not. As you read the chapter, see if you can solve the Case if the Disappearing Delivery or, as they say in Massachusetts, the Mystery of the Missing Merchandise. (See *Ninth Street East, Ltd. v. Harrison,* 259 A.2d 772, 5 Conn.Cir.Ct. 597 (Connecticut Circuit Court, First Circuit).)

**Opening Case Questions**

1. In the case of *Ninth Street East, Ltd. v. Harrison,* what does the notation "F.O.B. Los Angeles" mean?

2. At what point did the risk of loss pass to the buyer? Explain.

3. The bill of lading in this case noted that the shipment was to be "collect." How does this notation figure into the passage of risk? Explain.

4. Did the truck driver's refusal to deliver the cartons inside the store amount to a refusal to tender performance? Why or why not?

5. Is the shipper's refusal to honor the manufacturer's claim significant in this case? Why or why not?

 Learning Objectives

1. Describe what is meant by tender of performance.
2. Outline the rights and duties of sellers and buyers in a sales contract.
3. Explain the doctrine of anticipatory breach.
4. Discuss the seller's and the buyer's remedies in case of a breach.
5. Define the term *statute of limitations.*
6. Describe the three ways in which an express warranty may be created.
7. State the requirements of the Magnuson-Moss Warranty Act.
8. Differentiate among the implied warranties of fitness for a particular purpose, merchantability, and usage of trade.
9. Explain the meaning of a warranty of title.
10. Recognize the ways in which warranties may be excluded.

# 14-1 Rights and Duties of the Parties

The duties of the parties to a sales contract are simple and straightforward: The seller is obligated to turn the goods over to the buyer, and the buyer is obligated to accept and pay for the goods. In addition, all parties must act in good faith, which means that they must act honestly. The court need not enforce a contract or part of a contract that it finds to be unconscionable. An unconscionable contract is one that gives an unfair advantage to one of the parties. Unequal bargaining power, the absence of a meaningful choice by one party, and unreasonably one-sided terms, when put together, indicate unconscionability. When disputes arise between parties who have dealt together in the past, the court often looks to their past dealings to give meaning to the disputed transaction.

When interpreting the meaning of a contract, the court may also consider any usage of trade, that is, any particular methods of doing business, that are commonly used in that field and the way that the parties have dealt with one another in the past. Although terms that are expressly stated in a contract will usually control the contract's meaning, the parties' past dealings and usage of trade are often considered to supplement or qualify the express terms. Moreover, the UCC establishes a series of rights and duties that are key elements within all sales contracts. Most of these rights and duties are based on common sense and the practicality of commercial world. Others have been uniquely created by the NCUSL to ensure stability in the world of sales. These rights and duties include the tender

UCC 1-205 (see page 820)

of performance, the buyer's rights and duties of upon delivery of improper goods, and the seller's right to cure improper tender.

## Tender of Performance

When the seller offers to turn the goods over to the buyer and when the buyer offers to pay for them, **tender of performance** occurs. It is the offering by the parties to do what they have agreed to do under the terms of the contract. Tender is necessary to test the party's ability and willingness to perform his or her part of the bargain. The seller must make tender of delivery, and the buyer must make tender of payment. If one party fails to make tender and the other breaches the contract, the one not making tender cannot bring suit. To be in a position to bring suit on a sales contract, the seller of goods must make **tender of delivery**, that is, offer to turn the goods over to the buyer. Failure to make this offer is an excuse for buyers not to perform their part of the bargain.

UCC 2-507 (see page 833)

UCC 2-503(1)(b) (see page 832)

UCC 2-504 (see page 832)

UCC 2-503(4) (see page 832)

**Making Proper Tender** To make proper tender, the seller must put and hold conforming goods at the buyer's disposition during a reasonable hour of the day. Sometimes goods are in the possession of a warehouse and are to be turned over to the buyer without being moved. When this situation occurs, tender requires that the seller either tender a document of title covering the goods or obtain an acknowledgment by the warehouse of the buyer's right to their possession. In a **shipment contract**, the seller must put the goods in

## THE OPENING CASE *Revisited, Part I*
## The Case of the Disappearing Delivery: *Ninth Street East, Ltd. v. Harrison*, Round 2

In the Opening Case at the beginning of the chapter, the plaintiff, a Los Angeles clothing manufacturer, received an order from The Rage, a retailer in Connecticut. The clothing was packaged carefully and then released to a reliable and responsible shipping company known as the Denver-Chicago Shipping Company (Denver). Denver gave a *bill of lading* to the manufacturer and the manufacturer sent along *four separate invoices* to The Rage. The invoices stated explicitly that the shipment was *"F.O.B. Los Angeles,"* that the shipper was Denver-Chicago, and that the buyer bore the risk of loss. Moreover, the *bill of lading* stated quite clearly that the order was to be "collect," which meant that all shipping charges would be paid by The Rage. The plaintiff in this case, made all the proper moves and obtained or produced all of the proper paper work as required by the UCC. Therefore, the contract was clearly a *shipping contract*. Moreover, Connecticut court had no difficulty coming to this conclusion. The court simply referred to the official comments of the NCCUSL in explaining UCC

2-503, which note that all transactions carried out under the authority of the UCC are presumed to be shipment contracts unless proven otherwise. This meant that the risk of loss passed to buyer the moment that the clothing was delivered to the trucking company in Los Angeles. More specifically, the court referred to UCC 2-504, which states that it is the responsibility of the seller to "(a) put the goods in the possession of such a carrier and make such a contract for their transportation as may be reasonable having regard to the nature of the goods and other circumstances of the case; and (b) obtain and promptly deliver or tender in due form any document necessary to enable the buyer to obtain possession of the goods or otherwise required by the agreement or by usage of trade; and (c) promptly notify the buyer of the shipment." The seller had done all of this indicating that, if the buyer had any legal case at all, it would have to be levied against the trucking company, which had control of the goods, not the seller who relinquished control in Los Angeles.

the possession of a carrier and contract with that carrier for their transportation. Any necessary documents must be sent to the buyer, who must be promptly notified of the shipment.

## Tender of Payment by Buyer

Although the seller is obligated to deliver the goods to the buyer, this obligation stands on the condition that the buyer make tender of payment, unless otherwise agreed. **Tender of payment** means offering to turn the necessary money over to the seller. Such tender may be made by any means or in any manner that is commonly used in the ordinary course of business. The seller has the right to demand payment in legal tender but must give the buyer a reasonable time to obtain it. **Legal tender** is money that may be offered legally in satisfaction of a debt and that must be accepted by a creditor when offered. Payment by check is conditional under the UCC. If the check clears, the debt is discharged. If the check is dishonored, the debt is revived. When a contract requires payment before inspection, as when goods are shipped c.o.d., the buyer must pay for them first, even if they turn out to be defective when they are inspected. Of course, if the defect is obvious, the buyer would not have to accept or pay for the goods. Payment by the buyer before inspecting the goods does not constitute an acceptance of them. Upon discovering a defect and notifying the seller, the buyer may use any of the remedies that are mentioned later in the chapter against the seller for breach of contract.

UCC 2-511(1) (see page 833)

UCC 2-511(3) (see page 833)

UCC 2-512 (see page 833)

## Buyer's Rights and Duties

Except when goods are shipped c.o.d. or when the contract provides for payment against a document of title, the buyer has the right to inspect the goods before accepting or paying for them. The inspection may take place after the goods arrive at their destination. Expenses of inspection must be borne by the buyer but may be recovered from the seller if the goods do not conform to the contract and are rejected by the buyer. Goods conform to a contract when they are in accordance with the obligations under the contract. When defective goods or goods not of the kind specified in the contract are delivered, the buyer may elect to reject them all, accept them all, or accept any commercial unit or units and reject the rest. A **commercial unit** is a single whole for the purpose of sale, the division of which impairs its character or value on the market. For example, a commercial unit or a set of articles (e.g., suite of furniture, assortment of sizes). It may be a quantity (e.g., bale, gross, carload) or any other unit treated may be a single article (e.g., a machine) in the marketplace as a single whole item.

UCC 2-513 (see page 834)

UCC 2-106(2) (see page 822)

Failure of the buyer to inspect goods upon delivery results in an acceptance of the goods, even if nonconforming.

## Rejection of Goods by the Buyer

A rejection occurs when a buyer refuses to accept delivery of goods tendered. A rejection must be done within a reasonable time after delivery or tender to the buyer. After a rejection, the buyer may not claim ownership of the goods. In addition, the buyer must notify the seller of the particular defect in the goods so as to give the seller an opportunity to correct the defect. If the goods are in the buyer's possession, the buyer must hold them with reasonable care long enough for the seller to remove them.

UCC 2-601 (see page 834)

CISG Article 38 (see page 886)

UCC 2-602 (see page 834)

If the seller gives no instructions within a reasonable time after being notified of the rejection, the buyer may store the goods for the seller, reship them to the seller, or resell them for the seller. In all cases, the buyer is entitled to be reimbursed for expenses. A special duty comes into existence when a buyer who is a merchant rejects goods. Merchant buyers have a duty after the rejection of goods in their possession or control to follow any reasonable instructions received from the seller with respect to the goods. If there are no such instructions, they must make reasonable efforts to sell the goods for the seller if they

## THE OPENING CASE *Revisited, Part II*
The Case of the Disappearing Delivery: *Ninth Street East,*
*Ltd. v. Harrison,* Round 3

In the Opening Case at the beginning of the chapter, the Los Angeles clothing manufacturer appears to have done everything by the book. After receiving an order from The Rage in Connecticut, the manufacturer packaged the clothing in eight cartons and turned those cartons over to a reputable shipper named the Denver-Chicago Shipping Company (Denver). Denver then transferred a bill of lading to the manufacturer and the manufacturer then sent four separate invoices to The Rage. The invoices stated explicitly that the shipment was "F.O.B. Los Angeles," that the shipper was Denver-Chicago, and that the buyer bore the risk of loss. In addition, the bill of lading stated quite clearly that all shipping charges would be paid by The Rage. Later, Denver handed the shipment off to Old Colony Transportation which attempted to deliver the goods to The Rage. At that point, the buyer rejected the ship-

ment because the driver refused to deliver the goods inside of the store. The trucker then drove off, apparently still in possession of the shipment. At first blush, this may seem like a rejection under UCC 2-602 and 2-603, permitting the buyer to walk away from the contract with no liability. This interpretation, however, would be a misreading of the statute. In order for a rejection to be legally correct, the buyer must first notify the seller of the rejection [UCC 2-602 (1)] and then follow the reasonable instructions of the seller in relation to the goods [UCC 603 (1)]. The buyer in this case did neither. First, the buyer continued to demand that the missing shipment be delivered to The Rage, thus negating any claim under UCC 2-602 (1) and (2) the buyer refused to respond to the seller's attempts to contact the store with instructions about the goods, thus violating his duties under UCC 2-603 (1).

---

UCC 2-604 (see
page 835)

are perishable or threaten to decline speedily in value. Merchants who sell rejected goods are entitled to be reimbursed either by the seller or from the proceeds of the sale for reasonable expenses of caring for and selling the goods. They are also entitled to such commission as is usual in the trade or, if none, a reasonable sum not exceeding 10 percent of the proceeds of the sale. A buyer who is not a merchant has no other obligation regarding goods that are rightfully rejected.

UCC 2-603(1) (see
page 834)

UCC 2-603(2) (see
page 834)

UCC 2-606 (see
page 835)

**Acceptance of Goods by the Buyer** Once goods have been accepted, they cannot be rejected. Acceptance of goods takes place when the buyer, after a reasonable opportunity to inspect them, does any of the following:

- Signifies to the seller that the goods are conforming, that is, that they are in accordance with the obligations under the contract.
- Signifies to the seller a willingness to take them even though they are not conforming.
- Fails to reject them.
- Performs any act that is inconsistent with the seller's ownership.

UCC 2-607(3) (see
page 835)

When the buyer accepts goods and later discovers something wrong with them, the buyer must notify the seller within a reasonable time after the discovery. The failure to give proper notice will prevent the buyer from having recourse against the seller.

UCC 2-608 (see
page 835)

**Revocation of Acceptance** If a buyer has accepted goods on the assumption that their nonconformity would be corrected by the seller and the seller does not do so, the buyer may revoke the acceptance. This revocation must be made within a reasonable time after the buyer discovers the nonconformity. A revocation of an acceptance is not effective until the buyer notifies the seller of it. Buyers who revoke an acceptance have the same rights and duties with regard to the goods involved as if they had rejected them.

## Seller's Rights and Duties

Sellers may sometimes **cure** an improper tender or delivery of goods; that is, they may correct the defect that caused the goods to be rejected by the buyer. When the time for performance has not yet expired, the seller has the right to cure the defect and make a proper tender within the contract time. If the time for performance has expired, the seller is allowed to have an additional amount of time to substitute a conforming tender if the seller has reasonable grounds to believe that the goods that were delivered were acceptable. In all cases, sellers have a duty to notify buyers that they are going to cure the improper tender or delivery.

UCC 2-508 (see page 833)

> ### EXAMPLE 14-1: Cure of Improper Tender
>
> Caravan Motel ordered 10 dozen bath towels from samples shown by Fleming Towel Company's representative. The representative made a mistake in writing up the order. As a result, the towels that were delivered were inferior to those shown to Caravan at the time the order was given. Caravan rejected them. Because the Fleming Towel Company had reasonable grounds to believe that Caravan Motel would accept the towels that were delivered, it was allowed additional time to substitute correct towels for the ones that were delivered. When it learned of the rejection, Fleming Towel Company was required to notify the motel that it intended to cure the nonconforming delivery.

The seller does not have the right to cure improper tender when a buyer accepts nonconforming goods, even though the buyer may later sue the seller for breach of contract. The seller has this right only when the buyer either rejects the goods tendered or revokes an acceptance of the goods.

### quick quiz 14-1

| | | |
|---|---|---|
| 1. According to the law of sales contracts, all parties must act in good faith, which means they must act honestly. · | true \| false | |
| 2. Tender of performance is the offering by the parties to do what they have agreed to do under the terms of the contract. | true \| false | |
| 3. Buyers have no right to inspect goods before paying for them when they are shipped c.o.d. | true \| false | |

# 14-2 Breach of Contract

Breach of contract occurs when one of the parties fails to do what was agreed upon in the contract. When this happens, the other party to the contract has specific remedies available under the UCC. All parties must attempt to mitigate the damages, that is, to keep them as low as possible.

# Anticipatory Breach

UCC 2-610 (see page 836)

Sometimes, one of the parties will notify the other party before the time for performance that he or she is not going to conform. This notification is known as *anticipatory breach*. It is a breach committed before there is a present duty to perform the contract. Under older contractual law, the injured party in such a case had to wait until the actual time for performance before bringing suit or taking some other action. It was necessary to wait for the actual time for performance to know for sure that the other party was indeed not going to perform. Under the UCC, when either party repudiates the contract before the time for performance, the injured party may take action immediately if waiting would be unjust or cause a material inconvenience. Any of the remedies for breach of contract are available to the aggrieved party, in addition to the right to suspend his or her own performance.

## EXAMPLE 14-2: Anticipatory Breach

The Westwell Construction Company ordered 1000 steel I-beams to be made to order from the Anaconda Steel Corporation for use in a building that Westwell was going to begin building in six months. Anaconda Steel agreed to deliver the I-beams on or before that date. Two months before the delivery date, Anaconda Steel notified Westwell that it would not be able to fill the order. Westwell could treat the contract as having been breached and use any of the buyer's remedies that are available to him under the UCC.

# Seller's Remedies

When a buyer breaches a sales contract, the seller may select from a number of remedies. Table 14-1 lists six remedies that sellers may employ when the buyer breaches. These remedies include withholding the delivery of goods, stopping the delivery of the goods, reselling the goods, recovering damages, suing for the price of the goods, and simply canceling the contract. Of the six remedies, the last one, cancelling the contract, is the simplest and the most pain-free solution. However, from a financial perspective, it is often the most damaging. On the other hand, the most difficult and time-consuming is initiating a lawsuit. However, if it is handled properly, a lawsuit can be the fairest and the most effective remedy available in the law today.

UCC 2-703(a) (see page 837)

### Table 14-1   Seller's Remedies When the Buyer Breaches

1. Withhold delivery of any goods not yet delivered.
2. If the buyer is insolvent, stop delivery of any goods that are still in the possession of a carrier.
3. Resell any goods that have been rightfully withheld, and then sue the buyer for the difference between the agreed price and the resale price.
4. If the goods cannot be resold, sue the buyer for the difference between the agreed price and the market price.
5. Sue the buyer for the price of any goods that were accepted by the buyer.
6. Cancel the contract.

## Withhold or Stop the Delivery of Goods

If the goods have not been delivered, the seller has a right to keep them upon learning of the buyer's breach. If, after shipping the goods, the seller discovers that the buyer is insolvent (unable to pay debts), the seller may have the delivery stopped. This right is known as stoppage in transit and is permitted after goods have been shipped but before they have reached their destination. The seller must give information to the carrier (the transportation company) to satisfy the latter that the buyer is insolvent. In addition, the seller must accept responsibility for any damage suffered by the carrier for not completing the shipment. If the insolvency information is incorrect, both the seller and the carrier could be sued for damages. The seller may also stop delivery of a carload, truckload, planeload, or larger shipments of express or freight when the buyer repudiates or fails to make a payment that is due before delivery or otherwise breaches the contract. If the seller has issued a document of title, the seller can stop delivery only by surrendering the document to the carrier. If the buyer has received the document, delivery of the goods cannot be stopped in transit.

UCC 2-705 (see page 838)

## Resell the Goods

The seller may resell the goods or the undelivered balance of them. In the case of unfinished manufactured goods, a seller may either complete the manufacture and resell the finished goods or cease manufacture and resell the unfinished goods for scrap or salvage value. In such cases, the seller must use reasonable commercial judgment to avoid losses. After the sale, the injured party may sue the other for the difference between what the property brought on resale and the price the buyer had agreed to pay in the contract. Resale may be a public or private sale. If it is a private sale, the seller must give the buyer reasonable notice of its intention to resell the goods. If it is a public sale, it must be made at a place that is normally used for public sales, if such a place is available. In addition, if the goods are perishable or threaten to decline in value speedily, the seller must give the buyer reasonable notice of the time and place of resale. A purchaser who buys in good faith at a resale takes the goods free of any rights of the original buyer. Furthermore, the seller is not accountable to the buyer for any profit made on the resale. The seller who chooses to do so may buy the goods at resale.

UCC 2-706(1) (see page 838)

UCC 2-704(2) (see page 838)

UCC 2-706(4)(b) (see page 838)

UCC 2-706(4)(d) (see page 838)

## Damages

The seller may retain the merchandise and sue the buyer for either the difference between the contract price and the market price at the time the buyer breached the agreement or the profit (including overhead) that the seller would have made had the contract been performed. In either case, the seller is also entitled to *incidental damages*. These damages are reasonable expenses that indirectly result from the breach, such as expenses incurred in stopping delivery of goods, transporting goods, and caring for goods after the buyer's breach.

UCC 2-708 (see page 839)

UCC 2-710 (see page 839)

## Sue for Price

The seller may sue for the price of any goods that the buyer has accepted. Similarly, upon the buyer's breach, the seller may bring suit for the price of goods that cannot be resold at a reasonable price. In addition, the seller may sue the buyer for the price of any *lost* or damaged goods after the risk of their loss has passed to the buyer. In the commercial setting this remedy is sanctioned by the Uniform Commercial Code in UCC 2-709 (1) (a). The seller who sues the buyer for the price must hold for the buyer any goods that are under the seller's control. The goods may be sold, however, at any time resale is possible before the collection of a judgment in the case. The net proceeds of any resale must be credited to the buyer. Any goods that are not resold become the property of the buyer if the buyer pays for them as a result of a court judgment.

UCC 2-709 (see page 839)

## Cancel the Contract

The seller can cancel the contract. This cancellation occurs when the seller ends the contract because the other party breached. When cancellation takes place in this manner, the seller may use any of the remedies mentioned for breach of contract.

UCC 2-106 (see page 822)

## THE OPENING CASE *Revisited, Part III*
### The Case of the Disappearing Delivery: *Ninth Street East, Ltd. v. Harrison,* Round 4

Recall in the Opening Case at the beginning of the chapter that, when the Old Colony truck arrived at The Rage with eight cartons of clothing, the driver refused to deliver the goods inside of the store, preferring, instead, to leave them outside the premises. When the store manager refused to accept the eight cartons of clothing unless they were placed inside the store, the trucker drove off, still holding the shipment. The shipment was never seen again. The owner of The Rage protested this sorry state of affairs to the manufacturer, which filed a claim against Denver, which Denver did not honor. Back in Connecticut, the owner of The Rage continued to demand that the missing shipment be delivered inside the store. Yet, whenever the manufacturer tried to contact him, he was unavailable. When the manufacturer sued, the owner of The Rage argued that he could not possibly be liable for goods he never received. Instead, he claims that the manufacturer is responsible for the loss of the shipment because he chose an unreliable shipper who apparently absconded with the goods into the night. In turn, the manufacturer argues that, since the risk of loss passed to the retailer when the shipment was delivered to the trucker, and since the retailer refused to accept a shipment that was quite literally on his doorstep, he must pay for the eight cartons of clothing whether he actually received them or not. The court agreed with the manufacturer. To prove its point, the court referred directly to UCC 2-709 which says quite clearly that, "(1) When the buyer fails to pay the price as it becomes due the seller may recover . . . the price (a) * * * of conforming goods lost or damaged within a commercially reasonable time after the risk of their loss has passed to the buyer." (See UCC Section 2-709 *Ninth Street East, Ltd. v. Harrison*, 259 A.2d 772, 5 Conn.Cir.Ct. 597 (Connecticut Circuit Court, First Circuit).)

## Buyer's Remedies

UCC 2-711 (see page 839)

UCC 2-712 (see page 839)

When a seller breaches a sales contract, the buyer may select from a number of remedies. Table 14-2 lists six remedies that buyers may use whenever the seller breaches the sales contract. The first two remedies are relatively clear and straightforward. The buyer either [1] tells the seller that the deal is off or [2] demands a repayment of any money that has already been handed over to the seller as a down payment or some other type of monetary guarantee of performance. If the seller cooperates, there is no need to go any further.

**Table 14-2    Buyer's Remedies When the Seller Breaches**

1. Cancel the contract.

2. Sue the seller for the return of any money that has been paid.

3. Cover the sale—that is, buy similar goods from someone else and sue the seller for the difference between the agreed price and the cost of the purchase.

4. Sue the seller for the difference between the agreed price and the market price at the time the buyer learned of the breach.

5. If nonconforming goods have been accepted, notify the seller that they do not conform to the contract. Then, if no adjustment is made, sue the seller either for breach of contract or for breach of warranty.

6. When goods are unique or rare, sue for specific performance.

However, if the seller refuses to comply, the buyer has several additional options available. These include cover the sale, sue for breach, keep the goods and seek an adjustment, or, in some rare circumstances, sue for specific performance. Of these four remedies, the last one, suing for specific performance is the most difficult and the least applicable remedy because it can only be used when the subject matter of the sales contract is something unique, such as an original work of art, or when the subject is very rare, as with an antique, a family heirloom, or a vintage automobile. On the other hand, from a financial perspective, it is often a very rewarding process for buyers because, if they are successful, they receive exactly what they bargained for in the original contract.

### Cover the Sale or Sue for Breach

The buyer may **cover** the sale, that is, buy similar goods from someone else. The buyer may then sue the seller for the difference between the agreed pice and the cost of the purchase. Cover must be made without unreasonable delay. In the alternative, when a seller breaches a contract by not delivering the goods, the buyer may sue for damages if any were suffered. The measure of damages is the difference between the price that the parties agreed upon and the price of the same goods in the marketplace on the date the buyer learned of the breach. In addition, the buyer may sue for incidental and consequential damages. Damages for breach of contract may be liquidated, that is, agreed upon by the parties when they first enter into the contract. Liquidated damages will be allowed by the court if they are reasonable.

### EXAMPLE 14-3: Cover of a Sales Contract

Flamme Bros. contracted to deliver a specific quantity of corn to Farmers' Union Co-op Co., a cooperative grain elevator. When Flamme Bros. failed to deliver the corn, Farmers' Union bought corn from its members over a two-week period. The court held that this purchase was cover of the contract without unreasonable delay. Farmers' Union recovered the difference between the agreed price of the corn from Flamme Bros. and the price it paid to the farmers for the corn it bought. In the alternative, the Farmer's Union could have refrained from purchasing the grain from other suppliers and simply brought a lawsuit against Flamme Brothers for damages. The damages would be measured by the difference between the price that the parties agreed upon and the price of corn in the marketplace on the date the Farmer's Union learned of the breach. In addition, the Farmer's Union may sue for incidental and consequential damages.

### Keep Goods and Seek Adjustment

When improper goods are delivered, the buyer may keep them and ask the seller for an adjustment. If no adjustment is made, the buyer may sue the seller for either breach of contract or breach of warranty, whichever applies. The amount of the suit would be the difference between the value of the goods contracted for and the value of the goods received. Warranties are discussed in later in this chapter.

### EXAMPLE 14-4: Swimsuit Adjustment

The Jacobs Brothers Department chain of Omaha ordered 40 dozen swimsuits from Illumination Encore, Ltd, a clothing manufacturer in Fort Worth. The suits that were delivered were totally different from the samples shown by Illumination's sales rep. Because the Jacobs Brothers needed swimsuits for its spring trade show, Kenneth Jacobs, the CEO of the department chain, decided to keep them. If no adjustment is made by the manufacturer, Illumination Encore, Jacobs can sue the manufacturer for damages (including loss of profits) that were suffered because of the breach of the express warranty that the goods would be the same as the sample.

UCC 2-713 (see page 840)

UCC 2-715 (see page 840)

UCC 2-718(1) (see page 840)

UCC 2-714(2) (see page 840)

UCC 2-716(1) (see page 840)

## Sue for Specific Performance

**Sue for Specific Performance** When the goods are unique or rare, the buyer may ask the court to order the seller to do what he or she agreed to do under the contract terms. This request is known as an action for specific performance of the contract. A decree of specific performance, if granted by the court, would require the seller to deliver to the buyer the goods described in the sales agreement. This type of action is permitted only when an award of money will not give the buyer sufficient relief. Contracts for *objets d'art,* rare gems, antiques, and goods described as one-of-a-kind come within the scope of this type of action. Under the UCC, the decree of specific performance may include the payment of the price, damages, or other relief as the court may deem just. Buyers have a right of replevin for goods that have been identified to the contract if, after a reasonable effort, they are unable to buy the goods elsewhere. A **writ of replevin** is a court action that allows a person entitled to goods to recover them from someone who has them wrongfully.

## The Commercial Docket

Commercial cases have become so numerous recently that a few states have taken the extraordinary step of establishing a separate court docket dedicated exclusively to commercial cases. Those commentators who support establishing a commercial docket argue that commercial lawsuits can be handled more effectively if they are assigned to judges who have been trained to manage such cases. For example, the state of Ohio recently inaugurated a Commercial Docket Pilot Project. The goal of the project is to create a docket for commercial lawsuits that will be handled by judges and mediators who have received special education sessions devoted exclusively to commercial law. To implement the system, the chief justice of the Ohio Supreme Court chose five trial courts to lead the way by establishing a commercial docket within their jurisdictions. The chief justice then appointed several commercial docket judges who were assigned to handle every case that fit within the commercial docket in their court. The plan limits the commercial docket to cases that involve disputes among two or more businesses, although the court also handles a long list of similar lawsuits including such things as the formation or dissolution of a business, the rights and duties of business partners, and so on. Once a commercial docket is ready to begin operation, the commercial judge chooses a cadre of mediators, referred to in Ohio as special masters, who are trained to handle commercial lawsuits. The special masters are the first line of defense on the commercial docket. They handle cases and make rulings that are then passed onto the commercial judge for evaluation and approval. The commercial judge can uphold, reject, reverse, or resubmit the case to the special master. (See Ohio Sup. R. Temp. Rules 1.01 to 1.11).

UCC 2-716(3) (see page 840)

UCC 2-725 (see page 842)

### Self-Evident Truths: The Science Court v. The Commercial Docket

As noted earlier, a planned court system that is similar to the Ohio commercial docket is the proposed science court. The science court would act as a forum for cases involving scientific and technological disputes. Like commercial docket judges, the science court judges would be trained to deal exclusively with cases of a scientific and technological nature. The science court would focus on disputes involving genetic engineering; nuclear energy research; cyber-contract law; energy law; cloning; engineering, architectural, and technological projects; medical treatments; medical research; environmental law; birth control; health care wills; health care power of attorney disputes; abortion law disputes; intellectual property problems, surrogate parenting and so on. The plan is to use specially trained judges with scientific and technological backgrounds who will be equipped to handle the complexities of today's science related cases. The science court and the commercial court look good on paper, but would they actually work in the real world?

## Self-Evident Questions

1. What happens when a sales contract involves the purchase of scientific equipment? Would such a case fall under the jurisdiction of the commercial docket court or the science court?

2. What would we do with a case involving a surrogate parenting contract? Is that a job for the science court or the commercial docket? Explain.

3. Would commercial judges begin to lean toward the best interests of merchants rather than the consumer? Explain.

4. Would science court judges begin to lean toward the best interests of scientists and engineers rather than the public? Explain.

5. There is also the question of equal protection of the law. Does the commercial court violate equal protection by giving special treatment to business people? Explain. Does the science court violate equal protection by giving special treatment to scientists and engineers? Why or why not?

## Statute of Limitations

Nearly all lawsuits have a time limit within which a lawsuit must be brought. If the time limit is exceeded, the action is forever barred. In general, an action for breach of a sales contract must be brought within four years after the date of the breach. The parties may, if they wish to do so, provide for a shorter time period, not less than one year, in their sales agreement. They may not, however, agree to a period longer than four years.

CISG Article 49 (see page 888)

CISG Articles 61–64 (see page 889)

CISG Articles 74–77 (see page 891)

CISG Articles 79 (see page 891)

CISG Articles 81 (see page 891)

CISG Articles 85–88 (see page 892)

### quick quiz 14-2

1. If the goods have not been delivered, the seller has a right to keep them upon learning of the buyer's breach.      true | false

2. The seller may sue the buyer for the price of any *lost* or damaged goods after the risk of their loss has passed to the buyer.      true | false

3. When the goods are unique or rare, the buyer may ask the court to order the seller to do what he or she agreed to do under the contract terms.      true | false

# 14-3 Warranty Protection

Up until now, in this chapter we have focused on the actual sales agreement itself. We have looked at what constitutes performance, what constitutes nonperformance, and what happens when the seller does not deliver the goods, the buyer does not pay for the goods, or the trucking company loses the goods. Now we switch focus. Instead of looking at a contract that has not been performed, we will look at contracts that have been performed—sort of. Have you ever purchased an item that turned out to be damaged or broken when you opened the box? Have you ever paid for something that you wanted for a particular purpose, only to find that it would not do the job? Has a salesperson ever made a statement or a promise about a product that did not come true? Have you ever found an impurity or a foreign substance in food that you bought in a store or ate in a restaurant? The UCC gives you protection in all these situations under its law of warranties. A warranty is another name for a guarantee. Warranties come in all shapes and sizes. Still, in one way or another, all warranties fall into one of three categories: express warranties, implied warranties, and warranties of title.

## Express Warranties

An **express warranty** is an oral or written statement, promise, or other representation about the quality of a product. Express warranties arise in three different ways: by a statement of fact or promise, by a description of the goods, or by a sample or model. In states that have adopted Article 2A of the UCC, express warranties arise when goods are leased in exactly the same way that they arise when goods are sold.

### Statement of Fact or Promise
Whenever a seller of goods makes a statement of fact to a buyer about the goods, that seller has created an express warranty. The seller's statement is treated legally as a guarantee that the goods will be as "they were stated to be." *This guarantee exists whether the seller is a merchant or not.* If the goods are not as they were stated to be, the seller has breached an express warranty. An express warranty also occurs when a seller makes a promise about the goods to a buyer. The promise must relate to the goods and be part of the transaction. Manufacturers often include express warranties with the products they sell. They are usually found inside the package containing the product and are sometimes referred to as *guarantees*. Formal words such as *warranty* or *guarantee* do not have to be used to create an express warranty. A seller may not intend to make a warranty, but if the language used by the seller is a statement of fact or a promise about the goods and is part of the transaction, an express warranty is created. Advertisements often contain statements and promises about goods that are express warranties.

### Advertising Express Warranties
The Federal Trade Commission has established specific rules for advertising express warranties on goods that are sold in interstate commerce:

- An advertisement stating that a product is warranted must tell you how to get a copy of the warranty before you buy the product.

- Advertisers who use expressions such as "Satisfaction Guaranteed," "Money-Back Guarantee," and "Free Trial Offer" must refund the full purchase price of their product at the purchaser's request. Any conditions, such as those limiting the return of the product, must be stated in the ad.

- Advertisers who warrant products for a lifetime must fully explain the terms of their promises, such as "Good for as long as you own the car."

Warranties are based on statements of fact. Therefore, the opinions of salespersons and their exaggerated and persuasive statements do not create express warranties. Courts have long indulged the temptation of salespersons to use **sales puffery** to extol their merchandise beyond the point of fact. Buyers must use common sense to recognize the difference between a salesperson's statements of fact from statements that are opinion or puffery. Such statements as "this is the best Hi Def screen on the market" or "this GPS system is a great buy" are examples of sales talk or puffery. They are not express warranties. Such statements as "this car has never been in an accident" or "this desk is made of mahogany' are factual statements that do create an express warranty.

### Descriptions, Samples, and Models
Any description of the goods that is made part of the basis of the bargain creates an express warranty that the goods will be as described. It is a common practice of salespeople to show samples of their products to

prospective buyers. When a sample or model becomes part of the basis of the bargain, an express warranty is created. The seller warrants that the goods that will be delivered are the same as the sample or model.

### Magnuson-Moss Warranty Act

The federal Magnuson-Moss Warranty Act is designed to prevent deceptive warranty practices and provide consumers with more information about warranties that are made on products they buy. The act applies only when written warranties are made voluntarily for purchases of consumer products. These products are defined as tangible personal property normally used for personal, family, or household purposes. Because it is a federal law, the act affects only warranties on products that are sold in interstate commerce. Under the act, when a written warranty is given to a consumer on goods costing more than $10, the warranty must disclose whether it is a full or a limited warranty. When goods cost more than $15, the written warranty must be made available before the consumer decides to buy the product. The writing must express the terms and conditions of the warranty in simple and readily understood language.

A **full warranty** is one in which a defective product will be repaired without charge within a reasonable time after a complaint has been made about it. If it cannot be repaired within a reasonable time, the consumer may have either a replacement of the product or a refund of the purchase price. The consumer will not have to do anything unreasonable to get warranty service, such as ship a heavy product to the factory. A full warranty applies to anyone who owns the product during the warranty period, not only the original buyer. A full warranty must also state its duration, for example, a "full one-year warranty."

### EXAMPLE 14-5:  Full Warranty

Kienitz bought an electric range manufactured by a well-known firm. Attached to the box containing the range were several papers, one of which read as follows: "Full one-year warranty. If your range fails because of a manufacturing defect within one year from the date of original purchase, we will repair the product without charge to you. Parts and service labor are included. Service will be provided in your home in the forty-eight contiguous states, the state of Hawaii, or in the District of Columbia." This paper was a full warranty.

A **limited warranty** is any written warranty that does not meet all of the requirements for a full warranty. The consumer is not given the absolute, free-of-charge repair or replacement of a defective product, as in the full warranty. Something less than a complete remedy is given to the consumer. Examples of limited warranties are those that cover only parts, not labor; allow only pro rata (divided proportionately) refund or credit in the case of a defect rather than a full refund; require the buyer to return a heavy product to the store for service; or cover only the first purchaser.

## Implied Warranties

Under the UCC, an **implied warranty** is a warranty that is imposed by law rather than by statements, descriptions, or samples given by the seller. It arises independently and outside the contract. The law annexes it, by implication, into the contract that the parties have made. Implied warranties are designed to promote high standards in business and to discourage harsh dealings. There are three types of implied warranties: the implied warranty of merchantability, the implied warranty of fitness for a particular purpose, and the implied warranty that is derived from a course of dealing or usage of trade.

**Merchantability**  One of the most beneficial warranties, from the point of view of a buyer, is the implied **warranty of merchantability**. This warranty provides that, unless excluded in one of the ways discussed, whenever a merchant sells goods, the merchant warrants that the goods are **merchantable**, that is, they are reasonably fit for the purpose for which they are sold. For example, merchantability means that a lawnmower will cut grass, a sailboat will not sink, an automatic dishwasher will wash dishes, and so on. This warranty is given when the seller is a **merchant** with respect to goods of that kind. It is given by manufacturers, wholesalers, and retailers whenever they sell goods to give assurance that products sold by them are fit for the purpose for which the goods are to be used. The warranty of merchantability is not given by someone who is not a merchant. To be merchantable, goods must at least pass without objection in the trade under the contract description; if fungible goods, be of fair average quality; be fit for the ordinary purposes for which such goods are used; be of the same kind, quality, and quantity; be adequately contained, packaged, and labeled as the agreement may require; and be in conformance with any promises or statements of fact made on the container or label. A claim for breach of warranty of merchantability can be made only when a defect exists at the time the goods are purchased.

## EXAMPLE 14-6: No Defect at Time of Purchase

Haven Hills Farm purchased a truck tire from Sears, Roebuck. On a trip from Mississippi to Alabama, the tire blew out, causing the truck to turn on its side, destroying 11,862 dozen eggs. At the time of the blowout, the tire was four and one-half months old and had been driven 30,000 miles. Haven Hills claimed that Sears was liable for breach of the implied warranty of merchantability. It argued that Sears sold the tire in a defective condition. In finding in favor of Sears, Roebuck, the court held that there was no evidence of a defect in the tire at the time it left the control of the manufacturer or seller.

**Fitness for a Particular Purpose**  Sometimes buyers will have the seller select goods for them rather than select them themselves. They rely on the seller's knowledge and experience to choose the product after telling the seller of the particular use they have for the goods. This arrangement creates an implied **warranty of fitness for a particular purpose**. When the buyer relies on the seller's skill and judgment to select the goods, the seller implicitly warrants that the goods will be fit for the purpose for which they are to be used.

**Usage of Trade**  Other implied warranties may arise from the ways in which the parties have dealt in the past or by usage of trade. For example, when a person sells a pedigreed dog, there is an implied warranty that the seller will provide pedigree papers to demonstrate the conformity of the animal to the contract. The reason this implied warranty arises is that providing such papers has become a well-established custom or practice of the trade.

## Warranty of Title

Whenever goods are sold, either by a merchant or a private party, the seller warrants that the title being conveyed is good and that the transfer is rightful. This warranty is known as the **warranty of title**. It includes an implied promise that the goods will be delivered free of any liens (claims of others) about which the buyer has no knowledge. When anyone buys goods that turn out to be stolen, the rightful owner will be entitled to the return of those goods. The innocent purchaser may sue the seller for breach of warranty of title.

When the buyer is aware that the person selling the goods does not personally claim title to them, the warranty of title is not made by the seller. Such is the case, for example, in sheriff's sales and sales by personal representatives of estates. To recover money damages for breach of warranty, buyers of defective goods must notify the seller of the defect within a reasonable time either after the discovery or after the defect should have been discovered. Failure to do so will prevent them from recovering damages for breach of warranty.

## Warranty Exclusion

To exclude the implied warranty of merchantability in states that allow it, the word *merchantability* must be used in the disclaimer. If the exclusion is in writing, it must be in large, bold type so that it is conspicuous. To exclude the implied warranty of fitness for a particular purpose, the exclusion must be in writing and also be conspicuous. A common practice in the sale of used cars, lawnmowers, electrical appliances, and similar merchandise is for the seller to stipulate that the goods are being sold *as is*. The use of expressions such as *as is, with all faults,* and others is another way to exclude implied warranties. However, those words do not exclude express warranties or the warranty of title. Implied warranties may also be excluded under the UCC by having buyers examine the goods. When buyers have examined the goods, the sample, or the model as fully as they desire (or have refused to examine them when given the opportunity), there is no implied warranty as to defects that an examination would have revealed. Under the Magnuson-Moss Warranty Act, any clause purporting to exclude or limit consequential damages for breach of warranty must appear conspicuously on the face of the warranty. **Consequential damages** are losses that do not flow directly and immediately from an act but only from some of the consequences or results of the act.

## EXAMPLE 14-7: Consequential Damages

Souci bought a freezer made by a reputable manufacturer. The freezer carried a full one-year warranty. The following sentence appeared in boldface type on the face of the warranty: "In no event shall this company be liable for consequential damages." Shortly after buying the freezer, Souci filled it with $1,500 worth of meat. Several days later, the freezer stopped working owing to a defect in its manufacture. Under the warranty, the company would have to repair or replace the freezer, but it would not be responsible for the loss of the meat. This loss would be considered consequential damage, which the company had effectively disclaimed.

## Privity Not Required

Under earlier law, warranties extended only to the actual buyer of the product, that is, the one with whom the seller had dealt or was in privity of contract. People who were injured by defective products had no remedy against the seller for breach of warranty unless they themselves had purchased the goods. Thus, if children were injured by foreign objects in food that had been bought by their parents, the children could not recover for injuries because they had not purchased the goods. The UCC has abolished the requirement of privity. Instead, it provides three alternatives from which a state may choose. In all of the alternatives, warranties extend to people who would normally be expected to use the goods as well as to those who actually buy them.

*Alternative A*   A seller's warranty, whether express or implied, extends to any natural person who is in the family or household of his buyer or who is a guest in his home if it is reasonable to expect that such person may use, consume, or be affected by the goods and who is injured in person by breach of the warranty. A seller may not exclude or limit the operation of this section.

*Alternative B* A seller's warranty, whether express or implied, extends to any natural person who may reasonably be expected to use, consume, or be affected by the goods and who is injured in person by breach of the warranty. A seller may not exclude or limit the operation of this section.

*Alternative C* A seller's warranty, whether express or implied, extends to any person who may reasonably be expected to use, consume, or be affected by the goods and who is injured by breach of the warranty. A seller may not exclude or limit the operation of this section with respect to injury to the person of an individual to whom the warranty extends.

## quick quiz 14-3

1. An express warranty is an oral or written statement, promise, or other representation about the quality of a product.    true | false

2. An implied warranty is a warranty that is imposed by law rather than by statements, descriptions, or samples given by the seller.    true | false

3. A warranty of title mans that the seller warrants that the title for the goods being sold is good and that the transfer is rightful.    true | false

## Summary

**14.1** Sellers and buyers must follow the terms of their contract and act in good faith. Tender of performance is necessary to test the other party's ability and willingness to perform. Tender of delivery requires the seller to make conforming goods available to the buyer at a reasonable hour of the day. Tender of payment may be made by any means that is commonly used in the ordinary course of business. Except when goods are shipped c.o.d. or when the contract provides for payment against a document of title, the buyer has the right to inspect goods before accepting or paying for them. When improper goods are delivered, the buyer may elect to reject all of them, accept all of them, or accept any commercial unit or units and reject the rest. Sellers may cure defects or nonconformities that caused the goods to be rejected by the buyer.

**14.2** When a buyer breaches a sales contract, the seller may withhold delivery of any goods not yet delivered, stop goods that are in transit, resell the goods or the undelivered balance of them, retain the goods and bring suit for damages, bring suit for the price of any goods that the buyer has accepted, or cancel the contract. When a seller breaches a sales contract, the buyer may cancel the contract and recover any money paid out, buy similar goods from someone else and sue the seller for the difference in price, sue the seller for damages for nondelivery, keep the goods and deduct the cost of damages from any price still due, or sue for specific performance if the goods are rare or unique.

**14.3** Express warranties arise by a statement of fact or promise, by a description of the goods, and by a sample or model. Other warranties may arise from the ways in which parties have dealt in the past. When goods are sold, either by a merchant or a private party, the seller warrants that the title is good and that there are no liens on the goods. Except when express warranties are made, sellers may exclude the warranties of merchantability and fitness for a particular purpose. Such an exclusion must be in writing and conspicuous. The words *as is* and *with all faults* serve to disclaim implied warranties but not the warranty of title. Warranties extend to people who would normally be expected to use the goods as well as to those who actually buy them.

## Key Terms

| | | |
|---|---|---|
| carrier, 305 | implied warranty, 311 | tender of delivery, 300 |
| commercial unit, 302 | insolvent, 305 | tender of payment, 301 |
| consequential damages, 313 | legal tender, 301 | tender of performance, 300 |
| consumer products, 311 | limited warranty, 311 | unconscionable contract, 299 |
| cover, 307 | merchant, 312 | warranty of fitness for a |
| cure, 303 | merchantable goods, 312 | particular purpose, 312 |
| express warranty, 310 | sales puffery, 310 | warranty of merchantability, 312 |
| full warranty, 311 | shipment contract, 300 | warranty of title, 312 |
| good faith, 299 | stoppage in transit, 305 | writ of replevin, 308 |

## Questions for Review and Discussion

1. What is meant by tender of performance?
2. What are the rights and duties of sellers and buyers in a sales contract?
3. What is the doctrine of anticipatory breach?
4. What are the seller's and the buyer's remedies in case of a breach?
5. What is the statute of limitations?
6. In what three ways can an express warranty be created?
7. What are the requirements of the Magnuson-Moss Warranty Act?
8. What is the nature of each of the following warranties: merchantability, fitness for a particular purpose, and usage of trade?
9. What is meant by warranty of title?
10. How can warranties be excluded?

## Cases for Analysis

1. Kathleen Liarkos purchased a used Jaguar XJS automobile from Pine Grove Auto Sales. After experiencing various mechanical problems, she discovered that the vehicle's odometer had been turned back. Liarkos notified the seller that she revoked her acceptance of the vehicle. When is this remedy available to a buyer? *Liarkos v. Mello,* 639 N.E.2d 716 (MA).

2. P&F Construction Corporation ordered 338 door units for an apartment condominium project from Friend Lumber Corporation. The doors were delivered to the job site three weeks after they were ordered. Each door unit came wrapped in clear plastic. Three and one-half months after receiving the door units, P&F Construction notified Friend Lumber that the doors were one-quarter inch off size. P&F refused to pay Friend Lumber the balance due. What rule of law may Friend Lumber use to recover the money owed? *P&F Const. v. Friend Lumber Corp.,* 575 N.E.2d 61 (MA).

3. William Young had cut evergreen boughs and sold them exclusively to Frank's Nursery & Crafts, Inc., for 10 years. Upon receiving a $238,000 order for 360 tons of boughs from Frank's, Young obtained cutting rights from many farmers, repaired his machinery, and made 75 new hand tiers to tie the evergreen bundles. Several months later, Frank's reduced its order to less than $60,000 for about 70 tons of boughs. Young delivered the 70 tons of boughs and sued Frank's for breach of contract. How were Young's damages computed? *Young v. Frank's Nursery & Crafts, Inc.,* 569 N.E.2d 1034 (OH).

4. Herman Googe agreed to buy an automobile from Irene Schleimer. Later, Googe changed his mind and refused to buy the car. Schleimer, without making tender of delivery, brought suit against Googe for breach of contract. Did Schleimer recover damages? Explain. *Schleimer v. Googe,* 377 N.Y.S.2d 591 (NY).

5. Mr. and Mrs. Aldridge bought a motor home from Sportsman Travel Trailer Sales, located in Texas. Two years later, after traveling more than 14,000 miles on trips to Louisiana, Colorado, and California, they attempted to reject the motor home, claiming that it was defective. Could they return the vehicle and recover damages? Explain. *Explorer Motor Home Corp. v. Aldridge,* 541 S.W.2d 851 (TX).

6. DiCintio leased for a three-year period from Adzan Auto Sales a Jeep Grand Cherokee Laredo sport utility vehicle manufactured by DaimlerChrysler. Soon after accepting delivery, the automatic transmission failed to shift gears properly, and then the vehicle started to pull to the left while being driven, after which it began to "idle rough" and stall while stopped at traffic lights. DiCintio took the vehicle to authorized dealers for repairs on six or seven occasions, but the defects persisted. When Adzan Auto Sales refused to terminate the lease or give him another car, DiContio brought suit against DaimlerChrysler for breach of the Magnuson-Moss Warranty Act. Does DiCintio have a cause of action under this law? Explain. *Mark DiCintio v. DaimlerChrysler Corporation, et al,* 768 NE2d 1121 (NY).

7. Lohr bought a mobile home from Larry's Homes. The home was damaged during delivery and never fully set up on Lohr's property. Larry's Homes attempted some repairs, but they were insufficient. An arbitrator found that the intended repairs would not have been enough even if they had been carried out. Lohr took the case to arbitration on the grounds of a breach of the warranty of merchantability under the UCC. Does the UCC apply to this case? Why or why not? *Lohr v. Larry's Homes of Virginia.* Arbitrated by McCammon Group referred out of Cumberland County Circuit Court (VA).

8. Caswell bought a gas grill to give to his friend, Kile, as a birthday present. The grill exploded the first time it was used due to a factory defect, and Kile was injured. The manufacturer of the grill argued that it was not responsible for Kile's injuries because Kile had not purchased the grill. There was no privity of contract between Kile and the manufacturer. How would you decide?

9. Shaffer ordered a glass of rosé wine at the Victoria Station Restaurant. As he took his first sip of wine, the glass broke in his hand, causing permanent injuries. Shaffer brought suit against the restaurant for breach of warranty of merchantability. The restaurant's position was that because it did not sell the wine glass to Shaffer (only its contents), it was not a merchant with respect to the glass and therefore made no warranty. Do you agree with the restaurant? Why or why not? *Shaffer v. Victoria Station, Inc.,* 588 P.2d 233 (WA).

10. McCoy bought an antique pistol from the Old Fort Trading Post for $1,000. Later, the gun was taken from McCoy by the police when they learned that it was stolen property. The police turned the gun over to the rightful owner. McCoy notified the Old Fort Trading Post of what had happened and asked for the return of his money, but the owner of the business refused to give him a refund. What remedy, if any, did McCoy have against the owner of the trading post? Explain. *Trial v. McCoy,* 553 S.W.2d 199 (TX).

**quick quiz** Answers

| 14.1 | 14.2 | 14.3 |
| --- | --- | --- |
| 1. T | 1. T | 1. T |
| 2. T | 2. T | 2. T |
| 3. T | 3. T | 3. T |

# Chapter 15

## Product Liability and Consumer Protection

**THE OPENING CASE** Saving Consumers from Themselves: *Huff v. White Motor Co.*

Whether they admit to it or not, all legal professionals will, from time to time, use the law for social engineering purposes. One example of this social engineering function is found in the doctrine of product liability and one clear example of product liability is seen in the automotive industry. A case on point is *Huff v. White Motor Co.*, a lawsuit that started a trend toward a new standard of automotive product liability. Prior to this case, as strange as it may seem to us today, automotive manufacturers had successfully argued that "the intended purpose of an automobile does not include its participation in collisions." The pre-*Huff* rule stated that automobile makers had no responsibility to design and manufacture cars that would protect passengers and drivers from the effects of an accident. Since *Huff* started the ball rolling three decades ago, the courts and the legislatures have altered this standard and have declared that car manufacturers must now design vehicles that have a high level of "crashworthiness." Moreover, and perhaps more to the point, the crashworthiness standard is not based on warranties or negligence. Instead, the standard is based on strict liability. This means that the consumer in an automotive product liability lawsuit does not have to demonstrate that the manufacturer violated a warranty or behaved negligently. The simple fact that the automobile was unsafe beyond what would be expected by the ordinary consumer is enough to result in liability. Today the strict liability standard applies to all products not just vehicles. In addition, the standard extends beyond privity and can be used to hold both the manufacturer and the seller liable. Remember, though, that the law is a balancing act. The courts have also ruled, on the opposite end of the spectrum, that the manufacturers of dangerous products are permitted to promote the sale of their products even though they know that the products are dangerous (not unsafe, but dangerous; there is a difference). As long as the product itself is legal, the corporation can advertise and sell the product despite its dangerous nature. Thus, somewhere within the intangible dimension of legal niceties there exists an invisible, largely undetectable line between manufacturing products that are unsafe and selling products that are dangerous. Manufacturing "unsafe products" is wrong; selling "dangerous products" is not. As you read the chapter, see if you can detect just where that line might be drawn. (See *Huff v. White Motor Co.*, 565 F.2d 104 (7th Cir. App. Ct 1977); David Lauter, "Automakers Face Strict Liability," *The National Law Journal* (December 21, 1981), p. 18; and Charles H. Moellenberg, Jr., and Leon F. DeJulius, Jr., "Remove the Tort Liability Muzzle," *The National Law Journal,* (May 10, 2010), p. 34.)

**Opening Case Questions**

1. Is *Huff v. White Motors Co.* a tort case or a contract case? Explain.

2. What is the difference between a lawsuit based on negligence and one based on strict liability? Explain.

3. Is the "crashworthiness" standard found in sales law or tort law? Explain.

4. What is significant about the fact that the plaintiff in an automotive product liability case does not have to prove privity? Explain.

5. What is the difference between a "dangerous" product and an "unsafe" product? Explain.

 Learning Objectives

1. Describe the link between social engineering and the law.
2. Explain the difference between public interest and public policy.
3. Explain the difference between negligence and strict liability.
4. State the purpose of the Consumer Product Safety Act.
5. Explain the enforcement of the Federal Trade Commission Act.
6. Develop a list of unfair or deceptive practices.
7. Identify several FTC rules designed to protect the consumer.
8. Identify the function of the Truth-in-Lending Act.
9. Explain the latest amendments to the Truth-in-Lending Act.
10. Explain the requirements of the Consumer Leasing Act.

# 15-1 Product Liability

One of the fastest growing areas of consumer law is known as **product liability**. Under product liability standards, a person harmed by a product's unsafe condition may recover damages from the manufacturer, the seller, or the supplier of the product. Product liability results from the court's willingness to react to social problems and, at times, use the law to engineer social results. Because of the court's flexibility in this regard, product liability suits can now be based on one of two legal theories, negligence or strict liability, both of which are tort actions.

## Social Engineering and the Law

The German philosopher Max Weber saw the law as a combination of consensus and coercion. Consensus reveals the norms by which the people of a society live, while coercion clarifies the measures taken against those who violate the consensus. Some parts of the legal community, such as the legislature and the agencies, are designed to proactively shape social policy. Others, like the courts, passively deal with problems on a case-by-case basis. Nevertheless, both levels, active and passive alike, must understand consensus and must use coercion. To do this properly, the courts frequently call upon the doctrine of public policy, a concept of based on the assumption that no one should be permitted to do anything that harms the public interest (See Gerald Turkel, *Law and Society: Critical Approaches* (Boston: Allyn and Bacon, 1996), pp. 8–9.)

### Public Interest and Public Policy

Public policy is not the same as public interest, although the two terms are very similar. **Public interest** refers to the idea that certain activities affect the entire social structure and must, therefore, be regulated by the government. Public interest, then, is the equivalent of Weber's social consensus. It is in the best interests of society, for example, to have crime-free neighborhoods. **Public policy**, in contrast, seeks to implement behavior that promotes the public consensus and eliminates behavior that does not. Thus, any activity that somehow permits, encourages, or compels people to break the law and thus disrupt those crime-free neighborhoods would be against public policy and would, therefore, be outlawed. Public interest, then, is the ideal consensus, and public policy is the coercive social engineering strategy by which that consensus is implemented.

**Public Policy and Product Liability**     It is in the public interest to maintain a social structure that promotes health and safety and thus prevents illness and injury. To engineer this public interest goal, public policy promotes the making of safe products. To coerce this behavior, public policy demands that manufacturers, sellers, and distributors be held responsible for any injuries that result from their products. Therefore, public policy insists that manufacturers, sellers, and distributors compensate any innocent victim who is injured by an unsafe product, regardless of whether that victim purchased, used, or simply got in the way of that unsafe product. To meet the public interest goal of a safe society, the courts have produced two legal strategies, negligence and product liability. Nevertheless, of the two standards, strict liability is more effective in reaching that goal.

## Negligence and Product Liability

One legal theory available to people who are injured by faulty products is negligence. Negligence results when an individual fails to exercise the degree of care that a reasonable person would have exercised under the same circumstances. To recover for negligence in a product liability case, the victim must prove: (1) that the manufacturer or seller owed a duty to the victim; (2) that the manufacturer or the seller violated that duty by not following the appropriate standard of care; (3) that the victim suffered an injury because of that careless action; and (4) that the careless action was both the actual and the proximate cause of the victim's injury.

### THE OPENING CASE *Revisited, Part I*
Saving Consumers from Themselves: *Huff v. White Motor Co.,* Round 2

Before *Huff v. White Motor Co.,* the Opening Case at the beginning of this chapter, automobile makers had no responsibility to design and manufacture cars that would protect passengers and drivers from the effects of an accident. Looking at the elements that are needed to prove a negligence case, we can see just how powerful this rule was for the manufacturers. Think about it. If automobile makers had *no responsibility to design and manufacture cars that were crashworthy,* then the victim of an unsafe vehicle would be unable to prove even the first element of a negligence action, that is, that the manufacturer had a duty to ensure the safety of the

victim. Seen from this perspective, it's no wonder that automobile makers fought so hard against the new rule.

As noted above, it is difficult for an injured consumer to win a product liability case using negligence. This is true not only because the victim cannot prove the existence of duty, but also because the injured party can rarely demonstrate that the manufacturer was careless. The victim was not present when the goods were made and normally has very little information about the manufacturing process. Consequently, injured parties are often more successful when bringing a suit based on strict liability.

## THE OPENING CASE *Revisited, Part II*
## Saving Consumers from Themselves: *Huff v. White Motor Co.*, Round 3

After *Huff v. White Motor Co.*, the courts and the legislatures declared that car manufacturers must design vehicles that have a high level of "crashworthiness." More importantly, the crashworthiness standard is not based on warranties or negligence. Instead, the standard is based on strict liability. This means that the consumer in an automotive product liability lawsuit does not have to demonstrate that the manufacturer violated a warranty or behaved negligently. The simple fact that the automobile was unsafe beyond what would be expected by the ordinary consumer is enough to result in liability. Today the strict liability standard applies to all products not just vehicles. In addition, the standard extends beyond privity and can be used to hold both the manufacturer and the seller liable.

## Strict Liability and Product Liability

The doctrine of **strict liability** holds manufacturers or suppliers liable for selling goods that are unsafe, without regard to fault or negligence. The principal consideration under the doctrine of strict liability is the safety of the product, not the conduct of the manufacturer or supplier of the goods. Under this rule, manufacturers have the duty to design reasonably safe products. They must also give proper instructions for the product's use and provide warnings of possible danger. People who are injured or suffer property damage from a defective product may recover from the manufacturer or seller only if they can prove all of the following:

1. The manufacturer or seller sold the product in a defective condition.
2. The manufacturer or seller was engaged in the business of selling the product.
3. The product was unsafe to an unreasonable degree to the user or the consumer.
4. The defective condition was the proximate cause of the injury or damage.
5. The defective condition existed at the time it left the hands of the manufacturer or seller.
6. The consumer sustained physical harm or property damage by use or consumption of the product.

The defective condition may arise through faulty product design, faulty manufacturing, inadequate warning of danger, or improper instructions for the product's use. The manufacturer's and seller's liability extends to all persons who may be injured by the product. Injured bystanders, guests, or others who have no relationship to the product, the seller, or the manufacturer may seek damages caused by defects in the offending product.

**Duty to Warn**    Sometimes a duty is placed on manufacturers to warn consumers that harm may result from a product. Unavoidably dangerous products may require a warning to inform the consumer of possible harm. If the warning is adequate, consumers may be required to use the product at their own risk. A warning must specify the risk presented by the product and give a reason for the warning. When the danger that is presented by a product is obvious, however, no duty to warn exists because a warning will not reduce the likelihood of injury.

**Punitive Damages**    In addition to recovering damages to compensate them for their losses, injured parties in strict liability cases sometimes recover punitive damages. These are monetary penalties imposed as a punishment for a wrongdoing.

## Self-Evident Truths: Unsafe Products v. Dangerous Products

As we have seen many times throughout this text, the law is a balancing act. We have just examined how the courts have been willing (eager?) to use strict liability to hold manufacturers and distributors liable for injuries caused by unsafe products without any reference to negligence or warranties. Just how far will the courts go in this regard? What is the ultimate limit of strict liability as a coercive strategy of public policy? One answer to this question might be that there is no limit, that dangerous products, period, must be targeted by the law, at all cost no matter what. This is known as a *per se* rule. Literally translated from the Latin, *per se* means "in and of itself" and a rule that labels a product dangerous *per se* would assert that the product is dangerous in and of itself. In other words, such a product cannot be made "safe" because to make it "safe" would remove its basic function and render it useless. The prime target of the suggested "dangerous *per se*" rule has been handguns. However, the rule could apply to any firearm or explosive device (read "bomb"). The argument goes something like this. Handguns other firearms, and explosive devices are dangerous *per se* because their function is to kill. When a manufacturer designs, makes, and sells a handgun any other firearm or explosive device, that manufacturer knows that the product is designed to kill. Moreover, the only way to make a handgun safe is to render it unworkable, which makes it useless, and which, therefore, is not an option. Moreover, there is no social benefit to the firearm or the explosive device that outweighs the potential harm that it can cause. Therefore, when a manufacturer places a firearm or explosive device in circulation, he or she is well aware of its potential (inevitable?) criminal use and, when such an event occurs, that manufacturer must be held strictly liable for the injuries and the harm that results—period. Now there are counterarguments to this position which we will see later in the text. For now, however, consider the "dangerous *per se*" rule and answer the following questions. (See Donald E. Santarelli and Nicholas E. Calio, "Turning the Gun on Tort Law: Aiming at Courts to Take Products Liability to the Limit," *St. Mary's Law Journal* 14:3 (1983), pp. 471–508.)

## Self-Evident Questions

1.  Is the function of a firearm or explosive device to kill? If you believe that the function is to kill, then, what socially justifiable reason is there for continuing to manufacture them?

2.  If you believe that the function is *not* to kill, then what other socially redeeming functions does a firearm or explosive device possess? Explain.

3.  Max Weber believes that the law can be used to coerce the members of a society into conforming to the general consensus. Will the "dangerous *per se*" rule eliminate killing and, thus, create crime-free neighborhoods? Explain.

4.  The very first element of strict liability is that the plaintiff must prove that the manufacturer or seller sold the product in a defective condition. What is the defective condition of a firearm or explosive device that works exactly as it should? Explain.

5.  What other products might be outlawed using the "dangerous *per se*" rule? Explain.

**Aircraft Cases and Product Liability** Despite the court's willingness to impose strict liability in product liability cases involving automobiles and despite the fact that the doctrine could easily be applied to other products, there has been a curious lack of activity in this area of the law. For example, there has been a reluctance on the part of both the courts and the legislature to apply strict liability, especially as it is expressed in the crashworthiness test, to aviation accident cases. Several reasons may explain the lack of movement in this area. One reason for this apparent inactivity is that aviation crashes are rare, at least when compared to automobile accidents. Another reason may be that most aviation cases are settled out of court before litigation even begins. However, probably the most significant reason is that aviation cases tend to be more complex and difficult than automobile cases. Typically, aviation cases will require a more in-depth understanding of and appreciation for the complexity of aircraft design and operation. It may be that product liability arguments in aviation cases will have to wait for the establishment of a science court, one version of which is discussed at length in this text in "Chapter 4 Alternative Dispute Resolution and in the *Self-Evident Truths* feature in Chapter 14." (See Scott G. Lindvall, "Aircraft Crashworthiness: Should the Courts Set Standards?" *William and Mary Law Review,* 27:2 (1986), pp. 371–408.)

## The Consumer Product Safety Act

Product safety has not remained solely within the purview of the courts. Congress has also gotten into the act. In an attempt to protect consumers from dangerous products, Congress passed the Consumer Product Safety Act. The act established the Consumer Product Safety Commission (CPSC) to protect consumers from unreasonable risk or injury from hazardous products. The act covers products or component parts, American-made or imported, that are manufactured or distributed for sale to a consumer for personal use, consumption, or enjoyment. The commission can order the recall of products found to be inherently unsafe and dangerous. It has the authority to impose civil fines for violations of its standards and cease-and-desist orders. Private citizens, acting on their own behalf, may bring suit to establish or enforce a safety rule if the commission fails to act.

### quick quiz 15-1

| | | |
|---|---|---|
| 1. Public interest and public policy are the same thing. | true | false |
| 2. Negligence would usually be more effective as a legal theory in a product liability lawsuit than strict liability. | true | false |
| 3. In addition to recovering damages to compensate them for their losses, injured parties in strict liability cases sometimes recover punitive damages. | true | false |

# 15-2 Consumer Protection Laws

Consumer protection laws apply to transactions between business people and consumers. A **consumer** is someone who buys or leases real estate, goods, or services for personal, family, or household purposes. Thus, people who buy or rent things for personal use from a business are protected by consumer protection laws. However, if they buy the same things from another consumer or for business use, they are not, with some exceptions, protected by consumer protection law. State consumer protection offices provide information and help enforce state consumer protection laws. They sometimes assist consumers with individual problems. Consumer protection offices are located in state and county offices and, in some cities, the mayor's office.

Federal consumer protection law stems from the Federal Trade Commission Act (FTCA), which states that "unfair or deceptive acts or practices in . . . or affecting commerce are hereby declared unlawful." The act defines **commerce** as "commerce among the several states or with foreign nations or the District of Columbia." Thus, the act applies to businesses that sell real estate, goods, or services in interstate commerce or that somehow affect interstate commerce. **Interstate commerce** is business activity that touches more than one state. Purely local business activity, which has no out-of-state connections, called **intrastate commerce**, is not governed by the FTCA.

## The Federal Trade Commission

The Federal Trade Commission Act transferred certain powers to the Federal Trade Commission, giving it the authority to oversee and eliminate deceptive and unfair practices in commerce. These powers include:

1.  To conduct investigations into the practices of businesses.
2.  To investigate possible antitrust violations.
3.  To compel interstate businesses to file reports with the commission detailing their operations that fall within the FTC's jurisdiction.
4.  To publish the results of the commission's investigation of interstate businesses.
5.  To deal with disputes that emerge from the application of FTC regulations.
6.  To deal with disputes that emerge from the application of federal antitrust law.
7.  To make recommendations to Congress concerning new legislation.

In effect, the commission has become a coercive public policy instrument designed to promote the public interest. In doing so, the FTC must determine when a practice is unfair by balancing the harm that might affect consumers with the overall public good promoted by the activity under scrutiny.

If, after a thorough investigation, the FTC concludes that a violation of the law occurred, it may attempt to obtain voluntary compliance by entering into a consent order with the violating company. A **consent order** is an order under which the company agrees to stop the disputed practice without necessarily admitting that it violated the law. If an agreement cannot be reached, the FTC may issue a complaint. This action begins a formal hearing before an administrative law judge. If a violation of law is found, a cease-and desist order or other appropriate relief may be issued. Consumers may bring individual or class-action lawsuits against businesses for violating FTC rules. A **class-action lawsuit** is one that is brought by one or more plaintiffs on behalf of a class of persons. Usually, a suit must be brought within one year after the violation. Alternate dispute resolutions are also available for resolving this type of problem.

## Unfair or Deceptive Practices

The FTC Act prohibits unfair or deceptive practices. These practices include fraudulent misrepresentations, sending unordered merchandise, bait-and-switch schemes, and odometer tampering.

### Fraudulent Misrepresentation
It is unfair or deceptive for a seller to make a fraudulent misrepresentation, that is, a statement that is designed to mislead the buyer. A misrepresentation usually occurs when the seller misstates facts important to the consumer. Making false statements about the construction, durability, reliability, safety, strength, condition, or life expectancy of a product is a deceptive practice. It is also deceptive to fail to disclose to a buyer any fact that would cause the buyer to walk away from the contract. You may see ads like the following in newspapers and magazines: "Would you like to earn hundreds of dollars a week at home in your leisure time? Many people are supplementing their income in a very easy way. Let us tell you how. . . . " An offer like this may sound very attractive, particularly if you are unable to leave your home to work. Be cautious about work-at-home ads, especially ones that promise large profits in a short period of time. Although some work-at-home plans are legitimate, many are not. Home employment schemes are some of the oldest kinds of classified advertising fraud.

**Unordered Merchandise** Except for free samples clearly and conspicuously marked as such and merchandise mailed by charitable organizations soliciting contributions, it is a violation of the postal law and the FTCA to send merchandise through the mail to people who did not order it. Similarly, it is illegal to send a bill for such unordered merchandise or to send **dunning letters**, that is, letters requesting payments. People who receive unordered merchandise through the mail may treat it as a gift. They may keep the merchandise or dispose of it in any manner they see fit without any obligation whatsoever to the sender. In addition, senders of unordered merchandise must attach a statement to the package informing recipients of their right to keep and use the goods.

**Bait-and-Switch Schemes** A **bait-and-switch scheme** is an alluring but insincere offer to sell a product or service that the advertiser does not really intend to sell. Its purpose is to switch customers from buying the advertised merchandise to buying something else, usually at a higher price or on a basis more advantageous to the advertiser. There is no question that the FTCA prohibits bait-and-switch schemes. The very nature of the strategy is to trick unwary consumers into purchasing something that they neither want nor need and that is more expensive than the original bait that snagged their interest and pulled them into the store. The statute states quite specifically that: "No advertisement containing an offer to sell a product shall be made when the offer is not a *bona fide* effort to sell the advertised product." Any of the following activities could indicate a bait-and-switch scheme:

- A refusal to show, demonstrate, or sell the product offered in accordance with the terms of the offer.
- A "put-down" of the product by the acts or words of the seller.
- Failing to have available at all outlets listed in the advertisement a sufficient quantity of the advertised product to meet reasonably anticipated demands.
- Refusing to take orders for the advertised product to be delivered within a reasonable period of time.
- Showing a product that is defective, unusable, or impractical for the purpose represented in the advertisement.

**Odometer Tampering** The federal Odometer Law prohibits people from disconnecting, resetting, or altering the odometer of a motor vehicle in order to hide a vehicle's true mileage. Anyone who sells or gives away a car must provide the new owner with a written statement disclosing the odometer reading at the time of the transfer. If the seller believes that the mileage reading on the odometer is incorrect, the disclosure statement must indicate that the actual mileage is unknown. It is also a violation of the act to obtain a vehicle for resale without acquiring a finalized odometer statement from the seller. An odometer must be set at zero if it is repaired and cannot be adjusted to show the true mileage. In addition, the car owner must attach to the left doorframe a written notice showing the true mileage before the service, repair, or replacement and the date that the odometer was set at zero. It is illegal for anyone to alter or remove any such notice attached to the doorframe of a car.

## Trade Regulation Rules

To correct wrongdoings in the marketplace, the FTC has also established trade regulation rules to govern the activities of interstate companies. These rules include the Used Car Rule, the Cooling-Off Rule, the negative option rule, the Mail and Telephone Order Rule, the telemarketing sales rule, and the rules connected with 900 numbers. Other rules are established by the antispam and the antislamming laws.

## Used Car Rule

To remedy consumer complaints involving used car sales, the FTC established the **Used Car Rule**. This rule requires used car dealers to place a **Buyer's Guide** sticker in the window of each used car they offer for sale. The Buyer's Guide provides the following information:

- A statement that the car is sold *as is* if it is sold with no warranties. (Some states do not allow used cars to be sold as is by car dealers.)
- A statement that the car is sold with implied warranties only if that is the case.
- A statement telling whether the warranty is "full" or "limited" and citing the length of the warranty period if the car is sold with an express warranty. In addition, the guide must list the specific systems that are covered by the warranty and state the percentage of the repair costs that will be paid by the dealer.
- A statement that tells consumers not to rely on spoken promises.
- A suggestion that consumers ask whether they may have the vehicle inspected by their own mechanic either on or off the premises.
- A list of the 14 major systems of an automobile and some of the principal defects that may occur in these systems.
- Whenever the sale of a vehicle will be carried on in Spanish, a Spanish language version of the Buyer's Guide must be placed on the window before the vehicle is marketed.

A dealer is defined as anyone who sells more than five used cars in a 12-month period. The law covers the sale of automobiles, light-duty vans, and light-duty trucks. The Buyer's Guide sticker must be printed in black ink on a white sheet of paper that is at least $11 \times 7\frac{1}{4}$ inches in size. The guide becomes part of the sales contract and overrides any contrary provision that may be in the contract.

## Cooling-Off Rule

The FTC has established the **Cooling-Off Rule** to give consumers an opportunity to change their minds after signing contracts with people who come to their houses. Under this rule, sales of consumer goods or services over $25 made away from the seller's regular place of business, such as at a customer's home, may be canceled within three business days after the sale occurs. This rule requires the seller to give the buyer two copies of a **cancellation form**, one of which the buyer may send to the seller any time before midnight of the third business day after the contract was signed. The law also applies to consumer product parties given in private homes and to sales made in rented hotel rooms or restaurants. There are, however, several exceptions to the rule. The rule does not apply to:

- Sales that are less than $25.
- Sales that involve items used for something other than personal, household, or family reasons.
- Sales that are entered completely by phone or by mail.
- Sales that begin at the seller's regular place of business and then are simply concluded at the buyer's home.
- Sales that are made under emergency conditions.
- Sales that are involved in the repair or maintenance of personal property.

In addition, the Cooling-Off Rule does not cover insurance, securities, real estate, or craft items sold at fairs, civic centers, schools, or shopping malls. Finally, the rule does not cover vehicle sales when the seller has set up a temporary location away from his or her permanent place of business. Under the laws of some states, such as New York, the three-day right to cancel does not begin until the seller gives the buyer a written notice of the right to cancel. Until such notice is given, the buyer may use any means to notify the seller of the cancellation of the contract.

## Negative Option Rule

The negative option rule applies when a consumer subscribes to a magazine, joins a CD club, enrolls in a DVD club, or enters some other plan that sends products on a regular basis. Under such plans, the seller notifies the subscriber about the next selection before that selection is shipped. If the subscriber does nothing, the seller will ship the selection automatically. If the subscriber does not want the selection, he or she must tell the seller not to send the item before an agreed to deadline. The negative option rule does not outlaw such agreements but it does demand that sellers tell subscribers:

* The number of selections they must purchase, if any.
* The circumstances under which they can withdraw their membership.
* The notification process used to opt out of a selection.
* The timing for the return of the negative option cancellation forms.
* The circumstances under which subscribers qualify for credit in a return.
* The technique for determining postage and handling costs.
* The timing of each selection announcement.

The negative option rule does not apply to continuity plans. Under a **continuity plan**, the seller ships the goods to the subscriber on a regular basis without first sending an announcement of the upcoming delivery. While the negative option rule does not limit the use of such continuity plans, they are regulated by standard consumer protection rules. This means that the seller must notify the subscriber of all terms and conditions in a clear and unambiguous way.

## The Mail and Telephone Order Rule

The FTC has established a rule to protect consumers who order goods by mail, telephone, Internet, or fax machine. Under the **Mail and Telephone Order Rule (MTOR)**, sellers must ship orders within the time promised in their advertisements. If no time period is promised, sellers must either ship the order within 30 days or send the consumer an option notice. The option notice informs consumers of any shipping delay and gives them a chance to cancel and receive a refund. Instructions on how to cancel orders must be included in the notice. In addition, the seller must provide a free means for consumers to reply.

## Telemarketing Sales Rule

The FTC's Telemarketing Sales Rule is designed to protect consumers from abusive and unscrupulous telemarketers. The rule has established the *Do Not Call Registry* (see Figure 15-1) that makes it easier for consumers to reduce or eliminate unwanted sales calls. Under the Telemarketing Sales Rule:

* It is illegal for a telemarketer to call a consumer if the consumer has asked not to be called.
* Calling times are restricted to the hours between 8:00 A.M. and 9:00 P.M.
* Telemarketers must tell the consumer that it is a sales call, the name of the seller, and what they are selling before they make their pitch. If it is a prize promotion, they must tell the consumer that no purchase or payment is necessary to enter or win.

**NATIONAL
DO NOT CALL
REGISTRY**

Place your telephone number on the National Do Not Call Registry by calling toll-free 1-888-382-1222 (TTY: 1-866-290-4236) or going online to donotcall.gov. Registration is free.

Placing your telephone number on the Do Not Call Registry will stop all telemarketing calls except those from political organizations, charities, and people making surveys. You can expect fewer calls within three months of the date you sign up for the registry. Your number will stay in the registry for five years, until it is disconnected, or until you delete it from the registry. You may renew your registration after five years.

Telemarketers are required to search the registry every three months and avoid calling any phone numbers that are on the registry.

If you receive telemarketing calls after you have registered your telephone number and it has been in the registry for three months, you can file a complaint at donotcall.gov or by calling toll-free 1-888-382-1222 (TTY: 1-866-290-4236). You will need to provide the date of the call and the name or phone number of the company that called you. Telemarketers who disregard this law can be fined up to $11,000 for each call they make.

**Figure 15-1** Once your number is registered, how long will it remain in the National Do Not Call Registry?

- It is illegal for telemarketers to misrepresent any information, including facts about their goods or services, earnings potential, profitability, the risk or liquidity of an investment, or the nature of a prize in a prize-promotion scheme.

- Before consumers pay, telemarketers must tell them the total cost of the products or services offered and any restrictions on getting or using them or that a sale is final or nonrefundable.

Consumers who have the slightest doubt about a telephone offer should ask for written information about the product, service, investment opportunity, or charity that is the subject of the call. They should resist high-pressure sales tactics and talk to a family member or friend before responding to the call. Consumers should never give out their bank account or credit card number to anyone who calls them. Similarly, they should never send money by courier, overnight delivery, or wire to anyone who insists on immediate payment.

### 900-Telephone Number Rules
Telemarketers sometimes use 900 telephone numbers as part of their strategy, because the consumer, rather than the seller, pays the phone charge. To combat the abusive use of 900 telephone numbers, the Federal Trade Commission has established a series of 900-Telephone Number Rules. These rules require telemarketers who use 900 numbers to warn callers of the cost of the calls and to give those callers a chance to hang up before being charged. Under the rules, customers are also permitted to ask telephone companies to block all 900-prefix number calls. In addition, the rules require telephone companies to send customers pay-per-call disclosure statements. The FTC also prohibits the use of any prefix other than 900 as a pay-per-call service. Moreover, the FTC will not permit telephone companies to disconnect phone service to customers who refuse to pay for 900-number calls. Finally, the FTC has established a series of rules for resolving billing disputes.

### AntiSpam Law
The **Can Spam Act** is an attempt by the federal government to reduce the use of unsolicited commercial e-mail, commonly known as **spam**, on the Internet. Under the law, unsolicited commercial e-mail messages must be truthful and cannot use

misleading subject lines or incorrect return addresses. E-mail containing pornography must be specifically labeled in the subject line. In addition, spammers cannot harvest e-mail addresses from chat rooms and other sites without permission. The rule has also been amended to include messages that are intended for mobile phones, provided that a domain name is used as part of the Internet address. This ban does not include short phone-to-phone messages

**AntiSlamming Law**   The illegal practice of changing a consumer's telephone service without permission is referred to as **slamming**. New consumer protection rules created by the Federal Communications Commission (FCC) provide a remedy for consumers who have been slammed. With these rules, the FCC has taken the profit out of slamming and protected consumers from illegal charges.

---

### quick quiz 15-2

1. A consumer is someone who buys or leases real estate, goods, or services for personal, family, or household purposes.   true | false

2. The Federal Trade Commission Act transferred certain powers to the Federal Trade Commission, giving it the authority to oversee and eliminate deceptive and unfair practices in commerce.   true | false

3. To correct wrongdoings in the marketplace, the FTC has established trade regulation rules that must be followed by companies that transact business only in intrastate commerce.   true | false

---

# 15-3 Consumer Credit Laws

Consumers need just as much protection (some experts would argue more protection) in their credit transactions as in their consumer product contracts. Most Americans use credit cards as a matter of course on a daily basis, almost without thinking about it. In addition, the average American makes an installment payment on a car loan (perhaps even two) every month, almost as if it were a civic duty, like paying taxes or voting. Due to this extensive use of credit, Congress has found it necessary to pass federal laws to protect the consumer.

## The Federal Truth-in-Lending Act

Because lending institutions and businesses charge different rates of interest to consumers, it often pays to shop around before borrowing money or buying on credit. To help consumers know the truth about the cost of borrowing money, Congress passed the Truth-in-Lending Act. Under this act, lenders must disclose two important things to borrowers: the **finance charge** (the actual cost of the loan in dollars and cents) and the **annual percentage rate (APR)** (the true rate of interest of the loan). With this information, consumers can compare the cost of loans from different lenders before deciding from which to borrow. Surprisingly, the APR sometimes turns out to be greater than it would appear at first glance.

Most consumers today rely heavily on credit card transactions. For this reason, Congress has enacted several consumer credit protection laws.

## EXAMPLE 15-1: True Rate of Interest

Hana borrowed $100 for one year and agreed to pay a finance charge of $10. If she kept the $100 for the year and at the end of the year paid back the full amount, together with the $10 finance charge, the APR would be 10 percent. If, however, she paid the $110 in 12 monthly installments of $9.17 each, the APR would be 18 percent. The latter rate is higher because during the course of the year, she would have the use, on the average, of only about half of the $100.

## Equal Credit Opportunity

The Equal Credit Opportunity Act was passed by Congress, as amendment to the Truth-in-Lending Act, to ensure that all consumers are given an equal chance to receive credit. The law makes it illegal for banks and businesses to discriminate against credit applicants because of their sex, race, marital status, national origin, religion, or age or because they get public assistance income. The law must be followed by anyone who regularly extends credit, including banks, credit unions, finance companies, credit card issuers, and retail stores. Some of the rights to consumers under the act are as follows:

1. People who apply for credit may not be asked to reveal their sex, race, national origin, or religion; whether they are divorced or widowed; their marital status, unless they are applying for a joint account or a secured loan; information about their spouse, except in community property states, unless the spouse is also applying for credit or will use the account; their plans for having or raising children; and whether they receive alimony, child support, or separate maintenance payments if they will not be relying on that income.

2. When deciding to extend credit, creditors must not consider the applicant's sex, marital status, race, national origin, or religion; consider the applicant's age, unless the applicant is a minor or is considered favorably for being over 62; refuse to consider public assistance income in the same manner as other income; and refuse to consider income from part-time employment, pensions, or retirement programs.

3. Applicants may apply for credit under the name given to them at birth, their married name, or a combination of both. They may receive credit without a cosigner if they meet the creditor's standards. In addition, applicants have a right to know within 30 days whether their application for credit has been accepted or rejected. If rejected, they have a right to know the reasons for the rejection within 60 days.

## Unauthorized Use of Credit Cards

Sometimes credit cards are lost, stolen, or used by people who have no authority to use them. Under the Truth-in-Lending Act, credit cardholders are not responsible for any unauthorized charges made after the card issuer has been notified of the loss, theft, or possible unauthorized use of the card. Such notice may be given to the card issuer by telephone, letter, or any other means. Even then, credit cardholders are responsible only for the first $50 of any unauthorized charges. Debit cards do not have this built-in protection. The credit cardholder can avoid the $50 liability if the credit card issuer has not included on the card a method to identify the user of the card, such as a signature, a photograph, or other means of identification. Card issuers must notify cardholders in advance of the potential $50 liability. As an amendment to the Truth-in-Lending Act, Congress recently launched the Consumer Financial Protection Bureau, a new federal office that is deigned to act as a watchdog in the credit industry.

# Fair Credit Reporting

The Fair Credit Reporting Act was passed by Congress to ensure that consumers are treated fairly by credit bureaus and consumer reporting agencies. A consumer has the right to know all information (other than medical information) that is in his or her files. A consumer also has the right to know, in most cases, the source of the information on file. In addition, a consumer has the right to be told the name of anyone who received a credit report in the past year (or two years if the credit report relates to a job application). If errors are found, credit bureaus must investigate and then correct or delete information that is inaccurate, incomplete, or obsolete. If the credit bureau retains information that the consumer believes to be incorrect, the consumer's version of the facts must be inserted in the file. Also, creditors are required to tell consumers the specific reasons for the denial of credit.

# Billing, Collecting, and Leasing

Even with all of the consumer protection laws outlined above, there are still a variety of ways in which consumers can be victimized. The last of these areas include billing, collecting, and leasing. In billing, retail stores, credit card companies, and other businesses that extend credit sometimes make billing errors that threaten the reputation and the credit record of innocent consumers. To make it easier for billing errors to be corrected, Congress has passed the Fair Credit Billing Act (FCBA). Improper collection procedures can also hassle innocent consumers. Under the Fair Debt Collection Practices Act, specific rules must be followed by companies that are in the business of collecting debts for others. Finally, consumers who must rent or lease products sometimes find themselves victimized by unscrupulous leasing companies. The Consumer Leasing Act is a federal law requiring leasing companies to inform consumers of all of the terms of a lease of personal property.

**The Fair Credit Billing Act**  Under the Fair Credit Billing Act (FCBA), when consumers believe an error has been made in a bill, they must notify the creditor within 60 days after the bill was mailed. The notice must identify the consumer and give the account number, the suspected amount of error, and an explanation of why the consumer believes there is an error. The creditor must acknowledge the consumer's notice within 30 days. Then, within 90 days, the creditor must conduct an investigation and either correct the mistake or explain why the bill is believed to be correct. Another provision of the act gives consumers protection when they buy unsatisfactory goods or services with credit cards. If a consumer has a dispute with a credit card purchase, the consumer can disregard the bill for the disputed item and, instead, notify the credit card issuer of the error by telephone. The credit card issuer will put the disputed amount on hold and send the consumer a form to fill out explaining the dispute. The credit card issuer will attempt to resolve the dispute and inform the consumer of the results. Then, if the problem is not corrected and suit is brought by the credit card issuer, the consumer may use as a defense the fact that unsatisfactory goods or services were received. For this law to apply, the initial transaction must have taken place in the consumer's state or within 100 miles of the consumer's mailing address. Creditors may not give cardholders a poor credit rating for exercising their rights under this act.

**Fair Debt Collection Practices**  Under the Fair Debt Collection Practices Act, specific rules must be followed by companies that are in the business of collecting debts for others. Some of these rules are as follows:

1. When trying to locate someone, a debt collector may not communicate by postcard or tell others that the consumer owes money.

Under the Fair Debt Collection Practices Act, debt collectors must follow strict guidelines when contacting consumers.

2.   When the debt collector knows that the consumer is represented by an attorney, the debt collector may communicate only with the attorney.

3.   A debt collector may not communicate with the consumer at any unusual or inconvenient time or place. Unless there are circumstances to the contrary, the convenient time for communicating with a consumer is between the hours of 8:00 A.M. and 9:00 P.M.

4.   A debt collector may not communicate with the consumer at the consumer's place of employment if the debt collector knows that the employer prohibits such communication.

5.   A debt collector may not communicate, in connection with the collection of a debt, with any person other than the consumer, the consumer's attorney, the creditor's attorney, or a consumer reporting agency.

6.   If a consumer notifies a debt collector in writing that the consumer refuses to pay the debt or wishes the debt collector to cease further communication, the debt collector must cease communication, except to notify the consumer of a specific action.

7.   Debt collectors may not harass consumers or use abusive techniques to collect debts. The use or threatened use of violence or other criminal means to harm the person, property, or reputation of consumers is not allowed. In addition, debt collectors may not use obscene or profane language or publish a list of those who allegedly refuse to pay debts. It is also illegal for a debt collector to cause a telephone to ring or to engage in repeated telephone conversations with the intent to annoy the consumer.

Debt collectors who violate this law may be sued for actual damages, punitive damages, and attorneys' fees.

**The Consumer Leasing Act**  The Consumer Leasing Act is a federal law requiring leasing companies to inform consumers of all of the terms of a lease of personal property. Consumers can use the information to compare one lease with another or the cost of leasing with the cost of buying the same property. The law applies only to personal property leased by an individual for a period of more than four months for personal, family, or household use. It does not cover daily or weekly rentals, leases for apartments or houses, or leases to anyone for business purposes.

**EXAMPLE 15-2:** Businesses Not Protected

Guzman decided that her business could be managed much more efficiently if it had a computer. The cost of buying a computer, however, was more than Guzman could afford. She considered leasing one. The Consumer Leasing Act would not apply to Guzman's lease, because the computer was for business rather than personal use. She would be able to make a better decision, however, if she asked the leasing company for the same information the company would be required to provide to a consumer.

The law requires that consumers be given a written statement informing them of the full cost of the lease, including the cost of any necessary licenses, taxes, or other fees. Consumers must be informed of any insurance requirements and penalties for late payment. They must also be told who is responsible for maintaining and servicing the property. In addition, they must be told whether they can buy the property and, if so, when and at what price. The law also places a limit on the amount of a **balloon payment** (a very large final payment) to no more than three times the average monthly payments. Advertisements of leases are also regulated by law. If an advertisement mentions the amount or number of payments, specifies a particular down payment, or states that no down payment is required; it must also disclose the total of regular payments, the consumer's responsibility at the end of the lease, and whether the consumer may purchase the property.

## quick quiz 15-3

| | | |
|---|---|---|
| 1. Under the terms of the Truth-in-Lending Act. Lenders need disclose only things to the finance charge to lenders. | true | false |
| 2. If a credit card or a debit card is lost, the cardholder is responsible only for the first $50 of any unauthorized charges. | true | false |
| 3. Debt collectors who violate the Fair Debt Collection Practices cannot be sued. | true | false |

## Summary

**15.1** Public interest refers to the idea that certain activities affect the entire social structure and must, therefore, be regulated by the government. Public policy, in contrast, seeks to implement behavior that promotes the public consensus and eliminates behavior that does not. Both concepts are inherent within the legal doctrines of product liability. Under the theory of product liability, a buyer or user of a product who is injured because of the product's unsafe or defective condition may recover damages from the manufacturer, the seller, or the supplier of the goods. Product liability suits can now be based on one of two legal theories, negligence or strict liability, both of which are tort actions. Public policy has not remained solely within the purview of the courts. Congress has also entered the product safety arena by establishing the Consumer Product Safety Commission (CPSC) to protect consumers from unreasonable risk or injury from hazardous products.

**15.2** The Federal Trade Commission Act gave the Federal Trade Commission (FTC) the authority to oversee and eliminate deceptive and unfair practices in commerce. The FTC and the courts have determined that certain activities are unfair or deceptive. They include fraudulent misrepresentations, sending unordered merchandise, bait-and-switch schemes, and odometer tampering. To correct wrongdoings in

the marketplace, the FTC has also established trade regulation rules to govern the activities of interstate companies. These rules include the used-car rule, the cooling-off rule, the negative-option rule, the mail and telephone order rule, the telemarketing sales rule, and the rules connected with 900 numbers. Other rules are set up by the antispam law and the antislamming law.

**15.3** Under the Truth-in-Lending Act, lenders must disclose the true nature of finance charges and the annual percentage rate. The Equal Credit Opportunity Act ensures that all consumers have an equal chance to receive credit. The Fair Credit Reporting Act guarantees fair treatment by credit bureaus and consumer reporting agencies. Under the Truth-in-Lending Act, credit-card holders are not responsible for any unauthorized charges made after the card issuer has been notified of the loss, theft, or possible unauthorized use of the card. The Fair Credit Reporting Act promises that consumers will be treated fairly by credit bureaus and consumer reporting agencies. To make it easier to correct billing errors, Congress has passed the Fair Credit Billing Act (FCBA). Under the Fair Debt Collection Practices Act, specific rules must be followed by companies that are in the business of collecting debts for others. The Consumer Leasing Act requires leasing companies to inform consumers of all of the terms of a lease of personal property.

# Key Terms

annual percentage rate (APR), 329

bait-and-switch scheme, 325

balloon payment, 332

Buyer's Guide, 326

cancellation form, 326

Can Spam Act, 328

class-action lawsuit, 324

commerce, 323

consent order, 324

consumer, 323

continuity plan, 327

Cooling-Off Rule, 326

dunning letters, 325

finance charge, 329

interstate commerce, 323

intrastate commerce, 324

Mail and Telephone Order Rule, 327

product liability, 319

public interest, 319

public policy, 320

strict liability, 321

slamming, 329

spam, 328

Used Car Rule, 326

# Questions for Review and Discussion

1. What is the link between social engineering and the law?
2. What is the difference between the public interest and public policy?
3. What is the difference between negligence and strict liability?
4. What is the purpose of the Consumer Product Safety Act?
5. How is the Federal Trade Commission Act enforced?
6. What are some unfair or deceptive practices?
7. What are the FTC rules designed to protect the consumer?
8. What is the function of the Truth-in-Lending Act?
9. What are some of the latest amendments to the Truth-in-Lending Act?
10. What is required by the Consumer Leasing Act?

# Cases for Analysis

1. Paul and Cynthia Vance invited Carl and Jeanne Leichtamer to go for a ride in the Vances's four-wheel drive Jeep at an "off the road" recreation facility called the Hall of Fame Four-Wheel Club. The club had been organized by a Jeep dealer who showed films to club members of Jeeps traveling in hilly country. This activity was coupled with a national advertising program of American Motor Sales Corporation encouraging people to buy Jeeps that could drive up and down steep hills. As the Jeep went up a 33-degree sloped, double-terraced hill, it pitched over from front to back and landed upside-down. The Vances were killed, and the Leichtamers were severely injured. The Jeep was equipped with a factory-installed roll bar attached to the sheet metal that housed the rear wheels. When the vehicle landed upside down, the flat sheet metal gave way, causing the roll bar to move forward and downward 14 inches. The Leichtamers argued that the weakness of the sheet metal housing upon which the roll bar had been attached was the cause of their injuries. The manufacturer claimed that the roll bar was provided solely for side-roll protection, not pitchover, as occurred in this case. Did the Leichtamers recover against the manufacturer on a theory of strict liability? Why or why not? *Leichtamer v. American Motors Corp.*, 424 N.E.2d 568 (OH).

2. Michael P. Babine was injured when he was thrown from an "El Toro" mechanical bull that he rode at a nightclub. The club had placed mattresses around the bull to cushion the fall of riders, but the mattresses were not adequately pushed together. Babine was thrown off during his ride and hit his head on the floor where there was a gap between the mattresses. Before riding the bull, Babine had signed a form releasing the nightclub from liability for injuries sustained from the activity. The mechanical bull had been manufactured for the purpose of being a training device for rodeo cowboys, and it was purchased second-hand by the nightclub. Babine sought to recover damages from the manufacturer under the theory of product liability. Did he succeed? Why or why not? *Babine v. Gilley's Bronco Shop, Inc.*, 488 So.2d 176 (FL).

3. Harriet Glantz lost her job. She was unable to find work for several months and fell behind in the payment of her debts. A debt collector telephoned her at 11:45 P.M., used profanity, and threatened to "take care of her" if she didn't pay the amount owed. Were Glantz's rights violated? Explain.

4. Ingram went to a used car lot in a large city and bought a used car. On his way home from the lot, the car that he had purchased broke down. The engine stopped running altogether. The used car lot refused to fix the car because the salesperson had written "as is" on the sales slip. Ingram had not been informed that the car was sold to him as is. Was a consumer protection law violated? Explain.

5. Prior to his marriage, Edward Garber had been in financial difficulty and had a poor credit rating. His wife, Natalie, applied for a credit card in her family name, fearing that she would be turned down if she used her married name of Garber. She was told that she must use her married name on a credit application. Could Natalie have used her family name when she applied for credit? Explain.

6. Horack bought a used Mustang from a used car lot. The odometer showed that the car had been driven only 30,000 miles. Later, while cleaning her car, Horack found a service receipt showing that the actual mileage on the car a year earlier was 45,000 miles. Was a law violated? Explain.

7. Carboni's MasterCard bill contained several charges that she had not made. Upon investigation, she discovered that her credit card was missing from her wallet. She immediately notified the bank of the lost credit card. The unauthorized charges on the bill that she received amounted to $375. Did Carboni have to pay the full amount of the bill? Explain.

8. Delores Bierlein paid a $200 deposit toward the rental of the Silver Room at Alex's Continental Inn for her wedding reception. Later, Bierlein canceled the reception because her fiancé was transferred from Ohio to New York. The inn refused to refund Bierlein's deposit. The consumer protection law of that state requires suppliers to furnish receipts when they receive deposits. Bierlein was not given a receipt for her $200 deposit. When she sued for the return of the $200, the question arose as to whether this transaction fell within the consumer protection law. Do you think it does? Explain. *Bierlein v. Alex's Continental Inn, Inc.,* 475 N.E.2d 1273 (OH).

9. In response to a radio advertisement, Mr. and Mrs. Lancet telephoned Hollywood Decorators, Inc., and arranged for Mr. Wolff, a company representative, to visit their home. During Wolff's visit, the Lancets signed a contract for interior decoration and paid a $1,000 deposit. Two days later, the Lancets canceled the contract by telephone and asked for the return of their deposit. Twelve days after that, the Lancet's attorney wrote a letter to the company renewing the cancellation. Were they bound by the contract they signed? Why or why not? *Hollywood Decorators, Inc., v. Lancet,* 461 N.Y.S.2d 955 (NY).

10. After receiving an unsuccessful surgical procedure designed to facilitate weight loss, Gatten brought suit against the physician for violation of the state consumer protection law. That law read in part, "unfair methods of competition and deceptive practices in the conduct of any trade or commerce are unlawful." Gatten based her case on statements made to her about her course of treatment and the probable results of that treatment. Does the unsuccessful treatment by a physician fall within the consumer protection law? Explain. *Gatten v. Merzi,* 579 A.2d 974 (PA).

## quick quiz Answers

| 15.1 | 15.2 | 15.3 |
| --- | --- | --- |
| 1. F | 1. T | 1. F |
| 2. F | 2. T | 2. F |
| 3. T | 3. F | 3. F |

# Part 3 Case Study

**DiCenzo v. A-Best Products Company Inc.,**
Ohio State Supreme Court
120 Ohio St. 3d 149 (2008)

## Summary

Joseph DiCenzo worked for Wheeling-Pittsburgh Steel Corporation from the 1950s until 1993. He worked as a tin-line laborer, a tractor operator, a plier, a welding-machine operator, and a tin-line operator. During all of this time, without his knowledge or consent, he was surrounded by asbestos laden insulation products. A good portion of these products originated with George V. Hamilton, Inc. ("Hamilton"), a company which did not manufacture the asbestos filled insulation products but which did, nevertheless, supply many of them to the mill. Several years after leaving the mill, DiCenzo was diagnosed with mesothelioma. He passed away in 1999, as a direct result of this illness, which has been linked to asbestos. DiCenzo's widow joined together with several other plaintiffs in a lawsuit against Hamilton as well as approximately 90 additional defendants. The grounds for the suit included, among several additional claims, failure to warn, breach of warranty, design defects, and product liability, based on the theory of strict liability. Hamilton filed a summary judgment motion demanding a dismissal of the strict liability claim. To support the motion, Hamilton claimed that DiCenzo's strict liability argument could not be applied to Hamilton's pre-1977 behavior because the strict liability standard for product liability had not existed at the time. In fact the standard was not created until 1977 in the case of *Temple v. Wean* 590 Ohio St.2d 317 (1977). Consequently, the strict liability standard could not be applied retrospectively to outlaw conduct that had been perfectly legal at the time it was performed. The lower court agreed and the case was dismissed. The court of appeals, however, disagreed and reversed the lower court's dismissal. The Ohio Supreme Court agreed to hear the case. A good portion of the Ohio Supreme Court's opinion is based on *Chevron Oil Co. v. Huson,* 404 U.S. 97, 92 U.S. 349, 30 L.Ed.2d 296 (1971) a United States Supreme Court case that predates both *Temple* and *DiCenzo,* and that sets the standard for determining when cases are to be viewed as retrospective and when they are to be considered prospective only. To apply the *Chevron* case and to reach the decision that it does, the Ohio State Supreme Court discusses the origin of strict liability as it relates to product liability, as well as the nature of privity and the application of breach of warranty claims.

## The Court's Opinion

Lundberg, Stratton, J.

III. Analysis

### A. Chevron Oil Co. v. Huson

Because Chevron is central to the dispute before this court, we begin our analysis by examining its holding . . . The court held that the answers to three questions determine whether a decision should be applied prospectively only: (1) does the decision establish a new principle of law that not clearly foreshadowed? (2) does retroactive application of the decision promote or hinder the purpose behind the decision? and (3) does retroactive application of the decision cause an inequitable result? *Chevron Oil,* 404 U.S. at 106–107, 92 S.Ct. 349, 30 L.Ed.2d 296 . . . We now apply the *Chevron Oil* test to determine whether prospective-only application of *Temple* is justified.

1. Nonmanufacturing-Supplier Liability was an Issue of First Impression in *Temple v. Wean.*

(30) Historically, a lack of privity between consumers and manufacturers prevented consumers from recovering damages for a defective product under a breach of warranty claim against the product's manufacturer . . . However, in a series of cases issued from 1958 to 1966; this court gradually relaxed certain longstanding legal rules that made consumer actions against *manufacturers* more viable.

(31) In *Rogers v. Toni Home Permanent Co.* 167 Ohio St. 244, 4 O.O.2d 291. 147 N.E.2d 612, a hair product caused a consumer personal injuries. The consumer filed suit against the manufacturer, alleging negligence, breach of implied warranty, and a breach of express warranty based on the manufacturer's advertisements that the product was safe . . . The issue before then court was whether the consumer could maintain a claim for breach of an express warranty . . . The court recognized that he prevailing view was that privity of contract was required to bring an action alleging the breach of express warranty. However, the court held that the manufacturer's advertisements about its product safety effectively created an express warranty upon which the consumer could rely and that her breach of warranty claim could arise in tort . . . Thus, the court held that a lack of privity did not prevent her claim for breach of an express warranty against the manufacturer for the defective hair product.

(32) In *Inglis,* 3 Ohio St.2d 132, 32 O.O2d 136, 209 N.E.2d 583, the plaintiff succeeded in recovering damages for losses caused by a defectively manufactured automobile under a theory of breach of express warranty. This court affirmed, extending the rule it had announced in *Toni* (permitting express-warranty claim for personal injury to the consumer in *Inglis* for recovery of damages against the manufacturer caused by the defective automobile.)

(33) Finally, in *Lonzrick v. Republic Steel Corp.* (1966), 6 Ohio St.2d 227, 35 O.O.2d 404, 216 N.E.2d 185, the court held that even absent privity, a consumer could maintain a claim of breach of implied warranty against the manufacturer for injuries caused by its defective product.

(34) In *Lonzrick* the plaintiff was injured when steel joists collapsed and fell on him . . . The plaintiff sued the manufacturer of the steel joists in tort based upon a breach of an implied warranty . . . The issue was whether the plaintiff, who was injured by a defective product could maintain an action alleging breach of *implied* warranty based on tort, because unlike in *Toni* and *Inglis,* the manufacturer made no advertised representations about the metal beams. The court held that advertising was not relevant to determining whether a manufacturer should be liable. More critical to the analysis was that by placing the product into the stream of commerce, the manufacturer had implicitly represented the product to be of "good and merchantable quality, fit and safe for the ordinary purposes for which steel joists are used." . . . Thus the court held that the plaintiff could maintain a claim for breach of an implied warranty against the manufacturer based in tort.

(35) Thus, in *Toni, Inglis,* and *Lonzrick,* the court gradually relaxed the long-held legal requirement of privity, held that a breach-of-warranty claim could arise out of tort, and recognized that a claim for breach-of-warranty was viable when the manufacturer did not advertise. The gradual evolution in the products liability law was aimed at making manufacturers more accessible to consumer-product lawsuits. Indeed, it was the lack of a contractual relationship between consumers and manufacturers that spurred the products-liability evolution in the first place . . . These cases epitomized the, "slow, orderly and evolutionary development" of Ohio products-liability law against *manufacturers*.

(36) In contrast, *Temple v. Wean* marked a relatively large step in the further development of the products-liability law in its holding. *"One who sells any product* in a defective condition unreasonably dangerous to the user or consumer or to his property *is subject to liability* for physical harm thereby caused to the ultimate user or consumer, or to his property if

(37) "(a) the seller is engaged in the business of selling such a product, and

(38) "(b) it is expected to and does reach the consumer without substantial change in the condition in which it is sold."

(39) Although plaintiff's evidence in temple failed to prove liability against multiple defendants, the court's analysis makes clear that for the first time, the court defined a rule that allowed *nonmanufacturing* suppliers to be liable for defective products that they sell. We begin our review of the analysis in *Temple* by examining the facts.

(40) Betty Temple was injured by a punch press. Wean United Incorporated manufactured the punch press, which was sold to General Motors Corporation

("G.M."). G.M. in turn sold the punch press to Turner Industries, and Turner sold it to Wean, the plaintiff's employer. After her injury, Temple sued Wean United, as well as the subsequent punch-press vendors, G.M., and Turner.

(41) *Temple* adopted 2 Restatement of the Law 2d, Torts (1965), Section 402A, holding that "a plaintiff must prove that the product was defective at the time it left the seller's hands" for the seller to be held liable . . . However, the evidence showed that the press had been modified *after* it had been sold to the plaintiff's employer and that the modification was the cause of the plaintiff's injury . . . The circumstance "absolved the manufacturer, Wean, and the subsequent vendor G.M., from strict tort liability . . . G.M. was a nonmanufacturing seller of the press.

(42) Thus, *Temple* clearly defined a new rule that nonmanufacturing suppliers of products could be held liable for injuries caused by those products. Prior to *Temple,* no holding form this court had permitted the seller of a product who was not also the manufacturer to be liable for a defective product under breach of warranty theory based in tort absent privity, and none foreshadowed that such a holding was on the horizon. Clearly, *Temple* addressed an issue of first impression that had not been foreshadowed in prior cases.

2. Retroactive Application of temple Neither Promotes Nor Hinders the Purpose Behind the Products-Liability Law.

(43) The second prong of the test in *Chevron Oil* asks whether applying the decision retroactively promotes or hinders the purpose behind the rule stated in the decision . . . We conclude that retroactive application of temple will neither promote nor hinder the purpose behind products liability law.

(44) A primary "purpose of the strict liability doctrine is to induce manufacturers and suppliers to do everything possible to reduce the risk of injury and insure against what risk remains.". . .

(45) Products containing asbestos have not been manufactured or sold for approximately 30 years. The time for making these products safer has come and gone. Thus, retroactively applying temple to nonmanufacturing sellers of asbestos products will not promote the purpose of making those products safer.

(46) Moreover, one of the expressed reasons for the adoption of Section 402A of 2 Restatement of the Law 2d, Torts, in temple was that "there are virtually no distinction between Ohio's "implied warranty in tort' theory and the Restatement version of strict liability in tort and * * * the Restatement formulation, together with its numerous illustrative comments, greatly facilitates analysis in this area." . . . Again, applying Temple retroactively to impose liability on a nonmanufacturer supplier of asbestos products would neither promote nor impede the purpose of facilitating the analysis of products-liability law.

3. It Would Be Inequitable to Impose *Temple* on Nonmanufacturing Suppliers of Asbestos Products.

(47) As we noted in section I above, *Temple,* which was decided in 1977, marked the first time this court had held that a nonmanufacturing seller of a product could be held liable for injuries caused by a defective product. Thus, nonmanufacturing sellers of asbetstos, such as Hamilton, could not have foreseen that these products, distributed from the 1950s to the 1970s, could decades later result in Hamilton's being liable for injuries caused by that product. Imposing such a potential financial burden on these nonmanufacturing suppliers years after the fact for an obligation that was not foreseeable at the time would result in a great inequity

(48) Thus, the answer to the question posed in *Chevron Oil* collectively indicate that our decision in Temple should be applied prospectively only. Accordingly, we reverse the judgment of the court and reinstate the judgment of the trial court.

Judgment reversed.

O'Connor, O'Donnell, Lanzinger, and Cupp, JJ., concur.
Moyer, C.J., dissents without opinion.
Pfeifer, J. dissents with opinion.

# Questions for Analysis

1. What is the difference between an *express* and an *implied* warranty? How are express warranties created in sales law? Explain.

2. How are *implied* warranties created in sales law? What types of implied warranties are recognized in sales law? Explain.

3. The first step in the gradual evolution of the product liability theory involved a modification of *express* warranty. In general how is an express warranty created in sales law? In what way was the warranty made "express" in the case of *Rogers v. Toni Home Permanent?* Explain.

4. How did the case of *Inglis v. Am. Motors Corp.* extend the express warranty claim established by the court in the *Toni* case? Explain.

5. The next step in the development of the product liability theory involved a modification of *implied*

warranty. In general how is an implied warranty created in sales law? Which type of implied warranty is breached in the *Lonzrick* case? Explain.

6. The court notes that *"Temple v. Wean* marked a relatively large step in the further development of the products-liability law." What "relatively large step" was taken by the court in advance in the case of *Temple v. Wean?* Explain.

7. The court decided not to apply the rule created in the case of *Temple v. Wean* restrospectively. What does it mean to apply a rule restrospectively.?

What does it mean to apply a rule prospectively? Explain.

8. The court gives three reasons for not applying the rule created in *Temple v, Wean* retrospectively. What are those three reasons? Explain.

9. What is the public interest promoted by the courts in the line of cases discussed at length in *DiCenzo v. A-Best Products Company Inc.?* Explain.

10. What public policy tactic is at use in the case of *DiCenzo v. A-Best Products Company Inc.?* Explain.

# Part Four

## Negotiable Instruments and Banking

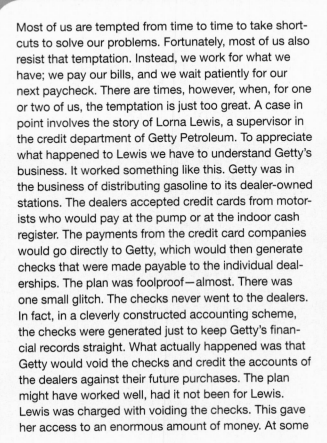

## THE OPENING CASE   Stolen Checks, Forgery, and Credit Card Debt: *Getty Petroleum v. American Express*

Most of us are tempted from time to time to take shortcuts to solve our problems. Fortunately, most of us also resist that temptation. Instead, we work for what we have; we pay our bills, and we wait patiently for our next paycheck. There are times, however, when, for one or two of us, the temptation is just too great. A case in point involves the story of Lorna Lewis, a supervisor in the credit department of Getty Petroleum. To appreciate what happened to Lewis we have to understand Getty's business. It worked something like this. Getty was in the business of distributing gasoline to its dealer-owned stations. The dealers accepted credit cards from motorists who would pay at the pump or at the indoor cash register. The payments from the credit card companies would go directly to Getty, which would then generate checks that were made payable to the individual dealerships. The plan was foolproof—almost. There was one small glitch. The checks never went to the dealers. In fact, in a cleverly constructed accounting scheme, the checks were generated just to keep Getty's financial records straight. What actually happened was that Getty would void the checks and credit the accounts of the dealers against their future purchases. The plan might have worked well, had it not been for Lewis. Lewis was charged with voiding the checks. This gave her access to an enormous amount of money. At some

point along the way, Lewis decided to keep the checks and forge the indorsement of the payees. She then sent the checks to the credit card companies to pay off her own credit card debt. The credit card companies forwarded the checks to Chemical Bank which was where Getty kept its accounts. Eventually Lewis's game was discovered and Getty sued the credit card companies for the lost money. Now a good portion of the blame for this entire fiasco would seem to fall on Getty's shoulders. After all, it was Getty that came up with scheme. It was Getty that hired Lewis in the first place, and it was Getty that failed to properly supervise her activities. Yet, Getty had no problem trying to get its money back from the credit card companies. Who is responsible for all of this and how would you decide if you were the judge? As you read the chapter, see if you can detect just how many of the rules of negotiable instruments were violated here. (See *Getty Petroleum Corp. v. American Express Travel Related Services, Co., Inc.* 683 N.E.2d 311 (New York Court of Appeals).)

### Opening Case Questions

1. What type of lawsuit did Getty bring against American Express? Was this a tort case or a contract case or something else? Explain.

2. Who is the legitimate payee on all of these checks? Explain.

3. Does the "fictitious payee" rule come into play in this case? Why or why not?

4. Which party was in the best possible position to prevent the losses from occurring? Explain.

Should the court consider Getty's responsibilities when it decides the case? Why or why not?

5. In most instances, what is the drawer's liability on a forged check? Does that rule apply here? Explain.

##  Learning Objectives

1. State the purpose of a negotiable instrument.
2. Explain those negotiable instruments that contain a promise to pay money.
3. Explain those negotiable instruments that contain an order to pay money.
4. Differentiate among the different types of checks and money orders.
5. Identify the requirements of a negotiable instrument.
6. Explain an assignment and a negotiation of an instrument.
7. Name and describe four kinds of indorsements.
8. Identify the implied warranties related to indorsements.
9. Explain the contract that is made when people indorse negotiable instruments.
10. Describe the legal effect of a forged indorsement.

# 16-1 The Essentials of Negotiable Instruments

Throughout history, people have had a need to transact business without carrying around large sums of money. In the Middle Ages, for example, merchants carried gold and silver with them as they traveled from one fair to another buying goods. They were in constant danger of being robbed and needed a safer and more convenient method of exchanging their gold and silver for the goods they bought. A system was developed by which merchants could deposit their precious metals with goldsmiths or silversmiths for safekeeping. When the merchants bought goods, instead of paying for them with gold or silver, they simply filled in a piece of paper, called a bill of exchange (now known as a draft). The bill of exchange ordered the goldsmith or silversmith to give a certain amount of the precious metal to the person who sold the goods. That person would then take the bill of exchange to the goldsmith or silversmith and receive payment. In a similar fashion throughout history, people have borrowed money from one another, necessitating an orderly system of procedures and laws to govern credit transactions.

The law of negotiable instruments has developed to meet these needs. Checks, drafts, and notes are used conveniently and safely as a substitute for money and to obtain credit in today's society. With the rapid development of cyber-commerce and electronic banking, online payments are now being used as a substitute for checks and other paper transactions, as well as for actual check processing through the banking system. As a result, it is estimated that the number of checks written in the United States will decline greatly during the next decade.

## Promise and Order Instruments

The law of negotiable instruments is found in Article 3 of the UCC. This article was originally drafted in 1952. Since that time, many new developments have occurred in the commercial

No. *381*    *Boston, Massachusetts, October 1,20 —*

On demand, the undersigned, for value received, promise(s) to pay to the order of
CAMBRIDGE TRUST COMPANY

*Two thousand four hundred and* °°/100 ————————Dollars,

at its offices in Boston, Massachusetts, together with interest thereon from the
date thereof until paid at the rate of __*6*__ percent per annum.

Address *100 Bedford Street*    *Victor Powell*
*Waltham, Massachusetts*

**Figure 16-1**  A demand note is payable whenever the payee demands payment.

UCC Revised (1990)
3-104(e)-(j) (see
page 864)

field. To adapt to modern technology and contemporary practices, Article 3 of the UCC has been extensively revised over the last six decades. Today under the UCC, a **negotiable instrument** is a written document signed by the maker that contains an unconditional promise *or* order to pay a fixed amount of money on demand or at a definite time to the bearer or to order. There are two basic kinds of negotiable instruments: promise instruments (including notes and certificates of deposit) and order instruments (including drafts and checks).

**Promise Instruments: Notes**  A **note** (often called a promissory note) is a written promise by one party, called the *maker,* to pay money to the order of another party, called the *payee.* People who loan money or extend credit use notes as evidence of debt. When two or more parties sign a note, they are called *comakers.* A **demand note**, as its name implies, is payable whenever the payee demands payment (Figure 16-1). A holder of a demand note may decide to collect the balance due at any time and for any reason. A time note, in contrast, is payable at some future time, on a date named in the instrument. Unless a note is payable in installments, the principal (face value) of the note plus interest must be paid on the date that it is due. In an **installment note**, the principal together with the interest on the unpaid balance is payable in a series of payments at specified times.

UCC Revised (1990)
3-104(e) (see page 864)

**Promise Instruments: Certificates of Deposit**  A **certificate of deposit (CD)** is an instrument containing an acknowledgment that a bank has received a sum of money and a promise by the bank to repay the sum of money. A CD is a note of the bank, and CDs are written for a specific time period, such as six months, one year, two years, or five years. Banks pay higher interest for longer-term CDs and more interest than regular savings accounts because the depositor cannot withdraw the money before the due date without penalty. Some banks allow a one-time early withdrawal from a CD without penalty.

UCC Revised (1990)
3-108(a) (see page 864)

UCC Revised (1990)
3-104(j) (see page 864)

**Order Instruments: Drafts**  In contrast to notes, which are *promises* to pay money, drafts are *orders* to pay money. They are more complicated than notes because they involve three parties rather than two. The most common type of draft in use today is the check, but this was not always the case. For example, in Ernest Hemingway's *A Farewell to Arms,* a novel set in Italy during World War I, one of the characters, an American major, discusses with his friend Rinaldi the possibility of going to Milan:

UCC Revised (1990)
3-104(e) (see page 864)

> The tickets are very expensive. I will draw a sight draft on my grandfather, I said. A what? A sight draft. He has to pay or I go to jail. Mr. Cunningham at the bank does it. I live by sight drafts. Can a grandfather jail a patriotic grandson who is dying that Italy may live? Live the American Garibaldi, said Rinaldi. Viva the sight drafts, I said.

A **draft** (also called a **bill of exchange**) is an instrument in which one party writes an instrument ordering a second party to pay money to a third party. The one who draws the draft (that is, the one who orders money to be paid) is called the *drawer*. The one who is ordered to pay the money is called the *drawee*. The one who is to receive the money is known as the *payee*.

UCC Revised (1990) 3-409 (see page 875)

## EXAMPLE 16-1:  Sight Draft

In Hemingway's novel, the major would be the drawer of the draft, and his grandfather would be the drawee. The story does not name the payee of the draft, but it could be the railroad ticket office or a bank in Italy—whoever is to receive the money. If this situation involved a check, the person who signed the check would be the drawer, the bank would be the drawee, and the one to whom the check were written would be the payee.

A draft may be presented by the holder to the drawee for payment or for acceptance. When a draft is presented for payment, the drawee may decline to pay it unless it has been accepted. If the drawee refuses to pay an unaccepted draft, the draft is dishonored, and the drawee has no liability for refusing to pay it. In contrast, when a draft is presented for acceptance, the drawee is asked to become liable on the instrument. **Acceptance** is the drawee's signed agreement to pay the draft as presented. If the drawee refuses to accept the draft, it is dishonored, and again, the drawee has no liability.

Drawees are liable on drafts only when they accept them, that is, agree to become liable on them. To accept a draft, the drawee need only sign the draft across the face of the instrument. It is customary, however, when accepting a draft, for the drawee to write "accepted" across the face of the instrument, followed by the date and signature. An acceptance must be written on the draft itself; it may not be written on a separate piece of paper. By accepting a draft, the drawee agrees to pay the instrument at a later date when it became due.

*Sight and Time Drafts*   A **sight draft** (Figure 16-2) is payable as soon as it is presented to the drawee for payment. A **time draft** (Figure 16-3) is not payable until the lapse of a particular time period stated on the draft. Drafts that are payable "thirty days after sight" and "sixty days after date" are examples of time drafts.

### About the Law

A **trade acceptance** is a draft used by a seller of goods to receive payment and extend credit. Drafts are often used in combination with bills of lading, which are receipts given by freight companies to people who ship goods. A seller will ship goods to a buyer and send a *(continued)*

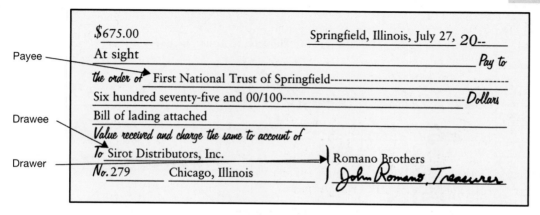

Figure 16-2   A sight draft is payable as soon as it is presented to the drawee for payment. How do you know that this draft has not been accepted by the drawee?

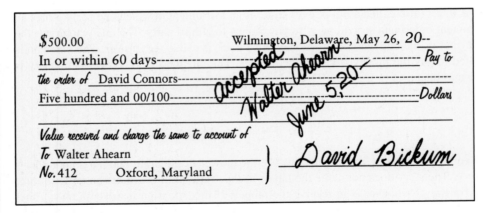

bill of lading, with a trade acceptance attached, to a bank in the buyer's city. The trade acceptance orders the buyer to pay money to the seller or another party. The buyer must either pay the money or accept the draft to receive the bill of lading from the bank. The freight company will not release the goods to the buyer unless the buyer has possession of the bill of lading.

UCC Revised (1990) 3-104(f) (see page 864)

**Figure 16-3** A time draft is not payable until the lapse of a particular time period stated on the draft. How do you know that this draft has been accepted by the drawee?

*Domestic and International Bills of Exchange* A **domestic bill of exchange** is a draft that is drawn and payable in the United States. A draft that is drawn in one country but payable in another is called an **international bill of exchange** or **foreign draft**.

## Order Instruments: Checks

A **check** is a draft drawn on a bank and payable on demand. It is the most common form of a draft. It is drawn on a bank by a drawer who has an account with the bank and is made to the order of a specified person or business named on the check or to the bearer. A check is a safe means of transferring money, and it serves as a receipt after it has been paid and canceled by the bank. In the check shown in Figure 16-4, Evans is the drawer; she has an account with the Western National Bank. Alicia Adams Fashions, Inc., is the payee. Western National Bank, on which the check is drawn, is the drawee. Ownership of a check may be transferred to another person by indorsement by the payee. In this manner, a check may circulate among several parties, taking the place of money. A bank must honor a check when it is properly drawn against a credit balance of the drawer. Failure to do so would make the bank liable to the drawer for resulting damages.

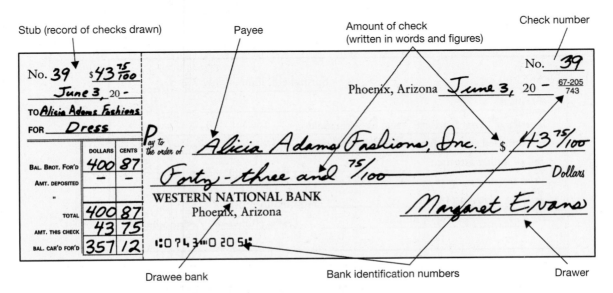

**Figure 16-4** All elements of a sample check are identified.

# A QUESTION OF ETHICS

Along with their bill, credit card companies often include blank checks for customers to make payable to anyone they wish, thus increasing the amount owed the credit card issuer, usually at an exceptionally high rate of interest. The practice is legal; is it ethical?

*Form for Checks*  Banks provide regular and special printed check forms. These check forms display a series of numbers printed in magnetic ink, which make it possible to process checks speedily and accurately by computer. The first set of figures is the bank's Federal Reserve number. This number is followed by the bank's own number. The second set of numbers is the depositor's account number. The use of printed forms is not required, however. Any writing, no matter how crude, may be used as a check if it is a draft drawn on a bank and payable on demand.

UCC Revised (1990) 3-409(d) (see page 875)

*Certified Checks*  A **certified check** is a check that is guaranteed by the bank. At the request of either the depositor or the holder, the bank acknowledges and guarantees that sufficient funds will be withheld from the drawer's account to pay the amount stated on the check. A prudent person will request a certified check rather than accept a personal check when involved in a business transaction with a stranger. A certified check, under the UCC, is "a check accepted by the bank on which it is drawn." The UCC places no obligation on a bank to certify a check if it does not want to do so, and the refusal to certify is not a dishonor of the check. When a check is certified, the drawer is discharged regardless of when it was done or who obtained the acceptance. Figure 16-5 illustrates a certified check.

UCC Revised (1990) 3-414(c) (see page 876)

UCC Revised (1990) 3-104(g)(h) (see page 864)

*Bank Drafts and Cashier's Checks*  A **bank draft**, sometimes called a **teller's check** or *treasurer's check*, is a check drawn by one bank on another bank in which it has funds on deposit in favor of a third person, the payee. Many banks deposit money in banks in other areas for the convenience of depositors who depend upon the transfer of funds when transacting business in distant places. When the buyer is unknown to the seller, such checks are more acceptable than personal checks. A **cashier's check** is a check drawn by a bank upon itself. The bank, in effect, lends its credit to the purchaser of the check. It is the equivalent

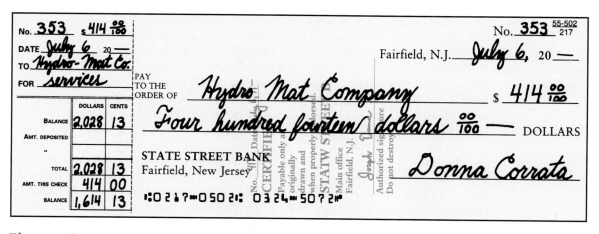

Figure 16-5  The State Street Bank became primarily liable when it certified this check.

Online banking and bill paying has replaced the need for paper transactions for many customers.

of a promissory note of the bank. Courts have held that payment cannot be stopped on a cashier's check because the bank, by issuing it, accepts the check in advance. People who will not accept personal checks will often accept cashier's checks. Such a check may be made payable either to the depositor, who purchases it from the bank, or to the person who is to cash it. If the check is made payable to the depositor, it must be indorsed to the person to whom it is transferred.

*Traveler's Checks*    A **traveler's check** is similar to a cashier's check, in that the issuing financial institution is both the drawer and the drawee. The purchaser signs the checks in the presence of the issuer when they are purchased. To cash a check, the purchaser writes the name of the payee in the space provided and countersigns it in the payee's presence. Only the purchaser can negotiate traveler's checks, and they are easily replaced by the issuing bank if they are stolen. Traveler's checks are issued in denominations of $10 and up, and the purchaser of the checks ordinarily pays a fixed fee to the issuer.

*Money Orders*    A **money order** is a type of draft that may be purchased from banks, post offices, telegraph companies, and express companies as a substitute for a check. Instead of being drawn on an individual's account as is a check, however, a money order is drawn on the funds of the organization that issues it. That organization promises payment from its own funds. Purchasers of money orders fill in their name and address and the name of the payee on the instrument. They are given a receipt along with the money order. If the money order is lost and the purchaser has the receipt, it will be replaced if it has not already been cashed. U.S. Postal Service money orders can be purchased for amounts up to $1,000. U.S. International Postal Service Money Orders are often used to send money to foreign countries. Telegraphic money orders may be used to send money quickly. Under the UCC, a *bank* money order is a check, even though it is described on its face as a money order, and payment can be stopped on it like an ordinary check.

UCC Revised
(1990) 3-104(i) (see
page 1000)

UCC Revised
(1990) 3-104(f) (see
page 1000)

# 16-2 Parties to Negotiable Instruments

The following are parties to negotiable instruments: maker or comaker; drawer; issuer; drawee; payee; bearer; holder; holder in due course; indorser; indorsee, and acceptor. One by one, step by step, this is what they look like. A **maker** is a person who signs a note, that is, a person who promises to pay. **Comakers** are two or more people who sign the same note promising to pay. A **drawer** is a person who signs a draft, that is, the one who orders payment. An **issuer** is either a maker or a drawer of an instrument. A **drawee** is a person ordered in a draft to make payment. A **payee** is a person to whom a note or draft is payable. A **bearer** is a person who is in possession of a negotiable instrument that is payable to the bearer or to cash. A person who is in possession of an instrument that has been indorsed in blank (by the payee's signature alone) is also a bearer.

A **holder** is a person who is in possession of a negotiable instrument that is issued or indorsed to that person's order or bearer. A **holder in due course** is a holder of a negotiable instrument who is treated as favored and given immunity from certain defenses. An **indorser** is a person who indorses a negotiable instrument, in most cases by signing one's name on the back of the paper. An **indorsee** is a person to whom a draft, note, or other negotiable instrument is transferred by indorsement. An **acceptor** is a drawee of a draft who has promised to honor the draft as presented by signing it on its face. (See Figure 16-6.)

UCC Revised (1990)
3-103 (see page 863)

UCC 1-201(5) (see
page 817)

UCC Revised
(1990) 3-109(a) (see
page 865)

UCC 1-201(20) (see
page 817)

UCC Revised (1990)
3-204 (see page 868)

**Parties to a note**

maker ——→ (promise to pay) ——————————→ payee
                                                ↓ (transfer)
                                            indorser
                                                ↓ (transfer)
                                            indorser
                                                ↓ (transfer)
                                            indorser

**Parties to a draft**

drawee
  ↑ (order to pay)
drawer ——→ (issued to) ——————————→ payee
                                            ↓ (transfer)
                                        indorser
                                            ↓ (transfer)
                                        indorser
                                            ↓ (transfer)
                                        indorser

**Parties to a check**

drawee (payor) bank
  ↑ (order to pay)
drawer ——→ (issued to) ——————————→ payee
                                            ↓ (transfer)
                                        indorser
                                            ↓ (transfer)
                                        indorser
                                            ↓ (transfer)
                                        indorser

**Figure 16-6**  This diagram illustrates the relationship of the principal parties to negotiable instruments.

# Requirements of Negotiable Instruments

To be negotiable, instruments must: (1) be in writing; (2) be signed by the maker or drawer; (3) contain an unconditional promise or order to pay; (4) be made out for a fixed amount of money; (5) be payable on demand or at a definite time, and (6) except for checks, be payable to order or to bearer. As will be discussed soon, instruments that do not meet all of these requirements can be transferred to others by assignment. They cannot, however, be transferred by negotiation. Let's look at these requirements one at a time.

**Written Instrument**  A negotiable instrument must be in writing (see Figure 16-7), which includes printing, word processing, pen or pencil writing, or any other tangible form of writing. Under the Uniform Electronic Transactions Act (UETA), an electronic record fulfills this requirement. Article 3 of the UCC has also been amended to permit electronic negotiable instruments. However, not all states have incorporated that amendment into their version of the statute and so it is best to check to see if your state has done so. Although it hardly seems worth mentioning, it is still a good idea to recognize that any negotiable instrument written in pencil is an invitation to alteration by forgery. If forgery should happen, the person who drew the instrument would be responsible for any loss caused by the negligent drawing of the instrument.

**Signature of Maker or Drawer**  To be negotiable, an instrument must be signed by the maker or drawer. Any writing, mark, or symbol is accepted as a signature as long as it is the writer's intent to be a signature. It may be handwritten, typewritten, printed, or produced by a machine. A signature may be made by an agent (one who represents and

UCC Revised (1990) 3-104(a) (see page 864)

UCC 1-201(46) (see page 819)

UCC Revised (1990) 3-401(a)(b) (see page 873)

UCC Revised (1990) 3-402 (see page 873)

UCC Revised (1990) 3-104(a) (see page 864)

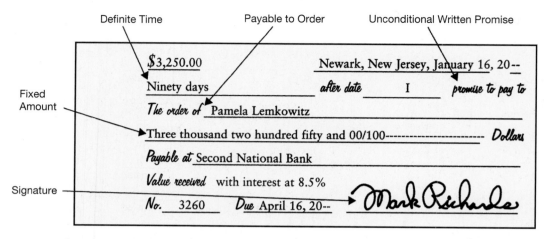

**Figure 16-7** The requirements of negotiability are indicated on this ninety-day note.

acts for another) or other representative. No particular form of appointment is necessary to establish such authority. Agents who sign their own names to an instrument are personally obligated if the instrument neither names the person represented nor shows that the agent signed in a representative capacity. The signature may appear in the body of the instrument as well as at the end.

UCC Revised (1990) 3-106(b) (see page 864)

UCC Revised (1990) 3-104(a) (see page 864)

### Unconditional Promise or Order to Pay

To be negotiable, an instrument must contain no conditions that might in any way affect its payment. Statements requiring that certain things be done or that specific events take place prior to payment make the instrument a simple contract rather than negotiable paper. An instrument is conditional, and thus not negotiable, if it states that it is subject to any other agreement. The same is true if an instrument states that it is to be paid only out of a particular fund. This latter rule does not apply to instruments issued by government agencies. An instrument may state that it "arises out of" another agreement without being conditional. Similarly, a negotiable instrument may indicate a particular account that is to be charged. In addition to being unconditional, a negotiable instrument must contain a promise to pay (as in a note) or an order to pay (as in a draft). A writing that says "Due Karen Osgood $600" or "IOU $600" is not negotiable because it is neither a promise nor an order to pay.

### Fixed Amount of Money

A negotiable instrument must be payable in a fixed amount or sum certain of money. This stipulation means an amount of money that is clearly known. *Money* is defined as a medium of exchange adopted by a domestic or foreign government as part of its currency. Thus, a fixed amount of money need not be American dollars.

### Payable on Demand or at a Definite Time

Negotiable instruments must be made payable on demand or at a definite time. This requirement makes it possible to determine when the debtor or promisor can be compelled to pay. Without this information, the present value of an instrument cannot be determined.

*Demand Paper* An instrument is payable *on demand* when it so states or when it is payable "on sight" or "on presentation." The key characteristic of demand instruments is that the holder can require payment at any time by making the demand upon the person who is obligated to pay.

*Definite-Time Paper* Certainty as to the time of payment of an instrument is satisfied if it is payable on or before a stated date. Instruments payable at a fixed period after a stated date or at a fixed period after sight are also considered payable at a definite time. In each instance, a simple mathematical calculation makes the maturity date certain. The expressions "one year after date" and "thirty days after sight" are definite as to time. An undated instrument payable 60 days after date is negotiable as a demand paper. A promise to pay only upon an act or event, the time of whose occurrence is uncertain, is not payable at a definite time. Thus, an instrument payable when a person marries, reaches a certain age, or graduates from college, or one payable within a specific period of time after a named person's death, is not negotiable.

UCC 1-201(24) (see page 818)

UCC Revised (1990) 3-107 (see page 865)

UCC Revised (1990) 3-108(a) (see page 865)

UCC Revised (1990) 3-108(b) (see page 865)

## Payable to Order or to Bearer

Negotiable instruments, except for checks, must be payable to order or to bearer. The terms *to the order of* and *to bearer* are called words of negotiability. The most recent version of Article 3 of the UCC allows checks (but not other instruments) that are not payable to order or to bearer to be negotiable. Thus, a check, but no other instrument, payable "to Mary Harris" is negotiable in all states except those that have yet to adopt the revised Article 3.

*Payable to Order* An instrument is payable to order when it states that it is payable to the order of any person with reasonable certainty. The maker or drawer may state "Pay to the order of Mary Doe," "Pay to Mary Doe or order," or "Pay to Mary Doe or her assigns." An instrument may be payable to the order of the maker or drawer; the drawee; a payee who is not the maker, drawer, or drawee; two or more payees; an estate, trust, or fund; an office or officer by title; or a partnership or an unincorporated association.

*Payable to Bearer* An instrument is payable to bearer when it states that it is payable to bearer or the order of bearer, a specified person or bearer, cash or the order of cash, or any other indication that does not designate a specific payee. An instrument is payable to bearer when it does not state a payee. An instrument made payable to both, such as "Pay to the order of Anthony Andrews or bearer," is payable to order unless the word "bearer" is handwritten or word processed.

## Dates and Controlling Words

The omission of the date does not affect the negotiability of an instrument. When the date is omitted, the date on which the instrument is received is considered to be the date of issue. An instrument may be predated or postdated without affecting its negotiability. Handwritten terms control word processed and printed terms, and word processed terms control printed terms. Words control figures, except when words are ambiguous (capable of being understood in more than one way). The numbering of, or the failure to number, an instrument does not affect its negotiability. The signature may appear in the body of the instrument as well as at the end.

## quick quiz 16-1

| | |
|---|---|
| 1. Notes are promises to pay money and drafts are orders to pay money. | true \| false |
| 2. Checks are the least common form of a draft. | true \| false |
| 3. Under the Uniform Electronic Transactions Act (UETA) an electronic record fulfills the requirement that a negotiable instrument be in writing. | true \| false |

# 16.3 Transferring Negotiable Instruments

When an instrument is first delivered by the maker or drawer for the purpose of giving rights to any person, it is said to be *issued*. When the person to whom it is issued delivers it to a third party, it is *transferred*. Instruments can be transferred by assignment or by negotiation. An **assignment** is the transfer of a contract right from one person to another. Negotiable instruments are assigned either when a person whose indorsement is required on an instrument transfers it without indorsing it or when it is transferred to another person and does not meet the requirements of negotiability. In all such transfers, the transferee has only the rights of an assignee and is subject to all defenses existing against the assignor. An assignment of negotiable instruments also occurs by operation of law when the holder of an instrument dies or becomes bankrupt. In such cases, title to the instrument vests in the personal representative of the estate or the trustee in bankruptcy.

A **negotiation** is the transfer of an instrument in such form that the transferee becomes a *holder* (a person in possession of an instrument issued or indorsed to that person, to that person's order, to bearer, or in blank). In contrast to an assignment, a negotiation gives greater rights to transferees. If an instrument is payable to order, such as "pay to the order of," it is known as **order paper**. To be negotiated, order paper must be indorsed by the payee and delivered to the party to whom it is transferred. If an instrument is payable to bearer or cash, it is called **bearer paper** and may be negotiated by delivery alone, without an indorsement. When order paper is indorsed with a blank indorsement, it is turned into bearer paper and may be further negotiated by delivery alone.

UCC Revised (1990) 3-104(c) (see page 864)

UCC Revised (1990) 3-109(b) (see page 865)

UCC Revised (1990) 3-109(a) (see page 865)

UCC Revised (1990) 3-113 (see page 866)

## The Concept of Negotiability

The concept of negotiability is one of the most important features of negotiable instruments. Largely because of this feature, negotiable instruments are highly trusted and used daily by millions of people. When an instrument is transferred by negotiation, the person receiving the instrument is provided with more protection than was available to the person from whom it was received. The person receiving the instrument is able, in many instances, to recover money on the instrument even when the person from whom the instrument was received could not have done so.

Instruments that do not meet all of the requirements of negotiability cannot be negotiated. However, they can be transferred by assignment, which is governed by the ordinary principles of contract law. People who receive instruments by assignment are not given the special protection provided those who receive instruments by negotiation, because they cannot be *holders in due course,* as explained in the next chapter.

The payee is never guaranteed to receive payment on a check, so some small businesses choose not to accept personal checks.

## Negotiation by Indorsement

An instrument is indorsed when the holder signs it, thereby indicating the intent to transfer ownership to another. Indorsements may be written in ink, typewritten, or stamped with a rubber stamp. They may be written or word processed on a separate paper (rider, or **allonge**), as long as the separate paper is so firmly affixed to the instrument that it becomes part of it. Although the UCC does not require indorsements to be on any particular side of the paper, for convenience, they are usually placed on the back of the instrument. Anyone who gives value for an instrument has the right to have the unqualified indorsement of the person who transferred it, unless it is payable to bearer.

Check Face

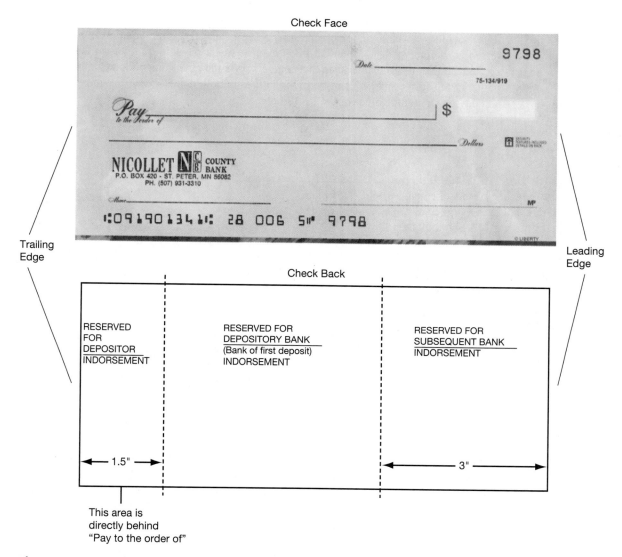

Figure 16-8   Regulation CC has issued check indorsement standards.

Regulation CC, issued by the Federal Reserve Board under the Competitive Banking Act, has established standards for check indorsements (Figure 16-8). Under the regulation, the back of a check is divided into specific sections designed to protect the indorsement of the depositor bank (the bank of first deposit). The first one-and-one-half inches from the trailing edge of the check is reserved for the payee's indorsement. Negotiation is effective to transfer an instrument, even when it is transferred by a minor, a corporation exceeding its powers, or any other person without capacity; obtained by fraud, duress, or mistake of any kind; part of an illegal transaction; or made in breach of duty. Any such negotiations, however, may be rescinded except as against a holder in due course (defined and explained in the next chapter), who is given special protection. There are four commonly used types of indorsements: blank indorsements, special indorsements, restrictive indorsements, and qualified indorsements.

## Blank Indorsements
A **blank indorsement** consists of the signature alone written on the instrument. No particular indorsee (person to whom an instrument is indorsed) is named. When an instrument is indorsed in blank, it becomes payable to the bearer and may be transferred by delivery alone. If the instrument is lost or stolen and gets into the hands of another holder, the new holder can recover its face value by delivery alone. For

this reason, a blank indorsement should be used only in limited situations, such as at a bank teller's window. A blank indorsement turns order paper into bearer paper and may be transferred by delivery alone. When an instrument is made payable to a person under a misspelled name or a name other than that person's own, the payee may indorse in the incorrect name, in the correct name, or in both. Signatures in both names may be required by a person paying or giving value for the instrument.

## EXAMPLE 16-2: Blank Indorsement

Carol Barcley received her first paycheck from the restaurant where she worked as a part time hostess. She took the check to the bank, where she indorsed it in blank at the teller's window. This was a proper time and place to use a blank indorsement because there was no likelihood that the check would get lost or stolen.

> **INDORSE HERE**
> *Carol Barcley*
>
> **BELOW THIS LINE**

> *February 29,* 20__
> *Carol Barcley* $ *85.00*
> *ty-five* 00/100 ___ DOLLARS
>
> Conrad's Restaurant
>
> By *Joseph Conrad*

**Special Indorsements**  A special indorsement (also called an indorsement in full) is made by writing the words *pay to the order of* or *pay to,* followed by the name of the person to whom it is to be transferred (the indorsee) and the signature of the indorser. When indorsed in this manner, the instrument remains an order instrument and must be indorsed by the indorsee before it can be negotiated further. The holder of an instrument may convert a blank indorsement into a special indorsement by writing the words *pay to the order of a person* or *pay to a person* above the indorser's signature.

## EXAMPLE 16-3: Special Indorsement

Frank Cully withdrew $3,500 from his savings account to buy a car from Glendale Motors, Inc. When he made the withdrawal, Cully received a check from the bank payable to him for $3,500. He took the check to Glendale Motors, indorsed it with a special indorsement, and received title to the car. A special indorsement (indorsement in full) creates order paper, which requires the signature of the indorsee. Because the check could not be legally transferred or negotiated further until Glendale indorsed it, all parties were protected.

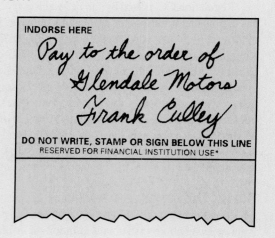

> **INDORSE HERE**
> *Pay to the order of*
> *Glendale Motors*
> *Frank Culley*
>
> **DO NOT WRITE, STAMP OR SIGN BELOW THIS LINE**
> RESERVED FOR FINANCIAL INSTITUTION USE*

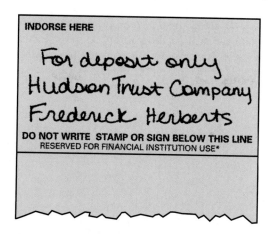

**INDORSE HERE**

*For deposit only*
*Hudson Trust Company*
*Frederick Herberts*

**DO NOT WRITE  STAMP OR SIGN BELOW THIS LINE**
RESERVED FOR FINANCIAL INSTITUTION USE*

**Figure 16-9**  A restrictive indorsement limits the subsequent use of the instrument.

**Restrictive Indorsements**  A restrictive indorsement limits the rights of the indorsee in some manner to protect the rights of the indorser. Indorsements for deposit or collection are restrictive indorsements designed to get an instrument into the banking system for the purpose of deposit or collection. When a check is indorsed "for deposit only," as in Figure 16-9, the amount of the instrument is credited to the indorser's account before it is negotiated further. Retail stores often stamp each check "for deposit only" when it is received. This wording provides protection in the event the check is stolen. Checks mailed to the bank for deposit should always be indorsed in this way. An indorsement that purports to prohibit further transfer, such as "pay Olga Peterson only," may be further negotiated after the directions in the indorsement are carried out. Thus, after Olga Peterson is paid, any holder of the instrument may continue to negotiate it. A restrictive indorsement does not prevent further transfer or negotiation of the instrument.

A conditional indorsement, a type of restrictive indorsement, purports to make the rights of the indorsee subject to the happening of a certain event or condition. A person paying the instrument or taking it for value, however, may disregard the condition.

## EXAMPLE 16-4:  Conditional Indorsement

Gallo wished to transfer a dividend check that he received to his grandson, James Ingram, as a birthday gift (see the indorsement in the illustration). Because Gallo did not want Ingram to cash the check before his eighteenth birthday, he issued a conditional indorsement. However, under the UCC, a bank or anyone else who gives Ingram money or value for the check will not be affected by the condition.

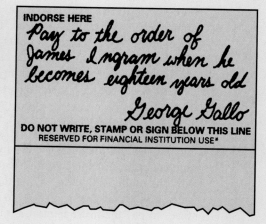

**INDORSE HERE**
*Pay to the order of*
*James Ingram when he*
*becomes eighteen years old*
*George Gallo*

**DO NOT WRITE, STAMP OR SIGN BELOW THIS LINE**
RESERVED FOR FINANCIAL INSTITUTION USE*

**Qualified Indorsements**   A **qualified indorsement** is one in which words have been added to the signature that limit the liability of the indorser. By adding the words *without recourse* to the indorsement, the indorser is not liable in the event the instrument is dishonored, that is, not paid by the maker or drawer.

## EXAMPLE 16-5: Qualified Indorsement

A $25,000 check was made payable to Attorney Samuel Brock in payment of a client's claim. Brock indorsed the check to the client, George Rose, "without recourse." By using this indorsement, Brock would not be responsible for payment if the check failed to clear, because a qualified indorsement limits the contractual liability of the indorser.

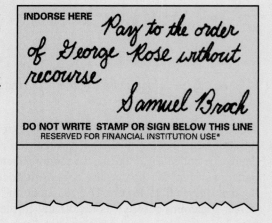

INDORSE HERE

*Pay to the order of George Rose without recourse*

*Samuel Brock*

**DO NOT WRITE  STAMP OR SIGN BELOW THIS LINE**
RESERVED FOR FINANCIAL INSTITUTION USE*

# Obligations of Indorsers

Indorsements have threefold significance. In addition to being necessary to negotiate order paper, they create obligations on the part of the indorser. These obligations come in the form of implied warranties and a contractual promise to pay subsequent holders of the instrument.

**Warranties of Indorsers**   An indorser who receives consideration for an instrument makes five warranties to subsequent transferees of the instrument. These five warranties are as follows. First, the indorser is entitled to enforce the instrument. This warranty gives assurances to subsequent holders that the person indorsing it did not steal it or come into possession of it in an unlawful manner. Second, the indorser warrants that all signatures are authentic and authorized. Third, the next warranty is that the instrument has not been altered. The indorser warrants that there has been no alteration or other irregularity. Fourth, the instrument is not subject to a defense of any party that can be asserted against the indorser. Fifth, the last warranty provides that the indorser has no knowledge of the bankruptcy of the maker, acceptor, or drawer.

**Contract of Indorsers**   Unless an indorsement states otherwise (e.g., by words such as *without recourse*), every indorser agrees to pay any subsequent holder the face amount of the instrument if it is **dishonored** (not paid by the maker or drawee). To enforce this obligation, it is necessary for the holder to do two things. The holder of an instrument must first present it for payment to the maker or drawee when it is due. If that person refuses to pay the instrument, it is said to be dishonored. The holder then must notify the indorser or indorsers of the dishonor. If the holder is a bank, notice must be given by midnight of the next banking day. Holders other than banks must give notice within 30 days after the dishonor. Failure by the holder to make presentment and give timely notice of dishonor to an indorser has the effect of discharging that indorser from liability on the contract to pay subsequent holders of the instrument.

## Multiple Payees, Missing and Forged Indorsements

If an instrument is payable to either of two payees, as in "pay to the order of Eric Foss *or* Betty Foss," the indorsement of only one of the payees is necessary to negotiate it. However, if an instrument is payable to both of two payees, as in "pay to the order of Eric Foss *and* Betty Foss," the indorsement of both payees is necessary for a proper negotiation. A bank that has taken an instrument from a customer to send through the bank collection process may supply any indorsement of the customer that is necessary to title. This rule is designed to speed up bank collections by eliminating the necessity to return to a depositor any items that were not indorsed. Such an indorsement may not be supplied by a bank, however, if the instrument contains the words *payee's indorsement required.*

## Unauthorized or Forged Indorsements

An unauthorized signature or indorsement is one made without actual, implied, or apparent authority. With three exceptions and unless ratified (approved afterward), an unauthorized or forged signature does not serve as the signature of the person whose name is signed. It has no effect. In addition, when an instrument is paid on a forged indorsement, the tort of conversion takes place. For example, when a bank pays proceeds to a forger and the payee's wishes are not carried out, the bank is held liable for converting the payee's funds. **Conversion** is the wrongful exercise of dominion and control over another's personal property.

## THE OPENING CASE *Revisited, Part I*
### Stolen Checks, Forgery, and Credit Card Debt: *Getty Petroleum v. American Express*, Round 2

Getty's dealer-owned stations accepted credit cards as payment from its customers. The payments from the credit card companies went to Getty which then generated checks payable to the individual dealerships. Of course, as we saw above, the checks never went to the dealers. Instead, Getty voided the checks and credited the accounts of the dealers against their future purchases. Lewis's job was to void the checks. Rather than voiding them, she forged the indorsement of the payees, and sent the checks to American Express and other credit card companies to pay off her own credit card debt. The credit card companies forwarded the checks through banking channels after crediting Lewis's accounts. The checks were then honored by Getty's bank. When the forgeries were discovered Getty sued the credit card companies for the lost money. Getty argued that, whenever a credit card company pays money to a forger, that credit card company is liable for the lost money. Getty was correct too, well almost. Had it not been for a very important exception to the rule, the petroleum company might have actually won the case.

## THE OPENING CASE *Revisited, Part II*
### Stolen Checks, Forgery, and Credit Card Debt: *Getty Petroleum v. American Express*, Round 3

In *Getty Petroleum v. American Express*, Getty argued that, when a credit card company pays money to a forger, that credit card company is liable for the lost money. Under this rule, Getty was "in like Flynn," or would have been, had it not been for the fictitious payee exception. The fictitious payee exception says that, when the maker or drawer of an instrument does not intend for the payee to have an interest in the instrument, any indorsement is effective. So, in this case, because the drawer (Getty) had no intent to transfer any interests to the payees (the service stations) anyone who signs those instruments (Lewis) has indorsed them properly and the loss falls on the shoulders of the drawer (Getty).

**Exceptions**   There are three exceptions to the general rule that an unauthorized indorsement has no effect. The exceptions, shown in the following list, are designed primarily to promote negotiability of negotiable instruments.

1. *Imposters*   An imposter is someone who impersonates another. When an instrument is issued to an imposter on the false belief that the imposter is the payee, the indorsement by any person in the name of the payee is treated as an effective indorsement. This rule places the loss, in such a case, on the one who is in the best position to prevent it—the maker or drawer of the instrument.

2. *Padded Payrolls*   When an agent or employee of the maker or drawer pads the payroll by supplying the employer with fictitious names, an indorsement by any person in the name of each fictitious payee is effective. This rule places the burden of preventing this type of fraud on the party who is in the best position to prevent it—either the drawer (if a draft) or the maker (if a note).

3. *No Interest Intended; Fictitious Payee*   When the maker or drawer of an instrument intends the payee to have no interest in the instrument or the payee is a fictitious person, an indorsement by any person in the name of the payee is effective.

### quick quiz 16-2

| | | |
|---|---|---|
| 1. An instrument is indorsed when the holder signs it, thereby indicating the intent to transfer ownership to another. | true \| false | |
| 2. Instruments that do not meet all of the requirements of negotiability cannot be negotiated nor transferred by assignment. | true \| false | |
| 3. An unauthorized signature or indorsement is one made without actual, implied, or apparent authority. | true \| false | |

## Summary

**16.1**   The law of negotiable instruments is found in Article 3 of the UCC. Under the UCC, a negotiable instrument is a written document signed by the maker that contains an unconditional promise or order to pay a fixed amount of money on demand or at a definite time to the bearer or to order. There are two basic kinds of negotiable instruments: promise instruments (including notes and certificates of deposit) and order instruments (including drafts and checks). The following are parties to negotiable instruments: maker or co-maker; drawer; issuer; drawee; payee; bearer; holder; holder in due course; indorser; indorsee, and acceptor. To be negotiable, instruments must: (1) be in writing; (2) be signed by the maker or drawer; (3) contain an unconditional promise or order to pay; (4) be made out for a fixed amount of money; (5) be payable on demand or at a definite time, and (6) except for checks, be payable to order or to bearer.

**16.2**   When an instrument is first delivered by the maker or drawer for the purpose of giving rights to any person, it is said to be *issued*. When the person to whom it is issued delivers it to a third party, it is *transferred*.

Instruments can be transferred by assignment or by negotiation. An instrument is indorsed when the holder signs it, thereby indicating the intent to transfer ownership to another. Indorsements may be written in ink, typewritten, or stamped with a rubber stamp. There are four commonly used types of indorsements: blank indorsements, special indorsements, restrictive indorsements, and qualified indorsements. Indorsements have threefold significance. In addition to being necessary to negotiate order paper, they create obligations on the part of the indorser. These obligations come in the form of implied warranties and a contractual promise to pay subsequent holders of the instrument. An unauthorized signature or indorsement is one made without actual, implied, or apparent authority.

## Key Terms

acceptance, 345

acceptor, 348

allonge, 352

assignment, 352

bank draft, 347

bearer, 348

bearer paper, 352

bill of exchange, 345

blank indorsement, 353

cashier's check, 347

certificate of
deposit (CD), 344

certified check, 347

check, 346

comakers, 348

conditional indorsement, 355

conversion, 357

demand note, 344

dishonored, 356

domestic bill of exchange, 346

draft, 345

drawee, 348

drawer, 348

foreign draft, 346

holder, 348

holder in due course, 348

indorsee, 348

indorsement in full, 354

indorser, 348

installment note, 344

international bill of
exchange, 346

issuer, 348

maker, 348

money order, 348

negotiable instrument, 344

negotiation, 352

note, 344

order paper, 352

payee, 348

qualified indorsement, 356

restrictive indorsement, 355

sight draft, 345

special indorsement, 354

teller's check, 347

time draft, 345

trade acceptance, 345

traveler's check, 348

## Questions for Review and Discussion

1. What is the purpose of a negotiable instrument?
2. Which negotiable instruments contain a promise to pay money?
3. Which negotiable instruments contain an order to pay money?
4. What are the different types of checks and money orders?
5. What are the requirements of a negotiable instrument?

6. What is the difference between an assignment and a negotiation of an instrument?

7. What are the four kinds of indorsements?

8. What are the implied warranties that are related to indorsements?

9. What contract is made when people indorse negotiable instruments?

10. What is the legal effect of a forged indorsement?

## Cases for Analysis

1. Haas deposited two checks totaling $42,000 into his account at the Meridian Bank and, at the same time, purchased a $35,000 money order. He then went to the Trump Plaza and Casino, where he received cash for the money order for gambling purposes. The next day, the two checks were returned to Meridian Bank unpaid with a notation "account closed." The bank put a stop-payment order on the money order and refused to pay it when it was presented by Trump Plaza for payment. Trump argued that payment could not be stopped on a money order. Do you agree with Trump? Why or why not? *Trump Plaza Associates v. Haas,* 692 A. 2d 86 (NJ).

2. Gail Sak wanted to give her niece, Kim Ryan, a gift of money for her twenty-first birthday, which was two weeks away. Because she was leaving for a trip to Europe the next day, Sak gave Ryan a check dated that day reading, "Pay to the order of Kim Ryan when she reaches the age of twenty-one (signed) Gail Sak." Was the check negotiable? Why or why not?

3. In exchange for legal services rendered to her by the law firm of Westmoreland, Hall, and Bryan, Barbara Hall wrote the following letter: "I agree to pay to your firm as attorney's fees for representing me in obtaining property settlement agreement and tax advice, the sum of $2,760, payable at the rate of $230 per month for twelve (12) months beginning January 1, 1970. Very truly yours, Barbara Hall Hodge." Was the letter a negotiable instrument? Give the reason for your answer. *Hall v. Westmoreland, Hall & Bryan,* 182 S.E.2d 539 (GA).

4. Barton signed a promissory note promising to pay to the order of Scott Hudgens Realty & Mortgage, Inc., the sum of $3,000. The note stated, "This amount is due and payable upon evidence of an acceptable permanent loan . . . and upon acceptance of the loan commitment." Was the note negotiable? Why or why not? *Barton v. Scott Hudgens Realty & Mortg.,* 222 S.E.2d 126 (GA).

5. Melanie E. Regan wrote the following words on a sheet of notebook paper in her own handwriting: "Twenty years from date, I, Melanie E. Regan promise to pay to the order of Ryan M. Brown $10,000 without interest." She did not sign the paper at the end. Is the instrument negotiable? Why or why not?

6. David Shin, a silver collector, ran short of cash. He borrowed $1,500 from Vinnie Gaff, giving Gaff the following note: "Thirty days from date, I promise to pay to the order of Vinnie Gaff $1,500 worth of silver (signed) David Shin." Gaff indorsed the note and gave it to Kia Lai in exchange for services rendered by Lai. What legal term describes the transfer of the note from Gaff to Lai? Explain your answer.

7. Powell, intending to write a check to Thompson Electric, Inc., instead made it payable to the order of "Tompson Electric." Thompson Electric, Inc., indorsed the check with its name correctly spelled. Was the indorsement valid? Why or why not? *State v. Powell,* 551 P.2d 902 (KS).

8. Tufi forged the payee's name on the front of a U.S. Treasurer's check. When convicted of a forgery, he appealed, contending that a signature on the front of a check cannot be an indorsement. May an indorsement be written on the front of an instrument? Explain. *United States v. Tufi,* 536 F.2d 855 (9th Cir.).

9. Morse wrote a check for $2,500 payable to Reynolds for services rendered. Reynolds fraudulently raised the check to $5,500, indorsed it "without recourse," and deposited it in her bank account. Later, when the alteration was discovered, Reynolds argued that she was not responsible because her indorsement was qualified. Do you agree with Reynolds? Why or why not? See also *Wolfram v. Halloway,* 361 N.E.2d 587 (IL).

10. Sanders borrowed $5,000 from Waskow, giving Waskow a promissory note that read, "One year

from date, I promise to pay to the order of James Waskow $5,000, without interest (signed) Mary Sanders." Six months later, Waskow died. The unindorsed note was in the possession of Waskow's landlord, who claimed that Waskow had given him the note in payment of back rent. Was the landlord a holder of the note? Why or why not? See also *Smathers v. Smathers*, 239 S.E.2d 637 (NC).

## quick quiz Answers

| 16.1 | 16.2 |
|------|------|
| 1. T | 1. T |
| 2. F | 2. F |
| 3. T | 3. T |

# Chapter 17

## Holders in Due Course, Defenses, and Liabilities

## THE OPENING CASE  All in a Day's Work: *Montalbano and Friends v. Scranton Bank and Trust*

This case is really three separate cases, each one adding a new twist to the life and times of Scranton Bank and Trust, a small banking firm in Scranton, Pennsylvania. In the first case, Norwalk Auto Mall sold a vintage Jaguar to George Montalbano for $34,000. In order to convince Montalbano to buy the vehicle, Jerry Morris, a sales rep for Norwalk, told him that the radiator was new and the brakes had been replaced three weeks earlier. Neither of these things had been done and everyone at Norwalk, including Harry Jameson, the owner, knew that. Montalbano gave Norwalk a check from his account at Scranton for the $34,000. While on his way to Plymouth, Massachusetts, the car's brakes failed and, after a quick investigation, Montalbano discovered the fraud. He immediately stopped payment on the check. However, back home in Scranton, Jameson had indorsed the check and given it to Calvin Calloway, a holder in due course. In the second case, in another part of town, Greg and Samantha Laszlo had contracted with Englehardt and Sons, Construction for the construction of their new home on the outskirts of Scranton. They financed their loan through a lending company named Lascher Loans which issued checks periodically as the construction continued. The checks were payable to Greg, Samantha, and Englehardt. By a strange twist of fate, on the day of the Montalbano fiasco, the last check was issued by

Lascher and was deposited in Englehardt's account at Scranton Bank and Trust without Samantha's indorsement. In the third and last case, Norwalk Auto Mall purchased three vintage autos at a car auction from Gary Thatcher, paying for them with two checks that totaled $78,453.00. Thatcher presented the checks and asked for cash because he was going to another auction and needed it. Lew Oswald, the teller on duty did so without getting the bank manager's okay, which was standard procedure at Scranton (and in the business for that matter). A little while later, on the same day as the Englehardt deposit, Norwalk stopped payment on the checks because the title to the three cars was not clear. Scranton later found itself embroiled in several lawsuits. In all three lawsuits, the bank argued that it was a holder in due course of the checks in its possession and, therefore, could collect from Montalbano, Englehardt, and Norwalk. Somewhere in this tangle of legal technicalities there exists a rule that will unravel all of these cases and will tell Scranton what it has to do. As you read the chapter see if you can detect just what that rule is and how the courts should decide each of these cases.

**Opening Case Questions**

1. What are the three characteristics of a holder in due course? Are all three necessary or will only

one or two satisfy the court that "holder status" exists? Explain.

2. What does *good faith* mean and how is it related to *honesty in fact*? Explain.

3. In the *Montalbano* case, does the fact that the Norwalk sales rep committed fraud affect Calloway's status as a holder in due course? Explain.

4. In the *Englehardt* case, does it matter that Samantha never indorsed the final check from Lascher? Explain.

5. In the *Norwalk* case, does the teller's failure to secure the manager's permission eliminate the bank's holder status? Why or why not?

 **Learning Objectives**

1. State the characteristics of being a holder in due course.
2. Describe the special protection given to a holder in due course.
3. Define holder.
4. Explain the protection given to a holder through a holder in due course.
5. Name six personal defenses.
6. Discuss the protection given to people who sign consumer credit contracts.
7. Name six real defenses and explain the significance of a real defense.
8. Explain primary liability.
9. Explain secondary liability.
10. Describe the conditions that must be met to hold a secondary party liable.

# 17-1 Holder in Due Course

A basic principle of contract law is that people cannot transfer greater rights than they have themselves. This rule, however, does not apply to the law of negotiable instruments. People who are *holders in due course* of negotiable instruments can receive even more rights than

## THE OPENING CASE *Revisited, Part I*
### All in a Day's Work: *Montalbano and Friends v. Scranton Bank and Trust*, Round 2

The Opening Case at the beginning of this chapter involves three separate cases. In the first case, Norwalk Auto Mall sold a vintage Jaguar to George Montalbano for $34,000. In order to convince Montalbano to buy the vehicle, Jerry Morris, a sales rep for Norwalk, told him that the radiator was new and that the brakes had been replaced three weeks earlier. Neither of these things had been done and everyone at Norwalk, including Harry Jameson, the owner, knew that. Montalbano gave Jameson a check drawn on his account at Scranton Bank and Trust for the $34,000. While on his way to

Plymouth, Massachusetts, the car's brakes failed and, after a quick investigation, Montalbano had discovered the fraud. He immediately stopped payment on the check. However, back home in Scranton, Jameson had indorsed and given it to Calvin Calloway, a holder in due course. Calloway can collect he full $34,000 from Montalbano. Even though Montalbano was defrauded, he cannot use that defense against a holder in due course, because holders are protected against this kind of fraud. His action would have to be against Morris, Jameson, and Norwalk because they committed the fraud.

## THE OPENING CASE *Revisited, Part II*
### All in a Day's Work: *Montalbano and Friends v. Scranton Bank and Trust, Round 3*

In the second case in the Opening Case at the beginning of this chapter, Greg and Samantha Laszlo contracted with Englehardt and Sons, Construction for the construction of their new home on the outskirts of Scranton. They financed their loan through a lending company named Lascher Loans which issued checks periodically as the construction continued. The checks were payable to Greg, Samantha, and Englehardt. By a strange twist of fate, on the day of the Montalbano

fiasco, the last check was issued by Lascher and was deposited in Englehardt's account at Scranton Bank and Trust without Samantha's indorsement. Unfortunately for the bank manager, Scranton Bank and Trust was not a holder because, without Samantha's indorsement, the check was not issued or indorsed to it, to bearer, or in blank. Because Scranton Bank and Trust was not a holder, it could not be a holder in due course.

UCC Revised (1990)
3-302(a)(2) (see
page 869)

those who held the instruments before them. Largely for this reason, negotiable instruments are used frequently and passed liberally from one person to another.

## The Elements of a Holder in Due Course

**LO2**

**LO3**

To be a holder in due course, the person in possession of the instrument must first be a **holder**. To be a holder means that the instrument must have been issued or indorsed to that person, to that person's order, or to bearer. A **holder in due course** is a *holder* who takes an instrument: (1) for value; (2) in good faith, and (3) without notice that anything is wrong with the underlying transaction.

A person must give value for an instrument to qualify as a holder in due course. Thus, if an instrument is transferred to a person as a gift, that person would not qualify as a holder in due course. To be a holder in due course, the holder must take the instrument in

UCC Revised (1990)
1-201(20) (see
page 817)

## THE OPENING CASE *Revisited, Part III*
### All in a Day's Work: *Montalbano and Friends v. Scranton Bank and Trust, Round 4*

In the third and last case, Norwalk Auto Mall purchased three vintage autos at a car auction from Gary Thatcher, paying for them with two checks that totaled $78,453.00. Thatcher presented the checks at Scranton Bank and Trust and asked for cash because he was going to another auction and needed it. Lew Oswald, the teller on duty did so without getting the manager's okay, which was standard procedure at Scranton Bank and Trust (and in the business for that matter). A little while later, on the same day as the Englehardt deposit, Norwalk stopped payment on the checks because the title to the three cars was not

clear. The lower court held that Scranton Bank and Trust was not a holder in due course because of the teller's negligence in failing to obtain the manager's approval before cashing the checks. The appellate court reversed the lower court's decision, holding that good faith means honesty in fact. The court said, "Nothing in the definition suggests that, in addition to being honest, the holder must exercise due care to be in good faith." Because the Scranton Bank and Trust was a holder in due course, it was able to recover the $78,453.00 from the drawer of the checks, Norwalk Auto Mall.

good faith. Good faith means *honesty in fact* and fair dealing. It requires that the taker of a commercial instrument act honestly. If the taker is negligent in not discovering that something was wrong with the paper, it does not establish lack of good faith.

To be a holder in due course, a holder must not have notice of any claim or defense to an instrument or notice that an instrument is overdue or has been dishonored. A holder has notice of a claim or defense if the instrument bears visible evidence of forgery or alteration. The same is true if the instrument is so incomplete or irregular as to make its legal acceptance doubtful. Notice of a claim or defense is also considered given if the holder knows that the obligation of any party is voidable. A holder has notice that a demand instrument is overdue when more than a reasonable length of time has elapsed since it was issued. A check is overdue 90 days after its date. For other instruments, such as a note or draft, a reasonable time depends on the circumstances of each case. Knowledge of some facts does not in itself give the holder notice of a defense or claim. For example, the fact that an instrument is postdated or antedated does not prevent someone from being a holder in due course; neither does completing an incomplete instrument constitute having such notice, unless the holder has notice of any improper completion.

## Holder through a Holder in Due Course

A holder who receives an instrument from a holder in due course acquires the rights of the holder in due course, even though he or she does not qualify as a holder in due course. This stipulation is called a **shelter provision**. It is designed to permit holders in due course to transfer all of the rights they have in the paper to others. The shelter does not apply to a holder who has committed fraud or an illegal act.

UCC Revised (1990) 3-304 (see page 870)

UCC Revised (1990) 3-203(b) (see page 867)

### EXAMPLE 17-1: Holder through a Holder in Due Course

Vance Wittmer gave Hillary Mullins a $225 check in payment for an antique vase. Mullins indorsed the check and gave it to Ellen Hudson in payment for a debt. Because Hudson took the check for value, in good faith, and without notice, he was a holder in due course of the instrument. Hudson indorsed the instrument with a special indorsement and gave it to his niece Alison as a graduation present. Alison was not a holder in due course because she did not give value for the instrument. However, she had the rights of a holder in due course, because she received the check from a holder in due course.

## A QUESTION OF ETHICS

Michael Carrington, the CEO of the Ice-Fire Security Corporation pushed his marketing division into developing a hard-hitting marketing campaign that included several new aggressive strategies. At one level the marketing executives launched a telemarketing promotion using a customer list that Ice-Fire had purchased from several publishers who kept track of buyers interested in the types services and products provided by Ice-Fire. Whenever a potential customer responded favorably to the telemarketer's call, he or she was placed on the company's direct mail advertising list. The direct mail department then generated a series of mailings, each of which included a document that cleverly produced a sheet of paper about the size of a dollar bill that appeared to be a valid check but which lacked one of the essential requirements of negotiability, such as the words, "Good only when applied to the purchase of . . ." Clearly then the entire direct mail campaign was designed to provoke the customer to open the mail, be duped by the imitation check, and make a purchase that ends up costing more than it appeared, because of the implied message induced by the fictitious check. Is this publishers' sale of the customer list ethical? Is Ice-Fire's purchase and use of the lists ethical? Is a campaign that targets susceptible customers ethical? Is the use of the simulated check ethical? Give reasons for each answer. Be consistent in your responses. If you have a difficult time being consistent, then your principle itself may be flawed. Try formulating a new guiding principle. If you're stumped on the nature of a guiding principle, look back to the first chapter in the book, "Ethics, Social Responsibility, and the Law." The information in that chapter should help you.

## quick quiz 17-1

1. A holder is a person who is in possession of a negotiable instrument that is issued or indorsed to that person's order or to bearer.    true | false

2. Able bought a book from Baker and gave Baker a $25 check. Baker indorsed the check and gave it to Charlie in payment of a debt. Charlie was not a holder in due course of the check.    true | false

3. Charlie indorsed the check he received in Question 2 from Baker and gave it to David as a birthday gift. David had the rights of a holder in due course of the check.    true | false

# 17-2 Personal Defenses

UCC Revised (1990) 3-305(b) (see page 870)

The favorable treatment that holders in due course receive ensures that they take instruments free from all claims to them on the part of any person and free from all personal defenses of any party *with whom they have not dealt.* **Personal defenses** (also called **limited defenses**) are defenses that can be used against a holder but not a holder in due course of a negotiable instrument. (The terms *personal defense* and *limited defense* come from common law and are not used in the UCC.) The most common personal defenses are breach of contract, failure or lack of consideration, fraud in the inducement, lack of delivery, and payment (see Table 17-1).

## Breach of Contract

Negotiable instruments are often issued in exchange for property, services, or some other obligation as part of an underlying contract. Sometimes, the party to whom the instrument was issued breaches the contract by failing to perform or by performing in an unsatisfactory manner. If suit is brought on the instrument by a holder against the maker or drawer, the latter may use breach of contract as a defense. Because breach of contract is a personal defense however, it may not be used if the holder of the instrument is a holder in due course unless the parties dealt with each other.

## Lack or Failure of Consideration

**Lack of consideration** is a defense that may be used by a maker or drawer of an instrument when no consideration existed in the underlying contract for which the instrument

| **Table 17-1**  Most Common Personal Defenses | |
|---|---|
| **Defense** | **Description** |
| Breach of contract | One of the parties to a contract has failed to do what he or she has previously agreed to do. |
| Failure of consideration | One of the parties to a contract has failed to furnish the agreed consideration. |
| Lack of consideration | No consideration existed in the underlying contract for which the instrument was issued. |
| Fraud in the inducement | The drawer or maker of an instrument is persuaded to enter negotiable instrument into a contract because of a misrepresentation of some fact regarding the item purchased. |
| Lack of delivery of a negotiable instrument | A payee forcibly, unlawfully, or conditionally takes an instrument from a maker or drawer. The maker or drawer did not intend to deliver the instrument. |
| Payment of a negotiable instrument | The drawer or maker of an instrument has paid the amount of the instrument. |

was issued. The ordinary rules of contract law are followed to determine the presence or absence of consideration in such a case.

## EXAMPLE 17-2: Lack of Consideration

Lowell, without any mention of payment, helped his friend Ransom move from Cambridge to Gambier. At the end of the day, after he was in his new apartment, Ransom told Lowell that he'd give him some money for helping him move. The next day, Ransom gave Lowell a $200 check. Lowell cashed the check at a local bar and promptly left town. Ransom then stopped payment on the check. Ransom's promise to pay Lowell was not enforceable because Lowell had completed the work when the promise was made—it was past consideration. The local bar could recover the $200 from Ransom, however, because it was a holder in due course and was not subject to the personal defense of lack of consideration.

Failure of consideration is not the same as a lack of consideration, although many people confuse the two. **Failure of consideration** is a defense that the maker or drawer may use when the other party breaches the contract by not furnishing the agreed consideration. Both lack of consideration and failure of consideration are personal defenses. They may not be used against a holder in due course.

## Fraud in the Inducement

There are two kinds of fraud: fraud in the inducement and fraud as to the essential nature of the transaction. The first is a personal defense; the second is a real defense, discussed later in the chapter. The five elements of fraud are explained in depth in the contract law unit. When someone is induced by a fraudulent statement to enter into a contract, that person may have the contract rescinded. However, he or she may not use that defense against a holder in due course. A holder in due course can cut through the defense of fraud in the inducement and collect from the person who was defrauded. In the Opening Case, Montalbano had to pay Calloway, a holder in due course of the check, even though he had been fraudulently induced by Morris and Jameson to write the check to Norwalk Auto Mall.

## Lack of Delivery, Payment, and Consumer Protection

Every commercial instrument may be revoked by its maker or drawer until it has been delivered to the payee. *Delivery* is the voluntary transfer of possession of an instrument from one person to another. If the transfer of possession is not voluntary, the instrument has not been "issued." Thus, in the event a payee forcibly, unlawfully, or conditionally takes an instrument from a drawer, the drawer has the defense of lack of delivery. The payee therefore may be denied the right to collect on the instrument. If the payee negotiates the instrument to a holder in due course, however, this defense is removed.

### EXAMPLE 17-3:  Lack of Delivery

Morse wrote out a check payable to the order of Smith, intending to give it to Smith after Smith had completed a certain amount of work. Smith discovered the check on Morse's desk and took it without doing any work at all. Smith was not entitled to the check; however, if she negotiated the check to a bank, store, or private party for value, in good faith, and without notice (a holder in due course), Morse would have to honor the check even though Smith failed to do the required work.

Payment of an instrument by a maker or drawee usually ends the obligations of the parties. However, if a negotiable instrument is negotiated to a holder in due course after it has been paid, it will have to be paid again. This rule exists because payment is a personal defense, which cannot be used against a holder in due course. Because of this rule, anyone who pays a demand instrument should have it marked "paid" and take possession of it. This requirement is not as important with a time instrument, unless it is paid before its due date, because no one can be a holder in due course of a past due instrument.

The protection that is given to holders in due course was not always fair to consumers who bought on credit in the past.

### EXAMPLE 17-4:  Former Law

In 1975, Ruby Merlin bought a car from a used car dealer. She paid a small amount down and signed a consumer sales contract agreeing to pay the balance in 24 monthly installments. The used car dealer negotiated the contract (which was actually a promissory note) to a finance company and received payment immediately. The next day, the car's transmission stopped working, and the dealer refused to fix it. Merlin would still have to pay the finance company the full amount due on the note because the finance company was a holder in due course and was not subject to personal defenses.

In 1976, the FTC adopted the **holder in due course rule**. Under this rule, holders of consumer credit contracts who are holders in due course are subject to all claims and defenses that the buyer could use against the seller, including personal defenses. Thus, if the situation described in Example 17-4 were to occur today, Merlin's defense that the car's transmission did not work could be used against the finance company, even though it was a holder in due course. When sellers of consumer products have arrangements with financial institutions to finance their customer's purchases, the financial institutions are subject to the customer's personal defenses. They lose their protection as holders in due course.

## quick quiz 17-2

1. Personal defenses are defenses that can be used against a holder in due course but not a holder of a negotiable instrument.   true | false

2. The most common personal defenses are infancy and illegality.   true | false

3. If a negotiable instrument is negotiated to a holder in due course after it has been paid, it will have to be paid again.   true | false

# 17-3 Real Defenses

Some defenses can be used against everyone, including holders in due course. These defenses are known as **real defenses** or **universal defenses**. The terms *real* and *universal defense* come from the common law and are not used in the UCC. No one is required to pay an instrument when they have a real defense. Real defenses include infancy and mental incompetence, illegality and duress, fraud as to the essential nature of the transaction, bankruptcy, unauthorized signature, and alteration (see Table 17-2).

UCC Revised (1990) 3-305(a)(1) (see page 870)

## Infancy and Mental Incompetence

A minor (person under the age of 18 years) or mental incompetent need not honor a negotiable instrument if it was given in payment for a contract that the minor or mental

## Table 17-2  Most Common Real Defenses

| Defense | Description |
| --- | --- |
| Infancy and mental incompetence | The maker or drawer of the instrument was a minor or mentally incompetent. |
| Illegality | The underlying contract for which the instrument was issued was illegal. |
| Duress | The instrument was drawn against the will of the maker or drawer because of threats of force or bodily harm. |
| Fraud as to the essential nature of the transaction | A false statement was made to the maker or drawer about the nature of the instrument being signed. |
| Bankruptcy | An order for relief was issued by the federal court that ended all the debtor's outstanding contractual obligations. |
| Unauthorized signature | Someone wrongfully signed another's name on an instrument without authority to do so. |
| Material alteration | The amount of the instrument or the payee's name was changed wrongfully after it was originally drawn by the maker or drawer. |

incompetent may disaffirm on the grounds of minority or incompetency. This rule is true even if the instrument comes into the hands of a holder in due course. Similarly, persons who have been found insane by a court are not liable on a negotiable instrument, because their contracts are void.

## Illegality and Duress

An instrument that is associated with duress or an illegal act, such as twisting one's arm or drug trafficking, would be void and uncollectible by anyone, even a holder in due course. This provision is true even if the holder in due course is unaware of the illegal acts or conditions.

### EXAMPLE 17-5: Illegality—a Real Defense

The Condado Aruba Caribbean Hotel loaned Tickel, who resided in Colorado, $20,000. The money was loaned for the purpose of gambling at the hotel's casino in Aruba, Netherlands Antilles, where gambling is legal. Tickel wrote two checks to repay the debt, each of which was returned for insufficient funds. When suit was brought on the checks, the Colorado court held that gambling debts are unenforceable in that state even against a holder in due course. Tickel was not liable on the checks that he had written to the hotel.

## Fraud as to the Essential Nature of the Transaction

Fraud as to the essential nature of the transaction is more serious than fraud in the inducement. When this type of fraud occurs, the defrauded party has no knowledge or opportunity to learn of the true character or terms of the matter. Because of its seriousness, it is a real defense and may be used against anyone, even a holder in due course.

### EXAMPLE 17-6: Fraud as to the Essential Nature of the Transaction

Duffy, who was almost blind, was asked by Ingram to sign a receipt. Duffy signed the paper without having had it read to him. The paper was actually a note promising to pay Ingram $2,500. Duffy would not be required to pay the note, even to a holder in due course, because this kind of fraud is more critical than fraud in the inducement.

## Bankruptcy

Bankruptcy may be used as a defense to all negotiable instruments, even those in the hands of a holder in due course. Holders of such instruments will receive treatment equal to that of other similar creditors when the debtor's assets are collected and divided according to the bankruptcy law.

## Unauthorized Signatures

UCC Revised (1990) 3-403(a) (see page 874)

Whenever someone signs another's name on an instrument without authority, it is a forgery. Unless ratified, it does not operate as the signature of the person whose name is signed. Instead, it operates as the signature of the person who signed it, that is, of the wrongdoer.

## EXAMPLE 17-7:  Forgery—a Real Defense

With no authority to do so, Parks signed Brown's name on a note, promising to pay Rivera $3,000 in 90 days. The note was negotiated by Rivera to a holder in due course. Brown would not have to pay the money to the holder in due course because the unauthorized signature is a real defense. Parks had committed a crime. The holder in due course could recover from Rivera who, in turn, could recover from the wrongdoer, Parks.

## Alteration

Sometimes negotiable instruments are altered after they leave the hands of the maker or drawer. Usually, the alteration involves changing the payee's name or increasing the amount of an instrument. The alteration of an instrument may be used as a real defense. Unless an instrument is written negligently so that it can be easily altered, makers and drawers are not required to pay altered amounts. They must pay only the amount for which the instrument was originally written.

Writing a check in pencil is legal, but not a good idea. It leaves the check vulnerable to alteration by a dishonest person.

## EXAMPLE 17-8:  Alteration—a Real Defense

Martinez wrote out a check in a proper manner for $315 and gave it to Video Sales in payment for a DVD player. Video Sales raised the check to read $815. Martinez's bank honored the altered check. Martinez could seek reimbursement from his bank for $500, the difference between the original and the altered amount.

Any person who negligently contributes to a material alteration of an instrument or an unauthorized signature may not exercise the defense of alteration or lack of authority against a holder in due course, a drawee, or other payor who pays the instrument in good faith. For example, using a pencil to write a check or not being careful to keep the figures compact and clear gives a dishonest holder an opportunity to alter the amount. The careless writer would be without defense.

UCC Revised (1990) 3-407 (see page 875)

UCC Revised (1990) 3-406 (see page 875)

### quick quiz 17-3

1. No one with a real defense is required to pay an instrument.              true | false

2. Fraud in the inducement is more serious than fraud as to the             true | false
   essential nature of the transaction.

3. If a check is written with an erasable pen and later altered by a        true | false
   wrongdoer, the drawer of the check would not be responsible for
   any loss because alteration is a real defense.

UCC Revised (1990) 3-401 (see page 873)

UCC Revised (1990) 3-412, 3-413 (see page 876)

# 17-4 Liability of the Parties

No person is liable on an instrument unless that person's signature or the signature of an authorized agent appears on the instrument. Parties to negotiable instruments have different liability depending on their function.

## Makers, Acceptors, and Certain Drawers

The following are obligated to pay an instrument without reservations of any kind. They are said to be primarily liable: (1) the maker of a note; (2) the issuer of a cashier's check or other draft in which the drawer and the drawee are the same person; and (3) the acceptor of a draft.

## Other Drawers and Indorsers

UCC Revised (1990) 3-414, 3-415 (a)(c) (see pages 876–887)

Other drawers and indorsers have limitations on their obligation to pay an instrument. They are said to be secondarily, or conditionally, liable. The drawer of a draft that has not been accepted is obligated to pay the draft to anyone who is entitled to enforce it; however, if a bank accepts a draft, the drawer is discharged. If a drawee other than a bank accepts a draft and it is later dishonored, the obligation of the drawer is the same as an indorser stated here.

Indorsers are obligated to pay an instrument only when the following conditions are met: (1) The instrument must be properly presented to the drawee or party obliged to pay the instrument, and payment must be demanded; (2) the instrument must be dishonored, that is, payment refused; and (3) notice of the dishonor must be given to the secondary party within the time and in the manner prescribed by the UCC. If all three of these conditions are not met, drawers of drafts and indorsers are discharged from their obligations.

UCC Revised (1990) 3-501 (see page 879)

**Presentment**    Presentment means a demand made by a holder to pay or accept an instrument. Presentment may be made by any commercially reasonable means, including oral, written, or electronic communication. If requested by the person to whom presentment is made, the person making presentment must exhibit the instrument and provide identification.

**Dishonor**    *Dishonor* means to refuse to pay a negotiable instrument when it is due or to refuse to accept it when asked to do so. An instrument is dishonored when proper presentment is made and acceptance or payment is refused. Dishonor also occurs when presentment

UCC Revised (1990) 3-502 (see page 879)

## EXAMPLE 17-9: Dishonor

A note was presented to Baker for payment on the date specified. Baker refused to honor it, claiming the note was a forgery. The holder would have to proceed against the indorsers to obtain payment. The note was dishonored when Baker refused to pay it.

is excused and the instrument is past due and unpaid. The presenting party has recourse against indorsers or other secondary parties after notice of dishonor has been given.

## Notice of Dishonor

Obligations of indorsers and drawers of instruments may not be enforced unless they are given notice of the dishonor or notice is excused. Notice of dishonor may be given by any reasonable means, including oral, written, or electronic communication, and is sufficient if it reasonably identifies the instrument and indicates that the instrument has been dishonored or has not been paid or accepted. The return of an instrument given to a bank for collection is sufficient notice of dishonor.

Nonbank holders must give notice of the dishonor to the drawer and indorsers within 30 days following the day of dishonor. Banks taking instruments for collection must give notice before midnight of the banking day following the day the bank was notified of the dishonor. Delay in giving notice of dishonor is excused when the holder has acted carefully and the delay is due to circumstances beyond the holder's control. Presentment and notice of dishonor are also excused when the party waived either presentment or notice of dishonor.

### quick quiz 17-4

1. Indorsers never have liability to pay.  true | false
2. Presentment can be made by oral, written, or electronic communication.  true | false
3. Notice of dishonor must be given by nonbank holders to indorsers within 30 days following the day of dishonor.  true | false

## Summary

**17.1**  A holder in due course is a holder who takes the instrument for value, in good faith, without notice that it is overdue or has been dishonored, and without notice of any defenses against it or claim to it. Good faith means honesty in fact. A holder who receives an instrument from a holder in due course receives all the rights of the holder in due course.

**17.2**  Personal defenses can be used against a holder but not a holder in due course. The most common personal defenses are breach of contract, lack or failure of consideration, fraud in the inducement, lack of delivery, and payment. Holders of consumer credit contracts who are holders in due course are subject to all claims and defenses that the buyer could use against the seller, including personal defenses.

**17.3**  Real defenses can be used against anyone, including a holder in due course. Real defenses are infancy and mental incompetence, illegality and duress, fraud as to the essential nature of the transaction, bankruptcy, unauthorized signature, and alteration.

**17.4**  Makers of notes and acceptors of drafts have an absolute liability to pay. Indorsers have a liability to pay only if an instrument is presented properly for payment, the instrument is dishonored, and proper notice of dishonor is given to the secondary party.

## Key Terms

failure of consideration, 367

holder, 364

holder in due course, 364

holder in due course rule, 368

lack of consideration, 366

limited defenses, 366

personal defenses, 366

presentment, 372

real defenses, 369

shelter provision, 365

universal defenses, 369

## Questions for Review and Discussion

1. What are the characteristics of being a holder in due course?
2. What special protection is given to a holder in due course?
3. What is a holder?
4. What protection is given to a holder through a holder in due course?
5. What are the six personal defenses?
6. What protection is given to people who sign consumer credit contracts?
7. What are the six real defenses and what is the significance of a real defense?
8. What is primary liability?
9. What is secondary liability?
10. What conditions must be met to hold a secondary party liable?

## Cases for Analysis

1. Without authority to do so, Allen signed Baker's name on a note, promising to pay Cohen $5,000 in 30 days. The note was negotiated to Davidson who was a holder in due course. Will Davidson be successful in recovering the $5,000 from Baker in court? Why or why not?

2. Refrigerated Transport Co., Inc., employed a collection agency to collect some of its overdue accounts. The collection agency indorsed, without authority, checks made payable to Refrigerated Transport and deposited them in the agency's own checking account. Was the bank that accepted the checks for deposit a holder in due course? Why or why not? *Nat'l Bank v. Refrigerated Transp.,* 248 S.E.2d 496 (GA).

3. Andersen entered into a franchise agreement with Great Lake Nursery, under which Andersen was to grow and sell nursery stock and Christmas trees. Great Lake was to provide trees, chemicals, and other items. Andersen signed an installment note that read in part, "For value received, Robert Andersen promises to pay to Great Lake Nursery Corp. $6,412." Great Lake indorsed the note and transferred it to First Investment Company. Later, Andersen stopped making payments because Great Lake filed bankruptcy and failed to perform its part of the franchise agreement. May Andersen use failure of consideration as a defense when sued by First Investment Company on the note? Why or why not? *First Inv. Co. v. Andersen,* 621 P.2d 683 (UT).

4. In exchange for an asphalt paving job, Paulick gave Bucci a note promising to pay to the order of Bucci $7,593 in six months with 10 percent per annum interest. Payment was not made on the due date, and Bucci brought suit. Paulick used failure of consideration as a defense, claiming that the paving job was improperly done. The court held that Bucci was a holder in due course because he had taken the instrument for value, in good faith, and without notice of any claims or defenses of Paulick's. Could Paulick use the defense of failure of consideration against Bucci? Why or why not? *Bucci v. Paulick,* 149 A.2d 1255 (PA).

5. Carolyn Brazil wrote a check to a contractor who agreed to make certain improvements on her home. She wrote the check in reliance on the contractor's false representation that the materials for the job had been purchased, when in fact, they had not. Brazil had the bank on which the check was drawn stop payment on it. Another bank, which cashed the check and became a holder in due course of the instrument, attempted to recover the amount of the check from Brazil. Could it do so?

Explain. *Citizens Nat'l Bank v. Brazil,* 233 S.E.2d 482 (GA).

6. As part of the purchase price for a 9,040-acre ranch, Kirby gave Bergfield a $20,000 check drawn on the Bank of Bellevue. Bergfield had her banker telephone the Bank of Bellevue to inquire about Kirby's account balance to be sure that the check was good. It was learned that there was not enough money in Kirby's account to cover the check. Bergfield continued to hold the check and did not present it to the Bank of Bellevue for payment. Later, Bergfield argued that the telephone call to the bank was a presentment and demand for payment of the check. Do you agree? Why or why not? *Kirby v. Bergfield,* 182 N.W.2d 205 (NE).

7. Haik transferred his stock in Petrocomp, an oil exploration company, to Rowley in exchange for five $10,000 promissory notes. The notes were signed by Rowley and indorsed by Rowley's son, Stephen. Rowley failed to pay the notes when they became due. No presentment for payment was made by Haik on the due date, nor was a timely notice of dishonor given to Rowley's son, Stephen. Could Haik hold Stephen liable on the notes as an indorser? Explain. *Haik v. Rowley,* 377 So.2d 391 (LA).

8. David and Nettie Weiner signed seven promissory notes, totaling $89,000, in their capacity as president and secretary of NMD Realty Co. In addition, they indorsed each note on the reverse side with their individual signatures. Each note contained the following provision: "The Maker and indorser or indorsers each hereby waives presentment, demand, and notice of dishonor." The Weiners claimed that, because they are secondarily liable, the bank may not proceed against them individually until after presentment, notice of dishonor, and protest have occurred. Do you agree with the Weiners? Explain. *Bank of Delaware v. NMD Realty Co.,* 325 A.2d 108 (DE).

9. Rutherford purchased real property from Ethel Stokes for $35,000. He paid $5,000 down and signed a promissory note for the balance. The note was secured by a deed of trust (a type of security interest, discussed in detail in Chapter 31). When payments on the note were overdue, Stokes considered foreclosing on the property. Prior to doing so, however, she negotiated the note to Craig, who purchased it at a discount with notice that it was in default. Was Craig a holder in due course of the note? Why or why not? *Matter of Marriage of Rutherford,* 573 S.W.2d 299 (TX).

10. Bolton wrote a check for $20,000 to his daughter, Joyce, intending to make a gift. The check was drawn on the State Bank of Wapello and mailed to Joyce in Maryland, where she was living. Joyce received the check, indorsed it, and mailed it to her bank in Baltimore with instructions to use it to establish a certificate of deposit in joint tenancy with her father. Was Joyce a holder in due course of the check? Explain. *Matter of Estate of Bolton,* 444 N.W.2d 482 (IA).

## quick quiz Answers

| 17-1 | 17-2 | 17-3 | 17-4 |
|------|------|------|------|
| 1. T | 1. F | 1. T | 1. F |
| 2. F | 2. F | 2. F | 2. T |
| 3. T | 3. T | 3. F | 3. T |

## THE OPENING CASE   The Greatest Good or Self-Interest: *Bentham v. Smith*

Toward the end of the 18th century, the British legal system had begun to stagnate. This stagnation was reflected in the legal system's ill-advised over-dependency on precedent. A Scottish philosopher named Jeremy Bentham suggested that the law could escape this unhealthy obsession with the past, if it adopted a more scientific approach to the law-making process. If the law simply promoted the greatest good for the greatest number of people, Bentham argued, then judges and members of Parliament would know exactly what to do when faced with a legal problem. In the day-to-day operation of the law, Bentham's plan would require law-makers to consider the good and the bad effects of any legal proposal and then, after weighing those effects, determine the correct action.

All of this sounds good in theory and it might even have worked, had it not been for a single fatal flaw, a flaw that had been anticipated a generation earlier by another philosopher, Adam Smith. In his famous work, *The Wealth of Nations,* Smith had considered an approach similar to Bentham's but rejected it as impractical for a simple reason. Human nature, Smith argued, led people to focus on their own self-interest rather than the interests of their fellow man. Self-interest, Smith realized, was the best way to build a legal

system. Unfortunately, self-interest has a weakness too. Even when people are focused on self-interest, Smith noted, they rarely, if ever, comprehend what that self-interest ought to be. Ironically, if they actually understood what was in their own self-interest, they would frequently make decisions that promoted the best interests of the group, because, as Smith believed, these two things often went hand in hand.

Interestingly enough for our purposes here, Smith targeted bankers as a classic example of a group of men who never really understood what was in their own self-interest and, as a result, frequently sabotaged their own industry. At one point Smith wrote, "Had every particular banking company always understood and attended to its own particular interest, the circulation never could have been overstocked with paper money. But every particular banking company has not always understood or attended to its own particular interest." Does this tendency to focus on self-interest still plague the banking industry or have bankers learned something over the last two centuries? As an experiment, answer that question now and then see if the chapter either changes your mind or confirms your answer. [See J. Bronowski and Bruce Mazlish, *The Western Intellectual Tradition* (New York: Harper Perennial, 1960), pp. 336–356, 436–449.]

## LO Learning Objectives

1. Clarify the bank's duties in the bank–depositor relationship.
2. Clarify the depositor's duties in the bank–depositor relationship.
3. Explain a drawer's rights in relation to a stop-payment order.
4. Explain the extent of the insurance protection provided by the FDIC.
5. List the different terms used to describe banks during the bank collection process.
6. Outline a check's life cycle.
7. Describe the principal features of the Check 21 Act.
8. Describe the consumer protection features of the Check 21 Act.
9. Describe the process of an electronic fund transfer.
10. Discuss the protection given to consumers by the Electronic Fund Transfer Act.

# 18-1 The Bank–Depositor Relationship

The relationship between the drawee bank and its customer is that of both debtor and creditor and agent and principal. The relationship arises out of the express or implied contract that occurs when the customer opens a checking account with the bank. The bank becomes a debtor when money is deposited in the bank by the customer. At this time, the customer is owed money by the bank and is therefore a creditor. When an **overdraft** occurs, that is, when the bank pays out more than the customer has on deposit, the debtor–creditor role reverses, and the bank becomes the creditor.

LO1

The bank acts as the customer's agent when it collects or attempts to collect checks or other negotiable instruments made payable to the customer. If the items are deposited in the customer's account, any settlement made by the bank with the customer is provisional. A provisional settlement may be revoked by the bank if an item that the bank is attempting to collect is dishonored. The bank may charge back the amount of any credit given for the item to its customer's account or obtain a refund from its customer.

UCC 4-201

UCC 4-212

## EXAMPLE 18-1: Provisional Settlement

Baker Company deposited in its checking account a check it had received in the mail from a customer. Baker Company's bank credited its account for the amount of the check and sent it through the clearinghouse for collection. The check was returned to the bank because of insufficient funds. Baker Company's bank charged back (debited) the amount it had credited to Baker Company's account.

# The Bank's Duties

The bank owes a duty to its depositors to honor orders and to protect funds. However, these duties carry strict limitations.

UCC 4-401
UCC 4-402

**Duty to Honor Orders**    The drawee bank is under a duty to honor all checks drawn by its customers when there are sufficient funds on deposit in the customer's account. If there are insufficient funds on deposit, the bank may charge the customer's account even if it creates an overdraft. If a bank fails to honor a check because of a mistake on its part, the bank is liable to the customer for any actual damages the customer suffers. The drawee bank has no liability to the holder of the check, however, unless it is certified.

## EXAMPLE 18-2: Bank's Liability Extends to Actual Damages Only

Rougier, who had $178 in her checking account, wrote out a check for $78.42 and mailed it to the telephone company in payment of a telephone bill. Due to a mistake on its part, Rougier's bank dishonored the check and returned it to the telephone company marked "insufficient funds." As soon as the error was discovered, the telephone company was notified, and the check was redeposited and honored by the bank. Because Rougier suffered no loss, the bank was not liable for dishonoring the check. Had Rougier's telephone been disconnected because of the dishonored check, the bank would have been liable to her for the cost of restoring service. The bank was not liable to the telephone company.

UCC 4-404

A bank is under no obligation to a customer to pay a stale check unless it is certified. A **stale check** is a check that is presented for payment more than six months after its date. A bank, however, may honor a stale check without liability to its customer if it acts in good faith.

## EXAMPLE 18-3: Bank Must Act in Good Faith

The Chemical Bank paid a check that had been written by New York Flameproofing Co. ten years earlier on a check form no longer used by that company. The account on which the check was drawn had been closed for seven years, and the company's address written on the check had changed seven years earlier. In holding against the bank for paying the check, the court said that such payment was a reckless disregard of due care, so much as to constitute bad faith. The bank was liable for the amount paid.

The drawee bank is not liable to a holder of a check for dishonoring the instrument unless it is certified. The holder's recourse is against the drawer or indorsers on their secondary liability.

UCC 4-405

**Death or Incompetence of Customer**    The drawee bank is not liable for the payment of a check before it has notice of the death or incompetence of the drawer. In any event, a bank may pay or certify checks for 10 days after the date of death of the drawer. This rule permits holders of checks that are drawn shortly before the drawer's death to cash them without the necessity of filing a claim with the court handling the deceased's estate.

## Forged and Altered Checks

A **forgery** is the fraudulent making or alteration of a writing. A forgery is committed when a person fraudulently writes or alters a check or other form of negotiable instrument to the injury of another. The commission of forgery is a crime, subject to a fine and imprisonment. The offering of a forged instrument to another person when the offeror knows it to be forged is also a crime, known as **uttering**. If a bank, in good faith, pays the altered amount of a check to a holder, it may deduct from the drawer's account only the amount of the check as it was originally written.

### EXAMPLE 18-4: Bank Responsible for Paying an Altered Check

Lane wrote out a $400 check, in a nonnegligent fashion, to the order of Robinson in payment for repairs to Lane's house. Robinson raised the check to $4,000. If Lane's bank pays the full $4,000 to Robinson, it can deduct $400 from Lane's account, but no more. The bank must either get the money back from the wrongdoer, Robinson, or suffer the loss. The bank would be able to deduct the full $4,000 from Lane's account if the alteration was facilitated by Lane's carelessness in writing the check.

The depositor is also protected against a signature being forged. When a checking account is opened, the depositor must fill out a signature card, which is permanently filed at the bank. Thereafter, the bank is held to know the depositor's signature. The bank is liable to the depositor if it pays any check on which the depositor's signature has been forged.

Despite this list of depositor rights, the banks are not without protection against forgery. For example, banks still control the contractual relationship that exists with their customers and can, thus, add a clause or two that protects them against certain types of forgery. For instance, a bank can add a clause to a contract stipulating that it will not be liable for forgeries that result from the customer's use of a facsimile or a nonmanual signature. So, if a customer uses a rubber stamp facsimile of his or her signature, as is a common practice among corporate executives, and that stamp is used in a forgery scheme, the bank would not be liable. This is a contractual matter, however, making it something that the customer agrees to when he or she opens an account with that bank. If the customer is unhappy with that treatment, he or she is free to shop around for a bank that makes no such stipulation on their contracts.

On the other hand, banks sometimes put themselves at risk by permitting tellers to cash checks without verifying the depositor's signature. Many, perhaps most, banks actually have a formal policy in place that permits their tellers to cash checks under $2,500 without comparing the signature on the check with the signature on file. Most of the time this works. The checks are cashed, the funds are available, the signature is genuine, the transaction is completed and, most of all, the customer is pleased with bank's overall efficiency. When it does not work and a forged check slips through, the bank is responsible. In the long run, however, the amount of money saved by permitting the tellers to cash checks without verification far outweighs the amount of money lost on the occasional forgery.

## Availability of Funds

In the past, banks were not uniform in the amount of time they required before they would make funds available to their depositors. Some banks held funds longer than others, and many banks did not disclose their holding policy to their customers.

To address the issue, Congress passed the Competitive Banking Act. Under the act, the Federal Reserve Board of Governors issued Regulation CC, which requires banks to make funds available to depositors according to a prescribed schedule (Table 18-1). With exceptions,

# THE OPENING CASE *Revisited, Part I*
## The Greatest Good or Self-Interest: *Bentham v. Smith*, Round 2

Recall that in the Opening Case at the beginning of this chapter, Adam Smith had rejected Jeremy Bentham's belief in the greatest good principle because Smith was convinced that human nature always led people to focus on their own self-interest rather than the interests of their fellow man. Self-interest, Smith argued, was the best way to build a legal system. Unfortunately, Smith added, in any given situation people rarely understand what that self-interest really is and, therefore, do things that, in the long run, do more harm than good. Ironically, if they actually understood what was in their own self-interest, Smith said, they would frequently make decisions that promoted the best interests of the group, because, as Smith believed, these two things often went hand in hand. The policy that permits bank tellers to cash some checks without verifying signatures may be an argument that proves Smith wrong, at least in part. Here we have banks doing their best to satisfy customers by skipping a long and involved step to save their customers' time. Does the bank pay the price for the occasional slip-up? Yes. But, apparently, banking executives have determined that their own long-term best interests, seen in customer satisfaction, is served by putting up with the inconvenience of an occasional forgery.

funds from checks drawn on the U.S. Treasury or any state or local government and any bank draft, cashier's check, or postal money order must be made available on the next business day following the banking day of deposit; funds from checks drawn on banks within the same Federal Reserve district must be made available within two business days

| **Table 18-1** Availability of Funds (Under $5,000) You Deposit in Your Bank | |
|---|---|
| **Type of Check** | **Funds Must Be Made Available for Withdrawal** |
| "On us" check [drawn on your bank] | 1st business day* after the banking day[†] of deposit |
| Local check (except $100[‡]) [drawn on a bank in same check-processing region] | 2nd business day* after the banking day[†] of deposit |
| Nonlocal (except $100[‡]) [drawn on a bank in a different check-processing region] | 5th business day* after the banking day[†] of deposit |
| Electronic payment | 1st business day* after the banking day[†] of deposit |
| Cashier's check | 1st business day* after the banking day[†] of deposit |
| Certified check | 1st business day* after the banking day[†] of deposit |
| Government check | 1st business day* after the banking day[†] of deposit |
| U.S. Postal Service money order | 1st business day* after the banking day[†] of deposit |

*Monday through Friday except most federal holidays.

[†]Any business day (up to the bank's cut-off hour) when the bank is open for substantially all of its banking activities.

[‡]The first $100 (or the total amount of the deposit if less than $100) must be made available on the 1st business day after the banking day of deposit.

following the banking day of deposit; and funds from checks drawn on banks outside the bank's Federal Reserve district must be made available within five business days following the banking day of deposit. A *business day* is defined under Regulation CC as Monday through Friday, except for most federal holidays. A *banking day* is any business day (up to the bank's cut-off hour) when the bank is open for substantially all of its banking activities.

## EXAMPLE 18-5: Fund Availability

Edna Chase deposited a $500 local check that was payable to her in her bank at 3:00 P.M. on Monday. The bank's cut-off hour for the day's transactions was 2:00 P.M. Because the deposit was made after the bank's cut-off hour, it was considered received on Tuesday. The first $100 must be made available to Chase by Wednesday, and the remaining $400 must be made available by Thursday, the second business day after the banking day of deposit.

Exceptions are made for new accounts, deposits greater than $5,000, accounts that are repeatedly overdrawn, deposits of a suspicious nature, and emergency conditions. In addition, some state laws require even shorter time periods for banks to make funds available. Regulation CC also requires banks to disclose in advance their policy for making funds available to depositors. Such disclosures must be made when the account is initially opened and on conspicuously visible notices at teller stations in the bank.

**Midnight Deadline** Payor banks are required to either settle or return checks  UCC 4-302
quickly. If they do not do so, they are responsible for paying them. If the payor bank is not the depositary bank, it must settle for an item by midnight of the banking day of receipt.

## EXAMPLE 18-6: Bank's Midnight Deadline

LaPierre wrote a check to Kimberly Motors for $2,500 in payment for a secondhand car. The payor of the check (the bank on which it was drawn) was the National Bank & Trust Co. Kimberly Motors deposited the check into its account in the Southwest Mutual Bank (the depositary bank), which sent it on for collection. LaPierre's car broke down before she reached home that evening. She immediately stopped payment on the check. The National Bank & Trust Company must return the check to the Southwest Mutual Bank, with a notation that payment has been stopped, before midnight of the day that it received the check. If it keeps the check longer than that, it will be liable for payment.

If the payor bank is also the depositary bank, it must either pay or return the check or  UCC 4-104(h)
send notice of its dishonor on or before its midnight deadline. In this case, the bank's **midnight deadline** is midnight of the next banking day following the banking day on which it receives the relevant item.

## EXAMPLE 18-7: Longer Deadline for Depository Bank

If the National Bank & Trust Company in Example 18-6 had also been the depositary bank, it would have had an extra day to handle the check. The bank would have had until midnight of the next banking day to return the check to Kimberly Motors with the notation that payment had been stopped.

## The Depositor's Duties

Depositors, in general, owe a duty to the banks in which they have checking accounts to have sufficient funds on deposit to cover checks that they write. They must also examine their bank statements and canceled checks promptly and with reasonable care and notify the bank quickly of any discrepancies.

Banks and their customers must both perform their responsibilities properly for the system to function effectively.

**Bad Checks** Most states have statutes making it larceny or attempted larceny for a person to issue a check drawn on a bank in which the person has insufficient funds. Such statutes usually have the following provisions that must be observed in the prosecution of anyone issuing a *bad check,* sometimes called an *NSF check:* The payee has the obligation of informing the drawer of the nonpayment of the check, together with notice of the provisions of the bad-check law and of the party's legal rights and obligations. After receiving notice of nonpayment, or dishonor, the drawer is given a specified number of days, usually five or ten, in which to make the check good, without fear of prosecution. Failure to make full payment of the check within the number of days allowed by statute serves as presumption of guilt that the drawer issued the check with full knowledge of the facts and with intent to defraud.

### EXAMPLE 18-8:  Bad Check Notice

State National Bank received Yoder's check for $120 due on an installment note it held. After it was deposited, the check was returned to State National with the notification "insufficient funds." The bank's collection department sent a certified letter to Yoder, which explained his responsibility under the bad-check statute. Failure on the part of Yoder to make the check good within the period of time indicated would result in a criminal complaint being lodged against Yoder through the office of the state's prosecuting attorney.

Bad-check statutes are effectively used as a means of collection. Most bad-check writers make an effort to make full payment of the check when advised that they are subject to prosecution. Many banks offer overdraft protection service to their depositors, which covers small overdrafts that are usually caused by the mistake of the drawer in balancing the checkbook. This service is important under the Check 21 Act, because checks may have a shorter float time than in the past. With this service, the bank honors small overdrafts and charges the depositor's account. This service saves the drawer the inconvenience and embarrassment of having a check returned to a holder marked "insufficient funds."

UCC 4-406

**Duty to Examine Accounts** The UCC imposes a duty on depositors to examine their bank statements and canceled checks promptly and with reasonable care when they are received from the bank. In the past, banks returned the canceled checks to their customers so that they could verify the authenticity of those checks and then balance their statements properly. Today, as we shall see shortly, as a standard operating procedure, banks send an electronic accounting to their customers. Banks will still send the paper checks to a customer if a customer demands that service; however, the bank will also charge the customer for that service. The electronic record that is sent to the customer will include the check number, the date the check was issued, and the amount charged to the customer's

## THE OPENING CASE *Revisited, Part II*
### The Greatest Good or Self-Interest: *Bentham v. Smith*, Round 3

The policy that permits a bank to provide customers with overdraft protection is another example of the banking industry's ability to see how, from time to time, their own long-term best interest is served by putting up with the small, immediate problems associated with overdrafts. Again, we have bank executives doing their best to satisfy customers by overlooking the occasional overdraft in exchange for customer satisfaction. In effect, customers protected by the overdraft policy often feel a sense of loyalty to their bank; loyalty that will result in continued patronage and the occasional recommendation. Does this necessarily prove that Adam Smith was wrong about bankers' inability to see beyond their own short-term self-interest. Perhaps, but perhaps not. As we shall see shortly, there are some instances in which the banks act exactly as predicted by Smith.

account. If, however, the customer pays bills online or has an automatic bill-paying plan in place, the bank statements will show the payees for each withdrawal.

After receiving and examining their statements, customers must report promptly to the bank any forged or altered checks. If they do not do so, depositors cannot hold the bank responsible for losses due to the bank's payment of a forged or altered instrument. The exact time within which a depositor must notify a bank is not established except in the case of the same wrongdoer forging or altering more than one check. In that case, the bank must be notified of the wrongdoing within 30 days after the depositor receives the bank statement. The absolute limit for notifying a bank of a forged or altered check is one year from the time the depositor receives the bank statement. The limit is three years, however, in the case of a forged indorsement on a check.

### Antedated and Postdated Checks

A check may be antedated or postdated. It is antedated when it is written and dated on one day and delivered at a later time. A check is postdated when the drawer delivers it before its stated date. However, a bank may charge a postdated check against a customer's account unless the customer has notified the bank of the postdated check within a reasonable time for the bank to act on it. Any such notice by a customer to a bank is effective for the same time periods allowed for stop-payment orders, discussed subsequently. If a check is undated, its date is the date that it was first given to someone.

UCC 4-401(c)

## Stop-Payment Rights

Drawers may order a bank to stop payment on any item payable on their account. The stop-payment order must be received in time and in such a manner as to afford the bank a reasonable opportunity to act on it. An oral order is binding upon the bank for 14 calendar days only, unless confirmed in writing within that period. A written order is binding for only six months, unless renewed in writing. The burden of establishing the fact and amount of loss resulting from the payment of an item contrary to a binding order to stop payment is on the customer.

UCC 4-403

UCC 4-403(3)

### Bank's Right of Subrogation

If a bank fails to stop payment on a check, it is responsible for any loss suffered by the drawer who ordered the payment stopped. The bank, however, may take the place of any holder, holder in due course, payee, or drawer who has rights against others on the underlying obligation. This right to be substituted for another is known as the bank's right of subrogation. It is designed to prevent loss to the bank and unjust enrichment to other parties.

UCC 4-407

| **Table 18-2** How a Husband, Wife, and One Child May Have Insured Accounts Totaling $1,000,000 | |
| --- | --- |
| **Individual Accounts:** | |
| Husband | $ 100,000 |
| Wife | $ 100,000 |
| Child | $ 100,000 |
| **Joint Accounts:** | |
| Husband and Wife | $ 100,000 |
| Husband and Child | $ 100,000 |
| Wife and Child | $ 100,000 |
| **Revocable Trust Accounts:** | |
| Husband as Trustee for Wife | $ 100,000 |
| Husband as Trustee for Child | $ 100,000 |
| Wife as Trustee for Child | $ 100,000 |
| Wife as Trustee for Husband | $ 100,000 |
| | $1,000,000 |

## EXAMPLE 18-9: Bank's Right of Subrogation

Jervey was induced by fraud to enter into a contract with Glidden. As part of the transaction, Jervey wrote and delivered a check to Glidden for $1,500. When Jervey discovered the fraud, she immediately ordered her bank to stop payment on the check. The bank, by mistake, ignored the stop-payment order and paid the $1,500 to Glidden. The bank must return the $1,500 to Jervey but may sue Glidden for fraud under its right of subrogation.

## Insured Accounts

The Federal Deposit Insurance Corporation (FDIC) insures deposits in banks as well as in savings and loan associations. The basic insurance coverage protects individual bank accounts for up to $100,000 and joint accounts for up to an additional $100,000. Revocable trust and payable-on-death bank accounts are protected for up to $100,000 for each beneficiary who is a close relative and named in the account records. (See Table 18-2.)

### quick quiz 18-1

1. The bank acts as the customer's principal when it collects checks or other negotiable instruments made payable to the customer.    true | false

2. The drawee bank has no liability to the holder of a check unless it is certified.    true | false

3. The commission of forgery is a crime, subject to a fine and imprisonment.    true | false

# 18-2 Bank Deposits and Collections

The tremendous number of checks handled by banks and the countrywide nature of the bank collection process require uniformity in the law of bank collections. For this reason, Article 4 of the UCC contains rules and regulations for handling bank deposits and collections.

## Bank Descriptions

During the bank collection process, banks are described by different terms, depending on their particular function in a transaction. Sometimes a bank takes a check for deposit. At other times, it pays a check as a drawee. At still other times, it takes a check for collection only. The different terms that are used to describe banks and their meanings are as follows: A **depositary bank** is the first bank to which an item is transferred for collection, even if it is also the payor bank. The term **payor bank** describes a bank by which an item is payable as drawn or accepted. It includes a drawee bank. **Intermediary bank** defines any bank to which an item is transferred in the course of collection, except the depositary or payor bank. The **collecting bank** is any bank handling the item for collection, except the payor bank, and the **presenting bank** is any bank presenting an item, except a payor bank. **Remitting bank** describes any payor or intermediary bank remitting for an item.

UCC 4-105

---

## A QUESTION OF ETHICS

Bethany Golemen was discharged from her job as an advertising executive at Farnsworth, Yardley, and Brook. Her credit cards were maxed out, her savings account depleted, and her rent was due. On the bright side, James Farnsworth, the senior partner in the advertising firm, had given Goleman a sizable severance check as she left the office on her last day. Goleman was feeling lucky until she tried to retrieve her car from the service station where Tommy Henderson had just finished fixing the brakes on her Saturn. When Goleman tried to pay by credit card her card was rejected. Henderson refused to allow her to take her car until she gave him some type of payment. To satisfy Henderson she wrote him a check for the new brakes, even though she knew that the account was empty. She fully intended to place the severance check into the account the next morning so that the check would not bounce. Unfortunately, when she arrived at her apartment, she found that the landlord had changed the locks because her rent was six months overdue. In order to get into her apartment, she signed the severance check over to the landlord. As a result she never deposited any money in her checking account and her check to Henderson bounced. Was it ethical for Goleman to write Henderson the check knowing there was no money in the account? Remember that, at the time she wrote the original check out to Henderson, she fully intended to place the severance check in the account the next day. From an ethical perspective, does her intent to deposit funds in her checking account tomorrow permit her to write the bad check today? Why or why not?

---

## A Check's Life Cycle

The life cycle of a check begins when the drawer writes a check and delivers it to the payee. The payee may take the check directly to the payor bank (the bank on which it was drawn) for payment. If that bank pays the check in cash, its payment is final, and the check is returned to the drawer with the next bank statement. However, it is more likely that the check will be deposited in the payee's own account in another bank. That bank,

UCC 4-213
UCC 4-201

known as the depository bank, acts as its customer's agent to collect the money from the payor bank. Any settlement given by the depository bank in this case is **provisional** (not final). It may be revoked if the check is later dishonored. The check is sent (sometimes through an intermediary bank) to a collecting bank, which presents the check to the payor bank for payment. If it is honored by the payor bank, the amount will be deducted from the drawer's account, and a substitute check will be returned to the drawer with the next bank statement. If the check is dishonored for any reason, a substitute check will be returned to the payee via the same route that it was sent, and all credits given for the item will be revoked (see Figure 18-1).

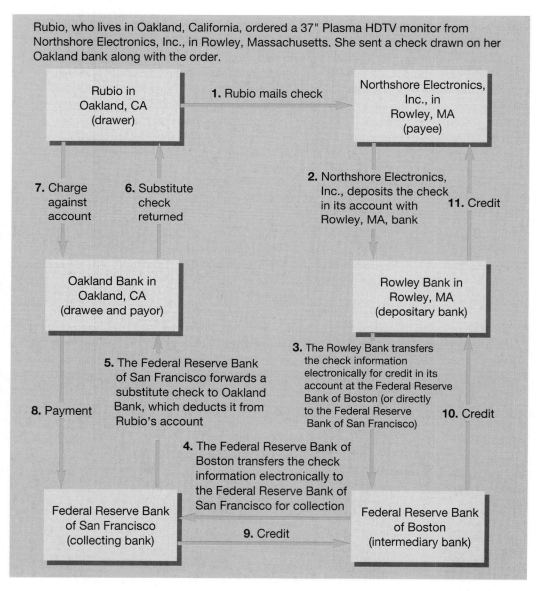

Figure 18-1   The life cycle of Rubio's check is traced through its collection and clearing-house routes. Before the Check 21 Act became effective in October 2004, the check in this example would have had to be physically transported by plane or truck around its entire route.

# 18-3 Cyber-Banking

Like all of us, the world of banking has been forced to adapt to the global electronic revolution. The Internet has made the transfer of funds and the record keeping associated with those funds, easier, faster, and more efficient than ever before. The new system, however, is also filled with problems. In fact, the new electronic transfer process is more precarious than the traditional process. This is because the new system is subject to sabotage, manipulation, and privacy problems. Consequently, as is true of all parts of the social system, the banking community has been forced to interface with several new statutes designed to monitor and influence its day-to-day operation. These statutes include but are not limited to the Check 21 Act and the Electronic Fund Transfer Act.

Some banks prefer that customers use ATMs for their regular banking transactions, even featuring accounts that charge a fee for the use of live tellers.

## The Check 21 Act

Named for the 21st century, the **Check 21 Act** brings the check-clearing method into the modern age by the use of electronic check processing. Such processing could not be done prior to this 2004 law, because of the legal requirement that original checks be presented to the drawee bank for payment. Under this law, a new negotiable instrument called a substitute

## THE OPENING CASE Revisited, Part III
## The Greatest Good or Self-Interest: Bentham v. Smith, Round 4

The banking industry has been very quick to adopt computer technology to help them to make long distance transactions and to keep track of those transactions. It is true, of course that the global computer network has made the transfer of funds easier, faster, and more efficient than ever before. The computer network, however, is also plagued by difficulties that make the new electronic transfer process more hazardous than the conventional process. This is because the network can be sabotaged, manipulated, and invaded.

Is this rush to the Internet an example of Adam Smith's principle that says that individuals and institutions (like banks, for instance) always look out for their best interests first? Have the banks made their own lives easier while placing the world's savings accounts, pension plans, checking accounts, and investment portfolios at risk? Does the bank's convenience outweigh the customer's peace of mind? Or have the banks stumbled on a system that benefits both customer and bank alike? Think about it.

check is used. A **substitute check** (also called an *image replacement document,* or *IRD*) is a paper reproduction of both sides of an original check that can be processed just like the original check. Under the new law, banks are not required to use substitute checks, but when they do so for consideration, they make the following warranties: (1) the substitute check contains an accurate image of the front and back of the original check; (2) it is the legal equivalent of the original check; and (3) no drawer, drawee, indorser, or depositary bank will be asked to pay a check that already has paid.

UCC 4-406 (a)(b)

**Original Checks No Longer Returned** As noted earlier in the chapter, many banks in the past automatically returned canceled checks with their monthly bank statements to their customers, even though the UCC does not require that original checks be returned unless a customer requests them. The Check 21 Act, which takes precedence over the UCC, changes this rule. Under the Check 21 Act, the customer has a right only to a paper substitute check that is a reproduction of the front and back of the original. Bank customers no longer have an absolute right to see their original canceled checks.

**Consumer Protection** To protect consumers from losses related to substitute checks, the Check 21 Act includes a consumer's right to claim an *expedited credit.* This right exists if the consumer asserts in good faith the following four facts:

LO8

- The bank charged the consumer's account for a substitute check that was given to the consumer.
- Either the check was not properly charged to the consumer's account, or the consumer has a warranty claim with respect to the substitute check.
- The consumer suffered a resulting loss.
- The production of the original check or a better copy of the original check is necessary to determine the validity of any claim.

If the consumer makes a claim within 45 days after receiving the bank statement or substitute check, the bank must investigate it and make any necessary recredit to the consumer's account. If the bank needs more than 10 days to investigate and resolve the complaint, it must recredit the consumer's account for an amount up to $2,500 while it completes its investigation. The bank must recredit any remaining balance greater than $2,500 no later than 45 days after the consumer submits the claim.

## Electronic Fund Transfers

LO9

Electronic banking (also called **electronic fund transfers** or **EFTs**) uses computers and electronic technology as a substitute for checks and other banking methods. People can go to automatic teller machines (ATMs) 24 hours a day to make bank deposits and withdrawals. They can pay bills by phone, have deposits made directly to their bank accounts, and pay for retail purchases directly from their bank accounts. Some banks have arrangements for payment by **e-check** (sometimes called *electronic check conversion*), which is a system in which funds are electronically transferred from a customer's checking account, eliminating the need to process a paper check. Under one system, the customer writes out an ordinary check and gives it to a merchant when making a purchase. After obtaining the customer's written authorization, the merchant passes the check through an instrument that reads the information on the check and converts the payment from a paper check to an electronic funds transfer. The merchant then voids the check and returns it to the customer with a receipt. Payment by e-check is faster and less expensive, thus saving time and money for everyone involved.

### ATM, Debit, and Combination Cards An **ATM card** is used together with a personal identification number (PIN) to gain access to an automatic teller machine either

on or off the bank premises. In contrast, a **debit card** (also called a *check card* or *cash card*) is used to subtract money electronically from a bank account to pay for goods or services. Debit cards are used at stores rather than at ATM machines and usually require the use of the customer's signature rather than a PIN. Many banks now use a combination ATM–debit card that performs both functions. There are two kinds of debit cards: online and offline. *Online* debit cards make an immediate transfer of money from the customer's bank account to the merchant's bank account. *Offline* debit cards record a debit against the customer's bank account, which is processed later. A debit card offers less protection than a credit card. Unlike a credit card, a debit card payment cannot be stopped if a purchase is defective or an order is not delivered. In addition, your liability for the unauthorized use of your ATM or debit card is limited to $50 only if you notify the issuer within two business days of the loss or theft of the card. Your liability increases to $500 if notice is delayed beyond that time, and it becomes unlimited when notice is not given within 60 days. The unauthorized use of an ATM card is a criminal offense punishable by a $10,000 fine and/or 10 years in prison.

## EXAMPLE 18-10: Stolen ATM Card

A thief stole Hockmeyer's purse from a grocery store shopping cart. Three days later, Hockmeyer notified the bank that her ATM card was missing. By then, however, the thief had found the card along with Hockmeyer's secret identification number and withdrawn $800 from her account. Because the bank was notified within three days of the theft, Hockmeyer lost $500. Had she notified the bank within two business days of the theft, she would have lost only $50.

## The Electronic Funds Transfer Act

**Regulation E**, issued by the Federal Reserve Board under the Electronic Funds Transfer Act, establishes the basic rights, liabilities, and responsibilities of consumers who use electronic fund transfer services and financial institutions that offer these services. Transactions covered under the regulation include:

UCC 4A-103-505

UCC 4A-104

UCC 4A-103

- Point-of-sale purchases.
- Automated teller machine transfers.
- Telephone-initiated transfers requiring an entry password (PIN).
- Transfers resulting from debit card transactions requiring an entry password (PIN).
- Internet banking.

Under the act, consumers are entitled to receive a written receipt whenever they use an ATM. In addition, the transaction must appear on the periodic statement sent to the consumer. The consumer has 60 days to notify the bank of any error on the periodic statement or terminal receipt. After being notified, the bank has 10 business days to investigate the error. If the bank needs more time, it may take up to 45 days to complete the investigation, but only if the money in dispute is returned to the consumer's account.

Because the Electronic Fund Transfer Act is a consumer protection law, it does not apply to transactions between banks and other businesses. A different law, Article 4A of the UCC, has been adopted by many states to govern EFTs made by banks and businesses. Under the UCC, a business that orders money to be sent electronically is called the *originator*. The business that is to receive the money is called the *beneficiary*. EFTs help businesses that deal with large sums of money make quick transfers to avoid a loss of interest.

### Did You Know?

- A *credit* card is like a loan. You agree to pay the money back later at a high interest rate unless you pay the full amount when the bill arrives. A *debit* card, in contrast, means "subtract"— when you use it, you subtract the money from your own bank account. *(continued)*

## EXAMPLE 18-11: Electronic Transfers by Banks

Data Control, Inc., sold a computer system to Western Sales, Inc., for $2 million. When the system was installed, Western Sales ordered its bank to pay $2 million to Data Control. Because both companies had accounts in the First National Bank, the bank simply debited Western Sales' account and credited Data Control's account for $2 million. Western Sales was the originator; Data Control was the beneficiary. If Data Control had used a different bank, the First National Bank would have ordered that bank, called the beneficiary's bank, to credit Data Control's account for $2 million.

- If your *credit* card is lost or stolen, you can't lose more than $50. In contrast, if someone uses your *ATM* or *debit* card without permission, you can lose much more unless you notify your bank quickly.

- A *debit* card is often easier to obtain than a credit card and allows you to spend what is in your bank account.

- A *debit* card gives you less protection than a credit card when you purchase items that are defective or never delivered.

- Using a *debit* card instead of writing checks saves you from showing identification or giving out personal identification at the time of a transaction.

# The Global Financial Cyber-Crisis

The Internet provides us with an enormous amount of flexibility and efficiency in the transfer of funds and with the record keeping associated with those funds. However, as noted above the system is also often at risk. Poorly written software, an incorrect file number, a solar storm, or inadequately maintained hardware can interrupt the operation of even the most secure system. Information technicians might enter an incorrect password, an inaccurate code, or the wrong PIN and the system might shut down or begin to act erratically. Most of these errors are handled easily enough. Other problems, those that are deliberate and knowingly target a computer system, are less easily solved.

**Global Level Problems**  For instance, a rival firm, an enemy nation or a crime syndicate, could send an e-mail with an attached PDF file that, when opened, will install a deadly virus into a corporate computer system. The software might command the system to shut down, delete data, or, perhaps worse, transfer control of the system to the hacker. What makes this type of attack so insidious is that no one knows about it until the damage is done. Thus, without so much as a digital alarm going off, a corporation might lose all of its data or a banking system might be wiped clean of all transactions. Constructing a plan for dealing with a deliberate computer attack is difficult at best. Nevertheless, steps must be taken to deal with such attacks. (See "Briefing Cyber-war: War in the Fifth Domain," *The Economist,* July 3, 2010, p. 25.)

**Global Cyber-Targets and Cyber-Tactics**  One step that has been suggested is to divide the data stream so that it travels along a variety of routes so that if one line is attacked the others can continue to transmit. This solution works most of the time. Unfortunately, there are bottlenecks along the global network at which the data streams intersect and fall under the control of a limited number of domain-name servers, making them tempting targets for cyber-criminals and cyber-terrorists. These main intersection points appear in the Middle East, in South East Asia, and along the Eastern seaboard of the United States, any one of which is an inviting target. (See "Briefing Cyber-war: War in the Fifth Domain," p. 25.)

**Cyber-Command (Cyber-com)**  The global response to such problems has been the establishment of a new cyber-command center. The task of the new command center is to protect the military's computer command system. This National Security Agency has been given control over this new center which has been officially named Cyber-Command or Cyber-com. Cyber-com is designed to protect the American cyber-system from attack and to formulate plans to undermine the computer systems of enemy nations. Two of its goals might be to protect the "chokepoints" in the submerged fiber-optic system and to uncover effective ways to use the system in a way that benefits the American military (See "Briefing Cyber-war: War in the Fifth Domain," p. 25.)

## Domestic Cyber-Targets and Cyber-Tactics

The tactics noted above are needed to protect the global Internet, but they do not protect individuals except in an indirect way. This is crucial because cyber-criminals also frequently target individuals. Such criminals can gain access to banks account, stock portfolios, and other financial records in order to drain funds from those accounts. Or they may steal an individual's identity in order to use that person's credit cards, debit cards, checking account, and other personal financial resources. Fortunately, the federal government has taken steps to protect your bank accounts and your identity from cyber-criminal attacks. These steps include the establishment of the Internet Crime Complaint Center and the passage of legislation aimed at protecting Internet transactions.

## Internet Crime Complaint Center (IC3)

The federal government has set up the Internet Crime Complaint Center (IC3) which connects the National White Collar Crime Center (NW3C) with the Federal Bureau of Investigation (FBI). The IC3 handles complaints involving cybercrimes such as identity theft, cyber-extortion, and Internet fraud. Individuals and businesses can file complaints with the IC3 by accessing their website online. The IC3 also works closely with administrative agencies as well as with local, state, and federal law enforcement agencies. (See *Internet Crime Complaint Center*, http://www.ic3.gov.)

## Domestic Cyber-Legislation

Congress has also passed legislation aimed at solving these problems. Two such acts are the Identity Theft and Assumption and Deterrence Act (ITDA) and the National Stolen Property Act (NSPA). ITADA, which was amended by the Identity Theft Penalty Enhancement Act, outlaws the unauthorized transfer, possession, or use of a means of identifying another person to violate federal law. The amendment adds a new crime, called *aggravated identity theft* to the original statute. The section on aggravated identity theft makes it clear that identity theft is much worse when it involves certain very serious felonies, including terrorism. Under the NSPA it is a federal crime to use interstate or foreign commerce to transport personal currency and securities that an individual is aware were stolen, were secured by fraud, or were taken by some other illegal method including an unauthorized electronic transfer.

## quick quiz 18-3

1. Consumers have 30 days to notify the bank of any error on the periodic statement received for the use of an ATM.   true | false

2. A consumer's liability for the unauthorized use of an ATM card is limited to $500 if notice of the loss or theft of a card is given the issuer within two business days.   true | false

3. The unauthorized use of an ATM card is a criminal offense punishable by a $500 fine and/or five years in prison.   true | false

# Summary

**18.1**   The drawee bank must honor all checks (except stale checks) drawn by its customers when there are sufficient funds on deposit. Failure to do so makes the bank liable to the customer for any actual damages the customer suffers. The drawee bank has no liability to the holder of a check unless it is certified. Banks are responsible for paying altered or forged checks. Banks must make funds available to depositors according to a specific schedule. In addition, banks must pay or return checks on or before their midnight deadline. Depositors must examine their bank statements and canceled checks promptly. It is a crime to write a check with insufficient funds in the bank. Oral stop-payment orders are binding upon the bank for 14 days; written orders to stop payment are binding for six months.

**18.2**   During the bank collection process, banks are described by different terms, depending on their particular function in a transaction. Sometimes a bank takes a check for deposit. At other times, it pays a check as a drawee. At still other times, it takes a check for collection only. The different terms that are used to describe banks and their meanings are as follows: depositary bank, payor bank, intermediary bank, collecting bank, presenting bank, and remitting bank. The life cycle of a check begins when the drawer writes a check and delivers it to the payee. If a payee cashes a check at a payor (drawee) bank, the payment is final. If, instead, the payee deposits a check in his or her bank, which sends it to the payor bank for collection, any payment is provisional.

**18.3**   The Check 21 Act establishes substitute checks, which may be returned to bank customers in place of the canceled original check and thus make check clearing much quicker through the use of electronic processing. Consumers who use EFTs have 60 days to notify the bank of an error; thereafter, the bank must investigate. A consumer's liability for the unauthorized use of an ATM card is limited to $50 if notice of the loss or theft of a card is given the issuer within 2 business days. Article 4A of the UCC governs EFTs made by banks and businesses. The federal government has set up the Internet Crime Complaint Center which handles complaints involving cybercrimes such as identity theft, cyber-extortion, and internet fraud. Congress has also passed legislation aimed at solving these problems. Two such acts are the Identity Theft and Assumption and Deterrence Act and the National Stolen Property Act.

# Key Terms

ATM card, 388

Check 21 Act, 387

collecting bank, 385

debit card, 389

depositary bank, 385

e-check, 388

electronic fund transfers (EFTs), 388

forgery, 379

intermediary bank, 385

midnight deadline, 381

overdraft, 377

payor bank, 385

presenting bank, 385

provisional, 386

Regulation E, 389

remitting bank, 385

stale check, 378

subrogation, 383

substitute check, 388

uttering, 379

# Questions for Review and Discussion

1. What are the bank's duties in the bank–depositor relationship?
2. What are the depositor's duties in the bank–depositor relationship?
3. What are a drawer's rights in relation to a stop-payment order?
4. What is the extent of the insurance protection provided by the FDIC?

5. What are the different terms used to describe banks during the bank collection process?
6. What are the steps in a check's life cycle?
7. What are the principal features of the Check 21 Act?
8. What consumer protection features are found in the Check 21 Act?

9. What happens during the process of an electronic funds transfer?
10. What protection is given to consumers by the Electronic Fund Transfer Act?

## Cases for Analysis

1. Arthur Woods died holding an annuity payable on his death to his wife, Dorothy. In payment of the annuity, a checking account for $24,900 was established in Dorothy Woods's name. The bank sent the checkbook and account statements to Woods's attorney, who had requested that the account be established for Woods. Six unauthorized checks bearing Dorothy Woods's forged signature were drawn on her checking account. Woods discovered the forgeries a year later when she received the checkbook and bank statements from her attorney. She notified the bank of the forgeries 15 months after they had been written. Was the bank responsible for paying the forged checks? Why or why not? *Woods v. MONY Legacy Life Insurance Company,* 84 N.Y.2d 290 (NY).

2. Kelco bought a truck from Felton, paying for it with a cashier's check she had obtained from her bank. On her way home, the truck broke down. Kelco immediately telephoned her bank and told it to stop payment on the cashier's check. Later, Kelco discovered that her bank had not stopped payment on the cashier's check and instead had paid it. Did Kelco have a claim against the bank? Explain. See also *Taboada v. Bank of Babylon,* 408 N.Y.S.2d 734 (NY).

3. Granite Corp. sent a check to Overseas Equipment Co. When the check was reported lost, Granite wrote to its bank telling it to stop payment on the check. Granite then sent the money to Overseas Equipment Co. by wire. Thirteen months later, the check turned up, and Granite's bank paid it. Did the bank violate its duty to stop payment on the check? Explain. *Granite Equip. Leasing Corp. v. Hempstead Bank,* 326 N.Y.S.2d 881 (NY).

4. While in the hospital during his final illness, Norris wrote out a check and gave it to his sister. She deposited it in her bank account. Norris died before the check cleared, and his bank refused to pay it. May a bank honor a check when it knows of the death of the drawer? Explain. *In re Estate of Norris,* 532 P.2d 981 (CO).

5. On June 18, Templeton deposited in his bank account a $5,000 check that was payable to his order. The check reached the drawee bank through normal banking channels on June 22. That bank had received a stop-payment order on the check on May 15 and, therefore, refused to honor it. It kept the check until June 28, when it returned it to Templeton with the notification that payment had been stopped. Did the drawee bank violate a duty it owed to Templeton? Explain. *Templeton v. First Nat'l Bank,* 362 N.E.2d 33 (IL).

6. In payment for services rendered, one of Stewart's clients gave him a check for $185.48 that had been drawn by the client's corporate employer and had been made payable to the order of the client. Although properly indorsed by the client, the drawee bank flatly refused to cash the check for Stewart. The bank acknowledged that the check was good, that is, that there were sufficient funds in the account. Could Stewart sue the bank for refusing to honor the check? Why or why not? *Stewart v. Citizens & Nat'l Bank,* 225 S.E.2d 761 (GA).

7. Fitting wrote an $800 check on her account with Continental Bank. A bank employee had mistakenly placed a hold on the account, causing the bank to dishonor the check when it was presented for payment. Fitting was unable to prove that she suffered damages because of the dishonor. Could she recover damages from the bank? Explain. *Continental Bank v. Fitting,* 559 P.2d 218 (AZ).

8. Roberta Lunt deposited a $625 nonlocal check payable to her with a teller at her bank at 10:30 A.M.

on Monday. The next day, Tuesday, she went to the bank to withdraw $300 and was told by the teller that she could have only $100 from the check she had deposited the day before. When must the funds be made available to Roberta? Explain why.

**quick quiz** Answers

| 18.1 | 18.2 | 18.3 |
|------|------|------|
| 1. F | 1. T | 1. F |
| 2. T | 2. T | 2. F |
| 3. T | 3. T | 3. F |

**Triffin v. Dillabough and American Express**
Supreme Court of Pennsylvania
670 A.2d 684; 716 A.2d 605

## Summary

Three American Express money orders were stolen from one of its agents, and 100 others were stolen while being shipped to a different agent. When stolen, all of the money orders contained the preprinted signature of the chairman of American Express, but they were blank as to the amount, sender, and date.

Stacy Anne Dillabough presented two of the stolen money orders for payment at Chuckie Enterprises, Inc. (Chuckie's), a check-cashing operation in Philadelphia. The money orders were in the amounts of $550 and $650 and listed Dillabough as the payee and David W. (last name undecipherable) as the sender. Two months later, Robert Lynn presented another one of the stolen money orders for payment at Chuckie's in the amount of $200, which listed himself as payee and Michael C. Pepe as the sender.

After being cashed at Chuckie's, the money orders traveled the regular bank collection routes and were returned to Chuckie's bearing the stamp "REPORTED LOST OR STOLEN—DO NOT REDEPOSIT." American Express refused to pay Chuckie's the face amounts of the money orders. Chuckie's then sold them to Triffin, a commercial discounter. By written agreements, Chuckie's assigned all of its right, title, and interest in the money orders to Triffin.

In court, Triffin obtained judgments by default against Dillabough and Lynn. In a trial with American Express, the court found that the money orders were not negotiable instruments and entered a judgment in favor of American Express. On appeal, the Superior Court reversed the trial court and held that the money orders were negotiable instruments and that Triffin had the status of a holder in due course, entitling him to recover the face amount of the money orders from American Express.

## The Court's Opinion

Madame Justice Newman

The Superior Court has described the purpose of negotiable instruments and the Commercial Code as follows:

> A negotiable instrument is an instrument capable of transfer by indorsement or delivery. Negotiability provides a means of passing on to the transferee the rights of the holder, including the right to sue in his or her own name, and the right to take free of equities as against the assignor/payee. [Citations omitted.] The purpose of the Commercial Code is to enhance the marketability of negotiable instruments and to allow bankers, brokers, and the general public to trade in confidence. [Citations omitted.] As a matter of sound economic policy, the Commercial Code encourages the free transfer and negotiability of commercial paper to stimulate financial interdependence.

*Manor Bldg. Corp. v. Manor Complex Assocs.,* 645 A.2d 843. With these principles in mind, we turn to a discussion of the American Express money orders at issue here.

The threshold question is whether the money orders qualify as negotiable instruments under Division Three of the Commercial Code, 3101, et seq., which governs negotiability.[1] Both parties agree that if the money orders are not negotiable instruments then Triffin's claims against American Express must fail. Initially, we note that the Commercial Code does not specifically define the term "money order," nor does it provide a descriptive list of financial documents that automatically qualify as negotiable instruments. Instead, 3104(a) sets forth the following four-part test to determine if a particular document qualifies as a negotiable instrument:

A. Requisites to negotiability. Any writing to be a negotiable instrument within this division must:

1. be signed by the maker or drawer;

2. contain an unconditional promise or order to pay a sum certain in money and no other promise, order, obligation or power given by the maker or drawer except as authorized by this division;

3. be payable on demand or at a definite time; and

4. be payable to order or to bearer.

The Superior Court described the face of the money orders in question as follows:

Prior to being stolen[,] the American Express money orders read: "AMERICAN EXPRESS MONEY ORDER . . . CHASE SAVINGS BANK . . . DATE (blank). PAY THE SUM OF (blank), NOT GOOD OVER $1,000, TO THE ORDER OF (blank). Louis V. Gerstner, Chairman. SENDER'S NAME AND ADDRESS (blank). Issued by American Express Travel Related Services Company, Inc., Englewood, Colorado. Payable at United Bank of Grand Junction, Downtown, Grand Junction, Colorado.

The first requisite of negotiability, a signature by the drawer or maker, "includes any symbol executed or adopted by a party with present intention to authenticate a writing." § 1201. "Authentication may be printed, stamped or written; it may be by initials or by thumbprint. . . . The question always is whether the symbol was executed or adopted by the party with

present intention to authenticate the writing." Additionally, section 3307(a)(2) states that when the effectiveness of a signature is challenged, it is presumed to be genuine or authorized unless the signer has died or become incompetent. Here, the drawer, American Express, affixed the pre-printed signature of Louis Gerstner, its then Chairman, to the money orders in question before forwarding them to its agents. American Express does not argue that Gerstner's signature was affixed to the money orders for any reason other than to authenticate them. Accordingly, the money orders satisfy the first requisite for negotiability.

The second requisite, American Express argues, is lacking because the money orders do not contain an unconditional promise or order to pay. Specifically, American Express claims that a legend it placed on the back of the money orders qualifies an otherwise unconditional order on the front directing the drawee to "PAY THE SUM OF" a specified amount "TO THE ORDER OF" the payee. The legend provides as follows:

IMPORTANT
DO NOT CASH FOR STRANGERS

THIS MONEY ORDER WILL NOT BE PAID IF IT HAS BEEN ALTERED OR STOLEN OR IF AN INDORSEMENT IS MISSING OR FORGED. BE SURE YOU HAVE EFFECTIVE RECOURSE AGAINST YOUR CUSTOMER.

---

PAYEE'S INDORSEMENT

According to American Express, this legend renders the order to pay conditional on the money order not being altered, stolen, unindorsed or forged and destroys the negotiability of the instrument.

We disagree. In a factually similar case, the Louisiana Court of Appeal construed a legend on the back of an American Express money order similar to the one at issue here. *Hong Kong Importers, Inc. v. American Express Co.,* 301 So.2d 707. The legend there stated "CASH ONLY IF RECOURSE FROM INDORSER IS AVAILABLE. IF THIS MONEY ORDER HAS NOT BEEN VALIDLY ISSUED OR HAS BEEN FRAUDULENTLY NEGOTIATED, IT WILL BE RETURNED." The money order also had the following language printed on its face: "KNOW YOUR INDORSER CASH ONLY IF RECOURSE IS AVAILABLE." The Louisiana Court held that the legend on the back and the language on the front did not convert the money order into a conditional promise to pay, but merely operated as a warning to the party cashing the money order to protect himself against fraud. Although *Hong Kong* was decided before Louisiana

[1] Although the Commercial Code has been revised since the transactions in this case occurred, its basic provisions survived the 1992 amendments. We expect that this Opinion will provide guidance for transactions conducted pursuant to the Commercial Code as amended in 1992.

adopted the Uniform Commercial Code, we find its rationale to be persuasive and applicable to § 3104.

American Express attempts to distinguish *Hong Kong* by asserting that the legend in this case is more specific because it explicitly conditions payment on the money orders not being altered, stolen, unindorsed or forged. This argument misses the point. "Any writing which meets the requirements of subsection [(a)] and is not excluded under Section [3103] is a negotiable instrument, and all sections of this [Division] apply to it, *even though it may contain additional language beyond that contemplated by this section.*" § 3104, Comment 4 (emphasis added). An otherwise unconditional order to pay that meets the section 3104 requirements is not made conditional by including implied or constructive conditions in the instrument. § 3105(a)(1). Moreover, purported conditions on an otherwise negotiable instrument, that merely reflect other provisions of the law, do not vitiate negotiability. *State v. Phelps*, 608 P.2d 51 (Ariz. Ct. App. 1979). Here, the alleged conditions on the back of the money orders are nothing more than a restatement of American Express' statutory defenses against payment because of alteration, absence of signature, and forgery. Contrary to American Express' claims, expressing those statutory defenses in a legend with the conditional phrase "THIS MONEY ORDER WILL NOT BE PAID IF . . ." does not elevate the legend to a condition for the purposes of 3104(a) because it is merely a restatement of the defenses present in the Commercial Code. The legend is simply a warning that American Express has reserved its statutory defenses. Whether these defenses are effective against Triffin is a separate question to be answered after resolving the issue of negotiability. We hold, therefore, that the money orders contain an unconditional order to pay, and satisfy the second requisite of negotiability.

The third requisite, that the writing be payable on demand or at a definite time, and the fourth requisite, that the writing be payable to order or bearer, are clear from the face of the money orders and are not disputed by the parties. Thus, the American Express money orders qualify as negotiable instruments pursuant to § 3104.

American Express contends that even if the money orders are facially negotiable, they should not be viewed as negotiable instruments because they were never issued or otherwise "placed in the stream of commerce." Issue is defined as "[t]he first delivery of an instrument to a holder or a remitter." § 3102. Delivery is defined as the "voluntary transfer of possession." § 1201. American Express argues that because the money orders were incomplete when stolen and subsequently completed without authorization, the money orders were never delivered and it should have no liability for them.

Authorized completion and delivery, however, are not listed as requisites to negotiability in section 3104. Moreover, section 3115 specifically permits the enforcement of incomplete and undelivered instruments and provides as follows:

A. General rule. When a paper whose contents at the time of signing show that it is intended to become an instrument is signed while still incomplete in any necessary respect it cannot be enforced until completed, but when it is completed in accordance with authority given it is effective as completed.

B. Unauthorized completion. *If the completion is unauthorized the rules as to material alteration apply (section 3407), even though the paper was not delivered by the maker or drawer,* but the burden of establishing that any completion is unauthorized is on the party so asserting [emphasis added].

Section 3407 provides that the defense of unauthorized completion discharges a party from liability to any person *other than a holder in due course.* § 3407(a)(2); § 3407(b). "A subsequent holder in due course may in all cases enforce the [negotiable] instrument according to its original tenor, and when an incomplete instrument has been completed, he may enforce it as completed." 3407(c). Additionally, section 3305 provides that a holder in due course takes a negotiable instrument free from the defense of non-delivery. § 3305, Comment 3.

When read together, sections 3115, 3407 and 3305 demonstrate that unauthorized completion and non-delivery do not prevent enforcement of an otherwise negotiable instrument. Instead, the three sections permit a holder in due course to enforce the undelivered instrument as completed. . . .

The next question then, is whether Triffin has the rights of a holder in due course who can enforce the negotiable money orders.

Section 3302(a) describes a holder in due course as follows:

A. General rule. A holder in due course is a holder who takes the instrument:

1. for value;

2. in good faith; and

3. without notice that it is overdue or has been dishonored or of any defense against or claim to it on the part of any person. § 3302(a).

Because the trial court held that the money orders were not negotiable instruments, it never answered the question of Triffin's status as a holder in due course. . . .

Triffin obtained the money orders from Chuckie's pursuant to a written agreement by which Chuckie's assigned all of its right, title and interest in the money orders to Triffin. Triffin could not become a holder in due course in his own name because he had notice of American Express' defenses when he took the money orders from Chuckie's. § 3302(a)(3). However, Triffin could acquire the status of a holder in due course from Chuckie's through the assignment if Chuckie's was a holder in due course because a transferee acquires whatever rights the transferor had, even if the transferee is aware of the defenses to enforcement. § 3201. Therefore, the focus of our inquiry is whether Chuckie's was a holder in due course.

The parties do not dispute that Chuckie's took the money orders for value. Paul Giunta, the owner of Chuckie's, testified that he paid Dillabough and Lynn the face value of the money orders, minus a two percent fee. Thus, section 3302(a)(1) is satisfied. The second element of section 3302(a), good faith, is defined as "honesty in fact in the conduct or transaction concerned." § 1201. The evidence established that Giunta recognized Dillabough and Lynn from previous transactions and required them to present photographic identification. Additionally, although the trial court did not discuss each element of Chuckie's holder in due course status, it did opine in a discussion of its legal conclusions on the record that Chuckie's acted in good faith. Moreover, American Express does not argue that Chuckie's failed to act in good faith. Based on Giunta's actions, we cannot say that the trial court erred in concluding that Chuckie's acted in good faith. Therefore, section 3302(a)(2) is satisfied. Regarding section 3302(a)(3), there was no evidence presented that Chuckie's had any notice that the Dillabough and Lynn money orders were stolen when he cashed them. Accordingly, the record demonstrates as a matter of law that Chuckie's was a holder in due course. Because Triffin stands in Chuckie's shoes as its assignee, Triffin has attained the status of a holder in due course. § 3201.

American Express further contends that even if Triffin qualifies as a holder in due course, the money orders are still not enforceable because the legend on their backs limits the "tenor" of the instruments. Pursuant to § 3413(a), American Express claims that it is only obligated to pay an instrument "according to its tenor." The 1979 Commercial Code does not define "tenor." The 1992 amendments to section 3413(a), however, substitute the word "terms" for the word "tenor." § 3413(a). Therefore, it appears that no substantive change was intended by the substitution of the word "terms" for the word "tenor" and we will treat

these words synonymously. Thus, American Express is essentially arguing that each money order should be enforced according to its terms, which state that the money order "WILL NOT BE PAID IF IT HAS BEEN ALTERED OR STOLEN OR IF AN INDORSEMENT IS MISSING OR FORGED."

As previously discussed, the legend on the back of the money orders is merely a warning that restates American Express' defenses against persons other than holders in due course in the event of alteration, theft, lack of indorsement or forgery. These defenses are ineffective against a holder in due course. § 3305; § 3407(c). Because Triffin has attained holder in due course status through the assignment of the money orders from Chuckie's, American Express cannot enforce the defenses against him. Accordingly, American Express is liable to Triffin for the face value of the money orders.

The Order of the Superior Court is affirmed.

# Dissenting Opinion

## Mr. Justice Castille

The majority concludes that appellee Robert J. Triffin ("appellee") is entitled to recover the value of the money orders at issue because the money orders were negotiable instruments and because appellee was a holder in due course of those negotiable instruments. However, since the money orders at issue contained express conditional language which precluded negotiability under the relevant statute, I must respectfully dissent from the majority's conclusion....

At issue here is the second of the four statutory prerequisites to negotiability, the requirement of an "unconditional" promise or order. Regarding this prerequisite, section 3105 provides:

A. Unconditional promise or order. A promise or order otherwise unconditional is not made conditional by the fact that the instrument:

 1. is subject to implied or constructive conditions;

. . .The comment to section 3105 states:

> 1. Nothing in [paragraph (a) subsection (1)] is intended to imply that language may not be fairly construed to mean what it says, but implications, whether of law or fact, are not to be considered in determining negotiability.

Thus, the statute clearly distinguishes between language which creates an implied condition and language which creates an express condition. The latter renders a promise or order non-negotiable while the former does not.

This conclusion derives further support from the revised § 3106(a), which provides that

> . . .a promise or order is unconditional unless it states (1) an express condition to payment. . . .

Here, the operative language in the money orders at issue clearly created an "express" condition and thereby rendered the money orders non-negotiable. The language at issue . . . explicitly conditions payments on the money orders' not being altered or stolen and the indorsements' not being missing or forged. The use of the word "if" renders the condition an express one, since "if" by definition means "on *condition* that; in case that; supposing that." Webster's New World Dict., 2d College ed. (emphasis added).

Furthermore, the official comment to revised section 3106 explains what the code intends by drawing the distinction between implied and express conditions:

> If the promise or order states an express condition to payment, the promise or order is not an instrument. For example, A states, "I promise to pay $100,000 to the order of John Doe if he conveys title to Blackacre to me." The promise is not an instrument because there is an express condition to payment. However, suppose a promise states, "In consideration of John Doe's promise to convey title of Blackacre I promise to pay $100,000 to the order of John Doe. That promise can be an instrument if [section 3104] is otherwise satisfied.

Accordingly, the use of the word "if" creates an express condition which otherwise might be lacking, and thereby precludes a money order from being a negotiable instrument under the statute. The language at issue in this case created the same type of express condition which is embodied in the Comment; consequently, the language precludes the money orders from being negotiable instruments.

The reasons proffered by the majority to justify its departure from this seemingly inescapable statutory logic are strained. First, the majority cites a case, decided by the Louisiana Court of Appeal in 1974, in which a condition incorporating the word "if" was construed not to bar negotiability. In that case, the Louisiana Court did not evaluate the significance of the word "if" or the significance of the condition which that word introduced. Moreover, in 1974, Louisiana had not yet adopted Article III of the Uniform Commercial Code ("UCC"). Hence, it appears that the Louisiana decision was decided against the backdrop of the Code of Napoleon. See *9 to 5 Fashions, Inc. v. Petr L. Spurney,* 538 So.2d 228, 233 (La. 1989) (discussing roots of Louisiana's civil code in the Napoleonic

code). Pennsylvania, on the other hand, has adopted Article III of the UCC, which speaks directly to the issue presented in this case, as explained supra. A decision by an intermediate Louisiana appellate court interpreting French legal principles should not override the explicit statutory guidance furnished by the Pennsylvania legislature on an issue of Pennsylvania law.

The majority also seizes on Comment 4 to § 3104, which states that "any writing which meets the requirements of subsection [(a)] and is not excluded under Section [3103] is a negotiable instrument, and all sections of this [Division] apply to it, *even though it may contain additional language beyond that contemplated by this section*" (emphasis added by majority). Since, as explained supra, the money orders contained language which precluded them from satisfying subsection (a), the quoted language from Comment 4 does not further the majority's argument.

Finally, the majority attempts to support its conclusion by referring to the principle that "purported conditions on an otherwise negotiable instrument, that merely reflect other provisions of the law, do not vitiate negotiability." The majority contends that the language at issue amounts merely to a restatement of appellant's statutory defenses against payment where there has been alteration (§ 3407), theft (§ 3306(4)), absence of signature (§ 3401) and forgery (§ 3404). The majority overlooks the fact that all of these statutory defenses are, by their own terms, ineffective against holders in due course. On the other hand, the language at issue here—which categorically states that the money order will not be paid if it was stolen—is operative even against holders who have taken in due course. As noted in the Comment to section 3105(a)(1), conditional language may be fairly construed to mean what it says. By its plain terms, the language at issue here sweeps beyond the scope of appellant's statutory defenses, and therefore does more than simply "reflect other provisions of the law."

In sum, the statute at issue in this case is devoid of ambiguity, and the application of that statute to these facts compels a conclusion contrary to that reached by the majority. Consequently, I respectfully dissent.

Mr. Justice Cappy joins this dissenting opinion.

# Questions for Analysis

1. What did the court say is the four-part test to determine whether a particular document qualifies as a negotiable instrument? Were these basic requirements changed by the 1990 UCC revision?

2. What does the definition of a signature on a negotiable instrument include?
3. How did the court respond to American Express's argument that the following words created a condition: "this money order will not be paid if it has been altered or stolen or if an indorsement is missing or forged"?
4. Why does the fact that the money orders were completed without authorization and not delivered have no effect on negotiation of an instrument?
5. Why could Triffin not become a holder in due course?
6. Why could Triffin acquire the status of a holder in due course?
7. In his dissenting opinion, what argument did Mr. Justice Castille use to try to persuade the other justices that the money orders were not negotiable?
8. Do you agree with the dissenting opinion? Why or why not?

# Part Five

## Insurance, Secured Transactions, and Bankruptcy

# Chapter 19 Insurance

## THE OPENING CASE We're Not in Mississippi Anymore: *Cosmopolitan Life Insurance v. Sanderson*

Often the day-to-day details of a relationship inter-fere with the big picture. Sometimes small things in life are overlooked; promises are broken; responsibili-ties put aside. Most of the time none of this matters. Someone picks up the slack and the job gets done one way or the other. Occasionally, though, some-thing slips through the cracks and lies dormant for years. Then, when we least expect it, the forgotten item emerges from the past and, depending on our situation, either pleases or horrifies us. This is exactly what happened to Alvin and Cynthia Sanderson. Cynthia and Alvin were married in 2004. It was Alvin's second marriage, and Cynthia's first. Both of them had saved a substantial amount of money. Alvin had a handsome investment portfolio and a house in Pas Christian, Mississippi. Cynthia had a small inheri-tance that she had managed well over the years. Af-ter their marriage, they sold Alvin's home and bought a newer house in another part of Pas Christian, which they insured with a homeowners' insurance policy that did not include flood insurance. The couple also took out life insurance policies, naming each other as beneficiaries. Cynthia continued to pay the premiums even after the couple was divorced in 2006. The di-vorce judgment contained an order that the couple's

late model Lexus that was registered and insured in their names jointly "shall belong to Alvin outright." Cynthia received the Pas Christian house in the set-tlement where she continued to live after the divorce. Then disaster hit in the form of Hurricane Katrina. First, the marital home was washed away in the storm. Then, while rushing back to Mississippi, Alvin was killed on the interstate. The state police reported that he was driving at a high rate of speed and was not wearing his seat belt at the time of the crash. The Lexus was totaled. It was at this point that those day-to-day details began to emerge. An investigation revealed that the couple had never removed Cyn-thia's name from the insurance policy as the co-owner of the car and that neither Alvin nor Cynthia had changed the beneficiaries on their life insurance. As for the house, Cynthia had simply continued the same homeowner's insurance policy with no changes in coverage. Cynthia filed claims under all three poli-cies. Madeline Sanderson, Alvin's mother, also filed a claim under Alvin's life insurance arguing that, after the divorce, Cynthia had no insurable interest that she could enforce. As you read this chapter on insurance, see if you can unravel who owes what to whom.

**Opening Case Questions**

1. Would a lawsuit like this be held in the state or the federal court? Explain.

2. Who will be able to recover the benefits on the life insurance? Madeline or Cynthia? Explain.

3. Does Cynthia have an insurable interest in the life insurance policy? Explain.

4. Will Cynthia be able to collect on the automobile insurance policy? Explain.

5. Will Cynthia be able to recover on the home-owner's policy for the loss of her home? Why or why not?

## LO Learning Objectives

1. Define risk management and explain the purpose of insurance.
2. Identify the contractual elements of an insurance agreement.
3. Make clear the importance of insurable interest.
4. Differentiate among the different types of life insurance.
5. Explain how insurable interest differs with life insurance and property insurance.
6. Explain the coinsurance clause in most property insurance policies.
7. Describe coverage given by fire, marine, homeowner's, renter's, and flood insurance.
8. Differentiate among the principal kinds of automobile insurance.
9. Describe the benefits included in health insurance policies.
10. List the steps in applying for, obtaining, and maintaining an insurance policy.

# 19-1 Risk Management

Although life has always been full of risks and uncertainties, it has become even more so since 9/11. A process called risk management is used by many businesses to identify, analyze, control, and communicate risks of all kinds, from the making of an accounting error to having the company's security compromised. Hazards such as accidents, fire, and illness pose a constant threat to our well-being. The principal protection against losses from such hazards is insurance. The purpose of insurance is to spread the losses among a great number of people. (See Table 19-1.) Insurance is a transfer of the risk of economic loss from the insured to the insurance company. Small contributions made by a large number of individuals can provide sufficient money to cover the losses suffered by a few as they occur each year. The function of insurance is to distribute each person's risk among all others who may or may not experience losses.

## Parties to an Insurance Contract

The parties to an insurance contract are the insurer (sometimes called *underwriter*), the insured, and the beneficiary. The insurer accepts the risk of loss in return for a premium (the consideration paid for a policy) and agrees to indemnify, or compensate, the insured against the loss specified in the contract. The insured is the party (or parties) protected by the insurance contract. The contract of insurance is called the policy. The period of time during which the insurer assumes the risk of loss is known as the life of the policy. A third party, to whom payment of compensation is sometimes provided by the contract, is called the beneficiary.

**Table 19-1**   Examples of Risk Management Strategies

| RISKS | | Strategies for Reducing Financial Impact |
| --- | --- | --- |
| **Personal Event** | **Financial Impact** | |
| Disability | • Loss of income<br>• Increased expenses | • Savings and investments<br>• Disability insurance |
| Death | • Loss of income | • Life insurance<br>• Estate planning |
| Property loss | • Catastrophic storm damage to property<br>• Repair or replacement<br>• Cost of theft | • Property repair and upkeep<br>• Auto insurance<br>• Homeowner's insurance<br>• Flood or earthquake insurance |
| Liability | • Claims and settlement costs<br>• Lawsuits and legal expenses<br>• Loss of personal assets and income | • Maintaining property<br>• Homeowner's insurance<br>• Auto insurance |

*Source:* Gordon W. Brown, *Understanding Business and Personal Law,* 11e, p. 752. Copyright © 2006 Glencoe/McGraw-Hill. Reprinted with permission.

## Contractual Elements

Insurance policies, like other contracts, require the four elements of a contract: mutual assent, capacity, consideration, and legality. The application filled in by an applicant is an offer to the insurer, which may then accept or reject the offer. When the insurer (the offeree) accepts the offer (the application) from the applicant (the offeror) mutual assent emerges between the parties. A party to a contract must also be capable of understanding the terms of the agreement. Consideration arises from the premiums paid by the insured and the promise of the insurer to pay money to the beneficiary if a certain event happens. Finally, the subject matter must not be tainted with illegality. For example, a fire insurance policy written on a building in which the owners permitted the illegal manufacture of fireworks would be void in the event of a fire.

## Insurable Interest

A person or business applying for insurance must have an insurable interest in the subject matter of the policy to be insured. An **insurable interest** is the financial interest that a policyholder has in the person or property that is insured. In the case of life insurance, all people have an insurable interest in their own lives as well as the lives of their spouses and dependents. Business partners have an insurable interest in each other because they could suffer a financial loss if a partner dies. A corporation can have a financial interest in its key employees for the same reason. In the case of property insurance, anyone who would suffer a financial loss from damage to property would have an insurable interest in that property. For life insurance, the insurable interest must exist at the time the insurance is purchased. In contrast, for property insurance, the insurable interest must exist at the time of loss.

## Subrogation

Insurance companies have the right to step into the shoes of the party they compensate and sue any party whom the compensated party could have sued. This substitution of one person in place of another relative to a lawful claim is known as **subrogation**.

## quick quiz 19-1

| | |
|---|---|
| 1. The purpose of insurance is to spread losses among people who can most afford it. | true \| false |
| 2. An application filled in by an insurance applicant is a binding contract on the insurer. | true \| false |
| 3. Anyone can obtain insurance on another person or property, regardless of their relationship. | true \| false |

# 19-2 Types of Insurance

It is possible to obtain insurance against almost any risk if an individual or business is willing to pay the price. The premium charged will depend on the risk involved. Life insurance, property insurance, and health insurance are discussed here.

## Life Insurance

**Life insurance** is an insurance contract that provides monetary compensation for losses suffered by another's death. Anyone has an insurable interest in the life of another if a financial loss will occur if the insured dies. For example, an insurable interest exists if the person who buys the insurance is dependent on the insured for education, support, business (partners), or debt collection. A life insurance policy will remain valid and enforceable

---

## THE OPENING CASE *Revisited, Part I*
### We're Not in Mississippi Anymore: *Cosmopolitan Life Insurance v. Sanderson,* Round 2

After they were married, Cynthia and Alvin Sanderson took out life insurance policies, naming each other as beneficiaries. The couple was divorced in 2006. Despite this, Cynthia continued to pay the premiums on both policies. The divorce agreement said nothing about the life insurance policies. While rushing back to Mississippi after Hurricane Katrina, Alvin was killed on the interstate. An investigation revealed that neither Alvin nor Cynthia had changed the beneficiaries on their life insurance policies. When Cynthia filed a claim for the insurance benefits, she discovered that Alvin's mother, Madeline had filed a similar claim. They both demanded that Cosmopolitan Life pay them the money owed under the policy. Madeline argued that Cynthia no longer had an insurable interest in Alvin's life and, in fact, had lost that interest when the divorce was finalized. The court said that Madeline's argument

was correct up to a point. However, what she missed was the fact that Cynthia had an insurable interest when the policy was issued. Since the law only requires that the beneficiary have an insurable interest at the time that the policy was originally issued, the court ruled in Cynthia's favor. (Note: Some states have statutes that expressly terminate a spouse's status as a beneficiary under a life insurance policy upon divorce, dissolution, or annulment. These states also usually terminate the death benefits under IRAs and employer death benefit plans upon divorce, dissolution, or annulment. Even in these states, however, the law generally permits the couple to preserve these beneficiary rights in their decree or judgment of divorce, dissolution, or annulment. See for example, Ohio Revised Code 5815.33 Termination of marriage revokes designation of spouse as beneficiary.)

even if the insurable interest terminates. It is necessary only that the insurable interest exists at the time the policy was issued.

Premiums for life insurance are based on several factors, including the age and health of the insured, the coverage, and the type of policy. It is less expensive to buy life insurance at a young age because the death rate for young people is very low, and their health is usually at its peak.

If an individual takes out insurance on him- or herself, it is not necessary for the beneficiary to have an insurable interest in the insured's life. However, if a person takes out life insurance on someone else, that person must have an insurable interest in the insured's life.

The principal types of life insurance are straight life, limited-payment life, term, and endowment insurance.

### Straight Life Insurance

**Straight life insurance**, which is also known as **ordinary life insurance** or **whole life insurance**, requires the payment of premiums throughout the life of the insured and pays the beneficiary the face value of the policy upon the insured's death. The amount of the premium is determined by the age of the insured at the time of purchase and normally stays the same throughout the life of the policy. The younger the insured, the lower the premium, because the company expects to collect many years' worth of premiums.

Straight life insurance contains an investment feature known as the *cash surrender value*. The cash surrender value usually builds up slowly at first but in later years approaches the face amount of the policy. At some stated point (usually at the age of 95 or 100 years), it equals the face value of the policy. An insured can cancel a straight life policy at any time and receive its cash surrender value. Straight life insurance also contains a feature called a *loan value,* which is an amount of money that may be borrowed against the cash surrender value of the policy, usually at a relatively favorable rate of interest. During inflationary times, when bank interest rates are high, insurance policies are often excellent sources of loans at low interest rates.

### EXAMPLE 19-1: Straight Life Insurance

At age 18 years, LaPlume purchased a straight life insurance policy with a face value of $20,000. The premiums were quite modest. At some later time, LaPlume could borrow on the policy or trade it in for its cash surrender value. Or, LaPlume could continue premium payments until death. If LaPlume died while a loan was outstanding, the insurance company would deduct the amount of the loan from the amount it paid to LaPlume's beneficiary.

A form of straight life insurance, called **universal life insurance**, allows the policy owner flexibility in choosing and changing terms of the policy. Within certain guidelines, the policy owner can modify the face value of the policy as well as the premiums in response to changing needs and circumstances in the policy owner's life. Under a typical universal life policy:

- Premiums may be increased or decreased within policy limits.
- The amount of insurance may be increased, subject to evidence of insurability, or decreased, subject to set minimums.
- The owner may borrow up to the maximum loan value at a prearranged interest rate. Policy loans reduce the cash surrender value and death benefit.
- Withdrawals may be made from the cash surrender value.

## Limited-Payment Life Insurance

**Limited-payment life insurance** provides that the payment of premiums will stop after a stated length of time—usually 10, 20, or 30 years. The amount of the policy will be paid to the beneficiary upon the death of the insured, whether the death occurs during the payment period or after. Because of the limited number of payments made by the insured, the premiums are proportionately higher than those for straight life; however, the cash surrender value grows faster than that of straight life insurance.

## Term Insurance

As the name suggests, **term insurance** is issued for a particular period, usually 10 or 20 years. The time period is known as the term. Term insurance is the least expensive kind of life insurance because term policies have no cash or loan value, as others do. Term insurance offers protection alone, in contrast to straight life, which combines protection with a savings plan. Term insurance can be renewable at the end of each period simply by paying the increased premium, without need for a new medical examination. *Convertible* term insurance policies can be converted to straight life policies without taking a new medical examination—allowing protection throughout the insured's lifetime. A modified form of term insurance is *decreasing term insurance*. The premium stays constant from year to year, but the amount of protection (death benefit) decreases over the years. This type of insurance is widely used to cover the outstanding balance of a home mortgage.

## Annuity

An **annuity** is guaranteed retirement income purchased by paying either a lump-sum premium or making periodic payments to an insurer. The insured may choose either (a) to receive an income for a certain fixed number of years, with a beneficiary receiving whatever is left of the annuity if the insured dies before the term expires, or (b) to receive payments as long as the insured lives and, upon death, relinquish whatever is left of the annuity, if anything.

## Exemptions from Risk

Many life insurance policies contain clauses that exempt the insurance company from liability in certain situations. For example, policies often do not cover the insured when riding in an airplane, violating the law, or working in certain dangerous occupations.

Most policies provide that beneficiaries can recover for a death caused by suicide if the suicide occurs more than two years after the policy was taken out. They may not recover, however, when the policy contains a provision preventing such recovery or when the life insurance was purchased by someone planning suicide or who was insane. One example of a named beneficiary who could recover would be a creditor of the insured.

Life insurance policies usually include an exemption from liability in times of war. The exemption states that the insurer will not be liable on the policy if the insured is killed while a member of the armed forces, generally outside the continental United States, or by service-connected causes.

## Optional Provisions

Life insurance policies have many optional provisions that may be purchased by the insured. Three popular options are double indemnity, waiver of premium, and guaranteed insurability.

For an additional premium, the insured may purchase a benefit known as **double indemnity**, or accidental death benefit. This option provides that if the insured dies from accidental causes, the insurer will pay double the amount of the

Insurance protects you and your family providing security for unexpected occurences.

## THE OPENING CASE *Revisited, Part II*
### We're Not in Mississippi Anymore: *Cosmopolitan Life Insurance v. Sanderson*, Round 3

Recall that in the Opening Case at the beginning of the chapter, Cynthia and Alvin were divorced in 2006. The divorce judgment contained an order that the couple's late model Lexus that was registered and insured in their names jointly. "shall belong to Alvin outright." While rushing back to Mississippi, Alvin was killed on the interstate and the Lexus was totaled. Cynthia then filed a claim for the insurance benefits that covered the car. The Greensboro Auto Insurance company refused to pay Cynthia anything for the totaled Lexus. The company was within its rights under the contract and under the law to do this. Cynthia's insurable interest ended when the court ruled that as a result of the divorce decree, the Lexus belonged solely to Alvin outright.

policy to the beneficiary. Death must occur within 90 days of the accident for this benefit to apply.

The *waiver of premium* option excuses the insured from paying premiums if he or she becomes disabled. Some insurance policies automatically include the waiver in their provisions; others offer it as an extra-cost option.

A *guaranteed insurability* option allows the insured to pay an extra premium initially in exchange for a guaranteed option to buy more insurance at certain specified times later. The additional insurance can be purchased with no questions asked; thus, no new medical examination is required even if the insured develops a serious illness before exercising the option.

## Property Insurance

Property insurance can be purchased to protect both real and personal property. To establish the existence of an insurable interest in property, the insured must demonstrate a monetary interest in the property. This monetary interest means that the insured will suffer a financial loss if the property is damaged or destroyed. Unlike life insurance, this insurable interest must exist when the loss occurs.

Property insurance can be made less expensive by the use of a deductible, which is an amount of any loss that is to be paid by the insured. It can be a specified dollar amount, a percentage of the claim amount, or a specified amount of time that must elapse before benefits are paid. The bigger the deductible, the lower is the premium charged for the same coverage.

### Coinsurance Clauses    Coinsurance is an insurance policy provision under which the insurer and the insured share costs, after the deductible is met, according to a specific formula. Most property and inland marine policies have a coinsurance clause, which limits the insurance company's liability for a loss if the property is not insured for its full replacement value. For example, if a homeowner's insurance policy has an 80 percent coinsurance clause, the building must be insured for 80 percent of its replacement value to receive full reimbursement for a loss (see Figure 19-1).

### Fire Insurance    A fire insurance policy is a contract in which the fire insurance company promises to pay the insured if some real or personal property is damaged or destroyed by fire. A fire insurance policy is effective on delivery to the insured, even before the premium is paid. Even an oral agreement will make fire insurance effective.

---

### TYPICAL COINSURANCE CLAUSE

---

"The insurance company will pay that part of a loss that the insurance carried bears to 80 percent of the replacement cost of the building."

It would cost $100,000 to replace Felipe Garcia's house. If he insured it for $60,000, the insurance company would pay only three-fourths of any loss, computed as follows:

$$\frac{\text{Amount of insurance carried}}{\text{Percent of replacement cost}} \quad \frac{\$60,000}{80\% \text{ of } \$100,000} \quad = \quad \frac{\$60,000}{\$80,000} \quad = \quad \frac{3}{4}$$

A fire partially destroys the building, causing $40,000 worth of damage. Because of the co-insurance clause, Garcia would recover $30,000 (¾ of the loss) from the insurance company.

**Figure 19-1**  Here is a typical coinsurance clause found in an insurance policy. It limits the insurer's liability for a loss if the property is not insured for full, or at least 80% of, replacement value.

The insurer's liability under a fire policy usually covers losses other than those directly attributed to fire. Under most policies, claims may also be made for losses from water used to fight the fire; scorching; smoke damage to goods; deliberate destruction of property as a means of controlling a spreading fire; lightning, even if there is no resultant fire; riot or explosion, if a fire does result; and losses through theft or exposure of goods removed from a burning building.

## Marine Insurance
Marine insurance is one of the oldest types of insurance coverage, dating back to Venetian traders who sailed the Mediterranean Sea. Ocean marine insurance covers ships at sea. Inland marine insurance covers goods that are moved by land carriers such as rail, truck, and airplane. Inland marine insurance also covers such items as jewelry, fine arts, musical instruments, and wedding presents. Customers' goods in the possession of bailees, such as fur-storage houses and dry cleaners, are also covered by inland marine insurance. A *floater policy* is one that insures property that cannot be covered by specific insurance because the property is constantly changing in either value or location. A personal property floater, for example, covers personal property in general, wherever it is located.

## Homeowner's and Renter's Insurance
Many of the leading insurance companies offer a combination policy known as the homeowner's policy. This insurance gives protection for all types of losses and liabilities related to home ownership. Among the items covered are losses from fire, windstorms, burglary, vandalism, and injuries suffered by other persons while on the property. Losses from flooding generally are not covered under a homeowner's policy. Renter's insurance protects tenants against the loss of personal property, liability for a visitor's personal injury, and liability for negligent destruction of the rented premises.

## Flood Insurance
Flooding can be caused by heavy rains, melting snow, inadequate drainage systems, failed protective devices such as levees and dams, and tropical storms and hurricanes. Nevertheless, most commercial, homeowner's, and renter's insurance policies do not cover flood damage. To obtain such coverage, special flood insurance must be obtained from an insurance agent.

Most flood insurance is backed by the National Flood Insurance Program (NFIP), established by Congress in response to the high cost of taxpayer-funded disaster relief for flood victims and the amount of damage caused by floods. Communities that agree to manage

## THE OPENING CASE *Revisited, Part III*
## We're Not in Mississippi Anymore: *Cosmopolitan Life Insurance v. Sanderson*, Round 4

Recall that when Cynthia and Alvin Sanderson were married in 2004, they had both saved a substantial amount of money. Alvin had a solid investment portfolio and a house in Pas Christian, Mississippi. Cynthia had a small inheritance that she had managed well over the years. After their marriage, they sold Alvin's house and bought a new home in another part of Pas Christian, which they promptly insured with homeowners' insurance that did not include flood insurance. Cynthia received the house in the divorce settlement and extended the same homeowner's policy with the same exact coverage. After Katrina, she tried to collect for her losses under the insurance policy. She argued

that the home was destroyed by the storm. The insurance company contended that the home was destroyed by the flood waters that had been caused by the storm not by the storm itself. As a result, because Cynthia did not have flood insurance, they were under no obligation to pay her anything under that policy. It is likely that the insurance company will prevail. Evidence that emerged in the aftermath of Katrina has shown that much of the damage to homes along Mississippi's Gulf Coast was caused by the storm surge of water rather than by wind. Her case could be reopened and reviewed, however, under the insurers' agreement with the state attorney general.

Without adequate insurance, most people would be unable to even approach status quo after suffering a catastrophic event.

flood hazard areas by adopting minimum standards can participate in the NFIP. However, communities that do not participate in the program cannot receive flood insurance, federal grants and loans, federal disaster assistance, or federal mortgage insurance for the acquisition or construction of structures located in flood hazard areas of their community. Most lending institutions require borrowers to obtain flood insurance when they buy, build, or improve structures in Special Flood Hazard Areas (SFHAs). Lending institutions that are federally regulated or federally insured must determine if the structure is located in an SFHA and provide written notice requiring flood insurance.

Following hurricane Katrina, one of the most destructive storms in recent memory, which devastated the Gulf Coast in 2005, many insurance claims were delayed, and others were not paid on the grounds that damages were caused by water rather than by wind, though most homeowners had little or no flood insurance. Hundreds of lawsuits were brought by disgruntled homeowners against insurance companies, and some million-dollar jury verdicts against the companies were settled out of court. Some of the jury awards were for punitive damages because the companies failed to pay the claims quickly enough. A federal appeals court found that many insurance policies covering property in New Orleans contained flood exclusions. The court said, "Regardless of what caused the failure of the flood-control structures that were put in place to prevent such catastrophe, their failure resulted in a widespread flood that damaged the plaintiffs' property. Their policies clearly excluded water damage caused by floods." One lower federal court case upheld the insurance company's view that homeowner policies cover damage from a hurricane's wind but not the rising water that ensues, including wind-driven surge. Several major insurers in Mississippi, which does not allow punitive damages in these cases, entered an agreement with the Mississippi Attorney General to pay about $80 million to 639 policyholders whose claims were denied following Katrina. As part of the agreement, insurers were required to reopen and review claims filed by policyholders who live in that state.

## Automobile Insurance

Automobile insurance provides for indemnity against losses resulting from fire, theft, or collision with another vehicle and damages arising out of injury by motor vehicles to the person or property of another. One thing to always remember about car insurance and about car accidents in general is that the law in relation to determining fault in such accidents differs a great deal from state to state. It is, therefore, always best to be very careful about choosing automobile insurance and in making certain that anyone involved in an accident contact an attorney in the state in which the accident occurs. This is because it is the law of that state that generally applies to the accident. The following are the most common types of automobile insurance:

- Bodily injury liability insurance.
- Fault-based insurance.
- No-fault insurance.
- Add-on coverage.
- Threshold guidelines and choice-based jurisdictions.
- Uninsured-motorist insurance.
- Underinsured-motorist insurance.
- Medical payments insurance.
- Property damage liability insurance.
- Collision insurance.
- Comprehensive coverage.
- Substitute transportation insurance.
- Towing and labor insurance.

**Bodily Injury Liability Insurance** The risk of bodily injury or death to pedestrians and the occupants of other cars arising from the negligent operation of the insured's motor vehicle is covered by **bodily injury liability insurance**. Under liability insurance, the insurer is liable for damages up to the limit of the insurance purchased. The insurance company must also provide attorneys for the insured's defense in any civil court action.

**Fault-Based Insurance** Most states still base their car insurance and, therefore, the handling of car accident claims, on tort law. **Fault-based insurance** means that liability in an automobile accident will be measured by the degree of fault that can be assigned to each driver based on negligence principles. The level of fault that can be attributed to each party in the accident forms the basis for the insurance company's payment. In such a state, lawsuits may be necessary to determine damages based on pain and suffering, hospital expenses, lost wages, and so on.

**No-Fault Insurance** Currently no-fault insurance is required, at least to some extent, in some states. **No-fault insurance** which is also called **personal injury protection (PIP)** places limitations on the insured's ability to sue other drivers but allows drivers to collect damages and medical expenses from their own insurance carriers, regardless of who

loss in 2005. Add investment income, and insurers had net income after taxes of nearly $64 billion, giving the industry its highest rate of return in 20 years. All that money expands the industry's underwriting wherewithal, driving down the price.

*Source*: Peter Coy and Adam Aston, "Hurricane Ahead, But Lower Insurance," *BusinessWeek,* May 14, 2007, pp. 68–69.

is at fault in an accident. This coverage helps cut down on fraudulent and excessively high claims. It also eliminates costly litigation needed to determine the negligence or lack of negligence of people involved in automobile accidents. On the other hand, even in no-fault states, a victim must sue if he or she wants to be compensated for actual property damage to the automobile itself, or to the items in the car. Some states alter the no-fault formula by adding a new element called a **threshold**. When the damages go beyond this threshold, which is defined by a set dollar amount, by injury description, or by time, the victim can file a negligence based lawsuit. Threshold injuries based on description include very serious ailments such as a permanent disability. In contrast, **time-based thresholds** are ascertained by measuring the time that the victim is incapacitated. Moreover, some jurisdictions permit both descriptive and time-based thresholds.

### Add-On Coverage

In some jurisdictions, add-on coverage is legally recognized. These jurisdictions currently include Arkansas, Delaware, Maryland, and the District of Columbia. **Add-on coverage** permits a driver to buy optional coverage such as personal injury insurance that would allow him or her to receive payment without bothering to determine fault. Add-on policies, however, would not prevent the insured from bringing a lawsuit for pain and suffering and other similar injuries. Generally, threshold provisions are included in these policies.

### Threshold Guidelines and Choice-Based Jurisdictions

Some no-fault jurisdictions set threshold guidelines that must be met by everyone regardless of the nature of their insurance policy. **Threshold guidelines** determine when victims can bring a lawsuit for injuries that result from an auto accident. Several states apply a strict monetary threshold while some no-fault jurisdictions have **descriptive thresholds**. A few states permit drivers to choose between no-fault and tort-law based insurance.

### Uninsured-Motorist Insurance

Essentially, **uninsured-motorist insurance** provides protection against the risk of being injured by an uninsured motorist. The coverage applies when the person who caused the accident was at fault and had no bodily injury liability insurance to cover the loss. It protects the insured, the insured's spouse, relatives in the same household, and any other person occupying an insured automobile. It also protects people who are injured by hit-and-run drivers. No coverage is provided to an automobile used without the permission of the insured or the insured's spouse. Uninsured motorist insurance provides no reimbursement for damages to the insured's property.

### Underinsured-Motorist Insurance

Basically, **underinsured-motorist insurance** provides protection against the risk of being injured by an underinsured motorist. For an insured to collect this insurance, someone without enough bodily injury coverage must have caused the accident.

### Medical Payments Insurance

In essence, **medical payments insurance** pays for medical (and sometimes funeral) expenses resulting from bodily injuries to anyone occupying the policyholder's car at the time of an accident. In some states, it pays for the medical bills of all family members who are struck by a car or who are riding in someone else's car when it is involved in an accident.

### Property Damage Liability Insurance

In brief, **property damage liability insurance** provides protection when other people bring claims or lawsuits against the insured for damaging property such as a car, fence, or tree. The person bringing the claim or suit must prove that the driver of the motor vehicle was at fault.

## Collision Insurance
Basically, **collision insurance** provides against any loss arising from damage to the insured's automobile caused by accidental collision with another object or with any part of the roadbed. Liability under collision insurance is limited to the insured's car.

## Comprehensive Coverage
In short, **comprehensive coverage** provides protection against loss when the insured's car is damaged or destroyed by fire, lightning, flood, hail, windstorm, riot, vandalism, or theft. The insurance company's liability is limited to the actual cash value of the vehicle at the time of the loss.

## Substitute Transportation Insurance
Essentially, **substitute transportation insurance** reimburses up to specified limits for car rental or transportation costs, including taxi, bus, and train fare, while the insured's car is undergoing covered repairs.

## Towing and Labor Insurance
In essence, **towing and labor insurance** reimburses up to specified limits for towing and labor charges whenever the insured's car breaks down, whether or not an accident is involved.

## Health Insurance

With the increasingly high costs of prescriptions, other medical products, and services, affordable health insurance is a foremost need in today's society. Many people obtain health insurance through a group insurance plan from the company for which they work. Others have individual plans that they purchase directly from an insurer. Still others have government health insurance plans through government employment, Medicare, and Medicaid (see Figure 19-2). Health insurance policies often include the following benefits:

- Physician care.
- Prescription drugs.
- Inpatient and outpatient hospital care.
- Surgery.
- Dental and vision care.
- Long-term care for the elderly.

*Major medical coverage* pays for expenses beyond those covered by a basic plan, including long-term hospitalization and catastrophic illness.

### HMOs and PPOs
Health Maintenance Organizations (HMOs) contract with doctors and other health care professionals to provide health care services for their members. Members pay monthly premiums and must choose from a list of doctors provided by the HMO. HMOs encourage their members to have regular checkups, immunizations, and other forms of early treatment. In this way, it is hoped that people will be less likely to require more expensive kinds of treatment. Many different kinds of organizations sponsor HMOs, including doctors, community groups, insurance companies, labor unions, and corporations.

A Preferred Provider Organization (PPO) is a group of health care providers, such as doctors or hospitals, that provide care for groups of employees at reduced rates. PPOs are usually sponsored as part of an employer's group health plan. Employees choose among the health care providers on the PPO list when they need treatment. Choosing a non-PPO provider reduces the benefits paid to the insured under the plan.

| Year of birth | Full retirement age |
|---|---|
| 1937 or earlier | 65 |
| 1938 | 65 and 2 months |
| 1939 | 65 and 4 months |
| 1940 | 65 and 6 months |
| 1941 | 65 and 8 months |
| 1942 | 65 and 10 months |
| 1943–1954 | 66 |
| 1955 | 66 and 2 months |
| 1956 | 66 and 4 months |
| 1957 | 66 and 6 months |
| 1958 | 66 and 8 months |
| 1959 | 66 and 10 months |
| 1960 and later | 67 |

**Note:** *People who were born on January 1 of any year should refer to the previous year.*

**Figure 19-2**  Age to Receive Social Security Benefits.
*Source:* Social Security Administration, SSA Publication No. 05-10035.

**Medicare and Medicaid**  Most people 65 years of age and older are eligible for Medicare a federally funded health insurance program. The age for eligibility began increasing in 2003 at two-month intervals over at 12-year period (see Figure 19-2). Medicare Part A helps pay for inpatient hospital care. Medicare Part B pays for 80 percent of doctors' and other medical services. Many people buy their own medigap insurance to cover the 20 percent not covered by Medicare. Medicaid is a health care plan for low-income people. State governments administer Medicaid, which is funded by both state and federal funds.

**Disability Insurance**  Disability insurance pays benefits when a person cannot work because of a disability. Total, or long-term, disability pays if the insured cannot perform normal job duties for a year or longer; partial, or short-term, disability pays for shorter periods of time.

**Long-Term Care Insurance**  Long-term care insurance helps cover care received in adult day care, assisted-living facilities, and nursing homes. Benefits are usually payable when an insured is unable to perform certain daily living activities without assistance, such as eating, bathing, dressing, or using the bathroom.

**Legal Protection**  A variety of state and federal laws help make it easier for people with preexisting conditions to obtain and keep health insurance. A federal law known as HIPAA (Health Insurance Portability and Accountability Act) sets national standards for all health plans.

# Health Care Reform

The new health care reform bill has altered taxes as they relate to certain health-related activities. For example, back in 2010 the new bill imposed a 10 percent tax on the price paid for an indoor tanning treatment. Also in 2010, the refundable tax credit permitted for expenses related to an adoption has risen to $13,170. That represents an increase of $1,000. Also, the maximum income exclusion permitted for employer assistance in adoption also went up to $13,170. The law also added an inflation adjustment factor that went into effect back in 2011. Also, as obvious reflection of changing family life styles, the new law permits parents to exclude the value of employer provided health care benefits for "children" who are still 27 years old at the end of the tax year. The same is true for those self-employed people who have paid out health care coverage for that 27 year old "child."

Back in 2011, another adjustment was made that eliminated over-the-counter medications as a qualified medical expense for flex plans, health savings accounts, Archer MSA, and health reimbursement arrangements. However, expenses for insulin and other over-the-counter medications prescribed by a physician remain eligible under such plans. In 2013, a new change affects taxpayers who itemize deductions. Such taxpayers will be to deduct unreimbursed medical expenses if they go over 10 percent of the taxpayers adjusted gross income. There are exceptions to this new rule.

High-income people are hit hard in 2013. In that unlucky year, married taxpayers who make over $250,000 jointly in wages ($200,000 for unmarried folks) will see an additional 0.9 percent added to their payroll withholding for Medicare. Individuals with over $200,000 in adjusted gross income and couples with over $250,000 are hit with an additional 3.8 percent Medicare tax on unearned income. The year 2014 also sees some changes. The changes will affect people with a household income that lies somewhere between 100 percent and 400 percent of the national poverty level as calculated by the federal government. These households can take advantage of a tax credit calculated based on their exact income for each year. The tax credit does not, however, affect employees who are covered by a health care plan at work. There are also exceptions to this rule. If the work-related plan is inadequate or overpriced, the employee might still qualify for the tax credit. In addition, a new cost-sharing subsidy for out-of-pocket expenses will be available for some of these same poverty level households.

Finally, United States citizens must have health care coverage by the year 2014. Those citizens without such coverage will be penalized come tax time. They will be forced to pay a penalty tax that will be calculated based on a set formula. The maximum amount of the penalty tax will be $95 for each adult not insured ($47.50 for each uninsured minor). The highest amount a household can be penalized is $285 until 2016 when $2085 becomes the highest household penalty possible. (Note: Health care reform is a volatile issue that is prone to sudden changes based on political and economic movements and so it is best to check for the most up-to-date laws in this area.)

## quick quiz 19-2

| | |
|---|---|
| 1. An insured can cancel a straight life policy at any time and receive its cash surrender value. | true \| false |
| 2. Term insurance is the most expensive kind of life insurance. | true \| false |
| 3. With property insurance, unlike life insurance, an insurable interest must exist when a loss occurs. | true \| false |

# 19-3 The Insurance Policy

In most states, the insurance policy (which is the insurance contract) comes in a standard form. These forms are carefully drafted by insurance commissioners with help from the states' legal advisers. In this way, the consumer-buyer is protected from deception or fraud. As an additional protection to consumers, some states now require that insurance contracts must be written in clear, understandable language and printed in a readable typeface. Insurance policies, nevertheless, are adhesion contracts—that is, contracts drawn by one party that must be accepted as is on a take-it-or-leave-it basis.

## Application

The first step in obtaining an insurance policy is to fill in an application. The application is an offer made by the applicant to the insurance company. As with any offer, the offeree, in this case the insurance company, may accept or reject the offer.

## Binders

The waiting period between the offer and the acceptance opens the insured to potential risk. To avoid this risk, the insured can arrange to have the insurer issue a binder. A binder, or binding slip, will provide temporary insurance coverage until the policy is formally accepted. The binder will include all of the usual terms that would be included in the actual policy to be issued.

## Premiums

An insurance contract differs from most other contracts in that it requires the payment of premiums. The amount of the premium is determined by the nature and character of the risk and by how likely the risk is to occur. The premium increases as the chance of loss increases. Thus, a premium on a fireproof building in a city with a fire department will be much lower than the premium on a barn located where firefighting equipment is not available.

## Lapse

When the insured stops paying premiums, an insurance contract is said to lapse. This feature may not mean, however, that the contract will terminate automatically on the date that the last premium is paid. It may also not lapse automatically if the insured makes a delayed payment. Although state laws differ, most states allow for a grace period in which the insured may make payments to keep life and health insurance policies in force. Beyond this period, however, the insurance contract will lapse, and the policy will terminate. Automobile and property insurance policies usually have no grace periods and will terminate when a premium is not paid when due.

---

### quick quiz 19-3

1. An insurance binder provides permanent insurance coverage.  true | false
2. Insurance premiums increase as the chance of loss increases.  true | false
3. An insurance contract will terminate automatically if a premium payment is not paid on time.  true | false

# 19-4 Cancellation of Insurance by Insurer

Under certain conditions, the insurer is given a legal right to forfeit, or cancel, an insurance policy. Proof of a forfeiture permits cancellation either before a loss or at the time the claim is made on a policy. Among the grounds permitting forfeiture are a breach of warranty and a concealment or misrepresentation of a material fact by the insured (Table 19-2). Neither the insured nor the insurer may deny statements or acts previously made or committed that might affect the validity of the policy.

## Warranties

A *warranty* is an insured's promise to abide by restrictions, especially those written into a policy that are intended to be conditions precedent to the existence of coverage. By statute in many states, an insurance company has the burden of proof in establishing that a warranty has been breached (broken) by the insured. If this breach is proved, the insurer may cancel the contract or refuse payment of loss to the insured or to a beneficiary.

### EXAMPLE 19-2:  Breach of Warranty

Nicole Duffy, a well-known NASCAR driver, applied for life insurance after being involved in several racing accidents. Community Life was aware of these accidents, and Duffy agreed not to race while the policy remained in force. Duffy was killed while racing in an important race. Community Life could rescind any obligation to pay Duffy's beneficiaries.

## Concealment

*Fraudulent concealment* is any intentional withholding of a fact that would be of material importance to the insurer's decision to issue a policy. The applicant need only give answers to questions asked. However, the insured may not conceal facts that would be material in acceptance of a risk.

**Table 19-2**  Cancellation of Insurance Policies

| Grounds for Cancellation | Explanation |
| --- | --- |
| Warranty violation | Insured fails to abide by restrictions especially written into the policy |
| Concealment | Insured deliberately withholds fact of material importance to insurer's decision to issue a policy |
| Misrepresentation | Insured gives false answers to questions in the insurance application that materially affect the insurer's risk |

## EXAMPLE 19-3: Concealment

VanDorn, an insurance agent for Canadian Life, inspected Kalintor's building before issuing a fire insurance policy. Kalintor did not show VanDorn the basement, which was filled with flammable chemicals. After the policy was issued, Kalintor's building burned to the ground. Canadian Life later learned of the secret lab and was permitted to cancel Kalintor's policy.

## Misrepresentation

If an insured party gives false answers, or *misrepresentations,* to questions in an insurance application that materially affect the risk undertaken by the insurer, the contract is voidable by the insurer. A representation is material if the facts represented influence the insurer's decision to issue the policy or the rate of premium to charge.

## EXAMPLE 19-4: Misrepresentation

The Clark family applied for fire insurance from the Alabama Farm Bureau Mutual Casualty Insurance Company. The Clarks answered no when asked whether they had ever been arrested. When their house was destroyed by fire and they attempted to collect under the policy, an investigation revealed that the Clarks had both been arrested on previous occasions. The court upheld the Farm Bureau's denial of benefits due to this deliberate material misrepresentation.

Although all jurisdictions agree on the effects of a deliberate deception, there is disagreement as to the effects of an innocent misrepresentation. A majority of the states hold that the intent of the insured is irrelevant. Even an innocent misrepresentation would make the policy voidable by the insurer. A minority of states would not allow the insurer to deny coverage to an insured whose misrepresentation was unintentional.

## EXAMPLE 19-5: Innocent Misrepresentation

Folk took out an insurance policy with Countryside Casualty. When asked if he had any physical impairments, Folk, who suffered from epilepsy, said no. When Folk was killed in an automobile accident, his estate attempted to collect the insurance. Countryside, which had discovered Folk's epilepsy, refused to pay, claiming he had misrepresented his physical health. Evidence indicated that Folk genuinely did not consider his epilepsy, which was controlled by drugs, to be a physical impairment. In a majority of states, Folk's belief would make no difference. The policy would still be voidable by Countryside. In a minority of states, Folk's innocent misrepresentation would not allow Countryside to deny recovery under the policy.

## Estoppel

An insurer may not deny acts, statements, or promises that are relevant and material to the validity of an insurance contract. This bar to denial is called an *estoppel.* When an insurer has given up the right to cancel a policy under certain circumstances by granting the insured a special dispensation, the insurer cannot deny that dispensation when the chance to cancel or deny liability arises.

## EXAMPLE 19-6: Estopped from Denying Liability

Maxwell, an insurance agent for Fidelity, called on MacLaine, who wanted fire insurance to cover her new cabin. The cabin was heated by a woodburning stove that, according to Fidelity's specifications, was located too close to a wooden wall. Maxwell told MacLaine not to worry about those specifications. He then falsified the measurements on the application. Two weeks later, MacLaine's cabin burned to the ground. Due to Maxwell's behavior, Fidelity would be estopped from denying its liability to MacLaine under the policy.

When the insurance company gives up one of its rights to help the insured, the company has made a *waiver*. A waiver, which is actually a form of estoppel, can be implied from the conduct of the insurance company. For example, when an insurance company cashes the check of a lapsed policy, it has, in effect, given up or waived its right to cancel that policy. Once a right has been waived, the insurer may not later deny its waiver.

---

### quick quiz 19-4

1. An insurance company may refuse to pay for a loss if it can prove that the insured breached a warranty to abide by certain restrictions.    true | false

2. If an insured gives false answers to questions in an insurance application, the insurance company can do nothing about it unless it discovers the fraud before any loss.    true | false

3. An insurer may not deny acts, statements, or promises that are relevant and material to the validity of an insurance contract.    true | false

---

## Summary

**19.1**  Insurance is a transfer of the risk of economic loss from the insured to the insurer. Insurance policies require the elements of a contract: offer, acceptance, mutual assent, capable parties, consideration, and legality. To be insured, one must have an insurable interest in the subject matter of the policy. The parties to an insurance contract include the insurer, the insured, and the beneficiary.

**19.2**  It is possible to obtain insurance for a variety of risks. Life insurance provides funds to a beneficiary on the death of the insured. A beneficiary must have an insurable interest when the policy is issued but need not have that interest when the insured dies. The principal types of life insurance are straight life, limited-payment life, term, and endowment insurance.

Principal types of property insurance include fire, marine, homeowner's, flood, and automobile insurance. In the case of property insurance, the insured must have an insurable interest when the loss occurs. Health insurance helps pay for such things as physician care, prescription drugs, inpatient and outpatient hospital care, surgery, dental and vision care, and long-term care for the elderly.

**19.3** The first step in obtaining an insurance policy is to fill in an application. A binder provides temporary insurance coverage between the time the application is made and the time the policy becomes effective. Premiums are the consideration or payment an insured gives the insurer for its acceptance of risk. A lapse occurs when the insured stops paying premiums.

**19.4** Under certain conditions, the insurer is given a legal right to cancel an insurance policy. Grounds permitting cancellation include breach of warranty, concealment of material facts, and misrepresentation on an application. Under the estoppel rule, an insurer is not allowed to deny certain statements, activities, or waivers.

## Key Terms

add-on coverage, 412

adhesion contracts, 416

annuity, 407

beneficiary, 403

binder, 416

bodily injury liability insurance, 411

coinsurance, 408

collision insurance, 413

comprehensive coverage, 413

deductible, 408

descriptive threshold, 412

double indemnity, 407

fault-based insurance, 411

homeowner's policy, 409

indemnify, 403

inland marine insurance, 409

insurable interest, 404

insurance, 403

insured, 403

insurer, 403

life insurance, 405

limited-payment life insurance, 407

Medicaid, 414

medical payments insurance, 412

Medicare, 414

monetary threshold, 412

no-fault insurance, 411

ocean marine insurance, 409

ordinary life insurance, 406

personal injury protection (PIP), 411

policy, 403

premium, 403

property damage liability insurance, 412

renter's insurance, 409

straight life insurance, 406

subrogation, 404

substitute transportation insurance, 413

term insurance, 407

threshold, 412

threshold guideline, 412

time-based threshold, 412

towing and labor insurance, 413

underinsured-motorist insurance, 412

uninsured-motorist insurance, 412

universal life insurance, 406

whole life insurance, 406

## Questions for Review and Discussion

1. What is risk management and what is the purpose of insurance?
2. What are the contractual elements of an insurance agreement?
3. Why is insurable interest so important?
4. What are the differences among types of life insurance?
5. How does insurable interest differ with life insurance and property insurance?
6. What is a coinsurance clause?
7. What coverage is given by fire, marine, homeowner's, renter's, and flood insurance?
8. What differences exist among the principal kinds of automobile insurance?
9. What benefits are included in health insurance policies?
10. What are the steps in applying for, obtaining, and maintaining an insurance policy?

# Cases for Analysis

1. Juan Ramos's wife, Maria, became concerned after a violent storm caused disastrous flooding in a community not too far down the river from where their house was located. She felt comforted when her husband told her that they were fully protected against flooding by their homeowner's insurance policy. The following spring, a flood caused serious damage to their home, and Juan's insurance agent told him that his homeowner's policy did not cover flood damage. What recourse do the Ramoses have against the insurance company?

2. Al Zuni Trading, Inc., purchased a $1 million life insurance policy on the life of one of its officers, Thomas McKee. Three months later, McKee resigned from the company. Two years later, McKee died. Did Al Zuni Trading, Inc., have an insurable interest in the life of McKee, and thus, was it entitled to the million dollars? Explain. *In re Al Zuni Trading, Inc.,* 947 F.2d 1403 (9th Cir.).

3. U.S. Aviation Underwriters issued an aircraft insurance policy to Cash Air, Inc., covering its employees. The policy stated that to be covered under the policy, the aircraft must be "flown only by a pilot or pilots described on the Coverage Summary page." Each policy coverage page stated that a pilot not named in the policy must be one who holds "an AA commercial pilot certificate with AA multi-engine and instrument ratings who has flown a minimum of 2,500 hours as pilot in command, at least 1,000 hours of which shall have been in multi-engine aircraft and at least 25 hours of which shall have been in Piper PA 31-350 aircraft." Peter Covich, an employee of Cash Air, Inc., did not meet the pilot experience requirements when the Piper Seneca airplane he was piloting crashed, causing personal injuries and property damage. Must the insurance company pay for the loss? Explain. *U.S. Aviation Underwriters v. Cash Air,* 568 N.E.2d 1150 (MA).

4. Victory Container Corporation was owned by the three Radin brothers. Two of those brothers also owned the Warrensburg Paper and Board Corporation. Victory had no direct ownership of the Warrensburg plant however. Nevertheless, Victory took out a fire insurance policy on the Warrensburg plant. When the Warrensburg property was damaged, Victory attempted to collect under the policy. Did Victory have an insurable interest in the Warrensburg property? Explain. *Victory Container Corporation v. Calvert Fire Insurance Company,* 486 N.Y.S.2d 211 (NY).

5. Avrit and Schuring entered an agreement to purchase a certain property. Each paid $1,000 as a down payment. They were later to pay an additional $25,000. The seller of the property was to maintain insurance until the deal was finalized. Avrit and Schuring also obtained an insurance policy on the property. Before the deal was finalized, fire damaged the property. Avrit and Schuring attempted to collect on their policy, but the insurance company claimed that Avrit and Schuring had no insurable interest at the time of the fire. Did Avrit and Schuring have an insurable interest between the time of the down payment and the time the deal was finalized? Explain. *Avrit v. Forest Industries Insurance Exchange,* 696 P.2d 583 (OR).

6. Martin Searle's life insurance policy contained a standard suicide clause. Under the clause, Allstate would not be liable to the beneficiary, Alice Searle, should Martin commit suicide within the first two years of the policy even if Martin were insane at the time of his death. Martin committed suicide ten months after the policy went into effect. Allstate refused to pay Alice any benefits under the policy. Alice sued the company, claiming that her husband had been mentally deranged at the time of the suicide and did not realize the consequences of his action. Allstate argued that the sanity clause removed the issue of mental incapacity from the case. Who would prevail in a majority of states? Explain. *Searle v. Allstate Life Insurance Company,* 212 Cal. Rptr. 466 (CA).

7. Bayer took his car to Whitaker's auto repair shop for repairs. Whitaker took the car for a test drive, with Bayer seated in the passenger seat. During the test drive, a car operated by another person drove on the wrong side of the road and collided with Bayer's vehicle, injuring Bayer. Neither Bayer's vehicle nor the vehicle owned by the wrongdoer was insured. Whitaker carried insurance on his own vehicles, including uninsured-motorist insurance. Could Bayer recover from Whitaker's insurance company under the uninsured-motorist provision of the policy?

Why or why not? *Bayer v. Travelers Indemnity Co.*, 267 S.E.2d 91 (VA).

8. Riggins contacted the Hartford Insurance Company and asked for an all-risk policy for his truck. An underwriter for Hartford agreed to the policy and issued a binder on March 28. On April 2, before the full policy had been executed, Riggins left on a trip, hauling liquor. Sometime during the trip, the liquor was stolen. Hartford refused to pay, arguing that the final policy that would have been issued would not have covered the hauling of liquor. Riggins argued that the all-risk binder was in effect at the time of the theft and that he was therefore covered, even though the final policy would not have covered him. Was Riggins correct? Explain. *Hilt Truck Lanes, Inc., v. Riggins,* 756 F.2d 676 (8th Cir).

9. When Sidney Henry applied for insurance with State Farm, he was asked whether he had ever had recurrent indigestion or a hernia. Henry answered no to each question. In fact, he had experienced recurring indigestion, and it had been diagnosed as either an ulcer or a hernia. The policy was issued. Eight months later, Henry died of cancer of the esophagus. When Eula Henry applied for benefits, State Farm denied her request. Eula argued that the misrepresentations were not material because her husband died from cancer, not the illnesses he was questioned about. Was Mrs. Henry correct? Explain. *Henry v. State Farm,* 465 So.2d 276 (LA).

10. On January 13, Lax made out a check to State Farm Insurance to pay for her automobile insurance, which had lapsed 62 days earlier. Unfortunately, she forgot to mail the check. On January 22, Lax was killed when trying to pass a truck. The check was found in the wreckage and taken to a State Farm agent who mailed it to the main office. The main office, with knowledge of the accident, cashed the check. The beneficiaries argued that State Farm's conduct in cashing the check with knowledge of the accident constituted a waiver of its right to cancel the policy due to her failure to pay by the due date. Were the beneficiaries correct? Explain. *VanHulle v. State Farm,* 254 N.E.2d 457 (IL).

| **quick quiz** Answers | | | |
|---|---|---|---|
| **19-1** | **19-2** | **19-3** | **19-4** |
| 1. F | 1. T | 1. F | 1. T |
| 2. F | 2. F | 2. T | 2. F |
| 3. F | 3. T | 3. F | 3. T |

# Mortgages and Security Interests

## THE OPENING CASE

Now You See It–Now You Don't: *Superior Savings Association v. City of Cleveland*

The Superior Savings Association, a reputable savings and loan institution with a long history of serving the Lithuanian community in Cleveland, owned a properly recorded first mortgage on a two-story brick building located at 6802 Superior Avenue in the city. The building was located just across the street from one of the branches of Superior Savings in the heart of the Lithuanian community, and one of the bank's officers passed the building every morning on his way to work. The building also held special significance in the neighborhood because it had once housed the main office of Cleveland's only Lithuanian newspaper. You can, therefore, imagine the banking officer's surprise when he arrived at work one morning to find that the building was, to say it bluntly, gone. As he pieced together the story, the officer learned that the mortgagor, Hughes, had failed to keep the building in an appropriate state of repair. As a result the city condemned the building. As a final warning, the city gave Hughes more than two months to make the needed repairs before the building would be demolished. When Hughes failed to comply, the building was torn down. At no time during the two-month grace period did anyone at Superior Savings receive any notice of the impending demolition by the city. Superior Savings sued, arguing that the city had violated the association's constitutional rights by "taking away" its property without giving it proper notice. Attorneys for Superior Savings argued that the city, as an agent of the state, had deprived the banking institution of its constitutional rights under the Due Process Clause of the Fourteenth Amendment to the U.S. Constitution. In addition, the city had also violated its own ordinances which also require that it give notice of the impending demolition to Superior Savings. Had the city followed its own procedures and complied with Constitutional law, the bank would have been properly notified and could have taken steps to save what had become a local landmark, despite its state of disrepair. As it is, there is no way to undo the damage that has been done. Therefore, Superior Savings asked the court to grant the institution a monetary award that would provide it with money damages that would be equal to the amount that the mortgage was worth just before it was torn down and its value after being destroyed. The measurement of that value would, of course, take some fancy calculating, given the historical nature of the building, but it would ultimately be worth it to Superior Savings. (See *Superior Savings Association v. City of Cleveland,* 501 F. Supp. 1244 (U.S. District Court, Northern District of Ohio).)

**Opening Case Questions**

1. Under what theory or legal argument can an institution like a savings and loan association claim constitutional rights? Explain.

2. Would it make a difference in this case if the savings and loan owned the mortgage but had not recorded it? Could the savings and loan use the same argument in that scenario? Why or why not?

3. Did Hughes violate any duty or duties to Superior Savings? Explain.

4. What if there was another mortgagee out there with a recorded mortgage? How would that fact affect this case (or would it)? Explain.

5. Has Superior Savings been fair and reasonable in its request for damages? Explain.

## LO Learning Objectives

1. Differentiate between a secured and an unsecured loan.
2. Identify the types of mortgages that are available to borrowers.
3. Explain the legal effect of recording a mortgage.
4. Describe the rights and duties of the mortgagor and those of the mortgagee.
5. Differentiate among Fannie Mae, Ginnie Mae, and Freddie Mac.
6. Define securitization and connect it to the financial crisis.
7. Explain the nature of a liar loan and a NINJA loan.
8. Describe how a security interest is created for personal property.
9. Decide whether security interests are perfected.
10. Determine priorities when parties claim a security interest in the same property.

# 20-1 Real Property as Security

Security is the assurance that a creditor will be paid back for any money loaned or for credit extended to a debtor. Debts are said to be secured when creditors know that somehow they will be able to recover their money. Lenders of money and people who extend credit often require a security device to protect their financial interests. A security device is a way for creditors to get their money back in case the borrower or debtor does not pay. A **secured loan** is one in which creditors have something of value, usually called *collateral,* from which they can be paid if the debtor does not pay. In general, if creditors are not paid the debt owed to them, they can legally gain possession of the collateral. The collateral is then sold, and the money is used to pay the debt. The right to use the collateral to recover a debt is called the creditor's **security interest**. If creditors lend money but do not require collateral, they have made an unsecured loan. An **unsecured loan** is one in which creditors have nothing of value that they can repossess and sell to recover the money owed to them by the debtor. Both real property and personal property can be used to secure a debt.

When real property is used as security for a loan, a device known as a mortgage is used to establish collateral for the loan. A **mortgage** is a transfer of an interest in property for the purpose of creating a security for a debt. The one who borrows the money (the **mortgagor**) conveys his or her interest in the property to the lender (the **mortgagee**) while at the same time retaining possession of the property. The borrower signs a promissory note as evidence of the loan in addition to a mortgage instrument.

The mortgage creates a legal claim to the property. This legal claim, also called a *lien,* gives the lender the right to have the property sold if the debt is not paid. Once the land is sold and the debt is paid, the mortgagor's obligation to the mortgagee is over. However, if the sale of the property does not satisfy the whole debt, the mortgagor will still owe the balance.

Did You Know?

The chances of a borrower defaulting on mortgage payments can increase dramatically with life-changing events. They jump:

- 54 percent if the borrower has an unexpected drop in income.

- 26 percent if the borrower gets divorced from his or her spouse.

- 6 percent for each additional household member after the first two.

## EXAMPLE 20-1: Mortgage Foreclosure

Mayo bought a house for $145,000. Of this sum, she put up $50,000 in cash. Mayo then took out a $95,000 loan from the Unicorp Bank to cover the rest of her purchase. When Mayo could not meet the mortgage payments, Unicorp foreclosed and sold the house for $6,593 less than what was owed. Mayo would be personally liable for the $6,593, plus interest, until the debt was paid.

## Mortgage Costs

Many costs are associated with obtaining a mortgage. Initially, a potential borrower must pay a mortgage application fee, an appraisal fee, a credit report fee, and an inspection fee. Once the loan is approved, the borrower often pays an origination fee, which is a charge for issuing the loan. Sometimes, the borrower pays interest in a lump sum upfront, called points, to get a lower rate of interest. A point is a one-time charge equal to 1 percent of the principal amount borrowed. Thus, if three points are charged on an $80,000 mortgage, the borrower will be required to pay a one-time fee of 3 percent of $80,000, which amounts to $2,400. If all IRS requirements are met, points are tax deductible. Other items charged to the borrower include charges for document preparation, attorney's fees, title insurance, surveyor fees, termite inspections, mortgage insurance, and homeowner's insurance.

## Types of Mortgages

There are many different types of real property mortgages (Table 20-1). Some of the most common mortgages are the conventional, the variable-rate, the graduated-payment, the balloon-payment, the reverse mortgage, the subprime mortgage, a participation loan, a construction loan, a deed of trust, and the subprime mortgage.

**Conventional Fixed-Rate Mortgage** A **conventional fixed-rate mortgage** involves no government backing by either insurance or guarantee. The loan is made by private lenders, and the risks of loss are borne exclusively by them. Conventional mortgages have interest rates that stay the same during the life of the mortgage, regardless of fluctuations in the economy. Changes in recent years, however, have resulted in the creation of variations to the fixed-interest rate mortgage, including the variable rate mortgage.

**Variable-Rate Mortgage** A **variable-** or **flexible-** or **adjustable-rate mortgage (ARM)** has a rate of interest that changes according to fluctuations in the index to which it is tied. The index rate may be the bank's prime rate or the Federal Reserve Board discount rate. As the index rate goes up and down, so does the rate of interest charged on the loan. This rate may be more or less than the index rate but always varies with it. The obvious advantage of the variable-rate mortgage is the drop in the amount of the mortgage payment when the rate drops. However, mortgage payments can also rise when the rate rises. In general, a change in payments, either up or down, does not occur without some advance warning. Also, ARM agreements must include a maximum rate that cannot be exceeded. In addition, the frequency of these changes in the rate is usually restricted by the terms of the mortgage agreement.

There are many different types of mortgages. Knowing which type fits your needs, both in the present and for the future, makes homeownership easier and more enjoyable.

**Interest-Only Mortgages** In some situations, a borrower might negotiate an **interest-only mortgage**. In such a situation, the borrower, who very often cannot afford a

## Table 20-1 Some Methods of Financing a House

| Types of Mortgages | Description |
| --- | --- |
| **Fixed-rate mortgage** | Conventional fixed-rate mortgages have interest rates that are permanent, regardless of fluctuations in the economy. |
| **Adjustable-rate mortgage** | A variable- or flexible- or adjustable-rate mortgage has a rate of interest that changes according to fluctuations in the index to which it is tied. |
| **Interest-only mortgage** | With an interest-only mortgage, the borrower pays only the interest for a period of time, between one and three years or so, set by the agreement. |
| **Graduated-payment mortgage** | A graduated-payment mortgage has a fixed interest rate during the life of the mortgage; however, the monthly payments made by the mortgagor increase over the term of the loan. |
| **Balloon-payment mortgage** | A balloon-payment mortgage has comparatively low fixed payments during the life of the mortgage, followed by one large final (balloon) payment. |
| **Reverse mortgage** | A reverse mortgage is a loan that allows older homeowners to convert some of the equity in their home into cash while retaining ownership of their home. |
| **Participation loans** | In a participation loan, the borrower will transfer certain ownership (or equity) rights to the lender and in exchange, the borrower will negotiate lower interest rates or a lower down payment. |
| **Construction loans** | Construction loans authorize staggered payments at various stages of the process of building a home. |
| **Subprime mortgages** | Subprime loans are offered when a borrower does not qualify for one of the regular loans. To compensate, the lender demands that the borrower pay a much higher interest rate than more qualified lenders are required to pay. |
| **Deed of trust** | Under a deed of trust, the mortgagor conveys his or her interest in the property to a trustee. |
| **Junior mortgages** | A junior mortgage, also called a second (or subsequent) mortgage, is a mortgage subject to a prior mortgage. |
| **Home equity loans** | A home equity loan is either an outright loan or a line of credit made available to homeowners based on the value of the property over and above any existing mortgages. Home equity loans are often used to consolidate credit card balances or other debts that have higher interest rates. |

**Did You Know?**

The more points you pay, the lower your interest rate will be. If given a choice, you need to decide which is best for you, paying more in points and a lower rate of interest, or paying less in points and a higher rate. To decide, you need to consider: (1) whether you can afford to make the upfront payment now for points and (2) the length of time you expect to have the mortgage. The longer you plan to have your mortgage, the more it makes sense to pay for points now, because you'll have a long time to benefit from the lower rate.

down payment on a house, will agree to pay only the interest on the loan for a set period of time, anywhere between one and three years or so, set by the agreement. The idea under this approach is to wait until the borrower's financial picture brightens allowing him or her to make the higher payments that will eventually come due.

## Graduated-Payment Mortgage A **graduated-payment mortgage** has a fixed interest rate during the life of the mortgage; however, the monthly payments made by the

## THE OPENING CASE *Revisited, Part I*
Now You See It–Now You Don't: *Superior Savings Association v. City of Cleveland,* Round 2

Recall that, in the Opening Case at the beginning of the chapter, Superior Savings Association owned a properly recorded first mortgage on a two-story brick building located at 6802 Superior Avenue in the city of Cleveland. There is no reason to believe from the content of the case that loan between Hughes and the S&L was anything other than a conventional fixed-rate mortgage. The fact that the building held special significance in the neighborhood because it had once housed the main office of Cleveland's Lithuanian newspaper would have lent no special significance to the mortgage loan unless it was specifically mentioned in the agreement. Still, the loan would have given Superior Savings a constitutional right to notice before the "taking" of the property by the city. The unlawful taking thus violated the S&L's rights under the Due Process Clause of the Fourteenth Amendment to the U.S. Constitution.

mortgagor increase over the term of the loan. In the first years of the mortgage, the payments are low. The payments gradually increase over time, usually reaching a plateau at which the payments remain fixed. This type of mortgage is advantageous for young people, whose income may be expected to increase as their mortgage payments increase.

### Balloon-Payment Mortgage
A **balloon-payment mortgage** has comparatively low fixed payments during the life of the mortgage, followed by one large final (balloon) payment. The mortgage has a fixed interest rate, but it is written for a short time period, such as five years. At the end of the time period, the mortgagor usually must find new financing, either with the same or with a different lender, at the current interest rate.

### Reverse Mortgage
A **reverse mortgage** is a type of loan that allows older homeowners, to convert some of the equity in their home into cash while retaining ownership of their home. The loan is repaid when the property is sold, or on the occurrence of some other specified event.

### Participation Loans
A borrower who is shopping for a loan with terms that are more favorable than usual, may request a **participation loan**. In such a loan, the borrower will transfer certain ownership (or equity) rights to the lender and in exchange, the borrower will negotiate lower interest rates or a lower down payment.

### Construction Loans
Sometimes a borrower wants to build a new home rather than to buy an existing one. In such a case, the borrower may wish to negotiate a **construction loan** that will authorize staggered payments at various stages of the building process. Thus, the loan will issue a payment at the time the borrower buys the land, when the foundation of the house is laid, when the framing is finished, when the exterior has been constructed, and when the entire house is completed. Construction loans come in a variety of flavors including both variable and fixed rate loans.

### Deeds of Trust
In some states, a deed of trust is used instead of a mortgage. In a conventional mortgage, the mortgagor conveys all or part of his or her interest in the property

directly to the mortgagee. Under a **deed of trust**, the mortgagor conveys his or her interest in the property to a disinterested third party, known as a trustee. The mortgagor remains on the property, but the trustee holds certain rights to that property as security for the mortgagor's creditors. If the debtor defaults, the trustee can sell the property for the benefit of those creditors. The provisions of many deeds of trust allow the trustee to sell the property without going to court. For this reason, some legal authorities do not consider a deed of trust a true mortgage, because true mortgages require a foreclosure action for the sale of the property.

### Subprime Mortgages

When a borrower does not qualify for one of the regular mortgages just covered, he or she might ask for and receive a subprime loan. Generally, these borrowers have been disqualified from conventional loan because of a bad credit history or because of a low debt-to-income ratio. These loans generally have a much higher default rate than most of the conventional loans and are thus disfavored by lenders. This is true now more than ever before because of the recent mortgage crisis that has occurred during the last few years. To compensate for the risk involved in a subprime loan, the lender demands that the borrower pay a much higher interest rate than more qualified lenders are required to pay.

### Junior Mortgages

Sometimes an owner of real property may execute a junior mortgage on the property. A **junior mortgage**, also called a **second** (or subsequent) **mortgage**, is a mortgage subject to a prior mortgage. For example, if a homeowner wants to improve the mortgaged property and needs another loan to do so, he or she may use the property as security for another loan. If this transaction occurs, the mortgagor is said to have executed a second mortgage on the property. Some people have three or more mortgages on one parcel of property. If all the mortgages are recorded, the holders of second and subsequent mortgages may exercise their rights against the property only after prior mortgages have been paid off. Thus, if the first mortgagee causes the property to be sold and is paid off in full, the second and subsequent mortgages are paid out of the proceeds that remain. The first mortgagee acts as a trustee of the surplus funds for the benefit of the junior mortgagees.

### Home Equity Loans

A **home equity loan** is an example of a junior mortgage. It is either an outright loan or a line of credit made available to homeowners based on the value of the property over and above any existing mortgages. Such a loan takes advantage of the equity that has built up in a home over a period of time. Home equity loans are often used to consolidate credit card balances or other debts that have higher interest rates. Unlike interest paid on a credit card balance, interest paid on a home equity loan is tax deductible.

## Recording the Mortgage

Like a deed, a mortgage must be in writing and delivered to the recorder's office in the county where the property is located. Recording a mortgage notifies any third party who may be interested in purchasing the property or in lending money to the owner that the mortgagee has an interest in the real property covered by the mortgage. If the mortgage is not recorded and a later mortgage is given on the same property, the new mortgage is superior to the first. The second mortgagee must not know about the first mortgage and must record the mortgage properly. A failure to record the first mortgage, however, would not remove the obligation of the mortgagor to the first mortgagee. The debt would simply be unsecured.

## THE OPENING CASE *Revisited, Part II*
Now You See It–Now You Don't: *Superior Savings Association v. City of Cleveland*, Round 3

Again recall that, in the Opening Case at the beginning of the chapter, Superior Savings Association owned a properly recorded first mortgage on a building located at 6802 Superior Avenue in Cleveland. Recording that mortgage notified all third parties that the mortgagee, Superior, had an interest in the building at that address. Had the mortgage not been recorded, and had Hughes taken out a later mortgage on the property which had been properly recorded by the second mortgagee, then the new mortgage would have taken precedence over the one held by Superior. The failure to record the first mortgage, however, would not remove any other obligations of Hughes to Superior Savings. The debt would simply be unsecured and Hughes would still be indebted to Superior.

## Rights and Duties of the Mortgagor

By law and by agreement, the mortgagor has certain rights and duties in conjunction with the mortgage. First, the mortgagor has the right to possess the property. Second, the mortgagor has the right to any income produced by the property. For instance, the mortgagor would be entitled to any rent proceeds gained from leasing all or part of the property. The mortgagor could, however, assign this right to the mortgagee, which is sometimes done as a condition of executing the original mortgage agreement. Third, the mortgagor has the right to use the property for a second or third mortgage. Fourth, the mortgagor has the **equity of redemption**, that is, the right to pay off the mortgage in full, including interest, and thus discharge the debt in total.

In addition to these rights, the mortgagor has certain duties. Chief among these duties is to make payments on time. Mortgagors must preserve and maintain the mortgaged property for the benefit of the mortgagee's interest and security. Similarly, the mortgagor is often required to insure the property to the benefit of the mortgagee for the amount of the mortgaged debt. The mortgagor also must pay all taxes and assessments

## THE OPENING CASE *Revisited, Part III*
Now You See It–Now You Don't: *Superior Savings Association v. City of Cleveland*, Round 4

Once more recall that, in the Opening Case at the beginning of the chapter, Superior Savings Association owned a properly recorded first mortgage on a building located in Cleveland. The mortgagor, Hughes, failed to keep the building in an appropriate state of repair. In fact, things got so bad inside the building that city inspectors condemned the building. The city gave Hughes more than two months to make the needed repairs before the building would be demolished. When Hughes failed to comply, the building was torn down. Hughes clearly violated his duty to the mortgagee, Superior Savings, by not preserving and maintaining the mortgaged property for the benefit of the mortgagee's interest and security.

that may be levied against the property. Frequently, the mortgagor will ease the burden of these obligations by paying a percentage of the insurance premium and taxes each month along with the mortgage payment. The mortgagee holds the money in an escrow account. An escrow account is a special account into which money is deposited before the payment of the insurance or taxes is due. The money stays in the account until the time comes to pay the insurance or tax. The mortgagee then takes the money out of the account and makes the payments.

## Rights and Duties of the Mortgagee

The mortgagee has the unrestricted right to sell, assign, or transfer the mortgage to a third party. Whatever rights the mortgagee had in the mortgage are then the rights of the assignee. The only way the mortgagor could stop the mortgagee from assigning the mortgage is to pay the mortgagee everything owed on the mortgage. Sometimes an assignment by the mortgagee to another mortgagee can cause unforeseen problems for the mortgagor.

### EXAMPLE 20-2: Mortgage Assignment

The Chamberlins financed the purchase of their house through the Midway Savings Bank, a local bank with only four branches, all in the city of Bromfield. The Chamberlins made their mortgage payments faithfully each month, in person, at the branch on their street. Without warning, they received notice that Midway had assigned their mortgage to the Unicorp Mortgage Corporation, a multimillion-dollar financial institution headquartered in New York. Although the Chamberlins had no desire to deal with Unicorp, they had no choice in the matter. The only way they could avoid dealing with Unicorp would be to make full payment of the mortgage debt.

Mortgagees have the right to receive each installment payment as it falls due. Frequently, mortgagees will include a term in the mortgage agreement allowing an **acceleration** of the debt if the mortgagor fails to meet an installment payment. This term means that a default on one installment payment will make the entire balance due immediately, giving the mortgagee the right to collect the full amount. In general, a clause allowing acceleration must be executed in good faith. In other words, before invoking the acceleration clause, the mortgagee must genuinely believe that the mortgagor will not be able to make good on the debt and that the mortgagee's security interest is therefore threatened. If the matter ends up in court, the mortgagor will have the burden of proving that the mortgagee did not act in good faith.

If the mortgagor has defaulted or has failed to perform some other agreement in the mortgage, the mortgagee has the right to apply to a court to have the property sold. This right is called **foreclosure**. It takes priority even when the mortgagor files for bankruptcy. Because, in a majority of jurisdictions, a mortgage is a lien on the land, a foreclosure is an equitable action. The mortgagor does not have a right to a jury trial in foreclosure action. A mortgage is foreclosed when the mortgagee proves the amount of the unpaid debt (including interest and other charges) and the property is sold by and under the direction of a court. The proceeds from the sale are then applied to the payment of the debt. Any money remaining after the claims of the mortgagee have been satisfied goes to the mortgagor or to the second and subsequent mortgagees. The mortgagee's financial interest in mortgaged property gives rise to certain constitutional rights. Under the Fourteenth Amendment to the U.S. Constitution, mortgagees cannot lose their interest in property without due process of law.

**Did You Know?**

Since it began in 1968, Fannie Mae has helped more than 63 million families achieve the American dream of home ownership. Ginnie Mae estimates that it has helped over 30 million American families since it began operation in 1968. Freddie Mac opened its doors two years later and has financed homes for 41 million families.

## THE OPENING CASE *Revisited, Part IV*
### Now You See It–Now You Don't: *Superior Savings Association v. City of Cleveland*, Round 5

One final time, recall that, in the Opening Case at the beginning of the chapter, Superior Savings Association owned a first mortgage on a building in Cleveland. Also recall that the city had condemned the building. As a final warning, the city gave Hughes more than two months to make the needed repairs before the building would be demolished. When Hughes failed to comply, the building was torn down. At no time during the two-month grace period, did anyone at Superior Savings receive any notice of the impending demolition by the city. Superior Savings sued, arguing that the city had violated the association's constitutional rights by "taking away" its property without giving it proper notice. Attorneys for Superior Savings argued correctly that the city, as an agent of the state, had deprived the banking

institution of its constitutional rights under the Due Process Clause of the Fourteenth Amendment to the U.S. Constitution.

Mortgagees also have certain duties imposed by law. Both state and federal legislation prohibits lenders from discriminating against borrowers because of race, creed, color, sex, or ethnic background. Such legislation imposes a duty to use nondiscriminatory criteria in approving and disapproving mortgage applications. For example, a lender may not refuse a mortgage to a prospective borrower simply because that borrower is a woman. Similarly, a lender could not refuse a mortgage to a borrower because that borrower is Hispanic. The mortgagee also has the duty to respect all rights properly claimed by the mortgagor.

## A QUESTION OF ETHICS

In the Opening Case at the beginning of the chapter, Superior Savings owned a properly executed and legally recorded mortgage on the building at 6802 Superior Avenue in Cleveland. The mortgagee, Hughes, abandoned the building and let it fall into a terrible state of disrepair. The city after warning Hughes several times, demolished the building without notifying Superior Savings first. The demolition of the bank was legal; however, failing to notify Superior was not. Was the failure to notify Superior unethical a well? Explain.

U.S. Const.
Amendment 14
(page 812)

## Purchase by Mortgage Takeover

Mortgages often contain a clause providing that if the property is sold, the mortgage becomes due and payable. If the mortgage does not contain such a clause, the property may be sold with the mortgage remaining on it. In such takeovers, the transfer of title to a new buyer is subject to the buyer's payment of the seller's mortgage at the existing rate of interest. In purchasing a property already mortgaged, the buyer will either **assume the mortgage** or take the property **subject to the mortgage**. When buyers decide to assume the mortgage, they agree to pay it. When they take the property subject to a mortgage, the seller agrees to continue paying the debt.

## quick quiz 20-1

| | |
|---|---|
| 1. A security device is a way for creditors to get their money back in case the borrower or debtor does not pay. | true \| false |
| 2. A home equity loan is an example of a junior mortgage. | true \| false |
| 3. The mortgagor has the right to possess the mortgaged property and to any income produced by the property unless otherwise assigned. | true \| false |

# 20-2 The 21st Century Financial Crisis

Now that we have discussed mortgage loans in general, and subprime loans in particular, it might be a good time to stop for a moment and consider the 21st century financial crisis. One of the causes of the crisis was the runaway real estate market. Speculation on property prices ran rampant; buyers rushed to invest in land; lenders (most of which were now deregulated) began to lend money to buyers, some of whom were, quite frankly, extremely bad credit risks. Some of these buyers used techniques like the balloon-payment mortgage or the graduated-payment mortgage to pay a small amount upfront, until the value of the property rose, at which time they planned to sell the property at an enormous profit. It was in this environment that the use of subprime loans skyrocketed. The popularity of subprime loans had a serious effect on the market. Still, it would be unwise, irresponsible, and just plain wrong, to say that subprime lending caused the 21st century financial crisis.

## The Causes of the Crisis

As Nouriel Roubini and Stephen Mihm point out in their book *Crisis Economics,* "Subprime mortgages were but the most obvious sign of a deep and systemic rot. This fact underscores a cardinal principle of crisis economics: the biggest and the most destructive financial disasters are not produced by something so inconsequential as subprime mortgages or a few reckless risk takers. Nor are they merely produced by the euphoria of a speculative bubble. Rather, much as with earthquakes, the pressures build for many years, and when the shock finally comes, it can be staggering." [See Nouriel Roubini and Stephen Mihm, *Crisis Economics* (New York: Penguin, 2010), p. 62.] The pressure in the current crisis resulted from several factors. These factors include the creation and later mismanagement of Fannie Mae and Freddie Mac, the development of securitization (including both mortgage backed securities and asset backed securities), and the increased use of faulty loans (including subprime loans, liar loans, and NINJA loans).

**Fannie Mae, Ginnie Mae, and Freddie Mac** The Federal National Mortgage Association (Fannie Mae) was chartered by the Reconstruction Finance Corporation during the Great Depression in 1938. Fannie Mae does not make mortgage loans. Rather, it purchases loans that were made based on strict guidelines set up by the Federal Housing Association (FHA) and the Veterans Administration (VA). Eventually Congress recognized a flaw in the Fannie Mae system caused by the fact that the agency had to borrow money to fund mortgages it purchased. That in and of itself was not the real problem, however. The real problem was that Congress had not properly anticipated the amount of debt that Fannie Mae would accumulate. To remedy this situation, Congress created another agency, the

Government National Mortgage Association (Ginnie Mae), which then took over much of Fannie's debt, freeing Fannie to buy mortgages insured by the government. Around this same time Congress created the Federal Home Loan Mortgage Corporation (Freddie Mac), another **government-sponsored enterprise (GSE)** to help support the mortgage market (See Phil Angelides, et al., *The Financial Crisis Inquiry Report* (New York: Public Affairs, 2011, pp. 38–39; and Roubini and Mihm, pp. 61–63.).

### Securitization and Mortgage Backed Securities
Slowly the government lifted some of the restrictions on Fannie and Freddie, first permitting them to buy loans that had not fallen within FHA or VA guidelines and then authorizing them to participate in securitization. The process of **securitization** works like this (Angelides, et al., pp. 38–39 and 70–71; and Roubini and Mihm, pp. 62–65). A bank or other lender lends money to a borrower who pays off the loan over time with interest. The lender makes money on the interest at a slow and steady rate over a period of years (decades actually when speaking of real property). Somewhere along the line some bright boy (or gal) decided that it would be better to bundle a bunch of these mortgages together and sell them as bonds (now called **mortgage-backed securities**) to big investors, like pension funds, which would then reap the benefit of the interest payments multiplied by the number of loans purchased in that bundle over a long period of time, while the lender received a big payment up front, allowing it to bundle more and more mortgages more and more rapidly (Roubini and Mihm, p. 65). As noted above, Fannie, Ginnie, and Freddie were all authorized to purchase these mortgage backed securities.

### Securitization and Asset-Backed Securities
Now three effects rolled off of this. First, another bright gal (or boy) decided that, what worked for mortgages would work for car loans, furniture loans, boat loans, home improvement loans, student loans, construction loans, and so on. Thus, we witness the growing popularity of **asset-backed securities**. Second, the original lenders began to care less and less about whether the borrowers were financially qualified to pay back the loans because, well, the lenders were passing the risk on to those who purchased the securities. It was at this point that subprime loans, as well as other radical loan practices like the so-called liar loans and the NINJA ("no income, no job or assets") loans began to appear (see discussion below). Third, everybody got into the act, not only government sponsored entities, like Fannie, Ginnie, and Freddie, but also commercial banks, investment banks, and dozens of private lending firms, such as Merit Financial, that appeared and vanished overnight. As a result the use of mortgage and asset backed securities grew by 230 percent between 2000 and 2006. This amounted to just about $2.7 trillion. [Charles Gasparino, *The Sellout* (New York: Harper, 2009), p. 158.] The final consequences were inevitable. The crash occurred when the high-risk borrowers could not make their payments. Land values collapsed and, in the wink of an eye, Roubini and Mihm's financial earthquake shook the very foundation of the economy.

### Subprime Loans (Revisited)
Before the collapse, however, the use of loans experienced huge resurgence in the middle of the first decade of the 21st century. Some of this was due to technology that allowed loans to be processed faster and for approval to be based on a mathematical probability of repayment rather than the traditional criteria of credit, capacity, capital, and collateral. (Angelides, pp. 67–72.) However, some of it was also caused by a push toward deregulation. This encouraged the banks and other lenders to issue subprime loans as a way to bring new homeowners into the market while simultaneously helping the lenders build handsome portfolios. (Roubini and Mihm, pp. 73–76.)

### Liar Loans and NINJA Loans

An unintended consequence of this strategy was an increase in the number of liar loans and NINJA loans that appeared on the scene with increased regularity. **Liar loans** are those that deliberately misstate the qualifications of a borrower to push a loan through the approval process. A **NINJA loan** is one that has been negotiated by a borrower with "no income, no job, and no assets." Liar loans and NINJA loans actually come in many different shapes and sizes. They include both adjustable-rate and interest-only mortgages. The idea is to somehow make it easier for someone with little or no buying power to negotiate a mortgage (Gasparino, p. 151; and Roubini and Mihm, pp. 65, 89). Securitization made such loans possible and, in a strange retroactive way, encouraged many others to jump on the securitization bandwagon, thus accelerating the securitization process. Clearly this was a recipe for disaster although only a few people realized it at the time.

## The Effects of the Crisis

The crisis erupted when so many of these borrowers could not make mortgage payments that the mortgage securities market began to collapse. This led to a decline in the value of real property which naturally accelerated the collapse. Those invested in the mortgage backed and asset backed securities began to experience a series of unprecedented losses. One of the most disheartening events that rolled off this crisis was the government takeover of Fannie Mae and Freddie Mac.

### The Fannie and Freddie Takeover
The risky mortgages purchased by Fannie and Freddie began to take their toll on the two GSEs. The purchasing power of the two GSEs had been exaggerated by the fact that their operation was supposedly supported by the U.S Treasury. The apparently risk-free purchases that they made were focused on mortgaged-backed and asset-backed securities both of which were much riskier than they had at first appeared. Then the bottom began to fall out from under them. The two GSEs were hit by enormous losses as the housing crisis hit and mortgages began to default. The fees that had been paid to Fannie and Freddie for backing these risky mortgages did not cover their losses. Nor could they cover those losses with insurance. Moreover, and perhaps more to the point here, their portfolios were filled to capacity with mortgages purchased by subprime borrowers, ARMs, and NINJAs, and everyone knew that, as those mortgages failed Fannie and Freddie's capital reserves would rapidly falling to zero. To prevent this disaster, and to restore confidence in the system, the government stepped in to save both institutions. Of course, as usual, the bailout came too late for many investors, but the overall confidence in those institution was restored at least temporarily (Roubini and Mihm, pp. 108–108; and Angelides, pp. 309–323; Gasparino, pp. 410–416.).

### Troubled Asset Relief Program (TARP)
Another government solution to the crisis was the **Troubled Asset Relief Program** (Note: Some people refer to it as the Toxic Asset Relief Program). This program was designed to allow the government to buy many of the so-called troubled assets that had resulted from the securitization epidemic. The program was funded at a level that reached beyond $700 billion. Not all of the assets, however, went to the purchase of these troubled assets, at least not directly. Instead, they went indirectly into the bailout of several large firms such as GM and Chrysler. Part of the funds also went to financial institutions such as AIG and Bank of America. Many people saw this as a move that bordered on a nationalization of these financial institutions (Roubini and Mihm, pp. 168–169.).

### Home Affordable Modification Program
The **Home Affordable Modification Program (HAMP)** was established by the Department of the Treasury to support the efforts of homeowners who, though in default, wished to continue to make payments on their mortgages. The program provides help to the private banks and other lenders who own the mortgages and who must be convinced of the need and the value of restructuring

the mortgages. Of course not every debtor will be qualified under the HAMP guidelines. In order to take advantage of HAMP, a debtor must owe no more than $729,750 on the mortgage. The property must be the debtor's primary residence and the mortgage must have been entered no later than January 1, 2009. Finally, the debtor must also be at least 60 days behind on payments or close to losing the home entirely.

### Dodd-Frank Wall Street Reform and Consumer Protection Act

Undoubtedly the most sweeping reform bill to pass Congress and to be signed into law by the President is the **Dodd-Frank Wall Street Reform and Consumer Protection Act (The Dodd-Frank Act)**. As mighty be expected, the Dodd-Frank Act is long, involved, and complicated. It consists of 16 separate titles many of which are often referred to as separate acts. Thus, Title XIV of the Dodd-Frank Act, is also called the Mortgage Reform and Anti-Predatory Lending Act. Title XIV is especially pertinent to our discussion of the 21st century financial crisis because the new act is designed to prevent the problems noted above. Some of the new provisions include the following.

1. Lenders are now required to make a good faith attempt to insure that all borrowers have the financial ability to repay the loan taken out to finance the mortgage.

2. Lenders must also make a good faith attempt to determine whether the borrower can also pay all taxes, insurance, and all other assessments.

3. A good faith attempt must include an examination of specifically defined documents that provide concrete verifiable evidence of the borrower's income stream, credit history, debt-to-income situation, employment, financial resources not (counting the equity in the real property involved in the current loan).

4. The Lender is required to use documentation supplied by the Internal Revenue Service (IRS) or some other comparable third party which is also regulated by the act.

5. Certain types of mortgage arrangements are either outlawed or limited by the act, including mortgages with balloon payments that more than double the previous payments.

On a more positive note, the act also creates a category of mortgages called **qualified mortgages** which have met the good faith requirements outlined in the act. Having a qualified mortgage bestows on the lender a safe harbor privilege that creates a presumption that the lender had ample evidence demonstrating that the borrower could satisfy the loan's repayment requirements. On the other hand, the act also outlaws certain types of lender-related compensation. Thus, mortgage originators cannot be compensated based on the loan's terms, except for terms related to the principal on the loan. Also, the mortgage originator cannot be paid an origination fee, with certain exceptions, unless that fee is paid by the borrower. [See "Dodd-Frank Act Ushers in New Regulations for Mortgage Originators," *Day Pitney, LLP* (August 24, 2010), pp. 1–3; John ReVeal, "Mortgage Reforms Under the Dodd-Frank Act," *Bryan Cave LLP* (August 3, 2010), http://www.bankbryancave.com; "Summary of Mortgage Related Provisions of the Dodd-Frank Wall Street Reform and Consumer Protection Act," *Mortgage Bankers Association* (July 21, 2010), p. 1; and William Sweet, "Dodd-Frank Becomes Law," *The Harvard Law School Forum on Corporate Governance and Financial Regulation* (July 21, 2010), p. 2, http://blogs.law.harvard.edu.]

These are only a few of the many modifications made by the new act. Other modifications include a new rule requiring institutions that engage in securitization to keep an economic stake in the assets that they securitize (Title IX); the formation of a Financial Stability Oversight Council (Title I); the elimination of the Office of Thrift Supervision and the transfer of some of its operations to the Office of Comptroller and others to the Federal Reserve, and the FDIC (Title III); the formation of the Office of Financial Research (Title I); and the establishment of a Bureau of Consumer Financial Protection (Title X).

---

## quick quiz 20-2

1. Subprime lending was the only cause of the 21st century finan-          true | false
   cial crisis.

2. Although the securitization process works very well for mortgage-       true | false
   backed securities, it has never been applied to other types
   of assets.

3. The federal government was forced to take over Fannie Mae but           true | false
   did not have to follow a similar strategy with Freddie Mac.

---

# 20-3 Personal Property as Security

Article 9 of the UCC brings all personal property security devices, or security interests, together under one law. The property that is subject to the security interest is called **collateral**. A security interest is created by a written agreement, called a **security agreement**, which identifies the goods and is signed by the debtor. The lender or seller who holds the security interest is known as the **secured party**. A security interest is said to attach when the secured party has a legally enforceable right to take that property and sell it to satisfy the debt. It is said to be **perfected** when the secured party has done everything that the law requires to give the secured party greater rights to the goods than others have.

The following definitions apply to secured transactions:

- **Consumer goods** are goods that are used or bought for use primarily for personal, family, or household purposes.
- **Equipment** are goods other than inventory, farm products, or consumer goods.
- **Farm products** are crops or livestock or supplies used or produced in farming operations.
- **Inventory** are goods other than farm products held for sale or lease or raw materials used or consumed in a business.                                       UCC 9-102(23)
- **Fixtures** are goods that are so related to real estate that an interest arises in them under real estate law.                                                  UCC 9-102(34)
- **Purchase money security interest** is a security interest taken by a lender or a seller of an item to secure its price.                                         UCC 9-102(41)
- **Buyer in the ordinary course of business** is a person who in good faith and without knowledge that the sale is in violation of ownership rights or security interest of a third party buys goods in ordinary course from a person in the business of selling goods of that kind, not including a pawnbroker.

UCC 9-102(33)
UCC 9-102(48)
UCC 9-103
UCC 1-201(9)
(see page 817)

## Security Agreement

A security agreement is an agreement that creates a security interest. It must be in writing, be       UCC 9-105(l)
signed by the debtor, and contain a description of the collateral that is used for security.

**EXAMPLE 20-3:** Security Agreement Must Describe Collateral

Moody Industries contracted to purchase certain robotics equipment from Universal. Moody's president signed a promissory note identifying Universal as a secured party. When Moody filed for bankruptcy, Universal claimed to have a security interest in the robotics equipment. Because the promissory note did not describe the collateral, Universal did not hold a valid security interest in the equipment.

If Universal had provided enough information about the collateral to allow the court to identify it without a detailed description, the result would have been different. Had Universal made reference to the equipment by including purchase order or invoice numbers, the court could have identified the equipment and would have upheld the validity of the security agreement.

## Attachment of a Security Interest

UCC 9-203

To be effective, a security interest must be legally enforceable against the debtor. This enforceability is known as **attachment**. Attachment occurs when three conditions are met. First, the debtor has some ownership or possessive rights in the collateral. Second, the secured party (or creditor) transfers something of value, such as money, to the debtor. Third, the secured party takes possession of the collateral or signs a security agreement that describes the collateral.

**EXAMPLE 20-4:** Attachment of Security Interest

Conroy loaned Lightfoot $5,000 for six months at 8 percent interest. Lightfoot secured the debt by giving Conroy several uncut diamonds that Lightfoot owned. Conroy agreed to return the diamonds when Lightfoot paid the debt. The security interest was legally enforceable because all three conditions were met. First, Lightfoot had ownership rights in the diamonds. Second, Conroy gave Lightfoot something of value (the $5,000). Third, Conroy took possession of the diamonds. The security interest would also have attached if Lightfoot had kept the diamonds but signed a security agreement describing them.

UCC 9-204

Creditors may obtain security interests in property acquired by the debtor after the original agreement is entered. The creditor does so by placing a provision in the security agreement that the security interest of the creditor also applies to goods the debtor acquires at a later time. It is known as a **floating lien**. This lien is important to creditors who take security interests in goods, such as food items, that are sold and replaced within short periods of time. The lien is lost when the goods are sold but regained as soon as the debtor takes possession of the new property.

## Perfection of a Security Interest

When a security interest attaches, it is effective only between debtor and creditor. Such creditors, however, want to make certain that no one else can claim that collateral before they do if the debtors fail to pay them back. To preserve the right to first claim on the collateral, creditors must perfect their interest. A security interest can be perfected in one of three ways: by filing a financing statement in the appropriate government office, by attachment alone, or by possession of the collateral.

**Perfection by Filing** Security interests in most kinds of personal property are perfected by filing a financing statement in a public office. The office may be a central one (secretary of state's office) or a local one (county recorder or city clerk) where the debtor resides or has a place of business. The proper office for filing depends on the type of collateral and varies from state to state.

A financing statement must give the names of the debtor and the secured party. It must be signed by the debtor and give the address of a secured party from which information regarding the security interest may be obtained. It must also give a mailing address of the debtor and contain a statement indicating the types, or describing the items, of collateral. When the financing statement covers such things as fixtures, crops, timber, minerals, oil, and gas, the statement must also contain a description of the real estate concerned.

*UCC 9-302*

**Perfection by Attachment Alone** A purchase money security interest in *consumer goods* is perfected the moment it attaches, with the exception of motor vehicles and fixtures. Security interests on motor vehicles are perfected by making a note of the lien on the certificate of title issued by the state government. Security interests on fixtures are perfected by filing a financing statement with the registry of deeds where the land is located.

*UCC 9-302(1)(d)*
*UCC 9-302(3)(b)*

## EXAMPLE 20-5: Perfection of Purchase Money Security Interest

Sabatini purchased a new 34" widescreen HDTV for $1,999.99 from Steinbeck's TV Outlet. To pay for the TV, she borrowed money from the Atlantic Finance Company, which took a security interest in the TV by entering into a security agreement with Sabatini. Because this interest was a purchase money security interest and the TV set was a consumer good, the security interest would become perfected the moment it attached, that is, when Sabatini signed the agreement and received the TV set, and Steinbeck received payment from the finance company.

**Perfection by Possession** A security interest may be perfected when the secured party (creditor) takes possession of the collateral. This possession is called a pledge. The borrower, or debtor, who gives up the property, is the pledgor. The secured party, or creditor, is the pledgee. A secured party who has possession of the collateral must take reasonable care of the property. The debtor must reimburse the secured party for any money spent to take care of the property.

*UCC 9-313*

## EXAMPLE 20-6: Pledge of Personal Property

After Sabatini paid off the debt to the Atlantic Finance Corporation, she decided to buy a Kindle. This time, she borrowed the money from her cousin, Colter, who agreed to lend Sabatini the money only if he could have her Kindle as security until she repaid him. Colter's security interest in the Kindle became perfected when he took possession of it.

## Priorities and Claims

UCC 9-312(3)

UCC 9-312(4)

UCC 9-307(1)

UCC 9-301(1)(c)

Collateral may be re-
possessed if the debtor
defaults, but the repos-
session may not breach
the peace.

Sometimes, two or more parties claim a security interest in the same collateral. At other times, unsecured parties claim that they have better rights than secured parties. The UCC helps resolve these conflicts. The following are some of the provisions, stating who prevails over whom in particular situations:

1. A perfected purchase money security interest in inventory has priority over a conflicting security interest in the same inventory.

2. A purchase money security interest in collateral other than inventory has priority over a conflicting security interest in the same collateral if it is perfected when the debtor receives the collateral or within 10 days thereafter.

3. Buyers of goods in the ordinary course of business (except farm products) prevail over security interests in the seller's inventory.

4. Buyers of farm products in the ordinary course of business, to the extent that they pay for and receive collateral without knowledge of the security interest, take precedence over nonperfected security interests.

5. Buyers of consumer goods are not affected by perfected security interests of which they have no knowledge.

6. In all other cases, a perfected security interest prevails over an unperfected security interest.

7. Conflicting security interests rank according to priority in time of filing or perfection.

8. When two or more parties have unperfected security interests in the same collateral, the first to attach prevails over the other parties.

## Default of the Debtor

UCC 9-307(2)

UCC 9-301

UCC 9-312(5)(a)

UCC 9-312(5)(b)

UCC 9-601

If a debtor defaults by failing to make payments when due, the secured party may satisfy the debt by taking possession of the collateral. Because of the difficulties of doing this, the perfection of a security interest by possession, as in a pledge, is better than other types of perfection. Collateral may be repossessed without going through the court if it can be done without causing a disturbance; otherwise, the creditor must use legal processes.

After repossessing the goods, the secured party (the creditor) may sell them at a public auction or private sale. The terms of the sale must be reasonable, and the debtor must be given notice of the time and place of any public auction so that he or she may bid on them personally. If the goods are consumer goods and the debtor has paid 60 percent or more of the cash price of a purchase money security interest, the secured party cannot keep the goods. They must be sold.

### quick quiz 20-3

1. A security interest is perfected when the secured party has a legally enforceable right to take that property and sell it to satisfy the debt.    true | false

2. Security interests in most kinds of personal property are perfected by filing a financial statement in a public office.    true | false

3. Buyers of goods in the ordinary course of business (except farm products) prevail over security interests in the seller's inventory.    true | false

# Summary

**20.1** Individuals and institutions that lend money need some assurance that they will have their money returned to them. Security devices serve as this means of assurance.

**20.2** Purchases of real property are generally secured by a mortgage. A mortgage is a transfer of an interest in property for the purpose of creating a security for a debt. Some common types of mortgages include the conventional mortgage, the variable-rate mortgage, the graduated-payment mortgage, the balloon-payment mortgage, FHA and VA mortgages, and deeds of trust. One of the causes of the 21st century financial crisis was the runaway real estate market. Speculation on property prices ran rampant; buyers rushed to invest in land; and deregulated lenders lent money to bad credit risks. One cause of the crisis was the popularity of mortgage-backed and asset-backed securities. The use of these securities meant that original lenders did not properly police the qualifications of borrowers. It was at this point that subprime loans, as well as other radical loan practices like "liar loans" and NINJA ("no income, no job or assets") loans began to appear. Soon government sponsored entities,

like Fannie Mae, Ginnie Mae, and Freddie Mac, as well as commercial banks, investment banks, and private lending firms got into the act causing a strain that led to the collapse. One of the most severe effects that rolled off this crisis was the government takeover of Fannie Mae and Freddie Mac. One government solution to the crisis was the Troubled Asset Relief Program and another was the Home Affordable Modification Program (HAMP).

**20.3** When personal property is purchased on credit, the seller frequently retains a security interest in the property. Property that is subject to a security interest is called collateral. A security interest is created by a written agreement called a security agreement, which identifies the goods and is signed by the debtor. To be effective between debtor and creditor, a security interest must be made legally enforceable. This legality is known as attachment. To be effective against third parties who might also claim the secured property, the creditor must perfect the security interest. Perfection is accomplished by filing a financing statement, by attachment alone in certain cases, or by taking possession of the collateral.

# Key Terms

acceleration, 431

adjustable-rate mortgage (ARM), 426

asset-backed security, 434

assume the mortgage, 432

attachment, 438

balloon-payment mortgage, 428

buyer in the ordinary course of business, 437

collateral, 437

construction loan, 428

consumer goods, 437

conventional fixed-rate mortgage, 426

deed of trust, 429

Dodd-Frank Wall Street Reform and Consumer Protection Act, 436

equipment, 437

equity of redemption, 430

farm products, 437

fixtures, 437

flexible-rate mortgage, 426

floating lien, 438

foreclosure, 431

government-sponsored enterprise (GSE), 434

graduated-payment mortgage, 427

Home Affordable Modification Program (HAMP), 435

home equity loan, 429

interest-only mortgage, 426

inventory, 437

junior mortgage, 429

liar loan, 434

mortgage, 425

mortgage-backed security, 434

mortgagee, 425

mortgagor, 425

NINJA loan, 435

participation loan, 428

perfected, 437

purchase money security interest, 437

qualified mortgage, 436

reverse mortgage, 428

second mortgage, 429

secured loan, 425

secured party, 437

## Questions for Review and Discussion

1. What is the difference between a secured and an unsecured loan?
2. What types of mortgages are available to borrowers?
3. What is the legal effect of recording a mortgage?
4. What are the rights and duties of the mortgagor and those of the mortgagee?
5. What are Fannie Mae, Ginnie Mae, and Freddie Mac?
6. What is securitization and how did it contribute to the financial crisis?
7. What are liar loans and NINJA loans?
8. How is a security interest is created for personal property?
9. When is a security interest perfected?
10. What priorities exist when parties claim a security interest in the same property?

## Cases for Analysis

1. Sanchez bought a house for $100,000, paying $10,000 down and financing the balance through a local bank. As part of the closing costs, Sanchez was required to take out private mortgage insurance to protect the bank in case she defaulted on the mortgage. She had an excellent credit rating and always paid her mortgage payments when they were due. Two years after buying the property, she received an inheritance and used the money to pay an additional amount of $10,000 to the bank toward the principal of the loan. Hoping to cut down on her monthly payments, she asked the bank to cancel the mortgage insurance, but the bank refused. Does Sanchez have any rights in this situation? Explain.

2. Robert and Sherrell Bergeron gave a first mortgage on their property to First Colonial Bank and a second mortgage to Ford Motor Credit Company. When the Bergerons were unable to pay the mortgage, the bank foreclosed. The property was sold at a foreclosure sale for more money than the Bergerons owed the bank. The Bergerons claim that they are entitled to the surplus funds from the sale. Do you agree? Explain. *First Colonial Bank for Savings v. Bergeron*, 646 N.E.2d 758 (MA).

3. When the Prestons took out a variable mortgage with the First Bank of Marietta, their interest rate was 9 percent. The agreement allowed First Bank to raise or lower the interest rate at any time,

provided that the Prestons received 30 days' advance notice. When the bank raised the interest rate to 11 percent, the Prestons refused to pay, arguing that the agreement was unenforceable, because it set no limit on what interest rate they might be forced to pay. Were the Prestons correct? Explain. *Preston v. First Bank of Marietta*, 473 N.E.2d 1210 (OH).

4. The Woolseys ran a mink farm that was mortgaged to the State Bank of Lehi. The agreement included provisions that allowed acceleration and foreclosure if the Woolseys failed to pay their obligations under the contract. The Woolseys defaulted on several payments, and the bank foreclosed. The couple demanded a jury trial on the foreclosure action. They also argued that the bank had not acted in good faith in its acceleration and foreclosure. Were the Woolseys entitled to a jury trial? Explain. Who had the burden of proof in demonstrating the bank's good faith in accelerating payments and demanding foreclosure? *State Bank of Lehi v. Woolsey*, 565 P.2d 413 (UT).

5. Bloom executed a real estate mortgage in favor of Lakeshore Commercial Finance Corporation on September 16. On October 4, Bloom executed another mortgage on the same described real estate in favor of Northridge Bank. Northridge, without notice of the mortgage to Lakeshore, recorded its mortgage at 9:28 A.M. on October 25. On that same date, at 3:07 P.M., the prior mortgage executed in

favor of Lakeshore was recorded. Bloom defaulted on the mortgages. The value of the real estate was insufficient to satisfy both mortgages fully. Which party had first rights to the property, Lakeshore or Northridge? Why? *Northridge Bank v. Lakeshore Com. Fin. Corp.,* 365 N.E.2d 382 (IL).

6. Cramer's mortgage contained a provision requiring her to pay monthly tax and insurance payments into an escrow account held by the bank in addition to principal and interest. Cramer paid the principal and interest regularly but refused to pay the tax and insurance escrow payments. The bank brought foreclosure proceedings. Did it have the right to foreclose on Cramer's mortgage? Explain. *Cramer v. Metro. Sav. & Loan Ass'n.,* 258 N.W.2d 20 (MI).

7. Matthews Motors sold a Buick Riviera to Jenkins for $11,500. Matthews then borrowed money from Averysboro National Bank, using the Buick as collateral. When Matthews defaulted on the loan, the bank attempted to repossess the Buick from Jenkins. Jenkins refused to surrender the automobile, claiming that he and not Matthews owned it. The bank brought suit, asking the court to force Jenkins to turn over the Buick. Should the court grant the bank's request? Why or why not? *Averysboro National Bank v. Jenkins,* 328 S.E.2d 399 (GA).

8. Giant Wholesale agreed to supply Hendersonville Food Center with groceries if the owner, William Page, would guarantee all debts incurred by Hendersonville. Page agreed, and a security agreement was drawn up. The security agreement gave Giant a security interest in Hendersonville's groceries and equipment. Giant failed to file a financing statement properly. When Hendersonville ran into financial difficulty, Page turned over the checking account to Giant. When this maneuver did not work, Giant repossessed all of Hendersonville's inventory. Page later went bankrupt. Gray, the bankruptcy trustee, brought a suit against Giant, claiming that the inventory was part of Page's property and thus subject to the bankruptcy proceeding. Gray argued that because the financing statement had not been filed, Giant's security interest had not been perfected. Was Gray correct? Explain. *Gray v. Giant Wholesale,* 758 F.2d 1000 (4th Cir.).

9. U.S. Electronics, a Missouri corporation with a place of business in DeKalb County, Georgia, borrowed money from a Missouri bank. The corporation gave the bank a security interest in all of its machinery and equipment. The bank filed a financing statement in Fulton County rather than in DeKalb County, as required by law. U.S. Electronics defaulted on the loan and fell behind on its rent. The corporation's landlord obtained a judgment against it for past due rent, becoming a lien creditor. The landlord claimed priority over the bank for the proceeds of a sheriff's sale of the machinery and equipment, arguing that the bank's security interest was not perfected. Do you agree? Why or why not? *United States v. Waterford No. 2 Office Center,* 271 S.E.2d 790 (GA).

10. Lallana bought a car on credit from a dealer who assigned the contract and the security agreement to Bank of America. When Lallana failed to make several payments, the bank repossessed the car. The bank notified Lallana that if she did not redeem the car or reinstate the contract within 15 days, it would sell the car. The bank then sold the car at a public auction for $5,000 and sued Lallana for $11,249, the balance due on her loan. The Kelly Blue Book's estimated retail value of the car at the time of the auction was $14,820. Did the bank give Lallana proper notice of the sale? Why or why not? *Bank of America v. Lallana,* 960 P.2d 1133 (CA).

## quick quiz Answers

| 20-1 | 20-2 | 20-3 |
|------|------|------|
| 1. T | 1. F | 1. F |
| 2. T | 2. F | 2. T |
| 3. T | 3. F | 3. T |

# Chapter 21 · Bankruptcy and Debt Adjustment

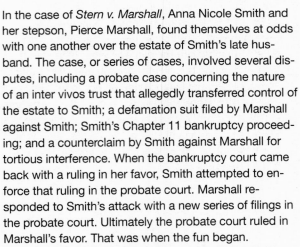

## THE OPENING CASE  State's Rights or Federal Supremacy: *Stern (Anna Nicole Smith) v. Pierce Marshall*

In the case of *Stern v. Marshall*, Anna Nicole Smith and her stepson, Pierce Marshall, found themselves at odds with one another over the estate of Smith's late husband. The case, or series of cases, involved several disputes, including a probate case concerning the nature of an inter vivos trust that allegedly transferred control of the estate to Smith; a defamation suit filed by Marshall against Smith; Smith's Chapter 11 bankruptcy proceeding; and a counterclaim by Smith against Marshall for tortious interference. When the bankruptcy court came back with a ruling in her favor, Smith attempted to enforce that ruling in the probate court. Marshall responded to Smith's attack with a new series of filings in the probate court. Ultimately the probate court ruled in Marshall's favor. That was when the fun began.

The federal bankruptcy court had ruled for Smith and the state probate court had ruled for Marshall. Which court's decision has precedence over the other? Ordinarily, the right answer would be the bankruptcy court because, by virtue of the Supremacy Clause of the Constitution, the federal court rulings trump state court rulings; however, and this is a big however, court cases extending as far back as 1923 have consistently

held that bankruptcy courts must follow the final rulings of state courts, rather than the other way around. Also, in a case involving a bankruptcy, we are dealing with a court created by Article I rather than Article III. This makes a difference because both the courts and a federal law [28 USC 157 (b) (2)] have consistently declared that bankruptcy courts cannot make final judgments on "noncore" issues.

A noncore issue does not really involve the approval or disapproval of a creditor's claim. In contrast, when an issue involves a core matter, the bankruptcy court can make a final judgment. Thus, in this case, the final decision turns on whether the counterclaim filed by Smith for tortious interference is a core or a noncore issue. This may not seem serious, but if the counterclaim is a noncore issue, then the power of the bankruptcy courts will be in question and the future of bankruptcy filings in doubt. Is it appropriate to always defer to the federal courts in bankruptcy matters or is it better to also consider states rights? Think about these issues as you explore bankruptcy law and debt adjustment in this chapter. [See Daniel H. Reiss, "Smith Case Could Transform Bankruptcy Litigation," *The National Law*

*Journal* (February 28, 2011), p. 22. See also: *Stern v. Marshall,* No. 10-179, United States Supreme Court, argued Jan. 18.]

**Opening Case Questions**

1. What article in the U.S. Constitution established the federal court system and which court is named in that article? Explain.

2. What article in the U.S. Constitution established federal bankruptcy courts? Explain.

3. What is the Supremacy Clause and where in the constitution is it located? Explain.

4. What is the difference between a bankruptcy court and a probate court? Explain.

5. Why does it make sense for the federal courts to have supremacy over the state courts? Explain.

## LO Learning Objectives

1. Summarize the history of bankruptcy law in the United States.
2. Discuss restoring credit following bankruptcy.
3. State the criteria necessary to be eligible to file voluntarily for Chapter 7 bankruptcy.
4. Explain the "means test" that is required for filing Chapter 7 bankruptcy.
5. State the criteria necessary for creditors to force debtors into involuntary bankruptcy.
6. Distinguish between an *order for relief* and *automatic stay* in the bankruptcy process.
7. List the federal exemptions debtors can exclude from the bankruptcy process.
8. Recognize those debts that have priority payment status under the Bankruptcy Code.
9. Explain Chapter 11 bankruptcy, emphasizing the reorganization process.
10. Discuss the requirements for Chapters 12 and 13 bankruptcy.

# 21-1 Bankruptcy's History

These objectives have not always been the priority in the history of bankruptcy law. Early laws favored creditors. In addition to losing all of their property, debtors were often put in debtor's prison and sometimes, though not in the United States, put to death. The first federal bankruptcy law in the United States was enacted in 1800. Under that law, only creditors could begin a bankruptcy proceeding, and only merchants could qualify as debtors. That law lasted only three years before Congress repealed it. In 1840, debtor's prisons were abolished in the United States, and a year later, Congress passed a bankruptcy law that lasted only two years. Following the turmoil of the Civil War, Congress enacted a third bankruptcy law in 1867 that lasted 11 years. It wasn't until 1898 that permanent bankruptcy legislation came about in the United States, with a law that gave businesses protection from creditors and lasted, with modifications during the Great Depression, for 80 years.

The Bankruptcy Reform Act of 1978 again brought major changes, making it easier for businesses and individuals to obtain bankruptcy relief. It was in 1978 that Chapters 11 and 13 of the Bankruptcy Code (discussed subsequently) were created, allowing businesses and individuals to reorganize and keep going. In addition, debtors were allowed to keep more of their assets, giving them a better chance to make a fresh start with their activities. The 1994 Bankruptcy Reform Act continued honing the law and created the National Bankruptcy Commission to study the subject and make recommendations. In 2005, following a period of easy credit with many people spending far above their means, Congress made it more difficult to declare bankruptcy by enacting far-reaching changes to the Bankruptcy Code. The current law is explained in this chapter.

## THE OPENING CASE *Revisited, Part I*
## State's Rights or Federal Supremacy: *Stern (Anna Nicole Smith) v. Pierce Marshall,* Round 2

The case of *Stern (Anna Nicole Smith) v. Marshall* involved a series of disputes, including a probate case concerning the nature of an inter vivos trust that allegedly transferred control of the estate to Smith; a defamation suit filed by Marshall against Smith; Smith's Chapter 11 bankruptcy proceeding; and a counterclaim by Smith against Marshall for tortious interference. The bankruptcy court ruled in favor of Smith, but when she tried to enforce that ruling in the probate court, her stepson, Marshall responded by initiating a new series of filings in the probate court. The probate court ruled in Marshall's favor creating a deadlock. The

federal bankruptcy court had ruled for Smith and the state probate court had ruled for Marshall. Which court's decision has precedence over the other? The case turned on whether Smith's counter claims for tortious interference was a core or a noncore issue. The decision was so important that the United States Supreme Court agreed to hear and decide the case. [See Daniel H. Reiss, "Smith Case Could Transform Bankruptcy Litigation," *The National Law Journal* (February 28, 2011), p. 22. See also: *Stern v. Marshall,* No. 10-179, United States Supreme Court, argued Jan. 18.]

## Constitutional Authority

U.S. Const., Article I, Sec. 8 (see page 808)

The U.S. Constitution gives the federal government jurisdiction over bankruptcy proceedings by stating that "Congress shall have the Power . . . To establish . . . uniform laws on the subject of Bankruptcies throughout the United States." Congress exercised this power when it enacted the Bankruptcy Code, which is found in Title 11 of the United States Code (USC). Unfortunately, as clear-cut as this may seem on the surface, sometimes federal and state jurisdictions overlap on these issues. One reason for this overlap is the fact that the bankruptcy courts were created by Congress under a power granted to the legislature under Article I rather than Article III. This makes a difference because both the courts and a federal law [28 USC 157 (b) (2)] have repeatedly ruled that bankruptcy courts can only make final judgments on core issues. A core issue is one that clearly involves the approval or disapproval of a creditor's claim. In contrast, when an issue involves a noncore matter, the bankruptcy court cannot make a final judgment. It is doubtful that either the courts or the legislature would have handled the jurisdiction of Article III courts in the same manner.

## Restoring Credit Following Bankruptcy

A personal bankruptcy filing remains on a debtor's credit report for 10 years and has a detrimental effect on the ability to establish a line of credit. However, most debtors who file bankruptcy have already established a poor credit rating anyway, and filing bankruptcy gives them an opportunity to begin anew. A good number of their debts become discharged, which improves their debt-to-income ratio—a factor that potential creditors look at carefully. The more time that elapses after the bankruptcy filing, the easier it is to reestablish credit.

Many people in this situation switch from credit cards to debit cards, which is like paying cash because instead of initiating a charge, debit cards withdraw money instantly from a bank account. Some banks offer *secured credit cards* in which customers deposit money in the bank to guarantee that their credit card charges will be paid. Until their credit is reestablished, their credit limit is the same as the amount of their bank deposit. Credit card issuers sometimes allow debtors to continue using their credit cards if they agree in writing, after the bankruptcy filing, to pay off the old debt. Often, this allowance also requires an agreement by the debtor to pay the credit card balance each month without carrying a balance. People who are able to make a down payment and have steady income may be eligible for a mortgage loan as soon as two years following a discharge in bankruptcy.

---

### quick quiz 21-1

1. The U.S. Constitution gives state courts jurisdiction over bankruptcy proceedings.    true | false

2. In 2005, Congress made it easier to declare bankruptcy by enacting far-reaching changes to the Bankruptcy Code.    true | false

3. A core issue is one that clearly involves the approval or disapproval of a creditor's claim.    true | false

---

# 21-2 Liquidation—Chapter 7, Bankruptcy Code

Chapter 7 of the Bankruptcy Code, sometimes referred to as ordinary bankruptcy, provides a system in which debtors are forced to sell much of their property and use the cash to pay their creditors a portion of the amount owed each one. This process is also called liquidation. See Table 21-1 for a summary of different types of bankruptcy procedures.

## Commencing the Action

Under Chapter 7 bankruptcy, the debtor may be an individual, partnership, corporation, or other type of business. The process may be either voluntary or involuntary. With voluntary bankruptcy, the debtor files the bankruptcy petition. With involuntary bankruptcy, creditors file the papers to force the debtor into bankruptcy and pay them off.

**Voluntary Proceedings** Debtors sometimes realize that their financial position can never improve without some drastic action and decide to file a bankruptcy petition on their own. Under the 2005 Bankruptcy Act, however, not everyone is allowed to file for Chapter 7 bankruptcy. To qualify, debtors must do all of the following:

- Satisfy the means test, discussed next.
- Meet with an approved nonprofit credit counselor before filing for bankruptcy.
- Provide a federal income tax return for the most recent tax year.
- Take a course in financial management after filing for bankruptcy.

**The Means Test** The means test consists of three steps, the passing of any one of which allows the debtor to file for Chapter 7 bankruptcy. The first step is to compare the debtor's average income during the previous six months with the median income for a family of that size in the debtor's state. If the debtor's income is less than the state's median income, the debtor is eligible to file for Chapter 7 bankruptcy. Every state's medium income is provided by the U.S. Census Bureau and can be found at www.census.gov.

## Table 21-1   Types of Bankruptcy Procedures

| Chapter | Who Can File? | When Used? | Special Features |
|---|---|---|---|
| Chapter 7: Ordinary Bankruptcy | Only those who (a) have income below the state's average family income for families of that size, (b) meet with an approved nonprofit credit counselor before filing, (c) provide a federal income tax return for the most recent tax year, and (d) take a course in financial management after filing. | Used when debtor wants to discharge most debts and begin with a clean slate | Debtor's property is liquidated; some property is exempt; some debts cannot be discharged |
| Chapter 11: Reorganization | Individuals, partnerships, and corporations can file; railroads can file; only commodity brokers and stockbrokers cannot; filing can be voluntary or involuntary. | Used when debtor, usually a business, wants to continue operating but needs to reorganize and liquidate debts | Debtor-in-possession feature; plan must be fair, equitable, and feasible; creditors can also file plans; confirmation needed |
| Chapter 12: Family Farmer or Fishing Business Debt Adjustment | Family farmer or fishing businesses that receive 50 percent of income from farming or fishing can file, including partnerships and corporations. | Used when debtor has a family farming or fishing business and needs a debt adjustment plan to keep running | Debtor-in-possession feature |
| Chapter 13: Individual Debt Adjustment | Individuals who meet with a credit counselor and have steady income only; no corporations or partnerships; no involuntary filings allowed. | Used when an individual debtor with a steady income voluntarily decides to adopt a debt adjustment plan | Only the debtor can file a plan; a few debts cannot be discharged; plan lasts three years (with two-year possible extension) |

## EXAMPLE 21-1: The Means Test—Step One

Raymond and Jessica Mattik lived with their two children in a house they owned in North Carolina. They were very much in debt. Not only were they behind in their payments for their late-model car and household furnishings, but they also owed the maximum amount on five different credit cards. When the interest on their adjustable-rate mortgage increased dramatically, they considered filing for bankruptcy. Together, they earned $42,178 annually. They would be eligible to file for Chapter 7 bankruptcy because their income was less than $43,229—the median income for a family of four in North Carolina. Because they qualified under this first step, they are finished with the means test.

Suppose Raymond and Jessica, in Example 21-1, had income that exceeded their state's median income for a family of four. Then, they would have to go to step two of the means test, which is more complicated. Step two requires debtors to determine whether they have enough income to pay off some of their unsecured debts. This determination requires subtracting certain deductions, which vary according to where they live, and arriving at a figure called their **disposable income**. If their disposable income is less then $110 a month, they pass the means test and will be allowed to file for Chapter 7 bankruptcy. If it is more than $183 a month, however, they fail the means test and cannot file for Chapter 7. They may, however, be able to convert the case to Chapters 11, 12, or 13 of the Bankruptcy Code discussed subsequently.

## EXAMPLE 21-2: The Means Test—Step Two

Robert and Carol Kling lived with their two children in Texas, where the median income for a family of four is $47,143. Because their combined income of $47,800 is greater than this median, they did not pass step one of the means test and had to go to step two. After deducting certain amounts prescribed for their geographical area, their disposable income was $120 a month—again, too high to pass the means test because it was over $110. They now must go to step three of the test.

The third step in the means test is taken only by debtors who do not qualify for Chapter 7 bankruptcy under the first two steps. Under this final step, a determination is made as to whether the debtor has the ability to pay unsecured debts over a five-year period. If a debtor's monthly disposable income is between $110 and $183 but not enough to pay more than 25 percent of outstanding unsecured debts over a five-year period, the debtor passes the means test and will be allowed to file for Chapter 7 bankruptcy. In contrast, if the disposable income is enough to pay those debts over five years, the debtor does not pass the means test and will be required to switch over to another bankruptcy chapter, such as Chapter 13, discussed later.

To petition for bankruptcy, debtors file official forms with the nearest U.S. Bankruptcy Court. These courts are attached to district courts within the federal court structure (see Chapter 3). Official forms for filing bankruptcy can be obtained at legal stationery stores as well as www.uscourts.gov. The form asks debtors to name all of their creditors and indicate how much money they owe those creditors. The form also requires a listing of their property and a statement of income and expenses. Finally, the form asks debtors to list all of the property that they feel should be exempt from the sale when it comes time later in the bankruptcy proceeding to sell what they own.

## Involuntary Proceedings
Under Chapter 7 of the Bankruptcy Code, creditors may be able to force debtors, other than farmers, into involuntary bankruptcy if the debtor fails to pay bills generally as they become due. Creditors must prove that the outstanding debts are not subject to a bona fide dispute. A single creditor who is owed a debt of more than $14,425 can file if the debtor has fewer than 12 creditors. If the debtor has 12 or more creditors, 3 of them must file the petition. The combined debt owed the 3 must exceed $14,425. This dollar amount, instituted in 2010, is adjustable every three years to reflect changes in the consumer price index.

## EXAMPLE 21-3: Involuntary Bankruptcy

Goodell had an excellent job with a high salary and a promise of continued advancement. However, he made several miscalculations in the stock market that severely damaged his financial picture. Consequently, though he owned a lot of property, he had little cash on hand. This situation caused him to fall behind on his payments to most of his 14 creditors. Three of those creditors, the Bromfield Department Store, the Mariano Oil Company, and the Financial Bank, filed an involuntary bankruptcy petition against Strasser in federal court. Because Strasser owed them more than $14,425, the petition was accepted.

## Order for Relief

An **order for relief** is the court's command that the liquidation begin. In a voluntary filing, the bankruptcy petition itself becomes the order for relief and is effective the moment it is filed with the court. In an involuntary case, the court does not issue the order immediately because the debtor is allowed to contest the filing, after which a hearing is held to determine whether an order for relief will be issued. When an order for relief is issued, a **case trustee** is named by the court. The trustee schedules a meeting of creditors, which the debtor is required to attend to answer questions about financial matters. Following the meeting, the trustee reports to the court as to whether the case should proceed.

The trustee is charged with the responsibility of liquidating the assets of the debtor for the benefit of all interested parties. Bank accounts, including debit cards, can no longer be used because they become the property of the bankruptcy trustee.

## A QUESTION OF ETHICS

Carol and Michael Rothko created a limited liability company partnership named Rosewood Acres, LLC to buy, renovate, and flip second and third generation homes in Sarasota, Florida. For the first four years of operation, the LLC made a neat little profit on each house flipped. At first the Rothkos had been cautious and had flipped one house at a time. Then when the market was at its peak, they purchased two homes to work on simultaneously. Then the market collapsed. Up until that time, contractors who worked for the Rothkos had been willing to let overdue payments slide because they knew that the Rothkos did a very good business and the contractor did not want to jinx a good thing. Similarly, the bankers who set up the mortgages in each case were willing to accept late payments because they also knew that the Rothkos had an excellent track record in the "flipping" business. However, when the market collapsed the contractors found themselves losing jobs left and right and so they all pressed the Rothkos for more timely payments. The bank was also less forgiving about late payments. Eventually, the Rothkos found that they could not pay the contractors, the bank, nor the utility companies. Nor could they pay property taxes on the three houses. Consequently, the Rothkos decided to file a voluntary petition for bankruptcy. The court appointed Arthur M. Dent as trustee to the debtor's bankruptcy estate. Dent decided to use his own real estate firm as a consultant to assist in the sale of the debtors' property. Consider each of the following ethical issues.

1. First, was it ethical for the Rothkos to delay payments to the contractors?
2. Second, was it ethical for the contractors to suddenly demand earlier payments just because the market had shifted?
3. Third, was it ethical for the bank to demand on-time payments, after being so generous with the Rothkos?
4. Fourth, was it ethical for the court to appoint a trustee to oversee the bankruptcy process of an LLC when the court knew that the trustee was a realtor?
5. Finally, was it ethical for Dent to accept the position as trustee and to then use his own firm to assist in the sale of the debtors' property? Explain each point using a consistent ethical standard.

## Automatic Stay

When a voluntary or involuntary petition is filed, an **automatic stay** goes into effect. This stay is a self-operating postponement of collection proceedings against the debtor. Further efforts by creditors against the debtor to collect debts must stop immediately, except for debts caused by fraud, amounts owed for back taxes, family support, and student loans that do not impose a hardship on the debtor. Among other things, the stay prohibits creditors from beginning or continuing:

- Lawsuits to collect debts incurred before the filing of the petition.
- Attempts to enforce a judgment against the debtor.
- Foreclosure sales.
- Collection proceedings.
- Repossession activities.

As noted above, automatic stays apply to both voluntary and involuntary petitions. Creditors who knowingly ignore the stay can be held in contempt of court.

## EXAMPLE 21-4: Order for Relief and Automatic Stay

Hilenbrand found herself so deeply in debt that she could pay very little on her bills. One of her creditors, Linden Musical Supplies, told her that it was about to file a lawsuit against her. At that point, being able to pass the means test, Hilenbrand filed a bankruptcy petition in federal court. Because she filed voluntarily, the petition was considered the order for relief. At this time, the automatic stay provision of the Bankruptcy Code went into effect. If Linden Musical Supplies carried out its planned action, it could be held in contempt of court.

# Federal Exemptions

As part of the fresh start approach under the Bankruptcy Code, debtors are permitted to exempt or exclude certain items of property from the bankruptcy process, which means that the property is kept by the debtor and cannot be sold to pay the debtor's outstanding bills. Exemptions can be doubled for married couples who file jointly.

**Federal Homestead and Household Exemptions** The Bankruptcy Code allows debtors to keep a maximum of $21,625 in equity in the debtor's place of residence and in property used as a burial ground. This allowance is known as the federal **homestead exemption**. Debtors can also keep a maximum of $550 for any single item of furniture, household goods, clothes, appliances, books, crops, animals, or musical instruments. The total of all exemptions taken in this category cannot exceed $11,525. Debtors are also allowed to exempt $1,450 in jewelry beyond the $9,850 set aside for the other household items mentioned previously. In addition, they may keep any other property not exceeding the value of $1,150, plus up to $10,825 of any unused amount of the $21,625 homestead exemption.

**Necessities** Congress allows debtors to maintain a minimum standard of living by exempting certain necessary items of property. For example, debtors are allowed to exclude a maximum of $2,175 in professional tools, instruments, and books. In addition, they can exempt up to $3,450 in a motor vehicle. Finally, medical supplies that have been prescribed for the health of the debtor can be excluded.

**Benefits and Support Payments** Again, to allow debtors to maintain a minimum standard of living, Congress allows the exclusion of certain benefits and support payments. For instance, alimony and child support payments can be excluded. Benefits received under Social Security or a disability program are also exempt. Profits that are due under profit-sharing, pension, and annuity plans may be excluded. Furthermore, debtors are allowed to protect payments due to them under certain court orders. For example, if someone owes a debtor damages resulting from a personal injury tort case, those damages are exempt up to $21,625. Life insurance contracts carried for the benefit of a relative or approved beneficiary that have yet to mature are also protected. Finally, tax-deferred retire-ment funds are exempt under the bankruptcy act.

## State Exemptions

The Bankruptcy Code allows states to use exemptions created by the state legislature rather than the federal exemptions (see Figure 21-1). Often, the dollar amounts included in the state statutes will be a more accurate assessment of property values within each state, be-cause the state legislators are more flexible in such matters than members of Congress, who must consider property values across the entire country. Every state has its own set of bankruptcy exemptions. States are permitted to give debtors a choice of using the state's exemptions or requiring debtors to take the state exemptions.

## Trustee's Duties

After the order for relief is granted, a trustee will be appointed to take control of the debt-or's property. One of the first things the trustee does is set aside, under the trustee's avoid-ing powers, certain sales and property transfers made by the debtor. The property is then returned to the estate of the debtor. Included in this "pull back" are any fraudulent transfers that the debtor might have made to temporarily hide property from creditors. If the debtor is a business, the bankruptcy court may authorize the trustee to operate the business for a limited period of time. In addition, the trustee sells the debtor's property to obtain cash. The trustee then distributes the cash among the creditors according to set priorities.

**Property Distribution**  The Bankruptcy Code provides a priority list that indi-cates which categories of debts are paid first (Table 21-2). Each category must be paid in

### Table 21-2  Payment Priorities

| Debt | Explanation |
|---|---|
| Secured debts | Creditors with security interests take their collateral first. |
| Domestic obligations | Support obligations owed to a spouse or child. |
| Administrative expenses | Bankruptcy trustee and others involved in bankruptcy process are paid next. |
| Certain unsecured debts | All unsecured debts after an involuntary petition has been filed, but before order for relief has been granted, are paid next. |
| Wages | Employees are paid next; a maximum is set for each employee. |
| Benefit plans | Contributions owed on employee benefit plans are paid next; again, a maximum is set. |
| Deposits and advances | Deposits made for purchase or lease of property are paid next, as are advances made for personal, family, and household services. |
| Taxes | Certain taxes are paid next. |
| Death or injury claims | Some claims for death or injury caused by debtor. |
| Remaining unsecured creditors | All other unsecured creditors are paid from any balance remaining. |
| Debtor | If anything is left, it goes back to the debtor. |

full before moving on to the next category. As explained in Chapter 20, secured creditors have the right to take their collateral to satisfy the debt, and that collateral is not sold by the trustee. Although there are some narrow exceptions to this rule, most secured creditors are protected.

## EXAMPLE 21-5: Secured Creditor Protected

Perez purchased a digital camera from Digicam Corp. Perez financed the deal by signing a security agreement with the company. Under the agreement, Digicam retained a security interest in the property, allowing it to repossess the camera if Perez defaulted on the loan. Digicam was a secured creditor. The digital camera was the collateral.

## Exceptions to Discharge

Once the trustee has run through all the aforementioned creditors, the debtor's debts are said to be discharged, which means that the debts are wiped away, and the debtor is allowed to begin again. If the bankruptcy debtor does not have enough money to cover the debts, they are nevertheless considered discharged. However, there are some exceptions to this general rule. Some debts cannot be discharged. In other words, even though the debtor has gone through the entire bankruptcy proceeding, money may still be owed to certain creditors.

**Debts Created by Misconduct**   Certain debts that have fallen into the debtor's lap because of misconduct cannot be charged in bankruptcy. For example, any debts that arose because of the debtor's fraudulent behavior cannot be discharged. Similarly, the debtor cannot escape legal liability for any debt that arose from willful and malicious misconduct. Finally, if the debtor knew about a debt that was not on the original list of debts, that unlisted debt cannot be discharged.

**Debts Enforced by the Government**   Certain debts that the debtor owes the government remain on the books even after the bankruptcy proceeding has ended. These include certain back taxes, student loans that do not impose a hardship on the debtor, and many government fines and penalties. Similarly, several types of court-enforced debts cannot be discharged, including alimony and child support or any legal liability that resulted from a court-ordered judgment for driving while intoxicated. Finally, any debts that were not discharged under a previous bankruptcy cannot be discharged under the new bankruptcy proceeding.

**Debts Created by Excessive Spending**   Congress also refuses to allow bankruptcy debtors to discharge any excessive expenditures that occur around the time of the bankruptcy filing. This measure prevents people from running up big bills unnecessarily because they think they will not have to pay the full amount due on these bills when their assets are finally distributed. Thus, debts for luxury items that exceed $600 in value cannot be discharged if those items were purchased within 90 days before the order for relief was granted. Likewise, the debtor cannot discharge any cash advances paid to a creditor under an open-ended credit plan that total more than $875 if those advances were made within 70 days of the relief order.

## EXAMPLE 21-6: Nondischargeable Debt

Caswell finally realized that his financial problems were out of control. Consequently, he decided to file for bankruptcy on the following Monday. That weekend, he charged $7,000 on his credit card on a weekend trip to Atlantic City before filing for bankruptcy on Monday. Caswell would not be allowed to discharge the $7,000 debt in bankruptcy.

### quick quiz 21-2

1. Congress no longer allows debtors to maintain a minimum stan-        true | false
   dard of living by exempting certain necessary items of property.

2. Under Chapter 7 Bankruptcy, debtors are forced to sell most of        true | false
   their property and use the cash to pay their creditors a portion of
   the amount owed each one.

3. The Bankruptcy Code allows states to use a list of exemptions        true | false
   created by the state legislature rather than the federal exemptions.

# 21-3 Reorganization—Chapter 11, Bankruptcy Code

Chapter 11 of the Bankruptcy Code provides a method for businesses to reorganize their financial affairs and still remain in business. If allowed to continue in operation, companies may be able to overcome their difficulties without having to sell most of their property. In a **reorganization**, a qualified debtor creates a plan that alters the repayment schedule. A Chapter 11 filing is available to sole proprietors, partnerships, and corporations and may be either voluntary or involuntary. Individuals who file must receive credit counseling from an approved credit counseling agency before doing so. Unlike Chapter 7, Chapter 11 also allows railroads to file. The only individuals specifically excluded from filing under Chapter 11 are commodity brokers and stockbrokers, who must use Chapter 7.

In February of 2011, Borders Group, Inc. announced that it was filing for Chapter 11 bankruptcy protection.

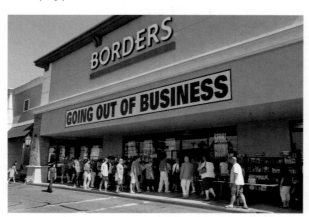

## Special Features of Chapter 11

One of the most attractive features of Chapter 11 for business debtors is that the business continues to operate after the filing. A debtor is referred to as a **debtor in possession** under Chapter 11 because the debtor keeps possession and control of the assets, continues to run the firm, and performs most of the functions that a trustee performs in other types of bankruptcy. However, if the problems of the business have been caused by poor judgment, mismanagement, or dishonesty, a case trustee may have to step in to examine the debtor's financial position and provide the court, creditors, and tax authorities with financial information as necessary.

## THE OPENING CASE *Revisited, Part II*
### State's Rights or Federal Supremacy: *Stern (Anna Nicole Smith) v. Pierce Marshall,* Round 3

The case of *Stern (Anna Nicole Smith) v. Marshall* involved a series of disputes, including a probate case concerning the nature of an inter vivos trust that allegedly transferred control of the estate to Smith and a defamation suit filed by Marshall against Smith. A major problem developed because the case was also entangled with Smith's Chapter 11 bankruptcy proceeding. It should be easy to see why Smith chose to file under Chapter 11 rather than Chapter 7. Given the size of the estate that was involved in the *Stern v. Marshall* case, it is highly unlikely that Smith could have passed the means test at any level of its application. Second, even if there was a way to pass the means test, it would be better for Smith to retain some control over her own financial affairs. Implementing a reorganization plan would have been infinitely preferable in her case.

As with a Chapter 7 voluntary case, the bankruptcy petition itself becomes the order for relief. The moment it is filed, the debtor assumes the position of "debtor in possession." At the same time, an automatic stay goes into effect, stopping collection proceedings against the debtor. In an involuntary case, the order for relief comes later, because the debtor is allowed time to contest the filing.

## The Reorganization Plan

When a Chapter 11 petition is filed, the debtor has 120 days, during which it has the exclusive right to file a reorganization plan. The 120-day period may be shortened or lengthened by the court. When the exclusive period ends, creditors (and the case trustee, if any) can file competing plans. The debtor also files a disclosure statement containing information about the debtor's assets, liabilities, and business affairs to allow creditors to make informed decisions about the reorganization plan. The disclosure statement must be approved by the court before there can be a vote by creditors on the reorganization plan.

### Creditors' Committee
A creditors' committee is appointed to investigate the operation of the business and assist the debtor in possession in developing and administering a reorganization plan. Membership on the committee normally consists of the creditors who hold the seven largest unsecured claims against the debtor.

### Plan Qualifications
The Bankruptcy Code requires fairness, equity, and feasibility in the creation of a reorganization plan. The plan will group claims against the debtor into the following classes:

- Secured creditors
- Unsecured creditors entitled to priority (for such things as taxes and bankruptcy costs)
- General unsecured creditors
- Equity security holders, such as shareholders and limited partners

The law requires equal treatment for all creditors grouped in a class. In addition, the plan must be feasible; that is, there must be a good chance that the plan will actually work. The law does not require an absolute guarantee of success. A plan may be difficult to implement because of labor or supply problems and still be feasible within the meaning of the law.

# Part 5 Case Study

**In re: Lisa A. Bloch, Debtor Plaintiff v. Windham Professionals, et al., Defendants**

United States Bankruptcy Court for the District of Massachusetts, 257 B.R. 374

## Summary

Lisa A. Bloch filed for bankruptcy relief, seeking a discharge of her student loan obligations. A 41-year-old woman with no dependents, Bloch attended a number of prestigious universities and colleges including Radcliffe, Cornell, Harvard, and Princeton. Her graduate education, a master's degree in public administration from Suffolk University in Boston, was financed through five promissory notes totaling $41,863, which had been assigned to the defendant, Educational Credit Management Corp. (ECMC).

While in Boston, she established a pattern of sporadic, full-time employment supplemented by part-time clerical assignments arranged by temporary employment agencies. The evidence at trial suggested that Bloch has an impressive educational résumé and an abundance of marketable skills, including considerable computer background and some management experience. After obtaining her master's degree, she moved to Seattle, Washington, without a job and incurred moving expenses of approximately $5,000. Her employment woes continued in Seattle, where she failed to obtain permanent work. Her testimony revealed that she survived for the last year by living with friends and paying expenses by accepting a gratuitous $4,000 loan. Bloch admitted she had no physical or mental disabilities that would hinder her from working full time, but for some unexplained reason, either a personality issue or perhaps wanderlust, she had not been employed in any one full-time position for longer than a year since attaining her master's degree.

At the time of the trial, Bloch worked less than 30 hours per week at $20 per hour, earning approximately $2,350 per month gross pay. She testified that she was reluctant to seek additional evening or weekend employment because it would impede her search for a permanent full-time position. She presented evidence showing her current monthly living expenses to be approximately $2,200.

At trial, Bloch expressed optimism about an improvement in her job prospects, a desire to repay her outstanding loans, and an acknowledgment that she only brought this action as a result of her frustration in dealing with the various student loan agencies.

## The Court's Opinion

Joel B. Rosenthal, United States Bankruptcy Judge

Section 523(a) (8) of the Bankruptcy Code states:

> A discharge under sections 727, 1141, 1228(a), 1228(b), or 1328(b) of this title does not discharge an individual debtor from any debt for an educational benefit, overpayment or loan made, insured or guaranteed by a governmental unit, or made under any program funded in whole or in part by a governmental unit or nonprofit institution, or for an obligation to repay funds received as an educational benefit, scholarship or

stipend unless excepting such debt from discharge under this paragraph will impose an undue hardship on the debtor and the debtor's dependents. . . .

(T)he issue . . . is whether the Debtor has met her burden of proving that excepting her student loan obligations from discharge will cause her "undue hardship."

This Court has adopted the "totality of the circumstances" test. . . . In *Dolan v. American Student Assistance, et al.*, 256 B.R. 230, this Court stated that a debtor seeking discharge of student loans under § 523(a)(8) "must prove by a preponderance of the evidence, that (1) his past, present, and reasonably reliable future financial resources; (2) his and his dependents' reasonably necessary living expenses, and; (3) other relevant facts or circumstances particular to the debtor's case are such that excepting the student loans from discharge will prevent the debtor from maintaining a minimal standard of living, even with the advantage of a discharge of his other pre-petition debts." By making specific findings as to each of these matters, the Court must then determine if excepting a debtor's student loans from discharge will impose an "undue hardship" on that debtor and the debtor's dependents. Having stated the applicable analysis for "undue hardship" in this Court, I now turn to this Debtor's request for relief.

## A. The Debtor's Past, Present and Reasonably Reliable Future Financial Resources

While it may be true the Debtor's past and present income are insufficient to pay her student loans and still maintain a minimal standard of living, the Debtor has nonetheless not proven to the Court's satisfaction that her prospects for increasing her future income are so bleak as to warrant a discharge of her student loans.... The Debtor currently makes $2,350 per month, and the Debtor's current living expenses suggest her past and present income have not been enough to service her student loans. The Court believes, though, that the Debtor could significantly enhance her future income by exploiting her educational credentials and the job skills she has acquired in past employment. Although highly educated, the Debtor's résumé and testimony indicate a presently unstable and uninspiring employment history, but the Court is convinced this will change, particularly in light of the favorable economic conditions present in Boston and Seattle, as well as the Debtor's portable credentials and job skills.

Furthermore, the Court believes the Debtor could do more to maximize her income by increasing the length of her work week. The Debtor admitted she works an average of only 29.5 hours per week. The Debtor has failed to show that this is reasonable given her economic circumstances and abilities. A 29.5 hour work week is a personal choice she has made and is not linked to any physical or mental disability, nor is it motivated by a need to care for any dependents. The Debtor stated her unwillingness to take part-time evening or weekend work because she says this would interfere with her job search. The Court finds this explanation unconvincing. It is not at all unreasonable to expect this Debtor to supplement her income by taking part-time weekend or evening work in order to meet her student loan obligations. . . . An increase in the Debtor's work hours, either at a part-time job or at her present temporary position, would raise her monthly income, possibly allowing her to make some effort at repayment of her student loans. The Debtor's strong educational background, coupled with her transferable skills and talents should assist her in her search for employment. Based on her education, and her articulate pro se presentation in this adversary proceeding, the Court is confident that the Debtor will bounce back by finding employment commensurate with her education. Therefore, the Court concludes the Debtor's past, present, and reasonably reliable future financial resources will allow her to pay her student loan obligations and still maintain a minimal standard of living.

## B. The Debtor's Reasonably Necessary Living Expenses

In addition to the Court's conclusion that the Debtor's future income prospects will allow her to repay her student loans without undue hardship, the Court likewise finds the Debtor has not done all she can to minimize her reasonably necessary living expenses, and as such the Court denies her the relief requested. . . . The Court's review of the Debtor's living expenses leads to the conclusion that her living expenses are, for the most part, modest. The Debtor could however reduce her substantial rent expense in some manner with a resultant monthly savings of perhaps hundreds of dollars. For example, the Debtor could reduce her rent expense by taking a more affordable apartment, or perhaps by taking in a roommate in her present home. Either of these options would help ease her present financial burdens. Thus, the Court finds the Debtor has not done all she can to minimize her reasonably necessary living expenses such that she is entitled to a discharge of her student loans for "undue hardship" under § 523(a)(8).

## C. The Debtor's Other Relevant Facts or Circumstances

While the Court has already concluded the Debtor has not taken steps to maximize her current income and minimize her expenses, the Court also looks to see if there are facts or circumstances unique to the Debtor's case that warrant granting a discharge of her student loans, notwithstanding the Court's conclusions above. In this case, the Debtor has failed to present evidence of any facts or circumstances that would lead this Court to conclude that excepting her student loans from discharge would impose an undue hardship. On the contrary, the Debtor's facts and circumstances militate against granting a discharge. For example, the Debtor has no dependents that might place a burden upon her monthly income or expenses. . . . Also, the Debtor is fortunately not burdened with any handicap or disability that precludes her from any of the vocational fields the Debtor is qualified to enter. Additionally, the Debtor has continually professed a willingness to repay her outstanding student loans, and but for the purported inflexibility of the lenders' policies would enter into a payment arrangement to meet those obligations.

As the Court can find no compelling reason to grant this Debtor a discharge of her student loans, the Court must find for the defendant, ECMC, and leave the prevailing party with the suggestion that it work with this Debtor to reach a transitional agreement until the Debtor's employment situation changes.

# Questions for Analysis

1. What must a debtor prove to be excepted from the rule that a student loan obligation cannot be discharged in bankruptcy?

2. What is the name of the test that the court has adopted to determine whether an exception exists?

3. What three points must a debtor prove to meet the test?

4. Summarize the court's opinion on each point.

5. What was the decision of the court?

# Part Six

## Agency and Employment

# Chapter 22    Agency Law

## THE OPENING CASE   Deprogramming For Profit: Scott v. Ross, Workman, Simpson, and the Cult Awareness Network

Kathy Tonkin and her six children were members of an organization known as the Life Tabernacle Church (Tabernacle). After 12 months within the Tabernacle, Tonkin left the church because she was convinced that it was a harmful cult. When she left the Tabernacle, she took her three youngest children with her, but the three oldest children, Scott, Thysen, and Matthew, decided not to leave. Tonkin called the Seattle Community Service hotline, which referred her to Shirley Landa, a high-profile anti-cult activist associated with a group called the Cult Awareness Network (CAN). Landa was one of the organizers of a group called the Citizens Freedom Foundation, the forerunner of CAN. She was also on CAN's list of contacts in Washington, received about five referrals from CAN every year, and formerly had been a member of the CAN board. The Cult Awareness Network relies primarily on contact people like Landa to act as their *field* agents; CAN expressly asks contact people to say that they are "assisting on behalf of CAN." In this case, after being contacted by Tonkin and reviewing the case, Landa recommended that Tonkin contact Rick Ross, a professional deprogrammer who frequently worked on behalf of CAN. Ross successfully deprogrammed Thysen and Matthew, the two younger Tonkin children, but did not succeed in deprogramming Scott. Ross,

along with two of his associates, Mark Workman and Charles Simpson, took custody of Scott and detained him for five days, in an effort to deprogram him. After pretending to be won over, Scott got away from his captors and eventually brought this lawsuit against Ross and CAN. Attorneys for CAN argued that the case against the network should be dismissed because Ross was not its agent. In turn, Scott argued that Ross was referred by Landa, who was an agent of CAN, and that she had both express and implied authority to make such referrals. Scott pointed out that CAN had many such contact agents, that it operated mostly through those contact agents, that those contact agents had the express authority to say that they assisted CAN, that CAN itself had a long history of using deprogrammers like Ross, and that CAN knew about the activities of Ross. Therefore, Scott concluded, Ross was working as an agent of CAN. Both the trial court and the appellate court agreed. (See *Scott v. Ross, Workman, Simpson, and the Cult Awareness Network,* Case No. 96-35050, U.S. Court of Appeals for the Ninth Circuit.)

**Opening Case Questions**

1. What is express and what is implied authority?

2. Does it make any difference to Scott's argument that Landon is a gratuitous agent? Explain.

3. Could Scott have argued that Landon's authority was apparent rather than express or implied? Explain.

4. If the case had been based on apparent authority, would the outcome have changed? Explain.

5. Why did CAN choose to disavow its relationship with Ross and Landon? Explain.

## **LO** Learning Objectives

1. Describe the nature of the agency relationship.
2. Outline the doctrine of vicarious liability.
3. Distinguish among the different types of principals.
4. Distinguish among the different types of agents.
5. Distinguish among express, implied, and apparent authority.
6. Outline the duties of an agent to the principal.
7. Clarify the duties that a principal has in relation to an agent.
8. Name the ways that an agency relationship can be terminated.
9. Identify who is entitled to a notice that an agency has ended.
10. Explain electronic agency.

# 22-1 The Nature of Agency Law

In an essay entitled, "How Culture Changes," the anthropologist George Peter Murdock of Yale University explains, "It is a fundamental characteristic of culture that, despite its essentially conservative nature, it does change over time and from place to place." The fact that the law is a part of this process of change has been a recurring theme throughout this book. The emergence of the law of agency within our culture is another example of this tendency toward change within the legal system. Many of the changes that we have seen throughout the book emerge because the law must adapt by striking a balance between or among competing interests.

## Agency and Other Relationships

The emergence of the agency law demonstrates how the legal system works as it attempts to strike a balance between doing business on your own and having other people conduct certain aspects of your business for you. To create this balance, agency law has developed its own principles, rules, doctrines, and concepts, all of which emerged independently and belong only to agency. As a result, agency law is said to be *sui generis,* that is, a law unto itself.

In July of 2010, Leon Rose negotiated a sizeable contract on behalf of LeBron James, with the Miami Heat.

**Principal-Agent Relationship**   **Agency** is a legal relationship in which one party, the **agent**, transacts business for and under the control of the second, the **principal**. The **third party** is that individual with whom the agent deals for the principal. The principal must indicate in some manner that the agent is to act for and under the control of the principal. An agency relationship is always **consensual** because the agent must agree to act for the principal. The agency relationship is

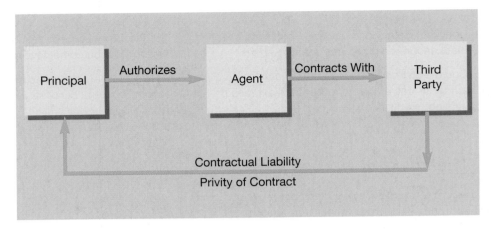

**Figure 22-1** The agent has the authority to represent the principal in an agency relationship.

*fiduciary* because the agent and principal trust each other. All agency relationships are fiduciary relationships, although not all fiduciary relationships are agency relationships.

**Employer–Employee Relationship** The legal principles governing the relationship of principal and agent and of employer and employee are very similar. In fact, the two areas frequently intersect. Still, there are agency relationships that are not employment relationships so the two must *not* be thought of as equivalent. There are also employment relationships that are not agency relationships. The main distinction between the two relationships is that agent–employees have the authority to, and usually do, deal with third parties on behalf of the principal. Generally, we say that agent–employees conduct business for the principal, whereas non-agent–employees do not.

**Master–Servant Relationship** The terms *master* (employer) and *servant* (employee) are not outdated but continue to be used in some legal circumstances. A **master** is a person who has the right to control the activities of another person. The person whose activities are controlled is called the **servant**. A servant who has the right to conduct the business of the master is also an agent. In common usage, the terms *employer* and *employee* refer to the master–servant relationship. The terms *master* and *servant* are used instead of *employer* and *employee* in a legal setting when questions of tort liability arise.

Independent contractors are not employees of the homeowner.

**Proprietor–Independent Contractor Relationship** An **independent contractor** is a party who agrees to do a job and retains complete control over the methods employed to obtain final completion. The party for which an independent contractor works is often referred to as an employer or a **proprietor**. Independent contractors are not subject to the control of the proprietor. They maintain all required business licenses and permits and pay all job-related expenses; they are obligated only to get the job done. The proprietor has the right to specify the results of the job in question. Moreover, he or she has the right to inspect and approve, or disapprove, the results of the independent contractor's performance. Independent contractors are not employees; however, they may be agents. The distinction depends on whether the independent contractor deals with third parties for the proprietor.

# The Question of Liability

The distinctions among these relationships frequently can be crucial in determining the nature and the extent of legal liability. It is important to note, however, that the names themselves are not controlling. Instead, it is the true nature of the relationship that is critical. Calling a servant an independent contractor does not transform the nature of the relationship if the master still controls the servant's conduct.

**Contract Liability**  An agent is appointed by a principal to negotiate and enter into contracts on behalf of the principal. Therefore, the principal is bound to the terms of those contracts. Unless an employee is also an agent, he or she has no power to negotiate and enter contracts for the employer. Moreover, an independent contractor has no power to bind the proprietor to a contract, unless expressly authorized to do so.

**Tort Liability**  The distinction between master–servant and proprietor–independent contractor relationships is especially critical in determining the nature and the extent of tort liability. This type of liability is called **vicarious liability**. Vicarious liability is based on the principle of *respondeat superior* (let the master, or the superior, respond). To apply the doctrine of *respondeat superior* in a tort case, two questions must be answered. First, is the alleged tortfeasor a servant? Second, was the servant's action within the scope of employment.

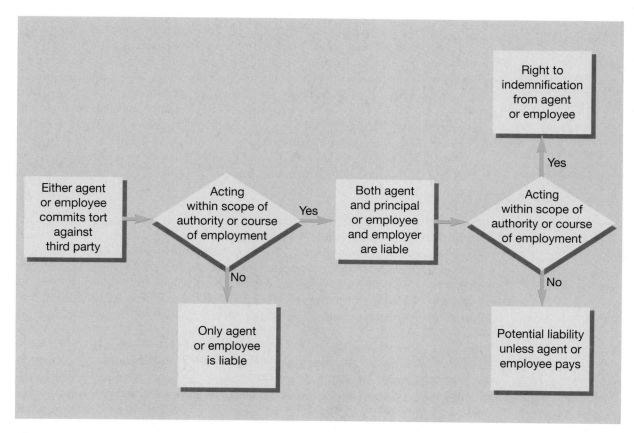

**Figure 22-2**  This chart shows the flow of principal/employer tort liability under the *respondeat superior* doctrine.

*Is the Alleged Tortfeasor a Servant?*    To establish the existence of the master–servant relationship, the court must decide whether the alleged tortfeasor (the hired person) is a servant or an independent contractor. The most widely accepted test for determining the existence of a master–servant relationship is the control test. The **control test** requires that we look at the degree of control, or right to control, that the hiring person exercises over the hired person. The more control, or right to control, that the hiring person has over the hired person, the more likely that the court will rule that a master–servant relationship exists.

When the degree of control is unclear or in dispute, the court has a series of factors that can be applied to bring the level of control into focus. These begin by reiterating the control test itself and then include the following additional factors:

1.  Who decides the time period in which the job is performed?
2.  Who owns the tools that are used on the job?
3.  Who selects the overall length of the hired person's employment?
4.  Who decides the method of compensating the hired person?
5.  Who decides how the job is to be done?
6.  What job skills are required to perform the tasks?
7.  How much freedom does the hired person possess on the job?
8.  Does the hired person operate a distinct business?
9.  What was the understanding that existed between the parties?
10. What is the nature of the written agreement (if one exists)?

The first five questions are fairly straightforward. If the answer to a question is the hired person, then it is likely that he or she is an independent contractor (IC) at least for that question. The final five questions require a bit more analysis. For instance, in question six, the more skill involved on the job, the more likely the hired party is an IC. In question seven, the more freedom, the more likely the hired person is an IC. In question eight, a distinct business is indicative of an IC. Finally, the ninth and the tenth questions examine what transpired between the parties themselves. While the terms set up between the parties may provide evidence of an IC, they cannot alone prove the existence of an IC. Thus, the court will accept evidence about what the parties called themselves, (IC or employee, for instance) but will not use it as final proof, absent some additional evidence.

*Did the Servant Act within the Scope of Employment?*    If the court determines that a master–servant relationship exists, it will turn to the next question, that is, "Did the servant act within the scope of employment?" The **scope of employment** involves the range of activities for which the servant is engaged. For the doctrine of *respondeat superior* to apply, a tort must be committed while the worker was performing a task for which he or she was hired, or at least one that he or she was authorized to perform by his or her employer. To determine whether a servant was operating within the scope of employment, ask the following questions:

1.  Was the action committed by the employee authorized by the employer?
2.  Where did the action take place?
3.  Were the employer's interests promoted by the action?
4.  Did the employer supply the instrumentality used in the action?
5.  Was this action performed by other employees on a regular basis?
6.  Was the action committed by the employee criminal?

**EXAMPLE 22-1:** From LaGuardia to the Marquis

Anne Rutgers works as a cabdriver for the Starshine Cab Company. While on a routine run transporting a passenger from New York's La Guardia Airport to the Marriott Marquis Hotel in Times Square, she collided with a car driven by Ian Harrington. Harrington wanted to sue both Rutgers and the Starshine Cab Company. He did so under the doctrine of vicarious liability because Rutgers was (a) an employee under the control of the cab company and (b) operating within the scope of her employment.

If we apply these six factors, the outcome of Example 22-1 becomes obvious. First, Rutgers's activity of driving a cab was authorized by her employer. Second, the incident took place in midtown Manhattan, where Rutgers is authorized to drive. Third, the business of her employer was advanced by transporting a passenger from the airport to a hotel. Fourth, she was using a cab owned by the company. Fifth, she was driving a cab, which was something that she did on a regular basis. Sixth, there was nothing criminal about her action. If several of the questions listed led to the opposite answers, a different decision might result. Consider, for instance, the following example.

**EXAMPLE 22-2:** From the Marquis to Jersey

Suppose in Example 22-1, after the accident in midtown, Rutgers got off work and, instead of returning the cab to the company garage as she was supposed to, drove the cab to New Jersey to visit some friends and to have a drink or two in a neighborhood bar to calm her nerves. If in that situation she were to leave the bar and collide with a pedestrian, or anyone else for that matter, she would be operating outside the scope of her employment, and the cab company would not be liable for her negligence.

*The Intentional Tort Factor* Most of the time, vicarious liability is applied to negligence cases, because workers are not usually hired to commit intentional torts. There are, of course, exceptions to this rule. If, for example, a servant commits a tort intending to further the master's business, as when a bouncer at a casino uses force to eject an unruly patron or when a security guard at a department store commits false imprisonment, the master may be liable. Moreover, if the master could reasonably foresee that the servant might commit the intentional tort, as might be the case with a bouncer in a casino or a security guard in a department store, the master may be liable for that tort.

*Independent Contractor Liability* In some situations, the court may hold the proprietor liable for the torts of the independent contractor. For instance, in some jurisdictions, if a proprietor is negligent in checking an independent contractor's qualifications and consequently hires someone who is incompetent, the proprietor may be held liable should an innocent third party be injured by the negligence of the incompetent independent contractor. In this case, the court may hold the proprietor liable for the **negligent hiring** of the incompetent independent contractor. Similarly, a proprietor may be liable for the **negligent retention** of an incompetent independent contractor if, after hiring the independent contractor, the proprietor learns that the contractor is incompetent and does not dismiss the contractor. A proprietor may also be open to liability when the independent contractor has been hired to perform a nondelegable duty. A **nondelegable duty** is one that the proprietor cannot delegate, or pass off, to another party. For example, an airline cannot delegate the responsibility it has for the safety of its passengers by hiring an independent contractor to do its maintenance work.

### Criminal Liability

The principal or employer ordinarily is not liable for an agent's or employee's crimes, unless the principal or employer actually aids or participates in their commission. The commission of a crime usually requires a state of mind that is specified in the criminal statute. Thus, if the principal or employer had not authorized the crime, the courts would conclude that the requisite mental state has not been shown. A principal or employer will be held criminally liable for acts done by an agent or employee to further an illegal business. In addition, most states have enacted statutes that hold a principal or employer liable for certain crimes committed by their agents or employees, even though they acted disobediently. Examples of such statutes are those that penalize the sale of impure foods or alcoholic beverages.

### Statutory Liability

One of the most heavily regulated segments of the social structure is employment. Both Congress and the state legislatures create agencies, commissions, and departments that make regulations governing workplace safety, wages and hours, unemployment compensation, workers' compensation, employment discrimination, health care, layoffs and plant closings, collective bargaining and labor unions, and so on. Such statutes include Title VII of the Civil Rights Act, the Age Discrimination in Employment Act, the Worker Adjustment and Retraining Notification Act, the Family and Medical Leave Act, ERISA, the American's with Disabilities Act, the Internal Revenue Code, the Fair Labor Standards Act, and statutes related to workers' compensation, among others. Frequently, these statutes will be written so that they apply to employees and not to independent contractors. Or, as in the case of the Internal Revenue Code, the regulations will treat employees one way and independent contractors another. This has prompted employers to simply label workers as ICs to escape or minimize the effects of the law. Consequently, the courts have created a test, called the *economic reality test,* to uncover the true nature of the employment relationship.

### The Economic Reality Test

The economic reality test is generally tailor made to reflect the goals of each statute and is, thus, a fairly flexible rule. Nevertheless, the rule is very similar to the control test used in *respondeat superior*. This is because the economic reality test considers many of the same factors that are applied in the control test. These factors include determining the hired party's autonomy on the job, the length of time involved in the employment situation, and the level of skill needed to do the job. However, the economic reality test also adds some factors of its own. For example, in an attempt to determine the true nature of the financial arrangement between the parties, the economic reality test also asks about the hired party's investment in the employer's business and the degree to which the hired person's services were integrated into the employer's commercial activity.

## A QUESTION OF ETHICS

Lou Sinclair, the owner, operator, and CEO of the Sinclair Security Firm, Inc., has over the last few years become increasingly concerned about the amount of workers' compensation that he must pay to the state of Winnemac in order to cover his employees. Most of his workers are security agents who are engaged in field work and rarely report in person to the office. In an economic move to cut costs, Sinclair orders Hal Kellogg, his human resources director, to restructure the contract of all field agents so that they are called "independent contractors" rather than "employees." Wary of this tactic, Kellogg takes a detailed look at the Winnemac state statute on workers' compensation. In his view the statute is flexible enough to permit Sinclair's scheme to work with a minimum of legal exposure. As a result, he complies with Sinclair's order and revamps every agent's contract. As word filters out to other security firms, this practice becomes an industrywide strategy. Senator Winston Arrowsmith, a member of the Winnemac state legislature, gets wind of this tactic and introduces a bill into the state senate that will reform the worker compensation law, expanding the definition of employee to such an extent that it actually includes workers who really are independent contractors. Arrowsmith justifies this move by saying that the security firms have gotten away with violating the original law so much that it serves them right to now have to pay for workers who really are ICs. Consider these questions: (1) Was Sinclair's original plan ethical? (2) Does the information uncovered by Kellogg on the original law make the original decision by Sinclair ethical? (3) Is Arrowsmith's plan to punish the security firms ethical? Make sure you give reasons for your answers here.

## Sovereign Immunity and the Federal Government
The doctrine of **sovereign immunity** prevents lawsuits against a government authority without the government's consent. The doctrine is no longer as important a defense for government torts as it once was. The Federal Tort Claims Act of 1946 limits the federal government's sovereign immunity. Whenever a federal employee harms a third party or private property while driving a motor vehicle in the course of employment, the federal government is liable. However, the 1946 law explicitly preserves governmental immunity for a vaguely defined category of "discretionary" actions by officials.

### EXAMPLE 22-3: Above-Ground Radioactive Fallout

In 1982, a federal district court judge held that radioactive fallout from above-ground nuclear tests had caused at least nine people and perhaps dozens of others to die of cancer. The judge ruled that the federal government must pay damages under the Federal Tort Claims Act, explaining that while the high-level decision to conduct the tests had been discretionary, and thus was immune from liability, officials had conducted the tests in a negligent manner by failing to monitor radiation adequately or warn residents of neighboring areas in Nevada, southern Utah, and northern Arizona who lived downwind from the test site about radiation hazards and how to reduce them. A federal appeals court, however, held that all aspects of the testing program were conducted in accordance with discretionary decisions of the Atomic Energy Commission and were thus immune from liability. The U.S. Supreme Court in 1988 refused to hear an appeal from the appellate decision.

## Sovereign Immunity, *Respondeat Superior,* and the States
The formula for determining when a state government is liable for its own torts and for the torts of its employees, and when it retains its immunity, is often difficult to unravel. Generally, the starting point is to determine whether the state has a statute for preserving or eliminating sovereign immunity. If a statute exists that preserves immunity, the next step would be to determine whether the state has established any exceptions to the elimination of sovereign immunity. These exceptions would override sovereign immunity and permit a plaintiff to sue the state. For instance, even if immunity has been preserved in most cases, it might be forfeited if the action complained about involves a government employee's negligence while working

for a state agency involved in the state's proprietary activities or its governmental functions. The final step would be to determine if any defenses are available to the state that would permit the state to escape liability, even though its sovereign immunity has been removed.

### Self-Evident Truths

Many states have special statutes that list the defenses that can be used by the state to reassert its sovereign immunity. Because a state government can only act through its employees, some of these defenses focus on the actions of those employees and echo the doctrine of *respondeat superior*. Generally, this criterion begins by establishing that in most situations, the employees of the state government or of a political subdivision of the state government are immune from litigation under the doctrine of sovereign immunity. Thus, the statute will generally preserve sovereign immunity if the actions of the employee were discretionary in nature but will impose liability if the actions were performed outside the scope of their employment or outside of their official duties, or if their actions were reckless, malicious, wanton, or in bad faith. Sometimes the legislature will also create special statutes that impose liability for certain specifically named activities. Thus, a state might make school bus drivers liable automatically for not stopping at railroad crossings. Or it might make school nurses liable for not reporting a case of suspected child abuse to the proper authorities, and so on.

### Self-Evident Questions

1. Do you believe that state governments should be permitted to insulate themselves from lawsuits simply by neglecting to enact a statute that eliminates sovereign immunity? Explain.

2. If a state elects to forgo sovereign immunity should individual employees be held liable for their own torts? Explain.

3. Should it make a difference whether the employee's acts are discretionary in nature? Explain.

4. Should state employees be held strictly liable, as is suggested above in the school bus driver and the school nurse examples? Why or why not?

5. Remember that when the state itself is forced to pay an award to a plaintiff, the money for that award comes out of tax money paid by citizens. Does this reminder change any of you answers here? Explain.

---

### quick quiz 22-1

| | |
|---|---|
| 1. An agency relationship is always consensual because the agent must agree to act for the principal. | true \| false |
| 2. All fiduciary relationships are agency relationships but not all agency relationships are fiduciary relationships. | true \| false |
| 3. Agency law is said to be *sui generis*, that is, a law unto itself. | true \| false |

---

## 22-2 Principles of Agency

Now that the different types of relationships involved in business have been discussed, the focus of the chapter can return to the principal–agent relationship. Several key guidelines help the courts distinguish among different types of principals and the different types of agents.

# Types of Principals and Agents

There are three types of principals. A **disclosed principal** is one whose identity is known by third parties dealing with that principal's agent. When an agent does not reveal the existence of an agency relationship but appears to act on his or her own behalf rather than for another, an **undisclosed principal** exists. A **partially disclosed principal** exists when the agent, in dealing with third parties, reveals the existence of an agency relationship but does not identify the principal. Agents are generally classified according to the scope of their responsibility. A **general agent** is a person who is given broad authority to act on behalf of the principal in conducting the bulk of the principal's business activity on a daily basis.

A **special agent** is a person who is authorized to conduct only a particular transaction, conduct a series of related transactions, or perform only a specified act for the principal. Examples are real estate brokers, lawyers, and accountants who are retained to do a specific job and whose authority is restricted to those acts necessary to accomplish it. A **factor**, or common merchant, is a special agent who is employed to sell merchandise consigned for that purpose. The factor has possession of the goods and sells them for and on behalf of a principal. A factor who guarantees the credit of a third party to a principal and guarantees the solvency of the purchaser and performance of the contract is known as a *del credere* **agent**. In the event of default, the *del credere* agent is liable to the principal.

## EXAMPLE 22-4: The Antique Agent

Edna Freeman hired Leonard Tenpenny to act as her agent in the sale of several antiques. The contract of agency included a promise by Tenpenny that Freeman would not suffer any loss because of any sales on credit that Tenpenny made with third parties. Shortly after, Tenpenny sold a rare first edition of one of Louis Bromfield's novels, valued at $50,000, to Robert Fisher on credit. Fisher later declared bankruptcy. As a *del credere* agent, Tenpenny had guaranteed the credit of Fisher and is liable to Freeman for the value of the book.

# Liability of Principals and Agents

The principal is liable for all contracts that a general or special agent may enter into with third parties, as long as the agent acts within the authority conferred by the principal. An undisclosed principal can be held liable for the acts of the agent once the identity of the principal is disclosed. Once the principal's identity is revealed, a third party may sue either the principal or the agent. Following this election however, the third party cannot later decide to sue the other, unless the principal was undisclosed at the time the choice was made.

When an agent is not known to be an agent and is acting as a principal, the agent can be held liable as a principal. When a person is known to be an agent, but it is not known for whom the agent acts, the third party can also hold the agent liable. In addition, when an agent exceeds the authority conferred by the principal, the agent can be made personally liable.

# Scope of an Agent's Authority

Agents may perform only acts that have been authorized by the principal. Agents who exceed their delegated authority become personally liable. Unauthorized actions do not bind the principal unless those actions can be reasonably assumed by a third party to be within the scope of the agent's authority. Authority granted to an agent may be express, implied, or apparent.

### Express, Implied, and Apparent Authority

An agency is created by some action or conduct on the part of the principal. A would-be agent cannot by conduct alone or by any statement establish an agency relationship. It is therefore wise for a third party, when dealing with an agent, to determine the nature and extent of the agent's authority. An agency relationship is generally created by the following methods:

By appointment and implication.

By necessity and operation of law.

By estoppel and ratification.

The first way that a principal can create an agency relationship is by appointment. This occurs when the principal either orally or in writing creates the agency relationship. The agent's **express authority** is created at the same time that the principal appoints the agent and creates the agency relationship. This happens when the principal writes down (word processes, types out, e-mails, faxes, texts, and so on) the instructions or instructs the agent orally. In either case, the principal uses words to transfer authority to the agent. Sometimes referred to as *actual authority*, express authority may also be indicated by conduct, as when a sales representative informs the principal of travel plans, and no objection to them is expressed.

### Implied authority

The agent's authority to perform acts that are necessary or customary to carry out expressly authorized duties is referred to as **implied authority**. It stems from the reasonable effort of an agent to understand the meaning of the principal's

---

## THE OPENING CASE *Revisited, Part I*
## Deprogramming for Profit: *Scott v. Ross, Workman, Simpson, and the Cult Awareness Network, Round 2*

In the Opening Case at the beginning of the chapter, Kathy Tonkin contacted Shirley Landa to help rescue her oldest son, Jason Scott, from the influence of the Life Tabernacle Church (Tabernacle). Landa was a gratuitous agent who was connected to a group known as the Cult Awareness Network (CAN), an organization that was formed to combat cults. Landa recommended that Tonkin contact Rick Ross, a deprogramming expert, who could rehabilitate Scott. Tonkin contacted Ross, who then took custody of Scott to begin the deprogramming procedure. Something went wrong, however, and Scott got away from Ross. Scott then brought this lawsuit against Ross and CAN. In turn, CAN attempted to distance itself from Ross by claiming that Ross was not its agent. The court, however, did not buy this argument. Instead, it took notice of the fact that Ross had been recommended by Landa, who had the implied, if not the express, authority to make such referrals in the

name of CAN. To prove this authority, the plaintiff had produced evidence demonstrating that CAN expressly told all of its contact agents, including Landa, to tell their clients that they assisted CAN in its work. The plaintiff had also verified that CAN was aware of Ross and his work and had on occasion used Ross directly. Finally, the plaintiff had established that CAN was aware that Landa recommended Ross for other deprogramming sessions. From all of this evidence, the court concluded that Landa had the express power to represent CAN and carry out its mission, part of which was to rescue young people who had been misled by cults. Within this express authority was the implied authority to do what was necessary to carry out that express authority. The express authority to assist CAN thus included the implied authority to recommend deprogramming agents such as Ross whom CAN had itself directly used in the past to carry out its anti-cult mission.

words describing what the agent is to do. Implied authority can be described as *incidental authority* when the acts performed are reasonably necessary to carry out an express authority. For example, an agent might have incidental authority to contract for the repair of the principal's van that broke down while being used to deliver perishable products that the agent had express authority to sell and deliver. Implied authority may be described as *customary authority* when the agent acts in conformity with the general trade or professional practices of the business.

## Apparent authority

When a principal, by words or actions, leads a third party to believe that a non-agent is an agent, that principal has clothed that non-agent with **apparent authority**. Apparent authority is sometimes referred to as *agency by estoppel, apparent agency,* and *ostensible agency.* The principal may make known to the third party in a variety of ways that such authority exists. For instance, it may be generated by making a direct statement to the third party, permitting someone to have a meaningful business title, enabling someone to occupy a position of authority, or allowing someone to perform duties that give a third party reason to believe that the person has the authority to act for the principal. Sometimes apparent authority can even arise because the principal fails to act in some way. For example, apparent authority may be created if the principal terminates an agent's actual authority but fails to give proper notice of that termination to those who are entitled to receive such notice. Such apparent authority is sometimes referred to as **lingering apparent authority**. The party with whom the agent is dealing must reasonably believe that the agent has authority to so act, have had no notice of a lack of such authority, and act or rely on the agent's appearance of authority.

## Agency by Ratification

Agents sometimes perform acts on behalf of the principal that exceed their authority. In such cases, the principal for whom the agent claimed to act may either ignore the transaction or affirm it by *ratification*. **Ratification** occurs when the principal approves the unauthorized act performed by an agent or by one who has no authority to act as an agent. Although an agent generally is personally liable to third parties for actions in excess of the agent's authority, this liability is not true when the third party knows that the agent has exceeded the proper level of authority. In addition to an intent to

## THE OPENING CASE *Revisited, Part II*

Deprogramming for Profit: *Scott v. Ross, Workman, Simpson, and the Cult Awareness Network,* Round 3

In the Opening Case at the beginning of the chapter, it was quite clear to the court that Landa had the actual authority to recommend deprogrammers like Ross to concerned parents like Tonkin. However, even if this had not been the case, there was enough evidence to hold CAN liable under the doctrine of apparent authority. Recall that apparent authority is created by something that the principal, in this case CAN, communicates to a third party, like Tonkin.

Because CAN was in the habit of referring concerned parents to deprogrammers like Ross and because CAN had actually recommended Ross for deprogramming purposes in the past, it would not be unreasonable for Tonkin and others to assume that Landa, an actual agent of CAN, had that same authority. Thus, even if Landa had not had the actual authority to recommend Ross, she did have the apparent authority to do so.

ratify, certain other conditions must be fulfilled for ratification to be valid. The principal must have the capacity to ratify and have knowledge of all the material facts. The act to be ratified must be legal and been done on behalf of the principal. Moreover, the ratification must apply to the entire act of the agent, and ratification must occur before the third party withdraws. The principal cannot accept the benefits of an unauthorized act and then refuse to accept the obligations that are part of it. The principal becomes bound as though the agent had authority to act.

**Authority by Statute**  In some cases, agency authority is bestowed upon employees by statutory law. Such authority carries with it the risk of liability for the illegal activities outlined by the statute. For example, the courts have held that some individual employees, such as corporate executives, who act as agents on behalf of the corporation, can be held personally liable for violations of the Fair Labor Standards Act. In contrast, despite the fact that the word "agent" is included in the statutory definition of "employee" the courts have held that individual employees are not liable for violations of the Americans with Disabilities Act or for violations of Title VII of the Civil Rights Act.

**Appointment of Subagents**  Agents are appointed by principals because of their assumed fitness to perform some particular job. Because principals rely on the agent's personal skill and integrity, they do not ordinarily give agents the power to delegate someone else to do the job they have agreed to do. Should an agent delegate authority without authorization, the acts of the subagent do not impose any obligation or liability on the principal to third parties. In some instances, the agent is permitted to delegate authority, even if the agency agreement does not contain an express power of delegation. Such an intention may be implied from the nature of the employment or custom and usage. A real estate broker, for example, has the implied authority to delegate authority to salespersons. The nature of the business is such that it is presumed that the principal (seller) contemplates that the authority given to the agent (broker) would be exercised through the broker's agents (subagents).

**Exceptions to the Delegation of Authority**  The purpose of agency cannot be criminal or contrary to public policy. In addition, some acts must be performed in person, not delegated to an agent. Nondelegable acts include, but are not limited to, voting, serving on juries, testifying in court, making a will, and holding public office. However, forms required by law, such as tax returns and license applications, may be executed by an agent provided that the identity of the principal, as well as the identity and capacity of the agent, are clearly shown.

## quick quiz 22-2

1. A disclosed principal is one whose identity is known by third parties dealing with that principal's agent.   true | false

2. A special agent is a person who is given broad authority to act on behalf of the principal in conducting the bulk of the principal's business activity on a daily basis.   true | false

3. A factor, or common merchant, is a special agent who is employed to sell merchandise consigned for that purpose.   true | false

# 22-3 Duties in Agency Law

The agency relationship between agent and principal establishes rights and obligations that may be expressed in the agreement or merely implied. An individual who acts as agent for another has a fiduciary relationship with the principal. This relationship implies the placement of trust and confidence in the agent that the agent will serve the principal's interests before all others. Thus, an agent may not enter any agency transaction in which the agent has a personal interest. An agent must also not take a position in conflict with the interest of the principal.

## Agent's Obligations to a Principal

In compliance with the agency contract and the fiduciary relationship, various obligations are imposed on the agent. These obligations generally involve the following duties:

1. To obey all instructions and be loyal to the principal.
2. To exercise reasonable judgment, prudence, and skill and account for all property.
3. To perform work personally and communicate fully with the principal.

### Obedience and Loyalty
The agent, whether being paid or acting gratuitously, must obey all reasonable and legal instructions issued by the principal that relate to the agency agreement. In obeying the instructions of the principal, the agent is duty-bound to remain within the **scope of authority** (i.e., the range of acts authorized by the principal). For example, if the agent were to sell equipment to a third party in violation of the principal's instructions, the agent would be liable for any injury suffered by the principal. An agent may not engage in any activity that would result in a conflict of interest with the business of the principal. This duty of loyalty implies strict and continuing faithfulness to the principal's best interests at all times. Hence, the agent must resist any temptation to use acquired confidential information to advance the agent's own interest at the expense of the principal's.

### Judgment, Prudence, Skill, and the Duty to Account
Agents imply that they possess the required knowledge, training, and skill to perform and carry out their agency obligations properly with reasonable care and diligence. Unless an agent claims to be an expert, the principal is entitled to expect that the agent has the degree of skill commonly displayed by others employed in similar work. An expert, such as a person in a profession requiring specific education and a special license, must use the expert judgment, prudence, and skill possessed by others who have been admitted to those professions. Whether an expert or not, the agent may be liable to the principal for losses resulting from personal neglect or incompetence.

The agent has a duty to keep a separate account of the principal's funds. Whatever money the agent receives during and as a result of the agency relationship is held in trust for the principal. An accounting must be given to the principal within a reasonable period of time after money or property is received or disbursed. Money collected by the agent must be held separate from funds belonging to the agent. If deposited in a bank, the money must be deposited in a separate account and so identified that a trust is apparent. Failure to keep such funds separate is known as *commingling,* and the agent may be held personally liable for any resulting losses.

### Personal Service and Communication
The agency relationship is usually one involving an agreement for personal services. In the absence of the authority to do so, an agent may not delegate duties to others unless such duties are purely mechanical in

nature and require no particular knowledge, training, skill, or responsibility. The agent is duty-bound to keep the principal fully informed of all facts that materially affect the subject matter of the agency because the law assumes that if an agent receives either notice or information, it was also communicated to the principal. Therefore, the rights and liabilities of the principal to any third party are the same as if the principal had personally received the notice or information that come to the agent's attention when acting within the agent's scope of authority.

### EXAMPLE 22-5: A Commitment to Communicate

Marcy Magliozzi instructed Barbara Harrison to purchase a particular furnished house on Catawba Island for her. While examining the final contract, Harrison discovered that several thousand books that were in the house would not be considered as part of the "furnishings" that went along with the sale. Despite this exception, Harrison completed the purchase for Magliozzi. A little later, Magliozzi discovered that the books did not come with the "furnished" house. Magliozzi demanded that the contract be voided. Because in the course of carrying out her duties and before buying the house, Harrison learned that the books were not part of the deal, the law assumes that Magliozzi had the same information. She cannot use the loss of the books as the basis for voiding the contract.

**Remedies Available to the Principal** Remedies are always available when an agent fails to observe a duty owed to a principal. For instance, the principal may do one or more of the following:

1. Terminate the agent's contract of employment.
2. Withhold compensation otherwise due the agent.
3. Recover profit the agent made in violation of agency obligations.
4. Recover money or property gained or held by the agent to which the principal is entitled.
5. Restrain the agent from continuing to breach the agency obligations.
6. Recover damages from the agent for breach of the contract of employment or assessed against the principal for the agent's wrongdoing.
7. Rescind a contract entered into by the agent based on an improper relationship between the agent and the third party.

## The Principal's Obligations to the Agent

The agreement between a principal and an agent creates the duties the principal owes to the agent. Even when the agency agreement is silent, there are implied obligations owed to the agent. Among the principal's actual and implied duties are the following obligations:

1. To compensate the agent.
2. To reimburse the agent.
3. To indemnify the agent.
4. To cooperate with the performance of the agent's duties.

**Compensation** The principal is under a duty to pay an agent an agreed amount or the fair value for work or services that the agent performs within the scope of authority or employment. In addition, the principal must make salary deductions and payments to the government as are required by law. All states have statutes that provide for the enforcement of the payment of wages and that place penalties on delinquent employers. The agent may not recover compensation for illegal services, even though they were rendered at the request of the principal. The agent may also forfeit rights to compensation when the agent breaches his or her duties to the principal. If an agency relationship does not result from a contract, it a **gratuitous agency**, and the agent is a **gratuitous agent**.

## Reimbursement

The principal is obligated to reimburse the agent for any reasonable expenses incurred while working on the principal's behalf and within the scope of the agent's authority or employment. The agent cannot recover for expenses due to the agent's own negligence. Recovery is also barred when expenses incurred by an agent are unnecessary or unreasonable in the discharge of the agency.

## Indemnification

Agents are also entitled to **indemnification** (i.e., payment for loss or damage suffered) if they incur a loss or are damaged as a result of a request made by the principal. The obligation to pay for the agent's personal loss or damage, which may occur in the future or is already suffered, is avoidable if the loss or damage results from an action the agent knew to be illegal or from the agent's negligence. Public policy also requires employers to indemnify employees for personal injury sustained in the course of employment, except for self-inflicted injury or intoxication. State workers' compensation laws hold that the cost of paying for such injury should be a part of the operating expense of the business.

## Cooperation with the Agent

The principal, having granted the agent the duty to perform certain tasks, must not interfere with the performance of those tasks. Should the principal make the agent's job difficult or impossible, the principal has breached the duty of cooperation.

## Remedies Available to the Agent

The remedies of an agent against a principal are based on the principal's breach of express or implied contract obligations. Where appropriate, the agent has the option of exerting one or more of the agent's rights:

1. Leave the principal's employ.
2. Recover damages for the principal's breach of contract.
3. Recover the value of services rendered.
4. Obtain reimbursement for payments made for the principal.
5. Secure indemnity for personal liability sustained while performing an authorized act for the principal.

---

## quick quiz 22-3

| | | |
|---|---|---|
| 1. In obeying the instructions of the principal, the agent is duty-bound to remain within the scope of authority. | true | false |
| 2. When the agency agreement is silent, there are no implied obligations owed to the agent. | true | false |
| 3. If an agency relationship does not result from a contract, it is a gratuitous agency and the agent is a gratuitous agent. | true | false |

# 22-4 A Final View of Agency Law

The agency agreement may be terminated by the acts of one or both parties to the agreement or by operation of the law. When the authority of the agent is terminated, the agent loses the right to act for the principal. The only exception to the rule that either the principal or the agent may terminate an agency relationship at any time arises in the situation of an agency coupled with an interest. The principal has the duty to inform certain third parties when an agency relationship is terminated.

## Termination by the Acts of the Parties

Both principal and agent may terminate an agency relationship by their acts. Most agency relationships are terminated when the parties have satisfied their contractual obligations. The relationship also may be discharged by mutual consent, as well as when either the agent or the principal breaches the agency contract.

**Fulfillment of Purpose or Mutual Agreement** When the purpose for which the agency was created is achieved, the agency is terminated. If an agent is appointed for a specific period of time, the arrival of that time terminates the agency. In short, when the contract is performed, the agency is at an end. The parties to an agency relationship may terminate it at any time by agreement, even before the contract is fully performed. This is referred to as mutual agreement.

**Revocation or Renunciation** The principal or the agent usually has the power (if not necessarily the right) at any time to terminate the agency relationship. Acting with or without cause, the principal may terminate the agreement by simply recalling the agent's authority to act (i.e., **revocation**). Even though the principal's act of revocation may be a violation of contract, the agent's authority is terminated. Agents may terminate by simply giving notice to principals that they are quitting (i.e., **renunciation**). Unless the terms of the agency agreement permit termination "at will," agents and principals who end their relationship may be liable for damages resulting from the violation of the contractual promise (see Figure 22-3). Nevertheless, one cannot be forced to work against one's will.

## Termination by Operation of Law

The termination of the agency agreement by operation of the law results when significant events make the continuance of the agency impossible or impractical. Termination by operation of the law occurs in instances of death, insanity, bankruptcy, or impossibility of performance.

**Death or Insanity** The death of the principal or agent ordinarily terminates the agency relationship automatically, even without notice. Hence, any agreement made between the agent and a third party is ineffective upon the death of the principal. Although the agent may be liable to third parties for breach of the implied warranty that the agent has authority to act, third parties cannot recover from the estate of the principal because the contract is not binding. The insanity of either the principal or the agent usually terminates the agent's authority. In some states, however, an agent has power to bind a principal who has become insane if the principal has not been legally declared insane and if the third party had no knowledge of the insanity. If the principal is only incapacitated briefly, the agent's authority may be suspended rather than terminated.

**Durable Power of Attorney** Generally, an agency relationship is terminated upon the incapacity of the principal. However, the trend in many states has been to enact statutes that permit the creation of a durable power of attorney. Under such statutes, a person can appoint an agent by signing a written durable power of attorney. A **durable power of attorney** preserves the authority of an agent should the principal become incapacitated. In some cases, the durable power of attorney may even activate the agent's power once the principal is incapacitated. The durable power of attorney should contain the following words: "This power of attorney shall not be affected by subsequent disability or incapacity of the principal," or "This power of attorney shall become effective upon the disability or incapacity of the principal." The National Conference of Commissioners on Uniform State Laws recently finalized a new **Uniform Durable Power of Attorney Act**. Many state legislatures are in the process of adopting either a complete or a modified version of this new act and so it is best to check the most up-to-date version of the law in your state.

## Bankruptcy

In the event of the bankruptcy of the principal, the agency is ended. All of the principal's ordinary contracts are canceled, and title to the principal's property passes to a trustee for the benefit of creditors. The bankruptcy of the agent sometimes terminates the agency for the same reasons, but the principal and the agent may continue the relationship if they choose. Usually, the bankruptcy of the agent does not prevent the agent from doing the job in the regular way, provided the agent is not using personal funds.

## Impossibility of Performance

An agency relationship terminates when it is impossible for the agent to accomplish the purpose of the agency for any reason. Destruction of a house by fire ends the real estate broker's agency to sell the property. A broker authorized to sell a principal's boat loses that authority if the boat is destroyed in a storm. An agent's loss of a license required to conduct the principal's business ends the authority of the agent. A change in the law that causes authorized acts to be illegal terminates the agent's authority. The authority of the agent is also terminated by notice or knowledge of a change in business conditions or values that substantially affects the agent's exercise of authority. For example, an agent hired to sell property at a specified price would have that authority terminated when the value of the property increases substantially because of zoning changes.

## Agency Coupled with an Interest

The only exception to the rule that either the principal or the agent may terminate an agency relationship at any time arises in the situation of an agency coupled with an interest. An **agency coupled with an interest** is an agency agreement in which the agent is given an interest in the subject matter of the agency, in addition to compensation for services rendered to the principal. The concept protects the agent's interest in specific property belonging to the principal. The principal lacks power to revoke agencies of this kind without the consent of the agent.

**EXAMPLE 22-6:** An Agency Coupled with a Lot of Interest

James Heilman borrowed $9,000 from the National Security Specialty Bank of Louisville. He put up as security 200 shares of stock in the Actors' Theatre Group of Louisville. Heilman then authorized the bank to sell the shares to satisfy the loan obligation should he default on that loan. In the event that it becomes necessary to sell the stock, the bank serves as Heilman's agent. Heilman may not terminate the agency except by paying off the $9,000 loan (plus interest, as per his agreement with the National Security Specialty Bank).

### Notice of Termination to Third Parties

The principal has the duty to notify third parties with whom the agent has done business when the agency relationship has been terminated by the act of the parties. The exception to this rule is when the agency is terminated by operation of the law. In such instances, the principal is not required to notify anyone, and no subsequent act by the agent will bind the principal. The type of notice required depends on how the former business relations were conducted. When the third party has given credit to the principal through the agent, the third party is entitled to actual notice of termination of authority, which may be done by regular mail or by telephone. The safest way, however, is by certified mail, because the post office provides a receipt of the notice. A notice in the classified advertisement section in a newspaper of general circulation is sufficient for third parties who have never given credit but who have had cash transactions with the agent or know that other persons have dealt with the principal through the agent. The failure to give third parties appropriate notice would make the principal liable on contracts made by a former agent with third parties.

## Cyber-Agency Statutes

The Uniform Computer Information Transactions Act (UCITA) is valuable because it clearly establishes the nature of an electronic agent. According to UCITA, an *electronic agent* (also referred to as a *cyber-agent* or *e-agent*) can be characterized as a computer program that acts without human intervention to begin an activity, answer cyber-messages, deliver or accept *electronic mail,* or enter electronic contracts as a representative of an individual who does not intervene in the action taken by the electronic agent at the actual time of the electronic agent's activity. It is clear then that a *bot* (*robot, shopping bot, cyberbot,* or *e-bot*) that searches cyberspace for the lowest price in a contract, sifts through the Internet for the best accommodations, hunts cyberspace for the most economical plan, or spontaneously responds to a bidding process during an electronic auction is an electronic agent. The UCITA makes it clear that a principal, now termed an *electronic principal,* who places authority in the "hands" of an electronic agent will be liable for the electronic contracts entered by that electronic agent, even if the electronic principal remains ignorant of what the electronic agent has done because the electronic principal either ignores or forgets about the automated process.

Another model act, the Uniform Electronic Transactions Act (UETA), has legitimized the use of electronic agents by certifying that contracts made by electronic agents have the same binding effect as contracts created by human agents. The net effect of these provisions is to guarantee that a company that has used an electronic agent to receive and process an order sent by an electronic agent will not be able to deny the effectiveness of that electronic contract. The provisions also state that once an individual has received an e-mail, he or she is considered to have received notice of an e-contract, even if that person ignores or trashes the e-mail without opening or reading it. The UETA also says that e-agents must be programmed to give the other party a confirmation that the electronic contract has been entered. Otherwise, the e-contract is voidable by that party.

---

### quick quiz 22-4

| | | |
|---|---|---|
| 1. | Most agency relationships are terminated when the parties have satisfied their contractual obligations. | true \| false |
| 2. | The termination of the agency agreement can never happen solely by operation of law. | true \| false |
| 3. | The principal has the duty to notify third parties with whom the agent has done business when the agency relationship has been terminated by the act of the parties. | true \| false |

# Summary

**22.1**   Agency is the legal fiduciary relationship that exists when the principal authorizes the agent to represent the principal. The courts are often called upon to distinguish among relationships between principal and agent, employer and employee, master and servant, and proprietor and independent contractor. The terms *master* (employer) and *servant* (employee) are used when questions of tort liability arise. Even though all people are responsible for their own tortuous conduct, there are times when the law will hold not only the actual tortfeasor but also the person who engaged the tortfeasor liable for the tort. The name given to this type of liability is vicarious liability. Other liability questions include contract liability, criminal liability, statutory liability, and sovereign immunity.

**22.2**   Any person legally capable of entering into a contract may be a principal. There are three kinds of principals—disclosed, undisclosed, or partially disclosed. Anyone may be appointed an agent. Agents are commonly classified as general agents, special agents, factor, and *del credere* agents. A principal is liable on all contracts that a general or special agent enters into, as long as the agent acts with the authority of the principal. An agent's authority may arise expressly from the written or spoken words of the principal to the agent or implied from the agent's reasonable effort to understand the meaning of the principal's words describing what the agent is to do. Apparent authority results from actions by the principal that give a third party reason to believe that an agent has the authority to act for the principal. Ratification by the principal of an unauthorized act by another person does not create agency, but it has the effect of agency.

**22.3**   As a result of the fiduciary relationship, the agent owes the principal the duty of obedience to instructions; loyalty; reasonable judgment, prudence, and skill; accounting for agency money and property; personal performance of agency work; and communication of all facts that affect the subject matter of the agency. In addition to the duties that the principal owes to the agent under the agency agreement, there are certain implied obligations. These obligations include the duty to compensate the agent, reimburse the agent for authorized expenses incurred, indemnify the agent for losses caused by the agency relationship through no fault of the agent, and comply with the terms of the agency contract.

**22.4**   An agency agreement generally terminates when its purposes are accomplished. The agency may also terminate at any time by the principal's revocation of the agent's authority or by the agent's renunciation of the agency relationship. If either party dies, becomes insane, goes bankrupt, or ceases to be qualified to act, the agency relationship is terminated by operation of the law. The principal has the duty to notify third parties with whom the agent has done business when the agency relationship has been terminated by acts of the parties. Actual notice is required when the third party has given credit to the principal through the agent. A public notice in a newspaper of general circulation is sufficient for third parties who have never given credit but who have had cash transactions with the agent.

# Key Terms

agency, 471
agency coupled with an interest, 487
agent, 471
apparent authority, 481
consensual, 471
control test, 474
*del credere* agent, 479
disclosed principal, 479
durable power of attorney, 487

economic reality test, 476
express authority, 480
factor, 479
general agent, 479
gratuitous agency, 485
gratuitous agent, 485
implied authority, 480
indemnification, 485
independent contractor, 472

lingering apparent authority, 481
master, 472
negligent hiring, 475
negligent retention, 475
nondelegable duty, 475
partially disclosed principal, 479
principal, 471

proprietor, 472

ratification, 481

renunciation, 486

revocation, 486

scope of authority, 483

scope of employment, 474

servant, 472

sovereign immunity, 477

special agent, 479

*sui generis*, 478

third party, 471

undisclosed principal, 479

Uniform Durable Power of
Attorney Act, 487

vicarious liability, 473

## Questions for Review and Discussion

1. What is an agency relationship?
2. What is vicarious liability?
3. What are the different types of principals?
4. What are the different types of agents?
5. What is express authority? Implied authority? Apparent authority?
6. What are the duties of an agent to the principal?
7. What are the duties that a principal has in relation to an agent?
8. How can an agency relationship be terminated?
9. Who is entitled to a notice that an agency has ended?
10. What are the major electronic agency laws?

## Cases for Analysis

1. During batting practice in the batting cages at Howland High School, while under the supervision of baseball coach Thomas Eschman, Jeffrey Elston was injured when a ball hit a protective screen, ricocheted, and struck him in the head. Elston was life-flighted to Cleveland by helicopter, where he was treated for head injuries at Rainbow Babies and Children's Hospital. Later Elston's parents brought suit against the high school. The school pointed to a state statute that granted state subdivisions, such as the school district, sovereign immunity. Elston's parents argued that the actions under scrutiny involved a school-related activity located on government-owned property, which clearly made it one of the exceptions to the sovereign immunity rule. The school district defended itself by arguing that the coach's actions not only represented a legitimate exercise of his professional discretion but were also carried out in good faith and were free from wanton, reckless, or malicious conduct. Should the school district escape liability here? Explain. *Elston v. Howland Local Schools,* 113 Ohio St.3d 314 (Ohio Supreme Court).

2. A delivery truck driver who worked for the *Evening Star* in Washington, D.C., was on his route when he was commanded by a police officer to follow a traffic violator to apprehend him. The police officer then jumped onto the side of the truck and held on for the duration of the chase. During the high-speed pursuit, Balinovic was injured when the truck collided with his car. Balinovic wanted to sue both the driver and the *Evening Star* under the theory of vicarious liability. Would vicarious liability apply here? Was the driver a servant of the *Evening Star?* Was the driver operating within the scope of employment? Explain. *Balinovic v. Evening Star Newspaper Co.,* 113 F.2d 505 (D.C. Cir.).

3. Janet Young worked in an administrative capacity for the International Brotherhood of Locomotive Engineers. She was given a 10-year contract by John Sytsma, the president of the union. The president regularly engaged in hiring union employees without consulting with either the executive committee or the advisory board of the union. In addition, the president entered into other contracts on behalf of the union. Although these powers were not specified in the constitution, the union knew that he dealt with the hiring of employees and that he routinely entered nonemployment contracts on behalf of the union. Sometime after Sytsma was defeated in a reelection bid, Larry McFather, the new president, discharged Young. McFather argued that Sytsma did not have the capacity to enter a 10-year employment contract with Young because the authority to do so was not specified in the union's constitution. In addition, McFather

pointed out that the contract had been entered during the union's convention, during which the power to govern the union falls to the delegates at the convention. In response, Young argued that the past practices of the union led her to the reasonable belief that the president had the power to grant her the employment contract. She also argued that even though the power to hire employees was not in the union constitution, the power to do so was implied by the powers of the president to preside over the union's administrative matters. Is Young correct on either of these points? Explain. *Young v. International Brotherhood of Locomotive Engineers,* 683 N.E.2d 420 (OH).

4. Mularchuk was employed as a part-time reserve police officer for the borough of Keansburg, New Jersey. He was never given any training, and he was not required to submit to any training with respect to the revolver he carried. A quarrel arose between McAndrew, who had car trouble, and a towtruck driver whom McAndrew had called for assistance. Mularchuk proceeded to make arrests and, in the course of events, shot and seriously injured McAndrew. Was the borough of Keansburg liable to McAndrew under the doctrine of *respondeat superior*? Explain. *McAndrew v. Mularchuk,* 162 A.2d 820 (NJ).

5. Food Caterers, Inc., had a franchise agreement with Chicken Delight, Inc. Carfiro was employed by Food Caterers to deliver hot chicken bearing the trademark "Chicken Delight." While making a delivery, Carfiro was involved in an accident that killed McLaughlin. In a suit naming Chicken Delight, the franchiser, as defendant, the McLaughlin estate argued that Carfiro was an agent of Chicken Delight, because Carfiro was acting for the benefit of the company. There was no evidence, however, that Carfiro was hired, paid, instructed by, or even known by Chicken Delight. The decision was for whom, and why? *Estate of McLaughlin v. Chicken Delight, Inc.,* 321 A.2d 456 (CT).

6. While Elliot was an inmate at the state-run Chillicothe Correctional Institution, he was hit in the face by Turner, a corrections officer at the institution and therefore a state employee. Elliot brought a lawsuit against the state under the doctrine of *respondeat superior*. The state argued that because Turner had acted recklessly in striking Elliot, his actions were outside the scope of his employment. Therefore, the state concluded, the court should dismiss Elliot's claim against it. Were Turner's actions outside the scope of his employment as a prison guard? Explain. *Elliot v. Ohio Department of Rehabilitation and Correction,* 637 N.E.2d 106 (OH).

7. On April 11, Fred Chapman discharged Anna Savant, the manager of his store, the Super Electronic Supply Outlet. On April 12, Chapman called *The Barnard Crossings Chronicle* and had a notice printed to the effect that Savant no longer worked for Super. On that same day, Savant ordered 12 electronic games, 2 computers, 2 laser printers, a fax machine, and a car stereo from the Global Electronic Components Corporation. As she had frequently done in the past while acting as manager for Super, she told George Pierce, the owner of Global, to send the bill to Super. Pierce did so. Savant then kept these items for herself. Pierce did not have actual notice of Savant's discharge until April 28, when he saw the notice as he was throwing out some old newspapers. Savant could not be located, so Pierce brought suit against Chapman and Super. Chapman argued that the newspaper notice was sufficient to warn Pierce not to deal with Savant. How would the court rule? Explain.

8. Stahl was having trouble with her Volkswagen. She brought it to the service station of LePage, where it was examined and the trouble was diagnosed. LePage informed Stahl that he would not be able to do the work, but that his employee Donley wanted to take the job on his own and could make use of the garage facilities for this purpose. A new engine was required, and Donley installed the wrong engine. The entire job had to be done over at a cost of hundreds of dollars. Stahl brought suit against LePage. She argued that she should be allowed to recover against LePage for the misdeed of Donley, because Donley had apparent authority to act as LePage's agent. LePage disputed this claim, arguing that the facts did not warrant a finding of agency under any theory. How did the court find in this dispute? Why? *Stahl v. LePage*, 352 A.2d 682 (VT).

9. Castle Fabrics, Inc., sold fabric to Fortune Manufacturers, Inc. A dispute arose as to the acceptability of the fabric received, and Fortune returned the fabric to Castle for full credit. Castle gave Fortune only partial credit and sued Fortune for recovery of its loss. In court, Fortune showed a credit memorandum from a Castle employee indicating that

both parties to end an unsatisfactory relationship or take advantage of new opportunities. Unfortunately, the principle can be abused by unscrupulous employers. Therefore, the law has created certain exceptions to the general rule. These exceptions fall into three categories: contractual exceptions; statutory exceptions; and court-created wrongful discharge exceptions. Some of these exceptions modify parts of the at-will doctrine as it applies to an employee or a group of employees. Others actually eliminate an employee's at-will status.

**Contractual Exceptions** Individuals with unique abilities, special talents, or a highly specialized education often have the flexibility to negotiate their own employment contracts. Such individuals would not be affected by employment-at-will. Generally, such people are in demand and can thus be selective in the choice of employers. Professional athletes, established scientists, top business executives, famous entertainers, and well-known artists and writers belong in this category. In contrast to an individual employment contract, a collective bargaining agreement is negotiated by the employer and the labor union. A collective bargaining agreement is a contract that covers all issues related to employment. Such agreements, which are authorized under the National Labor Relations Act (NLRA), prevent the unfair discharge of employees. The employer needs some legitimate, employment-related reason, or just cause, for the release. In general, collective bargaining contracts also provide a grievance procedure. Under a grievance procedure, employees have the right to appeal any employer's decision that they think violates just cause. Often, economic conditions force layoffs or plant closings. When such events occur, some or all employees may lose their jobs. Still, most collective bargaining agreements provide a negotiated procedure by which such layoffs occur. In this way, employees are at least guaranteed that the layoffs will be handled in as fair a manner as possible.

**Statutory Exceptions** The federal government has passed legislation that has altered the at-will doctrine in order to add a level of fairness to employment law that would not exist absent that legislation. In particular, the government has been interested in protecting employees from discrimination based on race, color, creed, national origin, and gender. Later,

---

**THE OPENING CASE** *Revisited, Part I*
Concerted Activities on Facebook: *In re American Medical Response of Connecticut, Inc.,* Round 2

The National Labor Relations Act (NLRA) was designed by Congress to protect not only those employees who are already in a union but also those who wish to form a union. In fact, when the law was first passed back in 1935, it was this right that was the most important because, at that time, unions and union members were few and far between. This is why Congress added a clause to the NLRA that states that, "[e]mployees shall have the right to self-organization, to form, join or assist labor organizations, to bargain collectively through representation of their own choosing, and to engage in other concerted activities for the purpose of collective bargaining or other mutual aid or protection." Moreover,

the right of employees to talk about employment conditions among themselves does not cease when the union has been formed. In the Opening Case at the beginning of this chapter, Sousa, the employee under fire, was not attempting to collectively bargain, to form a union, or to assist a labor union. She simply complained about the decisions made by her supervisor. The court ruled that, under the NLRA, the comments she made on *Facebook* were protected by law. The NLRB also chastised AMR for having a social media policy that was too open-ended. Such an open-ended policy would permit the employer to dismiss an employee for a simple complaint within earshot of a third party.

the legislature also developed statutory law to prevent discrimination based on age and disability. Finally, Congress stepped in to protect workers from the hardship that results when a firm decides to close or move a business.

*Protected Classes and Civil Rights Law* The rule that says that an employer can discharge an employee at any time for any reason or for no reason is also limited by civil rights legislation, such as the Civil Rights Act, the Age Discrimination in Employment Act, and the Americans with Disabilities Act. As the prototype, the Civil Rights Act of 1964 provides a template that the other acts generally follow. The Civil Rights Act of 1964 acknowledges the existence of certain protected classes, including race, color, creed, gender, and national origin, and makes it illegal to use membership in one of those

classes as a reason for employment-related decisions. Thus, it is not completely true to say that an employer can discharge an employee for "any reason or for no reason." Thanks to civil rights legislation, an employer cannot discharge an employee if the only reason for the discharge is membership in one or more of the protected classes. Civil rights legislation is covered at length later in this chapter.

*Worker Adjustment and Retraining Notification Act* Many employers who contemplate mass layoffs and/or plant closings must comply with the provisions of the Worker Adjustment and Retraining Notification Act (WARN). Under this federal statute, employers with more than 100 full-time employees must give written notice to a union official 60 days before any plant closing or mass layoff. If the employees are not represented by a union, the advance notice must go directly to all employees who will be affected by the layoff or closing. Written notice is not required if the layoff or closing is caused by a natural disaster, such as a flood or an earthquake. Notice is also not required if the closing is caused by an unpredictable business situation or if the notice might prevent the acquisition of business or capital that the employer is attempting to acquire.

Employers with 100 or more full-time employees must provide a 60-day notice to the union, or if there is no union, to the individual employees, regarding any planned layoffs or closings.

**Did You Know?**

The labor movement enjoyed early success in Germany, where union membership among unskilled workers rose phenomenally in the mid-1890s.

## Wrongful Discharge

**Wrongful discharge**, which is also referred to as *unjust dismissal* in some states, gives employees legal grounds for a lawsuit against employers who have dismissed them unfairly. The courts have used several theories to judge the injustice of a dismissal. These theories include promissory estoppel, fraud, implied contract, implied covenant, public policy tort, and the intentional inflection of emotional distress.

**Promissory Estoppel** To make a case based on promissory estoppel, the employee must demonstrate that the employer or a representative of the employer, generally a supervisor or department head, promised the employee job security despite the apparent at-will nature of the employment relationship. In promissory estoppel cases, what matters is that someone in authority made a promise to the employee that the employee believed and relied on, to his or her detriment. Promissory estoppel thus involves four elements:

1. The employer makes a promise.
2. The employer can reasonably expect the employee to rely on the promise.
3. The employee really does rely on the promise and, as a consequence, does something or refrains from doing something.
4. The employee in turn is hurt by the action or inaction in reliance on the promise.

tive if the employer has made some sort of specific promise. For instance, if an employer adds a disclaimer to a handbook that also includes a very specific plan for progressive discipline, that employer might still be required to follow that disciplinary plan. Employers who fail to follow their own progressive disciplinary plan may find themselves in the midst of a wrongful discharge lawsuit, despite the disclaimer.

## A QUESTION OF ETHICS

Beth Waid was to receive a 15 percent commission on all sales she made for her employer, the Jian Computer Corporation. Waid sold a $10,000,000 computer system to the Defense Department. To avoid paying $1,500,000 to Waid, Jian fired her, despite her record as a terrific salesperson. In an employment-at-will state that did not recognize the implied covenant exception, such a discharge would be legal. However, would such a termination be ethical? Explain.

**Public Policy Tort** In states that still adhere to the at-will doctrine, an employee who can prove that his or her discharge somehow violated public policy may recover damages in tort. Public policy is the broad legal principle that says that the courts will not allow anyone to do anything that injures the public at large. In many jurisdictions, if an employee is fired for refusing to violate the law, such a discharge would violate public policy. For example, if an employee refuses to dump toxic waste into a river and is then fired for insubordination, that employee would have public policy grounds for a wrongful discharge lawsuit.

Similarly, if the firing itself violates the law, public policy will provide a remedy for the employee. For instance, most jurisdictions have legislation that makes it illegal for an employer to terminate an employee for missing work in order to serve on a jury. Therefore, an employer who fires an employee for absenteeism, knowing that the absent employee is actually serving as a juror, would have violated public policy and could, therefore, be targeted in a wrongful discharge lawsuit.

To succeed in a wrongful discharge lawsuit grounded on the public policy tort exception to employment-at-will, the employee would have to prove clarity, jeopardy, causation, and the lack of an overriding business justification for the discharge:

1. Clarity requires the existence of a definite public policy, clearly created by the U.S. Constitution, the state constitution, a statute, an administrative regulation, a common law principle, or a general governmental policy.

2. Jeopardy requires that the public will be endangered if the court does not dissuade the type of firing involved in the case.

3. Causation requires that the discharge be induced by actions that are related to the stated public policy issue.

4. The lack of an overriding business justification means that the employer had no legitimate business reason for the discharge of the employee.

In a wrongful discharge lawsuit based on public policy, the judge is charged with determining whether the first two elements, clarity and jeopardy, exist. These two elements are considered questions of law. If the case is tried before a jury, the jurors, as the triers of fact, would determine the existence of causation and the absence of an overriding business justification. In the absence of a jury, the judge would make this determination.

**Implied Covenant** The final wrongful discharge exception, **implied covenant** holds that there is an implied promise in any employment relationship that the employer and the employee will be fair and honest with each other. Therefore, neither party will unfairly or dishonestly cheat the other out of anything due to the other party because of the employment relationship. The existence of an implied covenant has nothing to do with anything that the employer has said, written, or done. The implied covenant exists because the employment relationship exists. Several legal experts have argued convincingly that, once a jurisdiction embraces implied covenant, that jurisdiction is no longer an at-will jurisdiction. These experts contend that if a jurisdiction has said that a promise of fairness exists within any employment relationship, it becomes impossible to discharge an employee for "no reason" or "without notice." A discharge without cause or without notice would be inherently unfair and thus a clear violation of the ever-present, inescapable implied covenant.

**Intentional Infliction of Emotional Distress** Another tort claim that is being used more frequently in wrongful discharge lawsuits is the intentional infliction of emotional distress. An employee may attempt to recover damages for the intentional infliction of emotional distress if the conduct of the employer in the discharge of the employee caused serious mental and emotional suffering. To succeed in such a lawsuit, the plaintiff must prove that the employer's conduct was extreme, that the employer knew the conduct was extreme and would result in emotional distress, and that the conduct was the proximate cause of serious mental and emotional suffering.

## After-Acquired Evidence Defense

A relatively new defense that employers have used successfully in wrongful discharge cases is called the *after-acquired evidence defense*. This defense is applied when an employer uncovers evidence, usually during the discovery process, that reveals that the employer could have legitimately discharged the employee, even if the employee's claims of wrongful discharge prove to be true. The defense is often raised as the grounds for the granting of a summary judgment.

### EXAMPLE 23-3: An After-Acquired License Problem

Frank Handley was discharged from his position as a test pilot for Coastline Aviation, Inc., when he was absent from work on one occasion without notifying his superior. The company's employment manual, which had no disclaimer, indicated that an employee would receive three warnings, one oral and two in writing, for unexcused absences before being suspended. Only after a fourth unexcused absence could an employee be discharged. Handley filed a wrongful discharge suit against Coastline based on a breach of the implied contract created by the promises in the employment manual. During the discovery process, attorneys for Coastline found out that Handley's pilot's license had been suspended several years before he was hired and that Handley had lied about his license on his job application. The court ruled that even though the lack of a license had not been the reason that he was discharged, under the circumstances, because he had falsified his application and was not qualified to fly an airplane, which is clearly the function of a test pilot, he would not be entitled to receive any damages.

The after-acquired evidence defense has also been used by defendants in discrimination lawsuits. Consequently, the Equal Employment Opportunity Commission has issued a special rule that is to be applied when such a defense is raised. This rule is discussed later in the chapter.

# 23-2 Laws Regulating Employment Conditions

Employment conditions can be divided into two distinct areas: the actual physical situation in which employees must work and the compensation received by employees. Moreover, there is a national employment verification system that affects all newly hired employees. The federal government regulates these working conditions to protect workers.

## Health and Safety Laws

Various state and federal laws and administrative rules and regulations are designed to reduce preventable hazards to employees in the workplace and to provide for safe and helpful working conditions. On the state level, departments of labor and health may be charged with determining whether an employer is complying with state health and safety laws. On the federal level, the Occupational Safety and Health Act assures all workers in a business, in or affecting interstate commerce, a safe and healthful place of employment.

**Occupational Safety and Health Administration** The Occupational Safety and Health Administration (OSHA), an agency responsible to the Department of Labor, establishes and enforces occupational health and safety standards with which employers must comply. To withstand a court challenge, however, it must be shown that the OSHA standards and regulations reasonably reduce the frequency or severity of employee injuries or illnesses. Employers are required to keep records of illnesses, injuries, and deaths suffered by employees and submit requested reports to the secretary of labor.

A team of OSHA inspectors enforces compliance with its many and varied health and safety regulations. Employees are permitted to request an inspection if they believe that a violation exists. The U.S. Supreme Court has ruled that an OSHA inspector must produce a search warrant if the employer refuses to admit an inspector to the job site voluntarily. When a violation of a standard is observed, the inspector issues a citation. A citation is a notice commanding the appearance of the employer in a proceeding. Employers may contest citations before the OSHA's Review Commission. If this effort fails, they may seek relief in the U.S. Court of Appeals.

## Fair Labor Standards Act

The principal federal law affecting the wages and hours of employees is the Fair Labor Standards Act (FLSA), commonly referred to as the Wage-Hour Law. Frequently amended, the act provides that workers in interstate commerce or in an industry producing goods for sale in interstate commerce must be paid no less than a specified minimum wage. Furthermore, it specifies that employees cannot work for more than 40 hours per week unless they are paid time and a half for overtime. The act prohibits the employment of children under the age of 14 years or the employment of "oppressive child labor" in any enterprise engaged in commerce or in the production of goods for commerce. Provisions of the FLSA have been duplicated by a number of states to regulate intrastate commerce and industries not covered by the federal law.

**Wage and Hour Exceptions and Exemptions** The wage and hour provisions of the FLSA permit the employment of learners, apprentices, and messengers at less than the minimum wage. However, the employer must obtain express permission from the Wage and Hour Division of the Department of Labor and is subject to conditions set by it governing wages and hours. Full-time students are permitted to be employed under the same conditions in retail and service stores outside of school hours.

The wage and hour provisions of the FLSA, with certain exceptions, do not apply to people employed in an executive, administrative, or professional capacity. The exempt workers are generally identified as those who manage other employees. At least 50 percent of their primary duties must be in the performance of office or nonmanual work relating to the operations of the company or in the performance of work requiring scientific or specialized study. State, local, and federal employees; self-employed persons; and armed forces personnel are exempted from the wage and hour provisions. Also exempted are outside salespeople, employees of certain seasonal amusement or recreational businesses, and employees of small retail or service establishments.

## Identity and Employment Eligibility

The federal Immigration Reform Act of 1986 created a national employment verification system that placed responsibility for verification of the identity and employment of all employees on the employer. The act provided that alien workers hired on or before November 6, 1986, had until May 5, 1988, to seek temporary resident status. Those who do not have documentation of their right to work in this country are not entitled to help from the National Labor Relations Board (NLRB) in labor disputes.

Employers are required to request and examine documentation of identity and employment eligibility of all new hires and rehires, including U.S. citizens, permanent residents, and nonimmigrant visa holders. Job applicants must present original documentation. After the documents are reviewed by the employer, individuals who accept an offer of employment are required to complete and sign an employment eligibility verification form in the presence of a supervisor or a human resource officer.

## quick quiz 23-2

| | |
|---|---|
| 1. The Occupational Safety and Health Act is a model law created by the American Law Institute. | true \| false |
| 2. The minimum wage is set by OSHA. | true \| false |
| 3. The Immigration Reform Act of 1986 does not affect the job application process. | true \| false |

# 23-3 Worker Benefits

The law attempts to protect workers who have left a job because of retirement, injury, or disability. The law also assists workers who have been laid off or discharged. These objectives are accomplished through Social Security, unemployment insurance, and worker's compensation.

## Social Security

Federal and state governments participate in programs designed to reduce the financial risk to workers caused by their unemployment, disability, hospitalization, retirement, or death. The primary federal law covering these risks is the Social Security Act of 1935. Under the Federal Insurance Contributions Act (FICA), both employers and employees are taxed equally to help pay for the worker's loss of income on retirement. The law provides that the employee's contribution is held back by the employer, who then provides a matching contribution. The amount that an employee is assessed is based on the employee's annual wage base. Each year the annual wage base is raised to accommodate changes that occur because of increases in the cost of living. The Social Security Administration will pay benefits to retired workers who are eligible under the plan. Each retired worker's benefit payments are set by law but are also raised automatically to match cost-of-living increases. Table 23-1 outlines the age at which individuals can retire and receive full benefits under Social Security.

| Table 23-1  Age to Receive Full Social Security Benefits (AKA *full retirement age* or *normal retirement age*) | |
|---|---|
| **Year of Birth** | **Full Retirement Age** |
| 1937 or before | 65 years of age |
| 1938 | 65 and 2 months |
| 1939 | 65 and 4 months |
| 1940 | 65 and 6 months |
| 1941 | 65 and 8 months |
| 1942 | 65 and 10 months |
| 1943 to 1954 | 66 years of age |
| 1955 | 66 and 2 months |
| 1956 | 66 and 4 months |
| 1957 | 66 and 6 months |
| 1958 | 66 and 8 months |
| 1969 | 66 and 10 months |
| 1960 or later | 67 years of age |

(*Note:* Those born on January 1 of any year use the previous year as their mark.)

(*Note:* The earliest that anyone can actually claim Social Security retirement benefits is 62 years of age.)

# Unemployment Insurance

The unemployment insurance section of the Social Security Act provides for a joint federal and state system of unemployment insurance. Temporary financial assistance is available to individuals who are unemployed through no fault of their own and who have earned sufficient credits from prior employment. Under the Federal Unemployment Tax Act, each state operates its own unemployment insurance system, subject to conditions established by the federal government. In addition to meeting state requirements regarding length of time employed and amount of wages, former employees must be ready,

willing, and able to take suitable full-time employment should it become available. Thus, claimants are ineligible to receive unemployment benefits when they refuse to work without good cause. Good cause for refusing to work must be real, not imaginary; substantial, not trivial; and reasonable, not whimsical. For example, a desire to avoid a small cut in pay does not constitute good cause to refuse an employer's offer of employment in a reasonably similar position.

Unemployment benefits help those out of work, however, the recipient must be ready, willing, and able to work should suitable employment become available.

To recover for work-related injuries under workers' compensation, a worker must be injured on the job. A worker traveling to work, traveling home, or traveling to some other non-work-related destination cannot recover for injuries. This restriction is also true of lunches and breaks when a worker leaves the workplace. The result is different, however, when a worker leaves the work site on a *special mission* for the employer. Then the employee would be eligible to recover if he or she is injured, especially if the trip involved a business-related lunch that the employee was required to attend away from the job site.

An employee who quits a job without cause or is discharged for misconduct or theft generally does not qualify for unemployment benefits. Most states disqualify workers from receiving benefits if they are on strike because of a labor dispute. Domestic workers, agricultural workers, and state and local government employees are not governed by the federal–state program. Separate federal unemployment programs exist for railroad workers and federal civilian workers.

# Workers' Compensation

**Workers' compensation** laws are in effect in all states. These statutes compensate covered workers or their dependents for injuries, disease, or death that occur on the job or as a result of it. One form provides a fund operated only by the state government. Employers pay into a state-controlled fund. When employees suffer injuries, they apply to the state to receive their benefits.

In another form of workers' compensation, companies are required to carry insurance for their workforce, but they have the option of contributing to the state fund or purchasing insurance from a private insurer. In the third form, all employers are required to purchase workers' compensation insurance from private insurers.

If this worker is injured on the job, his state's workers' compensation insurance will pay benefits based on the severity and duration of the injury.

# Pension Plan Regulation

The Employee Retirement Income Security Act (ERISA) provides necessary supervision over employee pension plans that are established by many employers. Under the act, employers must place their pension contributions on behalf of the employees into a pension trust, independent of the employer. Under the rules of vesting, workers are guaranteed the right to receive pension benefits, regardless of whether they are working under the plan at the time of retirement. The law requires all pension plans to have minimum vested benefits. All pension plans must provide vested benefits after a worker has been on the job for five years.

# Family and Medical Leave Regulation

Under the provisions of the federal Family and Medical Leave Act (FMLA), employers who have 50 or more employees at the workplace (or within 75 miles of the workplace) must give those employees up to 12 weeks of leave time in a 12-month period for child, spousal, or parental care or for the employee's own serious medical condition if that condition necessitates either in-patient treatment or medical care on a continuing basis. The 12-month period can be calculated based on a calendar year or from the time the leave actually begins. The leave time may be unpaid, but it must not jeopardize the job of the employee. To qualify for the leave time guaranteed by the FLMA, the worker must have been employed by the firm for at least one year and worked for 1,250 hours over the 12-month period before the leave is requested. Employees can draw on the 12 weeks consecutively, at intervals, or as an adjusted work plan. For example, an employee might take a half-week of leave time now and another half-week later, or an employee might reduce his or her workweek from five to four days, or a worker might adjust his or her daily work schedule from eight to six hours, and so on.

**Employer Responsibilities**  Both the employee and the employer have responsibilities under the FMLA. For instance, the employer must keep the employee's group health insurance in effect while the employee is on leave. Furthermore, when the employee returns to work, the employer must reinstate the employee to his or her former job or a job equal to the former job. In addition, the employer must make certain that, upon returning to work, the employee receives the same pay and the same benefits that he or she received before going on leave. Employers are also forbidden to dismiss an employee or discriminate against a worker who exercises his or her leave rights under the FMLA. Similarly, the employer cannot retaliate against a worker who protests the employer's attempt to bypass the rights granted to employees under this act. Employers are also responsible for informing employees, in writing, when leave time under the FMLA has been activated.

**Employee Responsibilities**  The FMLA also imposes certain obligations on employees. For instance, employees are required by law to give notice of their intention to take an FMLA leave whenever they can foresee the need for the leave. This notice must be given to the employer at least 30 days before the employee intends to take the leave. If the need for a leave is unpredictable, the employee must give notice as soon as doing so is practical.

**Enforcement of FMLA Rules**  Employees who believe that their employer has violated FMLA rules can file complaints with the Labor Employment Standards Administration. Moreover, employees who believe that their rights have been violated may file a lawsuit against their employers. Finally, a state statute or a collective bargaining agreement that gives employees more comprehensive leave coverage would supersede FMLA.

**Military Amendments to the FMLA**  Congress amended the FMLA in 2009 to accommodate military caregivers. Under these new provisions, an employer must give an employee up to 26 weeks of leave time in a 12-month period to care for a family member who has sustained a serious illness or injury that occurred because of military service. This new type of leave has been labeled military caregiver leave. In addition, employees are permitted to use as much as 20 weeks to take care of certain nonmedical emergencies during the time that a spouse, child, or parent is on active duty in the military. This is referred to as qualifying exigency leave.

## Did You Know?

One of the earliest forms of public assistance for the poor was instigated in Antwerp in the fourteenth century. Citizens considered deserving of the city's assistance were given identification badges. No one could receive food without the appropriate identification badge.

---

**quick quiz** 23-3

1. Most states have eliminated workers' compensation laws because they are too expensive to maintain.    true | false

2. Under the Federal Unemployment Tax Act, all state unemployment compensation systems were dismantled.    true | false

3. The Family Medical Leave Act provides for 12 weeks of paid leave for all employees in any 12-month period.    true | false

---

# 23-4 Equal Employment Opportunity

As noted earlier in the chapter, in recent years, the government has attempted to address the problem of discrimination in the workplace by fashioning statutes that promote equal employment opportunities. The most prominent of these statutes include Title VII of the Civil Rights Acts, the Equal Pay Act, the Age Discrimination in Employment Act, the Uniformed Services Employment and Reemployment Rights Act, the Americans with Disabilities Act, and the Genetic Information Nondiscrimination Act (GINA).

## Title VII of the Civil Rights Act

Today we are so used to governmental efforts to promote equal employment opportunity that we forget that it was a long and hard struggle to reach the type of workplace equity that we enjoy today. Although the Civil Rights Act of 1964 is clearly the most important of these acts, it was not the first. The stage was set for the Civil Rights Act of 1964 by the Equal Pay Act of 1963. Under provisions of the federal Equal Pay Act, employers must pay women the same amount that they pay men for the same job. The underlying motto of those who support the Equal Pay Act was and is "equal pay for equal work." Such a rule is easy to follow when the work in question is exactly the same. Problems occur when the work done by the women in the workplace is comparable, but not identical, to the work done by the men. To deal with this issue, the courts have ruled that as long as the work in question requires the same level of effort, ability, and accountability and is rendered in a comparable work environment, it is considered substantially equal. Substantially equal work requires equal pay. Since 1979, the Equal Pay Act has been administered by the Equal Employment Opportunity Commission (EEOC).

## Title VII of the Civil Rights Act of 1964

The Civil Rights Act of 1964 covers more than employment. It also outlaws discrimination in such things as housing, travel accommodations, and education. One of its primary features is the creation of the original five protected classes. Simply stated the act prohibits discrimination on the basis of race, color, creed, gender, and national origin. Employees who believe that they have been discriminated against can file complaints with the Equal Employment Opportunity Commission (EEOC). Moreover, some state governments have equal employment agencies that have been designated as deferral agencies under Title VII. In those states, all discrimination charges filed with the EEOC must be sent by the EEOC to the state equal employment agency. Even so, an employee who has filed such a claim can ask the EEOC, rather than the state agency, to conduct the inquiry. Discrimination claims must be registered with the EEOC no later than 180 days after the prohibited activity. In states with deferral agencies, that deadline is lengthened to 300 days. Discrimination can be committed in one of two ways: disparate treatment and disparate impact.

**Disparate Treatment** In cases of **disparate treatment**, the employer intentionally discriminates against an individual or a group belonging to one of the protected classes. For instance, a business that advertises for "salesmen" or "saleswomen" rather than "salespersons" would be practicing this type of discrimination. The act has had a profound effect on the language of the workplace. Words and phrases that reveal a certain bias (usually a gender bias) have largely disappeared from the language. We no longer see advertisements for "waiters," "stewardesses," "actresses," "salesmen," "busboys," or "girl Fridays." Instead, we read about "servers," "flight attendants," "actors," "salespersons," "bussers," and "administrative assistants." Nevertheless, a common misconception still exists that this type of brazen discrimination has been eliminated from the workplace. Such is not the case. Even in the present day, the United States Supreme Court is still reviewing cases that dealt with companies that continued to discriminate in direct and obvious ways.

## EXAMPLE 23-4: The Johnson Battery Discrimination Case, Part I

Johnson Controls Inc., a battery manufacturer located in Wisconsin, had an employment policy that eliminated women younger than 70 years of age from performing certain jobs in the making of batteries unless they could produce proof that they were infertile. The company argued that it was just trying to protect its workers, because all the prohibited jobs involved prolonged exposure to lead. The U.S. Supreme Court disagreed and labeled the company's policy as a clear-cut example of sex discrimination.

**Bona Fide Occupational Qualification** Businesses have a defense against a charge of disparate treatment, called a *bona fide occupational qualification (BFOQ)*. The discrimination may be justified if the employer can prove that the job requirement is a BFOQ. Even so, a BFOQ defense can never be raised to justify racial discrimination. However, a BFOQ defense can work for some forms of sexual discrimination. For example, a requirement that all applicants for a job modeling women's bathing suits be female would be a BFOQ.

## EXAMPLE 23-5: The Johnson Battery Discrimination Case, Part II

Could Johnson Controls Inc., in Example 23-4, argue that infertility in a woman is a valid BFOQ? The U.S. Supreme Court said no. A BFOQ must be related to the job performance. Both men and women can be competent battery makers, so excluding one sex or the other from that job cannot be justified.

**Disparate Impact** In contrast to disparate treatment, disparate impact is a more subtle form of discrimination. Discrimination through **disparate impact** or adverse impact occurs when an employer has a policy that on the surface seems neutral but that has an unequal and unfair impact on the members of one or more of the protected classes. For instance, an employer who requires all employees who work in the warehouse to be six feet tall and weigh at least 180 pounds may have discriminated against women under the doctrine of disparate impact. Although the criteria seem neutral on the surface, they would exclude women disproportionately and thus have an unfair impact on them.

## Business Necessity

Business Necessity Businesses have a defense against a charge of disparate impact known as business necessity. A qualification may be permitted despite its disparate impact on a protected class if the employer can show that the qualification is needed to perform the job. For example, a requirement that all job applicants have a law degree for a job as an attorney might have a disparate impact on one or more of the protected classes. However, because a law degree is needed for the job, it will be allowed. Naturally, the claimant has an opportunity to demonstrate that the challenged practice is not really needed to perform the job in question.

## Workplace Harassment

Workplace Harassment In recent years, the courts have witnessed an increase in the number of workplace harassment claims. The first type of harassment claims that appeared before the EEOC were sexual harassment claims. There is no question that sexual harassment is a type of sexual discrimination and that it is forbidden by the Civil Rights Act. However, exactly what constitutes sexual harassment is misunderstood by many people. Although most people recognize *quid pro quo* harassment, they do not realize that the creation of a *hostile work environment* also constitutes sexual harassment. Quid pro quo sexual harassment occurs when a supervisor makes unwelcome sexual advances toward a subordinate or suggests that the subordinate trade sexual favors for preferential treatment or to avoid the threat of an adverse employment decision such as a demotion, a pay cut, or termination. The Supreme Court has also made it clear that this type of discrimination can occur between individuals of the same gender.

A hostile work environment occurs when misconduct, such as sexually explicit comments, photographs, pictures, text messages, e-mails, *Facebook* postings, cartoons, jokes, posters, or gestures, pervade the workplace to the extent that conditions become distressing, offensive, or hostile. In recent years, the law has begun to recognize that a hostile work environment need not be limited to sexual situations. In fact, a hostile workplace can be created by misconduct that creates an environment that is so offensive that it interferes with the employee's work performance. This type of harassment can result from comments, jokes, cartoons, text messages, voice mails, e-mails, *Facebook* postings, and so on based upon insults, attacks, sarcasm, complaints, or inappropriate jokes because of another worker's religion, color, creed, or national origin. The law expressly forbids employers from retaliating against employees who file harassment complaints.

## Affirmative Action and Reverse Discrimination

Affirmative Action and Reverse Discrimination The term affirmative action refers to a practice by which an employer actively pursues a policy that will reduce the effects of past discrimination in the workplace. The term *affirmative,* in this context, means to go forth actively, and the word *action* means a definitive plan. Affirmative action is neither mandated nor prohibited by the Civil Rights Act. Generally, affirmative action plans come from a court order but nothing prevents an employer from pursuing an affirmative action plan voluntarily. Some people are opposed to affirmative action because they see it as a form of reverse discrimination.

## Reverse Discrimination

Reverse Discrimination Any practice that is designed to eliminate discrimination against the members of a protected class but that has the opposite effect on other members of that class or on the members of another protected class is called reverse discrimination. To prevent this, the Supreme Court that affirmative action plans promote a "compelling state interest" and be finely drawn to minimize harm to those workers outside the plan. To preserve an affirmative action plan, the government must show the plan is necessary to fight past discrimination, has a termination date, and is the only way to reverse the discriminatory practice.

# Amendments to the Civil Rights Act

Congress has amended the Civil Rights Act many times since its original passage in 1964. One such amendment involving pregnancy occurred in 1978. Moreover, a major overhaul of the act took place in 1991. One goal of the 1991 amendments was to revitalize the doctrine of disparate impact. The second objective involves an expansion of the remedies available under Civil Rights legislation. The Equal Pay Act has also been amended recently.

### The Pregnancy Discrimination Act
This 1978 amendment to Title VII of the Civil Rights Act of 1964 makes it clear that employers cannot discriminate against women because of pregnancy or because they recently gave birth. Stated more positively, the act provides that pregnant women must be afforded the same treatment in all employment-related decisions, including health care, as any other employee.

### Strengthening Disparate Impact
The first goal of the 1991 amendments was to strengthen the doctrine of disparate impact that had been weakened by the U.S. Supreme Court. The amendments make it clear that in disparate impact cases, the employer has the burden of proving that a business necessity exists for the alleged discriminatory practice that forms the basis of the complaint. The law also makes it clear that the employer must prove that the hiring or promotion qualification is directly related to the specific job in question rather than to general business needs. The party who files a complaint in a disparate impact case may also be victorious if he or she can show that the same business goal can be reached by using a nondiscriminatory employment practice.

### Compensatory and Punitive Damages
A second objective was to expand the availability of compensatory and punitive damages. Prior to the passage of the new act, only victims of racial discrimination could collect compensatory and punitive damages. All other victims of discrimination were limited to collecting back pay only. Under the 1991 amendments, compensatory and punitive damages were made available to people who have been discriminated against because of their sex, religion, or national origin. Other remedies that are available under Title VII are back pay, reinstatement, and attorney fees.

### Other Effects of the 1991 Amendments
The 1991 amendments also added a few other critical provisions designed to reinstate the actual intent of Congress in creating the original statute in 1964. For instance, the new law mandates that American businesses must give U.S. citizens working abroad the same protection against discrimination that they give workers in the United States. In addition, the new act makes it clear that an employment practice is illegal even if only a portion of the practice is discriminatory.

### Amendment to the Equal Pay Act
The Equal Pay Act was designed to help women undo more than 45 years of continued paycheck discrimination. This discrimination had taken place, despite the passage of the Equal Pay Act in 1963. The new amendments clarify that employers cannot discriminate against women in any gender-related capacity that might be related to education, training, or background. Moreover, the new amendments also specify that the 180-day time limit for filing a claim with the EEOC begins to run every time the worker is paid. Thus, the paycheck is a continuing wrong that hurts the worker each time she receives it. Finally, the new statute also adds compensatory and punitive damages to the remedies available in a gender-based wage discrimination case.

### After-Acquired Evidence in Relation to Discrimination Cases
The EEOC has adopted an approach for discrimination cases in which after-acquired evidence reveals that the employer had a legitimate reason for discharging the employee. The

rule, which applies only to cases involving the EEOC, states that the commission will not require that the employer rehire the claimant, nor will the commission attempt to recover back pay or compensatory damages that arise after the time that the after-acquired evidence was obtained. However, to avoid squelching the effectiveness of the 1991 amendments, the EEOC will still seek punitive damages in such cases.

## Age Discrimination in Employment Act

The Age Discrimination in Employment Act (ADEA) prohibits discrimination on the basis of age. ADEA covers employment agencies, employers of 20 or more employees, and labor unions of more than 25 members. This act protects any person aged 40 years or older from discrimination in hiring, firing, promotion, or other aspect of employment. Like the Civil Rights Act, the ADEA is administered by the EEOC. Age discrimination claims must be registered with the EEOC no later than 300 days after the prohibited activity. Naturally, if age is a true job qualification, the law does not apply. For instance, if the job involves the modeling of junior miss fashions, it would not be discrimination to hire someone of suitable age to model the clothes. The courts, however, will carefully scrutinize all such requirements and generally be able to detect those that are merely a pretense covering age discrimination.

### EXAMPLE 23-6: Taggart, Time, and the ADEA

Thomas Taggart, aged 58 years, lost his position when the subsidiary he worked for was disbanded by Time, Inc., the parent corporation. All of the employees who were laid off as a result of the closing were promised preferential treatment for other jobs at Time, Inc. Taggart applied for more than 30 of these positions. He was never rehired. Most of the time the reason given for his rejection was that he was overqualified.

Taggart brought an age discrimination suit under the ADEA. Time, Inc., argued that Taggart was not rehired because of an overqualification barrier that had nothing to do with his age. The court disagreed. The court ruled that calling Taggart overqualified was just another way of saying he was too old.

In 1990, Congress amended the ADEA in response to a U.S. Supreme Court case that held that the original ADEA did not cover employee benefit plans. The amendment, which is called the Older Workers' Benefit Protection Act (OWBPA), makes it clear that the ADEA forbids discrimination against older workers in the handling of their employee benefit and retirement plans. In addition, OWBPA gives older workers legal recourse if they are forced or tricked into giving up their rights under the ADEA. Usually this situation occurs when the employee is asked to sign a waiver. A waiver of rights is valid only if it is given freely and without force or coercion. The employer has the job of proving that the waiver is valid if it is introduced as evidence in court.

## Uniformed Services Employment and Reemployment Rights Act

Under provisions of the Uniformed Services Employment and Reemployment Rights Act (USERA), an employee who has served in the armed forces and successfully completed his or her tour of duty is entitled, upon returning to work, to be reinstated in his or her previous position on the job. Unlike the Civil Rights Act, which is controlled by the EEOC, USERA is administered by the Office of Veterans' Employment and Training Service (VETS). Also unlike the Civil Rights Act, under USERA, employees may file a complaint with VETS, or they can take the case directly to court. No statute of limitations is connected to USERA. However, employees are not permitted to hold back on the filing of a case for an unreasonable length of time. Employees who succeed in a case might receive damages, an injunction to prevent their termination, and sometimes, at the discretion of the judge, attorneys' fees.

## Americans with Disabilities Act

The Americans with Disabilities Act (ADA) is designed to open the American workplace to this country's disabled citizens. The ADA is divided into several titles. Title I lays out the duties imposed on private-sector employers, whereas Title II covers public services and public transportation. The ADA is administered by the EEOC. The ADA carefully outlines what is considered a disability. It also explains who and what are covered by the act and what practices are specifically forbidden.

### Disabilities
The ADA defines **disability** as any physical or mental impairment that substantially limits one or more of the major life activities. This definition includes paralysis, blindness, deafness, cancer, mental retardation, learning disabilities, and AIDS, among others. Excluded from protection are people with kleptomania, pyromania, or gambling disorders. Nor does the act extend to people who use illegal drugs. The definition of disability also does not include homosexuality or bisexuality. However, because the act forbids discrimination against people who are associated with a particular disability, discrimination against homosexuals, on the basis of the claim that they are more likely to contract AIDS, would be forbidden.

### Activities and Individuals Covered by ADA
Discrimination is forbidden in the screening of applicants, initial hiring, and on-the-job treatment. This protection against discrimination also extends to apprenticeship programs, promotions, pay raises, and on-the-job-training opportunities. Individuals, including both employees and applicants for employment, cannot be segregated or classified because of a disability. The ADA also protects an individual from discrimination because that individual is associated with someone who has a disability. As is true of other situations, a state statute that gives individuals with disabilities more protection than the ADA would supersede the federal statute.

### Forbidden Practices
The ADA forbids discrimination on the basis of a disability if the disabled individual can do the essential functions of the job with "reasonable accommodations." Exactly what would qualify as a reasonable accommodation in a given set of circumstances is, at best, problematic. Nevertheless, the statute does give some guidance in determining the extent of a **reasonable accommodation**. An accommodation will be reasonable if it permits the disabled individual to accomplish the essential functions of the job without imposing an undue hardship on the employer. Factors used in determining whether a proposed accommodation will cause **undue hardship** include the type of accommodation needed, the expense involved in providing the accommodation, the financial ability of the company to provide the necessary accommodation, and the size and nature of the company involved. Because of the innovative nature of the law and the lack of precedent, the EEOC has decided to follow a case-by-case evaluation of all claims filed by disabled individuals against employers.

## Genetic Information Nondiscrimination Act

Congress has become increasingly disturbed over the unauthorized use of generic information to invade the privacy of employees or to make employment decisions based on that information. To combat this threat, Congress passed the **Genetic Information**

**Nondiscrimination Act (GINA).** GINA was written to protect employees by making it unlawful for employers and health insurance companies to make decisions based on any genetic information that they have acquired due to any type of genetic testing. Under the statute, the purpose of the test is immaterial. GINA targets health insurance companies, forbidding them to use genetic information to make changes in premiums or in employee contributions. On the other hand, the new statute does permit medical professionals, such as physicians, nurses, therapists, technicians, and the like, to use genetic tests and to compile genetic information for health care reasons. In fact, the law even permits health insurance providers to establish payment schedules for their clients based on genetic information. Still, GINA demands that insurers use as little of the genetic information as possible to make such decisions. In contrast, employers are forbidden to use genetic information to make hiring, firing, promotion, vacation, continuing education, professional development, transfer, budgetary, work schedule, and salary decisions. The law also forbids unions, employment agencies, and joint labor–management committees from discriminating against individuals in any employment-related decisions related to genetic information. In fact, all employment-related decisions must be made free of any influence from the genetic information. Moreover, employers, unions, employment agencies, and joint labor–management committees cannot request, require, or purchase genetic information, unless required by law, used to protect individuals from toxic substances, or as part of a forensic investigation for law enforcement purposes. [See David J. Kovach, "GINA," *Ohio State Bar Association: 2010 Annual Convention* (May 5-7, 2010): 6.1-6.5. See also "The Genetic Information Nondiscrimination Act," *Department of Health and Human Services* (April 6, 2009), 1, retrieved on September 25, 2010, from http://www.genome.gov; and "H.R. 493: Genetic Information Nondiscrimination Act of 2008," *Congressional Research Service,* 1, retrieved on August 20, 2010, from http://www.gov.track.us/congress/bill.]

## quick quiz 23-4

1. The term *affirmative action* refers to a practice by which an employer actively pursues a policy that will reduce the effects of past discrimination in the workplace.      true | false

2. American businesses working in other countries need not give U.S. citizens the same protection against discrimination under the Civil Rights Act as those afforded workers in the United States itself.      true | false

3. The Uniformed Services Employment and Reemployment Rights Act (USERA) is administered by the EEOC.      true | false

# 23-5 Social Media Policies

There is no way to escape the social media craze that has swept through the business world in the 21st century. Employees and employers use computers as part of their jobs and they expect everyone else, customers and suppliers alike, to do the same. In fact, computers have become so commonplace in business that it is possible, perhaps even likely, that most business people no longer even notice then. Nevertheless, it is crucial to remember that computers are all around us, even in places and in devices that we do not usually think of as computers. Moreover, it is also important to recall that when people become too accustomed to technology they can become careless.

## The Social Media Culture

Business people must remember that computers include not only mainframes, desktop PCs, tablet computers, and laptops, but also mobile phones, notebooks, personal digital assistants (PDAs), skype, digital recorders, GPS units, smartphones, scanners, fax machines, and wireless reading devices (WRDs). It would also be helpful to remember that to the business person it is not just the devices that are important—is the data itself. Keeping trade secrets and protecting a client's or an employee's privacy may also mean protecting data and, at times, metadata. **Metadata** is data about data and includes such things as archival metadata, administrative metadata, structural metadata, descriptive metadata, intellectual property rights, human resources metadata, planning metadata, management metadata, financial metadata, product metadata, architectural metadata, engineering metadata, research-related metadata, preservation metadata, and so on.

It is also crucial to see that employees have become so immersed in computers that they frequently act as if those computers have always been there and will always work flawlessly. They communicate with one another with customers, suppliers, wholesalers, and retailers online. They use conference calls and webinars on a daily basis. They make purchases, pay bills, and sell goods on line. They "talk" to one another on mobile phones, with text messages, by e-mail, and on Twitter. When they go home they jump on *Facebook, YouTube,* or *LinkedIn*. They make connections on dating Web sites; plan trips using *Orbitz, Priceline,* or *Travelocity;* purchase hard-to-get items on *e-Bay* or *craigslist* buy books from *Amazon.com* or *Barnes and Noble* online; they blog, read blogs, or tell others about their favorite blogs; and if that were not enough, they take college courses, attend webinars, take certification exams, and earn advanced degrees online.

## The Nature of a Social Media Policy

In some ways this makes conducting business easier, more economical, and more efficient. However, the social media craze also causes problems and, as a business person, you must be aware of the legal risks involved when your people use social media outlets and what to do about it when things go wrong. There is, therefore, no question that every business needs to write and enforce a social media policy. A **social media policy (SMP)** is a set of rules written by an employer telling employees what they can and cannot do when using electronic communication devices, formats, Web sites, and other electronic messaging techniques, such as blogs, text messages, tweets, skype transmissions, and e-mails. The only remaining questions are what are the risks involved in social media; what must be included in a SMP; what is the proper way to communicate an SMP to employees; and what is the most effective way to enforce an SMP?

## The Hazards Involved in Social Media

As noted above, social media has a very important role in the business world. It can be used to communicate effectively, to contact customers and suppliers, to store data, to write proposals and reports, to conduct video conferences and webinars, to pay company bills online, to disseminate information, and so on. The purposes are limited only by the imagination of the business person at the keyboard. However, there are also risks involved. Social media can be used to disclose trade secrets, customer lists, or other company information that is best kept confidential. It can be used to harass fellow workers or customers or to defame them or perhaps to invade their privacy. There are also legal limits set down by the Federal Trade Commission that might be violated inadvertently by the improper use of social media. For these reasons, among others, it is best for every company to write, publish, distribute, and enforce a social media policy.

### The Proper Way to Construct a Social Media Policy

A social media policy must include certain features. First, the policy must be written in a language and a style that is precise, exact, plain, and explicit. There must be no room for misinterpretation, because if the court has to interpret an ambiguous clause, its decision will likely be against the party who wrote the policy to begin with. Second, the policy must be given to the employees with the understanding that they will read and comprehend the details of the policy. Moreover, as part of this disclosure process, employees must be told up front that the employer intends to monitor their e-mail accounts and all additional online work.

### The Content of a Social Media Policy

First, in order to play fair with employees, the employer must let the employees know what activities are forbidden. Forbidden activities would include: sending out trade secrets, customer lists, and other private business related data; using sexual comments and discriminatory remarks about anyone, but especially other employees, supervisors, clients, and suppliers; making remarks that are libelous, invade privacy, create emotional distress, or constitute product or ownership disparagement; and distributing any communication about company products or services that is not accompanied by a clear statement distancing the company from the author. In addition, it would be helpful to also outline what activities are appropriate using social media in the workplace.

### The Procedures Associated with a Social Media Policy

Once the policy has been written and explained to the employees, each of them should be given two copies of the policy, one to sign and return for their personnel file and one to keep as a reminder of what is expected of them. The employer should reserve the right to make alterations in the policy as experience reveals situations and events that were not predicted by the original policy. It is also crucial for the employer to remember that, even after the policy is distributed and the employees have been warned, there are limits to what an employer can do about violations of the policy [Source for the above material on social media policies is Adrienne l. Rapp, "The Responsible Employer's Social Media Policy," *Labor and Employment Update*," Ohio State Bar Association Annual Conference, (Columbus, Ohio, May 6, 2011).]

## THE OPENING CASE *Revisited, Part II*
## Concerted Activities on Facebook: *In re American Medical Response of Connecticut, Inc., Round 3*

Recall how in the Opening Case at the beginning of the chapter, a disgruntled employee of American Medical Response (AMR) complained on *Facebook* about her boss. At one point the angry employee wrote that she loved "how the company allows a 17 to become a supervisor." (It was later revealed that the number 17 refers to psychiatric patients.) When AMR learned about the *Facebook* discussion, the employee was fired because she had disobeyed an AMR rule that forbids workers from making unflattering remarks about AMR online. The employee then filed a complaint with the National Labor Relations Board. Although AMR had a social media policy, the NLRB ruled against the company stating that the employee's remarks were protected by the National Labor Relations Act, precisely because she had discussed working conditions with co-workers. This activity is clearly protected by the NLRB as "concerted activities for the purpose of . . . mutual aid and protection." The NLRB also chastised AMR for having a social media policy that was just way too open-ended, which, as a result, violated the NLRA. So, it was not just the employee's termination that bothered the NLRB, it was also the entire social media policy that AMR had created. The lesson to learn from this case is that a social media policy must be tailored very carefully as a balance between protecting the company and protecting workers' rights.

## quick quiz 23-5

1. Metadata is data about data.    true | false

2. A social media policy must be given to the employees with the understanding that they will read and comprehend the details of the policy.    true | false

3. The employer should reserve the right to make alterations in the social media policy as experience reveals situations and events that were not predicted by the original policy.    true | false

## Summary

**23.1**   This doctrine means that an employer can dismiss an employee at any time for any reason. Employees who belong to labor unions and individuals with the power to negotiate their own employment contracts would not be affected by employment-at-will. Wrongful discharge gives employees legal grounds for a lawsuit against employers who have dismissed them unfairly. The courts have used several theories to judge the injustice of a dismissal. These include promissory estoppel, fraud, implied contract, implied covenant, public policy tort, and intentional inflection of emotional distress.

**23.2**   OSHA establishes and enforces occupational health and safety standards with which employers must comply. The principal federal law affecting the wages and hours of employees is the Fair Labor Standards Act. The act provides that workers in interstate commerce or in an industry that produces goods for sale in interstate commerce must be paid no less than a specified minimum wage. The federal Immigration Reform Act of 1986 created a national employment verification system that placed responsibility on the employer for verifying the identity and employment of all employees.

**23.3**   Federal and state governments participate in programs designed to reduce the financial risk to workers by reason of their unemployment, disability, hospitalization, retirement, and death. The principal federal law covering these risks is the Social Security Act of 1935. Under the Federal Unemployment Tax Act, each state operates its own unemployment insurance system, subject to conditions established by the federal government. Workers' compensation laws are in effect in all states. These statutes compensate covered workers or their dependents for injuries, disease, or death that occurred on the job or as a result of it. ERISA provides needed supervision over employee pension plans established by many employers. Under provisions of the Family and Medical Leave Act (FMLA), employers who have 50 or more employees must give those employees up to 12 weeks of leave time for child, spousal, or parental care.

**23.4**   The Civil Rights Act of 1964 prohibits discrimination based on race, color, creed, gender, and national origin. Employees who believe they have been discriminated against can file a complaint with the EEOC. Discrimination can be committed in one of two ways: disparate treatment or disparate impact. Other steps toward equality in employment include the Age Discrimination in Employment Act, the Uniformed Services Employment and Reemployment Rights Act, and the Americans with Disabilities Act.

**23.5**   A social media must be written in a language and a style that is precise, exact, plain, and explicit. The policy must also be given to the employees with the understanding that they will read and comprehend the details of the policy. Moreover, employees must be told that the employer intends to monitor their e-mail accounts and their online work. The employer must also let the employees know what activities are forbidden. In addition, it would be helpful to outline what activities are acceptable when using social media in the workplace. Once the policy has been written and explained to the employees, each of them should be given two copies of the policy. The employer should reserve the right to make alterations in the policy. The employer needs to remember that even after the policy is distributed and the employees have been warned, there are limits to what an employer can do about violations of the policy.

# Key Terms

affirmative action, 509

business necessity, 509

collective bargaining agreement, 496

disability, 512

disclaimer, 499

disparate impact, 508

disparate treatment, 508

employment-at-will, 495

employment contracts, 496

Genetic Information
Nondiscrimination Act (GINA), 512

grievance procedure, 496

hostile work environment, 509

implied contract, 498

implied covenant, 500

metadata, 513

military caregiver leave, 506

qualifying exigency leave, 506

*quid pro quo* sexual
harassment, 509

reasonable accommodation, 512

reverse discrimination, 509

social media policy
(SMP), 513

undue hardship, 512

workers' compensation, 505

wrongful discharge, 497

# Questions for Review and Discussion

1. What is the doctrine of employment-at-will?
2. What contractual situations fall outside employment-at-will?
3. What statutory situations fall outside employment-at-will?
4. What are the wrongful discharge exceptions to employment-at-will?
5. What is the after-acquired evidence rule?

6. What laws regulate employee working conditions?
7. What laws provide worker benefits?
8. What are the key provisions of the Civil Rights Act?
9. What protections are provided by the Age Discrimination in Employment Act?
10. What is the nature of and the need for a social media policy?

# Cases for Analysis

1. The Equal Employment Opportunity Commission (EEOC) recently has been hit with many newly filed cases that allege discrimination based on caregiver status. The cases involve, for example, a police officer who was not promoted because she had young children at home, a man who was fired for taking time off to care for his sick father, a class action case against an employer that discriminated against workers who had applied for FMLA leave, and a case filed by a man who took leave time to take care of his elderly parents. Caregiver discrimination, which is officially known as family responsibility discrimination, or FRD, has caused some experts to suggest that the EEOC should create guidelines that are specifically aimed at defining and outlining the elements of FRD. Others argue that there really is no such thing as FRD and that each case must be treated for what it really is, that is, gender discrimination, age discrimination, disabilities discrimination, family leave discrimination, or some other form of specifically delineated discrimination. What existing statutes could be called upon to handle FRD cases, even if those

cases must go by another, more traditional name? See Tresa Baldas, "EEOC Looks at Caregiver Bias: Suits Involving Family Care Rise," *The National Law Journal*, May 21, 2007, pp. 1 and 18.

2. Eugene Meade was offered a job by Cedarapids, Inc. The job required moving to Eugene, Oregon, where Cedarapids, Inc., had a facility called the El-Jay Plant. To entice Meade to join the Cedarapids staff, management representatives told him that business was improving, that they believed in the potential of the El-Jay plant, that El-Jay sales were growing, that production at the plant was also increasing, and that there were plans to bring in an even greater numbers of new employees. On the basis of these assurances, Meade left his job and moved to Oregon. He also signed an agreement that noted that he was an at-will employee who could be fired at any time. Meade later discovered that all of the statements about the financial health of the El-Jay plant were false. Furthermore, Meade believed that the management had known all along that the statements were false. Meade learned that the El-Jay plant was actually caught in a downward economic spiral and was

about to close. When Meade was discharged, he brought a lawsuit against Cedarapids, Inc., arguing that he had been defrauded into moving to Oregon. In response, the Cedarapids management team argued that they had no duty to disclose the plan to shut down the Oregon facility. The management team also pointed to the agreement that Meade had signed and concluded that, as an at-will employee, he could not complain about his firing. The trial court agreed and dismissed the case. Meade then filed an appeal. Is there enough evidence of fraud in this case to allow it to go to a jury? Explain. *Meade v. Cedarapids, Inc.* Case No. 97-35836 (The United States Court of Appeals for the Ninth Circuit).

3. Carla McFarland was an associate professor of English literature at Highland College. She was the only single person in her department. Consequently, she was frequently assigned classes late in the evening, on weekends, and during the summer semester. She was also called upon to pick up visiting professors and serve as their escort and guide during their stays at the college. She received extra duty as adviser to the *The Highland Review,* the college's literary magazine. When McFarland complained about the unequal treatment, she was told that the married professors had family responsibilities that she did not have, which took up much of their time and prevented them from having the flexibility that she had. Thus, she would continue to carry the extra load. McFarland filed a complaint with the EEOC. Can discrimination based on an employee's status as a single person be considered unlawful under the Civil Rights Act? Explain. Is this a case of disparate impact or disparate treatment? Explain. See Wilson, Robin. "Singular Mistreatment: Unmarried Professors Are Outsiders in the Ozzie and Harriet World of Academe." *The Chronicle of Higher Education* (23 April 2004): A10–A12.

4. Henderson worked as a chemical engineer for the Wannisky Chemical Corporation. McGuire, Henderson's supervisor, ordered him to remove the labels from several hundred steel drums that had once contained a severely corrosive acid. McGuire told Henderson that they intended to reuse the drums to ship a new chemical fertilizer. Henderson refused to remove the labels, because reusing the old drums would violate both state and federal laws. When McGuire told another employee to remove the labels and reuse the drums, Henderson reported the company's activities to the state and federal authorities.

Henderson was fired for his refusal to follow orders and for notifying the authorities. In a lawsuit against Wannisky, which legal exception to the employment-at-will doctrine did Henderson use? Explain.

5. Bennerson was employed by the Checker Garage Service Corporation as an auto mechanic. His duties included both assisting mechanics in the garage and making road calls to service vehicles owned and operated by his employer. During his lunch hour, Bennerson used one of his employer's taxi cabs to drive to a restaurant. En route to the restaurant, he was seriously injured when the taxi struck a pole. Bennerson filed a claim before the workers' compensation board. His claim was granted. Checker Garage appealed, arguing among other things that the taxi that Bennerson drove did not "go out of control" but that Bennerson had lost control. Was Checker correct? Explain. *Bennerson v. Checker Garage Service Corporation,* 388 N.Y.S.2d 374 (NY).

6. Nancy Barillaro and Nancy Fotia were employed in the inspection and trimming departments of Elwood Knitting Mills for approximately 16 years. Barillaro was laid off in September and Fotia in November. Both were offered the option of returning to work in March of the following year as knitting machine operators, but at an 18 percent reduction in pay. Neither accepted the offer. They argued that the offered work would have involved a loss in seniority and a substantial reduction in pay. In addition, Fotia claimed that she was not familiar with the operation of the machine. Barillaro claimed that she was too short to operate the machine. The Pennsylvania Unemployment Compensation Board decided that neither claimant was eligible to receive benefits because they refused offers of suitable work without good cause. Was the board correct in its ruling? Explain. *Barillaro v. Unemployment Compensation Bd. Of Review,* 387 A.2d 1324 (PA).

7. The Wynn Oil Company, which conducted an enormous amount of business with Latin American companies, argued that being male was a bona fide occupational qualification (BFOQ) for the position of sales executive. Wynn contended that because of certain Latin American customs, the hiring of a female sales executive would have a serious detrimental effect on the company's business. The contention was challenged in federal court. Will Wynn's argument succeed? Explain. *Fernandez v. Wynn Oil Co.,* 653 F.2d 1273 (9th Cir.).

8. The Spelling Entertainment Group hired actress Hunter Tylo to appear in the television show *Melrose Place*. Her role was to involve the seduction of another character's husband. When Tylo became pregnant, she dutifully reported her condition to Spelling. The entertainment company then discharged her, arguing that non-pregnancy was a bona fide occupational qualification (BFOQ) for the role designed for Tylo. Tylo challenged the contention that her condition disqualified her from performing her job. Can non-pregnancy be a BFOQ? Explain. *Tylo v. Superior Court*, 55 Cal. App. 4th 1379 (CA).

9. Rice, an African American woman, was denied employment as a public health representative by the city of St. Louis for lack of a college degree. Failing to obtain relief after filing a complaint with the EEOC charging racial discrimination, she filed a lawsuit in the federal district court. Rice took the position that the degree requirement had a disparate impact on African Americans and was invalid under the Civil Rights Act of 1964. She pointed out that blacks were only approximately 55 percent as likely as whites in the St. Louis area to have a college degree. Testimony showed that the satisfactory performance of public health representatives required the ability to communicate with others, frequently in emotional situations, and the ability to speak and write intelligibly. There was also a risk to the public health and safety in the employment of unqualified applicants. Did Rice prevail? Explain. *Rice v. The City of St. Louis*, 607 F.2d 791 (8th Cir).

10. The Commonwealth of Virginia required all applicants for state troopers to be between 21 and 29 years of age, at least 5 feet, 9 inches tall, and at least 156 pounds. The height and weight requirements eliminated 98 percent of the female applicants. The basic employment requirements also made it mandatory that all applicants, including applicants for civilian dispatcher positions, complete and pass written mental ability tests. The tests for dispatcher positions were not valid predictors of job performance. The tests for the trooper positions also were shown not to be predictors of job performance. The United States brought suit, charging that Virginia engaged in a pattern and practice of discrimination against African American applicants for the civilian positions and against both African American and women candidates for the trooper positions. Did the United States prevail? Explain. *United States v. Commonwealth of Virginia*, 620 F.2d 1018 (4th Cir).

11. Shirley Painter was the Chief Deputy Clerk in the Bookkeeping Department of the Civil Division of the Municipal Court of the City of Cleveland. She decided to run for city council and asked for a leave of absence to pursue that goal. At first she was granted the leave. However, two months later, she was terminated. Painter brought a wrongful discharge lawsuit against Charles Graley, the assistant personnel director in the municipal court clerk's office. Painter asked to be reinstated. She also asked for back pay and punitive damages. Her wrongful discharge suit was based on a violation of public policy. She argued that she had appropriate grounds for the suit because her termination violated the state constitution. Graley argued that a plaintiff can bring a wrongful discharge lawsuit based on public policy only if a statute exists that prohibits the firing in question. Has Painter stated sufficient legal grounds for her wrongful discharge lawsuit? Explain. *Painter v. Graley*, 639 N.E.2d 51 (OH).

## quick quiz Answers

| 23-1 | 23-2 | 23-3 | 23-4 | 23-5 |
|------|------|------|------|------|
| 1. F | 1. F | 1. F | 1. T | 1. T |
| 2. F | 2. F | 2. F | 2. F | 2. T |
| 3. F | 3. F | 3. F | 3. F | 3. T |

# Chapter 24 Labor Law

## THE OPENING CASE  Government Regulation or Creative Destruction: *Keynes v. The Austrians*

The two dominant schools of economic thought in academia today are the Keynesians and the Austrians. Predictably, the two schools agree on almost nothing and so there is a clear dialectic split between the two groups, a split which inevitably affects labor, labor law, and the labor union concept. The two schools of thought do agree on one premise, however, and that is a belief that capitalism is unstable. Unfortunately, they disagree on what to do about that instability.

At the risk of oversimplifying things (always a danger when speaking of economics) we can say that the Keynesians push for governmental intervention into the economy in order to protect the workers, to control debt, to provide support for industry, and to control the money supply. The basic idea is that the best way to control an inherently unstable economy is to intervene in a rational way. On the other side, the Austrian School, notably Friedrich Hayek and Joseph Schumpeter, argue that government intervention does more harm than good because it permits weak financial firms to survive, thus postponing, but not eliminating, an economic crisis, a crisis that, as strange as it may seem, is necessary for the economy to correct itself. To the Austrians the best route is to avoid interfering with what Schumpeter called the "creative destruction" of the capitalist system. To reiterate, the Keynesians see

instability as a harmful trend born of human emotion and badly in need of rational governmental correction; while the Austrians see it as the natural movement of events that must remain untouched by the government.

Labor, unfortunately falls in the middle of this mess and, at times, is victimized by both sides. The Austrians would suspend or eliminate labor unions so that the unprofitable companies will collapse to be replaced by profitable companies that rehire the unemployed workers of the collapsed firms. The Keynesians, in contrast, see unions as a necessary governmental control device, granting workers the power to determine their own wages and benefits, and thus permitting the government, in the form of the National Labor Relations Board, the Courts, and Congress, to lawfully interfere in the operation of that business.

Is there a balancing principle hidden somewhere in this conflict or is the Keynesian-Austrian dialectic unresolvable? Which side seems to have the correct approach? Would you rather see the government step in or step out of the economy? As you read this chapter on labor law, try to see the problem from both perspectives, that of the employee (easy enough for most of us) and from that of the employer. [See Nouriel Roubini and Stephen Mihm, *Crisis Economics* (New York: Penguin Books, 2010), 47–59.]

**Opening Case Questions**

1. Both the Keynesians and the Austrians believe that capitalism is inherently unstable. Do you agree or disagree with is joint premise? Explain.

2. Would you rather see the government step in or step out of the economy? Explain.

3. Do you support or oppose the establishment of labor unions in private business? Explain.

4. Do you support the establishment of labor unions in governmental agencies, such as police departments, fire departments, colleges, and schools? Why or why not?

5. Do you support the selective use of labor unions to bargain for working conditions but not money-related issues such as wages and benefits? Why or why not?

## LO  Learning Objectives

1. Relate the historical context in which unions developed.
2. Outline the congressional–judicial tug-of-war in union history.
3. Identify the major provision of the Norris-LaGuardia Act.
4. List the basic aims of labor unions.
5. Explain the nature of the 21st century crisis in labor law.
6. Indicate the primary tenets of the Wagner Act.
7. List the functions of the Taft-Hartley Act.
8. Explain the provisions of the Landrum-Griffin Act.
9. Describe the jurisdiction of the National Labor Relations Board.
10. Identify the possible results of a complaint filed with the NLRB.

# 24-1 Labor Law and the Economic Crisis

A **labor union** is an organization that acts on behalf of all employees in negotiations with the employer regarding the terms of their employment. It is a lawful assembly that is protected by the First Amendment to the United States Constitution and by federal and state statutes. Americans have always had a love–hate affair with unions. On the one hand, they recognize that the marketplace should be allowed to fluctuate without undue interference from the government. As noted in the Opening Case at the beginning of this chapter, this position is not unlike the economic theories of the Austrian school which believes that the government should be prohibited from getting involved in the internal affairs of any business. On the other hand, the American people, for the most part, acknowledge that businesses, when left unregulated, often take advantage of that freedom and exploit the labor market. Like Keynesian economists, many people recognize that, at times, the government must provide a rational plan for dealing with economic strife, even when that plan includes protecting unions. Still, most Americans also believe that business owners should be free to hire the people they want, when they want, and to pay those people what the market will bear. Yet, most also recognize that employers hold a great deal of power in the labor market and are, therefore, grateful when Congress creates a more level playing field by passing supportive union legislation. This seesaw-like relationship is evident in the historical development of the union movement in the United States and it provides a further example of the law as a balancing act.

John L. Lewis (left), founder of the Congress of Industrial Workers (CIO), and Samuel Gompers (right), founder of the American Federation of Labor (AFL), combined to form the AFL-CIO in 1955. Labor unions continue to shape the way companies operate.

## An Economic Tug-of-War

The history of union development in the United States provides us with a vivid example of the give and take between two economic theories: (1) the Keynesian strategy that approves of governmental control; and (2) the Austrian school that supports a *laissez-fair* approach to the economy. In this case, the legislature and the courts, were at odds for a long period of time and thus played off one another in a complicated tug-of-war as they attempted to reestablish a balance within the law. Although this legal tug-of-war really had no definitive beginning, for convenience, we can identify the passage of the Sherman Antitrust Act in 1890 as a logical starting point. This statute was designed to break up the great anticompetitive trusts of the 19th century. As such, the passage of the Sherman Antitrust Act was an Austrian-like tactic designed to encourage competition in the capitalist economy. Ironically, in fashioning the Sherman Act to promote Austrian-like competition, Congress used its power to interfere in the economic sector, a very Keynesian-like tactic. The Courts responded by issuing injunctions that permitted the corporations to use the Sherman Act to break up unions, another Keynesian tactic that, strangely, promoted Austrian principles (See The Opening Case *Revisited, Part I*).

**The Clayton Act of 1914**  Congress reacted to this example of judicial activism by passing the Clayton Act in 1914, another Keynesian-like tactic that forced companies to cooperate with union organizers and thus helped keep people employed. One of the goals of the Clayton Act was to hamper the federal courts' ability to issue injunctions to stop union activities. This would force businesses to recognize the role of unions as a way for employees to protect their rights. The federal judicial system, however, again reflecting an Austrian-like desire to pull the government out of the economic sector, effectively destroyed the Clayton Act when the Supreme Court created two criteria that allowed the courts to issue injunctions freely to stop labor activities. The first test was *the objectives test*. Under this test, a court could issue an injunction if it determined that the goal of a strike was unlawful. Under the second test, *the means test,* the courts could stop a strike if

---

## THE OPENING CASE *Revisited, Part I*
### Government Regulation or Creative Destruction:
### *Keynes v. The Austrians*, Round 2

Although the move by Congress in passing the Sherman Antitrust Act in 1890 took place some 46 years before Keynes wrote his groundbreaking book, *The General Theory of Employment, Interest, and Money,* the Sherman Act represents the use of the government to control the activities of business. Nevertheless, the action in its purest form is Austrian because the entire goal of the act was to promote Austrian-like competition. This internal contradiction may explain why the act backfired so badly. In what amounted to a brilliant counter move by big business, a few savvy corporate attorneys recognized this essential inconsistency within the act. Using this flaw, they argued that any union that organized a strike was engaged in an antitrust action that damaged a company's ability to compete with rival companies. As such, it was an illegal restraint of trade under the Sherman Act and had to be prevented by the courts. By creating an antitrust law, Congress had effectively shut down union activity, something the members of Congress had never intended to do. The courts, following an Austrian school approach, agreed with the corporate attorneys and willingly issued injunctions, even when a union simply threatened to strike against a company as a bargaining tactic. Yet, even in this action we see an internal contradiction. The courts (read "the government" here) used their power in a Keynesian way to promote Austrian-like competition (or so they said).

it was conducted in an unlawful manner. The two tests were easily manipulated by big business and the courts cooperated by routinely issuing injunctions in ways that had not been foreseen nor intended by Congress. Once again a pro-Keynesian strategy (court issued injunctions) had been used to reestablish an Austrian-like economy (a union-free, strike-free economic system).

### The Norris-LaGuardia Act of 1932

Not to be outdone, Congress reacted to this subterfuge by passing another pro-Keynesian law, the Norris-LaGuardia Act, in 1932, the net effect of which was to prohibit the federal courts from issuing injunctions against union-organized strikes, thus forcing companies to do what Congress had wanted all along, to cooperate with union organizers and thus keep people working. The law also supported union activities by forbidding the courts from using injunctions to stop picketing or boycotts organized by unions again forcing businesses to cooperate with union organizers.

## The Goals of Labor Organization

The Norris-LaGuardia Act was just one step down a long road of labor law development. Later labor laws both promoted the aims of labor unions while also preventing unions from becoming too powerful, thus perpetuating the Keynesian-Austrian balance (some might say tug-of-war). Many different types of unions have developed over the years since the advent of the Norris-LaGuardia Act. Whatever their form, however, labor unions have several objectives in common. These Keynesian-like goals include (1) creating a seniority system to protect workers' jobs from arbitrary layoffs and replacement with less demanding wage earners; (2) upgrading worker status through wage and fringe benefit increases; and (3) sponsoring laws that improve social, economic, and political conditions for worker.

## The 21st Century Labor Crisis

Over the last few years, the battle over unions has started once again. Stymied by the recent economic meltdown caused by subprime loans, falling real estate prices, and uncontrolled debt, state governments have elected to use an odd hybrid of Keynesian-Austrian tactics on

**THE OPENING CASE** *Revisited, Part II*
Government Regulation or Creative Destruction:
*Keynes v. The Austrians*, Round 3

This contradiction aside, we have to wonder just which economic theory is being pursued by the states. Are they promoting a Keynesian approach or an Austrian-school strategy here? Keynesian economics demands state intervention. Clearly we have the state intervening in the economy and so the strategy appears to be quite Keynesian. Yet, the antiunion laws are not directly interfering in the capitalist sector but in the political sector, and so the government is, in essence, regulating its own pocketbook. The net effect, however, does not stop there. The government's antiunion campaign clearly involves the private sector. By pulling money out of the pockets of employees, the government stifles the buying power of a large segment of the population, which has an impact on retail sales, investments, and other areas in which disposable income is used. Still, by eliminating collective bargaining, the state is also promoting competition by increasing the state's purchasing power. Thus, the state, by paying less into employee pension plans, health care benefits, and annual pay increases has more money to invest in state corporations, thus stimulating private competition, a clear promotion of Austrian principles—or is it? Perhaps the bottom line here is that the states in

*(continued)*

this crisis are applying both systems and neither system. They have, in effect, created a synthesis, a sort of Keynesian-Austrian hybrid, that regulates the economy when appropriate and stays out when intervention would be ineffective. On the other hand, it may be more correct to say that any interference, even ineffective interference, is Keynesian. After all, the Austrian school, or at least the Schumpeter wing of that school, believes in *creative destruction,* the idea that the economy must be allowed to regulate itself completely even when that means that many corporations and even

state governments crash and burn so that out of the ashes can arise a stronger and more effective economy. Of course, all of this theoretical analysis may be giving the state politicians a bit too much credit. Perhaps they have not even considered any of this and are, instead, simply trying to get reelected by hitting a few easy targets (teachers, firefighters, and police officers), so that they can continue to take their own chunk of state tax money. After all, none of the governors or state legislators in these fiscally strapped states work for free. Or do they?

themselves. In a strangely schizophrenic pattern of activity, the state governments have decided that labor unions that represent state workers must be eliminated. In essence, the governors and the state legislatures of several midwestern states, notably Wisconsin, Ohio, and Michigan, created and passed legislation that was deliberately and unapologetically designed to eliminate the collective bargaining power of those unions that represent state workers (see Table 24-1). In theory, this plan would save the state governments a great deal of money, money that will not be paid in raises, health care benefits, and pension contributions. Of course, this would also mean fewer dollars in the pockets of almost 360,000 workers in Ohio alone which, of course, decreases the buying power of state citizens, citizens who will no longer be spending quite as much money in stores, restaurants, hotels, and shops in their home states. (See The Opening Case *Revisited, Part II.*) (Note: Ohio voters rejected the antiunion law by a 61-39% margin in November 2011.)

### Table 24-1    Provisions of Ohio's Antiunion Law (2011)

| Provision | Explanation |
| --- | --- |
| Health Insurance | Employers cannot pay more than 80% into the cost of employee health insurance benefits. |
| Pension Plans | Stops public employers from paying employee contributions to state retirement systems. |
| Merit Pay | Mandates merit pay; takes step increases and all other automatic pay increases off the negotiating table. |
| Strikes and Mediation | Eliminates public employees' right to strike and to submit disputes to any agreed upon dispute resolution procedure. |
| Collective Bargaining I | Eliminates the collective bargaining rights of K-12 teachers in relation to class size, workload, and workforce size. |
| Collective Bargaining II | Eliminates collective bargaining completely for college and university faculty members. |
| Fiscal Emergencies | Municipalities, counties, school districts in fiscal emergency status can ignore past collective bargaining agreements. Also occurs if the state itself is in a fiscal emergency. |

*Sources:* Nick Thomas, "Sub. S.B. 5 of the 129th G.A.," *Fiscal Note and Impact Statement: State and Local Fiscal Highlights, Ohio Legislative Service Commission* (Feb. 2011); and Amanda Garrett, "Ohio's Senate Bill 5 Could End Collective Bargaining for Many Public College Professors," *Cleveland.com* (March 2011). See also Bill Analysis, Legislative Service Commission, Sub. S.B. 5, http://www.legislature.state.oh.us.)

### quick quiz 24-1

1. A labor union is an organization that acts on behalf of all employees in negotiations with the employer regarding the terms of their employment.  true | false

2. Labor union activity is not protected by the First Amendment.  true | false

3. One of the first successful union organizing efforts took place in 1886, when Samuel Gompers organized the Congress of Industrial Workers.  true | false

# 24-2 Major Federal Labor Legislation

After the Norris-LaGuardia Act was passed by Congress in 1932, several tough labor laws were enacted. The three most important legislative enactments are the National Labor Relations Act of 1935 (generally referred to as the Wagner Act); the Labor-Management Relations Act of 1947 (popularly referred to as the Taft-Hartley Act); and the Labor Management Reporting and Disclosure Act of 1959 (often simply called the Landrum-Griffin Act). The first of these was designed to support labor's attempt to organize. The last two were designed to curb some unanticipated problems that accompanied the growth of unions in the United States. (See Table 24-2.)

## The Wagner Act

The passage of the National Labor Relations Act in 1935 (commonly known as the Wagner Act) opened the door for the rapid growth of the union movement. It is probably the most significant labor relations statute, in that it expressly sets forth the unfair labor practices prohibited for both employers and unions.

**LO6**

The Wagner Act gives workers the right to organize by allowing them to form, join, or aid labor unions. It also establishes procedures for representative elections and collective bargaining. After a union has been chosen to represent the employees of a business, only that union can bargain with management. After the union has been set up at a business, individual workers cannot, on their own initiative, negotiate with management. The union has the exclusive right to bargain with the management of the business, even if the employees do not agree with how the union is handling a matter. The Wagner Act is also known for its creation of the National Labor Relations Board (NLRB), which hears and rules on charges that unfair labor practices have been committed by employers or by unions.

Various activities are prohibited by the Wagner Act as **unfair labor practices**, that is, improper employment practices by either an employer or union. These activities include the following:

- Interference with employees' right to organize.
- Domination or interference with the formation or administration of any union.
- Discrimination to encourage or discourage union membership.
- Discharge for charges filed or testimony given.
- Refusal to bargain collectively.

**Table 24-2** Federal Laws Governing Labor-Management Relations

| Year | Law | Major Provisions |
|------|-----|------------------|
| 1914 | Clayton Act | Exempted union activity from the antitrust laws |
| 1926 | Railway Labor Act | Provided for supervision of collective bargaining for railroads and airlines<br>Established the National Mediation Board to conduct union elections and mediate employer-union disputes |
| 1932 | Norris-LaGuardia Act | Outlawed yellow-dog contracts<br>Limited the power of federal courts to issue injunctions to halt labor disputes<br>Guaranteed employees the right to organize into unions and to engage in collective bargaining |
| 1935 | Wagner Act | Created the National Labor Relations Board (NLRB)<br>Authorized NLRB to conduct representative elections and to determine the bargaining unit<br>Outlawed certain conduct by employers as unfair labor practices<br>Authorized NLRB to hold hearings on unfair labor practice petitions |
| 1947 | Taft-Hartley Act | Outlawed certain practices by unions as unfair labor practices<br>Allowed states to legislate right-to-work laws<br>Provided an 80-day cooling-off period in strikes that endangered national health or safety<br>Created a mediation and conciliation service to assist in the settlement of labor disputes |
| 1959 | Landrum-Griffin Act | Established a bill of rights for union members<br>Required unions to adopt constitutions and bylaws<br>Required unions to submit annual reports detailing assets, liabilities, payments, and loans<br>Added further provisions to the list of unfair labor practices |

## Self-Evident Truths

No two intellectuals appear to be further apart than Adam Smith, the spiritual founder of capitalism, and Karl Marx, the principal architect of communism. Yet if we read the following two excerpts from their most influential treatises, they appear to be in agreement on at least one point: the propensity of workers to unite in a common cause and eventually become violent as a result.

> Such combinations, however, are frequently resisted by a contrary defensive combination of the workmen; who sometimes too, without any provocation of this kind, combine of their own accord to raise the price of their labour. Their usual pretences are, sometimes the high price of provisions; sometimes the great profit which their masters make by their work. But whether their combinations be offensive or defensive, they are always abundantly heard of. In order to bring the point to a speedy decision, they have always recourse to the loudest clamour, and sometimes to the most shocking violence and outrage.
>
> —Adam Smith, *Wealth of Nations,* p. 71.

> The unceasing improvement of machinery, ever more rapidly developing, makes their livelihood more and more precarious. The collisions between individual workmen and individual bourgeois take more

and more the character of collisions between two classes. Thereupon the workers begin to form combinations (trade unions) against the bourgeois; they join together in order to keep up the rate of wages; they form permanent associations in order to make provision beforehand for these occasional revolts. Here and there the contest breaks out into riots.

—Karl Marx and Frederick Engels, *Essential Works of Marxism,* p. 21.

It is curious that both of them believe that workers will eventually revolt against their capitalist bosses. This may result from the theories of an earlier philosopher, Thomas Hobbes, who believed that human nature was inherently depraved and that, when placed in a state of nature, the instinctive tendency of human beings is to engage in war. This view, of course, runs counter to the view of Jean Jacques Rousseau, who believed that humans in state of nature were fundamentally good.

## Self-Evident Questions

1. Looking back from a historical perspective, were Marx and Smith correct in their predictions that unionization leads to violence? Is such violence ever justifiable from a moral perspective? Why or why not?

2. If these two philosophers are convinced that unionization leads to violence, at what point do you suppose they part company? Explain.

3. Do the words of Smith and Marx seem to call for a Keynesian or an Austrian interpretation of violence? Explain.

4. Which of the two theories about human nature, that of Hobbes or that of Rousseau, do you believe? Explain.

5. Do the activities of the governments of Wisconsin, Ohio, and Michigan reflect Hobbes or Rousseau? Smith or Marx? Explain. What about the public employees in each state? Do their activities reflect Hobbes or Rousseau? Smith or Marx? Explain.

*See* Karl Marx and Frederick Engels, "The Communist Manifesto," in *Essential Works of Marxism,* Arthur P. Mendel, ed. (New York: Bantam Books, 1961); and Adam Smith, *An Inquiry into the Nature and Causes of The Wealth of Nations* (Amherst, NY: Prometheus Books, 1991).

**Interference with Employees' Right to Organize** An employer cannot interfere with employees when they are forming a union, selecting their representatives, voting, striking, picketing, or engaging in any other protected and legal acts. For example, an employer cannot threaten to fire or discipline a worker for union activity or reward workers who do not participate in union activities. Threats to eliminate certain benefits or privileges, to close down the business, or to discharge workers for union activity also are prohibited.

## EXAMPLE 24-1: Insubordination or Inconsistency: Which One Trumps the Other?

In his 10 years as a chef at the Imperial National Hotel in Houston, James Kirby might have been fired several times for violating work rules. He frequently refused to follow orders, disobeying direct instructions from his supervisor. When a union began organizing the kitchen service and housekeeping staff, Kirby strongly supported the effort. During the organizing campaign, Kirby apparently acted in an insubordinate manner and was discharged. At a subsequent NLRB hearing, his discharge was found to be tainted. On appeal, the court reasoned that, though Kirby was far from the valued and trusted employee the union claimed he was, the hotel had tolerated his insubordination for 10 years. The court held that Kirby's discharge was more the result of his union activities than his work performance and reinstated him with back pay.

### Domination or Interference with the Formation or Administration of Any Union

An employer cannot form a company-run union for its employees. The purpose of this prohibition is to bar company-owned unions from bowing to the wishes of management. It is also an unfair practice to aid one union over another, place employer spies at union meetings, reward some union officials, or agree with a union that a closed shop will be maintained. A closed shop is a work site in which the employer, by agreement, hires only union members in good standing. It is usually lawful, however, to have a provision allowing a union shop in the employment contract. A union shop is a place of employment in which nonunion workers may be employed for a trial period of not more than 30 days, after which the nonunion workers must join the union or be discharged.

### Discrimination to Encourage or Discourage Union Membership

Intentional discrimination by the employer toward an employee to encourage or discourage union membership is an unfair labor practice. Such discrimination may involve assigning an employee to less desirable work or denying an employee the opportunity to participate in overtime work. Also viewed as discriminatory is constructive discharge, which occurs when an employee is demoted to a job with lesser pay or authority or poorer working conditions than a previously held job or when the employee is subjected to supervisory harassment. To avoid employee complaints of intentional discrimination, employers must rely on meaningful business reasons when bestowing or denying employment opportunities.

### EXAMPLE 24-2: Constructive Discharge: Nothing Trivial About It

Teresa Remington was chosen by union members to serve as their representative in collective bargaining meetings with the Harrisburg Construction Company. After her selection, Remington was harassed by the general manager of her department for trivial matters pertaining to scheduled lunch breaks and the cleanliness of her locker in the break room. Remington has the right to file a complaint with the NLRB, charging constructive discharge due to her union activities.

### Discharge for Charges Filed or Testimony Given

It is unlawful for employers to discharge or otherwise discriminate against employees because they file charges or give testimony under the Wagner Act. The courts interpret discrimination under this provision to include discharge, layoff, failure to rehire or recall, and transfer of covered employees.

### Refusal to Bargain Collectively

An employer must negotiate with employee representatives over wages, hours, the effects of business changes on employees, grievance procedures, health benefits, seniority systems, dues checkoffs, and vacations. Issues must be discussed willingly, free of delaying tactics, coercion, or harassment by both sides. The employer has no duty to agree to any union demands but must meet with employee representatives at reasonable times and places to bargain in good faith. Neither party can bargain about a closed shop contract, politics, religious issues, management functions, or foreign affairs. The NLRB has no jurisdiction over religious schools, both on labor relations grounds and by virtue of the religion clauses of the First Amendment of the U.S. Constitution. The U.S. Supreme Court has ruled that the requirements of collective bargaining would represent an encroachment upon the freedom of church authorities to shape and direct teaching in accordance with the requirements of their religion. Finally, it is important to recall that the Wagner Act does not apply to most federal employees. Nor does it apply to state government or local government employees. This is why it is possible, even easy, for the state governments in Wisconsin, Ohio, and Michigan to alter and/or eliminate the collective bargaining rights of firefighters, police officers, and teachers.

## The Taft-Hartley Act

The Labor-Management Relations Act of 1947, popularly named the Taft-Hartley Act, established a means to protect employers in collective bargaining and labor organization matters. The act also prohibits union officials from using coercive or abusive tactics against its own members. A detailed list of unfair labor activities that unions, as well as employers, were forbidden to practice was added to those of the Wagner Act.

### State Right-to-Work Laws
State laws that prohibit labor–management agreements requiring union membership as a condition of getting or keeping a job are called **right-to-work laws**. These laws, in effect, outlaw both the closed shop and the union shop. Ordinarily, state labor laws have not applied to unions and businesses that are involved in interstate commerce and that are governed by federal labor laws. In fact, as noted earlier in the chapter, state labor laws generally focus only on those employees whose union activities are not regulated by federal labor law, such as state government workers. Nevertheless, the Taft-Hartley Act has created special rules with regard to state right-to-work laws. It provides that union shop contracts are legal only in states that do not forbid them. As a result, state right-to-work laws, where they exist, are applicable to most unions and businesses (see Table 24-3). All employees in the bargaining unit (i.e., a unit formed for the purpose of collective bargaining) are benefited by the collective bargaining agreement negotiated by the union, even if they have not paid union dues. However, nonunion employees lose all right to vote on union officers or collective bargaining agreements.

### Limiting the Power of the NLRB
Some members of Congress recently proposed limiting the power of the National Labor Relations Board to pressure an employer into keeping his or her business located in a particular state. Recall that some states have passed right-to-work laws that allow employees to opt out of union membership when a union is formed or presently operates in their workplace. This feature makes such states attractive to businesses that would rather keep union membership in their business to a minimum. Some businesses have gone so far as to decide to move a plant or office from a non-right-to-work state into a state with a right-to-work law. In one case, the National Labor Relations Board issued an order that would have prevented a business from setting up a new facility in a right-to-work state. This order by the NLRB prompted some members of Congress to mount a campaign to amend the Wagner Act to limit the power of the board to frame such orders. Like the actions by the governors and the state legislatures in Wisconsin, Ohio, and Michigan, a proposal like this one in Congress, further demonstrates the antiunion sentiment that has been growing within the government in the 21st century.

## Table 24-3    Right-To-Work States

**The following states have enacted right-to-work statutes**

| | |
|---|---|
| 1. Alabama | 12. Nevada |
| 2. Arkansas | 13. North Carolina |
| 3. Arizona | 14. North Dakota |
| 4. Florida | 15. Oklahoma |
| 5. Georgia | 16. South Carolina |
| 6. Idaho | 17. South Dakota |
| 7. Iowa | 18. Tennessee |
| 8. Kansas | 19. Texas |
| 9. Louisiana | 20. Utah |
| 10. Mississippi | 21. Virginia |
| 11. Nebraska | 22. Wyoming |

*Sources:* National Right to Work Committee; and Sean Higgins, "Congress May Bar NLRB from Grounding Boeing," *Investor's Business Daily,* May 10, 2011, p. 1.

**Free Speech Provision** The Taft-Hartley Act includes a free speech provision that allows employers to comment freely on union organizing activities. The provision states that employers do not commit an unfair labor practice by speaking to employees about unions unless they threaten reprisal or promise some benefit to employees. For instance, an employer might properly inform its employees that they should not vote for a union, but a threat to fire anyone for favoring a union shop would be an unfair labor practice.

**Employee Anti-Coercion Provision** It is also an unfair labor practice for a labor union to try to coerce employees to join the union, block the employment of individuals who refuse to support a union, or encourage an employee to withdraw an unfair labor practice charge. A union can set rules for its internal operations and punish any member who refuses to follow them, but it cannot use force, violence, or intimidation against an employee. A union is also not permitted to discipline one of its members without good cause. The union has a duty to represent all of its members on an equal basis.

**Secondary Boycott** It is also prohibited for a union to engage in a **secondary boycott**. This action is a conspiracy in which a union places pressure on a neutral customer or supplier with whom the union has no dispute to cause the neutral entity to cease doing business with the employer with whom the union has a dispute. Under the Taft-Hartley Act provision, it is an unfair labor practice for a union (1) to strike against an employer because another employer uses nonunion employees, (2) to strike against a general contractor to force the contractor to stop dealing with a subcontractor, (3) to ask employees of another company not to load trucks carrying the products of a company the union is striking, or (4) to refuse to work on products made by nonunion employees.

EXAMPLE **24-3:** Secondary Boycotts: Of Primary Concern

The Benning Oil Company sold fuel oil to the Monarchy Empire Hotel chain. The oil was shipped on tankers owned by the Metroliner Transport Corporation, whose employees were nonunion. The union representing Benning instructed its members to refuse to ship the fuel oil to the docks where the Metroliner tankers were docked to force Benning to stop using a nonunion shipper. This form of secondary boycott is an unfair labor practice, because it involved an innocent employer in a union tactic intended to harm another employer.

**National Emergency Strikes**  The Taft-Hartley Act gives the president of the United States special powers to deal with actual or threatened strikes that affect interstate commerce or that endanger the nation's health and safety. On the basis of a board of inquiry's findings, the president can order the attorney general to petition a federal district court to issue an injunction, stopping the strike for 60 days. The board of inquiry may then require the union members to vote on the most recent offer within an additional 15-day period and to send the results to the attorney general within 5 days after balloting. When the injunction ends after this 80-day period, the employees may strike. However, the president can then make legislative recommendations to Congress that would resolve the dispute.

**Other Prohibited Union Practices**  Under other provisions of the Taft-Hartley Act, unions cannot refuse to bargain collectively with an employer and must give notice to the employer of an intention to strike prior to the termination date of a collective bargaining contract. It is also an unfair labor practice for a labor union to require an employer to keep unneeded employees, pay employees for not working, or assign more employees to a given job than are needed (i.e., **featherbedding**). Another provision of the law prohibits a union from requiring employees who join a union to pay excessively high dues, fees, and related expenses. To determine what is excessive, the courts consider the amounts other unions charge and the employee's wages.

## The Landrum-Griffin Act

The Labor Management Reporting and Disclosure Act of 1959, known as the Landrum-Griffin Act, is a tough anticorruption law. It is designed to clean up the corruption and violence that had been uncovered in the internal affairs of unions. The law requires all unions to adopt constitutions and bylaws and to register them with the secretary of labor. In addition, unions are required to submit annual reports detailing assets, liabilities, receipts, sources, payments to union members exceeding $10,000, loans to union members and businesses, and other monies paid out.

**Bill of Rights Provision**  An important part of the Landrum-Griffin Act is the bill of rights provision for union members. This provision assures all union members of the opportunity to participate in the internal affairs of their union. They are guaranteed the right to vote in union elections, to speak at union meetings, and to receive union financial reports.

**Hot-Cargo Agreement**  The Landrum-Griffin Act amended the Taft-Hartley Act, making it an unlawful labor practice to become involved in a **hot-cargo contract**. In this type of agreement, an employer voluntarily agrees with a union not to handle, use, or deal in nonunion-produced goods of another employer.

# 24-3 The Collective Bargaining Process

The Taft-Hartley Act established a system for helping labor and management settle their disputes without causing a major disruption in the economy or endangering the public health and safety. Central to this collective bargaining process is the NLRB and the procedures it follows in settling labor–management disputes.

## The National Labor Relations Board

The NLRB is a governmental commission that has the exclusive jurisdiction to enforce the Taft-Hartley Act and related laws. It has the power to act when cases are brought before it, but only in cases in which the employer's operation or the labor dispute affects commerce. Like most government regulatory agencies, the NLRB has investigative, regulatory, administrative, enforcement, and judgmental powers. It can make its own rules of procedure, conduct investigations into unfair labor practice charges, compel individuals to appear with papers relevant to the controversy, hold hearings, and issue orders. Appeals from the five-member board go first to the appropriate U.S. Court of Appeals and then to the U.S. Supreme Court.

## Unfair Labor Practice Procedure

A person, union, or employer can file notice with the NLRB of an alleged unfair labor practice within six months after it occurs. It is important to remember that unfair labor practices include not only those practices that occur between management and the labor union but also those between a union and its own members. This point is a crucial part of the union representation process, because once a collective bargaining unit is formed, the employees have only one recourse when they have a grievance, and that is through the union. Consequently, the law imposes an affirmative duty on the unions to be fair in their representation of all members. This rule does not mean that the union cannot monitor its own internal affairs, nor does it mean that unions must represent those outside of the bargaining unit. However, once a worker becomes a member of a union, he or she has the right to expect fair and equal treatment, and the union has the duty to deliver such treatment or be liable for not doing so.

If the charge has merit, a complaint is issued to notify the offending party that a hearing is to be held concerning the charges. Efforts are made through arbitration to resolve the dispute before the hearing date. **Arbitration** involves the submission of the dispute to selected persons and the substitution of their decision for the judgment of the NLRB. If arbitration efforts fail, the hearing is held. In the event that the complaint is found to be valid, a cease-and-desist order may be issued, restoring the parties to the state that existed before the unfair practice began. For example, wrongfully discharged employees may be reinstated with or without back pay. Evidence at the hearing that does not support the complaint is dismissed. Either party to the hearing may subsequently appeal the NLRB action to the appropriate U.S. Court of Appeals and then to the Supreme Court.

**Mediation**   The Taft-Hartley Act encourages labor and management to agree freely on the settlement of disputes. To further this effort to preserve labor peace and promote prompt settlements, Congress has formed the Federal Mediation and Conciliation Service. This body can act by itself or upon the request of either side to a labor dispute. Its mediation role is to offer nonbinding suggestions for settling the dispute, require the parties to negotiate, and force a vote by employees on an employer's offers.

Strikes, like the 2010 nurses' strike in Minnesota, can cause major inconvenience and hardship for the general public. Unions often count on public pressure to get favorable concessions from management.

## The Right to Strike in the Public Sector

In the public sector, when the general welfare, safety, health, and morals of the public are involved, the right to strike is restricted. Consequently, strikes by police, firefighters, refuse collectors, air traffic controllers, postal workers, and other public employees who perform vital services are generally illegal, unless specifically authorized by statute. The U.S. Code states that "an individual may not accept or hold a position in the government of the United States or the government of the District of Columbia if he participates in a strike or asserts the right to strike against the government." The U.S. Supreme Court has affirmed lower court rulings that there is no constitutional right to strike against the federal government. Thus, strikes by federal employees are substantially more than merely unfair labor practices; they are crimes.

---

**EXAMPLE 24-4:**  Air Traffic Controllers: To Strike or Not To Strike

The air traffic controllers, employees of the Federal Aviation Administration, went on strike. The controller's union, the Professional Air Traffic Controllers Organization, demanded that the controllers be removed from the civil service designation that prohibited them from striking. They argued that prohibition of the right to strike was a violation of a fundamental civil liberty. A federal district court ruled that government employees did not have the right to strike because Congress had not given them such a right. The controllers persisted in their strike. As a result, all striking controllers were fired, and the union was fined $100,000 an hour for the duration of the strike. The union was subsequently decertified, removing its rights to bargain on behalf of the controllers.

---

## A QUESTION OF ETHICS

The air traffic controllers in Example 24-4 simply wanted rights that are guaranteed to many similarly situated workers. They argued that prohibition of the right to strike was a violation of a fundamental civil liberty. Nevertheless, the Court held that Congress had the authority to deny them that right. Consequently, the firing of the striking air traffic controllers was legal. Now consider whether the firing was ethical. Explain your response.

**quick quiz** 24-3

1. There is no appeal permitted after a decision has been rendered by the National Labor Relations Board.  true | false

2. If a complaint is found valid under the NLRB procedures, a cease-and-desist order may be issued, restoring the parties to the state that existed before the unfair labor practice began.  true | false

3. The United States Supreme Court has repeatedly affirmed that federal employees have a constitutionally protected right to strike.  true | false

## Summary

**24.1** The first federal statute relating to labor was the Clayton Act, which attempted to prohibit federal courts from forbidding activities such as picketing and strikes. The Norris-LaGuardia Act specified acts, such as striking, picketing, and boycotting, that were not subject to federal injunctions.

**24.2** The Wagner Act opened the door for the growth of labor unions. It set forth specific labor practices that were prohibited for employers and unions, established procedures for representative elections and collective bargaining, and created the NLRB. The Taft-Hartley Act outlaws specific conduct by unions as unfair labor practices and provides for an 80-day cooling off period in strikes that endanger national health or safety. The Act also provides a mediation and conciliation service to assist in the settlement of labor disputes. The Landrum-Griffin Act provides a bill of rights for union members, requires unions to report to the secretary of labor, and has added to the list of unfair labor practices.

**24.3** The NLRB has exclusive jurisdiction to enforce labor–management relations laws with investigative, regulatory, administrative, enforcement, and judgment powers. Any person, union, or employer can file notice with the NLRB of an alleged unfair labor practice. If the complaint has merit, a hearing is held before the NLRB. If the complaint is found to be valid, an order may be issued restoring the parties to the state existing prior to the unfair practice. Appeals of NLRB actions can be taken to the appropriate U.S. Circuit Court of Appeals and then to the U.S. Supreme Court. The Federal Mediation and Conciliation Service was formed to encourage labor and management to agree freely on the settlement of their disputes. Its mediation role is to offer nonbinding suggestions for settling the dispute, require the parties to negotiate, and force a vote by employees on employers' offers. In the public sector, the right to strike is restricted. The U.S. Code states that "an individual may not accept or hold a position in the government of the United States or the government of the District of Columbia if he participates in a strike or asserts the right to strike against the government."

## Key Terms

arbitration, 532
bargaining unit, 529
closed shop, 528
constructive discharge, 528

featherbedding, 531
hot-cargo contract, 531
labor union, 521
right-to-work laws, 529

secondary boycott, 530
unfair labor practices, 525
union shop, 528

## Questions for Review and Discussion

1. What is the historical context in which unions developed?

2. What is the congressional-judicial tug-of-war in union history?

3. What are the major provisions of the Norris-LaGuardia Act?
4. What are the basic aims of labor unions?
5. What is the nature of the 21st century crisis in labor law?
6. What are the primary tenets of the Wagner Act?
7. What are the functions of the Taft-Hartley Act?
8. What are the provisions of the Landrum-Griffin Act?
9. What is the jurisdiction of the National Labor Relations Board?
10. What are the possible results of a complaint filed with the NLRB?

## Cases for Analysis

1. Nine longshoremen, all of whom were members of Local 13 of the International Longshoremen's and Warehousemen's Union, found that they were having difficulty getting jobs. The problem seemed to be that Local 13 had refused to place them on a hiring list at the union's hiring hall. Because this list was the only way that union members could get jobs as longshoremen, the nine union members were in effect being boycotted by the union and, as a result, by all potential employers. When the out-of-work union members filed grievances with Local 13, they were effectively ignored. To challenge these actions (as well as others not covered here), the out-of-work longshoremen filed a complaint with the National Labor Relations Board (NLRB). The NLRB and the District Court dismissed the complaint, and the longshoremen appealed. The union argued that the question of whether to place certain members on the hiring list was a purely internal union affair that could not be challenged by the NLRB or the courts. The longshoreman contended that by refusing to place them on the list and ignoring their grievances, the union was being unfair to them. Should the appeals court overturn this ruling by the NLRB and the District Court? Explain. *Richard Diaz, et al. v. International Longshoremen's and Warehousemen's Union, Local 13*, Case No. 04-56957 (U.S. Court of Appeals for the Ninth Circuit).

2. The union representing employees of the Consolidated Manufacturing Company elected Franco and Allanson to act on their behalf at a collective bargaining session with management. At the session, Franco and Allanson demanded that the new collective bargaining agreement include terms that would require management to hire only union members in good standing. Management disagreed with this proposal. Instead, management offered a term in the agreement that would allow the company to hire nonunion workers for a trial period lasting no more than 30 days. After the 30-day trial period, the nonunion worker would have to join a union. Which of these terms in the proposed collective bargaining agreement would be allowed under federal labor law? Explain. Management also proposed that the employee union be disbanded and replaced by a company-run union. Management argued that the new company-run union would not only be more efficient but also more economical than the current union. Would this proposal be allowed under federal labor law?

3. An employee was discharged for violating the company's no-solicitation rule in its factory and offices. The employee had persisted in soliciting union membership on company property during lunch periods. The company argued that its no-solicitation rule would have been enforced against not merely union solicitation but any solicitation. How would you decide? Why? *Republic Aviation Corp. v. NLRB*, 324 U.S. 793 (U.S. Sup. Ct.).

4. Having advised Exchange Parts Co. that it was conducting an organizational campaign, the union petitioned the NLRB for an election to determine whether it would be certified as the bargaining agent of the company's employees. During the organizational campaign, while the granted certification election was pending, the company announced five additional benefits for the employees, two of which were announced only a few days before the election. In the election, the employees voted against being represented by a union. The union then filed a complaint with the NLRB, charging the company with an unfair labor practice because it granted benefits while the campaign was taking place and the election was pending. The union argued that the company's actions interfered with the freedom of choice of the employees to determine whether they wished to be represented by the union. For whom would you decide? Why? *NLRB v. Exchange Parts Co.*, 375 U.S. 405 (U.S. Sup. Ct.).

5. Darlington Manufacturing Co. operated one textile mill that was controlled by Deering Milliken, which operated 27 other such mills. The union began an organizational campaign, which Darlington resisted. The employees filed charges of unfair labor practices with the NLRB. The board found in a subsequent hearing that the different mills controlled by Deering Milliken represented an integrated enterprise and that the closing of the Darlington mill was due to the antiunion hostility of Deering Milliken. The NLRB ordered Deering Milliken to provide back pay to the workers until they obtained similar work. The court of appeals denied enforcement of the NLRB order, holding that an independent employer has an absolute right to close a business, regardless of notice. On review by the U.S. Supreme Court, how should the Court rule on the question of whether an employer has the absolute right to close part of a business, no matter what the reason? Why? *Textile Worker's Union v. Darlington Mfg. Co.,* 380 U.S. 263 (U.S. Sup. Ct.).

6. The NLRB conducted an election among employees of Savair Manufacturing Co. to determine whether the union would represent the employees. During the election, recognition slips were distributed. The employees were told by the union that if they signed the slips before the election, they would not have to pay an initiation fee if the union won. At least 35 employees signed the slips before the election, which the union won by a vote of 22 to 20. The company refused to bargain with the union, contending that the union, by offering possible benefits to employees for signing the recognition slips, was guilty of an unfair labor practice. Did the practice of the union prevent a fair and free choice of a bargaining representative? Why or why not? *NLRB v. Savair Mfg. Co.,* 414 U.S. 270 (U.S. Sup. Ct.).

7. The Department Store Employees Union (union) was selected by the employees of the Emporium Capwell Company (company) as their exclusive bargaining unit. Charges of discrimination in the workplace were levied against the company through the union. The union followed the grievance procedure, as established in the collective bargaining agreement. Some of the employees became dissatisfied with the union's handling of the case. Accordingly, they asked the union to begin to picket the company. Union officials advised these dissatisfied employees that according to the collective bargaining agreement, the union was bound to follow the established grievance procedure. The employees refused to cooperate with the grievance procedure and demanded that company management deal with them directly to establish an overall anti-discrimination policy. Later the employees also picketed the store. Written notices were given to the picketing employees, telling them that they could be discharged if they repeated the conduct. The employees ignored the notices and, after picketing on the following weekend, were discharged. The employees filed a complaint with the National Labor Relations Board, which found that it could not support the employees. The NLRB believed that such support would challenge the exclusive bargaining power of the union and thereby subvert the statutory intent of Congress. The appeals court hearing the case reversed the Board's findings, stating its belief that discrimination cases had a special position and thus fell outside the guarantee to the union of exclusive bargaining power. The case was appealed to the United States Supreme Court. Should the Supreme Court uphold the union's exclusive right to engage in collective bargaining with the company? Explain. *Emporium Capwell, Co. v. Western Addition Community Organization,* 420 U.S. 50. (U.S. Sup. Ct.).

## quick quiz Answers

| 24-1 | 24-2 | 24-3 |
|------|------|------|
| 1. T | 1. F | 1. F |
| 2. F | 2. F | 2. T |
| 3. F | 3. T | 3. F |

## Summary

A group of employees who worked for the Duke Power Company were upset about the promotion policies of their employer, Dan River steam station, a power-generating plant owned and operated by the Duke Power Company of Draper, North Carolina. The requirements for advancement included a high school education or successful completion of a standardized general education examination. The argument made by the petitioners was that neither of these requirements was actually related to doing an effective job at the plant; that both of the requirements had the adverse effect of eliminating black employees from hiring and promotions in a proportion that was at a substantially higher rate than white employees; and the positions that required the diploma or the test were filled only by white employees and had been dominated by white employees as part of a deliberate strategy to exclude blacks. The case went to the district court which found that the company had indeed followed a deliberately discriminatory hiring and promotion process that was consciously designed to exclude blacks from the higher-paying positions. The plant had five departments: labor, coal handling, operations, maintenance, and the laboratory. Blacks worked exclusively in the labor department, which meant that all the high-paying jobs in the other departments were occupied by whites. Promotions in all departments were based on seniority alone. Starting in 1955 a high school diploma was needed for an initial assignment to any department except labor. After the Civil Rights Act went onto effect in 1965, the company eliminated its deliberately discriminatory hiring policies. However, at that time, a high school diploma became a requirement for moving out of labor into any of the higher-paying departments. On July 2, 1965, the date that the Civil Rights Act went into effect, the company installed a new policy. The new policy required applicants to any department but the Labor Department to achieve a satisfactory score on two aptitude tests and to have a high school diploma. Later the requirement was modified somewhat to allow a transfer from the Labor Department or the Coal Department to a higher-paying department based on test scores alone. The district court ruled that the Civil Rights Act was not designed to pass judgment on past transgressions. The appeals court believed that the case should be decided based on the intent of the employer rather than on the actual results and, finding no intent to discriminate on the part of Duke, rejected the employees' charge of discrimination. At that point the case landed in the lap of the United States Supreme Court.

## The Court's Opinion

### Chief Justice Burger

We granted in the writ in this case to resolve the question whether an employer is prohibited by the Civil Rights Act of 1964, Title VII, from requiring a high school education or passing of a standardized general intelligence test as a condition of employment or transfer to jobs when (a) neither standard is shown to be significantly related to successful job performance . . . All the petitioners are employed at the Company's Dan River Steam Station, a power generating facility located at Draper, North Carolina . . . The District Court found that prior to July 2, 1965, the effective date of the Civil Rights Act of 1964, the Company openly discriminated on the basis of race in the hiring and assigning of employees at its Dan River plant. The plant was organized into five operating departments: (1) Labor, (2) Coal Handling, (3) Operations, (4) Maintenance, and (5) Laboratory and Test . . . Promotions were normally made within each department on the basis of job seniority. Transferees into a department usually began in the lowest position.

In 1955 the Company instituted a policy of requiring a high school education for initial assignment to any department except Labor, and for transfer to the Coal handling to any "inside" department (operations, maintenance, or laboratory) . . . From the time the high school requirement was instituted to the time of trial, however, white employees hired before the time of the high school education requirement continued to perform satisfactorily and achieve promotions in the "operating" departments.

The Company added a further requirement for new employees on July 2, 1965, the date on which Title VII became effective. To qualify for placement in any but the Labor Department it became necessary to registered satisfactory scores on two professionally prepared aptitude tests, as well as to have a high school education. Completion of high school alone continued to render employees eligible for transfer to the four desirable departments . . . employees who lacked a high school education to qualify for transfer from labor to coal handling to an "inside" job by passing two tests— the Wonderlic Personnel Test, which purports to measure general intelligence, and the Bennett Mechanical Comprehension Test. Neither was directed or intended to measure the ability to learn or perform a particular job or category of jobs. The requisite scores used for both initial hiring and transfer approximated the national median for high school graduates.

The District Court had found that while the Company previously followed a policy of overt racial discrimination in a period prior to the Act, such conduct had ceased. The District Court also concluded that Title VII was intended to be prospective only and, consequently, the impact of prior inequities was beyond the reach of corrective action authorized by the Act.

The Court of Appeals was confronted with a question of first impression, as are we, concerning the meaning of Title VII. After careful analysis a majority of that court concluded that a subjective test of the employer's intent should govern, particularly in a close case that there was no showing of a discriminatory purpose in the adoption of the diploma and test requirements. On this basis the Court of Appeals concluded that there was no violation of the Act.

The objective of Congress in the enactment of Title VII was to achieve equality of employment opportunities and remove barriers that have operated in the past to favor an identifiable group of white employees over other employees. Under the Act, the practices, procedures, or tests, neutral on their face, and even neutral in terms of intent, cannot be maintained if they operate to "freeze" the status quo of prior discriminatory employment practices . . .

Congress did not intend by Title VII, however, to guarantee a job to every person regardless of qualifications. In short, the Act does not command that any person be hired simply because he was formerly the subject of discrimination, or because he is a member of a minority group. Discriminatory preference for any group, minority or majority, is precisely and only what Congress has proscribed. What is required by Congress is the removal of artificial, arbitrary, and unnecessary barriers to employment when the barriers operate invidiously to discriminate on the basis of racial or other impermissible classification.

The Act proscribes not only overt discrimination, but also practices that are fair in form, but discriminatory in operation. The touchstone is *business necessity* (italics added). . .

On the record before us, neither in the high school completion or in the general intelligence test is shown to bear a demonstrable relationship to job performance ability. Rather, a vice president of the company testified, the requirements were instituted on the Company's judgment that they would generally improve the overall quality of the workforce.

The evidence, however, shows that employees who have not completed high school or taken the tests have continued to perform satisfactorily and make progress in departments for which the high school and test criteria are now used. The promotion record of present employees who would not be able to meet the new criteria that suggests the possibility that the requirements may not be needed even for the limited purpose of preserving the avowed policy of advancement within the Company.

The Court of Appeals held that the Company had adopted the diploma and test requirements without any "intention to discriminate . . . We do not suggest that either the District Court or the Court of Appeals erred in examining the employer's intent; but good intent or the absence of discriminatory intent does not redeem reemployment procedures or testing mechanisms that operate as built in headwinds for minority groups and are unrelated to measuring job capability.

The Company's lack of discriminatory intent is suggested by special efforts to help the undereducated employees through the Company financing of two-thirds the cost of tuition for high school training. But Congress directed the thrust of the Act to the consequences of employment practices, not simply the motivation. More than that, Congress has placed on the employer the burden of showing that any given requirement must have a manifest relationship to the employment in question.

The Company contends that its general intelligence tests are specifically permitted by Section 703(h) of the Act. That section authorizes the use of "any professionally developed ability test" that is not "designed, intended or used to discriminate because of race."

The Equal Employment Opportunity Commission having enforcement responsibility, has issued guidelines interpreting section 703(h) to permit only the use of job-related tests. The administrative interpretation of the Act and its legislative history support the guidelines as expressing the will of Congress.

Nothing in the Act precludes the use of testing or measuring procedures: obviously they are useful. What Congress has forbidden is giving these devices and mechanisms controlling force unless they are demonstrably a reasonable measure of job performance. Congress has not commanded that the less qualified be preferred over the better qualified simply because of minority origins. Far from disparaging job qualifications as such, Congress has made such qualifications the controlling factor, so that race, religion, nationality, and sex become irrelevant. What Congress has commanded is that any tests used must measure the person for the job and not the person in the abstract.

The judgment of the court of appeals is, as to that portion of the judgment appealed from, reversed.

Judgment reversed.

Mr. Justice Brennan took no part in the consideration or decision of this case

# Questions for Analysis

1. The test used in *Griggs v. Duke Power* established the Disparate Impact test in employment discrimination law. The test emerged from within a race discrimination case. Can you imagine how the test might apply in a gender discrimination case? Explain.

2. The District Court did not believe that the Civil Rights Act was designed to correct past discrimination. What developments in the law since then have proven this position incorrect? Explain.

3. The obvious, open, and deliberate disparate treatment that was applied by Griggs in this case is virtually unheard of today in race discrimination cases. Is this also true in gender discrimination? Explain.

4. The obvious, open, and deliberate disparate treatment that was applied by Griggs in this case is virtually unheard of today in race discrimination cases. Is this also true in religious discrimination? Explain.

5. The obvious, open and deliberate disparate treatment that was applied by Griggs in this case is virtually unheard of today in race discrimination cases. Is this also true in age discrimination? Explain.

6. What is the *business necessity* defense that is mentioned in the *Griggs v. Duke Power* case? Explain.

7. Should intent to discriminate be in issue in a case of disparate impact? Explain.

8. Sometimes the disparate impact test is referred to as the "disproportionate exclusionary impact" doctrine. Examine this phrase and demonstrate how it might be a more accurate designation than "disparate impact." Explain.

9. How does the proof needed in a disparate impact case differ from the proof needed in a disparate treatment case? Explain.

10. Explain what the Court meant when it wrote that "What Congress has commanded is that any tests used must measure the person for the job and not the person in the abstract."

# Chapter 25

# Sole Proprietorships and Partnerships

## THE OPENING CASE  Ignorance of the Law Is No Excuse: *Robinson v. Kleinfeld*

In 1985 Josef Kleinfeld purchased a building in the East Village and opened a video rental store on the ground floor. Unfortunately, Kleinfeld lost a great deal of money during his first year. Things were so bad that he decided to fire his clerk, a New York University student named Dawn Robinson. Robinson pleaded with Kleinfeld to keep her on as his clerk by promising to give up her hourly wages and instead take a percentage of the store's profits every two weeks. Kleinfeld would not have to pay her anything if the store made no money during any two-week period. Kleinfeld, who could see that Robinson knew about the video market and was very skillful in handling customers, gave her more and more responsibility in store matters. Eventually, Robinson ran the business. She hired and fired clerks, ordered tapes, set prices, balanced the books, handled payroll, wrote the firm's policy and procedure manual, and filled out the firm's tax returns every year. Her business acumen led her to move Kleinfeld's store away from Beta tapes and into an exclusive VHS business before any other rental store in the neighborhood. Later, she was quick to see that the DVD market would overtake the VHS market and moved the store into DVDs, again ahead of all local competition,

and then into Blu-ray discs. The store expanded until it occupied all three floors of Kleinfeld's building. During all of this time, Robinson continued to draw a percentage of the profits, periodically negotiating increases until the percentage reached 45 percent. Meanwhile, Kleinfeld did little more than check on Robinson's progress every two weeks—and sometimes not even then. Her work at the store enabled him to use his own profits to engage in other ventures. While working on one of these ventures, Kleinfeld met Gerry Ackerman, who offered to purchase Kleinfeld's business and his building for $50 million. Kleinfeld agreed. When Robinson was told about the deal, she expected to get a share of the sale price, based on her percentage of the profits. Kleinfeld was offended by Robinson's demand and refused to comply. Robinson sued Kleinfeld, claiming that she had been a partner in the video business in everything but name. She ran the business; she contributed her expertise in technology, customer relations, and business matters to the running of the store; and for 20 years she had taken only a fair share of the profits for pay. As you read the chapter see if you can figure out how the judge ruled in this case.

Learning Objectives

1. List the most common forms of business associations.
2. Outline the advantages and disadvantages of a sole proprietorship.
3. Identify the two model acts that govern partnership law.
4. Describe the differences between the aggregate and the entity theories of partnership.
5. Explain the nature of a partnership agreement.
6. Explain when profit sharing does not create a partnership.
7. Explain what constitutes a person in partnership law.
8. Identify the different views of specific partnership property in partnership law.
9. Distinguish between dissociation and dissolution in partnership law.
10. Distinguish between a registered limited liability partnership and a limited partnership.

# 25-1 Sole Proprietorships

There are several forms of doing business available to people who are about to enter the economic arena for the first time. Here are some of the most common forms:

- Sole proprietorships
- General partnerships
- Registered limited liability partnerships
- Limited partnerships
- Corporations
- Limited liability companies

## Formation of a Sole Proprietorship

The easiest business organization to form is a **sole proprietorship**. In most cases, businesspeople can initiate a sole proprietorship by simply opening their doors for business. Depending on the nature, location, and extent of the business, the sole proprietor may have to check zoning restrictions, licensing laws, and filing requirements. For example, some states require a formal filing if a sole proprietor chooses to use a fictitious name.

## Advantages and Disadvantages of a Sole Proprietorship

Perhaps the greatest advantage to a sole proprietorship is that the owner has complete control over the business. Another major advantage is that the owner may keep all of the profits made by the sole proprietorship. A third advantage is that a sole proprietorship is relatively simple to begin and to end.

A major disadvantage to this type of business is that the owner of a sole proprietorship is subject to unlimited liability. For example, the sole proprietor is responsible for all of the debts incurred in running the business. This liability may even extend to the owner's personal assets. Another disadvantage is that the sole proprietorship's existence depends entirely upon the sole proprietor. Finally, owners of sole proprietorships often find it difficult to raise a lot of cash quickly for expansion purposes.

## quick quiz 25-1

1. Businesspeople can form a sole proprietorship only by going through the attorney general's office in the state capital.    true | false

2. The greatest advantage of a sole proprietorship is that the owner has complete control over the operation of the business.    true | false

3. A major disadvantage of a sole proprietorship is unlimited liability.    true | false

# 25-2 General Partnership Characteristics

Often a sole proprietor will decide to extend his or her business venture by joining with other people to create a partnership. The law of partnership has integrated principles associated with tort law, contract law, and agency law. However, because of its unique characteristics, it has also developed its own separate and distinct legal principles.

## Revised Uniform Partnership Act

One of the most dependable sources of law affecting partnerships has been the National Conference of Commissioners on Uniform State Laws (NCCUSL), which developed the Uniform Partnership Act (UPA) in 1914. The UPA was so successful that it was put into practice by every state in the union but one. Only Louisiana, which is devoted to the Napoleonic Code, did not adopt the UPA. Nevertheless, the UPA has been the mainstay of partnership law, in relation to general partnerships, for more than 90 years. It does, however, have its limitations and shortcomings. For instance, it never made it clear whether a partnership should be considered an entity with an existence separate from the partners or whether it was in fact simply an aggregate of all of the partners. These problems motivated two agents within the complex adaptive legal system, the NCCUSL and the American Bar Association (ABA), to collaborate to develop an updated set of rules for partnerships, named the Revised Uniform Partnership Act (RUPA).

The NCCUSL offers several reasons to support states' adoption of the RUPA. Chief among those reasons is that the new act solves several problems with the UPA, not the least of which is the old act's ambiguity about the status of a partnership as an entity or an aggregate. The new act also clarifies the nature of a partner's interest in partnership property, explains the duties partners have in relation to one another, and gives partners the power to pursue a remedy when those duties are violated. It grants partnerships continuity of life, a feature that is similar but not identical to the one enjoyed by corporations. Finally, the revised act solves one of the most troubling problems of the old partnership structure, that of joint and several liability. For these reasons, among others, the RUPA has been implemented in more than half the states. The RUPA will therefore be the basis of discussion for the remainder of this chapter.

## Elements of a Partnership

The RUPA says that a **partnership** is "an association of two or more persons to carry on as co-owners a business for profit." The RUPA definition emphasizes the two most essential elements of a partnership. First, partnerships must involve at least two persons. As is often the case with legal terms, "person" can have multiple meanings. In this case, the term "person" can refer to a flesh-and-blood individual, a corporation, other partnerships, joint ventures, trusts, estates, and other commercial or legal institutions. Second, a partnership must involve a sharing of profits. This last point is so crucial that the sharing of profits is considered *prima facie* evidence of the existence of a partnership. *Prima facie* evidence in this context means that the law presumes, in the absence of evidence to the contrary, that an individual receiving profits is a partner.

## Entity and Aggregate Theories

Under the Uniform Partnership Act, there was room to dispute whether a partnership should be considered an aggregate or an entity. According to the **entity theory**, a partnership exists as an individual person with its own separate identity. This unique, individual entity is separate from the identities of the partners. In contrast, under the **aggregate theory**, the partnership is seen simply as an assembly or collection of the partners who do business together. The RUPA has settled this dispute. Under the RUPA, a partnership is considered an entity in most situations. Thus, a partnership is an entity in its ability to own title to property, to sue or be sued, and to have its own separate bank accounts in its own name. Under the RUPA, partnerships also have continuity of existence. **Continuity of existence** permits a partnership to continue to operate as an entity even after the individual partners are no longer associated with it. In addition, the partners are considered agents of the partnership. However, the RUPA still considers a partnership an aggregate in relation to liability. Thus, even under the RUPA, partners still have unlimited liability for the obligations of the partnership. It is, however, possible to avoid even this problem if the partners elect to form a registered limited liability partnership. The concept of registered limited liability partnerships is discussed subsequently in this chapter.

### quick quiz 25-2

| | | |
|---|---|---|
| 1. The Revised Uniform Partnership Act has yet to be adopted by any state legislature. | true | false |
| 2. Under the RUPA, a partnership is an aggregate. | true | false |
| 3. Under the RUPA, partners are considered to be agents of the partnership. | true | false |

# 25-3 Partnership Formation

The problem with a partnership is that it can emerge simply because of the way that two or more parties are doing business with one another. That is why it is essential that businesspeople be aware of their relationships with other businesspeople with whom they work on

| **Table 25-1** Partnership Formation | |
| --- | --- |
| **Form** | **Definition** |
| Partnership by contract | Express agreement drawn up by partners<br>Articles of partnership |
| Partnership by proof of existence | Individuals form partnership because of their method of doing business<br>Sharing of profits is *prima facie* evidence |

a daily basis (see Table 25-1). Certainly the best way to form a partnership is to enter a contractual relationship by drawing up a partnership agreement. Consequently, we will examine this approach first. However, we will also look at the circumstances that can automatically create a partnership as a matter of law.

## Formation of a Partnership by Contract

One of the most common ways to form a partnership is by an express agreement between the parties. Although the agreement can be oral, it is generally best to put the terms in writing to prevent misunderstanding and disputes that might arise later in the life of the partnership. The written agreement that establishes a partnership is called a partnership agreement. The RUPA is quite specific about the nature of a partnership agreement. In fact, the RUPA defines a partnership contract as "the agreement, whether written, oral, or implied, among the partners concerning the partnership, including amendments to the partnership agreement." It is of course still possible for the partners to enter agreements subsequent to the creation of a partnership that would not be considered part of the partnership agreement. Thus, partners might enter a loan or a rental agreement that would be separate from the partnership agreement itself.

Both the RUPA and UPA are default statutes, which means that the partners are free to enter any type of agreement that they desire. However, if the partners neglect to include something in the agreement or are unsure of the interpretation of some point, the RUPA (or UPA in those states that still follow it) will "fill in the gaps." It is advisable for a partnership agreement to include the following provisions:

1. The name and duration of the partnership.
2. The names of the partners.
3. The amount of capital that each partner has contributed to the partnership.
4. The character and the extent of the business of the partnership.
5. The way that profits will be divided.
6. The way that any loss will be shared.
7. The duties of the partners.
8. Any limitations placed on the partners.
9. A section on salaries, if so desired.
10. An explanation of the dissolution process, if it is to be different from the process outlined in the RUPA.
11. A provision for determining the value of a partner's interest in the partnership.

It is also wise to recall that, though the RUPA does not require that a partnership agreement be in writing, the Statute of Frauds does dictate that certain types of contracts, such as those that will take longer than one year to complete, must be in writing. Thus, it is best to cross-reference with the Statute of Frauds just to make certain that none of those provisions apply.

# Formation of a Partnership by Proof of Existence

The definition of a partnership offered by the RUPA establishes the parameters within which a partnership will be formed. The definition states that a business arrangement will be considered a partnership if it involves two or more persons, in association with one another, who are carrying on a business as co-owners for profit. Therefore, to show that a business is operating as a partnership by proof of existence, we must be able to point to three elements: (1) an association of two or more persons, (2) who are co-owners of (3) a business for profit.

### An Association of Two or More Persons
In the case of a partnership, a "person" can be a living flesh-and-blood individual, a corporation, another partnership, a joint venture, a trust, an estate, or some other commercial enterprise or legal institution. Any two of these persons working together would be sufficient to create an association.

### Co-Ownership of the Business
There are certain signs that indicate that the parties in a venture are co-owners. One such sign is the existence of management power. Of course, management power by itself is not enough. Employees who are not partners and even independent contractors who have control over certain projects conducted for the business may have management power without being co-owners. Still, the power to make

## THE OPENING CASE *Revisited, Part I*
## Ignorance of the Law Is No Excuse: *Robinson v. Kleinfeld*, Round 2

The lawsuit between Robinson and Kleinfeld at the opening of this chapter is a classic case of the formation of a partnership by proof of existence. As is often true in a situation like this, neither Kleinfeld nor Robinson ever used the term "partnership" to describe their business relationship, except perhaps in the most casual and off-handed way. Nor had they drawn up a contract to delineate their roles and responsibilities in the running of the video outlet. Instead, the business simply evolved from one between an employer and his employee to one between partners. The most telling piece of evidence was, of course, the sharing of profits. This sharing was never questioned by either party. In fact, profit sharing was so ingrained in their relationship that the percentage that Robinson received grew annually until it reached an almost equal arrangement. The court also noted, however, that Robinson brought more to the table than just the profit-sharing arrangement. She also brought several valuable assets to the enterprise—her time, her talent, and her expertise. It is quite likely that Kleinfeld would never have made the video outlet a success without Robinson's business know-how, her grasp of the video marketplace, her easygoing way with customers, and her powers of persuasion. Kleinfeld could not profit from that talent and energy for 20 years without realizing that their association had made a quantum leap from an employer–employee relationship to one of partners.

management decisions is a persuasive piece of evidence that is helpful in establishing co-ownership. Co-ownership is also established by the sharing of profits among the partners. However, the RUPA also says that certain types of profit sharing, though real enough, will not rise to the level needed to create a partnership. These profit-sharing activities include the following:

1. The repayment of a debt.

2. Wages to an employee.

3. Payments to an independent contractor.

4. Rent payments to a landlord.

5. Annuity payments or health benefit payments to a beneficiary, representative, or designee of a retired or deceased partner.

6. Interest payments on a loan, even if the level of payments is tied to profit fluctuations.

7. Consideration for the sale of goodwill or for the sale of other property even if the payments are made in installments.

Although the sharing of profits is *prima facie* evidence of the existence of a partnership, parties can receive profits in any of the ways on this list without being saddled with the label of partner.

### Carrying on a Business for Profit

Finally, it is not enough for two or more persons to simply be co-owners of property, even if the property does make a profit. The association must also have the goal of running the business together. It is, of course, essential that the business in question be run for a profit. This point means that the venture cannot involve an unincorporated nonprofit venture. It is also unlikely that a solitary profit-making business transaction by itself will be enough to establish a partnership.

## THE OPENING CASE *Revisited, Part II*
## Ignorance of the Law Is No Excuse: *Robinson v. Kleinfeld*, Round 3

Once Robinson has demonstrated to the court's satisfaction that she and Kleinfeld were sharing profits, the burden would shift to Kleinfeld. He would then have a chance to show that the sharing of profits was of a type not associated with partnership activity and that it therefore could not be used by Robinson as proof of the partnership's existence. However, to accomplish this, he would have to demonstrate that Robinson's profit sharing was located on the list outlined above. A quick look at that list reveals that none of them, save one, even remotely relates to the type of payments that

Robinson received. The one that comes the closest is the payment of wages. Unfortunately for Kleinfeld, the payments that Robinson received were clearly not wages, which was apparent from the original conversation between Robinson and Kleinfeld. During that discussion, she expressly gave up the right to receive an hourly wage in exchange for the right to receive profits. Moreover, the fluctuations in the amount of money that Robinson actually took home would verify that the payments that she received could not possibly be wages.

# 25-4 Partnership Property Rights and Duties

Property is an extremely critical element in partnership law, because virtually every decision made by a partner deals with the disposition of partnership property. Decisions involving the use of partnership property, such as machinery, equipment, furniture, and vehicles; the purchase of raw materials; and the sale of finished products all involve the disposition of property. Even service-oriented partnerships such as shipping firms and restaurants involve the disposition of property in one way or another. Therefore, partnership duties and rights always involve partnership property. This point is also why it is critical to determine whether a given piece of property belongs to the partnership entity or to an individual partner as his or her personal property. At times it is relatively easy to distinguish between partnership property and property that belongs to individual partners. For instance, the capital contributions of all partners are considered the property of the partnership. **Capital contributions** are sums that are contributed by the partners as permanent investments and that the partners are entitled to have returned when the partnership is dissolved. In contrast, loans or later advances that partners make to the partnership and accumulated but undivided profits belong to the partners on an individual basis. Other forms of partnership property belong only to the partnership in its status as an entity.

## Partnership Property

The fact that the RUPA has established the existence of a partnership as an entity has alleviated some of the difficulties once associated with identifying partnership property. The RUPA states that partnership property is any and all property that has been obtained by the partnership itself. For instance, if the property was obtained in the partnership's name, it is partnership property. If the property was obtained by a partner in his or her role as a partner, it is partnership property. If the instrument of title for the property includes the name of the partnership, it is partnership property. Finally, if the instrument of transfer indicates that the property was obtained by a partner in his or her role as a partner or if the partnership is referred to in the instrument, the property belongs to the partnership.

When it is difficult to determine whether a piece of property belongs to the partnership or to a partner, the court may ask the following questions: Has the partnership included the property in its account books? Has the partnership expended its own funds to improve or repair the property? Has the partnership paid taxes on the property? Has the partnership paid other expenses, such as maintenance costs, for the property? The more of these questions that can be answered in the affirmative, the more likely it is that the property is partnership property.

# Specific Partnership Property

The RUPA has made a significant change in the rule with regard to individual pieces of partnership property. Under the UPA, each partner had a property interest in all specific items of partnership property. Each partner was therefore a co-owner of that property. This form of ownership was known as tenancy in partnership. Under the UPA, a tenancy in partnership had the following characteristics:

1. A partner had an equal right with all other partners to possess and use specific partnership property for partnership purposes but not for that partner's personal use.

2. A partner's interest in partnership property could not be assigned (i.e., transferred by sale, mortgage, pledge, or otherwise) to a nonpartner, unless the other partners agreed to the transfer.

3. Partners' rights in partnership property were not subject to attachment (i.e., taking a person's property and bringing it into the custody of the law) for personal debts or claims against the partners themselves.

4. A deceased partner's interest in real property held by the partnership passed to the surviving partners.

5. Partners' rights in specific partnership property were not subject to any allowances or rights to widows, heirs, or next of kin.

Under the RUPA, all of this has changed. The RUPA states that "A partner is not co-owner of partnership property and has no interest in partnership property which can be transferred, either voluntarily or involuntarily." Of course, partners will still be able to use partnership property. However, their right to hold and use such property is limited to partnership purposes. This significant change in relation to partnership law actually brings partnership property rights in relation to individual pieces of partnership property in line with the way property rights operate for other business associations, such as corporations.

# Interest in the Partnership

The RUPA establishes that a partner has an interest in the partnership as a firm. That right consists of two parts: (1) a transferable economic interest and (2) a nontransferable interest in management rights.

### Transferable Economic Interest
The partner's economic interest is his or her share of the profits and losses and his or her share of the surplus. **Surplus** includes any funds that remain after the partnership has been dissolved and all other debts and prior obligations have been paid. Partners can voluntarily assign their economic interest to another party. The assignee in such an action, however, is not entitled to take part in the management of the partnership. The assignee also cannot gain access to the partnership books or the partnership financial records. Nor can an assignee demand to receive information concerning the transactions of the partnership.

### Management of the Firm
Participation in management decision making is not limited to the partner's proportional share of the firm. Instead, all partners have equal rights in the management of the partnership business. The day-to-day decisions of the firm are decided by a majority vote of the partners. If a vote is split evenly, then the status quo remains. If such deadlocks persist, and the very operation of the business is threatened, it may be time to dissolve the partnership. Occasionally, a unanimous vote is required in a business decision. However, such decisions must involve actions that fall outside the regular, daily operation of the business. Decisions that involve amendments to the partnership agreement also require unanimous consent.

It is, of course, possible for a partner to reduce his or her part in management voluntarily by becoming a silent partner. A silent partner is one who does not participate in the day-to-day business of the firm. This role is in contrast to a secret partner, whose identity and existence are not known outside the firm but who nevertheless can participate in the management of the firm. Some partnerships create their own hierarchy of partners. Thus, a firm may be divided into *junior* and *senior partners* or into *managing* and *nonmanaging partners*.

## Partnership Rights and Duties

We have already pinpointed most of the individual rights that partners possess by virtue of their participation in the partnership. These rights include: (1) the right to use partnership property, as long as the property is held and used for partnership purposes; (2) the right to receive the partner's share of the profits (and losses) and his or her share of the surplus; (3) the right to manage the regular day-to-day operation of the partnership business; (4) the right to approve of serious matters outside the ordinary course of business; and (5) the right to approve of amendments to the partnership agreement. In addition, partners have certain enforcement rights, should the need arise to implement the other rights.

**Enforcement Rights** Under the UPA, a partner's enforcement rights are few. In fact, partners have only three enforcement rights: (1) the right to see the firm's financial records, (2) the right to compel an accounting, and (3) the right to compel a dissolution of the entire partnership. Under the RUPA, those enforcement rights are enhanced. The three rights previously noted are retained, but in addition, a partner can sue another partner directly or, under the entity theory, the partnership itself to enforce his or her partnership rights as expressed in the RUPA or granted by the partnership agreement. In such an action, the partner can ask for damages or for an equitable remedy, such as an injunction or specific performance. Of course, the reverse is also true; that is, the partner can be sued by another partner or by the partnership itself.

**Partnership Duties** The RUPA notes that partners have three critical duties: (1) loyalty, (2) obedience and (3) due care. The first of these three, the duty of loyalty, is based on the fact that the partners are in a fiduciary relationship.

**The Duty of Loyalty** The duty of loyalty has become centrally important under the RUPA, unlike its position under the UPA, which devoted only a very small amount of space to the topic. According to the RUPA, the duty of loyalty includes the following items:

1. To account to the partnership for any property, profits, or benefit that comes from the partner's use of partnership property or from the winding up process after dissolution.

2. To refrain from dealing with people who may have an interest that is adverse to the best interests of the partnership.

3. To refrain from entering any competition with the partnership in the operation of partnership business.

A partner does, however, retain the right to look after himself or herself during the formation of the partnership, because the duty of loyalty does not arise until the partnership entity actually exists.

**The Duty of Obedience** Simply stated, the duty of obedience means that a partner must follow faithfully all the arrangements made in the partnership agreement. The partner must also honor all decisions made by the partnership, provided those decisions were made following proper protocols. If a partner disobeys the partnership agreement or disregards a decision lawfully made by the other partners, he or she will be liable for any loss that befalls the partnership as a result of that disobedience.

### About the Law

Because each partner in a partnership is an agent for all of his or her partners, any knowledge about the business of the firm that one partner has is imputed to all other partners.

## Self-Evident Truths

One of the premiere economists of the last century was a Harvard professor named Joseph Schumpeter, who wrote a treatise entitled *Capitalism, Socialism, and Democracy* in which he foretold the ultimate end of the capitalist economic system. Oddly, Schumpeter was himself a confirmed capitalist, so when he predicted the end of the capitalist economy, it was without joy or pleasure. In fact, it was more of a warning than a prediction, offered with the hope that something could be done to divert the path away from destruction. Schumpeter's affection for capitalism is described in the following passage, penned by Allen M. Sievers in his study, *Revolution, Evolution, and the Economic Order:*

> The capitalist, for one thing, wishes to provide for his family, and indeed capitalism is really not individual-centered but family-centered. Further, the capitalist shares in lesser degree the romantic adventuresomeness which characterized feudal society, or there would be no risky innovation or entrepreneurial exploit. Capitalism also requires a kind of symbiosis with the aristocracy and other non-bourgeois elements to run the state, and this depends on a kind of loyalty by these classes to capitalism. The masses must also be awed by the glamor or prestige of capitalist success in order to submit to the discipline necessary for business production. The business classes themselves must have an *esprit de corps* and a devotion to their way of life, as well as a code of ethics if the contract and property system is to work. We might say in sum, that Schumpeter believed that capitalist civilization is based on a rationalism qualified just a bit by other human qualities.
>
> Allen M. Sievers, *Revolution, Evolution, and the Economic Order,* p. 41

We can distill from this quotation five essential qualities of the capitalist: (1) family-centeredness, (2) a willingness to take risks, (3) loyalty to the capitalist ideal, (4) awe at the success of capitalistic ventures, and (5) a code of ethics that permits the rules of contract and property law to work.

## Self-Evident Questions

1. Which of the business organizations described in this chapter is best suited for realizing Sievers's capitalistic ideals? Explain.

2. According to Sievers, capitalism requires an integration of the aristocratic and the working class elements of society. Is such an integration promoted or hampered by the partnership form of doing business? Explain.

3. Take another look at the Opening Case at the beginning of this chapter. In that case, a working class clerk manages to become a member of the capitalistic aristocracy. Does a case like *Robinson v. Kleinfield* disprove Sievers's theory? Why or why not?

4. Do the alternate forms of partnership such as the limited partnership structure prove or disprove Sievers's theory? Explain.

5. Recall that Schumpeter, like F.A. Hayek, opposes governmental interference in the economy. Does this not mean that the sole proprietorship would be the perfect Schumpeter business? Why or why not?

**The Duty of Due Care** Basically, the duty of due care means that partners must do their best in the business, based on their talents, education, and abilities. It does not mean that partners must be infallible. On the contrary, the standard recognizes that a partner may make mistakes and allows for those mistakes, provided the partner acted with an ordinary level of skill and competence and in the best interests of the partnership.

---

## quick quiz 25-4

1. Under the RUPA, each partner has a property interest in all specific items of partnership property.      true | false

2. The RUPA states that partnership property is any and all property that has been obtained by the partnership itself.      true | false

3. A partner's economic interest in the partnership is nontransferrable.      true | false

---

# 25-5 Dissociation and Dissolution

One of the objectives of the National Conference of Commissioners on Uniform State Laws and the American Bar Association in rewriting the UPA and developing the RUPA was to make certain that the new law coincided as much as possible with commercial realities. Under the UPA, whenever a partner ceased to be associated with the partnership, technically, that partnership went through the dissolution process. In present commercial realities, it no longer makes sense for partners to have to deal with the dissolution technicalities when the only thing that is really happening is the buyout of a partner who wants to leave the firm. Consequently, the RUPA now includes two methods by which a partner becomes dissociated with partnership: dissociation and dissolution.

## Dissociation of a Partnership

Under RUPA, a **dissociation** takes place whenever a partner is no longer associated with the running of the firm. It is always possible for partners to leave a partnership firm when they want. However, sometimes, a partner leaves the firm wrongfully when he or she does not have the legal right to do so. A partner's right to withdraw from a partnership may depend on whether the partnership is a term partnership or a partnership at will. A **term partnership** is one that has been set up to run for a certain set time period or to accomplish a task of some sort. A partner who leaves a term partnership before the term expires or before the task is accomplished has acted wrongfully. A **partnership at will** is one that any partner may leave without liability. The RUPA establishes the circumstances in which it is proper to leave a partnership. Some rules affect both types of partnerships; others apply only to partnerships at will. These include (1) a partner's death in either type of partnership; (2) a partner's leave-taking from a partnership at will; (3) a partner's leave-taking from either type of partnership under the rules set up by the partnership agreement; or (4) a partner's leave-taking from either type of partnership, if a court has decided that a partner cannot do what he or she is supposed to do under the partnership agreement.

## Dissolution of a Partnership

The **dissolution** of a partnership occurs when a partner ceases to be associated with the partnership and the partnership ends. The dissolution of a partnership can occur in one of three ways: (1) by an action committed by the partners, (2) by operation of law, or (3) by the decree of a court of law.

**An Action by the Partners** Whenever a partnership at will exists, that partnership can be dissolved whenever a partner notifies the other partners that he or she intends to leave the firm. Partnerships at will, however, are not dissolved when a partner dies or enters bankruptcy. Whenever a term partnership is involved, the RUPA says that there are

This partnership is in the "winding up" stage and is selling its assets and inventory to satisfy creditors and hopefully distribute surplus to the former partners.

several ways to dissolve the firm: (1) when the time limit has passed; (2) when the task of the partnership has been accomplished; (3) when there is express agreement among all partners to end the partnership; (4) when a partner dies; (5) when a partner becomes incapacitated; (6) when a partner goes bankrupt; and (7) when a partner produces a wrongful dissociation from the partnership and, within 90 days of that leave-taking, at least half the other partners agree to end the business.

**By Operation of Law** Dissolution becomes effective by operation of law if some event occurs that makes it illegal to continue the business of the firm. If, for instance, at some time in the distant future it became illegal to manufacture and sell tobacco products, a partnership formed to produce and market cigarettes would dissolve by operation of law.

**By a Court Order** When a partner has engaged in some sort of wrongdoing and, on those grounds, another partner petitions the court for a dissolution, the court may dissolve the partnership by court order. When a continuation of the business would be economically foolish, the court may dissolve the firm. Finally, when a partner does something that makes it impractical to continue the business with that partner, the court may order the dissolution of the business.

**Winding Up the Partnership Business** When a partnership terminates, there must be a winding up of the partnership affairs. This action includes the orderly sale of the partnership's assets, the payment of creditors, and the distribution, if any, of the remaining surplus to partners according to their profit-sharing rations.

## quick quiz 25-5

| | | |
|---|---|---|
| 1. | The RUPA includes two methods by which a partner becomes dissociated with a partnership: dissociation and dissolution. | true \| false |
| 2. | A partnership at will is one that any partner may leave without liability. | true \| false |
| 3. | When partnership terminates, there must be a winding up of the partnership affairs. | true \| false |

# 25-6 Other Forms of Partnership Business

The changing needs of the modern marketplace and the development of new ideas in the law have combined to allow for a new form of partnership, the registered limited liability partnership. Those same forces have also cooperated to update one of the more traditional forms of the partnership business, the limited partnership.

# Registered Limited Liability Partnerships

Statutory developments in several states have produced a new type of business organization known as the registered limited liability partnership (RLLP or LLP). A **registered limited liability partnership** is a general partnership in all respects except one—liability. In a traditional general partnership, the liability for the torts committed by a partner or an employee of the partnership is joint and several. This stance means that each partner is liable and may be sued in a separate action or in a joint action. A judgment may be levied against one or more partners. The release of one partner in one action does not necessarily release the others.

The statutes usually require that the registration statement be filed by all of the partners or at least by those partners holding a majority interest in the partnership. Limited liability partnerships must update their registration statement each year or risk the loss of registration. As far as the tax laws are concerned, LLPs are considered general partnerships. When an LLP has been created, partners can no longer be held jointly or severally liable for the torts, wrongful acts, negligence, or misconduct committed by another partner or by any representative of the partnership. Naturally, partners would still be liable for their own wrongful acts and for the wrongful acts committed by other partners or employees who are under the direct control of that partner. The Revised Uniform Partnership Act includes the provisions necessary for obtaining limited liability status. Thus, states that have adopted the RUPA in its entirety do not need to pass a separate statute to allow for the creation of an LLP.

# Limited Partnerships

Limited partnerships are governed by the Revised Uniform Limited Partnership Act (RULPA). The revised act defines a **limited partnership** as "a partnership formed by two or more persons . . . having one or more general partners and one or more limited partners." **General partners** take an active part in the management of the firm and have unlimited liability for the firm's debts. **Limited partners** are nonparticipating investors. They contribute cash, property, or services to the partnership but do not take part in the management of the firm.

A limited partnership is advantageous for both the limited partner and the general partner. The general partner can accumulate additional capital without admitting another general partner who would be entitled to management rights. Thus, the general partner maintains control while strengthening the firm's treasury. The limited partner also benefits because a limited partnership means limited liability. **Limited liability** in turn means that the limited partner's nonpartnership property cannot be used to satisfy any debts owed by the partnership. Thus, limited partners receive a return on their investment while risking only that original investment.

Limited partnerships must follow strict filing requirements. Usually, a certificate of limited partnership must be filed with the secretary of state's office. The purpose of the certificate is to warn third parties of the limited liability of some partners. However, some state statutes indicate that neither the names of the limited partners nor the amounts of their capital contributions must be included in the certificate. This provision simplifies the formation of a limited partnership because it allows limited partners to remain anonymous.

Failure to file a certificate of limited partnership will deprive a limited partner of limited liability if third parties attempting to hold the limited partner liable did not know that they were dealing with a limited partnership. Moreover, if in the certificate of limited partnership, a limited partner is incorrectly identified as a general partner, he or she would not have limited partner status. To correct such an error, the limited partner would have to refile an amended certificate of limited partnership or leave the limited partnership altogether. Such drastic actions would be necessary unless the state statute under which the

**Did You Know?**

Because the dissolution of a partnership occurs whenever a partner becomes disassociated with the carrying on of partnership business, the dissolution of every partnership is inevitable. Therefore, the dissolution of a partnership is not a question of "if" but of "when."

limited partnership was formed allows a limited partner who has been incorrectly named as a general partner to file with the appropriate state office a unilateral **disclaimer of general partner status**. Limited partners must also guard against becoming too involved in the business. A limited partner who exercises too much control over partnership affairs may lose the protective mantle of limited liability. Recently, however, many state legislatures have greatly expanded the types of activities that a limited partner can perform without losing the shelter provided by limited partnership status.

---

**quick quiz** 25-6

1. A registered limited liability partnership is like a general partner-     true | false
   ship in all respects except liability.

2. In most states, to become a registered limited liability partnership, the     true | false
   partners must file with the auditor's office in the county courthouse.

3. Limited partnerships must have at least three limited partners     true | false
   and no general partners.

---

## Summary

**25.1**  The easiest business organization to form is a sole proprietorship. All that businesspeople have to do is open their doors for business, and a sole proprietorship is created. The greatest advantage to a sole proprietorship is that the owner has complete control over the business. The major disadvantage is that the sole proprietor is subject to unlimited liability.

**25.2**  The Revised Uniform Partnership Act states that a partnership is "an association of two or more persons to carry on as co-owners a business for profit." Under the RUPA, a partnership is considered an entity, or an individual unit that exists separate from the partners. A partnership is an entity in its ability to own title to property, sue or be sued, and have its own separate bank accounts in its own name. Under the RUPA, partnerships also have continuity of existence.

**25.3**  One of the most common ways to form a partnership is by an express agreement between the parties. It is generally best to put the terms in writing to prevent misunderstanding and disputes that might arise later in the life of the partnership. The written agreement that establishes a partnership is called a partnership agreement. To show that a business is operating as a partnership by proof of existence, three elements

must exist: (1) an association of two or more persons (2) who are co-owners of (3) a business for profit.

**25.4**  Capital contributions are sums that are contributed by the partners as permanent investments and that the partners are entitled to have returned when the partnership is dissolved. Loans or later advances that partners make to the partnership and accumulated but undivided profits belong to the partners on an individual basis. Other forms of partnership property belong only to the partnership in its status as an entity. The RUPA states that "A partner is not co-owner of partnership property and has no interest in partnership property which can be transferred, either voluntarily or involuntarily." Partners can use a partnership only for partnership purposes. The RUPA establishes that a partner has an interest in the partnership as a firm. That interest consists of two parts: (1) a transferable economic interest and (2) a nontransferable interest in management rights.

**25.5**  Under the RUPA, a dissociation takes place whenever a partner is no longer associated with the running of the firm. Partners can leave a partnership firm whenever they want. A partner leaves a firm wrongfully if he or she does not have the legal right to do so. The dissolution of a partnership occurs when a partner ceases to be associated with the partnership and the partnership ends. The dissolution of a partnership can occur in one of three ways: (1) by an action committed by the partners, (2) by operation of law, or (3) by the decree of a court of law.

**25.6**   The changing needs of the modern marketplace and the development of new ideas in the law have combined to allow for a new form of partnership, the registered limited liability partnership. Those same forces have cooperated to update one of the more traditional forms of the partnership business, the limited partnership.

## Key Terms

aggregate theory, 545

capital contribution, 549

continuity of existence, 545

disclaimer of general partner status, 556

dissociation, 553

dissolution, 553

entity theory, 545

general partner, 555

limited liability, 555

limited partner, 555

limited partnership, 555

partnership, 545

partnership at will, 553

registered limited liability partnership, 555

Revised Uniform Partnership Act (RUPA), 544

secret partner, 551

silent partner, 551

sole proprietorship, 543

surplus, 550

term partnership, 553

Uniform Partnership Act (UPA), 544

## Questions for Review and Discussion

1. What are the most common forms of business associations?
2. What are the advantages and disadvantages of a sole proprietorship?
3. What are the two model acts that govern partnership law?
4. What are the differences between the aggregate and entity theories of partnership?
5. What is the nature of a partnership agreement?
6. When does profit sharing not create a partnership?
7. What constitutes a person in partnership law?
8. What are the different views of specific partnership property in partnership law?
9. What is the difference between dissociation and dissolution in partnership law?
10. What is the difference between a registered limited liability partnership and a limited partnership?

## Cases for Analysis

1. Jennifer Yauger owned a loft in uptown Silverton. Robert Tomba and Gary Jorgen were partners in a mail-order business in Middletown called NASCAR Collectibles. To open an outlet in Silverton, Tomba and Jorgen leased the loft from Yauger. As part of the agreement, Yauger received $2,650 in rent each month. Later Tomba and Jorgen set up a Web site and began an online auction house for NASCAR collectibles, similar to eBay. They were successful beyond their highest expectations, making over $2 million in their first year of operation. When another online auction house offered Tomba and Jorgen $60 million for their site, they accepted the offer without hesitation. When Yauger heard about the deal, she claimed that she was a partner and demanded a $20 million payment, a sum equal to a one-third share of the sale price. When the case went to court, Yauger pointed to her monthly payments and labeled those payments a share of the profits. She argued that this payment demonstrated that she was a partner, based on proof of existence. Should the court grant Yauger partner status and give her a share of the proceeds from the sale of the business? Explain.

2. Kerry Taylor owned a warehouse in the industrial flats of Parke Central City. Yale Roberts and William Hull were partners in a chain of restaurants called Pirate's Seafood Carousel. Roberts and Hull leased Taylor's warehouse for their restaurant. As part of the agreement, Taylor received $7,500 in rent each month. Taylor retained office space on the top floor of the warehouse. She also agreed to allow Roberts and Hull to remodel the rest of the warehouse to meet the needs of their new restaurant. Taylor occasionally offered advice about the remodeling of the warehouse. In addition, after the restaurant opened for business, Taylor frequently signed for shipments that Roberts and Hull had ordered for the restaurant. After five years in this location, and after selling their other restaurants, Roberts and Hull decided to dissolve their partnership. During the winding up process, they were surprised to learn that Taylor claimed that she should receive a share of the surplus cash after the dissolution of the partnership, because she claimed to be a partner in Pirate's Seafood Carousel. Is Taylor correct in her claim? Will Roberts and Hull have to pay her a share of their surplus cash? Explain.

3. When the father of Stephen and Chris Nuss died, the two boys, aged 15 and 12 years, began to work the family farm. While the boys were still under the age of majority, their mother, Lois, kept the books for the farm. As the boys grew older, they took more and more responsibility in running the farm. They also rented and worked additional acres of farmland. They financed these rental agreements on their own, but their mother cosigned for the arrangements. The boys also purchased additional farmland. Again, their mother helped in this purchase by cosigning. When Chris decided to leave farming, Stephen paid him $100,000, and in exchange, Chris signed over the deed to the newly purchased land. Lois was not involved in this transaction. Stephen's farming business grew. He eventually amassed more than 1,200 acres. He and his wife, Linda, kept their own financial records and maintained their own checking account for the running of the farm. Stephen's mother was not involved in any of this detail. However, Stephen continued to pay many of the expenses involved on the original farm, where his mother still maintained her residence. Stephen also paid the insurance, maintenance, and repair expenses on all buildings and equipment on the original farm. Because Stephen continued to farm this land, in addition to the land he had subsequently purchased, these payments were always characterized as rent. No other payments went to Stephen's mother. When Stephen died, Linda, his widow and executor, claimed that a partnership existed and that the farm equipment on the original acreage and original acreage itself belonged to that partnership. Lois argued that no partnership between Stephen and her existed. Is Linda or Lois correct? Did a partnership exist? Explain. *In re Estate of Nuss,* 646 N.E.2d 504 (OH).

4. McCoy and Gugelman borrowed money from State Security Bank for their partnership, Antiques, Etc. When McCoy and Gugelman failed to pay back the debt, the bank sued them as individuals. At trial, McCoy and Gugelman argued that their partnership, Antiques, Etc., was an entity, not an aggregate, of the partners. Therefore, they concluded, the bank would have to show that the partnership funds were insufficient to answer the judgment before it could proceed against them individually. Are they correct? Why or why not? *Security State Bank v. McCoy,* 361 N.W.2d 514 (NE).

5. Shane ran a liquid fertilizer business. As part of the operation of the business, Shane paid Svoboda a specified amount per acre to spread the fertilizer on his clients' crops. Svoboda's per acre payments remained steady, despite Shane's profits or losses. Frisch was injured while filling a tank truck that was supposed to haul the fertilizer to Svoboda's tractor. Frisch sued both Shane and Svoboda, claiming that Svoboda was sharing in Shane's profits and was therefore a partner. Was Frisch correct? Explain. *Frisch v. Svobada,* 157 N.W.2d 774 (NE).

6. Summers and Dooley formed a partnership for the purpose of operating a trash collection business. The business was operated by the two men, and when either was unable to work, the nonworking partner provided a replacement at his own expense. Summers approached Dooley and requested that they hire a third worker. Dooley refused. Notwithstanding Dooley's refusal, Summers, on his own initiative, hired a worker. Summers paid the employee out of his own pocket. Dooley, upon discovery that a third

person had been hired, objected. He stated that the additional labor was not necessary and refused to allow partnership funds to be used to pay the new employee. After paying out more than $11,000 in wages without any reimbursement from either partnership funds or his partner, Summers brought suit in the Idaho state courts. The trial court held that Summers was not entitled to reimbursement for the wages he had paid the employee. On appeal, did the Supreme Court of Idaho uphold the trial court's decision? Explain. *Summers v. Dooley,* 481 P.2d 318 (ID).

## quick quiz Answers

| 25-1 | 25-2 | 25-3 | 25-4 | 25-5 | 25-6 |
|------|------|------|------|------|------|
| 1. F | 1. F | 1. T | 1. F | 1. T | 1. T |
| 2. T | 2. F | 2. T | 2. T | 2. T | 2. F |
| 3. T | 3. T | 3. T | 3. F | 3. T | 3. F |

## THE OPENING CASE   "Alter Egos" and "Alter-Alter Egos"—*Lehman, Hudson Castle, and Fenway*

The story of the alter ego with an alter ego, begins in 2001 when the financial giant Lehman Brothers used $7 million to purchase an existing corporation named Ibex Capital Markets. Almost immediately, for reasons that will become obvious in a moment, Lehman changed the name of Ibex to Hudson Castle. Despite the name change, Hudson remained a legally incorporated entity with its own separate identity and its own independent corporate status—well, sort of. It had incorporation papers, its own board, and its own employees—well, almost. It looked, acted, and operated like a stand-alone corporate entity, as long as no one looked closely at what it was doing. If someone had looked closely, however, a different picture would have emerged. That picture would have revealed that Hudson was almost totally dedicated to supporting Lehman Brothers. Apparently, this was no accident. A memo written by a Lehman executive, the same Lehman executive who later became CEO of Hudson, revealed that one of Lehman's reasons for buying Hudson was to use it as a shield that would protect Lehman from a public relations disaster if any of Lehman's financial deals collapsed. The close relation-

ship between Lehman and Hudson was hidden from Lehman's shareholders but was well known by Lehman employees, especially since the new CEO at Hudson brought several Lehman employees along with him. The close relationship between Lehman and the Hudson alter ego was cemented by Lehman's control of Hudson's board of directors; by its ownership of 25 percent of Hudson's stock; by a contract that prevented Hudson from working with Lehman's competition, and by a series of alter-alter egos which worked for Hudson as it worked for Lehman. One of its key alter-alter egos was a Hudson alter ego named Fenway, which Hudson operated to benefit Lehman. Under Hudson's control Fenway would borrow money in order to lend that money to Lehman. In one interesting deal, Lehman purchased Fenway notes that were worth more than $3 billion. Then Lehman used the notes to support a loan that Fenway made to Lehman that was secured by a Lehman investment in a West Coast firm that eventually failed. The use of alter egos is not wrong in and of itself. In fact, it can be a very creative process that permits a parent corporation to do a wide variety of things that it would not ordinarily be able to do on its own. Sometimes the alter ego even benefits if it maintains just enough independence to eventually step away from the parent. This is, in fact, what happened to Hudson which lives on even today, brokering the same kind of deals for other firms that it originally fashioned for Lehman, but in a much more independent way. (See Louise Story and Eric Dash, "Lehman Channeled Risks Through 'Alter Ego' Firm," *The New York Times*, April 13, 2010, p. 1.)

**Opening Case Questions**

1. What makes an alter ego an alter ego? Does the definition actually fit the Hudson entity discussed above? Why or why not?

2. Is the Fenway corporation an alter ego of Hudson or of Lehman and what difference would the difference make in this case? Explain.

3. Generally in a veil-piercing case, a plaintiff pierces the veil of the alter ego to reach the parent. In this situation, the alter ego has survived. Can veil piercing be reversed? Can a plaintiff pierce the veil of an insolvent parent to reach a financially healthy alter ego? Explain.

4. Would the instrumentality test work in this case to reach Lehman through Hudson? Why or why not?

5. Would the instrumentality test work in this case to reach Lehman through Fenway? Why or why not? Would a plaintiff be forced to go through Fenway, to Hudson, to Lehman, or could Lehman be reached directly through Fenway? Explain.

## LO Learning Objectives

1. Describe the evolution of associative corporativism.
2. Explain the nature of a corporation.
3. List the constitutional rights of a corporation.
4. Describe the differences among a private, a public, and a quasi-public corporation.
5. Distinguish between a close and an S corporation.
6. List the typical elements within the articles of incorporation.
7. Distinguish between the articles of organization and the operating agreement of a limited liability company.
8. Distinguish between a *de jure* and a *de facto* corporation.
9. Identify the objective of piercing the corporate veil.
10. Distinguish between common and preferred stock.

# 26-1 The Theory of Corporativism

A **corporation** is a legal entity created under the authority of a state or federal statute that gives certain individuals the capacity to operate an enterprise. As such, corporations are products of capitalism. Although capitalism originated in Europe, it flourished in the United States in the 19th century, because the American economic system at that time provided the perfect engine for capitalistic progress. Much of this progress occurred because there was an enormous amount of land that needed to be developed in the United States and an influx of energetic immigrants who were willing to improve that land. Capitalism grew in response, because those businesspeople who worked the land as farms, factories, railroads, and stores needed an efficient and rapid way to raise capital to finance land development projects. The corporation was the perfect means of raising capital quickly and using it effectively. The corporation of today, however, bears little resemblance to the corporation as it was born in the 19th century. Nevertheless, the corporate structure that exists today is a good example of the balancing act that is the law.

# The Corporate Balancing Act

As we have seen at various intervals throughout the text, the law must balance several opposing factors: the letter of the law must be balanced with its spirit; the language of the law must be balanced with its interpretation; abstract legal principles must be balanced with the concrete application of those principles; and the intent of the law must be balanced with the results that emerge from the work of the lawmakers. In many ways, the corporate structure is a vivid manifestation of these balancing acts. Corporations are governed by their own bylaws which must be balanced with state corporate law and with federal statutes and regulations that govern the operation of those corporations. As a direct result of this, corporate officers will at times follow the letter of the law while skirting its spirit as when they make corporate decisions that technically ought to go to the board of directors for a vote. Or they will at times interpret that language of the law to their own advantage as the big corporations did in the 19th century, when they used the Sherman Antitrust, a law specifically designed to end corporate monopolies, to break up union organizing activities, and thus protect their corporate structure.

None of this is to say that corporations or their officers are lawless or unethical. On the contrary, most of them are doing what they are supposed to do. They are protecting their own best interests and the best interests of their shareholders. Much of this is expressed in the balancing act between the Model Business Corporation Act, which is the key statute that governs the creation and operation of corporations in the states, and common law, which is made by state courts in cases involving corporate mishaps.

**The Model Business Corporation Act** As noted above, a corporation is a legal entity created under the authority of a state or federal statute that gives certain individuals the capacity to operate an enterprise. The statutory template that most states follow in developing their corporate law statutes is the Model Business Corporation Act, often referred to as the Model Corporation Act and sometimes simply as the MBCA. The MBCA is a relatively young statute and is therefore not quite as settled as older, more traditional statutes, such as the Uniform Commercial Code and the original Uniform Partnership Act. In addition, the model act has been revised since its original inception, making some of its provisions even more recent and therefore less fully developed than similar provisions in other comparable statutes.

**State Common Law** Also, many states have a long history of common law decisions in relation to corporate law, some of which must be preempted when a state legislature adopts the MBCA. Even in the face of explicit instances of preemption however, some state courts have been reluctant to surrender long-term common law principles and sometimes have found creative ways to interpret the MBCA within the context of that state's long-standing legal tradition. Therefore, the study of corporate law must always be tempered by a look at the state law of the jurisdiction in which a dispute is located. The process of doing business as a self-governing business association, that is, as a corporation, is called **associative corporativism**, or simply **corporativism**. In the 19th century, each corporation was individually created by a unique legislative enactment. Each corporation had its own charter that outlined the powers and abilities of that corporation.

# Balancing Corporate Legal Principles

The theory of associative corporativism has ensured that corporations are protected in a variety of ways. However, the basis of that protection lies within four fundamental legal principles that are designed to protect the corporate structure. These four principles are limited liability, corporate status as an entity, corporate constitutional rights, and corporate citizenship.

## THE OPENING CASE *Revisited, Part I*
### "Alter Egos" and "Alter-Alter Egos"—*Lehman, Hudson Castle, and Fenway,* Round 2

Recall that in the Opening Case at the beginning of the chapter, Lehman Brothers purchased an existing corporation named Ibex Capital Markets and changed its name to Hudson Castle. As an existing corporation, Hudson remained a legally incorporated entity with its own separate identity and its own independent corporate status. It had incorporation papers; its own board, and its own employee. It looked, acted, and operated like a stand-alone corporate entity. One of the advantages to Lehman Brothers in the purchase of Hudson is that the corporation would have limited liability. It also had its own corporate existence. Like any corporation it was, and still is for that matter, a legal person. In order for Lehman to take advantage of this arrangement, Lehman as the parent corporation would have to permit Hudson to have a certain degree of independence so that, if they were ever asked to account for Hudson's actions they could legitimately claim that, throughout all of the financial maneuvering that went on, Hudson remained an independent entity.

**Corporate Limited Liability**  Today one of the most attractive features of the corporate way of doing business is its limited liability. **Limited liability** means that the corporate investors cannot be held personally liable for the debts of the corporation. Thus, the most that an investor can lose is the amount of money used to purchase his or her **shares** of the corporation.

**Corporate Entity Status**  A corporation exists apart from its owners and is taxed directly on the income it earns. As a legal entity, a corporation can own property and sue or be sued, just as an individual can. Moreover, the existence of a corporation is not affected by the death, incapacity, or bankruptcy of a manager or shareholder.

**Corporate Constitutional Rights**  Under provisions of the U.S. Constitution, a corporation is also considered an artificially created legal person. Within the context of the Fourteenth Amendment, a corporation—like a natural person—may not be deprived of life, liberty, or property without due process of law. Also, a corporation may not be denied equal protection of the laws within the jurisdiction of a state.

**Corporate Citizenship**  A corporation is considered a citizen of both the state in which it is incorporated and the state where it has its principal place of business. It can also be sued as a citizen of both these states. By virtue of the due process clause of the Fourteenth Amendment, a state court may also exercise jurisdiction over a noncitizen corporate defendant, as long as that corporation has had an appropriate contact with that state. Such contact can include owning property within the state, doing business in the state, or committing a tort within the state.

U.S. Const.
Amendment 14

## Self-Evident Truths

Corporations are interesting legal constructs. They are totally artificial; they do not have any type of corporal existence. There is no way to see a corporation, talk to one, or watch one in action. Even when we speak of Lehman purchasing Ibex Capital Markets and transforming it into Hudson Castle, for example, we know that Lehman did no such thing. Lehman cannot act. Lehman has no existential exis-tence. Similarly, when we talk about BP's liability in the disaster in the Gulf, we know that there really is no BP to arrest, arraign, indict, and hold without bail. Yet, we not only continue to speak of Lehman and BP as if they were made of flesh and blood, but we also provide them with constitutional rights and give them state citizenship. We also grant them something that the flesh and blood citizens among us do not have—perpetual existence.

Corporations outlive their founders, their officers, their directors, their employees, and their share-holders, well, at least their human shareholders. Perpetual existence, however, does not mean eternal existence. Corporations can and do "pass away." Most actually pass away rather quickly, largely be-cause their incorporators, officers, and directors have mismanaged their resources, mishandled their corporate agenda, or mistreated their employees. At least that is the judgment offered by John Steele Gordon, a financial historian, who in an article entitled "How Long Is a Corporate Lifespan?" also notes that, occasionally, a goliath appears on the corporate horizon whose life seems to be eternal. Still, Gordon argues that all corporate entities, even the goliaths among them, have a life cycle. "They are born," he writes, and they "mature, age, and die." To prove his point he discusses the long, ambitious, and highly successful life of the great railroads, which dominated the transportation industry in the 19th century and far into the 20th only to die from the most common ailment that eventually attacks all the goliaths, "they become," he says, "fat, dumb, lazy, and uninnovative." The American automobile industry is the latest of the goliaths to enter a stage of rapid decline and the next group on the list may be the great investment banks like Lehman Brothers, and all the Lehman clones who are also on the verge of becoming "fat, dumb, lazy, and uninnovative."

## Self-Evident Questions

1.  Is perpetual existence a good idea from a legal and financial perspective or should we limit the life span of corporations? Explain.

2.  According to Gordon, all corporations, even the great goliaths like GM and Chrysler, "become fat, lazy, dumb, and uninnovative." Is he correct in this judgment? Why or why not?

3.  Take another look at the Opening Case at the beginning of this chapter. In that case, Lehman tries to hide some of its financial activities by passing them off to Hudson, thus avoiding what is called "headline risk." Is manipulating corporate ownership to avoid headline risk an ethical practice? Why or why not?

4.  Does Lehman exercise too much control over Hudson, or is Hudson really independent? Explain.

5.  Is there any justifiable reason for granting corporations citizenship and constitutional rights? Why or why not?

## quick quiz 26-1

1.  A corporation is a legal entity created by either a state or federal statute authorizing individuals to operate an enterprise.          true | false

2.  A corporation may not be deprived of life, liberty, or property without due process of law.          true | false

3.  A corporation is considered a citizen of only the state in which it is incorporated.          true | false

# 26-2 Types of Corporate Entities

Corporations may be classified in various ways to emphasize a purpose or characteristic. For clarity, this chapter is limited mainly to a discussion of the major kinds of corporations created by statute and authorized by state-granted charters to incorporate.

## Private, Public, and Quasi-Public

A **private corporation** is a corporation formed by private persons to accomplish a task best undertaken by an entity that can raise large amounts of capital quickly or that can grant the protection of limited liability. Private corporations can be organized for a profit-making business purpose or for a nonprofit charitable, educational, or scientific purpose. If the corporation is organized for profit-making purposes, those profits may be distributed to the shareholders in the form of dividends. **Dividends** are the net profits, or surplus, set aside for the shareholders. **Shareholders** (or stockholders, as they are also known) are the persons who own units of interest (shares of stock) in a corporation.

Large private corporations generally sell their stock to the public at large and are therefore often referred to as public corporations. When the owners of a private corporation decide to sell stock to the public at large, financial experts report that the corporation is about to "go public." This designation can be confusing because the term **public corporation** is more properly used to describe a corporation created by the federal, state, or local government for governmental purposes. When used in the latter sense, the term includes incorporated cities, sanitation districts, school districts, transit districts, and so on. Corporations that are privately organized for profit but also provide a service on which the public depends are generally referred to as **quasi-public corporations**. In most instances, they are public utilities, which provide the public with such essentials as water, gas, and electricity. (Note: Unless specified otherwise, the discussion in this chapter and those that follow will focus on private corporations.)

Google, Inc., headquartered in Menlo Park, California, maintains 17 corporate offices in the United States and 38 corporate offices in 23 countries throughout Asia, Europe, and North and South America.

## Domestic, Foreign, and Alien

A corporation is a **domestic corporation** in the state that grants its charter. It is a **foreign corporation** in all other states. The right to do business in other states (subject to reasonable regulation) is granted by the commerce clause of the U.S. Constitution. To qualify to do business in another state, a foreign corporation must obtain a certificate of authority by providing information similar to the information provided by a domestic corporation applying for a charter. A **certificate of authority** is a document that grants a foreign corporation permission to do business in another state. A registered office and agent must be maintained within the state upon which service of process (notice of a lawsuit) may be made on behalf of the corporation. An **alien corporation** is one that, though incorporated in a foreign country, is doing business in the United States.

## Close and S Corporations

A business corporation may be designated as a **close corporation** when the outstanding shares of stock and managerial control are closely held by fewer than 50 shareholders (often members of the same family) or by one person. State business corporation statutes generally accommodate closely held corporations by allowing them to have a few directors or a sole director and president, with no voting shares in the hands of the public.

The Subchapter S Revision Act of 1982 gives small, closely held business corporations the option of obtaining special tax advantages by becoming an S corporation. An **S corporation** is a corporation in which shareholders have agreed to have the profits (or losses) of the corporation taxed directly to them rather than to the corporation. In this way, they avoid double taxation. There are, however, several restrictions on S corporations. These restrictions include limits on the number and types of owners that can be involved in such an entity. Consequently, many individuals now look to limited liability companies to escape double taxation.

## Limited Liability Companies

The **limited liability company (LLC)** is best thought of as a cross between a partnership and a corporation. Like a corporation, the LLC offers the protection of limited liability to its owners. However, unlike a corporation, the LLC's tax liability flows through the LLC and to the owners. In this way, an LLC, like a partnership and an S corporation, escapes the double taxation penalty that falls on corporate entities. In addition, LLCs are statutory, which means that they may come into existence only if the owners follow the precise steps laid out in the state code by the state legislature. The owners of an LLC are called members. The people who run the LLC are called managers. Later in this chapter, we discuss the formation details of an LLC. Chapter 27 also includes a discussion of the duties and responsibilities of the members and the managers of an LLC.

### quick quiz 26-2

1. A private corporation is one that is formed under the authority of a state statute to perform a governmental function.  true | false
2. A certificate of authority is issued only to S corporations that have passed the test of associative liability.  true | false
3. Limited liability companies have been outlawed in most states because they limit the tax revenue that is due to the government.  true | false

# 26-3 Corporate Formation

A corporation may be incorporated in any state that has a general incorporation statute. Keep in mind that corporations are also subject to court decisions and the state constitution. Federal agencies such as the Securities and Exchange Commission (SEC) also regulate corporate activity. A proper understanding of effective corporate formation necessitates an examination of promoters, the articles of incorporation, the corporate name, the approval of the articles, and commencement of business. Figure 26-1 illustrates the steps of the incorporation process.

## Promoters

The people who want to begin a new corporation or incorporate an existing business are called **promoters**. These people do the actual day-to-day work involved in the incorporation process. **Incorporators** are the people who actually sign the articles of incorporation and submit them to the appropriate state officials. The promoters may also be the incorporators, who later become shareholders and directors of the corporation. Promoters occupy

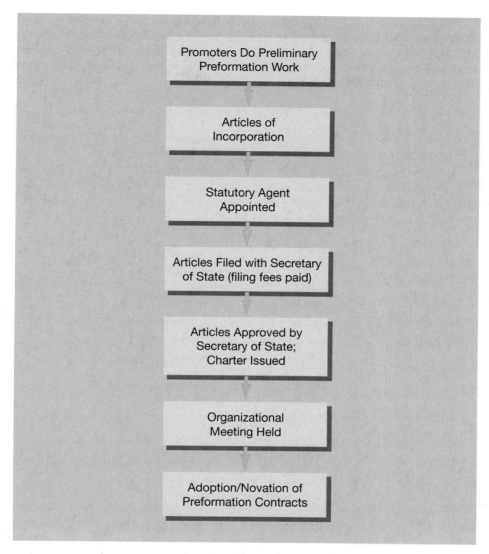

**Figure 26-1** This chart shows the steps in the incorporation process.

a fiduciary relationship with the nonexistent corporation and its future shareholders. Therefore, the promoter must act in the best interests of the new corporation and its shareholders. The promoter must be honest and loyal and fully reveal all information about any contracts made for the corporation.

**Preformation Contracts** Often, promoters will enter contracts for the unborn corporation. For example, it may be necessary to lease office and warehouse space, purchase equipment, and hire employees as preliminary steps in preparing the way for the new corporation. A corporation is not bound by any of the promoter's contracts unless it adopts those contracts. Adoption occurs expressly if the directors pass a resolution agreeing to be bound by a contract. Adoption can also occur implicitly if the corporation accepts the benefits of a contract or makes any payments called for by the agreement.

**Novation** Even after adoption of the contracts, promoters are still potentially liable under the preincorporation contracts. One way for promoters to escape potential liability is to have the corporation and the third party agree to release them. The agreement releasing a promoter is known as a **novation**. The promoter may also include an automatic release clause in all contracts negotiated for the unborn corporation. However, the release clause must do more than simply include the corporation as a party to the contract. It must also specifically release the promoters from liability.

## Articles of Incorporation

The **articles of incorporation** are the written applications to the state for permission to incorporate. This written application is prepared by the corporation's incorporators. The articles, together with the status of incorporation, represent the legal boundaries within which a corporation must conduct its business. Some state incorporation statutes are very strict, requiring detailed information in the articles of incorporation. Typically this information includes the following:

- The corporation's name
- The duration of the corporation
- The purpose(s) of the corporation
- The number and classes of shares
- The shareholders' rights in relation to shares, classes of shares, and special shares
- The shareholders' right to buy new shares
- The addresses of its original registered (statutory) office and its original registered (statutory) agent
- The number of directors plus the names and addresses of the initial directors
- Each incorporator's name and address

### A QUESTION OF ETHICS

Frank Klesner served as a promoter for the formation of a corporation that eventually came to be known as Aerospin, Inc. The board of directors of Aerospin, Inc., held an initial organization meeting at which they were asked to ratify several contracts that Klesner had made on behalf of the corporation before the corporation had actually been formed. One of the contracts involved the purchase of an office building in downtown Billings, Montana. Rudy Lawnbridge, one of the directors, knew of an office building that Aerospin, Inc., could get for much less than the price paid for the building purchased by Klesner. Lawnbridge also knew that because the contract for the Billings building did not include a release clause, Aerospin, Inc., did not have to adopt the contract. Legally, Lawnbridge is correct, but is it ethical for the board of Aerospin, Inc., to abandon Klesner in this manner? Explain.

The newer version of the MBCA has simplified this list somewhat, requiring only the name of the corporation, the number of shares originally authorized, the address of the original registered (statutory) office, the address of the original registered agent, and the incorporators' names and addresses.

## The Corporate Name

One of the first steps in forming a corporation is to choose a corporate name. Usually, the words or an abbreviation of the words *corporation, company,* or *incorporated* must appear somewhere in the corporate name. Also, the corporation cannot choose a name that some other corporation already uses or a name that would confuse the new corporation with one already in existence. Even in situations in which a specific state statute does not prohibit the use of similar names, the courts will prevent such duplication if confusion or unfair competition results. Often the secretary of state's office can tell promoters whether a name has been taken. It is also possible to reserve a name. Usually, there is a small fee for this service. Promoters also must make certain that they check the availability of a corporate name in not only the state of incorporation but also any state within which they plan to have the corporation do business.

## Approval of Articles

After the articles of incorporation are submitted to the state, the appropriate state officer, often the secretary of state, will examine them to make certain that they meet all legal requirements. The secretary of state will also make certain that all filing fees have been paid and that a registered or statutory office and a registered or statutory agent have been appointed. The registered or **statutory agent** is an individual who is designated to receive service of process when a lawsuit is filed against the corporation. Once satisfied that all legal formalities have been met, the secretary of state will issue the corporation's charter, or certificate of incorporation. The charter, or **certificate of incorporation**, is the corporation's official authorization to do business in the state. After the charter is issued, the corporation becomes a fully and legally incorporated entity. The work of the promoters and incorporators ends, unless they become directors or officers of the corporation.

**Did You Know?**

A quick reference to corporate law is a book entitled *Corporations: Laws of the United States,* published by Nova Publishing.

## Commencement of the Business

Most state statutes provide that the first order of business upon incorporation is holding an organizational meeting. Some states require that the meeting be run by the initial directors designated in the articles. In contrast, those states that do not require naming the directors in the articles allow the organizational meeting to be run by the incorporators. Nevertheless, the first order of business at an incorporator-run meeting is to elect the directors. In addition to the appointment of the first directors, the adoption of bylaws, or regulations, also occurs at the organizational meeting. **Bylaws** or **regulations** are the rules that guide the corporation's day-to-day internal affairs. Bylaw provisions usually stipulate the time and place of shareholders' and directors' meetings, quorum requirements, qualifications and duties of directors and officers, and procedures for filling board vacancies.

## Formation of a Limited Liability Company

Similar to a corporation, a limited liability company requires only one person to incorporate. However, the term "person" is liberally defined to include not only people but also corporations and other legal entities, such as partnerships, limited partnerships, trusts, estates, and so on. The term "person" can even include another LLC. Because not all states recognize the tax advantage usually granted to limited liability companies, it is wise for persons contemplating the formation of an LLC to check the legal status of such entities in all of the states in which they intend to do business.

**The Articles of Organization** The **articles of organization** are the written application to the state for permission to form a limited liability company. These articles must include the name of the LLC, the duration of the LLC, and the address where the LLC's operating agreement and bylaws are to be kept. If neither the articles nor the operating agreement, as discussed below, include a duration statement, then some state statutes set an automatic duration period, generally of 30 years. In contrast, in the absence of a duration statement, other state statutes set an unlimited duration. The name of the LLC must include the term "Limited Liability Company" or those words abbreviated, followed by the word "Limited" or the abbreviation "Ltd." In addition, the name of the LLC must not be the same as the name of another LLC or corporation.

However, a problem may arise when a general partnership is transformed into an LLC. An existing general partnership may discover that it has been using a name that is reserved for a corporation or for an already existing LLC. This transformation will require changing the name of the existing partnership before it becomes an LLC. Such a change can be bothersome and complicated, not to mention expensive. The only other alternatives in such a situation would be to acquire authorization to use the common name or to abandon the effort to form an LLC. In addition, a statutory agent for the service of process must be named at the time that the articles are filed in the office of the secretary of state. Finally, proper filing fees must also be paid. Such fees are generally not exorbitant.

**The Operating Agreement** It is also beneficial for the members of an LLC to draw up an **operating agreement**. Such an agreement, though not required by law in all states, is still very helpful in establishing the bylaws of the LLC, which outline the structure and operation of an LLC. Typically the articles of organization include formation provisions, operating provisions, the nature of the business to be conducted by the LLC, distribution of profits and losses, the powers of the managers, voting rights of the members, admission and withdrawal procedures, provisions regarding the transfer of a member's interest in the LLC, and provisions involving the termination of the LLC, among others. Provisions not covered by the operating agreement are determined by the statute authorizing the creation of LLCs in that state.

**Oral Modifications of the Operating Agreement** Some state LLC statutes specify that operating agreements can be oral. Under such a provision, certain procedures may inadvertently be added to the operating relationship between the members simply because of a conversation among those members. For this reason, operating agreements should be written even if state law does not require a writing. Moreover, it is wise to add a provision to the written operating agreement that asserts there can be no oral modifications to the agreement. Fortunately, even those statutes that allow oral additions to the operating agreement specify that certain things, such as an agreement to make a capital contribution to the LLC, must be in writing to be binding on the members.

**Taxation of an LLC** Under Internal Revenue Service (IRS) regulations, the status of a business under state law is not the determining factor in establishing whether a firm, such as an LLC, should be taxed as a partnership or a corporation. Rather, the tax status of such an entity depends on an election made by the owners of that entity. Under the regulations, an entity with two or more members can elect to be treated for tax purposes as an association or as a partnership. An entity owned by one person can elect either association status or a status that will, in effect, hold that the owner and the entity are identical. Election as an association in either situation means that the entity will be taxed as a corporation. The other choice will avoid the corporate tax status.

## quick quiz 26-3

| | |
|---|---|
| 1. An agreement that releases a promoter is called a novation. | true \| false |
| 2. Bylaws are the rules that guide the corporation's day-to-day internal affairs. | true \| false |
| 3. Operating agreements for LLCs are required in all states. | true \| false |

# 26-4 Corporate Identity

Corporations have a life of their own; or at least they are supposed to have such a life. That life begins when they are incorporated by their owners and continues through the choosing of a name, the appointment of an agent for service of process, the election of directors, the hiring or the appointment of managers, the selling of shares, and the paying of dividends. As we have seen, corporations have constitutional rights, citizenship (sometimes even dual citizenship), and limited liability. They are entities that can own property, buy and sell that property, sue and be sued. All of this is true, of course, provided that they are legally formed and are permitted by their owners to develop their own corporate identities. A legally formed corporation is referred to as a *de jure* corporation. A *de jure* corporation is one that has been formed properly by incorporators who followed all of the steps outlined by the state incorporation statute. Most corporations are *de jure* corporations. There are times, however, when the incorporation process is flawed or when the corporation loses its corporate standing. In those cases, the corporation may or may not be a *de facto* corporation, that is, one that exists in fact, but not in law. As strange as it may seem, there are even times when a group of people never intends to incorporate but acts like a corporation to such an extent that they create a corporation by estoppel. Finally, there are situations when a corporation is created legally but is held back by its owners and prevented from becoming an independent entity. In that case, if the subsidiary commits a wrongful act the victim may want to pierce the corporate veil of the subsidiary to reach the parent.

## De Jure and De Facto Corporation

A corporation whose existence is the result of the incorporators having fully or substantially complied with the relevant corporation statutes is a *de jure* corporation. Its status as a corporation cannot be challenged by private citizens or the state. Sometimes an error is made in the incorporation process. When this occurs, the corporation does not exist legally. Nevertheless, as long as the following conditions have been met, a *de facto* corporation (a corporation in fact) will exist:

1. A valid state incorporation statute must be in effect.
2. The parties must have made a *bona fide* (good faith) attempt to follow the statute's requirements for incorporation.
3. The business must have acted as if it were a corporation.

Usually, if only some minor requirement has been left unsatisfied, the court will hold that there has been a good faith attempt to incorporate. Only the state can directly challenge the existence of a *de facto* corporation. Thus, a *de facto* corporation has the same rights, privileges, and duties as a *de jure* corporation as far as anyone other than the state is concerned. The doctrine of *de facto* corporation is in a state of flux at the present time. The doctrine is itself a common law principle and, as such, can be altered by the courts and by statutory law. Moreover, it seems that the Model Business Corporation Act eliminates the doctrine altogether. Nevertheless, some states have either altered that proposition or ignored it. Montana, for example, has added a section to its version of the MBCA, which states that a corporation that forfeits its corporate status, and then recovers it, will be treated as a corporation retroactively to the day that it lost its corporate status. In effect, what this statute does is to validate the use of the *de facto* doctrine when the secretary of state retroactively reactivates a corporation's corporate status. This application is not exactly the reestablishment of the *de facto* doctrine, but it is a reasonable facsimile. Other states have found other ways around the MBCA by reinstituting a frequently ignored doctrine called corporation by *estoppel*. Given the uncertainty surrounding this issue, however, it is best to check the most recent version of a state's corporate law statute should the question ever arise.

## Corporation by Estoppel

In some states, if a group of people act as if they are a corporation when in fact and in law they are not, any parties who have accepted that counterfeit corporation's existence will not be allowed to deny that acceptance. Similarly, individuals who acted as if they were a corporation will not be able to deny that the corporation exists. This doctrine has been labeled corporation by estoppel. Corporation by estoppel does not create a real corporation. Instead, it is a legal fiction used by the courts on a case-by-case basis to prevent injustice. Generally, but not always, it is applied in contract cases rather than in tort cases. Some states may have also abolished corporation by estoppel, and so, as with *de facto* corporation, it is best to check the most recent version of a state's corporate law statute.

### EXAMPLE 26-1 *Valley Victory Church v. Darvin Struck and Bonnie Struck*

The Valley Victory Church lost its *de jure* corporate standing when the attorney who was responsible for filing the church's yearly reports with the secretary of state's office left the state without filing that crucial report. When the report was not filed, the secretary of state revoked Valley Victory's corporate standing and sent a letter to that effect to the truant attorney. The attorney, of course, neither received the letter nor alerted church officials, who continued to act as if the church were a corporation. In the middle of a lawsuit involving the church, Darvin Stock, one of the parties to the suit, discovered this oversight. He argued that the church had no corporate existence at the time of his gift and so the property at the heart of the dispute was still his. Church officials made two counterarguments. First, they said that at the time of the gift, they had a good faith belief that the church was a corporation operating under the authority of a valid state incorporation statute. Therefore, under the doctrine of *de facto* corporation, they continued to operate as a corporation. Second, church officials argued that the Strucks had given the land to the congregation, not to the church. Although the court clearly wanted to accept the church's first argument, it reluctantly rejected that line of reasoning. The court, however, did decide that, under Montana statutory law, once the secretary of state had restored the church's corporate status, all previous corporate acts were ratified. That meant that the church's acceptance of the land was valid when it had occurred. The court also supported the Church's second argument as far as it could, saying that under corporation by estoppel, the Strucks could not recognize the church as a corporation when they transferred the land and then change their minds when it suited them.

## Piercing the Corporate Veil

Sometimes the court will disregard corporate status to impose personal liability on those who have used the corporation to commit fraud or crimes or to harm the public. In such cases, the court will **pierce the corporate veil** and hold the wrongdoers (usually the controlling shareholders) personally liable for activities committed in the corporation's name. The shareholders of close corporations are more likely to fall victim to piercing the corporate veil than are the shareholders of large corporations, because the shareholders of a close corporation are often also the original incorporators, as well as the directors and officers of the corporation, and thus may neglect to follow the corporate formalities required by statute and/or fail to keep corporate property and business separate from their personal property and business. Thus, the court will sometimes find that the corporation is nothing more than the **alter ego** (other self) of the original incorporators. Veil piercing by the courts is less likely to occur with an LLC because corporate formalities are not required by law for LLCs as they are with a corporation. However, in many states, the shareholders of a small corporation can enter a close corporation agreement, which would allow them to escape the need to follow many corporate formalities.

## EXAMPLE 26-2: Jamestown Beauty and Tanning's Alter Ego

For 12 years, Laurie Bostic and Shelley Hershey ran the Jamestown Beauty and Tanning Salon by themselves. On advice from their financial planner, they decided to incorporate. They named themselves president and chairperson of the board respectively. They were also the sole shareholders. Despite the incorporation of Jamestown, Bostic and Hershey continued to run their salon as if it were not incorporated. They failed to keep a separate bank account for the salon and usually simply commingled their personal funds with funds that actually belonged to the corporation. They also used all of the property in the salon as her own personal property. They held no directors' meetings and kept no corporate records. When they were sued by a creditor, the court allowed that creditor to pierce the corporate veil and hold Bostic and Hershey personally liable. Bostic and Hershey had failed to maintain a distinction between themselves and the corporation so that, even though on paper in the secretary of state's office, they appeared to be different, in reality, they were not. Therefore, the court concluded that the Jamestown Beauty and Tanning Salon was actually Bostic and Hershey's alter ego. Bostic and Hershey could have avoided this problem if they had created an LLC rather than a corporation or if they had executed a close corporation agreement.

Large corporations can also fall victim to piercing the corporate veil if they set up subsidiaries, completely control those subsidiaries, and then commit fraud through the subsidiary. In such cases, however, it is the parent corporation, rather than the individual shareholders, that the courts will hold liable. The test used to determine whether the corporate veil should be pierced to reach the parent corporation is called the *instrumentality test*.

## THE OPENING CASE *Revisited, Part II*
## "Alter Egos" and "Alter-Alter Egos"—*Lehman, Hudson Castle, and Fenway*, Round 3

When Lehman brothers purchased Ibex Capital Markets and renamed it Hudson Castle, the investment firm created an unusual alter ego veil-piercing problem. It was clear that, despite the name change, Hudson remained a legally incorporated entity with its own separate identity and its own independent corporate status. It had incorporation papers; its own board, and its own employees. Nevertheless, Hudson was almost totally dedicated to supporting Lehman Brothers. The close relationship between Lehman and the Hudson alter ego was solidified by Lehman's control of Hudson's board; by its ownership of 25 percent of Hudson's stock; by a contract that prevented Hudson from working with Lehman's competition, and by a series of alter-alter egos that worked for Hudson as it worked for

Lehman. Usually, in these circumstances, the alter ego collapses, and a plaintiff who has lost money as a result asks the court to pierce the corporate veil to reach the protected parent, which has a rich treasury filled with money made off the now insolvent alter ego. In this case we have the opposite situation. Hudson, the alter ego, benefited from its relationship with Lehman. Moreover, Hudson maintained just enough independence to eventually step away from Lehman. Today Hudson, which lives on is brokering the same kind of deals it did for Lehman but in a much more independent way. Might it be possible for a disgruntled investor to ask the court to perform a "reverse veil-piercing operation" going through Hudson's veil to reach Lehman? Think about it.

This test requires that the parent corporation so dominate the subsidiary that the subsidiary has become a "mere instrumentality of the parent." In this situation, the courts will allow the veil of the instrumentality to be pierced to reach the dominant corporation and to hold that corporation liable for any harm that has been committed through the instrumentality. The courts, however, do not engage in such veil piercing lightly. Still, while the courts respect the separate corporate identity of most subsidiaries, they cannot allow a subsidiary to be used by the parent so that the parent can escape liability, especially if the instrumentality was set up in the first place to commit fraud. When a corporation is set up as a mere instrumentality of a parent, it is sometimes referred to as a **dummy corporation** or a **corporate shell**.

## quick quiz 26-4

| | |
|---|---|
| 1. The doctrine of the *de facto* corporation requires that there be a *bona fide* attempt to incorporate under an existing incorporation statute and an exercise of corporate power. | true \| false |
| 2. Corporation by estoppel does not create a real corporation. | true \| false |
| 3. The standard used to determine whether the corporate veil should be pierced to reach the parent corporation is called the instrumentality test. | true \| false |

# 26-5 Corporate Financing

Corporate financing begins when the original investments are made to set up the corporation. Once the corporation is operating, additional corporate financing may be obtained from earnings, loans, and the issuance of additional shares of stock. The issuing and selling of shares of stock to raise capital is known as *equity financing,* and equity securities give their owners a legal interest in the assets, earnings, and control of the corporation. The part of a corporation's net profits or surplus set aside for the shareholders is known as dividends.

## Classes of Corporate Stock

The number of shares and classes of stock that a corporation is authorized to issue are established in its certificate of incorporation. A shareholder who purchases corporate stock invests money or property in the corporation and receives a stock certificate. A **stock certificate** is written evidence of ownership of a unit of interest in the corporation.

## Dividends

The most common type of dividend is the **cash dividend**, declared and paid out of current corporate earnings or accumulated surplus at regular intervals. A corporation's board of directors has the sole authority to determine the amount, time, place, and manner of dividend payment. Typically, the directors' declaration of a dividend sets a cutoff date—the date by which a shareholder must hold corporate stock of record to receive payment. In a few instances, a distribution of earnings is made in shares of capital stock, called a **stock dividend**.

**Common Stock**    The most usual type of corporate stock is **common stock**. Common stock carries with it all the risks of the business, inasmuch as it does not guarantee its holder the right to profits. The shareholder is usually entitled to one vote for each share of stock held. The holders of common stock are paid dividends when the corporation elects to make such a distribution. Holders of common stock risk whatever they invest.

## Preferred Stock
Those classes of stock that have rights or preferences over other classes of stock are known as **preferred stock**. These preferences generally involve the payment of dividends and/or the distribution of assets on the dissolution of the corporation. Preferred stock may be either cumulative or noncumulative. Generally, dividends on cumulative preferred stock are paid every year. However, if the dividends are not paid in one year, they will be paid in later years if any dividends at all are paid by the corporation. Dividends on noncumulative preferred stock are also usually paid each year. However, with noncumulative preferred stock, dividends that are not paid in one year are lost forever.

## Stock Valuation
**Par value** is the value placed on the shares of stock at incorporation. This value, which is the same for each share of stock of the same issue, is stated on the corporation's certificate of incorporation. In the case of par value shares, the amount of the capital stock or stated capital is the total par value of all the issued stock.

The practice of placing a par value on a share of stock has been criticized as misleading. Uninformed buyers often interpret par value printed on the face of the certificate as the actual market value of the shares. To correct this condition, all states have authorized the issuance of no par value stock. *No par value stock* is corporate stock issued without any stated price. In fact, par value stock has been eliminated completely under provisions found in the newest version of the MBCA.

---

### quick quiz 26-5

1. Corporate financing cannot begin until six months after the certificate of incorporation has been issued.      true | false

2. The most common type of dividend is the stock dividend.      true | false

3. The practice of placing a par value on a share of stock has been approved of and is now mandated by the American Federated Banking Commission.      true | false

---

## Summary

**26.1**   The process of doing business as a self-governing business association, that is, as a corporation, is called associative corporativism, or simply corporativism. A corporation is a legal entity (also referred to as a legal person), the creation of which is empowered by a state or a federal statute authorizing individuals to operate an enterprise. A corporation is a legal person and therefore has certain constitutional rights, such as the right to equal protection of the law and the right not to be deprived of property without due process. Corporations also have dual citizenship. They are citizens of the states in which they are incorporated and in which they have their principal place of business.

**26.2**   Corporations can be classified in many ways, including private, public, and quasi-public corporations; domestic and foreign corporations; and close and S corporations. The limited liability company offers the protection of limited liability but allows tax liability to flow through the LLC and to its owners.

**26.3** A corporation can be incorporated in any state that has a general incorporation statute. The people who actually start the corporation are the promoters. Promoters are liable on preformation contracts until those contracts are adopted by the corporation. The articles of incorporation are drawn up by the corporation's incorporators. After reviewing the articles of incorporation, the secretary of state will issue a corporate charter, and the corporation becomes a legally incorporated entity. The members of a limited liability company must also follow precise formation procedures.

**26.4** A *de jure* corporation is a legally formed corporation. Two doctrines, *de facto* corporation and corporation by estoppel, have been developed to deal with the problem of defective incorporation. A *de facto* corporation exists if there has been a good faith attempt to comply with an existing incorporation statute and an exercise of corporate power. The doctrine of corporation by estoppel prevents later denial of corporate existence by parties willing to deal with an entity as if it were a corporation. Under the doctrine of piercing the corporate veil, courts can refuse to recognize a legally formed corporation to prevent injustice and to impose liability on the wrongdoers.

**26.5** Corporate financing begins when the incorporators give money to set up the business. Subsequent financing takes many forms. The issuing and selling of shares of stock to raise capital is called equity financing. The two most popular classes of stock are common stock and preferred stock. Stock can also be par value or no par value stock. Dividends can be issued as cash or as stock.

## Key Terms

alien corporation, 565
alter ego, 572
articles of incorporation, 568
articles of organization, 569
associative corporativism, 562
bylaws, 569
cash dividend, 574
certificate of authority, 565
certificate of incorporation, 569
close corporation, 565
common stock, 574
corporate shell, 574
corporation, 561
corporation by estoppel, 571

corporativism, 562
*de facto* corporation, 571
*de jure* corporation, 571
dividends, 565
domestic corporation, 565
dummy corporation, 574
foreign corporation, 565
incorporators, 566
limited liability, 563
limited liability company (LLC), 566
novation, 568
operating agreement, 570
par value, 575

pierce the corporate veil, 572
preferred stock, 575
private corporation, 565
promoters, 566
public corporation, 565
quasi-public corporation, 565
regulations, 569
S corporation, 566
share, 563
shareholders, 565
statutory agent, 569
stock certificate, 574
stock dividend, 574

## Questions for Review and Discussion

1. How did the concept of corporativism evolve?
2. What is the nature of a corporation?
3. What are the constitutional rights of a corporation?
4. What are the differences among a private, a public, and a quasi-public corporation?
5. What is the difference between a close and an S corporation?
6. What are the typical elements within the articles of incorporation?

7. What is the difference between the articles of organization and the operating agreement of a limited liability company?
8. What is the difference between a *de jure* and a *de facto* corporation?
9. What is the objective of piercing the corporate veil?
10. What is the difference between common and preferred stock?

# Cases for Analysis

1. Dr. Steven A. Pottschmidt was employed by Dr. Thomas J. Klosterman, who was doing business as a corporation named Thomas J. Klosterman, M.D., Inc. Once Pottschmidt's original employment agreement ended, he decided to bring a breach of contract suit against Klosterman alleging that he, Pottschmidt, had not been paid the amount that was actually owed him under the agreement. Within two months of the lawsuit, Klosterman created a new corporation, called Klosterman Family Practice, Inc. Klosterman Family Practice, however, did not employ anyone other than the staff of the first corporation, Thomas J. Klosterman, M.D., Inc. In addition, the second corporation had not moved from the original office, had not changed its phone number, had not purchased new equipment or new furniture, and had not taken on any new patients. For a while, the two corporations held separate accounts at one bank. Eventually, however, the first company's bank account was terminated, and income for bills sent out by the first company were placed in the account of the second company. Pottschmidt wants the court to permit him to pierce the corporate veil of both Thomas J. Klosterman, M.D., Inc., and Klosterman Family Practice, Inc., to hold Dr. Klosterman directly liable for the money owed to him. Is there enough evidence here to permit the veil piercing requested by the plaintiff? Explain. *Pottschmidt v. Thomas J. Klosterman, M.D., Inc.,* 169 Ohio App.3d 824 (Court of Appeals of Ohio, Ninth District, Medina County).

2. The Aerenthal Financial Loan Corporation lent $578,000 to Raymond Viviani and secured the loan with a mortgage on Viviani's ski lodge, which was located south of Burlington, Vermont. Vermont decided to build a new state highway along a route that cut right through Viviani's lodge. Viviani contested the state's decision and attempted to get the highway rerouted. After several months of unsuccessful battles with the state, Viviani decided to settle for the offer from the government. The state then paid Viviani the market value for the property. Unfortunately, the state failed to notify Aerenthal Financial Loan Corporation about the transaction. When Aerenthal discovered that it had not been notified, it filed a formal protest with the state. The state sent its apologies but argued that Aerenthal had no right to be notified about what was essentially a contractual matter between Viviani and the government. Aerenthal disagreed, arguing that the government had violated its constitutional right not to be deprived of property without due process of law. The state responded by noting that under the state constitution, it had operated properly and Aerenthal was not entitled to due process. Who is correct here? Explain.

3. General Housing Assistance was incorporated as a nonprofit organization that provides low-cost housing for families who have been economically dislocated because of the downsizing of a company or the outsourcing of jobs. One year after the formation of General Housing Assistance, General Mutual Housing Assistance was incorporated in the same state. General Mutual Housing Assistance sold housing shares in condominiums to subscribers. General Mutual ran an aggressive, often obnoxious advertising campaign. After this campaign, General Housing found that people were confusing the two entities. The resulting mix-up damaged General Housing Assistance's image and threatened its charitable funding sources. Consequently, it filed suit to stop General Mutual from using the name because of the confusion between the two entities. Are the names similar enough to cause the court to order General Mutual to change its name? Explain.

4. Through Langham Engineering, Michael Langham marketed his invention, the cross-slope monitor (CSM), as an accessory to John Deere equipment. He had a plan to expand his business to include the CSM as an accessory to Caterpillar Tractor (CAT) equipment. To do this, Langham and Clark Balderson of Balderson, Inc., entered a preincorporation agreement (PIA), in which Langham agreed to contribute his technical abilities, and Balderson agreed to contribute his leadership capabilities to manufacture and market the CSM to CAT. No release clause was included in the PIA. The resulting corporation was named Illinois Controls, Inc. Balderson was designated the president and chairman of the board, and Langham was named vice president. Over the next two years, Balderson failed to train and motivate the sales staff about the proper techniques for selling the CSM to CAT dealers. Balderson also neglected to arrange

demonstrations and consignment sales, failed to employ properly trained personnel, and disregarded the need to develop, print, and distribute installation manuals for the CSM. Finally, Balderson set up another corporation named the Dymax Corporation, which dealt with CAT's competitors, thereby undermining Illinois Control's relationship with CAT. As a result, Illinois Controls was forced to shut down operations. Langham sued Balderson personally for the losses that he incurred as a result of Balderson's failure to meet his obligations as outlined in the PIA. Balderson argued that the PIA was a promoter's contract and that the corporation had adopted it. Therefore, Illinois Controls should be held liable. Was Balderson correct? Explain. *Illinois Controls, Inc., v. Langham,* 639 N.E.2d 771 (OH).

5. Harry and Kay Robinson of New York purchased a new Audi automobile from World Wide Volkswagen (WWV) in New York. After having an accident in Oklahoma, they brought a product liability action against WWV. The case was brought to court in Oklahoma. The Robinsons claimed that the injuries they suffered were caused by the defective design and placement of their automobile's gas tank and fuel system. WWV, which was incorporated in New York and did business there, contended that the Robinsons could not sue WWV in Oklahoma because it was not a citizen of Oklahoma. WWV further contended that it performed no services, owned no property, and closed no sales in Oklahoma. It solicited no business in Oklahoma either through salespersons or through advertising. It also did not indirectly through others serve or seek to serve the Oklahoma market. Did the Oklahoma state court have jurisdiction over WWV? Explain. *World Wide Volkswagen Corporation v. Woodson,* 100 S.Ct. 559 (U.S. Sup. Ct.).

6. Spence was a promoter in the incorporation of a new business. The new corporation had not yet been formed when he bought Huffman's employment agency to serve as the nucleus of that corporation. Eventually, the corporation was formed, but it never generated enough cash to pay Huffman for the employment agency. Huffman sued Spence, attempting to hold him personally liable for the amount due. Spence claimed that the corporation was liable and that his personal assets were not a proper target of the suit. Was Spence correct? Explain. *Spence v. Huffman,* 486 P.2d 211 (AZ).

7. MBI filed its original articles of incorporation under the name Montana Public Employees Benefit Services Co., Inc. After filing the articles, the corporation entered a contract with the Montana Department of Administration. Under the contract, the new corporation would have exclusive administrative control over Montana's public employee deferred-payment pension plan. The articles were not approved by the secretary of state, who requested a name change. After the corporation's name was changed to MBI, the charter was issued, and the corporation became a legal entity. The Montana Association of Underwriters, a private corporation that wanted a share in administering the state pension plan, challenged the validity of the contract, arguing that at the time the contract was signed, MBI did not legally exist. Was the Montana Association of Underwriters correct? Explain. *Montana Association of Underwriters v. Department of Administration and MBI,* 563 P.2d 577 (MT).

8. Lamas Company, Inc., was incorporated in Georgia. Baldwin negotiated with Lamas, sole owner of Lamas Company, Inc., to finish some electrical work on a construction site. When Baldwin was dissatisfied with the work, he decided to sue. Unfortunately, the statute of limitations ran out before he could sue Lamas Company, Inc., so he sued Lamas individually. Baldwin argued that he had dealt only with Lamas, that he did not know Lamas was an agent of the company, that Lamas did not tell him about the company, and that he understood the contract to be with Lamas individually. Lamas pointed out that Baldwin made out and sent checks directly to Lamas Company, Inc., and that Lamas Company, Inc., always appeared as the payee on those checks. Lamas claimed that this evidence alone would be enough to stop Baldwin from denying that he had dealt with Lamas Company, Inc. The trial court rendered judgment against Lamas. On appeal, did the appellate court reverse? Explain. *Lamas v. Baldwin,* 230 S.E.2d 13 (GA).

9. Boafo was allegedly injured while giving birth at Parkway Regional Hospital. Boafo sued both Parkway Regional and Hospital Corporation of America (HCA), asking the court to pierce the corporate veil to reach HCA, which Boafo claimed was a parent company. Boafo showed that the two corporations shared the same offices, that they purchased hospital equipment together, that HCA owned 100 percent of Parkway stock, that major

financing for Parkway was performed by HCA through a national accounting system, and that Parkway was insured by another wholly owned subsidiary of HCA. In answer, HCA emphasized that Parkway handled its own daily financing, that it was free to negotiate and enter its own contracts, that it had an adequate amount of money in its treasury, and that it was not formed to promote fraud, conceal crime, or evade legal liability. The trial court granted summary judgment, dismissing the claim against HCA. Did the appellate court uphold the trial court's ruling? Explain. *Boafo v. Hospital Corporation of America,* 338 S.E.2d 477 (GA).

10. The Northeastern Corporate Institute of Technology (NCIT), a profit-oriented corporation engaged in nuclear research projects, owned and operated an experimental station in a remote region of Alaska. The Alaskan Chemical Disposal Corporation, a subsidiary of NCIT, disposed of all chemical and nuclear waste products produced by NCIT's experimental station. On a routine disposal route, an Alaskan Chemical Disposal transport convoy collided with a North Coast moving van.

The lead truck in the convoy spilled chemical waste into a lake owned by Kenneth Ridgeway. Ridgeway sued both NCIT and Alaskan Chemical Disposal. NCIT argued that the disposal of NCIT's chemical was the sole responsibility of Alaskan Chemical Disposal, which it characterized as an independent contractor. Ridgeway's attorney, however, had discovered that Alaskan Chemical Disposal had no business other than providing waste disposal services to NCIT. The attorney also discovered that Alaskan Chemical Disposal was listed as a division of NCIT, was financed by NCIT, and shared the same board of directors and officers as NCIT. Moreover, the attorney found out that Alaskan Chemical Disposal was badly undercapitalized. In addition, all decisions in the running of Alaskan Chemical Disposal were made by NCIT. In light of all of this evidence, Ridgeway's attorney began to suspect that Alaskan Chemical Disposal might have been formed to allow NCIT to escape liability in just this type of situation. Will Ridgeway be allowed to maintain its suit against NCIT? Explain.

## quick quiz Answers

| 26-1 | 26-2 | 26-3 | 26-4 | 26-5 |
|------|------|------|------|------|
| 1. T | 1. F | 1. T | 1. T | 1. F |
| 2. T | 2. F | 2. T | 2. T | 2. F |
| 3. F | 3. F | 3. F | 3. T | 3. F |

# Chapter 27 · Corporate Governance

## THE OPENING CASE
### Winners, Losers, and Innocent Victims—BP, Transocean, and Anadarko

The story of the Great Gulf Oil Spill is the stuff of epic movies, television specials, and congressional hearings. It is also the stuff of lawsuits and financial disasters. Part of this great epic is deciding who is to blame for the disaster. That decision would not be difficult were it not for the innocent victims involved in the tragedy. Sometimes it is even challenging to determine just who those victims might be. Certainly, some of the victims include those who suffered because of the initial explosion. Identifying and compensating these victims and their families should be uncomplicated. However, there are other people who, through no fault of their own, were victims of the Great Gulf Spill, but who are often overlooked in the rush to judgment that generally surrounds these situations. Among those people are the shareholders of the main corporate players in the disaster—BP, Transocean, and Anadarko. Technically, the shareholders are the real owners of these corporations. They hold shares in each enterprise and they expect to profit from those shares. For some of these shareholders that profit comes from dividends, while for others it comes from the sale of the stock. When the value of the shares drops, that potential profit drops accordingly, regardless of its source. A case in point would involve the shareholders of BP who, within a month of the disaster, saw the value of their shares drop eight points. Similarly, Transocean shareholders saw a drop of 16 points and Anadarko experienced a drop of 12 points. The most interesting aspect about these losses is that they were not issued as punishment by a court of law or a congressional committee but resulted, instead, from random market forces within the economy, forces that react to rumors, innuendo, and lies. Thus, as soon as investors learned that the oil spill would take at least three months to fix, BP stock dropped in value, and the shareholders of BP had to absorb that loss. Is this not an excellent argument for increasing the power of the shareholders? Should they not be more involved in corporate decision-making? Should they not have more power to sue corporate managers? The manger-control theory of corporate power suggests that corporate managers should be insulated from shareholders because the managers know what is going on in the corporation while the shareholders do not. How convincing does that argument sound in the wake of the Great Gulf Oil Spill? (See Andrew Bary, "BP, Transocean Priced for Disaster," *Barron's*, May 3, 2010, p. 26. See also

Thomas G. Donlan, "In the Face of Disaster," *Barron's,* May 10, 2010, p. 62.)

**Opening Case Questions**

1. Is it fair for corporate shareholders to be penalized for decisions that they had no hand in making? Why or why not?

2. Some experts argue that both groups—shareholders and corporate managers—are too biased by self-interest to make corporate decisions properly. Does this argument mean that the government should control corporate decision making? Explain.

3. Is permitting shareholders easier access to the courts for the purpose of suing corporate managers a good solution to the problem of corporate decision making? Explain. Would increasing the shareholders' voting power be a more effective, less disruptive strategy? Explain.

4. No one believes for a moment that drilling for oil from ocean platforms will cease because of the Great Gulf Oil Spill. Why then should anyone be penalized for the accident in the Gulf? Explain.

5. Individuals who support special interest group control would like to see representatives from employees' unions, consumer protection organizations, and environmental protection groups on corporate boards. Would this have helped prevent the Great Gulf Oil Spill? Why or why not?

 Learning Objectives

1. Explain the central dilemma of corporate governance.
2. Describe the functions of directors, officers, and shareholders.
3. List the five theories of corporate governance.
4. Describe cumulative voting and proxy solicitation.
5. Explain shareholder proposals.
6. Distinguish between voting trusts and pooling agreements.
7. Contrast shareholder direct suits with shareholder derivative suits.
8. Contrast the business judgment rule with the fairness rule.
9. List the rights that belong to shareholders.
10. Explain the management of a limited liability company.

# 27-1 Management of the Corporation

Most state incorporation statutes provide that a corporation's business affairs are to be managed under the direction of a board of directors. The board of directors establishes broad policies, and the officers and other employees implement those policies. The shareholders are the owners of the corporation. How to keep the role of the board separate from that of executive management and that of shareholders is related to the challenge of how best to organize the board and select its members. The issues are even more complex today because a single individual often functions as a director, an officer, and a shareholder. Nevertheless, the three roles have distinct functions and should be examined separately.

## Directors of the Corporation

The business affairs of a corporation are managed by a board of directors elected by the shareholders. The board's responsibility is to take whatever actions are appropriate, in keeping with the corporation's rules and regulations, to further the corporation's business. Individual board members are supposed to use their own judgment in the corporate decision-making process.

## Qualifications of Directors

State law and corporate rules set up the qualifications that a person must have to be a corporate director. Unless prohibited by the corporation's certificate of incorporation, membership on the board of directors can be extended to anyone, including aliens, minors, and nonshareholders. Often the certificate stipulates that at least one director must be a state resident and at least one must be a shareholder.

## Time Commitment of Directors

Directors are elected at the annual meeting of the shareholders. Generally, directors hold office for one or two years. The number of directors on the board varies between eight and twelve. Usually, several directors are elected as a group to maintain continuity; this procedure permits one-third of the board to be elected annually. The basic time commitment for a director is approximately 30 days per year, but depending upon need, availability, and interest, it can be 40, 60, 80, or even more days. Naturally, directors can resign from the board. However, many states require written notice of the director's resignation to the corporation.

## Meetings of Directors

The directors of most large corporations meet on a regular basis at a precise time and place of their choosing. The directors of many smaller corporations meet only when specific items are to be considered. Some states allow small corporations with fewer than 50 shareholders to eliminate the board of directors entirely, as long as someone is assigned the duties that the board would have performed.

Directors are not entitled to be notified about regular board meetings unless notice is required by the corporation's bylaws. (The bylaws, or regulations of a corporation, determine how that corporation will operate.) However, directors must be notified of special meetings of the board. For example, a special meeting of the directors might be called to decide whether the corporation should institute a lawsuit. If any director is not notified of a special meeting, all actions taken at the meeting are void. A director may not specify another person to vote in her or his place. The quorum, or minimum number of directors necessary to conduct business, is usually one more than half of the total number of directors. Bylaws may require more than a quorum, perhaps 70 percent of the directors, to conduct certain types of business. This supermajority might be needed, for instance, to remove a director or sell a significant portion of the business. Generally though, the actions of a quorum constitute the official actions of the board.

### EXAMPLE 27-1: Meeting the Quorum

The board of directors of Barber Enterprises, Inc., consisted of seven persons. At a properly called meeting, one of the directors presented a motion calling for a stock-option purchase plan for Barber's president, vice presidents, secretary, and treasurer. Five directors attended the meeting. This constituted a quorum. Three of the five voted for the plan. This vote would constitute an official act by the board.

## Officers of the Corporation

Directors are not expected to spend all of their time and energy managing the corporation. They have the authority to appoint officers and agents to run the day-to-day affairs of the corporation. By statute, the usual officers are a president, several vice presidents, a secretary, and a treasurer. Other officers, such as a comptroller, cashier, and general counsel, are often provided. The bylaws of the corporation describe the duties of each officer. Officers have the authority of general agents for the operation of the normal business of the corporation. They in turn delegate duties to various department heads. Although the roles of directors and officers differ, they are frequently assumed by the same people. An individual may be both chief executive officer and chair of the board of the same corporation. Directors and officers can also be shareholders in the corporation.

## Shareholders of the Corporation

The shareholders are the owners of the corporation. The more shares that a shareholder owns, the more voting power that shareholder has in the running of the corporation. Therefore, the most effective way for a shareholder to obtain corporate power is to purchase more stock. Unfortunately, purchasing additional stock is not always possible, either because the shareholder does not have the financial leverage needed to purchase enough shares to gain corporate control or because there are no shares available to purchase. Another way to gain operating power is to work with the shares that the shareholder already owns but increase voting power in other ways. Before looking at those voting techniques, it is important to remember that though many shareholders are individuals, others are large institutions such as union pension funds that have invested large sums of money in corporate stock to gain a return for their retirees.

---

### quick quiz 27-1

| | | |
|---|---|---|
| 1. | The business affairs of a corporation are managed by a board of directors elected by the shareholders. | true \| false |
| 2. | Membership on a board of directors can never be extended to aliens, minors, or nonshareholders. | true \| false |
| 3. | Directors have authority to appoint officers and agents to run the day-to-day affairs of the corporation. | true \| false |

---

# 27-2 Issues in Corporate Governance

Under the original concept of a corporation, the shareholders are the primary reason that a corporation exists. This image has evolved over the years, so that now shareholders often take a back seat to consumers, employees, environmentalists, politicians, social science engineers, and economists. For this reason, the corporate landscape has come to resemble a battlefield in recent years. There are those who believe that the battle is a good thing because it helps make corporations more responsible. There are others, however, who believe that the battle has weakened, and in some cases completely dismantled, corporate power.

## The Corporate Balancing Act Revisited

A more productive way of looking at the issue might be to see, not a battlefield, but an extension of the corporate balancing act that we discussed in the last chapter. We have noted repeatedly throughout the text that the law must balance several opposing factors. For instance, we have noted that the intent of the law must be balanced against the results that emerge from the work of lawmakers; the letter of the law must be balanced with its spirit; the language of the law must be balanced with its interpretation; abstract legal principles must be balanced with the concrete application of those principles, and so on. The

**Did You Know?**

Although the shareholders of a corporation are the actual owners of the corporation, they are not agents of the corporation, as are the directors and officers, and therefore cannot commit the corporation to any contractual arrangements.

issue of corporate leadership is just one more aspect of this legal balancing act. Thus, in this case, the needs of the shareholders must be balanced against the needs of the local community, while the needs of the local community must be balanced against needs of the economic agenda of the state and the nation. Similarly, the expertise of the managers must be balanced against the profit motive of the shareholders, the regulatory agenda of the government, and the individual needs of special interest groups. Each group has offered a different solution to the problem. Which group, if any, has correctly diagnosed the problem remains to be seen. For the present, we can examine five different corporate control paradigms. These paradigms include special interest group control, governmental control, independent director control, managerial control, and shareholder democratic control.

## Theories of Corporate Governance

As noted previously, five theories have been put forth by legal scholars and business experts regarding how corporations should be managed: special interest group control, governmental control, independent director control, managerial control, and shareholder democracy.

**Special Interest Group Control** Special interest group control is based on the idea that corporate decision making affects more individuals and groups than just the shareholders and the managers of the corporation. The people who support special interest group control argue that many corporate decisions, such as a decision to open or close a factory, affect the community through consumers, suppliers, employees, and community neighbors. Consequently, all of these groups and more should be represented on the boards of directors of all major corporations. Individuals who support special interest group control would like to see representatives from employees' unions, consumer protection organizations, and environmental protection groups on these boards. Opponents of the theory point out the impracticality of this approach to corporate management.

**Governmental Control** Support for the governmental control theory of corporate management is based on the belief that because corporate decision making influences more individuals and groups than just the shareholders and the managers, corporate decisions should be made by an impartial group of corporate outsiders. Usually, the corporate outsiders named are government officials. These specially educated government officials would make corporate decisions in an objective manner, based on the needs of the entire society and the economy as a whole. Opponents of this theory label such an approach socialistic and point to the relatively poor record of many socialist economies as evidence of the impracticality of this approach.

Of course, those who support governmental control do not always go so far as to demand that the government have a seat in every corporate boardroom in America. A less dramatic and perhaps more effective technique is to use governmental control indirectly through regulatory legislation. One particularly effective piece of congressional legislation in this regard is the Sarbanes-Oxley (SarbOx) Act of 2002. SarbOx was passed by Congress in the wake of a series of corporate scandals, some of which were caused by the failure of the board and the chief corporate officers to oversee activities properly within their corporations. Thus, Congress placed certain strict requirements on officers and directors and added severe penalties for the failure to meet those requirements. For example, under SarbOx, chief executive officers (CEOs), chief operating officers (COO's), and chief financial officers (CFOs) are required to present declarations that confirm the accuracy of their corporation's financial statements. They must indicate that the statements do not misrepresent the company's economic situation. The penalties for violating this particular provision include possible incarceration and monetary penalties that run into the millions.

Not everyone in the corporate community is happy about the passage of SarbOx or about the extra regulatory responsibilities that it places on corporate directors, officers, and auditors. Some financial experts, for instance, predict that the United States will soon experience a loss of foreign business because of the strict rules enforced under SarbOx. These pundits fear that some global alien corporations that have the chance to place their stock for sale on an American stock exchange will move instead to a foreign exchange in search of a more lenient approach to corporate governance. Although some evidence of this trend has been detected, other causes may explain why a foreign corporation might choose to list in London rather than New York. Some analysts argue that the epidemic of anti-corporate lawsuits rather than regulatory legislation is what actually drives foreign firms away from the United States. Others suggest that the American insistence that all disputes be fashioned under American law, a trend known as legal imperialism, makes listing in the United States unpopular today. In contrast, some experts see no crisis at all, and still others suggest that the problem of attracting foreign firms to an American exchange is less troublesome than dealing with the type of widespread corruption that sparked the passage of SarbOx in the first place.

## Self-Evident Truths

The Sarbanes-Oxley Act (SarbOx) includes a long list of regulations that outlaw actions and procedures that most people would see as ethical problems rather than legal issues. For instance, SarbOx prevents individual loans from the corporation to board members or officers. It is difficult to see how anyone with a well-developed moral compass would even think about making or receiving such loans, let alone actually do it. Yet, here we have a federal statute that outlaws a clearly unethical practice. Another SarbOx provision requires that the corporate audit team include an impartial, outside director. Again, such an obvious ethical safeguard should be self-evident. Yet, Congress felt the need to include that provision in the act. As if this were not surprising enough, Congress also felt the need to include a provision that expressly prohibits both altering evidence and revising, destroying, or suppressing any records needed in a government investigation of the corporation. Essentially, this is a statutory provision that tells corporate directors not to lie. It is sad to see that the Congress of the United States, of all bodies, must tell corporate managers that it is immoral to lie. Possibly even more disheartening is that the penalties for lying include incarceration. Perhaps most telling of all is that Congress believed it necessary to encourage corporate executives to develop ethical rules and regulations, as if corporate executives had never heard of the word *ethics* pre-SarbOx. Incredibly, Congress also found it necessary to remind executives that employees who provide information to federal authorities about any corporate violations are protected by the act. Finally, Congress did not trust corporate managers to follow the law on their own, and so SarbOx also set up a Public Company Accounting Oversight Board to regulate corporate auditing procedures.

## Self-Evident Questions

1. In what way, if any, is the Sarbanes-Oxley Act a reflection of general trends in this country concerning ethics and morality? Explain.

2. Should Congress also pass laws to regulate other institutions such as schools, churches, synagogues, and mosques, in the same way that Sarbanes-Oxley regulates corporations? Why or why not?

3. Take another look at the Opening Case at the beginning of this chapter. In that case, we discussed how shareholders are victimized by financial trends sometimes prompted by rumors, innuendo, and lies. Many of these rumors are generated by the media. Should Congress protect shareholders from the media and from the reaction of the financial community to the media? Why or why not?

4. The text suggests that Sarbanes-Oxley is an example of government control over the corporate culture. In what way does SarbOx also promote independent director control and special interest group control? Explain.

5. Is there any justifiable reason for congressional intervention into the world of ethics and morality, especially considering the Congress's poor track record in ethics? Explain.

**Independent Director Control** A third theory of corporate control involves the establishment of independent directors. Those theorists who support the use of independent directors argue that the most effective way to ensure that corporate decisions are made in the best interests of those affected is to make certain that the decision makers themselves are not affected by those decisions. Some groups have already implemented requirements to ensure the addition of independent directors to the boards of many corporations. **Independent directors** are defined as directors who have no family members employed by the corporation, who are not themselves employed by the corporation, or, if they were at one time employed by the corporation, have not been on the staff for at least three years. There is, of course, an "opt out" rule that permits some corporations to sidestep the independent directors' rule if they are a "controlled" company. A **controlled company** is one that has more than half its voting power concentrated in one person, or a small group of persons, who always vote together. The opt out provision is designed to give parent companies that are already controlled by independent boards a technique for eliminating a duplication of the independence restriction in their subsidiaries.

**Managerial Control** The fourth approach to corporate governance is **managerial control**. Those who favor managerial control point out that the officers and the directors of a corporation are in the best position for judging not only the needs of the corporation but also the needs of the community and the needs of society at large. Individuals who favor managerial control would insulate the managers from shareholders by limiting the shareholders' power to vote and making it difficult for shareholders to sue managers. Opponents of managerial control argue that corporate managers may tend to be self-interested and, as a result, make relatively short-sighted decisions.

**Shareholder Democracy** Individuals who favor **shareholder democracy**, or **corporate democracy** as it is also known, believe that the shareholders have the right to run the corporation, because without their money, the corporation would not be able to survive. As the real owners of the corporation, the shareholders have a right to say how their money and their property should be used. Supporters of shareholder democracy would make management more responsive to shareholders by giving shareholders greater voting control and making it easier for them to take managers to court. Opponents of this theory point out that most shareholders are removed from the center of corporate activity and therefore cannot make the same type of informed decisions that the managers can make.

Today there is a delicate balance between the theories of managerial control and shareholder democracy. Therefore, this chapter will focus on the battle between these two positions as it examines the subject of corporate control. The two most significant areas of this conflict lie in shareholder voting control and shareholder lawsuits. Shareholders can influence corporate decision making through their voting powers and through their right to initiate a lawsuit against managers (see Table 27-1).

## Table 27-1  Shareholder Control

| Votes and Lawsuits | Explanation |
| --- | --- |
| *Voting control:* | |
| Cumulative voting | Each share of stock has as many votes as there are directors to be elected |
| Proxy voting | The right to vote another shareholder's stock |
| Voting trusts | An agreement among shareholders to transfer their voting rights to a trustee |
| Pooling agreements | Shareholders join together in a temporary arrangement, agreeing to vote the same way on a particular issue |
| Shareholder proposals | A suggestion about a broad company policy or procedure submitted by a shareholder and included in management's proxy solicitation |
| *Shareholder suits:* | |
| Direct suit | A suit brought by shareholders who have been deprived of a right |
| Derivative suit | A suit brought by shareholders based on an injury to the corporation |

## Shareholder Voting Control

Shareholders usually receive one vote per share of common stock held. Shareholders who are dissatisfied with management can attempt to buy more shares to increase their voting power. With this increased voting power, the dissatisfied or dissident shareholders can influence the election of the board of directors. However, shareholders are not always able to buy more shares of the corporation, either because they cannot afford them or because the

### THE OPENING CASE *Revisited, Part I*

Winners, Losers, and Innocent Victims—BP, *Transocean, and Anadarko,* Round 2

In the Opening Case at the beginning of this chapter we explored the ramifications of the Great Gulf Oil Spill. In that case we noted that there are many people who, through no fault of their own, were indirect victims of the Great Gulf Spill, including, but not limited to, the shareholders of the main corporate players in the disaster—BP, Transocean, and Anadarko. While we were careful to admit that the shareholders are the real owners of these corporations and that they expect to profit from that position of ownership, we also noted that it does not seem quite fair for them to lose out be-

cause of the mistakes of a few corporate managers. Remember that these shareholders did not lose because of their own actions but because of the actions of the managers and the whimsical unpredictable trends in the financial marketplace. Is this not an excellent argument for promoting shareholder democracy? Think about this as you read about shareholder voting power and shareholder lawsuits. (See Andrew Bary, "BP, Transocean Priced for Disaster," *Barron's*, May 3, 2010, p. 26. See also Thomas G. Donlan, "In the Face of Disaster," *Barron's,* May 10, 2010, p. 62.)

other shareholders are not willing to sell. In such cases, shareholders can resort to one of the other voting methods available:

- Cumulative voting
- Proxy solicitation
- Shareholder proposals
- Voting trusts
- Pooling agreements
- Shareholder nominations
- Unanimous voting restrictions

**Cumulative Voting** Ordinarily, each share of common stock is worth one vote. Therefore, only a majority of shareholders can elect directors of the corporation. To give minority shareholders an opportunity to elect one or more directors, some states permit **cumulative voting**. This system allows shareholders to multiply the number of their voting shares by the number of directors to be elected. All these votes may be cast for one candidate or distributed among several candidates. This procedure allows minority shareholders an opportunity to be represented on the board of directors.

**EXAMPLE 27-2:** Cumulative vs. Straight Voting

Beth General, James Garrett, Ken Collins, and Heather Gilliam were presented to the shareholders as candidates for the board of directors of Shopton Enterprises, Inc. Three of the four were to be chosen. Because cumulative voting was authorized, the minority shareholders cast all their weighted votes for Gilliam, who had promised to represent the minority voice in corporate affairs. Had the minority voters been allowed only one vote for each share instead of three, they might have failed in their effort to elect a favored director.

**Proxy Voting** A **proxy** is the authority given to one shareholder to cast another shareholder's votes. **Proxy solicitation** is the process by which one shareholder asks another for his or her voting right. Proxy solicitation also refers to the actual document that is used to request the right to vote the other shareholders' votes. The minority shareholder's voting power increases as the number of proxies held rises. Because majority shareholders, including management, can also solicit proxies, a struggle between the two groups, known as a **proxy contest**, often results. Proxy contests involving large, publicly held corporations are closely regulated by the Securities and Exchange Commission (SEC). The primary federal law that controls the operation of a proxy contest is Section 14 (a) of the Securities Exchange Act of 1934. Section 14 (a) is designed to prevent fraud by requiring a complete revelation of certain facts by any individual or group that gets involved in the proxy solicitation process. Specifically, the law requires that anyone soliciting a proxy must disclose the identity of the solicitor, the reason behind the solicitation, and all other crucial facts that the shareholders will need to make an informed decision about the proxy. The document that communicates this information to the shareholders is called a **proxy statement**, which is delivered to SEC and then sent to shareholders before the shareholders' annual meeting. Generally, the solicitation includes a card called a proxy card that can be returned to the solicitor. Rule 14 (a) of the Securities Exchange Act has recently become the focus of heated debate among shareholders and management alike. The dispute covers the question of what corporate management can and cannot exclude from proxy materials that are to be sent to shareholders.

The Securities and Exchange Commission recently enacted several new proxy solicitation rules that have answered a few of these questions. Specifically, the SEC now requires proxies to include additional information about manager-level compensation packages. This information includes (1) risk-related elements in corporate compensation packages; (2) equity awards added to corporate compensation packages; and (3) any conflicts of interest involved in the pay packages earned by compensation consultants. The first of these reflects the fact that corporate compensation packages sometimes involve risky investment opportunities that might have a long-term effect on the value of the shareholders' shares. Such risks must now be disclosed but only if the risks might have a "material adverse effect" on shareholders. The second disclosure reflects a change in the way that equity rewards are reported in proxy statements. Rather than the dollar figure called for under the old rules, the new rules require that the "fair value" of the award be reported. The final

Stockholders exercise their control through votes at annual meetings and through proxies.

change requires the reporting of any money paid to consultants hired to evaluate nonexecutive-related salaries. The fear is that such consultants might be caught in a conflict of interest between the managers who pay their fees and the nonexecutives whose compensation packages are being evaluated. Not everyone believes that these changes will be helpful to shareholders. The fear is that the very nature of the new information (risk management, equity awards, and conflicts of interest) and the complex language needed to communicate the required facts might, at the very least, be useless to the shareholders and, at the worst, might confuse and mislead them, thus causing more harm than good. (See Arden T. Phillips, "SEC Rules Bolster Compensation Disclosure," *The National Law Journal,* February 8, 2010, p. 7.)

**Shareholder Proposals** Another way for shareholders to exercise their voting power to shape corporate decision making is the shareholder proposal. Because shareholder proposals are placed in the proxy materials that are sent from corporate management to shareholders, they are closely allied with the proxy solicitation process and also governed by the Securities Exchange Act of 1934. A shareholder proposal allows shareholders to influence corporate affairs because, under SEC guidelines, shareholders of large, publicly owned corporations can compel management to include their proposals in management's proxy solicitation prior to the next shareholder meeting. A **shareholder proposal** is a suggestion about a broad company policy or procedure that is submitted by a shareholder. The proposal cannot be about the ordinary business operation of the corporation. It must concern something that affects all shareholders. A proposal to hire or fire a particular employee would not qualify, whereas a proposal to amend the corporate charter would. The rules also prohibit proposals that concern only dividend payments.

To qualify as a valid shareholder proposal under SEC rules, the proposal must be no more than 500 words long and must be submitted to management at least 120 days before the shareholders' meeting. In addition, the shareholder must have owned at least 1 percent or $2,000 in market value of the voting stock of the corporation for one year and may submit only one proposal at a time. Even then, managers can reject the proposal if they feel that it does not qualify as a valid shareholder proposal according to a lengthy list of disqualifying characteristics cataloged by the SEC. Included on this list are proposals that are personal grievances, those beyond the corporation's power, and proposals that relate to a corporate election. However, some of these limitations recently have been challenged in a series of lawsuits filed by high-powered corporate shareholders.

Shareholder proposals, sometimes referred to as **shareholder resolutions**, have traditionally been among the weakest of shareholder voting tactics. One reason is that for many years, such proposals were not taken seriously by the directors and officers of most corporations, a situation that was exacerbated by the fact that the courts did not appear to take them seriously either. Much of this attitude was caused by the open-ended nature of the

## A QUESTION OF ETHICS

In the 21st century, it has become increasingly popular for shareholders to press their corporate demands through the use of shareholder proposals. Many of these proposals are filed by large institutional shareholders. Nevertheless, corporate boards continue to resist such proposals. Is it ethical for corporate directors to resist the will of the shareholders in this way? Explain your position by referring to the section on corporate social responsibility in Chapter 1.

### Table 27-2    Strengthening Shareholders

| >> End supermajority votes, the rule that up to 80% of owners back some proposals: | >> Reelect all directors each year rather than hold staggered elections: | >> Let shareholders approve golden parachutes if they exceed three times pay: | >> Allow investors to cast a nonbinding vote on executive pay: | >> Link executive pay to performance of the company: |
|---|---|---|---|---|
| 2006 **63%** | 2006 **66%** | 2006 **52%** | 2006 **40%** | 2006 **30%** |
| 2007 **73%** | 2007 **72%** | 2007 **66%** | 2007 **43%** | 2007 **35%** |

*Data:* Institutional Shareholder Services. 2007 averages are based on preliminary vote counts and are not final.

*Source:* Jena McGregor, "Activist Get More Respect: Boards Are Listening, and Shareholder Proposals Are Making Headway," *BusinessWeek,* June 11, 2007, pp. 34–35.

### Table 27-3    Shareholder Proposals

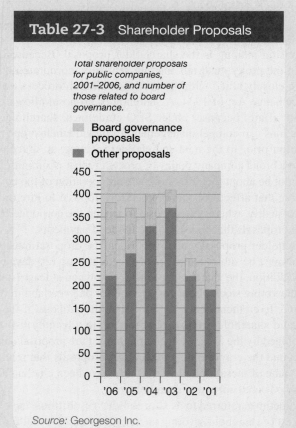

Total shareholder proposals for public companies, 2001–2006, and number of those related to board governance.

- Board governance proposals
- Other proposals

*Source:* Georgeson Inc.

*Source:* Sheri Qualters, "Dissident Shareholders Up Demands," *The National Law Journal,* March 5, 2007, pp. 1 and 9.

rules which permitted the corporate directors to reject most proposals made by shareholders. Moreover, many of the proposals that did make it to the ballot were filed by people with a political agenda and demanded such things as a cessation of business dealings with South African companies, a boycott of Defense Department contracts, or a campaign to redistribute shareholder dividends among needy Third World nations.

The law of balancing forces has operated over the last few years to increase the power of shareholder proposals and decrease the ability of corporate managers to short circuit such proposals. Part of this has emerged because the shareholder proposal itself has become less a soapbox for political dissidents and more a tool for large institutional shareholders, thus resetting a balance that had moved too heavily toward politics. Institutional shareholders, such as the American Federation of State County and Municipal Employees or Boston Common Asset Management, have pressed claims against corporations asking not for political action but for a share in corporate governance (see Table 27-2). Typically, such proposals demand that the corporation make some sort of amendment in voting procedures, such as a change in the bylaws to require a majority rather than a plurality vote on directors, to allow shareholders to cast advisory votes on executive salaries, or to permit shareholders to vote on antitakeover tactics, such as the use of a white knight or a lockup agreement strategy (see Chapter 28). Corporate directors have become more amenable to such shareholder proposals in light of the Sarbanes-Oxley Act and the outside support that has been provided by newly formed expert support groups, such as the Institutional Shareholder Services and Global Advisors, Inc., to help shareholder activists.

## Voting Trusts
A voting trust is an agreement among shareholders to transfer their voting rights to a trustee. A trustee is a person who is entrusted with the management and control of another's property or the rights associated with that property. Sometimes, the trustee is one of the shareholders; at other times, the trustee is an outsider. The trustee votes those shares at the annual shareholders' meeting at the direction of the shareholders. Shareholders surrender only their voting rights. All other rights, including the right to receive profits, remain with them. Generally, once a voting trust has been created, it cannot be ended until the specified time period has run its course. However, state statutes usually place a maximum time limit on the duration of a voting trust. Most state time limits run from 10 to 21 years. Voting trusts must be in writing and must be filed with the corporation.

## Pooling Agreements
Sometimes, shareholders join together in a temporary arrangement and agree to vote the same way on a particular issue. Such agreements are known as pooling agreements, shareholder agreements, or voting agreements. They differ from proxies and voting trusts because the shareholders retain control of their own votes. In this sense, pooling agreements are also the weakest voting arrangement because shareholders can change their votes at the last minute. If a member of a pooling agreement changes her or his vote, however, the other members may bring a lawsuit against the shareholder who broke the agreement. In general, pooling agreements are interpreted by the court under the principles of contract law.

## Shareholder Nominations
Another way to increase the voting power of shareholders is to augment their ability to elect a director or directors who will represent their point of view in crucial issues facing the company. Several ways to do this include enacting state statutes, altering SEC rules, or changing stock exchange regulations so that certain events will trigger the ability of shareholders to elect board members. One such triggering event might be coupled with a shareholder proposal to permit shareholders to nominate their own directors. The rules might permit this nomination process to go forward as long as 50 percent of the votes cast (not 50 percent of the available votes, but 50 percent of those votes actually used in an election) support such a proposal. Another triggering event might

## THE OPENING CASE *Revisited, Part II*
### Winners, Losers, and Innocent Victims—BP, *Transocean, and Anadarko,* Round 3

In the Opening Case at the beginning of this chapter we looked at the legal complications that have flowed from the Great Gulf Oil Spill. The case demonstrated, quite clearly, that there were many individuals who, regardless of their lack of direct involvement, were victimized by the Great Gulf Spill. These people included the shareholders of the main corporations involved in the spill—BP, Transocean, and Anadarko. The shareholders were hurt by management action or, in some cases, nonaction. Would it not be better to prevent this behavior in the future by making the board and the executives more answerable to the shareholders thorough the vote or in the courts? We have just explored several ways to increase the board's accountability to the shareholders through the vote. We will now look at a similar strategy in the courts. Keep an open mind as you read and decide which strategy would be the most effective tactic to take. (See Andrew Bary, "BP, Transocean Priced for Disaster," *Barron's,* May 3, 2010, p. 26. See also Thomas G. Donlan, "In the Face of Disaster," *Barron's,* May 10, 2010, p. 62.)

be the ability of the minority shareholders to reach a 35–50 percent (depending on how the rule is worded) margin of voters who block the election of a management-nominated board candidate. Should either of these events occur, the minority shareholders would be permitted to place their own director on the next ballot at the expense of the corporation.

**Unanimous Voting Restrictions**  An additional approach to strengthening the power of the shareholders involves a change in the corporate bylaws that makes it more difficult for the board to approve crucial issues that affect the fate of the corporation. The new voting bylaws would require unanimous agreement among all directors when the issue before the board involves a critical matter such as a merger, the sale of corporate assets, or a large increase in the salary of a top officer. Under current bylaws, one director with one vote on a board of 12 persons is of little consequence. However, under the revised regulations that require the unanimous approval of the board when major issues are decided, a single board member would have the power to block any material change contemplated by the rest of the board. The fact that a single director would have the power to stop major changes in corporate structure and policy might encourage minority shareholders to join forces in a campaign to elect their own director to the board.

**Combinations**  Although each of these voting techniques has been discussed separately, in practice, they can be combined to increase shareholder voting power. For example, a group of minority shareholders could enter a pooling agreement in which they all agree to cast their cumulative votes for a single board candidate. It is even possible for one of the voting techniques to be used to institute another of those techniques.

## Shareholder Lawsuits

The battle between management and dissident shareholders may also be waged on a front other than the annual shareholders' meeting. That front is the courtroom. Shareholders can sue management to compel a change in direction or to force management to overturn a decision. The two types of suits available to shareholders are direct suits and derivative suits.

**Direct Suits**  A **direct suit** is brought by shareholders who have been deprived of a right that belongs to them as shareholders. These rights include the right to vote, the right

THE OPENING CASE *Revisited, Part III*
Winners, Losers, and Innocent Victims—BP,
*Transocean, and Anadarko, Round 4*

In the Opening Case at the beginning of this chapter we examined the legal complications that have surrounded the Great Gulf Oil Spill including, especially, the complications for indirect victims such as the corporate shareholders involved in BP, Transocean, and Anadarko. We have since suggested that one strategy for stopping the problem from happening again might be to make the board of directors and the corporate officers more accountable to the shareholders through shareholder lawsuits. If the shareholders of BP, Transocean, and Anadarko decided to sue the directors and the officers of their respective corporations, would the suits be direct or derivative? Explain what would be required of the shareholders in each case. (See Andrew Bary, "BP, Transocean Priced for Disaster," *Barron's*, May 3, 2010, p. 26. See also Thomas G. Donlan, "In the Face of Disaster," *Barron's*, May 10, 2010, p. 62.)

to receive dividends, the right to transfer shares, the right to purchase newly issued stock, and the right to examine corporate books and records. If shareholders have been denied any of these rights, they can bring a direct suit to make up for any loss they have suffered.

**Derivative Suits** A **derivative suit** allows shareholders to sue corporate management on behalf of the corporation. Unlike a direct suit, a derivative suit is not based on a direct injury to a shareholder. Instead, the injury is to the corporation. The shareholders' right to sue is derived from the corporate injury. Shareholders who bring a successful derivative suit are entitled to recover attorney fees. To bring a derivative suit, shareholders must meet certain prerequisites. One prerequisite is the exhaustion of internal remedies. Before bringing suit, the shareholder must attempt to solve the problem by communicating with the board of directors and with other shareholders. In their original complaint commencing the derivative action, the shareholders must state the steps that they took to exhaust all internal remedies. If the shareholders have not exhausted internal remedies and still insist on bringing the lawsuit, the court will dismiss the case and deny any request from the shareholders for the payment of attorney fees.

To bring a derivative suit, a shareholder must own stock at the time of the injury and at the time of the suit. This requirement is known as the **rule of contemporary ownership**. Frequently, state corporate laws also require derivative suit plaintiffs to pay a security deposit to cover the corporation's potential expenses in defending the derivative suits. All of these requirements make it difficult for a shareholder to bring a derivative lawsuit.

## quick quiz 27-2

1. Under the original concept of the corporation, the shareholders are the primary reason that a corporation exists.          true | false

2. Pooling agreements have been outlawed in all states.          true | false

3. A controlled company is one that has more than half its voting power concentrated in one person, or a small group of persons, who always vote together.          true | false

| Table 27-4 | Management Responsibilities | |
|---|---|---|
| **Rule** | **Situation** | **Explanation** |
| Business judgment rule | Manager does not profit from decision | The decision stands if it is made (1) in good faith, (2) with due care within the law, and (3) in the corporation's best interests. |
| Fairness rule | Manager profits from decision | The decision must be fair to the corporation because managers must remain loyal to the corporation. |

# 27-3 Governance Responsibilities

When the court hears a case challenging a manager's decision, it will turn to one of two rules in judging that conduct: the business judgment rule or the fairness rule (see Table 27-4).

## The Business Judgment Rule

Under the **business judgment rule**, the court will not interfere with most business decisions. The rule protects managers who act with due care and in good faith, as long as their decisions are lawful and in the best interests of the corporation. The rule results from the commonsense belief that, based on their education, experience, and knowledge, managers are in the best position to run the corporation. In contrast, shareholders and judges are far removed from the day-to-day operations of the business and should not be allowed to second-guess most management decisions. Protecting directors and officers in this way encourages people to become corporate managers and reassures them that they will be protected when they make difficult business decisions. The business judgment rule emerges from the duty of due diligence that a manager owes to the corporation. The **duty of due diligence** consists of three parts. It says that when acting on behalf of the corporation, a manager must act (1) in good faith, (2) using the same level of care that an ordinarily prudent individual would use in a comparable situation, and (3) in the reasonable belief that the best interests of the company are being met.

### EXAMPLE 27-3: The Business Judgment Rule in Action

Donald Young was chair of the board and chief executive officer of the Sterling Software Corporation. On September 9, a Connecticut software company went on the market for $590 million. The Connecticut company appeared to be a guaranteed money-maker. In considering the plant's purchase, Young had to act before September 12. After careful examination of the plant's financial records, consultation with the corporation's legal and financial experts, and a detailed study of the marketplace, Young decided to buy. According to the business judgment rule, if the Connecticut software company proves to be an unprofitable investment, Young will be protected because he acted (1) with due care, (2) in good faith, (3) within the law, and (4) in the best interests of the corporation.

## The Fairness Rule

The business judgment rule assumes that managers do not personally profit from business decisions. If managers do profit, then the decision is suspect, because all managers owe a

**duty of loyalty** to the corporation. To fulfill this duty, managers must place the corporation's interests above their own. When managers enter contracts with the corporation or when they are on the boards of two corporations that do business with each other, a different standard is used to judge their conduct. This standard, known as the **fairness rule**, requires managers to be fair to the corporation when they personally benefit from their business decisions. Managers who benefit from their own decisions are said to be self-dealing. The fairness rule does not automatically declare managers disloyal if they profit from a corporate decision. Rather, it allows the court to examine the decision to determine its basic fairness to the corporation. How to measure fairness is, at best, problematic. At a minimum, it requires corporate managers to disclose all crucial information when they enter contracts with the corporation.

## EXAMPLE 27-4: Upholding Corporate Fairness

Amy Myers was the chair of the board of the Ural-Orenburg Shipping Corporation. The corporation leased a shipping depot from Denikin, Inc. Myers was also the majority shareholder and CEO of Denikin. Before finalizing the lease agreement, Myers revealed her relationship with Denikin to the other board members of Ural-Orenburg. The rental rate for the warehouse was in keeping with current market rates. Consequently, if the lease were challenged by shareholders of either corporation, a court, using the fairness rule, would uphold its validity.

Two rules that are offshoots of the fairness rule and the duty of loyalty are the insider trading rule and the corporate opportunity doctrine. Both rules give specific ways to measure a corporate manager's fairness in certain types of situations.

**The Insider Trading Rule**  Because of their role in corporate affairs, directors and officers often possess inside information. **Inside information** is material, nonpublic, factual data that can be used to buy or sell securities at a profit. Directors, officers, and other key individuals in a corporation, such as major shareholders, who are not directors or officers, qualify as insiders. In fact, under current SEC rules, any individual who holds such information, including corporate employees such as administrative assistants, researchers, public relations executives, human resource personnel, marketing directors, and so on, can be insiders. Even nonemployees such as financial planners, accountants, auditors, and attorneys who, by virtue of their contact with a company, have material nonpublic data about the company's stock can be insiders. Corporate "outsiders," such as spouses, family members, and friends, may be considered insiders if they receive corporate information about corporate stock without being involved in any actual business need to have the information. Such "outside" insiders are generally referred to as **tippees**. Nevertheless, the most common actual corporate insiders are directors and officers.

Inside information clearly gives directors and officers an advantage over corporate outsiders in the buying and selling of stock. This advantage must not be abused when dealing with the corporation or with individuals outside the corporation. Corporate managers act unfairly when they use their inside information to either cheat the corporation or take unfair advantage of corporate outsiders. Such transactions, which are referred to as **insider trading**, are forbidden by law. According to the **insider trading rule**, when managers possess important inside information, they are obligated to reveal that information before trading on it themselves. The rule also states that when inside information is revealed, the managers must use that information when trading with the corporation or with those outside the corporation.

**The Corporate Opportunity Doctrine** As noted previously, along with the duty of due diligence and the duty of actual authority (see the next section), corporate managers also owe a duty of loyalty to the corporation. The duty of loyalty requires that corporate managers place the corporation's well-being ahead of their own interests. One offshoot of this duty is the idea of the corporate opportunity doctrine. The corporate opportunity doctrine states that corporate managers cannot take a corporate business opportunity for themselves if they know that the corporation would be interested in that opportunity as well. Before taking such an opportunity, a manager must first offer it to the corporation by informing other managers and shareholders. If the corporation rejects the opportunity, then the manager is free to take that opportunity.

## The Actual Authority Rule

Corporate managers are also held to a third duty, that is, the duty to act within actual authority. The authority spoken of here includes those powers that have been granted to managers by virtue of their position within the corporation. The duties of the directors and officers of the corporation are outlined in the appropriate state statutes, in the articles of incorporation, in the regulations issued by government bodies such as the SEC, in relevant case law, and in the bylaws of the company. The actual authority rule states that a manager may be held liable if he or she exceeds his or her authority and the corporation is harmed as a result. Some states say that the managers will be liable for any violation of the limits of their authority on the basis of absolute or strict liability; some jurisdictions will consider the managers responsible only if the violation results in negligent or intentional conduct. This duty is also sometimes referred to as the duty of obedience. It is, of course, possible for a vote of the board or of the shareholders to approve a previously unauthorized act by a manager through the process of ratification.

**Efforts to Limit Liability** Corporate managers have come under very close scrutiny by regulators and the courts in recent years. As a result, many otherwise well-qualified individuals have avoided serving as corporate managers in general but, in particular, as corporate directors. To counteract this trend, some states have enacted legislation that is designed to help protect the good faith and due diligent activities of such managers. These legislative enactments take three forms: (1) voluntary protective measures, (2) automatic protective measures, and (3) protective measures that limit the amount of damages that can be recovered against directors. A voluntary protective measure is one that permits corporate shareholders to fashion their bylaws so as to limit or eliminate the liability of directors for decisions made while carrying out their duties. Such measures would allow recovery of damages only if the director deliberately broke the law, deliberately violated the duty of loyalty, deliberately violated the duty of good faith, or improperly benefited from the transaction in question. Automatic protective measures grant the same type of immunity by state law, regardless of the action or inaction of corporate shareholders. The final measure would allow lawsuits against managers even in the cases noted above but would place a cap on the amount of money damages that can be recovered against directors.

**Efforts to Increase Responsibility** At the same time that state governments are attempting to ease the liability of directors, the federal government has enacted efforts to increase director responsibilities for catching and stopping the wrongdoing of others within the corporation. One such measure is the Sarbanes-Oxley Act, which places an affirmative duty on the directors of publicly traded corporations to monitor whether their corporation is conforming to all legal requirements. A second measure involves the United States Sentencing Commission, which has issued a set of rules that control the discretion of the federal courts in issuing fines against corporations found guilty of criminal activities. Under the new rules, if the directors of a corporation did not do their best to discover and stop illegal activities, the court can place very severe penalties on the corporation, once it has been found guilty of those violations. The idea behind the new rules is to force directors to pay more attention to what is going on within their own companies, especially in relation to crime-stopping activities.

The new rules have led some legal commentators to suggest a series of steps that corporate directors should take when faced with suspected wrongdoing within their company. Seven steps are recommended: (1) Once a legal violation has been uncovered (or even suspected), the activity must cease instantly; (2) any and all consequences that have flowed from the violation should be uncovered and stopped immediately; (3) any attempt to engage in a cover-up, and in fact any actions that can be remotely perceived as a cover-up, must be avoided religiously; (4) notification of the violation must be made to the proper authorities; (5) investigations must be made to uncover any similar or related activities that may be illegal; (6) the cause or causes of the legal violations must be determined; and (7) an action plan must be created and executed to punish the violators and to prevent any future violations.

---

## quick quiz 27-3

1. The business judgment rule states that a manager's decision will stand as long as it was legal, was made with due care and in good faith, and was made in the best interests of the corporation.     true | false

2. The fairness rule states that a decision made by a manager will stand if it is fair to the corporation.     true | false

3. The business judgment rule is used by the courts when the manager is disinterested, that is, he or she does not personally gain from the decision.     true | false

---

# 27-4 Shareholder Rights

In addition to their voting rights and their right to sue, shareholders are entitled to examine certain corporate records, share in dividends, transfer shares of stock, and buy newly issued stock.

## Right to Examine Corporate Records

A shareholder's right by statute to inspect the records of the corporation is usually limited to inspections for proper purposes at an appropriate time and place. Idle curiosity and an intent that unreasonably interferes with or embarrasses corporate management would prompt officers or directors to refuse shareholders' requests to examine corporate accounts, minutes, and records. When the purpose of inspection is proper, it may be enforced by a court order.

## Right to Share in Dividends

Shareholders have the right to share in dividends after they have been declared by the board of directors. Once declared, a dividend becomes a debt of the corporation and enforceable by law, as is any other debt. However, shareholders cannot force the directors to declare a dividend unless the directors are not acting in good faith in refusing to do so. Courts are not inclined to order directors to meet and declare a dividend if the court must substitute its own business judgment for that of the directors.

## Right to Transfer Shares of Stock

Shareholders have the right to sell or transfer their shares of stock. The person to whom stock shares are transferred has the right to have the stock transfer entered on the corporate books. The transferee becomes a **shareholder of record** and is entitled to vote, receive dividends, and enjoy all other shareholder privileges.

## Preemptive Rights

Unless the right is denied or limited by the corporate charter or by state law, shareholders have the right to purchase a proportionate share of every new offering of stock by the corporation. This right is known as the shareholder's **preemptive right**. Preemptive rights are more prevalent in small, closely held corporations than in large, publicly owned corporations. This right prevents management from depriving shareholders of their proportionate control of a corporation simply by increasing the number of shares in the corporation.

### quick quiz 27-4

1. Assuming a request by a shareholder to inspect the corporate books is a proper one, the courts will enforce that request.          true | false

2. Today the courts will readily substitute their own judgment and declare a dividend on corporate stock, even when the directors of the corporation have voted against such a move.          true | false

3. Preemptive rights are more common in large, publicly held corporations than in small, closely held corporations.          true | false

# 27-5 Governance of a Limited Liability Company

The members of a limited liability company can choose to manage the business themselves, or they can hire outside management. An LLC that is run by the members themselves is called a member-managed LLC, whereas one operated by outside managers is referred to as a manager-managed LLC.

## Member-Managed LLCs

If the managers choose to run the LLC on their own, management rights are apportioned among the members, according to the capital contributions made by each member to the LLC. Like the partners in a general partnership, the members of the LLC act as agents of the LLC. Accordingly, whenever a member performs a function within his or her apparent authority, the LLC will be bound by that action. However, as is true of a partnership, some actions fall outside the member's apparent authority. These include but are not limited to disposing of the firm's goodwill and submitting a claim of the LLC to arbitration. Naturally, the operating agreement can alter any of these statutory provisions.

## Manager-Managed LLCs

If the members hire outside managers, then the LLC is run like a corporation. In the absence of an operating agreement, a single manager operates much like the CEO of a corporation, while a group of managers acts as a board of directors. Nevertheless, regardless of the number of managers involved in an LLC, both the business judgment rule and the fairness rule apply to their decisions in the same way that those rules apply to the directors of a corporation.

## Fiduciary Duties

Regardless of whether the members or the managers ultimately run the LLC, both groups have a fiduciary duty to the LLC and to its members. However, as noted in the previous chapter, it would be wise to outline the specific management duties in the written operating agreement.

---

### quick quiz 27-5

1. The members of an LLC have no choice in the matter of who will manage their firm.  true | false

2. An operating agreement established by the LLC is not permitted to alter statutory provisions regarding governance in any way.  true | false

3. Regardless of whether the members or the managers ultimately run the LLC, fiduciary duties have been suspended by provisions outlined in the latest version of the Uniform Limited Liability Company Act.  true | false

---

## Summary

**27.1**  The business affairs of a corporation are managed by a board of directors elected by the shareholders. The directors have the authority to appoint officers and agents to run the day-to-day affairs of the corporation.

**27.2**  Five theories have been put forth by legal scholars and business experts concerning how corporations should be managed. These theories are special interest group control, governmental control, independent director control, managerial control, and shareholder democracy. Shareholders can increase their voting power by purchasing additional stock. If they cannot purchase additional stock, they may use another device to increase their voting power, such as cumulative voting, proxies, voting trusts, pooling agreements, shareholder proposals, shareholder nominations, and unanimous voting restrictions. Shareholders can also sue the corporation. Direct suits are brought by shareholders to protect their own rights. Derivative suits are brought by shareholders when they feel that the corporation has been damaged by a management decision.

**27.3**  Under the business judgment rule, the court will not interfere with most management decisions as long as those decisions are made with due care, in good faith, within the law, and in the best interests of the corporation. If the manager profits personally from a business decision, then the court will use the fairness rule to judge the manager's conduct.

**27.4**  Shareholder rights include the right to examine corporate records, the right to share dividends, the right to transfer shares of stock, and the right to buy newly issued stock.

**27.5**  The members of a limited liability company can choose to manage the business themselves or hire outside management. Regardless of whether the members or the managers ultimately run the LLC, both groups have a fiduciary duty to the LLC and to the members of the LLC. Nevertheless, it would be wise to outline specific management duties in the operating agreement.

## Key Terms

actual authority rule, 596

business judgment rule, 594

controlled company, 586

corporate democracy, 586

corporate opportunity doctrine, 596

cumulative voting, 588

derivative suit, 593

direct suit, 592

duty of due diligence, 594

duty of loyalty, 595

duty of obedience, 596

fairness rule, 595

governmental control, 584

independent director, 586

inside information, 595

insider trading, 595

insider trading rule, 595

legal imperialism, 585

managerial control, 586

pooling agreement, 591

preemptive rights, 598

proxy, 588

proxy contest, 588

proxy solicitation, 588

proxy statement, 588

ratification, 596

rule of contemporary ownership, 593

Sarbanes-Oxley Act, 596

shareholder democracy, 586

shareholder of record, 598

shareholder proposal, 589

shareholder resolutions, 589

special interest group control, 584

tippee, 595

trustee, 591

United States Sentencing Commission, 596

voting trust, 591

## Questions for Review and Discussion

1. What is the central dilemma of corporate governance?
2. What are the functions of directors, officers, and shareholders?
3. What are the five theories of corporate governance?
4. What is the difference between cumulative voting and proxy solicitation?
5. What is a shareholder proposal?
6. What is the difference between a voting trust and a pooling agreement?
7. What is the difference between a shareholder direct suit and a shareholder derivative suit?
8. What is the difference between the business judgment rule and the fairness rule?
9. What are the rights that belong to shareholders?
10. How does the management of a limited liability company operate?

## Cases for Analysis

1. United Missionary Baptist Church, a not-for-profit corporation, held an election for the new church pastor. Several members of the church were dissatisfied with the results of the election and with the procedures that were followed during the election. They claimed that the inclusion of absentee balloting violated the church's constitution. Without making any parliamentary moves to correct the alleged misapplication of the constitution, and despite the fact that they had used their own absentee ballots during the election, these unhappy members brought a derivative lawsuit, asking the court to compel the church to follow its own constitution. The suit was dismissed. However, the members who brought the lawsuit claimed that because the lawsuit was a derivative action, they were entitled to attorney's fees, just as the shareholders of a profit corporation were entitled to attorney's fees. The court agreed that the same rules that apply to profit corporations in derivative actions apply to derivative suits brought for nonprofit corporations. However, the court still refused to grant the request for attorney's fees. Why? *Russell v. United Missionary Baptist Church*, 637 N.E.2d 82 (OH).

2. The bylaws of Jameson Enterprises, Inc., required a 70 percent supermajority to establish a quorum sufficient to hold a meeting to remove a director from the board. The bylaws also designated a meeting with such a purpose as a special meeting. The board consisted of ten directors. Six showed

up at the meeting. Of the four who failed to attend, three were in Europe. The fourth, Weinberger, was not notified of the meeting because he was the one to be removed. The six directors attending the meeting first voted to change the bylaws to require only 60 percent of the directors to establish a quorum sufficient to hold a special meeting. The six directors then unanimously voted to remove Weinberger. When Weinberger found out about the meeting, he objected to the vote and claimed that the entire procedure was void. Was Weinberger correct? Explain.

3. Smith, a shareholder, filed suit against the board of directors of a corporation in which he had owned stock. Smith claimed that he and other shareholders had not received top dollar for their shares when their corporation had merged with another. Consequently, they sought either a reversal of the merger or payment from the directors to make up for their losses. The directors, Smith argued, had violated their duty of due care because they based their decision on a 20-minute speech by the CEO. Also, the directors had not even looked at the merger documents, let alone studied them. Furthermore, the directors had not sought any independent evaluation by outside experts. For their part, the directors argued that because their decision was made in good faith and was legal, they were protected by the business judgment rule. Were the directors correct? *Smith v. VanGorkon,* 488 A.2d 858 (DE).

4. Donald Lewis was a shareholder in S.L.&E., Inc., a corporation that owned land and a complex of buildings in Rochester, New York. The land and buildings were leased to LGT, a tire manufacturer. Donald's brothers were shareholders and directors of both S.L.&E. and LGT. Donald had no financial or managerial interest in LGT. S.L.&E. leased the land to LGT at a rate that Donald considered damaging to S.L.&E. He pointed out that S.L.&E. collected only $14,000 per year in rent from LGT while paying out $11,000 in taxes. This rate, he argued, meant that S.L.&E. could never be a profit-making corporation. Should the directors of LGT and S.L.&E. be judged by the business judgment rule or the fairness rule? Explain. *Lewis v. S.L.&E., Inc.,* 629 F.2d 764 (2nd Cir.).

5. Jackson set up a trust for his seven children. Most of the assets in the trust consisted of stock in the two newspapers owned and run by Jackson. Over

the course of 18 years, Jackson transferred all but two shares of voting stock in the newspapers. The trustee was given full power to manage the assets in the fund and sell or otherwise dispose of the newspaper stock. State law places a strict 10-year limit on voting trusts. The plaintiffs claimed that the trust, which had lasted 18 years, was no longer valid, having passed the 10-year limit. The defendants claimed that the 10-year limit did not apply to this trust. Were the defendants correct? Explain. *Jackson v. Jackson,* 402 A.2d 893 (CT).

6. Klinicki and Lundgren incorporated to form an air taxi service known as Berlinair, Inc. Each of them owned one-third interest in the corporation. The final third was owned by Lelco, Inc., a company owned by Lundgren. In his capacity as president of Berlinair, Lundgren learned that the Berlinair Flug Ring (BFR), a business association of Berlin's travel agents, was looking for an air charter service. Lundgren incorporated a new corporate entity called Air Berlin Charter (ABC). ABC then negotiated an air charter contract with BFR. Klinicki brought suit, demanding that Lundgren reimburse Berlinair for any profits made by ABC on the BFR contract. Was this a direct or derivative suit? Explain. Should the business judgment rule or the fairness rule be used by the court to measure Lundgren's performance? Explain. Who should have won the suit? Defend your choice. *Klinicki v. Lundgren,* 695 P.2d 906 (OR).

7. Naquin, Dubois, and Hoffpauir incorporated to form Air Engineered Systems and Services, Inc. Dubois became president and Hoffpauir became secretary-treasurer. Naquin was employed by the company. Conflicts among the three caused a breakdown in the working relationship. Dubois and Hoffpauir offered Naquin $2,000 a month for 10 years for his share of the business if he would sign a noncompetition agreement. Naquin refused to sell until he could examine the corporate records. Dubois and Hoffpauir refused to allow Naquin to see the books until he signed the noncompetition agreement. Could Dubois and Hoffpauir attach such a condition to Naquin's request? Explain. *Naquin v. Air Engineered Systems and Services, Inc.,* 463 So.2d 992 (LA).

8. Snodgrass, a minority shareholder in the 21st Century Broadcasting Network, Inc., was dissatisfied with management's decision to cancel several long-running news shows and replace them

with several sitcoms and talk shows. She was also disturbed that management had decided to discharge several editorial writers and newscasters, including one who had recently won a major award for investigative journalism. Finally, she believed that a change in policy that would phase out foreign broadcast efforts would eventually cost the company an enormous amount of money. Assuming that Snodgrass does not want to sue the corporation, what options does she have if she wants to increase her influence over the board of directors of 21st Century Broadcasting Network, Inc.? Explain.

9. Keith Harris, a shareholder of Fastway Airlines, Inc., discovered that Donald Fleure, chief executive officer of Fastway, had sold some of his own land to the corporation at what Harris believed to be excessive prices. Can Harris bring a direct or a derivative suit in this situation? Explain. Would the fairness rule or the business judgment rule be used to evaluate the activities of Fleure? Explain.

## quick quiz Answers

| 27-1 | 27-2 | 27-3 | 27-4 | 27-5 |
|------|------|------|------|------|
| 1. T | 1. T | 1. T | 1. T | 1. F |
| 2. F | 2. F | 2. T | 2. F | 2. F |
| 3. T | 3. T | 3. T | 3. F | 3. F |

# Government Regulation of Corporate Business

## THE OPENING CASE  Single Entity or Collection Point—*American Needle, Inc. v. National Football League*

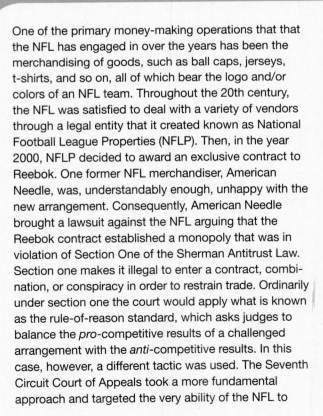

One of the primary money-making operations that that the NFL has engaged in over the years has been the merchandising of goods, such as ball caps, jerseys, t-shirts, and so on, all of which bear the logo and/or colors of an NFL team. Throughout the 20th century, the NFL was satisfied to deal with a variety of vendors through a legal entity that it created known as National Football League Properties (NFLP). Then, in the year 2000, NFLP decided to award an exclusive contract to Reebok. One former NFL merchandiser, American Needle, was, understandably enough, unhappy with the new arrangement. Consequently, American Needle brought a lawsuit against the NFL arguing that the Reebok contract established a monopoly that was in violation of Section One of the Sherman Antitrust Law. Section one makes it illegal to enter a contract, combination, or conspiracy in order to restrain trade. Ordinarily under section one the court would apply what is known as the rule-of-reason standard, which asks judges to balance the *pro*-competitive results of a challenged arrangement with the *anti*-competitive results. In this case, however, a different tactic was used. The Seventh Circuit Court of Appeals took a more fundamental approach and targeted the very ability of the NFL to

enter a contract of any sort. The court ruled that the NFL was not a collection point around which a group of 32 different team joined forces but was, instead, a single entity. As a single entity, the NFL could not make any type of contract with itself, let alone a contract to restrain trade. This ruling means that section one did not apply to the case and, as a result, the case was dismissed. The United States Supreme Court disagreed with the appellate court, however, and ruled that the NFL is not a single entity. The Court said that, under corporate law, the NFL might be a single entity, but under antitrust law, it is not. The NFL turns out to be, at least for purposes of antitrust law, a collection of 32 distinct constituent parts, referred to as teams and headquartered in different cities, that make financial decisions on their own for their own purposes and benefit. (See *American Needle, Inc. v. National Football League*, 130 S.Ct. 2201 (2010). See also Gabriel Feldman, "The NFL Is Not a Single Entity," *The National Law Journal*, February 1, 2010, p. 35; and Michael P. Waxman, "*American Needle Inc. v. National Football League:* Surprise! The Supreme Court Upholds an Existing Antitrust Doctrine," *Marquette University Law School Faculty Blog*, October 29, 2010, http://law.marquette.edu.)

**Opening Case Questions**

1. In *American Needle, Inc. v. National Football League,* the U.S. Supreme Court seems to admit that, under corporate law, the NFL might be a single entity. Is it appropriate to have two different areas of the law come to two entirely different outcomes when judging the same set of facts? Why or why not?

2. In relation to antitrust law, what is significant about the Supreme Court's ruling that the NFL is not a single entity? Explain.

3. What is the rule-of-reason test in antitrust law and how is it carried out? Explain.

4. What other test, besides the rule-of-reason test, is available in antitrust law? Explain.

5. Now that the U.S. Supreme Court has remanded the case, what happens next? Explain.

## LO Learning Objectives

1. Explain the development of the federal government's power to regulate business.
2. Describe the source of state power to regulate business.
3. Explain how the Securities and Exchange Commission prevents unfair practices.
4. Explain *per se* antitrust violations of antitrust law.
5. Explain the rule-of-reason standard in antitrust law.
6. Outline the general provisions of all Post-Sherman antitrust laws.
7. Define the various techniques of corporate expansion.
8. Contrast the interest of the Securities and Exchange Commission with that of the Federal Trade Commission in corporate expansion.
9. Identify the two ways that a corporation may undergo dissolution.
10. Explain the circumstances under which a limited liability company may undergo dissolution.

# 28-1 Business and the Constitution

Despite the beliefs of many theorists, it is not possible to separate the world of the law from the world of economics. In the real world, the two systems interact with each other in such a way that they become, at times, one single system, the **judicial–economic system**.

## The Commerce Clause of the Constitution

Sometimes the law must adapt to economic realities, as seen in the way the law has adjusted to economic realities to give the federal courts the power to regulate economic activity. The process worked something like this: The **Commerce Clause** is found in Article I, Section 8, Clause 3, of the Constitution. Clause 3 states that "Congress shall have the Power . . . To regulate Commerce with foreign nations, and among the several States." At first the courts interpreted this clause to mean that Congress could only regulate commercial activity if the activity passed between two or more states.

**LO1**

U.S. Const. Article I
(see page 807)

However, changing economic needs demanded a revision of this narrowly drawn interpretation. The federal government, which had entered the land-granting business, determined that it needed a way to enforce the distribution of this land. To meet this and other related economic needs, the Supreme Court in an 1824 case, *Gibbons v. Ogden,* held that any commercial activity that affected commerce among the states could be regulated by the federal government. This ruling included the activity that occurred within a single state, so long as that completely in-state activity affected interstate commerce. The extent of this interpretation was not felt until 1942, when in the case of *Wickard v. Filburn,* the Supreme Court upheld the doctrine so thoroughly that a farmer's production of wheat for use only on his own farm was held to affect interstate commerce. The Court reasoned that if the farmer used his own wheat, he would not buy wheat in interstate commerce, thus weakening the entire interstate market. The justices emphasized that it was the cumulative effect of many such farmers that concerned them rather than the effect of a single farmer.

## The Judicial–Economic System

Several dynamic factors work together in the judicial–economic system to make this type of revolutionary adjustment to the realities of the marketplace palatable to the culture as a whole. These factors include (1) the need to reason by analogy in the common law system, (2) the desire to balance individual justice with regulatory justice, and (3) the inclination on the part of jurists to control legal change so that the revolutionary process is almost imperceptible from case to case.

### Reasoning by Analogy
Whenever a judge must decide a case, he or she is faced with a conflict that involves real people embroiled in a series of real events. In such cases, the judge must make a decision based on precedent. When a judge applies the law of an old case to the facts of the new case, the match between the two is rarely exact. Therefore, the judge must reason by analogy. Reasoning by analogy gives the judge a certain degree of flexibility. Generally, if there is a deviation from precedent, the judge will justify this slight change in the law by explaining how the present case can be distinguished from the past case.

### Balancing Individual and Regulatory Justice
The inclination to reason by analogy is driven by the perceived need to balance individual justice with regulatory justice. **Individual justice** is justice meted out to the people in the case before the judge. It is important that the parties in the case believe that the judge has entered a fair ruling that is tailor-made to their situation. However, the judge must also promote regulatory justice. **Regulatory justice** is a fair and balanced interpretation of the law that evolves from and is consistent with previous law. When a judge deviates too much from regulatory justice, he or she risks a political upheaval. As a result, in most cases, the judge balances the two goals and creates a new ruling that is in line with regulatory justice but that fine-tunes the rule enough to fit the particular case, thus introducing a small measure of change into the system.

### Controlling Legal Change
What results from the judge's need to reason from analogy and his or her desire to balance individual justice with regulatory justice is a system that promotes change at a slow and measured rate. For this reason, it is possible for the judicial–economic system to adjust legal rules to changing economic realities. The parties to the case welcome change because it reassures them that the law is flexible enough to deal with their individual problems. Other jurists welcome the new precedent as an added weapon in their arsenal of past cases. Legislators welcome the new case as long as it offers a change that is so small it manages to preserve the judicial–economic status quo.

**EXAMPLE 28-1:** The Interstate Effects of Intrastate Commerce

The Lafayette Nuclear Research and Development Corporation owned and operated DeBroglie Plutonium Processing Plant, Inc. Both corporations were based in Louisiana. DeBroglie supplied Lafayette with about 25 percent of its plutonium needs and did no other plutonium business with anyone. The other 75 percent of Lafayette's plutonium came from one in-state producer and two out-of-state suppliers. When the federal government imposed new safety regulations on all plutonium processing plants, DeBroglie argued that the regulations did not apply to it because its business was totally within the borders of Louisiana. The court disagreed. The court said that the fact that 25 percent of Lafayette's plutonium was purchased from DeBroglie meant that Lafayette did not buy that 25 percent from other corporations, including the two corporations from outside Louisiana. Because the two corporations outside Louisiana could have sold more plutonium to Lafayette had DeBroglie not sold its plutonium to Lafayette, DeBroglie's business was affecting interstate commerce, and could therefore be regulated by Congress.

## A QUESTION OF ETHICS

The Framers of the U.S. Constitution clearly wanted to limit the legislative power of the national government. They made this desire quite clear by enumerating the powers that Congress would possess and by specifically starting Article I of the Constitution with the following words, "All legislative Powers herein granted shall be vested in a Congress of the United States." Now reread Example 28-1. In that case, the court allowed Congress to regulate DeBroglie, a corporation that did business totally within a single state. Is it ethical for the courts, in their interpretation of the Commerce Clause, to ignore the deliberate attempt by the Framers to limit congressional power to the regulation of commerce "among the several states" and to extend that power, allowing Congress to regulate a commercial activity that takes place completely within one state? Explain.

## State Regulatory Power

In contrast to the convoluted and indirect way that the judicial–economic system has developed federal commerce power, the system had no problem accommodating state economic power, because the states automatically have the power to regulate economic activities. This power comes from a state's police power. **Police power** is the state's authority to restrict private rights to promote and maintain public health, safety, welfare, and morals. A state has police power simply by virtue of its existence as a legitimate governmental authority. Today we take for granted that all business activity, even that of the sole proprietor, is subject to state regulation. The state government and the various subdivisions of the state government, from countries to cities to zoning districts, all play a role in this regulatory process.

## quick quiz 28-1

1. The world of the law and the world of economics often interact in such a way that the two become, at times, one single system, the judicial–economic system.   true | false

2. Police power is the state's authority to restrict private rights to promote and maintain public health, safety, welfare, and morals.   true | false

3. The Contracts Clause is found in Article I, Section 8, Clause 3, of the Constitution.   true | false

# 28-2 Securities Regulation

Two pieces of federal legislation that affect business are the Securities Act of 1933 and the Securities Exchange Act of 1934 (see Table 28-1). The primary purpose of these acts is to protect business investors by making certain that they are informed about the securities they purchase. The independent regulatory agency that carries out this function is the Securities and Exchange Commission (SEC). The SEC regulates the issuance of securities by corporations and partnerships. A **security** has been defined as a monetary investment that expects a return solely because of another person's efforts. As the following example demonstrates, a security is a security even if it is called something else.

### EXAMPLE 28-2: A Security by Any Other Name

Osgood Minerals, Inc., had to raise an enormous amount of capital quickly. One of the directors devised a scheme whereby Osgood would sell to investors parcels of land owned by the corporation and used for mining purposes. In return, the investors would be entitled to a return on their investment. The return would be calculated in relation to the amount of land owned by each investor. To avoid having to comply with SEC regulations, Osgood labeled each sale a land contract rather than a security. Because the sales were land contracts, Osgood argued, it did not have to follow SEC regulations. The SEC disagreed and brought suit to stop the sale of unregulated securities. The court held that because each investor's profits would be derived solely from the efforts of others, the investments were securities and therefore subject to SEC regulations.

## Securities Act of 1933

The Securities Act of 1933 regulates the issuance of new securities by corporations and partnerships. Offers of securities by mail or through interstate or foreign commerce must be registered with the SEC. A registration statement and a prospectus must be filed with the SEC. A **registration statement** contains detailed information about the corporation, including data about its management, capitalization, and financial condition. A **prospectus** contains much of the same information but in a condensed and simplified form. The registration statement is designed for the experts at the SEC, whereas the prospectus is designed for potential investors.

The Securities and Exchange Commission (SEC) regulates the issuance of securities by corporations and partnerships and assures that the public is protected by enforcing mandatory reporting requirements and other 1933 and 1934 Act mandates.

## Securities Exchange Act of 1934

The Securities Exchange Act of 1934, which actually established the SEC, deals with the subsequent trading in securities. It requires periodic reports of financial information concerning registered securities, and it prohibits manipulative and deceptive actions in the sale and purchase of securities. The act prohibits insiders, including officers and directors, from realizing profit from any purchase and sale of securities within any period of less than six months. The courts have held that insiders are not permitted to trade on information until that information has been made available to the public.

According to Section 14 (a) of the 1934 act, shareholders, including majority shareholders, who solicit proxies (see Chapter 27) must also follow strict reporting requirements. The SEC requires a written proxy solicitation to include the identity of the individual or

| Table 28-1   Securities and Antitrust Regulations | |
| --- | --- |
| **Regulation** | **Explanation** |
| Securities regulation: Securities Act of 1933 | Regulates the issuance of new securities |
| Securities Exchange Act of 1934 | Established the Securities and Exchange Commission; act deals with subsequent trading in securities |
| Dodd-Frank Act Title VII | Title VII now requires that certain swaps be registered with the SEC and that they comply with certain principles enumerated in the act. |
| Dodd-Frank Act Title IX | Title IX creates the Office of Investor Advocate and authorizes the office to appoint an ombudsman; improves the regulation of credit rating institutions; alters the use of asset-backed securities; improves shareholder democracy; and enhances whistleblowing opportunities. |
| Antitrust regulation: Sherman Antitrust Act | Prohibits contracts, combinations in restraint of trade; also prohibits monopolies, attempts to monopolize, and conspires to monopolize |
| Clayton Act | Prohibits specific practices such as tying agreements and interlocking directorates |
| Robinson-Patman Act | Deals with product pricing, advertising, and promotional allowances |
| Federal Trade Commission Act | Established the Federal Trade Commission |

individuals seeking the proxy, any potential conflicts of interest, and specific information about any corporate changes to be voted on. When management solicits proxies, the solicitation must also include information about management salaries. The SEC regulations also state quite specifically that all material information must be stated in readable language and be displayed prominently, rather than buried in small type somewhere in the back of the document. The regulations also explicitly forbid false or misleading information.

# Dodd-Frank Wall Street Reform and Consumer Protection Act

In Chapter 20 we learned that, in response to the 21st century financial crisis, Congress passed several pieces of legislation, including the **Dodd-Frank Act**, aimed at fixing current economic problems and preventing such events from happening again in the future. The problems that we discussed in Chapter 20 were related to mortgages. The mortgage industry, however, was only part of the problem. Another industry involved in the crisis was the securities industry. For that reason, Congress also included provisions in the Dodd-Frank Act to deal with the shortcomings and the errors of the securities industry. As might be expected, the Dodd-Frank Act is long, involved, and complicated. It is in fact divided into 16 different titles, many of which are named as individual acts. Two titles that affect the Securities Exchange Commission are Title VII, the Wall Street Transparency and Accountability Act, and Title IX, the Investor Protection and Securities Reform Act of 2010.

Financial institutions on Wall Street have come under increased regulation and scrutiny due to their reckless practices.

## The Wall Street Transparency and Accountability Act

The 21st century financial crisis was caused in part by the reckless use of a financial instrument known as the derivative. A **derivative** (sometimes called a derivative contract and sometimes a derivative instrument) is a financial tool the value of which emerges from a variable item, such as an interest rate, a stock index, or a commodity like fuel or crops. Derivatives can be used to manage risk as long as they are handled properly. In contrast, the misuse of derivatives can be disastrous as was demonstrated during the 21st century financial crisis. A swap transaction (or simply, a swap) is a derivative that is made in an over-the-counter market. The SEC has the power to regulate security-based swaps that are traded on the exchanges. According to the SEC, **security-based swaps** are "swaps based on (1) a single security, (2) a loan, (3) a narrow-based group or index of securities, or (4) events relating to a single issuer or issuers of securities in a narrow-based security index." The problem has been that, before Title VII of Dodd-Frank, the swap process was not well regulated. There was little or no transparency before, during, or after such transactions. The law now requires that certain swaps be registered with the SEC and that they comply with certain principles enumerated in the act. The SEC and its sister regulating body, the Commodity Futures Exchange Commission, now have the power to make rules in consultation with one another on the swaps over which each agency has jurisdiction. (See "SEC Proposes Rules for Securities-Based Swap Execution Facilities," *U.S. Securities and Exchange Commission* (February 2, 2011), http://www.sec.gov/news/press/2011/2011-35/htm; and Marl Jickling and Kathleen Ann Ruane, "The Dodd-Frank Wall Street Reform and Consumer Protection Act: Title VII Derivatives," *Congressional Research Service,* August 30, 2010, pp. i, 1–2.)

## Title XI Investor Protection and Securities Reform Act

The second area that Dodd-Frank now regulates more directly involves the day-to-day activities of corporations. Under Title XI, which is also known as the Investor Protection and Securities Reform Act, the rules governing the SEC have been revised so that the agency can better monitor the areas under its jurisdiction and provide more effective protection for investors. The act does several things: creates the Office of Investor Advocate and authorizes the office to appoint an ombudsman; improves the regulation of credit rating institutions; alters the use of asset-backed securities; improves shareholder democracy; and enhances whistle-blowing opportunities.

*The Office of Investor Advocate* Subtitle A of Title XI of the Dodd-Frank Act creates a new agency, referred to as the **Office of Investor Advocate (OIA)**, the purpose of which is to help make the work of broker–dealers and investment advisors (IAs) more transparent. The law also gives the SEC the power to make new regulations that will define the fiduciary relationship between IAs and broker–dealers, on the one hand, and their clients, on the other. Section A also empowers the OIA to appoint an ombudsman and reactivates the Investor Advisory Committee, which was originally authorized in 2009.

*Regulation of Credit Rating Institutions* Subtitle C of Title XI authorizes the SEC to develop a new agency known as the **Office of Credit Ratings**, the purpose of which is to watchdog those organizations that issue credit ratings. These organizations, known in the industry as Nationally Recognized Statistical Rating Organizations or NRSROs, are key elements in the financial structure of the U.S. economy because they open or close the door on the ability of investors and borrowers to enter the marketplace. Section C provides for better internal controls that will eliminate conflicts of interest and promote the reporting of irregularities, among other things.

*Asset-Backed Securities* Subtitle D of Title XI of Dodd-Frank mandates more effective control over the issuance of asset-backed securities. Securitization became an issue during the 21st century financial crisis because many institutions that issued asset-backed securities sold them off almost immediately. This meant that they were unconcerned about the borrower's ability to pay back the loan. To minimize the risks associated with this practice, the new law requires institutions that engage in securitization to maintain an economic stake in the assets that they securitize. More specifically, the rules now state that institutions issuing asset-backed securities must keep a minimum of 5 percent of the credit risk, although there are exceptions to this rule built into the law.

*Shareholder Democracy* One of the primary goals of Title XI of the Dodd-Frank Act is to enhance shareholder democracy. Recall that shareholder democracy demands that the shareholders of a corporation have more input into the decision making process of the corporation, specifically as those decisions relate to the board of directors. To improve shareholder democracy the following changes have been mandated by the act. The SEC is now required to make rules to ensure that shareholders have a continuing opportunity to review executive compensation. Moreover, the act specifically permits the shareholders to review and reject golden parachute contracts with executives. A **golden parachute** is a compensation package that protects executives who might lose their positions following a merger or consolidation, and so on. The SEC is also authorized to make new regulations that will empower shareholders to use management proxies to nominate board members in election contests (See David S. Huntington, "Summary of Dodd-Frank Financial Regulation Legislation," *The Harvard Law Forum on Corporate Governance and Financial Regulation* (July 7, 2010); and "Brief Summary of the Dodd-Frank Wall Street Reform and Consumer Protection Act," *U.S. Senate Committee on Banking, Housing, and Urban Affairs,* http://banking.senate.gov/public.)

*Whistleblowing Enhancement* Perhaps the most controversial provision included in the new act is Subtitle B of Title XI which permits the SEC to make regulations that will improve its enforcement powers by establishing rules to implement a "whistleblowing bounty" program analogous to the one that the IRS implemented in 2006. Whistleblowers, or SEC "bounty-hunters," must meet certain minimum requirements to qualify for their "bounty." For instance, it is necessary that the evidence provided by a bounty-hunter concern a security law violation and include original information. (Apparently, *original* in this situation means that the SEC did not have the new evidence until the friendly neighborhood bounty-hunter showed up on their doorstep.) Bounty hunting can be very lucrative, which is, of course, the point since successful hunters can pull in somewhere between 10 and 30 percent of a sanction that is over $1 million. Naturally, there is some disagreement about how the new rules should be structured. Corporations believe that the rules should require whistleblowing bounty hunters to exhaust internal remedies first, before going to the SEC. They argue that since Sarbanes-Oxley required that such reporting mechanisms be put in to place, it makes sense to require whistleblowers to go through those reporting systems first. On the other hand, those attorneys who have whistleblowing clients argue that such internal remedies are rarely, if ever, effective since the people who receive the complaints work for and report to the people accused in the complaint. This would be a little like requiring mugging victims to talk to a mugger's accomplice before going to the police, or so the argument goes. (See David Ingram, "SEC Weighing How to Award Tipsters," *The National Law Journal,* May 16, 2011, pp. 1 and 4.)

# 28-3 Antitrust Regulation

Both the federal government and the states have antitrust laws to preserve the values of competition and to discourage monopolies. A **monopoly** is the exclusive control of a market by a business enterprise. At the federal level, the four principal antitrust statutes are the Sherman Antitrust Act, the Clayton Act, the Robinson-Patman Act, and the Federal Trade Commission Act.

## Sherman Antitrust Act

The Sherman Antitrust Act (1890) prohibits contracts, combinations, and conspiracies in restraint of trade. It also prohibits monopolization, attempts to monopolize, and combinations or conspiracies to monopolize any part of interstate or foreign commerce. Violations of the Sherman Antitrust Act must involve at least two parties acting together. The courts use two tests to judge antitrust offenses: *per se* violations and the rule-of-reason standard. The two tests, however, sometimes represent moving targets that are easy to articulate but difficult to implement in a consistent and fair fashion. In fact, the line of distinction between the two standards is sometimes so small that the two tests can, at times, seem as indistinguishable from each other as a set of identical twins.

**Per Se Violations**  Some restraint-of-trade practices are so serious that they are prohibited, whether or not they harm anyone. These practices are labeled *per se* **violations**, which means that the practice is so contrary to antitrust policy that harm is presumed, and the practice is prohibited. For example, price fixing is inherently unreasonable and therefore considered a *per se* violation. An agreement between competitors to divide territories among themselves to minimize competition would also be unlawful, even if the agreement helps the parties compete against other parties outside the agreement. Similar unlawful activities include agreements among competitors to stop competing with one another in prices, customers, or products.

**Rule-of-Reason Standard**  If an alleged antitrust practice is not considered a *per se* violation, then the courts will judge the legality of that practice with the rule-of-reason approach. The **rule-of-reason standard** will stop certain practices only if they are an unreasonable restriction of competition. As a result, some practices that in fact limit competition may be legal. To determine if an anticompetitive practice is legal, the court considers such facts as the history of the restraint, the harm that results, the reason for the practice, and the purpose to be attained.

**The Evolving Nature of the Twin Standards**  The *per se* and rule-of-reason standards have been part of antitrust law for decades, so the line of distinction between the

## THE OPENING CASE *Revisited, Part I*
### Single Entity or Collection Point—*American Needle, Inc. v. National Football League*, Round 2

Recall that in the Opening Case at the beginning of this chapter, the NFL through its subsidiary, National Football League Properties (NFLP) awarded an exclusive contract to Reebok to handle all official NFL merchandise. Recall also that a former NFL merchandiser, American Needle, was justifiably displeased with the new agreement. As a result, American Needle brought a lawsuit against the NFL. American Needle argued that the Reebok contract created an illegal monopoly violating the Sherman Antitrust Law. Now logically, as the next step, the court should have applied the rule-of-reason test, as noted above. However, it did not do so. Instead it tackled a more fundamental question and that was, "Is the NFL a collection point around which a group of 32 different teams have joined forces or is the league itself a single entity?" This is not an idle question.

If the NFL is a single entity, then it could not make any type of contract with itself, let alone a contract to restrain trade, and it would be home free. However, if it were a collection of separate enterprises then it could make a contract or a series of contracts and could, therefore, be in violation of the Sherman Act. The question went all the way to the Supreme Court which ruled that the NFL is not a single entity. The Court said that, under corporate law, the NFL might be a single entity, but under antitrust law, it was not. The NFL turns out to be, at least for purposes of antitrust law, a collection of 32 distinct constituent parts, referred to as teams and headquartered in different cities, that make financial decisions on their own for their own purposes and benefit. [See *American Needle, Inc. v. National Football League*, 130 S.Ct. 2201 (2010).]

two is usually very clear. However sometimes, as the law evolves, that line of distinction becomes less and less distinct. A case in point involves the court's distinction between resale price maintenance (RPM) agreements and quasi-RPM arrangements. An **RPM agreement** occurs when a retailer and a manufacturer decide that the retailer will sell certain products at a price set by the manufacturer. These RPMs have been outlawed by the court as a *per se*

## THE OPENING CASE *Revisited, Part II*
### Single Entity or Collection Point—*American Needle, Inc. v. National Football League*, Round 3

Let's look at the Opening Case one more time. The fact that the Supreme Court has decided that the National Football League is not a single entity does not end the case. On the contrary, now the case will go back to the trial court which will have to decide whether the NFL teams (remember under antitrust law according to the Supreme Court, the NFL is really just a collection of teams) made a contract that restrains trade. Now since the contract under consideration here does not appear to be a *per se* violation of the law, the court will then apply the rule-of-reason standard, which asks judges to balance the pro-competitive results of a

challenged arrangement with the anti-competitive results. Take a moment to speculate on this. What might the pro-competitive results be from the single contract with Reebok? What might the anti-competitive results be? Now balance the two and predict how the court will rule. [Note: Of course, if you can find no appropriate balance here, you might just want to settle the case before going any further. (Despite Jack McCoy's winning record on *Law and Order*, sometimes surrendering is an option.) (See *American Needle, Inc. v. National Football League*, 130 S.Ct. 2201 (2010).]

violation of antitrust law. In contrast, a **quasi-RPM arrangement** occurs when a manufacturer lets retailers know the price that it expects to see on an item and then declines to sell that item to any retailer that does not list the item at that price. Such arrangements are legally permissible under antitrust law because the law cannot take away the rights of manufacturers to pick those sellers with which they want to deal. While the distinction between the two seems, at best, artificial and, at worst, nonexistent, it is, nevertheless, the law.

## Post-Sherman Antitrust Legislation

Three principal antitrust statues made the Sherman Act more specific and, as a result, more effective. The Clayton Act of 1914, the Robinson-Patman Act of 1936, the Foreign Trade Antitrust Improvements Act, and the Federal Trade Commission Act of 1914 sought to prevent practices that reduced competition or favored the creation of monopolies.

**Clayton Act** Congress passed the Clayton Act to police specific business practices that could be used to create a monopoly. One practice outlawed by the act is tying agreements. A **tying agreement** occurs when one party refuses to sell a product unless the buyer also purchases another product tied to the first product. The issue is the effect of the tie-in on the seller's competitors. Interlocking directorates are also outlawed by the Clayton Act. **Interlocking directorates** occur when individuals serve as directors of two corporations that are competitors. This provision is not entirely foolproof, however, because banks and common carriers are exempt. To fall under this part of the Clayton Act, at least one of the corporations must have an aggregate worth (capital, surplus, and individual profits) of more than $1 million.

**Robinson-Patman Act** The Robinson-Patman Act deals with product pricing, advertising, and promotional allowances. It specifically prohibits a seller from charging different prices to different customers for the same product when such differences might injure competition. However, nothing in the law is intended to prevent price differences due to cost of manufacture, sale, delivery, or bulk purchases.

**Federal Trade Commission Act** In addition to establishing the Federal Trade Commission (FTC), the Federal Trade Commission Act, as amended, declares that "unfair methods of competition, and unfair or deceptive practices in or affecting commerce are hereby declared unlawful." The act did not name specific unfair methods of competition. Instead, it has allowed the courts and the FTC to determine those unfair practices. The Federal Trade Commission Act was amended by the Wheeler-Lea Act and amendments in 1938 and 1975. This legislation authorized the FTC to act against unfair or deceptive acts without first proving the existence of anticompetitive behavior. The FTC was also granted the power to challenge false advertising of food, drugs, and cosmetics, regardless of the advertiser's knowledge of the advertisement's truth or falsity.

**The Foreign Trade Antitrust Improvements Act (FTAIA)** Another antitrust measure passed by Congress is the Foreign Trade Antitrust Improvements Act (FTAIA). Unlike the other antitrust provisions supported by Congress, the FTAIA is designed to circumvent some of the restrictions placed on American companies by the Sherman Antitrust Act. The objective of the FTAIA is to permit American companies operating in foreign markets to have a fighting chance against foreign competitors that are not subject to the strict antimonopoly provisions of the act. Under terms of the bill, if an American company is operating totally in a foreign market, that company is not subject to American antitrust law.

## Self-Evident Truths

In his treatise, *Overcoming Law,* the legal scholar Richard Posner spends a great deal of time exploring the relationship between economics and the law. In doing so, he focuses on the ideas of two economists, Ronald Coase, who won the Nobel Memorial Prize for Economic Sciences in 1991, and George Stigler, the author of *The Citizen and the State: Essays on Regulation.* Posner explains their diverse points of view in the following way:

> The Swedish Academy had also emphasized Stigler's theory of regulation . . . as "treating *political behavior as utility-maximizing* [and] *political parties as firms supplying regulation,* with *what is supplied being what is wanted* by those groups (or coalitions) which are able to outbid others in the political market.
>
> —Posner, *Overcoming Law,* pp. 411–412 (italics added)

> These terms, and the vast bodies of formal theory that have grown up around them, assume the *fragility of markets* and the *robustness of government,* whereas Coase believes that careful observation of markets and government discloses the *robustness of markets* and the *fragility of government.*
>
> —Posner, *Overcoming Law,* p. 413 (italics added)

To summarize, Stigler proposes that the government is the only institution that can regulate the economy successfully, while Coase argues that the government is a fragile obstacle that cripples rather than promotes economic activity. By pointing to these two positions, Posner has suggested another area of the law that needs a proper balance. In fact, he is repeating the arguments of Keynes and Hayek discussed earlier in the book. So the debate continues. Do we need the government in the economy or do we need an economy that is free from governmental interference?

## Self-Evident Questions

1. What brief argument does Stigler offer for his position in favor of government intervention in the economy? Explain.

2. What is the major objection that Coase has for opposing government intervention into the economy? Explain.

3. Which view supports the idea that the judicial–economic system is a flexible and responsive system? Explain.

4. How would you suggest that we balance the views of Stigler and Coase? Explain.

5. In the real world of the 21st century, which system has prevailed? The Stiglerian interventionist system? Or the Coasist *laissez-faire* system? Explain.

In contrast, consumer advocates want to make it easier for plaintiffs to bring antitrust lawsuits against certain types of defendants, but especially against manufacturers. Plaintiffs frequently complain that retailers rarely bring antitrust claims against manufacturers, because retailers can avoid the effects of any antitrust scheme, such as a price-fixing conspiracy, by passing the increased cost of doing business on to the consumers. The consumers, who under current rules are frequently barred from bringing lawsuits against manufacturers, have no recourse other than to pay the higher prices. For this reason, consumer advocacy groups favor making it easier for plaintiffs to file class-action lawsuits against all manufacturing firms that violate antitrust law but especially against those large cartels that are the worst offenders. Finally, state and local regulators would also like to see changes in the law. These regulators favor changes that would transfer more antitrust enforcement authority from the federal government to the states.

# 28-4 Tactics of Corporate Expansion

No other area of corporate activity has been scrutinized by the government more closely in recent years than the area of corporate expansion (see Table 28-2). As noted previously, several governmental agencies may be involved in any given corporate expansion venture, including the Department of Justice and the Federal Communications Commission. However, the two agencies that have the primary responsibility for regulating this activity are the SEC and the FTC. The two commissions have different interests in the expansion process. The SEC is concerned with regulating the expansion tactics themselves, whereas the FTC is more concerned with the competitive effects of those expansion tactics.

## Expansion Tactics and Securities Law

All corporations change in size. Some grow and expand, while others shrink until they dissolve completely or are absorbed by a larger, more successful enterprise. Like all other corporate activities, corporate expansions are looked at very closely by government. The primary expansion techniques include mergers and acquisitions (M&A).

### Merger and Consolidation
Traditionally, a merger involves two corporations, one of which is absorbed by the other. One of the two corporations continues to carry on business under its original name, and the other simply disappears into the first. In contrast,

---

**Table 28-2**   Securities Law and Corporate Expansion

| Technique | Explanation | Regulation |
|---|---|---|
| Merger and consolidation | In a merger, one company is absorbed by another; in a consolidation, two companies join and a new company results. | Most antifraud provisions of the SEC apply here. |
| Asset acquisition | One corporation buys all the property of another. | Antifraud provisions of the SEC apply here if a proxy solicitation is involved or if insider information is used to profit from the sale. |
| Stock acquisition (takeover) | One corporation (suitor) makes a tender offer to the shareholders of another corporation (target). | Whenever a suitor makes an offer to acquire more than 5 percent of the target, the suitor must file with the SEC. |

in a **consolidation**, both companies disappear, and a new company carries on the business under a new name. Today, most legal scholars do not make any distinction between merger and consolidation. In fact, many state incorporation statutes make no reference to consolidation, preferring the term *merger* instead. A merger requires advance approval from the boards and shareholders of both corporations. In general, a two-thirds majority vote of the shareholders will be required before a merger can be approved, though some states require a supermajority of four-fifths. Shareholders who dissent are entitled to be paid for their stock if they do not wish to be a part of the merger. Written notice of a dissent is required so that the cost of purchasing the dissenter's stock can be figured as a part of the expense involved in the merger.

Most antifraud provisions of the SEC apply to the merger process. Often the merger vote will be preceded by a proxy solicitation battle. All material facts about the merger must be included in the proxy solicitation. In addition, the solicitation must not contain any false or misleading information. Similarly, the SEC prohibits insiders who know of merger plans from taking advantage of that knowledge to profit personally before the knowledge is revealed to the public.

Some state statutes apply different rules to mergers that involve a limited liability company (LLC). Under some state statutes, a merger involving an LLC requires the unanimous approval of the members rather than the two-thirds majority required of corporations. However, as is true in other circumstances, the operating agreement of an LLC could cancel this unanimous vote requirement. If the operating agreement specifies that a merger vote may be approved by less than a unanimous vote, many states give those members who are opposed to the merger the right to withdraw from the LLC and receive the cash value of their investment. However, once again, the operating agreement can alter this statutory right.

## Asset Acquisition

In an **asset acquisition**, one corporation purchases all the property of a second corporation. However, as in the case of mergers, SEC antifraud regulations can be applied to asset acquisitions if a proxy solicitation process is involved or if insider information is used to profit from the sale. Asset acquisition is easy and efficient, because the only formality required is approval by the directors and shareholders of the corporation that is selling its assets. A second advantage is that the buyer need not purchase all of the assets of the seller. The buyer may choose to purchase some assets while rejecting others.

Another advantage of asset acquisition is that, in general, no debts or other liabilities are transferred from seller to buyer. There are exceptions to this rule however. In certain situations, the debts of the selling corporation will transfer to the buying corporation. For instance, if the buyer is simply a continuation of the selling corporation, the buyer will not escape the liabilities of the seller. Similarly, if the sale is structured fraudulently to escape the liabilities of the selling corporation, the debts will transfer to the buyer. It is also possible for the buyer to either expressly or implicitly assume the debts and liabilities of the seller. Finally, if, despite its label as an asset acquisition, the sale is actually a merger, the liabilities will transfer to the buyer.

## Stock Acquisition

In a **stock acquisition**, the buyer purchases enough stock in a corporation to gain voting control of that corporation. Stock acquisitions come in many shapes and sizes (see Table 28-3). One type of stock acquisition is the leveraged buyout (LBO). In a **leveraged buyout**, a controlling portion of the stock in a corporation is purchased by a group of shareholders, often several outsiders but sometimes a team of officers and directors of the company. The potential buyers can then collect the money needed to purchase the outstanding shares by enlisting the support of a bank. The bank will lend a good portion of the money to the buyers, taking an enormous payment to support that loan. If the amount produced by the bank proves inadequate, the buyers will seek the assistance of an investment firm. The investment firm produces the remainder of the needed money

| Table 28-3 | Stock Acquisition Techniques |
|------------|------------------------------|
| **Technique** | **Explanation** |
| Leveraged buyout | A controlling portion of stock purchased by shareholders; leveraged by loans and junk bonds. |
| Tender offer | Suitor makes a public offer to buy voting stock in a target corporation. |
| Takeover bid | Tender offer opposed by the management of the target corporation. |
| Corporate raid | Takeover bid opposed by management of target because corporate raider intends to dismantle target. |

by issuing **junk bonds**, or bonds that are unstable but offer an elevated level of return to large, powerful investors. Because the stock purchase is made possible by these high-stakes loans, the buyout is referred to as "leveraged." The shareholders are motivated to sell because the buyout team offers them an inflated price for their shares. Sometimes after the buyers have purchased control of the corporation, they ensure their continued control by transforming the company into a private corporation. This action is referred to as "taking the company private."

A second form of stock acquisition is the tender offer. In a **tender offer**, the buyer or suitor, whether it is an individual, a consortium of like-minded individuals, or another corporation, makes a public offer to buy voting stock in a **target corporation**. A successful tender offer occurs once the buyer or buyers have purchased enough of the voting stock to satisfy the original goal, whatever that might have been. One advantage of the stock acquisition process is that it sidesteps the board of directors. The buyer deals directly with the shareholders. Again, the shareholders are motivated to sell because the buyer has made an offer that is above the current market price of the stock.

Sometimes a tender offer is welcomed by the directors and the officers of the target because they see it as a way to strengthen the corporation and enhance their own positions within the company. At other times, however, the tender offer is seen as a corporate **takeover bid** by an **unfriendly buyer**. In a takeover bid, the unfriendly buyer, also known as an **unfriendly suitor** or a **hostile bidder**, intends to purchase enough stock to control the corporation. Often the goal of the hostile bidder is to change management and shake up the corporation after the takeover. If the suitor intends to dismantle the corporation totally or somehow integrate the target into an existing corporation to such an extent that the target ceases to exist, the suitor is referred to as a **corporate raider** and the tender offer a **corporate raid**. In both cases, hostile bidder and corporate raider, the target's management is expected to fight the takeover with every tactic available.

To avoid being taken over by a hostile bidder, the management of a corporation can institute both post-offer and pre-offer tactics. Post-offer tactics include, but are not limited to, public relations initiatives, greenmail, the white knight gambit, lockup agreements, and targeted shareholder agreements (see Table 28-4). In contrast, pre-offer tactics could involve supermajority voting and accelerated loans, among others (see Table 28-5).

## Post-Offer Techniques

Probably the least problematic post-offer technique is the public relations initiative. Such an initiative is aimed at convincing shareholders that it is in their best interests not to sell their shares to the hostile bidder. News releases, advertisements, press conferences, and even personal letters would attempt to convince shareholders that present management should be retained. The difficulty with this approach is that many

**Table 28-4**  Post-Offer Antitakeover Tactics

| Post-Offer Tactics | Explanations |
| --- | --- |
| Public relations campaign | Target corporation uses news releases, advertisements, and press conferences to convince shareholders to retain present management. |
| Greenmail | Target corporation offers to buy target's stock already owned by suitor. |
| White knight | Target corporation invites friendly suitor to outbid a hostile bidder. |
| Lockup agreement | Target corporation tags irreplaceable property for sale when hostile bidder succeeds in takeover. |
| Targeted shareholder agreement | Target corporation makes deal with suitor to protect management of target. |

arguments pale to insignificance when placed alongside a bid that is above the current market price of the stock.

Sometimes the most effective way for a target to shake off a bidder's hostile suit is to offer the bidder greenmail. A corporation that activates the greenmail defense has offered to buy the portion of the target's stock that the bidder already owns. Naturally, such an approach will work only if the target's offer is significantly higher than the amount that the bidder paid for the stock in the first place. Such an approach is disfavored because it robs the shareholders of the opportunity to make a profit by selling their shares and may seriously devalue the target's remaining stock, thereby victimizing the shareholders a second time.

Another post-offer technique that can be used by the target company is the white knight gambit. To implement this tactic, the target invites another suitor to outbid the hostile bidder. The second suitor is known as a friendly suitor or a white knight, because the invited suitor agrees that it will retain existing management. The white knight also frequently agrees not to disrupt the smooth running of the target by selling off key assets, closing down plants, or laying off employees. A takeover battle usually follows. The winner is generally the suitor that can offer the highest price for the target's outstanding stock.

A fourth post-offer technique is the lockup agreement. A lockup agreement might be used by target management if the target owns an irreplaceable piece of property, the sale of which would seriously devalue the overall worth of the target. Such property might include rich timberland or an extremely productive coal mine. Provided that the sale of that property

**Table 28-5**  Pre-Offer Antitakeover Tactics

| Pre-Offer Tactic | Explanation |
| --- | --- |
| Supermajority provision— for takeover bids | Target corporation rewrites bylaws to require 90 percent vote to approve any takeover. |
| Supermajority provision— for amendments | Target corporation rewrites bylaws to require 90 percent vote to amend the bylaws. |
| Accelerated loans | Target corporation enters loan agreements which are due in full when the target is subject to a successfull takeover. |

does not deplete virtually all the assets of the target, management could enter a contract with a white knight, giving the knight an option to buy that valuable piece of property should the hostile bidder gain control of the target corporation. The idea is to discourage the hostile bidder from buying the now-devalued target.

A fifth post-offer technique is the **targeted shareholder agreement**. Strictly speaking, a targeted shareholder agreement is not an anti-acquisition tactic as much as it is an executive protection strategy. Under the provisions of a targeted shareholder agreement, the suitor negotiates a deal with certain targeted shareholders, generally the CEO, the CFO, the CTO, and other high-ranking officers. These agreements will provide the officers/shareholders with handsome employment-related deals that supplement the price that they will receive for the sale of their stock. Such deals might include a salary increase, a severance package, a non-compete agreement, and so on. The strategy behind negotiating a targeted shareholder agreement is not to stop the acquisition but to protect key employees who might be financially damaged or even discharged in the post-acquisition culture.

Targeted shareholder agreements were hampered in the late 1990s and early in the twenty-first century by two rules instituted by the SEC. These rules, known collectively as the **best-price rule**, prohibited suitors from offering different prices to different shareholders during a tender offer process. Unfortunately, the best-price rule was interpreted differently by different federal courts. Some courts, using what was called the **integral-part test**, decided that any type of price enhancement, including employment-related packages, would violate the best-price rule—period. The other rule, known as the **bright-line test**, was used by those courts that saw a violation of the best-price rule only during the actual tender offer. Thus, if an employment agreement was negotiated with a targeted shareholder before or after the actual tender offer, and the actual price that the suitor paid for the stock remained unaffected, then there was no violation of the best-price rule. The SEC eventually amended the rule to make it clear that targeted shareholder agreements that involved *only* employment-related agreements would not be subject to the best-price rule. This decision is likely to pave the way for the increased use of the targeted shareholder agreement in the future.

**Pre-Offer Techniques**  Sometimes post-offer techniques are instituted too late to prevent takeover. For this reason, many corporations plan ahead by instituting certain pre-offer measures even before any unfriendly suitors have appeared on the horizon (see Table 28-5). For example, a corporation could institute a supermajority provision into its bylaws that would require a 90 percent affirmative vote by all shareholders for the approval of any merger. Such a move would mean that any suitor would have to acquire 90 percent of the stock of the target to assure a takeover. A back-up provision requiring a supermajority to change the supermajority bylaws would also be necessary to ensure that the suitor does not simply take 51 percent of the target and then use that majority control to eliminate the supermajority merger vote provision.

An additional pre-offer technique involves the corporation in a series of accelerated loans. Under the provisions of an accelerated loan program, all major loans taken out by the corporation are due in full immediately upon the takeover of the target by an unfriendly suitor. The plan is to place the suitor in a precarious financial position because, once the target has been acquired, the suitor would be forced to pay off a series of expensive loans, thus straining the treasury of the target. The accelerated loan gambit is often unsuccessful because the financial institutions that made the loans are often willing to renegotiate the terms of the accelerated loans with the target's new owner to avoid getting a poor return on their investments.

**Takeover Bids and the SEC**  Takeover bids are closely scrutinized by the SEC. Under recent amendments to federal securities law, whenever a suitor makes an offer to acquire more than 5 percent of a target, that suitor must file a statement with the SEC. The statement must indicate (1) where the money for the takeover originates, (2) why the suitor is buying the stock, and (3) how much of the target the suitor already owns. These procedures are designed to let shareholders know the identity and intention of a takeover bidder. Bidders who falsify any information on their statement may find their takeover bid stopped by a court order.

# Expansion Tactics and Antitrust Law

As noted previously, antitrust law is designed to preserve competition and discourage monopolies. One way that companies can create monopolies is through a corporate expansion effort. Antitrust law does not focus on corporate expansion techniques. Instead, it looks at how an expansion attempt will affect competition in the marketplace (see Table 28-6). Section 7 of the Clayton Act forbids any corporate expansion if that expansion sets up a monopoly or otherwise hurts competition. The Clayton Act applies to horizontal, vertical, or conglomerate expansion attempts.

**Expansion Attempts** Because horizontal expansion occurs between companies that are involved in the same business, such attempts often result in monopolies. Consequently, horizontal expansion schemes are closely scrutinized by the FTC and are more likely to be labeled illegal. A vertical expansion occurs between companies that were in a customer–supplier relationship. If a manufacturer of designer jeans were to buy a chain of department stores that carried its jeans, a vertical expansion would result. A conglomerate expansion joins two companies that were not in competition with each other, either because they dealt in different products or services or because they operated in different geographical areas.

**Hart-Scott-Rodino Antitrust Act** Like the SEC, the FTC has a chance to step into expansion situations even before they become an established fact. This opportunity is provided by the Hart-Scott-Rodino Antitrust Act. Hart-Scott-Rodino is designed to police any expansion attempts that might harm competition in the marketplace. The act requires corporations that are setting up an expansion attempt to notify the FTC before the deal is completed. This advance notice allows the FTC to investigate the anticompetitive effects of the planned expansion. Should the FTC decide that the expansion will hurt competition, it can go to court and ask for an injunction to prevent the expansion.

**The Tunney Antitrust Act** The federal government also regulates corporate expansion through the activities of the Antitrust Division of the Department of Justice (DOJ) and through the activities of specialized agencies, such as the Federal Communications Commission (FCC). The DOJ's Antitrust Division is charged with policing mergers

**Table 28-6** Antitrust Law and Corporate Expansion

| Technique | Explanation | Regulation |
|---|---|---|
| Horizontal expansion | Occurs between companies that are involved in the same business | Closely scrutinized by the FTC because of the likelihood of a monopoly |
| Vertical expansion | Occurs between companies that are in a customer–supplier relationship | Less likelihood of monopoly, therefore less FTC scrutiny |
| Conglomerate expansion | Occurs between two companies that are not in competition with each other | Least likelihood of monopoly, therefore least FTC scrutiny |

that affect antitrust law to ensure that in carrying out a corporate combination, the participants have not violated those laws. The primary goal of the DOJ, however, is not to stop such mergers outright but instead to help the parties negotiate a merger that can be completed without violating the law. Such agreements are referred to as **consent decrees**. The Justice Department's antitrust consent decrees are, in turn, regulated by a federal statute known as the **Antitrust Procedures and Penalties Act** or simply as the **Tunney Act**.

The Tunney Act requires that the DOJ defend its support of a consent decree by sending the decree to the federal court along with a complaint and a **competitive impact statement (CIS)**. The CIS is a document that clarifies any potential antitrust problems inherent within the expansion and the solutions to those problems suggested by the decree. The law requires that 60 days before concluding the agreement, the DOJ publish the complaint, the decree, and the CIS in the *Federal Register*. Publishing the documents gives people a chance to have input into the nature, purpose, and effects of the agreement. The *Federal Register* will then print these statements and observations. A judge must also approve the decree. In doing so, the judge takes into account two elements: (1) the effect of the decree on competition and (2) the decree's effect on the community and on any parties who might be hurt separately. The Tunney Act was amended in 2004 to make it clear that the courts have the authority to challenge consent decrees negotiated by the Justice Department.

The corporate expansion process is sometimes regulated by specialty agencies that are charged with overseeing the socioeconomic activities of the corporations involved in the expansion process. Thus, for instance, the Federal Communications Commission would be responsible for reviewing merger plans proposed by corporations involved in the communications industry. Some agency officials take this responsibility very seriously and use their power to negotiate concessions within merger agreements that permit the agency to engage in an unofficial, but effective, brand of social engineering. The FCC is one such agency. In recent years, it has exercised its review power in merger cases to protect consumers, set prices, and return jobs to the United States. Agencies that use their regulatory powers to advance social agendas that are technically outside their legislative authority are referred to as **activist agencies**.

---

### quick quiz 28-4

| | | |
|---|---|---|
| 1. | Most antifraud provisions of the Securities and Exchange Commission apply to the merger process. | true \| false |
| 2. | Greenmail is the least effective anti-hostile takeover technique. | true \| false |
| 3. | The Hart-Scott-Rodino Act is designed to police any expansion attempts that might harm competition in the marketplace. | true \| false |

---

# 28-5 The Government and Corporate Dissolution

Just as the government is involved in the birth and growth (expansion) of a corporation, it is also involved in its death, or dissolution. Whether a corporation ends involuntarily or voluntarily, the government is somehow involved.

## Involuntary Dissolution

If a corporation has repeatedly conducted business in an unlawful manner, the secretary of state can ask the state attorney general to bring a *quo warranto* action against that corporation.

Under a *quo warranto* proceeding, the state revokes the corporation's charter. Common examples of illegal actions forming the grounds for revocation include a failure to file annual reports, a failure to pay franchise taxes, or a failure to maintain a registered or statutory agent for service of process. Corporations formed fraudulently and those exceeding their authority may also be subject to a *quo warranto* proceeding.

Courts have the power to liquidate the assets of a corporation when an action is brought by a shareholder. Grounds for involuntary dissolution at the request of a shareholder include the following:

- Evidence of illegal, oppressive, or fraudulent acts.
- A misapplication or waste of corporate assets.
- A deadlock of directors that threatens irreparable harm.
- Evidence that a dissolution is necessary to protect the rights of the complaining shareholder.

## Voluntary Dissolution

Because the government grants corporate charters and regulates corporate activity, it must be informed when a corporation voluntarily dissolves. A corporation can be dissolved voluntarily by the unanimous approval of the shareholders or by a positive vote of the directors with the approval of two-thirds of the shareholders. Once the decision to dissolve has been approved, a statement of intent must be filed with the state government. The corporation will then cease business and notify creditors (by certified mail) and the public (by publication). After all claims have been received, corporate assets will be used first to pay creditors, with the surplus going to shareholders. If the existing assets cannot meet all claims, a receiver may be called in to handle matters. A *receiver* is a person appointed by law to hold property subject to diverse claims. The receiver would divide assets fairly among creditors. Following the distribution of all assets, the corporation must prepare articles of dissolution and present them to the secretary of state.

| | |
|---|---|
| **quick quiz 28-5** | |
| 1. If a corporation has repeatedly conducted business in an unlawful manner, the secretary of state can require the Federal Justice Department to revoke its charter. | true \| false |
| 2. Courts no longer have any power to liquidate the assets of a corporation when an action is brought by a shareholder. | true \| false |
| 3. Corporations are no longer permitted to engage in voluntary dissolution. | true \| false |

# 28-6 Dissolution of a Limited Liability Company

Because limited liability companies are created by state statutory law, the dissolution of a LLC is also regulated by state statutory law. Most state LLC statutes outline the circumstances that will trigger the dissolution of an LLC.

late business develop?

2. What is the source of state power to regulate business?

sion prevent unfair practices?

4. What is a *per se* antitrust violation of antitrust law?

# Part 7 Case Study

**Gries Sports Enterprises, Inc. v. Cleveland Browns Football Co., Inc.**

Supreme Court of Ohio 496 N.E.2d 959

## Summary

Arthur Modell, president, CEO, and a director of the Cleveland Browns Football Co., Inc., (Browns) owned 53 percent of that corporation. Other members of the board at that time included Pat Modell, Modell's wife; James Bailey, who was also chief counsel for and an employee of the Browns; James Berick, who was outside counsel representing the corporation and a Browns shareholder; Richard Cole; and Nate Wallack, who was also an employee of the Browns. The final member of the board of directors was Robert Gries, who owned 43 percent of the Browns and also owned Gries Sports Enterprises, Inc. (GSE). Modell also owned 80 percent of the Cleveland Stadium Corporation (CSC), which leased Cleveland Stadium from the city and which then subleased the Stadium to the Browns and the Cleveland Indians. Other shareholders of CSC included Berick, Bailey, Cole, Wallack, Gries, and GSE. Modell was also president of CSC, and Bailey was both secretary and general counsel of that corporation.

CSC purchased 190 acres of land in Strongsville, Ohio, from Modell for $3,000,000 in cash and a promissory note for $1,000,000. Although Modell later canceled the $1,000,000 note, CSC still had debts exceeding $4,000,000. Modell decided that it would be expedient for the Browns to purchase CSC. Accordingly, he had CSC appraised by the brokerage and investment banking firm of McDonald and Company. Modell and Bailey, along with Michael Poplar, chief financial officer of CSC, determined that the Browns should pay $6,000,000 for the purchase of CSC. After this decision had been made, Modell, Bailey, Berick, and Poplar told Gries and Cole that CSC would be purchased by the Browns for $6,000,000. The purchase plan involved a payment of $120 per share of CSC to the minority shareholders, among whom were Berick, Bailey, Wallack, and Cole. Modell, the majority shareholder in CSC, was to receive a payment of $4,800,000 for his shares.

Subsequently, Gries did his own investigation into the value of CSC and concluded that Modell, Bailey, and Poplar had seriously overvalued the worth of that corporation. When the board met to consider the purchase, Modell made a presentation in support of the plan, and Gries explained his opposition. When the matter came to a vote, Bailey, Berick, Cole, and Wallack all voted for the plan. Neither Arthur nor Pat Modell participated in the vote, and Gries voted against the transaction. The following day, Gries filed a derivative lawsuit, the objective of which was to compel a reversal of the decision to purchase CSC. Gries stated that the transaction was unfair to the corporation, in that CSC was worth only $2,000,000 at the time that the Browns purchased it for $6,000,000. Gries argued that the fairness rule rather than the business judgment rule should be used to evaluate the directors' conduct because the directors who voted for the purchase were either "interested" directors due to their stock ownership or were dominated by Modell and had simply "rubber stamped" his decision.

Moreover, Gries contended that the overvaluation of CSC was prompted by Modell's need to secure the money to pay off outstanding debts to several banks.

Modell and the other directors argued that the decision to buy CSC should be evaluated by the business judgment rule. The trial court agreed with Gries, but the appeals court reversed that decision. The case then went to the Ohio Supreme Court.

# The Court's Opinion

## Justice Wise

The appellees-directors herein claim that they are protected by the presumption of good faith and fair dealing that arises from the business judgment and, therefore, they do not have the burden of proving that their decision to purchase CSC was intrinsically fair to the Browns' minority shareholders.

The issue before us, then, centers on the applicability of the business judgment rule. The business judgment rule is a principle of corporate governance that has been part of the common law for at least one hundred fifty years. It has traditionally operated as a shield to protect directors from liability for their decisions. If the directors are entitled to the protection of the rule, then the courts should not interfere with or second-guess their decisions. If the directors are not entitled to the protection of the rule then the courts scrutinize the decision as to its intrinsic fairness to the corporation and the corporation's minority shareholders. . . . A party challenging a board of directors' decision bears the burden of rebutting the presumption that the decision was a proper exercise of the business judgment of the board. . . .

In a stockholders' derivative action challenging the fairness of a transaction approved by a majority of directors of a corporation a director must be (1) disinterested, (2) independent, and (3) informed in order to claim benefit of the business judgment rule. If a director fails to pass muster as to any one of these three, he is not entitled to the business judgment presumption. This does not mean that the director's decision is necessarily wrong; it only removes the protection provided by the business judgment presumption. Once this presumption is removed, the court must then inquire into the fairness of the director's decision.

(A) [A] director is interested if (1) he appears on both sides of the transaction or (2) he has or expects to derive a personal financial benefit not equally received by the stockholders; (B) a director is independent if his decision is based on the corporate merits of the subject before the board rather than extraneous considerations or influences; a director is not independent when he is dominated by or beholden to another person through personal or other relationship; and (C) a director is informed if he makes a reasonable effort to become familiar with the relevant and reasonably available facts prior to making a business judgment.

Browns' directors Modell, Gries, Bailey, Berick, Cole, and Wallack, were all stockholders in CSC. Modell was the fifty-three percent majority stockholder in the Browns and the eighty percent majority stockholder in CSC (one hundred percent after March 2, 1982). [These facts convinced the court that the directors were interested in the challenged decision and were therefore not entitled to the protection of the business judgment rule. The court then went on to apply the fairness rule to the purchase of CSC by the Browns.]

(W)hen the transaction ". . . involves insiders dealing with their corporation the test of validity of the transaction is fairness. That our courts have frequently so held is without question . . . the substance of our decisions that 'when the persons, be they stockholders or directors, who control the making of a transaction and the fixing of its terms, are on both sides, then the presumption and deference to sound business judgment are no longer present.'"

In the instant case, no arms length negotiations as to price, terms, the elements to be included (or not to be included), or any other aspect of the proposed acquisition ever took place between the Browns and CSC. The $6,000,000 price was arrived at by Messrs. AMA (Modell), Bailey and Poplar . . . prior to any disclosure to plaintiffs of the possibility of such an acquisition, and never changed despite plaintiff's objections and despite the valuations furnished the defendants by plaintiffs. The manner in which the subject transaction was initiated, structured and disclosed to plaintiffs therefore did not satisfy the reasonable concept of fair dealing. . . .

The judgment of the court of appeals is reversed, and the judgment of the trial court is reinstated.

Judgment reversed.

# Questions for Analysis

1. Which party had the burden of proof in this case?

2. According to the court's opinion, what factors should be taken into consideration in determining whether a director has an interest in a transaction that is challenged by a shareholder in a derivative lawsuit?

3. According to the court's opinion, when is a director independent, and under what circumstances does the director lose that independence?

4. What circumstances does the court say will make a director informed?

5. When the business judgment rule cannot be used, as occurred in this case, what standard is applied by the court to determine whether to reverse a challenged decision made by the directors?

6. Did the court consider the purchase of the Cleveland Stadium Corporation by the Cleveland Browns to be fair to the corporation and the minority shareholders in this case? Why or why not?

# Part Eight

## Property Law

# Personal Property and Bailments

## THE OPENING CASE   Footsteps in the Night, Footprints in the Morning: *Melling v. Los Alamos Inn and Suites*

Often the best intentions and the most well-laid plans are not enough to prevent misfortune. Sometimes chance intervenes and sometimes people just fail to see the significance of their actions (or nonaction as the case may be). Psychologists and sociologists have a name for this phenomenon. They call it the law of unintended consequences. Rarely do unintended consequences cause a disaster, but when they do, the law is there to pick up the pieces. This is what happened in the case of *Melling v. Los Alamos Inn and Suites*. The Los Alamos Inn was owned and operated by the Rosier Hospitality Corporation, a company incorporated in Delaware and operating in 17 states and 3 Canadian provinces. The Mellings arrived in Los Alamos to attend Mr. Melling's nephew's wedding. The couple checked into the inn and unpacked their luggage. After settling in, Mr. Melling decided to shower while his wife was out shopping. After taking a shower, he opened the bathroom door and discovered a couple bringing suitcases into his room. The desk clerk had assigned the room to another couple by mistake. Following the incident, Mr. Melling was embarrassed, humiliated, and angry with the inn's employees for making such a silly mistake, but there was nowhere else in town with vacancies and so the couple decided to stay. Meanwhile, while shopping, Mrs. Melling purchased a diamond

ring which she placed in the Inn's safe deposit vault. Later, Mrs. Melling withdrew the ring from the vault to wear that evening at the rehearsal dinner. When she went to return the ring to the vault later that night, she was told by the desk clerk that the vault was closed until the next morning. Before retiring for the night, the Mellings locked their outside door but did not secure the chain latch. At about 5:30 AM, they awoke to find a ski-masked burglar in the room at the foot of their bed. The burglar escaped with Mrs. Melling's new diamond ring and Mr. Melling's wallet. After the police had been called and a report filed, the Mellings went off to the wedding. Although they were advised to lock their room before going to the church, Mr. Melling was so upset with the staff at the Inn that he just stormed off and drove away, leaving the room unlocked. While the couple was at the wedding and the reception, their luggage disappeared from their room at the Inn. Later the couple brought this suit against the Rosier Hospitality Corporation. How many legal problems can you spot here and what will the outcome be in each case?

**Opening Case Questions**

1. What is the Inn's liability, if any, for Mr. Melling's embarrassment and distress caused by room assignment error? Explain.

2. Does the Inn have any responsibility for the stolen diamond ring and the stolen wallet? Explain.

3. Is there any limit to the Inn's liability for the Mellings' stolen property or must it pay for the full amount of the loss? Explain.

4. Does the Inn have any responsibility for the Mellings' missing luggage? Why or why not?

5. Is there any difference between the Inn's liability for the stolen rings, the stolen wallet, and the missing luggage? Explain.

 ## Learning Objectives

1. Give examples of tangible and intangible personal property.
2. Describe the methods of owning property with others.
3. Differentiate among lost property, misplaced property, and abandoned property.
4. Identify the requirements of a completed gift.
5. Explain the law that applies to stolen property.
6. Determine when a bailment occurs.
7. Name and describe the principal types of bailments.
8. Discuss the burden of proof as it relates to bailments.
9. Make clear an innkeeper's duty to accept all guests.
10. Explain innkeepers' duties of care to their guests and their guests' property.

# 29-1 Personal Property

Broadly defined, **personal property** is everything that can be owned other than real estate. It is divided into two kinds, tangible and intangible. *Tangible* personal property is property that has substance and can be touched, such as a book, a pair of jeans, or a cell phone. Also called goods, or **chattels**, tangible personal property is movable and includes animals and crops. *Intangible* personal property, in contrast, is property that is not perceptible to the senses and cannot be touched. Accounts receivables and stock certificates are examples of intangible personal property. Another name for this type of property is **chose in action**, which means evidence of the right to property but not the property itself. In addition to the items mentioned, chose in action includes money due on a note or contract, damages due for breach of contract or tort, and rights under insurance policies.

## Ownership of Personal Property

When personal property is owned solely by one person, it is said to be owned in **severalty**. When it is owned by more than one person, it is said to be held in **cotenancy**. The types of cotenancies discussed here are tenancy in common, joint tenancy, and community property. When two or more people own personal property as **tenants in common**, each cotenant's share of the property passes to his or her heirs upon death. In contrast, when two or more people own personal property as **joint tenants** (sometimes referred to as **joint tenants with the right of survivorship**), each cotenant's share of the property passes to the surviving joint tenants upon death. Nine states recognize **community property**, which is property (except a gift or inheritance) that is acquired by the personal efforts of either spouse during marriage and that, by law, belongs to both spouses equally. The states that recognize community property are: Arizona, California, Idaho, Louisiana, Nevada, New Mexico, Texas, Washington, and Wisconsin. Spouses can leave their half of the community property by will to whomever they choose. If they die without a will, their share passes to their surviving spouse.

## Lost, Misplaced, and Abandoned Property

The finder of lost property has a legal responsibility, usually fixed by statute, to make an effort to learn the identity of the owner and return the property to that person. Advertising the property in a general circulation newspaper is usually evidence of the finder's honest effort to locate the owner, although today some sort of Internet posting might be even more effective. Statutes in many states provide that if the finder of lost property has made an effort to locate the owner and has not been successful within a period specified by law, the property belongs to the finder.

If lost property is found on the counter of a store, on a table in a restaurant or hotel, on a chair in a washroom, or in some similar public or semipublic place, it is considered not to be *lost* but to have been *misplaced*. It is reasonable to suppose that the owner will remember leaving it there and return for it. For this reason, the finder may not keep possession of the article but must leave it with the proprietor or manager to hold for the owner. If the property is found on the floor or in the corridor or any other place that would indicate it was not placed there intentionally, the finder may retain possession of the article while looking for the true owner. In this case, it is not likely that the owner would recall where it was lost.

### EXAMPLE 29-1: Misplaced Property

While walking along a beach one morning, Carlow noticed a plastic bag near the edge of the water. She opened the bag and discovered that it contained a large sum of money. In the bag with the money was a bank deposit slip made out in the name of a nearby seafood restaurant. Carlow had a legal duty to return the money to the restaurant. Suppose the bank deposit slip had not been in the bag and Carlow was unsuccessful in an attempt to find the rightful owner. After making a sincere effort to locate the real owner, and after the period of time set by state statute, Carlow would become the owner of the money.

When property is found and turned over to officials of a state, without any claim registered by the finder, the property becomes the property of the state after a period of time set by statute. The same rule applies to bank deposits and other claims that have been abandoned by persons in whose names such claims were registered. In these latter instances, a period of up to 20 years may be required to establish the right of the state to take title. In some states, gift certificate money that is unclaimed after a certain number of years is supposed to be transferred to the state under the abandoned property law. When property reverts to the state, it is said to escheat. Some states have statutes that remove gift certificates from their abandoned property law, treating them in different ways.

Abandoned property is property that has been discarded by the owner without the intent to reclaim ownership of it. Courts require clear and convincing evidence of both the desertion of the property by the owner as well as the owner's intent not to return to it before determining that property was indeed abandoned. With some exceptions, anyone who finds abandoned property has the right to keep it and obtains good title to it, even against the original owner.

Old shipwrecks are often the subject of abandoned property cases. If an abandoned shipwreck is found outside the boundaries of a state, either the law of finds or the law of salvage applies under admiralty law. The *law of finds* gives ownership to the finder if all of the following apply: (a) the property is abandoned, (b) the finder intends to acquire the property, and (c) the finder has possession of the property. The *law of salvage* gives a salvor (one who salvages) the right to compensation for assisting a foundering vessel. **Salvage** is the reward given to persons who voluntarily assist a sinking ship or recover its cargo from peril or loss. In addition, the United Nations Convention on the Law of the Sea (UNCLOSIII) requires salvors to protect the historical character of shipwrecks. If an abandoned shipwreck is found in the submerged land of any state of the United States, the Abandoned Shipwreck Act of 1987 applies rather than the *law of finds* or the *law of salvage*. This Act gives states the right of ownership to shipwrecks found beneath their waters.

## EXAMPLE 29-2: Law of Finds

In 2004, the federal court awarded full ownership of a Civil War–era shipwreck to Odyssey Marine Exploration. The salvage company agreed to pay $1.6 million to an insurance company that had paid claims when the ship sank. The *SS Republic* was a side-wheel steamer that went down in 1865 while en route from New York to New Orleans after fighting a hurricane for two days. The salvage company discovered the shipwreck 1,700 feet below the surface of the Atlantic Ocean approximately 100 miles off the Georgia coast. Among other relics, the ship contained $400,000 (face value) of gold and silver coins, which may now be worth up to $180 million.

## Gifts of Personal Property

People often make gifts of personal property. There are three requirements for a gift to be completed: the **donor** (the one giving the gift) must intend to make a gift, the gift must be delivered to the **donee** (the one receiving it), and the donee must accept the gift. Once all three requirements are met, the gift cannot be taken back by the donor. It is known as an absolute gift, or **gift** *inter vivos* (between the living).

The gift of an engagement ring is a conditional gift, given in contemplation of marriage. Most courts hold that the donor of an engagement ring is entitled to its return if the engagement is broken by mutual agreement or by the donee. A few courts allow the return of the ring even when the donor breaks the engagement. These courts theorize that it is better to break the engagement without penalty than to have an unhappy marriage.

### Uniform Transfers to Minors Act

Problems can easily arise when gifts are given to minors. Sometimes, parents or guardians use such gifts for themselves rather than for the minor. At other times, donors make gifts to minors and then change their minds and take the gifts back. Gifts to minors are often used as tax shelters. Formerly, wealthy parents in high tax brackets often made gifts to their minor children as a way to shift unearned income to lower-bracket taxpayers. The IRS has changed this practice with the so-called kiddie tax. Effective January 1, 2008, unearned income (dividends and interest) of a child under the age of 19 up to $1,700 is taxed at the child's income tax rate and, above that, at the parent's income tax rate. This rule also applies to college students under the age of 24 unless they provide over half of their own support from earned income (wages and salaries).

The Uniform Transfer to Minors Act (UTMA), which has been adopted by most states, also prevents some of these problems. The act establishes a procedure for gifts to be made to minors. Under the procedure, minors are assured that gifts to them will either be used for their benefit or made available to them when they become adults. The income from gifts that are given to minors is taxable according to the kiddie tax rules mentioned previously. The UTMA allows money, securities, real property, and tangible and intangible personal property to be transferred to a custodian for the minor's benefit. The age of 21 rather than 18 years is used as the age when the custodianship terminates, because the IRS uses that age to terminate certain trusts.

**Gift in Causa Mortis**  A gift given during one's lifetime, in contemplation of death from a known cause, is a gift *in causa mortis*. A gift *in causa mortis* is conditional, and it is ineffective if the donor does not die as expected or if death is caused by circumstances other than those feared.

---

**EXAMPLE 29-3:** Void Gift *in Causa Mortis*

Rossano was seriously ill following an abdominal operation. Realizing that death might be near, Rossano signed over a savings account to Hall, giving Hall the savings book with necessary notations of assignment. Rossano did die three weeks later, not because of the surgery but because of an automobile accident. Rossano's executor may declare the gift *in causa mortis* void and demand the return of Rossano's savings for the benefit of the estate.

---

**Anatomical Gifts**  With so many medical advancements in recent years, there is an increased need in society for gifts of human bodies, tissues, and organs for medical education, research, and transplantation. The Uniform Anatomical Gift Act was revised in 2006 to help meet present-day needs.

## Stolen Personal Property

Although a presumption of title to goods usually follows possession of them, it is possible for a person to have possession of goods without having title, just as it is possible for a person to have title without having possession. Thus, a thief acquires no title to goods that are stolen and therefore cannot convey a good title. The true owner never relinquished title to the goods, and even an innocent purchaser who acquired the goods in good faith and for value would be obliged to return the goods to the owner. Title to stolen goods never left the true owner, and possession can always be regained by that owner if the goods can be found, no matter in whose possession they may be at the time.

---

**quick quiz** 29-1

1. If lost property is found on a table in a restaurant, it is considered to be misplaced rather than lost.    true | false

2. Under the kiddie tax, a child's unearned income over $1,500 is taxable at the parent's income tax rate if the child has not reached age 14 years.    true | false

3. An innocent purchaser who buys stolen goods from a thief acquires good title to the stolen goods.    true | false

---

# 29-2 Bailments

A **bailment** is the transfer of possession and control of personal property to another with the intent that the same property will be returned later. Renting a film or a television series on a DVD from a rental shop, borrowing a friend's car, and leaving clothes at the cleaners

are examples of bailments. The person who transfers the property is the **bailor**. The person to whom the property is transferred is the **bailee**.

## Principles of Bailment

In a bailment, neither the bailor nor the bailee intends that title to the property should pass. The bailee has an obligation to return the same property to the bailor, or to someone the bailor designates, at a later time. A bailment does not occur when the person in possession of the property has no control over it. For example, it is not a bailment when someone parks a car in an unattended parking area.

### EXAMPLE 29-4:  Not a Bailment

Sewall parked his car in the same parking lot he used each day. He paid the attendant, locked the car, and took the keys with him. The attendant remained on duty only in the morning and left the lot unattended for the rest of the day. There were several entrances and exits to the lot. When Sewall returned for his car, he discovered that it had been stolen. The court held that this scenario was not a bailment. The attendant had exercised no control over the vehicle whatsoever. Instead, it was simply a rental of a parking space. Sewall lost the case against the parking lot owner because he could not prove that the employees had committed a negligent act.

In contrast, courts have held it to be a bailment when someone parks a car in a garage or lot that has an attendant present at all times to check cars going in and out.

### EXAMPLE 29-5:  Bailment

Eduardo drove his car to the entrance of the public parking garage at Logan International Airport in Boston. He entered the garage through a gate by taking a ticket from a machine, drove into the garage, parked and locked his car, and took the keys with him. The exit from the garage was attended at all times. When Eduardo returned four days later, he discovered that his car had been stolen. The court held that this situation was a bailment because the parking garage had possession and control of the vehicle. Eduardo recovered the value of the car from the parking garage because the garage could not prove that it had used reasonable care to prevent the theft of the car.

When an individual loans goods to another with the intention that the goods may be used and later replaced with an equal amount of different goods, it is not a bailment. Instead, it is known as *mutuum*.

### EXAMPLE 29-6:  *Mutuum*

Susan Chin borrowed a cup of flour from her neighbor. She used the flour in a cake that she made that evening. She returned a cup of flour to her neighbor the next day after shopping at a grocery store. The loan of the flour was a *mutuum* rather than a bailment because the parties did not intend that the identical particles of flour that were borrowed would be returned.

## Bailments for Sole Benefit of Bailor

There are three principal types of bailments: bailments for the sole benefit of the bailor, bailments for the sole benefit of the bailee, and mutual-benefit bailments. In the first two types, called **gratuitous bailments**, property is transferred to another person without either party giving or asking for payment of any kind. Such bailments lack consideration; therefore, they may be rescinded at any time by either party. Parties to such agreements usually consider them only as favors. In reality, however, definite legal responsibilities are placed upon both the bailor and the bailee.

When possession of personal property is transferred to another for purposes that will benefit only the bailor, *bailments for the sole benefit of the bailor* result. In a bailment for the sole benefit of the bailor, the bailee owes a duty to use only *slight care,* because the bailee is receiving no benefit from the arrangement. The bailee is required only to refrain from **gross negligence**, or very great negligence—much more serious than ordinary negligence. In a bailment for the sole benefit of the bailor, the bailor has a duty to reimburse the bailee for any expenses the bailee might have in the care of the property.

However, the bailee has no implied right to use the bailor's property in a bailment for the sole benefit of the bailor. Use without permission is technically a tort of conversion on the part of the bailee; it would make the bailee liable for any damages that might result, even if the bailee had used great care and was not guilty of negligence. (Conversion is the civil wrong that arises when one unlawfully treats another's property as one's own.)

### EXAMPLE 29-7: Unauthorized Use

Lindstrom agreed to care for Holbart's car while Holbart was absent from the city. Although permission to use the car had not been given, Lindstrom drove the car many times to save having to walk. If Lindstrom is involved in an accident as a result of the unauthorized use of Holbart's car, he would have been liable to Holbart for damages. In a case like this, it would *not* even be necessary for the Holbart, the bailor, to prove lack of care by the Lindstrom, the bailee.

## Bailments for Sole Benefit of Bailee

Transactions in which the possession of personal property is transferred for purposes that will benefit only the bailee are gratuitous *bailments for the sole benefit of the bailee.* In a bailment for the sole benefit of the bailee, the bailee is required to use *great care* because possession of the goods is solely for the bailee's benefit. The bailee is responsible for **slight negligence**, which is the failure to use that degree of care that persons of extraordinary prudence and foresight are accustomed to use. In this type of bailment, the bailee has the right to use the property for the purposes for which the bailment was created. Use for other purposes or over a longer period of time than provided for in the agreement will make the bailee responsible for any damages that may result to the property, regardless of the amount of care exercised.

### EXAMPLE 29-8: Unpermitted Use

Robbins used Castro's chainsaw to cut up a small tree that fell during a storm. The cutting of the tree was all that Castro had agreed to allow Robbins to do with the saw. Robbins decided to cut up another piece of timber awaiting the fireplace. Through no fault of Robbins's, the saw's engine caught fire. Even though Robbins was not responsible for the fire, he was obligated to reimburse Castro for the damage because he used the saw for a purpose other than that to which was agreed.

Any *ordinary* and *expected expense* incurred in the use of another's property must be borne by the bailee. For example, gas and oil for the operation of the chainsaw in Example 29-8 should be paid for by Robbins. However, repairs and adjustments not caused by ordinary use or damages not attributed to the bailee's negligence become the responsibility of the bailor. The bailee is not obligated to replace parts that break down because of the gradual use and depreciation of the other's property over an extended period. If the chainsaw had simply worn out through no fault of Robbins, he would not have been responsible.

## EXAMPLE 29-9: Unusual and Unexpected Expense

Swanson, with Oberly's permission, took Oberly's motorcycle on a trial ride. Every precaution was taken to avoid damage. Nevertheless, on the way home, the front tire blew, and Swanson found it necessary to buy a new tire. The old tire had been badly worn in many places. The blowout was not caused by Swanson's negligent use. Oberly, the bailor, would be responsible for any *unusual* and *unexpected* expenses resulting from the tire blowout, including the obligation of reimbursing Swanson for the tire.

## Mutual-Benefit Bailments

When personal property is transferred to a bailee with the intent that both parties will benefit, a *mutual-benefit bailment* results. Ordinary bailments involving business transactions are usually mutual-benefit bailments in which the businessperson is paid for his or her services. Renting an item such as a car or a DVD, leaving a car at a garage to be repaired or a suit to be cleaned at a cleaners, placing one's property in storage, and leaving a diamond ring at a pawn shop (a *pledge*) in exchange for a loan of money are examples of mutual benefit bailments.

## EXAMPLE 29-10: Pledge

Cohen borrowed $7,400 from the American Arlington Bank. As security for the loan, the parties signed a bailment agreement making the bank the bailee of Cohen's valuable painting of King George III of England, allegedly one of three portraits of the king by the 18th century painter George Ramsey. The painting was hung in the office of the bank's vice president. This agreement was a pledge because the bank had possession and complete control over the painting while the loan was outstanding.

A **consignment contract** is a type of mutual benefit bailment in which the **consignor** entrusts goods to the **consignee** for the purpose of selling them. If the goods are sold, the consignee, known as the *factor,* will forward the proceeds, less a fee, to the consignor. If they are not sold, they will be returned. In a mutual-benefit bailment, the bailee owes a duty to use *reasonable care*. Reasonable care means the degree of care that a reasonably prudent person would use under the same circumstances and conditions. The bailee is responsible for **ordinary negligence**, which is the failure to use the care that a reasonable person would use under the same circumstances.

## EXAMPLE 29-11: Reasonable Care Required

Champine stored his boat, motor, and trailer in Field's building for the winter for $1,000. Champine expressed some doubts about the soundness of the building, particularly concerning the structure of the roof. Field assured him that the building was safe. The roof collapsed after a winter snowstorm, damaging Champine's boat. In allowing Champine to recover from Field, the court said that the relationship imposed a duty on the bailee to use reasonable care, which he failed to do.

Many courts today apply the reasonable care standard to all types of bailments, including bailments for the sole benefit of the bailor and bailments for the sole benefit of the bailee. In a mutual-benefit bailment, the bailee must use the property only for the express purposes permitted by the bailor, as provided for in the contract of bailment. The rental of a car, tools, or formal wear, for example, implies the right of reasonable use. Failing to use the property as agreed makes the bailee responsible for any damages that might result, regardless of the degree of care exercised.

## EXAMPLE 29-12: Duty to Use Reasonable Care

Smith rented a tuxedo from the Valet Shop. While wearing it, he crawled under a friend's car to make an adjustment to the brakes. Smith was liable to the Valet Shop for the resulting damage to the suit. The bailed property had not been used for the purposes permitted by the bailor. A reasonably prudent person would know that one does not crawl under a car while wearing a rented tuxedo.

## Burden of Proof

Sometimes items are damaged, lost, or stolen when they are in the possession of a bailee. In the past, the bailor had to prove that the bailee was negligent to recover against the bailee for damages. This proof was very difficult to obtain because the bailor was not in a position to know what caused the loss, because the bailee had possession of the property at the time. Most courts today shift the burden of proof in bailment cases to the one who is in the best position to know what happened—that is, to the bailee. Today, when items in the possession of a bailee are damaged, lost, or stolen, the burden is on the bailee to prove that it was not negligent.

## EXAMPLE 29-13: Failure to Use Reasonable Care

Edwards took her Toyota Rav4 automobile to the Crestmont Toyota-Chevy Auto Mall garage to have a tire changed and the wheels aligned. When she returned later to pick up the car, she learned that it had been stolen from the garage. The court held Crestmont responsible. It had not used reasonable care in preventing the car from being stolen. The court said that a bailee is presumed to be negligent when it fails to redeliver the bailed property, unless it can prove that it was not negligent.

Refer again to Examples 29-4 and 29-5. In the former example, which was not a bailment, the burden was on Sewall to prove that the parking lot owner was negligent. In contrast, Example 29-5 involved a bailment, placing the burden on the parking garage (the bailee), to prove that it was not negligent.

# Innkeepers, Carriers, Warehousers

Certain types of bailees, including innkeepers, common carriers, and warehousers, have extraordinary obligations in addition to the duties imposed on all bailees.

**Innkeepers**   An **innkeeper** is the operator of a hotel, motel, or inn that holds itself out to the public as being ready to entertain travelers, strangers, and transient guests. A **transient** is a guest whose length of stay is variable. To assist travelers in obtaining accommodations, common law imposed the duty upon innkeepers to accept all people who requested a room if one was available. In addition, innkeepers were considered insurers of their guests' property. With some exceptions, these standards are still the law today. The Civil Rights Act of 1964 prohibits discrimination in the selection of guests for reasons of race, creed, color, gender, or ethnic background. People may be turned away when all rooms are occupied or reserved. In addition, innkeepers may refuse to accommodate people whose presence might endanger the health, welfare, or safety of other guests or the safety of the establishment itself.

*Innkeeper's Duty of Care*   Innkeepers must use reasonable care in protecting their guests from harm. They are responsible for injuries to their guests caused by the inn's negligence or the negligence of employees. Innkeepers must respect their guests' rights to privacy. Guests are guaranteed exclusive and undisturbed privacy of rooms assigned by the hotel. Interruption of the guests' privacy through unpermitted entry by hotel employees or other guests creates a liability in tort for invasion of privacy.

*Innkeepers' Eliminated Liability*   Innkeepers are not liable as insurers in four situations:

1. Losses caused by a guest's own negligence.
2. Losses to the guest's property due to acts of God or acts of the public enemy.

Hotels hold great responsibility and must meet obligations when it comes to their guests and travelers.

## THE OPENING CASE *Revisited, Part I*
Footsteps in the Night, Footprints in the Morning:
*Melling v. Los Alamos Inn and Suites*, Round 2

Recall that in the Opening Case at the beginning of the chapter, after settling into his room at the Los Alamos Inn and Suites, Mr. Melling decided to shower while his wife was out shopping. After taking a shower, he opened the bathroom door and discovered a couple bringing suitcases into his room. The desk clerk had assigned the room to another couple by mistake. Following the incident, Mr. Melling was embarrassed, humiliated, and angry with the inn's employees for making such a silly mistake. Melling may seek damages against the Los Alamos Inn and

Suites and its corporate parent Rosier Hospitality Corporation for invasion of privacy.

Innkeepers have a greater duty of care toward their guests' property than is imposed in a usual mutual-benefit bailment. With exceptions (as described subsequently), innkeepers are held by law to be insurers of their guests' property. The insured property includes all personal property brought into the hotel for the convenience and purpose of the guests' stay. In the event of loss, the hotelkeeper may be held liable, regardless of the amount of care exercised in the protection of the guests' property.

## THE OPENING CASE *Revisited, Part II*
### Footsteps in the Night, Footprints in the Morning:
### *Melling v. Los Alamos Inn and Suites*, Round 3

Let's look back again at the Opening Case. Recall that Mrs. Melling purchased a new diamond ring which she placed in the Inn's safe deposit vault. Later, Mrs. Melling withdrew the ring from the vault to wear that evening at the rehearsal dinner. When she went to return the ring later that night, she was told by the desk clerk that the vault was closed until the next morning. At about 5:30 AM, the Mellings awoke to find a ski-masked burglar in the room at the foot of their bed. The burglar escaped with Mrs. Melling's new diamond ring. The Inn will be held liable for the loss of the ring because it did not provide a place for its safekeeping.

3. Losses of property due to accidental fire in which no negligence may be attributed to the hotelkeeper. This exception also includes fires caused by other guests staying at the hotel at the same time. Such persons, even though on other floors, are called fellow guests.

4. Losses arising out of characteristics of the property that cause its own deterioration.

*Innkeeper's Lien and Credit Card Blocking* Innkeepers have a lien on their guests' property. A lien is a claim that one has against the property of another. If a guest cannot pay the bill, the innkeeper is permitted to take possession of the guest's property as security for payment at some later date. Payment of the bill releases the property and terminates the right of lien. Credit card blocking is a common method used by hotels to secure payment for a room. Under this system, guests are asked for a credit card when they register. The hotel then contacts the card issuer electronically with the estimated cost of the bill. If the card issuer approves the transaction, the guest's available line of credit is reduced by the estimated amount. This procedure is known as a block (or authorization). The final actual charge for the room will replace the block within a day or two after the guest checks out. If the guest pays the final charge with cash, check, or a different credit card, however, the block can remain on the original credit card for as long as 15 days.

## THE OPENING CASE *Revisited, Part III*
### Footsteps in the Night, Footprints in the Morning:
### *Melling v. Los Alamos Inn and Suites*, Round 4

Let's take one last look at the Opening Case. Recall that on the morning of his nephew's wedding, Mr. Melling was warned by the Inn's staff to lock his room door. Although he had been so advised, Mr. Melling was so upset with the staff at the Inn that he just stormed off and drove away, leaving the room unlocked. While the couple was at the wedding and the reception, their luggage disappeared from their room at the Inn. The Inn will not be liable for this loss.

In most states, innkeepers are further protected by laws limiting the amount of claim any guest may make for a single loss. The limit is usually $500 or less, depending on the state in which the hotel is located. These laws also give the innkeeper the right to provide a safe or vault for the better protection of the guests' valuables. A guest who does not use the safe provided for valuables will be personally responsible for losses and may not seek recovery from the innkeeper.

## Carriers

**Carriers** The Transportation Security Administration (TSA) within the Department of Homeland Security protects the nation's transportation systems to ensure freedom of movement for people and commerce. Soon after the establishment of the TSA, Congress set up the Department of Homeland Security, which oversees the Coast Guard, Customs Service, Immigration and Naturalization Service, and TSA. Collectively, these organizations are responsible for protecting the nation's transportation system and supervising the entry of people and goods into the United States. **Carriers** are businesses that undertake to transport persons, goods, or both.

*Common Carriers* If a carrier holds itself out to the general public to provide transportation for compensation, it is called a **common carrier**. Like hotels, common carriers cannot turn away people who ask for their services, with exceptions for security reasons. Common carriers of goods are insurers of all goods accepted for shipment. They are liable as insurers regardless of whether they have been negligent. The Carmack Amendment to the Interstate Commerce Act states that a carrier is liable for damages to goods transported by it unless there is proof that the damage occurs because of one of the following exceptions:

- Acts of God (e.g., floods, tornadoes, cyclones, volcanoes, asteroid collisions, earthquakes).
- Acts of the public enemy (wartime enemies, terrorists, and the like).
- Acts of public authorities.
- Acts of the shipper.
- The inherent nature of the goods (e.g., perishable goods, evaporating and fermenting liquids, diseased animals).

### EXAMPLE 29-14: Insurer of Goods

Whitehall Packing Co. engaged Amway Truck Lines to transport 40 barrels of fresh meat from its plant in Wisconsin to Howard Johnson's in New York. The federal government required plastic liners in the barrels, and Howard Johnson's would not allow dry ice in them. The refrigerator unit in Amway's truck operated properly. The truck experienced delays and took longer than its normal running time for the trip. When it arrived in New York, the meat in the barrels had a gassy odor and was not considered acceptable by the U.S. government inspector (no kidding!). An expert meat inspector testified that the barreled meat was smothered because of the use of the plastic liners and the absence of dry ice. Some hanging meat in the same truck was found to be in perfect condition. Although there was no evidence that Amway was negligent, the court held it responsible, saying that it was an insurer of the meat.

*Antidiscrimination Provisions* In addition to being insurers, common carriers of goods must accept *without discrimination* all goods offered to them for shipment. Under the Interstate Commerce Act, discrimination through either the selection of customers or the use of preferential rates is illegal. Exceptions to the rule against discrimination are as follows:

1. A common carrier is not required to accept goods of a type that it is not equipped to carry.
2. The carrier may refuse goods that are inherently dangerous and that would create hazard beyond the control of the carrier's usual safety facilities.
3. The common carrier may refuse goods that it does not represent itself as hauling.

4.  The carrier may refuse goods that are improperly packed. Proper packaging is determined by the type of goods being shipped, the length of the haul, and the usual custom of the trade.

5.  The carrier may refuse goods that are not delivered at the proper place and time.

Common carriers will not be excused from liability for losses due to strikes, mob violence, fire, and similar causes. Labor unions are required to give notice of impending strikes weeks in advance of the strike dates to allow carriers to reject shipments that might be damaged by delays caused by strikes. The carrier is required to ship goods by the proper route, protect them during shipment, and deliver them to the proper person. Carriers may limit the amount of their liability to the value stated on the bill of lading, which is the written contract between a common carrier and a shipper.

## EXAMPLE 29-15: Failure to Read Contract

Bratton hired Allied Van Lines, Inc., to transport her household goods from Ohio to Florida. When the goods were picked up, Bratton signed a bill of lading that contained a provision limiting the carrier's liability to $1.25 per pound (which amounted to $4,500) or the actual value of the goods as written on the bill of lading. There was a place on the bill of lading for Bratton to fill in the actual value of the goods ($10,630). She failed to do so. The shipment was destroyed in transit. Bratton argued that because she did not read the document and was unaware of any provision affecting the carrier's liability, she was not bound by the words in the bill of lading. The court held that a bill of lading containing a limitation of the carrier's liability is binding, even though the shipper had not read it.

*Carrier's Lien on Goods Shipped*  A common carrier has the right to the payment of fees agreed upon for the shipment of the goods and a lien on all goods shipped for the amount of the shipping charges due. Should the shipper or the party receiving the goods fail to pay the charges, the carrier has the right to sell the goods at public sale.

## EXAMPLE 29-16: *Swift and Sure Shipping v. Harrison Printing*

The Harrison Printing Company ordered paper from the Metropolis Paper Company. The paper was shipped from Metropolis, Illinois, under terms that transferred title to the paper when delivered to the carrier, Swift and Sure Shipping. Harrison Printing refused to pay shipping costs when informed of the arrival of the shipment. Notice was finally given to both firms of the carrier's intention to sell the paper to recover shipping charges. At a public sale, the paper brought a high bid of $2,237. The carrier deducted shipping costs and turned over the balance to the Harrison Printing Company.

*Common Carriers of Passengers*  A **passenger** is defined as a person who enters the premises of a carrier with the intention of buying a ticket for a trip. One continues to be a passenger as long as one continues the trip. This relationship is terminated after the person has reached the destination printed on the ticket and left the premises of the carrier. Prior to 9/11, common carriers had an obligation to accept all passengers who sought passage over their lines. This rule has changed. By order of the U.S. Congress, the Federal Aviation Administration (FAA) has established regulations that require the screening of passengers and property before they enter an aircraft to search for dangerous weapons, explosives, and other destructive substances. Passengers who do not consent to the screening must be refused transportation.

Functioning under the Department of Homeland Security, the TSA's mission is to prevent terrorist attacks and protect the U.S. transportation network. Its work encompasses all sectors of transportation, from container ships in harbors to trucks on highways to commuter trains in subways. The approach to security on aircraft includes thorough screening of baggage and passengers by highly trained screeners, fortified cockpit doors in all airliners, thousands of federal air marshals aboard a record number of flights, and armed federal flight deck officers. A list of items that cannot be taken on board an aircraft can be found on the Internet.

*More Antidiscrimination Provisions* Common carriers may not discriminate in the selection of passengers on the basis of race, color, national origin, religion, sex, or ancestry. **Racial profiling**, the act of targeting a person for criminal investigation primarily because of racial or ethnic characteristics, may not be a motivating factor in a carrier's decision to refuse transportation. However, carriers may refuse passengers (1) when all available space is occupied or reserved; (2) if they are disorderly, intoxicated, insane, or infected with a contagious disease; or (3) since 9/11, when the carrier decides a passenger "is or might be inimical to safety." Moreover, a passenger who has boarded a plane that has not taken off must leave the plane if told to do so by an authorized airline representative. This is because a carrier must exercise reasonable care in the protection of passengers. Injuries that are reasonably foreseeable or preventable and that result from the carrier's negligence give the passenger a right to sue for damages. However, if injuries are not reasonably foreseeable or preventable, the carrier is not responsible.

## EXAMPLE 29-17: Carrier's Duty to Protect Passengers

Three men who were intoxicated boarded a commuter train around midnight. They were talking loudly and making a lot of noise. A conductor saw them and told them not to bother passengers. At the next stop, while the conductor let passengers on and off the train, the men went to another car. There, they assaulted, hit, and kicked a passenger. As soon as the conductor reboarded the train, he sought out the three men, discovered what they had done, and had them arrested. In a suit brought by the injured passenger against the carrier, the court held in favor of the carrier. The court said that the incident occurred so quickly and unexpectedly that the conductor, acting with the highest degree of care under the circumstances, could not have averted it.

*Bumped Airline Passengers* When an airline flight is overbooked, the airline must first find volunteers willing to give up their seats for ones on the next available flight. If there are not enough volunteers, other passengers may be denied a seat in accordance with the airline's priority rules. Airlines are required to establish and publish priority rules for determining which passengers holding confirmed reservation space will be denied boarding on an oversold flight.

Passengers who are denied boarding involuntarily, that is, bumped, may be entitled to compensation. If the airline can arrange alternate transportation that is scheduled to arrive at the passenger's destination within one hour of the original arrival time, there is no compensation. However, if the alternate flight gets to the destination between one and two hours late, the passenger is entitled to a cash payment. Passengers may refuse all compensation and bring private legal action. Federal regulations state: "The passenger may decline the payment and seek to recover damages in a court of law or in some other manner." The

U.S. Supreme Court has confirmed that passengers who are bumped from a scheduled flight may sue the carrier for damages.

*Passengers' Baggage*  Since 9/11, dangerous weapons, explosives, destructive items, and items that may be deemed to present a potential threat cannot be carried on board an aircraft. Many items that cannot be hand-carried may, however, be carried in the luggage compartment of planes. The law has no requirement for returning banned items that are left at airport security checkpoints. In addition, those who attempt to bring banned items through airport checkpoints are subject to civil penalties and criminal penalties. Passengers must declare any hazardous materials that they are carrying. Violators of federal hazardous materials regulations may be subject to a civil and criminal penalties. In conjunction with the carrying of passengers, a carrier is obliged to accept a reasonable amount of baggage. Excess baggage may be shipped by a passenger or through payment of additional fees. Baggage limits vary with different airlines. Personal luggage carried aboard an airline and kept at one's seat does not generally fall within the baggage weight limits permitted each passenger. When a baggage car or baggage compartment is available for checking luggage, the carrier is considered an insurer of the luggage checked by the passengers and left in these places. Property kept by passengers at their seats or in overhead compartments places upon the carrier the obligation of exercising ordinary care for its safety. Federal rules place limits on the liability of airlines for lost luggage.

Warehousers  When goods are stored in a warehouse, the relationship of bailor and bailee is created between the owner of the goods and the warehouser. The UCC defines a **warehouser** as a person engaged in the business of storing goods for hire. A **warehouse** is a building or structure in which any goods, but particularly wares or merchandise, are stored. A *warehouse receipt* is a receipt issued by a person engaged in the business of storing goods for hire. Although both common carriers and warehousers are mutual-benefit bailees, they perform different functions. Common carriers are engaged in moving goods. Warehousers keep goods in storage. At times, however, one or the other will perform both functions.

Warehousers may be classified as public or private. A *public warehouser* is one that owns a warehouse in which any member of the public who is willing to pay the regular charge may store goods. Grain elevators in the Midwest, used to store farmers' grain, are sometimes established as public warehouses. A warehouser whose warehouse is not for general public use is a *private warehouser*. Most warehousers fall into this latter category. Sometimes, businesspeople will borrow money using goods that they have stored in a warehouse as security for the loan. The one who lends the money is given the warehouse receipt. If the debt is not paid, the holder of the receipt may obtain possession of the goods in storage. This practice is called *field warehousing*. A warehouser must use the amount of care that a reasonably careful person would use under similar circumstances. Failure to use such care is negligence and makes the warehouse liable for losses or damages to the goods.

## EXAMPLE 29-18:  Reasonable Care Required

Bekins Warehouse stored Keefe's household goods in its warehouse beneath some sprinkler system pipes. It did not inspect the area before placing the goods there. One of the pipes was unconnected, and water from the pipes leaked onto Keefe's goods, damaging them. Bekins's failure to inspect the area of storage was a negligent act that made Bekins responsible for the loss. The parties may limit the amount of liability of the warehouser by including terms to that effect in the storage agreement or warehouse receipt.

## EXAMPLE 29-19: Contract Limitation

The warehouse receipt given by Bekins to Keefe in Example 29-18 limited Bekins's liability to 50 cents per pound per article. The limitation was enforceable even though it was not specifically called to Keefe's attention when the warehouse receipt was signed.

If goods are not removed from a warehouse at the end of a storage period, the warehouser may sell them. Before doing so, however, the warehouser must notify the owner that they are going to be sold and give that person the right to redeem them. If no time for storage is fixed in the agreement, the warehouser must give at least 30 days' notice to the owner before selling the goods. A warehouser has a lien on the goods that are in the warehouser's possession. A **warehouser's lien** is the right to retain possession of the goods until the satisfaction of the charges imposed on them. The lien is for the amount of money owed for storage charges, transportation charges, insurance, and expenses necessary for the preservation of the goods. The lien is a possessory one. It is lost when the warehouser voluntarily delivers the goods or unjustifiably refuses to deliver them. If the owner of the goods owes the warehouse money for the storage of other goods, the warehouser has a lien for the other debt only if it is so stated in the warehouse receipt.

If the person who stored the goods is a merchant in the course of business, the warehousers's lien may be enforced by a public or private sale at any time or place and on any terms that are commercially reasonable. Notice must be given to all persons known to claim an interest in the goods. The notice must include a statement of the amount due, the nature of the proposed sale, and the time and place of any public sale. If the person who stored the goods is not a merchant, more complicated rules must be followed to enforce the warehouser's lien. In addition to giving notice to all persons known to claim an interest in the goods, the nonmerchant must advertise the pending sale in a local newspaper. Notices and advertisements must contain specific information set forth in the UCC.

### quick quiz 29-2

1. A bailment is the transfer of possession and control of personal property to another with the intent that the same property will be returned later.    true | false

2. An innkeeper is the operator of a hotel, motel, or inn that holds itself out to the public as being ready to entertain travelers, strangers, and transient guests.    true | false

3. If a carrier holds itself out to the general public to provide transportation for compensation, it is called a common carrier.    true | false

## Summary

29.1   Personal property is everything that can be owned except real estate. Anyone who finds lost property must make a reasonable effort to find the owner. Misplaced property must be turned over to the manager

of the place where it is found. Abandoned property is property that has been intentionally discarded by the owner and may be kept by a finder. The Abandoned Shipwreck Act gives states the right to shipwrecks beneath their waters. For a gift to be completed, the donor must intend to make a gift, it must be delivered to the donee, and the donee must accept the gift. A thief acquires no title to goods that are stolen and therefore cannot convey a good title to others.

29.2    Bailment occurs whenever someone transfers possession and control of personal property to another with the intent that the same property will be returned later. The principal types of bailments are: bailments for the sole benefit of the bailor, bailments for the sole benefit of the bailee, and mutual-benefit bailments. Under modern law, bailees owe a duty to use reasonable care with the goods in their possession. When goods are lost or damaged while in the possession of a bailee, the burden is on the bailee to prove that no negligence was involved; if this proof cannot be made, the bailee will be held responsible for the loss, Innkeepers are required to accept all guests unless there are no vacancies. They must respect their guests' right of privacy. With some exceptions, innkeepers are insurers of their guests' property. The Transportation Security Administration (TSA), under the Department of Homeland Security, is responsible for protecting the United States' transportation system. Common carriers of goods are liable as insurers of the goods they ship regardless of whether they have been negligent. Public warehousers must accept goods for storage by any member of the public willing to pay for the service. Private warehouses are not for general public use.

## Key Terms

abandoned property, 636

bailee, 639

bailment, 638

bailor, 639

carrier, 645

chattels, 635

chose in action, 635

common carrier, 645

community property, 635

consignee, 641

consignment contract, 641

consignor, 641

cotenancy, 635

donee, 637

donor, 637

escheat, 636

gift *in causa mortis,* 638

gift *inter vivos,* 637

gratuitous bailment, 640

gross negligence, 640

innkeeper, 643

joint tenants, 635

joint tenants with the right of survivorship, 635

*mutuum,* 639

ordinary negligence, 641

passenger, 646

personal property, 635

racial profiling, 647

salvage, 637

salvor, 636

severalty, 635

slight negligence, 640

tenants in common, 635

transient, 643

warehouse, 648

warehouser, 648

warehouser's lien, 649

## Questions for Review and Discussion

1. What are some examples of tangible and intangible personal property?
2. What are the methods of owning property with others?
3. What are the differences among lost property, misplaced property, and abandoned property?
4. What are the requirements of a completed gift?
5. How does the law apply to stolen property?
6. When does a bailment occur?
7. What are the principal types of bailments?
8. What is the burden of proof as it relates to bailments?
9. What is an innkeeper's duty in relation to accepting guests?
10. What are innkeepers' duties of care to their guests and their guests' property?

# Cases for Analysis

1. Susan Lacroix's Yerf-Dog go-kart was stolen from her driveway one evening when she went inside to have dinner. The thief placed an advertisement in the newspaper and sold it to Ronald Casey for half what it was worth. Later, Lacroix recognized the kart in Casey's yard and identified it as hers through its serial number. In a suit brought by Lacroix for the return of the go-kart, Casey argued that he now had title to the kart because he paid for it without knowledge that it had been stolen. Is Casey's argument sound? Explain.

2. David Bess rented three outdoor booth spaces at the Traders World flea market to display his inventory of Beanie Babies for sale. He stored his inventory in a locked trailer, which he left parked at the flea market overnight. When he returned the next morning, he discovered that the padlock on his trailer had been changed. Upon forcing the trailer open, he found that his entire inventory of Beanie Babies, which he estimated had a value of $60,000 to $75,000, was missing. In a suit against Traders World, Bess argued that the transaction was a bailment. Do you agree with Bess? Why or why not? *Bess v. Traders World, Inc.,* CA2001-06-063 (OH).

3. Schaeffer boarded a 30-passenger, single-aisle turboprop airplane carrying two pieces of baggage. When asked by a flight attendant to surrender one carry-on for proper storage, he refused and became verbally abusive. The captain of the plane decided not to depart with the disruptive passenger on board because he was concerned about the safety of the flight. When asked to leave the plane, Schaeffer refused, and the Port Authority police were called to remove him. Must a passenger who has boarded a plane that has not taken off leave the plane when told to do so by an authorized representative? Explain. *Schaeffer v. Cavallero,* 54 F. Supp.2d 350 (S.D.N.Y.).

4. Pollard found a valuable first edition that someone had dropped on the street. She took the book home, placing it with others in a collection of first editions. The owner's name could not be found in the lost book, and Pollard made no effort to locate the owner. Did she thus have title to the book? Explain. See also *Doe v. Oceola,* 270 N.W.2d 254 (MI).

5. Vincent Hartwell admired a valuable book collection on his uncle's bookshelf. To Hartwell's surprise, his uncle said that he planned to give the books to Hartwell as a gift and that he could have them at that moment. Hartwell replied that he was living in a dormitory and had no place to keep the collection. His uncle said, "Consider the books yours. I'll keep them here, and when you're ready for them, come and get them." Hartwell thanked his uncle and left for school. His uncle died a week later. Hartwell's cousin, Kathleen Lane, inherited the uncle's entire estate. She claimed that the valuable book collection belonged to her. Who was the legal owner, Hartwell or Lane? Explain.

6. Torczyner, a diamond salesman, registered as a guest at the Hilton Hotel in Denver, Colorado. He placed his diamonds in the hotel safe when he did not need them for business purposes. On the last day of his visit, he removed the gems from the safe, left the hotel to make some business calls, and returned for the purpose of packing and checking out. Instead of placing the diamonds in the hotel safe, Torczyner carried them to his room. There, he was assaulted by two men who beat him and robbed him of the diamonds. Is the hotel responsible for the loss of the diamonds? Explain. *Pacific Diamond Co. v. Superior Ct.,* 85 Cal. App. 3rd 871 (CA).

7. In his will, Gavegnano left all his tangible personal property to his daughter, Caroline. At the time of his death, he owned 19 thoroughbred horses. In addition, a cashier's check made payable to him for $33,000 was found among his belongings. The lower court judge held that the horses and the check were tangible personal property and should be given to Caroline under the terms of the will. Caroline's brothers appealed the decision, claiming that neither the horses nor the check were tangible personal property. Were Caroline's brothers correct? Explain. *Pagiarulo v. National Shawmut Bank,* 233 N.E.2d 213 (MA).

8. Joe Scott left his automobile with Purser Truck Sales, Inc., to be repaired. Purser Truck Sales turned the automobile over to Lonz Radford to

make the repairs. The car was demolished while in the possession of Radford. In a suit brought by Scott against Purser, the trial court held in favor of Purser, because Scott presented no evidence indicating that Purser was negligent. Was the trial court correct? Why or why not? *Scott v. Purser Truck Sales, Inc.*, 402 S.E.2d 354 (GA).

## quick quiz Answers

| 29-1 | 29-2 |
|------|------|
| 1. T | 1. T |
| 2. T | 2. T |
| 3. F | 3. T |

## THE OPENING CASE  Eminent Domain and All the King's Men: *Kelo v. City of New London*

Generally speaking, when the United States Supreme Court hears a case it involves some sort of major league controversy, like the establishment of a defendant's rights in court, or a review of the constitutionality of an abortion statute, or an analysis of a college's limitation on the free speech of its faculty and students. Sometimes, however, even the Supreme Court must deal with matters that seem mundane and ordinary. A case on point is the dispute in *Kelo v. City of New London*. This controversy started when the city fathers of New London, Connecticut, agreed to help the Pfizer Corporation which had decided to build a research and manufacturing center in the city. To do this, the city activated the New London Development Corporation (NLDC) which began to buy up the land in that area of town. Many residents in the targeted area did not want to sell or leave their homes. Therefore, many of them simply refused to sell. Then unexpectedly, some bright boy or gal in the city's legal department recommended invoking the city's power to confiscate land for public use under eminent domain as found in the Fifth Amendment of the Constitution. Then somebody else in the city's legal department discovered that the power to exercise eminent domain in economic

development situations was granted to the City by a Connecticut statute. A homeowner named Susette Kelo, along with several other owners, sued to end the unconstitutional seizure of their property. The homeowners argued that the taking of their land for private development purposes did not fall under the heading of "public use" as visualized by the Founding Fathers when they wrote the Fifth Amendment. The property owners also argued in the alternative that, even if the annexation of their property did qualify as public use, the city had to prove with "reasonable certainty" that the appropriation of their land really would result in the public benefits predicted by the development corporation. The suit was filed in the state court of Connecticut and eventually reached the Supreme Court of Connecticut which supported the city. In the end, the case was heard by the United States Supreme Court which granted a *writ of certiorari*. After considering the arguments from both sides, the Court, in a 5–4 ruling, held that the city's seizure of the land really was public use. The Court also disagreed with the homeowner's contention that the city could be forced to show with reasonable certainty that the benefits would be actualized by the city and by the local neighborhood.

[See *Kelo v. City of New London,* 125 S.Ct. 2655 (U.S. Supreme Court).]

**Opening Case Questions**

1. What types of rights are associated with the ownership of real property? Explain.

2. What is eminent domain and how does it apply in this case? Explain.

3. What is unusual about the Supreme Court's interpretation of eminent domain in this case? Explain.

4. Did the Supreme Court overstep its authority in this case when it used eminent domain to support a private real estate development corporation? Explain.

5. How might the city use its zoning powers in this case? Explain.

## LO Learning Objectives

1. Explain what constitutes real property.
2. Differentiate between freehold and leasehold estates.
3. Describe the different types of co-ownership of real property.
4. Identify the methods of acquiring title to real property.
5. Explain eminent domain.
6. List the five elements necessary to create a landlord–tenant relationship.
7. Identify the essential requirements of a lease.
8. Clarify rent control and security deposits.
9. Make clear the duties of landlords and tenants.
10. Discuss tort liability as it applies to landlords and tenants.

# 30-1 The Rights Related to Real Property

Real property and real estate are not really the same thing, although they are often treated as if they were. When real estate agents, bankers, and attorneys use the term **real estate**, they are generally referring to the actual land itself as well as everything permanently attached to it. This would include buildings, fences, and trees on the surface; earth, rocks, and minerals under the surface; and the airspace above the surface. In contrast, the term **real property** refers to the ownership rights that go along with the real estate. The problem is that very few people know about this difference, and those who do know really do not care to make the distinction. For that reason, the two terms will be used alternately in the rest of the chapter, just as if they mean the same thing. The rights that are associated with real property generally include those rights related to trees and other vegetation, air rights, subterranean rights, water rights, and the rights associated with fixture and easements

## Trees and Vegetation

Trees, flowers, shrubs, vineyards, and field crops that grow each year without replanting (perennials) are considered real property. These plants have been planted and cultivated with the intention that they remain part of the real estate. Once planted and growing, such improvements to the land are called *fructus naturales* (fruit of nature). In contrast, crops or garden plantings that produce flowers, vegetables, or other harvest only for the year in which they are planted (annuals) are called *fructus industrials.* A tree belongs to the person on whose land the trunk is located. People who own adjoining land have the right to cut off trespassing tree branches in their airspace and trespassing roots at the boundary line of their property. Whenever property owners dig down at the very edge of their own property, however, they must provide support to their neighbor's land so that it does not cave in.

## Air Rights, Subterranean Rights, and Water Rights

In medieval England, landowners owned the airspace above their property to "as high as the heavens." This law changed with the increased use of the aircraft. Modern courts have held that landowners own the airspace above their land to as high as they can effectively possess or reasonably control. This height usually extends as high as the highest tree or structure on their property. It is a trespass for anyone to run wires through someone else's airspace or to use another's airspace in any way without permission. Electric and telephone companies must obtain easements for the right to run wires through the airspace of property owners.

Congress has enacted legislation that gives the public the right of freedom of transit through the navigable airspace of the United States. The **navigable airspace**, subject to FAA regulations, is the space above 1,000 feet over populated areas and above 500 feet over water and unpopulated areas. In airport cases involving planes landing and taking off, the courts try to strike a balance between the landowners' rights to the exclusive possession of their airspace, free from noise and exhaust fumes, and the public need for air travel.

Air rights are valuable and often sold to interested buyers, particularly in land-depleted metropolitan areas. For example, in New York City, developers bought air rights over the access to the George Washington Bridge and constructed multistory buildings. Two privately owned buildings have been constructed in the airspace over the Massachusetts Turnpike near Boston. Use of air rights becomes important when land is no longer available for new buildings. The private use of airspace also becomes a tax source for otherwise untaxable land owned by a city or state government.

Unless excluded in the deed, the owner of land has exclusive title to material below the surface of the land. The right extends to the point determined to be the exact center of the earth. These subterranean rights are often sold to corporations exploring for coal, oil, or other mineral deposits. Taking out oil or minerals from below the surface would constitute trespass if such rights were not obtained from their owners. A landowner must not dig a cellar or other excavation so close to the boundary of a neighbor as to cause the neighbor's land to cave in or the neighbor's building to be damaged. A person excavating who fails to shore up the adjoining land is liable to the neighbor for damages.

People who own land along the bank of a river or stream are called **riparian owners**. They have certain rights and duties with respect to the water that flows over, under, and beside their land. Owners of land through which a stream flows own the soil beneath the water. If a nonnavigable stream is a boundary line between two parcels of land, the owner on each side owns to the center of the stream. If the stream is navigable, however, each owner owns only to the bank of the stream, and the bed is owned by the state. A navigable stream in some states is defined as one that ebbs and flows with the tide. In other states, it is defined as a stream that is capable of being navigated by commercial vessels. Although property owners may own the land under a stream, they do not own the water itself. Their right to the use of the water depends on the doctrine followed in their state.

## Fixtures and Easements

Personal property attached to real property is known as a **fixture** and becomes part of the real property. Built-in stoves and dishwashers, kitchen cabinets, and ceiling light fixtures are examples of fixtures. If there is a question as to whether an item is a fixture, the courts ask the following questions: Has there been a temporary or permanent installation of the personal property? Can it be removed without damaging the real property? Has it been adapted to the intended use of the real property? Also, the court would ask what the intent of the party was at the time the personal property was attached to the real property. Trade fixtures are those items of personal property brought upon the premises by the tenant that are necessary to carry on the trade or business to which the premises will be devoted. Contrary to the general rule, trade fixtures remain the personal property of the tenant or occupier of the property and are removable at the expiration of the term of occupancy. Trade fixtures are not treated as part of the real property.

An easement (also called a right of way) is the right to use another's land for a particular purpose. Easements are used to give people the right to pass over another's land, to run wires through another's airspace, to drain water onto another's property, or to run pipes underneath someone else's ground. The one who enjoys the easement and to whom it attaches is called the dominant tenement. In contrast, the one on whom the easement is imposed is called the servient tenement.

## EXAMPLE 30-1: Parties to an Easement

Hatfield owned a long, narrow strip of land that ran between a lake and a highway. She decided to sell the front half of the lot that bordered the highway to McCoy and keep the back half that bordered the lake for her own use. To give McCoy the ability to reach the lake, an easement was placed in the deed granting McCoy the right to "pass and repass" over Hatfield's property to reach the lake. In this easement, McCoy is the dominant tenement and Hatfield is the servient tenement. Also, to give Hatfield the ability to reach the highway, an easement was placed in the deed, reserving to Hatfield the right to "pass and repass" over McCoy's property to reach the highway. In this easement, Hatfield is the dominant tenement and McCoy is the servient tenement.

An easement may be created in three ways: by grant, by reservation, and by prescription. To create an easement by grant, the owner of the land signs a deed, giving the easement to the dominant tenement, and keeps the remainder of the land. To create an easement by reservation, the owner of the land grants to another person the entire parcel of land except for the easement that he or she keeps. An easement by prescription is an easement that is obtained by passing over another's property without permission, openly and continuously for a period of time set by state statute (20 years in many states). People claiming easements by prescription must show that they used (but did not possess) part of another's property openly, notoriously, and in a hostile manner for the prescribed period. This proof is similar to that used in adverse possession, discussed later in this chapter. A legal easement may exist even if it isn't written. For example, the law allows people access to their homes so, if the only access is by crossing through another land owner's property, the court may grant permission through an "easement by necessity." Once an easement is created, it runs with the land. This condition means that future owners will have the right to use the easement unless one of them gives it up by a deed or by not using it for a long period of time.

## EXAMPLE 30-2: Easement Runs with Land

Jesse Horney conveyed the northern portion of his real estate to Wayne County Lumber Company by warranty deed in 1907. That deed included the following provision: "Said Jesse Horney hereby conveys to Wayne County Lumber Company the right of ingress and egress for teams and wagons in conducting their business through an open driveway along the South line to South Main Street." The property was conveyed to a different lumber company in 1930 and to a third lumber company in 1943. Later, in a dispute over the easement, the court held that the easement ran with the land and belonged to the third lumber company. In this case, Horney's property was the servient tenement. The lumber company's property was the dominant tenement. A profit *à prendre* is a special type of easement with the added privilege of removing something of value from the servient property. For example, the right to enter another's property and remove sand, gravel, soil, or the like is called a profit *à prendre*. This right may be created by deed, will, or adverse use.

## EXAMPLE 30-3: Profit *à Prendre*

The Bates Company and Sawyer executed an agreement that provided Bates could enter upon Sawyer's land and remove sand, gravel, and stone. Bates agreed to pay Sawyer a set rate per cubic yard or short ton for all the sand removed. The agreement stated, "Sawyer will not grant to anyone else the privilege of removing sand and stone from said parcel during the period hereof . . . but Sawyer reserves to herself, her successors and assigns, the right during said period . . . to go on and use said tract of land for any purpose they may desire, but without unreasonable interference with the rights of said Bates." The court held that Bates possessed a profit *à prendre* under the agreement.

### quick quiz 30-1

1. Real property and real estate mean exactly the same thing.    true | false

2. In medieval England, landowners owned the airspace above their property to "as high as the heavens."    true | false

3. When personal property is attached to real property, it is known as a fixture and becomes part of the real property.    true | false

# 30-2 Estates in and Co-Ownership of Real Property

Most of the basic ownership rules regarding real property in the United States actually had their origin a millennium ago in England. After William the Conqueror won the English throne in the Battle of Hastings in 1066, he realized that he had an enormous amount of land to preserve and protect. Although he would have preferred to maintain and defend all the land on his own, he knew that he could not, and so he established a system by which he could retain the ownership of all the land in England while parceling out its maintenance and defense to the nobility. Those nobles who received large tracts of land from the king were said to hold estates, a term derived from the Latin word *status*. Although the rules that apply today emerged centuries ago on the other side of the Atlantic, they still affect us because of our English legal heritage. This heritage influences the rules that govern modern estates as well as those that relate to the co-ownership of land.

## The Law of Estates

Most of the estates that were passed on to the nobility in medieval England could last infinitely because the nobles who held them were empowered to pass them on to their heirs. These estates were called **freehold estates**. Anyone with a freehold estate may transfer that interest to another by sale, gift, will, or by dying without a will. Freehold estates are either estates in fee simple or life estates.

**Estates in Fee Simple** Anyone owning real property outright—that is, forever—is said to have an **estate in fee simple**. The estate descends, on the death of the owner, to the owner's heirs. The owner of an estate in fee simple has absolute ownership in the real estate, with the right to use or dispose of it as desired, so long as the use of it does not interfere with others' rights.

### EXAMPLE 30-4: Fee Simple Estate

When the Landers bought the land on which to build their house, they received an estate in fee simple from the former owners. They thus received full rights to the property. They may sell it, give it away, or use it as they wish. The only restrictions are those contained in the deed or required of them by law.

**Life Estates** A person who owns real property for life or for the life of another owns an interest in real property called a **life estate**. Such an estate may be created by deed, by will, or by law. When the terms of a deed or will state that the property is to pass at the end of a life estate to someone other than the grantor or the grantor's heirs, the future interest is a **remainder estate**.

### EXAMPLE 30-5: Life Estate

Rosengard deeded her farm to Kinkaid for life. The deed stated that upon Kinkaid's death, the property was to pass to Honig in fee simple. Kinkaid owns a life estate in the farm. Honig owns a remainder estate until Kinkaid's death, then an estate in fee simple. The owner of a life estate may convey that interest to another. Thus, if Kinkaid conveys his interest to Jenkins, Jenkins will own a life estate for the duration of Kinkaid's life, after which the property will belong to Honig. When the terms of a deed or a will state that property is to return to the grantor or the grantor's heirs at the expiration of a life estate, the future interest is a **reversion estate**.

# The Law of Co-Ownership

Often only one person owns a tract of real estate. This type of ownership is referred to as ownership in **severalty**. It is also very common, however, for two or more people to own the same tract of land. This type of ownership is referred to as **concurrent ownership**, although the more common term is **co-ownership**. Real property may be owned individually or by two or more persons known as **cotenants**. Cotenant relationships include: tenancy in common, joint tenancy, community property, and tenancy by the entirety.

**Tenancy in Common** When two or more persons own real property as **tenants in common**, each person owns an undivided share of the whole property. A cotenant's share of the property transfers to that cotenant's heirs upon his or her death rather than to the surviving cotenants. Each cotenant is entitled to possession of the entire premises. This rule is known as unity of possession. Tenants in common have the right to sell or deed away as a gift their share in the property without the permission of the other cotenants. When this action occurs, any new owner becomes a tenant in common with the remaining cotenants. One cotenant's interest is not necessarily the same as another cotenant's interest.

## EXAMPLE 30-6: Tenants in Common

Ingalls and Carpenter owned a parcel of real property as tenants in common. When Ingalls died, his three children inherited his estate equally. The children became tenants in common (each owning a one-sixth interest) with Carpenter, who owned a one-half interest in the property.

Tenants in common may separate their interests in the property by petitioning the court for a partition of the property. If the court allows the petition, either it will divide the property into separate parcels so that each cotenant will own a particular part outright, or it will order the property sold and divide the proceeds of the sale among the cotenants. Creditors may reach the interest of a tenant in common by bringing a lawsuit against that particular cotenant and, if successful, having that cotenant's interest sold to pay the debt. By statute in most states, co-ownership of property by two or more persons is considered tenancy in common unless the relationship is expressly indicated as a joint tenancy or a tenancy by the entirety.

**Joint Tenancy** When two or more persons own real property as **joint tenants**, the estate created is a single estate with multiple ownership. Each tenant owns the entire estate, subject to the equal rights of the other joint tenants. Four unities must be present to create a joint tenancy: time, title, interest, and possession:

1. The unity of time means that all owners must take title at the same time.
2. The unity of title means that all owners must derive title from the same source.
3. The unity of interest means that all owners must have equal interests in the property.
4. The unity of possession means that all owners must have the equal right to possess the property.

Upon the death of one joint tenant, the entire ownership remains with the other joint tenants and does not pass to the heirs or devisees of the deceased cotenant. For this reason, joint tenants are often identified as joint tenants with the right of survivorship.

## EXAMPLE 30-7: Joint Tenants

If Ingalls and Carpenter, in Example 30-6, had owned the parcel of real property as joint tenants instead of as tenants in common, Carpenter would have owned the entire property outright when Ingalls died. Ingalls's three children would not have been entitled to any interest in the real property whatsoever.

A joint tenant may deed away his or her interest to a new owner without permission of the other joint tenants. The new owner, in such a case, becomes a tenant in common with the remaining joint tenants. As in the case of a tenant in common, a joint tenant may petition the court for a partition of the estate, which would end the joint tenancy. Creditors may levy upon the interests of a joint tenant on execution and take over that particular joint tenant's interest as a tenant in common with the remaining joint tenants. To levy on execution means to collect a sum of money by putting into effect the judgment of a court.

**Community Property** Property (except a gift or inheritance) that is acquired by the personal efforts of either spouse during marriage is called **community property**. By law community property belongs to both spouses equally. The law originated in Spain, was embraced by Mexico, and is presently followed in Puerto Rico, in some Southern states, such as Texas and Louisiana, and in many Western states, such as California and Nevada. Although state laws differ, they all operate on the theory that both spouses contribute equally to the marriage—that all property acquired during the marriage is the result of the combined efforts of both of them. Although one spouse may earn all the money to acquire the property, all the property acquired is considered community property.

**Tenancy by the Entirety** A **tenancy by the entirety** may be held only by a husband and wife and is based upon the common law doctrine known as unity of person. Under this very old doctrine, a husband and wife were regarded, under the law, as one. In theory, each spouse owned the entire estate, and neither could destroy it by any separate act. The husband, however, had the entire control over the estate, including the exclusive right to possession and the right to all rents and profits. Many states have done away with the statute of tenancy by the entirety. Other states have enacted statutes giving equal rights to husbands and wives who own property as tenants by the entirety. Still other states require both spouses to consent to a valid mortgage on property owned as tenants by the entirety. See Table 30-1.

### quick quiz 30-2

1. Most of the basic ownership rules regarding real property in the United States actually had their origin a millennium ago in France.   true | false

2. A person who owns real property for life or for the life of another owns an interest in real property called a life estate.   true | false

3. When two or more persons own real property as tenants in common, each person owns an undivided share of the whole property.   true | false

**Table 30-1** Cotenant Relationships

| | Tenants in Common | Joint Tenants | Tenants by Entirety | Community Property |
|---|---|---|---|---|
| 1. Who can be cotenants | Any number of people | Any number of people | Only husband and wife | Only husband and wife |
| 2. At death, deceased's share goes | To deceased's heirs* | To surviving cotenants | To surviving spouse | To deceased's heirs* |
| 3. Title | Separate title for each cotenant | One title to the entire property | Husband has title (under the doctrine of unity)† | Title is in the community |
| 4. Division of ownership interests | Cotenants can have equal or unequal interests | All interests must be equal | Interests equal; husband has the right to control and manage† | Both interests equal |
| 5. Right to possession of entire premises | Equal with all cotenants | Equal with all cotenants | Husband only† | Equal with both spouses |
| 6. Right to convey ownership interest | May convey to another without permission of cotenant | May convey to another but will end joint tenancy relationship | Husband may convey to anyone; wife's interest is protected† | May convey personal property without spouse's permission; must have written permission to convey real property |
| 7. Right to partition the property | Yes | Yes | No | No |
| 8. Owner's separate interest reachable by creditors | Yes | Yes | Husband's only† | No. Whole community only, depending on state law |

*Either by will or the law of intestate succession if the deceased had no will.

†At common law. States have either abolished this type of tenancy or amended it to give equal rights to men and women.

# 30-3 Acquiring Title to and Managing Real Property

Most of the time property owners, unless they are causing a nuisance of a danger to others, get to decide to use, manage, and transfer the title to their own property without undue interference from the government, except, of course, for the payment of taxes and fees. Sometimes, however, the government will decide how property will be used in certain parts of a city or town, and at other more extreme times, the government may actually confiscate property for the public good. Such governmental management is exercised through zoning ordinances and eminent domain. See Figure 30-1.

## Title to Real Property

Title to real property refers to the ownership of that property. Saying that someone has title to a piece of property is really just a quick way of saying that a person has the evidence needed to demonstrate that he or she is entitled to possess, use, and convey that property to another. Title to real property may be acquired by sale or gift, will or descent, or by neglect.

A house deed is one example of a title to real property.

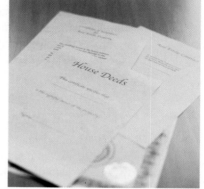

### Title by Sale or Gift
Ownership and title to real property are most frequently transferred from one owner to another by sale or by gift. This action is done by transferring a written instrument called a *deed*. The person transferring title is the **grantor**. The person to whom the title is transferred is the **grantee**. A deed becomes effective when it is delivered to the grantee. A deed to real property may be bestowed as a gift from the owner or through a sale. In the case of a gift, consideration is not given by the grantee for the deed. There are four types of deeds:

1. General warranty deed
2. Special warranty deed

Foreigners spent a record $37.7 billion on U.S. commercial property in 2006, says a reprot by real estate firm Jones Lang LaSalle. All major metro markets except San Francisco and L.A. had gains in foreign investment. Why the Left Coast snub? Asian investors are buying closer to home, and California is too long a plane ride for Europeans, says JLI. – Michael Arndt, *BusinessWeek,* March 12, 2007.

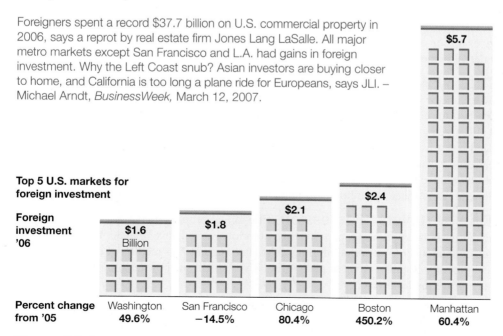

**Top 5 U.S. markets for foreign investment**

| Foreign investment '06 | Washington | San Francisco | Chicago | Boston | Manhattan |
|---|---|---|---|---|---|
| | $1.6 Billion | $1.8 | $2.1 | $2.4 | $5.7 |
| **Percent change from '05** | 49.6% | −14.5% | 80.4% | 450.2% | 60.4% |

**Figure 30-1**  Real property investment by foreigners in the United States.

3. Bargain-and-sale deed

4. Quitclaim deed

*General Warranty Deed*   A **general warranty deed**, sometimes called a *full covenant and warranty deed,* contains express warranties under which the grantor guarantees the property to be free of encumbrances created by the grantor or by others who had title previously. It is the most desirable form of deed from the point of view of the grantee because it warrants (gives assurances) that title is good.

*Special Warranty Deed*   A **special warranty deed** contains express warranties under which the grantor guarantees that no title defect arose during the time that the grantor owned the property, but not otherwise. No warranties are made as to defects that arose *before* the grantor owned the property.

---

## EXAMPLE 30-8: Special Warranty Deed

Grant sold a vacant lot to Tuttle. The lot had been left to Grant through the will of a distant relative. Grant had never had the title searched, but she could guarantee Tuttle that no liens or claims against the property had been created since she inherited the property. Grant would be safe in granting title under a special warranty deed. The buyer would be protected only by making a title search that would disclose claims not covered by the seller's warranty.

---

*Bargain-and-Sale Deed*   A **bargain-and-sale deed** is one that transfers title to property but contains no warranties. The form of the deed is the same as that of a warranty deed except that the warranties are omitted. Because a bargain and sale necessarily involves the idea of a valuable consideration, this type of deed is not valid without consideration. It could not be used to convey a gift of real property.

*Quitclaim Deed*   A **quitclaim deed** (also called a *deed without covenants*) transfers to the buyer only the interest that the seller may have in a property. This type of deed merely releases a party's rights to the property. It contains no warranties. It is used when the seller gives up some right in the property, such as an easement or dower and courtesy, or to cure a defect in the chain of title.

## Title by Will or Descent
When people die owning real property solely in their own name or with others as tenants in common, title passes to their heirs at the moment of death. If they die with a will, title passes to the people named in the will. If they die without a will, title passes to the heirs, as tenants in common, according to the laws of intestacy. A deed is not used when title passes to heirs in this manner. Instead, the records of the probate court establish title to the property. A deed may be used, however, by the personal representative of an estate to transfer title to real property to another. This transfer may be done in many states by authority granted in a will or by a license issued by the court.

## Title by Adverse Possession
Title to real property may be obtained by taking actual possession of the property openly, notoriously, exclusively, under a claim of right, and continuously for a period of time set by state statute. This method of obtaining title to real property is called **adverse possession**. To establish such ownership rights, claimants must prove the following:

- They have had continuous use of the property for 20 years (or a period set by state statute).
- This use has been without interruption by the owner.
- It was without the owner's permission.
- It was with the owner's knowledge.

Proof of these facts in court will give a person superior rights over the one in whose name a deed is recorded. A court of equity has the power to declare the one claiming under adverse possession to be the new owner.

## EXAMPLE 30-9: Adverse Possession

Wilhelm and Kupersmith were next-door neighbors. Not realizing where the true property line was, Wilhelm built a garage and driveway two feet onto Kupersmith's land. He used the garage and driveway continuously, with Kupersmith's knowledge, for the next 22 years. The error was discovered when Kupersmith sold her property to a new owner, who had it surveyed. Wilhelm, through court action, was able to obtain title to the land on which the garage and driveway were located by adverse possession.

## Governmental Management of Real Property

Thomas Jefferson once said that "the care of human life and happiness, and not their destruction, is the first and only legitimate object of good government." Ideally, the governmental management of real property should promote the "care of human life and happiness." Zoning laws, on the surface at least, have as their purpose the regulation, limitation, and planning of real property for the good of the entire society. Eminent domain goes a step further declaring that there are some instances in which the "care of human life and happiness" demands the confiscation of one person's property for the preservation and the promotion of the general good.

**Zoning Laws** Municipal zoning laws regulate the uses that may be made of properties within specified geographical areas or districts. Residential zoning prohibits properties from being used for commercial purposes within a given area. Multifamily zoning permits construction of apartment buildings. Limited-commercial zoning allows the construction of small stores but restricts the building of large shopping malls and commercial centers. Industrial zoning allows the building of factories, and agricultural zoning allows farming in a particular area. Zoning laws help keep property values from declining and protect against the undesirable use of neighboring property.

Newly passed zoning laws do not apply to existing uses of the land. Such uses are called nonconforming uses if they are not allowed under the new zoning law. They may continue in existence but may not be enlarged or changed in kind. By appeal to the local zoning board, variances may be given to individuals or businesses when justified and reasonable. A variance is an exemption or exception that permits a use that differs from those allowed under the existing ordinance. Variances are granted in special circumstances to protect property owners who might otherwise suffer a hardship if zoning laws were applied and enforced arbitrarily. Decisions of a local zoning commission may be appealed to county commissioners, a county court, or the highest court in the state.

**Eminent Domain** All ownership of private property is subject to the government's superior rights if property is needed for a public purpose. Eminent domain, also called condemnation, is the right of federal, state, and local governments, or other public bodies, to take private lands, with compensation to their owners, for a public purpose. The right is exercised for such purposes as new highway construction, public parks, and state hospitals, as well as to reinvigorate depressed areas.

Eminent domain is at times extended to public utilities when it can be shown that denial of a right of way for electric, telephone, gas, or other lines may interrupt construction of installations that provide needed services to an entire community. When private property is taken by eminent domain proceedings, the owner must be paid the fair value of what has

## THE OPENING CASE *Revisited, Part I*
### Eminent Domain and All the King's Men:
*Kelo v. City of New London,* Round 2

Recall that in the Opening Case at the beginning of this chapter, the United Sates Supreme Court had agreed to hear the case of *Kelo v. City of New London*. Recall also that several home owners sued the city to end the unconstitutional seizure of their property. The home-owners argued that the taking of their land for private development purposes did not fall under the heading of public use as visualized by the Founding Fathers when they wrote the Fifth Amendment. After considering the arguments from both sides, the Court in a 5–4 ruling, held that the city's seizure of the land really was public use. The Court ruled that the government could take private property to promote private economic development. The Court said that an increased tax base, higher-paying jobs, and other benefits fulfilled a public

purpose. In its decision, the Court further noted, "nothing in our opinion precludes any State from placing further restrictions on its exercise of the takings power."

Within two years after the unpopular decision in the Kelo Case, more than 80 percent of U.S. states changed their laws on the subject, making it more difficult to take private property by eminent domain. Some states, including Florida, have taken a broad approach, such as forbidding the use of eminent domain for any kind of private development. Others, including Missouri, have made guarded changes, such as not allowing farmland to be classified as "blighted." In 2007, the New Jersey high court held that before invoking eminent domain, a municipality must prove a site is truly "blighted," not simply "not fully productive."

been taken. The owner is not required to accept an amount offered by those assessing the value of the property. In fact, homeowners can also contest the government's decision to take their land, when they have reason to believe that the "taking' is not really for public purposes but is actual for private profit. This is precisely what happened in the *Kelo* Case, the Opening Case at the beginning of this chapter.

### quick quiz 30-3

1. Title to real property may be acquired by sale or gift, will or descent, or by neglect.    true | false

2. Municipal zoning laws that regulate the uses that may be made of properties within specified geographical areas or districts have been declared unconstitutional.    true | false

3. Eminent domain is the right of federal, state, and local governments, or other public bodies, to take private lands, with compensation to their owners, for a public purpose.    true | false

## 30-4 The Landlord–Tenant Relationship

The landlord–tenant relationship is a contractual arrangement in which the owner of real property allows another to have temporary possession and control of the premises in ex-change for consideration. The agreement that gives rise to the landlord–tenant relationship is called a **lease**. The property owner who gives the lease is the **lessor** or **landlord**, and the person to whom the lease is given is the **lessee** or **tenant**. Five elements are necessary for the creation of a landlord–tenant relationship:

1. Consent of the landlord to the occupancy by the tenant
2. Transfer of possession and control of the property to the tenant in an inferior position (in subordination) to the rights of the landlord
3. The right by the landlord to the return of the property, called the right of reversion
4. The creation of an ownership interest in the tenant known as a leasehold estate
5. Either an express or implied contract between the parties that satisfies all the essentials of a valid contract (mutual assent, capacity, consideration, legality)

Although rent is usually paid by the tenant to the landlord for the arrangement, it is not essential to the creation of the landlord–tenant relationship.

## Leasing versus Other Relationships

Sometimes people confuse leasing with other relationships that are similar but which convey different rights and, therefore, limit certain activities that would be permissible under a leasing arrangement. The two most common relationships that may be compared with the landlord–tenant relationship are licensing and lodging.

**Leasing Compared with Licensing**  A lease differs from a license in that a lease gives an interest in real property and transfers possession, whereas a **license** gives no property right or ownership interest in the property but merely allows the licensee to do certain acts that would otherwise be a trespass.

### EXAMPLE 30-10:  License Rather than Lease

The city of Topeka was given a gift of 80 acres of land for use as a public park by the heirs of Guilford G. Gage. The deed signed by the heirs contained a condition that the property would revert to them if the property were ever deeded or leased to a third party. After the park was established, the city granted the exclusive right to McCall to construct and operate, for a period of five years, a miniature train on the premises. Under the agreement, McCall was subject in virtually all respects to the control of the city, and either party could terminate the arrangement by giving 30 days' notice. The heirs of Gage claimed that the transaction was a lease and that the property should be returned to them. In holding that McCall had a license rather than a lease, the court said that all McCall had was "the exclusive right to operate as the City may dictate."

Because a license confers a personal privilege to act and not a present possessory estate, it does not run with the land and is usually not transferable. It may be made orally or in writing and may be given without consideration. In addition, a license need not delineate the specific space to be occupied. In contrast, a lease gives the tenant exclusive possession of the premises as against all the world, including the owner. It describes the exact property leased and states the term of the tenancy and the rent to be paid. In addition, in some states, a lease must be in writing. Permission to sell Christmas trees at a gas station, to hold dance parties in a hall, and to place a sign on the outside of a building have all been held to be licenses rather than leases.

**Leasing Compared with Lodging** A **lodger** is one who has the use of property without actual or exclusive possession of it. A lodger is a type of licensee, with a mere right to use the property. The landlord retains control of the premises and is responsible for its care and upkeep. Unlike a tenant, a lodger has no right to bring suit for trespass or to eject an intruder from the premises. One who lives in a spare room of a house, for example, whose owner retains direct control and supervision of the entire house, is a lodger.

## Types of Leasehold Interests

The interest conveyed by a lease is called a **leasehold estate** or a **tenancy**. There are four kinds of leasehold estates:

1.   Tenancy at will
2.   Tenancy for years
3.   Periodic tenancy
4.   Tenancy at sufferance

**Tenancy at Will** A **tenancy at will** is an ownership interest (estate) in real property for an indefinite period of time. No writing is required to create this tenancy, and it may be terminated at the will of either party by giving proper notice. The notice requirement to terminate a tenancy at will varies from state to state. It ranges from the time between rent periods to 30 days' written notice from the next day that rent is due. The rule generally followed in this country is that a tenancy at will comes to an end when the property is sold by the landlord to a third party. The notice required by state law must be given to the tenant in any event.

**Tenancy for Years** A **tenancy for years** is an ownership interest (estate) in real property for a definite or fixed period of time. It may be for one week, six months, one year, five years, 99 years, or any period of time, as long as it is definite. Such a tenancy automatically terminates on the expiration of the stated term. A tenancy for 100 years or more creates an estate in fee simple, transferring absolute ownership to the tenant. For this reason, leases are sometimes written for 99-year periods. In some states, a tenancy for years may be oral if the term is shorter than one year; otherwise, it must be in writing. Other states require all tenancies for years to be in writing. A tenant who remains in possession of the premises at the expiration of the term with permission of the landlord, but without a new lease, is a tenant at will in some states. In other states, such a tenant is known as a periodic tenant.

**Periodic Tenancy** A **periodic tenancy**, which is also known as a **tenancy from year to year** (or month to month or week to week), is a fixed-period tenancy that continues for successive periods until one of the parties terminates it by giving notice to the other party. Unless the landlord or tenant gives advance notice of an intention to terminate the lease, it will be automatically renewed at the end of each fixed period for the same term. Advance notice varies from state to state, but it generally is defined as a period of three months for periodic tenancies of one year or longer and "one period" for periodic terms of less than a year.

The death of a tenant who holds a periodic tenancy does not terminate the tenancy. Rather, the interest of the tenant passes to the personal representative of the deceased's estate. A periodic tenancy may be created impliedly by a landlord accepting rent from a tenant for years whose lease has expired or who is wrongfully in possession. Some states treat the latter situation as a tenancy at will.

**Tenancy at Sufferance**  A **tenancy at sufferance** arises when tenants wrongfully remain in possession of the premises after their tenancy has expired. It often comes about at the expiration of the term of a tenancy for years or when a tenancy at will has been properly terminated and the tenant remains in possession. Such a tenant is a wrongdoer, having no estate or other interest in the property. A tenant at sufferance is not entitled to notice to vacate and is liable to pay rent for the period of occupancy. A periodic tenancy or a tenancy at will may come about, however, instead of a tenancy at sufferance if a landlord accepts rent from a tenant whose tenancy has expired.

## The Lease Agreement

The agreement between a lessor and a lessee, called a lease, creates the landlord–tenant relationship. It provides the tenant with exclusive possession and control of the real property

---

LEASE

This lease made the 20th day of August, 2012, between ROBERT VICKERS, herein called Landlord, and ETHEL LOPAZ, herein called Tenant, witnesseth:

The Landlord leases to the Tenant the following described premises: Four rooms and a bath on the first floor of the premises located at 17 Rosebud Terrace, Ashmont, New Hampshire, for the term of one year commencing at noon on the first day of September 2012 and ending at noon on the 31st day of August, 2013.

The Tenant agrees to pay to the Landlord the sum of $6,000 for the said term, in eleven (11) monthly payments as follows: The first and last months' rent of $1,000, plus a security deposit of $500, payable on September 1, 2012, and $500 on the first day of each month thereafter.

The Landlord agrees that the Tenant on paying the said rent and performing the covenants herein contained shall peaceably and quietly have, hold, and enjoy the premises for said term.

The Tenant agrees that at the expiration of the time mentioned in this lease she will give peaceable possession of the said premises to the Landlord in as good a condition as they now are, the usual wear, unavoidable accidents, and loss by fire excepted, and will not make or suffer any waste thereof, nor assign this lease, nor sublet, nor permit any person to occupy the same, nor make or suffer to be made any alteration therein, without the consent of the Landlord in writing having first been obtained, and that the Landlord may enter to view and make improvements, and to show the premises to prospective tenants or purchasers.

The covenants herein shall extend to and be binding upon heirs, executors, and administrators of the parties to this lease.

IN WITNESS WHEREOF, the parties have hereunto set their hands and seals the day and year first above written.

_Robert Vickers_
Robert Vickers

_Ethel Lopaz_
Ethel Lopaz

---

**Figure 30-2**  This is an example of a lease.

of the landlord. Because the lease is a contract, the general rules of contract law apply to it. The essential requirements of a lease are: (1) a definite agreement as to the extent and bounds of the leased property, (2) a definite and agreed term, and (3) a definite and agreed price of rental and manner of payment.

### Rent Control
Some large communities have passed rent control laws to keep rents within an affordable range. These laws limit what landlords can charge for rental property and often contain procedures that must be followed before tenants may be evicted. In a number of areas, rent control laws have caused landlords to turn their apartments into condominiums, leading to shortages in rental apartments. Such laws differ from place to place. Some states, including Massachusetts, have done away with rent control laws altogether.

### Security Deposits
In addition to the first month's rent, landlords often require either a security deposit or the last month's rent, or both, to be paid at the beginning of a tenancy. The deposit protects landlords against damages to their property as well as nonpayment of rent. Due to abuses of such deposits by landlords, state legislatures have passed laws regulating security deposits on residential property. Such laws spell out the rights of tenants and make it easier for tenants to prevail in court. Although these laws differ from state to state, most states limit security deposits to one, one and one-half, two, or two and one-half months' rent, and most states require that security deposits be placed in interest-bearing accounts. The interest is either paid to tenants on an annual basis or accrued in their favor. Security deposits may not be commingled with other money belonging to the landlord. Also, the landlord is given a specific period, usually 30 days after the lease ends, to account for the security deposit and return the balance due to a tenant. Many states have now "put teeth" into the law, providing for double or triple damages, court costs, and attorney's fees for tenants whose security deposits are wrongfully withheld.

### EXAMPLE 30-11: Double Damages
Santos rented a $450-per-month apartment from Hollis for a term of two years. When Santos's tenancy ended, Hollis refused to return any of the $450 security deposit to Santos, claiming that the damages to the apartment fully offset the amount of the deposit. Santos hired a lawyer, who brought suit against Hollis. The landlord was able to demonstrate only $70 in damages to Santos's apartment. The court found that Hollis had wrongfully withheld $380 of Santos's security deposit. The court awarded Santos a judgment for double damages of $760 plus attorney's fees of $200. With court costs, the landlord was forced to pay over $1,000.

### Option to Renew or to Purchase
Many leases contain a provision allowing the lessee to have the option to renew the lease for one or more additional periods. An option to renew gives the lessee the right, at the end of the lease, to a new lease for an additional period. The new lease is on the same terms as the old one, with the possible exception of an increase in the rent. To exercise the option, the lessee must notify the lessor on or before the date set forth in the lease to do so. A lessee may, if the lease so provides, be given an option to purchase the property. This option is an agreement by the lessor to sell the property to the lessee for a stated price. To exercise the option, the lessee must notify the lessor, within the time period stated in the lease, of the decision to purchase the property.

**EXAMPLE 30-12:** Option to Purchase

Larson purchased a parcel of real property for $191,140 and leased it to the Panhandle Rehabilitation Center. The lease was for 10 years and contained an option to buy for $200,000. After leasing the premises for five years and spending $25,000 to improve it, Panhandle notified Larson of its intention to exercise its option. By this time, the property was worth $238,000. Larson refused to sell the property to Panhandle for $200,000. The court ordered her to do so.

**Assignment and Subletting** An assignment of a lease occurs when the interest in the leased premises is transferred by the lessee to another person for the balance of the term of the lease. The new party, called the *assignee,* steps into the shoes of the tenant, or assignor, and is liable for all of the original tenant's obligations and entitled to all the original tenant's rights under the lease. In contrast, it is called a sublease or underlease if the transfer is for a part of the term but not for the remainder of it. A lease may be assigned or sublet unless the lease states otherwise. Many leases are written so that they require landlord approval for an assignment or a sublease. However, in some states, the landlord cannot withhold such approval unreasonably. An assignment or sublease will be held valid if the landlord accepts rent over a period of time from either an assignee or a subtenant.

---

### quick quiz 30-4

1. A license is just like a lease because it bestows upon the licensee the same type of property rights and ownership interests as those bestowed on a party with a lease.   true | false

2. A tenancy at will is an ownership interest (estate) in real property for a definite period of time.   true | false

3. An option to renew gives the lessee the right, at the end of the lease, to a new lease for an additional period.   true | false

---

# 30-5 Duties of the Landlord and the Tenant

Like most of the legal relationships that we have examined in the book thus far, the landlord–tenant relationship is a balancing act that offsets the rights of one side against the duties of the other. In this case the rights are inherent within the very nature of the landlord–tenant relationship. The tenant is given the right to have temporary possession of the premises and the landlord has the right to receive consideration. The duties, in contrast, are not quite that clear.

## The Landlord's Duties

A good lease agreement will carefully spell out the respective rights and duties of the landlord and the tenant. However, state and local laws may restrict or expand upon what is set forth in the lease.

## Duty to Refrain from Discrimination

A landlord may not discriminate in selecting tenants on the grounds of race, creed, color, national origin, or gender. In most states, a landlord may restrict rentals to persons without children but may not restrict a married couple's freedom to bear children during the leasehold. It is permissible, however, for landlord to set up a housing complex that is open only to people 62 years of age and older and not run counter to age discrimination prohibitions. Although not directly applicable to a lease agreement, the Americans with Disabilities Act does require that owners of public accommodations such as motels and hotels have handicapped accessibility.

## Duty to Maintain the Premises

When real property is rented for dwelling purposes, there is an implied warranty, called the **warranty of habitability**, that the premises are fit for human habitation. This provision means that the landlord warrants there are no defects vital to the use of the premises for residential purposes. Examples of defects are unsafe electrical wiring, a malfunctioning heating or cooling system, broken windows, a leaking roof, and infestation of insects. Many municipalities have adopted ordinances to protect tenants from unsafe or unhealthy conditions created by a landlord's refusal to make necessary repairs. Building inspectors, health authorities, and other public officials are empowered to make inspections and demand improvements when they are contacted by dissatisfied tenants. In many cases, ordinances permit the tenant to cease payment of rent for the period during which the landlord fails to make the repairs or improvements needed. The majority of states hold that a landlord has a duty to clear common entryways of natural accumulations of snow and ice. Some states, nevertheless, still follow the older rule that the landlord owes no duty to tenants to clean common entryways of ice and snow unless there is an agreement on the part of the landlord to do so.

Landlords must ensure that the property they rent out to tenants is habitable.

## Duty to Deliver Peaceful Possession

The tenant is entitled to the exclusive peaceful possession and quiet enjoyment of the rental premises. **Quiet enjoyment** is the right of a tenant to the undisturbed possession of the property. The landlord may not interfere with the tenant's rights of possession as long as the tenant abides by the conditions of the lease and those imposed by law.

### EXAMPLE 30-13: Breach of Quiet Enjoyment

Smith Grocery & Variety, Inc., leased one store in a two-store mall from Northern Terminals, Inc. The lease entitled Smith to the use of the parking areas (between 14 and 20 spaces) abutting the leased premises. Five months after Smith opened for business, Northern Terminals added an additional store to the mall without increasing the mall's parking facilities. Smith's business declined due to the severe parking shortage caused by the opening of a Triple-S Blue Stamp Redemption Center in the new addition. The court held that Northern Terminals, Inc., breached the covenant of quiet enjoyment. There was a substantial interference with the lessee's use of the premises, which was caused by the lessor's taking away of the parking spaces.

The right to exclusive possession by the tenant makes the landlord a trespasser should there be any unauthorized entry by the landlord into the rented premises.

## EXAMPLE 30-14: Trespass

Benson & Childs rented a skylight suite for their architecture offices. The lease gave the owner permission to enter only when a request had been made or in the event of extreme emergency. The landlord entered the offices late one evening for what he termed was his regular safety and fire inspection. Benson & Childs may treat the landlord's trespass as a breach of their right to sole possession, giving them the right to terminate the lease and charge the landlord in either a civil or a criminal complaint.

A tenant who is wrongfully evicted is not required to return and may consider the lease as ended. An **eviction** is an act of the landlord that deprives the tenant of the enjoyment of the premises. It is called an **actual eviction** when the tenant is physically deprived of the leasehold. When the tenant is deprived of something of a substantial nature that was called for under the lease, it is termed a **constructive eviction**. The tenant is justified in abandoning the premises without paying rent when a wrongful eviction occurs. The tenant must mitigate (lessen) any damages, however, if possible.

## EXAMPLE 30-15: Constructive Eviction

Sound City, U.S.A., was interested in renting space in a shopping center. An inspection of the premises disclosed portions of the ceiling tile missing or hanging loose, water marks on the ceiling, and bare fluorescent light fixtures. As a result, Sound City included in its one-year lease an addendum (addition), whereby the landlord agreed to repair and paint the ceiling tile, cover the light bulb fixtures, panel the south wall, and erect a partition. Sound City moved into the shopping center, but after three months and many complaints, the repairs were never completed. It then moved out. The landlord brought suit for the remaining nine months' rent. The court held against the landlord, saying that there had been a constructive eviction. The physical appearance of the store was an important factor in the successful operation of Sound City's business. The failure to repair the premises properly in accordance with the lease rendered the premises unsuitable for the purpose for which they were rented.

## The Tenant's Duties

The tenant has the duty to pay rent to the landlord. In addition, the landlord has the right to remove, through court procedures, a tenant for nonpayment of rent, disorderliness, or illegal or unpermitted use of the premises. A tenant has the duty to observe the valid restrictions contained in the lease. Leases may impose duties of all kinds as long as they are legal and do not deny a tenant's constitutional rights. Failure to abide by the restrictions agreed to at the time of the signing of the lease gives the landlord the right to seek the eviction of the tenant. Unless agreed otherwise, the tenant must turn over to the landlord all fixtures (except trade fixtures belonging to a business) that have been made a permanent part of the real property by the tenant during the leasehold. Tenants also have a duty to avoid damaging or destroying the property, that is, commit waste. **Waste** is defined as substantial damage to premises that significantly decreases the value of the property.

## Tort Liability

When a person is injured on leased property, the one who is in control of the part of the premises where the injury occurs usually is responsible if the injury was caused by that person's negligence. The landlord, for example, is responsible for injury to others that may be caused by a defect in the common areas, such as hallways and stairways. Although landlords are not guarantors of the safety of persons in a building's common area, they are not free to ignore reasonably foreseeable risks of harm to tenants and others lawfully on the premises. Landlords must take reasonable steps to guard against foreseeable criminal acts of third parties.

## Eviction Proceedings

States today do not allow landlords to use force to evict tenants. Instead, they must make use of statutory remedies that are available to them. Some states do, however, recognize the right of landlords to enter wrongfully held premises and take over possession if it can be done peacefully. **Ejectment** is the common law name given to the lawsuit brought by the landlord to have the tenant evicted from the premises. This older remedy is still available in many states; however, it is time consuming, expensive, and subject to long delays. **Unlawful detainer** is a legal proceeding that provides landlords with a quick method of evicting a tenant. The proceeding is referred to by different names in different states, including the following: summary process, summary ejectment, forcible entry and detainer, and dispossessory warrant proceedings. The remedy provides landlords with a quick method of regaining possession of their property and protects tenants from being ousted by force and violence. Strict notice requirements must be followed by the landlord, after which both parties are given their day in court. If a forcible eviction becomes necessary, it is done by the sheriff under the supervision of the court.

---

### quick quiz 30-5

| | | |
|---|---|---|
| 1. | A landlord may not discriminate in selecting tenants on the grounds of race, creed, color, national origin, or gender. | true \| false |
| 2. | Tenants also have a duty to avoid damaging or destroying the property, that is, commit waste. | true \| false |
| 3. | States today do not allow landlords to use force to evict tenants. | true \| false |

---

## Summary

**30.1** Real property is the ground and everything permanently attached to it. It includes the airspace above the surface to as high as the owner can use and the ground under the surface. Fixtures are personal property that are so permanently attached to real property that they become part of the real property. Easements give people the right to pass over another's land, to run wires through another's airspace, to drain water onto another's property, and to run pipes underneath another's ground. Easements run with the land.

**30.2** An estate in fee simple is the greatest interest that one can have in real property. It descends to one's heirs upon death and can be disposed of in any manner during one's lifetime. In contrast, a life estate lasts only for someone's life. People may own real property individually or with others. When two or more people own real property as tenants in common, the interest of a deceased owner's share passes to the heirs upon death. In contrast, when two or more people own real property as joint tenants or tenants by the entirety, the interest of the deceased owner's share passes to any other cotenants upon death.

**30.3**   A deed is used to transfer real property by sale or gift. The records of the probate court, instead of a deed, establish title to property when an owner dies. Title to real property may also be gained by adverse possession. Zoning laws regulate the uses that may be made of properties within specified geographical areas. Eminent domain is the right of federal, state, and local governments, or other public bodies, to take private lands for a public purpose. Owners must be paid the fair value of the property taken.

**30.4**   The landlord–tenant relationship is a contractual arrangement whereby the owner of real property allows another to have temporary possession and control of the premises in exchange for consideration. A lease is different from a license and from an agreement with a lodger. A tenancy at will is an ownership interest (estate) in real property for an indefinite period of time.

A tenancy for years is an estate for a definite period of time, no matter how long or how short. A periodic tenancy is a tenancy that continues for successive periods until one of the parties terminates it by giving notice to the other party. A tenancy at sufferance arises when tenants wrongfully remain in possession of the premises after their tenancy has expired. A lease creates the landlord–tenant relationship. Because it is a contract, the general rules of contract law apply to it.

**30.5**   A landlord may not discriminate in selecting tenants on the grounds of race, creed, color, or gender. Landlords have the right to evict tenants for nonpayment of rent, disorderliness, and unpermitted use of the premises. Tenants must observe the valid restrictions in a lease and not commit waste. When someone is injured, the person in control of that part of the premises where the injury occurs is responsible if negligent. Peaceable entry, ejectment, and unlawful detainer are the principal methods available to landlords to regain possession of their premises.

## Key Terms

# Questions for Review and Discussion

1. What constitutes real property?
2. What is the difference between freehold and lease-hold estates?
3. What are the different types of co-ownership of real property?
4. What are the methods of acquiring title to real property?
5. What is eminent domain?
6. What are the five elements necessary to create a landlord–tenant relationship?
7. What are the essential requirements of a lease?
8. What are rent control and security deposits?
9. What are the duties of landlords and tenants?
10. How does tort liability apply to landlords and tenants?

# Cases for Analysis

1. Aloi sold a section of her land to Bell, including in the deed an easement allowing Bell to cross Aloi's property to reach the newly acquired parcel. Three years later, Aloi sold his property to Cadd. Shortly thereafter, following an argument, Cadd put a chain across Bell's right of way, saying that he had not given permission for Bell to cross his land. How should the court rule on this case and why?

2. Alfonso DiFilippo and his brother, Pasquale, owned a parcel of real property as tenants in common. Pasquale died in 1961, leaving a life estate in the property to his widow, Annie, with the remainder estate when Annie dies to Alfonso. Annie died in 1985. Alfonso died in 1969, leaving his interest in the property to his wife, Maria. What interest did Maria own in the property when she died in 1981? *DiFilippo v. DiFilippo,* 640 N.E.2d 1120 (MA).

3. When its lease expired, Kingston Frameworks made plans to move to another building. Preparations were made to remove shelving, mat and glass cutters, display boards, benches, and other fixtures that had been built into the store when the lease first started. All the shelves and fixtures were specially designed for the picture-framing business. The landlord told the owners of Kingston Frameworks to stop removing the items from the property. Could they remove the shelves and other fixtures that were paid for and installed by them during their tenancy? Why or why not? See also *George v. Town of Calais,* 373 A.2d 553 (VT).

4. Smith and Dudley are next-door neighbors. The branches of a large maple tree on Smith's property hangs over Dudley's driveway, dripping sap onto Dudley's car. Smith refuses to trim the branches overhanging Dudley's driveway, saying that she does not want to spoil the beauty of the tree. What are Dudley's legal rights in this situation?

5. Two years after Jean Russell was divorced from Billy Russell, Jean signed a quitclaim deed conveying her interest in their jointly owned real property to Billy. Later, she tried to have the deed set aside on the ground that Billy gave her no consideration. Was she successful? Why or why not? *Russell v. Russell,* 361 So.2d 1053 (AL).

6. Bech owned a building in which Cuevas resided as a tenant at will. Alleging that Cuevas had committed waste, Bech delivered a letter to Cuevas ordering her to vacate the premises in two days. The law of that state required 30-day notice to evict a tenant at will. Must Cuevas vacate the premises? Explain. *Bech v. Cuevas,* 534 N.E.2d 1163 (MA).

7. The following language was in a handwritten agreement signed by Harold and Saul and their respective wives: "Saul & Zelda get the option to rent the lower level of the Hope Chest store when their lease expires. If they do take it, they will pay the same rate of rent per square foot that Harold is paying for his store. Saul & Zelda will do all the fixing up at their expense. Entrance to upper level has to be maintained from Newbury Street—similar to how it is now. Saul and Zelda have to let Harold know six months ahead of time: (lease expires by May 31, 1987, so that Saul and Zelda have to let Harold know by Nov. 31, 1986). Saul and Zelda cannot use the name Simon or Simon's or anything with the Simon name as a name for their store. Too confusing." Does the language contain the essential elements of a lease? Explain. *Simon v. Simon,* 625 N.E.2d 564 (MA).

8. Goldstein rented an apartment from Dunbar as a tenant at will. She paid her rent on time and took good care of the premises; she was never disorderly. Dunbar decided to evict Goldstein and rent the apartment to a college friend who was moving to the area. He sent Goldstein a proper notice to quit. Goldstein claimed that she could not be asked to leave because she had done nothing wrong. Do you agree with Goldstein? Explain. See also *Ralo, Inc., v. Jack Graham, Inc.,* 362 So.2d 310 (FL).

9. Sarah H. Brown and Sandy F. Soverow agreed to rent separate apartments from Osborn, the owner of an apartment complex called Nob Hill Apartments, which was being constructed. Because their single apartments were not yet completed, Brown and Soverow agreed to rent one larger apartment in the complex and live in that until their separate apartments were finished. A fire occurred in the apartment shortly after Brown put some leftover liver and gizzards for her dogs on the electric stove and left the apartment. In the lawsuit that followed, the contention was made that Brown and Soverow were lodgers rather than tenants. Do you agree with the contention? Explain. *Osborn v. Brown,* 361 So.2d 82 (AL).

10. Alabama Outdoor Advertising Co., Inc., leased part of a lot from All State Linen Service Co. to erect a commercial advertising sign. The term of the lease was for "indefinite years, beginning 1st day of January, 1973, and ending year to year thereafter." When All State sold the lot, it was argued that Alabama's lease was a tenancy at will and therefore came to an end when the lot was sold. Do you agree with this argument? Why or why not? *Industrial Mach., Inc., v. Creative Displays, Inc.,* 344 So.2d 743 (AL).

## quick quiz Answers

| 30-1 | 30-2 | 30-3 | 30-4 | 30-5 |
|------|------|------|------|------|
| 1. F | 1. F | 1. T | 1. F | 1. T |
| 2. T | 2. T | 2. F | 2. F | 2. T |
| 3. T | 3. T | 3. T | 3. T | 3. T |

# Chapter 31

# Wills, Trusts, and Advanced Directives

## THE OPENING CASE — Balancing the Right to Die with Federal Control: *Gonzales, Attorney General v. Oregon*

Sometimes the United States Supreme Court must dive into a controversy that has implications beyond the actual facts and issues in the case. In such situations, the court may decide a case on what seems to be a narrow legal technicality, but which is actually a major policy shift that will shape the future of generations to come. A case in point is the dispute in *Gonzales, Attorney General v. Oregon.* This controversy started when the citizens of Oregon authorized the establishment of a radical new measure legalizing physician-assisted suicide. The unconventional measure, which had been dubbed the Oregon Death with Dignity Act (ODWDA), protected physicians from prosecution under criminal law and from litigation under civil law, for prescribing drugs for terminally ill patients who wished to commit suicide. So far so good. The problem arose because the drugs that would have been prescribed under the law were listed on the Controlled Substances Act (CSA) and are thus subject to federal scrutiny. The situation was, in fact, scrutinized by the United States attorney general (AG), who issued an interpretive ruling that stated that any physician who prescribed such drugs under the authority of the act and with the intent to have those drugs used for suicide could lose his or her license to practice

medicine. The attorney general reasoned that drugs controlled by the CSA were to be used only for legitimate medical purposes and suicide is not a legitimate medical purpose. Moreover, such activities were deemed by the AG to be "inconsistent with the public interest." A lawsuit was filed by several interested parties in the federal district court in Oregon which ruled in favor of the plaintiffs, and which then enjoined the AG from enforcing his interpretation of the CSA. The appeals court agreed. The AG filed an appeal which ended up in the United States Supreme Court. Now 16 years earlier in another case, this one a ground-breaker known as *Cruzon v. Director, Missouri Department of Health* 110 S.Ct. 2841 (1990), the Supreme Court had ruled that the right to die was constitutionally preserved by the Due Process Clause. Consequently, it had little problem in this case telling the attorney general to, in effect, "mind his own business." The CSA is supposed to stop physicians from trafficking in illegal drugs. It is not supposed to give the federal government the power to police a state's authority to regulate the practice of medicine. Consequently, the AG clearly overstepped his authority when he tried to short circuit the Oregon law. [See *Gonzales, Attorney General v. Oregon,* 126 S.Ct. 904 (United States Supreme Court).]

**Opening Case Questions**

1. What is the central issue in this case? Explain.

2. In what way does the central issue not reflect the real issue in the case? Explain.

3. In what way might the court's previous ruling in the *Cruzon* case have affected the decision making in this case? Explain.

4. How might this case affect advanced directives and living wills? Explain.

5. How might this case affect future generations? Explain.

 Learning Objectives

1. Give details about the sources of probate law and its relevance to business entities.
2. Explain the formal requirements for executing a will.
3. Determine whether a person who makes a will has the capacity to do so.
4. Compare the protection of children with the protection of spouses under the law of wills.
5. Identify the different methods of revoking or changing a will.
6. Explain the three grounds for contesting a will.
7. Describe who will inherit the property of someone who dies without a will.
8. Describe the steps to be taken by an executor or administrator in settling an estate.
9. Discuss the types and purposes of advance directives.
10. Differentiate among the various types of trusts and determine when they might be used.

# 31-1 Sources and Relevance of Probate Law

The term **probate** refers to the process of handling the will and the estate of a deceased person. Each state has its own laws passed by its legislature, different from other states, governing the writing of wills and the settling of estates. For this reason, it is necessary to check one's own state law to ascertain the rules for writing a will and to determine how property passes when someone dies. In an attempt to standardize and modernize the different state laws on this subject, the Uniform Probate Code (UPC) has been set up by the National Conference of Commissioners on Uniform State Laws (NCCUSL). However, the UPC does not enjoy the popularity and universal applicability of other model laws created by the NCCUSL such as the Uniform Commercial Code and the Revised Uniform Partnership Act, and so not all states have made it part of their law at this time. This may be due to the fact that each state jealously guards its own way of handling the distribution of the estates of its own citizens and is, thus, reluctant to pitch all of that in favor of a uniform standard, which may or may not reflect the traditions of that state. Moreover, unlike commercial law which cannot operate without crossing state lines, issues in probate law can often be handled without leaving a jurisdiction and, thus, need not fit as neatly into the network of interstate legal matters.

## Relevance of Probate to Business

Because probate matters deal with the handling of people's estates, and because all businesses are owned by people in one way or another, the subject of probate law is relevant to all forms of business entities. When sole proprietors die, for example, the assets of their businesses pass to their heirs according to their states' probate laws. When owners of a corporation—that is, stockholders—die, their solely owned shares of stock pass to their heirs in a similar fashion. The death of a partner in a partnership form of business automatically dissolves the partnership. In such event, the deceased partner's estate has the right to either be paid the value of the partner's share or have the partnership ended.

## Probate Terminology

It is not uncommon for people to prepare for possible future misfortune by making advance arrangements while they are still mentally and physically able to do so. One such advanced arrangement is the making of a will. A **will**, also called a **last will and testament**, is a formal document that governs the transfer of property at death. A person who dies with a will is said to die **testate**. A person who dies without a will is said to die **intestate**. The giving away of one's property by will is known as testamentary disposition. A person who makes a will is called a **testator** if a man or a **testatrix** if a woman. (The masculine forms of terms like *testator* are used for purposes of discussion here. They refer to people of either sex.) Personal property that is left by will is called a **bequest** or legacy, except in states that have adopted the Uniform Probate Code.

Real property that is left by will is known as a **devise**. Those who receive property by will are referred to as beneficiaries. They are also known as **legatees** if they receive personal property and **devisees** if they receive real property under a will. In states that have adopted the Uniform Probate Code, the term *devise* refers to both real and personal property, and the term *devisee* refers to a person who receives a gift of either real or personal property. The term **heir** is a broader term referring to a person who inherits property either under a will or from a person dying without a will. A **durable power of attorney** is a document authorizing another person to act on one's behalf with words stating that it is to either survive one's incapacity or become effective when one becomes debilitated. This authorization is not the same as an ordinary *power of attorney* which would have questionable effect upon one's incapacity.

**Did You Know?**

It can be risky to draft one's own will or even to use a preprinted generic will found in a stationery store. The law of wills is very technical, and unique language is often used in the drafting of wills that may not be fully understood by laypeople. In addition, the law of wills varies considerably from state to state, making a generic will unreliable in many cases.

### quick quiz 31-1

| | true \| false |
|---|---|
| 1.  The Uniform Probate Code (UPC) has been adopted by all 50 states and Puerto Rico. | true \| false |
| 2.  A person who dies without a will is said to die testate. | true \| false |
| 3.  A person who makes a will is called a *testator* if a woman or a *testatrix* if a man. | true \| false |

## 31-2 The Law of Wills

President John F. Kennedy once said, "Our problems are man-made; therefore, they can be solved by man. For in the final analysis, our most common link is that we all inhabit this small planet; we all breathe the same air; we all cherish our children's future, and we are all mortal." Kennedy was correct. As human beings we do cherish our children's future and we are all mortal. There is little we can do about the second proposition. However, the law of wills does give us some control over the first. As long as we are willing to follow the conditions set down by the law of wills, we should be able to transfer a good portion of our property to our spouse, to our children, and to others that we choose to remember.

# Requirements for Executing a Will

First, it is important to remember that the law governing the making and signing of wills is not uniform throughout the United States. Nevertheless, a will that is properly executed according to the laws of one state will be given full faith and credit in other states. The laws are highly technical and require strict adherence to detailed formalities. Many lawsuits have occurred over the years because people have attempted to make their own wills without consulting a lawyer. Often, in such cases, a technicality causes the will to be disallowed by the court, and the true wishes of the deceased are not carried out.

**Soundness of Mind** Any person who has reached the age of adulthood (18 years) and is of sound mind may make a will. The issue of soundness of mind is raised only when someone contests a will on that ground. In determining whether a testator was of sound mind when making a will, the court asks the following questions: When making the will, did the testator know, in a general way, the nature and extent of the property he or she owned? Did the testator know who would be the natural recipients of the estate? Was the testator free from delusions that might influence the disposition of the property? Did the testator know that he or she was making a will? If all of these questions are answered in the affirmative, the court will find that the testator was of sound mind when making a will.

## EXAMPLE 31-1: Soundness of Mind

At the time of the execution of his will, Stein was suffering from loss of memory. His son observed his father's failing health and mental illness over a period of time. He once observed his father's failure to recognize his own wife. Stein's daughter once observed her father's failure to recognize her and another relative, both of whom he saw frequently. The court disallowed the will, saying, "The testator did not have mind and memory sound enough to know and understand the businesses upon which he was engaged at the time of execution."

**Formal Requirements** With the exception of a nuncupative will, discussed later, a will must be in writing, signed by the testator, and attested to in the testator's presence by the number of witnesses established by state law (see Figure 31-1). Each of the particular statutory requirements of the state where the will is made must be met for a will to be valid.

## EXAMPLE 31-2: Improperly Signed and Witnessed

Dugan's will contained the following clause: "All United States Savings Bonds in safety deposit box #559 Farmers Bank 10th and Market Sts., Wilmington, Del., to be given to the people and places as marked." When Dugan died, a number of U.S. Savings Bonds were found in his safe deposit box. There was also a handwritten list of the names of various individuals and organizations and, next to each name, serial numbers, dates, and face amounts corresponding to specific bonds. Further specific notations were written on small slips of paper and attached to each bond with a rubber band. The court held that there was no effective testamentary transfer of the bonds. Neither the list nor the envelopes nor the small slips of paper satisfied the statutory requirements for executing a will. They were not properly signed and witnessed. Dugan's wishes as stated in the will were never carried out.

LAST WILL AND TESTAMENT
OF
JUDITH M. DORE

I, JUDITH M. DORE, of Salem, County of Essex, Commonwealth of Massachusetts, make this my Last Will and Testament, hereby revoking all earlier wills and codicils.

ARTICLE I

I give, devise, and bequeath all my estate, real, personal, and mixed and wherever situated to my husband, PETER DORE, if he is living on the thirtieth day after my death.

ARTICLE II

If my husband, PETER DORE, is not living on the thirtieth day after my death, I give and devise all of my property of every kind and wherever located which I own at the time of my death or to which I am then in any way entitled in equal shares to my children, ALAINA DORE and DAVID DORE, but if either of them shall not be living, his or her share thereof shall pass to his or her issue then living by right of representation, and in default of such issue then his or her share shall pass to the survivor of them.

I, the undersigned testator, do hereby declare that I sign and execute this instrument as my last will, that I sign it willingly in the presence of each of said witnesses, and that I execute it as my free and voluntary act for the purposes herein expressed, this 15th day of January, 2005.

_____
Judith M. Dore

We, the undersigned witnesses, each do hereby declare in the presence of the aforesaid testator that the testator signed and executed this instrument as her last will in the presence of each of us, that she signed it willingly, that each of us hereby signs this will as witness in the presence of the testator, and that to the best of our knowledge the testator is eighteen (18) years of age or over, of sound mind, and under no constraint or undue influence.

_____        _____
(Witness)                               (address)

_____        _____
(Witness)                               (address)

COMMONWEALTH OF MASSACHUSETTS
COUNTY OF ESSEX

On this 15th day of January, 2005, before me, the undersigned notary public, personally appeared JUDITH M. DORE, proved to me through satisfactory evidence of identification, which was a current Massachusetts driver's license, to be the person whose name is signed on this instrument, and acknowledged to me that she signed it voluntarily for its stated purpose.

_____
Charles E. Jones, Notary Public

**Figure 31-1**  These are sample portions of a formal will drafted according to Massachusetts law. The laws of each state are not the same on the subject of wills.

A will may be typewritten or handwritten, or it may consist of a filled-in form. It need not be under seal. The will offered for probate must be the original and not a copy. In a case in which a testator executed both an original and a carbon copy of a will and later canceled only the carbon, the court has held that it could be presumed that the testator also intended to cancel the original. Problems of this nature can be avoided by executing only an original will.

A will must be signed by the testator. The place of the signature on the will and the requirement as to who must be present at the signing vary from state to state. In some states, a will must be signed at the end of the instrument; in other states, the signature may be placed anywhere on the paper. Similarly, some states require a will to be signed in the presence of witnesses, whereas others allow a will to be signed privately if the testator acknowledges to the witnesses when they sign that it is his or her signature. Testators who are not able to write may make a mark, such as an X, attested to by the required number of witnesses. If the testator's condition makes movement impossible, as in paralysis, another person may sign for the testator. This signing must be done at the request of the testator, in the testator's presence, and in the presence of witnesses.

With the exception of some wills that are handwritten, wills must be witnessed by the number of witnesses prescribed by state law. Almost every state today requires that a will be witnessed by two witnesses. Witnesses must sign in the presence of the testator and, in some states, each other's presence. Because the witnesses may be called upon to attest to the genuineness of the testator's signature and soundness of mind, it is advisable that witnesses be younger than the testator. In some states, no age requirements are given for witnesses. Instead, minors may witness a will as long as they are of sufficient understanding and competent to testify in court as to the facts relating to the execution of the will. In other states, witnesses must have reached a certain age, such as 14, 16, or 18 years, to qualify as a witness. In many states, persons and their spouses who witness a will may not receive gifts under the will unless there are still other witnesses. The failure to observe this provision may result in their being disinherited. Some states protect beneficiaries who witness a will by allowing them to inherit up to the amount that they would have inherited had the deceased died without a will.

## Need for Accuracy

Certain words often used in wills may have a legal interpretation that is different from their everyday meaning. Care must be taken to describe each bequest and devise in a manner that will satisfy the legal definition. For instance, a testator may use the word *heirs* when really meaning *children*. The differences in the meanings of the two words could result in much dispute and expensive litigation. It is also important to avoid ambiguous language.

## Informal Wills

A *holographic will* is one that is not witnessed but is written entirely in the handwriting of the testator. About half the states in the United States treat holographic wills as valid. The other half do not recognize them because of the lack of witnesses.

## EXAMPLE 31-3: Holographic Will

Sedmak resided in Pennsylvania. The following handwritten document was found among his papers when he died:

My Brother Mil
Please see that Zella Portenar receives $15,000 from my savings account it is in the Western Savings Bank.
George A. Sedmak
or Alexander Sedmak
Oct 6, '02

The Pennsylvania court held the unwitnessed document to be a valid holographic will.

Oral wills made by persons in their last illness or by soldiers and sailors in actual combat are nuncupative wills. *Nuncupative wills* are valid only in some states and are restricted to the giving of personal property only. Testators must indicate their bequests and state that those hearing the statements are to be considered witnesses to the oral will.

## Protection of Spouses and Children

**LO4**

Even though the law of wills differs from state to state, some provisions are consistent from jurisdiction to jurisdiction. Many of these identical provisions deal with the portion of an estate left to a spouse and that which is left to the children of the deceased. Most state laws contain a series of provisions that will protect the spouse. Similarly, most states have legal provisions that will protect the children. One major stipulation here is that children must have evidence that they were inadvertently left out of a parent's will. If they can do this, they will be are protected by state law in most jurisdictions.

Wills provide for the smooth transfer of property and assure the rights of the heirs and beneficiaries.

**Protection of Spouses** As noted above, most state laws include various devices that are designed to protect all family members, but especially the spouse of the deceased. Some states provide for a family allowance, sometimes called a widow's allowance, which is an amount of money taken from the decedent's estate and given to the family to meet its immediate needs while the estate is being probated. The amount of the allowance is either a fixed, statutory amount or discretionary with the court and is not chargeable against other benefits given to the family members. Another family protection is the homestead exemption, which puts the family home beyond the reach of creditors up to a certain limit. Still another protective device provided by some states is known as exempt property, which is certain property of a decedent that passes to the surviving spouse or children and is beyond the reach of creditors. In some states, for example, $3,500 worth of personal property passes automatically to the surviving spouse or, if none, to surviving children equally. The rights of dower (for a widow) and curtesy (for a widower) are also available in some states, providing the surviving spouse with certain property rights in real property owned by the deceased spouse.

In addition to the rights mentioned, surviving spouses are assured a share of a deceased spouse's estate. A surviving spouse who does not like the provisions of a deceased spouse's will may choose to take a portion of the estate set by state statute rather than accept the amount provided in the will. In some states, this sum is referred to as a spouse's forced share. In other states, it is called a spouse's elective share. The amount the surviving spouse will receive varies from state to state. In some states, it is the amount the spouse would have received had the deceased spouse died without a will. In other states, the amount is computed by the use of a different formula.

**Protection of Children** As mentioned above, children who can prove that they were mistakenly (rather than intentionally) left out of a parent's will are protected by the laws of most states. Forgotten children will receive the same share that they would have received had their parent died without a will. This situation does not mean that a parent may not disinherit a child. Parents are not obligated to leave children anything, but to avoid litigation, such an intention should be shown in the will. A testator who wishes to disinherit a child should name the child in the will and make the statement that the child was intentionally omitted. By doing so, the omitted child cannot claim to have been mistakenly omitted from the will. Adopted children, under modern laws, are given the same legal rights as natural children. They inherit from their adopting parents. In contrast, stepchildren, unless they have been adopted by a stepfather or stepmother, do not inherit from a stepparent. Children who have been taken into the family for one reason or another but never legally adopted have no right of inheritance.

## Revoking, Changing, and Contesting a Will

People often make promises that are later broken, forgotten, or ignored. Broken promises come with consequences, of course, many of them unpleasant. Nevertheless, when those consequences result in fines for overdue library books, late fees for tardy car payments, or low grades for forgotten homework, the pain is bearable. However, when the broken promises relate to a will, the consequences are far more hurtful and sometimes irreparable. This is why the law has a way for handling situations that involve revoking, changing, and contesting wayward wills.

**Revoking a Will** With variations from state to state, a will may be revoked (canceled) in any of the following ways: (1) burning, tearing, canceling, or obliterating the will with the intent to revoke it; (2) executing a new will; and (3) in some states, the subsequent marriage of the testator.  In most states, the divorce or annulment of a marriage revokes all gifts made under a will to the former spouse and revokes the appointment of the former spouse as executor of the will.

**Changing a Will** Sometimes testators wish to make slight changes in a will. They may do so by executing a new will or executing a codicil, which is a formal document used to supplement or change an existing will. A codicil must be executed with the same formalities as a will. It must be signed by the testator and properly witnessed. In addition, it must refer to the existing will to which it applies.

## EXAMPLE 31-4: Properly Executed Codicil

Rueda made a will giving her entire estate to her husband. Later, Rueda enjoyed unusual financial success and felt inclined to leave $100,000 toward a new church building under construction in her parish. Rueda's attorney prepared a codicil, which Rueda formally executed in the presence of two witnesses. The bequest to the church contained in the codicil became an integral part of the will itself.

A properly executed codicil has the effect of republishing a will. It is said that a codicil breathes new life into a will, which means that the codicil will reestablish a will that had been formerly revoked or improperly executed. If, for example, a will is witnessed by only one person in a state that requires two witnesses, the will is invalid. However, if a properly signed and witnessed codicil is added at a later date, the will becomes valid.

**Contesting a Will** Only persons who would inherit under an earlier made will or under the law of intestacy (described later in this chapter) are allowed to contest a will. A will may be contested on any of three grounds: improper execution, unsound mind, and undue influence. *Improper execution* occurs when an individual has attempted to make a will but has not followed the formal requirements. Because laypeople are not usually aware of the formal requirements for executing a will, it can be risky for them to make their own. Another grounds to contest a will is to allege that the testator was of *unsound mind*. When such an allegation is made, the burden is on the person presenting the will to the court to prove that the testator was of sound mind. This proof may occur by testimony and affida-vits of witnesses and by testimony of the deceased's physician. A will may also be attacked and held invalid if a probate court finds that the testator made the will under circumstances of *undue influence*. When persons come under the influence of another to the degree that they are unable to express their real intentions in a will, the will may be declared invalid. The court must distinguish between undue influence and the kindness, attention, advice, guidance, and friendliness shown toward the testator by the one named in the will.

### EXAMPLE 31-5: Undue Influence

Smolak executed a will prepared by a lawyer whom he had selected and with whom he had conferred several times before the date on which the will was signed. His niece, Sandra, was the major benefi-ciary under that will. A week later, he executed another will under which his nephew Michael and Michael's brother were named principal beneficiaries. This will was executed at the same time that Smolak executed a deed conveying his farm to Michael and Michael's brother (which conveyance he later sought to rescind, claiming that it was procured by fraud). The second will was executed at the office of a lawyer employed by Michael. Michael had made arrangements for a conference between his lawyer and Smolak. Michael attended that conference and also attended the execution of the resulting will. Smolak never conferred privately with Michael's lawyer concerning the second will and therefore never had an opportunity to express his true intentions out of earshot of his nephew. The court held that the second will was procured through undue influence and was therefore void.

## Dying without a Will

When people die without a will, they are said to have died **intestate**. The property of a person who dies intestate passes to others according to the various state laws of **intestate succession**. (See an example in Figure 31-2.) These state laws, which differ from state to state, contain the rules governing the allocation of intestate property. Personal property is treated differently from real property. *Personal property* is dispersed according to the law of the state where the deceased permanently resided (his or her domicile) at the time of death and passes to the personal representative to be distributed to the heirs. In contrast, *real property* passes according to the law where the property is located and passes directly to the heirs upon the death of the owner. The personal representative receives title to real property only when it must be sold to pay debts of the estate. The following steps are taken to ascertain who will inherit from someone who dies without a will:

- Determine the rights of the surviving spouse, if any.
- Determine the rights of the other heirs.

**Rights of the Surviving Spouse**   Under a typical state statute, if a person dies intestate, the rights of the surviving spouse are as follows: If the deceased is survived by **issue** (children, grandchildren, great-grandchildren), the surviving spouse is entitled to one-half of the estate. If the deceased is survived by no issue but by blood relatives, the surviving spouse is entitled to $200,000 plus one-half of the remainder of the estate. If the deceased is survived by no issue and no blood relatives, the surviving spouse is entitled to the entire estate. Keep in mind that this particular formula will differ from state to state.

**Rights of Other Heirs**   Under the same typical state statute, if a person dies intes-tate, the property will pass, subject to the rights of the surviving spouse, as follows: If the

| If the Deceased Is Survived by: | A Surviving Spouse (if any) Receives: | Any Remainder Is Distributed: |
|---|---|---|
| *Issue* (lineal descendants such as children, grandchildren, great-grandchildren) | One-half of the estate | Equally to the deceased's children. If any children are also deceased, their children divide their deceased parents' share equally. |
| No issue but by kindred (blood relatives) | $200,000 plus one-half of the remainder of the estate | Equally between the deceased's father and mother or to the survivor of them. *However, if both parents are deceased, then:* Equally among the deceased's brothers and sisters. If any brothers or sisters are also deceased, their children divide their deceased parents' share equally. *However, if there are no living brothers or sisters or nieces or nephews, then:* Equally among the deceased's *next of kin* (those who are most nearly related by blood, including aunts, uncles, and cousins). |
| No issue and no kindred | The entire estate *However, if there is no surviving spouse, issue, or kindred, then:* The entire estate *escheats* to (becomes the property of) the state. | |

**Figure 31-2** This is an example of the way intestate property is distributed under a typical state statute (Massachusetts).

deceased is survived by issue, the property passes in equal shares to the deceased's children, with the issue of any deceased child taking that child's share. If the deceased is survived by no issue, the property passes in equal shares to the deceased's father and mother or the survivor of them. If the deceased is survived by no issue and no father or mother, the property passes to the deceased's brothers and sisters, with the issue of any deceased brother or sister taking that brother's or sister's share. If the deceased is survived by no issue and no father, mother, brother, or sister, or issue of any deceased brother or sister, the property passes to the deceased's **next of kin** (those who are most nearly related by blood).

## Simultaneous Death

When two people die in a common disaster so that it is impossible to determine who died first, the Uniform Simultaneous Death Act often comes into play. This law contains rules that are adhered to when the inheritance of property depends upon the time of death, and there is nothing to indicate that the parties died other than at the same time. The following rules are obeyed:

1. The separately owned property of each person passes as if he or she had survived unless a will or trust provides otherwise. For example, if a husband and wife die together in a plane crash, the husband's individually owned property passes to his heirs as

though his wife were not living at the time of his death. Similarly, the wife's individually owned property passes to her heirs as though her husband were not living at the time of her death.

2. Property owned jointly by both of the deceaseds is distributed equally. In this example, half of the couple's jointly owned property passes to the husband's heirs; the other half passes to the wife's heirs.

3. When the beneficiary of an insurance policy dies at the same time as the insured, the proceeds of the insurance policy are payable as if the insured had survived the beneficiary. Suppose, in the example, the wife was the beneficiary on the husband's life insurance policy. The wife would be regarded as deceased at the time of the husband's death. The proceeds of the policy would go to the husband's estate unless an alternate beneficiary is named in the policy.

## EXAMPLE 31-6: Simultaneous Death Act Not Applicable

John F. Kennedy, Jr., and his wife, Carolyn Bessette Kennedy, were killed in 1999 when their plane crashed into the ocean off the coast of Martha's Vineyard. The Uniform Simultaneous Death Act did not apply because the gifts to the spouses in each will were prefaced by the phrase "if she (or he) is living on the thirtieth day after my death."

## Settling an Estate

When people die owning assets, their estates must be probated, that is, settled under the supervision of the court. The court that supervises the procedure is called a probate court in some states and a surrogate court, or orphan's court, in others. The first step in probating an estate is to determine whether the deceased left a will. If a will exists, it usually names a personal representative called an executor (male) or executrix (female) who is the person named in the will to carry out its terms. If there is no will, or if the executor named in the will fails to perform, someone must petition the court to settle the estate. That person, if appointed, is called an administrator (male) or administratrix (female). In states that have adopted the Uniform Probate Code, executors and administrators are called personal representatives.

Before an executor or administrator is appointed, notice of the petition for appointment is published in a newspaper and sent to all heirs, legatees, and devisees. Anyone with grounds to object may do so. Witnesses are sometimes asked to testify or sign affidavits about their knowledge of the execution of the will. Testimony is not necessary when all heirs and next of kin assent to the allowance of the will and no one contests it.

To ensure faithful performance, the executor or administrator is required to post a bond. A bond is a promise by the executor or administrator (and the sureties, if any) to pay the amount of the bond to the probate court if the duties of the position are not faithfully performed. Sureties are persons or insurance companies that stand behind executors or administrators and become responsible for their wrongdoing. In some states, a bond is not required if the will indicates that the executor or administrator need not post bond. In other states, a bond is always necessary, but sureties are not required if the will so dictates.

When a satisfactory bond has been filed, the court issues a certificate of appointment, called letters testamentary, to an executor or letters of administration to an administrator. The executor or administrator, called a fiduciary (one in a position of trust), is then authorized to proceed. The fiduciary's job consists of gathering the assets, paying the debts and taxes, and distributing the remaining assets in accordance with the will or the law of intestate succession.

| | |
|---|---|
| **quick quiz** 31-2 | |
| 1. A will may be typewritten or handwritten, or it may consist of a filled-in form and, whatever the case, it must be under seal and notarized. | true \| false |
| 2. A will may be contested for only one reason: unsound mind. | true \| false |
| 3. When people die owning assets, their estates must be probated, that is, settled, under the supervision of the court. | true \| false |

# 31-3 Advanced Directives

It is not uncommon for people to prepare for possible future misfortune by making advance arrangements while they are still mentally and physically able to do so. A good time to do this is when a will is executed, because all the necessary documents can be prepared, signed, and witnessed simultaneously. Part of this procedure can involve advanced directives that include the making of a living will and the execution of a health care proxy.

## Living Wills and Health Care Proxies

**Advance directives** are written statements in which people give instructions for their future medical care if they become unable to do so themselves. The most common type of advance directive is the **living will**, which is a written expression of a person's wishes to be allowed to die a natural death and not kept alive by heroic or artificial methods. Another vehicle that is used for this purpose is the **health care proxy**—a written statement authorizing an agent to make medical treatment decisions for another in the event of incapacity.

## The Right to Die and the Supreme Court

In 1990, in the case known as *Cruzon v. Director, Missouri Department of Health,* the United States Supreme Court ruled that the right to die was guaranteed by the Due Process Clause of the United States Constitution. This was not the first time that the Supreme Court got into the business of mixing the law and science in relation to decisions regarding life and death.

**The Government's Compelling Interest in Life** Perhaps one of the most critical instances was the case of *Roe v. Wade,* in which the United States Supreme Court decided that the government does not have a compelling interest for interfering with a mother's own choices in relation to her pregnancy until the fetus becomes viable, that is, capable of living outside the mother's womb. At that point, the point of viability, the government has a compelling interest in preserving the life of the fetus that outweighs the mother's right to have an abortion. In 1972, the year of *Roe v. Wade,* the point of viability was after the pregnancy entered the third trimester. In a later case, the case of *Planned Parenthood v. Casey,* the Supreme Court eliminated the redline at the third trimester because medical advances allowed the fetus to become viable at an earlier time, one that could not now be drawn with any certainty. Indeed, because of scientific advances, the moment of viability had become a moving target.

**Living Wills and the Right to Die** Now there is a curious disconnect that exists among the use of a living will, the right to die, and the government's compelling interest

## THE OPENING CASE *Revisited, Part I*
## Balancing the Right to Die with Federal Control:
## *Gonzales, Attorney General v. Oregon*, Round 2

Recall that in the Opening Case at the beginning of this chapter, the citizens of Oregon authorized the establishment of a radical new measure legalizing physician-assisted suicide. The Oregon Death with Dignity Act (ODWDA) protects physicians from criminal prosecution and civil litigation for prescribing drugs for terminally ill patients who wish to commit suicide. The problem arose because the drugs that would have been prescribed under the law were listed on the Controlled Substances Act (CSA) and are thus subject to federal scrutiny. The situation was, in fact, scrutinized by the United States attorney general (AG), who issued an interpretive ruling that stated that any physician who prescribed such drugs under the authority of the act and with the intent to have those drugs used for suicide could lose his or her license to

practice medicine. The attorney general argued that drugs controlled by the CSA were to be used only for legitimate medical purposes and suicide is not a legitimate medical purpose. Moreover, such activities were deemed by the AG to be "inconsistent with the public interest." If we take a close look at this argument it appears to be in line with the Supreme Court's ruling in *Roe v. Wade* (and *Planned Parenthood v. Casey*, for that matter). In that case the Supreme Court said that the government has a compelling interest in preserving life. In this case the AG said that the government cannot have a hand in facilitating suicide because to do so would be inconsistent with the public interest. From this perspective it is easy to see why the AG might have been surprised when the Supreme Court ruled against him.

in the preservation of life. On the one hand, the Supreme Court has said that the government has a compelling interest in preserving life and can, therefore, enact sanctions to stop the taking of a life by abortion while, on the other, it has said that the government has an interest in due process and cannot, therefore, enact sanctions that stop the taking of life by passive euthanasia. In short, the government cannot prevent passive euthanasia in accordance with a living will because it must protect due process, but it can prevent abortion because it has a compelling interest in preserving life. The next step in this controversy is represented by the case of *Gonzales, Attorney General v. Oregon*.

Of course, in one sense the court in *Gonzales, Attorney General v. Oregon* avoided addressing the real issue because the ruling was actually based on two other issues, the issue of the real purpose of the Controlled Substances Act (CSA), which is to prevent drug trafficking by physicians, and the issue of the state's right to control the activities of the medical profession within its own borders. Therefore, the balancing act between the government's compelling interest in life and the rights guaranteed by due process is still open to debate.

## A QUESTION OF ETHICS

The future that is outlined in the novel *Unisave* by Axel Madsen is dark, depressing, and discouraging. The novel is set in the 22nd century at a time when the planet's natural resources, its energy reserves, its agriculture, and its fresh water are depleted. Demographically the total population of Earth has surpassed the 24 billion mark. There is very little hope held out for the salvation of humanity. The planet has reached a tipping point beyond which there seems to be no hope. In a desperate attempt to stall the inevitable and perhaps reverse the slide toward total disaster, the United Nations has come up with several plans. One of the chief plans is established under the authority of an all-powerful global agency known as Unisave. This agency has been granted the authority to enforce a population control program that will affect everyone on Earth. There are several aspects to this program. First, the agency is equipped with the power to set quotas to control the number of children permitted to each couple. That, however, is the least strict of the new controls implemented by Unisave. Second, the agency has developed a compulsory sterilization program for some people under some circumstances. Third, it has ordered the use of drugs to suppress the sex drive urge among young people. Fourth, it has instituted a global program of electronic surveillance to prevent the violation of its strict anti-sex laws. Finally, it has mandated a program of compulsory gericide, which involves the systematic killing of the elderly. Consider each of the following ethical and legal issues.

1. First, when the people of Oregon supported the so-called Death with Dignity Act, did they legalize *gericide* in Oregon? Explain.

2. Second, can the Supreme Court's "compelling interest" standard be used to argue that the United States *cannot* cooperate with Unisave? Explain.

3. Third, could that same standard be used to compel U.S. cooperation with Unisave? Explain.

4. Fourth, can the due process standard that upheld the right to die in *Cruzan v. Director, Missouri Department of Health* be used to argue that the United States must cooperate with the gericide program? Why or why not?

5. Finally, in what way can the ruling in *Gonzales, Attorney General v. Oregon* be used to support the implementation of a gericide program? Explain.

**The Science Court Revisited** In Chapter 4 on alternative dispute resolution, we discussed a proposal by the governor of Minnesota for the creation of a science court to resolve legal issues related to science, medicine, engineering, and technology. The science court would be made up of scientists, engineers, and other experts educated in the discipline and the industry involved in the dispute, thus allowing them to use their expertise in deciding the case. The science court would also permit the parties to avoid the long and involved process of litigation. Since living wills, the right to die, physician-assisted suicide, and gericide involve medical issues related to life and death, cases involving them would be perfect candidates for the future science court.

## Self-Evident Truths

In a recent book entitled *Dark Age Ahead,* Jane Jacobs argues that Western Civilization in general and the United States in particular stand on the verge of cultural collapse. As the cause of this collapse she focuses on the decline of five essential mainstays of society: the family and the community; colleges and universities; the productive use of science; the government and its taxing power; and the self-regulation of the learned professions. She ends her book with a final prognosis of our culture:

> Ironically, societies (including our own) that were great cultural winners in the past are in special peril of failing to adapt successfully in the face of new realities. This is because nothing succeeds like success, and it follows that nothing hangs on past its prime like past success. Formerly vigorous cultures typically fall prey to arrogant self-deception for which the Greeks had a word, *hubris,* which we still use. Because a culture is all of a piece, tolerance of commercial false accounting for gaining profit has military equivalents in inflated reports or enemy casualties, along with wishful intelligence about disaffection in

enemy ranks. The falsities merely feed hubris; the enemy is a "public" that knows quickly whether wartime false accounting and wishful intelligence are empty bragging. The Bay of Pigs fiasco in Cuba and false body counts in the Vietnam War demonstrated an American proclivity for deception. Worse, the incentives for deception—success at sycophancy and pursuit of specious careerism—imply civilian cultural expectations that are shameful whether or not they infect military capability.

—Jane Jacobs, *Dark Age Ahead* (New York: Vintage Books, 2005), p. 175.

## Self-Evident Questions

1. When Attorney General Gonzales in the *Oregon* case argues that the government cannot be involved in supporting physicians who prescribe lethal drugs for terminally ill patients, is he "failing to successfully adapt in the face of new realities"? Explain.

2. When the Supreme Court supported the right to die in the *Cruzan* case was it exhibiting the type of self-deceptive *hubris,* of which Jacobs writes in *Dark Age Ahead?* Why or why not?

3. Some people have argued that the Supreme Court justices used a "technicality" to avoid the real issue in Oregon and in doing so managed to support governmentally approved suicide without actually "sticking their necks out" in the *Gonzales* case. Is this action by the justices on the Supreme Court an example of the "American proclivity for self-deception"? Explain.

4. Are the rulings in *Roe v. Wade* and *Planned Parenthood v. Casey* two examples adapting successfully to changing circumstances or another case of self-deception? Explain.

5. Both *Roe v. Wade* and *Planned Parenthood v. Casey* use a standard for personhood based on science's ability to push viability closer and closer to conception. Is this faith in science not an excellent example of hubris? Explain.

### quick quiz 31-3

| | | |
|---|---|---|
| 1. Advance directives are oral statements in which people give instructions for their future medical care if they become unable to do so themselves. | true | false |
| 2. A living will is a written expression of a person's wishes to be kept alive using heroic and artificial methods. | true | false |
| 3. United States Supreme Court has ruled that the right to die is guaranteed by the Due Process Clause of the United States Constitution. | true | false |

# 31-4 The Law of Trusts

A **trust** is a legal device by which property is held by one person (the **trustee**) for the benefit of another (the beneficiary). The person who sets up the trust is called the *settlor.* The property that is held in trust is the *corpus,* or *trust fund.*

When a trust is established, title is split between the trustee, who holds legal title, and the beneficiary, who holds equitable or beneficial title. This separation allows the trustee to manage the trust property for the benefit of the beneficiary. Trusts are established to save taxes, provide for the needs of young children, and prevent money from being squandered, among other reasons.

Property is often placed in trust so that it will be preserved for future generations. In such cases, only the income is given out during the life of the trust, with the principal held in relatively safe investments. The rule against perpetuities prevents trusts (except charitable trusts) from lasting indefinitely. This rule in many states requires trust property to become owned by the beneficiary outright not later than 21 years after the death of some person alive at the creation of the trust.

## Types of Trusts

The two principal types of trusts are testamentary trusts and living trusts. A **testamentary trust** is a trust that is created by a will. It comes into existence only upon the death of the testator. The terms of the trust, together with the names of the trustee and beneficiaries, are set out in the body of the will itself.

## EXAMPLE 31-7: Spendthrift Trust

Emile Hanson died, leaving four grown sons and daughters. His children had never demonstrated any real ambition and had depended heavily on their prospects of receiving large legacies from the estate. Hanson feared that his heirs would quickly spend their inheritances and have nothing to support themselves in the years ahead. He therefore provided for this possibility in his will by placing all assets in trust. The assets would remain intact, safely invested, and a small income would be paid from the trust income to the children. Hanson's purpose was realized in that the estate would be preserved and the surviving children would not squander their inheritance.

In a trust, such as the one illustrated in Example 31-6, provision must be made for final distribution of the trust's assets when the purpose of the trust has been served. For example, Hanson could have the trust property go to a church, college, or some other worthy nonprofit organization on the death of the last surviving child. He also could have designated a grandchild or grandchildren as the ultimate beneficiaries.

A **living trust**, also called an *inter vivos* trust, comes into existence while the settlor is alive. It is established by either a conveyance in trust or a declaration of trust. In a **conveyance in trust**, the settlor conveys away the legal title to a trustee to hold for the benefit of either the settlor or another as a beneficiary. In a **declaration of trust**, the settlor holds the legal title to the property as trustee for the benefit of some other person (the beneficiary) to whom the settlor now conveys the equitable title. A living trust may be either irrevocable or revocable. If it is *irrevocable,* the settlor loses complete control over the trust and cannot change it. The advantage of an irrevocable trust is that the income from the trust is not taxable to the settlor, and estate and inheritance taxes are avoided. The disadvantage of such a trust is that it can never be rescinded. The settlor can never get back that which has been put in an irrevocable trust, regardless of the circumstances. A *revocable* living trust may be taken back or changed at any time during the settlor's lifetime. It has neither estate tax nor income tax advantages; however, it can serve the purpose of relieving the cares of management of money or property, as well as other purposes.

A spendthrift is one who spends money profusely and improvidently. A *spendthrift trust* is designed to provide a fund for the maintenance of a beneficiary and, at the same time, secure the fund against that person's improvidence or incapacity. In some states, all trusts are considered to be of this type. In others, a clause must be placed in the trust instrument to the effect that the beneficiary cannot assign either the income or the principal of the trust and neither the income nor the principal can be reached by the beneficiary's creditors. Spendthrift trusts are not permitted in some states.

A charitable, or public, trust is one established for charitable purposes, such as the advancement of education; relief to the aged, ill, or poor; or the promotion of religion. For the trust to be valid, the identity of the person to be benefited must be uncertain. The rule against perpetuities does not apply to a charitable trust.

A *sprinkling trust,* or *spray trust,* allows the trustee to decide how much will be given to each beneficiary rather than have the settlor make the decision. The advantage of this type is that the trustee can compare the tax brackets of the beneficiaries long after the settlor is dead and cause a smaller tax liability to occur by giving more money to those beneficiaries in the lowest tax brackets. It also has built-in spendthrift provisions. The chief objection to this type of trust is that it gives the trustee too much control.

## Obligations of the Trustee

The trustee is obligated by law to use a high standard of care and prudence in the investment of funds held by the trust. If real property is held in trust, it is the trustee's obligation to supervise and care for the property. When economic and other reasons indicate the need to shift trust assets to safer areas of investment, it becomes the duty of the trustee to make such changes. If investments selected by the trustee fail, the trustee is held liable unless a court rules that the action was taken with prudence and caution.

The trustee relationship is one of great and continuing responsibility. Appointment as a trustee should not be accepted by those without the knowledge and background that would afford prudent and good management. Banks, trust companies, and other kinds of fiduciary corporations offer professional services in the administration of trusts. They provide professional investment services and generally give maximum security and benefit for the fees charged.

### quick quiz 31-4

| | | |
|---|---|---|
| 1. | When a trust is established, title to the trust property is held completely by the trustee. | true \| false |
| 2. | A *spendthrift* is one who is frugal and careful about spending money. | true \| false |
| 3. | Trustees are obligated by law to use an average standard of care when investing funds for the trust. | true \| false |

## Summary

31.1  Because each state's law is different on the subject of probate law, it is necessary to check one's own state law when dealing with probate matters. Furthermore, the subject of probate law is relevant to all forms of business entities.

31.2  The terms *will, last will and testament, testate, intestate, testator, testatrix, bequest, devise, legatees,* *devisees,* and *heir* are frequently used in the field of probate law.

Any person who has reached adulthood and is of sound mind may make a will. Wills must be in writing, signed by the testator, and attested to in the testator's presence by two witnesses in most states. In some states, no formalities are necessary when a holographic will is made.

Surviving spouses are given protection through such provisions as a family allowance, a homestead exemption, exempt property, and the rights of dower and curtesy. Children who can prove that they were mistakenly (rather than intentionally) omitted from a parent's will may be able to receive an intestate share of their parent's estate.

A will may be revoked by burning, tearing, canceling, or obliterating the will with the intent to revoke it; by executing a new will; and in some states, by the subsequent marriage of the testator. A will may be contested on the grounds of improper execution, unsound mind, and undue influence.

When people die without a will, their property passes to others according to the law of intestate succession, which varies from state to state.

Special rules apply when people die simultaneously. Separately owned property passes as if its owner had survived the other person. Property owned jointly by both decedents is distributed equally. Insurance proceeds are payable as if the insured survived the beneficiary when they both die at the same time.

When people die owning assets, their estates must be probated. Heirs are notified, and an executor or administrator is appointed by the probate court.

**31.3**   Advance directives are written statements in which people give instructions for their future medical care if they become unable to direct their care themselves. The most common type of advance directive is the living will, which is a written expression of a person's wishes to be allowed to die a natural death and not kept alive by heroic or artificial methods. Another vehicle that is used for this purpose is the health care proxy—a written statement authorizing an agent to make medical treatment decisions for another in the event of incapacity.

**31.4**   Trusts are used, among other reasons, to save taxes, provide for the needs of young children, and prevent money from being squandered easily. They may be created to take effect while a person is alive or after a person dies. When a trust is established, title is split between the trustee, who holds legal title, and the beneficiary, who holds equitable or beneficial title. The trustee manages the trust fund for the beneficiary.

## Key Terms

administrator, 688

administratrix, 688

advance directives, 689

bequest, 680

bond, 688

codicil, 685

conveyance in trust, 693

declaration of trust, 693

devise, 680

devisees, 680

durable power of attorney, 680

elective share, 684

executor, 688

executrix, 688

exempt property, 684

family allowance, 684

fiduciary, 688

forced share, 684

gericide, 691

health care proxy, 689

heir, 680

homestead exemption, 684

intestate, 686

intestate succession, 686

issue, 686

last will and testament, 680

legatees, 680

living trust, 693

living will, 689

next of kin, 687

personal representatives, 688

probate, 679

probated, 688

sureties, 688

testamentary trust, 693

testate, 680

testator, 680

testatrix, 680

trust, 692

trustee, 692

widow's allowance, 684

will, 680

## Questions for Review and Discussion

1. What are the sources of probate law and why is it relevant to business entities?

2. What are the formal requirements for executing a will?

3. When does a person who makes a will have the capacity to do so?
4. What are the protections given to the spouse and the children of a testator?
5. What are the different methods of revoking or changing a will?
6. What are the three grounds for contesting a will?

7. Who inherits the property of someone who dies without a will?
8. What are the steps to be taken by an executor or administrator in settling an estate?
9. What are the types and purposes of advance directives?
10. What are the various types of trusts and when might they be used?

## Cases for Analysis

1. Miguel Ruiz, who had a wife and two small children, did not have a will. A friend told Miguel that he should have a will because if he died without one, everything he owned would go to the state. Was the friend correct? Explain.

2. Ling Lee, who had two children, made a will leaving $1 to her husband, Seung, and the balance in equal shares to her two children. When Ling died, her husband, Seung, claimed that he was legally entitled to more than $1. Do you agree with Seung? Explain.

3. D.W. Elmer, a hospital patient, was seriously ill and unable to write his name. He executed his will, however, by making a belabored *X* on the paper in the presence of witnesses. Can a signature on a will made by an *X* be valid? Explain. *In re Estate of Elmer,* 210 N.W.2d 815 (ND).

4. James and Wanda Barns, husband and wife, were killed in a head-on automobile collision. It was impossible to determine who died first, and neither one had a will. The couple owned the following items as joint tenants: the house in which they resided and its furnishings, a savings account, and a checking account. James owned a car and some Lucent stock separately in his name. Wanda owned a car and a certificate of deposit separately in her name. James was survived by two children of another marriage; Wanda was survived by one child of another marriage. Who will inherit their property?

5. Julia Dejmal executed her will while a patient in St. Joseph's Hospital. The will was witnessed by Lucille and Catherine Pechacek. Catherine was 19 years old and employed as an assistant X-ray technician at the hospital. The age of majority at the time in that state was 21. It was contended that the will was not valid because one of the witnesses to it was a minor. Do you agree with the contention?

Why or why not? *Matter of Estate of Dejmal,* 289 N.W.2d 813 (WI).

6. Lazer, a wealthy 17-year-old, learned that he was suffering from AIDS. He wrote a will leaving everything he owned to a friend he had met in school. Two years later, when Lazer died, his parents claimed that the will was not valid. Do you agree with Lazer's parents? Explain.

7. Santiago, a widower, made a will leaving $1 to his son, Carlos, and the balance in equal shares to his other children, Benito and Angelita. The estate, after deducting debts, taxes, and expenses, amounted to $90,000. When Santiago died, Carlos claimed that he was legally entitled to $30,000 from his father's estate. Was Carlos correct? Why or why not?

8. Evidence was introduced in court to show that, at the time she executed her will, Blanch Robinson suffered from schizophrenia. She had delusions about having had a love affair with Nelson Eddy and was suspicious, mistrustful, and perhaps deluded about her friends and acquaintances. Dixon, who had been left out of the will, contended that Robinson lacked the mental capacity to make a will. Do you agree with Dixon? Explain. *Dixon v. Fillmore Cemetery,* 608 S.W.2d 84 (MO).

9. Walsh, as settlor, executed a declaration of trust, naming himself as trustee and giving himself the income from the trust during his lifetime. After his death, the income was to be paid to his second wife for her life, and upon her death, to his two children, Edward and Margot. Upon their deaths, the income was to be paid to the children of Edward and Margot, after which it terminated. The trust expressly provided that the settlor had not made any provisions for his third child, Patricia, because "previous provisions had been made in her behalf." After executing the instrument, Walsh

transferred to the trust the family residence, three farms, and a checking account. Patricia argued that the trust was testamentary and therefore invalid because it failed to comply with the statute of wills. Was this a testamentary or an *inter vivos* trust? Explain. *First Nat'l Bank v. Hampson,* 410 N.E.2d 1109 (IL).

10. Whitman Winsor's will read in part: "I give, devise, and bequeath all my property, real and personal, to my daughter Lucy T. Winsor. . . . I deem it only right and just that my said daughter Lucy T. Winsor shall have all my property . . . because she has lived with me and cared for me for many years, and it is my will that all shall be hers." Winsor had another daughter, Caroline, who was not provided for in the will. Is Caroline entitled to an intestate share of her father's estate? Why or why not? *Hauptman v. Conant,* 400 N.E.2d 272 (MA).

## quick quiz Answers

| 31-1 | 31-2 | 31-3 | 31-4 |
|------|------|------|------|
| 1. F | 1. F | 1. F | 1. F |
| 2. F | 2. F | 2. F | 2. F |
| 3. F | 3. T | 3. T | 3. F |

# Part 8 Case Study

**Estate of Saueressig v. Goff**
Supreme Court of California
136 P3rd 201 (CA)

## Summary

Timothy Saueressig typed his will, which left his property to his friends, Scott Smith, Harry Ernst, and Cliff Thomas, and named Smith as his executor. Saueressig had no brothers or sisters, and his parents were deceased. He never married and had no children. To his beneficiaries' knowledge, he had "no known next of kin."

Saueressig took the will to his friends Joongok Shin and her husband Theodore Boody at the Mail Boxes Etc. franchise that Shin owned to have Shin notarize his will. Saueressig explained to them that he had drafted his will to eliminate one of the beneficiaries under a previous will. Boody watched as Saueressig signed the will, and Shin notarized his signature.

The lower court disallowed the will, finding that it did not qualify as a holographic will because its material terms were typed, and it did not qualify as a formal will because it was signed by only one witness, the notary Shin, rather than two witnesses as required by the Probate Code.

One week later, the Court of Appeals decided a different case (*Estate of Eugene*, 104 Cal.App.4th 907) in which it held that a witness may sign the will after the death of the testator. In light of this new authority, Saueressig's will was resubmitted to probate with a declaration from Boody that both he and Shin had watched Saueressig sign the will and that he was prepared to sign the will as the necessary second witness. The lower court again disallowed the will, but the Court of Appeals reversed, stating: "We find nothing in the language of the statute to preclude an otherwise qualified witness from signing a will after the death of the testator." This case is an appeal from that decision.

## The Court's Opinion

Corrigan, J.

A will that meets statutory requirements is effective upon the testator's death. Probate Code section 6110 requires a will be signed by two witnesses. The question here is whether the signature of a witness affixed after the testator's death satisfies the statute. We conclude that such postdeath subscription is not permitted, and reverse the contrary Court of Appeal judgment.

Before 1985, a formal will required attestation by two witnesses in the presence of the testator. The required presence of the testator foreclosed any argument that a witness's signature affixed after the testator's death would satisfy the statute.

That year the Legislature substantially revised the Probate Code [to read] a will "shall be witnessed by being signed by at least two persons each of whom (1) being present at the same time, witnessed either the signing of the will or the testator's acknowledgment of the signature or of the will and (2) understand that the instrument they sign is the testator's will."

The issue here is the scope of the legislative intent in eliminating the requirement that the witnesses sign the will in the testator's presence. Plainly, [the statute] contains no express temporal limitation on when the witnesses must sign the will in order for the document to be valid. Thus, it is ambiguous as to whether it permits postdeath attestation.

A number of states have construed statutes similar to [this] as prohibiting postdeath attestation. In *re Estate of Flicker* (1983) 215 Neb. 495 [339 N.W.2d 914], construed Nebraska's statute "to require that the witnesses to a will must sign it before the testator's death. A line must be drawn, and we believe that it is unreasonable to follow the alternative of permitting witnesses to sign a will at any time after the testator's death and prior to the 3-year statute of limitations for probate or testacy proceedings. . . . As a practical matter, we can think of no good reason for a delay in signing by witnesses until after the testator's death. Permitting witnesses to sign a will after the death of a testator would erode the efficacy of the witnessing requirement as a safeguard against fraud or mistake. We must bear in mind that we are dealing with an instrument allegedly signed or acknowledged by a man who is now dead. He is not present to confirm or reject it. Requiring completion of formalities of execution prior to death is likely to minimize miscarriages of justice." Other states have made similar observations. "[I]f the will speaks as of the date of the testator's death, it follows that the document should be complete at that time. Consequently, we adopt the bright line rule that witnesses' signatures should be affixed to the document at least by the time it becomes operative, the death of the testator." (*Matter of Estate of Royal* (Colo. 1992) 826 P.2d 1236; *Matter of Estate of Mikeska* (1985) 362 N.W.2d 906; *Rogers v. Rogers* (1984) 691 P.2d 114)

We find *Crook,* 95 Cal.App.4th 1194, and the cases from other states following a similar rule, to be persuasive. Such an interpretation is consistent with the critical principle that a will is operative following the death of the testator. It is not effective a week or a year later, or whenever purported witnesses manage to comply with the statutory requirement. While the dissent superficially acknowledges this rule, it nonetheless maintains that postdeath attestation is permitted.

The dissent relies on the fact that the Uniform Probate Code, through a comment regarding the actual statutory language, allows postdeath attestation. However, we are governed by section 6110(c) of [our statute], not the Uniform Probate Code.

In addition, while the Legislature did not expressly address the question of whether section 6110(c) permitted postdeath attestation, comments in the legislative history regarding a related area are instructive. As originally introduced, section 6110(c) required "at least two persons" be "present at the same time" to witness "either the signing of the will or the testator's acknowledgement of the signature or of the will." The

section was amended to delete the requirement that the witnesses be "present at the same time."

Our conclusion regarding the legislative intent is consistent with sound public policy. As the Cal. Law Commission observed, "The formalities for execution of an attested will are to ensure that the testator intended the instrument to be a will, to minimize the opportunity for fraudulent alteration of the will or substitution of another instrument for it, and to provide witnesses who can testify that the testator appeared to be of sound mind and free from duress at the time the testator signed or acknowledged the will." The opportunity for fraud is obviously greater once the testator is dead. The lack of any requirement that the testator be living when the witness signs the will would deprive the testator of the chance to dispute the attestation and the consequent validity of the will. Only if he is still alive can the testator say, "This will is not mine," or "I did not ask this person to witness my will." Interpreting section 6110(c) to allow postdeath attestation would, for example, permit a witness to validate a will that the deceased testator executed, but deliberately did not have signed because of changed intent.

. . . A rule allowing postdeath attestation would essentially substitute oral testimony for the Legislature's requirement of a written signature. It would encourage will contests and put witnesses, not the testator, in control of the disposition of an estate. As one court observed decades ago, if witnesses could sign after the testator's death, " '[t]he final disposition of the estate would thereby be made to depend, not solely upon the intention of the testator, but upon the will or caprice of one who had been requested to perform the very simple act of becoming a witness. The legislature never intended to give to subscribing witnesses such power. . . . A will must be a valid, perfect instrument at the time of the death of the testator. It takes effect at the instant testator dies. If invalid then, life cannot be given to it by the act of a third party.' "

. . . The dissent expresses the concern that by concluding postdeath attestation is not permitted by the statute, we are "supplying language the Legislature omitted." Similarly, the dissent states, "The majority apparently concludes that the Legislature must have made a mistake in removing the requirement that a witness sign a will in the presence of the testator without inserting a requirement that the witness sign the will before the testator's death."

In fact, the opposite is true. Section 6110(c) requires that the will "be witnessed by being signed by at least two persons." If we were to conclude that postdeath attestation is available, we would be adding the language "before or after the testator's death" to the current statutory requirement. We agree that it is not for us to draft statutes in the Legislature's stead. Rather, the task here is to discern what the Legislature meant by the language it has chosen. The Legislature may at some point conclude that postdeath attestation offers sufficient safeguards against fraud to allow it. That is its prerogative. However, in the absence of any evidence the Legislature has added this option to the Probate Code, it is not up to this court to do so. Given the history and context of section 6110(c), the most reasonable interpretation of the statutory language is that postdeath attestation is not an act the Legislature has authorized.

The Court of Appeal's judgment is reversed. The matter is remanded to that court with instructions to direct the trial court to reinstate its previous order denying probate of Saueressig's will.

George, C.J., Kennard, J., Baxter, J., and Chin, J., concurred.

# Dissenting Opinion

Moreno, J.

I agree with the Court of Appeal. If Boody is permitted to sign the will as the second witness, which he is prepared to do, the requirements of section 6110, subdivision (c) will be satisfied. The statute requires that the will be signed by two persons who were present at the same time to witness the signing or acknowledgment of the will, but the statute places no restrictions on when the witnesses must sign the will. Boody and Shin were "present at the same time" and "witnessed . . . the signing of the will." Nothing in the statute requires that Boody must have signed the will before Saueressig died.

In interpreting a statute, we are guided first and foremost by its language. "We begin by examining the statutory language, giving the words their usual and ordinary meaning." [citation omitted] "If the plain, commonsense meaning of a statute's words is unambiguous, the plain meaning controls." Nothing in the language of section 6110, subdivision (c) states or even suggests that there is a limit upon when the witnesses may sign the will.

. . . I fail to see how the circumstance that the statute does not limit when a witness may sign a will renders the statute ambiguous with respect to postdeath attestation. But even if we assume for purposes of argument that section 6110, subdivision (c) is ambiguous, the majority's review of the legislative history of the statute does not support its conclusion that the Legislature meant to require witnesses to sign a will before the testator dies.

The majority concludes that "nothing in the language or legislative history of section 6110 indicates that by modifying the execution requirements, the Legislature intended to permit postdeath attestation." I disagree. The Legislature's repeal of the only provision in the former statute that required, as a practical matter, that the witnesses sign the will while the testator was alive is a strong indication that the Legislature intended to permit a witness who was present when the testator signed the will to sign the will at any time, even after the testator has died. This conclusion is supported by the fact that section 6110, subdivision (c) was patterned in large part upon the Uniform Probate Code, which since has been interpreted to permit a witness to sign a will after the death of the testator.

In 1990, the Uniform Probate Code was amended to provide that a witness to a will must sign the will "within a reasonable time" after witnessing the signing or acknowledgement of the will. The comment to the amended provision states: "The witnesses must . . . sign within a reasonable time after having witnessed the signing or acknowledgment. There is, however, no requirement that the witnesses sign before the testator's death; in a given case, the reasonable-time requirement could be satisfied even if the witnesses sign after the testator's death."

The Arizona Court of Appeals relied upon the above quoted comment in *In re Estate of Jung* 109 P.3d 97, to hold that an Arizona statute that codified this provision of the Uniform Probate Code did not require that a witness sign the will prior to the death of the testator, noting that the statute required only that the witness sign the will "within a reasonable time" and adding: "The language of the statute does not limit that reasonable time to a time before the decedent's death and the comment to the [Uniform Probate Code] provision on which it is based expressly notes that a witness signing after the testator's death is not prohibited."

The majority's conclusion that this court should read into section 6110, subdivision (c) an unstated requirement that the witnesses must sign the will while the testator is alive also is based upon the fact that "a will is operative following the death of the testator."

But another of our sister states reached the opposite conclusion based upon reasoning that I find more convincing. *In Matter of Estate of Peters* (1987) 107 N.J. 263 [526 A.2d 1005], the testator signed his will in the presence of several witnesses, including two persons who had come for the express purpose of witnessing the signing of the will, but the witnesses inadvertently failed to sign the will. The testator died 15 months later. Eighteen months after the testator died, the trial court ruled that the witnesses who were present when the testator signed the will could sign the will at that time, because the governing statute, like section 6110,

# Chapter 32   Professional Liability

## THE OPENING CASE   Unconstitutional or Unethical: *State of Florida, et al. v. U.S. Department of Health and Human Services*

Almost immediately after the Patient Protection and Affordable Care Act became law, the attorney general of Florida, joined by AGs from 12 other states, filed a lawsuit asking the courts to declare the act unconstitutional. In essence, the AGs claimed that the law was an unconstitutional extension of federal power that violated the Commerce Clause, the Tenth Amendment, and Article I, Sections 2 and 9 of the Constitution. Probably the most effective argument said that penalizing someone for inactivity (not having health insurance) could not be used to support a congressional invasion of the states. This might have been the end of it, had it not been for the fact some experts began to suspect the AGs had no legal justification for bringing the lawsuit in the first place. In fact, some experts even argued that the AGs should be made to pay for the cost of the lawsuit out of their own pockets and perhaps even be disbarred because they had violated Rule 11 of the Federal Rules of Civil Procedure. Rule 11 demands that an attorney certify that, in any lawsuit filed in federal court, the "claims, defenses, and other legal contentions are warranted by existing

law." The claims brought in this case were not only unwarranted but also patently false, or so the argument goes. For one thing the AGs had grossly misstated the law and had no evidence to support their factual contentions. The new law would not eliminate Medicare in noncomplying states, as the AGs contend; it would not require states to create an agency to help insurance consumers as the AGs said, and it would not impose a financial burden on the states, as the AGs argued, but would, instead, result in a huge savings for some states due to new federal money flowing into those states. Moreover, and perhaps more to the point, the very filing of the lawsuit in the first place was an illegal exercise of state power since, as long ago as 1923, the Supreme Court ruled in *Massachusetts v. Mellon,* 262 U.S. 447, that the states have no standing to attack federal statutes on constitutional grounds. The consequences of this lawsuit go beyond the declaratory action requested by the AGs. It will cost a fortune in the taxpayers' money to argue the case, it can delay the law's implementation, and it could eliminate many needed programs that would disappear along with any truly unconstitutional parts (if there really are any). [See *State of Florida, et al. v. U.S. Department of Health and Human Services,* 3:10-CV-91 RV/EMT; and Timothy Stoltzfus Jost, "Sanction the 18 State AGs," *The National Law Journal* (April 12, 2010).]

**Opening Case Questions**

1. Should the state AGs in this case be held liable for the cost of the lawsuit based on their alleged violation of Rule 11? Should they face disbarment? Is the suit unethical? Explain.

2. Should the states be given standing to attack federal statutes on constitutional grounds? Explain.

3. Should it be possible for a party to attack one part of a law as unconstitutional without attacking all parts of that same law? Explain.

4. Should a judge be sanctioned for allowing a lawsuit that violates Rule 11 and a Supreme Court precedent? Why or why not?

5. Who will ultimately end up paying for this lawsuit and is that a fair and just outcome no matter what the status of the law itself? Explain.

 Learning Objectives

1. Distinguish between a certified public accountant and a public accountant.
2. Differentiate between generally accepted accounting principles and generally accepted auditing standards.
3. Identify the types of auditing opinions that can be issued by auditors.
4. Indicate the duties that accountants owe to their clients.
5. Outline the registration requirements imposed on architects by the state.
6. Identify the duties that an architect owes to his or her clients.
7. Determine the duties that an attorney owes to his or her clients.
8. State the standard of care used to judge health care professionals.
9. Contrast the locality rule with the national standard in determining a health care provider's liability.
10. Explain the circumstances in which hospitals can be held liable for the torts of independent contractor physicians.

# 32-1 The Liability of Accountants

As we've seen in the commercial world, the legal system and the economic culture interact with each other in such a way that they become, at times, one single system, the judicial–economic system. In the last chapter, we also examined how the judicial–economic system acts as another aspect of the balancing process within the law. Now we turn our attention to one of the key players in the judicial–economic system, the accountant.

## The Regulation of Accounting and Auditing

Accountants, like all professionals, must meet certain basic standards that are defined by the nature of their profession. A **professional** is a person who can perform a highly specialized task because of his or her special abilities, education, experience, and knowledge. Often the term professional is reserved for those individuals who perform a service for the public good. An **accountant** is a professional who can plan, direct, and evaluate a client's financial affairs. Although many accountants are charged with keeping a client's financial records, their responsibilities often go far beyond such routine tasks. Moreover, the nature of accounting means that an accountant's activities may have an impact on investors who exist outside the accountant's inner circle of clients. For these reasons, among others, accountants are regulated by the government. The federal government's power to regulate business, in general, and accounting, in particular, emerges from the Commerce Clause of the Constitution. The regulation of accounting by the state is part of the state's police power. The state's police power permits the state to regulate various activities to promote the general health, safety, welfare, and morals of the people.

## Accountant Registration

The regulation of accounting is part of the state's police power. There are many different types of accountants. Some accountants work only for one employer. British Petroleum, for example, employs hundreds of accountants to chart the financial fortunes of the corporation. Other accountants hire themselves out to work for a wide variety of different clients. Regardless of where they work, however, accountants generally belong to one of two categories: certified public accountants or public accountants.

**Certified public accountants (CPAs)** have met certain age, character, education, experience, and testing requirements. These requirements are generally established by the state. For example, the state government may require CPAs to be at least 18 years of age and of good moral character. The state may also require a bachelor's degree, two or more years of experience, and a passing score on a written examination that covers accounting, auditing, and other related subject areas. **Public accountants (PAs)** are accountants who work for a variety of clients but are not certified. Frequently, states will not allow individuals to call themselves public accountants unless they have met certain requirements that are not as strict as the requirements for CPAs. State registration requirements are designed to shield citizens against people who practice accounting without the education or experience necessary to do a competent job. The state cannot, however, prevent someone from practicing accounting as a profession. The state can only stop such individuals from calling themselves CPAs, PAs, or any other title that might mislead a client into thinking the nonregistered accountant is registered.

## Accounting and Auditing

Accountants perform a number of functions for their clients. They may balance accounts, reconcile bank records with account books, handle the payroll, fill out income tax returns, and handle other tax matters. Another important job that falls to the accountant is the task of auditing.

**Did You Know?**

Because there is a tendency among accountants to settle cases out of court, many lawsuits against them never make it to trial. A lawsuit against the mega-accounting firm of Ernst & Young, for instance, was settled in the 1990s for $400 million.

**Auditing** An **audit** is an examination of the financial records of an organization to determine whether those records are a fair representation of the actual financial health of the institution. To be effective, an audit is usually conducted by an outside, independent auditor. An **auditor** is an accountant who conducts an audit. The dilemma that auditors face is that they are responsible at two levels of accountability. Traditionally, auditors are hired by and work for the organization that is being audited. This is the first level of accountability. At the second level of accountability, auditors are responsible to the investors, lenders, shareholders, and others who rely on the financial statements made by those auditors. Ideally, auditors ought to be loyal to both groups of individuals. Realistically, auditors do not always overlook the fact that the organization is the one that hired them and that writes out their paycheck. As a result, there is a tendency, probably unconscious in most cases, to help the organization rather than the outside investors.

**Accounting Principles** An independent group known as the Financial Accounting Standards Board (FASB) has established generally accepted accounting principles (GAAP). The rules established by the FASB are followed by the American Institute of Certified Public Accountants (AICPA). The rules outline the procedures that accountants must use in accumulating financial data and preparing financial statements. In general, the procedures facilitate the preparation of reports that are useful, understandable, reliable, verifiable, and comparable.

## Auditing Standards

The Auditing Standards Board of the AICPA has set up **generally accepted auditing standards (GAAS)**. These auditing standards measure the quality of the performance of auditing procedures. In short, the auditing standards explain how an auditor can determine whether proper accounting procedures have been used. There are ten auditing standards. Three of them relate to the auditors, three relate to their work in the field, and four relate to the opinions that they issue.

## Types of Opinion

An auditor's opinions may be unqualified or qualified. When auditors conclude that the financial records of the company are an accurate reflection of the company's financial status, they will issue an **unqualified opinion**. When auditors issue a **qualified opinion**, they are saying that the books represent the company's financial health as of a given date. However, auditors may qualify the opinion in one of two ways. One type of qualified opinion is the "subject to" opinion. In this case, auditors state that the books represent the company's financial health subject to some uncertainty, such as a pending lawsuit, which may affect the company in the future. The second type of qualified opinion is an "except for" opinion. Such an opinion indicates that the financial statements are an accurate reflection of the company's financial health except for some minor deviation from GAAP, not serious enough to warrant an adverse opinion. Auditors may also issue adverse opinions and disclaimers. An **adverse opinion** is rendered when the deviations from GAAP are so serious that an unqualified opinion is impossible and a qualified opinion is not justified. An adverse opinion would be rendered in the following cases:

- The financial statements do not fairly present the financial health of the organization.
- Generally accepted accounting principles are consistently ignored.
- Financial information has not been adequately disclosed.
- There are major uncertainties that could have a serious impact on the organization, and the auditor disagrees with management's presentation of those uncertainties.

A **disclaimer** declares that the auditor has decided not to give any opinion on the company's financial records. This situation generally occurs because the auditor has not had enough time to examine the books properly or was denied access to crucial records. An auditor might also issue a disclaimer if the books indicate that the organization exercised no control over the accounting process.

## Ethical Rules of Accountants

The AICPA has also established a **Code of Professional Ethics**, which outlines rules that govern the ethical conduct of accountants. These rules are frequently used by the courts to determine whether an accountant has breached a duty to the client in nontechnical matters not covered by GAAP and GAAS. For example, the AICPA's code has established that accountants owe their clients a duty of confidentiality even after the relationship has terminated. In this regard, an accountant cannot reveal information about a client's business to anyone outside of the accountant–client relationship unless authorized to do so by the client.

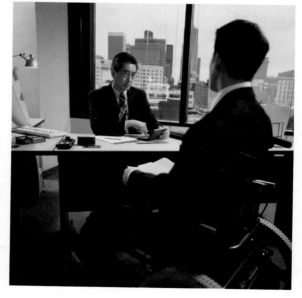

Accountants have a fiduciary duty with their clients and must adhere to the AICPA Code of Professional Ethics as well as GAAP and GAAS standards for the profession.

Although this privilege does not extend to a court's request for information, it does cover most other situations. The ethical code also encompasses contingent fees, the independence of the auditor, promotional practices, operational practices, and quality reviews by peers.

## The Sarbanes-Oxley Act

In response to some of the difficulties that can be traced to the dual identity that auditors must assume, Congress enacted the **Sarbanes-Oxley Act**. Although the Sarbanes-Oxley Act has many targets, one of the most crucial is to restore the confidence of the investment community. A key feature of the act is the creation of the **Public Company Accounting Oversight Board (PCAOB)**. This new regulatory agency is charged with the task of making certain that correct, unbiased, and comprehensive data find their way to potential investors, so that they can make informed decisions about investment opportunities. To accomplish this task, Congress gave the board responsibility for the supervision of public accounting firms. With this power came the ability to set up practical instructions for auditing procedures and philosophical canons for the ethical values that such firms must follow. To give the new federal board proper authority, the act requires the registration of all public accounting firms that are involved in auditing publicly traded corporations. The board has the authority to inspect those companies and their procedures on a regularly established schedule. The board consists of five members, only two of whom are permitted to be certified public accountants. The hope is that this approach will keep the agency objective and unbiased as it evaluates both the accounting firms and the procedures by which they operate.

The Sarbanes-Oxley Act also enacted several additional features. For example, the act specifically prohibits conflicts of interest that might arise when former auditors are hired by a company, if that company is still being audited by the same firm that once employed the former auditor. The prohibition lasts for one year and covers only the uppermost management positions of the audited company. Sarbanes-Oxley also requires that corporate audit committees receive timely and comprehensive reports from the accounting firm that is auditing the company. Alternative approaches to the way that financial data are packaged must be included in these regular reporting sessions. Under the provisions of the act, Congress has probed the mergers that have occurred among various major accounting firms. The aim such a probe would be to find out what led to the mergers, what fallout will result from the new configuration, and what ways exist to improve the competitive atmosphere in the accounting profession.

## Conflicting Jurisdictional Problems

Although auditors and accountants are regulated by several different authorities, those authorities coexist peacefully as long as they agree with one another. Trouble results, however, when different agencies promote different agendas. This problem is further complicated whenever accountants interact with other professionals. Many of these professionals, notably attorneys, are also regulated by professional authorities, some of which promote duties that conflict with those of the accounting profession. Thus, for example, the FASB might require auditors to perform a task that calls for information that is in the hands of a client's attorney. The AICPA might support the auditor's need to obtain such information from their clients' attorneys, but the American Bar Association (ABA) might direct attorneys to withhold information from auditors to preserve attorney–client privilege or the work product privilege or both. At that point, no matter what happens, someone will violate his or her professional code and someone—the auditor, the attorney, or the client—will have to suffer the consequences.

## EXAMPLE 32-1: The Hazards of Serving Too Many Masters

In the mid-1970s, in the midst of a growing litigation epidemic, the FASB released a decision that required auditors to make sure that they accrued certain losses to income while auditing any client's books, including losses that might result from possible lawsuits. To do this properly, the auditors had to get information from their clients' attorneys. To help auditors accomplish this task, the AICPA announced that auditors were now permitted to ask clients to obtain certain information from their attorneys. In reaction, the ABA declared that attorneys ought to be very careful about providing auditors with too much information, lest they violate the attorney–client or the work product privilege or both. The AICPA responded by assuring the ABA that their auditors would never go so far as to violate either the attorney–client or the work product privilege. Everything might have rested there, had the Public Company Accounting Oversight Board (PCAOB) of Sarbanes-Oxley not gotten into the act. The PCAOB muddied the waters considerably by warning auditors that they would be severely disciplined for not insisting that attorneys provide them with the necessary information, regardless of whatever arguments those attorneys might make. Does this conflict give the auditors a license to demand that attorneys violate the attorney–client privilege and the work product privilege? Certainly the ABA does not think so, but the PCAOB insists that it does. Whatever the ultimate outcome of this dispute might be, it serves to illustrate the problems that arise when too many governmental agencies regulate the same activity. (See Peggy A. Heeg, "Auditors Are Increasingly at Odds with Attorneys," *The National Law Journal,* November 20, 2006, pp. S-1 and S-6–S-7.)

## The Dodd-Frank Act

In Chapters 20 and 29 we learned that Congress attempted to deal with the 21st century financial crisis by passing the Dodd-Frank Act, the purpose of which is to rectify present economic problems and, thus, head off any future crisis. The problems that we discussed in Chapter 20 were related to mortgages. The problems that we looked at in Chapter 29 involved corporations. So far so good. However, mortgage lenders and corporate officers were not the only ones guilty of wrongdoing in the crisis. Accountants and auditors also had a hand in the mess. For that reason, Congress also included provisions in the Dodd-Frank Act for dealing with the problems peculiar to the accounting profession. As noted earlier in the book, the Dodd-Frank Act is a long, complex, and intricate statute covering over 2,000 pages of text. The provisions that we will concentrate on now are those that affect the potential liability of accountants.

**Securities Exchange Commission Jurisdiction** The Securities and Exchange Commission (SEC) has been charged with investigating the information that is given to investors. The goal of the study is to determine if such disclosures actually help investors. The ultimate goal of this program is to develop a new generation of literate investors who actually know what they are doing when they invest their money. (What a novel idea.) The SEC will report to Congress, specifically to the Senate Banking Committee and the House Financial Services Committee. As part of this investigation, the SEC will also look at the possibility of adding a Private Rights Action section to the law, with an explanation of how such a proposal would affect institutional investors, among others.

**Government Accountability Office/Public Company Accounting Oversight Board** The Government Accountability Office (GAO) has been charged with investigating how to regulate financial planners, including especially those planners who perform income tax planning services. Similarly, the Public Company Accounting Oversight Board (PCAOB) has been empowered to develop a plan to regulate and register auditors of nonpublic broker dealers. Accordingly, the PCAOB is also now considering the development of a fresh set of audit standards.

**Consumer Financial Protection Bureau**  Under provisions of the new act, certified public accountants (CPAs) and non-CPA partners are not under the authority of the Consumer Financial Protection Bureau as long as they are performing routine and traditional tasks. However, should such firms extend their operations to include such things as loans made in anticipation of tax refunds, they can be regulated by the CFPB. [See Sukanya Mitra, "What's the Brouhaha Over the Frank-Dodd Act," *American Institute of CPAs* (September 7, 2010), http://www.aicpa.org.]

## Duties Owed by the Accountant to the Client

A client often hires an accountant to take care of all the client's financial affairs. Therefore, the client and the accountant have a contractual arrangement. If an accountant fails to fulfill the terms of the contract, the client could bring a breach of contract suit against the accountant. For this reason, it is very important that the terms of the contract include express duties that outline the task of the accountant and the time limits, if any, within which the tasks must be performed. Naturally, certain implied duties are included in any contract between an accountant and the client. These implied duties arise because the relationship exists. Thus, the accountant's agreement to work for the client implies an agreement to use the appropriate level of skill and due care that would be expected of any similarly situated accountant. An accountant might also be liable to clients under common law for negligence and fraud.

**Negligence/Malpractice**  The client has the right to expect the accountant to do a good job in whatever task has been assigned. From this right arises the accountant's duty of due care. The duty of due care means that the accountant must perform the job with the same skill and competence that a reasonable accounting professional would use in the same situation. Negligence or malpractice occurs whenever an accountant fails to meet his or her duty of due care. Although the term malpractice is usually reserved for health care professionals and attorneys, it could also be applied to any form of professional negligence. How a reasonable accounting professional would handle a given situation, and thus avoid a charge of malpractice, would be determined by reference to GAAS or GAAP.

Whenever accountants ignore the rules established by GAAS and GAAP, they do so at their own risk. It is fairly certain that ignoring or remaining ignorant of these principles and procedures is a one-way ticket to a malpractice suit, and there is little question that in such circumstances, the accountant would be found liable for negligence. Unfortunately, the opposite precept is not always true; that is, just because an accountant follows the GAAS or GAAP guidelines does not automatically lead to his or her vindication in a court of law. It is always possible that an accountant can follow the proper principles and procedures yet still make other errors that lead to liability. Thus, an accountant might follow GAAS, yet file a return after a required deadline, or the accountant might make a calculation error, or send the forms to the wrong agency, and so on.

**Fraud**  Accountants must perform their duties with the best interests of their client in mind. If an accountant *deliberately* misrepresents the client's financial condition or in some way *deliberately* falsifies a statement or an auditing report, that accountant may be liable to the client for fraud. Accountants may also be liable for fraud if they compile a

## A QUESTION OF ETHICS

Samuel Sorrell works as a CPA for the accounting firm of Morris, Miller, and Kierns. He has just completed an audit of the Randall-Cassidy Sports Wear Corporation. The audit revealed that Randall-Cassidy is in serious financial difficulty. Moreover, Sorrell feels obligated to issue an adverse opinion because Randall-Cassidy's financial statements do not fairly reflect the financial status of the corporation, generally accepted accounting principles have not been followed properly, and major uncertainties about the sportswear market could cause a serious slump in corporate sales. Sorrell learns that Thomas Keifer, the CEO of Randall-Cassidy, plans to make a presentation to a group of potential investors. The presentation contains figures that are technically accurate but that will actually mislead the investors as to the true financial state of the corporation. Ethically, what should Sorrell do now? Would your answer change if one of the investors directly asked Sorrell about the company's financial condition? Why or why not?

financial report or conduct an audit recklessly. To make a proper case for fraud, it is not enough for the plaintiff to show that the accountant deliberately or recklessly attempted to falsify records and statements. In addition, the plaintiff must demonstrate that he or she actually relied on the false statements or reports. The extra effort is worth it, however, because if the plaintiff succeeds in proving that he or she was defrauded by the accountant, that plaintiff can ask for and will often be awarded punitive damages.

## The Accountant's Liability to Third Parties

Under common law, an accountant can be held liable to some third parties who are damaged by a negligently prepared financial statement. Accountants are also liable to some third parties if they deliberately make fraudulent statements.

**Negligence/Malpractice** The right to bring suit for a negligently prepared financial statement will always extend to actually named third parties. Most states also extend this right to any limited classes of specifically foreseen third parties. A few states extend the right to bring suit protection to reasonably foreseeable classes of third parties (see Table 32-1).

**Actually Named Third Parties** If an accountant prepares a financial statement with the actual knowledge that the client is going to show the statement to a particular third party, then the accountant is clearly liable to that *known* third party. If, for example, the client tells the accountant that the statement is for Mr. X, then Mr. X can recover if he suffers actual financial loss due to the accountant's negligence.

**Specifically Foreseen Third Parties** Most states have extended this rule even further, holding that accountants are also liable to the limited class of third parties that is specifically foreseen when the financial statement is drawn up. Thus, an accountant who prepares a financial statement knowing that the client intends to show it to investors would be liable to any investor in that same class of specifically foreseen third parties. To recover from the accountant, the investors would have to rely on the statements and suffer financial loss.

**Reasonably Foreseeable Third Parties** Some courts have become very strict in holding accountants liable to third parties. These jurisdictions have adopted a test that depends on whether the plaintiff in the case was foreseeable as a possible recipient of the accountant's report. For instance, if it is reasonable for the accountant to foresee that the financial statement would be shown to bankers, suppliers, and potential investors, then

**Table 32-1** . Accountants' Liability to Third Parties Under Common Law

| Liability Theory | Explanation |
|---|---|
| Actually named third parties | When accountants prepare financial statements knowing that the client will show the statement to a named third party, then those accountants will be liable to that known third party if through their negligence the third party is injured. Only a few states limit recovery to actually named third parties. |
| Specifically foreseen third parties | Accountants may also be liable to certain third parties for negligently prepared financial statements if those third parties are members of a limited class that is specifically foreseen when the financial statement is drawn up. Most states follow this theory. |
| Reasonably foreseeable third parties | Accountants may also be liable for negligently prepared financial statements if those third parties can be reasonably foreseen as recipients of the statements. Only a few states extend recovery this far. |

the accountant is liable to anyone of these reasonably foreseeable classes of individuals. This ruling would be true even if the class were not specifically mentioned when the accountant was hired by the client. This version is the strictest of the three tests that the courts have adopted for determining the extent of an accountant's liability to third parties in negligence cases.

**Fraud** Because fraud involves a deliberate deception, the courts have no difficulty extending protection to a wide class of third parties. Thus, an accountant who prepares a fraudulent financial statement is liable to anyone who can be reasonably foreseen as relying on that statement.

## EXAMPLE 32-2: Foreseeing the Effects of the Specifically Foreseen Rule

Isaac Berryman brought suit against the accounting firm of Dowling, Krueger, and McBride when it failed to detect the poor financial condition of New Design Software, Inc. Berryman was an investor who lost his life savings when New Design collapsed. The accountants argued that Berryman could not sue them because New Design, not Berryman, was their client. Under the named third party test, the accountants would be correct because Berryman was not actually named as a recipient of the financial reports prepared by the accountants. However, under the specifically foreseen rule, the accountants would be wrong because Berryman is a member of a limited class of third parties that was specifically foreseen as a recipient of the information. Significantly, if Berryman could show fraud, it would not matter whether he was actually named as a recipient or simply the member of a specifically foreseen class. If fraud is involved, anyone who can be reasonably foreseen as a recipient of those reports could hold Dowling, Krueger, and McBride liable for any actual loss caused by reliance on those reports.

## An Accountant's Statutory Liability

Accountants may also be sued for violating statutory laws governing their activities. Such suits can arise under the Securities Act of 1933, the Securities Exchange Act of 1934, and various state laws.

**Securities Act of 1933** Under the Securities Act of 1933, the first time a corporation issues stock for sale, it must file a registration statement (see Chapter 28). Such statements are prepared by accountants. The 1933 act allows purchasers who have lost money after buying corporate stock based on misleading or false registration statements to sue the accountants who prepared the statements. To succeed in such a lawsuit, the plaintiff must show that the registration statement included a false or misleading statement about a material matter and that he or she suffered a measurable financial setback as a result of relying on that statement. However, the accountant has a defense in such cases. Usually, if the accountant can show that he or she used due diligence in preparing the report, he or she will escape liability. Due diligence is generally demonstrated by reference to the proper application of GAAS and GAAP standards. However, the accountant will also have to show that he or she committed no additional negligent actions and made no other avoidable mistakes.

**Securities and Exchange Act of 1934** A second federal law, the Securities and Exchange Act of 1934, also contains some provisions that affect accountants. These provisions are designed to prevent the fraudulent filing of various documents with the SEC and the fraudulent manipulation of the securities market. Both acts also contain provisions that impose criminal liability on accountants in some situations.

**State Statutes** In addition to these federal statutes, most states have enacted similar statutes regulating the activities of accounts as they relate to the sale of stock. State statutes that regulate the sale of stock are frequently referred to as blue sky laws because they are set up to stop the sale of securities that are as empty as several feet of blue sky.

---

### quick quiz 32-1

1. An accountant is a professional who can plan, direct, and evaluate a client's financial affairs.   true | false

2. An auditor's report and the accompanying financial statements will always guarantee an institution's financial health.   true | false

3. Whenever certified public accountants ignore the rules established by GAAS and GAAP, they do so with little or no risk, because of their certified status.   true | false

---

# 32-2 The Liability of Architects and Attorneys

In addition to accountants, two other frequently contracted business professionals are architects and attorneys. Both are regulated by the states, and both must follow certain clearly stated duties.

## The Liability of Architects

An architect is a professional who plans the construction or alteration of a variety of structures, from small, single-family dwellings to enormous skyscrapers. Generally, architects do not actually construct the building. However, they may manage the construction according to their detailed plans.

**State Regulation** Under its police power, the state can regulate the conduct of architects. States often establish an agency that makes the rules that architects must follow to be officially recognized as professionals in their field of expertise. The state will usually establish age, character, education, experience, and testing requirements. Often a state will maintain a list of all architects officially registered as having met all of these legal requirements.

**Duties of the Architect** Like any other professional, an architect owes a duty to exercise due care and skill in carrying out professional duties. This standard of care requires the architect to use the same methods, techniques, and procedures that any architect of ordinary skill would use in a similar situation. The standard does not demand that the architect's design be perfect or that the execution of the design be faultless. Architects can make mistakes, as long as those mistakes do not result from a failure to use appropriate skill and good judgment according to accepted professional standards.

**Contractual Liability** Sometimes the final version of a building differs from the original plan at the time the contract was made. If the deviation is actually an error caused by the architect's failure to use due care and skill, the architect may have to reimburse the client for any extra money spent to correct the error. This requirement is known as the **cost of repair rule**. A different rule is followed if the design is so defective that the structure is unusable for its originally intended purpose. In such situations, the court may declare that the architect owes the client the difference between the market value of the building as it stands and the market value of the intended structure.

**Tort Liability** Unlike mistakes made by accountants, errors made by architects may injure people or damage property. If the architect has failed to exercise the appropriate standard of care and if, as a result, property is damaged or people are injured, the architect may have to compensate the victims. Note, however, that the architect's mistake must cause injury or damage.

### EXAMPLE 32-3: The Ironic Puzzle of Causation

Architects Lefkowitz and Rudman were hired to plan the new Convention Center to be located in Las Vegas. Rudman failed to check the stress specs on a balcony on the second level of the convention center's main exhibition floor. Had he made the check, his inspection would have revealed that an error had been made that could cause the balcony to collapse under its own weight. The construction firm of McMahon-Fulton, Inc., ignored the Lefkowitz-Rudman specs and used their own plans. However, the McMahon-Fulton plan contained the same error that the architects' plan had contained. On the night that the convention center opened, the balcony suffered a partial collapse that injured several people. Because the contractor had ignored the Lefkowitz-Rudman plan, the architects were not held liable, despite their error.

## The Liability of Attorneys

Next to the accountant, one of the most sought-after professionals by a businessperson is the attorney. An attorney is a professional because of expert knowledge, ability, and education in finding, understanding, interpreting, and, ultimately, applying the law. Attorneys advise their clients in a variety of different ways, all of which require good faith, loyalty, and the exercise of due care.

**State Regulation of Attorneys** Like accountants and architects, attorneys are regulated by the state's police power. Also like accountants and architects, attorneys are normally required to be of a certain age (usually 18) and of good moral character. They are required to possess a certain educational background and to pass a special examination, demonstrating minimum competency. Unlike architects and accountants, attorneys often do not have any experience requirements, because architects and accountants usually are required to have only a bachelor's degree, whereas attorneys obtain an advanced degree in law. This extra education often takes three to four years beyond the bachelor's degree. The experience requirement of architects and accountants frequently amounts to two years.

## Self-Evident Truths

In his essay, "The Chaotic Indeterminacy of Tort Law: Between Formalism and Nihilism," Denis J. Brion, professor of law at Washington and Lee University School of Law, explains that two very distinct interpretations of the law have existed side by side for a number of years. He calls one of these two theories *formalism* and the other *nihilism*. Brion explains the two theories in the following way:

> In "Legal Formalism: On the Immanent Rationality of Law," Ernest Weinrib offers . . . the idea that the law can be accurately described in terms of . . . its "inner coherence." He argues that the law is altogether distinct from politics and that it can only be understood from within itself. The function of judges is to "make transactions and distributions" in the social world conform to the "latent unity" of the law. The function of legal scholars is to make explicit the internal coherence and intelligibility of the law.
>
> In *The Disorder of Law: A Critique of Legal Theory*, Charles Sampford sets out to criticize the various theories of law that seek to describe it as systematic. His principal thesis is that society itself is without system—his term is the "social melee"—and that the law, as an integral part of society, is correspondingly disordered—the "legal melee." He concludes that, because of this disorder, the impact of legal doctrine on social and individual practices is strongly attenuated.

A third alternative is offered by Lawrence Friedman in his treatise *Law in America*. The law, Friedman says, is not a separate autonomous system. Rather, the law "is, essentially, a product of society; and as society changes, so does its legal system. Feudal societies have feudal legal systems; socialist societies have socialist systems; tribal societies have tribal systems; capitalist societies have capitalist legal systems. How could it be otherwise?"

## Self-Evident Questions

1. Of the three theorists, which one has the more accurate view of the legal system? Explain.
2. Which view supports the idea that the judicial–economic system is a balancing act that aims at creating a flexible and responsive system? Explain.
3. Which view is supported by the evidence in this chapter concerning the regulation of the legal profession? Explain.
4. Of the three theorists, which one reflects your own personal view? Explain.
5. Of the three views, which one best explains the need for laws like Sarbanes-Oxley and Dodd-Frank? Explain.

**Ethical Rules of Attorneys** The American Bar Association has established a set of ethical standards entitled the ABA Model Rules of Professional Conduct. These rules have been officially adopted and implemented in 47 states. Only California, New York, and Maine have rejected the new rules. California and Maine elected to create rules peculiar to their own jurisdictions, while New York prefers to operate under the old Model Code of Professional Responsibility. The new Model Rules of Professional Conduct simplify the old rules by dividing professional responsibility into eight different areas. These areas include the client–lawyer relationship, the lawyer's duty as a counselor, the lawyer's responsibilities as an advocate, the lawyer's obligations to third parties, the responsibilities of lawyers to one another in law firms and in partnerships, the lawyer's duty to perform public service, and the lawyer's responsibilities in relation to the legal profession.

**Ethical Problems in Dodd-Frank**  One the most hotly debated provisions in the Dodd-Frank Act is Subtitle B of Title XI which permits the SEC to develop regulations that will create a "whistleblowing bounty program" analogous to the one used by the IRS. Whistleblowers, or SEC "bounty hunters" as they are sometimes called, must qualify for their "bounty" by providing original evidence of a securities law violation. This is not always easy. Nevertheless, bounty hunters can be a very determined group because successful hunters can earn 10 to 30 percent of a penalty over $1 million. Unfortunately, for attorneys, there are ethical problems associated with bounty hunting. If an in-house counsel discovers evidence of an in-house securities violation, and if the SEC rules demand that bounty hunters circumvent internal remedies, then the attorney has an ethical choice to make. Does the attorney remain loyal to the client and not report the violation or does the attorney help the SEC and the public-at-large by reporting the violation according to "the new whistleblower rule system"?  The answer should be obvious. Client loyalty always comes before any other loyalty. However, the whistleblowing system does place an enormous temptation in the path of the unsuspecting attorney. It will be interesting to see how this all plays out in the future. [See David Ingram, "SEC Weighing How to Award Tipsters," *The National Law Journal* (May 16, 2011), pp. 1 and 4.]

**Negligence/Malpractice**  An attorney has the duty to represent clients with good faith, loyalty, and due care. An attorney who does not fulfill these duties may be liable for malpractice. Usually, however, an attorney is not liable to a third party who is not a client.

**Duties of the Attorney**  When a client hires an attorney, the client has the right to expect the attorney to act in *good faith,* which means that the attorney's duty is to act in the best interests of the client. In the absence of such good faith conduct, the attorney may face a lawsuit brought by the client and disciplinary action brought by the state.

An attorney also has a duty of *loyalty* to protect the client and to make certain that the client receives advice and representation that is free of conflicting interests. Thus, an attorney cannot represent two clients on opposite sides of the same dispute, unless both sides have been completely informed of the dual representation and consent to it. Similarly, an attorney violates the duty of loyalty if he or she takes advantage of a client for personal profit. The duty of loyalty also gives rise to certain privileges that exist between clients and their attorneys. One of the most fundamental privileges is the attorney–client privilege. The **attorney–client privilege** guarantees that information that passes between clients and their attorneys will remain secret. The rationale that supports the attorney–client privilege is the belief that clients must feel free to tell their attorneys everything that is involved in a case so that the attorney can do his or her best as an advocate of that client. The privilege can be waived if a third party unrelated to the client is present during a discussion with the attorney, provided that third party is not a person involved in the case, such as another attorney in the firm, a paralegal, or a legal assistant.

Closely related to attorney-client privilege is the work product privilege. The **work product privilege** protects all notes, recordings, research documents, Q&As, voice mails, faxes, e-mails, computer records, memos, letters, flash drives, disks, DVDs, CDs, and so on that are prepared in anticipation of litigation. So, for instance, if an attorney interviews a client about the facts in a pending lawsuit and takes notes during that interview, those notes are protected by the work product privilege. Or if a client sends an e-mail to his or her attorney after an interview, saying something like, "Oh, by the way, when we talked yesterday, I forgot to tell you this or that about the lawsuit," that e-mail is also protected by the work product privilege. Like the attorney–client privilege, the work product privilege can be waived if the work product is revealed to a third party not related to the client or not involved in the preparation of the client's case. Moreover, the work product privilege is not an absolute privilege. This distinction means that the content of the work product may have to be disclosed if a party who needs the information wrapped up in that work product can convince a judge that he or she has a substantial need for that information and cannot obtain that information some other, more legitimate, less intrusive way.

Like all other professionals, an attorney owes a duty of *due care* to clients. This duty means that in giving legal advice, negotiating claims, litigating suits, making out wills, negotiating divorce settlements, and performing any number of other legal tasks, an attorney must exercise the same skill and care that would be expected of other attorneys in the same situation.

## Steps in a Legal Malpractice Case

For a plaintiff to succeed in a malpractice case against an attorney, that plaintiff must demonstrate the existence of four specifically drawn elements. First, the plaintiff must show that the attorney owed a duty to that plaintiff. Generally, this proof is not a problem, because when the client consults the attorney, a contract is created by which the attorney assumes the duty to represent that client with the appropriate level of care. The question of duty can arise, however, when there is a factual discrepancy about whether the client actually hired the attorney to represent him or her. Thus, the duty clearly arises when the client comes to the attorney's office and asks the attorney to help him or her deal with a legal problem. In contrast, if a student were to ask a law professor a hypothetical question during

---

### THE OPENING CASE *Revisited, Part I*
### Unconstitutional or Unethical: *State of Florida, et al. v. U.S. Department of Health and Human Services,* Round 2

Recall that, in the Opening Case at the beginning of this chapter, the attorney general of Florida, joined by AGs from 12 other states, filed a lawsuit asking the courts to declare the Patient Protection and Affordable Care Act unconstitutional. The AGs argued that the new act is an unconstitutional extension of federal power. Unfortunately for the AGs, many legal experts now believe that the AGs themselves had no legal justification to bring the lawsuit in the first place. Some of these experts have even gone so far as to claim that the AGs should be forced to cover the cost of the suit and perhaps even be disbarred for violating the Federal Rules of Civil Procedure by bringing an unwarranted lawsuit for political reasons. It does appear, however

that, even under the new Model Rules of Professional Conduct, an attorney faces an ethical dilemma in a case like this. The Ohio version of the Model Rules, for instance, demands that an attorney act as an advocate for his or her clients and, at the same time, "advance the administration of justice." When a lawyer is the attorney general of a state, which duty comes first? Is the public-at-large the AG's client? Is the AG's home state the client? None of these questions have clear answers, which is why attorneys often end up in controversies like this one. [See "Preamble: A Lawyers Responsibilities," *Ohio Rules of Professional Conduct* (Columbus: Ohio Bar Liability Insurance Company, 2010), p. 1.]

a class discussion, then no duty has arisen because there is no client-attorney relationship created in such a situation.

Second, the attorney must have breached the duty that is owed to the client. The attorney's duty is measured by his or her compliance with a standard that holds that an attorney must represent a client in a way that demonstrates enthusiasm and dedication to the client's best interests. The attorney cannot, however, file claims or advance arguments that have no realistic chance of succeeding or that are not firmly grounded in acceptable legal principles. The attorney must act as a reasonable professional would in the same circumstances. This standard does not mean that attorneys are not permitted to make mistakes. On the contrary, mistakes are tolerated as an inevitable part of the legal profession, just as a long as they do not result from carelessness, inattention, laziness, or ignorance. Third, the plaintiff must show that the attorney's questionable behavior caused the resulting harm to the plaintiff. Moreover, it is not enough that there is a factual connection between the behavior and the injury. There must also be a legal connection between the two. Such a legal connection requires foreseeability. Fourth, the plaintiff must show that he or she suffered actual harm as a result of the attorney's breach of duty.

Because attorneys are professionals and because the intricacies of the law are often mystifying to the layperson, the law requires that the elements of malpractice must be supported by expert testimony. Expert testimony can only be overlooked when the relationship between the injury suffered by the client and the behavior by the attorney is so obvious that the experience of the plaintiff is within the everyday experience of the jury. As we shall see, a very similar—in fact, an almost identical—standard is used to guide the question of whether expert testimony is needed in the case of malpractice claims that are filed against health care professionals.

### Third-Party Liability

In contrast to accountants and architects, attorneys are rarely held liable to third parties because the attorney's responsibilities are tied closely to the interests of the client. On the other hand, this does not mean that an attorney can be disrespectful, cruel, or vindictive to a third party. In fact, in one instance, the Ohio Version of the Model Rules of Professional Conduct state quite specifically that an attorney cannot, "embarrass, harass, delay, or burden a third person." The rules also stipulate that an attorney cannot with knowledge "make a false statement of material fact or law to a third person." [See "Rule 4.1 Truthfulness in Statements to Others" and "Rule 4.4 Respect for Rights of Third Persons," *Ohio Rules of Professional Conduct* (Columbus: Ohio Bar Liability Insurance Company, 2010), pp. 133 and 139.]

### Court-Driven Protection

As we've seen, attorneys who are negligent can be the target of a civil suit brought by a wronged client. There are other safeguards within the legal system, however, that are designed to make certain that attorneys do not file phony lawsuits, promote unwarranted legal arguments, conduct unnecessary investigations, file unjustifiable motions, or make allegations that lack evidentiary support. The Federal Rules of Civil Procedure, for example, specifically forbid such objectionable conduct and impose severe penalties should that rule be broken. Many states have similar civil rules that are designed to deter unprofessional conduct on the part of unscrupulous attorneys. Penalties can include a payment of money to the court or to the other party. These payments may even include attorneys' fees in appropriate cases.

### Criminal Liability

Attorneys are not immune to criminal liability, especially when they act in collusion with their clients. Fortunately, most of the time, attorneys know what is going on within the attorney-client relationship because they are responsible for most, if not all, of the legal decisions made in that relationship. Sometimes, however, an attorney, especially an in-house attorney, might not know everything about a transaction that he or she is handling for a client. An **in-house attorney** is one who is part of the officer corps of a business and, as an employee of that business, does what he or she is told to do by his or her supervisor. Therefore, the attorney might know very little about the details behind a particular deal. Thus, the attorney might draft a contract between a manufacturer and a retailer that appears legitimate but involves a series of unrecorded kickbacks about which the attorney knows nothing. Or an attorney might transcribe the details of a contract that involves a stock transaction based on insider trading without knowing anything about that insider's involvement in the deal. In the past, prosecuting attorneys were willing to give attorneys the benefit of the doubt. Today, however, such favoritism is fast becoming a thing of the past. In the current climate, prosecutors are less likely to be forgiving when an attorney should have known better about a suspicious contract or should have asked certain crucial questions that remained unspoken.

---

## quick quiz 32-2

1. An architect is a professional who plans the construction or alteration of a variety of structures from single-family dwellings to enormous skyscrapers.    true | false

2. For a plaintiff to fail in a malpractice case against an attorney, that attorney must disprove the existence of all four elements of malpractice.    true | false

3. Because attorneys are professionals and because the intricacies of the law are often mystifying to the layperson, the law requires that the elements of malpractice be supported by expert testimony.    true | false

---

# 32-3 The Liability of Health Care Providers

Health care providers are professionals who possess the specialized knowledge, abilities, education, and experience that make it possible for them to answer some aspect of a patient's health care needs. Some businesspeople must deal with health care providers on a daily basis. Such contact is routine for hospital administrators, risk-management experts, pharmaceutical salespeople, hospital accountants, insurance adjusters, and biomedical equipment salespeople. Even individuals who do not deal regularly with health care providers in the business world may one day have to deal with them as patients. Knowledge of the liability of such professionals may be helpful in these situations.

## The Professional Status of Health Care Providers

It should be obvious that physicians are professionals, because they must possess the specialized knowledge, abilities, education, and experience needed to perform their jobs. However, dentists, podiatrists, chiropractors, nurses, nurse practitioners, nurse technicians, radiologic technologists, respiratory therapists, and laboratory technicians are also considered health care professionals. All these professions are regulated by the state. In addition, most are regulated by independent professional organizations such as the American Society of Clinical Pathologists.

## The Health Care Standard of Care

Unlike accountants, architects, and attorneys, health care professionals frequently must physically touch their patients. This physical touching can involve routine tests and examinations, as well as dangerous and painful procedures. To avoid liability for the intentional tort of battery, health care providers frequently must obtain the patient's written consent. In addition to intentional torts, health care providers might be vulnerable to charges of negligence if they do not follow the appropriate standard of care.

Consent Patients who undergo tests and treatment have the right to know about those procedures and the right to refuse to undergo them if they so desire. These rights impose a duty on the health care professional to seek the patient's consent. Consent takes two forms: general consent and informed consent. Upon entering a hospital, a patient automatically gives general consent for the routine tests and procedures that are needed for diagnosis and treatment. Although such consent is implied in the situation, many hospitals require patients to sign general consent forms (see Figure 32-1).

When a diagnostic test or a procedure will be dangerous or painful, the treating physician must obtain the patient's informed consent. For this type of consent, the physician must tell the patient in advance about the procedure and the risks involved. Informed consent must be in writing on a form that is signed by the patient and witnessed by a third party. Generally, a written consent form is considered valid by the court and precludes any suit based on battery, unless the patient can prove a lack of understanding of the information on the form or a deliberate misrepresentation as to its content.

---

**CONSENT UPON ADMISSION TO HOSPITAL**

Patient _____   Date _____ a.m. _____ p.m. _____

(or _____ for _____ )
knowing that I, or the patient (am) (is) suffering from an illness requiring hospital care do hereby voluntarily consent to such hospital care requiring an operation, diagnostic tests or therapeutic treatment by Dr. _____ , his/her assistant or his/her designee or as necessary according to his/her judgment.

I also recognize that during the course of my operation, tests, or therapy unforeseen conditions may necessitate additional or different procedures and I am aware that inasmuch as the practice of medicine and surgery is not an exact science, there have been no guarantees made to me as the result of treatments or examinations to be performed in this hospital.

I have read the above statements and I certify that I understand them.

_____         _____
Witness                                                    Signature of Patient

---

Figure 32-1   Many hospitals today require patients to sign general consent forms like this one upon admission.

## Negligence

**Negligence** For a patient to succeed in a negligence case against a health care professional, the patient must show that the four elements of negligence exist in the case. First, the patient must demonstrate that the health care provider owed a duty to that patient. Usually, the question of duty is not at issue in such cases. However, the question will arise whenever the relationship between the patient and the health care provider is not clear-cut or obvious. In such cases, the court may be asked to determine whether the health care provider owed a duty to the plaintiff.

Second, after establishing the existence of a duty between the health care provider and the patient, the plaintiff must show that the health care professional breached that duty. The health care professional's duty is measured by his or her compliance with a standard of care. The health care provider must act with the same level of skill, care, and knowledge that any reasonable health care provider would display in a similar situation. Determining how a reasonable health care provider would act in a given situation can be determined in several ways. One way is to refer to the hospital's policy and procedure manual. When professionals follow the standard policies and procedures as written in the manual, they are performing as any reasonable professional would, unless the procedure in the manual can be shown to be out of date, incompetently written, or incomplete in some way.

If a hospital's manual does not address a situation, if the manual is outdated, if the procedure is incompetently written, or if the steps in the procedure are incomplete, the court may judge the performance by going outside the hospital and looking at the manuals or procedures used at other hospitals. Many states today use a rule called the locality rule. The **locality rule** judges a health care provider's behavior on the basis of how other health care professionals in the same community would have acted in the same situation. Thus, rural physicians are compared to other rural physicians in the same rural community, city physicians with other city physicians in the same city, and so on. The rationale behind the locality doctrine is the commonsense notion that it is unfair to judge the professional conduct of a small-town general practitioner (GP) who is involved in a case involving a heart attack victim by comparing him or her to a big city cardiologist involved in a similar case. In such a comparison, the small-town GP will always be judged poorly, because he or she will have neither the educational opportunities nor the up-to-date facilities that are available to the big city cardiologist.

Despite the widespread use of the term "locality rule," there is no single locality doctrine. Instead, there are variations on the same theme. The most rigorous version of the doctrine is the true locality rule. The **true locality rule** requires the court to look at the standard of care used in the exact locality of the physician. This standard makes it very difficult for the plaintiff, who must use an expert witness from the same area as the defendant. Such experts are rarely forthcoming because the fraternity of local physicians is generally a closed group. A second variation on the locality rule is the **similar locality rule**. This rule permits the court to judge the actions of a local physician against those of a physician in a community of comparable size and socioeconomic character. Thus, a physician in New York would be compared to one in Chicago or Los Angeles, a physician in Cleveland with one in Pittsburgh or Buffalo, and a physician in Green Bay, Wisconsin, with one in South Bend, Indiana, or Dayton, Ohio. This rule permits the plaintiff to find an expert in one of those analogous localities an easier task because there are fewer fraternal ties among that class of physicians.

The third version of the locality rule is the **same state locality rule**. This rule, perhaps the least logical of the four variations, ignores the socioeconomic character of the physician's home base and concentrates instead on the geographical limits of a state border. Thus, a plaintiff who finds him- or herself in a state that honors the same state locality rule (there are only three: Arizona, Virginia, and Washington) can call an expert from any region in that state to testify as an expert witness. The final variation of the locality rule is known as the **similar practitioner rule**. This rule actually rests on a double standard that permits GPs to be judged by one criterion and specialists by another. Thus, GPs, who are apparently expected to stay close to home, are judged by other GPs in the same community, whereas specialists, who are expected to be more cosmopolitan and therefore more educated, more up-to-date, and more competent, are judged by a standard that can be applied anywhere in the country.

Those states that no longer use the locality rule have adopted another rule called the national rule or the national standard. These states have recognized that with the advent of continuing education requirements and the presence of mass communication, online continuing education programs, and the like, there is rarely any good reason for a health care professional to be unaware of the development of medical trends on a national, or, at times, even an international basis.

### Causation in a Malpractice Suit

A crucial element in any malpractice case is the issue of causation. In such a case, the plaintiff must prove not only that the defendant's conduct did not conform to acceptable medical practices but also that this failure to follow acceptable procedures was the cause of the plaintiff's injury. Much of the difficulty in supplying this proof arises because the fact finder in a malpractice case must attempt to understand medical evidence that is frequently beyond his or her experience.

### Expert Testimony

Because many of the tasks performed by the health care provider are highly specialized, determining how the professional should act often requires expert testimony. However, expert testimony is not required if the action under examination is within the common knowledge of all people.

## EXAMPLE 32-4: Experts Need Not Apply

Nurse Noel Grady was called away from Kurt Yarborough's room by another nurse. Yarborough was sedated but restless. He was thrashing about and had attempted to leave the bed several times. Despite this state, Grady left him alone, failing to raise the siderails or restrain Yarborough in any way. While Grady was absent, Yarborough tried to get out of bed. He fell and broke his leg. At Grady's negligence trial, the judge ruled that no expert testimony was needed to measure Grady's standard of care. The judge felt that the issue of whether a sedated and restless patient should be left unsupervised and unrestrained was well within the common knowledge of the jurors.

## Medical Records and the Patient's Rights

In recent years, concerns about privacy matters have come to the forefront of the law. In no area of the law is this truer than in health care law. Physicians once effectively guarded the secrecy of their files by arguing that patients were apt to misinterpret or misunderstand notations made in medical jargon or hospital shorthand. These arguments are no longer acceptable. To ensure the patient's right to see his or her records, Congress passed the Health Insurance Portability and Accountability Act (HIPAA). Under HIPAA, Congress has guaranteed that patients have the right to see their medical records and parents have the right to see the medical records of their children. The act also gives both groups the right to obtain duplicates of the records. There are, of course, exceptions to this rule. For instance, records that result from psychotherapy sessions receive a higher level of protection under the act. Patients are permitted to see such records only if the patient has the physician's permission. Even with permission, the patient must look through the records along with the physician. These extra limitations are placed on psychotherapy records because they are seen as somewhat emotional and open to a wide variety of false impressions.

## The Patient Protection and Affordable Care Act

Under provisions included in the federal Patient Protection and Affordable Care Act, the Department of Health and Human Services has developed a set of new regulations on a trial basis to help support physicians, hospitals, clinics, and other health care establishments in the creation of a system of coordinated health care institutions for Medicare patients, known as accountable care

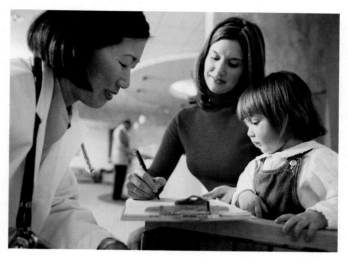

The Health Insurance Portability and Accountability Act (HIPAA) gives patients the right to review their medical records and the records of their children.

organizations (ACOs). Under the new rules, an ACO can consist of a variety of formats including (1) ACO professionals, including physicians and hospitals in group practice arrangements; (2) networks of individual practices of ACO professionals; (3) partnerships or joint ventures between hospitals and ACO professionals; (4) hospitals employing ACO professionals; and (5) other Medicare providers and suppliers as determined by the secretary of health and human services.

The new regulations will measure the quality of an ACO under five criteria: (1) patient and caregiver experience; (2) care coordination; (3) patient safety; (4) preventative health, and (5) the handling of at-risk populations including the frail and elderly. The ACO program is administered by the Center for Medicare and Medicaid Services (CMMS). Under the new rules, an ACO must have a board of governors with a wide-ranging membership including representatives of all the people affected by its operation. Specifically, the rules call for a membership that involves health care providers, suppliers, and Medicare beneficiaries. To be properly certified by the CMMS a new ACO must take responsibility for at least 5,000 beneficiaries for three years.

## THE OPENING CASE *Revisited, Part II*
### Unconstitutional or Unethical: *State of Florida, et al. v. U.S. Department of Health and Human Services,* Round 3

One more time recall that the Opening Case at the beginning of this chapter involved a lawsuit filed by the AG of Florida along with 12 additional state AGs all of whom attacked the constitutionality of the Patient Protection and Affordable Care Act. When the case reached the district court, the judge decided that the act was indeed unconstitutional, at least in part. Unfortunately, the judge also ruled that the unconstitutional portions could not be separated from the constitutional ones. Consequently, should one part of the act be lost, the entire act will be lost, including provisions like the one discussed above. What would then be the fate of an already established and operating accountable care organization? Explain your answer. [See *State of Florida, et al. v. U.S. Department of Health and Human Services,* 3:10-CV-91 RV/EMT; and Timothy Stoltzfus Jost, "Sanction the 18 State AGs," *The National Law Journal* (April 12, 2010).]

# 32-4 Hospital Liability

Hospitals can be held liable for the negligence of a physician, even if that physician is not an employee of the hospital. Hospitals routinely grant physicians, who are not employed by the hospital, the privilege to treat their patients at that hospital. The granting of such **staff privileges** can be troublesome for the hospital if the staff physician becomes the defendant in a malpractice lawsuit, because the patient frequently sues not only the physician but also the hospital. Two legal theories that have been used successfully to add the hospital to the list of defendants in a malpractice lawsuit are ostensible authority and negligent credentialing.

## Ostensible Authority and Hospital Liability

Ostensible authority, also known as agency by estoppel and apparent authority, has been successfully used by plaintiffs to hold the hospital, as well as the physician, liable for malpractice. **Ostensible authority** is created when a hospital presents itself to the public at large as a provider of health care services and in some way leads the patient to believe that a physician with staff privileges is an employee of the hospital. This authority can be shown if the hospital allows the physician to wear a hospital identification tag, use hospital equipment, dispense medication at the hospital, issue orders to hospital employees, and so on. Under such circumstances, the courts have been willing to hold that, because it is reasonable to believe that these representations would lead the patient to the conclusion that the physician is an employee of the hospital, the patient can add the hospital to the malpractice suit as a defendant.

## Negligent Credentialing by Hospital Authorities

**Negligent credentialing** occurs if the hospital has retained a physician that the governing body of the hospital knew or should have known was incompetent. Another form of negligent credentialing occurs if a previously competent physician with staff privileges loses that competence and the hospital governing body knows or should have known about the changed circumstances but takes no remedial action. This form of negligent credentialing is sometimes referred to as **negligent retention**. In either situation, a patient injured by the malpractice of the incompetent physician can also hold the hospital liable.

# Tort Reform and Litigation

In recent years, some states have attempted to lessen the burden placed on hospitals by ostensible authority and negligent credentialing. This movement has been motivated by the belief that such lawsuits frequently pull the hospital into a lawsuit unjustly. To alleviate this injustice, tort reform provisions often place the burden of proof on the plaintiff to prove both ostensible authority and negligent credentialing. For instance, in the area of ostensible authority, some states say that the plaintiff must prove that the hospital held itself out to the public at large as a provider of health care services and that the hospital gave no notice that nonemployee staff physicians, rather than hospital employees, would render services to the patient. Moreover, these statutes also allow the hospital to escape liability by posting notices that inform patients of the independent status of staff physicians. In states that have established such a statutory protection for hospitals, a patient can hold a hospital that posts such notices liable only if the hospital directed the negligent actions that injured the patient. In negligent credentialing, some states have created a rebuttable presumption that says a hospital is presumed to have properly credentialed staff physicians if the hospital is accredited by the Joint Commission of Accreditation of Health Care Organizations. If the hospital can show that it is accredited, the burden of proof shifts to the plaintiff to show that the hospital did not follow the credentialing procedures of the Joint Commission, that the hospital knew or should have known of the physician's incompetence and did nothing to limit the physician's privileges, or that the credentialing process did not apply to this hospital, this physician, or the type of case that formed the basis for the lawsuit.

## quick quiz 32-4

1. A hospital can never be held liable for the torts of a physician   true | false
   unless that physician is an employee of that hospital.

2. Ostensible authority applies only to hospitals in large urban areas.   true | false

3. Negligent credentialing and negligent retention have been   true | false
   outlawed under the Restatement (Second) of Torts.

# Summary

**32.1**   Accountants are business professionals who can plan, direct, and evaluate the complex financial affairs of their clients. The most common types of accountants are certified public accountants and public accountants. Accountants must follow generally accepted accounting principles. Auditors must follow generally accepted auditing standards. They must also follow the Code of Professional Ethics of the AICPA. Accountants may be liable to both their clients and third parties.

**32.2**   Architects and attorneys are considered professionals and are regulated by the state. Architects may find themselves liable to clients and to third

parties, whereas attorneys are generally responsible to their clients alone. Both architects and attorneys must exercise due care and skill in carrying out their professional duties.

**32.3**   The term *health care provider* includes not only physicians but also dentists, chiropractors, podiatrists, nurses, nurse practitioners, nurse technicians, radiologic technologists, respiratory therapists, and laboratory technicians. Like other professionals, health care providers must act with the same skill, care, and level of knowledge that a reasonable health care professional would display in a similar situation.

**32.4**  Hospitals can be held liable for the negligence of a physician, even if that physician is not an employee of the hospital. The granting of staff privileges can be troublesome for the hospital if the staff physician becomes the defendant in a malpractice lawsuit, because the patient can sue both the physician and the hospital. Two legal theories that have been used successfully to add the hospital to the list of defendants in a malpractice lawsuit are ostensible authority and negligent credentialing.

## Key Terms

accountant, 705

adverse opinion, 707

attorney–client privilege, 716

audit, 706

auditor, 706

certified public accountant (CPA), 706

Code of Professional Ethics, 707

cost of repair rule, 714

disclaimer, 707

general consent, 720

generally accepted accounting principles (GAAP), 706

generally accepted auditing standards (GAAS), 707

Health Insurance Portability and Accountability Act (HIPAA), 722

informed consent, 720

in-house attorney, 719

locality rule, 721

malpractice, 710

national rule, 722

national standard, 722

negligence, 710

negligent credentialing, 724

negligent retention, 724

ostensible authority, 724

professional, 705

public accountant (PA), 706

Public Company Accounting Oversight Board (PCAOB), 708

qualified opinion, 707

same state locality rule, 721

Sarbanes-Oxley Act, 708

similar locality rule, 721

similar practitioner rule, 721

staff privileges, 724

true locality rule, 721

unqualified opinion, 707

work product privilege, 716

## Questions for Review and Discussion

1. What is the difference between a certified public accountant and a public accountant?
2. What is the difference between generally accepted accounting principles and generally accepted auditing standards?
3. What are the various types of auditing opinions that can be issued by auditors?
4. What duties do accountants owe to their clients?
5. What are the registration requirements imposed on architects?
6. What are the duties that an architect owes to his or her clients?
7. What are the duties that an attorney owes to his or her clients?
8. What is the standard of care used to judge health care professionals?
9. What is the difference between the locality rule and the national standard in determining a health care provider's liability?
10. What are the circumstances in which hospitals can be held liable for the torts of independent contractor physicians?

## Cases for Analysis

1.  While she was under investigation by a grand jury, Martha Stewart penned an e-mail that explained the circumstances that led to the ImClone scandal. Stewart then dispatched the e-mail to her attorney, and sent a copy to her daughter, Alexis Stewart. The e-mail was inadvertently provided to the government, along with a number of other files that had been delivered in response to a subpoena.

When the e-mail was identified, government attorneys went back to the court and asked the judge to decide whether they could use the e-mail as evidence. Stewart's attorneys argued that the e-mail was under the protection of the attorney–client privilege and the work product privilege. On the other side of that argument, it is clear that the intended recipient of the e-mail was Stewart's daughter, not her attorney. Should the judge uphold the protection granted by the attorney–client privilege and the work product privilege, or should she allow the government to use the e-mail, because Stewart sent it to a third party? Explain. *United States v. Stewart,* 03 Cr. 717 (United States District Court Southern District of New York).

2. Fred Stern and Company applied to the Ultramares Loan Corporation for a credit advance in support of its import business. As was its custom, Ultramares asked Stern for a detailed financial statement that included an audited balance sheet. Stern agreed and supplied Ultramares with a report from its auditors, Touche, Niven, and Company. When Stern went to Touche, Niven, and Company, the import corporation did not reveal to the accounting firm that Ultramares would see the report. The only thing that the importers told the auditors was that the report would be shown to some possible creditors. Touche, Niven, and Company filed an audit report that stated Stern had a net worth of $1 million. Satisfied with the statement, Ultramares loaned the money to Stern. The report turned out to be completely false. Fred Stern and Company was not only worth less than $1 million; it was actually completely worthless. The auditors had filed the erroneous report because Stern had shown them a phony set of books that misrepresented the company's value. The importer, of course, could not hope to pay Ultramares back for the money it had borrowed, so the loan company went after someone who actually had enough money to make up for their loss, and that was the accounting firm of Touche, Niven, and Company. The firm argued that the report had been prepared for Stern, and because it had no knowledge that Ultramares would see the report, it could not be liable to the loan company. Apply each of the standards used to evaluate an accounting firm's liability to third parties and report on the results for each test in this case. *Ultramares Corp. v. Touche,* 255 N.Y. 70, 174 N.E. 441.

3. The Consolidata Services Company (CDS) was established to provide small businesses with payroll services. All CDS clients were required to provide CDS with an advance deposit equal to the amount of one payroll. When CDS got into a cash flow problem, it tapped into some of this deposit money to cover its own debts. Eventually, the accounting firm of Alexander Grant, which had been hired by CDS to advise it on taxes and other financial matters, discovered that the deposit account was $150,000 short. CDS assured Grant that it was devising a plan to cover the missing $150,000. Accordingly, CDS asked Grant not to reveal the deficit. Nevertheless, Grant informed several of its own clients using the CDS payroll services and other nonclients of CDS's problem. Was Alexander Grant correct in revealing the information? What guidelines did the court use to answer this question? Explain. *Wagenheim v. Alexander Grant and Co.,* 482 N.E.2d 955 (OH).

4. Burke, an energy tycoon, hired the accounting firm of Arthur Young and Company to audit several of his operations. The SEC brought an action against Burke for fraud and for failure to meet certain SEC reporting requirements. The SEC also named Arthur Young as a defendant, claiming that the accounting firm should have discovered the fraud. Arthur Young argued that it had followed GAAS when it had audited Burke. The accounting firm concluded that this strict adherence to GAAS immunized it from liability under securities law. The SEC argued that Arthur Young should have done more to discover the fraud than what was required under GAAS. Was the SEC correct? Explain. *Securities and Exchange Commission v. Arthur Young and Company,* 590 F.2d 785 (9th Cir.).

5. Hutchins and O'Neil, as general partners in the Haddon View Investment Co., became limited partners in Car Wash Investments. The general partner in Car Wash was the Minit Man Development Company. Coopers and Lybrand were the accountants who handled the accounting work for both Minit Man and Car Wash. They performed audits and prepared financial statements that allegedly revealed two healthy companies. Nevertheless, both Car Wash and Minit Man went out of business. As a result, Hutchins and O'Neil lost a total of $252,000. They sued Coopers and Lybrand, alleging malpractice, breach of contract, concealment, fraud, and deceit in the accoun-

## THE OPENING CASE  "To be or not to be": *JCVI and Patent Application US2007 0264688*

When members of the J. Craig Venter Institute filed patent #US 2007 0264688 with the U.S. Patent Office, they expected to be met with a flurry of protests. In fact, the tone of the news release sent out by the JCVI PR Department on the day of the filing makes it clear that they anticipated opposition from religious groups, academia, and perhaps even from the Patent Office itself. This opposition was inevitable because patent #US 2007 0264688 was an attempt to patent synthetic life. No, it was not Dr. Frankenstein's creature, or *Star Trek's* Mr. Data, but it was the next best thing. What JCVI had produced was a self-replicating bacterial cell completely under the control of a synthetic genome. The development of the synthetic self-replicating cell proved that such organisms can be planned by a computer, constructed chemically in a laboratory, and then placed in a bacterium from which the original DNA had been removed. The new cell then replicated itself one billion times. The process will make DNA synthesis more economical and more affordable leading to possible breakthroughs in the development of new vaccines, innovative pharmaceuticals, clean water, new food products, innovative pollution filters, and possibly even revolutionary new biofuel derivatives. Not everyone was happy with this development, however. Some religious groups charged Venter with trying to "play

God," while others urged him to slow down and reconsider the implications of his actions. Venter expected this, however, which is why JCVI continues to consult with ethicists, policy makers, and the public at large about the ethical concerns and social consequences of its genetic research. What may have been unexpected was the backlash from other scientists, some of whom accused Venter of trying to corner the market with the patent application. The main objection to the JCVI patent application is that it is too broad. Venter is not attempting to patent the synthetic self-replicating bacterium that his team actually created, but the process of planning, constructing, and creating any synthetic cell imaginable. One critic remarks that what Venter wants is a patent for the wheel so he can claim that he owns the patent rights to aircraft tires, tank treads, and inline skates. Several questions come to mind here, not the least of which is the most basic one of all. Can an inventor patent a living thing? Think about it. [See J. Craig Venter Institute, "First Self-Replicating Synthetic Bacterial Cell Constructed by J. Craig Venter Institute Researchers," *News Release* (May 20, 2010), http://www.jcvi.org; and Boonsi Dickinson, "Will Patents Give Craig Venter a Monopoly Over Synthetic Life?" *Smart Planet* (May 28, 2010), http://www.smartplanet.com].

**Opening Case Questions**

1. What is the purpose of patent law? Explain.

2. Why would the competition oppose JCVI's application for a patent? Explain.

3. What advantages would JCVI have after it obtains a patent for its synthetic cell? Explain. What

disadvantages, if any, would JCVI have after obtaining a patent? Explain.

4. What part of the U.S. Constitution authorizes Congress to enact patent law? Explain.

5. What ethical arguments can you imagine might be used against JCVI's obtaining a patent for its synthetic cell? Explain.

## LO Learning Objectives

1. Explain how the law permits the government to regulate science and technology.
2. Describe the function of the Office of Science and Technology Policy.
3. Outline the role of the National Science Foundation.
4. Define the function of the National Institutes of Health.
5. List the three challenges that face the modern world.
6. Identify the purpose of the Federal Energy Regulatory Commission.
7. Define the role of the Nuclear Regulatory Commission.
8. Describe the functions of the Clean Air Act and the Clean Water Act.
9. Explain how the law protects patents, trade secrets, and copyrights.
10. Describe four main issues that must be considered in developing a science policy.

# 33-1 Regulating Science and Technology

The law involves rules made by the government to promote order, stability, and justice. Science is an academic discipline that studies the natural universe with the goal of understanding the physical laws that guide the operation of the universe. Technology is the process of developing ways to enhance human control of those physical laws with the goal of extending human abilities. Science and technology, then, are involved in developing ways to create order and stability in the universe. For this reason, among others, science, technology, and the law often interact with one another. The point at which these three disciplines intersect is often referred to as **juriscience**. Because, the government actualizes the law, we must look to the sources of governmental power to determine just how much power the law has to control science and technology.

## National, State, and International Authority

The power to regulate science and technology in the United States is shared by the national government and the state governments. There are some functions that only the federal government is empowered to handle, such as granting patents and copyrights. There are also some functions that the two levels of government share, such as establishing departments, supporting education, and funding research programs. The national power emerges from the United States Constitution; the state power emerges from the state's police power. International power depends upon the type of international institution that is charged with oversight responsibilities. Depending upon which level a scientist has entered, he or she may find the road to governmental or international funding easy or difficult.

## National Authority

**National Authority** The Constitution revolves around two fundamental principles: (1) the separation of national powers among three distinct branches of government and (2) a system of checks and balances. The principle of the separation of powers set up the three branches of the national government: the executive branch, the legislative branch, and the judicial branch. The principle of checks and balances allows each branch to share in the power of the other two branches. Congress is the legislative branch and is, therefore, the branch that makes statutory law. Statutory law regulates the social system by telling people what they can and cannot do. For this reason, any legislature has an enormous amount of power that can be used or misused depending on the predilections of the men and women in office. It was such an abuse of power that the Founding Fathers objected to under Parliament. For this reason, the Framers, after experimenting with the Articles of Confederation, made certain that the legislative branch was strictly controlled by the new Constitution. Thus, the powers granted to Congress are enumerated in Article I of the Constitution. That means that they are specifically listed, there. If a power is listed, it belongs to Congress. If it is not listed, Congress has no power in that area. Now this does cause some ambiguity at times. For example, the power to regulate science and technology is not specifically listed in Article I. How then did Congress obtain that power? The answer is found in several areas including the general welfare clause, the commerce clause, and the necessary and proper clause.

*The General Welfare Clause* The fact that Congress is the branch of enumerated powers does not mean that there is nothing in Article I that can be used to discern the existence of some ancillary powers, including ancillary powers that can be used to enhance the power to regulate science and technology. For example, the power over weights and measures, the power to raise an army and a navy, the power to grant patents and copyrights, and the power to take the census have all been used in this way at one time or another. Nevertheless, one of the most useful clauses in this regard has been the general welfare clause. The general welfare clause is found in Article I, Section 8, Clause 1, which reads in part that Congress is empowered to "lay and collect taxes, Duties, Imposts, and Excises, to pay the Debts and provide for the common defense and general welfare of the United States." Under that clause, Congress set up the Department of Agriculture in 1862 and, as part of the operation of that department, used federal money collected by taxes to hire scientists (botanists and chemists in particular) to work in that department. The power was challenged in the courts and, when the case, known as *United States v. Butler,* reached the Supreme Court, it was upheld, thus verifying Congressional authority to regulate science under the general welfare clause

*The Commerce Clause* By far the most powerful clause in Article I is the commerce clause (Article I, Section 8, Clause 3). The commerce clause has been used over the last two centuries to give Congress the power to create a national police force, the FBI; to prevent employment discrimination, The Civil Rights Act of 1964; and to regulate union activity, The Wagner Act. It has also been used to empower Congress to regulate science and technology. The actual text of the commerce clause is deceptively simple and innocuous. It says that Congress has the power "(T)o regulate Commerce with foreign Nations, and among the several States, and with the Indian Tribes." Early in the development of Constitutional law, the courts created a very narrow interpretation of this clause, arguing that Congress could only regulate commercial dealings if they passed between two or more states.

This interpretation, however, did not last long. The growth of the nation and the economic shift from an agrarian to a manufacturing economy demanded that the courts grant Congress more flexibility in handling economic issues. Part of this shift involved a distribution of land under the government's land-granting program. This program demanded that Congress have the power to enforce the allocation of this land. As a result, in a case known as *Gibbons v. Ogden,* the Supreme Court ruled that any commercial operation that touched on commerce among the states could be regulated by the federal government. The implications of this ruling were not immediately clear. However, eventually, lawmakers began to realize that this meant that any commercial activity affecting commerce, even an activity that took place totally within the borders of one state could be controlled by Congress. The outer limits of this activity were met when, in a 1942 case known as *Wickard v. Filburn,* the Supreme Court ruled that a farmer's production of wheat for consumption on his own property had an impact on interstate commerce. The Court concluded that because farmer used only home-grown wheat, he was not out purchasing wheat from other farmers which meant that those other out-of-state farmers were not selling as much wheat as they would absent the in-state farmer's self-dealing. The Court did recognize that the effect of one farmer's self-dealing was minimal at best. That, however, was not the point. The point was that, if everybody did the same thing, the cumulative effect would collapse the interstate wheat market.

## EXAMPLE 33-1: The Outer Limits of Interstate Commerce

Despite the revolutionary, expansive ruling by the Supreme Court in *Wickard v. Filburn,* we may not have yet reached the outer limits of the commerce clause. The outer limit may come in a case known as *State of Florida, et al. v. U.S. Department of Health and Human Services.* The case emerged in the wake of the passage of the Patient Protection and Affordable Care Act. In that case, the Attorney General of Florida, joined by AGs from 12 other states, filed a lawsuit asking the courts to declare the act unconstitutional. In essence, the AGs claimed that the law was an unconstitutional extension of federal power that violated the Commerce Clause, the Tenth Amendment, and Article I, Sections 2 and 9 of the Constitution. Probably the most effective argument said that penalizing someone for inactivity (not having health insurance) could not be used to support a Congressional invasion of the states. Under *Wickard v. Filburn* growing wheat in your own back yard and baking your own bread affected interstate commerce. Under *State of Florida, et al. v. U.S. Department of Health and Human Services,* sitting at your kitchen table doing nothing at all (well, more specifically sitting there and not buying health insurance) may be ruled by the court to affect interstate commerce. That would truly be the outer limits of the Commerce clause. (Note: When this book went to press *State of Florida, et al. v. U.S. Department of Health and Human Services* was still in the courts. Do an Internet search to find out how the Supreme Court ruled.)

*The Necessary and Proper Clause*  Whenever the authors of a bill, or some other legislative act, are not quite sure that they have thought of everything that should be included in a statute or regulation, they will throw in a "kitchen sink" clause. Basically, the kitchen-sink clause is a device that empowers those who will interpret the law in the future to search beyond that actual letter of the law and find its spirit. This is part of the balancing act that is the law. It is also what the Framers intended when they added the necessary and proper clause to Article I of the Constitution. The **necessary and proper clause**, which is found in Article I, Section 8, Clause 18, of the U.S. Constitution, says that Congress has the power "(T)o make all Laws which shall be necessary and proper for carrying into Execution the foregoing Powers, and all other Powers vested by this Constitution in the Government of the United States, or any Department or Officer thereof." Generally, when Congress invokes the necessary and proper clause, it specifically says so in the preamble to the legislative action. Thus, when Congress enacted the War Powers Resolution in 1973, the resolution stated quite specifically that Congress was authorized to do so under the necessary and proper clause.

**State Police Power** There is no need for the state legislature to mimic the convoluted and indirect way that Congress has used to develop its power to regulate science and technology, because a state's power to regulate scientific activities is inherent within its police power. **Police power** is the state's authority to promote public health, safety, welfare, and morals. Police power exists simply because the state exists. Today it is self-evident that most scientific activity can be regulated by the state. The state government and the various subdivisions of the state government play a role in this regulatory process.

**International Power** On the other side of the ledger we find the exercise of power on the international level. While we will discuss international law in detail in the next chapter, it will be helpful to look at it briefly before moving on. In short, there are three types of nongovernmental international organizations (NIOs). First, there are NIOs that are completely dependent upon the nation states that make up their membership. Such NIOs are completely dependent upon their member nations and would be unable to do anything without their support. Basically such international entities are simple aggregates or conglomerates of the membership. An organization such as the G-8, which is made up of the most powerful industrial nations of the world and which has a floating leadership element that changes from year to year is an excellent example of an aggregate NIO. The second type of NIO is a semi-autonomous organization that is initially made up of nation-states but which is actually more than the membership and is, therefore, capable of carrying out actions absent the consent of, and, in fact, sometimes in defiance of, the members. Member nations might opt out of an action of which they disapprove, but the action might continue nevertheless. Still, there might be some actions that the member states or some of the member states might be able to stop, depending on the structure of the organization. The United Nations is probably the best example of this type of semi-autonomous NIO.

The third type of NIO is one that achieves or is initially granted entity status. NIOs with entity status act independently because they are not at the mercy of the member states. Some NIOs are not even formed by members states but perhaps by an independent membership, or by corporations, or by other NIOs. The International Red Cross is a good example of an entity level NIO. Some commentators also take an evolving view of NIOs. Basically, this view says that NIOs are moving targets. They may be originally formed as conglomerates but as they operate, they may evolve into semi-autonomous organizations or even into entities. If in its early history the United States could have been conceived of as an NIO, then we can see how what was originally a loose confederation of independent states, under the Articles of Confederation, gradually evolved into a semi-autonomous organization (before the Civil War the nation was referred to in the plural as in "the United States are…") and eventually became an entity (after the Civil War it becomes singular as in "the United States is…"). The European Union (EU) now appears to be going through a similar evolution. [See Richard W. Mansbach and Kirsten L. Rafferty *Introduction to Global Politics* (London: Routledge, 2008), pp. 403-404.] Finally, there are also some commentators that would add a fourth category to the NIOs–the "trans-nats." Trans-nats, or trans-national organizations, are outlaw, or rogue, organizations such as terrorist groups, drug cartels, slave traders, and pirates. Trans-nats are unsanctioned bodies, such as al Qaeda, whose power comes from a willingness to break international law, and who must, therefore, be taken into consideration when political leaders make strategic moves.

**The United Nations** Despite the fact that the United Nations is a semi-autonomous NIO, it nevertheless wields a great deal of soft power on the international scene. *Soft power,* in contrast to *hard power* which consists mostly of military force and economic influence, is waged at the emotional and psychological level. Soft power is used to persuade people, institutions, and nations that they have the same goals and objectives as the agency or person wielding the power. During the Vietnam Era in the 1960s and 70s, soft power was described as the ability to earn the "hearts and minds" of the people. The United Nations has the ability to win the hearts and minds of many people in the international community. From an organizational perspective, the UN consists of three central governing agencies all located in New York City at its headquarters on the East River: the General Assembly, the Security Council, and the Secretary General.

The General Assembly consists of all UN member-states. Each nation-state is empowered with a single vote on all matters presented to the assembly. The UN Security Council handles any crisis that threatens global peace. The Security Council is made up of 15 members. Five member states hold permanent seats: China, France, Russia, the United Kingdom, and the United States. The General Assembly elects the remaining 10 members for two-year terms. The Secretary General is the chief administrator of the United Nations. He or she heads up the Secretariat, which is the administrative bureaucracy of the UN. The Secretary General also takes a leading role in promoting world peace. The Security Council recommends a candidate for the position of Secretary General, but the General Assembly votes that person into office.

**International Problems** The United Nations, even during its early years, was and still is a complicated and diverse organization. Many juriscientific issues related to international problems are handled by the Economic and Social Council. (ECOSOC). This part of the UN is so big and so powerful that, after it takes its cut of the annual budget, only 30% is left to divide among the remainder of the agencies. Another key agency is the UN Educational, Scientific, and Cultural Organization (UNESCO). UNESCO promotes integrated activities in science, education, and culture and is responsible for urging nations to preserve their cultural heritage. ECOSOC has an indirect non-reporting relationship with UNESCO and with the World Health Organization (WHO). The WHO evolved out of a similar organization that was run under the auspices of the League of Nations, the precursor of the UN. WHO's job is to promote international health care and to help prevent the spread of illness and disease. It also supports programs in medical and health research in much the same way as the National Institutes of Health in the United States. The International Atomic Energy Commission (IAEC) is an independent agency that has oversight responsibilities in relation to nuclear energy programs, while the United Nations Environment Program, another independent agency, deals with pollution issues. The World Intellectual Property Organization is a specialized agency that has the job of shielding intellectual property from copyright infringement, patent violations, and IP theft. All these organization have parallels in the federal systems and all deal with the juriscientific problems of the 21st century outlined below.

## Funding Science and Technology

The federal government has been funding scientific and medical research for the last 150 years. That funding comes in many forms for a variety of purposes and with an enormously high price tag. Nevertheless, Congress and the president have agreed that the expenditure is necessary to provide for national security, to promote the health and welfare of American citizens, and to ensure the economic and social well-being of the nation. For this reason, the federal government has established a number of agencies and institutes that support, assess, coordinate, and fund scientific, medical, and technological research. The chief national scientific agencies for scientific, medical, and technological research are the Office of Science and Technology Policy, the National Science Foundation, and the National Institutes of Health. The primary international organizations under the umbrella of the UN are the UNESCO and the World Health Organization.

**Office of Science and Technology Policy** The Office of Science and Technology Policy originated in 1961 as the Office of Science and Technology under President John F. Kennedy. The primary purpose of the office under Kennedy was to keep the president apprised of developments in the space program. Eventually the purpose expanded, however, to ensure that the president was informed about overall advances in technology and science as well as the impact that these developments might have on U.S. policy. In 1976 Congress expanded the scope and function of the office when it set up the Office of Science and Technology Policy under the National Science and Technology Policy Organization and Priorities Act. The goal of the new office is to advise the president on technological and scientific matters so that he can make informed decisions about federal programs that impact science and technology. The office is also responsible for managing science and technology policy especially as that policy impacts the federal budget. In addition, the office integrates science policy at every level of governmental planning from the federal to the local level. This effort also includes coordinating governmental efforts with private industry to develop productive and efficient partnerships between government and the private sector. Finally, its job is to assess the effectiveness of the overall federal science and technology program (See "About OSTP," Office of Science and Technology Policy, The White House, http://www.whitehouse.gov/.)

### Chief Technology Officer of the United States

In 2009, a new position was added to the office of the president known officially as the assistant to the president, associate director for the Office of Science and Technology Policy, but referred to generally as the chief technology officer of the United States. The primary job of the chief technology officer is to coordinate advances in technology and engineering as they relate to the practical jobs of improving the American economy, managing medical and health care costs, and preserving national security. The chief technology officer works side by side with the United States chief information officer. The job of the chief information officer is to build an integrated technology policy especially designed to meet the needs of the national government. The position was created by Congress under the authority of the E-Government Act of 2002. All of these moves may seem new. However, even though none of these offices existed until recently, the president of the United States has had some sort of science and technology advisor on hand ever since Vannevar Bush worked for Franklin Delano Roosevelt and Harry S. Truman from 1939 to 1951. (See "Chief Technology Officer," Office of Science and Technology Policy, The White House, http://www.whitehouse.gov/.)

### National Science Foundation

The National Science Foundation (NSF) is a federally funded agency that was created by Congress in 1950 to support scientific research, to stimulate the national economy, and to safeguard national security. The National Science Foundation has an annual budget that runs close to $7 billion. A substantial portion of that money is spent on scientific research in American colleges and universities. Grants for the National Science Foundation are available for practitioners in all fields of science, mathematics, and computer technology. The NSF, which is based in Arlington, Virginia, authorizes over 120,000 grants annually. These grants are approved by a merit-based assessment process. Most of these grants fund individuals or small teams of researchers. Some grants, however, are set aside for large institutions for the purchase of equipment, facilities, and hardware. Projects that are likely to be funded are those that are clearly on the cutting edge of scientific research and development. The goal of the NSF, however, is not only to support scientific research but also to enhance scientific education, while at the same time building a globally competent and internationally competitive scientific labor force. Over the last 30 years, NSF researchers have been awarded more than 180 Nobel Prizes. One of the most recent Nobel Prizes went to Richard Heck of the University of Delaware, Eiichi Negishi of Purdue University, and Skira Suzuki of Hokkaido University in Japan. They won the 2010 Nobel prize for chemistry for developing an innovative technique for joining carbon atoms together to construct effective practical complex molecules ("NSF at a Glance," and "Nobel Prizes: The NSF Connection," National Science Foundation, http://nsf.gov).

## National Institutes of Health

The National Institutes of Health operate under the auspices of the Public Health Service of the Department of Health and Human Services. Their operational mission is to conduct research into all aspects of human life and health and to apply that understanding to cure illnesses, to alleviate disabilities, and to lengthen human life. The National Institutes also promote practical research that will reduce health care costs in order to improve the economic stability of the United States. The institutes also provide funding for research into the origin, prevention, and cure of diseases related to environmental problems. The institutes now invest over $21 billion each year in medical research. Eighty percent of that figure is awarded as grants to 350,000 recipients at over 3,000 universities, medical schools, and research organizations in the United States and around the globe. Ten percent of the original figure goes to funding the institutes' own operational laboratory in Bethesda, Maryland. The National Institutes consist of over 27 different segments designated as institutes or as centers, each of which has an individualized research program. For example, the National Cancer Institute is charged with conducting cancer research. All but a few of these independent institutes receive their money directly from the legislature. Nevertheless, the institutes handle their own administration. Funding decisions are delegated to institutes themselves because such decisions are better handled by the experts who know how the money should be spent within their own areas of expertise. The system has the added benefit of preventing Congress form trying to use its influence to control the projects, the universities, and the individual scientists who receive the funding. The objective is to make sure the funds are spent where they should be spent. (See "Mission," National Institutes of Health, United States Department of Health and Human Services, http://nih.gov.)

## A National Science Court

So far we have witnesses how the president, Congress, and the bureaucracy are involved in regulating science and technology. The courts are also involved in science and technology when a case involving such an issue comes before a judge. The issue may involve the right to die, the division of patent rights, a question of copyright law, or the legality of certain policies in relation to genetic engineering or some other cutting-edge technology. Most of the time when such cases come before a judge at the trial level, the judge must unravel technical and scientific concepts for which he or she is neither educated nor experienced. This is a time-consuming and error-filled process. That is why some commentators have suggested the creation of a national science court. The legislature took a step in this direction when it created the Court of Appeals for the Federal Circuit. This appeals court is limited in its jurisdiction, part of which covers patent and copyright law. This is an effective institution, and so, some experts have proposed extending the principle to the trial level. At that level the legislature might consider creating a national science trial court.

The national science court would have exclusive jurisdiction over issues involving scientific, engineering, medical, and technological cases. All judges who sit on the national science court would be expected to have a scientific background or would be required to undergo a special training session to get him or her up to speed on science and engineering matters. Each judge would be required to attend an internship program during which he or she would shadow a full-time science court judge to learn the ins and outs of all procedural and substantive issues peculiar to that court in regard to science and technology. The national science court would deal with a wide variety of cases such as those involving nuclear power; cyber-terrorism; genetic engineering projects; medical malpractice suits; medical research issues; environmental protection law; intellectual property problems; and so on. As things develop, the court might even be subdivided into layers, each of which would be responsible for a different discipline. Thus, there might be a medical division, a scientific division, a technology division, and an engineering division.

Commentators who support the national science court argue that the complex nature of today's scientific case load is beyond the expertise of most judges who sit on the bench at the trial level. These experts argue that it would be more effective and economical to build up an entirely new profession of science judges to deal with these complexities. Those who oppose the national science court contend that the training sessions to bring judges up to speed would be cost prohibitive. Moreover, the proposed subdivision of the court into subcourts handling different disciplines would create unnecessary and expensive duplication. As you read the following issues in relation to the juriscience, see if you can decide whether the science court would be a help or a hindrance. [See Barry Casper and Paul Wellstone, *Powerline: The First Battle of America's Energy War* (Amherst: University of Massachusetts Press, 1981); and Barry Casper and Paul Wellstone, "Science Court on Trial in Minnesota," *Science in Context: Readings in the Sociology of Science,* ed. Barry Barnes and David Edge (Cambridge: MIT Press, 1982).]

### UN Educational, Scientific, and Cultural Organization UNESCO

is a specialized agency of the United Nations run under the auspices of the ECOSOC. UNESCO is responsible for creating outreach efforts to develop educational, cultural, and scientific ties among the member nations of the UN. Initially, the objectives of UNESCO were seen as a function of the United Nations and were thus supported by the entire membership. Evidence of its key importance is the fact that the first head of UNESCO was the world famous British author Julian Huxley. Unfortunately, because UNESCO's mission was to allocate funds to projects run by various member states, some of these states saw themselves being marginalized while others were being rewarded. This situation fostered jealousy and resentment. As a result, UNESCO became a highly politicized organization. Eventually it even went so far as to demand the redistribution of global resources from the developed to the underdeveloped world.

In his book, *The Future of the United Nations,* Joshua Muravchik, resident scholar at the American Enterprise Institute, explains that UNESCO became more and more politicized when its leadership became tied to a bloc of underdeveloped nations within the UN. These underdeveloped nations referred to themselves as the Group of Seventy-Seven (or just G-77). The G-77 appeared on the international stage after certain delegates attended a meeting sponsored by the United Nations Conference on Trade and Development (UNCTAD). At the time of that meeting, UNCTAD was under the leadership of the Argentine economist Raul Prebisch. Prebisch is best known as the father of dependency theory, an economic picture of the world which holds the developed world responsible for poverty in the underdeveloped world. Eventually, dependency theory became the official political position of the G-77, UNCTAD, and the United Nations itself. The result was a group of organizations that convinced the underdeveloped nations to adopt socialist economic structures. The G-77 also developed a manifesto called the New International Economic Order (NIEO) which was endorsed by UNESCO. [See Linda Fasulo, *An Insider's Guide to the UN,* (New Haven: Yale UP, 2004), p. 182. Robert Speaight, *Teilhard de Chardin: A Biography* (London: Collins, 1967), pp. 290-291. Joshua Muravchik, *The Future of the United Nations: Understanding the Past to Chart a Way Forward* (Washington, D.C.: The American Enterprise Institute Press, 2005), pp. 69-72.]

## A QUESTION OF ETHICS

The controversy surrounding UNESCO's politicization has caused an enormous amount of difficulty for the organization throughout the years. Of course, there are those commentators who say that UNESCO's bias in favor of the poorer nations is justified. These experts support UNESCO's critique of the developed world for exploiting the underdeveloped world, its support for dependency theory, and its adoption of the New International Economic Order (NIEO), including its demand that the rich nations compensate the poor nations. There is another side to the issue, however. The rich nations and the corporations who actually entered the underdeveloped world and drilled for oil, mined for diamonds, cut down timber, and dug for coal, argue, rather convincingly, that it was their money, their equipment, and their workers that did the actual work. Their workers, with corporate money, built roads, harbors, communication systems, oil fields, refineries and so on. Moreover, the governments of these nations were all handsomely compensated for their fair share of the profits, or so the argument goes. Therefore, it is the government's fault, that is, the governments of the underdeveloped nations, who failed to properly distribute the profit to their citizens.

Who is correct here from an ethical perspective? Do the rich nations owe the underdeveloped nations because they, the rich, created the underdeveloped world's dependency on the developed world? Or does the fault lie in the hands of the governments of the underdeveloped world? Explain. By the way, there is an interesting parallel situation in the operation of the National Institutes of Health and the National Science Foundation. In those institutions the complaint is that the best and the most lucrative grants go to researchers from the big, powerful, rich mega-universities, while the small schools and the unknown researchers are largely ignored. The other side of this argument states that the unknown researchers from the small schools actually self-select themselves out of the process, either by not applying or by giving up and withdrawing their applications before the final awards are made. Who is correct here from an ethical perspective? Do the referees from the big schools owe the representatives from small schools special attention because they, the rich, created a peer review merit-based process that favors the big schools and the big names? Or does the fault lie in the hands of the inexperienced researchers from the small schools who "get cold feet"? Explain.

## The World Health Organization

In 1948 the constitution of the World Health Organization (WHO) was ratified by the member nations of the United Nations. WHO's mission is to improve the health care available to all the people of the world, but especially to those most at risk because of poverty or special health-related threats. WHO's program is based on eight basic component parts: nutrition and food; sanitation and a healthy water supply; protection against contagious diseases; containment of local illnesses; effective handling of everyday injuries and familiar diseases; adequate supplies of critical pharmaceuticals, and family planning efforts including especially the care of mothers and children. A good portion of the work done by the WHO is aimed at building up the medical and health care facilities and health care professionals in the poor nations of the world so that those nations can better handle the delivery of health care and medical services to the local people.

Moreover, like the National Institutes of Health at the national level, the WHO supports health and medical research programs at the international level, all of which are aimed at promoting its eight basic component parts of medical and health care. More specifically, the WHO has a special research program aimed at eradicating tropical diseases that it runs in cooperation with the UN Development Program (UNDP) and the World Bank. In addition, the WHO also works with the Food and Agriculture Organization of the UN, the World Bank, and the UNDP to fight a disease known as *onchocerciasis,* or river blindness, in West Africa. The WHO is also responsible for coordinating a global effort to control infection with human immunodeficiency virus (HIV) in an attempt to eradicate the acquired immune deficiency syndrome (AIDS). [See *Basic Facts about the United Nations* (New York: The United Nations Department of Public Relations 1992).]

Like UNESCO, the WHO has also had its fair share of controversy. In *The Future of the United Nations* (cited above), Muravchik, reports a case involving allegations that, in the 1990s, the director of WHO had granted contracts to institutions that were tied directly to members of the WHO executive board. There were also allegations at the time that threats of economic sanctions were made against certain countries if the chief of the WHO, who had been charged with these irregularities, were not to be re-elected. Muravchik also reports, however, that the WHO has had its share of successes and has accomplished a great deal in a variety of arenas. Specifically, he praises the WHO for dealing quickly with severe acute respiratory syndrome (SARS) crisis in 2002–03 and thus preventing what could have been a devastating global epidemic. The WHO can also lay claim to playing a large role in the global elimination of both smallpox and polio.

---

### quick quiz 33-1

| | |
|---|---|
| 1. The point at which science, technology, and the law intersect is often referred to as *juriscience*. | true \| false |
| 2. Congressional power to regulate science and technology is found in the general welfare clause, the commerce clause, and the necessary and proper clause. | true \| false |
| 3. The National Science Foundation (NSF) is a federally funded agency that was created to support scientific research and education, to stimulate the national economy, and to safeguard national security. | true \| false |

---

# 33-2 Facing the Global Challenges

The American bureaucratic system frequently appears complex and convoluted. The operation of the bureaucracy often seems erratic and directionless. The day-to-day activities appear to be designed to stall and block progress rather than to enhance it. The Federal Register, which produces a daily record of agency business, is so complex that it must include one section on rules and regulations, another on proposed rules, and one on notices of hearings, meetings, application deadlines, and administrative orders. There is also a section devoted to presidential orders and proclamations. The high level of activity within the bureaucracy could lead to the conclusion that the activity has become an end in itself, rather than the means to the end of running an efficient and effective government. While this evaluation may be discouraging, it may also be the price we pay for demanding a democratic government. Nevertheless, underneath, or perhaps above, all the activity is a series of challenges that funnel this activity in productive directions. All of the work done by the government, outside of the work needed to collect the money used to deal with the other problems themselves (think IRS here), relate in some way to four challenges (1) the possibility of war, (2) the volatility of the marketplace, (3) the twin dangers of environmental deterioration and energy depletion, and (4) the demographic crisis. Dealing with all of these problems is part of the balancing act that is the law.

## Heilbroner's Global Challenges

In 1974, the economist, author, and political scientist, Robert Heilbroner, wrote a book entitled *An Inquiry into the Human Prospect*. In this pioneering book, Heilbroner argued that the planet Earth is faced with three challenges that must be met if humanity expects to continue into the 21st and the 22nd centuries. If these three problems are not handled, Heilbroner says with some degree of confidence, then humanity is, well, doomed. The problems he focuses on are the possibility of war, especially nuclear war; the challenge of uncontrolled population growth (demographics), and the destruction of the environment. The list is slightly different from the one we compiled above. The one challenge he appears to miss is the challenge of a volatile economy. That challenge, however, is not actually missing from *An Inquiry into the Human Prospect*. In fact, the economy actually permeates the book because Heilbroner sees economic volatility as the challenge that underlies each of the other three and, ironically, is also the ultimate solution. In a sense, then, the economy is Heilbroner's mega-crisis [See Robert Heilbroner, *An Inquiry Into the Human Prospect* (New York: Norton, 1991).] We have dealt with the legal handling of the economy since we began talking about contract law back in Chapter 7. Moreover, and more to the point, we focused on much of it in Chapter 30 and 31 when we discussed the government's regulation of the economy especially as it relates to the stock market, the housing market, and corporate misconduct. In the Chapter 34, International Law, we will deal, at length, with the challenge of war. It remains, then, for us to discuss the twin challenges of energy and the environment and the inescapable problem of overpopulation.

## Regulating Energy Problems

The Arab Oil Embargo of 1973 and the subsequent energy crisis focused national attention on the power industry. In answer to these concerns, Congress created the Department of Energy and the Federal Energy Regulatory Commission. National concerns with the problems of nuclear energy, especially after the disasters involving nuclear energy in Japan, have also recently focused attention on the Nuclear Regulatory Commission. The regulation of nuclear energy for peaceful uses on a global scale is charged to the United Nations International Atomic Energy Agency (IAEA).

**The Federal Energy Regulation Commission** The Federal Energy Regulatory Commission (FERC) is responsible for regulating the transportation and the wholesale price of natural gas and electricity sold for use in interstate commerce. State utility commissioners regulate intrastate prices. Rates are calculated to allow companies a specific rate of return on investments (earnings divided by total assets), which they may not exceed. When utilities are confronted with increased costs due to higher fuel prices, they can apply to the commission for permission to pass these increased costs on to customers through fuel adjustment charges. The commission also licenses hydropower project proposals for the construction of interstate gas pipelines and liquefied natural gas terminals. In brief, a few of the additional duties of the FERC include regulating pipelines used in the interstate transport of oil; reviewing and approving interstate locations for natural gas lines; reviewing and approving the location of natural gas storage containers; reviewing applications for the placement of electricity transmission projects on a limited basis; licensing private and governmental (state and city) hydroelectric projects; producing mandatory standards for high-voltage interstate transmission systems; acting as a watchdog and overseeing accounting and financial reporting rules for companies regulated by the FERC; monitoring environmental risks in relation to hydroelectric and natural gas projects; and imposing civil penalties for violations of FERC regulations.

In 2005 Congress passed the Energy Policy Act which added a series of new tasks to the FRFC's already packed agenda. One of the top initiatives in the 2005 act involves the modernization of the nation's electric power grid. Specifically, the FERC is charged with the development of a smart grid that will make optimal use of state-of-the-art technology. The goal is to apply digital technology to the nation's power network to ensure a reliable, secure, and efficient electric grid. In addition, the FERC will ensure peak operation of the grid with protection from cyber-attacks of all kinds. Moreover, the FERC is charged with the task of implementing "smart technology in grid operations, including metering, communication, and distribution automation." Other new tasks involve removing unnecessary roadblocks that are currently preventing the implementation of the smart grid and developing standards for the interoperability of equipment connected to the grid, among many others. Congress also outlined the FERC's 2009–2014 strategic plan. In brief the mission under the plan is to help consumers receive dependable, effective, and economical energy service. The two main objectives are to make certain that rates and terms are reasonable and equitable and to ensure the creation of safe dependable and effective system that will serve the needs of the American citizenry. (See "Top Initiatives," "Smart Grid," and "Strategic Plan," Federal Energy Regulatory Commission http://ferc.gov.)

### Nuclear Regulatory Commission

Mandated by the Energy Reorganization Act, the Nuclear Regulatory Commission (NRC) is responsible for the licensing, construction, and operation of nuclear reactors. It is also responsible for regulating the possession, use, transportation, handling, and disposal of nuclear material. The NRC develops and implements rules and regulations governing licensed nuclear activities. Nuclear regulation actually began under the auspices of the Atomic Energy Commission which was established by Congress under the Atomic Energy Act of 1946. The 1946 law was superseded by the Atomic Energy Act of 1954 which was designed to encourage the development of safe and reliable nuclear power plants. The AEC came under fire in the 1960s (What government agency didn't in the 1960s?) for developing lenient regulations regarding radiation protection, plant location, reactor safety, and protection of the environment. The AEC was eliminated in 1974 and replaced by a new agency, the current Nuclear Regulatory Commission under the authority of the Energy Reorganization Act of 1974. The NRC was charged with overseeing various aspects of the nuclear power industry, including especially radiation shielding and reactor safety. The Three Mile Island incident in Pennsylvania in1979 focused attention on the need for stricter regulations in relation to personnel training, energy planning, plant operation, plant operational records, and human involvement in plant operations, among several other things.

The NRC has evolved into an agency of rules and regulations for the security of nuclear materials to prevent the theft of that material, especially theft of that material, by potential terrorists. The commission is also charged with developing and enforcing safety regulations in relation to radioactive waste materials. It also does its fair share of work in radiation medicine, developing standards and protecting patients from radiation overdoses. The NRC currently employs over 4,000 employees in Maryland and four regional offices in Georgia, Illinois, Pennsylvania, and Texas. NRC inspectors also visit nuclear power plant sites and various fuel facilities across the nation. It is important to note that the NRC does not regulate nuclear weapons, military reactors, or space vehicle reactors. It does not lobby Congress and it does not, contrary to popular opinion, operate its own reactors or its own power plants. It does, however, impose penalties for violations of its regulations. Penalties can be severe, up to $140,000 per day, per violation. Licenses can also be revoked, changed, or suspended for especially egregious violations. It is even possible that a wrongdoer's violation is so severe that the violator's case is sent to the Justice Department for possible criminal proceedings (See "About NRC," United States Nuclear Regulatory Commission, http://www.nrc.gov.)

### International Atomic Energy Agency

On the international scene, the United Nations has an agency with oversight responsibility for matters dealing with nuclear power. The International Atomic Energy Agency (IAEA), which was created in 1957, is responsible for making certain that, on a global basis, nuclear energy is used only for peaceful purposes. Thus, under the statute creating the agency, there is an assumption that nuclear energy is both a useful and necessary source of energy production, especially for developing nations. Nevertheless, the IAEA also exhibits a healthy respect for the dangers associated with nuclear power. IAEA's program is based on four basic component parts: setting up guidelines for the effective, economical, and environmentally safe production of nuclear energy; promoting the peaceful application of nuclear science technology; providing technical and engineering support on nuclear energy to member nations; and distributing scientific and technological knowledge about nuclear power. The agency must guard against the misplacement, loss, or theft of nuclear materials and equipment and make certain that such equipment and materials do not fall into the hands of those who would use them for military (or terrorist) operations. Much of this oversight is maintained by inspections, and by record-keeping procedures that can be verified by those inspectors. Such inspection and record-keeping strategies are involved in a variety of international agreements including: the Treaty for the Prohibition of Nuclear Weapons in Latin America and the Treaty on the Non-Proliferation of Nuclear Weapons, among others [See *Basic Facts about the United Nations* (New York: The United Nations Department of Public Relations, 1992).]

Unfortunately, in *The Future of the United Nations* (cited above), Muravchik notes that such inspections and record-keeping processes are not foolproof. In fact, the IAEA inspection process has been less than 100 percent effective on a number of occasions, notably in the cases of Iraq, Iran, and North Korea. On a more positive note, other governments, in the peaceful pursuit of nuclear power, have come directly to the IAEA for equipment, for technical assistance, and for the education of its personnel. The IAEA is also responsible for setting up regulations that guide the requirements for radiation shielding and for the safe and efficient transport of nuclear materials. The agency also handles emergency operations in the case of a nuclear accident. The IAEA is also a clearinghouse of information, research, and data on all phases of nuclear energy. The clearinghouse, which is known officially as the International Nuclear Information System, is located in Vienna. The IAEA also runs the International Centre for Theoretical Physics in conjunction with the United Nations, Educational, Scientific, and Cultural Organization. [See *Basic Facts about the United Nations* (New York: The United Nations Department of Public Relations, 1992).]

## Regulating Environmental Problems

In his book, *An Inquiry into the Human Prospect,* Robert Helibroner provides a succinct but poignant explanation for the nature of the environmental challenges that face the global community in the 21st century. Heilbroner writes: "Here we come to a crucial stage in our inquiry. For unlike the threats posed by population growth or war, there is an ultimate certitude about the problem of environmental deterioration that places it in a different category from the dangers we have previously examined. Nuclear attacks may be indefinitely avoided; population growth may be stabilized; but ultimately there is an absolute limit to the ability of the environment to support or tolerate the process of industrial activity, and there is a reason to believe that we are now moving to that limit very rapidly" (Heilbroner, 47). This is a scary thought. One that should give us pause. On the national level, the responsibility for the environment has been delegated to the Environmental Protection Agency. Important subsidiary legislation includes the Clean Air Act, the Clean Water Act, and the Oil Pollution Act. The regulation of the environment on a global scale is charged to the United Nations Environment Program (UNEP).

### The Environmental Protection Agency
The Environmental Protection Agency (EPA) is an independent agency in the executive branch of the federal government. It was created to carry out the provisions of the National Environmental Policy Act and other major environmental laws and executive orders dealing with air, water, solid waste, toxic substance, and noise pollution. The purpose of the 1969 National Environmental Policy Act is to establish a national policy that will combat pollution and improve the environment. The legislation encourages efforts that prevent or eliminate damage to the environment and that stimulate the health and welfare of the public. The act requires a detailed statement of environmental consequences in every recommendation or proposal for legislation and other major federal actions significantly affecting the quality of the

human environment. These environmental impact statements describe in detail the expected adverse environmental consequences of a proposed action. The alternatives to the action are also described.

All major antipollution programs dealing with air, noise, solid wastes, toxic substances, and pesticides were placed under the administrative control of the Environmental Protection Agency in 1970. The EPA's primary responsibilities are to conduct research on all aspects of pollution, set and enforce pollution control standards, monitor programs to determine whether pollution abatement standards are being met, and administer grants to assist states in controlling pollution. The EPA has the power to enforce the standards and programs it initiates. It encourages voluntary compliance by industry and communities and supports state and local governments' efforts to conduct enforcement actions of their own. When such efforts fail, the EPA conducts enforcement proceedings. Moreover, state laws and local ordinances must be in line with federal regulatory policies and standards. The states and their subdivisions are not permitted to skirt federal law by creating statutes and ordinances that establish more lenient standards than those provided for in the federal statute. Congress can intentionally and expressly pass a statute or empower an agency to create regulations that are designed to preempt state law. On the other hand, it is permissible for states and their subdivisions to impose restrictions that are different from and perhaps stricter than those imposed by the federal government. Thus, it is legally permissible for a state to require special standards on resold vehicles or commercial vehicles, or to impose procedures enforcing federal standards.

## EXAMPLE 33-2: *Allway Taxi, Inc. v. City of New York*

The City of New York passed an ordinance ordering the installation of emission control devices in all taxis as a new licensing requirement. Fifteen New York taxi companies filed this case in Federal District Court, asking the court to declare the new ordinance invalid and to prevent its enforcement. The taxi companies argued that federal law, which had no such requirement, was meant by Congress to supersede and replace any state or local ordinance related to vehicle pollution control measures. The court responded initially by noting that a federal law like the Clean Air Act (see below) will preempt state and local law only in two cases: first, if the state or local law clearly introduces a conflict between the state or local law and the federal law, or, second, when the federal law specifically and expressly declares that Congress intends to preempt other laws. In this case, neither situation applies. There is no conflict with federal law. In fact, the New York ordinance appears to provide tighter regulation requirements than the federal act. In relation to preemption, it was true that the federal law intended to preempt any state or local law related to exhaust emission control standards and new vehicles but not vehicles after they are in use and on the roads in local communities. The taxi companies, therefore, did not prevail in the case. [*Allway Taxi, Inc. v. City of New York,* 340 F. Supp. 1120 (Southern District of New York, 1972).]

**The Clean Air Act** In order to enforce the details of its overall environmental policy Congress has, over the years, passed subsidiary legislation regarding individual pollution problems. The three most visible acts are the Clean Air Act, the Clean Water Act, and the Oil Pollution Act. The **Clean Air Act**, for example, is designed to limit pollution from vehicles and from stationary sources such factories and manufacturing centers. The act authorizes the EPA to initiate regulations to limit air pollution. Over the years, the government has added new standards that have gradually reduced the amount of pollution that can be released by vehicles. New emission control requirements were issued in 1990, regarding nitrogen oxide, hydrocarbon, and carbon monoxide. Additional emission control limits were introduced in 2009 ordering a reduction in pollution from a variety of vehicles including SUVs that must reach an 80 percent reduction level within 40 years. The penalties for violating the act are severe. Congress also added a unique feature to the Clean Air Act, which emphasizes the legislature's serious intent to see that the law is enforced. Under provisions in the act, private parties are empowered to sue violators. Private parties are also permitted to sue the act's administrator for not enforcing the act properly. There are limits to this right to bring a citizen's suit, however. The citizen bringing the suit must point to a definite violation by the perpetrator and must give advance notice to the administrator so that he or she has a chance to correct the problem before the lawsuit is initiated.

**The Clean Water Act** The Clean Water Act which was passed by Congress in 1972 as an amendment to the Federal Water Pollution Control Act of 1948, sets requirements for limiting the pollution of the nation's water sources according to a schedule and based on the most effective technology currently available. The regulations set up a system for obtaining permits for the release of pollutants into the waterways. Permits are issued provided that the pollution emissions are within legal limits. Violations of the act are punished by fines up to $25,000 daily. Often the EPA must act against companies that pollute the environment, even if the pollution activity is unintentional. The courts have interpreted this broad prohibition to include even accidental pollution, because to hold otherwise would weaken the statute. The Clean Water Act also permits citizens suits against violators and against the administrator of the act for not properly carrying out his or her responsibilities under the act. The same definitive violation and notice provisions are applicable under this act as they are under the Clean Air Act. There is a difference between the two acts however. Under the Clean Water Act, the party bringing the citizen's suit must be a person "having an interest which is or may be adversely affected" by the violation of the act. No such limit exists in the Clean Air Act.

**EXAMPLE 33-3:** *Natural Resources Defense Council, Inc. v. Train*

In this case, the plaintiff, an organization known as the Natural Resources Defense Council, brought a citizen's suit under the authority of the Clean Water Act asking the court to issue an order that would compel the administrator of the act to perform specific duties enumerated in the suit. The administrator argued that the plaintiff did not give him the 60 days' notice required under the act. The plaintiff argued that it was not necessary to give the administrator notice because he had issued a clear edict indicating that he had no intention of performing the action that the plaintiffs were demanding. The court reviewed the facts in the case and then examined the legislative history of the act including a comparison to the Clean Air Act which has a similar citizen's suit provision. The court decided that, given the fact that the administrator had made it clear that he did not intend to perform the action requested by the plaintiffs, there was no need for them to give him notice and the case against him could be pursued by the Natural Resources Defense Council. [*Natural Resources Defense Council, Inc. v. Train* 510 F.2d 692 (U.S. Court of Appeals, District of Columbia Circuit, 1974).]

**The Oil Pollution Act** The Oil Pollution Act was passed by Congress in 1990 in the wake of the 1989 Exxon Valdez Alaskan oil spill tragedy. The act is designed to encourage companies that ship, drill for, and store oil to develop and use the most up-to-date equipment and the most effective safety measures possible. Sometimes the act will require that specifically named technological and engineering steps be taken. For instance, the act mandates that, by 2011, any oil tanker that wants to enter an American port must be equipped with double hulls to minimize any pollution damage should a spill occur. Under the act's provisions, any company responsible for a spill will be compelled to pay all expenses related to the clean-up and will, in addition, be subject to a heavy fine. Depending on certain factors, such as the source of the spill, violators could end up paying up to $350 million.

## United Nations Environment Program

The United Nations Environment Program (UNEP) was created in 1972 as a consequence of work done at the United Nations Conference on the Human Environment in Stockholm that year. The UNEP, which has its central offices in Kenya, was the first UN institution located in a developing nation-state. The agency is responsible for stimulating global awareness of environmental issues and for coordinating international efforts to solve the tough problems associated with environmental deterioration. It organizes the efforts of several UN agencies as they interface with governments and private establishments, such as youth groups and women's organizations. UNEP's programs are based on 10 fundamental areas of concentration: (1) climate change; (2) the vanishing ozone layer; (3) atmospheric activity; (4) fresh water supplies; (5) desertification; (6) deforestation; (7) biological variety; (8) oceanic activity; (9) biotechnology and bioengineering; and (10) chemical safety and security. The UNEP works in a variety of ways to fulfill its environmental mission. A key activity is the Global Environmental Monitoring System (GEMS). This program controls an international system of monitoring centers run by over 30,000 scientists located in over 140 nation-states. GEM's job is to monitor environmental activity in the oceans, in the atmosphere, in climate, in renewable resources. It also monitors pollution and pollution-related illnesses.

UNEP also monitors the work of INFOTERRA, a decentralized data clearing house that provides environmental information to institutions and individuals. Another source of environmental data monitored by UNEP is the Industry and Environment Office (IEO) which provides data to governments and industry. The IEO also promotes information and technology transfer between governments and industry dealing with environmental matters. The UNEP also develops Action Plans for dealing with problems in marine biology aimed at preserving marine resources. Such action plans have dealt with problems in the Mediterranean Sea, the Pacific Ocean, and the Black Sea. The UNEP also monitors a series on international agreements on the environment including the Vienna Convention and Montreal Protocol, the London Amendment to the Montreal Protocol, the Basel Convention on the Control of Transboundary Movements of Hazardous Wastes and their Disposal, and the Convention on International Trade in Endangered Species. [See *Basic Facts about the United Nations* (New York: The United Nations Department of Public Relations 1992).]

## United Nations Conference on Environment and Development

The UN has also taken steps to combine environmental and energy concerns together under the auspices of the United Nations Conference on Environment and Development (UNCED). UNCED, known more popularly as the Earth Summit program, is designed to integrate economic development and environmental protection into a single well-coordinated strategy that will promote sustainable development in developing nations with the assistance and cooperation of the developed nations of the globe. The first UNCED Conference (Earth Summit I), which was held in Rio de Janeiro in 1992, resulted in an international agreement known as Agenda 21. The provisions of Agenda 21 established an in-depth set of tactics designed to activate sustainable development plans across the globe. Earth Summit I also resulted in the Rio Declaration, which defines a set of standards outlining the duties and the rights of nations in sustainable development. The summit also led to the creation of the Commission on Sustainable Development (CSD) which coordinates efforts to activate Agenda 21. The CSD also serves as a central clearing-house for nations to report progress in the implementation of sustainable development plans.

A second international conference, known as the UN Framework Conference on Climate Change (UNFCCC) was held in Berlin in 1995. This conference involved 120 nations working to create a global strategy to stabilize growing levels of carbon dioxide and other greenhouse gases (GHGs) in the atmosphere. A plan was developed based on balancing (1) a timetable that will not endanger existing ecosystems; (2) a scientific strategy that will permit an adequate production of food; and (3) an economically feasible strategy that will support sustainable development. The plan, which was dubbed the Berlin Mandate, sets out a timetable for the reduction of carbon dioxide and other GHGs for various governments. A second Earth Summit was held in 1997 which revealed that very little progress had been made since the first conference. As a result Earth Summit II reconfirmed the goals, objectives, and plans of Agenda 21 and added a reconfirmation of the need to partner economic development with environmental protection. The new program, which was named, Development Reconciling Environmental and Material Success (DREAMS), set a new set of priorities for the next five years.

A second meeting in 1997, under the auspices of UNFCCC, was held in Kyoto to discuss the lowering of greenhouse gas emissions during the first decades of the 21st century. Under terms of the agreement, known as the Kyoto Protocol, the primary industrial nations would be mandated to reduce carbon dioxide emissions below levels recorded in 1900. Unfortunately, the three major industrial nations on the planet, the United States, China, and India refused to go along with the protocol. [See *Basic Facts about the United Nations* (New York: The United Nations Department of Public Relations 1992); Derek Osborn and Tom Bigg, *Earth Summit II: Outcomes and Analysis* (London: Earthscan, 1998); and Christopher Flavin, "Facing Up to the Risks of Climate Change," In *State of the World 1996,* ed. Lester Brown (New York: Norton, 1996).]

**The Copenhagen Accord** A new meeting under the auspices of the UN Framework Conference on Climate Change (UNFCCC) was held in Copenhagen in 2011. The meeting produced a new pact known as the Copenhagen Accord which was negotiated by five nation-states, including the key nations that did not sign the Kyoto Protocol, the United States, China, and India. The accord will actually operate outside the jurisdiction of the United Nations. In brief, the Copenhagen Accord includes a pledge made by the signatories to reduce greenhouse gases and to provide $30 billion annually to a fund designed to help developing nations balance sustainable development and environmental protection especially as it relates to GHGs. If things go according to plan, the Copenhagen Green Climate Fund will increase gradually, reaching $100 billion annually by the year 2020. There are, however, several weaknesses in the accord. First, the accord does not actually reduce any GHG emissions, at least before 2020. Second, the accord does absolutely nothing to reduce the Earth's future temperature problems. Third, from a legal perspective, the accord lacks "teeth." There is no way to enforce its provisions because it lies outside UN control. In this way, the Copenhagen Accord demonstrates the inherent drawbacks of semi-autonomous organizations like the United Nations. Such international organizations are incapable of carrying out actions absent the consent of the members. In this case, the United States, China, and India, all member states of the UN, decided, on their own authority, to ignore the Kyoto Protocol, to defy the other members of the UNFCC, and to set up their own accord which they may or may not follow based on their own choice. (See Lawrence Demase and Jennifer Smokelin, "After Copenhagen, It Is Clear There Will be Winners and Losers," *The National Law Journal* (February 2010), pp. 15 and 18.)

## Self-Evident Truths

In a review of the Earth II Summit by Derek Osborn of the United Nations Environment and Development UK Committee (UNED-UK) and Tom Bigg also of the UNED-UK, several prominent global figures comment on the environmental/energy crisis facing the planet. As might be expected, the views on the crisis and the summit vary tremendously. Two dramatically different views are offered by Wangari Maathai of the Women's Environmental and Developmental Organization and Bill Jordan, General Secretary of the International Confederation of Free Trade Unions, both of whom addressed the General Assembly Plenary Session.

> It is possible for poor countries to demand that international companies and governments refrain from testing nuclear technology, dumping toxic materials in other people's neighborhoods, that they do not exploit human and material resources, that they practice fair and just trade, respect the culture and values of host communities and they compensate those they aggrieve. It is possible and reasonable for such companies and governments to reinvest some of the profits in communities where they operate and therefore contribute to sustainable development instead of contributing to poverty and dehumanization of marginalized groups.
>
> —Wangari Maathai
>
> A massive education drive must explain to people why consumption patterns have to change drastically, in domestic life and in the workplace, and how it can be done. The Workplace Eco-Audit, which we have been promoting since 1993, is getting the message through bringing the workers and employers together to tackle a host of production problems, including the reduction of $CO_2$ emissions. It also provides a mechanism for monitoring and evaluating progress, and feeding into the national reporting process called for by the CSD.
>
> —Bill Jordan

Clearly Maathai and Jordan do not see eye to eye. They both perceive the problem accurately. Yet they each offer different, even conflicting causes, and propose different solutions. Much of this difference has to do with the speaker's view on the cause of the problem. Examine each quote again and then answer the following questions.

## Self-Evident Questions

1. What position is held by Maathi? How accurate is her take on the crisis? Explain. What position is held by Jordan? How accurate is his take on the crisis? Explain.

2. What organization does each speaker represent? Explain how the speaker's affiliation matches his or her opinion.

3. Which view seems to be have been adopted by the international community and by most Nongovernmental International Organizations like the UN? Explain.

4. Which view seems to be supported by most Americans? Explain. Which view seems to be in line with American energy and environmental policies in the twenty-first century? Explain.

5. Which view is morally correct? Explain.

[*See:* Derek Osborn and Tom Bigg, *Earth Summit II: Outcomes and Analysis* (London" Earthscan, 1998), pp. 31 and 35.]

## Regulating Population Growth

The third (our fourth) challenge that Heilbroner records in his book, *An Inquiry into the Human Prospect,* is the demographic challenge of runaway population growth. Heilbroner predicts that the population will pass its tipping point within a few generations. The tipping point will be reached when the planet can no longer support its people. What follows that tipping point is a downward slide characterized by famine, fresh water shortages, skyrocketing infant mortality rates, wars of redistribution, mega-city collapse, rolling blackouts, and a global economic depression. Heilbroner argues, rather convincingly, that this unchecked population explosion will continue unless two things happen: (1) those areas with the highest population growth rates impose strict birth control programs and (2) strong "iron" governments rise to deal with the issues of birth control and social unrest.

## Population Growth Figures

First, if we look at population growth figures, the United States, with a population of 300 million, a growth rate of 0.9 percent, and vast amounts of unsettled land, is not a threat. Neither is much of the developed world, including the EU which has an even smaller growth rate of only 0.21 percent. In contrast, the least developed nations of the world have a population growth rate that reaches almost 2.32 percent. Moreover, if we put the growth rates together and project into the future, we can see that by the year 2050 (which by the way is closer to us right now than 1950) the population will reach 9.5 billion. [See "International Data Base World Population 1950-2050," International, U.S. Census Bureau (June 2011), http://www.census.gov.] The significance of these figures in relation to population growth rates is difficult to imagine. So, it might be helpful to make some reverse comparisons. If we look back to the 19th century, we would find that the Earth reached its first billion in the year 1825. By 1925, 100 years later, humans had managed to add a second billion. By 1976, the population doubled again, reaching 4 billion. [See Paul Kennedy, *Preparing for the Twenty-First Century* (New York: Random House, 1993).]

## Consequences of Uncontrolled Population Growth

What are the consequences of uncontrolled population growth? The first and the most obvious consequence of more people is fewer job holders as the workforce increases but the job openings decrease. By the year 2050, predictions indicate a labor force of 3 billion. To employ the members of that labor pool, which is mostly in the developing world, would require the addition of 38 to 40 million jobs per year. [See Paul Kennedy, *Preparing for the Twenty-First Century* (New York: Random House, 1993).] The result will be more workers than job openings. This leads to poverty in the mega-cities of the developing world. Poverty leads to disease as problems develop with sanitation and waste disposal. More out of work people means a higher crime rate, an increase in violence, and a threat of social disorder. For a while, science and technology may be able to feed and provide water for these people, but at some point the numbers will outstrip the scientific ability to provide sufficient food and water. Famine follows as well as wars of redistribution. The wars of redistribution are waged when a nation (or tribe or ethnic group or revolutionary movement or terrorist organization) looks across the border to another nation and, seeing the crops and the water that they need, simply moves in and takes what it can. Depending on who is doing what to whom, the struggle my even led to a nuclear confrontation, as might happen if the Arab states attack Israel again, Pakistan attacks India, or North Korea attacks South Korea.

## The American Response

In light of all of this, we might believe that the United States would impose some legal incentives to participate in a birth control program that would, if nothing else, lead by example. Such a move, however, is not forthcoming. Return for a moment to Heilbroner's two solutions: (1) increased birth control and (2) the rise of iron governments to enforce both birth control and the civil peace. Neither of these is likely to emerge in the United States. First, the United States is not going to enforce birth control limitations on its citizens. The courts have a long and consistent tradition of avoiding any intrusion into the reproductive freedom of its citizens. The right to procreate without governmental interference was first recognized by the United States Supreme Court in the case of *Griswold v. Connecticut* when the justices ruled that the government could not prevent married couples from obtaining and using contraceptives. That right was extended to unmarried couples in the case of *Eisenstadt v. Baird*. In that case the Court wrote that "[i]f the right of privacy means anything it is the right of the individual , married or single to be free from unwarranted governmental intrusion into matters so fundamentally affecting a person as the decision whether to bear or beget a child." The cap was put on the bottle, so to speak, when, in *Carey v. Population Services International,* the High Court ruled that selling and distributing contraceptives was protected by law. It is very important to note that the procreative freedom referred to by the High Court in all of these cases includes not only the right to avoid reproduction but also to have children without any interference by the government. Thus it is unlikely, first, that the United States will enforce birth control or, second, that it will evolve into one of Heilbroner's "iron" governments willing to violate those rights. [See *Griswold v, Connecticut,* 381 U.S. 479, 85 S.Ct. 1678 (1965); *Eisenstadt v. Baird,* 405 U.S. 438 (1972); and *Carey v. Population Services International,* 431 U.S. 678 (1977).]

Nevertheless, there is always a difference between saying that the government *will not* do something and saying that it *cannot* do something. The flip side of the statement that the government *will not* interfere in procreative rights is that, given the right set of circumstances and the correct motivation, the government *can* interfere in procreative rights. Oddly enough that position was made clear in the case of *Roe v. Wade.* In that case the High Court supported laws that permit abortion as long as the abortion did not occur after the fetus becomes viable. In *Roe v. Wade* viability emerged in the third trimester, so laws that allowed abortion after that time were not permitted. According to *Planned Parenthood v. Casey,* viability comes earlier in a woman's pregnancy primarily because medical technology has pushed viability back further toward conception. Nevertheless, both cases say that the government can interfere in a woman's right to control her own body and both define that moment as the time at which the state has a compelling interest in the life of the child. In fact, *Planned Parenthood v. Casey* goes just a bit further noting that the state might even have an interest in the life of the fetus *before* viability and might even be able to pass legislature limiting the rights of the woman before viability, as long as those legal limits do not cause an undue burden on the woman. The important thing to note here is that the Supreme Court has said that the government *can* interfere in the child-bearing decision of a woman if it has a compelling interest to do so. Now, up until the present time, this has been assumed to mean that the government has a compelling interest to *stop* abortion. However, this same rationale could be made to enforce the idea that the government has a compelling interest in stopping runaway birth rates, that is, by forcing an abortion, or birth control or perhaps even compulsory sterilization. If, for example, there is a national, or a global crisis in relation to uncontrolled population growth, the government might find that it has a compelling interest in limiting population growth by any means available including coerced abortion, forced birth control, and so on. [See *Planned Parenthood v. Casey,* 112 S.Ct. 2791 (1992).]

## The International Response

The international community seems more ready, willing, and able to deal with runaway population growth than the United States. In fact, the United Nations has been involved in such work since 1947 when the Population Commission (PC) was created under the auspices of the Economic and Social Council. The PC investigates demographic concerns and then consults with ECOSOC on a variety of population issues. These issues include compiling accurate demographic data; developing strategies to control population growth; and gauging the relationship between a growing population, on the one hand, and economic and social issues, on the other. The authority for the commission comes from the top down, flowing as it does through the Population Division of the Department of Economic and Social Development. Moreover, and perhaps more to the point, the PC is charged with helping to implement the UN World Population Plan of Action, which was first developed in 1974 at the World Population Conference on Bucharest. The plan developed strategies based on the relationships between population growth and socio-economic factors. The plan has been revised since that time and now publishes an extensive list of recommendations that suggest action in relation to population-related questions. To provide funding for population-related government projects, the United Nation's Population Fund (UNPF) was set up in 1966. The UNPF provides money for family planning projects and other work in population management. [See *Basic Facts about the United Nations* (New York: The United Nations Department of Public Relations 1992).]

### quick quiz 33-2

1. The Federal Energy Regulatory Commission (FERC) is responsible for regulating the transportation and the wholesale price of natural gas alone.  true | false

2. The Nuclear Regulatory Commission owns and operates 104 civilian nuclear power plants and 63 military reactors.  true | false

3. The Clean Air Act is designed to limit pollution from vehicles but not from stationary sources such factories and manufacturing centers.  true | false

# 33-3 Protecting Innovation and Creativity

Unlike the regulatory powers discussed earlier in the chapter, the authority of the government in the area of intellectual property has never been in doubt. However, as they say, "the devil is in the details." This is especially true of patents and copyrights because the very nature of an invention and a recorded work is originality. Originality means that every copyright and every patent application will present a new question for the patent office and, possibly, for the courts. For that reason alone the law of intellectual property is complicated and diverse. Nevertheless, the law of intellectual property plays an enormously important role in the development of scientific and technological advances that will help to combat Heilbroner's global challenges. In its most fundamental form, the entire idea behind the legal framework supporting intellectual property is that inventors, scientists, engineers, and writers must be encouraged to pursue their crafts so that the entire socio-economic system can benefit from the advances that they produce. What the people at General Electric used to say about their own research and development applies equally well, perhaps even better, to the entire scientific community: "Progress is our most important product."

## The Nature of Intellectual Property

Intellectual property involves an intangible ownership right in an invention, a process, a computer program, a chemical formula, an original recorded work such as a book or an article, and so on. The ownership rights bestowed on a person holding the property includes the right to give permission to use the property in exchange for some sort of consideration. This consideration is usually referred to as a **royalty**. The power of the government to grant the exclusive rights to intellectual property is expressly mentioned in Article I, Section 8, Clause 8 of the Constitution, where the Framers gave Congress the authority to grant patents and copyrights. The clause reads that Congress has the power to "promote the Progress of Science and the useful Arts, by securing for limited Times to Authors and Inventors the exclusive Right to their respective Writings and Discoveries." The granting of patents and copyrights is one of the most direct and obvious entanglements of science and the law in jurisicence.

## THE OPENING CASE *Revisited, Part I*
### "To be or not to be": *JCVI and Patent Application US2007 0264688, Round 2*

Recall in the Opening Case at the beginning of the chapter that members of the J. Craig Venter Institute filed patent #US 2007 0264688 with the U.S. Patent Office, in an attempt to patent synthetic life. What JCVI had produced was a self-replicating bacterial cell completely under the control of a synthetic genome. The development of the synthetic self-replicating cell proved that such organisms can be planned by a computer, constructed chemically in a laboratory, and then placed in a bacterium from which the original DNA had been removed. The new cell then replicated itself 1 billion times. The process will make DNA synthesis more economical and more affordable, leading to possible breakthroughs in the development of new vaccines, innovative pharmaceuticals, clean water, new food products, innovative pollution filters, and possibly even revolutionary new biofuel derivatives. This is not the first time that the legal system has faced this issue. In the case of *Diamond v. Chakrabarty,* the United States Supreme Court had decided that it was possible to patent a life-form. Nevertheless, the issue of patenting a self-replicating completely synthetic life form presents a new twist on that original theme. This is what intellectual property law is all about. [See *Diamond v. Chakrabarty,* 447 U.S 303, 100 S.Ct. 204 (1980).]

## Protecting Patents

A **patent** is a property right granted by the federal government to an inventor. A patent gives the inventor the exclusive right to make, use, and sell that invention for a period of 20 years (14 years if the patent covers a process). A patent is, in effect, a deal with the government. The inventor reveals the details of the invention in the patent application. In exchange, the inventor receives a guarantee from the government that it will protect the inventor's exclusive right to produce and profit from that invention for a specified period of time. As we shall see below, a trade secret is not revealed in any way in the open marketplace; the holder of the trade secret receives no guaranteed protection from the government. A copyright differs from a patent in that a copyright protects only the expression of an idea, whereas a patent protects the idea itself.

**The Patent Application Process** Each patent application requires the creation of a unique technical document. The document is then filed with the Patent Office. To qualify for a patent, an invention must meet three requirements. First, the invention must fall within the limits defined by the statute as "patentable subject matter." Second, the invention must consist of some nonobvious, new, and useful feature not known or understood before the invention of this particular device. Third, the patent application must be so specific that individuals who are educated and experienced in the field can create the device on their own.

**Patentable Subject Matter** The law states that for the subject of a patent application to be patentable, it must be a "process, machine, manufacturer or composition of matter." In contrast, such things as laws of nature, natural phenomena, and abstract ideas cannot be patented. Neither mathematical formulas nor mathematical algorithms are patentable because they are actually laws of nature. An algorithm is a series of steps that, if followed properly, will reach a desired goal. Because many computer software programs are based on mathematical algorithms, problems arose when inventors first attempted to patent computer software. In fact, when patent applications for computer software programs began to appear in the Patent Office in the 1970s, most software programs were eventually found to be unpatentable. However, during the 1980s and the 1990s, the trend reversed itself. Today, more than 80 percent of all patent claims involving computers have been upheld, including those involving software alone. However, the law in this area remains somewhat unclear. Fortunately, some general guidelines can be laid down. For example, if a software program is only one part of a larger, more conventional process, the courts will allow patent protection for the whole process.

## EXAMPLE 33-4: Alison's Shatter-Proof Patent Problem

Alison Louise, the owner, operator, and CEO of Alison, Inc., "Home of the Best Shatter-Proof Glass Products in America," developed a new process for mass producing shatterproof glass goods. The new process allowed Alison, Inc. to produce a better quality glass at about half the cost of its closest competitors. Part of Alison's success was due to the use of lasers in the process. However, the lasers had to be timed so precisely that each one was controlled by a computer, following the directions of a computer program. This portion of the process was only about one-fourth of the entire operation, the rest of which was relatively conventional. The patent examiner denied Alison's patent application because part of the process involved an unpatentable computer program. A federal court reversed the refusal because the process itself was new and could be patented. The use of the program was only one part of that process.

However, if the software stands alone, the question of whether the patent application will be granted is more difficult. The Court of Appeals for the Federal Circuit has addressed the issue in several cases and tends to affirm such patent applications. The appellate court generally upholds the patentability of software, even if it is based on a mathematical algorithm, because the software actually changes the operation of the computer. Thus, the software can be viewed as either a process or a change in the physical nature of the computer itself. To deal with the issue, the U.S. Patent and Trademark Office established a set of guidelines for computer-related inventions. The objective of the guidelines is to help eliminate ambiguity in the law regarding the patentability of software.

## EXAMPLE 33-5: Cole's Infinity Bucks Tracker Tracks a Win.

Cole Christopher, the owner-operator of Cole's Infinity Bucks, Inc., developed Cole's Infinity Bucks Tracker, a software program that allowed the user to overlay on a computer screen all available trajectories for any stocks that he or she wished to purchase or sell in the near future while simultaneously displaying all changes in the data related to each pictured stock. Such a program would be invaluable to investors as they planned investment strategies. The patent examiner refused to issue a patent, arguing that Cole's program was simply the expression of a mathematical algorithm. The Board of Patent Appeals supported the examiner's position. The Court of Appeals for the Federal Circuit, however, reversed the decision and stated that in effect, Cole's program transformed an ordinary, all-purpose computer into a specialized computer. Thus, the all-purpose computer had in effect become a new computer, capable of performing a new function by following the commands of the software program. Cole's Infinity Bucks Tracker can be viewed as either a process creating a change or an alteration in the physical nature of the computer itself.

Until recently a **business system** was also considered unpatentable because it was not a "process, machine, manufacturer, or composition of matter." However, in a recent court

## THE OPENING CASE *Revisited, Part II*
## "To be or not to be": *JCVI and Patent Application US2007 0264688*, Round 3

Let's return for a moment to the requirement of "usefulness" and the case of the J. Craig Venter Institute and patent #US 2007 0264688. Recall that the application filed with the Patent Office was an attempt to patent synthetic life. The development of the synthetic self-replicating cell proved that such organisms can be planned by a computer, constructed chemically in a laboratory, and then placed in a bacterium from which the original DNA had been removed. The new cell then replicated itself 1 billion times. All that is nice, but . . . so what? What can the synthetic life do that, well, "real" life cannot? The answer is that JCVI's new process will make DNA synthesis more economical and more affordable leading to possible breakthroughs in the development of new vaccines, innovative pharmaceuticals, clean water, new food products, innovative pollution filters, and possibly even revolutionary new biofuel derivatives.

case, a computer system for analyzing information about a group of mutual funds was declared patentable by a federal court. This decision culminated in a slow erosion of the business systems category of unpatentable subjects. Even so, a computerized business system must still consist of some nonobvious, new, and useful feature not known or understood before the invention of this system. It must also be so specific that people who are educated and experienced in the field can recreate the system on their own.

### Usefulness, Novelty, and Nonobviousness
The objective of patent law is to encourage inventiveness and promote progress for the benefit of all society. Thus, a device, to be patentable, must be useful. Many processes involving computer programs would pass the usefulness test. Passing the usefulness test alone, however, is not enough to qualify for a patent. The new invention must also be novel and nonobvious. To pass the novelty test, the new device or process must be original. Copying someone else's innovation, even unintentionally, will disqualify an invention from patent eligibility. Similarly, to pass the nonobviousness test, the changes or improvements must not be obvious to a person of ordinary skill in the field. If the changes are obvious, then a patent will not be issued.

### Recent Developments in the Nonobviousness Test
The patent review process became more difficult for patent holders recently when the United States Supreme Court revised the traditional test of nonobviousness. The traditional test, which was referred to as the **teaching, suggestion, or motivation test** or the **TSM standard**, compelled those who challenged a patent to demonstrate that the so-called innovation would have been obvious to anyone exposed to the same *teaching* session, the same off-hand *suggestion,* or the same *motivation* as the inventor had been exposed to. In essence, the test rests on the belief that any small innovation based on prior art in the field would not be patentable but that other innovations, even small ones beyond prior art, would be (see Table 33-1). **Prior art** refers to all relevant technical knowledge about the field to which the invention belongs. The test was difficult, however, because it also required the challenger to produce some sort of hard evidence to support the TSM challenge. Generally, the only factual data that the court would accept as hard evidence was information that had been printed in a professional journal or data that rose to that level of credibility.

| Table 33-1   Recent Developments in Patent Law | |
|---|---|
| **Standard** | **Explanation** |
| Teaching, suggestion, motivation | An invention is obvious and not patentable if anyone exposed to the same teaching, suggestion, or motivation would have come up with the same invention. |
| Obvious-to-try standard | An invention is obvious and not patentable if the innovation was so obvious that anyone of ordinary skill could see that it was obvious to try that innovation. |
| Possible legislative changes | Some *possible* legislative changes slated for the future may be (1) increased ease in obtaining injunctions; (2) an 18-month publication rule; and (3) a change in the burden of proof |

The Supreme Court has made it clear that previous courts had been too uncompromising in their use of TSM. Accordingly, the Court suggested that challengers ought to consider using other types of evidence to contest the validity of a patent claim. Such evidence might include economic requirements, the knowledge of other inventors in the same field, or progress in the relevant technology that might show that a person of ordinary skill could easily have developed the same innovation introduced in the challenged patent. If any of these features exist, the innovation is not patentable. In addition, the Supreme Court reintroduced a variation on the TSM test called the obvious-to-try standard, a test that had been outlawed by previous precedent. Under the newly reinstated obvious-to-try standard, if the challenger can demonstrate that anyone of ordinary skill could see that it would have been obvious to try such an innovation, the innovation would be labeled as obvious, and the invention would not be patentable.

## Nonobviousness and Cyber-Inventions
The new rulings make it more difficult for inventors to obtain patents and easier for challengers to demonstrate that an innovation is obvious and therefore not patentable. The decision to make the test of patentability harder will have a direct effect on computer-related cyber-inventions. Many innovations in computer technology that might have been patentable under the old rules will not be patentable under the new obviousness tests. For instance, under the old rules that dealt exclusively with TSM, a small innovation in the component parts of a laptop or a PDA might have been patentable if the new component was not made clear by teaching, suggestion, or motivation. Now, if the challenger can show that trends in engineering made the innovation a logical next step, or that it was obvious to try the change in the component parts of that PDA or laptop, the innovation, no matter how clever, will be unpatentable.

## Specificity in the Application
Federal law states that a patent application must describe the nature of the invention in "full, clear, concise, and exact terms." In fact, the application must be so clear that any person educated and experienced in that field can recreate the invention without having to engage in an extensive trial-and-error period. This requirement causes some difficulty in computer software patent applications, because the surest way to guarantee that someone else will be able to recreate the invention is to provide the source code in the patent application. However, many inventors are reluctant to include source code because such codes often contain trade secrets that they are unwilling to dump into the public domain. The usual compromise is to include in the patent application either a flowchart or some other visual diagram that reveals the details of the process.

# THE OPENING CASE *Revisited, Part III*
## "To be or not to be": *JCVI and Patent Application US2007 0264688, Round 4*

Let's refer to the Opening Case again. Recall that the members of the J. Craig Venter Institute were attempting to patent synthetic life. Also recall that JCVI had produced a self-replicating bacterial cell completely under the control of a synthetic genome. The development of the synthetic self-replicating cell proved that such organisms can be planned by a computer, constructed chemically in a laboratory, and then placed in a bacterium from which the original DNA had been removed. Not everyone was happy with this development, however. Some of JCVI's competitors accused Venter of trying to corner the market with the patent application. The main objection to the JCVI patent application is that it is too broad. Venter is not attempting to patent the synthetic self-replicating bacterium that his team actually created, but the process of planning, constructing, and creating any synthetic cell imaginable. Some legal experts argue that the problem may be that JCVI's patent application lacked appropriate specificity. These experts predict that JCVI will get its patent, but not the way that it was originally written. Instead, what the Institute will receive is a patent for the process involving the bacterium that they used in the original process, or more likely, bacteria in general. What JCVI will not earn is a blank check to use the process on any cell imaginable.

## A QUESTION OF ETHICS

Let's go back to the Opening Case at the beginning of the chapter once again. Recall that members of the J. Craig Venter Institute filed patent #US 2007 0264688 with the U.S. Patent Office in an attempt to patent synthetic life. Recall also that JCVI had produced a self-replicating bacterial cell completely under the control of a synthetic genome. The development of the synthetic self-replicating cell proved that such organisms can be planned by a computer, constructed chemically in a laboratory, and then placed in a bacterium from which the original DNA had been removed. Also recall that this was not the first time that the legal system had faced this issue. In the case of *Diamond v. Chakrabarty,* the United States Supreme Court decided that it was possible to patent a life-form. As is often the case in sensitive issues like this, no one was happy with the High Court's decision except, perhaps, the new patent holder. Some experts felt compelled to criticize the High Court for stepping outside the bounds of its authority. Others accused the Court of a thoughtless ruling that would open the door to abusive use of biotechnology. However, one of the most interesting points was made when a commentator noted that it was strange that the Supreme Court was willing to grant a patent for a new life form when, in a previous case, the case of *Roe v. Wade,* the court had refused to define life. Is it ethical for the justices of the Supreme Court to avoid the definition of life when it comes to the rights of women and then turn around and permit a megacorporation, like General Electric, to reap potential profit from their decision. (Note: The microbiologist who developed the DNA plasmid that was the subject of *Diamond v. Chakrabarty,* was employed by General Electric.) Think about it and try to come up with a rationale for each side of the issue. [See *Diamond v. Chakrabarty,* 447 U.S 303, 100 S.Ct. 204 (1980); and *Roe V. Wade,* 410 S. Ct. 113, 93 S.Ct. 705 (1973).]

# The America Invents Act (AIA) of 2011

Congress amended the patent law for the first time in over sixty years when, in 2011, it passed the America Invents Act (AIA). The new act is designed to do several things, not the least of which is to bring U.S. patent law in line with international patent law. The AIA does several important things in this regard. First, it has changed the basic principle of American patent law. The act adopts the "first-to-file" patent process, which replaces the "first-to-invent" process which had been the American standard for decades. Second, the new act has set up a series of innovative ways to dispute previous or pending patent claims.

### The First-to-File Provision
As noted above, this is a key provision that will help bring U.S. patent law in line with international patent law. Congress set March of 2013 as the date for the activation of this new process. Some experts predict that this change will probably increase the practice of provisional filing. Provisional filing permits an inventor or company to "hold his or her place" in line as a first filer, without having to deal with some of the formalities involved in a full fledged filing. The net effect will be that inventors and the companies that they represent will likely file more patents earlier rather than later. The point of the early filing strategy will be to jump in line ahead of any other inventors who might be close to developing the same type of process or device that the first filer has developed, thus trumping the claims of all other inventors. The provision clearly gives the advantage to large corporate R&D departments which can move in lock step toward the Patent Office. In contrast, those inventors who work in the family garage or in the basement of the family home who are more engrossed in the science and the technology than day-to-day business matters are likely to lose the race to the patent office.

### The New Dispute Resolution Process
As indicated previously, the new law also sets up several new ways to call into question previous patent filings, including both those that have been completed and those that are still in the processing stage. There are several new ways to mount such challenges; however, the two most important, however, are the (1) pre-issuance submission challenge and (2) the post grant review process. The pre-submission disputes are permitted before the patent has been granted the Patent Office. They can be submitted anonymously by third parties who seek to block the issuance of the patent. Naturally, proper documentation must be presented to demonstrate that the patent should not be granted. The new law also permits a post grant review which must be filed within nine months of the patent issuance. To be accepted for review the post grant challenge must show either (a) that the invention did not meet the requirements of patentability or that (b) there are legal questions involved in the patent that will affect other patents and other patent applications that must be handled before proceeding further with the sale of distribution of the invention or process that is the subject of the challenged patent. (See Ronald Abramson, et al., "First Major Revision in Nearly Six Decades Changes the Patent Landscape," *Hughes Hubbard and Reed, LLP,* (30 September 2011), retrieved on 11 October 2011 from http://www.mondaq.com; and Chris Dixon, "Summary of New Patent Act," *Business Insider* (16 September 2011), retrieved on 11 October 2011 from http://www.businessinsider.com.)

# Protecting Trade Secrets

Sometimes an inventor or a discoverer refuses to apply for a patent. At first glance this may seem strange. After all, the patent protects the invention or the discovery so that no one else can use it except with the patent holder's permission, and then according to the owner's terms, which will generally include royalty payments of some sort. There are disadvantages to holding patent, however. First, a patent expires at the end of a 20-year period, and for design patents, that period is only 14 years. At the end of that period the invention or the discovery is in the public domain and anyone can use and profit from it. Second, to be awarded a patent, the patent applicant must fill out the patent application with great specificity. This means that anyone can access the patent and see exactly what the inventor has developed. Certainly, most people will honor the patent. However, there are people who will try to copy the process or the invention and benefit from the patent owner's work without having to pay royalties. Finally, once the patent is a public record it is possible that someone who examines the patent might be clever enough to see the next leap in technology or science before the patent owner sees it. Thus, the work of the patent owner may inspire a competitor to take the next developmental leap before the original owner sees it, leaving the owner holding an outdated patent almost before it is approved by the Patent Office. For all of these reasons and probably more, many scientists and engineers who have invented or discovered something may try to keep that discovery or that invention as secret as possible. Juriscientific principles protect these efforts as long as the holder of the secret takes certain relatively easy but very important steps.

### A Primer on Trade Secrets
A trade secret is a plan, process, device, procedure, formula, pattern, compilation, technique, program, design, method, or improvement used in a business and disclosed only to those employees who need to know it to do their jobs. The Uniform Trade Secrets Act sets up two conditions that must be met for a plan, process, program, and so on to gain trade secret status. First, the plan, process, or program must gain financial worth simply because it is a secret and cannot be applied by others who might use it to compete with the owner of the secret. Second, the alleged secret must be the subject of reasonable attempts to protect it from those who would use it in a way that would financially hurt the owner of the secret.

### State Statutory Trade Secret Protection
Various states have enacted trade secret statutes designed to protect trade secrets within the state's borders. Many of these statutes are patterned after the Uniform Trade Secrets Act, written by the National Conference of Commissioners on Uniform State Laws. Typically, these statutes define a trade secret, describe transgressions of the act, and provide for both damages and injunctive relief when there has been a trade secret infringement. The statutes also generally include a statute of limitations, typically about four years, and indicate that continuing use of a trade secret is a single rather than a series of transgressions. Some state statutes also allow for attorney's fees.

### The Economic Espionage Act
The federal government also entered the trade secrets' arena with the passage of the Economic Espionage Act in 1996. The Espionage Act does not provide for any civil actions but instead outlines criminal sanctions for the theft of trade secrets and the use of fraud to obtain trade secrets. Persons convicted under the statute can face up to 10 years of imprisonment and fines that may reach as much as $500,000. The statute forbids the theft of trade secrets for distribution to a foreign government or an agent of a foreign government or for economic gain that does not benefit the actual owner of the trade secret.

### Establishing Trade Secret Status
In the 21st century, many of the inventors, scientists, and engineers who apply for patents know that part of the patent application will include a step involving computers. For example the synthetic life process outlined in the Opening Case at the beginning of the chapter involves a computerized stage wherein the computer actually designs the synthetic genome before it is produced chemically and then placed in the bacterium. Scientists who are not overly concerned about the time limit placed on patents or with the specificity required in the patent application, might go ahead and file the patent application knowing full well that they have placed it at risk. Why do it then? The advantage to pursuing patent protection rather than trade secret protection is that

the patent applicant can be almost certain that a patent can include a computer program. The same is not true of an engineer or a technician who wants to keep a computer program as a trade secret. The law at the moment is filled with ambiguities about the trade secret status of a computer program.

The right to characterize a computer program as a trade secret depends on the way the owners of the program treat it in relation to other people. In general, the easier it is for people to gain access to the program, the less likely it is that the program will be considered a secret should the matter be contested in court. Therefore, to protect trade secret status, the owners of a program must make certain that the program is treated as a secret from the very beginning. The goal is to grant access to the secret only to those people who need to know it to carry out their duties in the ordinary course of business. Steps that can be taken to increase the likelihood that a court will rule that a program is a trade secret include the following: (1) label the program as secret in all documents related to the program; (2) limit employee access to the program on a need-to-know basis; (3) maintain tight security in the business in general but especially in any area where the program is required to be out in the open for business purposes; (4) keep the program and all related material under lock and key when it is not in use; (5) require employees who work with the program to sign secrecy agreements; (6) require customers who purchase the use of the program to sign licensing agreements; and (7) be especially vigilant in limiting any access to the program by competitors.

### Computer Programs Denied Trade Secret Status
Computer programs that have been transferred to software and then placed on the open market for wide distribution cannot claim trade secret status. Software that is widely distributed can be easily copied. Thus, it becomes difficult to demonstrate that the company has taken extensive measures to protect the information on the software. Moreover, because the purpose of placing the software on the open market is to sell it to as many people as possible, the seller must make the software readily available in bookstores and video outlets. This availability on the open market defeats the whole trade secret concept.

### Computer Programs Granted Trade Secret Status
Trade secret status is available to companies that distribute their software on a limited, highly selective basis. For example, a computer company that produces and sells a program used to control the distribution of drugs by pharmaceutical firms might be able to call that program a trade secret. Such a company would not actually sell the program to the pharmaceutical firm but would instead allow the firm to use the program through a licensing agreement. A licensing agreement occurs when the producer of a product, in this case a computer program, allows a purchaser to use the product only if the purchaser agrees to respect the producer's desire for secrecy. In this situation, to use the program, the pharmaceutical company would have to agree to respect the computer company's desire for secrecy. In this type of highly selective, strictly controlled transaction, trade secret status works.

### Trademark Protection
Before moving on to copyright law, it would be a good idea to pause momentarily just to distinguish between trade secrets and trademarks. A trademark is a symbol, picture, image, name, device, color, or word that a business uses to distinguish itself from its competitors. Once a business has established that it owns a trademark, that business has the exclusive right to use that mark to identify its products and services, as well as the business itself. The law provides businesspeople with several ways to establish trademark ownership: common law, state law, and federal law. To claim that trademark ownership has been established by common law, the alleged owner must show that the trademark has been used with such intensity and for such a long time that the mark

has come to be identified not only with the business's products but also with the business itself. Every state legislature has also passed state trademark laws to protect the use of trademarks in intrastate commerce. Despite the use of common law and state law to protect trademarks, most of the legal action in this area takes place at the federal level. The Trademark Protection Act, also known as the Lanham Act, was passed in 1946 to provide for the registration of trademarks with the federal government. The registration authority is the U.S. Office of Patents and Trademarks. Under the Lanham Act, once a trademark is properly registered with the office, it cannot be used by any other business. The act also protects trademark owners from businesses that use symbols, pictures, words, and so on that are so similar to the protected mark that consumers might be confused into thinking that the secondary mark is actually the original mark, thus leading those consumers from the owner's product to those of the competitor.

**Trademark Dilution**  In 1995 Congress passed the Trademark Dilution Act to establish a standard for trademark infringement that would not involve direct and obvious consumer confusion. Unfortunately, the act has not always worked as well as it was supposed to, mainly because of the courts' often perplexing rules about how it ought to be interpreted. To remedy this situation, Congress amended the act in 2006. The new act, referred to as the Trademark Dilution Revision Act, established several new provisions. First, the new act allows trademark owners to obtain an injunction to stop the use of a trademark, simply by demonstrating that the effectiveness of the original mark would probably be diminished. Second, the act strengthens the eligibility of certain marks for protection, especially expressive trademarks such as Quick Lube, Fresh Way Cleaners, or Complete Comfort Heating. Third, the act provides a series of characteristics that the courts can apply to determine if the unauthorized use of a trademark really does obscure the effectiveness of the original mark.

## Protecting Copyright

Copyright law is much more expansive than patent law because copyrights also protect the rights of nonscientific work. Therefore it encompasses an area of the law that goes beyond the bounds of normal juriscience. Nevertheless, there are two areas on which juriscience and copyright law intersect dramatically. The first is in the area of scientific writing. Perhaps more than any other academic discipline save perhaps law and literature, science communicates using the written word. Scientific ideas, claims, theories, antitheories, and arguments are all communicated by the written word. Scientific books, periodicals, articles, news releases, new stories, and conference poster presentations are the mainstay of the scientific community. Therefore, a clear connection exists between science and copyright law. The second, and perhaps more contemporary, way that science and copyright law intersect is in the world of computer advances. The law has had to play catch-up with scientific advances in computer technology. Scientists are responsible for these advances; they then communicate information about these advances using the advances themselves. The law must decide if the advances themselves and the way that those advances are communicated deserve copyright protection. A clear case exactly on point is the development and evolution of the computer program, something that scientists and information technologists took for granted but which the law struggled with for decades, literally.

**A Primer on Copyright**  A copyright is an intangible property right granted to authors of literary, artistic, and musical compositions. A copyright gives the owner the exclusive right to reproduce, publish, and sell his or her work in a fixed, tangible medium of expression. Although it was not immediately obvious to lawmakers and judges 30 year ago, a computer program is a fixed medium of expression and is, therefore, subject to copyright protection. Today, the federal Copyright Act specifically lists the following as works that are subject to copyright protection: literary works, dramatic works, musical works, pantomimes, pictorial works, sculptures, graphic works, motion pictures, audiovisual works, sound recordings, architectural works, and choreographic works. Computer programs are also specifically covered by the Copyright Act of 1980, which includes computer programs in the category of "writings" or "literary" works to which exclusive rights can be granted.

Juriscience has finally responded to the unprecedented changes that have occurred in computer technology. To make up for lost time, many of the recent alterations in the law were specifically designed to keep abreast of the effects of electronic communication on copyright privileges. Despite this effort, the high-speed, global, interactive nature of the Internet has caused unforeseen problems in copyright law. For example, computer technology now makes it possible for a single copy of a computer program or an individual copy of a scientific paper to be made available to millions of computer users, simply by placing that single copy on a Web site that is accessible to other users. This advance in computer technology may have been predictable to cyberneticists, but it went virtually unnoticed for quite some time by jurists and legislators. Nevertheless, despite the unpredictability of the problem, juriscience has provided a few solutions.

## The No Electronic Theft Act
One such solution came from Congress in the form of the **No Electronic Theft Act (NET Act)**, a federal law that granted limited immunity to persons who duplicate copyrighted works on the Internet, as long as those users do not profit from the copying process. The statute does not simply grant immunity to infringers, however. Instead, it imposes criminal penalties for the violation of certain provisions. Specifically, it makes it illegal to create a duplication (including an electronic duplication) of a copyrighted work for commercial profit or private financial gain by copying or handing out one or more copies of one or more copyrighted productions within a single 180-day period, if the productions in question have a complete retail value of over $1,000. Penalties can include fines of up to $100,000 and imprisonment of up to 10 years.

## The Digital Millennium Copyright Act
To defend their copyright privileges, copyright holders have developed computer protection programs that prevent users from duplicating their copyrighted works. Thus, the copyright owner of a film or television show might place a protective program on a DVD to prevent users from creating a copy of that film or television show from the DVD. Not to be outdone, infringers then created software that would allow a user to sidestep the protective program and create a duplicate of the scrambled work. In response to this technological tug-of-war, Congress passed the **Digital Millennium Copyright Act (DMCA)**. The DMCA is designed to combat scientific advances that permit users to override protection systems. The law makes it illegal to use technological means to bypass or override programs designed to prevent access to a copyrighted work. Another provision of the DMCA makes it illegal to use any means to circumvent a program intended to frustrate the copying of a copyrighted work. First-time offenders can be fined up to $500,000 and imprisoned for up to five years. Second-time offenders can be fined up to $1 million and receive a prison sentence that can reach as long as 10 years.

## The World Intellectual Property Organization
It would be unfair and incomplete to close any discussion of the Digital Millennium Copyright Act without mentioning its connection to the **World Intellectual Property Organization (WIPO)**. WIPO is part of the United Nations and supported the development of two international treaties specifically designed to deal with electronic copyright problems. Two separate but closely related treaties resulted from the efforts of the WIPO. The first treaty is known as

the **World Intellectual Property Organization Copyright Treaty**. This treaty guarantees that copyright holders will be allowed to use the Internet to post their works with full copyright protection. The second WIPO treaty, the **World Intellectual Property Organization Phonograms Treaty**, gives copyright holders the right to copy, publish, and distribute their works in any way, including by making video copies, audio copies, and encrypted copies. The DMCA was written to implement the provisions of these treaties into law in the United States.

## quick quiz 33-3

| | | |
|---|---|---|
| 1. | A patent gives the inventor the exclusive right to make, use, and sell that invention for a period of 20 years (14 years if the patent covers a process). | true \| false |
| 2. | A trade secret is a plan, process, device, procedure, formula, pattern, compilation, technique, program, design, method, or improvement used in a business and disclosed only to those employees who need to know it to do their jobs. | true \| false |
| 3. | A copyright is an intangible property right granted to authors of literary, artistic, and musical compositions. | true \| false |

# 33-4 Developing Global Solutions

The goal of this chapter has been to explore the relationship between science and the law and to look at how the law helps promote discoveries in science so that those discoveries can be directed toward social and economic improvements. A central function of the law is to contribute to the civic peace by securing order, stability, and justice. There can be no more serious threat to the global social system than the challenges that Heilbroner notes above. Some of these challenges can be met by promoting and awarding innovation and originality in science and technology by protecting intellectual property through patents, copyrights, and trade secrets. However, there is another way to help deal with these problems and that is to actively restructure the law to direct scientific and technological activities toward solving the problems.

## Four Basic Requirements

In order to solve any problem, the first thing that the government must do is to identify the parameters of the problem. At the close of the 20th century, there was an enormous amount of work done by colleges and universities, governmental institutions, corporations, and private think tanks to identify the problems that will face humanity in the 21st century. One such study was conducted by the New York Academy of Sciences (NYAS). As a result, the NYAS published a report based on 20 case studies that examined the results of government-supported science and technology polices in the United States and around the globe. The studies examined a series of successful and "less-than-successful" projects in an attempt to identify those factors that made things work and those that made them fail. The results were compiled in an article entitled "Lessons from Global Experiences in Policy for Science Based Development," by Susan U. Raymond, Director of the Policy Programs at NYAS. In the article Raymond pinpoints six issues that became the focal point of these studies. There are, however, four main issues that we will examine here. They are (1) the necessity of focusing on long-range results; (2) the need to create partnerships among government, business, and the academic community; (3) the need to appreciate the key role played in these projects by human resources, and (4) the need to develop inventive ways to obtain capital investments in science and related projects. [See Susan U. Raymond. "Lessons from Global Experiences in Policy for Science-Based Development," in *Science Based Economic Development: Case Studies Around the World* (New York: New York Academy of Sciences, 1996).]

## Developing Long-Range Plans

For decades American science and technology programs were based on the conclusions that were contained in a blue ribbon report compiled by a committee headed by Vannevar Bush, who served as the director of the White House Office of Scientific Research and Development under Presidents Franklin D. Roosevelt and Harry S. Truman. The report, which was cleverly dubbed *Science: The Endless Frontier,* emphasized the need for pure research, the kind conducted at colleges and universities and national thinks tanks. Pure research, or basic research as it is generally called, is aimed at understanding the laws of nature and the principles of the physical universe without any practical goals in mind [See Richard Nelson, "Why the Bush Report Has Hindered an Effective Civilian Technology Policy," in *Science for the 21st Century: The Bush Report Revisited* (Washington D.C.: AEI, 1997.) The Bush Report promoted pure research because the committee believed that it would contribute to American economic independence, promote technological developments, while, at the same time preserving the cultural and artistic aspects of human life. [See Claude E. Barfield, "Introduction and Overview," and David C. Mowery, "The Bush Report After 50 Years—Blueprint or Relic?" in *Science for the 21st Century: The Bush Report Revisited* (Washington D.C.: AEI, 1997.)]

The problem is that pure research is often underfunded because it is seen as impractical and unusable. As a result, for pure research to work it must be tied clearly to a set of long-range goals that show how such research can be applied in a practical real world setting. This is absolutely necessary in a capitalist democracy in which business people, politicians, consumers, and voters tend to look only as far as the next billing cycle or the next election. One way to do this is to create hybrid projects that include both short-terms results and long-term goals. The immediate gains satisfy the politician and the business people while the long-range goals serve to stimulate the researchers. Thus, the short-term gratification fuels support for the more long-range goals of the pure research program. Perhaps it will be of no surprise that this was the very technique used by the Benjamin Franklin Programs in Pennsylvania. Under the BF Programs, governmental long-term planning projects were designed to produce immediate results in entrepreneurship and education. The short-term accomplishments produced results that calmed critics and permitted the long-term goals to play themselves out successfully. [See Walter H. Plosila and Susan U. Raymond, "Policies for Science Based Economic Development: The Experiences of Pennsylvania and Ohio," and Susan U. Raymond. "Lessons from Global Experiences in Policy for Science-Based Development," in *Science Based Economic Development: Case Studies Around the World* (New York: New York Academy of Sciences, 1996).]

## Developing Partnerships

The second requirement for a successful marriage between science and government is to develop partnerships among government, business, and the academic community. Such partnerships are valuable because they make use of the talents, abilities, and experience of researchers at various levels of the scientific community and in a wide variety of settings. This mixture promotes innovation, stimulates creativity, and ensures some level of success no matter what the task. Also a cross fertilization of ideas takes place when scientists, engineers, and technicians are compelled to work

from nine other institutions of higher education, the government, and several financial institutions. The two foundations disperse funds for projects run by the university and by local businesses. [See Susan U. Raymond. "Lessons from Global Experiences in Policy for Science-Based Development," in *Science Based Economic Development: Case Studies Around the World* (New York: New York Academy of Sciences, 1996).]

# UN Economic Security Council

While all of these projects are admirable and while many of them succeed, they all lack one thing. There is no centralized control point for the vast array of projects underway at any one time, at least not on the international scene. Some commentators insist that what is needed is a new way of integrating international efforts to pool global resources and to direct those resources toward solving Heilbroner's central modern challenges: environment, war, and unchecked population growth. A model of this type of organization exists if we combine the work of the Commission on Sustainable Development with the work done by the UN Security Council. The proposed institution that emerges from the marriage of these two institutions has been named the UN Economic Security Council. If we take a close look at how these two present day institutions, the Commission on Sustainable Development (CSD) and the UN Security Council, work we will see how the proposed Economic Security Council might operate. First, recall how the CSD was created. The CSD was established after the first Earth Summit in 1992 in Brazil to administer Agenda 21, which established a set of tactics designed to activate sustainable development plans across the globe. The CSD also serves as a central clearing-house for nations to report progress in the implementation of sustainable development plans. In this way the CSD just might be able to deal with the Heilbroner challenges were it not for two obvious drawbacks. First, the CSD deals only with the environment, while the Heilbroner's challenges also deal with war, energy, and population. Second, the CSD lacks the power to enforce its recommendations under AGENA 21. In other words, the CSD has no "teeth." [See Commission on Global Governance, *Our Global Neighborhood: The Report of the Commission on Global Governance* (Oxford: Oxford University Press, 1995).]

The second agency, the UN Security Council, provides a model for those missing teeth. The Security Council has the power to pass resolutions that have consequences for those who break those resolutions. Those consequence must be carried out by the military forces of member nations or by NATO, to be sure. However, the threat of those consequences is often enough to prevent a rogue or failed state from ignoring the decisions of the Security Council and its members. Some commentators have suggested that the UN Charter be amended to create a new Economic Security Council (ESC) that would utilize the best parts of the CSD and the Security Council to coordinate science and technology policy in order to solve the economic, environmental, and demographic problems of the globe. The ESC would first diagnose the condition of the world especially as it relates to the issues of environment, energy, and population. The council would then draw up some long-range plans that would involve specific projects for sustainable development, environmental clean-up, population control, and energy enrichment. Those plans would outline the roles that each member nation of the UN would play in the development plan, plus deadlines for those goals, plus funding resources and, finally, consequences for noncompliance, consequences that would be carried out much like those carried out by the agents of the present Security Council.

Thus, the ESC would run much like the CSD in its planning and coordinating activities and much like the Security Council its enforcement function, except that, instead of responding to short-range crises, as the Security Council does, the ESC would deal with long-range problems and long-range solutions. The ESC would be autonomous, much like the CSD and the Security Council. It would consist of the largest economic blocs on the planet. The blocks might be made up of a single nation such as China, India, or the United States, or by conglomerates such as the EU, or unified regions such as the Association of

## THE OPENING CASE *Revisited, Part V*
### "To be or not to be": *JCVI and Patent Application US2007 0264688, Round 6*

Recall that in the Opening Case at the beginning of this chapter members of the J. Craig Venter Institute filed patent #US 2007 0264688 with the U.S. Patent Office, as their attempt to patent synthetic life. What JCVI had produced was a self-replicating bacterial cell completely under the control of a synthetic genome. The development of the synthetic self-replicating cell proved that such organisms can be planned by a computer, constructed chemically in a laboratory, and then placed in a bacterium from which the original DNA had been removed. The new cell then replicated itself 1 billion times. The process will make DNA synthesis more economical and more affordable leading to possible breakthroughs in the development of new vaccines, innovative pharmaceuticals, clean water, new food products, innovative pollution filters, and possibly even revolutionary new biofuel derivatives. Now let's suppose that the United Nations Economic Security Council had become a reality. Suppose further that the ESC has instituted an action plan that sets up a timetable for the reclamation of farm land, the recovery of clean drinking water, and the eradication of disease in a series of developing nations we will call the G-10 of the G-77. We know that the JCVI can probably use its patented process to create synthetic bacteria that can develop new vaccines and innovative pharmaceuticals to cure disease. It might also be able to develop an organism to purify the water supply and perhaps to develop crops that can grow in and revitalize the depleted soil of the G-10. In other words, all of the problems targeted by the ESC in the G-10 might be solved by the JCVI's miracle synthetic life forms. Would the ESC have the authority to force JCVI to hand over its work to activate the G-10 Action Plan? What if the ESC passed a resolution that it was ready to back up by military force to compel JCVI to cooperate? Does any of this seem fair to JCVI which has put so much effort and energy into developing the synthetic life forms using their own funds? What should the United States do in such a situation? What should JCVI do? What recourse, if any, might JCVI have, if any, in the United States court system? The international court system? [See J. Craig Venter Institute, "First Self-Replicating Synthetic Bacterial Cell Constructed by J. Craig Venter Institute Researchers," *News Release* (May 20, 2010), http://www. jcvi.org; and Boonsi Dickinson, "Will Patents Give Craig Venter a Monopoly Over Synthetic Life?" *Smart Planet* (May 28, 2010), http://www.smartplanet.com.]

Southeast Asian Nations. The charter amendment creating the ESC would also include a provision to ensure that both developed and developing nations are represented proportionately based on a set formula agreed to by all member states. The ESC would not replace existing UN agencies, such as the ECOSOC. Rather, it would serve as a support mechanism that would make the projects and the plans of all agencies a reality. It might even take the UN from the level of a semi-autonomous NIO to a completely autonomous entity by giving it the teeth that it needs to be successful in its goals and objectives. [See Commission on Global Governance, *Our Global Neighborhood: The Report of the Commission on Global Governance* (Oxford: Oxford University Press, 1995).]

## A QUESTION OF ETHICS

One of the problems that the ESC would be forced to deal with early on would be uncontrolled population growth. Remember that one of the reasons for modeling the ESC after the Security Council and not the CSD alone, is to provide "teeth" for the ESC's resolutions. Suppose that the ESC decided to enforce a vigorous program of population control and to use the power of the member nation's military forces to enforce its resolutions in this regard. This is what some critics of the ESC fear. They suspect that the inauguration of the ESC might usher in the same type of world that Axel Madsen imagined in his novel *Unisave*. The novel is set in the 22nd century at a time when the planet's natural resources, its energy reserves, its agriculture, and its fresh water are depleted. The Earth's population is more than 24 billion. The planet has reached a tipping point beyond which there seems to be nowhere to go. In a desperate attempt to reverse the slide toward total disaster, the United Nations establishes an agency called Unisave. If we look at Unisave closely, we will see that it resembles a runaway ESC. First, Unisave has the authority to set quotas for family size. Second, Unisave has developed a compulsory sterilization program for some people under some circumstances. Third, it has ordered the use of drugs to suppress the sex drive among young people. Fourth, it has instituted a global program of electronic surveillance to prevent the violation of its strict anti-sex laws. Finally, Unisave has mandated a program of compulsory gericide, which involves the systematic killing of the elderly. What would have to be done to prevent the ESC from transforming itself into Unisave? Is there any way to effectively stop it? Is it better not to start in that direction in the first place? Or is there a justification, perhaps based upon the Utilitarian principles outlined in Chapter 1 of this text, that would approve of, or perhaps even champion the work of the ESC and that of Unisave? Think about it.

**Positive Action Plans by the ESC** The *Opening Case Revisited* and the *Question of Ethics* exercise above paint a dark, dismal, and dangerous image of the proposed ESC. However, there is a positive side to the ESC proposal. An agency that is run by unbiased, well-trained, independent, and responsible individuals would be able to draw up tough-minded but fair action plans that must be implemented to save the planet. Let's face it; the task would be difficult and thankless. However, at some time in the future (the very near future if we listen to Heilbroner) such drastic measures may be needed. Remember that it was Heilbroner who stated clearly and unapologetically that drastic measures by "iron" governments might be needed to save the planet. Suppose, for instance, that we return to the Opening Case in Chapter 27 concerning the Great Gulf Oil Spill and combine it with the JCVI case in this chapter. What if another great oil spill occurs under the watchful eye and the global jurisdiction of the ESC? Suppose further that the ESC has instituted an action plan that sets up a timetable for removing the oil spill and recovering clean drinking water in the Gulf. We know that the JCVI can probably use its patented process to create synthetic bacteria that can filter and eliminate the pollutants in the Gulf and that can purify the water supply. To put it simply, all of the problems caused by the oil spill might be solved by the JCVI's genetically engineered synthetic life forms. In this case, the ESC might pass a resolution compelling the responsible parties to cooperate with JCVI and to compensate the Institute accordingly for the use of its patented process. Since, the ESC has the necessary military might to enforce the order; it is likely that the project would be carried out in record time, unlike the way it was handled in "real" life. The gulf would be cleaned up, JCVI would be justly compensated, and the environment would be safe again. The same technique could be used to compel a clean-up after a rogue military action such as the one carried out by the Saddam Hussein with the burning of the Kuwaiti oil facilities in the Gulf. Or such an action might be taken to force a dictator to rebuild the houses, schools, and hospitals that his military forces have destroyed in his own nation. The point is that it is not the structure of the ESC that matters quite as much as the people who run it. It takes people with the proper motivation, the appropriate experience, the courage of their convictions, and just the right level of power to carry it off.

## Summary

**33.1**   The point at which science, technology, and the law intersect can be referred to as juriscience. The power to regulate science and technology in the United States is shared by the national government and the state governments. International authorities also regulate science and technology. The national power emerges from the United States Constitution. The three specific clauses that relate to the national power are the general welfare clause, the commerce clause, and the necessary and proper clause. State power emerges from the state's police power. International power depends upon the nature of the nongovernmental international organization (NIO) itself. The federal government has set up a number of agencies and institutes that support, assess, coordinate, and fund scientific, medical, and technological research. The chief national scientific agencies for scientific, medical, and technological research are the Office of Science and Technology Policy, the National Science Foundation, and the National Institutes of Health. The primary international organizations under the umbrella of the UN are the UNESCO and the World Health Organization.

**33.2**   All of the work done by the government relates in some way to four challenges (1) the possibility of war, (2) the volatility of the marketplace, (3) the twin dangers of environmental deterioration and energy depletion, and (4) the demographic crisis. Dealing with all of these problems is part of the balancing act that is the law. The Federal Energy Regulatory Commission (FERC) is responsible for regulating the transportation and the wholesale price of natural gas and electricity sold for use in interstate commerce. State utility commissioners regulate intrastate prices. The Nuclear Regulatory Commission (NRC) is responsible for the licensing, construction, and operation of nuclear reactors. On the international scene, the International Atomic Energy Commission (IAEA) has oversight responsibility for matters dealing with nuclear power. On the national level, the responsibility for the environment has been delegated to the Environmental Protection Agency. Important subsidiary legislation includes the Clean Air Act, the Clean Water Act, and the Oil Pollution Act. The regulation of the environment on a global scale is charged to the United Nations Environment Program (UNEP).

**33.3**   Intellectual property involves an intangible ownership right in an invention, a process, a computer program, a chemical formula, an original recorded work such as a book or an article, and so on. A patent is a property right granted by the federal government to an inventor. A patent gives the inventor the exclusive right to make, use, and sell that invention for a period of 20 years (14 years if the patent covers a process). A trade secret is a plan, process, device, procedure, formula, pattern, compilation, technique, program, design, method, or improvement used in a business and disclosed only to those employees who need to know it to do their jobs. A copyright is an intangible property right granted to authors of literary, artistic, and musical compositions. A copyright gives the owner the exclusive right to reproduce, publish, and sell his or her work in a fixed, tangible medium of expression.

**33.4**  There are four factors to consider when attempting to solve the four Heilbroner challenges. They are (1) the necessity of focusing on long range results; (2) the need to create partnerships among government, business, and the academic community; (3) the need to appreciate the key role played in these projects by human resources, and (4) the need to develop inventive ways to obtain capital investments in science and related projects. The primary job of the proposed UN Economic Security Council would be to assess the condition of the world economy especially as it relates to the issues of environment, energy, and population. The council would then draw up some long range plans that would involve specific projects for sustainable development, environmental clean-up, population control, and energy enrichment.

## Key Terms

business system, 753

Clean Air Act, 744

Clean Water Act, 745

commerce clause, 732

compelling interest, 750

Copenhagen Accord, 747

copyright, 760

Digital Millennium Copyright Act (DMCA), 761

Economic Espionage Act, 758

General Assembly, 735

general welfare clause, 732

juriscience, 731

licensing agreement, 759

necessary and proper clause, 733

No Electronic Theft Act (NET Act), 761

obvious-to-try standard, 755

Oil Pollution Act, 745

patent, 752

police power, 734

Population Commission (PC), 750

prior art, 754

royalty, 751

Secretariat, 735

Secretary General, 735

Security Council, 735

teaching, suggestions, or motivation test (TSM standard), 754

trade secret, 758

trademark, 759

Uniform Trade Secrets Act, 758

World Intellectual Property Organization (WIPO), 735, 761

World Intellectual Property Organization Copyright Treaty, 762

World Intellectual Property Organization Phonograms Treaty, 762

## Questions for Review and Discussion

1. How does the law permit the government to regulate science and technology?
2. What is the function of the Office of Science and Technology Policy?
3. What is the role of the National Science Foundation?
4. What is the function of the National Institutes of Health?
5. What are the three major challenges facing the modern world?
6. What is the purpose of the Federal Energy Regulatory Commission?
7. What is the role of the Nuclear Regulatory Commission?
8. What are the functions of the Clean Air Act and the Clean Water Act?
9. How does the law protect trademarks, trade secrets, and copyrights?
10. What are the four main issues that must be considered in developing a science policy?

## Cases for Analysis

1. Earth Sciences, Inc., conducted gold-leaching operations in Colorado. The process involved spraying gold ore with a toxic substance. To prevent pollution, Earth Sciences had installed a reserve sump to catch any toxic runoff. An unexpected early thaw melted a snow bank, covering

the ore heap. As a result, the reserve sump over-flowed, dumping toxic waste into the Rito Seco Creek. The United States brought suit, alleging that Earth Sciences had violated pollution laws. Earth Sciences argued that it should not be held liable for an unintentional pollution accident. Was Earth Sciences correct? Explain. *United States v. Earth Sciences, Inc.,* 559 F.2d 368 (10th Cir.).

2. Gaskin, Ohio is the home of Ransom College. Each August the population of the small village triples as the students return. When this happens, the traffic in the middle of town becomes con-gested and the exhaust from the cars chokes the entire "downtown" area. This year the Village Council of Gaskin passed an ordinance that required the installation of emission control devices in all vehicles as a new licensing require-ment. A dozen students brought suit in the U.S. District Court in Columbus, asking the court to declare the new ordinance invalid and to prevent its enforcement. The students contended that the Clean Air Act, which did not make such demands, preempted the Village ordinance. Under what circumstances will a federal law like the Clean Air Act preempt state and local law? Explain. Who will prevail in this case, the village or the students? Explain.

3. Under the authority of the Clean Water Act, the Global Environment Resistance Movement (GERM) initiated a citizen's suit under the authority of the Clean Water Act asking the court to issue an order that would shut down a plant on the Kokosing River that was dumping waste into the navigable waterways of that river. The administrator responded that GERM had acted in haste and did not meet the statutory requirement of giving him 60 days' notice. GERM responded by noting that the notice requirement had been waived by the admin-istrator when he announced in a press conference that he did not intend to shut down the Kokosing plant . . . ever! In their argument, GERM pointed to the Clean Air Act and used that as the template for its lawsuit. Do the Clean Air Act and the Clean Wa-ter Act have identical citizen suit provisions? If they are the same, why is this so? If they are different, what are the differences? Who should win this case, GERM or the administrator? Why?

4. Officials at Semco, Inc., believed that some of their most important computer files, which they characterized as trade secrets, had been appropri-ated by Terry Hildreth, a former vice president of Semco. Semco officials accused Hildreth of using these programs to run his new limited liability company, Hildreth Manufacturing, LLC. Semco engaged in a series of harassing tactics designed to stop Hildreth's use of the alleged trade secrets. To protect himself and his new firm, Hildreth brought a lawsuit asking for a declaratory judg-ment that no trade secrets had been taken, despite Semco's allegations to the contrary. Semco then brought a second lawsuit alleging, among other things, that trade secrets had indeed been misap-propriated by Hildreth. After the suits were de-cided in favor of Hildreth, the results were appealed. During both suits, the following facts came to light: Material that described the manu-facturing steps that Semco now claimed were trade secrets had been routinely made available to vendors. Semco also regularly provided infor-mation about its "secret" manufacturing pro-cesses to people outside the company. Semco did not require employees to file nondisclosure or se-crecy agreements. Visitors were not screened, the building was locked only after regular business hours, and the plant was open for public tours. On the basis of these facts, how should the ap-peals court rule on the issue of trade secrets? Explain. *Hildreth Mfg., LLC. v. Semco, Inc.,* 151 Ohio App. 3d 693.

5. Parrish and Chlarson worked for J&K Computer Systems, Inc. Parrish was a computer programmer, and Chlarson was a trainee. In his capacity as programmer, Parrish wrote an accounts receivable program. Customers of J&K were granted licenses to use the program. A label on the program noted that it was J&K's property and that it could not be used without authorization under a licensing agreement. Parrish, Chlarson, and all other J&K employees were informed that the program was a secret. Nevertheless, Parrish copied it, left J&K's employ, and, along with Chlarson, opened a business similar to J&K. Parrish and Chlarson then sold the copied program to various custom-ers. When J&K sued, Parrish and Chlarson argued that the fact that J&K had revealed the program to their customers meant it was no longer a trade secret. Were Parrish and Chlarson correct? Explain. *J&K Computer Systems, Inc., v. Parrish,* 642 P.2d 732 (UT).

6. Diehr and Latton applied for a patent to protect their development of a new process for molding raw, uncured synthetic rubber into cured products. Diehr and Latton argued that their unique contribution was to measure the temperature inside the mold and feed that temperature into a computer that was programmed to calculate the exact time needed for the curing process. The computer would then activate a mechanism to open the mold. The process, as conceived by Diehr and Latton, eliminated the guesswork usually associated with measuring the length of time for the mold to remain closed. The patent office denied the patent because it used a computer program in the process. The office said that the program was essentially a mathematical idea and was therefore unpatentable. Diehr and Latton argued that the mere fact that a computer program was used as part of a process did not mean that the whole process would be unpatentable. Were Diehr and Latton correct? Why or why not? *Diamond v. Diehr,* 101 S.Ct. 1048 (U.S. Sup. Ct.).

7. Hiroyuki Iwahashi, Yoshiki Nishioka, and Mitsuhiro Hakaridani applied for a patent for an autocorrelation unit for use in computers for pattern recognition, in this case to aid in voice recognition. To achieve this type of pattern recognition, computers must perform a lengthy multiplication cycle that requires intricate circuitry and a costly multiplier unit. The computer hardware involved in this process is also large and cumbersome. The purpose of the new invention is to streamline the multiplication cycle. The elimination of the multiplier and the intricate circuitry is made possible by an algorithm that allows the computer to obtain the needed result by detouring the time-consuming multiplication cycle and using instead the electronic equivalent of a multiplication table. The U.S. Patent and Trademark Office rejected the patent application, and the Board of Patent Appeals and Interferences upheld that decision. Both concluded that the alleged invention was nothing more than an algorithm and could not therefore be patented. The inventors appealed the decision, arguing that the algorithm is simply part of the apparatus, which altered the operation of the computer and was therefore subject to patentability. Can a patent be rejected solely on the argument that the invention involves an algorithm? Explain. *In re Iwahashi,* 888 F.2d 1370 (Fed. Cir.).

8. Stern Electronics, Inc., entered a licensing agreement with Konami Industry Co., Ltd., granting Stern exclusive rights to market the video game Scramble in the United States. Omni Video Games, Inc., wrote a new program that duplicated the sights and sounds of Scramble. Stern sued Omni in federal court, asking for an injunction to prevent Omni from marketing its knockoff of Scramble. Omni argued that Stern could not get a copyright for the Scramble audiovisual display because every time a player plays the game, the display is different. The display is not fixed in a tangible medium, as required by law. Because Omni had written its own program, Stern could not stop it from marketing the duplicate Scramble games. Was Omni correct? Explain. *Stern Electronics, Inc., v. Kaufman and Omni Video Games, Inc.,* 669 F.2d 852 (2nd Cir.).

9. In *Kelo v. City of New London* the city fathers of New London agreed to help the Pfizer Corporation which had decided to build a research and manufacturing center in the city. To do this, the city began to buy up the land in that area of town. Many residents in the targeted area, refused to sell. The city invoked the government's power to confiscate land for public use under eminent domain. Kelo, along with several other owners, sued to end the unconstitutional seizure of their property. The homeowners argued that the taking of their land for private development purposes did not fall under the heading of "public use" as visualized by the Founding Fathers when they wrote the Fifth Amendment. The Court in a 5–4 ruling held that the city's seizure of the land really was public use. Now jump ahead in time and imagine that the ESC has been created under the UN. Could the ESC use this case as a precedent that would permit it to seize private land in the developed countries and then pass the rights and the possession of that land over to the underdeveloped countries? Explain your response. [See *Kelo v. City of New London,* 125 S.Ct. 2655 (U.S. Supreme Court).]

10. The citizens of Oregon authorized the establishment of the Oregon Death with Dignity Act (ODWDA), which protected physicians from prosecution under criminal law and from litigation under civil law for prescribing drugs for terminally ill patients who wished to commit suicide. The drugs would have to be prescribed under the

Controlled Substances Act (CSA). The U.S. attorney general (AG) stated that any physician who prescribed such drugs with the intent to have those drugs used for suicide could lose his or her medical license. The attorney general argued that drugs controlled by the CSA could not be used for suicide because suicide is not a legitimate medical purpose. A lawsuit was filed by several interested parties in the federal district court in Oregon which ruled in favor of the plaintiffs, and which then enjoined the AG from enforcing his interpretation of the CSA. Could this case be used as precedent to promote or to fight government-enforced population control as imagined by Axel Madsen in *Unisave?* Explain. [See *Gonzales, Attorney General v. Oregon*, 126 S.Ct. 904 (United States Supreme Court).]

## quick quiz Answers

| 33-1 | 33-2 | 33-3 | 33-4 |
|------|------|------|------|
| 1. T | 1. F | 1. T | 1. T |
| 2. T | 2. F | 2. T | 2. T |
| 3. T | 3. F | 3. T | 3. F |

# Chapter 34 — International Law

## THE OPENING CASE  Congress, International Law, and Military Force: *The United States v. Bin Laden*

When United States military forces entered Pakistan for the express purpose of invading the al Qaeda compound in Abbottabad and either capturing or killing Osama bin Laden, they were not concerned with legal niceties. They had a mission to accomplish and that was all that concerned them. Nevertheless, once the job was done, the legal questions emerged. In global operations such as the bin Laden mission, two legal spheres of influence must be addressed: the national and the international. In the international arena, there is the question of whether the uninvited use of American troops on foreign soil is legally permissible. This question can be handled in two ways. First, it can be answered by direct reference to international law, specifically the United Nations Charter. Chapter VII, Article 51 of the UN Charter clearly states that, despite earlier articles that limit the use of force against or within a sovereign state, nothing in those articles is intended to "impair the inherent right or individual or collective self-defence." Second, the question can also be answered by reference to the just war theory. The just war theory uses six tests for deciding whether a war is morally justified: (1) just cause, (2) right intention, (3) competent authority, (4) probability of success, (5) proportionality, and (6) last resort. As we shall

see, the bin Laden operation passes each of these tests. In the national arena, there is the question of whether the president can use American forces without a congressional declaration of war. This question can be answered by reference to the Authorization for the Use of Military Force, an act passed by Congress in the wake of the 9/11 attacks. The act empowers the president of the United States to utilize "all necessary and appropriate force against those nations, organizations, or persons" who are found to have been involved in the 9/11 attacks. Like the action authorized by UN Article 51, the Authorization Act relies upon self-defense as justification for the use of forces, so long as that military force is used "to prevent any future acts of international terrorism" against the United States. As we shall see, these are not the only legal justifications for the recent operation in Pakistan, but they will do for now. [See Dionne Searcey, "Killing Was Legal Under U.S. and International Law, Many Experts Say," *The Wall Street Journal* (May 6, 2011), p. A6; Jenna Greene, et al., "In Bin Laden Killing, Legal Clarity," *The National Law Journal* (May 9, 2011), pp. 1 and 4-5; Michael Byers, *War Law: Understanding International Law and Armed Conflict* (New York: Grove Press, 2005), p. 7.]

**Opening Case Questions**

1. Why should the United States care about international law in a situation like the operation in Pakistan? Explain.

2. Had bin Laden been captured alive, would he have been tried in the United States or by the International Criminal Court? Explain.

3. Had bin Laden been captured alive and tried in the United States, would he have been tried

by a civilian court or by a military tribunal? Explain.

4. Did the president overstep his authority in this case when he ordered a military operation within a sovereign nation-state? Why or why not?

5. How is the military action in Pakistan like the recent NATO military action in Libya? How is it unlike that action? Explain.

 Learning Objectives

1. Differentiate among the major new world orders.
2. List the criteria for a just war.
3. Explain the jurisdiction of the International Court of Justice.
4. Describe the mission of the International Criminal Court.
5. Identify the main goal of UNCITRAL.
6. State the differences between the UCC and the CISG.
7. Outline the structure of the World Trade Organization.
8. Relate the objectives of the Dispute Settlement Understanding.
9. Determine the major purpose of NAFTA.
10. Clarify the goals of the European Union.

# 34-1 The New World Order

The phrase *new world order* was used during the Paris peace talks in 1919 to describe the remaking of the world map following the Great War, and then again decades later by George H.W. Bush in the development of his Defense Planning Document. It is a phrase frequently used to describe situations on the global stage that are unusual and unfamiliar. For that reason, among others, the phrase can be used to describe the situation in which we find ourselves today. A **new world order** is a set of initial conditions that describes how nation-states relate to one another on a global scale. The use of the word *new* to describe that order reveals that these initial conditions have just emerged from a tectonic shift in international relations. Generally, because the conditions are so new, no one is exactly certain what those conditions are and how they work. [See M. MacMillan, *Paris 1919: Six Months that Changed the World* (New York: Random House, 2001); and Zbibniew Brzezinski, *Second Chance: Three Presidents and the Crisis of American Superpower* (New York: Basic Books, 2007).]

## Patterns within the New World Order

This description is not to say that global conditions do not follow certain patterns, but in the new world order, those patterns have yet to be determined. These patterns are not rules exactly, but neither are they unpredictable chance events. They instead have the status of indicators that are right more often than wrong. The trick then is to determine what the global initial conditions really are and what pattern those conditions can be expected to follow. What makes this trick so difficult is that the international players do not come into the game fresh but instead are steeped in their own expectations of what the pattern should be. When the pattern shifts, sometimes the players do not, which causes diplomatic errors, international incidents, and global conflicts, some of which can be solved easily but most of which cannot.

## EXAMPLE 34-1:  The Global Shift on 9/11

One of the reasons that many government officials were slow to act in response to the hijackings that began the terror attacks of 9/11 was that they expected the hijackers to follow a set pattern. Up until that moment in time, hijackers, at least those who had taken American hostages on American planes, had had some sort of political bargaining in mind. Thus, they would demand political asylum in Cuba the release of political prisoners being held in American prisons, a ransom to be paid to some foreign political party, or airtime during which they could broadcast their grievances against the United States. What American officials did not realize was that while they were looking in one direction, the world had moved in another. They were no longer facing hijackers with an agenda based on political bargaining but terrorists who had an entirely different plan in mind.

Our job during the remainder of this chapter will be to determine the nature of this new world order. It is not an easy task, because not everyone agrees about what that order might be. In fact, there are almost as many new world orders as there are political commentators to talk about them. Still, even within this confusing collection of political theories, common themes exist. Accordingly, we will divide our study in this chapter into four parts: (1) economic new world order theories; (2) civilizational new world order theories, (3) ideological new world order theories, and (4) globalized new world order theories. It is crucial to consider what each of these theories offers before looking at international law itself. To examine international law without taking a moment to understand the environment in which it operates is a little like trying to teach the rules of baseball to someone who has never seen a baseball diamond. Sure, it can be done—but why try, especially if there is a real diamond on the next block?

## The World Order of Westphalia

Regardless of whether we ultimately adopt an economic, civilizational, international, or globalized new world order as a model, one thing is clear: Every one of these "new world orders" must work within the Westphalia system. The Westphalia system, as reflected originally in the terms of the Treaty of Westphalia, which ended the Thirty Years' War in 1648, describes the existence of nation-states as the central performers on the international scene. It describes certain qualities that functioning nation-states must have to be recognized as legitimate international players. These characteristics include the following:

1.  Nation-states will govern a recognized area of land on the map. In other words, it is possible to point to a place on a world map and say something like, "There is Lithuania." It is also possible to travel to and enter a nation-state because it is a physical, geographical reality.

2.  Nation-states have sovereignty. Sovereignty is the exclusive power of a nation-state to govern what happens within its own borders. Therefore, nation-states can create their own governing systems to run their own territory. They can also establish an

internal police force to ensure domestic tranquility and a military arm to protect their people and territory from attack and invasion from other nation-states.

3.   Nation-states have the sole and absolute ability to raise money within their own borders in the form of taxes, tariffs, bonds, fines, and investments. They also have the sole legal power to coin money and set its value.

4.   Nation-states have a responsibility to provide for and play fair with their own citizens. Thus, a nation-state is responsible for providing or at least supporting the development of an infrastructure (i.e., a transportation system [roads, bridges, harbors, airports], a communication system [telephones, radio, television, Internet access, and so on], a sanitation system, an education system, and a health care system) for the safe and profitable operation of the economy of the state.

Although not explicitly part of the Westphalia formula, implied within this picture is the idea that nation-states exist because they are nation-states. In other words, nation-states control territory and govern the people of that territory, and then, if they have done this successfully, they are worthy of the title nation-state. It is not enough just to yell, "Hey! From now on, the six-block area on the east side of Cleveland from 66th Street on the west to 72nd Street on the east, and from St. Clair Ave. on the north to Superior Ave. on the south is now a nation-state." It just does not work that way. In fact, most of the time a nation-state is a nation-state before it calls itself a nation-state. As Lee Harris demonstrates in his perceptive study, *Civilization and Its Enemies: The Next Stage of History,* until the 20th century this requirement was not much of a problem. However, at times over the last 100 years or so, nation-states have been created by other nations-states or by the United Nations simply by cobbling parts of the map together like a jigsaw puzzle, or by giving territory to a group of people. Sometimes this works as it did with Israel in 1948, and sometimes, as in other parts of the Middle East, it does not. In fact, it would not be inaccurate to declare that earning the rank of a nation-state is what marks a functioning nation-state from a failed nation-state, or worse yet, a rogue nation-state. A true nation-state is answerable for its actions. Other entities, which are sometimes referred to as **worldwide organizations** like the World Trade Organization and the World Bank, and outlaw bands such as Al Qaeda and the Red Brigade, do not have the same rank, the same power, or the same respectability as nation-states, because they have neither earned their position nor demonstrated the ability, or even the willingness, to be answerable for their actions on the world stage. For this reason all of the following New World Order theories, save one, assume that nation-states are the key players on the international stage. [For a detailed analysis of the demise of the traditional nation-state see Lee Harris, *Civilization and Its Enemies: The Next Stage of History* (New York: Free Press, 2004), pp. 28–31.]

## 21st Century New World Order Theories

As noted previously, political pundits have offered four new world orders for our consideration: the economic, the civilizational, the ideological, and the globalized. Each of these new world orders has several incarnations, each slightly different from the others. Nevertheless, within each category, the variations share more characteristics than differences, so we will focus on those common denominators.

**LO1**

### The Economic New World Order
The economic new world order sees the international community as divided into two sectors: (1) those nations that have matured economically and thus have healthy, functioning, though not perfect economies and (2) those nation-states that are economically dysfunctional. Thomas Barnett, senior strategic researcher at the naval war college and author of *The Pentagon's New Map,* calls the

functioning nations the Core and the dysfunctional nations the Gap. Richard Haass of the Council on Foreign Relations and author of *The Opportunity* refers to the economically secure nations as the "21st Century Concert," or simply, the Concert. Haass does not directly name the economically unstable nations. However, given his overall theoretical bend, calling them the unintegrated nations would not be out of line. Traditionally, economically sound nations have been referred to as developed nations and economically fragile nations as developing nations. Developed nations include such nation-states as the United States, the countries in Western Europe, China, Russia, Japan, Australia, New Zealand, Canada, South Africa, Israel, and India. The developing nations include nation-states in the Middle East, the Balkans, all of Africa except South Africa, South and Central America, Indonesia, and Southeast Asia.

Both Barnett and Haass insist that developed nation-states must find ways to overcome or eliminate disconnectedness (Barnett's word) or to integrate (Haass's term) the developing nation-states with the Core or Concert. Adopting this perspective dramatically alters the political map and therefore demands a change in tactics. Some nation-states, such as China and Russia, are no longer seen by the United States as "the enemy" as they were during the Cold War. Instead, they are seen as allies within the Concert, and as such, they share a common set of goals with all other Core nations. In contrast, the enemy is any individual, group, or set of circumstances that somehow separates a nation from the Concert or prevents it from developing to the extent that it can become a self-sufficient member of the Core. Under this version of the new world order, international law has certain clear and decisive objectives, namely (1) to protect the Core nations from economic instability and political disruption; (2) to promote the integration of developing nations within the functioning Core; and (3) to fight the forces that keep nation-states underdeveloped, whether those forces are terrorists in Al Qaeda, warlords in Somalia, drug runners in Columbia, or rogue governments in Iran and North Korea. [See T. Barnett, *The Pentagon's New Map: War and Peace in the Twenty-first Century,* (New York: Berkley Books, 2004); and R.N. Haass, *The Opportunity: America's Moment to Alter History's Course,* (New York: Public Affairs, 2005).]

### The Civilizational New World Order

The civilizational new world order was so named by Samuel Huntington in his book, *The Clash of Civilizations.* This view sees the globe as divided into eight distinct civilizations that are more or less autonomous and more or less incapable of successfully cooperating with more than one, or at the most two, other civilizations at the same time. A **civilization** is a group of people in a series of different nation-states that share certain common characteristics, including their history, religion, traditions, beliefs, often language, and sometimes ancestry. The eight civilizations are Western Civilization (the United States, Canada, Western Europe, Israel, South Africa, Australia, and New Zealand); the Sinic Civilization (China, North and South Korea, and most of Southeast Asia); the Orthodox Civilization (Russia and other states in Eastern Europe); the Latin American Civilization (South and Central America); the Islamic Civilization (Middle Eastern nation-states, the nation-states of northern Africa, and Indonesia); the African Civilization (the sub-Saharan regions of Africa); the Hindu Civilization (India and Sri Lanka); and the Japanese Civilization.

Some of these civilizations contain powerful central states that serve as a sort of international "big brother" to the lesser states within a civilization. A civilization with a recognized central state is generally more stable, less war-like, and more economically prosperous than one without. The civilizations with central states include Western Civilization (the United States); the Sinic Civilization (China); the Hindu Civilization (India); the Orthodox Civilization (Russia); and the Japanese Civilization (Japan). Since most international conflicts occur between rather than within Civilizations, each Civilization is better off if it can limit its contact with other Civilizations. To this end, Huntington has outlined a number of rules that each civilization should follow in dealing with all other civilizations. These rules include (1) the prime directive of the civilizational world order, that is, that each civilization should never interfere with the internal affairs of another civilization; (2) the rule of collective mediation, which calls for dialogue and compromise whenever a dispute arises between civilizations; (3) the commonalities rule which encourages civilizations to emphasize those ideals that draw them together rather than those that drive them apart. Thus, it is healthier for Western Civilization, for instance, to share its focus on self-determination rather than to insist that all nations adopt Western-style democracy. Under this version of the New World Order, international law has two goals: to promote civilizational autonomy and to protect civilizational rights. [See S.P. Huntington, *The Clash of Civilizations and The Remaking of World Order* (New York: Simon & Schuster 1996).]

### The Ideological New World Order

Unlike the economic new world order and the civilizational new world order, the ideological new world order sees the nations of the world grouped together based on politics. This view is promoted by Robert Kagan in his book, *The Rebirth of History and the End of Dreams*. Kagan believes that the fall of the Soviet Union in 1991 led some political theorists to erroneously conclude that the ideological struggle among political systems had ended and that democracy had been victorious. These overly optimistic theorists declared the "end of history" and the triumph of democracy. They pointed to the transformation of the Soviet Union and the conversion of countries such as Poland, Lithuania, Latvia, and Estonia into democracies as evidence of this revolution. On the international scene, the United States, as the sole superpower, would keep the peace and would usher in a new age of goodwill and prosperity. These theorists, Kagan says, were wrong. The period of peace and prosperity in the 1990s was illusory at best. It represented a temporary respite in the eternal international struggle, a respite that would end as soon as the "losers" of the Cold War had a chance to pause, reassess their situation, regroup, and emerge as global powers once again.

This, Kagan argues, is precisely what happened when the Russian people, after their failed attempt at democracy, surrendered to the *de facto* dictatorship of a new Russian oligarchy and to the promise of a return to past days of glory. Russia, Kagan argues, believes that it was victimized by the United States and the European Union during the 1990s and is now determined to regain its place of power in the international community. Similarly, China, which also sees itself as victimized by the West, has decided to use its economic strength, its military power, and its political influence to rebuild alliances with third world nations that need its help to resist the temptation of Western corporate domination. Both of these great powers, Kagan argues, have returned to a 19th century strategy of empire-building and both have the ideological structure to see those plans of empire succeed. Thus, Kagan envisions the globe divided into two political camps: (1) the democracies, led by the United States and the EU, and (2) the autocracies, led by Russia and China. In this international environment, the job of international law is to build a modern concert of democracies which will join together for mutual protection and which will act as a counterbalance to the new autocratic empires. [See Robert Kagan, *The Rebirth of History and the End of Dreams* (New York: Public Affairs, 2005).]

### The Globalized New World Order

The globalized new world order is the only theory that has abandoned the notion that the nation-state is the primary actor on the international stage. In the globalized world, the multinational corporation, not the nation-state, becomes the seat of ultimate economic, political, and military power. Globalization as a concept sees the world as having become more interconnected because of advances in transportation and communication that make instantaneous contact between parties on a global basis as easy, or perhaps even easier, than it ever was on a local basis. The growth of this instantaneous interconnectedness is the wellspring of all other forms of expansion, not least of which is the use of the Internet as a way to conduct business. Global interconnectedness has greatly benefited international businesses, which can now trade quickly, make contracts instantly, and ship raw materials and finished products from one part of the globe to another in hours.

This level of global integration has fueled other forms of interconnectedness as well. Because orders can be filled instantly and goods shipped almost as fast, products no longer have to be manufactured in the place where they are to be used. Thus, products manufactured in Beijing, China, on Monday can be on the shelves of stores in Willowick, Ohio, on Tuesday. This movement permits the manufacturer to outsource jobs to foreign countries such as China, where wages are lower, working conditions less regulated, and raw materials cheaper. For this reason, firms that moved onto the global scene early in the globalization process have grown rapidly and continued to do well in the international marketplace. Some of these corporations, or mega-corporations as they are sometimes called, have become as economically independent, if not as powerful, as some of the nation-states of the world. Moreover, the mega-corporations do not always suffer the same restraints placed on nation-states. Instead, they can operate on a global level without having to be tied down to a particular place or a particular set of national rules. Under this version of the new world order, international law has a set of unambiguous goals, all of which must ensure the smooth operation of the multinational mega-corporation.

## quick quiz 34-1

| | | |
|---|---|---|
| 1. A world order is a set of initial conditions that describes how nation-states relate to one another on a global scale. | true | false |
| 2. The Westphalia system is based on the existence of nation-states as the primary actors on the international scene. | true | false |
| 3. The democracies have won the ideological battle and history has ended. | true | false |

# 34-2 International Law and War

Karl von Clausewitz, a nineteenth-century Prussian soldier and political scientist, is credited with one of the most often-quoted definitions of war. "War," Clausewitz claims, "is a continuation of politics by other means." In today's world of complex multinational corporations, delicate international relationships, and instantaneous Internet transactions, Clausewitz might have added that war is also the continuation of international business by other means. As we have seen recently, international business can be affected profoundly by war, especially when it is an unpopular war that lacks international legal authorization and when it results in a protracted campaign of attrition that drags on for months with no clear goals and no end in sight. Such a situation can increase costs, cause shortages of raw materials, endanger shipping, and render the execution of a contract commercially impracticable, if not impossible to perform. This scenario may be true even if the parties to a war are not citizens of the nations that are at war. Some of these problems can be solved by the internal law of a particular nation-state.

## EXAMPLE 34-2: The *S.S. Christos* and the Suez Crisis

The Transatlantic Financing Corporation operated the *S.S. Christos,* a cargo ship carrying wheat from Texas to Iran, for the United States government. While the *S.S. Christos* was en route to Iran, Israel invaded Egypt. Two days later, France and Great Britain invaded the Suez Canal Zone. The invasion and subsequent closing of the Suez Canal made it impossible for the *S.S. Christos* to use the canal. A 3,000-mile detour around the southern coast of Africa cost Transatlantic an unexpected $44,000 above the original estimated cost of $305,842.92. When the United States government refused to pay the additional amount, the company brought a lawsuit. Although the United States and Transatlantic were not directly involved in the Suez hostilities, their contract had been affected by the conflict. Nevertheless, the federal court did not allow Transatlantic to recover the additional payment from the government of the United States. The court's decision was based on a traditional rule of contract law in the United States. The court declared, "While it may be an overstatement to say that increased cost and difficulty of performance never constitute impracticability, to justify relief there must be more of a variation between the expected costs and the cost of performing by an available alternative than is present in this case."

The lesson to be learned from the case in Example 34-2 is a simple one: When entering a contract that relies on the international marketplace, it is wise for all parties to be aware of the international conditions in all areas of the globe that may affect the contract. This approach is crucial because courts in the United States will take into account the foreseeability of any international crisis, including not only war but also war-related events, such as blockades, quarantines, and border closings. If the court deems that the international crisis was foreseeable, the loss suffered by the parties affected by the crisis will not be offset by the court.

## Self-Evident Truths

In her influential study of World War I, *The Guns of August,* the historian Barbara W. Tuchman writes that in 1910 two very different, yet equally popular, views on the prospect of future wars existed on both sides of the Atlantic. One of these views was represented by a book by Norman Angell entitled *The Great Illusion.* War, Angell argued, had become an untenable option because of the economic connections among the nations of the global community. Any war would have such devastating consequences that nations could no longer afford to engage in any sort of armed conflict.

In support of this view, a key British military leader, Viscount Esher, contended that a combination of factors, including "commercial disaster, financial ruin and individual suffering," made war in the 20th century "more difficult and improbable" than ever before in the history of civilization (Tuchman, p. 10).

A contradictory position was represented by a German general named Friedrich von Bernhardi who, in a work entitled *Germany and the Next War,* argued that war was inevitable. In fact, Bernhardi argued, war was a consequence of "natural law." Bernhardi insisted that war was a "biological necessity" and actually the human expression of "the struggle for existence." Bernhardi wrote that, among nation-states, "there can be no standing still." He concluded that any country that fails to move up the evolutionary ladder of development, faces inevitable destruction (Tuchman, pp. 10–11).

## Self-Evident Questions

1. Of the two positions, which has been supported by the weight of world history in the 20th century? Explain.
2. Which view continues to be popular in the 21st century? Explain.
3. Which view seems to have been adopted by the international community? Explain.
4. Which view seems to be supported by most Americans? Explain. Which view seems to be in line with American political and military policy in the 21st century? Explain.
5. Which view is morally correct? Explain.

(*See:* Barbara Tuchman, "A Funeral," *The Guns of August* (New York: The MacMillan Company, 1962), pp. 10–11.)

## The Just War Theory

One central question that cannot be answered solely by the law of a single nation-state is whether a war is just. Ethical and legal philosophers in the West have developed criteria for determining when a war can be considered legally and morally correct. This theory, termed the **just war theory**, has been invoked to defend and question the morality of many armed conflicts. In its traditional form, the theory focuses on two main areas. First, it establishes the criteria that would justify going to war. Second, it institutes criteria for the proper conduct of a war that is already in progress. A third modern feature of justifiability adds a set of criteria that establish the rules of conduct that must be followed after a war ends.

**Criteria for Going to War**  The just war theory endorses six criteria for deciding whether a war can be morally justified: (1) just cause, (2) right intention, (3) competent authority, (4) probability of success, (5) proportionality, and (6) last resort. The first criterion, **just cause**, says that to be morally permissible, a war must be waged for honorable motives. Included among these motives are self-defense and the defense of a fellow sovereign nation-state that has been targeted by an aggressor and is unable to defend itself properly. The second criterion, **right intention**, declares that a war must be waged only if the combatant has the correct objective. The difference between the first and the second criteria is the difference between an objective justification for war and the subjective intent of the actual combatants. A war may have an objectively justifiable cause and yet be fought for the wrong reasons. This situation could happen, for instance, if one country goes to the defense of another country but then uses that defensive campaign as a pretext to destroy the government and subjugate the civilian population of the aggressor nation-state.

The third criterion, **competent authority**, states that war can be initiated only by legitimately recognized nation-states. This standard does not mean, however, as some people have suggested, that the United Nations must declare a war for that war to have been declared by competent authority. In fact, from a legal perspective, the UN cannot declare war at all. The UN Charter is founded on the belief that all member nations maintain their sovereign authority, including the authority to declare war. This criterion also means that it is not ethically permissible for individuals such as the late Osama

## THE OPENING CASE *Revisited, Part I*
## Congress, International Law, and Military Force: *The United States v. Bin Laden, Round 2*

Recall in the Opening Case at the beginning of this chapter that United States military forces entered Pakistan to either capture or kill Osama bin Laden, the leader of the terrorist group al Qaeda. Recall also that bin Laden and al Qaeda were responsible for the 9/11 attacks on the World Trade Center and the Pentagon, which killed over 3,000 people. In the international arena, the question has been asked as to whether the uninvited use of American troops in Pakistan in this case was legally and morally justifiable. Under the conditions set up by the just war theory, the answer is simple—yes, the action was legally and morally permissible. According to the just war theory, a military action is legally and morally correct, as long as it passes six tests: (1) just cause, (2) right intention, (3) competent authority, (4) probability of success,

(5) proportionality, and (6) last resort. The bin Laden operation passes each of these tests. First, it was just in that it targeted the self-proclaimed mastermind of the 9/11operation, Second, the action was fought with the right intention, bringing the man responsible for 9/11 to justice. Third, the operation was initiated by competent authority, in this case the authority of the president of the United States. Fourth, the operation had a great probability of success, given the experience, the training, and the planning used by the elite military team charged with mission. Fifth, the action was a limited operation with one primary objective in mind, the capture or elimination of bin Laden. Sixth, and finally, the action was a last resort, since all other efforts aimed at bringing bin Laden to justice had been for naught.

bin Laden or his successor in al Qaeda, Ayman al-Zawahiri, to declare war on anyone, let alone the United States. War is a function of nation-states in their relationships with one another, not the purview of individuals, no matter how much individuals like Zawahiri think otherwise.

The fourth criterion, probability of success, declares that at the outset of a war, there must be a reasonable chance that the war will be successful; a suicidal war would fall outside this criterion. Fifth, proportionality holds that the good advanced by the war must exceed the negative consequences of entering the conflict. Thus, a war fought over an imaginary diplomatic insult must be considered unjust, because the objective of vindicating a spurious affront to national honor is not proportional to the death and destruction caused by war. Finally, the criterion of last resort means that a war can be fought only after all other means for the resolution of the dispute have been tried and failed. If both nations still have diplomatic options available for ending the crisis in a nonviolent way; if an international organization, such as the United Nations, is still willing to explore a negotiated settlement; or if time still exists to pursue a nonviolent solution, war cannot be waged as a solution to the conflict, and if one side insists on declaring war, that war will be an unjust conflict. However, the fact that all options have not been implemented is not decisive. What matters is that the nation-state that began the war gave authentic consideration to each available option, short of war.

## Criteria for the Proper Conduct of War   It is not enough to advocate a set of ethical and legal criteria for entering war and then ignore the criteria for conducting the war or for conduct that must be followed after the end of a war. For this reason, many modern, legal, and moral theorists suggest several additional criteria that should guide conduct during a war and behavior after a war. The first of the criteria for conducting a war

requires that the warring factions use only those military means that are proportional to the ends that they wish to achieve. Thus, because it was possible for the international coalition to subdue and eject the invading Iraqi army from Kuwait in Gulf War I by using conventional weapons, the use of nuclear weapons would have been considered a disproportionate tactic. The second criterion states that the war must be fought with discrimination. This restriction means that only combatants should be targeted in the war and that civilians must be kept out of harm's way.

### Criteria for Proper Postwar Conduct

Three just war principles have been established for gauging the morality of conduct following the cessation of hostilities. The first of these principles is the principle of repentance. The **principle of repentance** calls for a genuine expression of remorse by the combatants for the death and destruction caused by war. Conduct that expresses either joy or satisfaction at the death of enemy combatants, even combatants involved in a war of aggression, would violate this principle. The second criterion, the **principle of honorable surrender**, requires the victor in a war to accept the surrender of the enemy and treat the defeated combatants with dignity and respect. Refusing a genuine offer of surrender, violating that surrender after it has been implemented, or mistreating enemy combatants after surrender would all be violations of this principle. Actions that are motivated by revenge or retribution would also violate the principle of honorable surrender, as would conduct that injures or humiliates prisoners of war. Finally, the **principle of restoration** requires that the victor in a conflict act responsibly in rebuilding the defeated nation's physical environment, economy, and governmental structure.

## Preemptive and Protective War

A nation-state starts a **preemptive war** to stop another nation-state's imminent attack on the first nation-state. A preemptive war is not the same as a preventative war, though the terms are often used as synonyms. A preemptive war is waged to stop an attack before it can begin. In contrast, a nation-state begins a **preventative war** to stop another nation-state from reaching a point that it would be capable of attacking the first nation. The doctrine adopted by the United States in 2002 was a doctrine of preemptive war, not one of preventative war. The concept of preemptive war goes back 500 years to Thomas More, who in his work *Utopia* noted that it would be wise to attack preemptively a force that was about to attack you. In the United States, two major military figures, General Leslie Groves, the head of The Manhattan Project, which developed the atomic bomb during World War II, and General Curtis LeMay, former commander of the Strategic Air Command (SAC), advocated preemptive war against the Soviet Union. In the 1950s, the Joint Chiefs of Staff commissioned a study that also recommended a preemptive strike against the Soviet Union. In all of these cases, cooler heads prevailed, and preemptive war was not at that time advocated as a strategic policy of the United States.

Times changed, however, when in 2002, preemptive war became an active strategic policy of the United States and was the primary stated motivation for the invasion of Iraq in 2003. Although it is difficult to pinpoint the exact moment of this shift in policy, the move toward preemptive war as the national policy of the United States seems to have come about less than three months after September 11, 2001, when, in the aftermath of the attacks on the World Trade Center and the Pentagon, President George W. Bush asked then-Secretary of Defense Donald Rumsfeld about war plans for an attack against Iraq. Evidence indicates that President Bush had similar strategic planning discussions with Vice President Richard Cheney and National Security Advisor Condoleezza Rice. Nevertheless, the first conscious public declaration of this change in policy occurred in a presidential address to the graduating class of West Point on June 1, 2002.

Times changed again nine years later when, during the administration of President Barack Obama, the United States, in response to a series of human rights violations by the late Col. Muammar Gaddafi in Libya, launched a new type of war, a protective war aimed at providing aid and assistance to innocent civilians who are being victimized by the military of their own nation-state. Unlike preemptive war, which is designed as a tactic to shield one nation from the unwarranted and deadly attacks of another, a protective war is waged by a nation or a coalition of nations as an intervention in the internal affairs of a sovereign state to protect the civilians of that state from their own government. This is a crucial step away from the traditions inherent within the Treaty of Westphalia which recognized the almost sacred right of a nation-state to do what it pleased within its own borders. Even the United Nations Charter, a document aimed at unifying the nation-states of the world in a global community, still holds sovereignty as one of its central premises. Consequently, while the theory is still in its formative stages, it might be a good idea to subject it to the tests of the just war theory as well as the test of international law and, in the case of the United States, to the test of domestic legality.

## Protective War and the Just War Theory
The just war theory is designed to help individuals and governments make judgments about the justifiability of particular wars, rather than about the morality of war in general. Indeed, the very existence of a just war theory presumes that some wars are in fact justifiable and some are not. Therefore, it is difficult to characterize the morality of a war-making strategy, such as the strategy of protective war, without reference to the war's actual historical context. Nevertheless, all protective wars share certain characteristics that make it possible to judge such wars in theory. For example, all protective wars involve a situation in which the government of a rogue or failed nation-state has somehow victimized its own people. This victimization might involve genocide, as in Rwanda, anarchy as in Somalia, or, as in the case of Libya, the use of the nation-state's military in an operation that targets its own people. Using this common context we can build a case in support of protective war using the just war theory. We will examine the criteria in reverse order: (1) last resort, (2) proportionality, (3) probability of success, (4) competent authority, (5) right intention, and (6) just cause.

First, the protector nations who initiate a protective war must demonstrate that the use of military force is a last resort. Basically, this would require the protector nations to use diplomatic channels and economic pressure to alter the behavior of the rogue nations before resorting to war. Second, a protective war should be, by definition, a war of proportional response. The object of such a war is to protect innocent civilians who have been victimized by their government. Thus, the war is not aimed at toppling the rogue government, gaining territory, aiding the rebels, or expanding the influence of the protector nations. Third, because protective wars are generally fought by coalitions with limited objectives, the probability of success is almost always ensured. Fourth, at least in the modern context, most protective wars will be channeled through the United Nations Security Council, which has a mechanism in place for dealing with such contingencies. Thus, there is little reason for a protective war to be launched outside competent authority. Fifth and sixth, as in the case of proportionality, the requirements of right intention and just cause are inherent within the reason for going to war in the first place. Protective wars, by definition "protect the innocent," a goal that involves both right intention and just cause. Thus, it is clear that a protective war like the one in Libya in 2011 met the criteria of the just war. However, this is only one-third of the battle. It is also necessary to examine the war from the perspective of international law and, in the case of the United States, from the perspective of domestic law.

### Protective War and International Law

In the 21st century, when dealing with questions of the legality of a war, it is necessary to defer to the judgment of the United Nations. Immediately following the Second World War, the founders of the UN wrote a charter that provided for the possibility of future military action. The mechanism is found in Chapter VII of the United Nations Charter. Chapter VII places most of the decision-making process in the hands of the UN Security Council. Although the authority granted to the Security Council in Chapter VII falls short of permitting the UN to actually declare war on a sovereign state, it does outline a process that *approximates* that power. Chapter VII empowers the Security Council to first ascertain that a genuine danger exists that threatens the civil peace of a nation-state and then determine what actions must be initiated "to maintain or restore international peace and security" (UN Chapter VII). Before these actions can be taken, however, the charter stipulates that diplomatic and economic sanctions must be put into effect before resorting to military force. If such sanctions do not work, then member states may be authorized to carry out whatever military measures are deemed appropriate to restore order and stability within the nation-state and to the region affected by the actions of the rogue or failed state.

In authorizing the protective war in Libya, the United Nations Security Council followed these steps religiously. First, the Security Council investigated the activities of the government in Libya and, following that investigation, issued UN Security Council Resolution 1970 which initiated economic and diplomatic sanctions against the Libyan government and referred the situation to the International Criminal Court. The next day the European Union, officially approved the sanctions outlined in Resolution 1970. One day later the UN General Assembly, recognizing the human rights violations being carried out by the government of Libya, temporarily revoked Libyan membership in the Human Rights Council. Fifteen days after the initial resolution was passed and once it was clear that the diplomatic and economic sanctions had failed to deter Gaddafi and his governmental forces, the Security Council passed UN Resolution 1973. This new resolution authorized NATO forces to take every means needed to protect civilians who had been endangered by the military onslaught carried out by Libyan governmental forces. The resolution included the establishment of a no-fly zone over Libya. Thus, it is quite clear that NATO's protective war in Libya is legal based on international law. The final question remains. Is it legal under American domestic law? It is to that question that we now turn.

### Protective War and U.S. Domestic Law

In the 1970s after the problems associated with a president of the United States waging war without Congressional approval, Congress enacted a law that would prevent a repeat of that type of activity. The War Powers Resolution is designed to limit the power of the president as Commander-in-Chief of the Armed Forces to commit American troops to the field and to maintain those troops in the field contrary to congressional approval. The resolution also requires the president to communicate to Congress on a regular basis about the military action, once that action is approved by Congress. More specifically, the War Powers Resolution requires that the president inform Congress of his use of American troops within 48 hours of doing so. The notice must be in writing and must be delivered to the Speaker of the House *and* the President Pro Tempore of the Senate. If Congress does, in fact, approve of the president's use of troops, he has 60 days to accomplish the mission. At that time, 60 days after the initial written notice was given to Congress, he must withdraw the troops within 30 days unless Congress authorizes a continuation of the action. All of this assumes, of course, that Congress can actually meet and has not somehow been compromised or eliminated by enemy action on American soil. In such a case, the president is authorized to continue whatever action is needed to protect the United States.

## THE OPENING CASE *Revisited, Part II*
## Congress, International Law, and Military Force: *The United States v. Bin Laden, Round 3*

Recall again that, in the Opening Case at the beginning of this chapter, the United States military entered Pakistan to capture or kill Osama bin Laden. There is one question left unanswered in the bin Laden operation. Can the president of the United States use American forces *without* a congressional declaration of war in an operation aimed at capturing or killing a terrorist on foreign soil? The question can be answered by looking at the Authorization for the Use of Military Force, an act passed by Congress in the wake of the 9/11 attacks. The proper designation of the act is Public Law 107-40 [S.J. Res. 23]. Officially, it is a joint resolution passed by both the House and the Senate. The Joint Resolution begins by stating that the United States is justified in using self-defense to protect its citizens and territory. The resolution also recognizes that the 9/11 attacks were an instance of the "unusual and extraordinary threat to the national security and foreign policy of the United States" and that the president has the authority, "under the Constitution to take action to deter and prevent acts of international terrorism against the United States." Given these preliminary conditions, Congress declared that "The President is authorized to use all necessary and appropriate force against those nations, organizations, or persons, he determines planned, authorized, committed or aided the terrorist attack that occurred on September 11, 2001, or harbored such organizations or persons, in order to prevent any future acts of international terrorism against the United States by such nations, organizations, or persons." The Resolution cites the War Powers Resolution [Section 8 (A) (1)] as the statutory authority upon which the new resolution is built. Like the action authorized by UN Article 51, the Authorization Act relies upon self-defense as justification for the use of force, so long as that military force is used "to prevent any future acts of international terrorism" against the United States. So was the bin Laden operation legal under domestic law? In a word, the answer is yes. [See Dionne Searcey, "Killing Was Legal Under U./S and International Law, Many Experts Say," *The Wall Street Journal* (May 6, 2011), p. A6; Jenna Greene, et al., "In Bin Laden Killing, Legal Clarity," *The National Law Journal* (May 9, 2011), pp. 1 and 4-5; and Michael Byers, *War Law: Understanding International Law and Armed Conflict* (New York: Grove Press, 2005), p. 7.]

In joining NATO forces in the protective war in Libya, the president of the United States faithfully followed the requirements of the War Powers Resolution. Within the required 48 hours, he notified Congress by sending a written report to the Speaker of the House and the President Pro Tempore of the Senate. At the end of that period, he again contacted Congress with a written request to extend the time period for another 60 days as required by the War Powers Resolution. Clearly then, as was true of NATOs protective war in Libya, the American use of the United States military in that protective war was carried out according to the law.

## Substantive and Procedural Issues

Most of these just war requirements were established before the advent of contemporary warfare. In the modern age, the face of war has changed. Along with these changes have come alterations in the conduct of war, including ways of dealing with prisoners of war, occupation forces, and war crimes.

### Substantive Legal Changes   Following World War II, in 1949, a major
effort involving most of the nations of the world and sponsored by the American Red

Cross was held in Geneva, Switzerland, to address the issues of prisoners of war, occupation forces, and war crimes. Out of this series of international meetings came the Geneva Conventions. These conventions attempt to deal with many of the problems brought on by the nature of warfare in the modern era. For instance, the first, second, and third conventions are concerned with prisoners of war, and the fourth deals with occupation forces.

**Procedural and Analytical Problems**   Substantive changes in the law of war and international relations, such as the Geneva Conventions, are frequently complicated by procedural and analytical questions. The mere fact that a convention has been written and adopted does not mean that it will be applied properly and consistently by the nations that signed the convention. Analytical questions nearly always plague any court faced with the application of an international agreement. To facilitate this analytical process, the U.S. courts have established some guidelines for interpreting international agreements such as the Geneva Conventions.

For instance, in determining the applicability of such international pacts, the courts will first look at the literal language of the agreement, especially any definitions contained within the agreement. Second, the court will examine any supporting documentation, such as the Red Cross Commentaries in the case of the Geneva Conventions, for assistance in interpreting the settlement. Third, U.S. courts will take a liberal view in the interpretation of such agreements. This guideline means that the court will broadly and openly interpret the convention to include as many cases and situations as are justly warranted.

---

## quick quiz 34-2

1. One central question that cannot be answered solely by the law of a single nation-state is whether a war is just.     true | false

2. The just war theory was developed in the twenty-first century to deal with problems of modern warfare.     true | false

3. The Geneva Conventions attempt to establish rules involving occupation forces and prisoners of war.     true | false

---

# 34-3 International Law and the United Nations

As World War II drew to a close, representatives of 50 nations met in San Francisco to work out the details of the formation of the United Nations. At that meeting, called the United Nations Conference on International Organization, the 50 nations adopted a charter that on June 26, 1945, established the United Nations. The stated purposes of the United Nations are to advance human rights, to end war, to enhance human achievement, to support peaceful international coalitions, and to promote truth, justice, and the rule of law. The promotion of international law has taken many forms within the structure of the United Nations, including the International Law Commission, International Court of Justice, the UN Commission on International Trade Law, and the UN Convention on Contracts for the International Sale of Goods. Although the International Criminal Court stands outside the official system of the UN, it nevertheless has an important role to play in the administration of global justice

# The Structure of the United Nations

The United Nations is an enormous, complicated organization that consists of many agencies, organizations, courts, and commissions (see Table 34-1). The three major governing bodies are the Secretary General, the General Assembly, and the Security Council. The Secretary General is the chief administrator of the United Nations. He or she heads up the Secretariat, which is the administrative bureaucracy of the UN. The Secretary General also takes a leading role in promoting world peace. The Security Council recommends a candidate for the position of Secretary General, but the General Assembly votes that person into office. The General Assembly is made up of all the member nations of the UN. Each nation has one vote on resolutions and other matters presented to the assembly. The UN Security Council deals with crises that involve threats to international peace. The Council consists of 15 members. Five of these members hold permanent seats: China, France, Russia, the United Kingdom, and the United States. The General Assembly elects the remaining 10 members for two-year terms.

The United Nations Headquarters in New York City.

# International Law and the United Nations

One of the strengths of the United Nations is that it is based on a platform that continues to respect the sovereignty of each member state. Without this express guarantee built into its founding principles, it is doubtful that the United Nations Charter would have been ratified in the first place, let alone developed into the symbol for international unity that it stands for today. As is often the case with such organizations, however, the UN's main strength is also its main weakness. The sovereign nature of each member state often means that the UN's power to enforce its decrees is a matter of voluntary acquiescence. Thus, the UN must make use of its soft power more than its hard power. The UN's soft power resides in its moral authority as a platform that speaks for all nations with equal objectivity. As we saw in Chapter 33, whether this unbiased attitude exists in reality is open to debate. Nevertheless, the ideal of objective representation stands as a central core belief of the UN, one that its various organizations cannot ignore, even when they want to. The legal organizations within the UN have a special duty to be as unbiased and impartial as possible. Those legal organizations include the International Law Commission, the International Court of Justice (known more popularly as the World Court), and the International Criminal Court.

### The International Law Commission
The authority to codify international law is the official mission of the International Law Commission. Because all UN member nations retain their sovereign identities, the codifications drawn up by the commission must be joined voluntarily by each nation-state. The commission meets every year at a time authorized by the General Assembly. A legal topic can make its way to the commission in one of two ways. Either the General Assembly submits a legal issue to the commission or the commission itself decides to pursue a legal problem. After the commission has examined a legal topic in depth, it may draw up a draft on that aspect of international law. That draft then goes to the General Assembly for further consideration. Once the General Assembly has accepted a draft, it is codified into a convention. That convention is then submitted to the member states for their adoption. Some of the conventions that have been suggested by the commission and adopted by the General Assembly include the Convention on the Law of Treaties and the Convention on Diplomatic Relations. The General Assembly elects each of the 34 members of the International Law Commission, who each remain on the commission for five years. [See *Basic Facts about the United Nations* (New York: United Nations, 2003), pp. 269–270.]

## Table 34-1 The United Nations System

# THE UNITED NATIONS SYSTEM

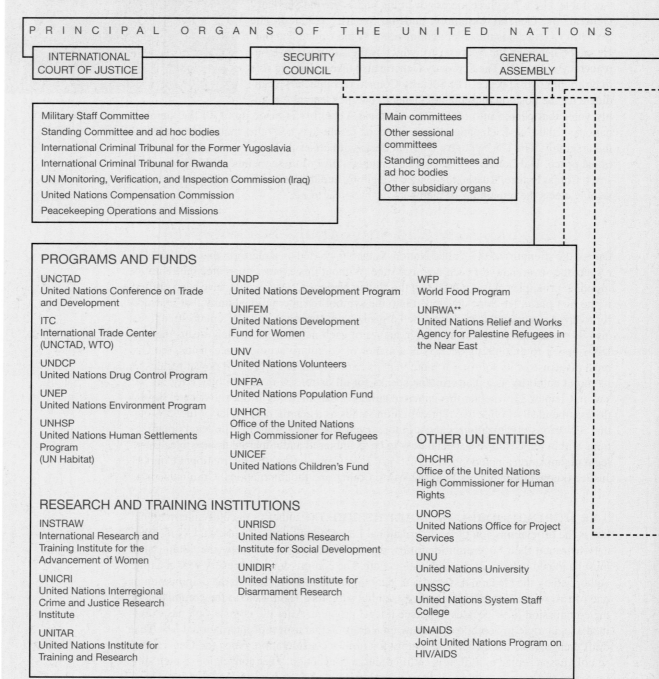

PRINCIPAL ORGANS OF THE UNITED NATIONS

**INTERNATIONAL COURT OF JUSTICE**

**SECURITY COUNCIL**

**GENERAL ASSEMBLY**

Military Staff Committee
Standing Committee and ad hoc bodies
International Criminal Tribunal for the Former Yugoslavia
International Criminal Tribunal for Rwanda
UN Monitoring, Verification, and Inspection Commission (Iraq)
United Nations Compensation Commission
Peacekeeping Operations and Missions

Main committees
Other sessional committees
Standing committees and ad hoc bodies
Other subsidiary organs

### PROGRAMS AND FUNDS

**UNCTAD**
United Nations Conference on Trade and Development

**ITC**
International Trade Center (UNCTAD, WTO)

**UNDCP**
United Nations Drug Control Program

**UNEP**
United Nations Environment Program

**UNHSP**
United Nations Human Settlements Program
(UN Habitat)

**UNDP**
United Nations Development Program

**UNIFEM**
United Nations Development Fund for Women

**UNV**
United Nations Volunteers

**UNFPA**
United Nations Population Fund

**UNHCR**
Office of the United Nations High Commissioner for Refugees

**UNICEF**
United Nations Children's Fund

**WFP**
World Food Program

**UNRWA\*\***
United Nations Relief and Works Agency for Palestine Refugees in the Near East

### OTHER UN ENTITIES

**OHCHR**
Office of the United Nations High Commissioner for Human Rights

**UNOPS**
United Nations Office for Project Services

**UNU**
United Nations University

**UNSSC**
United Nations System Staff College

**UNAIDS**
Joint United Nations Program on HIV/AIDS

### RESEARCH AND TRAINING INSTITUTIONS

**INSTRAW**
International Research and Training Institute for the Advancement of Women

**UNICRI**
United Nations Interregional Crime and Justice Research Institute

**UNITAR**
United Nations Institute for Training and Research

**UNRISD**
United Nations Research Institute for Social Development

**UNIDIR†**
United Nations Institute for Disarmament Research

\*Autonomous organizations working with the United Nations and each other through the coordinating machinery of the Economic and Social Council.

†Report only to the General Assembly.

*Source:* Department of Public Information, *Basic Facts about the United Nations*, New York: 2003, p. 24.

| ECONOMIC AND SOCIAL COUNCIL | TRUSTEESHIP COUNCIL | SECRETARIAT |

## FUNCTIONAL COMMISSIONS

Commission for Social
  Development
Commission on Human Rights
Commission on Narcotic Drugs
Commission on Crime Prevention
  and Criminal Justice
Commission on Science and
  Technology for Development
Commission on Sustainable
  Development
Commission on the Status of
  Women
Commission on Population and
  Development
Statistical Commission

## REGIONAL COMMISSIONS

Economic Commission for Africa (ECA)
Economic Commission for Europe (ECE)
Economic Commission for Latin
  America and the Caribbean (ECLAC)
Economic Commission for Asia
  and the Pacific (ESCAP)
Economic Commission for
  Western Asia (ESCWA)
United Nations Forum on Forestry
  Sessional and Standing
Committees Expert, ad hoc, and
  related bodies

## RELATED ORGANIZATIONS

IAEA
International Atomic Energy Agency

WTO (trade)
World Trade Organization

WTO (tourism)
World Tourism Organization

CTBTO
Preparatory Commission for the
Comprehensive Nuclear-Test-Ban-
Treaty Organization

OPCW
Organization for the Prohibition of
Chemical Weapons

## SPECIALIZED AGENCIES*

ILO
International Labor Organization

FAO
Food and Agriculture
Organization of the United Nations

UNESCO
United Nations Educational, Scientific,
and Cultural Organization

WHO
World Health Organization

WORLD BANK GROUP

  IBRD
  International Bank for Reconstruction
  and Development

  IDA
  International Development Association

  IFC
  International Finance Corporation

  MIG
  Multilateral Investment Guarantee
  Agency

  ICSID
  International Center for Settlement of
  Investment Disputes

IMF
International Monetary Fund

ICAO
International Civil Aviation Organization

IMO
International Maritime Organization

ITU
International Telecommunications Union

UPU
Universal Postal Union

WMO
World Meteorological Organization

WIPO
World Intellectual Property Organization

IFAD
International Fund for Agricultural
Development

OSG
Office of the Secretary-General

OIOS
Office of Internal Oversight
Services

OLA
Office of Legal Affairs

DPA
Department of Political Affairs

DDA
Department for Disarmament
Affairs

DPKO
Department of Peacekeeping
Operations

OCHA
Office for the Coordination of
Humanitarian Affairs

DESA
Department of Economic and
Social Affairs

DGAACS
Department of General
Assembly Affairs and Conference
Services

DPI
Department of Public Information

DM
Department of Management

OIP
Office of the Iraq Program

UNSECOORD
Office of the United Nations
Security Coordinator

ODC
Office on Drugs and Crime

UNOG
UN Office at Geneva

UNOV
UN Office at Vienna

UNON
UN Office at Nairobi

**The International Court of Justice** One of the principal vehicles for the establishment of international law and justice is the International Court of Justice (ICJ). Like many of the agencies of the UN, the ICJ, which is popularly referred to as the World Court, is not located in New York City (see Figure 34-1). Situated at The Hague in the Netherlands, the ICJ was established under provisions within the UN Charter. Key features of the court include its structure and its jurisdiction.

*The Structure of the ICJ* The ICJ is made up of 15 judges. The Security Council and the General Assembly of the United Nations are jointly responsible for electing these judges, each of whom serves a nine-year term. All of the judges are also eligible for reelection. To ensure as much impartiality as possible, the UN Charter also specifies that no two judges can be citizens of the same country and that the judges may not have any additional employment while they sit on the court. Ideally, the judges are chosen because of their legal qualifications. Every attempt is also made to ensure that the judges exemplify the foremost legal institutions in the world. When a nation is involved in a case presented to the ICJ, that nation is permitted to appoint a single judge to the court on a temporary basis.

*Standing within the ICJ* Only sovereign nations have legal standing to initiate a case before the ICJ. Included within this category are nations that are member states of the United Nations. Nations that are not member states, however, may also have cases heard before the court. Questions on the legal standing of nonmember states are left up to the determination of the General Assembly and the Security Council.

**Figure 34-1**    The Principal Offices of the United Nations.

*Source:* Department of Public Information, *Basic Facts about the United Nations* (New York: United Nations, 2003), p. 24.

*Subject Matter Jurisdiction in the ICJ*  Subject matter jurisdiction in the ICJ is outlined within the UN Charter. This jurisdiction includes legal questions specifically referred to within the charter, as well as any legal question raised by a member nation before the court. Such legal questions may involve the interpretation of treaties and international conventions. Unlike the courts of the United States, which can render opinions only when faced with an actual case, the ICJ is permitted to issue advisory opinions when requested by nation-states, the General Assembly, the Security Council, or other authorized agencies within the structure of the United Nations. Those judges who disagree with the advisory opinion of the majority are empowered to issue dissenting opinions. In an advisory case, sometimes a dissenting opinion can be just as vital as the majority opinion, because the dissenter's rationale may be used in other venues.

## EXAMPLE 34-3: Jurisdiction, Advisory Opinions, and the ICJ

One source of advisory opinions involves the question of how the corporate body of the United Nations relates to individual member nations. For instance, in 1949, the General Assembly solicited an advisory opinion from the ICJ concerning the assassination of a UN mediator. The mediator had been killed on a mission to Palestine. The issue before the court was whether the United Nations could hold a member state liable for any harm that befell an agent of the United Nations. The Court found that the UN did indeed have that capacity.

**The International Criminal Court**  To deal with crimes against humanity, an official **International Criminal Court (ICC)** was set up by the Rome Statute of the International Criminal Court in 1998. Unlike the ICJ, the ICC is not an official agency of the United Nations, though the UN was instrumental in its establishment. The objective of the new court, which actually began operation in 2002, is to preside over trials involving genocide, war crimes, and other human rights violations. The International Criminal Court itself and its prison are physically situated in The Hague, along with the International Court of Justice. Eighteen judges, no two of whom may be citizens of a single country, serve on the ICC for a term of nine years. The judges are elected by the states who are parties to the statute. The Court also names one of the judges as president, as well as a registrar and an official prosecutor.

One of the key differences between the ICJ and the ICC is that the ICC has jurisdiction over individual defendants. On the other hand, the ICC does not have *original* jurisdiction over a defendant who has been charged with war crimes, genocide, or other offenses against humanity. Rather, the defendant's own government must prosecute the defendant before the ICC can claim original jurisdiction. Should the government fail to bring legal action against the defendant, the ICC can then step into the case. This feature has caused some concern among critics of the ICC, who argue that nation-states can protect their own citizens from prosecution in the ICC by prosecuting them in a home-grown court that would intentionally acquit the defendant regardless of that defendant's real guilt or innocence. Supporters counter this concern by pointing out that the weight of world opinion will generally counteract this tendency of a nation-state to protect one of its own. Moreover, even though the ICC is not an official arm of the UN, the UN Security Council is empowered to intervene in a wrongful legal procedure perpetrated within or by the court. This safeguard should reassure a defendant's home nation that, once a defendant has been indicted, a strong case against that defendant has already been developed. One major drawback is that the court has very limited authority. Specifically, it can hear only cases

## THE OPENING CASE *Revisited, Part III*
### Congress, International Law, and Military Force: *The United States v. Bin Laden*, Round 4

The United States has repeatedly refused to ratify the Rome Statute of the International Criminal Court. Supporters of the international new world order might see this refusal as a puzzling development. After all, if the United States must act to defend itself and others in protective wars, it ought to benefit from any additional law enforcement support it can get. However, a closer look at this situation will reveal that this interpretation is not quite the case. If the United States must engage in protective wars from time to time and must, at other times, act as the *de facto* world government, the United States military must act as a *de facto* world police force. A police force, by its very nature, must enter dangerous, volatile, and potentially hazardous situations. Some of these police actions call for split-second decision making. Others may involve decisions that many people in the international community, especially those who see the United States as the enemy, do not support, and might even

condemn. A case in point is the situation in the Opening Case at the beginning of this chapter. Recall again that, in the Opening Case, the United States sent military personnel into Pakistan with orders to capture or kill Osama bin Laden. There are many individuals, groups, and nations that opposed this action. However, this is often the case when the police, even the *de facto* global police, must perform unpopular actions. If the United States were a party to the Rome Treaty, the Navy Seals who risked their lives to bring a sworn enemy of the United States to justice, would be in danger of a politically motivated prosecution under the authority of the ICC. If, as the international order scenario suggests, the United States must at times act as a global police force, then the members of its military, like the Navy Seals in the bin Laden operation, need the type of legal protection from political retribution that the ICC cannot now promise to deliver.

that involve the citizens of those countries that ratified the original treaty that created the court. Several major countries, including the United States, have not ratified the treaty, which places their citizens outside the court's jurisdiction. (See L. Fasulo, *An Insider's Guide to the UN* (New Haven, CT: Yale University Press, 2004) pp. 100–104; *Basic Facts about the United Nations* (New York: United Nations, 2003), 279.)

## Economic Regulation and the United Nations

The United Nations does some of its best work in the area of economics and trade. It serves as a central clearing house for international treaties, trade proposals, conventions, and trade agreements, as well as for the development of the law as it relates to the making of international contracts. Some of the chief organizations and institutions of the UN that are involved in economics and trade include the UN Commission on International Trade, the UN Convention on Contracts for the International Sale of Goods, and the Division for Science and Technology.

### The UN Commission on International Trade Law
In 1996, the General Assembly of the United Nations authorized the creation of the UN Commission on International Trade Law (UNCITRAL). The commission consists of 36 nations chosen to represent the primary social, economic, legal, and geographical areas of the globe. The goal of the commission is to cultivate the organization and integration of international law in relation to international trade. To this end, it coordinates the activities of institutions involved in international trade, encourages continued commitment to current treaties and conventions, and constructs new agreements for the community of international trade.

### The UN Convention on CISG

One of these agreements is the **UN Convention on Contracts for the International Sale of Goods (CISG)**. This agreement became effective in 1988. It applies only to sales between businesses located in different countries. The agreement specifically excludes contracts involving goods purchased for use by individuals or families. The CISG affects the formation of an international trade contract, as well as the rights and duties that arise under such contracts. However, it deals neither with the validity of such contracts nor with the liability of the seller for harm caused by the goods. Application of the CISG is limited to businesses that are located in countries that have ratified the agreement or those that create contracts that expressly stipulate that the CISG will apply to the agreement.

The CISG governs contracts for goods within the international community in much the same way that the Uniform Commercial Code (UCC) applies to sale-of-goods contracts within the United States. There are some significant differences, however. For example, the UCC applies to contracts between merchants and to those that involve nonmerchants. The CISG, in contrast, involves only contracts between merchants. The UCC also involves not only sale-of-goods contracts but also other commercial agreements, such as leases. The CISG, in contrast, applies only to sale-of-goods contracts. Also, the UCC has modified the traditional mirror image rule to overcome problems caused by the battle of the forms. The CISG still applies the mirror image rule to the acceptance of a contractual offer. Finally, the UCC has a provision that says that any contract for the sale of goods valued at over $500 must be in writing to be enforceable. The CISG has no such provision.

### Additional UN Economic Agencies

The efforts extended by the United Nations to monitor and regulate economic conditions in the global marketplace are evident in the existence of various organizations, each of which has its own mission in the financial structure of the worldwide economy. These agencies include global councils and conferences such as the Economic and Social Council (ECOSOC) and the UN Conference on Trade and Development (UNCTAD), as well as regional agencies such as the Economic Commission for Africa and the Economic Commission for Europe. Other agencies include the International Labor Organization; the World Health Organization; the United Nations Educational, Scientific, and Cultural Organization (UNESCO); the World International Property Organization (WIPO); and the Food and Agriculture Organization. Each organization makes assessments and enters judgments that influence how international business is conducted. One such organization that has special significance in this regard is the Division for Science and Technology of UNCTAD.

### The Division for Science and Technology

The **Division for Science and Technology** was created in response to recommendations made by the eighth conference of UNCTAD and the Ad Hoc Working Group of the International Commission on Science and Technology. Both of these groups saw the need to improve the international sharing of science and technology among governments, businesses, and educational institutions, especially between developed and developing nations. The Division of Science and Technology was created to coordinate the activities of several agencies that previously had been charged with handling issues of international cooperation in the sharing of science and technology for economic development. Many experts see this creation as a step in the right direction but urge an even more unified response in this regard.

## The Economic Security Council

The Commission on Global Governance, a 26-member international organization, has suggested streamlining the surveillance of international economic efforts under the auspices of an **Economic Security Council (ESC)**. The ESC would be a single, unified international agency under the management of the United Nations that would monitor the economic activities of the member nations of the UN. The ESC would evaluate the state of the international economy and implement long-term strategic planning to promote sustainable development across the planet. However, the ESC would not take the place of existing international agencies, such as the Economic and Social Council or the UN Conference on Trade and Development, but instead would coordinate their efforts in an efficient, effective, and economic manner.

## quick quiz 34-3

1. The secretary general is the chief administrator of the United Nations.        true/false

2. When a nation is involved in a case presented to the ICJ, that        true/false
   nation must voluntarily eliminate any judge on the panel that is a
   citizen of that nation.

3. The UCC and the CISG are identical in every way.        true/false

# 34-4 International Law, Finance, and Trade

Not everyone who wants to enter a local business transaction has the ready cash to do so. This hurdle, however, does not necessarily prevent them from looking for ways to expand their financial base. Therefore, by their very nature, business transactions often involve buying on credit, borrowing money, and investing in risky ventures designed to make a fast profit. The same thing can be said about international business transactions. To deal with issues of finance and trade on a worldwide scale, several international organizations and agreements have emerged that are designed to make global dealings work as smoothly as local ones.

## The International Monetary Fund and the World Bank

Two organizations that emerged in the aftermath of the Great Depression and World War II were the International Monetary Fund and the World Bank. Both institutions came out of a series of meetings held in Bretton Woods, New Hampshire, in the final months of World War II. The **International Monetary Fund (IMF)** is designed to serve as a way for financially strapped nations to secure loans that will help them engage in programs of sustainable economic growth and development. The IMF has 184 members, each of which has pledged to act responsibly in the pursuit of economic and developmental goals.

The **World Bank** has a mission that is quite similar to the mission of the IMF. The difference is that the IMF is dedicated to helping all nations, developed, developing, and undeveloped, with fiscal problems, whereas the World Bank works exclusively with the poorest nations in the international community. Even this mission is split between the two arms of the World Bank. The International Bank for Reconstruction and Development (IBRD) handles more conventional loans based on normal market provisions, whereas the International Development Association (IDA) handles loans to the world's most economically challenged nations.

## The World Trade Organization

After the end of World War II, the primary trading nations of the international community met to work out the details of a major trade agreement. The agreement, named the

**General Agreement on Tariffs and Trade (GATT)**, had as part of its original plan the creation of an International Trade Organization (ITO). Although the ITO was never established, GATT continued to function, frequently holding international conferences on the formation and execution of international trade law. The eighth conference, which came to be known as the Uruguay Round Agreements, resulted in the creation of the **World Trade Organization (WTO)**.

**The Structure of the World Trade Organization** The World Trade Organization was designed to serve as the corporate nucleus for the management of international trade relationships. As such, the WTO replaced GATT as the focus of world

trade talks. However, all agreements, treaties, and trade obligations created under GATT have been included in the WTO and thus remain in force. The structure of the WTO involves three levels: the Ministerial Conference, the General Council, and the Secretariat. The power to make key determinations under the authority of multinational trade agreements falls to the Ministerial Conference, which meets every two years. The responsibilities of the Ministerial Conference pass to the General Council whenever the Ministerial Conference is not assembled. Finally, the Secretariat, which is headed by a Director General, is responsible for the administration of the WTO.

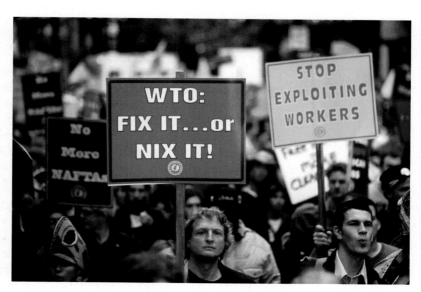

The World Trade Organization is a constant target of controversy and its summits are frequently targeted by hostile and aggressive protesters.

**The World Trade Organization Principles** The WTO has established certain overall principles that regulate how member nations must treat one another in the world of international trade. The first principle, the **national treatment principle**, states that WTO nations must apply the same standards to imports that they apply to domestic goods. The second principle, the **most-favored nation principle**, maintains that all member nations must apply the same privileges, advantages, and benefits to all other member nations in relation to similar imports. The third principle, the **tariff-based principle**, asserts that the only way that member nations can regulate the imports of other nations is through tariffs. This rule eliminates the use of more drastic techniques, such as boycotts, quotas, and quantitative limits.

**The Dispute Settlement Board** The **Dispute Settlement Board (DSB)** of the WTO was established to provide a forum for settling trade disputes among member nations. The DSB follows a commonly adopted procedure known as the **Dispute Settlement Understanding (DSU)**. All member nations can be held accountable under DSU regulations. According to those regulations, only member nations have standing to initiate a case. The DSU implements a number of measures designed to improve the way that quarrels are handled. For instance, the DSU has set up a series of precise time limits for the stages in a trade conflict. The DSU ensures that a network of comprehensive guidelines is followed consistently in all such controversies. The DSU also allows effective retaliatory measures that can be implemented by one nation against another if the offending nation refuses to adhere to a decision rendered under the DSU.

Did You Know?

As of 1997, the World Trade Organization (WTO) had a membership that includes 151 nations. The United States joined on January 1, 1995.

## EXAMPLE 34-4: The WTO, Germany, and the Korean Retaliation

Germany and Korea were involved in a dispute concerning trade in electronic appliances and automobiles. Korea claimed that in violation of trade agreements, Germany imposed a tariff on certain electronic appliances manufactured in Korea and imported to Germany. Korea followed proper DSU procedures and received a ruling from a panel that was supported by an appellate board. The ruling indicated that Germany had indeed violated the agreement. The WTO could not directly sanction Germany. Instead, it allowed Korea to impose an enormous tariff on luxury and sports model automobiles imported from Germany to Korea. This form of sanction is known as retaliation.

## The North American Free Trade Agreement

The United States and many other similarly situated nations have entered comprehensive trade coalitions designed to open their borders to the free flow of international trade. The most famous of these comprehensive coalitions is the **North American Free Trade Agreement (NAFTA)**, a trading coalition that includes the United States, Canada, and Mexico. The goal of the coalition is to establish a trading market in North America, free from the burdens imposed by internal tariff barriers. Thus, each country within the agreement can take advantage of this free market by importing those goods that it cannot produce itself in exchange for the tariff-free exportation of the goods that it can produce.

## The European Union

One of the most significant events to affect international law and commerce lately has been the inauguration of the **European Union (EU)**. The creation of the European Union, the attempt to formulate a common European economic policy, and the introduction of a common currency for most of Europe may transform the EU into a major competitor with the power to challenge American business interests in the global marketplace. Moreover, because many businesses within the EU have embraced cyber-commerce, American firms may face unique challenges in that arena.

The euro became the common currency used by European Union member states in 2002, replacing many of the individual currencies and providing consistency for the EU.

**The Introduction of the Euro** To adopt the euro, Europe's common currency, a country must first belong to the European Union. Membership in the EU alone, however, is not enough to allow a nation to adopt the euro. In addition, a nation must have a stable inflation rate, a history of interest rate convergence that falls within certain guidelines, and a pattern of fiscal responsibility. Of those nations that have qualified, eleven, including Austria, Belgium, France, Germany, Ireland, Italy, Luxembourg, the Netherlands, and Spain, elected to join the effort. Several nations, including the United Kingdom, Denmark, and Sweden, opted out of the program. The use of the euro is designed to lower costs by eliminating the need to change currencies when firms in the member states deal with one another across national boundaries.

**Electronic Commerce and the European Union** The EU has been active in the development of cyber-commerce directives in an attempt to head off proposed legislative initiatives in the individual member nations. Such individualized rules would complicate the rules of European cyber-commerce and defeat the purpose of a unified EU economic policy. One example of a unified directive is the Data Protection Directive. This directive assures all citizens of Europe that they will enjoy certain definitive privacy rights when they engage in cyber-commerce. Among the rights held by consumers in Europe are the right to obtain any computer data stored about them, the right to adjust any incorrect data, the right to deny another party the use of computer data, and the right to a legal remedy for any unlawful activities in relation to computer data. Another EU directive that affects cyber-commerce is the Directive on the Protection of Consumers in Respect of Distance Contracts (ECD). This directive gives specifically enumerated privileges to consumers who deal with companies selling goods and services within the EU by electronic means. The ECD allows consumers to cancel any electronic commerce transaction without penalty within seven working days.

## EXAMPLE 34-5: The Case of the Dissatisfied European Cyber-Consumer

Clay Joseph, a British citizen, was in the process of creating a new corporation that he hoped would revolutionize the comic book industry. To implement his business plan, he ordered a set of display cases from Volkmann Displays Unlimited, a German firm. On the same day, he also ordered a set of office furniture from IKEA in Sweden. When Joseph received the package from Volkmann, he discovered that the display cases could not hold the material that he wanted to store. One day later, the IKEA shipment arrived. Again he was dissatisfied, not because of any flaw in the furniture but because he had misjudged how the color of the chairs would fit into his office decor. As a European cyber-consumer, Clay Joseph's purchase of the books and the office furniture would be protected by the Directive on the Protection of Consumers in Respect of Distance Contracts (ECD), and he could rescind both deals within seven business days with no penalty whatsoever.

**National and International Law** One final word of warning is worth mentioning before we leave this chapter. Despite the importance of focusing on international law and the laws of other countries, businesses involved in international trade must always focus on the laws of their own nation. Sometimes national law will reach into the jurisdiction of a foreign country. Although such instances are rare, they may occur when one or more of the parties to a lawsuit are citizens of the country exercise jurisdiction and when the foreign activity somehow affects the welfare of that country.

**Did You Know?**

The official symbol for the euro looks like this: $\epsilon$. The symbol itself is usually printed in yellow with a blue background.

### quick quiz 34-4

1. Two organizations that emerged in the aftermath of the Great Depression and World War II were the International Monetary Fund and the World Bank.    true | false

2. None of the agreements, treaties, or trade obligations created under GATT have been included in the WTO.    true | false

3. NAFTA is a trading coalition that includes the United States, the United Kingdom, and Greenland.    true | false

# Summary

**34.1** It is important to define the new world order and explain how it works because international law exists within that global order. The problem of defining the new world order is made more difficult because it is unfamiliar and difficult to understand. Four theories have been offered to describe the new world order: (1) the economic new world order, (2) the civilizational new world order, (3) the ideological new world order, and (4) the globalized new world order.

**34.2** War has many significant effects on the transaction of business in the international marketplace. One of the key questions concerning the nature of war as it relates to international business is whether the war is just. Ethical and legal philosophers in the West have developed criteria for determining when a war can be considered legally and morally correct. This theory is termed the just war theory.

**34.3** The stated purposes of the United Nations are to advance human rights, to end war, to enhance human achievement, to support peaceful international coalitions, and to promote international fidelity to truth, justice, and the rule of law. The promotion of international law has taken many forms within the structure of the United Nations, including the International Court of Justice, the UN Commission on International Trade Law, and the UN Convention on Contracts for the International Sale of Goods. The International Criminal Court also plays a key role in policing international justice.

**34.4** To deal with issues of finance and trade on a worldwide scale, several international organizations and agreements have emerged that are designed to make global dealings work as smoothly as local ones. These include the International Monetary Fund, the World Bank, the World Trade Organization, the North American Free Trade Agreement, and the European Union.

# Key Terms

civilization, 778

competent authority, 782

Dispute Settlement Board (DSB), 797

Dispute Settlement Understanding (DSU), 797

Division for Science and Technology, 795

Economic Security Council (ESC), 795

euro, 798

European Union (EU), 798

General Agreement on Tariffs and Trade (GATT), 797

General Assembly, 789

Geneva Conventions, 788

International Court of Justice (ICJ), 792

International Criminal Court (ICC), 793

International Monetary Fund (IMF), 796

just cause, 782

just war theory, 782

last resort, 783

most-favored nation principle, 797

national treatment principle, 797

nation-state, 776

new world order, 775

North American Free Trade Agreement (NAFTA), 798

preemptive war, 784

preventative war, 784

principle of honorable surrender, 784

principle of repentance, 784

principle of restoration, 784

probability of success, 783

proportionality, 783

protective war, 785

right intention, 782

Secretariat, 789

Secretary General, 789

Security Council, 789

tariff-based principle, 797

UN Commission on International Trade Law (UNCITRAL), 794

UN Convention on Contracts for the International Sale of Goods (CISG), 795

Westphalia system, 776

World Bank, 796

World Trade Organization (WTO), 797

Worldwide organization, 777

# Questions for Review and Discussion

1. What are the four new world order theories?
2. What are the criteria for a just war?
3. What is the extent of the jurisdiction of the International Court of Justice?
4. What is the mission of International Criminal Court?
5. What is the main goal of UNCITRAL?
6. What are the differences between the UCC and the CISG?
7. What is the structure of the World Trade Organization?
8. What are the objectives of the Dispute Settlement Understanding?
9. What is the major purpose of NAFTA?
10. What is the European Union?

# Cases for Analysis

1. After General Manuel Noriega had come under the authority of the United States forces following the invasion of Panama, his attorneys argued that he should be treated as a prisoner of war (POW) under the Geneva Conventions. The United States government agreed to treat Noriega as a POW but refused to give him official POW status. Noriega's attorneys argued that this treatment as POW could be withdrawn by the government at any time. They asked the court to declare their client a POW under the Geneva Conventions. The government argued that the events in Panama were considered hostilities rather than a war. Consequently, the government pointed out, Noriega could not be a POW. Article II of Geneva Convention III states that "the present convention shall apply to all cases of declared war and of any other armed conflict which may arise between two or more of the High Contracting Parties, even if the state of war is not recognized by one of them." Moreover, the International Red Cross Commentary on Convention III says, "Any difference between two states leading to the intervention of the armed forces is an armed conflict within the meaning of Article II." Finally, Article IV of the Convention defines POWs as "persons belonging to one of the following categories, who have fallen into the power of the enemy: (1) members of the armed forces of a Party to the conflict. . . ." Taking all of this into account, as well as the United States courts' intent to construe the Geneva Conventions liberally, should the court declare Noriega a POW? Explain. *United States of America v. Manuel Antonio Noriega,* 808 F. Supp. 791 (S.D. FL).

2. American Rice, Inc., a U.S. corporation, sold its goods in Saudi Arabia under the trade name of ABU BINT, which means "of the girl." Another American corporation, the Arkansas Rice Growers Cooperative Association, marketed similar products in Saudi Arabia using the name BINT ALARAB, which in English means "Gulf Girl." American Rice sued Arkansas in federal district court under the Lanham Act, alleging an infringement by Arkansas of American Rice's exclusive trademark. None of the Arkansas rice products that American Rice complained of had entered any market within the United States. Arkansas argued that the federal district court had no extraterritorial power to mediate this international trade dispute. Was Arkansas correct? Explain. *American Rice, Inc., v. Arkansas Rice Growers Coop. Ass'n,* 701 F.2d 414 (5th Cir.).

3. Gulf Oil Corporation and Eastern Air Lines entered a contract under the terms of which Gulf Oil was obligated to supply Eastern with jet fuel according to an established pricing system. In 1973, the Organization for Petroleum Exporting Countries (OPEC) established an oil embargo that precipitated the now-famous energy crisis of the 1970s. As a result of the oil embargo and the energy crisis, the price of crude oil skyrocketed. Gulf Oil asked Eastern to consent to a price increase over the price agreed to under the original contract. Eastern refused to comply with the increase. Gulf Oil then vowed to stop all jet fuel shipments to Eastern unless Eastern would reconsider its refusal to go along with the price increase. Eastern filed a lawsuit in federal district court alleging a breach of contract on Gulf Oil's part. Did the American court have jurisdiction over an exclusively American contract affected by an international incident, such as the 1973 oil embargo? Did

the court agree that Gulf breached its contract with Eastern Airlines? Explain. *Eastern Air Line, Inc., v. Gulf Oil Corporation*, 415 F. Supp. 429 (S.D. FL).

4. Kenneth Armstrong, an American citizen, purchased the component parts of computers in Germany, Japan, and the United States. He took those parts to Bolivia, where he constructed the computers, stamped them with the name Starlight Computers, and sold them. Armstrong had a Bolivian registration that allowed him to use the trade name Starlight. Although none of the computers were imported into the United States by Armstrong himself, many of the counterfeit computers eventually found their way into the U.S. marketplace. Starlight Computers, Inc., an American corporation, brought a lawsuit against Armstrong in United States District Court under the Lanham Act. Armstrong moved for a dismissal of the case, arguing that the American court did not have the authority to enforce the Lanham Act against his Bolivian operation. Is Armstrong correct? Explain.

5. France and Japan are involved in a dispute regarding trade in aircraft parts. France claims that in violation of certain trade agreements, Japan is imposing a tariff on certain types of aircraft parts that are manufactured in France and imported to Japan. France follows proper DSU procedures and receives a ruling from a panel that is supported by an appellate board. The ruling indicates that Japan has indeed violated the agreement. France asks the WTO to apply punitive sanctions directly against Japan. Will France's request be granted? Explain.

6. Helga Godel, a German citizen, placed an order for certain software items from Pascal Enterprises, a French firm. On the same day, she ordered a silverware set from Silverwings Ltd., an Austrian company. When Godel received the package from Pascal, she unwrapped the software and attempted to download the program into her computer. When she accessed the program, however, she found that though the program worked well, it was not what she had expected. Later that day, she received the silverware set. Again she was dissatisfied, this time with the quality of the product. As a European e-consumer, what rights does Godel have under the EU Directive on the Protection of Consumers in Respect of Distance Contracts? Explain.

## quick quiz Answers

| 34-1 | 34-2 | 34-3 | 34-4 |
|------|------|------|------|
| 1. T | 1. T | 1. T | 1. T |
| 2. T | 2. F | 2. F | 2. F |
| 3. F | 3. T | 3. F | 3. F |

# Part 9 Case Study

**Legal Consequences of the Construction of a Wall in the Occupied Palestinian Territory (Request for Advisory Opinion)**
The International Court of Justice
Order of 30 January 2004

## Summary

The International Court of Justice is an agency of the United Nations, established under a statute within the UN Charter. Fifteen judges sit on the ICJ. The judges are elected by the Security Council and the General Assembly of the United Nations for nine years. The judges are also eligible for reelection. To ensure as much impartiality as possible, no nation-state can have more than a single judge on the Court at the same time. The statute also says that judges must work exclusively for the Court during their term on the bench. Ideally, the judges on the Court are chosen because of their legal qualifications. Every attempt is also made to make certain that the judges exemplify the foremost legal institutions in the world.

The statute establishing the ICJ also includes provisions to ensure the impartiality of the judges. One such provision is Article 17, paragraph 2, which states, "No Member [of the ICJ] may participate in the decision of any case in which he has previously taken part as agent, counsel, or advocate for one of the parties, or as a member of a national or international court, or of a commission of enquiry, or in any other capacity."

The present case involves the question of whether one of the judges on the ICJ ought to be permitted to participate in the case or be disqualified under this provision because of his previous involvement in the issue before the Court. The case was brought to the ICJ by the Government of Israel in a letter addressed to the Court Registrar, dated December 31, 2003. In that letter, the government asserted:

> Resolution A/RES/ES-10/14 requesting the advisory opinion locates the request squarely in the context of the wider Arab-Israeli/Israeli-Palestinian dispute. The essentially contentious nature of the proceedings is also recognised by the Court's invitation to Palestine to participate in the case. It is inappropriate for a Member of the Court to participate in decisions in a case in which he has previously played an active, official and public role as an advocate for a cause that is in contention in this case. Israel will be writing to the President of the Court separately on this matter pursuant to Article 34 (2) of the Rules of Court.

Israel objected to the connection that Judge Nabil Elaraby of Egypt had to the case because of his involvement in a number of initiatives that touched on several sensitive issues involved in the dispute. Specifically, Israel pointed to the judge's contributions to the Tenth Emergency Session of the General Assembly of the United Nations, his employment as a legal counselor to the Egyptian Ministry of Foreign Affairs, his work as a legal consultant to the Egyptian Delegates to the Middle East Peace Initiative at Camp David in 1978, and his connection to certain actions resulting from the 1979 Israeli–Egypt Peace Treaty, especially the development of independent West Bank and Gaza Strip territories. Finally, and perhaps most significantly, the government of Israel pointed to an interview printed in a newspaper in Egypt in which the judge discussed his personal political views in relation to the nation-state of Israel.

A majority of the judges on the ICJ saw no problem with Judge Elaraby's involvement in the activities to which Israel objected. Specifically, they saw no problem in his role as legal advisor for Egypt, because in that capacity, the judge had been speaking and acting as an agent of his government. In relation to the published interview, the majority pointed to the fact that Article 17, paragraph 2, detailed certain roles that a judge was prohibited from performing in a case that was before the court. Nothing on the list, the Court concluded, mentioned giving interviews or publishing private political views. Therefore, the majority upheld the judge's participation in the case.

The sole dissenter was Judge Thomas Buergenthal of the United States. While Judge Buergenthal agreed with the court in relation to Judge Elaraby's official governmental roles, he disagreed about the private interview and objected to the Court's strict and limited interpretation of Article 17, paragraph 2. This point is critical because, as noted previously, in an advisory case, a dissenting opinion can sometimes be just as vital as the majority opinion, because the dissenter's rationale may be used in other venues.

# Dissenting Opinion of Judge Buergenthal

1. I have voted against the instant Order because I believe that the Court's decision is wrong as a matter of legal principle.

2. Israel challenges Judge Elaraby's participation in these proceedings on the ground that his previous professional involvement and personal statements on matters which go to the substance of the question before the Court in this advisory opinion request require that he not participate in these proceedings.

3. As far as Judge Elaraby's professional activities as diplomatic representative of his country and its legal adviser are concerned, the Court rejects Israel's objection by concluding that these activities, having been performed many years before the question of the construction of the wall now submitted to the Court first arose, do not fall within the activities contemplated by Article 17, paragraph 2, of the Statute to justify that he be precluded from participation in the case.

4. With regard to the newspaper interview that Judge Elaraby gave two months before his election to this Court at a time when he was no longer his country's diplomatic representative, the Court finds no basis for precluding Judge Elaraby's participation in these proceedings, because Judge Elaraby "expressed no opinion on the question put in the present case."

5. Israel seeks Judge Elaraby's disqualification on the ground, *inter alia*, that the views expressed by Judge Elaraby in the interview bear directly on issues that will have to be addressed in the advisory opinion request and that, given their nature, they create an appearance of bias incompatible with the fair administration of justice.

6. In principle, I share the Court's opinion that Judge Elaraby's prior activities, performed in the discharge of his diplomatic and governmental functions, do not fall within the scope of Article 17, paragraph 2, of the Statute of the Court so as to prevent his participation in these proceedings. . . .

7. I part company with the Court's conclusions, however, with regard to the interview Judge Elaraby gave in August of 2001, two months before his election to the Court, when he was no longer an official of his Government and hence spoke in his personal capacity. See *Al-Ahram Weekly Online*, 16–22 August 2001, issue No. 547. . . .

10. It is clear, of course, that the language of Article 17, paragraph 2, does not apply in so many words to the views Judge Elaraby expressed in the above interview. That does not mean, however, that this provision sets out the exclusive basis for the disqualification of a judge of this Court. It refers to what would generally be considered to be the most egregious violations of judicial ethics were a judge falling into one of the categories therein enumerated to participate in a case. At the same time, Article 17, paragraph 2, reflects much broader conceptions of justice and fairness that must be observed by courts of law than this Court appears to acknowledge. Judicial ethics are not matters strictly of hard and fast rules—I doubt that they can ever be exhaustively defined—they are matters of perception and of sensibility to appearances that courts must continuously keep in mind to preserve their legitimacy.

11. A court of law must be free and, in my opinion, is required to consider whether one of its judges has expressed views or taken positions that create the impression that he will not be able to consider the issues raised in a case or advisory opinion in a fair and impartial manner, that is, that he may be deemed to have prejudged one or more of the issues bearing on the subject-matter of the dispute before the court. That is what is meant by the

dictum that the fair and proper administration of justice requires that justice not only be done, but that it also be seen to be done. In my view, all courts of law must be guided by this principle, whether or not their statutes or other constitutive documents expressly require them to do so. That power and obligation is implicit in the very concept of a court of law charged with the fair and impartial administration of justice. To read them out of the reach of Article 17, paragraph 2, is neither legally justified nor is it wise judicial policy.

12. In paragraph 8 of this Order, the Court declares that, "whereas in the newspaper interview of August 2001, Judge Elaraby expressed no opinion on the question put in the present case; whereas consequently Judge Elaraby could not be regarded as having 'previously taken part' in the case in any capacity."

13. What we have here is the most formalistic and narrow construction of Article 17, paragraph 2, imaginable, and one that is unwarranted on the facts of this case. It is technically true, of course, that Judge Elaraby did not express an opinion on the specific question that has been submitted to the Court by the General Assembly of the United Nations. But it is equally true that this cannot be examined by the Court without taking account of the context of the Israeli/Palestinian conflict and the arguments that will have to be advanced by the interested parties in examining the "Legal Consequences of the Construction of a Wall in the Occupied Palestinian Territory." Many of these arguments will turn on the factual validity and credibility of assertions bearing directly on the specific question referred to the Court in this advisory opinion request. And when it comes to the validity and credibility of these arguments, what Judge Elaraby has to say in the part of the interview I quoted above creates an appearance of bias that in my opinion requires the Court to preclude Judge Elaraby's participations in the proceedings.

14. What I consider important in reaching the above conclusion is the appearance of bias. That, in my opinion, is what Article 17, paragraph 2, properly interpreted, is all about and what judicial ethics are all about. And that is why I dissent from this Order, even though I have no doubts whatsoever about the personal integrity of Judge Elaraby for whom I have the highest regard, not only as a valued colleague but also a good friend.

(*Signed*) Thomas Buergenthal

# Questions for Analysis

1. Why did Israel bring this case rather than a private party? Explain.

2. What is the central issue in this case?

3. What legal statutory provision provided grounds for the complaint lodged by Israel?

4. What was the decision of the majority? Explain.

5. On what point did the dissent contest the majority opinion? Explain.

# Appendix A   The Constitution of the United States

## Preamble

We the People of the United States, in Order to form a more perfect Union, establish Justice, insure domestic Tranquility, provide for the common defence, promote the general Welfare, and secure the Blessings of Liberty to ourselves and our Posterity, do ordain and establish this Constitution for the United States of America.

## Article I

Section 1. All legislative Powers herein granted shall be vested in a Congress of the United States, which shall consist of a Senate and House of Representatives.

Section 2. [1] The House of Representatives shall be composed of Members chosen every second Year by the People of the several States, and the Electors in each State shall have the Qualifications requisite for Electors of the most numerous Branch of the State Legislature.

[2] No Person shall be a Representative who shall not have attained to the Age of twenty-five Years, and been seven Years a Citizen of the United States, and who shall not, when elected, be an Inhabitant of that State in which he shall be chosen.

[3] Representatives and direct Taxes shall be apportioned among the several States which may be included within this Union, according to their respective Numbers, which shall be determined by adding to the whole Number of free Persons, including those bound to Service for a Term of Years, and excluding Indians not taxed, three fifths of all other Persons. The actual Enumeration shall be made within three Years after the first Meeting of the Congress of the United States, and within every subsequent Term of ten Years, in such Manner as they shall by Law direct. The Number of Representatives shall not exceed one for every thirty Thousand, but each State shall have at Least one Representative; and until such enumeration shall be made, the State of New Hampshire shall be entitled to chuse three, Massachusetts eight, Rhode Island and Providence Plantations one, Connecticut five, New York six, New Jersey four, Pennsylvania eight, Delaware one, Maryland six, Virginia ten, North Carolina five, South Carolina five, and Georgia three.

[4] When vacancies happen in the Representation from any State, the Executive Authority thereof shall issue Writs of Election to fill such Vacancies.

[5] The House of Representatives shall chuse their Speaker and other Officers; and shall have the sole Power of Impeachment.

Section 3. [1] The Senate of the United States shall be composed of two Senators from each State, chosen by the Legislature thereof, for six Years; and each Senator shall have one Vote.

[2] Immediately after they shall be assembled in Consequence of the first Election, they shall be divided as equally as may be into three Classes. The Seats of the Senators of the first Class shall be vacated at the Expiration of the Second Year, of the second Class at the Expiration of the fourth Year, and of the third Class at the Expiration of the sixth Year, so that one third may be chosen every second Year; and if Vacancies happen by Resignation, or otherwise, during the Recess of the Legislature of any State, the Executive thereof may make temporary Appointments until the next Meeting of the Legislature, which shall then fill such Vacancies.

[3] No Person shall be a Senator who shall not have attained to the Age of thirty Years, and been nine Years a Citizen of the United States, and who shall not, when elected, be an Inhabitant of that State for which he shall be chosen.

[4] The Vice President of the United States shall be President of the Senate, but shall have no Vote, unless they be equally divided.

[5] The Senate shall chuse their other Officers, and also a President pro tempore, in the Absence of the Vice President, or when he shall exercise the Office of President of the United States.

[6] The Senate shall have the sole Power to try all Impeachments. When sitting for that Purpose, they shall be on Oath or Affirmation. When the President of the United States is tried, the Chief Justice shall preside: And no Person shall be convicted without the Concurrence of two thirds of the Members present.

[7] Judgment in Cases of Impeachment shall not extend further than to removal from Office, and disqualification to hold and enjoy any Office of honor, Trust, or Profit under the United States: but the Party convicted shall nevertheless be liable and subject to Indictment, Trial, Judgment, and Punishment, according to Law.

Section 4. [1] The Times, Places and Manner of holding elections for Senators and Representatives, shall be prescribed in each State by the Legislature thereof; but the Congress may at any time by Law make or alter such Regulations, except as to the Places of chusing Senators.

[2] The Congress shall assemble at least once in every Year, and such Meeting shall be on the first Monday in December, unless they shall by Law appoint a different Day.

Section 5. [1] Each House shall be the Judge of the Elections, Returns, and Qualifications of its own Members, and a Majority of each shall constitute a Quorum to do Business; but a smaller Number may adjourn from day to day, and may be authorized to compel the Attendance of absent Members, in such Manner, and under such Penalties as each House may provide.

[2] Each House may determine the Rules of its Proceedings, punish its Members for disorderly Behavior, and, with the Concurrence of two thirds, expel a Member.

**[3]** Each House shall keep a Journal of its Proceedings, and from time to time publish the same, excepting such parts as may in their Judgment require Secrecy; and the Yeas and Nays of the Members of either House on any question shall, at the Desire of one fifth of those Present, be entered on the Journal.

**[4]** Neither House, during the Session of Congress, shall, without the Consent of the other, adjourn for more than three days, nor to any other Place than that in which the two Houses shall be sitting.

Section 6. **[1]** The Senators and Representatives shall receive a Compensation for their Services, to be ascertained by Law, and paid out of the Treasury of the United States. They shall in all Cases, except Treason, Felony and Breach of the Peace, be privileged from Arrest during their Attendance at the Session of their respective Houses, and in going to and returning from the same; and for any Speech of Debate in either House, they shall not be questioned in any other Place.

**[2]** No Senator or Representative shall, during the Time for which he was elected, be appointed to any civil Office under the Authority of the United States, which shall have been created, or the Emoluments whereof shall have been increased during such time; and no Person holding any Office under the United States, shall be a Member of either House during his Continuance in Office.

Section 7. **[1]** All Bills for raising Revenue shall originate in the House of Representatives; but the Senate may propose or concur with Amendments as on other Bills.

**[2]** Every Bill which shall have passed the House of Representatives and the Senate, shall, before it becomes a Law, be presented to the President of the United States; If he approve he shall sign it, but if not he shall return it, with his Objections to the House in which it shall have originated, who shall enter the Objections at large on their Journal, and proceed to reconsider it. If after such Reconsideration two thirds of that House shall agree to pass the Bill, it shall be sent together with the Objections, to the other House, by which it shall likewise be reconsidered, and if approved by two thirds of that House, it shall become a Law. But in all such Cases the Votes of both Houses shall be determined by yeas and Nays, and the Names of the Persons voting for and against the Bill shall be entered on the Journal of each House respectively. If any Bill shall not be returned by the President within ten Days (Sundays excepted) after it shall have been presented to him, the Same shall be a Law, in like Manner as if he had signed it, unless the Congress by their Adjournment prevent its Return in which Case it shall not be a Law.

**[3]** Every Order, Resolution, or Vote, to Which the Concurrence of the Senate and House of Representatives may be necessary (except on a question of Adjournment) shall be presented to the President of the United States; and before the Same shall take Effect, shall be approved by him, or being disapproved by him, shall be repassed by two thirds of the Senate and House of Representatives, according to the Rules and Limitations prescribed in the Case of a Bill.

Section 8. **[1]** The Congress shall have Power To lay and collect Taxes, Duties, Imposts and Excises, to pay the Debts and provide for the common Defence and general Welfare of the United States; but all Duties, Imposts and Excises shall be uniform throughout the United States;

**[2]** To borrow money on the credit of the United States;

**[3]** To regulate Commerce with foreign Nations, and among the several States, and with the Indian Tribes;

**[4]** To establish an uniform Rule of Naturalization, and uniform laws on the subject of Bankruptcies throughout the United States;

**[5]** To coin Money, regulate the Value thereof, and of foreign Coin, and fix the Standard of Weights and Measures;

**[6]** To provide for the Punishment of counterfeiting the Securities and current Coin of the United States;

**[7]** To Establish Post Offices and Post Roads;

**[8]** To promote the Progress of Science and useful Arts, by securing for limited Times to Authors and Inventors the exclusive Right to their respective Writings and Discoveries;

**[9]** To constitute Tribunals inferior to the supreme Court;

**[10]** To define and punish Piracies and Felonies committed on the high Seas, and Offenses against the Law of Nations;

**[11]** To declare War, grant Letters of Marque and Reprisal, and make Rules concerning Captures on Land and Water;

**[12]** To raise and support Armies, but no Appropriation of Money to that Use shall be for a longer Term than two Years;

**[13]** To provide and maintain a Navy;

**[14]** To make Rules for the Government and Regulation of the land and naval Forces;

**[15]** To provide for calling forth the Militia to execute the Laws of the Union, suppress Insurrections and repel Invasions;

**[16]** To provide for organizing, arming, and disciplining, the Militia, and for governing such Part of them as may be employed in the Service of the United States, reserving to the States respectively, the Appointment of the Officers, and the Authority of training the Militia according to the discipline prescribed by Congress;

**[17]** To exercise exclusive Legislation in all Cases whatsoever, over such District (not exceeding ten Miles square) as may, by Cession of particular States, and the Acceptance of Congress, become the Seat of the Government of the United States, and to exercise like Authority over all Places purchased by the Consent of the Legislature of the State in which the Same shall be, for the Erection of Forts, Magazines, Arsenals, dock-Yards and other needful Buildings;—And

**[18]** To make all Laws which shall be necessary and proper for carrying into Execution the foregoing Powers, and all other Powers vested by this Constitution in the Government of the United States, or in any Department or Officer thereof.

Section 9. [1] The Migration or Importation of Such Persons as any of the States now existing shall think proper to admit, shall not be prohibited by the Congress prior to the Year one thousand eight hundred and eight, but a Tax or duty may be imposed on such Importation, not exceeding ten dollars for each Person.

[2] The privilege of the Writ of Habeas Corpus shall not be suspended, unless when in Cases of Rebellion or Invasion the public Safety may require it.

[3] No Bill of Attainder or ex post facto Law shall be passed.

[4] No Capitation, or other direct, Tax shall be laid, unless in Proportion to the Census or Enumeration herein before directed to be taken.

[5] No Tax or Duty shall be laid on Articles exported from any State.

[6] No Preference shall be given by any Regulation of Commerce or Revenue to the Ports of one State over those of another: nor shall Vessels bound to, or from, one State be obliged to enter, clear, or pay Duties in another.

[7] No money shall be drawn from the Treasury, but in Consequence of Appropriations made by Law; and a regular Statement and Account of the Receipts and Expenditures of all public Money shall be published from time to time.

[8] No Title of Nobility shall be granted by the United States: And no Person holding any Office of Profit or Trust under them, shall, without the Consent of the Congress, accept of any present, Emolument, Office, or Title, of any kind whatever, from any King, Prince, or foreign State.

Section 10. [1] No State shall enter into any Treaty, Alliance, or confederation; grant Letters of Marque and Reprisal; coin Money; emit Bills of Credit; make any Thing but gold and silver Coin a Tender in Payment of Debts; pass any Bill of Attainder, ex post facto Law, or Law impairing the Obligation of Contracts, or grant any Title of Nobility.

[2] No State shall, without the Consent of the Congress, lay any Imposts or Duties on Imports or Exports, except what may be absolutely necessary for executing its inspection Laws: and the net Produce of all Duties and Imposts, laid by any State on Imports or Exports, shall be for the Use of the Treasury of the United States; and all such Laws shall be subject to the Revision and Control of the Congress.

[3] No State shall, without the Consent of Congress, lay any Duty of Tonnage, keep Troops, or Ships of War in time of Peace, enter into any Agreement or Compact with another State, or with a foreign Power, or engage in War, unless actually invaded, or in such imminent Danger as will not admit of delay.

# Article II

Section 1. [1] The executive Power shall be vested in a President of the United States of America. He shall hold his Office during the Term of four Years, and, together with the Vice President, chosen for the same Term, be elected, as follows:

[2] Each State shall appoint, in such Manner as the Legislature thereof may direct, a Number of Electors, equal to the whole Number of Senators and Representatives to which the State may be entitled in the Congress; but no Senator or Representative, or Person holding an Office of Trust or Profit under the United States, shall be appointed an Elector.

[3] The Electors shall meet in their respective States, and vote by Ballot for two Persons, of whom one at least shall not be an Inhabitant of the same State with themselves. And they shall make a List of all the Persons voted for, and of the Number of Votes for each; which List they shall sign and certify, and transmit sealed to the Seat of the Government of the United States, directed to the President of the Senate. The President of the Senate shall, in the Presence of the Senate and House of Representatives, open all the Certificates, and the Votes shall then be counted. The Person having the greatest Number of Votes shall be the President, if such Number be a Majority of the whole Number of Electors appointed; and if there be more than one who have such Majority, and have an equal Number of Votes, then the House of Representatives shall immediately chuse by Ballot one of them for President; and if no Person have a Majority, then from the five highest on the List the said House shall in like Manner chuse the President. But in chusing the President, the Votes shall be taken by States the Representation from each State having one Vote; A quorum for this Purpose shall consist of a Member or Members from two thirds of the States, and a Majority of all the States shall be necessary to a Choice. In every Case, after the Choice of the President, the Person having the greater Number of Votes of the Electors shall be the Vice President. But if there shall remain two or more who have equal Votes, the Senate shall chuse from them by Ballot the Vice President.

[4] The Congress may determine the Time of chusing the Electors, and the Day on which they shall give their Votes; which Day shall be the same throughout the United States.

[5] No person except a natural born Citizen, or a Citizen of the United States, at the time of the Adoption of this Constitution, shall be eligible to the Office of President; neither shall any Person be eligible to that Office who shall not have attained to the Age of thirty-five Years, and been fourteen Years a Resident within the United States.

[6] In case of the removal of the President from Office, or of his Death, Resignation or Inability to discharge the Powers and Duties of the said Office, the Same shall devolve on the Vice President, and the Congress may by Law provide for the Case of Removal, Death, Resignation or Inability, both of the President and Vice President, declaring what Officer shall then act as President, and such Officer shall act accordingly, until the Disability be removed, or a President shall be elected.

[7] The President shall, at stated Times, receive for his Services, a Compensation, which shall neither be increased nor diminished during the Period for which he shall have been elected, and he shall not receive within that Period any other Emolument from the United States, or any of them.

[8] Before he enter on the Execution of his Office, he shall take the following Oath or Affirmation: "I do solemnly swear (or affirm) that I will faithfully execute the Office of President of the United States, and will to the best of my Ability, preserve, protect, and defend the Constitution of the United States."

Section 2. [1] The President shall be Commander in Chief of the Army and Navy of the United States, and of the militia of the several States, when called into the actual Service of the United States; he may require the Opinion, in writing, of the principal Officer in each of the Executive Departments, upon any subject relating to the Duties of their respective Offices, and he shall have Power to grant Reprieves and Pardons for Offenses against the United States, except in Cases of Impeachment.

[2] He shall have Power, by and with the Advice and Consent of the Senate to make Treaties, provided two thirds of the Senators present concur; and he shall nominate, and by and with the Advice and Consent of the Senate, shall appoint Ambassadors, other public Ministers and Consuls, Judges of the supreme Court, and all other Officers of the United States, whose Appointments are not herein otherwise provided for, and which shall be established by Law; but the Congress may by Law vest the Appointment of such inferior Officers, as they think proper, in the President alone, in the Courts of Law, or in the Heads of Departments.

[3] The President shall have Power to fill up all Vacancies that may happen during the Recess of the Senate, by granting commissions which shall expire at the End of their next Session.

Section 3. He shall from time to time give to the Congress Information of the State of the Union, and recommend to their Consideration such Measures as he shall judge necessary and expedient; he may, on extraordinary Occasions, convene both Houses, or either of them, and in Case of Disagreement between them, with Respect to the Time of Adjournment, he may adjourn them to such Time as he shall think proper; he shall receive Ambassadors and other public Ministers; he shall take Care that the Laws be faithfully executed, and shall commission all the Officers of the United States.

Section 4. The President, Vice President and all civil Officers of the United States, shall be removed from Office on Impeachment for, and Conviction of, Treason, Bribery, or other high Crimes and Misdemeanors.

# Article III

Section 1. The judicial Power of the United States, shall be vested in one supreme Court, and in such inferior Courts as the Congress may from time to time ordain and establish. The Judges, both of the supreme and inferior Courts, shall hold their Offices during good Behaviour, and shall, at stated Times, receive for their Services a Compensation, which shall not be diminished during their Continuance in Office.

Section 2. [1] The judicial Power shall extend to all Cases, in Law and Equity, arising under this Constitution, the Laws of the United States, and Treaties made, or which shall be made, under their Authority;—to all Cases affecting Ambassadors, other public Ministers and Consuls;—to all Cases of admiralty and maritime Jurisdiction;—to Controversies to which the United States shall be a Party;—between a State and Citizens of another State; between Citizens of different States;—between Citizens of the same State claiming Lands under the Grants of different States, and between a State, or the Citizens thereof, and foreign States, Citizens or Subjects.

[2] In all Cases affecting Ambassadors, other public Ministers and Consuls, and those in which a State shall be a Party, the supreme Court shall have original Jurisdiction, In all the other Cases before mentioned, the supreme Court shall have appellate Jurisdiction, both as to Law and Fact, with such Exceptions, and under such Regulations as the Congress shall make.

[3] The trial of all Crimes, except in Cases of Impeachment, shall be by Jury; and such Trial shall be held in the State where the said Crimes shall have been committed; but when not committed within any State, the Trial shall be at such Place or Places as the Congress may by Law have directed.

Section 3. [1] Treason against the United States, shall consist only in levying War against them, or, in adhering to their Enemies, giving them Aid and Comfort. No Person shall be convicted of Treason unless on the Testimony of two Witnesses to the same overt Act, or on Confession in open Court.

[2] The Congress shall have Power to declare the Punishment of Treason, but no Attainder of Treason shall work Corruption of Blood, or Forfeiture except during the Life of the Person attainted.

# Article IV

Section 1. Full Faith and Credit shall be given in each State to the public Acts, Records, and judicial Proceedings of every other State. And the Congress may by general Laws prescribe the Manner in which such Acts, Records and Proceedings shall be proved, and the Effect thereof.

Section 2. [1] The Citizens of each State shall be entitled to all Privileges and Immunities of Citizens in the several States.

[2] A Person charged in any State with Treason, Felony, or other Crime, who shall flee from Justice, and be found in another State, shall on demand of the executive Authority of the State from which he fled, be delivered up, to be removed to the State having Jurisdiction of the Crime.

**[3]** No Person held to Service or Labour in one State, under the Laws thereof, escaping into another, shall, in Consequence of any Law or Regulation therein, be discharged from such Service or Labour, but shall be delivered up on Claim of the Party to whom such Service or Labour may be due.

Section 3. **[1]** New States may be admitted by the Congress into this Union; but no new State shall be formed or erected within the Jurisdiction of any other State; nor any State be formed by the Junction of two or more States, or Parts of States, without the Consent of the Legislatures of the States concerned as well as of the Congress.

**[2]** The Congress shall have Power to dispose of and make all needful Rules and Regulations respecting the Territory or other Property belonging to the United States; and nothing in this Constitution shall be so construed as to Prejudice any Claims of the United States, or of any particular State.

Section 4. The United States shall guarantee to every State in this Union a Republican Form of Government, and shall protect each of them against Invasion; and on Application of the Legislature, or of the Executive (when the Legislature cannot be convened) against domestic Violence.

## Article V

The Congress, whenever two thirds of both Houses shall deem it necessary, shall propose Amendments to this Constitution, or, on the Application of the Legislatures of two thirds of the several States, shall call a Convention for proposing Amendments, which, in either case, shall be valid to all Intents and Purposes, as part of this Constitution, when ratified by the Legislatures of three fourths of the several States, or by Conventions in three fourths thereof, as the one or the other Mode of Ratification may be proposed by the Congress; Provided that no Amendment which may be made prior to the Year One thousand eight hundred and eight shall in any Manner affect the first and fourth Clauses in the Ninth Section of the first Article; and that no State, without its Consent, shall be deprived of its equal Suffrage in the Senate.

## Article VI

**[1]** All Debts contracted and Engagements entered into, before the Adoption of this Constitution shall be as valid against the United States under this Constitution, as under the Confederation.

**[2]** This Constitution, and the Laws of the United States which shall be made in Pursuance thereof; and all Treaties made, or which shall be made, under the Authority of the United States, shall be the supreme Law of the Land; and the Judges in every State shall be bound thereby, any Thing in the Constitution or Laws of any State to the Contrary notwithstanding.

**[3]** The Senators and Representatives before mentioned, and the Members of the several State Legislatures, and all executive and judicial Officers, both of the United States

and of the several States, shall be bound by Oath or Affirmation, to support this Constitution; but no religious Test shall ever be required as a Qualification to any Office or public Trust under the United States.

## Article VII

The Ratification of the Conventions of nine States shall be sufficient for the Establishment of this Constitution between the States so ratifying the Same.

# Amendments

*Articles in addition to, and in amendment of, the Constitution of the United States of America, proposed by Congress, and ratified by the Legislatures of the several States pursuant to the Fifth Article of the original Constitution.*

## Amendment 1 [1791]

Congress shall make no law respecting an establishment of religion, or prohibiting the free exercise thereof; or abridging the freedom of speech, or of the press; or the right of the people peaceably to assemble, and to petition the Government for a redress of grievances.

## Amendment 2 [1791]

A well regulated Militia, being necessary to the security of a free State, the right of the people to keep and bear Arms, shall not be infringed.

## Amendment 3 [1791]

No Soldier shall, in time of peace be quartered in any house, without the consent of the Owner, nor in time of war, but in a manner to be prescribed by law.

## Amendment 4 [1791]

The right of the people to be secure in their persons, houses, papers, and effects, against unreasonable searches and seizures, shall not be violated, and no Warrants shall issue, but upon probable cause, supported by Oath or affirmation, and particularly describing the place to be searched, and the persons or things to be seized.

## Amendment 5 [1791]

No person shall be held to answer for a capital, or other infamous crime, unless on a presentment or indictment of a Grand Jury, except in cases arising in the land or naval forces, or in the Militia, when in actual service in time of War or public danger; nor shall any person be subject for the same offence to be twice put in jeopardy of life or limb; nor shall be compelled in any criminal case to be a witness against himself, nor be deprived of life, liberty, or property, without due process of law; nor shall private property be taken for public use, without just compensation.

# Amendment 6 [1791]

In all criminal prosecutions, the accused shall enjoy the right to a speedy and public trial, by an impartial jury of the State and district wherein the crime shall have been committed, which district shall have been previously ascertained by law, and to be informed of the nature and cause of the accusation; to be confronted with the witnesses against him; to have compulsory process for obtaining witnesses in his favor, and to have the Assistance of Counsel for his defence.

# Amendment 7 [1791]

In Suits at common law, where the value in controversy shall exceed twenty dollars, the right of trial by jury shall be preserved, and no fact tried by jury, shall be otherwise re-examined in any Court of the United States, than according to the rules of common law.

# Amendment 8 [1791]

Excessive bail shall not be required, nor excessive fines imposed, nor cruel and unusual punishments inflicted.

# Amendment 9 [1791]

The enumeration in the Constitution, of certain rights, shall not be construed to deny or disparage others retained by the people.

# Amendment 10 [1791]

The powers not delegated to the United States by the Constitution, nor prohibited by it to the States, are reserved to the States respectively, or to the people.

# Amendment 11 [1798]

The Judicial power of the United States shall not be construed to extend to any suit in law or equity, commenced or prosecuted against one of the United States by Citizens of another State, or by Citizens or Subjects of any Foreign State.

# Amendment 12 [1804]

The Electors shall meet in their respective states and vote by ballot for President and Vice President, one of whom, at least, shall not be an inhabitant of the same state with themselves; they shall name in their ballots the person voted for as President, and in distinct ballots the person voted for as Vice President, and they shall make distinct lists of all persons voted for as President, and of all persons voted for as Vice President, and of the number of votes for each, which lists they shall sign and certify, and transmit sealed to the seat of the government of the United States, directed to the President of the Senate;—The President of the Senate shall, in the presence of the Senate and House of Representatives, open all the certificates and the votes shall then be counted;—The person having the greatest number of votes for President, shall be the President, if such number be a majority of the whole number of Electors appointed; and if no person have such majority, then from the persons having the highest numbers not exceeding three on the list of those voted for as President, the House of Representatives shall choose immediately, by ballot, the President. But in choosing the President, the votes shall be taken by states, the representation from each state having one vote; a quorum for this purpose shall consist of a member or members from two thirds of the states, and a majority of all states shall be necessary to a choice. And if the House of Representatives shall not choose a President whenever the right of choice shall devolve upon them before the fourth day of March next following, then the Vice President shall act as President, as in the case of the death or other constitutional disability of the President.—The person having the greatest number of votes as Vice President, shall be the Vice President, if such number be a majority of the whole number of Electors appointed, and if no person have a majority, then from the two highest numbers on the list, the Senate shall choose the Vice President; a quorum for the purpose shall consist of two thirds of the whole number of Senators, and a majority of the whole number shall be necessary to a choice. But no person constitutionally ineligible to the office of President shall be eligible to that of Vice President of the United States.

# Amendment 13 [1865]

Section 1. Neither slavery nor involuntary servitude, except as a punishment for crime whereof the party shall have been duly convicted, shall exist within the United States, or any place subject to their jurisdiction.

Section 2. Congress shall have power to enforce this article by appropriate legislation.

# Amendment 14 [1868]

Section 1. All persons born or naturalized in the United States, and subject to the jurisdiction thereof, are citizens of the United States and of the State wherein they reside. No State shall make or enforce any law which shall abridge the privileges or immunities of citizens of the United States; nor shall any State deprive any person of life, liberty, or property, without due process of law; nor deny to any person within its jurisdiction the equal protection of the laws.

Section 2. Representatives shall be apportioned among the several States according to their respective numbers, counting the whole number of persons in each State, excluding Indians not taxed. But when the right to vote at any election for the choice of electors for President and Vice President of the United States, Representatives in Congress, the Executive and Judicial officers of a State, or the members of the Legislature thereof, is denied to any of the male inhabitants of such State, being twenty-one years of age, and citizens of the United States, or in any way abridged, except for participation in rebellion, or other crime, the basis of representation therein shall be reduced in the proportion which the number of such male citizens shall bear to the whole number of male citizens twenty-one years of age in such State.

Section 3. No person shall be a Senator or Representative in Congress, or elector of President and Vice President, or hold any office, civil or military, under the United States, or under any State, who having previously taken an oath, as a member of Congress, or as an officer of the United States, or as a member of any State legislature, or as an executive or judicial officer of any State, to support the Constitution of the United States, shall have engaged in insurrection or rebellion against the same, or given aid or comfort to the enemies thereof. But Congress may by a vote of two thirds of each House, remove such disability.

Section 4. The validity of the public debt of the United States, authorized by law, including debts incurred for payment of pensions and bounties for services in suppressing insurrection or rebellion, shall not be questioned. But neither the United States nor any State shall assume or pay any debt or obligation incurred in aid of insurrection or rebellion against the United States, or any claim for the loss or emancipation of any slave; but all such debts, obligations and claims shall be held illegal and void.

Section 5. The Congress shall have power to enforce, by appropriate legislation, the provisions of this article.

# Amendment 15 [1870]

Section 1. The right of citizens of the United States to vote shall not be denied or abridged by the United States or by any State on account of race, color, or previous condition of servitude.

Section 2. The Congress shall have power to enforce this article by appropriate legislation.

# Amendment 16 [1913]

The Congress shall have power to lay and collect taxes on incomes, from whatever source derived, without apportionment among the several States, and without regard to any census or enumeration.

# Amendment 17 [1913]

[1] The Senate of the United States shall be composed of two Senators from each State, elected by the people thereof, for six years; and each Senator shall have one vote. The electors in each State shall have the qualifications requisite for electors of the most numerous branch of the State legislatures.

[2] When vacancies happen in the representation of any State in the Senate, the executive authority of such State shall issue writs of election to fill such vacancies: *Provided,* That the legislature of any State may empower the executive thereof to make temporary appointments until the people fill the vacancies by election as the legislature may direct.

[3] This amendment shall not be so construed as to affect the election or term of any Senator chosen before it becomes valid as part of the Constitution.

# Amendment 18 [1919]

Section 1. After one year from the ratification of this article the manufacture, sale, or transportation of intoxicating liquors within, the importation thereof into, or the exportation thereof from the United States and all territory subject to the jurisdiction thereof for beverage purposes is hereby prohibited.

Section 2. The Congress and the several States shall have concurrent power to enforce this article by appropriate legislation.

Section 3. This article shall be inoperative unless it shall have been ratified as an amendment to the Constitution by the legislatures of the several States, as provided in the Constitution, within seven years from the date of the submission hereof to the States by the Congress.

# Amendment 19 [1920]

[1] The right of citizens of the United States to vote shall not be denied or abridged by the United States or by any State on account of sex.

[2] Congress shall have power to enforce this article by appropriate legislation.

# Amendment 20 [1933]

Section 1. The terms of the President and Vice President shall end at noon on the twentieth day of January, and the terms of Senators and Representatives at noon on the third day of January, of the years in which such terms would have ended if this article had not been ratified; and the terms of their successors shall then begin.

Section 2. The Congress shall assemble at least once in every year, and such meeting shall begin at noon on the third day of January, unless they shall by law appoint a different day.

Section 3. If, at the time fixed for the beginning of the term of the President, the President elect shall have died, the Vice President elect shall become President. If the President shall not have been chosen before the time fixed for the beginning of his term, or if the President elect shall have failed to qualify, then the Vice President elect shall act as President until a President shall have qualified; and the Congress may by law provide for the case wherein neither a President elect nor a Vice President elect shall have qualified, declaring who shall then act as President, or the manner in which one who is to act shall be selected, and such person shall act accordingly until a President or Vice President shall have qualified.

Section 4. The Congress may by law provide for the case of the death of any of the persons from whom the House of Representatives may choose a President whenever the right of choice shall have devolved upon them, and for the case of the death of any of the persons from whom the Senate may choose a Vice President whenever the right of choice shall have devolved upon them.

Section 5. Sections 1 and 2 shall take effect on the fifteenth day of October following the ratification of this article.

Section 6. This article shall be inoperative unless it shall have been ratified as an amendment to the Constitution by the legislatures of three fourths of the several States within seven years from the date of its submission.

# Amendment 21 [1933]

Section 1. The eighteenth article of amendment to the Constitution of the United States is hereby repealed.

Section 2. The transportation or importation into any State, Territory, or possession of the United States for delivery or use therein of intoxicating liquors, in violation of the laws therefore, is hereby prohibited.

Section 3. This article shall be inoperative unless it shall have been ratified as an amendment to the Constitution by conventions in the several States, as provided in the Constitution, within seven years from the date of the submission hereof to the States by the Congress.

# Amendment 22 [1951]

Section 1. No person shall be elected to the office of the President more than twice, and no person who has held the office of President, or acted as President, for more than two years of a term to which some other person was elected President shall be elected to the office of President more than once. But this Article shall not apply to any person holding the office of President when this Article was proposed by the Congress, and shall not prevent any person who may be holding the office of President, or acting as President, during the term within which this Article becomes operative from holding the office of President or acting as President during the remainder of such term.

Section 2. This article shall be inoperative unless it shall have been ratified as an amendment to the Constitution by the legislatures of three fourths of the several States within seven years from the date of its submission to the States by the Congress.

# Amendment 23 [1961]

Section 1. The District constituting the seat of Government of the United States shall appoint in such manner as the Congress may direct:

A number of electors of President and Vice President equal to the whole number of Senators and Representatives in Congress to which the District would be entitled if it were a State, but in no event more than the least populous state;

they shall be in addition to those appointed by the states, but they shall be considered, for the purposes of the election of President and Vice President, to be electors appointed by a state; and they shall meet in the District and perform such duties as provided by the twelfth article of amendment.

Section 2. The Congress shall have power to enforce this article by appropriate legislation.

# Amendment 24 [1964]

Section 1. The right of citizens of the United States to vote in any primary or other election for President or Vice President, for electors for President or Vice President, or for Senator or Representative in Congress, shall not be denied or abridged by the United States, or any State by reason of failure to pay any poll tax or other tax.

Section 2. The Congress shall have power to enforce this article by appropriate legislation.

# Amendment 25 [1967]

Section 1. In case of the removal of the President from office or of his death or resignation, the Vice President shall become President.

Section 2. Whenever there is a vacancy in the office of the Vice President, the President shall nominate a Vice President who shall take office upon confirmation by a majority vote of both Houses of Congress.

Section 3. Whenever the President transmits to the President pro tempore of the Senate and the Speaker of the House of Representatives his written declaration that he is unable to discharge the powers and duties of his office, and until he transmits to them a written declaration to the contrary, such powers and duties shall be discharged by the Vice President as Acting President.

Section 4. Whenever the Vice President and a majority of either the principal officers of the executive departments or of such other body as Congress may by law provide, transmit to the President pro tempore of the Senate and the Speaker of the House of Representatives their written declaration that the President is unable to discharge the powers and duties of his office, the Vice President shall immediately assume the powers and duties of the office as Acting President.

Thereafter, when the President transmits to the President pro tempore of the Senate and the Speaker of the House of Representatives his written declaration that no inability exists, he shall resume the powers and duties of his office unless the Vice President and a majority of either the principal officers of the executive department or of such other body as Congress may by law provide, transmit within four days to the President pro tempore of the Senate and the Speaker of the House of Representatives their written declaration and the President is unable to discharge the powers and duties of his office. Thereupon Congress shall decide the issue, assembling within forty-eight hours for that purpose if not in session. If the

Congress, within twenty-one days after receipt of the latter written declaration, or, if Congress is not in session, within twenty-one days after Congress is required to assemble, determines by two thirds vote of both Houses that the President is unable to discharge the powers and duties of his office, the Vice President shall continue to discharge the same as Acting President; otherwise, the President shall resume the powers and duties of his office.

## Amendment 26 [1971]

Section 1. The right of citizens of the United States, who are eighteen years of age or older, to vote shall not be denied or abridged by the United States or by any State on account of age.

Section 2. The Congress shall have power to enforce this article by appropriate legislation.

## Amendment 27 [1992]

No law varying the compensation for the services of Senators and Representatives shall take effect, until an election of Representatives shall have intervened.

# Appendix B    Uniform Commercial Code (Articles 1, 2, 2a, and 3)

## Article 1: General Provisions

### Part 1: Short Title, Construction, Application and Subject Matter of the Act

**§1-101. Short Title.** This act shall be known and may be cited as Uniform Commercial Code.

**§1-102. Purposes; Rules of Construction; Variation by Agreement.**

(1) This Act shall be liberally construed and applied to promote its underlying purposes and policies.

(2) Underlying purposes and policies of this Act are

   (a) to simplify, clarify and modernize the law governing commercial transactions;

   (b) to permit the continued expansion of commercial practices through custom, usage and agreement of the parties;

   (c) to make uniform the law among the various jurisdictions.

(3) The effect of provisions of this Act may be varied by agreement, except as otherwise provided in this Act and except that the obligations of good faith, diligence, reasonableness and care prescribed by this Act may not be disclaimed by agreement but the parties may by agreement determine the standards by which the performance of such obligations is to be measured if such standards are not manifestly unreasonable.

(4) The presence in certain provisions of this Act of the words "unless otherwise agreed" or words of similar import does not imply that the effect of other provisions may not be varied by agreement under subsection (3).

(5) In this Act unless the context otherwise requires

   (a) words in the singular number include the plural, and in the plural include the singular;

   (b) words of the masculine gender include the feminine and the neuter, and when the sense so indicates words of the neuter gender may refer to any gender.

**§1-103. Supplementary General Principles of Law Applicable.** Unless displaced by the particular provisions of this Act, the principles of law and equity, including the law merchant and the law relative to capacity to contract, principal and agent, estoppel, fraud, misrepresentation, duress, coercion, mistake, bankruptcy or other validating or invalidating cause shall supplement its provisions.

**§1-104. Construction Against Implicity Repeal.** This Act being a general act intended as a unified coverage of its subject matter, no part of it shall be deemed to be impliedly repealed by subsequent legislation if such construction can reasonably be avoided.

**§1-105. Territorial Application of the Act; Parties' Power to Choose Applicable Law.**

(1) Except as provided hereafter in this section, when a transaction bears a reasonable relation to this state and also to another state or nation the parties may agree that the law either of this state or of such other state or nation shall govern their rights and duties. Failing such agreement this Act applies to transactions bearing an appropriate relation to this state.

(2) Where one of the following provisions of this Act specifies the applicable law, that provision governs and a contrary agreement is effective only to the extent permitted by the law (including the conflict of laws rules) so specified:

   Rights of creditors against sold goods. Section 2-402.

   Applicability of the Article on Leases. Sections 2A-105 and 2A-106.

   Applicability of the Article on Bank Deposits and Collections. Section 4-102.

   Bulk transfers subject to the Article on Bulk Transfers. Section 6-102.

   Applicability of the Article on Investment Securities. Section 8-106.

   Perfection provisions of the Article on Secured Transactions. Section 9-103.

**§1-106. Remedies to Be Liberally Administered.**

(1) The remedies provided by this Act shall be liberally administered to the end that the aggrieved party may be put in as good a position as if the other party had fully performed but neither consequential or special nor penal damages may be had except as specifically provided in this Act or by other rule of law.

(2) Any right or obligation declared by this Act is enforceable by action unless the provision declaring it specifies a different and limited effect.

**§1-107. Waiver or Renunciation of Claim or Right After Breach.** Any claim or right arising out of an alleged breach can be discharged in whole or in part without consideration by a written waiver or renunciation signed and delivered by the aggrieved party.

**§1-108. Severability.** If any provision or clause of this Act or application thereof to any person or circumstances is held invalid, such invalidity shall not affect other provisions or applications of the Act which can be given effect without the invalid provision or application, and to this end the provisions of this Act are declared to be severable.

**§1-109. Section Captions.** Section captions are parts of this Act.

## Part 2: General Definitions and Principles of Interpretation

**§1-201. General Definitions.** Subject to additional definitions contained in the subsequent Articles of this Act which are applicable to specific Articles or Parts thereof, and unless the context otherwise requires, in this Act.

(1) "Action" in the sense of a judicial proceeding includes recoupment, counterclaim, set-off, suit in equity and any other proceedings in which rights are determined.

(2) "Aggrieved party" means a party entitled to resort to a remedy.

(3) "Agreement" means the bargain of the parties in fact as found in their language or by implication from other circumstances including course of dealing or usage of trade or course of performance as provided in this Act (Sections 1-205 and 2-208). Whether an agreement has legal consequences is determined by the provisions of this Act, if applicable; otherwise by the law of contracts (Section 1-103). (Compare "Contract".)

(4) "Bank" means any person engaged in the business of banking.

(5) "Bearer" means the person in possession of an instrument, document of title, or certificated security payable to bearer or indorsed in blank.

(6) "Bill of lading" means a document evidencing the receipt of goods for shipment issued by a person engaged in the business of transporting or forwarding goods, and includes an airbill. "Airbill" means a document serving for air transportation as a bill of lading does for marine or rail transportation, and includes an air consignment note or air waybill.

(7) "Branch" includes a separately incorporated foreign branch of a bank.

(8) "Burden of establishing" a fact means the burden of persuading the triers of fact that the existence of the fact is more probable than its non-existence.

(9) "Buyer in ordinary course of business" means a person who in good faith and without knowledge that the sale to him is in violation of the ownership rights or security interest of a third party in the goods buys in ordinary course from a person in the business of selling goods of that kind but does not include a pawnbroker. All persons who sell minerals or the like (including oil and gas) at wellhead or minehead shall be deemed to be persons in the business of selling goods of that kind. "Buying" may be for cash or by exchange of other property or on secured or unsecured credit and includes receiving goods or documents of title under a pre-existing contract for sale but does not include a transfer in bulk or as security for or in total or partial satisfaction of a money debt.

(10) "Conspicuous": A term or clause is conspicuous when it is so written that a reasonable person against whom it is to operate ought to have noticed it. A printed heading in capitals (as: NON-NEGOTIABLE BILL OF LADING) is conspicuous. Language in the body of a form is "conspicuous" if it is in larger or other contrasting type or color. But in a telegram any stated term is "conspicuous". Whether a term or clause is "conspicuous" or not is for decision by the court.

(11) "Contract" means the total legal obligation which results from the parties' agreement as affected by this Act and any other applicable rules of law. (Compare "Agreement".)

(12) "Creditor" includes a general creditor, a secured creditor, a lien creditor and any representative of creditors, including an assignee for the benefit of creditors, a trustee in bankruptcy, a receiver in equity and an executor or administrator of an insolvent debtor's or assignor's estate.

(13) "Defendant" includes a person in the position of defendant in a cross-action or counterclaim.

(14) "Delivery" with respect to instruments, documents of title, chattel paper or certificated securities means voluntary transfer of possession.

(15) "Document of title" includes bill of lading, dock warrant, dock receipt, warehouse receipt or order for the delivery of goods, and also any other document which in the regular course of business or financing is treated as adequately evidencing that the person in possession of it is entitled to receive, hold and dispose of the document and the goods it covers. To be a document of title a document must purport to be issued by or addressed to a bailee and purport to cover goods in the bailee's possession which are either identified or are fungible portions of an identified mass.

(16) "Fault" means wrongful act, omission or breach.

(17) "Fungible" with respect to goods or securities means goods or securities of which any unit is, by nature or usage of trade, the equivalent of any other like unit. Goods which are not fungible shall be deemed fungible for the purposes of this Act to the extent that under a particular agreement or document unlike units are treated as equivalents.

(18) "Genuine" means free of forgery or counterfeiting.

(19) "Good faith" means honesty in fact in the conduct or transaction concerned.

(20) "Holder" means a person who is in possession of a document of title or a certificated instrument or an investment security drawn, issued or indorsed to him or to his order or to bearer or in blank.

(21) To "honor" is to pay or to accept and pay, or where a credit so engages to purchase or discount a draft complying with the terms of the credit.

(22) "Insolvency proceedings" includes any assignment for the benefit of creditors or other proceedings intended to liquidate or rehabilitate the estate of the person involved.

(23) A person is "insolvent" who either has ceased to pay his debts in the ordinary course of business or cannot pay his debts as they become due or is insolvent within the meaning of the federal bankruptcy law.

(24) "Money" means a medium of exchange authorized or adopted by a domestic or foreign government as part of its currency.

(25) A person has "notice" of a fact when

    (a) he has actual knowledge of it; or

    (b) he has received a notice or notification of it; or

    (c) from all the facts and circumstances known to him at the time in question he has reason to know that it exists.

A person "knows" or has "knowledge" of a fact when he has actual knowledge of it. "Discover" or "learn" or a word or phrase of similar import refers to knowledge rather than to reason to know. The time and circumstances under which a notice or notification may cease to be effective are not determined by this Act.

(26) A person "notifies" or "gives" a notice or notification to another by taking such steps as may be reasonably required to inform the other in ordinary course whether or not such other actually comes to know of it. A person "receives" a notice or notification when

    (a) it comes to his attention; or

    (b) it is duly delivered at the place of business through which the contract was made or at any other place held out by him as the place for receipt of such communications.

(27) Notice, knowledge or a notice or notification received by an organization is effective for a particular transaction from the time when it is brought to the attention of the individual conducting that transaction, and in any event from the time when it would have been brought to his attention if the organization had exercised due diligence. An organization exercises due diligence if it maintains reasonable routines for communicating significant information to the person conducting the transaction and there is reasonable compliance with the routines. Due diligence does not require an individual acting for the organization to communicate information unless such communication is part of his regular duties or unless he has reason to know of the transaction and that the transaction would be materially affected by the information.

(28) "Organization" includes a corporation, government or governmental subdivision or agency, business trust, estate, trust, partnership or association, two or more persons having a joint or common interest or any other legal or commercial entity.

(29) "Party", as distinct from "third party", means a person who has engaged in a transaction or made an agreement within this Act.

(30) "Person" includes an individual or an organization (See Section 1-102).

(31) "Presumption" or "presumed" means that the trier of fact must find the existence of the fact presumed unless and until evidence is introduced which would support a finding of its non-existence.

(32) "Purchase" includes taking by sale, discount, negotiation, mortgage, pledge, lien, issue or re-issue, gift or any other voluntary transaction creating an interest in property.

(33) "Purchaser" means a person who takes by purchase.

(34) "Remedy" means any remedial right to which an aggrieved party is entitled with or without resort to a tribunal.

(35) "Representative" includes as agent, an officer of a corporation or association, and a trustee, executor or administrator of an estate, or any other person empowered to act for another.

(36) "Rights" includes remedies.

(37) "Security interest" means an interest in personal property or fixtures which secures payment or performance of an obligation. The retention or reservation of title by a seller of goods notwithstanding shipment or delivery to the buyer (Section 2-401) is limited in effect to a reservation of a "security interest". The term also includes any interest of a buyer of accounts or chattel paper which is subject to Article 9. The special property interest of a buyer of goods on identification of those goods to a contract for sale under Section 2-401 is not a "security interest", but a buyer may also acquire a "security interest" by complying with Article 9. Unless a consignment is intended as security, reservation of title thereunder is not a "security interest", but a consignment in any event is subject to the provisions on consignment sales (Section 2-326).

Whether a transaction creates a lease or security interest is determined by the facts of each case; however, a transaction creates a security interest if the consideration the lessee is to pay the lessor for the right to possession and use of the goods is an obligation for the term of the lease not subject to termination by the lessee, and

    (a) the original term of the lease is equal to or greater than the remaining economic life of the goods,

    (b) the lessee is bound to renew the lease for the remaining economic life of the goods or is bound to become the owner of the goods,

(c) the lessee has an option to renew the lease for the remaining economic life of the goods for no additional consideration or nominal additional consideration upon compliance with the lease agreement, or

(d) the lessee has an option to become the owner of the goods for no additional consideration or nominal additional consideration upon compliance with the lease agreement.

A transaction does not create a security interest merely because it provides that

(a) the present value of the consideration the lessee is obligated to pay the lessor for the right to possession and use of the goods is substantially equal to or is greater than the fair market value of the goods at the time the lease is entered into,

(b) the lessee assumes risk of loss of the goods, or agrees to pay taxes, insurance, filing, recording or registration fees, or service or maintenance costs with respect to the goods,

(c) the lessee has an option to renew the lease or to become the owner of the goods,

(d) the lessee has an option to renew the lease for a fixed rent that is equal to or greater than the reasonably predictable fair market rent for the use of the goods for the term of the renewal at the time the option is to be performed, or

(e) the lessee has an option to become the owner of the goods for a fixed price that is equal to or greater than the reasonably predictable fair market value of the goods at the time the option is to be performed.

For purposes of this subsection (37):

(x) Additional consideration is not nominal if (i) when the option to renew the lease is granted to the lessee the rent is stated to be the fair market rent for the use of the goods for the term of the renewal determined at the time the option is to be performed, or (ii) when the option to become the owner of the goods is granted to the lessee the price is stated to be the fair market value of the goods determined at the time the option is to be performed. Additional consideration is nominal if it is less than the lessee's reasonably predictable cost of performing under the lease agreement if the option is not exercised;

(y) "Reasonably predictable" and "remaining economic life of the goods" are to be determined with reference to the facts and circumstances at the time the transaction is entered into; and

(z) "Present value" means the amount as of a date certain of one or more sums payable in the future, discounted to the date certain. The discount is determined by the interest rate specified by the parties if the rate is not manifestly unreasonable at the time the transaction is entered into; otherwise, the discount is determined by a commercially reasonable rate that takes into account the facts and circumstances of each case at the time the transaction was entered into.

(38) "Send" in connection with any writing or notice means to deposit in the mail or deliver for transmission by any other usual means of communication with postage or cost of transmission provided for and properly addressed and in the case of an instrument to an address specified thereon or otherwise agreed, or if there be none to any address reasonable under the circumstances. The receipt of any writing or notice within the time at which it would have arrived if properly sent has the effect of a proper sending.

(39) "Signed" includes any symbol executed or adopted by a party with present intention to authenticate a writing.

(40) "Surety" includes guarantor.

(41) "Telegram" includes a message transmitted by radio, teletype, cable, any mechanical method of transmission or the like.

(42) "Term" means that portion of an agreement which relates to a particular matter.

(43) "Unauthorized" signature or indorsement means one made without actual, implied or apparent authority and includes a forgery.

(44) "Value". Except as otherwise provided with respect to negotiable instruments and bank collections (Sections 3-303, 4-208 and 4-209) a person gives "value" for rights if he acquires them

(a) in return for a binding commitment to extend credit or for the extension of immediately available credit whether or not drawn upon and whether or not a chargeback is provided for in the event of difficulties in collection; or

(b) as security for or in total or partial satisfaction of a pre-existing claim; or

(c) by accepting delivery pursuant to a pre-existing contract for purchase; or

(d) generally, in return for any consideration sufficient to support a simple contract.

(45) "Warehouse receipt" means a receipt issued by a person engaged in the business of storing goods for hire.

(46) "Written" or "writing" includes printing, typewriting or any other intentional reduction to tangible form. As amended 1962 and 1972.

## §1-201. General Definitions (1977 Amendments).
Subject to additional definitions contained in the subsequent Articles of this Act which are applicable to specific Articles or Parts thereof, and unless the context otherwise requires, in the Act:

* * *

1. (5) "Bearer" means the person in possession of an instrument, document of title or certificated security payable to bearer or indorsed in blank.

* * *

2.  (14) "Delivery" with respect to instruments, documents of title chattel paper or certificated securities means voluntary transfer of possession.

\* \* \*

3.  (20) "Holder" means a person who is in possession of a document of title or an instrument or a certificated investment security drawn, issued or indorsed to him or his order or to bearer or in blank.

\* \* \*

## §1-202. Prima Facie Evidence by Third Party Documents.
A document in due form purporting to be a bill of lading, policy or certificate of insurance, official weigher's or inspector's certificate, consular invoice or any other document authorized or required by the contract to be issued by a third party shall be prima facie evidence of its own authenticity and genuineness and of the facts stated in the document by the third party.

## §1-203. Obligation of Good Faith.
Every contract or duty within this Act imposes an obligation of good faith in its performance or enforcement.

## §1-204. Time; Reasonable Time; "Seasonably".

(1) Whenever this Act requires any action to be taken within a reasonable time, any time which is not manifestly unreasonable may be fixed by agreement.

(2) What is a reasonable time for taking any action depends on the nature, purpose and circumstances of such action.

(3) An action is taken "seasonably" when it is taken at or within the time agreed or if no time is agreed at or within a reasonable time.

## §1-205. Course of Dealing and Usage of Trade.

(1) A course of dealing is a sequence of previous conduct between the parties to a particular transaction which is fairly to be regarded as establishing a common basis of understanding for interpreting their expressions and other conduct.

(2) A usage of trade is any practice or method of dealing having such regularity of observance in a place, vocation or trade as to justify an expectation that it will be observed with respect to the transaction in question. The existence and scope of such a usage are to be proved as facts. If it is established that such a usage is embodied in a written trade code or similar writing the interpretation of the writing is for the court.

(3) A course of dealing between parties and any usage of trade in the vocation or trade in which they are engaged or of which they are or should be aware give particular meaning to and supplement or qualify terms of an agreement.

(4) The express terms of an agreement and an applicable course of dealing or usage of trade shall be construed wherever reasonable as consistent with each other; but when such construction is unreasonable express terms control both course of dealing and usage of trade and course of dealing controls usage of trade.

(5) An applicable usage of trade in the place where any part of performance is to occur shall be used in interpreting the agreement as to that part of the performance.

(6) Evidence of a relevant usage of trade offered by one party is not admissible unless and until he has given the other party such notice as the court finds sufficient to prevent unfair surprise to the latter.

## §1-206. Statute of Frauds for Kinds of Personal Property not Otherwise Covered.

(1) Except in the cases described in subsection (2) of this section a contract for the sale of personal property is not enforceable by way of action or defense beyond five thousand dollars in amount or value of remedy unless there is some writing which indicates that a contract for sale has been made between the parties at a defined or stated price, reasonably identifies the subject matter and is signed by the party against whom enforcement is sought or by his authorized agent.

(2) Subsection (1) of this section does not apply to contracts for the sale of goods (Section 2-201) nor of securities (Section 8-319) nor to security agreements (Section 9-203).

## §1-207. Performance or Acceptance Under Reservation of Rights.
A party who with explicit reservation of rights performs or promises performance or assents to performance in a manner demanded or offered by the other party does not thereby prejudice the rights reserved. Such words as "without prejudice", "under protest" or the like are sufficient.

## §1-208. Option to Accelerate at Will.
A term providing that one party or his successor in interest may accelerate payment or performance or require collateral or additional collateral "at will" or "when he deems himself insecure" or in words of similar import shall be construed to mean that he shall have power to do so only if he in good faith believes that the prospect of payment or performance is impaired. The burden of establishing lack of good faith is on the party against whom the power has been exercised.

## §1-209. Subordinated Obligations.
An obligation may be issued as subordinated to payment of another obligation of the person obligated, or a creditor may subordinate his right to payment of an obligation by agreement with either the person obligated or another creditor of the person obligated. Such a subordination does not create a security interest as against either the common debtor or a subordinated creditor. This section shall be construed as declaring the law as it existed prior to the enactment of this section and not as modifying it. Added 1966.

**Note:** *This new section is proposed as an optional provision to make it clear that a subordination agreement does not create a security interest unless so intended.*

# Article 2: Sales

## Part 1: Short Title, General Construction and Subject Matter

**§2-101. Short Title.** This Article shall be known and may be cited as Uniform Commercial Code—Sales.

**§2-102. Scope; Certain Security and Other Transactions Excluded from This Article.** Unless the context otherwise requires, this Article applies to transactions in goods; it does not apply to any transaction which although in the form of an unconditional contract to sell or present sale is intended to operate only as a security transaction nor does this Article impair or repeal any statute regulating sales to consumers, farmers or other specified classes of buyers.

**§2-103. Definitions and Index of Definitions.**

(1) In this Article unless the context otherwise requires

   (a) "Buyer" means a person who buys or contracts to buy goods.

   (b) [Reserved.]

   (c) "Receipt" of goods means taking physical possession of them.

   (d) "Seller" means a person who sells or contracts to sell goods.

(2) Other definitions applying to this Article or to specified Parts thereof, and the sections in which they appear are:

   "Acceptance". Section 2-606.

   "Banker's credit". Section 2-325.

   "Between merchants". Section 2-104.

   "Cancellation". Section 2-106(4).

   "Commercial unit". Section 2-105.

   "Confirmed credit". Section 2-325.

   "Conforming to contract". Section 2-106.

   "Contract for sale". Section 2-106.

   "Cover". Section 2-712.

   "Entrusting". Section 2-403.

   "Financing agency". Section 2-104.

   "Future goods". Section 2-105.

   "Goods". Section 2-105.

   "Identification". Section 2-501.

   "Installment contract". Section 2-612.

   "Letter of Credit". Section 2-325.

   "Lot". Section 2-105.

   "Merchant". Section 2-104.

   "Overseas". Section 2-323.

   "Person in position of seller". Section 2-707.

   "Present sale". Section 2-106.

   "Sale". Section 2-106.

   "Sale on approval". Section 2-326.

   "Sale or return". Section 2-326.

   "Termination". Section 2-106.

(3) "Control" as provided in Section 7-106 and the following definitions in other Articles apply to this Article:

   "Check". Section 3-104.

   "Consignee". Section 7-102.

   "Consignor". Section 7-102.

   "Consumer goods". Section 9-102

   "Dishonor". Section 3-502.

   "Draft". Section 3-104.

(4) In addition Article 1 contains general definitions and principles of construction and interpretation applicable throughout this Article.

**§2-104. Definitions: "Merchant"; "Between Merchants"; "Financing Agency".**

(1) "Merchant" means a person who deals in goods of the kind or otherwise by his occupation holds himself out as having knowledge or skill peculiar to the practices or goods involved in the transaction or to whom such knowledge or skill may be attributed by his employment of an agent or broker or other intermediary who by his occupation holds himself out as having such knowledge or skill.

(2) "Financing agency" means a bank, finance company or other person who in the ordinary course of business makes advances against goods or documents of title or who by arrangement with either the seller or the buyer intervenes in ordinary course to make or collect payment due or claimed under the contract for sale, as by purchasing or paying the seller's draft or making advances against it or by merely taking it for collection whether or not documents of title accompany or are associated with the draft. "Financing agency" includes also a bank or other person who similarly intervenes between persons who are in the position of seller and buyer in respect to the goods (Section 2–707).

(3) "Between merchants" means in any transaction with respect to which both parties are chargeable with the knowledge or skill of merchants.

**§2-105. Definitions: Transferability; "Goods"; "Future" Goods; "Lot"; "Commercial Unit".**

(1) "Goods" means all things (including specially manufactured goods) which are movable at the time of identification to the contract for sale other than the money in which the price is to be paid, investment securities (Article 8) and things in action. "Goods" also includes the unborn young of animals and

growing crops and other identified things attached to realty as described in the section on goods to be severed from realty (Section 2–107).

(2) Goods must be both existing and identified before any interest in them can pass. Goods which are not both existing and identified are "future" goods. A purported present sale of future goods or of any interest therein operates as a contract to sell.

(3) There may be a sale of a part interest in existing identified goods.

(4) An undivided share in an identified bulk of fungible goods is sufficiently identified to be sold although the quantity of the bulk is not determined. Any agreed proportion of such a bulk or any quantity thereof agreed upon by number, weight or other measure may to the extent of the seller's interest in the bulk be sold to the buyer who then becomes an owner in common.

(5) "Lot" means a parcel or a single article which is the subject matter of a separate sale or delivery, whether or not it is sufficient to perform the contract.

(6) "Commercial unit" means such a unit of goods as by commercial usage is a single whole for purposes of sale and division of which materially impairs its character or value on the market or in use. A commercial unit may be a single article (as a machine) or a set of articles (as a suite of furniture or an assortment of sizes) or a quantity (as a bale, gross, or carload) or any other unit treated in use or in the relevant market as a single whole.

## §2-106. Definitions: "Contract"; "Agreement"; "Contract for Sale"; "Sale"; "Present Sale"; "Conforming" to Contract; "Termination"; "Cancellation".

(1) In this Article unless the context otherwise requires "contract" and "agreement" are limited to those relating to the present or future sale of goods. "Contract for sale" includes both a present sale of goods and a contract to sell goods at a future time. A "sale" consists in the passing of title from the seller to the buyer for a price (Section 2–401). A "present sale" means a sale which is accomplished by the making of the contract.

(2) Goods or conduct including any part of a performance are "conforming" or conform to the contract when they are in accordance with the obligations under the contract.

(3) "Termination" occurs when either party pursuant to a power created by agreement or law puts an end to the contract otherwise than for its breach. On "termination" all obligations which are still executory on both sides are discharged but any right based on prior breach or performance survives.

(4) "Cancellation" occurs when either party puts an end to the contract for breach by the other and its effect is the same as that of "termination" except that the can-

celling party also retains any remedy for breach of the whole contract or any unperformed balance.

## §2-107. Goods to Be Severed From Realty: Recording.

(1) A contract for the sale of minerals or the like (including oil and gas) or a structure or its materials to be removed from realty is a contract for the sale of goods within this Article if they are to be severed by the seller but until severance a purported present sale thereof which is not effective as a transfer of an interest in land is effective only as a contract to sell.

(2) A contract for the sale apart from the land of growing crops or other things attached to realty and capable of severance without material harm thereto but not described in subsection (1) or of timber to be cut is a contract for the sale of goods within this Article whether the subject matter is to be severed by the buyer or by the seller even though it forms part of the realty at the time of contracting, and the parties can by identification effect a present sale before severance.

(3) The provisions of this section are subject to any third party rights provided by the law relating to realty records, and the contract for sale may be executed and recorded as a document transferring an interest in land and shall then constitute notice to third parties of the buyer's rights under the contract for sale.

## Part 2: Form, Formation and Readjustment of Contract

### §2-201. Formal Requirements; Statute of Frauds.

(1) Except as otherwise provided in this section a contract for the sale of goods for the price of $500 or more is not enforceable by way of action or defense unless there is some writing sufficient to indicate that a contract for sale has been made between the parties and signed by the party against whom enforcement is sought or by his authorized agent or broker. A writing is not insufficient because it omits or incorrectly states a term agreed upon but the contract is not enforceable under this paragraph beyond the quantity of goods shown in such writing.

(2) Between merchants if within a reasonable time a writing in confirmation of the contract and sufficient against the sender is received and the party receiving it has reason to know its contents, it satisfies the requirements of subsection (1) against such party unless written notice of objection to its contents is given within 10 days after it is received.

(3) A contract which does not satisfy the requirements of subsection (1) but which is valid in other respects is enforceable

(a) if the goods are to be specially manufactured for the buyer and are not suitable for sale to others in the ordinary course of the seller's business and the seller, before notice of repudiation is received and under circumstances which reasonably indicate that the goods are for the buyer, has made either a substantial beginning of their manufacture or commitments for their procurement; or

(b) if the party against whom enforcement is sought admits in his pleading, testimony or otherwise in court that a contract for sale was made, but the contract is not enforceable under this provision beyond the quantity of goods admitted; or

(c) with respect to goods for which payment has been made and accepted or which have been received and accepted (Sec. 2–606).

## §2-202. Final Written Expression: Parol or Extrinsic Evidence.

Terms with respect to which the confirmatory memoranda of the parties agree or which are otherwise set forth in a writing intended by the parties as a final expression of their agreement with respect to such terms as are included therein may not be contradicted by evidence of any prior agreement or of a contemporaneous oral agreement but may be explained or supplemented

(a) by course of performance, course of dealing, or usage of trade (Section 1-303); and

(b) by evidence of consistent additional terms unless the court finds the writing to have been intended also as a complete and exclusive statement of the terms of the agreement.

## §2-203. Seals Inoperative.

The affixing of a seal to a writing evidencing a contract for sale or an offer to buy or sell goods does not constitute the writing a sealed instrument and the law with respect to sealed instruments does not apply to such a contract or offer.

## §2-204. Formation in General.

(1) A contract for sale of goods may be made in any manner sufficient to show agreement, including conduct by both parties which recognizes the existence of such a contract.

(2) An agreement sufficient to constitute a contract for sale may be found even though the moment of its making is undetermined.

(3) Even though one or more terms are left open a contract for sale does not fail for indefiniteness if the parties have intended to make a contract and there is a reasonably certain basis for giving an appropriate remedy.

## §2-205. Firm Offers.

An offer by a merchant to buy or sell goods in a signed writing which by its terms gives assurance that it will be held open is not revocable, for lack of consideration, during the time stated or if no time is stated for a reasonable time, but in no event may such period of irrevocability exceed three months; but any such term of assurance on a form supplied by the offeree must be separately signed by the offeror.

## §2-206. Offer and Acceptance in Formation of Contract.

(1) Unless otherwise unambiguously indicated by the language or circumstances

(a) an offer to make a contract shall be construed as inviting acceptance in any manner and by any medium reasonable in the circumstances;

(b) an order or other offer to buy goods for prompt or current shipment shall be construed as inviting acceptance either by a prompt promise to ship or by the prompt or current shipment of conforming or non-conforming goods, but such a shipment of non-conforming goods does not constitute an acceptance if the seller seasonably notifies the buyer that the shipment is offered only as an accommodation to the buyer.

(2) Where the beginning of a requested performance is a reasonable mode of acceptance an offeror who is not notified of acceptance within a reasonable time may treat the offer as having lapsed before acceptance.

## §2-207. Additional Terms in Acceptance or Confirmation.

(1) A definite and seasonable expression of acceptance or a written confirmation which is sent within a reasonable time operates as an acceptance even though it states terms additional to or different from those offered or agreed upon, unless acceptance is expressly made conditional on assent to the additional or different terms.

(2) The additional terms are to be construed as proposals for addition to the contract. Between merchants such terms become part of the contract unless:

(a) the offer expressly limits acceptance to the terms of the offer;

(b) they materially alter it; or

(c) notification of objection to them has already been given or is given within a reasonable time after notice of them is received.

(3) Conduct by both parties which recognizes the existence of a contract is sufficient to establish a contract for sale although the writings of the parties do not otherwise establish a contract. In such case the terms of the particular contract consist of those terms on which the writings of the parties agree, together with any supplementary terms incorporated under any other provisions of this Act.

## §2-208. [Reserved.]

## §2-209. Modification, Rescission and Waiver.

(1) An agreement modifying a contract within this Article needs no consideration to be binding.

(2) A signed agreement which excludes modification or rescission except by a signed writing cannot be otherwise modified or rescinded, but except as between merchants such a requirement on a form supplied by the merchant must be separately signed by the other party.

(3) The requirements of the statute of frauds section of this Article (Section 2–201) must be satisfied if the contract as modified is within its provisions.

(4) Although an attempt at modification or rescission does not satisfy the requirements of subsection (2) or (3) it can operate as a waiver.

(5) A party who has made a waiver affecting an executory portion of the contract may retract the waiver by reasonable notification received by the other party that strict performance will be required of any term waived, unless the retraction would be unjust in view of a material change of position in reliance on the waiver.

## §2-210. Delegation of Performance; Assignment of Rights.

(1) A party may perform his duty through a delegate unless otherwise agreed or unless the other party has a substantial interest in having his original promisor perform or control the acts required by the contract. No delegation of performance relieves the party delegating of any duty to perform or any liability for breach.

(2) Except as otherwise provided in Section 9-406, unless otherwise agreed all rights of either seller or buyer can be assigned except where the assignment would materially change the duty of the other party, or increase materially the burden or risk imposed on him by his contract, or impair materially his chance of obtaining return performance. A right to damages for breach of the whole contract or a right arising out of the assignor's due performance of his entire obligation can be assigned despite agreement otherwise.

(3) The creation, attachment, perfection, or enforcement of a security interest in the seller's interest under a contract is not a transfer that materially changes the duty of or increases materially the burden or risk imposed on the buyer or impairs materially the buyer's chance of obtaining return performance within the purview of subsection (2) unless, and then only to the extent that, enforcement actually results in a delegation of material performance of the seller. Even in that event, the creation, attachment, perfection, and enforcement of the security interest remain effective, but (i) the seller is liable to the buyer for damages caused by the delegation to the extent that the damages could not reasonably be prevented by the buyer, and (ii) a court having jurisdiction may grant other appropriate relief, including cancellation of the contract for sale or an injunction against enforcement of the security interest or consummation of the enforcement.

(4) Unless the circumstances indicate the contrary a prohibition of assignment of "the contract" is to be construed as barring only the delegation to the assignee of the assignor's performance.

(5) An assignment of "the contract" or of "all my rights under the contract" or an assignment in similar general terms is an assignment of rights and unless the language or the circumstances (as in an assignment for security) indicate the contrary, it is a delegation of performance of the duties of the assignor and its acceptance by the assignee constitutes a promise by him to perform those duties. This promise is enforceable by either the assignor or the other party to the original contract.

(6) The other party may treat any assignment which delegates performance as creating reasonable grounds for insecurity and may without prejudice to his rights against the assignor demand assurances from the assignee (Section 2–609).

# Part 3: General Obligation and Construction of Contract

## §2-301. General Obligations of Parties.
The obligation of the seller is to transfer and deliver and that of the buyer is to accept and pay in accordance with the contract.

## §2-302. Unconscionable Contract or Clause.

(1) If the court as a matter of law finds the contract or any clause of the contract to have been unconscionable at the time it was made the court may refuse to enforce the contract, or it may enforce the remainder of the contract without the unconscionable clause, or it may so limit the application of any unconscionable clause as to avoid any unconscionable result.

(2) When it is claimed or appears to the court that the contract or any clause thereof may be unconscionable the parties shall be afforded a reasonable opportunity to present evidence as to its commercial setting, purpose and effect to aid the court in making the determination.

## §2-303. Allocation or Division of Risks.
Where this Article allocates a risk or a burden as between the parties "unless otherwise agreed", the agreement may not only shift the allocation but may also divide the risk or burden.

## §2-304. Price Payable in Money, Goods, Realty, or Otherwise.

(1) The price can be made payable in money or otherwise. If it is payable in whole or in part in goods each party is a seller of the goods which he is to transfer.

(2) Even though all or part of the price is payable in an interest in realty the transfer of the goods and the

seller's obligations with reference to them are subject to this Article, but not the transfer of the interest in realty or the transferor's obligations in connection therewith.

## §2-305. Open Price Term.

(1) The parties if they so intend can conclude a contract for sale even though the price is not settled. In such a case the price is a reasonable price at the time for delivery if

   (a) nothing is said as to price; or

   (b) the price is left to be agreed by the parties and they fail to agree; or

   (c) the price is to be fixed in terms of some agreed market or other standard as set or recorded by a third person or agency and it is not so set or recorded.

(2) A price to be fixed by the seller or by the buyer means a price for him to fix in good faith.

(3) When a price left to be fixed otherwise than by agreement of the parties fails to be fixed through fault of one party the other may at his option treat the contract as cancelled or himself fix a reasonable price.

(4) Where, however, the parties intend not to be bound unless the price be fixed or agreed and it is not fixed or agreed there is no contract. In such a case the buyer must return any goods already received or if unable so to do must pay their reasonable value at the time of delivery and the seller must return any portion of the price paid on account.

## §2-306. Output, Requirements and Exclusive Dealings.

(1) A term which measures the quantity by the output of the seller or the requirements of the buyer means such actual output or requirements as may occur in good faith, except that no quantity unreasonably disproportionate to any stated estimate or in the absence of a stated estimate to any normal or otherwise comparable prior output or requirements may be tendered or demanded.

(2) A lawful agreement by either the seller or the buyer for exclusive dealing in the kind of goods concerned imposes unless otherwise agreed an obligation by the seller to use best efforts to supply the goods and by the buyer to use best efforts to promote their sale.

## §2-307. Delivery in Single Lot or Several Lots.

Unless otherwise agreed all goods called for by a contract for sale must be tendered in a single delivery and payment is due only on such tender but where the circumstances give either party the right to make or demand delivery in lots the price if it can be apportioned may be demanded for each lot.

## §2-308. Absence of Specified Place for Delivery.

Unless otherwise agreed

   (a) the place for delivery of goods is the seller's place of business or if he has none his residence; but

   (b) in a contract for sale of identified goods which to the knowledge of the parties at the time of contracting are in some other place, that place is the place for their delivery; and

   (c) documents of title may be delivered through customary banking channels.

## §2-309. Absence of Specific Time Provisions; Notice of Termination.

(1) The time for shipment or delivery or any other action under a contract if not provided in this Article or agreed upon shall be a reasonable time.

(2) Where the contract provides for successive performances but is indefinite in duration it is valid for a reasonable time but unless otherwise agreed may be terminated at any time by either party.

(3) Termination of a contract by one party except on the happening of an agreed event requires that reasonable notification be received by the other party and an agreement dispensing with notification is invalid if its operation would be unconscionable.

## §2-310. Open Time for Payment or Running of Credit; Authority to Ship Under Reservation.

Unless otherwise agreed

   (a) payment is due at the time and place at which the buyer is to receive the goods even though the place of shipment is the place of delivery; and

   (b) if the seller is authorized to send the goods he may ship them under reservation, and may tender the documents of title, but the buyer may inspect the goods after their arrival before payment is due unless such inspection is inconsistent with the terms of the contract (Section 2-513); and

   (c) if delivery is authorized and made by way of documents of title otherwise than by subsection (b) then payment is due regardless of where the goods are to be received (i) at the time and place at which the buyer is to receive delivery of the tangible documents or (ii) at the time the buyer is to receive delivery of the electronic documents and at the seller's place of business or if none, the seller's residence; and

   (d) where the seller is required or authorized to ship the goods on credit the credit period runs from the time of shipment but post-dating the invoice or delaying its dispatch will correspondingly delay the starting of the credit period.

## §2-311. Options and Cooperation Respecting Performance.

(1) An agreement for sale which is otherwise sufficiently definite (subsection (3) of Section 2–204) to be a contract is not made invalid by the fact that it leaves particulars of performance to be specified by one of the parties. Any such specification must be made in good faith and within limits set by commercial reasonableness.

(2) Unless otherwise agreed specifications relating to assortment of the goods are at the buyer's option and except as otherwise provided in subsections (1)(c) and (3) of Section 2–319 specifications or arrangements relating to shipment are at the seller's option.

(3) Where such specification would materially affect the other party's performance but is not seasonably made or where one party's cooperation is necessary to the agreed performance of the other but is not seasonably forthcoming, the other party in addition to all other remedies

    (a) is excused for any resulting delay in his own performance; and

    (b) may also either proceed to perform in any reasonable manner or after the time for a material part of his own performance treat the failure to specify or to cooperate as a breach by failure to deliver or accept the goods.

## §2-312. Warranty of Title and Against Infringement; Buyer's Obligation against Infringement.

(1) Subject to subsection (2) there is in a contract for sale a warranty by the seller that

    (a) the title conveyed shall be good, and its transfer rightful; and

    (b) the goods shall be delivered free from any security interest or other lien or encumbrance of which the buyer at the time of contracting has no knowledge.

(2) A warranty under subsection (1) will be excluded or modified only by specific language or by circumstances which give the buyer reason to know that the person selling does not claim title in himself or that he is purporting to sell only such right or title as he or a third person may have.

(3) Unless otherwise agreed a seller who is a merchant regularly dealing in goods of the kind warrants that the goods shall be delivered free of the rightful claim of any third person by way of infringement or the like but a buyer who furnishes specifications to the seller must hold the seller harmless against any such claim which arises out of compliance with the specifications.

## §2-313. Express Warranties by Affirmation, Promise, Description, Sample.

(1) Express warranties by the seller are created as follows:

    (a) Any affirmation of fact or promise made by the seller to the buyer which relates to the goods and becomes part of the basis of the bargain creates an express warranty that the goods shall conform to the affirmation or promise.

    (b) Any description of the goods which is made part of the basis of the bargain creates an express warranty that the goods shall conform to the description.

    (c) Any sample or model which is made part of the basis of the bargain creates an express warranty that the whole of the goods shall conform to the sample or model.

(2) It is not necessary to the creation of an express warranty that the seller use formal words such as "warrant" or "guarantee" or that he have a specific intention to make a warranty, but an affirmation merely of the value of the goods or a statement purporting to be merely the seller's opinion or commendation of the goods does not create a warranty.

## §2-314. Implied Warranty: Merchantability; Usage of Trade.

(1) Unless excluded or modified (Section 2–316), a warranty that the goods shall be merchantable is implied in a contract for their sale if the seller is a merchant with respect to goods of that kind. Under this section the serving for value of food or drink to be consumed either on the premises or elsewhere is a sale.

(2) Goods to be merchantable must be at least such as

    (a) pass without objection in the trade under the contract description; and

    (b) in the case of fungible goods, are of fair average quality within the description; and

    (c) are fit for the ordinary purposes for which such goods are used; and

    (d) run, within the variations permitted by the agreement, of even kind, quality and quantity within each unit and among all units involved; and

    (e) are adequately contained, packaged, and labeled as the agreement may require; and

    (f) conform to the promise or affirmations of fact made on the container or label if any.

(3) Unless excluded or modified (Section 2–316) other implied warranties may arise from course of dealing or usage of trade.

## §2-315. Implied Warranty: Fitness for Particular Purpose.
Where the seller at the time of contracting has reason to know any particular purpose for which the goods are required and that the buyer is relying on the seller's skill or judgment to select or furnish suitable goods, there is unless excluded or modified under the next

section an implied warranty that the goods shall be fit for such purpose.

## §2-316. Exclusion or Modification of Warranties.

(1) Words or conduct relevant to the creation of an express warranty and words or conduct tending to negate or limit warranty shall be construed wherever reasonable as consistent with each other; but subject to the provisions of this Article on parol or extrinsic evidence (Section 2–202) negation or limitation is inoperative to the extent that such construction is unreasonable.

(2) Subject to subsection (3), to exclude or modify the implied warranty of merchantability or any part of it the language must mention merchantability and in case of a writing must be conspicuous, and to exclude or modify any implied warranty of fitness the exclusion must be by a writing and conspicuous. Language to exclude all implied warranties of fitness is sufficient if it states, for example, that "There are no warranties which extend beyond the description on the face hereof."

(3) Notwithstanding subsection (2)

(a) unless the circumstances indicate otherwise, all implied warranties are excluded by expressions like "as is", "with all faults" or other language which in common understanding calls the buyer's attention to the exclusion of warranties and makes plain that there is no implied warranty; and

(b) when the buyer before entering into the contract has examined the goods or the sample or model as fully as he desired or has refused to examine the goods there is no implied warranty with regard to defects which an examination ought in the circumstances to have revealed to him; and

(c) an implied warranty can also be excluded or modified by course of dealing or course of performance or usage of trade.

(4) Remedies for breach of warranty can be limited in accordance with the provisions of this Article on liquidation or limitation of damages and on contractual modification of remedy (Sections 2–718 and 2–719).

## §2-317. Cumulation and Conflict of Warranties Express or Implied. 
Warranties whether express or implied shall be construed as consistent with each other and as cumulative, but if such construction is unreasonable the intention of the parties shall determine which warranty is dominant. In ascertaining that intention the following rules apply:

(a) Exact or technical specifications displace an inconsistent sample or model or general language of description.

(b) A sample from an existing bulk displaces inconsistent general language of description.

(c) Express warranties displace inconsistent implied warranties other than an implied warranty of fitness for a particular purpose.

## §2-318. Third Party Beneficiaries of Warranties Express or Implied.
**Note:** *If this Act is introduced in the Congress of the United States this section should be omitted. (States to select one alternative.)*

**Alternative A**—A seller's warranty whether express or implied extends to any natural person who is in the family or household of his buyer or who is a guest in his home if it is reasonable to expect that such person may use, consume or be affected by the goods and who is injured in person by breach of the warranty. A seller may not exclude or limit the operation of this section.

**Alternative B**—A seller's warranty whether express or implied extends to any natural person who may reasonably be expected to use, consume or be affected by the goods and who is injured in person by breach of the warranty. A seller may not exclude or limit the operation of this section.

**Alternative C**—A seller's warranty whether express or implied extends to any person who may reasonably be expected to use, consume or be affected by the goods and who is injured by breach of the warranty. A seller may not exclude or limit the operation of this section with respect to injury to the person of an individual to whom the warranty extends.

## §2-319. F.O.B. and F.A.S. Terms.

(1) Unless otherwise agreed the term F.O.B. (which means "free on board") at a named place, even though used only in connection with the stated price, is a delivery term under which

(a) when the term is F.O.B. the place of shipment, the seller must at that place ship the goods in the manner provided in this Article (Section 2–504) and bear the expense and risk of putting them into the possession of the carrier; or

(b) when the term is F.O.B. the place of destination, the seller must at his own expense and risk transport the goods to that place and there tender delivery of them in the manner provided in this Article (Section 2–503);

(c) when under either (a) or (b) the term is also F.O.B. vessel, car or other vehicle, the seller must in addition at his own expense and risk load the goods on board. If the term is F.O.B. vessel the buyer must name the vessel and in an appropriate case the seller must comply with the provisions of this Article on the form of bill of lading (Section 2–323).

(2) Unless otherwise agreed the term F.A.S. vessel (which means "free alongside") at a named port, even though used only in connection with the stated price, is a delivery term under which the seller must

   (a) at his own expense and risk deliver the goods alongside the vessel in the manner usual in that port or on a dock designated and provided by the buyer; and

   (b) obtain and tender a receipt for the goods in exchange for which the carrier is under a duty to issue a bill of lading.

(3) Unless otherwise agreed in any case falling within subsection (1)(a) or (c) or subsection (2) the buyer must seasonably give any needed instructions for making delivery, including when the term is F.A.S. or F.O.B. the loading berth of the vessel and in an appropriate case its name and sailing date. The seller may treat the failure of needed instructions as a failure of cooperation under this Article (Section 2–311). He may also at his option move the goods in any reasonable manner preparatory to delivery or shipment.

(4) Under the term F.O.B. vessel or F.A.S. unless otherwise agreed the buyer must make payment against tender of the required documents and the seller may not tender nor the buyer demand delivery of the goods in substitution for the documents.

## §2-320. C.I.F. and C. & F. Terms.

(1) The term C.I.F. means that the price includes in a lump sum the cost of the goods and the insurance and freight to the named destination. The term C. & F. or C.F. means that the price so includes cost and freight to the named destination.

(2) Unless otherwise agreed and even though used only in connection with the stated price and destination, the term C.I.F. destination or its equivalent requires the seller at his own expense and risk to

   (a) put the goods into the possession of a carrier at the port for shipment and obtain a negotiable bill or bills of lading covering the entire transportation to the named destination; and

   (b) load the goods and obtain a receipt from the carrier (which may be contained in the bill of lading) showing that the freight has been paid or provided for; and

   (c) obtain a policy or certificate of insurance, including any war risk insurance, of a kind and on terms then current at the port of shipment in the usual amount, in the currency of the contract, shown to cover the same goods covered by the bill of lading and providing for payment of loss to the order of the buyer or for the account of whom it may concern; but the seller may add to the price the amount of the premium for any such war risk insurance; and

   (d) prepare an invoice of the goods and procure any other documents required to effect shipment or to comply with the contract; and

   (e) forward and tender with commercial promptness all the documents in due form and with any indorsement necessary to perfect the buyer's rights.

(3) Unless otherwise agreed the term C. & F. or its equivalent has the same effect and imposes upon the seller the same obligations and risks as a C.I.F. term except the obligation as to insurance.

(4) Under the term C.I.F. or C. & F. unless otherwise agreed the buyer must make payment against tender of the required documents and the seller may not tender nor the buyer demand delivery of the goods in substitution for the documents.

## §2-321. C.I.F. or C. & F.: "Net Landed Weights"; "Payment on Arrival"; Warranty of Condition on Arrival.
Under a contract containing a term C.I.F. or C. & F.

(1) Where the price is based on or is to be adjusted according to "net landed weights", "delivered weights", "out turn" quantity or quality or the like, unless otherwise agreed the seller must reasonably estimate the price. The payment due on tender of the documents called for by the contract is the amount so estimated, but after final adjustment of the price a settlement must be made with commercial promptness.

(2) An agreement described in subsection (1) or any warranty of quality or condition of the goods on arrival places upon the seller the risk of ordinary deterioration, shrinkage and the like in transportation but has no effect on the place or time of identification to the contract for sale or delivery or on the passing of the risk of loss.

(3) Unless otherwise agreed where the contract provides for payment on or after arrival of the goods the seller must before payment allow such preliminary inspection as is feasible; but if the goods are lost delivery of the documents and payment are due when the goods should have arrived.

## §2-322. Delivery "Ex-Ship".

(1) Unless otherwise agreed a term for delivery of goods "ex-ship" (which means from the carrying vessel) or in equivalent language is not restricted to a particular ship and requires delivery from a ship which has reached a place at the named port of destination where goods of the kind are usually discharged.

(2) Under such a term unless otherwise agreed

   (a) the seller must discharge all liens arising out of the carriage and furnish the buyer with a direction which puts the carrier under a duty to deliver the goods; and

   (b) the risk of loss does not pass to the buyer until the goods leave the ship's tackle or are otherwise properly unloaded.

## §2-323. Form of Bill of Lading Required in Overseas Shipment; "Overseas".

(1) Where the contract contemplates overseas shipment and contains a term C.I.F. or C. & F. or F.O.B. vessel, the seller unless otherwise agreed must obtain a negotiable bill of lading stating that the goods have been loaded in board or, in the case of a term C.I.F. or C. & F., received for shipment.

(2) Where in a case within subsection (1) a tangible bill of lading has been issued in a set of parts, unless otherwise agreed if the documents are not to be sent from abroad the buyer may demand tender of the full set; otherwise only one part of the bill of lading need be tendered. Even if the agreement expressly requires a full set

    (a) due tender of a single part is acceptable within the provisions of this Article on cure of improper delivery (subsection (1) of Section 2–508); and

    (b) even though the full set is demanded, if the documents are sent from abroad the person tendering an incomplete set may nevertheless require payment upon furnishing an indemnity which the buyer in good faith deems adequate.

(3) A shipment by water or by air or a contract contemplating such shipment is "overseas" insofar as by usage of trade or agreement it is subject to the commercial, financing or shipping practices characteristic of international deep water commerce.

## §2-324. "No Arrival, No Sale" Term. Under a term "no arrival, no sale" or terms of like meaning, unless otherwise agreed,

(a) the seller must properly ship conforming goods and if they arrive by any means he must tender them on arrival but he assumes no obligation that the goods will arrive unless he has caused the non-arrival; and

(b) where without fault of the seller the goods are in part lost or have so deteriorated as no longer to conform to the contract or arrive after the contract time, the buyer may proceed as if there had been casualty to identified goods (Section 2–613).

## §2-325. "Letter of Credit" Term; "Confirmed Credit".

(1) Failure of the buyer seasonably to furnish an agreed letter of credit is a breach of the contract for sale.

(2) The delivery to seller of a proper letter of credit suspends the buyer's obligation to pay. If the letter of credit is dishonored, the seller may on seasonable notification to the buyer require payment directly from him.

(3) Unless otherwise agreed the term "letter of credit" or "banker's credit" in a contract for sale means an irrevocable credit issued by a financing agency of good repute and, where the shipment is overseas, of good repute. The term "confirmed credit" means that the credit must also carry the direct obligation of such an agency which does business in the seller's financial market.

## §2-326. Sale on Approval and Sale or Return; Rights of Creditors.

(1) Unless otherwise agreed, if delivered goods may be returned by the buyer even though they conform to the contract, the transaction is

    (a) a "sale on approval" if the goods are delivered primarily for use, and

    (b) a "sale or return" if the goods are delivered primarily for resale.

(2) Goods held on approval are not subject to the claims of the buyer's creditors until acceptance; goods held on sale or return are subject to such claims while in the buyer's possession.

(3) Any "or return" term of a contract for sale is to be treated as a separate contract for sale within the statute of frauds section of this Article (Section 2–201) and as contradicting the sale aspect of the contract within the provisions of this Article on parol or extrinsic evidence (Section 2–202).

## §2-327. Special Incidents of Sale on Approval and Sale or Return.

(1) Under a sale on approval unless otherwise agreed

    (a) although the goods are identified to the contract the risk of loss and the title do not pass to the buyer until acceptance; and

    (b) use of the goods consistent with the purpose of trial is not acceptance but failure seasonably to notify the seller of election to return the goods is acceptance, and if the goods conform to the contract acceptance of any part is acceptance of the whole; and

    (c) after due notification of election to return, the return is at the seller's risk and expense but a merchant buyer must follow any reasonable instructions.

(2) Under a sale or return unless otherwise agreed

    (a) the option to return extends to the whole or any commercial unit of the goods while in substantially their original condition, but must be exercised seasonably; and

    (b) the return is at the buyer's risk and expense.

## §2-328. Sale by Auction.

(1) In a sale by auction if goods are put up in lots each lot is the subject of a separate sale.

(2) A sale by auction is complete when the auctioneer so announces by the fall of the hammer or in other customary manner. Where a bid is made while the hammer is falling in acceptance of a prior bid the

auctioneer may in his discretion reopen the bidding or declare the goods sold under the bid on which the hammer was falling.

(3) Such a sale is with reserve unless the goods are in explicit terms put up without reserve. In an auction with reserve the auctioneer may withdraw the goods at any time until he announces completion of the sale. In an auction without reserve, after the auctioneer calls for bids on an article or lot, that article or lot cannot be withdrawn unless no bid is made within a reasonable time. In either case a bidder may retract his bid until the auctioneer's announcement of completion of the sale, but a bidder's retraction does not revive any previous bid.

(4) If the auctioneer knowingly receives a bid on the seller's behalf or the seller makes or procures such a bid, and notice has not been given that liberty for such bidding is reserved, the buyer may at his option avoid the sale or take the goods at the price of the last good faith bid prior to the completion of the sale. This subsection shall not apply to any bid at a forced sale.

## Part 4: Title, Creditors and Good Faith Purchasers

### §2-401. Passing of Title; Reservation for Security; Limited Application of This Section.
Each provision of this Article with regard to the rights, obligations and remedies of the seller, the buyer, purchasers or other third parties applies irrespective of title to the goods except where the provision refers to such title. Insofar as situations are not covered by the other provisions of this Article and matters concerning title become material the following rules apply:

(1) Title to goods cannot pass under a contract for sale prior to their identification to the contract (Section 2–501), and unless otherwise explicitly agreed the buyer acquires by their identification a special property as limited by this Act. Any retention or reservation by the seller of the title (property) in goods shipped or delivered to the buyer is limited in effect to a reservation of a security interest. Subject to these provisions and to the provisions of the Article on Secured Transactions (Article 9), title to goods passes from the seller to the buyer in any manner and on any conditions explicitly agreed on by the parties.

(2) Unless otherwise explicitly agreed title passes to the buyer at the time and place at which the seller completes his performance with reference to the physical delivery of the goods, despite any reservation of a security interest and even though a document of title is to be delivered at a different time or place; and in particular and despite any reservation of a security interest by the bill of lading

(a) if the contract requires or authorizes the seller to send the goods to the buyer but does not require him to deliver them at destination, title passes to the buyer at the time and place of shipment; but

(b) if the contract requires delivery at destination, title passes on tender there.

(3) Unless otherwise explicitly agreed where delivery is to be made without moving the goods,

(a) if the seller is to deliver a tangible document of title, title passes at the time when and the place where he delivers such documents and if the seller is to deliver an electronic document of title, title passes when the seller delivers the document; or

(b) if the goods are at the time of contracting already identified and no documents are to be delivered, title passes at the time and place of contracting.

(4) A rejection or other refusal by the buyer to receive or retain the goods, whether or not justified, or a justified revocation of acceptance revests title to the goods in the seller. Such revesting occurs by operation of law and is not a "sale".

### §2-402. Rights of Seller's Creditors Against Sold Goods.

(1) Except as provided in subsections (2) and (3), rights of unsecured creditors of the seller with respect to goods which have been identified to a contract for sale are subject to the buyer's rights to recover the goods under this Article (Sections 2–502 and 2–716).

(2) A creditor of the seller may treat a sale or an identification of goods to a contract for sale as void if as against him a retention of possession by the seller is fraudulent under any rule of law of the state where the goods are situated, except that retention of possession in good faith and current course of trade by a merchant-seller for a commercially reasonable time after a sale or identification is not fraudulent.

(3) Nothing in this Article shall be deemed to impair the rights of creditors of the seller

(a) under the provisions of the Article on Secured Transactions (Article 9); or

(b) where identification to the contract or delivery is made not in current course of trade but in satisfaction of or as security for a pre-existing claim for money, security or the like and is made under circumstances which under any rule of law of the state where the goods are situated would apart from this Article constitute the transaction a fraudulent transfer or voidable preference.

## §2-403. Power to Transfer; Good Faith Purchase of Goods; "Entrusting".

(1) A purchaser of goods acquires all title which his transferor had or had power to transfer except that a purchaser of a limited interest acquires rights only to the extent of the interest purchased. A person with voidable title has power to transfer a good title to a good faith purchaser for value. When goods have been delivered under a transaction of purchase the purchaser has such power even though

    (a) the transferor was deceived as to the identity of the purchaser, or

    (b) the delivery was in exchange for a check which is later dishonored, or

    (c) it was agreed that the transaction was to be a "cash sale", or

    (d) the delivery was procured through fraud punishable as larcenous under the criminal law.

(2) Any entrusting of possession of goods to a merchant who deals in goods of that kind gives him power to transfer all rights of the entruster to a buyer in ordinary course of business.

(3) "Entrusting" includes any delivery and any acquiescence in retention of possession regardless of any condition expressed between the parties to the delivery or acquiescence and regardless of whether the procurement of the entrusting or the possessor's disposition of the goods have been such as to be larcenous under the criminal law.

*[Legislative Note: If a state adopts the repealer of Article 6—Bulk Transfers (Alternative A), subsec. (4) should read as follows:]*

(4) The rights of other purchasers of goods and of lien creditors are governed by the Articles on Secured Transactions (Article 9) and Documents of Title (Article 7).

*[Legislative Note: If a state adopts Revised Article 6—Bulk Sales (Alternative B), subsec. (4) should read as follows:]*

(4) The rights of other purchasers of goods and of lien creditors are governed by the Articles on Secured Transactions (Article 9), Bulk Sales (Article 6) and Documents of Title (Article 7).

*For material relating to the changes made in text in 1988, see section 3 of Alternative A (Repealer of Article 6—Bulk Transfers) and Conforming Amendment to Section 2–403 following end of Alternative B (Revised Article 6—Bulk Sales).*

## Part 5: Performance

## §2-501. Insurable Interest in Goods; Manner of Identification of Goods.

(1) The buyer obtains a special property and an insurable interest in goods by identification of existing goods as goods to which the contract refers even though the goods so identified are non-conforming and he has an option to return or reject them. Such identification can be made at any time and in any manner explicitly agreed to by the parties. In the absence of explicit agreement identification occurs

    (a) when the contract is made if it is for the sale of goods already existing and identified;

    (b) if the contract is for the sale of future goods other than those described in paragraph (c), when goods are shipped, marked or otherwise designated by the seller as goods to which the contract refers;

    (c) when the crops are planted or otherwise become growing crops or the young are conceived if the contract is for the sale of unborn young to be born within twelve months after contracting or for the sale of crops to be harvested within twelve months or the next normal harvest season after contracting whichever is longer.

(2) The seller retains an insurable interest in goods so long as title to or any security interest in the goods remains in him and where the identification is by the seller alone he may until default or insolvency or notification to the buyer that the identification is final substitute other goods for those identified.

(3) Nothing in this section impairs any insurable interest recognized under any other statute or rule of law.

## §2-502. Buyer's Right to Goods on Seller's Repudiation, Failure to Deliver, or Insolvency.

(1) Subject to subsections (2) and (3) and even though the goods have not been shipped a buyer who has paid a part or all of the price of goods in which he has a special property under the provisions of the immediately preceding section may on making and keeping good a tender of any unpaid portion of their price recover them from the seller if:

    (a) in the case of goods bought for personal, family, or household purposes, the seller repudiates or fails to deliver as required by the contract; or

    (b) in all cases, the seller becomes insolvent within ten days after receipt of the first installment on their price.

(2) The buyer's right to recover the goods under subsection (1)(a) vests upon acquisition of a special property, even if the seller had not then repudiated or failed to deliver.

(3) If the identification creating his special property has been made by the buyer he acquires the right to recover the goods only if they conform to the contract for sale.

## §2-503. Manner of Seller's Tender of Delivery.

(1) Tender of delivery requires that the seller put and hold conforming goods at the buyer's disposition and

give the buyer any notification reasonably necessary to enable him to take delivery. The manner, time and place for tender are determined by the agreement and this Article, and in particular

 (a) tender must be at a reasonable hour, and if it is of goods they must be kept available for the period reasonably necessary to enable the buyer to take possession; but

 (b) unless otherwise agreed the buyer must furnish facilities reasonably suited to the receipt of the goods.

(2) Where the case is within the next section respecting shipment tender requires that the seller comply with its provisions.

(3) Where the seller is required to deliver at a particular destination tender requires that he comply with subsection (1) and also in any appropriate case tender documents as described in subsections (4) and (5) of this section.

(4) Where goods are in the possession of a bailee and are to be delivered without being moved

 (a) tender requires that the seller either tender a negotiable document of title covering such goods or procure acknowledgment by the bailee of the buyer's right to possession of the goods; but

 (b) tender to the buyer of a non-negotiable document of title or of a record directing to the bailee to deliver is sufficient tender unless the buyer seasonably objects, and except as otherwise provided in Article 9 receipt by the bailee of notification of the buyer's rights fixes those rights as against the bailee and all third persons; but risk of loss of the goods and of any failure by the bailee to honor the non-negotiable document of title or to obey the direction remains on the seller until the buyer has had a reasonable time to present the document or direction, and a refusal by the bailee to honor the document or to obey the direction defeats the tender.

(5) Where the contract requires the seller to deliver documents

 (a) he must tender all such documents in correct form, except as provided in this Article with respect to bills of lading in a set (subsection (2) of Section 2–323); and

 (b) tender through customary banking channels is sufficient and dishonor of a draft accompanying or associated with the documents constitutes non-acceptance or rejection.

**§2-504. Shipment by Seller.** Where the seller is required or authorized to send the goods to the buyer and the contract does not require him to deliver them at a particular destination, then unless otherwise agreed he must

 (a) put the goods in the possession of such a carrier and make such a contract for their transportation as may be reasonable having regard to the nature of the goods and other circumstances of the case; and

 (b) obtain and promptly deliver or tender in due form any document necessary to enable the buyer to obtain possession of the goods or otherwise required by the agreement or by usage of trade; and

 (c) promptly notify the buyer of the shipment.

Failure to notify the buyer under paragraph (c) or to make a proper contract under paragraph (a) is a ground for rejection only if material delay or loss ensues.

## §2-505. Seller's Shipment Under Reservation.

(1) Where the seller has identified goods to the contract by or before shipment:

 (a) his procurement of a negotiable bill of lading to his own order or otherwise reserves in him a security interest in the goods. His procurement of the bill to the order of a financing agency or of the buyer indicates in addition only the seller's expectation of transferring that interest to the person named.

 (b) a non-negotiable bill of lading to himself or his nominee reserves possession of the goods as security but except in a case of conditional delivery (subsection (2) of Section 2–507) a non-negotiable bill of lading naming the buyer as consignee reserves no security interest even though the seller retains possession or control of the bill of lading.

(2) When shipment by the seller with reservation of a security interest is in violation of the contract for sale it constitutes an improper contract for transportation within the preceding section but impairs neither the rights given to the buyer by shipment and identification of the goods to the contract nor the seller's powers as a holder of a negotiable document of title.

## §2-506. Rights of Financing Agency.

(1) A financing agency by paying or purchasing for value a draft which relates to a shipment of goods acquires to the extent of the payment or purchase and in addition to its own rights under the draft and any document of title securing it any rights of the shipper in the goods including the right to stop delivery and the shipper's right to have the draft honored by the buyer.

(2) The right to reimbursement of a financing agency which has in good faith honored or purchased the draft under commitment to or authority from the buyer is not impaired by subsequent discovery of defects with reference to any relevant document which was apparently regular.

## §2-507. Effect of Seller's Tender; Delivery on Condition.

(1) Tender of delivery is a condition to the buyer's duty to accept the goods and, unless otherwise agreed, to his duty to pay for them. Tender entitles the seller to acceptance of the goods and to payment according to the contract.

(2) Where payment is due and demanded on the delivery to the buyer of goods or documents of title, his right as against the seller to retain or dispose of them is conditional upon his making the payment due.

## §2-508. Cure by Seller of Improper Tender or Delivery; Replacement.

(1) Where any tender or delivery by the seller is rejected because non-conforming and the time for performance has not yet expired, the seller may seasonably notify the buyer of his intention to cure and may then within the contract time make a conforming delivery.

(2) Where the buyer rejects a non-conforming tender which the seller had reasonable grounds to believe would be acceptable with or without money allowance the seller may if he seasonably notifies the buyer have a further reasonable time to substitute a conforming tender.

## §2-509. Risk of Loss in the Absence of Breach.

(1) Where the contract requires or authorizes the seller to ship the goods by carrier

  (a) if it does not require him to deliver them at a particular destination, the risk of loss passes to the buyer when the goods are duly delivered to the carrier even though the shipment is under reservation (Section 2–505); but

  (b) if it does require him to deliver them at a particular destination and the goods are there duly tendered while in the possession of the carrier, the risk of loss passes to the buyer when the goods are there duly so tendered as to enable the buyer to take delivery.

(2) Where the goods are held by a bailee to be delivered without being moved, the risk of loss passes to the buyer

  (a) on his receipt of possession or control of a negotiable document of title covering the goods; or

  (b) on acknowledgment by the bailee of the buyer's right to possession of the goods; or

  (c) after his receipt of possession or control of a non-negotiable document of title or other direction to deliver in a record, as provided in subsection (4)(b) of Section 2–503.

(3) In any case not within subsection (1) or (2), the risk of loss passes to the buyer on his receipt of the goods if the seller is a merchant; otherwise the risk passes to the buyer on tender of delivery.

(4) The provisions of this section are subject to contrary agreement of the parties and to the provisions of this Article on sale on approval (Section 2–327) and on effect of breach on risk of loss (Section 2–510).

## §2-510. Effect of breach on Risk of Loss.

(1) Where a tender or delivery of goods so fails to conform to the contract as to give a right of rejection the risk of their loss remains on the seller until cure or acceptance.

(2) Where the buyer rightfully revokes acceptance he may to the extent of any deficiency in his effective insurance coverage treat the risk of loss as having rested on the seller from the beginning.

(3) Where the buyer as to conforming goods already identified to the contract for sale repudiates or is otherwise in breach before risk of their loss has passed to him, the seller may to the extent of any deficiency in his effective insurance coverage treat the risk of loss as resting on the buyer for a commercially reasonable time.

## §2-511. Tender of Payment by Buyer; Payment by Check.

(1) Unless otherwise agreed tender of payment is a condition to the seller's duty to tender and complete any delivery.

(2) Tender of payment is sufficient when made by any means or in any manner current in the ordinary course of business unless the seller demands payment in legal tender and gives any extension of time reasonably necessary to procure it.

(3) Subject to the provisions of this Act on the effect of an instrument on an obligation (Section 3–310), payment by check is conditional and is defeated as between the parties by dishonor of the check on due presentment.

## §2-512. Payment by Buyer before Inspection.

(1) Where the contract requires payment before inspection non-conformity of the goods does not excuse the buyer from so making payment unless

  (a) the non-conformity appears without inspection; or

  (b) despite tender of the required documents the circumstances would justify injunction against honor under this Act (Section 5–109(b)).

(2) Payment pursuant to subsection (1) does not constitute an acceptance of goods or impair the buyer's right to inspect or any of his remedies.

## §2-513. Buyer's Right to Inspection of Goods.

(1) Unless otherwise agreed and subject to subsection (3), where goods are tendered or delivered or identified to the contract for sale, the buyer has a right before payment or acceptance to inspect them at any reasonable place and time and in any reasonable manner. When the seller is required or authorized to send the goods to the buyer, the inspection may be after their arrival.

(2) Expenses of inspection must be borne by the buyer but may be recovered from the seller if the goods do not conform and are rejected.

(3) Unless otherwise agreed and subject to the provisions of this Article on C.I.F. contracts (subsection (3) of Section 2–321), the buyer is not entitled to inspect the goods before payment of the price when the contract provides

    (a) for delivery "C.O.D." or on other like terms; or

    (b) for payment against documents of title, except where such payment is due only after the goods are to become available for inspection.

(4) A place or method of inspection fixed by the parties is presumed to be exclusive but unless otherwise expressly agreed it does not postpone identification or shift the place for delivery or for passing the risk of loss. If compliance becomes impossible, inspection shall be as provided in this section unless the place or method fixed was clearly intended as an indispensable condition failure of which avoids the contract.

## §2-514. When Documents Deliverable on Acceptance; When on Payment.
Unless otherwise agreed documents against which a draft is drawn are to be delivered to the drawee on acceptance of the draft if it is payable more than three days after presentment; otherwise, only on payment.

## §2-515. Preserving Evidence of Goods in Dispute.
In furtherance of the adjustment of any claim or dispute

(a) either party on reasonable notification to the other and for the purpose of ascertaining the facts and preserving evidence has the right to inspect, test and sample the goods including such of them as may be in the possession or control of the other; and

(b) the parties may agree to a third party inspection or survey to determine the conformity or condition of the goods and may agree that the findings shall be binding upon them in any subsequent litigation or adjustment.

## Part 6: Breach, Repudiation and Excuse

## §2-601. Buyer's Rights on Improper Delivery.
Subject to the provisions of this Article on breach in installment contracts (Section 2–612) and unless otherwise agreed under the sections on contractual limitations of remedy (Sections 2–718 and 2–719), if the goods or the tender of delivery fail in any respect to conform to the contract, the buyer may

(a) reject the whole; or

(b) accept the whole; or

(c) accept any commercial unit or units and reject the rest.

## §2-602. Manner and Effect of Rightful Rejection.

(1) Rejection of goods must be within a reasonable time after their delivery or tender. It is ineffective unless the buyer seasonably notifies the seller.

(2) Subject to the provisions of the two following sections on rejected goods (Sections 2–603 and 2–604),

    (a) after rejection any exercise of ownership by the buyer with respect to any commercial unit is wrongful as against the seller; and

    (b) if the buyer has before rejection taken physical possession of goods in which he does not have a security interest under the provisions of this Article (subsection (3) of Section 2–711), he is under a duty after rejection to hold them with reasonable care at the seller's disposition for a time sufficient to permit the seller to remove them; but

    (c) the buyer has no further obligations with regard to goods rightfully rejected.

(3) The seller's rights with respect to goods wrongfully rejected are governed by the provisions of this Article on Seller's remedies in general (Section 2–703).

## §2-603. Merchant Buyer's Duties as to Rightfully Rejected Goods.

(1) Subject to any security interest in the buyer (subsection (3) of Section 2–711), when the seller has no agent or place of business at the market of rejection a merchant buyer is under a duty after rejection of goods in his possession or control to follow any reasonable instructions received from the seller with respect to the goods and in the absence of such instructions to make reasonable efforts to sell them for the seller's account if they are perishable or threaten to decline in value speedily. Instructions are not reasonable if on demand indemnity for expenses is not forthcoming.

(2) When the buyer sells goods under subsection (1), he is entitled to reimbursement from the seller or out of the proceeds for reasonable expenses of caring for and selling them, and if the expenses include no selling commission then to such commission as is usual

in the trade or if there is none to a reasonable sum not exceeding ten per cent on the gross proceeds.

(3) In complying with this section the buyer is held only to good faith and good faith conduct hereunder is neither acceptance nor conversion nor the basis of an action for damages.

## §2-604. Buyer's Options as to Salvage of Rightfully Rejected Goods.

Subject to the provisions of the immediately preceding section on perishables if the seller gives no instructions within a reasonable time after notification of rejection the buyer may store the rejected goods for the seller's account or reship them to him or resell them for the seller's account with reimbursement as provided in the preceding section. Such action is not acceptance or conversion.

## §2-605. Waiver of Buyer's Objections by Failure to Particularize.

(1) The buyer's failure to state in connection with rejection a particular defect which is ascertainable by reasonable inspection precludes him from relying on the unstated defect to justify rejection or to establish breach

    (a) where the seller could have cured it if stated seasonably; or

    (b) between merchants when the seller has after rejection made a request in writing for a full and final written statement of all defects on which the buyer proposes to rely.

(2) Payment against documents made without reservation of rights precludes recovery of the payment for defects apparent in the documents.

## §2-606. What Constitutes Acceptance of Goods.

(1) Acceptance of goods occurs when the buyer

    (a) after a reasonable opportunity to inspect the goods signifies to the seller that the goods are conforming or that he will take or retain them in spite of their non-conformity; or

    (b) fails to make an effective rejection (subsection (1) of Section 2–602), but such acceptance does not occur until the buyer has had a reasonable opportunity to inspect them; or

    (c) does any act inconsistent with the seller's ownership; but if such act is wrongful as against the seller it is an acceptance only if ratified by him.

(2) Acceptance of a part of any commercial unit is acceptance of that entire unit.

## §2-607. Effect of Acceptance; Notice of Breach; Burden of Establishing Breach after Acceptance; Notice of Claim or Litigation to Person Answerable Over.

(1) The buyer must pay at the contract rate for any goods accepted.

(2) Acceptance of goods by the buyer precludes rejection of the goods accepted and if made with knowledge of a non-conformity cannot be revoked because of it unless the acceptance was on the reasonable assumption that the non-conformity would be seasonably cured but acceptance does not of itself impair any other remedy provided by this Article for non-conformity.

(3) Where a tender has been accepted

    (a) the buyer must within a reasonable time after he discovers or should have discovered any breach notify the seller of breach or be barred from any remedy; and

    (b) if the claim is one for infringement or the like (subsection (3) of Section 2–312) and the buyer is sued as a result of such a breach he must so notify the seller within a reasonable time after he receives notice of the litigation or be barred from any remedy over for liability established by the litigation.

(4) The burden is on the buyer to establish any breach with respect to the goods accepted.

(5) Where the buyer is sued for breach of a warranty or other obligation for which his seller is answerable over

    (a) he may give his seller written notice of the litigation. If the notice states that the seller may come in and defend and that if the seller does not do so he will be bound in any action against him by his buyer by any determination of fact common to the two litigations, then unless the seller after seasonable receipt of the notice does come in and defend he is so bound.

    (b) if the claim is one for infringement or the like (subsection (3) of Section 2–312) the original seller may demand in writing that his buyer turn over to him control of the litigation including settlement or else be barred from any remedy over and if he also agrees to bear all expense and to satisfy any adverse judgment, then unless the buyer after seasonable receipt of the demand does turn over control the buyer is so barred.

(6) The provisions of subsections (3), (4) and (5) apply to any obligation of a buyer to hold the seller harmless against infringement or the like (subsection (3) of Section 2–312).

## §2-608. Revocation of Acceptance in Whole or in Part.

(1) The buyer may revoke his acceptance of a lot or commercial unit whose non-conformity substantially impairs its value to him if he has accepted it

    (a) on the reasonable assumption that its non-conformity would be cured and it has not been seasonably cured; or

(b) without discovery of such non-conformity if his acceptance was reasonably induced either by the difficulty of discovery before acceptance or by the seller's assurances.

(2) Revocation of acceptance must occur within a reasonable time after the buyer discovers or should have discovered the ground for it and before any substantial change in condition of the goods which is not caused by their own defects. It is not effective until the buyer notifies the seller of it.

(3) A buyer who so revokes has the same rights and duties with regard to the goods involved as if he had rejected them.

## §2-609. Right to Adequate Assurance of Performance.

(1) A contract for sale imposes an obligation on each party that the other's expectation of receiving due performance will not be impaired. When reasonable grounds for insecurity arise with respect to the performance of either party the other may in writing demand adequate assurance of due performance and until he receives such assurance may if commercially reasonable suspend any performance for which he has not already received the agreed return.

(2) Between merchants the reasonableness of grounds for insecurity and the adequacy of any assurance offered shall be determined according to commercial standards.

(3) Acceptance of any improper delivery or payment does not prejudice the aggrieved party's right to demand adequate assurance of future performance.

(4) After receipt of a justified demand failure to provide within a reasonable time not exceeding thirty days such assurance of due performance as is adequate under the circumstances of the particular case is a repudiation of the contract.

## §2-610. Anticipatory Repudiation.
When either party repudiates the contract with respect to a performance not yet due the loss of which will substantially impair the value of the contract to the other, the aggrieved party may

(a) for a commercially reasonable time await performance by the repudiating party; or

(b) resort to any remedy for breach (Section 2–703 or Section 2–711), even though he has notified the repudiating party that he would await the latter's performance and has urged retraction; and

(c) in either case suspend his own performance or proceed in accordance with the provisions of this Article on the seller's right to identify goods to the contract notwithstanding breach or to salvage unfinished goods (Section 2–704).

## §2-611. Retraction of Anticipatory Repudiation.

(1) Until the repudiating party's next performance is due he can retract his repudiation unless the aggrieved party has since the repudiation cancelled or materially changed his position or otherwise indicated that he considers the repudiation final.

(2) Retraction may be by any method which clearly indicates to the aggrieved party that the repudiating party intends to perform, but must include any assurance justifiably demanded under the provisions of this Article (Section 2–609).

(3) Retraction reinstates the repudiating party's rights under the contract with due excuse and allowance to the aggrieved party for any delay occasioned by the repudiation.

## §2-612. "Installment Contract"; Breach.

(1) An "installment contract" is one which requires or authorizes the delivery of goods in separate lots to be separately accepted, even though the contract contains a clause "each delivery is a separate contract" or its equivalent.

(2) The buyer may reject any installment which is non-conforming if the non-conformity substantially impairs the value of that installment and cannot be cured or if the non-conformity is a defect in the required documents; but if the non-conformity does not fall within subsection (3) and the seller gives adequate assurance of its cure the buyer must accept that installment.

(3) Whenever non-conformity or default with respect to one or more installments substantially impairs the value of the whole contract there is a breach of the whole. But the aggrieved party reinstates the contract if he accepts a non-conforming installment without seasonably notifying of cancellation or if he brings an action with respect only to past installments or demands performance as to future installments.

## §2-613. Casualty to Identified Goods.
Where the contract requires for its performance goods identified when the contract is made, and the goods suffer casualty without fault of either party before the risk of loss passes to the buyer, or in a proper case under a "no arrival, no sale" term (Section 2-324) then

(a) if the loss is total the contract is avoided; and

(b) if the loss is partial or the goods have so deteriorated as no longer to conform to the contract the buyer may nevertheless demand inspection and at his option either treat the contract as avoided or accept the goods with due allowance from the contract price for the deterioration or the deficiency in quantity but without further right against the seller.

## §2-614. Substituted Performance.

(1) Where without fault of either party the agreed berthing, loading, or unloading facilities fail or an agreed type of carrier becomes unavailable or the agreed manner of delivery otherwise becomes commercially impracticable but a commercially reasonable substitute is available, such substitute performance must be tendered and accepted.

(2) If the agreed means or manner of payment fails because of domestic or foreign governmental regulation, the seller may withhold or stop delivery unless the buyer provides a means or manner of payment which is commercially a substantial equivalent. If delivery has already been taken, payment by the means or in the manner provided by the regulation discharges the buyer's obligation unless the regulation is discriminatory, oppressive or predatory.

## §2-615. Excuse by Failure of Presupposed Conditions.
Except so far as a seller may have assumed a greater obligation and subject to the preceding section on substituted performance:

(a) Delay in delivery or non-delivery in whole or in part by a seller who complies with paragraphs (b) and (c) is not a breach of his duty under a contract for sale if performance as agreed has been made impracticable by the occurrence of a contingency the non-occurrence of which was a basic assumption on which the contract was made or by compliance in good faith with any applicable foreign or domestic governmental regulation or order whether or not it later proves to be invalid.

(b) Where the causes mentioned in paragraph (a) affect only a part of the seller's capacity to perform, he must allocate production and deliveries among his customers but may at his option include regular customers not then under contract as well as his own requirements for further manufacture. He may so allocate in any manner which is fair and reasonable.

(c) The seller must notify the buyer seasonably that there will be delay or non-delivery and, when allocation is required under paragraph (b), of the estimated quota thus made available for the buyer.

## §2-616. Procedure on Notice Claiming Excuse.

(1) Where the buyer receives notification of a material or indefinite delay or an allocation justified under the preceding section he may by written notification to the seller as to any delivery concerned, and where the prospective deficiency substantially impairs the value of the whole contract under the provisions of this Article relating to breach of installment contracts (Section 2–612), then also as to the whole,

   (a) terminate and thereby discharge any unexecuted portion of the contract; or

   (b) modify the contract by agreeing to take his available quota in substitution.

(2) If after receipt of such notification from the seller the buyer fails so to modify the contract within a reasonable time not exceeding thirty days the contract lapses with respect to any deliveries affected.

(3) The provisions of this section may not be negated by agreement except in so far as the seller has assumed a greater obligation under the preceding section.

## Part 7: Remedies

### §2-701. Remedies for Breach of Collateral Contracts Not Impaired.
Remedies for breach of any obligation or promise collateral or ancillary to a contract for sale are not impaired by the provisions of this Article.

### §2-702. Seller's Remedies on Discovery of Buyer's Insolvency.

(1) Where the seller discovers the buyer to be insolvent he may refuse delivery except for cash including payment for all goods theretofore delivered under the contract, and stop delivery under this Article (Section 2–705).

(2) Where the seller discovers that the buyer has received goods on credit while insolvent he may reclaim the goods upon demand made within ten days after the receipt, but if misrepresentation of solvency has been made to the particular seller in writing within three months before delivery the ten day limitation does not apply. Except as provided in this subsection the seller may not base a right to reclaim goods on the buyer's fraudulent or innocent misrepresentation of solvency or of intent to pay.

(3) The seller's right to reclaim under subsection (2) is subject to the rights of a buyer in ordinary course or other good faith purchaser under this Article (Section 2–403). Successful reclamation of goods excludes all other remedies with respect to them.

### §2-703. Seller's Remedies in General.
Where the buyer wrongfully rejects or revokes acceptance of goods or fails to make a payment due on or before delivery or repudiates with respect to a part or the whole, then with respect to any goods directly affected and, if the breach is of the whole contract (Section 2-612), then also with respect to the whole undelivered balance, the aggrieved seller may

(a) withhold delivery of such goods;

(b) stop delivery by any bailee as hereafter provided (Section 2–705);

(c) proceed under the next section respecting goods still unidentified to the contract;

(d) resell and recover damages as hereafter provided (Section 2–706);

(e) recover damages for non-acceptance (Section 2–708) or in a proper case the price (Section 2–709);

(f) cancel.

## §2-704. Seller's Right to Identify Goods to the Contract Notwithstanding Breach or to Salvage Unfinished Goods.

(1) An aggrieved seller under the preceding section may

(a) identify to the contract conforming goods not already identified if at the time he learned of the breach they are in his possession or control;

(b) treat as the subject of resale goods which have demonstrably been intended for the particular contract even though those goods are unfinished.

(2) Where the goods are unfinished an aggrieved seller may in the exercise of reasonable commercial judgment for the purposes of avoiding loss and of effective realization either complete the manufacture and wholly identify the goods to the contract or cease manufacture and resell for scrap or salvage value or proceed in any other reasonable manner.

## §2-705. Seller's Stoppage of Delivery in Transit or Otherwise.

(1) The seller may stop delivery of goods in the possession of a carrier or other bailee when he discovers the buyer to be insolvent (Section 2–702) and may stop delivery of carload, truckload, planeload or larger shipments of express or freight when the buyer repudiates or fails to make a payment due before delivery or if for any other reason the seller has a right to withhold or reclaim the goods.

(2) As against such buyer the seller may stop delivery until

(a) receipt of the goods by the buyer; or

(b) acknowledgment to the buyer by any bailee of the goods except a carrier that the bailee holds the goods for the buyer; or

(c) such acknowledgment to the buyer by a carrier by reshipment or as warehouseman; or

(d) negotiation to the buyer of any negotiable document of title covering the goods.

(3) (a) To stop delivery the seller must so notify as to enable the bailee by reasonable diligence to prevent delivery of the goods.

(b) After such notification the bailee must hold and deliver the goods according to the directions of the seller but the seller is liable to the bailee for any ensuing charges or damages.

(c) If a negotiable document of title has been issued for goods the bailee is not obliged to obey a notification to stop until surrender of possession or control of the document.

(d) A carrier who has issued a non-negotiable bill of lading is not obliged to obey a notification to stop received from a person other than the consignor.

## §2-706. Seller's Resale Including Contract for Resale.

(1) Under the conditions stated in Section 2–703 on seller's remedies, the seller may resell the goods concerned or the undelivered balance thereof. Where the resale is made in good faith and in a commercially reasonable manner the seller may recover the difference between the resale price and the contract price together with any incidental damages allowed under the provisions of this Article (Section 2–710), but less expenses saved in consequence of the buyer's breach.

(2) Except as otherwise provided in subsection (3) or unless otherwise agreed resale may be at public or private sale including sale by way of one or more contracts to sell or of identification to an existing contract of the seller. Sale may be as a unit or in parcels and at any time and place and on any terms but every aspect of the sale including the method, manner, time, place and terms must be commercially reasonable. The resale must be reasonably identified as referring to the broken contract, but it is not necessary that the goods be in existence or that any or all of them have been identified to the contract before the breach.

(3) Where the resale is at private sale the seller must give the buyer reasonable notification of his intention to resell.

(4) Where the resale is at public sale

(a) only identified goods can be sold except where there is a recognized market for a public sale of futures in goods of the kind; and

(b) it must be made at a usual place or market for public sale if one is reasonably available and except in the case of goods which are perishable or threaten to decline in value speedily the seller must give the buyer reasonable notice of the time and place of the resale; and

(c) if the goods are not to be within the view of those attending the sale the notification of sale must state the place where the goods are located and provide for their reasonable inspection by prospective bidders; and

(d) the seller may buy.

(5) A purchaser who buys in good faith at a resale takes the goods free of any rights of the original buyer even though the seller fails to comply with one or more of the requirements of this section.

(6) The seller is not accountable to the buyer for any profit made on any resale. A person in the position of a seller (Section 2–707) or a buyer who has rightfully rejected or justifiably revoked acceptance must account for any excess over the amount of his security interest, as hereinafter defined (subsection (3) of Section 2–711).

## §2-707. "Person in the Position of a Seller".

(1) A "person in the position of a seller" includes as against a principal an agent who has paid or become responsible for the price of goods on behalf of his principal or anyone who otherwise holds a security interest or other right in goods similar to that of a seller.

(2) A person in the position of a seller may as provided in this Article withhold or stop delivery (Section 2–705) and resell (Section 2–706) and recover incidental damages (Section 2–710).

## §2-708. Seller's Damages for Non-acceptance or Repudiation.

(1) Subject to subsection (2) and to the provisions of this Article with respect to proof of market price (Section 2–723), the measure of damages for non-acceptance or repudiation by the buyer is the difference between the market price at the time and place for tender and the unpaid contract price together with any incidental damages provided in this Article (Section 2–710), but less expenses saved in consequence of the buyer's breach.

(2) If the measure of damages provided in subsection (1) is inadequate to put the seller in as good a position as performance would have done then the measure of damages is the profit (including reasonable overhead) which the seller would have made from full performance by the buyer, together with any incidental damages provided in this Article (Section 2–710), due allowance for costs reasonably incurred and due credit for payments or proceeds of resale.

## §2-709. Action for the Price.

(1) When the buyer fails to pay the price as it becomes due the seller may recover, together with any incidental damages under the next section, the price

   (a) of goods accepted or of conforming goods lost or damaged within a commercially reasonable time after risk of their loss has passed to the buyer; and

   (b) of goods identified to the contract if the seller is unable after reasonable effort to resell them at a reasonable price or the circumstances reasonably indicate that such effort will be unavailing.

(2) Where the seller sues for the price he must hold for the buyer any goods which have been identified to the contract and are still in his control except that if resale becomes possible he may resell them at any time prior to the collection of the judgment. The net proceeds of any such resale must be credited to the buyer and payment of the judgment entitles him to any goods not resold.

(3) After the buyer has wrongfully rejected or revoked acceptance of the goods or has failed to make a payment due or has repudiated (Section 2–610), a seller who is held not entitled to the price under this section shall nevertheless be awarded damages for non-acceptance under the preceding section.

## §2-710. Seller's Incidental Damages. Incidental damages to an aggrieved seller include any commercially reasonable charges, expenses or commissions incurred in stopping delivery, in the transportation, care and custody of goods after the buyer's breach, in connection with return or resale of the goods or otherwise resulting from the breach.

## §2-711. Buyer's Remedies in General; Buyer's Security Interest in Rejected Goods.

(1) Where the seller fails to make delivery or repudiates or the buyer rightfully rejects or justifiably revokes acceptance then with respect to any goods involved, and with respect to the whole if the breach goes to the whole contract (Section 2–612), the buyer may cancel and whether or not he has done so may in addition to recovering so much of the price as has been paid

   (a) "cover" and have damages under the next section as to all the goods affected whether or not they have been identified to the contract; or

   (b) recover damages for non-delivery as provided in this Article (Section 2–713).

(2) Where the seller fails to deliver or repudiates the buyer may also

   (a) if the goods have been identified recover them as provided in this Article (Section 2–502); or

   (b) in a proper case obtain specific performance or replevy the goods as provided in this Article (Section 2–716).

(3) On rightful rejection or justifiable revocation of acceptance a buyer has a security interest in goods in his possession or control for any payments made on their price and any expenses reasonably incurred in their inspection, receipt, transportation, care and custody and may hold such goods and resell them in like manner as an aggrieved seller (Section 2–706).

## §2-712. "Cover"; Buyer's Procurement of Substitute Goods.

(1) After a breach within the preceding section the buyer may "cover" by making in good faith and without unreasonable delay any reasonable purchase of or contract to purchase goods in substitution for those due from the seller.

(2) The buyer may recover from the seller as damages the difference between the cost of cover and the contract price together with any incidental or consequential damages as hereinafter defined (Section 2–715), but less expenses saved in consequence of the seller's breach.

(3) Failure of the buyer to effect cover within this section does not bar him from any other remedy.

## §2-713. Buyer's Damages for Non-delivery or Repudiation.

(1) Subject to the provisions of this Article with respect to proof of market price (Section 2–723), the measure of damages for non-delivery or repudiation by the seller is the difference between the market price at the time when the buyer learned of the breach and the contract price together with any incidental and consequential damages provided in this Article (Section 2–715), but less expenses saved in consequence of the seller's breach.

(2) Market price is to be determined as of the place for tender or, in cases of rejection after arrival or revocation of acceptance, as of the place of arrival.

## §2-714. Buyer's Damages for Breach in Regard to Accepted Goods.

(1) Where the buyer has accepted goods and given notification (subsection (3) of Section 2–607) he may recover as damages for any non-conformity of tender the loss resulting in the ordinary course of events from the seller's breach as determined in any manner which is reasonable.

(2) The measure of damages for breach of warranty is the difference at the time and place of acceptance between the value of the goods accepted and the value they would have had if they had been as warranted, unless special circumstances show proximate damages of a different amount.

(3) In a proper case any incidental and consequential damages under the next section may also be recovered.

## §2-715. Buyer's Incidental and Consequential Damages.

(1) Incidental damages resulting from the seller's breach include expenses reasonably incurred in inspection, receipt, transportation and care and custody of goods rightfully rejected, any commercially reasonable charges, expenses or commissions in connection with effecting cover and any other reasonable expense incident to the delay or other breach.

(2) Consequential damages resulting from the seller's breach include

(a) any loss resulting from general or particular requirements and needs of which the seller at the time of contracting had reason to know and which could not reasonably be prevented by cover or otherwise; and

(b) injury to person or property proximately resulting from any breach of warranty.

## §2-716. Buyer's Right to Specific Performance or Replevin.

(1) Specific performance may be decreed where the goods are unique or in other proper circumstances.

(2) The decree for specific performance may include such terms and conditions as to payment of the price, damages, or other relief as the court may deem just.

(3) The buyer has a right of replevin for goods identified to the contract if after reasonable effort he is unable to effect cover for such goods or the circumstances reasonably indicate that such effort will be unavailing or if the goods have been shipped under reservation and satisfaction of the security interest in them has been made or tendered. In the case of goods bought for personal, family, or household purposes, the buyer's right of replevin vests upon acquisition of a special property, even if the seller had not then repudiated or failed to deliver.

## §2-717. Deduction of Damages From the Price.

The buyer on notifying the seller of his intention to do so may deduct all or any part of the damages resulting from any breach of the contract from any part of the price still due under the same contract.

## §2-718. Liquidation or Limitation of Damages; Deposits.

(1) Damages for breach by either party may be liquidated in the agreement but only at an amount which is reasonable in the light of the anticipated or actual harm caused by the breach, the difficulties of proof of loss, and the inconvenience or nonfeasibility of otherwise obtaining an adequate remedy. A term fixing unreasonably large liquidated damages is void as a penalty.

(2) Where the seller justifiably withholds delivery of goods because of the buyer's breach, the buyer is entitled to restitution of any amount by which the sum of his payments exceeds

(a) the amount to which the seller is entitled by virtue of terms liquidating the seller's damages in accordance with subsection (1), or

(b) in the absence of such terms, twenty per cent of the value of the total performance for which the buyer is obligated under the contract or $500, whichever is smaller.

(3) The buyer's right to restitution under subsection (2) is subject to offset to the extent that the seller establishes

    (a) a right to recover damages under the provisions of this Article other than subsection (1), and

    (b) the amount or value of any benefits received by the buyer directly or indirectly by reason of the contract.

(4) Where a seller has received payment in goods their reasonable value or the proceeds of their resale shall be treated as payments for the purposes of subsection (2); but if the seller has notice of the buyer's breach before reselling goods received in part performance, his resale is subject to the conditions laid down in this Article on resale by an aggrieved seller (Section 2–706).

## §2-719. Contractual Modification or Limitation of Remedy.

(1) Subject to the provisions of subsections (2) and (3) of this section and of the preceding section on liquidation and limitation of damages,

    (a) the agreement may provide for remedies in addition to or in substitution for those provided in this Article and may limit or alter the measure of damages recoverable under this Article, as by limiting the buyer's remedies to return of the goods and repayment of the price or to repair and replacement of non-conforming goods or parts; and

    (b) resort to a remedy as provided is optional unless the remedy is expressly agreed to be exclusive, in which case it is the sole remedy.

(2) Where circumstances cause an exclusive or limited remedy to fail of its essential purpose, remedy may be had as provided in this Act.

(3) Consequential damages may be limited or excluded unless the limitation or exclusion is unconscionable. Limitation of consequential damages for injury to the person in the case of consumer goods is prima facie unconscionable but limitation of damages where the loss is commercial is not.

## §2-720. Effect of "Cancellation" or "Rescission" on Claims for Antecedent Breach.
Unless the contrary intention clearly appears, expressions of "cancellation" or "rescission" of the contract or the like shall not be construed as a renunciation or discharge of any claim in damages for an antecedent breach.

## §2-721. Remedies for Fraud.
Remedies for material misrepresentation or fraud include all remedies available under this Article for non-fraudulent breach. Neither rescission or a claim for rescission of the contract for sale nor rejection or return of the goods shall bar or be deemed inconsistent with a claim for damages or other remedy.

## §2-722. Who Can Sue Third Parties for Injury to Goods.
Where a third party so deals with goods which have been identified to a contract for sale as to cause actionable injury to a party to that contract

    (a) a right of action against the third party is in either party to the contract for sale who has title to or a security interest or a special property or an insurable interest in the goods; and if the goods have been destroyed or converted a right of action is also in the party who either bore the risk of loss under the contract for sale or has since the injury assumed that risk as against the other;

    (b) if at the time of the injury the party plaintiff did not bear the risk of loss as against the other party to the contract for sale and there is no arrangement between them for disposition of the recovery, his suit or settlement is, subject to his own interest, as a fiduciary for the other party to the contract;

    (c) either party may with the consent of the other sue for the benefit of whom it may concern.

## §2-723. Proof of Market Price: Time and Place.

(1) If an action based on anticipatory repudiation comes to trial before the time for performance with respect to some or all of the goods, any damages based on market price (Section 2–708 or Section 2–713) shall be determined according to the price of such goods prevailing at the time when the aggrieved party learned of the repudiation.

(2) If evidence of a price prevailing at the times or places described in this Article is not readily available the price prevailing within any reasonable time before or after the time described or at any other place which in commercial judgment or under usage of trade would serve as a reasonable substitute for the one described may be used, making any proper allowance for the cost of transporting the goods to or from such other place.

(3) Evidence of a relevant price prevailing at a time or place other than the one described in this Article offered by one party is not admissible unless and until he has given the other party such notice as the court finds sufficient to prevent unfair surprise.

## §2-724. Admissibility of Market Quotations.
Whenever the prevailing price or value of any goods regularly bought and sold in any established commodity market is in issue, reports in official publications or trade journals or in newspapers or periodicals of general circulation published as the reports of such market shall be admissible in evidence. The circumstances of the preparation

of such a report may be shown to affect its weight but not its admissibility.

## §2-725. Statute of Limitations in Contracts for Sale.

(1) An action for breach of any contract for sale must be commenced within four years after the cause of action has accrued. By the original agreement the parties may reduce the period of limitation to not less than one year but may not extend it.

(2) A cause of action accrues when the breach occurs, regardless of the aggrieved party's lack of knowledge of the breach. A breach of warranty occurs when tender of delivery is made, except that where a warranty explicitly extends to future performance of the goods and discovery of the breach must await the time of such performance the cause of action accrues when the breach is or should have been discovered.

(3) Where an action commenced within the time limited by subsection (1) is so terminated as to leave available a remedy by another action for the same breach such other action may be commenced after the expiration of the time limited and within six months after the termination of the first action unless the termination resulted from voluntary discontinuance or from dismissal for failure or neglect to prosecute.

(4) This section does not alter the law on tolling of the statute of limitations nor does it apply to causes of action which have accrued before this Act becomes effective.

## Part 1: General Provisions

### §2A-101. Short Title. This Article shall be known and may be cited as the Uniform Commercial Code—Leases.

### §2A-102. Scope. This Article applies to any transaction, regardless of form, that creates a lease.

### §2A-103. Definitions and Index of Definitions.

(1) In this Article unless the context otherwise requires:

(a) "Buyer in ordinary course of business" means a person who in good faith and without knowledge that the sale to him [or her] is in violation of the ownership rights or security interest or leasehold interest of a third party in the goods buys in ordinary course from a person in the business of selling goods of that kind but does not include a pawnbroker. "Buying" may be for cash or by exchange of other property or on secured or unsecured credit and includes receiving goods or documents of title under a pre-existing contract for sale but does not include a transfer in bulk or as security for or in total or partial satisfaction of a money debt.

(b) "Cancellation" occurs when either party puts an end to the lease contract for default by the other party.

(c) "Commercial unit" means such a unit of goods as by commercial usage is a single whole for purposes of lease and division of which materially impairs its character or value on the market or in use. A commercial unit may be a single article, as a machine, or a set of articles, as a suite of furniture or a line of machinery, or a quantity, as a gross or carload, or any other unit treated in use or in the relevant market as a single whole.

(d) "Conforming" goods or performance under a lease contract means goods or performance that are in accordance with the obligations under the lease contract.

(e) "Consumer lease" means a lease that a lessor regularly engaged in the business of leasing or selling makes to a lessee who is an individual and who takes under the lease primarily for a personal, family, or household purpose [, if the total payments to be made under the lease contract, excluding payments for options to renew or buy, do not exceed $_____].

(f) "Fault" means wrongful act, omission, breach, or default.

(g) "Finance lease" means a lease with respect to which:

(i) the lessor does not select, manufacture, or supply the goods;

(ii) the lessor acquires the goods or the right to possession and use of the goods in connection with the lease; and

(iii) one of the following occurs:

(A) the lessee receives a copy of the contract by which the lessor acquired the goods or the right to possession and use of the goods before signing the lease contract;

(B) the lessee's approval of the contract by which the lessor acquired the goods or the right to possession and use of the goods is a condition to effectiveness of the lease contract;

(C) the lessee, before signing the lease contract, receives an accurate and complete statement designating the promises and warranties, and any disclaimers of warranties, limitations or modifications of remedies, or liquidated damages, including those of a third party, such as the manufacturer of the goods, provided to the lessor by the person supplying the goods in connection with or as part of the contract by which the lessor acquired the goods or the right to possession and use of the goods; or

(D) if the lease is not a consumer lease, the lessor, before the lessee signs the lease contract, informs the lessee in writing (a) of the identity of the person supplying the goods to the lessor, unless the lessee has selected that person and directed the lessor to acquire the goods or the right to possession and use of the goods from that person, (b) that the lessee is entitled under this Article to the promises and warranties, including those of any third party, provided to the lessor by the person supplying the goods in connection with or as part of the contract by which the lessor acquired the goods or the right to possession and use of the goods, and (c) that the lessee may communicate with the person supplying the goods to the lessor and receive an accurate and complete statement of those promises and warranties, including any disclaimers and limitations of them or of remedies.

(h) "Goods" means all things that are movable at the time of identification to the lease contract, or are fixtures (Section 2A–309), but the term does not include money, documents, instruments, accounts, chattel paper, general intangibles, or minerals or the like, including oil and gas, before extraction. The term also includes the unborn young of animals.

(i) "Installment lease contract" means a lease contract that authorizes or requires the delivery of goods in separate lots to be separately accepted, even though the lease contract contains a clause "each delivery is a separate lease" or its equivalent.

(j) "Lease" means a transfer of the right to possession and use of goods for a term in return for consideration, but a sale, including a sale on approval or a sale or return, or retention or creation of a security interest is not a lease. Unless the context clearly indicates otherwise, the term includes a sublease.

(k) "Lease agreement" means the bargain, with respect to the lease, of the lessor and the lessee in fact as found in their language or by implication from other circumstances including course of dealing or usage of trade or course of performance as provided in this Article. Unless the context clearly indicates otherwise, the term includes a sublease agreement.

(l) "Lease contract" means the total legal obligation that results from the lease agreement as affected by this Article and any other applicable rules of law. Unless the context clearly indicates otherwise, the term includes a sublease contract.

(m) "Leasehold interest" means the interest of the lessor or the lessee under a lease contract.

(n) "Lessee" means a person who acquires the right to possession and use of goods under a lease. Unless the context clearly indicates otherwise, the term includes a sublessee.

(o) "Lessee in ordinary course of business" means a person who in good faith and without knowledge that the lease to him [or her] is in violation of the ownership rights or security interest or leasehold interest of a third party in the goods, leases in ordinary course from a person in the business of selling or leasing goods of that kind but does not include a pawnbroker. "Leasing" may be for cash or by exchange of other property or on secured or unsecured credit and includes receiving goods or documents of title under a pre-existing lease contract but does not include a transfer in bulk or as security for or in total or partial satisfaction of a money debt.

(p) "Lessor" means a person who transfers the right to possession and use of goods under a lease. Unless the context clearly indicates otherwise, the term includes a sublessor.

(q) "Lessor's residual interest" means the lessor's interest in the goods after expiration, termination, or cancellation of the lease contract.

(r) "Lien" means a charge against or interest in goods to secure payment of a debt or performance of an obligation, but the term does not include a security interest.

(s) "Lot" means a parcel or a single article that is the subject matter of a separate lease or delivery, whether or not it is sufficient to perform the lease contract.

(t) "Merchant lessee" means a lessee that is a merchant with respect to goods of the kind subject to the lease.

(u) "Present value" means the amount as of a date certain of one or more sums payable in the future, discounted to the date certain. The discount is determined by the interest rate specified by the parties if the rate was not manifestly unreasonable at the time the transaction was entered into; otherwise, the discount is determined by a commercially reasonable rate that takes into account the facts and circumstances of each case at the time the transaction was entered into.

(v) "Purchase" includes taking by sale, lease, mortgage, security interest, pledge, gift, or any other voluntary transaction creating an interest in goods.

(w) "Sublease" means a lease of goods the right to possession and use of which was acquired by the lessor as a lessee under an existing lease.

(x) "Supplier" means a person from whom a lessor buys or leases goods to be leased under a finance lease.

(y) "Supply contract" means a contract under which a lessor buys or leases goods to be leased.

(z) "Termination" occurs when either party pursuant to a power created by agreement or law puts an end to the lease contract otherwise than for default.

(2) Other definitions applying to this Article and the sections in which they appear are:

"Accessions". Section 2A–310(1).

"Construction mortgage". Section 2A–309(1)(d).

"Encumbrance". Section 2A–309(1)(e).

"Fixtures". Section 2A–309(1)(a).

"Fixture filing". Section 2A–309(1)(b).

"Purchase money lease". Section 2A–309(1)(c).

(3) The following definitions in other Articles apply to this Article:

"Account". Section 9–106.

"Between merchants". Section 2–104(3).

"Buyer". Section 2–103(1)(a).

"Chattel paper". Section 9–105(1)(b).

"Consumer goods". Section 9–109(1).

"Document". Section 9–105(1)(f).

"Entrusting". Section 2–403(3).

"General intangibles". Section 9–106.

"Good faith". Section 2–103(1)(b).

"Instrument". Section 9–105(1)(i).

"Merchant". Section 2–104(1).

"Mortgage". Section 9–105(1)(j).

"Pursuant to commitment". Section 9–105(1)(k).

"Receipt". Section 2–103(1)(c).

"Sale". Section 2–106(1).

"Sale on approval". Section 2–326.

"Sale or return". Section 2–326.

"Seller". Section 2–103(1)(d).

(4) In addition Article 1 contains general definitions and principles of construction and interpretation applicable throughout this Article.

## §2A-104. Leases Subject to Other Law.

(1) A lease, although subject to this Article, is also subject to any applicable:

(a) certificate of title statute of this State: (list any certificate of title statutes covering automobiles, trailers, mobile homes, boats, farm tractors, and the like);

(b) certificate of title statute of another jurisdiction (Section 2A–105); or

(c) consumer protection statute of this State, or final consumer protection decision of a court of this State existing on the effective date of this Article.

(2) In case of conflict between this Article, other than Sections 2A–105, 2A–304(3), and 2A–305(3), and a statute or decision referred to in subsection (1), the statute or decision controls.

(3) Failure to comply with an applicable law has only the effect specified therein.

## §2A-105. Territorial Application of Article to Goods Covered by Certificate of Title.
Subject to the provisions of Sections 2A-304(3) and 2A-305(3), with respect to goods covered by a certificate of title issued under a statute of this State or of another jurisdiction, compliance and the effect of compliance or noncompliance with a certificate of title statute are governed by the law (including the conflict of laws rules) of the jurisdiction issuing the certificate until the earlier of (a) surrender of the certificate, or (b) four months after the goods are removed from that jurisdiction and thereafter until a new certificate of title is issued by another jurisdiction.

## §2A-106. Limitation on Power of Parties to Consumer Lease to Choose Applicable Law and Judicial Forum.

(1) If the law chosen by the parties to a consumer lease is that of a jurisdiction other than a jurisdiction in which the lessee resides at the time the lease agreement becomes enforceable or within 30 days thereafter or in which the goods are to be used, the choice is not enforceable.

(2) If the judicial forum chosen by the parties to a consumer lease is a forum that would not otherwise have jurisdiction over the lessee, the choice is not enforceable.

## §2A-107. Waiver or Renunciation of Claim or Right After Default. Any claim or right arising out of an alleged default or breach of warranty may be discharged in whole or in part without consideration by a written waiver or renunciation signed and delivered by the aggrieved party.

## §2A-108. Unconscionability.

(1) If the court as a matter of law finds a lease contract or any clause of a lease contract to have been unconscionable at the time it was made the court may refuse to enforce the lease contract, or it may enforce the remainder of the lease contract without the unconscionable clause, or it may so limit the

application of any unconscionable clause as to avoid any unconscionable result.

(2) With respect to a consumer lease, if the court as a matter of law finds that a lease contract or any clause of a lease contract has been induced by unconscionable conduct or that unconscionable conduct has occurred in the collection of a claim arising from a lease contract, the court may grant appropriate relief.

(3) Before making a finding of unconscionability under subsection (1) or (2), the court, on its own motion or that of a party, shall afford the parties a reasonable opportunity to present evidence as to the setting, purpose, and effect of the lease contract or clause thereof, or of the conduct.

(4) In an action in which the lessee claims unconscionability with respect to a consumer lease:
   (a) If the court finds unconscionability under subsection (1) or (2), the court shall award reasonable attorney's fees to the lessee.
   (b) If the court does not find unconscionability and the lessee claiming unconscionability has brought or maintained an action he [or she] knew to be groundless, the court shall award reasonable attorney's fees to the party against whom the claim is made.
   (c) In determining attorney's fees, the amount of the recovery on behalf of the claimant under subsections (1) and (2) is not controlling.

## §2A-109. Option to Accelerate at Will.

(1) A term providing that one party or his [or her] successor in interest may accelerate payment or performance or require collateral or additional collateral "at will" or "when he [or she] deems himself [or herself] insecure" or in words of similar import must be construed to mean that he [or she] has power to do so only if he [or she] in good faith believes that the prospect of payment or performance is impaired.

(2) With respect to a consumer lease, the burden of establishing good faith under subsection (1) is on the party who exercised the power; otherwise the burden of establishing lack of good faith is on the party against whom the power has been exercised.

## Part 2: Formation and Construction of Lease Contract

### §2A-201. Statute of Frauds.

(1) A lease contract is not enforceable by way of action or defense unless:
   (a) the total payments to be made under the lease contract, excluding payments for options to renew or buy, are less than $1,000; or
   (b) there is a writing, signed by the party against whom enforcement is sought or by that party's

authorized agent, sufficient to indicate that a lease contract has been made between the parties and to describe the goods leased and the lease term.

(2) Any description of leased goods or of the lease term is sufficient and satisfies subsection (1)(b), whether or not it is specific, if it reasonably identifies what is described.

(3) A writing is not insufficient because it omits or incorrectly states a term agreed upon, but the lease contract is not enforceable under subsection (1)(b) beyond the lease term and the quantity of goods shown in the writing.

(4) A lease contract that does not satisfy the requirements of subsection (1), but which is valid in other respects, is enforceable:
   (a) if the goods are to be specially manufactured or obtained for the lessee and are not suitable for lease or sale to others in the ordinary course of the lessor's business, and the lessor, before notice of repudiation is received and under circumstances that reasonably indicate that the goods are for the lessee, has made either a substantial beginning of their manufacture or commitments for their procurement;
   (b) if the party against whom enforcement is sought admits in that party's pleading, testimony or otherwise in court that a lease contract was made, but the lease contract is not enforceable under this provision beyond the quantity of goods admitted; or
   (c) with respect to goods that have been received and accepted by the lessee.

(5) The lease term under a lease contract referred to in subsection (4) is:
   (a) if there is a writing signed by the party against whom enforcement is sought or by that party's authorized agent specifying the lease term, the term so specified;
   (b) if the party against whom enforcement is sought admits in that party's pleading, testimony, or otherwise in court a lease term, the term so admitted; or
   (c) a reasonable lease term.

### §2A-202. Final Written Expression: Parol or Extrinsic Evidence. 
Terms with respect to which the confirmatory memoranda of the parties agree or which are otherwise set forth in a writing intended by the parties as a final expression of their agreement with respect to such terms as are included therein may not be contradicted by evidence of any prior agreement or of a contemporaneous oral agreement but may be explained or supplemented:

(a) by course of dealing or usage of trade or by course of performance; and

(b) by evidence of consistent additional terms unless the court finds the writing to have been intended also as a complete and exclusive statement of the terms of the agreement.

**§2A-203. Seals Inoperative.** The affixing of a seal to a writing evidencing a lease contract or an offer to enter into a lease contract does not render the writing a sealed instrument and the law with respect to sealed instruments does not apply to the lease contract or offer.

### §2A-204. Formation in General.

(1) A lease contract may be made in any manner sufficient to show agreement, including conduct by both parties which recognizes the existence of a lease contract.

(2) An agreement sufficient to constitute a lease contract may be found although the moment of its making is undetermined.

(3) Although one or more terms are left open, a lease contract does not fail for indefiniteness if the parties have intended to make a lease contract and there is a reasonably certain basis for giving an appropriate remedy.

**§2A-205. Firm Offers.** An offer by a merchant to lease goods to or from another person in a signed writing that by its terms gives assurance it will be held open is not revocable, for lack of consideration, during the time stated or, if no time is stated, for a reasonable time, but in no event may the period of irrevocability exceed 3 months. Any such term of assurance on a form supplied by the offeree must be separately signed by the offeror.

### §2A-206. Offer and Acceptance in Formation of Lease Contract.

(1) Unless otherwise unambiguously indicated by the language or circumstances, an offer to make a lease contract must be construed as inviting acceptance in any manner and by any medium reasonable in the circumstances.

(2) If the beginning of a requested performance is a reasonable mode of acceptance, an offeror who is not notified of acceptance within a reasonable time may treat the offer as having lapsed before acceptance.

### §2A-207. Course of Performance or Practical Construction.

(1) If a lease contract involves repeated occasions for performance by either party with knowledge of the nature of the performance and opportunity for objection to it by the other, any course of performance accepted or acquiesced in without objection is relevant to determine the meaning of the lease agreement.

(2) The express terms of a lease agreement and any course of performance, as well as any course of

dealing and usage of trade, must be construed whenever reasonable as consistent with each other; but if that construction is unreasonable, express terms control course of performance, course of performance controls both course of dealing and usage of trade, and course of dealing controls usage of trade.

(3) Subject to the provisions of Section 2A–208 on modification and waiver, course of performance is relevant to show a waiver or modification of any term inconsistent with the course of performance.

### §2A-208. Modification, Rescission and Waiver.

(1) An agreement modifying a lease contract needs no consideration to be binding.

(2) A signed lease agreement that excludes modification or rescission except by a signed writing may not be otherwise modified or rescinded, but, except as between merchants, such a requirement on a form supplied by a merchant must be separately signed by the other party.

(3) Although an attempt at modification or rescission does not satisfy the requirements of subsection (2), it may operate as a waiver.

(4) A party who has made a waiver affecting an executory portion of a lease contract may retract the waiver by reasonable notification received by the other party that strict performance will be required of any term waived, unless the retraction would be unjust in view of a material change of position in reliance on the waiver.

### §2A-209. Lessee under Finance Lease as Beneficiary of Supply Contract.

(1) The benefit of a supplier's promises to the lessor under the supply contract and of all warranties, whether express or implied, including those of any third party provided in connection with or as part of the supply contract, extends to the lessee to the extent of the lessee's leasehold interest under a finance lease related to the supply contract, but is subject to the terms of the warranty and of the supply contract and all defenses or claims arising therefrom.

(2) The extension of the benefit of a supplier's promises and of warranties to the lessee (Section 2A–209(1)) does not: (i) modify the rights and obligations of the parties to the supply contract, whether arising therefrom or otherwise, or (ii) impose any duty or liability under the supply contract on the lessee.

(3) Any modification or rescission of the supply contract by the supplier and the lessor is effective between the supplier and the lessee unless, before the modification or rescission, the supplier has received notice that the lessee has entered into a finance lease related to the supply contract. If the modification or rescission is effective between the supplier and the lessee,

the lessor is deemed to have assumed, in addition to the obligations of the lessor to the lessee under the lease contract, promises of the supplier to the lessor and warranties that were so modified or rescinded as they existed and were available to the lessee before modification or rescission.

(4) In addition to the extension of the benefit of the supplier's promises and of warranties to the lessee under subsection (1), the lessee retains all rights that the lessee may have against the supplier which arise from an agreement between the lessee and the supplier or under other law.

## §2A-210. Express Warranties.

(1) Express warranties by the lessor are created as follows:

(a) Any affirmation of fact or promise made by the lessor to the lessee which relates to the goods and becomes part of the basis of the bargain creates an express warranty that the goods will conform to the affirmation or promise.

(b) Any description of the goods which is made part of the basis of the bargain creates an express warranty that the goods will conform to the description.

(c) Any sample or model that is made part of the basis of the bargain creates an express warranty that the whole of the goods will conform to the sample or model.

(2) It is not necessary to the creation of an express warranty that the lessor use formal words, such as "warrant" or "guarantee," or that the lessor have a specific intention to make a warranty, but an affirmation merely of the value of the goods or a statement purporting to be merely the lessor's opinion or commendation of the goods does not create a warranty.

## §2A-211. Warranties against Interference and against Infringement; Lessee's Obligation Against Infringement.

(1) There is in a lease contract a warranty that for the lease term no person holds a claim to or interest in the goods that arose from an act or omission of the lessor, other than a claim by way of infringement or the like, which will interfere with the lessee's enjoyment of its leasehold interest.

(2) Except in a finance lease there is in a lease contract by a lessor who is a merchant regularly dealing in goods of the kind a warranty that the goods are delivered free of the rightful claim of any person by way of infringement or the like.

(3) A lessee who furnishes specifications to a lessor or a supplier shall hold the lessor and the supplier harmless against any claim by way of infringement or the like that arises out of compliance with the specifications.

## §2A-212. Implied Warranty of Merchantability.

(1) Except in a finance lease, a warranty that the goods will be merchantable is implied in a lease contract if the lessor is a merchant with respect to goods of that kind.

(2) Goods to be merchantable must be at least such as

(a) pass without objection in the trade under the description in the lease agreement;

(b) in the case of fungible goods, are of fair average quality within the description;

(c) are fit for the ordinary purposes for which goods of that type are used;

(d) run, within the variation permitted by the lease agreement, of even kind, quality, and quantity within each unit and among all units involved;

(e) are adequately contained, packaged, and labeled as the lease agreement may require; and

(f) conform to any promises or affirmations of fact made on the container or label.

(3) Other implied warranties may arise from course of dealing or usage of trade.

## §2A-213. Implied Warranty of Fitness for Particular Purpose. 
Except in a finance lease, if the lessor at the time the lease contract is made has reason to know of any particular purpose for which the goods are required and that the lessee is relying on the lessor's skill or judgment to select or furnish suitable goods, there is in the lease contract an implied warranty that the goods will be fit for that purpose.

## §2A-214. Exclusion or Modification of Warranties.

(1) Words or conduct relevant to the creation of an express warranty and words or conduct tending to negate or limit a warranty must be construed wherever reasonable as consistent with each other; but, subject to the provisions of Section 2A–202 on parol or extrinsic evidence, negation or limitation is inoperative to the extent that the construction is unreasonable.

(2) Subject to subsection (3), to exclude or modify the implied warranty of merchantability or any part of it the language must mention "merchantability", be by a writing, and be conspicuous. Subject to subsection (3), to exclude or modify any implied warranty of fitness the exclusion must be by a writing and be conspicuous. Language to exclude all implied warranties of fitness is sufficient if it is in writing, is conspicuous and states, for example, "There is no warranty that the goods will be fit for a particular purpose".

(3) Notwithstanding subsection (2), but subject to subsection (4),

(a) unless the circumstances indicate otherwise, all implied warranties are excluded by expressions like "as is," or "with all faults," or by other language that in common understanding calls the lessee's attention to the exclusion of warranties and makes plain that there is no implied warranty, if in writing and conspicuous;

(b) if the lessee before entering into the lease contract has examined the goods or the sample or model as fully as desired or has refused to examine the goods, there is no implied warranty with regard to defects that an examination ought in the circumstances to have revealed; and

(c) an implied warranty may also be excluded or modified by course of dealing, course of performance, or usage of trade.

(4) To exclude or modify a warranty against interference or against infringement (Section 2A–211) or any part of it, the language must be specific, be by a writing, and be conspicuous, unless the circumstances, including course of performance, course of dealing, or usage of trade, give the lessee reason to know that the goods are being leased subject to a claim or interest of any person.

## §2A-215. Cumulation and Conflict of Warranties Express or Implied.
Warranties, whether express or implied, must be construed as consistent with each other and as cumulative, but if that construction is unreasonable, the intention of the parties determines which warranty is dominant. In ascertaining that intention the following rules apply:

(a) Exact or technical specifications displace an inconsistent sample or model or general language of description.

(b) A sample from an existing bulk displaces inconsistent general language of description.

(c) Express warranties displace inconsistent implied warranties other than an implied warranty of fitness for a particular purpose.

## §2A-216. Third-Party Beneficiaries of Express and Implied Warranties.
**Alternative A**—A warranty to or for the benefit of a lessee under this Article, whether express or implied, extends to any natural person who is in the family or household of the lessee or who is a guest in the lessee's home if it is reasonable to expect that such person may use, consume, or be affected by the goods and who is injured in person by breach of the warranty. This section does not displace principles of law and equity that extend a warranty to or for the benefit of a lessee to other persons. The operation of this section may not be excluded, modified, or limited, but an exclusion, modification, or limitation of the warranty, including any with respect to rights and remedies, effective against the lessee is also effective against any beneficiary designated under this section.

**Alternative B**—A warranty to or for the benefit of a lessee under this Article, whether express or implied, extends to any natural person who may reasonably be expected to use, consume, or be affected by the goods and who is injured in person by breach of the warranty. This section does not displace principles of law and equity that extend a warranty to or for the benefit of a lessee to other persons. The operation of this section may not be excluded, modified, or limited, but an exclusion, modification, or limitation of the warranty, including any with respect to rights and remedies, effective against the lessee is also effective against the beneficiary designated under this section.

**Alternative C**—A warranty to or for the benefit of a lessee under this Article, whether express or implied, extends to any person who may reasonably be expected to use, consume, or be affected by the goods and who is injured by breach of the warranty. The operation of this section may not be excluded, modified, or limited with respect to injury to the person of an individual to whom the warranty extends, but an exclusion, modification, or limitation of the warranty, including any with respect to rights and remedies, effective against the lessee is also effective against the beneficiary designated under this section.

## §2A-217. Identification.
Identification of goods as goods to which a lease contract refers may be made at any time and in any manner explicitly agreed to by the parties. In the absence of explicit agreement, identification occurs:

(a) when the lease contract is made if the lease contract is for a lease of goods that are existing and identified;

(b) when the goods are shipped, marked, or otherwise designated by the lessor as goods to which the lease contract refers, if the lease contract is for a lease of goods that are not existing and identified; or

(c) when the young are conceived, if the lease contract is for a lease of unborn young of animals.

## §2A-218. Insurance and Proceeds.
(1) A lessee obtains an insurable interest when existing goods are identified to the lease contract even though the goods identified are nonconforming and the lessee has an option to reject them.

(2) If a lessee has an insurable interest only by reason of the lessor's identification of the goods, the lessor, until default or insolvency or notification to the lessee that identification is final, may substitute other goods for those identified.

(3) Notwithstanding a lessee's insurable interest under subsections (1) and (2), the lessor retains an insurable interest until an option to buy has been exercised by the lessee and risk of loss has passed to the lessee.

(4) Nothing in this section impairs any insurable interest recognized under any other statute or rule of law.

(5) The parties by agreement may determine that one or more parties have an obligation to obtain and pay for insurance covering the goods and by agreement may determine the beneficiary of the proceeds of the insurance.

### §2A-219. Risk of Loss.

(1) Except in the case of a finance lease, risk of loss is retained by the lessor and does not pass to the lessee. In the case of a finance lease, risk of loss passes to the lessee.

(2) Subject to the provisions of this Article on the effect of default on risk of loss (Section 2A–220), if risk of loss is to pass to the lessee and the time of passage is not stated, the following rules apply:

(a) If the lease contract requires or authorizes the goods to be shipped by carrier

(i) and it does not require delivery at a particular destination, the risk of loss passes to the lessee when the goods are duly delivered to the carrier; but

(ii) if it does require delivery at a particular destination and the goods are there duly tendered while in the possession of the carrier, the risk of loss passes to the lessee when the goods are there duly so tendered as to enable the lessee to take delivery.

(b) If the goods are held by a bailee to be delivered without being moved, the risk of loss passes to the lessee on acknowledgment by the bailee of the lessee's right to possession of the goods.

(c) In any case not within subsection (a) or (b), the risk of loss passes to the lessee on the lessee's receipt of the goods if the lessor, or, in the case of a finance lease, the supplier, is a merchant; otherwise the risk passes to the lessee on tender of delivery.

### §2A-220. Effect of Default on Risk of Loss.

(1) Where risk of loss is to pass to the lessee and the time of passage is not stated:

(a) If a tender or delivery of goods so fails to conform to the lease contract as to give a right of rejection, the risk of their loss remains with the lessor, or, in the case of a finance lease, the supplier, until cure or acceptance.

(b) If the lessee rightfully revokes acceptance, he [or she], to the extent of any deficiency in his [or her] effective insurance coverage, may treat the risk of loss as having remained with the lessor from the beginning.

(2) Whether or not risk of loss is to pass to the lessee, if the lessee as to conforming goods already identified to a lease contract repudiates or is otherwise in default under the lease contract, the lessor, or, in the case of a finance lease, the supplier, to the extent of any deficiency in his [or her] effective insurance coverage may treat the risk of loss as resting on the lessee for a commercially reasonable time.

### §2A-221. Casualty to Identified Goods. If a lease contract requires goods identified when the lease contract is made, and the goods suffer casualty without fault of the lessee, the lessor or the supplier before delivery, or the goods suffer casualty before risk of loss passes to the lessee pursuant to the lease agreement or Section 2A-219, then:

(a) if the loss is total, the lease contract is avoided; and

(b) if the loss is partial or the goods have so deteriorated as to no longer conform to the lease contract, the lessee may nevertheless demand inspection and at his [or her] option either treat the lease contract as avoided or, except in a finance lease that is not a consumer lease, accept the goods with due allowance from the rent payable for the balance of the lease term for the deterioration or the deficiency in quantity but without further right against the lessor.

## Part 3: Effect of Lease Contract

### §2A-301. Enforceability of Lease Contract. Except as otherwise provided in this Article, a lease contract is effective and enforceable according to its terms between the parties, against purchasers of the goods and against creditors of the parties.

### §2A-302. Title to and Possession of Goods. Except as otherwise provided in this Article, each provision of this Article applies whether the lessor or a third party has title to the goods, and whether the lessor, the lessee, or a third party has possession of the goods, notwithstanding any statute or rule of law that possession or the absence of possession is fraudulent.

### §2A-303. Alienability of Party's Interest Under Lease Contract or of Lessor's Residual Interest in Goods; Delegation of Performance; Transfer of Rights.

(1) As used in this section, "creation of a security interest" includes the sale of a lease contract that is subject to Article 9, Secured Transactions, by reason of Section 9–102(1)(b).

(2) Except as provided in subsections (3) and (4), a provision in a lease agreement which (i) prohibits the voluntary or involuntary transfer, including a transfer by sale, sublease, creation or enforcement of a security interest, or attachment, levy, or other judicial process, of an interest of a party under the lease

contract or of the lessor's residual interest in the goods, or (ii) makes such a transfer an event of default, gives rise to the rights and remedies provided in subsection (5), but a transfer that is prohibited or is an event of default under the lease agreement is otherwise effective.

(3) A provision in a lease agreement which (i) prohibits the creation or enforcement of a security interest in an interest of a party under the lease contract or in the lessor's residual interest in the goods, or (ii) makes such a transfer an event of default, is not enforceable unless, and then only to the extent that, there is an actual transfer by the lessee of the lessee's right of possession or use of the goods in violation of the provision or an actual delegation of a material performance of either party to the lease contract in violation of the provision. Neither the granting nor the enforcement of a security interest in (i) the lessor's interest under the lease contract or (ii) the lessor's residual interest in the goods is a transfer that materially impairs the prospect of obtaining return performance by, materially changes the duty of, or materially increases the burden or risk imposed on, the lessee within the purview of subsection (5) unless, and then only to the extent that, there is an actual delegation of a material performance of the lessor.

(4) A provision in a lease agreement which (i) prohibits a transfer of a right to damages for default with respect to the whole lease contract or of a right to payment arising out of the transferor's due performance of the transferor's entire obligation, or (ii) makes such a transfer an event of default, is not enforceable, and such a transfer is not a transfer that materially impairs the prospect of obtaining return performance by, materially changes the duty of, or materially increases the burden or risk imposed on, the other party to the lease contract within the purview of subsection (5).

(5) Subject to subsections (3) and (4):

(a) if a transfer is made which is made an event of default under a lease agreement, the party to the lease contract not making the transfer, unless that party waives the default or otherwise agrees, has the rights and remedies described in Section 2A–501(2);

(b) if paragraph (a) is not applicable and if a transfer is made that (i) is prohibited under a lease agreement or (ii) materially impairs the prospect of obtaining return performance by, materially changes the duty of, or materially increases the burden or risk imposed on, the other party to the lease contract, unless the party not making the transfer agrees at any time to the transfer in the lease contract or otherwise, then, except as limited by contract, (i) the transferor is liable to the party not making the transfer for damages caused by the transfer to the extent that the damages could not reasonably be prevented by the party not making the transfer and (ii) a court having jurisdiction may grant other appropriate relief, including cancellation of the lease contract or an injunction against the transfer.

(6) A transfer of "the lease" or of "all my rights under the lease", or a transfer in similar general terms, is a transfer of rights and, unless the language or the circumstances, as in a transfer for security, indicate the contrary, the transfer is a delegation of duties by the transferor to the transferee. Acceptance by the transferee constitutes a promise by the transferee to perform those duties. The promise is enforceable by either the transferor or the other party to the lease contract.

(7) Unless otherwise agreed by the lessor and the lessee, a delegation of performance does not relieve the transferor as against the other party of any duty to perform or of any liability for default.

(8) In a consumer lease, to prohibit the transfer of an interest of a party under the lease contract or to make a transfer an event of default, the language must be specific, by a writing, and conspicuous.

## §2A-304. Subsequent Lease of Goods by Lessor.

(1) Subject to Section 2A–303, a subsequent lessee from a lessor of goods under an existing lease contract obtains, to the extent of the leasehold interest transferred, the leasehold interest in the goods that the lessor had or had power to transfer, and except as provided in subsection (2) and Section 2A–527(4), takes subject to the existing lease contract. A lessor with voidable title has power to transfer a good leasehold interest to a good faith subsequent lessee for value, but only to the extent set forth in the preceding sentence. If goods have been delivered under a transaction of purchase, the lessor has that power even though:

(a) the lessor's transferor was deceived as to the identity of the lessor;

(b) the delivery was in exchange for a check which is later dishonored;

(c) it was agreed that the transaction was to be a "cash sale"; or

(d) the delivery was procured through fraud punishable as larcenous under the criminal law.

(2) A subsequent lessee in the ordinary course of business from a lessor who is a merchant dealing in goods of that kind to whom the goods were entrusted by the existing lessee of that lessor before the interest of the subsequent lessee became enforceable against that lessor obtains, to the extent of the leasehold interest transferred, all of that lessor's and the existing

lessee's rights to the goods, and takes free of the existing lease contract.

(3) A subsequent lessee from the lessor of goods that are subject to an existing lease contract and are covered by a certificate of title issued under a statute of this State or of another jurisdiction takes no greater rights than those provided both by this section and by the certificate of title statute.

## §2A-305. Sale or Sublease of Goods by Lessee.

(1) Subject to the provisions of Section 2A–303, a buyer or sublessee from the lessee of goods under an existing lease contract obtains, to the extent of the interest transferred, the leasehold interest in the goods that the lessee had or had power to transfer, and except as provided in subsection (2) and Section 2A–511(4), takes subject to the existing lease contract. A lessee with a voidable leasehold interest has power to transfer a good leasehold interest to a good faith buyer for value or a good faith sublessee for value, but only to the extent set forth in the preceding sentence. When goods have been delivered under a transaction of lease the lessee has that power even though:

(a) the lessor was deceived as to the identity of the lessee;

(b) the delivery was in exchange for a check which is later dishonored; or

(c) the delivery was procured through fraud punishable as larcenous under the criminal law.

(2) A buyer in the ordinary course of business or a sublessee in the ordinary course of business from a lessee who is a merchant dealing in goods of that kind to whom the goods were entrusted by the lessor obtains, to the extent of the interest transferred, all of the lessor's and lessee's rights to the goods, and takes free of the existing lease contract.

(3) A buyer or sublessee from the lessee of goods that are subject to an existing lease contract and are covered by a certificate of title issued under a statute of this State or of another jurisdiction takes no greater rights than those provided both by this section and by the certificate of title statute.

## §2A-306. Priority of Certain Liens Arising by Operation of Law.
If a person in the ordinary course of his [or her] business furnishes services or materials with respect to goods subject to a lease contract, a lien upon those goods in the possession of that person given by statute or rule of law for those materials or services takes priority over any interest of the lessor or lessee under the lease contract or this Article unless the lien is created by statute and the statute provides otherwise or unless the lien is created by rule of law and the rule of law provides otherwise.

## §2A-307. Priority of Liens Arising by Attachment or Levy on, Security Interests in, and Other Claims to Goods.

(1) Except as otherwise provided in Section 2A–306, a creditor of a lessee takes subject to the lease contract.

(2) Except as otherwise provided in subsections (3) and (4) and in Sections 2A–306 and 2A–308, a creditor of a lessor takes subject to the lease contract unless:

(a) the creditor holds a lien that attached to the goods before the lease contract became enforceable;

(b) the creditor holds a security interest in the goods and the lessee did not give value and receive delivery of the goods without knowledge of the security interest; or

(c) the creditor holds a security interest in the goods which was perfected (Section 9–303) before the lease contract became enforceable.

(3) A lessee in the ordinary course of business takes the leasehold interest free of a security interest in the goods created by the lessor even though the security interest is perfected (Section 9–303) and the lessee knows of its existence.

(4) A lessee other than a lessee in the ordinary course of business takes the leasehold interest free of a security interest to the extent that it secures future advances made after the secured party acquires knowledge of the lease or more than 45 days after the lease contract becomes enforceable, whichever first occurs, unless the future advances are made pursuant to a commitment entered into without knowledge of the lease and before the expiration of the 45-day period.

## §2A-308. Special Rights of Creditors.

(1) A creditor of a lessor in possession of goods subject to a lease contract may treat the lease contract as void if as against the creditor retention of possession by the lessor is fraudulent under any statute or rule of law, but retention of possession in good faith and current course of trade by the lessor for a commercially reasonable time after the lease contract becomes enforceable is not fraudulent.

(2) Nothing in this Article impairs the rights of creditors of a lessor if the lease contract (a) becomes enforceable, not in current course of trade but in satisfaction of or as security for a pre-existing claim for money, security, or the like, and (b) is made under circumstances which under any statute or rule of law apart from this Article would constitute the transaction a fraudulent transfer or voidable preference.

(3) A creditor of a seller may treat a sale or an identification of goods to a contract for sale as void if as against the creditor retention of possession by the seller is fraudulent under any statute or rule of law, but retention of possession of the goods pursuant to a lease contract entered into by the seller as lessee and

the buyer as lessor in connection with the sale or identification of the goods is not fraudulent if the buyer bought for value and in good faith.

## §2A-309. Lessor's and Lessee's Rights When Goods Become Fixtures.

(1) In this section:

    (a) goods are "fixtures" when they become so related to particular real estate that an interest in them arises under real estate law;

    (b) a "fixture filing" is the filing, in the office where a mortgage on the real estate would be filed or recorded, of a financing statement covering goods that are or are to become fixtures and conforming to the requirements of Section 9–402(5);

    (c) a lease is a "purchase money lease" unless the lessee has possession or use of the goods or the right to possession or use of the goods before the lease agreement is enforceable;

    (d) a mortgage is a "construction mortgage" to the extent it secures an obligation incurred for the construction of an improvement on land including the acquisition cost of the land, if the recorded writing so indicates; and

    (e) "encumbrance" includes real estate mortgages and other liens on real estate and all other rights in real estate that are not ownership interests.

(2) Under this Article a lease may be of goods that are fixtures or may continue in goods that become fixtures, but no lease exists under this Article of ordinary building materials incorporated into an improvement on land.

(3) This Article does not prevent creation of a lease of fixtures pursuant to real estate law.

(4) The perfected interest of a lessor of fixtures has priority over a conflicting interest of an encumbrancer or owner of the real estate if:

    (a) the lease is a purchase money lease, the conflicting interest of the encumbrancer or owner arises before the goods become fixtures, the interest of the lessor is perfected by a fixture filing before the goods become fixtures or within ten days thereafter, and the lessee has an interest of record in the real estate or is in possession of the real estate; or

    (b) the interest of the lessor is perfected by a fixture filing before the interest of the encumbrancer or owner is of record, the lessor's interest has priority over any conflicting interest of a predecessor in title of the encumbrancer or owner, and the lessee has an interest of record in the real estate or is in possession of the real estate.

(5) The interest of a lessor of fixtures, whether or not perfected, has priority over the conflicting interest of an encumbrancer or owner of the real estate if:

    (a) the fixtures are readily removable factory or office machines, readily removable equipment that is not primarily used or leased for use in the operation of the real estate, or readily removable replacements of domestic appliances that are goods subject to a consumer lease, and before the goods become fixtures the lease contract is enforceable; or

    (b) the conflicting interest is a lien on the real estate obtained by legal or equitable proceedings after the lease contract is enforceable; or

    (c) the encumbrancer or owner has consented in writing to the lease or has disclaimed an interest in the goods as fixtures; or

    (d) the lessee has a right to remove the goods as against the encumbrancer or owner. If the lessee's right to remove terminates, the priority of the interest of the lessor continues for a reasonable time.

(6) Notwithstanding subsection (4)(a) but otherwise subject to subsections (4) and (5), the interest of a lessor of fixtures, including the lessor's residual interest, is subordinate to the conflicting interest of an encumbrancer of the real estate under a construction mortgage recorded before the goods become fixtures if the goods become fixtures before the completion of the construction. To the extent given to refinance a construction mortgage, the conflicting interest of an encumbrancer of the real estate under a mortgage has this priority to the same extent as the encumbrancer of the real estate under the construction mortgage.

(7) In cases not within the preceding subsections, priority between the interest of a lessor of fixtures, including the lessor's residual interest, and the conflicting interest of an encumbrancer or owner of the real estate who is not the lessee is determined by the priority rules governing conflicting interests in real estate.

(8) If the interest of a lessor of fixtures, including the lessor's residual interest, has priority over all conflicting interests of all owners and encumbrancers of the real estate, the lessor or the lessee may (i) on default, expiration, termination, or cancellation of the lease agreement but subject to the agreement and this Article, or (ii) if necessary to enforce other rights and remedies of the lessor or lessee under this Article, remove the goods from the real estate, free and clear of all conflicting interests of all owners and encumbrancers of the real estate, but the lessor or lessee must reimburse any encumbrancer or owner of the real estate who is not the lessee and who has not otherwise agreed for the cost of repair of any physical injury, but not for any diminution in value of the real estate caused by the absence of the goods removed or by any necessity of replacing them. A person entitled to reimbursement may refuse permission to remove until the party seeking removal gives adequate security for the performance of this obligation.

(9) Even though the lease agreement does not create a security interest, the interest of a lessor of fixtures, including the lessor's residual interest, is perfected by filing a financing statement as a fixture filing for leased goods that are or are to become fixtures in accordance with the relevant provisions of the Article on Secured Transactions (Article 9).

## §2A-310. Lessor's and Lessee's Rights When Goods Become Accessions.

(1) Goods are "accessions" when they are installed in or affixed to other goods.

(2) The interest of a lessor or a lessee under a lease contract entered into before the goods became accessions is superior to all interests in the whole except as stated in subsection (4).

(3) The interest of a lessor or a lessee under a lease contract entered into at the time or after the goods became accessions is superior to all subsequently acquired interests in the whole except as stated in subsection (4) but is subordinate to interests in the whole existing at the time the lease contract was made unless the holders of such interests in the whole have in writing consented to the lease or disclaimed an interest in the goods as part of the whole.

(4) The interest of a lessor or a lessee under a lease contract described in subsection (2) or (3) is subordinate to the interest of

   (a) a buyer in the ordinary course of business or a lessee in the ordinary course of business of any interest in the whole acquired after the goods became accessions; or

   (b) a creditor with a security interest in the whole perfected before the lease contract was made to the extent that the creditor makes subsequent advances without knowledge of the lease contract.

(5) When under subsections (2) or (3) and (4) a lessor or a lessee of accessions holds an interest that is superior to all interests in the whole, the lessor or the lessee may (a) on default, expiration, termination, or cancellation of the lease contract by the other party but subject to the provisions of the lease contract and this Article, or (b) if necessary to enforce his [or her] other rights and remedies under this Article, remove the goods from the whole, free and clear of all interests in the whole, but he [or she] must reimburse any holder of an interest in the whole who is not the lessee and who has not otherwise agreed for the cost of repair of any physical injury but not for any diminution in value of the whole caused by the absence of the goods removed or by any necessity for replacing them. A person entitled to reimbursement may refuse permission to remove until the party seeking removal gives adequate security for the performance of this obligation.

## §2A-311. Priority Subject to Subordination.
Nothing in this Article prevents subordination by agreement by any person entitled to priority.

## Part 4: Performance of Lease Contract: Repudiated, Substituted and Excused

## §2A-401. Insecurity: Adequate Assurance of Performance.

(1) A lease contract imposes an obligation on each party that the other's expectation of receiving due performance will not be impaired.

(2) If reasonable grounds for insecurity arise with respect to the performance of either party, the insecure party may demand in writing adequate assurance of due performance. Until the insecure party receives that assurance, if commercially reasonable the insecure party may suspend any performance for which he [or she] has not already received the agreed return.

(3) A repudiation of the lease contract occurs if assurance of due performance adequate under the circumstances of the particular case is not provided to the insecure party within a reasonable time, not to exceed 30 days after receipt of a demand by the other party.

(4) Between merchants, the reasonableness of grounds for insecurity and the adequacy of any assurance offered must be determined according to commercial standards.

(5) Acceptance of any nonconforming delivery or payment does not prejudice the aggrieved party's right to demand adequate assurance of future performance.

## §2A-402. Anticipatory Repudiation.
If either party repudiates a lease contract with respect to a performance not yet due under the lease contract, the loss of which performance will substantially impair the value of the lease contract to the other, the aggrieved party may:

(a) for a commercially reasonable time, await retraction of repudiation and performance by the repudiating party;

(b) make demand pursuant to Section 2A–401 and await assurance of future performance adequate under the circumstances of the particular case; or

(c) resort to any right or remedy upon default under the lease contract or this Article, even though the aggrieved party has notified the repudiating party that the aggrieved party would await the repudiating party's performance and assurance and has urged retraction. In addition, whether or not the aggrieved party is pursuing one of the foregoing remedies, the aggrieved party may suspend performance or, if the aggrieved party is the lessor, proceed in accordance with the provisions of this Article on the lessor's right to identify goods to the lease contract notwithstanding default or to salvage unfinished goods (Section 2A–524).

## §2A-403. Retraction of Anticipatory Repudiation.

(1) Until the repudiating party's next performance is due, the repudiating party can retract the repudiation unless, since the repudiation, the aggrieved party has cancelled the lease contract or materially changed the aggrieved party's position or otherwise indicated that the aggrieved party considers the repudiation final.

(2) Retraction may be by any method that clearly indicates to the aggrieved party that the repudiating party intends to perform under the lease contract and includes any assurance demanded under Section 2A–401.

(3) Retraction reinstates a repudiating party's rights under a lease contract with due excuse and allowance to the aggrieved party for any delay occasioned by the repudiation.

## §2A-404. Substituted Performance.

(1) If without fault of the lessee, the lessor and the supplier, the agreed berthing, loading, or unloading facilities fail or the agreed type of carrier becomes unavailable or the agreed manner of delivery otherwise becomes commercially impracticable, but a commercially reasonable substitute is available, the substitute performance must be tendered and accepted.

(2) If the agreed means or manner of payment fails because of domestic or foreign governmental regulation:

  (a) the lessor may withhold or stop delivery or cause the supplier to withhold or stop delivery unless the lessee provides a means or manner of payment that is commercially a substantial equivalent; and

  (b) if delivery has already been taken, payment by the means or in the manner provided by the regulation discharges the lessee's obligation unless the regulation is discriminatory, oppressive, or predatory.

## §2A-405. Excused Performance. Subject to Section 2A-404 on substituted performance, the following rules apply:

(a) Delay in delivery or nondelivery in whole or in part by a lessor or a supplier who complies with paragraphs (b) and (c) is not a default under the lease contract if performance as agreed has been made impracticable by the occurrence of a contingency the nonoccurrence of which was a basic assumption on which the lease contract was made or by compliance in good faith with any applicable foreign or domestic governmental regulation or order, whether or not the regulation or order later proves to be invalid.

(b) If the causes mentioned in paragraph (a) affect only part of the lessor's or the supplier's capacity to perform, he [or she] shall allocate production and deliveries among his [or her] customers but at his [or her] option may include regular customers not then under contract for sale or lease as well as his [or her] own requirements for further manufacture. He [or she] may so allocate in any manner that is fair and reasonable.

(c) The lessor seasonably shall notify the lessee and in the case of a finance lease the supplier seasonably shall notify the lessor and the lessee, if known, that there will be delay or nondelivery and, if allocation is required under paragraph (b), of the estimated quota thus made available for the lessee.

## §2A-406. Procedure on Excused Performance.

(1) If the lessee receives notification of a material or indefinite delay or an allocation justified under Section 2A–405, the lessee may by written notification to the lessor as to any goods involved, and with respect to all of the goods if under an installment lease contract the value of the whole lease contract is substantially impaired (Section 2A–510):

  (a) terminate the lease contract (Section 2A–505(2)); or

  (b) except in a finance lease that is not a consumer lease, modify the lease contract by accepting the available quota in substitution, with due allowance from the rent payable for the balance of the lease term for the deficiency but without further right against the lessor.

(2) If, after receipt of a notification from the lessor under Section 2A–405, the lessee fails so to modify the lease agreement within a reasonable time not exceeding 30 days, the lease contract lapses with respect to any deliveries affected.

## §2A-407. Irrevocable Promises: Finance Leases.

(1) In the case of a finance lease that is not a consumer lease the lessee's promises under the lease contract become irrevocable and independent upon the lessee's acceptance of the goods.

(2) A promise that has become irrevocable and independent under subsection (1):

  (a) is effective and enforceable between the parties, and by or against third parties including assignees of the parties; and

  (b) is not subject to cancellation, termination, modification, repudiation, excuse, or substitution without the consent of the party to whom the promise runs.

(3) This section does not affect the validity under any other law of a covenant in any lease contract making the lessee's promises irrevocable and independent upon the lessee's acceptance of the goods.

## Part 5: Default

### A. In General

### §2A-501. Default: Procedure.

(1) Whether the lessor or the lessee is in default under a lease contract is determined by the lease agreement and this Article.

(2) If the lessor or the lessee is in default under the lease contract, the party seeking enforcement has rights and remedies as provided in this Article and, except as limited by this Article, as provided in the lease agreement.

(3) If the lessor or the lessee is in default under the lease contract, the party seeking enforcement may reduce the party's claim to judgment, or otherwise enforce the lease contract by self-help or any available judicial procedure or nonjudicial procedure, including administrative proceeding, arbitration, or the like, in accordance with this Article.

(4) Except as otherwise provided in Section 1–106(1) or this Article or the lease agreement, the rights and remedies referred to in subsections (2) and (3) are cumulative.

(5) If the lease agreement covers both real property and goods, the party seeking enforcement may proceed under this Part as to the goods, or under other applicable law as to both the real property and the goods in accordance with that party's rights and remedies in respect of the real property, in which case this Part does not apply.

### §2A-502. Notice after Default. Except as otherwise provided in this Article or the lease agreement, the lessor or lessee in default under the lease contract is not entitled to notice of default or notice of enforcement from the other party to the lease agreement.

### §2A-503. Modification or Impairment of Rights and Remedies.

(1) Except as otherwise provided in this Article, the lease agreement may include rights and remedies for default in addition to or in substitution for those provided in this Article and may limit or alter the measure of damages recoverable under this Article.

(2) Resort to a remedy provided under this Article or in the lease agreement is optional unless the remedy is expressly agreed to be exclusive. If circumstances cause an exclusive or limited remedy to fail of its essential purpose, or provision for an exclusive remedy is unconscionable, remedy may be had as provided in this Article.

(3) Consequential damages may be liquidated under Section 2A–504, or may otherwise be limited, altered, or excluded unless the limitation, alteration, or exclusion is unconscionable. Limitation, alteration, or exclusion of consequential damages for injury to the person in the case of consumer goods is prima facie unconscionable but limitation, alteration, or exclusion of damages where the loss is commercial is not prima facie unconscionable.

(4) Rights and remedies on default by the lessor or the lessee with respect to any obligation or promise collateral or ancillary to the lease contract are not impaired by this Article.

### §2A-504. Liquidation of Damages.

(1) Damages payable by either party for default, or any other act or omission, including indemnity for loss or diminution of anticipated tax benefits or loss or damage to lessor's residual interest, may be liquidated in the lease agreement but only at an amount or by a formula that is reasonable in light of the then anticipated harm caused by the default or other act or omission.

(2) If the lease agreement provides for liquidation of damages, and such provision does not comply with subsection (1), or such provision is an exclusive or limited remedy that circumstances cause to fail of its essential purpose, remedy may be had as provided in this Article.

(3) If the lessor justifiably withholds or stops delivery of goods because of the lessee's default or insolvency (Section 2A–525 or 2A–526), the lessee is entitled to restitution of any amount by which the sum of his [or her] payments exceeds:

(a) the amount to which the lessor is entitled by virtue of terms liquidating the lessor's damages in accordance with subsection (1); or

(b) in the absence of those terms, 20 percent of the then present value of the total rent the lessee was obligated to pay for the balance of the lease term, or, in the case of a consumer lease, the lesser of such amount or $500.

(4) A lessee's right to restitution under subsection (3) is subject to offset to the extent the lessor establishes:

(a) a right to recover damages under the provisions of this Article other than subsection (1); and

(b) the amount or value of any benefits received by the lessee directly or indirectly by reason of the lease contract.

### §2A-505. Cancellation and Termination and Effect of Cancellation, Termination, Rescission, or Fraud on Rights and Remedies.

(1) On cancellation of the lease contract, all obligations that are still executory on both sides are discharged, but any right based on prior default or performance

survives, and the cancelling party also retains any remedy for default of the whole lease contract or any unperformed balance.

(2) On termination of the lease contract, all obligations that are still executory on both sides are discharged but any right based on prior default or performance survives.

(3) Unless the contrary intention clearly appears, expressions of "cancellation," "rescission," or the like of the lease contract may not be construed as a renunciation or discharge of any claim in damages for an antecedent default.

(4) Rights and remedies for material misrepresentation or fraud include all rights and remedies available under this Article for default.

(5) Neither rescission nor a claim for rescission of the lease contract nor rejection or return of the goods may bar or be deemed inconsistent with a claim for damages or other right or remedy.

## §2A-506. Statute of Limitations.

(1) An action for default under a lease contract, including breach of warranty or indemnity, must be commenced within 4 years after the cause of action accrued. By the original lease contract the parties may reduce the period of limitation to not less than one year.

(2) A cause of action for default accrues when the act or omission on which the default or breach of warranty is based is or should have been discovered by the aggrieved party, or when the default occurs, whichever is later. A cause of action for indemnity accrues when the act or omission on which the claim for indemnity is based is or should have been discovered by the indemnified party, whichever is later.

(3) If an action commenced within the time limited by subsection (1) is so terminated as to leave available a remedy by another action for the same default or breach of warranty or indemnity, the other action may be commenced after the expiration of the time limited and within 6 months after the termination of the first action unless the termination resulted from voluntary discontinuance or from dismissal for failure or neglect to prosecute.

(4) This section does not alter the law on tolling of the statute of limitations nor does it apply to causes of action that have accrued before this Article becomes effective.

## §2A-507. Proof of Market Rent: Time and Place.

(1) Damages based on market rent (Section 2A–519 or 2A–528) are determined according to the rent for the use of the goods concerned for a lease term identical to the remaining lease term of the original lease agreement and prevailing at the times specified in Sections 2A–519 and 2A–528.

(2) If evidence of rent for the use of the goods concerned for a lease term identical to the remaining lease term of the original lease agreement and prevailing at the times or places described in this Article is not readily available, the rent prevailing within any reasonable time before or after the time described or at any other place or for a different lease term which in commercial judgment or under usage of trade would serve as a reasonable substitute for the one described may be used, making any proper allowance for the difference, including the cost of transporting the goods to or from the other place.

(3) Evidence of a relevant rent prevailing at a time or place or for a lease term other than the one described in this Article offered by one party is not admissible unless and until he [or she] has given the other party notice the court finds sufficient to prevent unfair surprise.

(4) If the prevailing rent or value of any goods regularly leased in any established market is in issue, reports in official publications or trade journals or in newspapers or periodicals of general circulation published as the reports of that market are admissible in evidence. The circumstances of the preparation of the report may be shown to affect its weight but not its admissibility.

## B. Default by Lessor

## §2A-508. Lessee's Remedies.

(1) If a lessor fails to deliver the goods in conformity to the lease contract (Section 2A–509) or repudiates the lease contract (Section 2A–402), or a lessee rightfully rejects the goods (Section 2A–509) or justifiably revokes acceptance of the goods (Section 2A–517), then with respect to any goods involved, and with respect to all of the goods if under an installment lease contract the value of the whole lease contract is substantially impaired (Section 2A–510), the lessor is in default under the lease contract and the lessee may:

(a) cancel the lease contract (Section 2A–505(1));

(b) recover so much of the rent and security as has been paid and is just under the circumstances;

(c) cover and recover damages as to all goods affected whether or not they have been identified to the lease contract (Sections 2A–518 and 2A–520), or recover damages for nondelivery (Sections 2A–519 and 2A–520);

(d) exercise any other rights or pursue any other remedies provided in the lease contract.

(2) If a lessor fails to deliver the goods in conformity to the lease contract or repudiates the lease contract, the lessee may also:

(a) if the goods have been identified, recover them (Section 2A–522); or

(b) in a proper case, obtain specific performance or replevy the goods (Section 2A–521).

(3) If a lessor is otherwise in default under a lease contract, the lessee may exercise the rights and pursue the remedies provided in the lease contract, which may include a right to cancel the lease, and in Section 2A–519(3).

(4) If a lessor has breached a warranty, whether express or implied, the lessee may recover damages (Section 2A–519(4)).

(5) On rightful rejection or justifiable revocation of acceptance, a lessee has a security interest in goods in the lessee's possession or control for any rent and security that has been paid and any expenses reasonably incurred in their inspection, receipt, transportation, and care and custody and may hold those goods and dispose of them in good faith and in a commercially reasonable manner, subject to Section 2A–527(5).

(6) Subject to the provisions of Section 2A–407, a lessee, on notifying the lessor of the lessee's intention to do so, may deduct all or any part of the damages resulting from any default under the lease contract from any part of the rent still due under the same lease contract.

## §2A-509. Lessee's Rights on Improper Delivery; Rightful Rejection.

(1) Subject to the provisions of Section 2A–510 on default in installment lease contracts, if the goods or the tender or delivery fail in any respect to conform to the lease contract, the lessee may reject or accept the goods or accept any commercial unit or units and reject the rest of the goods.

(2) Rejection of goods is ineffective unless it is within a reasonable time after tender or delivery of the goods and the lessee seasonably notifies the lessor.

## §2A-510. Installment Lease Contracts: Rejection and Default.

(1) Under an installment lease contract a lessee may reject any delivery that is nonconforming if the nonconformity substantially impairs the value of that delivery and cannot be cured or the nonconformity is a defect in the required documents; but if the nonconformity does not fall within subsection (2) and the lessor or the supplier gives adequate assurance of its cure, the lessee must accept that delivery.

(2) Whenever nonconformity or default with respect to one or more deliveries substantially impairs the value of the installment lease contract as a whole there is a default with respect to the whole. But, the aggrieved party reinstates the installment lease contract as a whole if the aggrieved party accepts a nonconforming delivery without seasonably notifying of cancellation or brings an action with respect only to past deliveries or demands performance as to future deliveries.

## §2A-511. Merchant Lessee's Duties as to Rightfully Rejected Goods.

(1) Subject to any security interest of a lessee (Section 2A–508(5)), if a lessor or a supplier has no agent or place of business at the market of rejection, a merchant lessee, after rejection of goods in his [or her] possession or control, shall follow any reasonable instructions received from the lessor or the supplier with respect to the goods. In the absence of those instructions, a merchant lessee shall make reasonable efforts to sell, lease, or otherwise dispose of the goods for the lessor's account if they threaten to decline in value speedily. Instructions are not reasonable if on demand indemnity for expenses is not forthcoming.

(2) If a merchant lessee (subsection (1)) or any other lessee (Section 2A–512) disposes of goods, he [or she] is entitled to reimbursement either from the lessor or the supplier or out of the proceeds for reasonable expenses of caring for and disposing of the goods and, if the expenses include no disposition commission, to such commission as is usual in the trade, or if there is none, to a reasonable sum not exceeding 10 percent of the gross proceeds.

(3) In complying with this section or Section 2A–512, the lessee is held only to good faith. Good faith conduct hereunder is neither acceptance or conversion nor the basis of an action for damages.

(4) A purchaser who purchases in good faith from a lessee pursuant to this section or Section 2A–512 takes the goods free of any rights of the lessor and the supplier even though the lessee fails to comply with one or more of the requirements of this Article.

## §2A-512. Lessee's Duties as to Rightfully Rejected Goods.

(1) Except as otherwise provided with respect to goods that threaten to decline in value speedily (Section 2A–511) and subject to any security interest of a lessee (Section 2A–508(5)):

(a) the lessee, after rejection of goods in the lessee's possession, shall hold them with reasonable care at the lessor's or the supplier's disposition for a reasonable time after the lessee's seasonable notification of rejection;

(b) if the lessor or the supplier gives no instructions within a reasonable time after notification of rejection, the lessee may store the rejected goods for the lessor's or the supplier's account or ship them to the lessor or the supplier or dispose of them for the lessor's or the supplier's account with reimbursement in the manner provided in Section 2A–511; but

(c) the lessee has no further obligations with regard to goods rightfully rejected.

(2) Action by the lessee pursuant to subsection (1) is not acceptance or conversion.

## §2A-513. Cure by Lessor of Improper Tender or Delivery; Replacement.

(1) If any tender or delivery by the lessor or the supplier is rejected because nonconforming and the time for performance has not yet expired, the lessor or the supplier may seasonably notify the lessee of the lessor's or the supplier's intention to cure and may then make a conforming delivery within the time provided in the lease contract.

(2) If the lessee rejects a nonconforming tender that the lessor or the supplier had reasonable grounds to believe would be acceptable with or without money allowance, the lessor or the supplier may have a further reasonable time to substitute a conforming tender if he [or she] seasonably notifies the lessee.

## §2A-514. Waiver of Lessee's Objections.

(1) In rejecting goods, a lessee's failure to state a particular defect that is ascertainable by reasonable inspection precludes the lessee from relying on the defect to justify rejection or to establish default:

  (a) if, stated seasonably, the lessor or the supplier could have cured it (Section 2A–513); or

  (b) between merchants if the lessor or the supplier after rejection has made a request in writing for a full and final written statement of all defects on which the lessee proposes to rely.

(2) A lessee's failure to reserve rights when paying rent or other consideration against documents precludes recovery of the payment for defects apparent on the face of the documents.

## §2A-515. Acceptance of Goods.

(1) Acceptance of goods occurs after the lessee has had a reasonable opportunity to inspect the goods and

  (a) the lessee signifies or acts with respect to the goods in a manner that signifies to the lessor or the supplier that the goods are conforming or that the lessee will take or retain them in spite of their nonconformity; or

  (b) the lessee fails to make an effective rejection of the goods (Section 2A–509(2)).

(2) Acceptance of a part of any commercial unit is acceptance of that entire unit.

## §2A-516. Effect of Acceptance of Goods; Notice of Default; Burden of Establishing Default After Acceptance; Notice of Claim or Litigation to Person Answerable Over.

(1) A lessee must pay rent for any goods accepted in accordance with the lease contract, with due allowance for goods rightfully rejected or not delivered.

(2) A lessee's acceptance of goods precludes rejection of the goods accepted. In the case of a finance lease, if made with knowledge of a nonconformity, acceptance cannot be revoked because of it. In any other case, if made with knowledge of a nonconformity, acceptance cannot be revoked because of it unless the acceptance was on the reasonable assumption that the nonconformity would be seasonably cured. Acceptance does not of itself impair any other remedy provided by this Article or the lease agreement for nonconformity.

(3) If a tender has been accepted:

  (a) within a reasonable time after the lessee discovers or should have discovered any default, the lessee shall notify the lessor and the supplier, if any, or be barred from any remedy against the party not notified;

  (b) except in the case of a consumer lease, within a reasonable time after the lessee receives notice of litigation for infringement or the like (Section 2A–211) the lessee shall notify the lessor or be barred from any remedy over for liability established by the litigation; and

  (c) the burden is on the lessee to establish any default.

(4) If a lessee is sued for breach of a warranty or other obligation for which a lessor or a supplier is answerable over the following apply:

  (a) The lessee may give the lessor or the supplier, or both, written notice of the litigation. If the notice states that the person notified may come in and defend and that if the person notified does not do so that person will be bound in any action against that person by the lessee by any determination of fact common to the two litigations, then unless the person notified after seasonable receipt of the notice does come in and defend that person is so bound.

  (b) The lessor or the supplier may demand in writing that the lessee turn over control of the litigation including settlement if the claim is one for infringement or the like (Section 2A–211) or else be barred from any remedy over. If the demand states that the lessor or the supplier agrees to bear all expense and to satisfy any adverse judgment, then unless the lessee after seasonable receipt of the demand does turn over control the lessee is so barred.

(5) Subsections (3) and (4) apply to any obligation of a lessee to hold the lessor or the supplier harmless against infringement or the like (Section 2A–211).

## §2A-517. Revocation of Acceptance of Goods.

(1) A lessee may revoke acceptance of a lot or commercial unit whose nonconformity substantially impairs its value to the lessee if the lessee has accepted it:

(a) except in the case of a finance lease, on the reasonable assumption that its nonconformity would be cured and it has not been seasonably cured; or

(b) without discovery of the nonconformity if the lessee's acceptance was reasonably induced either by the lessor's assurances or, except in the case of a finance lease, by the difficulty of discovery before acceptance.

(2) Except in the case of a finance lease that is not a consumer lease, a lessee may revoke acceptance of a lot or commercial unit if the lessor defaults under the lease contract and the default substantially impairs the value of that lot or commercial unit to the lessee.

(3) If the lease agreement so provides, the lessee may revoke acceptance of a lot or commercial unit because of other defaults by the lessor.

(4) Revocation of acceptance must occur within a reasonable time after the lessee discovers or should have discovered the ground for it and before any substantial change in condition of the goods which is not caused by the nonconformity. Revocation is not effective until the lessee notifies the lessor.

(5) A lessee who so revokes has the same rights and duties with regard to the goods involved as if the lessee had rejected them.

## §2A-518. Cover; Substitute Goods.

(1) After a default by a lessor under the lease contract of the type described in Section 2A–508(1), or, if agreed, after other default by the lessor, the lessee may cover by making any purchase or lease of or contract to purchase or lease goods in substitution for those due from the lessor.

(2) Except as otherwise provided with respect to damages liquidated in the lease agreement (Section 2A–504) or otherwise determined pursuant to agreement of the parties (Sections 1–102(3) and 2A–503), if a lessee's cover is by a lease agreement substantially similar to the original lease agreement and the new lease agreement is made in good faith and in a commercially reasonable manner, the lessee may recover from the lessor as damages (i) the present value, as of the date of the commencement of the term of the new lease agreement, of the rent under the new lease agreement applicable to that period of the new lease term which is comparable to the then remaining term of the original lease agreement minus the present value as of the same date of the total rent for the then remaining lease term of the original lease agreement, and (ii) any incidental or consequential damages, less expenses saved in consequence of the lessor's default.

(3) If a lessee's cover is by lease agreement that for any reason does not qualify for treatment under subsection (2), or is by purchase or otherwise, the lessee may recover from the lessor as if the lessee had elected not to cover and Section 2A–519 governs.

## §2A-519. Lessee's Damages for Non-delivery, Repudiation, Default, and Breach of Warranty in Regard to Accepted Goods.

(1) Except as otherwise provided with respect to damages liquidated in the lease agreement (Section 2A–504) or otherwise determined pursuant to agreement of the parties (Sections 1–102(3) and 2A–503), if a lessee elects not to cover or a lessee elects to cover and the cover is by lease agreement that for any reason does not qualify for treatment under Section 2A–518(2), or is by purchase or otherwise, the measure of damages for non-delivery or repudiation by the lessor or for rejection or revocation of acceptance by the lessee is the present value, as of the date of the default, of the then market rent minus the present value as of the same date of the original rent, computed for the remaining lease term of the original lease agreement, together with incidental and consequential damages, less expenses saved in consequence of the lessor's default.

(2) Market rent is to be determined as of the place for tender or, in cases of rejection after arrival or revocation of acceptance, as of the place of arrival.

(3) Except as otherwise agreed, if the lessee has accepted goods and given notification (Section 2A–516(3)), the measure of damages for non-conforming tender or delivery or other default by a lessor is the loss resulting in the ordinary course of events from the lessor's default as determined in any manner that is reasonable together with incidental and consequential damages, less expenses saved in consequence of the lessor's default.

(4) Except as otherwise agreed, the measure of damages for breach of warranty is the present value at the time and place of acceptance of the difference between the value of the use of the goods accepted and the value if they had been as warranted for the lease term, unless special circumstances show proximate damages of a different amount, together with incidental and consequential damages, less expenses saved in consequence of the lessor's default or breach of warranty.

## §2A-520. Lessee's Incidental and Consequential Damages.

(1) Incidental damages resulting from a lessor's default include expenses reasonably incurred in inspection, receipt, transportation, and care and custody of goods rightfully rejected or goods the acceptance of which is justifiably revoked, any commercially reasonable charges, expenses or commissions in connection with effecting cover, and any other reasonable expense incident to the default.

(2) Consequential damages resulting from a lessor's default include:

(a) any loss resulting from general or particular requirements and needs of which the lessor at the time of contracting had reason to know and which could not reasonably be prevented by cover or otherwise; and

(b) injury to person or property proximately resulting from any breach of warranty.

## §2A-521. Lessee's Right to Specific Performance or Replevin.

(1) Specific performance may be decreed if the goods are unique or in other proper circumstances.

(2) A decree for specific performance may include any terms and conditions as to payment of the rent, damages, or other relief that the court deems just.

(3) A lessee has a right of replevin, detinue, sequestration, claim and delivery, or the like for goods identified to the lease contract if after reasonable effort the lessee is unable to effect cover for those goods or the circumstances reasonably indicate that the effort will be unavailing.

## §2A-522. Lessee's Right to Goods on Lessor's Insolvency.

(1) Subject to subsection (2) and even though the goods have not been shipped, a lessee who has paid a part or all of the rent and security for goods identified to a lease contract (Section 2A–217) on making and keeping good a tender of any unpaid portion of the rent and security due under the lease contract may recover the goods identified from the lessor if the lessor becomes insolvent within 10 days after receipt of the first installment of rent and security.

(2) A lessee acquires the right to recover goods identified to a lease contract only if they conform to the lease contract.

## C. Default by Lessee

## §2A-523. Lessor's Remedies.

(1) If a lessee wrongfully rejects or revokes acceptance of goods or fails to make a payment when due or repudiates with respect to a part or the whole, then, with respect to any goods involved, and with respect to all of the goods if under an installment lease contract the value of the whole lease contract is substantially impaired (Section 2A–510), the lessee is in default under the lease contract and the lessor may:

(a) cancel the lease contract (Section 2A–505(1));

(b) proceed respecting goods not identified to the lease contract (Section 2A–524);

(c) withhold delivery of the goods and take possession of goods previously delivered (Section 2A–525);

(d) stop delivery of the goods by any bailee (Section 2A–526);

(e) dispose of the goods and recover damages (Section 2A–527), or retain the goods and recover damages (Section 2A–528), or in a proper case recover rent (Section 2A–529);

(f) exercise any other rights or pursue any other remedies provided in the lease contract.

(2) If a lessor does not fully exercise a right or obtain a remedy to which the lessor is entitled under subsection (1), the lessor may recover the loss resulting in the ordinary course of events from the lessee's default as determined in any reasonable manner, together with incidental damages, less expenses saved in consequence of the lessee's default.

(3) If a lessee is otherwise in default under a lease contract, the lessor may exercise the rights and pursue the remedies provided in the lease contract, which may include a right to cancel the lease. In addition, unless otherwise provided in the lease contract:

(a) if the default substantially impairs the value of the lease contract to the lessor, the lessor may exercise the rights and pursue the remedies provided in subsections (1) or (2); or

(b) if the default does not substantially impair the value of the lease contract to the lessor, the lessor may recover as provided in subsection (2).

## §2A-524. Lessor's Right to Identify Goods to Lease Contract.

(1) After default by the lessee under the lease contract of the type described in Section 2A–523(1) or 2A–523(3)(a) or, if agreed, after other default by the lessee, the lessor may:

(a) identify to the lease contract conforming goods not already identified if at the time the lessor learned of the default they were in the lessor's or the supplier's possession or control; and

(b) dispose of goods (Section 2A–527(1)) that demonstrably have been intended for the particular lease contract even though those goods are unfinished.

(2) If the goods are unfinished, in the exercise of reasonable commercial judgment for the purposes of avoiding loss and of effective realization, an aggrieved lessor or the supplier may either complete manufacture and wholly identify the goods to the lease contract or cease manufacture and lease, sell, or otherwise dispose of the goods for scrap or salvage value or proceed in any other reasonable manner.

## §2A-525. Lessor's Right to Possession of Goods.

(1) If a lessor discovers the lessee to be insolvent, the lessor may refuse to deliver the goods.

(2) After a default by the lessee under the lease contract of the type described in Section 2A–523(1) or 2A–523(3)(a) or, if agreed, after other default by the lessee, the lessor has the right to take possession of the goods. If the lease contract so provides, the lessor

may require the lessee to assemble the goods and make them available to the lessor at a place to be designated by the lessor which is reasonably convenient to both parties. Without removal, the lessor may render unusable any goods employed in trade or business, and may dispose of goods on the lessee's premises (Section 2A–527).

(3) The lessor may proceed under subsection (2) without judicial process if it can be done without breach of the peace or the lessor may proceed by action.

## §2A-526. Lessor's Stoppage of Delivery in Transit or Otherwise.

(1) A lessor may stop delivery of goods in the possession of a carrier or other bailee if the lessor discovers the lessee to be insolvent and may stop delivery of carload, truckload, planeload, or larger shipments of express or freight if the lessee repudiates or fails to make a payment due before delivery, whether for rent, security or otherwise under the lease contract, or for any other reason the lessor has a right to withhold or take possession of the goods.

(2) In pursuing its remedies under subsection (1), the lessor may stop delivery until

   (a) receipt of the goods by the lessee;

   (b) acknowledgment to the lessee by any bailee of the goods, except a carrier, that the bailee holds the goods for the lessee; or

   (c) such an acknowledgment to the lessee by a carrier via reshipment or as warehouseman.

(3) (a) To stop delivery, a lessor shall so notify as to enable the bailee by reasonable diligence to prevent delivery of the goods.

   (b) After notification, the bailee shall hold and deliver the goods according to the directions of the lessor, but the lessor is liable to the bailee for any ensuing charges or damages.

   (c) A carrier who has issued a nonnegotiable bill of lading is not obliged to obey a notification to stop received from a person other than the consignor.

## §2A-527. Lessor's Rights to Dispose of Goods.

(1) After a default by a lessee under the lease contract of the type described in Section 2A–523(1) or 2A–523(3)(a) or after the lessor refuses to deliver or takes possession of goods (Section 2A–525 or 2A–526), or, if agreed, after other default by a lessee, the lessor may dispose of the goods concerned or the undelivered balance thereof by lease, sale, or otherwise.

(2) Except as otherwise provided with respect to damages liquidated in the lease agreement (Section 2A–504) or otherwise determined pursuant to agreement of the parties (Sections 1–102(3) and 2A–503), if the disposition is by lease agreement substantially similar to the original lease agreement and the new lease agreement is made in good faith and in a commercially reasonable manner, the lessor may recover from the lessee as damages (i) accrued and unpaid rent as of the date of the commencement of the term of the new lease agreement, (ii) the present value, as of the same date, of the total rent for the then remaining lease term of the original lease agreement minus the present value, as of the same date, of the rent under the new lease agreement applicable to that period of the new lease term which is comparable to the then remaining term of the original lease agreement, and (iii) any incidental damages allowed under Section 2A–530, less expenses saved in consequence of the lessee's default.

(3) If the lessor's disposition is by lease agreement that for any reason does not qualify for treatment under subsection (2), or is by sale or otherwise, the lessor may recover from the lessee as if the lessor had elected not to dispose of the goods and Section 2A–528 governs.

(4) A subsequent buyer or lessee who buys or leases from the lessor in good faith for value as a result of a disposition under this section takes the goods free of the original lease contract and any rights of the original lessee even though the lessor fails to comply with one or more of the requirements of this Article.

(5) The lessor is not accountable to the lessee for any profit made on any disposition. A lessee who has rightfully rejected or justifiably revoked acceptance shall account to the lessor for any excess over the amount of the lessee's security interest (Section 2A–508(5)).

## §2A-528. Lessor's Damages for Non-acceptance, Failure to Pay, Repudiation, or Other Default.

(1) Except as otherwise provided with respect to damages liquidated in the lease agreement (Section 2A–504) or otherwise determined pursuant to agreement of the parties (Sections 1–102(3) and 2A–503), if a lessor elects to retain the goods or a lessor elects to dispose of the goods and the disposition is by lease agreement that for any reason does not qualify for treatment under Section 2A–527(2), or is by sale or otherwise, the lessor may recover from the lessee as damages for a default of the type described in Section 2A–523(1) or 2A–523(3)(a), or, if agreed, for other default of the lessee, (i) accrued and unpaid rent as of the date of default if the lessee has never taken possession of the goods, or, if the lessee has taken possession of the goods, as of the date the lessor repossesses the goods or an earlier date on which the lessee makes a tender of the goods to the lessor, (ii) the present value as of the date determined under clause (i) of the total rent for the then remaining lease

term of the original lease agreement minus the present value as of the same date of the market rent at the place where the goods are located computed for the same lease term, and (iii) any incidental damages allowed under Section 2A–530, less expenses saved in consequence of the lessee's default.

(2) If the measure of damages provided in subsection (1) is inadequate to put a lessor in as good a position as performance would have, the measure of damages is the present value of the profit, including reasonable overhead, the lessor would have made from full performance by the lessee, together with any incidental damages allowed under Section 2A–530, due allowance for costs reasonably incurred and due credit for payments or proceeds of disposition.

## §2A-529. Lessor's Action for the Rent.

(1) After default by the lessee under the lease contract of the type described in Section 2A–523(1) or 2A–523(3)(a) or, if agreed, after other default by the lessee, if the lessor complies with subsection (2), the lessor may recover from the lessee as damages:

(a) for goods accepted by the lessee and not repossessed by or tendered to the lessor, and for conforming goods lost or damaged within a commercially reasonable time after risk of loss passes to the lessee (Section 2A–219), (i) accrued and unpaid rent as of the date of entry of judgment in favor of the lessor, (ii) the present value as of the same date of the rent for the then remaining lease term of the lease agreement, and (iii) any incidental damages allowed under Section 2A–530, less expenses saved in consequence of the lessee's default; and

(b) for goods identified to the lease contract if the lessor is unable after reasonable effort to dispose of them at a reasonable price or the circumstances reasonably indicate that effort will be unavailing, (i) accrued and unpaid rent as of the date of entry of judgment in favor of the lessor, (ii) the present value as of the same date of the rent for the then remaining lease term of the lease agreement, and (iii) any incidental damages allowed under Section 2A–530, less expenses saved in consequence of the lessee's default.

(2) Except as provided in subsection (3), the lessor shall hold for the lessee for the remaining lease term of the lease agreement any goods that have been identified to the lease contract and are in the lessor's control.

(3) The lessor may dispose of the goods at any time before collection of the judgment for damages obtained pursuant to subsection (1). If the disposition is before the end of the remaining lease term of the lease agreement, the lessor's recovery against the lessee for damages is governed by Section 2A–527 or Section 2A–528, and the lessor will cause an appropriate credit to be provided against a judgment for damages to the extent that the amount of the judgment exceeds the recovery available pursuant to Section 2A–527 or 2A–528.

(4) Payment of the judgment for damages obtained pursuant to subsection (1) entitles the lessee to the use and possession of the goods not then disposed of for the remaining lease term of and in accordance with the lease agreement.

(5) After default by the lessee under the lease contract of the type described in Section 2A–523(1) or Section 2A–523(3)(a) or, if agreed, after other default by the lessee, a lessor who is held not entitled to rent under this section must nevertheless be awarded damages for non-acceptance under Section 2A–527 or Section 2A–528.

## §2A-530. Lessor's Incidental Damages. 
Incidental damages to an aggrieved lessor include any commercially reasonable charges, expenses, or commissions incurred in stopping delivery, in the transportation, care and custody of goods after the lessee's default, in connection with return or disposition of the goods, or otherwise resulting from the default.

## §2A-531. Standing to Sue Third Parties for Injury to Goods.

(1) If a third party so deals with goods that have been identified to a lease contract as to cause actionable injury to a party to the lease contract (a) the lessor has a right of action against the third party, and (b) the lessee also has a right of action against the third party if the lessee:

(i) has a security interest in the goods;

(ii) has an insurable interest in the goods; or

(iii) bears the risk of loss under the lease contract or has since the injury assumed that risk as against the lessor and the goods have been converted or destroyed.

(2) If at the time of the injury the party plaintiff did not bear the risk of loss as against the other party to the lease contract and there is no arrangement between them for disposition of the recovery, his [or her] suit or settlement, subject to his [or her] own interest, is as a fiduciary for the other party to the lease contract.

(3) Either party with the consent of the other may sue for the benefit of whom it may concern.

## §2A-532. Lessor's Rights to Residual Interest. 
In addition to any other recovery permitted by this Article or other law, the lessor may recover from the lessee an amount that will fully compensate the lessor for any loss of or damage to the lessor's residual interest in the goods caused by the default of the lessee.

# Article 3: Negotiable Instruments (Revised 1990)

## Part 1: General Provisions and Definitions

### §3-101. Short Title.— This Article may be cited as Uniform Commercial Code—Negotiable Instruments.

### §3-102. Subject Matter.—

(a) This Article applies to negotiable instruments. It does not apply to money, to payment orders governed by Article 4A, or to securities governed by Article 8.

(b) If there is conflict between this Article and Article 4 or 9, Articles 4 and 9 govern.

(c) Regulations of the Board of Governors of the Federal Reserve System and operating circulars of the Federal Reserve Banks supersede any inconsistent provision of this Article to the extent of the inconsistency.

**Note:** The previous version of Article 3, Commercial Paper, is found in the Instructor's Resource Guide. You may wish to photocopy it for your students' use.

### §3-103. Definitions.—

(a) In this Article:

(1) "Acceptor" means a drawee who has accepted a draft.

(2) "Drawee" means a person ordered in a draft to make payment.

(3) "Drawer" means a person who signs or is identified in a draft as a person ordering payment.

(4) "Good faith" means honesty in fact and the observance of reasonable commercial standards of fair dealing.

(5) "Maker" means a person who signs or is identified in a note as a person undertaking to pay.

(6) "Order" means a written instruction to pay money signed by the person giving the instruction. The instruction may be addressed to any person, including the person giving the instruction, or to one or more persons jointly or in the alternative but not in succession. An authorization to pay is not an order unless the person authorized to pay is also instructed to pay.

(7) "Ordinary care" in the case of a person engaged in business means observance of reasonable commercial standards, prevailing in the area in which the person is located, with respect to the business in which the person is engaged. In the case of a bank that takes an instrument for processing for collection or payment by automated means, reasonable commercial standards do not require the

bank to examine the instrument if the failure to examine does not violate the bank's prescribed procedures and the bank's procedures do not vary unreasonably from general banking usage not disapproved by this Article or Article 4.

(8) "Party" means a party to an instrument.

(9) "Promise" means a written undertaking to pay money signed by the person undertaking to pay. An acknowledgment of an obligation by the obligor is not a promise unless the obligor also undertakes to pay the obligation.

(10) "Prove" with respect to a fact means to meet the burden of establishing the fact (Section 1-201(8)).

(11) "Remitter" means a person who purchases an instrument from its issuer if the instrument is payable to an identified person other than the purchaser.

(b) Other definitions applying to this Article and the sections in which they appear are:

| | |
|---|---|
| "Acceptance" | Section 3-409 |
| "Accommodated party" | Section 3-419 |
| "Accommodation party" | Section 3-419 |
| "Alteration" | Section 3-407 |
| "Anomalous indorsement" | Section 3-205 |
| "Blank indorsement" | Section 3-205 |
| "Cashier's check" | Section 3-104 |
| "Certificate of deposit" | Section 3-104 |
| "Certified check" | Section 3-409 |
| "Check" | Section 3-104 |
| "Consideration" | Section 3-303 |
| "Draft" | Section 3-104 |
| "Holder in due course" | Section 3-302 |
| "Incomplete instrument" | Section 3-115 |
| "Indorsement" | Section 3-204 |
| "Indorser" | Section 3-204 |
| "Instrument" | Section 3-104 |
| "Issue" | Section 3-105 |
| "Issuer" | Section 3-105 |
| "Negotiable instrument" | Section 3-104 |
| "Negotiation" | Section 3-201 |
| "Note" | Section 3-104 |
| "Payable at a definite time" | Section 3-108 |
| "Payable on demand" | Section 3-108 |
| "Payable to bearer" | Section 3-109 |
| "Payable to order" | Section 3-109 |
| "Payment" | Section 3-602 |
| "Person entitled to enforce" | Section 3-301 |
| "Presentment" | Section 3-501 |
| "Reacquisition" | Section 3-207 |

(c) The following definitions in other Articles apply to this Article:

(d) In addition, Article 1 contains general definitions and principles of construction and interpretation applicable throughout this Article.

## §3-104. Negotiable Instrument.—

(a) Except as provided in subsections (c) and (d), "negotiable instrument" means an unconditional promise or order to pay a fixed amount of money, with or without interest or other charges described in the promise or order, if it:

(1) is payable to bearer or to order at the time it is issued or first comes into possession of a holder;

(2) is payable on demand or at a definite time; and

(3) does not state any other undertaking or instruction by the person promising or ordering payment to do any act in addition to the payment of money, but the promise or order may contain (i) an undertaking or power to give, maintain, or protect collateral to secure payment, (ii) an authorization or power to the holder to confess judgment or realize on or dispose of collateral, or (iii) a waiver of the benefit of any law intended for the advantage or protection of an obligor.

(b) "Instrument" means a negotiable instrument.

(c) An order that meets all of the requirements of subsection (a), except paragraph (1), and otherwise falls within the definition of "check" in subsection (f) is a negotiable instrument and a check.

(d) A promise or order other than a check is not an instrument if, at the time it is issued or first comes into possession of a holder, it contains a conspicuous statement, however expressed, to the effect that the promise or order is not negotiable or is not an instrument governed by this Article.

(e) An instrument is a "note" if it is a promise and is a "draft" if it is an order. If an instrument falls within the definition of both "note" and "draft", a person entitled to enforce the instrument may treat it as either.

(f) "Check" means (i) a draft, other than a documentary draft, payable on demand and drawn on a bank or (ii) a cashier's check or teller's check. An instrument may be a check even though it is described on its face by another term, such as "money order".

(g) "Cashier's check" means a draft with respect to which the drawer and drawee are the same bank or branches of the same bank.

(h) "Teller's check" means a draft drawn by a bank (i) on another bank, or (ii) payable at or through a bank.

(i) "Traveler's check" means an instrument that (i) is payable on demand, (ii) is drawn on or payable at or through a bank, (iii) is designated by the term "traveler's check" or by a substantially similar term, and (iv) requires, as a condition to payment, a countersignature by a person whose specimen signature appears on the instrument.

(j) "Certificate of deposit" means an instrument containing an acknowledgment by a bank that a sum of money has been received by the bank and a promise by the bank to repay the sum of money. A certificate of deposit is a note of the bank.

## §3-105. Issue of Instrument.—

(a) "Issue" means the first delivery of an instrument by the maker or drawer, whether to a holder or nonholder, for the purpose of giving rights on the instrument to any person.

(b) An unissued instrument, or an unissued incomplete instrument that is completed, is binding on the maker or drawer, but nonissuance is a defense. An instrument that is conditionally issued or is issued for a special purpose is binding on the maker or drawer, but failure of the condition or special purpose to be fulfilled is a defense.

(c) "Issuer" applies to issued and unissued instruments and means a maker or drawer of an instrument.

## §3-106. Unconditional Promise or Order.—

(a) Except as provided in this section, for the purposes of Section 3-104(a), a promise or order is unconditional unless it states (i) an express condition to payment, (ii) that the promise or order is subject to or governed by another writing, or (iii) that rights or obligations with respect to the promise or order are stated in another writing. A reference to another writing does not of itself make the promise or order conditional.

(b) A promise or order is not made conditional (i) by a reference to another writing for a statement of rights with respect to collateral, prepayment, or acceleration, or (ii) because payment is limited to resort to a particular fund or source.

(c) If a promise or order requires, as a condition to payment, a countersignature by a person whose specimen signature appears on the promise or order, the condition does not make the promise or order conditional for the purposes of Section 3-104(a). If the person whose specimen signature appears on an instrument fails to countersign the instrument, the failure to countersign is a defense to the obligation of the issuer, but the failure does not prevent a transferee of the instrument from becoming a holder of the instrument.

(d) If a promise or order at the time it is issued or first comes into possession of a holder contains a statement, required by applicable statutory or administrative law, to the effect that the rights of a holder or transferee are subject to claims or defenses that the issuer could assert the original payee, the promise or order is not thereby made conditional for the purposes of Section 3-104(a); but if the promise or order is an instrument, there cannot be a holder in due course of the instrument.

## §3-107. Instrument Payable in Foreign Money.—

Unless the instrument otherwise provides, an instrument that states the amount payable in foreign money may be paid in the foreign money or in an equivalent amount in dollars calculated by using the current bank-offered spot rate at the place of payment for the purchase of dollars on the day on which the instrument is paid.

## §3-108. Payable on Demand or at Definite Time.—

(a) A promise or order is "payable on demand" if it (i) states that it is payable on demand or at sight, or otherwise indicates that it is payable at the will of the holder, or (ii) does not state any time of payment.

(b) A promise or order is "payable at a definite time" if it is payable on elapse of a definite period of time after sight or acceptance or at a fixed date or dates or at a time or times readily ascertainable at the time the promise or order is issued, subject to rights of (i) prepayment, (ii) acceleration, (iii) extension at the option of the holder, or (iv) extension to a further definite time at the option of the maker or acceptor or automatically upon or after a specified act or event.

(c) If an instrument, payable at a fixed date, is also payable upon demand made before the fixed date, the instrument is payable on demand until the fixed date and, if demand for payment is not made before that date, becomes payable at a definite time on the fixed date.

## §3-109. Payable to Bearer or to Order.—

(a) A promise or order is payable to bearer if it:
   (1) states that it is payable to bearer or to the order of bearer or otherwise indicates that the person in possession of the promise or order is entitled to payment;

   (2) does not state a payee; or

   (3) states that it is payable to or to the order of cash or otherwise indicates that it is not payable to an identified person.

(b) A promise or order that is not payable to bearer is payable to order if it is payable (i) to the order of an identified person or (ii) to an identified person or order. A promise or order that is payable to order is payable to the identified person.

(c) An instrument payable to bearer may become payable to an identified person if it is specially indorsed pursuant to Section 3-205(a). An instrument payable to an identified person may become payable to bearer if it is indorsed in blank pursuant to Section 3-205(b).

## §3-110. Identification of Person to Whom Instrument is Payable.—

(a) The person to whom an instrument is initially payable is determined by the intent of the person, whether or not authorized, signing as, or in the name or behalf of, the issuer of the instrument. The instrument is payable to the person intended by the signer even if that person is identified in the instrument by a name or other identification that is not that of the intended person. If more than one person signs in the name or behalf of the issuer of an instrument and all the signers do not intend the same person as payee, the instrument is payable to any person intended by one or more of the signers.

(b) If the signature of the issuer of an instrument is made by automated means, such as a check-writing machine, the payee of the instrument is determined by the intent of the person who supplied the name or identification of the payee, whether or not authorized to do so.

(c) A person to whom an instrument is payable may be identified in any way, including by name, identifying number, office, or account number. For the purpose of determining the holder of an instrument, the following rules apply:
   (1) If an instrument is payable to an account and the account is identified only by number, the instrument is payable to the person to whom the account is payable. If an instrument is payable to an account identified by number and by the name of a person, the instrument is payable to the named person, whether or not that person is the owner of the account identified by number.

   (2) If an instrument is payable to:
      (i) a trust, an estate, or a person described as trustee or representative of a trust or estate, the instrument is payable to the trustee, the representative, or a successor of either, whether or not the beneficiary or estate is also named;

(ii) a person described as agent or similar representative of a named or identified person, the instrument is payable to the represented person, the representative, or a successor of the representative;

(iii) a fund or organization that is not a legal entity, the instrument is payable to a representative of the members of the fund or organization; or

(iv) an office or to a person described as holding an office, the instrument is payable to the named person, the incumbent of the office, or a successor to the incumbent.

(d) If an instrument is payable to two or more persons alternatively, it is payable to any of them and may be negotiated, discharged, or enforced by any or all of them in possession of the instrument. If an instrument is payable to two or more persons not alternatively, it is payable to all of them and may be negotiated, discharged, or enforced only by all of them. If an instrument payable to two or more persons is ambiguous as to whether it is payable to the persons alternatively, the instrument is payable to the persons alternatively.

## §3-111. Place of Payment.— 
Except as otherwise provided for items in Article 4, an instrument is payable at the place of payment stated in the instrument. If no place of payment is stated, an instrument is payable at the address of the drawee or maker stated in the instrument. If no address is stated, the place of payment is the place of business of the drawee or maker. If a drawee or maker has more than one place of business, the place of payment is any place of business of the drawee or maker chosen by the person entitled to enforce the instrument. If the drawee or maker has no place of business, the place of payment is the residence of the drawee or maker.

## §3-112. Interest.—

(a) Unless otherwise provided in the instrument, (i) an instrument is not payable with interest, and (ii) interest on an interest-bearing instrument is payable from the date of the instrument.

(b) Interest may be stated in an instrument as a fixed or variable amount of money or it may be expressed as a fixed or variable rate or rates. The amount or rate of interest may be stated or described in the instrument in any manner and may require reference to information not contained in the instrument. If an instrument provides for interest, but the amount of interest payable cannot be ascertained from the description, interest is payable at the judgment rate in effect at the place of payment of the instrument and at the time interest first accrues.

## §3-113. Date of Instrument.—

(a) An instrument may be antedated or postdated. The date stated determines the time of payment if the instrument is payable at a fixed period after date. Except as provided in Section 4-401(c), an instrument payable on demand is not payable before the date of the instrument.

(b) If an instrument is undated, its date is the date of its issue or, in the case of an unissued instrument, the date it first comes into possession of a holder.

## §3-114. Contradictory Terms of Instrument.— 
If an instrument contains contradictory terms, typewritten terms prevail over printed terms, handwritten terms prevail over both, and words prevail over numbers.

## §3-115. Incomplete Instrument.—

(a) "Incomplete instrument" means a signed writing, whether or not issued by the signer, the contents of which show at the time of signing that it is incomplete but that the signer intended it to be completed by the addition of words or numbers.

(b) Subject to subsection (c), if an incomplete instrument is an instrument under Section 3-104, it may be enforced according to its terms if it is not completed, or according to its terms as augmented by completion. If an incomplete instrument is not an instrument under Section 3-104, but, after completion, the requirements of Section 3-104 are met, the instrument may be enforced according to its terms as augmented by completion.

(c) If words or numbers are added to an incomplete instrument without authority of the signer, there is an alteration of the incomplete instrument under Section 3-407.

(d) The burden of establishing that words or numbers were added to an incomplete instrument without authority of the signer is on the person asserting the lack of authority.

## §3-116. Joint and Several Liability; Contribution.—

(a) Except as otherwise provided in the instrument, two or more persons who have the same liability on an instrument as makers, drawers, acceptors, indorsers who indorse as joint payees, or anomalous indorsers are jointly and severally liable in the capacity in which they sign.

(b) Except as provided in Section 3-419(e) or by agreement of the affected parties, a party having joint and several liability who pays the instrument is entitled to receive from any party having the same joint and several liability contribution in accordance with applicable law.

(c) Discharge of one party having joint and several liability by a person entitled to enforce the instrument does not affect the right under subsection (b) of a party having the same joint and several liability to receive contribution from the party discharged.

### §3-117. Other Agreements Affecting Instrument.

— Subject to applicable law regarding exclusion of proof of contemporaneous or previous agreements, the obligation of a party to an instrument to pay the instrument may be modified, supplemented, or nullified by a separate agreement of the obligor and a person entitled to enforce the instrument, if the instrument is issued or the obligation is incurred in reliance on the agreement or as part of the same transaction giving rise to the agreement. To the extent an obligation is modified, supplemented, or nullified by an agreement under this section, the agreement is a defense to the obligation.

### §3-118. Statute of Limitations.—

(a) Except as provided in subsection (e), an action to enforce the obligation of a party to pay a note payable at a definite time must be commenced within six years after the due date or dates stated in the note or, if a due date is accelerated, within six years after the accelerated due date.

(b) Except as provided in subsection (d) or (e), if demand for payment is made to the maker of a note payable on demand, an action to enforce the obligation of a party to pay the note must be commenced within six years after the demand. If no demand for payment is made to the maker, an action to enforce the note is barred if neither principal nor interest on the note has been paid for a continuous period of 10 years.

(c) Except as provided in subsection (d), an action to enforce the obligation of a party to an unaccepted draft to pay the draft must be commenced within three years after dishonor of the draft or 10 years after the date of the draft, whichever period expires first.

(d) An action to enforce the obligation of the acceptor of a certified check or the issuer of a teller's check, cashier's check, or traveler's check must be commenced within three years after demand for payment is made to the acceptor or issuer, as the case may be.

(e) An action to enforce the obligation of a party to a certificate of deposit to pay the instrument must be commenced within six years after demand for payment is made to the maker, but if the instrument states a due date and the maker is not required to pay before that date, the six-year period begins when a demand for payment is in effect and the due date has passed.

(f) An action to enforce the obligation of a party to pay an accepted draft, other than a certified check, must be commenced (i) within six years after the due date or dates stated in the draft or acceptance if the obligation of the acceptor is payable at a definite time, or (ii) within six years after the date of the acceptance if the obligation of the acceptor is payable on demand.

(g) Unless governed by other law regarding claims for indemnity or contribution, an action (i) for conversion of an instrument, for money had and received, or like action based on conversion, (ii) for breach of warranty, or (iii) to enforce an obligation, duty, or right arising under this Article and not governed by this section must be commenced within three years after the [cause of action] accrues.

### §3-119. Notice of Right to Defend Action.—

In an action for breach of an obligation for which a third person is answerable over pursuant to this Article or Article 4, the defendant may give the third person written notice of the litigation, and the person notified may then give similar notice to any other person who is answerable over. If the notice states (i) that the person notified may come in and defend and (ii) that failure to do so will bind the person notified in an action later brought by the person giving the notice as to any determination of fact common to the two litigations, the person notified is so bound unless after reasonable receipt of the notice the person notified does come in and defend.

## Part 2: Negotiation, Transfer, and Indorsement

### §3-201. Negotiation.—

(a) "Negotiation" means a transfer of possession, whether voluntary or involuntary, of an instrument by a person other than the issuer to a person who thereby becomes its holder.

(b) Except for negotiation by a remitter, if an instrument is payable to an identified person, negotiation requires transfer of possession of the instrument and its indorsement by the holder. If an instrument is payable to bearer, it may be negotiated by transfer of possession alone.

### §3-202. Negotiation Subject to Rescission.—

(a) Negotiation is effective even if obtained (i) from an infant, a corporation exceeding its powers, or a person without capacity, (ii) by fraud, duress, or mistake, or (iii) in breach of duty or as part of an illegal transaction.

(b) To the extent permitted by other law, negotiation may be rescinded or may be subject to other remedies, but those remedies may not be asserted against a subsequent holder in due course or a person paying the instrument in good faith and without knowledge of facts that are a basis for rescission or other remedy.

### §3-203. Transfer of Instrument; Rights Acquired by Transfer.—

(a) An instrument is transferred when it is delivered by a person other than its issuer for the purpose of giving to the person receiving delivery the right to enforce the instrument.

(b) Transfer of an instrument, whether or not the transfer is a negotiation, vests in the transferee any right of the transferor to enforce the instrument, including any right as a holder in due course, but the transferee cannot acquire rights of a holder in due course by a transfer, directly or indirectly, from a holder in due course if the transferee engaged in fraud or illegality affecting the instrument.

(c) Unless otherwise agreed, if an instrument is transferred for value and the transferee does not become a holder because of lack of indorsement by the transferor, the transferee has a specially enforceable right to the unqualified indorsement of the transferor, but negotiation of the instrument does not occur until the indorsement is made.

(d) If a transferor purports to transfer less than the entire instrument, negotiation of the instrument does not occur. The transferee obtains no rights under this Article, and has only the rights of a partial assignee.

## §3-204. Indorsement.—

(a) "Indorsement" means a signature, other than that of a signer as maker, drawer, or acceptor, that alone or accompanied by other words is made on an instrument for the purpose of (i) negotiating the instrument, (ii) restricting payment of the instrument, or (iii) incurring indorser's liability on the instrument, but regardless of the intent of the signer, a signature and its accompanying words is an indorsement unless the accompanying words, terms of the instrument, place of the signature, or other circumstances unambiguously indicate that the signature was made for a purpose other than indorsement. For the purpose of determining whether a signature is made on an instrument, a paper affixed to the instrument is a part of the instrument.

(b) "Indorser" means a person who makes an indorsement.

(c) For the purpose of determining whether the transferee of an instrument is a holder, an indorsement that transfers a security interest in the instrument is effective as an unqualified indorsement of the instrument.

(d) If an instrument is payable to a holder under a name that is not the name of the holder, indorsement may be made by the holder in the name stated in the instrument or in the holder's name or both, but signature in both names may be required by a person paying or taking the instrument for value or collection.

## §3-205. Special Indorsement; Blank Indorsement; Anomalous Indorsement.—

(a) If an indorsement is made by the holder of an instrument, whether payable to an identified person or payable to bearer, and the indorsement identifies a person to whom it makes the instrument payable, it is a "special indorsement". When specially indorsed, an instrument becomes payable to the identified person and may be negotiated only by the indorsement of that person. The principles stated in Section 3-110 apply to special indorsements.

(b) If an indorsement is made by the holder of an instrument and it is not a special indorsement, it is a "blank indorsement". When indorsed in blank, an instrument becomes payable to bearer and may be negotiated by transfer of possession alone until specially indorsed.

(c) The holder may convert a blank indorsement that consists only of a signature into a special indorsement by writing, above the signature of the indorser, words identifying the person to whom the instrument is made payable.

(d) "Anomalous indorsement" means an indorsement made by a person who is not the holder of the instrument. An anomalous indorsement does not affect the manner in which the instrument may be negotiated.

## §3-206. Restrictive Indorsement.—

(a) An indorsement limiting payment to a particular person or otherwise prohibiting further transfer or negotiation of the instrument is not effective to prevent further transfer or negotiation of the instrument.

(b) An indorsement stating a condition to the right of the indorsee to receive payment does not affect the right of the indorsee to enforce the instrument. A person paying the instrument or taking it for value or collection may disregard the condition, and the rights and liabilities of that person are not affected by whether the condition has been fulfilled.

(c) If an instrument bears an indorsement (i) described in Section 4-201(b), or (ii) in blank or to a particular bank using the words "for deposit", "for collection", or other words indicating a purpose of having the instrument collected by a bank for the indorser or for a particular account, the following rules apply:

(1) A person, other than a bank, who purchases the instrument when so indorsed converts the instrument unless the amount paid for the instrument is received by the indorser or applied consistently with the indorsement.

(2) A depositary bank that purchases the instrument or takes it for collection when so indorsed converts the instrument unless the amount paid by the bank with respect to the instrument is received by the indorser or applied consistently with the indorsement.

(3) A payor bank that is also the depositary bank or that takes the instrument for immediate payment over the counter from a person other than a collecting bank converts the instrument unless the proceeds of the instrument are received by the indorser or applied consistently with the indorsement.

(4) Except as otherwise provided in paragraph (3), a payor bank or intermediary bank may disregard the indorsement and is not liable if the proceeds of the instrument are not received by the indorser or applied consistently with the indorsement.

(d) Except for an indorsement covered by subsection (c), if an instrument bears an indorsement using words to the effect that payment is to be made to the indorsee as agent, trustee, or other fiduciary for the benefit of the indorser or another person, the following rules apply:

(1) Unless there is notice of breach of fiduciary duty as provided in Section 3-307, a person who purchases the instrument from the indorsee or takes the instrument from the indorsee for collection or payment may pay the proceeds of payment or the value given for the instrument to the indorsee without regard to whether the indorsee violates a fiduciary duty to the indorser.

(2) A subsequent transferee of the instrument or person who pays the instrument is neither given notice nor otherwise affected by the restriction in the indorsement unless the transferee or payor knows that the fiduciary dealt with the instrument or its proceeds in breach of fiduciary duty.

(e) The presence on an instrument of an indorsement to which this section applies does not prevent a purchaser of the instrument from becoming a holder in due course of the instrument unless the purchaser is a converter under subsection (c) or has notice or knowledge of breach of fiduciary duty as stated in subsection (d).

(f) In an action to enforce the obligation of a party to pay the instrument, the obligor has a defense if payment would violate an indorsement to which this section applies and the payment is not permitted by this section.

### §3-207. Reacquisition.— Reacquisition of an instrument occurs if it is transferred to a former holder, by negotiation or otherwise. A former holder who reacquires the instrument may cancel indorsements made after the reacquirer first became a holder of the instrument. If the cancellation causes the instrument to be payable to the reacquirer or to bearer, the reacquirer may negotiate the instrument. An indorser whose indorsement is canceled is discharged, and the discharge is effective against any subsequent holder.

## Part 3: Enforcement of Instruments

### §3-301. Person Entitled to Enforce Instrument.—
"Person entitled to enforce" an instrument means (i) the holder of the instrument, (ii) a nonholder in possession of the instrument who has the rights of a holder, or (iii) a person not in possession of the instrument who is entitled to enforce the instrument pursuant to Section 3-309 or

3-418(d). A person may be a person entitled to enforce the instrument even though the person is not the owner of the instrument or is in wrongful possession of the instrument.

### §3-302. Holder in Due Course.—

(a) Subject to subsection (c) and Section 3106(d), "holder in due course" means the holder of an instrument if:

(1) the instrument when issued or negotiated to the holder does not bear such apparent evidence of forgery or alteration or is not otherwise so irregular or incomplete as to call into question its authenticity; and

(2) the holder took the instrument (i) for value, (ii) in good faith, (iii) without notice that the instrument is overdue or has been dishonored or that there is an uncured default with respect to payment of another instrument issued as part of the same series, (iv) without notice that the instrument contains an unauthorized signature or has been altered, (v) without notice of any claim to the instrument described in Section 3-306, and (vi) without notice that any party has a defense or claim in recoupment described in Section 3-305(a).

(b) Notice of discharge of a party, other than discharge in an insolvency proceeding, is not notice of a defense under subsection (a), but discharge is effective against a person who became a holder in due course with notice of the discharge. Public filing or recording of a document does not of itself constitute notice of a defense, claim in recoupment, or claim to the instrument.

(c) Except to the extent a transferor or predecessor in interest has rights as a holder in due course, a person does not acquire rights of a holder in due course of an instrument taken (i) by legal process or by purchase in an execution, bankruptcy, or creditor's sale or similar proceeding, (ii) by purchase as part of a bulk transaction not in ordinary course of business of the transferor, or (iii) as the successor in interest to an estate or other organization.

(d) If, under Section 3-303(a)(1), the promise of performance that is the consideration for an instrument has been partially performed, the holder may assert rights as a holder in due course of the instrument only to the fraction of the amount payable under the instrument equal to the value of the partial performance divided by the value of the promised performance.

(e) If (i) the person entitled to enforce an instrument has only a security interest in the instrument and (ii) the person obliged to pay the instrument has a defense, claim in recoupment, or claim to the instrument that may be asserted against the person who granted the security interest, the person entitled to enforce the instrument may assert rights as a holder in due course only to an amount payable under the instrument which, at the time of enforcement of the instrument, does not exceed the amount of the unpaid obligation secured.

(f) To be effective, notice must be received at a time and in a manner that gives a reasonable opportunity to act on it.

(g) This section is subject to any law limiting status as a holder in due course in particular classes of transactions.

## §3-303. Value and Consideration.—

(a) An instrument is issued or transferred for value if:

    (1) the instrument is issued or transferred for a promise of performance, to the extent the promise has been performed;

    (2) the transferee acquires a security interest or other lien in the instrument other than a lien obtained by judicial proceeding;

    (3) the instrument is issued or transferred as payment of, or as security for, an antecedent claim against any person, whether or not the claim is due;

    (4) the instrument is issued or transferred in exchange for a negotiable instrument; or

    (5) the instrument is issued or transferred in exchange for the incurring of an irrevocable obligation to a third party by the person taking the instrument.

(b) "Consideration" means any consideration sufficient to support a simple contract. The drawer or maker of an instrument has a defense if the instrument is issued without consideration. If an instrument is issued for a promise of performance, the issuer has a defense to the extent performance of the promise is due and the promise has not been performed. If an instrument is issued for value as stated in subsection (a), the instrument is also issued for consideration.

## §3-304. Overdue Instrument.—

(a) An instrument payable on demand becomes overdue at the earliest of the following times:

    (1) on the day after the day demand for payment is duly made;

    (2) if the instrument is a check, 90 days after its date; or

    (3) if the instrument is not a check, when the instrument has been outstanding for a period of time after its date which is unreasonably long under the circumstances of the particular case in light of the nature of the instrument and usage of the trade.

(b) With respect to an instrument payable at a definite time the following rules apply:

    (1) If the principal is payable in installments and a due date has not been accelerated, the instrument becomes overdue upon default under the instrument for nonpayment of an installment, and the instrument remains overdue until the default is cured.

    (2) If the principal is not payable in installments and the due date has not been accelerated, the instrument becomes overdue on the day after the due date.

    (3) If a due date with respect to principal has been accelerated, the instrument becomes overdue on the day after the accelerated due date.

(c) Unless the due date of principal has been accelerated, an instrument does not become overdue if there is default in payment of interest but no default in payment of principal.

## §3-305. Defenses and Claims in Recoupment.—

(a) Except as stated in subsection (b), the right to enforce the obligation of a party to pay an instrument is subject to the following:

    (1) a defense of the obligor based on (i) infancy of the obligor to the extent it is a defense to a simple contract, (ii) duress, lack of legal capacity, or illegality of the transaction which, under other law, nullifies the obligation of the obligor, (iii) fraud that induced the obligor to sign the instrument with neither knowledge nor reasonable opportunity to learn of its character or its essential terms, or (iv) discharge of the obligor in insolvency proceedings;

    (2) defense of the obligor stated in another section of this Article or a defense of the obligor that would be available if the person entitled to enforce the instrument were enforcing a right to payment under a simple contract; and

    (3) a claim in recoupment of the obligor against the original payee of the instrument if the claim arose from the transaction that gave rise to the instrument; but the claim of the obligor may be asserted against a transferee of the instrument only to reduce the amount owing on the instrument at the time the action is brought.

(b) The right of a holder in due course to enforce the obligation of a party to pay the instrument is subject to defenses of the obligor stated in subsection (a)(1), but is not subject to defenses of the obligor stated in subsection (a)(2) or claims in recoupment stated in subsection (a)(3) against a person other than the holder.

(c) Except as stated in subsection (d), in an action to enforce the obligation of a party to pay the instrument, the obligor may not assert against the person entitled to enforce the instrument a defense, claim in recoupment, or claim to the instrument (Section 3-306) of another person, but the other person's claim to the instrument may be asserted by the obligor if the other person is joined in the action and personally asserts the claim against the person entitled to enforce the instrument. An obligor is not obliged to pay the instrument if the person seeking enforcement of the instrument does not have rights of a holder in due course and the obligor proves that the instrument is a lost or stolen instrument.

(d) In an action to enforce the obligation of an accommodation party to pay an instrument, the accommodation party may assert against the person entitled to enforce the instrument any defense or claim in recoupment under subsection (a) that the accommodated party could assert against the person entitled to enforce the instrument, except the defenses of discharge in insolvency proceedings, infancy, and lack of legal capacity.

## §3-306. Claims to an Instrument.—
A person taking an instrument, other than a person having rights of a holder in due course, is subject to a claim of a property or possessory right in the instrument or its proceeds, including a claim to rescind a negotiation and to recover the instrument or its proceeds. A person having rights of a holder in due course takes free of the claim to the instrument.

## §3-307. Notice of Breach of Fiduciary Duty.—

(a) In this section:

(1) "Fiduciary" means an agent, trustee, partner, corporate officer or director, or other representative owing a fiduciary duty with respect to an instrument.

(2) "Represented person" means the principal, beneficiary, partnership, corporation, or other person to whom the duty stated in paragraph (1) is owed.

(b) If (i) an instrument is taken from a fiduciary for payment or collection or for value, (ii) the taker has knowledge of the fiduciary status of the fiduciary, and (iii) the represented person makes a claim to the instrument or its proceeds on the basis that the transaction of the fiduciary is a breach of fiduciary duty, the following rules apply:

(1) Notice of breach of fiduciary duty by the fiduciary is notice of the claim of the represented person.

(2) In the case of an instrument payable to the represented person or the fiduciary as such, the taker has notice of the breach of fiduciary duty if the instrument is (i) taken in payment of or as security for a debt known by the taker to be the personal debt of the fiduciary, (ii) taken in a transaction known by the taker to be for the personal benefit of the fiduciary, or (iii) deposited to an account other than an account of the fiduciary, as such, or an account of the represented person.

(3) If an instrument is issued by the represented person or the fiduciary as such, and made payable to the fiduciary personally, the taker does not have notice of the breach of fiduciary duty unless the taker knows of the breach of fiduciary duty.

(4) If an instrument is issued by the represented person or the fiduciary as such, to the taker as payee, the taker has notice of the breach of fiduciary duty if the instrument is (i) taken in payment of or as security for a debt known by the taker to be the personal debt of the fiduciary, (ii) taken in a transaction known by the taker to be for the personal benefit of the fiduciary, or (iii) deposited to an account other than an account of the fiduciary, as such, or an account of the represented person.

## §3-308. Proof of Signatures and Status as Holder in Due Course.—

(a) In an action with respect to an instrument, the authenticity of, and authority to make, each signature on the instrument is admitted unless specifically denied in the pleadings. If the validity of a signature is denied in the pleadings, the burden of establishing validity is on the person claiming validity, but the signature is presumed to be authentic and authorized unless the action is to enforce the liability of the purported signer and the signer is dead or incompetent at the time of trial of the issue of validity of the signature. If an action to enforce the instrument is brought against a person as the undisclosed principal of a person who signed the instrument as a party to the instrument, the plaintiff has the burden of establishing that the defendant is liable on the instrument as a represented person under Section 3-402(a).

(b) If the validity of signatures is admitted or proved and there is compliance with subsection (a), a plaintiff producing the instrument is entitled to payment if the plaintiff proves entitlement to enforce the instrument under Section 3-301, unless the defendant proves a defense or claim in recoupment. If a defense or claim in recoupment is proved, the right to payment of the plaintiff is subject to the defense or claim, except to the extent the plaintiff proves that the plaintiff has rights of a holder in due course which are not subject to the defense or claim.

## §3-309. Enforcement of Lost, Destroyed, or Stolen Instrument.—

(a) A person not in possession of an instrument is entitled to enforce the instrument if (i) the person was in possession of the instrument and entitled to enforce it when loss of possession occurred, (ii) the loss of possession was not the result of a transfer by the person or a lawful seizure, and (iii) the person cannot reasonably obtain possession of the instrument because the instrument was destroyed, its whereabouts cannot be determined, or it is in the wrongful possession of an unknown person or a person that cannot be found or is not amenable to service of process.

(b) A person seeking enforcement of an instrument under subsection (a) must prove the terms of the instrument and the person's right to enforce the instrument. If that proof is made, Section 3-308 applies to the case as if the person seeking enforcement had produced the instrument. The court may not enter judgment in favor of the person seeking enforcement unless it finds that the person required to pay the instrument is adequately protected against loss that might occur by reason of a claim by another person to enforce the instrument. Adequate protection may be provided by any reasonable means.

## §3-310. Effect of Instrument on Obligation for Which Taken.—

(a) Unless otherwise agreed, if a certified check, cashier's check, or teller's check is taken for an obligation, the obligation is discharged to the same extent discharge would result if an amount of money equal to the amount of the instrument were taken in payment of the obligation. Discharge of the obligation does not affect any liability that the obligor may have as an indorser of the instrument.

(b) Unless otherwise agreed and except as provided in subsection (a), if a note or an uncertified check is taken for an obligation, the obligation is suspended to the same extent the obligation would be discharged if an amount of money equal to the amount of the instrument were taken, and the following rules apply:

(1) In the case of an uncertified check, suspension of the obligation continues until dishonor of the check or until it is paid or certified. Payment or certification of the check results in discharge of the obligation to the extent of the amount of the check.

(2) In the case of a note, suspension of the obligation continues until dishonor of the note or until it is paid. Payment of the note results in discharge of the obligation to the extent of the payment.

(3) Except as provided in paragraph (4), if the check or note is dishonored and the obligee of the obligation for which the instrument was taken is the person entitled to enforce the instrument, the obligee may enforce either the instrument or the obligation. In the case of an instrument of a third person which is negotiated to the obligee by the obligor, discharge of the obligor on the instrument also discharges the obligation.

(4) If the person entitled to enforce the instrument taken for an obligation is a person other than the obligee, the obligee may not enforce the obligation to the extent the obligation is suspended. If the obligee is the person entitled to enforce the instrument but no longer has possession of it because it was lost, stolen, or destroyed, the obligation may not be enforced to the extent of the amount payable on the instrument, and to that extent the obligee's rights against the obligor are limited to enforcement of the instrument.

(c) If an instrument other than one described in subsection (a) or (b) is taken for an obligation, the effect is (i) that stated in subsection (a) if the instrument is one on which a bank is liable as maker or acceptor, or (ii) that stated in subsection (b) in any other case.

## §3-311. Accord and Satisfaction by Use of Instrument.—

(a) If a person against whom a claim is asserted proves that (i) that person in good faith tendered an instrument to the claimant as full satisfaction of the claim, (ii) the amount of the claim was unliquidated or subject to a bona fide dispute, and (iii) the claimant obtained payment of the instrument, the following subsections apply.

(b) Unless subsection (c) applies, the claim is discharged if the person against whom the claim is asserted proves that the instrument or an accompanying written communication contained a conspicuous statement to the effect that the instrument was tendered as full satisfaction of the claim.

(c) Subject to subsection (d), a claim is not discharged under subsection (b) if either of the following applies:

(1) The claimant, if an organization, proves that (i) within a reasonable time before the tender, the claimant sent a conspicuous statement to the person against whom the claim is asserted that communications concerning disputed debts, including an instrument tendered as full satisfaction of a debt, are to be sent to a designated person, office, or place, and (ii) the instrument or accompanying communication was not received by that designated person, office, or place.

(2) The claimant, whether or not an organization, proves that within 90 days after payment of the instrument, the claimant tendered repayment of the amount of the instrument to the person against whom the claim is asserted. This paragraph does not apply if the claimant is an organization that sent a statement complying with paragraph (1)(i).

(d) A claim is discharged if the person against whom the claim is asserted proves that within a reasonable time before collection of the instrument was initiated, the claimant, or an agent of the claimant having direct responsibility with respect to the disputed obligation, knew that the instrument was tendered in full satisfaction of the claim.

## §3-312. Lost, Destroyed, or Stolen Cashier's Check, Teller's Check, or Certified Check.—

(a) In this section:

 (1) "Check" means a cashier's check, teller's check, or certified check.

 (2) "Claimant" means a person who claims the right to receive the amount of a cashier's check, teller's check, or certified check that was lost, destroyed, or stolen.

 (3) "Declaration of loss" means a written statement, made under penalty of perjury, to the effect that (i) the declarer lost possession of a check, (ii) the declarer is the drawer or payee of the check, in the case of a certified check, or the remitter or payee of the check, in the case of a cashier's check or teller's check, (iii) the loss of possession was not the result of a transfer by the declarer or a lawful seizure, and (iv) the declarer cannot reasonably obtain possession of the check because the check was destroyed, its whereabouts cannot be determined, or it is in the wrongful possession of an unknown person or a person that cannot be found or is not amenable to service of process.

 (4) "Obligated bank" means the issuer of a cashier's check or teller's check or the acceptor of a certified check.

(b) A claimant may assert a claim to the amount of a check by a communication to the obligated bank describing the check with reasonable certainty and requesting payment of the amount of the check, if (i) the claimant is the drawer or payee of a certified check or the remitter or payee of a cashier's check or teller's check, (ii) the communication contains or is accompanied by a declaration of loss of the claimant with respect to the check, (iii) the communication is received at a time and in a manner affording the bank a reasonable time to act on it before the check is paid, and (iv) the claimant provides reasonable identification if requested by the obligated bank. Delivery of a declaration of loss is a warranty of the truth of the statements made in the declaration. If a claim is asserted in compliance with this subsection, the following rules apply:

 (1) The claim becomes enforceable at the later of (i) the time the claim is asserted, or (ii) the 90th day following the date of the check, in the case of a cashier's check or teller's check, or the 90th day following the date of the acceptance, in the case of a certified check.

 (2) Until the claim becomes enforceable, it has no legal effect and the obligated bank may pay the check or, in the case of a teller's check, may permit the drawee to pay the check. Payment to a person entitled to enforce the check discharges all liability of the obligated bank with respect to the check.

 (3) If the claim becomes enforceable before the check is presented for payment, the obligated bank is not obliged to pay the check.

 (4) When the claim becomes enforceable, the obligated bank becomes obliged to pay the amount of the check to the claimant if payment of the check has not been made to a person entitled to enforce the check. Subject to Section 4-302(a)(1), payment to the claimant discharges all liability of the obligated bank with respect to the check.

(c) If the obligated bank pays the amount of a check to a claimant under subsection (b)(4) and the check is presented for payment by a person having rights of a holder in due course, the claimant is obliged to (i) refund the payment to the obligated bank if the check is paid, or (ii) pay the amount of the check to the person having rights of a holder in due course if the check is dishonored.

(d) If a claimant has the right to assert a claim under subsection (b) and is also a person entitled to enforce a cashier's check, teller's check, or certified check which is lost, destroyed, or stolen, the claimant may assert rights with respect to the check either under this section or Section 3-309.

## Part 4: Liability of Parties

### §3-401. Signature.—

(a) A person is not liable on an instrument unless (i) the person signed the instrument, or (ii) the person is represented by an agent or representative who signed the instrument and the signature is binding on the represented person under Section 3-402.

(b) A signature may be made (i) manually or by means of a device or machine, and (ii) by the use of any name, including a trade or assumed name, or by a word, mark, or symbol executed or adopted by a person with present intention to authenticate a writing.

### §3-402. Signature by Representative.—

(a) If a person acting, or purporting to act, as a representative signs an instrument by signing either the name of the represented person or the name of the signer, the represented person is bound by the signature to the same extent the represented person would be bound if the signature were on a simple contract. If the represented person is bound, the signature of the representative is the "authorized signature of the represented person" and the represented person is liable on the instrument, whether or not identified in the instrument.

(b) If a representative signs the name of the representative to an instrument and the signature is an authorized signature of the represented person, the following rules apply:

(1) If the form of the signature shows unambiguously that the signature is made on behalf of the represented person who is identified in the instrument, the representative is not liable on the instrument.

(2) Subject to subsection (c), if (i) the form of the signature does not show unambiguously that the signature is made in a representative capacity or (ii) the represented person is not identified in the instrument, the representative is liable on the instrument to a holder in due course that took the instrument without notice that the representative was not intended to be liable on the instrument. With respect to any other person, the representative is liable on the instrument unless the representative proves that the original parties did not intend the representative to be liable on the instrument.

(c) If a representative signs the name of the representative as drawer of a check without indication of the representative status and the check is payable from an account of the represented person who is identified on the check, the signer is not liable on the check if the signature is an authorized signature of the represented person.

## §3-403. Unauthorized Signature.—

(a) Unless otherwise provided in this Article or Article 4, an unauthorized signature is ineffective except as the signature of the unauthorized signer in favor of a person who in good faith pays the instrument or takes it for value. An unauthorized signature may be ratified for all purposes of this Article.

(b) If the signature of more than one person is required to constitute the authorized signature of an organization, the signature of the organization is unauthorized if one of the required signatures is lacking.

(c) The civil or criminal liability of a person who makes an unauthorized signature is not affected by any provision of this Article which makes the unauthorized signature effective for the purposes of this Article.

## §3-404. Impostors; Fictitious Payees.—

(a) If an impostor, by use of the mails or otherwise, induces the issuer of an instrument to issue the instrument to the impostor, or to a person acting in concert with the impostor, by impersonating the payee of the instrument or a person authorized to act for the payee, an indorsement of the instrument by any person in the name of the payee is effective as the indorsement of the payee in favor of a person who, in good faith, pays the instrument or takes it for value or for collection.

(b) If (i) a person whose intent determines to whom an instrument is payable (Section 3-110(a) or (b)) does not intend the person identified as payee to have any interest in the instrument, or (ii) the person identified as payee of an instrument is a fictitious person, the following rules apply until the instrument is negotiated by special indorsement:

(1) Any person in possession of the instrument is its holder.

(2) An indorsement by any person in the name of the payee stated in the instrument is effective as the indorsement of the payee in favor of a person who, in good faith, pays the instrument or takes it for value or for collection.

(c) Under subsection (a) or (b), an indorsement is made in the name of a payee if (i) it is made in a name substantially similar to that of the payee or (ii) the instrument, whether or not indorsed, is deposited in a depositary bank to an account in a name substantially similar to that of the payee.

(d) With respect to an instrument to which subsection (a) or (b) applies, if a person paying the instrument or taking it for value or for collection fails to exercise ordinary care in paying or taking the instrument and that failure substantially contributes to loss resulting from payment of the instrument, the person bearing the loss may recover from the person failing to exercise ordinary care to the extent the failure to exercise ordinary care contributed to the loss.

## §3-405. Employer's Responsibility for Fraudulent Indorsement by Employee.—

(a) In this section

(1) "Employee" includes an independent contractor and employee of an independent contractor retained by the employer.

(2) "Fraudulent indorsement" means (i) in the case of an instrument payable to the employer, a forged indorsement purporting to be that of the employer, or (ii) in the case of an instrument with respect to which the employer is the issuer, a forged indorsement purporting to be that of the person identified as payee.

(3) "Responsibility" with respect to instruments means authority (i) to sign or indorse instruments on behalf of the employer, (ii) to process instruments received by the employer for bookkeeping purposes, for deposit to an account, or for other disposition, (iii) to prepare or process instruments for issue in the name of the employer, (iv) to supply information determining the names or addresses of payees of instruments to be issued in the name of the employer, (v) to control the disposition of instruments to be issued in the name of the employer, or (vi) to act otherwise with respect to instruments in a responsible capacity. "Responsibility" does not include authority that merely

allows an employee to have access to instruments or blank or incomplete instrument forms that are being stored or transported or are part of incoming or outgoing mail, or similar access.

(b) For the purpose of determining the rights and liabilities of a person who, in good faith, pays an instrument or takes it for value or for collection, if an employer entrusted an employee with responsibility with respect to the instrument and the employee or a person acting in concert with the employee makes a fraudulent indorsement of the instrument, the indorsement is effective as the indorsement of the person to whom the instrument is payable if it is made in the name of that person. If the person paying the instrument or taking it for value or for collection fails to exercise ordinary care in paying or taking the instrument and that failure substantially contributes to loss resulting from the fraud, the person bearing the loss may recover from the person failing to exercise ordinary care to the extent the failure to exercise ordinary care contributed to the loss.

(c) Under subsection (b), an indorsement is made in the name of the person to whom an instrument is payable if (i) it is made in a name substantially similar to the name of that person or (ii) the instrument, whether or not indorsed, is deposited in a depositary bank to an account in a name substantially similar to the name of that person.

## §3-406. Negligence Contributing to Forged Signature or Alteration of Instrument.—

(a) A person whose failure to exercise ordinary care substantially contributes to an alteration of an instrument or to the making of a forged signature on an instrument is precluded from asserting the alteration or the forgery against a person who, in good faith, pays the instrument or takes it for value or for collection.

(b) Under subsection (a), if the person asserting the preclusion fails to exercise ordinary care in paying or taking the instrument and that failure substantially contributes to loss, the loss is allocated between the person precluded and the person asserting the preclusion according to the extent to which the failure of each to exercise ordinary care contributed to the loss.

(c) Under subsection (a), the burden of proving failure to exercise ordinary care is on the person asserting the preclusion. Under subsection (b), the burden of proving failure to exercise ordinary care is on the person precluded.

## §3-407. Alteration.—

(a) "Alteration" means (i) an unauthorized change in an instrument that purports to modify in any respect the obligation of a party, or (ii) an unauthorized addition of words or numbers or other change to an incomplete instrument relating to the obligation of a party.

(b) Except as provided in subsection (c), an alteration fraudulently made discharges a party whose obligation is affected by the alteration unless that party assents or is precluded from asserting the alteration. No other alteration discharges a party, and the instrument may be enforced according to its original terms.

(c) A payor bank or drawee paying a fraudulently altered instrument or a person taking it for value, in good faith and without notice of the alteration, may enforce rights with respect to the instrument (i) according to its original terms, or (ii) in the case of an incomplete instrument altered by unauthorized completion, according to its terms as completed.

## §3-408. Drawee Not Liable on Unaccepted Draft.— A check or other draft does not of itself operate as an assignment of funds in the hands of the drawee available for its payment, and the drawee is not liable on the instrument until the drawee accepts it.

## §3-409. Acceptance of Draft; Certified Check.—

(a) "Acceptance" means the drawee's signed agreement to pay a draft as presented. It must be written on the draft and may consist of the drawee's signature alone. Acceptance may be made at any time and becomes effective when notification pursuant to instructions is given or the accepted draft is delivered for the purpose of giving rights on the acceptance to any person.

(b) A draft may be accepted although it has not been signed by the drawer, is otherwise incomplete, is overdue, or has been dishonored.

(c) If a draft is payable at a fixed period after sight and the acceptor fails to date the acceptance, the holder may complete the acceptance by supplying a date in good faith.

(d) "Certified check" means a check accepted by the bank on which it is drawn. Acceptance may be made as stated in subsection (a) or by a writing on the check which indicates that the check is certified. The drawee of a check has no obligation to certify the check, and refusal to certify is not dishonor of the check.

## §3-410. Acceptance Varying Draft.—

(a) If the terms of a drawee's acceptance vary from the terms of the draft as presented, the holder may refuse the acceptance and treat the draft as dishonored. In that case, the drawee may cancel the acceptance.

(b) The terms of a draft are not varied by an acceptance to pay at a particular bank or place in the United States, unless the acceptance states that the draft is to be paid only at that bank or place.

(c) If the holder assents to an acceptance varying the terms of a draft, the obligation of each drawer and indorser that does not expressly assent to the acceptance is discharged.

## §3-411. Refusal to Pay Cashier's Checks, Teller's Checks, and Certified Checks.—

(a) In this section, "obligated bank" means the acceptor of a certified check or the issuer of a cashier's check or teller's check bought from the issuer.

(b) If the obligated bank wrongfully (i) refuses to pay a cashier's check or certified check, (ii) stops payment of a teller's check, or (iii) refuses to pay a dishonored teller's check, the person asserting the right to enforce the check is entitled to compensation for expenses and loss of interest resulting from the nonpayment and may recover consequential damages if the obligated bank refuses to pay after receiving notice of particular circumstances giving rise to the damages.

(c) Expenses or consequential damages under subsection (b) are not recoverable if the refusal of the obligated bank to pay occurs because (i) the bank suspends payments, (ii) the obligated bank asserts a claim or defense of the bank that it has reasonable grounds to believe is available against the person entitled to enforce the instrument, (iii) the obligated bank has a reasonable doubt whether the person demanding payment is the person entitled to enforce the instrument, or (iv) payment is prohibited by law.

## §3-412. Obligation of Issuer of Note or Cashier's Check.—

The issuer of a note or cashier's check or other draft drawn on the drawer is obliged to pay the instrument (i) according to its terms at the time it was issued or, if not issued, at the time it first came into possession of a holder, or (ii) if the issuer signed an incomplete instrument, according to its terms when completed, to the extent stated in Sections 3-115 and 3-407. The obligation is owed to a person entitled to enforce the instrument or to an indorser who paid the instrument under Section 3-415.

## §3-413. Obligation of Acceptor.—

(a) The acceptor of a draft is obliged to pay the draft (i) according to its terms at the time it was accepted, even though the acceptance states that the draft is payable "as originally drawn" or equivalent terms, (ii) if the acceptance varies the terms of the draft, according to the terms of the draft as varied, or (iii) if the acceptance is of a draft that is an incomplete instrument, according to its terms when completed, to the extent stated in Sections 3-115 and 3-407. The obligation is owed to a person entitled to enforce the draft or to the drawer or an indorser who paid the draft under Section 3-414 or 3-415.

(b) If the certification of a check or other acceptance of a draft states the amount certified or accepted, the obligation of the acceptor is that amount. If (i) the certification or acceptance does not state an amount, (ii) the amount of the instrument is subsequently raised, and (iii) the instrument is then negotiated to a holder in due course, the obligation of the acceptor is the amount of the instrument at the time it was taken by the holder in due course.

## §3-414. Obligation of Drawer.—

(a) This section does not apply to cashier's checks or other drafts drawn on the drawer.

(b) If an unaccepted draft is dishonored, the drawer is obliged to pay the draft (i) according to its terms at the time it was issued or, if not issued, at the time it first came into possession of a holder, or (ii) if the drawer signed an incomplete instrument, according to its terms when completed, to the extent stated in Sections 3-115 and 3-407. The obligation is owed to a person entitled to enforce the draft or to an indorser who paid the draft under Section 3-415.

(c) If a draft is accepted by a bank, the drawer is discharged, regardless of when or by whom acceptance was obtained.

(d) If a draft is accepted and the acceptor is not a bank, the obligation of the drawer to pay the draft if the draft is dishonored by the acceptor is the same as the obligation of an indorser under Section 3-415(a) and (c).

(e) If a draft states that it is drawn "without recourse" or otherwise disclaims liability of the drawer to pay the draft, the drawer is not liable under subsection (b) to pay the draft if the draft is not a check. A disclaimer of the liability stated in subsection (b) is not effective if the draft is a check.

(f) If (i) a check is not presented for payment or given to a depositary bank for collection within 30 days after its date, (ii) the drawee suspends payments after expiration of the 30-day period without paying the check, and (iii) because of the suspension of payments, the drawer is deprived of funds maintained with the drawee to cover payment of the check, the drawer to the extent deprived of funds may discharge its obligation to pay the check by assigning to the person entitled to enforce the check the rights of the drawer against the drawee with respect to the funds.

## §3-415. Obligation of Indorser.—

(a) Subject to subsections (b), (c), and (d) and to Section 3-419(d), if an instrument is dishonored, an indorser is obliged to pay the amount due on the instrument (i) according to the terms of the instrument at the time it was indorsed, or (ii) if the indorser indorsed an incomplete instrument, according to its terms when completed, to the extent stated in Sections 3-115 and 3-407. The obligation of the indorser is owed to a person entitled to enforce the instrument or to a subsequent indorser who paid the instrument under this section.

(b) If an indorsement states that it is made "without recourse" or otherwise disclaims liability of the indorser, the indorser is not liable under subsection (a) to pay the instrument.

(c) If notice of dishonor of an instrument is required by Section 3-503 and notice of dishonor complying with that section is not given to an indorser, the liability of the indorser under subsection (a) is discharged.

(d) If a draft is accepted by a bank after an indorsement is made, the liability of the indorser under subsection (a) is discharged.

(e) If an indorser of a check is liable under subsection (a) and the check is not presented for payment, or given to a depositary bank for collection, within 30 days after the day the indorsement was made, the liability of the indorser under subsection (a) is discharged.

## §3-416. Transfer Warranties.—

(a) A person who transfers an instrument for consideration warrants to the transferee and, if the transfer is by indorsement, to any subsequent transferee that:

(1) the warrantor is a person entitled to enforce the instrument;

(2) all signatures on the instrument are authentic and authorized;

(3) the instrument has not been altered;

(4) the instrument is not subject to a defense or claim in recoupment of any party which can be asserted against the warrantor; and

(5) the warrantor has no knowledge of any insolvency proceeding commenced with respect to the maker or acceptor or, in the case of an unaccepted draft, the drawer.

(b) A person to whom the warranties under subsection (a) are made and who took the instrument in good faith may recover from the warrantor as damages for breach of warranty an amount equal to the loss suffered as a result of the breach, but not more than the amount of the instrument plus expenses and loss of interest incurred as a result of the breach.

(c) The warranties stated in subsection (a) cannot be disclaimed with respect to checks. Unless notice of a claim for breach of warranty is given to the warrantor within 30 days after the claimant has reason to know of the breach and the identity of the warrantor, the liability of the warrantor under subsection (b) is discharged to the extent of any loss caused by the delay in giving notice of the claim.

(d) A [cause of action] for breach of warranty under this section accrues when the claimant has reason to know of the breach.

## §3-417. Presentment Warranties.—

(a) If an unaccepted draft is presented to the drawee for payment or acceptance and the drawee pays or accepts the draft, (i) the person obtaining payment or acceptance, at the time of presentment, and (ii) a previous transferor of the draft, at the time of transfer, warrant to the drawee making payment or accepting the draft in good faith that:

(1) the warrantor is, or was, at the time the warrantor transferred the draft, a person entitled to enforce the draft or authorized to obtain payment or acceptance of the draft on behalf of a person entitled to enforce the draft;

(2) the draft has not been altered; and

(3) the warrantor has no knowledge that the signature of the drawer of the draft is unauthorized.

(b) A drawee making payment may recover from any warrantor damages for breach of warranty equal to the amount paid by the drawee less the amount the drawee received or is entitled to receive from the drawer because of the payment. In addition, the drawee is entitled to compensation for expenses and loss of interest resulting from the breach. The right of the drawee to recover damages under this subsection is not affected by any failure of the drawee to exercise ordinary care in making payment. If the drawee accepts the draft, breach of warranty is a defense to the obligation of the acceptor. If the acceptor makes payment with respect to the draft, the acceptor is entitled to recover from any warrantor for breach of warranty the amounts stated in this subsection.

(c) If a drawee asserts a claim for breach of warranty under subsection (a) based on an unauthorized indorsement of the draft or an alteration of the draft, the warrantor may defend by proving that the indorsement is effective under Section 3-404 or 3-405 or the drawer is precluded under Section 3-406 or 4-406 from asserting against the drawee the unauthorized indorsement or alteration.

(d) If (i) a dishonored draft is presented for payment to the drawer or an indorser or (ii) any other instrument is presented for payment to a party obliged to pay the instrument, and (iii) payment is received, the following rules apply:

(1) The person obtaining payment and a prior transferor of the instrument warrant to the person making payment in good faith that the warrantor is, or was, at the time the warrantor transferred the instrument, a person entitled to enforce the instrument or authorized to obtain payment on behalf of a person entitled to enforce the instrument.

(2) The person making payment may recover from any warrantor for breach of warranty an amount equal to the amount paid plus expenses and loss of interest resulting from the breach.

(e) The warranties stated in subsections (a) and (d) cannot be disclaimed with respect to checks. Unless notice of a claim for breach of warranty is given to the warrantor within 30 days after the claimant has reason to know of the breach and the identity of the warrantor, the liability of the warrantor under subsection (b) or (d) is discharged to the extent of any loss caused by the delay in giving notice of the claim.

(f) A [cause of action] for breach of warranty under this section accrues when the claimant has reason to know of the breach.

## §3-418. Payment or Acceptance by Mistake.—

(a) Except as provided in subsection (c), if the drawee of a draft pays or accepts the draft and the drawee acted on the mistaken belief that (i) payment of the draft had not been stopped pursuant to Section 4-403 or (ii) the signature of the drawer of the draft was authorized, the drawee may recover the amount of the draft from the person to whom or for whose benefit payment was made or, in the case of acceptance, may revoke the acceptance. Rights of the drawee under this subsection are not affected by failure of the drawee to exercise ordinary care in paying or accepting the draft.

(b) Except as provided in subsection (c), if an instrument has been paid or accepted by mistake and the case is not covered by subsection (a), the person paying or accepting may, to the extent permitted by the law governing mistake and restitution, (i) recover the payment from the person to whom or for whose benefit payment was made or (ii) in the case of acceptance, may revoke the acceptance.

(c) The remedies provided by subsection (a) or (b) may not be asserted against a person who took the instrument in good faith and for value or who in good faith changed position in reliance on the payment or acceptance. This subsection does not limit remedies provided by Section 3-417 or 4-407.

(d) Notwithstanding Section 4-215, if an instrument is paid or accepted by mistake and the payor or acceptor recovers payment or revokes acceptance under subsection (a) or (b), the instrument is deemed not to have been paid or accepted and is treated as dishonored, and the person from whom payment is recovered has rights as a person entitled to enforce the dishonored instrument.

## §3-419. Instruments Signed for Accommodation.—

(a) If an instrument is issued for value given for the benefit of a party to the instrument ("accommodated party") and another party to the instrument ("An accommodation party") signs the instrument for the purpose of incurring liability on the instrument without being a direct beneficiary of the value given for the instrument, the instrument is signed by the accommodation party "for accommodation".

(b) An accommodation party may sign the instrument as maker, drawer, acceptor, or indorser and, subject to subsection (d), is obliged to pay the instrument in the capacity in which the accommodation party signs.

The obligation of an accommodation party may be enforced notwithstanding any statute of frauds and whether or not the accommodation party receives consideration for the accommodation.

(c) A person signing an instrument is presumed to be an accommodation party and there is notice that the instrument is signed for accommodation if the signature is an anomalous indorsement or is accompanied by words indicating that the signer is acting as surety or guarantor with respect to the obligation of another party to the instrument. Except as provided in Section 3-605, the obligation of an accommodation party to pay the instrument is not affected by the fact that the person enforcing the obligation had notice when the instrument was taken by that person that the accommodation party signed the instrument for accommodation.

(d) If the signature of a party to an instrument is accompanied by words indicating unambiguously that the party is guaranteeing collection rather than payment of the obligation of another party to the instrument, the signer is obliged to pay the amount due on the instrument to a person entitled to enforce the instrument only if (i) execution of judgment against the other party has been returned unsatisfied, (ii) the other party is insolvent or in an insolvency proceeding, (iii) the other party cannot be served with process, or (iv) it is otherwise apparent that payment cannot be obtained from the other party.

(e) An accommodation party who pays the instrument is entitled to reimbursement from the accommodated party and is entitled to enforce the instrument against the accommodated party. An accommodated party who pays the instrument has no right of recourse against, and is not entitled to contribution from, an accommodation party.

## §3-420. Conversion of Instrument.—

(a) The law applicable to conversion of personal property applies to instruments. An instrument is also converted if it is taken by transfer, other than a negotiation, from a person not entitled to enforce the instrument or a bank makes or obtains payment with respect to the instrument for a person not entitled to enforce the instrument or receive payment. An action for conversion of an instrument may not be brought by (i) the issuer or acceptor of the instrument or (ii) a payee or indorsee who did not receive delivery of the instrument either directly or through delivery to an agent or a co-payee.

(b) In an action under subsection (a), the measure of liability is presumed to be the amount payable on the instrument, but recovery may not exceed the amount of the plaintiff's interest in the instrument.

(c) A representative, other than a depositary bank, who has in good faith dealt with an instrument or its proceeds on behalf of one who was not the person entitled to enforce the instrument is not liable in conversion to that person beyond the amount of any proceeds that it has not paid out.

## Part 5: Dishonor

### §3-501. Presentment.—

(a) "Presentment" means a demand made by or on behalf of a person entitled to enforce an instrument (i) to pay the instrument made to the drawee or a party obliged to pay the instrument or, in the case of a note or accepted draft payable at a bank, to the bank, or (ii) to accept a draft made to the drawee.

(b) The following rules are subject to Article 4, agreement of the parties, and clearing-house rules and the like:

　(1) Presentment may be made at the place of payment of the instrument and must be made at the place of payment if the instrument is payable at a bank in the United States; may be made by any commercially reasonable means, including an oral, written, or electronic communication; is effective when the demand for payment or acceptance is received by the person to whom presentment is made; and is effective if made to any one of two or more makers, acceptors, drawees, or other payors.

　(2) Upon demand of the person to whom presentment is made, the person making presentment must (i) exhibit the instrument, (ii) give reasonable identification and, if presentment is made on behalf of another person, reasonable evidence of authority to do so, and (iii) sign a receipt on the instrument for any payment made or surrender the instrument if full payment is made.

　(3) Without dishonoring the instrument, the party to whom presentment is made may (i) return the instrument for lack of a necessary indorsement, or (ii) refuse payment or acceptance for failure of the presentment to comply with the terms of the instrument, an agreement of the parties, or other applicable law or rule.

　(4) The party to whom presentment is made may treat presentment as occurring on the next business day after the day of presentment if the party to whom presentment is made has established a cut-off hour not earlier than 2 p.m for the receipt and processing of instruments presented for payment or acceptance and presentment is made after the cut-off hour.

### §3-502. Dishonor.—

(a) Dishonor of a note is governed by the following rules:

　(1) If the note is payable on demand, the note is dishonored if presentment is duly made to the maker and the note is not paid on the day of presentment.

　(2) If the note is not payable on demand and is payable at or through a bank or the terms of the note require presentment, the note is dishonored if presentment is duly made and the note is not paid on the day it becomes payable or the day of presentment, whichever is later.

　(3) If the note is not payable on demand and paragraph (2) does not apply, the note is dishonored if it is not paid on the day it becomes payable.

(b) Dishonor of an unaccepted draft other than a documentary draft is governed by the following rules:

　(1) If a check is duly presented for payment to the payor bank otherwise than for immediate payment over the counter, the check is dishonored if the payor bank makes timely return of the check or sends timely notice of dishonor or nonpayment under Section 4-301 or 4-302, or becomes accountable for the amount of the check under Section 4-302.

　(2) If a draft is payable on demand and paragraph (1) does not apply, the draft is dishonored if presentment for payment is duly made to the drawee and the draft is not paid on the day of presentment.

　(3) If a draft is payable on a date stated in the draft, the draft is dishonored if (i) presentment for payment is duly made to the drawee and payment is not made on the day the draft becomes payable or the day of presentment, whichever is later, or (ii) presentment for acceptance is duly made before the day the draft becomes payable and the draft is not accepted on the day of presentment.

　(4) If a draft is payable on elapse of a period of time after sight or acceptance, the draft is dishonored if presentment for acceptance is duly made and the draft is not accepted on the day of presentment.

(c) Dishonor of an unaccepted documentary draft occurs according to the rules stated in subsection (b)(2), (3), and (4), except that payment or acceptance may be delayed without dishonor until no later than the close of the third business day of the drawee following the day on which payment or acceptance is required by those paragraphs.

(d) Dishonor of an accepted draft is governed by the following rules:

　(1) If the draft is payable on demand, the draft is dishonored if presentment for payment is duly made to the acceptor and the draft is not paid on the day of presentment.

　(2) If the draft is not payable on demand, the draft is dishonored if presentment for payment is duly made to the acceptor and payment is not made on the day it becomes payable or the day of presentment, whichever is later.

(e) In any case in which presentment is otherwise required for dishonor under this section and presentment is excused under Section 3-504, dishonor occurs without presentment if the instrument is not duly accepted or paid.

(f) If a draft is dishonored because timely acceptance of the draft was not made and the person entitled to demand acceptance consents to a late acceptance, from the time of acceptance the draft is treated as never having been dishonored.

## §3-503. Notice of Dishonor.—

(a) The obligation of an indorser stated in Section 3-415(a) and the obligation of a drawer stated in Section 3-414(d) may not be enforced unless (i) the indorser or drawer is given notice of dishonor of the instrument complying with this section or (ii) notice of dishonor is excused under Section 3-504(b).

(b) Notice of dishonor may be given by any person; may be given by any commercially reasonable means, including an oral, written, or electronic communication; and is sufficient if it reasonably identifies the instrument and indicates that the instrument has been dishonored or has not been paid or accepted. Return of an instrument given to a bank for collection is sufficient notice of dishonor.

(c) Subject to Section 3-504(c), with respect to an instrument taken for collection by a collecting bank, notice of dishonor must be given (i) by the bank before midnight of the next banking day following the banking day on which the bank receives notice of dishonor of the instrument, or (ii) by any other person within 30 days following the day on which the person receives notice of dishonor. With respect to any other instrument, notice of dishonor must be given within 30 days following the day on which dishonor occurs.

## §3-504. Excused Presentment and Notice of Dishonor.—

(a) Presentment for payment or acceptance of an instrument is excused if (i) the person entitled to present the instrument cannot with reasonable diligence make presentment, (ii) the maker or acceptor has repudiated an obligation to pay the instrument or is dead or in insolvency proceedings, (iii) by the terms of the instrument presentment is not necessary to enforce the obligation of indorsers or the drawer, (iv) the drawer or indorser whose obligation is being enforced has waived presentment or otherwise has no reason to expect or right to require that the instrument be paid or accepted, or (v) the drawer instructed the drawee not to pay or accept the draft or the drawee was not obligated to the drawer to pay the draft.

(b) Notice of dishonor is excused if (i) by the terms of the instrument notice of dishonor is not necessary to enforce the obligation of a party to pay the instrument, or (ii) the party whose obligation is being enforced waived notice of dishonor. A waiver of presentment is also a waiver of notice of dishonor.

(c) Delay in giving notice of dishonor is excused if the delay was caused by circumstances beyond the control of the person giving the notice and the person giving the notice exercised reasonable diligence after the cause of the delay ceased to operate.

## §3-505. Evidence of Dishonor.—

(a) The following are admissible as evidence and create a presumption of dishonor and of any notice of dishonor stated:

(1) a document regular in form as provided in subsection (b) which purports to be a protest;

(2) a purported stamp or writing of the drawee, payor bank, or presenting bank on or accompanying the instrument stating that acceptance or payment has been refused unless reasons for the refusal are stated and the reasons are not consistent with dishonor;

(3) a book or record of the drawee, payor bank, or collecting bank, kept in the usual course of business which shows dishonor, even if there is no evidence of who made the entry.

(b) A protest is a certificate of dishonor made by a United States consul or vice consul, or a notary public or other person authorized to administer oaths by the law of the place where dishonor occurs. It may be made upon information satisfactory to that person. The protest must identify the instrument and certify either that presentment has been made or, if not made, the reason why it was not made, and that the instrument has been dishonored by nonacceptance or nonpayment. The protest may also certify that notice of dishonor has been given to some or all parties.

## Part 6: Discharge and Payment

### §3-601. Discharge and Effect of Discharge.—

(a) The obligation of a party to pay the instrument is discharged as stated in this Article or by an act or agreement with the party which would discharge an obligation to pay money under a simple contract.

(b) Discharge of the obligation of a party is not effective against a person acquiring rights of a holder in due course of the instrument without notice of the discharge.

### §3-602. Payment.—

(a) Subject to subsection (b), an instrument is paid to the extent payment is made (i) by or on behalf of a party obliged to pay the instrument, and (ii) to a person entitled to enforce the instrument. To the extent of the payment, the obligation of the party obliged to pay the instrument is discharged even though payment is made with knowledge of a claim to the instrument under Section 3-306 by another person.

(b) The obligation of a party to pay the instrument is not discharged under subsection (a) if:

(1) a claim to the instrument under Section 3-306 is enforceable against the party receiving payment and (i) payment is made with knowledge by the payor that payment is prohibited by injunction or similar process of a court of competent jurisdiction, or (ii) in the case of an instrument other than a cashier's check, teller's check, or certified check, the party making payment accepted, from the person having a claim to the instrument, indemnity against loss resulting from refusal to pay the person entitled to enforce the instrument; or

(2) the person making payment knows that the instrument is a stolen instrument and pays a person it knows is in wrongful possession of the instrument.

## §3-603. Tender of Payment.—

(a) If tender of payment of an obligation to pay an instrument is made to a person entitled to enforce the instrument, the effect of tender is governed by principles of law applicable to tender of payment under a simple contract.

(b) If tender of payment of an obligation to pay an instrument is made to a person entitled to enforce the instrument and the tender is refused,. . . .

## §3-604. Discharge by Cancellation or Renunciation.—

(a) A person entitled to enforce an instrument, with or without consideration, may discharge the obligation of a party to pay the instrument (i) by an intentional voluntary act, such as surrender of the instrument to the party, destruction, mutilation, or cancellation of the instrument, cancellation or striking out of the party's signature, or the addition of words to the instrument indicating discharge, or (ii) by agreeing not to sue or otherwise renouncing rights against the party by a signed writing.

(b) Cancellation or striking out of an indorsement pursuant to subsection (a) does not affect the status and rights of a party derived from the indorsement.

## §3-605. Discharge of Indorsers and Accommodation Parties.—

(a) In this section, the term "indorser" includes a drawer having the obligation described in Section 3-414(d).

(b) Discharge, under Section 3-604, of the obligation of a party to pay an instrument does not discharge the obligation of an indorser or accommodation party having a right of recourse against the discharged party.

(c) If a person entitled to enforce an instrument agrees, with or without consideration, to an extension of the due date of the obligation of a party to pay the instrument, the extension discharges an indorser or accommodation party having a right of recourse against the party whose obligation is extended to the extent the indorser or accommodation party proves that the extension caused loss to the indorser or accommodation party with respect to the right of recourse.

(d) If a person entitled to enforce an instrument agrees, with or without consideration, to a material modification of the obligation of a party other than an extension of the due date, the modification discharges the obligation of an indorser or accommodation party having a right of recourse against the person whose obligation is modified to the extent the modification causes loss to the indorser or accommodation party with respect to the right of recourse. The loss suffered by the indorser or accommodation party as a result of the modification is equal to the amount of the right of recourse unless the person enforcing the instrument proves that no loss was caused by the modification or that the loss caused by the modification was an amount less than the amount of the right of recourse.

(e) If the obligation of a party to pay an instrument is secured by an interest in collateral and a person entitled to enforce the instrument impairs the value of the interest in collateral, the obligation of an indorser or accommodation party having a right of recourse against the obligor is discharged to the extent of the impairment. The value of an interest in collateral is impaired to the extent (i) the value of the interest is reduced to an amount less than the amount of the right of recourse of the party asserting discharge, or (ii) the reduction in value of the interest causes an increase in the amount by which the amount of the right of recourse exceeds the value of the interest. The burden of proving impairment is on the party asserting discharge.

(f) If the obligation of a party is secured by an interest in collateral not provided by an accommodation party and a person entitled to enforce the instrument impairs the value of the interest in collateral, the obligation of any party who is jointly and severally liable with respect to the secured obligation is discharged to the extent the impairment causes the party asserting discharge to pay more than that party would have been obliged to pay, taking into account rights of contribution, if impairment had not occurred. If the party asserting discharge is an accommodation party not entitled to discharge under subsection (e), the party is deemed to have a right to contribution based on joint and several liability rather than a right to reimbursement. The burden of proving impairment is on the party asserting discharge.

(g) Under subsection (e) or (f), impairing value of an interest in collateral includes (i) failure to obtain or maintain perfection or recordation of the interest in collateral, (ii) release of collateral without substitution of collateral of equal value, (iii) failure to perform a duty to preserve the value of collateral owed, under Article 9 or other law, to a debtor or surety or other person secondarily liable, or (iv) failure to comply with applicable law in disposing of collateral.

(h) An accommodation party is not discharged under subsection (c), (d), or (e) unless the person entitled to enforce the instrument knows of the accommodation or has notice under Section 3-419(c) that the instrument was signed for accommodation.

(i) A party is not discharged under this section if (i) the party asserting discharge consents to the event or conduct that is the basis of the discharge, or (ii) the instrument or a separate agreement of the party provides for waiver of discharge under this section either specifically or by general language indicating that parties waive defenses based on suretyship or impairment of collateral.

# Appendix C

# United Nations Convention on Contracts for the International Sale of Goods

THE STATES PARTIES TO THIS CONVENTION, BEARING IN MIND the broad objectives in the resolutions adopted by the sixth special session of the General Assembly of the United Nations on the establishment of a New International Economic Order,

CONSIDERING that the development of international trade on the basis of equality and mutual benefit is an important element in promoting friendly relations among States,

BEING OF THE OPINION that the adoption of uniform rules which govern contracts for the international sale of goods and take into account the different social, economic and legal systems would contribute to the removal of legal barriers in international trade and promote the development of international trade,

HAVE AGREED as follows:

## Part I Sphere of Application and General Provisions

### Chapter I Sphere of Application

#### Article 1

(1) This Convention applies to contracts of sale of goods between parties whose places of business are in different States:

    (a) when the States are Contracting States; or

    (b) when the rules of private international law lead to the application of the law of a Contracting State. [Pursuant to the reservation permitted by Article 95, the United States has excluded applicability of the Convention under this subparagraph.]

(2) The fact that the parties have their places of business in different States is to be disregarded whenever this fact does not appear either from the contract or from any dealings between, or from information disclosed by, the parties at any time before or at the conclusion of the contract.

(3) Neither the nationality of the parties nor the civil or commercial character of the parties or of the contract is to be taken into consideration in determining the application of this Convention.

#### Article 2 This Convention does not apply to sales:

(a) of goods bought for personal, family or household use, unless the seller, at any time before or at the conclusion of the contract, neither knew nor ought to have known that the goods were bought for any such use;

(b) by auction;

(c) on execution or otherwise by authority of law;

(d) of stocks, shares, investment securities, negotiable instruments or money;

(e) of ships, vessels, hovercraft or aircraft;

(f) of electricity.

#### Article 3

(1) Contracts for the supply of goods to be manufactured or produced are to be considered sales unless the party who orders the goods undertakes to supply a substantial part of the materials necessary for such manufacture or production.

(2) This Convention does not apply to contracts in which the preponderant part of the obligations of the party who furnishes the goods consists in the supply of labour or other services.

#### Article 4 This Convention governs only the formation of the contract of sale and the rights and obligations of the seller and the buyer arising from such a contract. In particular, except as otherwise expressly provided in this Convention, it is not concerned with:

(a) the validity of the contract or of any of its provisions or of any usage;

(b) the effect which the contract may have on the property in the goods sold.

#### Article 5 This Convention does not apply to the liability of the seller for death or personal injury caused by the goods to any person.

#### Article 6 The parties may exclude the application of this Convention or, subject to Article 12, derogate from or vary the effect of any of its provisions.

### Chapter II General Provisions

#### Article 7

(1) In the interpretation of this Convention, regard is to be had to its international character and to the need to promote uniformity in its application and the observance of good faith in international trade.

(2) Questions concerning matters governed by this Convention which are not expressly settled in it are to be settled in conformity with the general principles on which it is based or, in the absence of such principles, in conformity with the law applicable by virtue of the rules of private international law.

#### Article 8

(1) For the purposes of this Convention statements made by and other conduct of a party are to be interpreted according to his intent where the other party knew or could not have been unaware what that intent was.

(2) If the preceding paragraph is not applicable, statements made by and other conduct of a party are to be interpreted according to the understanding that a reasonable person of the same kind as the other party would have had in the same circumstances.

(3) In determining the intent of a party or the understanding a reasonable person would have had, due consideration is to be given to all relevant circumstances of the case including the negotiations, any practices which the parties have established between themselves, usages and any subsequent conduct of the parities.

## Article 9

(1) The parties are bound by any usage to which they have agreed and by any practices which they have established between themselves.

(2) The parties are considered, unless otherwise agreed, to have impliedly made applicable to their contract or its formation a usage of which the parties know or ought to have known and which in international trade is widely known to, and regularly observed by, parties to contracts of the type involved in the particular trade concerned.

**Article 10** For the purposes of this Convention:

(a) if a party has more than one place of business, the place of business is that which has the closest relationship to the contract and its performance, having regard to the circumstances known to or contemplated by the parties at any time before or at the conclusion of the contract;

(b) if a party does not have a place of business, reference is to be made to his habitual residence.

**Article 11** A contract of sale need not be concluded in or evidenced by writing and is not subject to any other requirement as to form. It may be proved by any means, including witnesses.

**Article 12** Any provision of Article 11, Article 29 or Part II of this Convention that allows a contract of sale or its modification or termination by agreement or any offer, acceptance or other indication of intention to be made in any form other than in writing does not apply where any party has his place of business in a Contracting State which has made a declaration under Article 96 of this Convention. The parties may not derogate from or vary the effect of this article.

**Article 13** For the purposes of this Convention "writing" includes telegram and telex.

# Part II Formation of the Contract

## Article 14

(1) A proposal for concluding a contract addressed to one or more specific persons constitutes an offer if it is sufficiently definite and indicates the intention of the offeror to be bound in case of acceptance. A proposal is sufficiently definite if it indicates the goods and expressly or implicitly fixes or makes provision for determining the quantity and the price.

(2) A proposal other than one addressed to one or more specific persons is to be considered merely as an invitation to make offers, unless the contrary is clearly indicated by the person making the proposal.

## Article 15

(1) An offer becomes effective when it reaches the offeree.

(2) An offer, even if it is irrevocable, may be withdrawn if the withdrawal reaches the offeree before or at the same time as the offer.

## Article 16

(1) Until a contract is concluded an offer may be revoked if the revocation reaches the offeree before he has dispatched an acceptance.

(2) However, an offer cannot be revoked:

(a) if it indicates, whether by stating a fixed time for acceptance or otherwise, that it is irrevocable; or

(b) if it was reasonable for the offeree to rely on the offer as being irrevocable and the offeree has acted in reliance on the offer.

**Article 17** An offer, even if it is irrevocable, is terminated when a rejection reaches the offeror.

## Article 18

(1) A statement made by or other conduct of the offeree indicating assent to an offer is an acceptance. Silence or inactivity does not in itself amount to acceptance.

(2) An acceptance of an offer becomes effective at the moment the indication of assent reaches the offeror. An acceptance is not effective if the indication of assent does not reach the offeror within the time he has fixed or, if no time is fixed, within a reasonable time, due account being taken of the circumstances of the transaction, including the rapidity of the means of communication employed by the offeror. An oral offer must be accepted immediately unless the circumstances indicate otherwise.

(3) However, if, by virtue of the offer or as a result of practices which the parties have established between themselves or of usage, the offeree may indicate assent by performing an act, such as one relating to the dispatch of the goods or payment of the price, without notice to the offeror, the acceptance is effective at the moment the act is performed, provided that the act is performed within the period of time laid down in the preceding paragraph.

### Article 19

(1) A reply to an offer which purports to be an acceptance but contains additions, limitations or other modifications is a rejection of the offer and constitutes a counter-offer.

(2) However, a reply to an offer which purports to be an acceptance but contains additional or different terms which do not materially alter the terms of the offer constitutes an acceptance, unless the offeror, without undue delay, objects orally to the discrepancy or dispatches a notice to that effect. If he does not so object, the terms of the contract are the terms of the offer with the modifications contained in the acceptance.

(3) Additional or different terms relating, among other things, to the price, payment, quality and quantity of the goods, place and time of delivery, extent of one party's liability to the other or the settlement of disputes are considered to alter the terms of the offer materially.

### Article 20

(1) A period of time for acceptance fixed by the offeror in a telegram or a letter begins to run from the moment the telegram is handed in for dispatch or from the date shown on the letter or, if on such date is shown, from the date shown on the envelope. A period of time for acceptance fixed by the offeror by telephone, telex or other means of instantaneous communication, begins to run from the moment that the offer reaches the offeree.

(2) Official holidays or non-business days occurring during the period for acceptance are included in calculating the period. However, if a notice of acceptance cannot be delivered at the address of the offeror on the last day of the period because that day falls on an official holiday or a non-business day at the place of business of the offeror, the period is extended until the first business day which follows.

### Artcle 21

(1) A late acceptance is nevertheless effective as an acceptance if without delay the offeror orally so informs the offeree or dispatches a notice to that effect.

(2) If a letter or other writing containing a late acceptance shows that it has been sent in such circumstances that if its transmission had been normal it would have reached the offeror in due time, the late acceptance is effective as an acceptance unless, without delay, the offeror orally informs the offeree that he considers his offer as having lapsed or dispatches a notice to that effect.

### Article 22
An acceptance may be withdrawn if the withdrawal reaches the offeror before or at the same time as the acceptance would have become effective.

### Article 23
A contract is concluded at the moment when an acceptance of an offer becomes effective in accordance with the provisions of this Convention.

### Article 24
For the purposes of this Part of the Convention, an offer, declaration of acceptance or any other indication of intention "reaches" the addressee when it is made orally to him or delivered by any other means to him personally, to his place of business or mailing address or, if he does not have a place of business or mailing address, to his habitual residence.

# Part III Sale of Goods

## Chapter I General Provisions

### Article 25
A breach of contract committed by one of the parties is fundamental if it results in such detriment to the other party as substantially to deprive him of what he is entitled to expect under the contract, unless the party in breach did not foresee and a reasonable person of the same kind in the same circumstances would not have foreseen such a result.

### Article 26
A declaration of avoidance of the contract is effective only if made by notice to the other party.

### Article 27
Unless otherwise expressly provided in this Part of the Convention, if any notice, request or other communication is given or made by a party in accordance with this Part and by means appropriate in the circumstances, a delay or error in the transmission of the communication or its failure to arrive does not deprive that party of the right to rely on the communication.

### Article 28
If, in accordance with the provisions of this Convention, one party is entitled to require performance of any obligation by the other party, a court is not bound to enter a judgment for specific performance unless the court would do so under its own law in respect of similar contracts of sale not governed by this Convention.

### Article 29

(1) A contact may be modified or terminated by the mere agreement of the parties.

(2) A contact in writing which contains a provision requiring any modification or termination by agreement to be in writing may not be otherwise modified or terminated by agreement. However, a party may be precluded by his conduct from asserting such a provision to the extent that the other party has relied on that conduct.

## Chapter II Obligations of the Seller

### Article 30
The seller must deliver the goods, hand over any documents relating to them and transfer the property in the goods, as required by the contract and this Convetion.

## Section I. Delivery of the goods and handing over of documents

**Article 31** If the seller is not bound to deliver the goods at any other particular place, his obligation to deliver consists:

(a) if the contract of sale involves carriage of the goods—in handing the goods over to the first carrier for transmission to the buyer;

(b) if, in cases not within the preceding subparagraph, the contract relates to specific goods, or unidentified goods to be drawn from a specific stock or to be manufactured or produced, and at the time of the conclusion of the contract the parties knew that the goods were at, or were to be manufactured or produced at, a particular place—in placing the goods at the buyer's disposal at the place;

(c) in other cases—in placing the goods at the buyer's disposal at the place where the seller had his place of business at the time of the conclusion of the contract.

## Article 32

(1) If the seller, in accordance with the contract or this Convention, hands the goods over to a carrier and if the goods are not clearly identified to the contract by markings on the goods, by shipping documents or otherwise, the seller must give the buyer notice of the consignment specifying the goods.

(2) If the seller is bound to arrange for carriage of the goods, he must make such contracts as are necessary for carriage to the place fixed by means of transportation appropriate in the circumstances and according to the usual terms for such transportation.

(3) If the seller is not bound to effect insurance in respect of the carriage of the goods, he must, at the buyer's request, provide him with all available information necessary to enable him to effect such insurance.

**Article 33** The seller must deliver the goods:

(a) if a date is fixed by or determinable from the contract, on that date;

(b) if a period of time is fixed by or determinable from the contract, at any time within that period unless circumstances indicate that the buyer is to choose a date; or

(c) in any other case, within a reasonable time after the conclusion of the contract.

**Article 34** If the seller is bound to hand over documents relating to the goods, he must hand them over at the time and place and in the form required by the contract. If the seller has handed over documents before that time, he may, up to that time, cure any lack of conformity in the documents, if the exercise of this right does not cause the buyer unreasonable inconvenience or unreasonable expense. However, the buyer retains any right to claim damages as provided for in this Convention.

## Section II. Conformity of the goods and third party claims

### Article 35

(1) The seller must deliver goods which are of the quantity, quality and description required by the contract and which are contained or packaged in the manner required by the contract.

(2) Except where the parties have agreed otherwise, the goods do not conform with the contract unless they:
(a) are fit for the purposes for which goods of the same description would ordinarily be used;

(b) are fit for any particular purpose expressly or impliedly made known to the seller at the time of the conclusion of the contract, except where the circumstances show that the buyer did not rely, or that it was unreasonable for him to rely, on the seller's skill and judgment;

(c) possess the qualities of goods which the seller has held out to the buyer as a sample or model;

(d) are contained or packaged in the manner usual for such goods or, where there is no such manner, in a manner adequate to preserve and protect the goods.

(3) The seller is not liable under subparagraphs (a) to (d) of the preceding paragraph for any lack of conformity of the preceding paragraph for any lack of conformity of the goods if at the time of the conclusion of the contract the buyer knew or could not have been unaware of such lack of conformity.

### Article 36

(1) The seller is liable in accordance with the contract and this Convention for any lack of conformity which exists at the time when the risk passes to the buyer, even though the lack of conformity becomes apparent only after that time.

(2) The seller is also liable for any lack of conformity which occurs after the time indicated in the preceding paragraph and which is due to a breach of any of his obligations, including a breach of any guarantee that for a period of time the goods will remain fit for their ordinary purpose or for some particular purpose or will retain specified qualities or characteristics.

**Article 37** If the seller has delivered goods before the date for delivery, he may, up to that date, deliver any missing part or make up any deficiency in the quantity of the goods delivered, or deliver goods in replacement of any non-conforming goods delivered or remedy any lack of conformity in the goods delivered, provided that the exercise of this right does not cause the buyer unreasonable inconvenience or unreasonable expense. However, the buyer retains any right to claim damages as provided for in this Convention.

### Article 38

(1) The buyer must examine the goods, or cause them to be examined, within as short a period as is practicable in the circumstances.

(2) If the contract involves carriage of the goods, examination may be deferred until after the goods have arrived at their destination.

(3) If the goods are redirected in transit or redispatched by the buyer without a reasonable opportunity for examination by him and at the time of the conclusion of the contract the seller knew or ought to have known of the possibility of such redirection or redispatch, examination may be deferred until after the goods have arrived at the new destination.

## Article 39

(1) The buyer loses the right to rely on a lack of conformity of the goods if he does not give notice to the seller specifying the nature of the lack of conformity within a reasonable time after he has discovered it or ought to have discovered it.

(2) In any event, the buyer loses the right to rely on a lack of conformity of the goods if he does not give the seller notice thereof at the latest within a period of two years from the date on which the goods were actually handed over to the buyer, unless this time-limit is inconsistent with a contractual period of guarantee.

**Article 40** The seller is not entitled to rely on the provisions of Articles 38 and 39 if the lack of conformity relates to facts of which he knew or could not have been unaware and which he did not disclose to the buyer.

**Article 41** The seller must deliver goods which are free from any right or claim of a third party, unless the buyer agreed to take the goods subject to that right or claim. However, if such right or claim is based on industrial property or other intellectual property, the seller's obligation is governed by Article 42.

## Article 42

(1) The seller must deliver goods which are free from any right or claim of a third party based on industrial property or other intellectual property, of which at the time of the conclusion of the contract the seller knew or could not have been unaware, provided that the right or claim is based on industrial property or other intellectual property:

  (a) under the law of the State where the goods will be resold or otherwise used, if it was contemplated by the parties at the time of the conclusion of the contract that the goods would be resold or otherwise used in that State; or

  (b) in any other case, under the law of the State where the buyer has his place of business.

(2) The obligation of the seller under the preceding paragraph does not extend to cases where:

  (a) at the time of the conclusion of the contract the buyer knew or could not have been unaware of the right or claim; or

  (b) the right or claim results from the seller's compliance with technical drawings, designs, formulae or other such specifications furnished by the buyer.

## Article 43

(1) The buyer loses the right to rely on the provisions of Article 41 or Article 42 if he does not give notice to the seller specifying the nature of the right or claim of the third party within a reasonable time after he has become aware or ought to have become aware of the right or claim.

(2) The seller is not entitled to rely on the provisions of the preceding paragraph if he knew of the right or claim of the third party and the nature of it.

**Article 44** Notwithstanding the provisions of paragraph (1) of Article 39 and paragraph (1) of Article 43, the buyer may reduce the price in accordance with Article 50 or claim damages, except for loss of profit, if he has a reasonable excuse for his failure to give the required notice.

### *Section III. Remedies for breach of contract by the seller*

## Article 45

(1) If the seller fails to perform any of his obligations under the contract or this Convention, the buyer may:

  (a) exercise the rights provided in Articles 46 to 52;

  (b) claim damages as provided in Articles 74 to 77.

(2) The buyer is not deprived of any right he may have to claim damages by exercising his right to other remedies.

(3) No period of grace may be granted to the seller by a court or arbitral tribunal when the buyer resorts to a remedy for breach of contract.

## Article 46

(1) The buyer may require performance by the seller of his obligations unless the buyer has resorted to a remedy which is inconsistent with this requirement.

(2) If the goods do not conform with the contract, the buyer may require delivery of substitute goods only if the lack of conformity constitutes a fundamental breach of contract and a request for substitute goods is made either in conjunction with notice given under Article 39 or within a reasonable time thereafter.

(3) If the goods do not conform with the contract, the buyer may require the seller to remedy the lack of conformity by repair, unless this is unreasonable having regard to all the circumstances. A request for repair must be made either in conjunction with notice given under Article 39 or within a reasonable time thereafter.

## Article 47

(1) The buyer may fix an additional period of time of reasonable length for performance by the seller of his obligations.

(2) Unless the buyer has received notice from the seller that he will not perform within the period so fixed, the buyer may not, during that period, resort to any remedy for breach of contract. However, the buyer is not deprived thereby of any right he may have to claim damages for delay in performance.

## Article 48

(1) Subject to Article 49, the seller may, even after the date for delivery, remedy at his own expense any failure to perform his obligations, if he can do so without unreasonable delay and without causing the buyer unreasonable inconvenience or uncertainty of reimbursement by the seller of expenses advanced by the buyer. However, the buyer retains any right to claim damages as provided for in this Convention.

(2) If the seller requests the buyer to make known whether he will accept performance and the buyer does not comply with the request within a reasonable time, the seller may perform within the time indicated in his request. The buyer may not, during that period of time, resort to any remedy which is inconsistent with performance by the seller.

(3) A notice by the seller that he will perform within a specified period of time is assumed to include a request, under the preceding paragraph, that the buyer make known his decision.

(4) A request or notice by the seller under paragraph (2) or (3) of this article is not effective unless received by the buyer.

## Article 49

(1) The buyer may declare the contract avoided:

    (a) if the failure by the seller to perform any of his obligations under the contract or this Convention amounts to a fundamental breach of contract; or

    (b) in case of non-delivery, if the seller does not deliver the goods within the additional period of time fixed by the buyer in accordance with paragraph (1) of Article 47 or declares that he will not deliver within the period so fixed.

(2) However, in cases where the seller has delivered the goods, the buyer loses the right to declare the contract avoided unless he does so:

    (a) in respect of late delivery, within a resonable time after he has become aware that delivery has been made;

    (b) in respect of any breach other than late delivery, within a reasonable time:

        (i) after he knew or ought to have known of the breach;

        (ii) after the expiration of any additional period of time fixed by the buyer in accordance with paragraph (1) of Article 47, or after the seller

has declared that he will not perform his obligations within such an additional period; or

        (iii) after the expiration of any additional period of time indicated by the seller in accordance with paragraph (2) of Article 48, or after the buyer has declared that he will not accept performance.

## Article 50

If the goods do not conform with the contract and whether or not the price has already been paid, the buyer may reduce the price in the same proportion as the value that the goods actually delivered had at the time of the delivery bears to the value that conforming goods would have had at that time. However, if the seller remedies any failure to perform his obligations in accordance with Article 37 or Article 48 or if the buyer refuses to accept performance by the seller in accordance with those articles, the buyer may not reduce the price.

## Article 51

(1) If the seller delivers only a part of the goods or if only a part of the goods delivered is in conformity with the contract, Articles 46 to 50 apply in respect of the part which is missing or which does not conform.

(2) The buyer may declare the contract avoided in its entirety only if the failure to make delivery completely or in conformity with the contract amounts to a fundamental breach of the contract.

## Article 52

(1) If the seller delivers the goods before the date fixed, the buyer may take delivery or refuse to take delivery.

(2) If the seller delivers a quantity of goods greater than that provided for in the contract, the buyer may take delivery or refuse to take delivery of the excess quantity. If the buyer takes delivery of all or part of the excess quantity, he must pay for it at the contract rate.

## Chapter III Obligations of the Buyer

**Article 53** The buyer must pay the price for the goods and take delivery of them as required by the contract and this Convention.

### Section I. Payment of the price

**Article 54** The buyer's obligation to pay the price includes taking such steps and complying with such formalities as may be required under the contract or any laws and regulations to enable payment to be made.

**Article 55** Where a contract has been validly concluded but does not expressly or implicitly fix or make provision for determining the price, the parties are considered, in the absence of any indication to the contrary, to have impliedly made reference to the price generally charged at the time of the conclusion of the contract for such goods sold under comparable circumstances in the trade concerned.

**Article 56**  If the price is fixed according to the weight of the goods, in case of doubt it is to be determined by the net weight.

## Article 57

(1) If the buyer is not bound to pay the price at any other particular place, he must pay it to the seller:

   (a) at the seller's place of business; or

   (b) if the payment is to be made against the handing over of the goods or of documents, at the place where the handing over takes place.

(2) The seller must bear any increase in the expenses incidental to payment which is caused by a change in his place of business subsequent to the conclusion of the contract.

## Article 58

(1) If the buyer is not bound to pay the price at any other specific time, he must pay it when the seller places either the goods or documents controlling their disposition at the buyer's disposal in accordance with the contract and this Convention. The seller may make such payment a condition for handling over the goods or documents.

(2) If the contract involves carriage of the goods, the seller may dispatch the goods on terms whereby the goods, or documents controlling their disposition, will not be handed over to the buyer except against payment of the price.

(3) The buyer is not bound to pay the price until he has had an opportunity to examine the goods, unless the procedures for delivery or payment agreed upon by the parties are inconsistent with his having such an opportunity.

**Article 59**  The buyer must pay the price on the date fixed by or determinable from the contract and this Convention without the need for any request or compliance with any formality on the part of the seller.

### Section II. Taking delivery

**Article 60**  The buyer's obligation to take delivery consists:

(a) in doing all the acts which could reasonably be expected of him in order to enable the seller to make delivery; and

(b) in taking over the goods.

### Section III. Remedies for breach of contract by the buyer

## Article 61

(1) If the buyer fails to perform any of his obligations under the contract or this Convention, the seller may:

   (a) exercise the rights provided in Articles 62 to 65;

   (b) claim damages as provided in Articles 74 to 77.

(2) The seller is not deprived of any right he may have to claim damages by exercising his right to other remedies.

(3) No period of grace may be granted to the buyer by a court or arbitral tribunal when the seller resorts to a remedy for breach of contract.

**Article 62**  The seller may require the buyer to pay the price, take delivery or perform his other obligations, unless the seller has resorted to a remedy which is inconsistent with this requirement.

## Article 63

(1) The seller may fix an additional period of time of reasonable length for performance by the buyer of his obligations.

(2) Unless the seller has received notice from the buyer that he will not perform within the period so fixed, the seller may not, during that period, resort to any remedy for breach of contract. However, the seller is not deprived thereby of any right he may have to claim damages for delay in performance.

## Article 64

(1) The seller may declare the contract avoided:

   (a) if the failure by the buyer to perform any of his obligations under the contract or this Convention amounts to a fundamental breach of contract; or

   (b) if the buyer does not, within the additional period of time fixed by the seller in accordance with paragraph (1) of Article 63, perform his obligation to pay the price or take delivery of the goods, or if he declares that he will not do so within the period so fixed.

(2) However, in cases where the buyer has paid the price, the seller loses the right to declare the contract avoided unless he does so:

   (a) in respect of late performance by the buyer, before the seller has become aware that performance has been rendered; or

   (b) in respect of any breach other than late performance by the buyer, within a reasonable time:

     (i) after the seller knew or ought to have known of the breach; or

     (ii) after the expiration of any additional period of time fixed by the seller in accordance with paragraph (1) of Article 63, or after the buyer has declared that he will not perform his obligations within such an additional period.

## Article 65

(1) If under the contract the buyer is to specify the form, measurement or other features of the goods and he fails to make such specification either on the date agreed upon or within a reasonable time after receipt of a request from the seller, the seller may, without

prejudice to any other rights he may have, make the specification himself in accordance with the requirements of the buyer that may be known to him.

(2) If the seller makes the specification himself, he must inform the buyer of the details thereof and must fix a reasonable time within which the buyer may make a different specification. If, after receipt of such a communication, the buyer fails to do so within the time so fixed, the specification made by the seller is binding.

## Chapter IV Passing of Risk

**Article 66** Loss of or damage to the goods after the risk has passed to the buyer does not discharge him from his obligation to pay the price, unless the loss or damage is due to an act or omission of the seller.

### Article 67

(1) If the contract of sale involves carriage of the goods and the seller is not bound to hand them over at a particular place, the risk passes to the buyer when the goods are handed over to the first carrier for transmission to the buyer in accordance with the contract of sale. If the seller is bound to hand the goods over to a carrier at a particular place, the risk does not pass to the buyer until the goods are handed over to the carrier at that place. The fact that the seller is authorized to retain documents controlling the disposition of the goods does not affect the passage of the risk.

(2) Nevertheless, the risk does not pass to the buyer until the goods are clearly identified to the contract, whether by markings on the goods, by shipping documents, by notice given to the buyer or otherwise.

**Article 68** The risk in respect of goods sold in transit passes to the buyer from the time of the conclusion of the contract. However, if the circumstances so indicate, the risk is assumed by the buyer from the time the goods were handed over to the carrier who issued the documents embodying the contract of carriage. Nevertheless, if at the time of the conclusion of the contract of sale the seller knew or ought to have known that the goods had been lost or damaged and did not disclose this to the buyer, the loss or damage is at the risk of the seller.

### Article 69

(1) In cases not within Article 67 and 68, the risk passes to the buyer when he takes over the goods or, if he does not do so in due time, from the time when the goods are placed at his disposal and he commits a breach of contract by failing to take delivery.

(2) However, if the buyer is bound to take over the goods at a place other than a place of business of the seller, the risk passes when delivery is due and the buyer is aware of the fact that the goods are placed at his disposal at that place.

(3) If the contract relates to goods not then identified, the goods are considered not to be placed at the disposal of the buyer until they are clearly identified to the contract.

**Article 70** If the seller has committed a fundamental breach of contract, Articles 67, 68 and 69 do not impair the remedies available to the buyer on account of the breach.

## Chapter V Provisions Common to the Obligations of the Seller and of the Buyer

### Section 1. Anticipatory breach and installment contracts

### Article 71

(1) A party may suspend the performance of his obligations if, after the conclusion of the contract, it becomes apparent that the other party will not perform a substantial part of his obligations as a result of:

   (a) a serious deficiency in his ability to perform or in his creditworthiness; or

   (b) his conduct in preparing to perform or in performing the contract.

(2) If the seller has already dispatched the goods before the grounds described in the preceding paragraph become evident, he may prevent the handing over of the goods to the buyer even though the buyer holds a document which entitles him to obtain them. The present paragraph relates only to the rights in the goods as between the buyer and the seller.

(3) A party suspending performance, whether before or after dispatch of the goods, must immediately give notice of the suspension to the other party and must continue with performance if the other party provides adequate assurance of his performance.

### Article 72

(1) If prior to the date for performance of the contract it is clear that one of the parties will commit a fundamental breach of contract, the other party may declare the contract avoided.

(2) If time allows, the party intending to declare the contract avoided must give reasonable notice to the other party in order to permit him to provide adequate assurance of his performance.

(3) The requirements of the preceding paragraph do not apply if the other party has declared that he will not perform his obligations.

### Article 73

(1) In the case of a contract for delivery of goods by installments, if the failure of one party to perform any of his obligations in respect of any installment constitutes a fundamental breach of contract with respect to that installment, the other party may declare the contract avoided with respect to that installment.

(2) If one party's failure to perform any of his obligations in respect of any installment gives the other party good grounds to conclude that a fundamental breach of contract will occur with respect to future installments, he may declare the contract avoided for the future, provided that he does so within a reasonable time.

(3) A buyer who declares the contract avoided in respect of any delivery may, at the same time, declare it avoided in respect of deliveries already made or of future deliveries if, by reason of their interdependence, those deliveries could not be used for the purpose contemplated by the parties at the time of the conclusion of the contract.

### Section II. Damages

**Article 74** Damages for breach of contract by one party consist of a sum equal to the loss, including loss of profit, suffered by the other party as a consequence of the breach. Such damages may not exceed the loss which the party in breach foresaw or ought to have foreseen at the time of the conclusion of the contract, in the light of the facts and matters of which he then knew or ought to have known, as a possible consequence of the breach of contract.

**Article 75** If the contract is avoided and if, in a reasonable manner and within a reasonable time after avoidance, the buyer has bought goods in replacement or the seller has resold the goods, the party claiming damages may recover the difference between the contract price and the price in the substitute transaction as well as any further damages recoverable under Article 74.

### Article 76

(1) If the contract is avoided and there is a current price for the goods, the party claiming damages may, if he has not made a purchase or resale under Article 75, recover the difference between the price fixed by the contract and the current price at the time of avoidance as well as any further damages recoverable under Article 74. If, however, the party claiming damages has avoided the contract after taking over the goods, the current price at the time of such taking over shall be applied instead of the current price at the time of avoidance.

(2) For the purposes of the preceding paragraph, the current price is the price prevailing at the place where delivery of the goods should have been made or, if there is no current price at that place, the price at such other place as serves as a reasonable substitute, making due allowance for differences in the cost of transporting the goods.

**Article 77** A party who relies on a breach of contract must take such measures as are reasonable in the circumstances to mitigate the loss, including loss of profit, resulting from the breach. If he fails to take such measures, the party in breach may claim a reduction in the damages in the amount by which the loss should have been mitigated.

### Section III. Interest

**Article 78** If a party fails to pay the price or any other sum that is in arrears, the other party is entitled to interest on it, without prejudice to any claim for damages recoverable under Article 74.

### Section IV. Exemptions

### Article 79

(1) A party is not liable for a failure to perform any of his obligations if he proves that the failure was due to an impediment beyond his control and that he could not reasonably be expected to have taken the impediment into account at the time of the conclusion of the contract or to have avoided or overcome it or its consequences.

(2) If the party's failure is due to the failure by a third person whom he has engaged to perform the whole or a part of the contract, that party is exempt from liability only if:

(a) he is exempt under the preceding paragraph; and

(b) the person whom he has so engaged would be so exempt if the provisions of that paragraph were applied to him.

(3) The exemption provided by this article has effect for the period during which the impediment exists.

(4) The party who fails to perform must give notice to the other party of the impediment and its effect on his ability to perform. If the notice is not received by the other party within a reasonable time after the party who fails to perform knew or ought to have known of the impediment, he is liable for damages resulting from such non-receipt.

(5) Nothing in this article prevents either party from exercising any right other than to claim damages under this Convention.

**Article 80** A party may not rely on a failure of the other party to perform, to the extent that such failure was caused by the first party's act or omission.

### Section V. Effects of avoidance

### Article 81

(1) Avoidance of the contract releases both parties from their obligations under it, subject to any damages which may be due. Avoidance does not affect any provision of the contract for the settlement of disputes or any other provision of the contract governing the rights and obligations of the parties consequent upon the avoidance of the contract.

(2) A party who has performed the contract either wholly or in part may claim restitution from the other party

of whatever the first party has supplied or paid under the contract. If both parties are bound to make restitution, they must do so concurrently.

## Article 82

(1) The buyer loses the right to declare the contract avoided or to require the seller to deliver substitute goods if it is impossible for him to make restitution of the goods substantially in the condition in which he received them.

(2) The preceding paragraph does not apply:

(a) if the impossibility of making restitution of the goods or of making restitution of the goods substantially in the condition in which the buyer received them is not due to his act or omission;

(b) if the goods or part of the goods have perished or deteriorated as a result of the examination provided for in Article 38; or

(c) if the goods or part of the goods have been sold in the normal course of business or have been consumed or transformed by the buyer in the course of normal use before he discovered or ought to have discovered the lack of conformity.

**Article 83** A buyer who has lost the right to declare the contract avoided or to require the seller to deliver substitute goods in accordance with Article 82 retains all other remedies under the contract and this Convention.

## Article 84

(1) If the seller is bound to refund the price, he must also pay interest on it, from the date on which the price was paid.

(2) The buyer must account to the seller for all benefits which he has derived from the goods or part of them:

(a) if he must make restitution of the goods or part of them; or

(b) if it is impossible for him to make restitution of all or part of the goods or to make restitution of all or part of the goods substantially in the condition in which he received them, but he has nevertheless declared the contract avoided or required the seller to deliver substitute goods.

### Section VI. Preservation of the goods

**Article 85** If the buyer is in delay in taking delivery of the goods or, where payment of the price and delivery of the goods are to be made concurrently, if he fails to pay the price, and the seller is either in possession of the goods or otherwise able to control their disposition, the seller must take such steps as are reasonable in the circumstances to preserve them. He is entitled to retain them until he has been reimbursed his reasonable expenses by the buyer.

## Article 86

(1) If the buyer has received the goods and intends to exercise any right under the contract or this Convention to reject them, he must take such steps to preserve them as are reasonable in the circumstances. He is entitled to retain them until he has been reimbursed his reasonable expenses by the seller.

(2) If goods dispatched to the buyer have been placed at his disposal at their destination and he exercises the right to reject them, he must take possession of them on behalf of the seller, provided that this can be done without payment of the price and without unreasonable inconvenience or unreasonable expense. This provision does not apply if the seller or a person authorized to take charge of the goods on his behalf is present at the destination. If the buyer takes possession of the goods under this paragraph, his rights and obligations are governed by the preceding paragraph.

**Article 87** A party who is bound to take steps to preserve the goods may deposit them in a warehouse of a third person at the expense of the other party provided that the expense incurred is not unreasonable.

## Article 88

(1) A party who is bound to preserve the goods in accordance with Article 85 or 86 may sell them by any appropriate means if there has been an unreasonable delay by the other party in taking possession of the goods or in taking them back or in paying the price or the cost of preservation, provided that reasonable notice of the intention to sell has been given to the other party.

(2) If the goods are subject to rapid deterioration or their preservation would involve unreasonable expense, a party who is bound to preserve the goods in accordance with Article 85 or 86 must take reasonable measures to sell them. To the extent possible he must give notice to the other party of his intention to sell.

(3) A party selling the goods has the right to retain out of the proceeds of sale an amount equal to the reasonable expenses of preserving the goods and of selling them. He must account to the other party for the balance.

## Part IV Final Provisions

**Article 89** The Secretary-General of the United Nations is hereby designated as the depositary for this Convention.

**Article 90** This Convention does not prevail over any international agreement which has already been or may be entered into and which contains provisions concerning the matters governed by this Convention, provided that the parties have their places of business in States parties to such agreement.

## Article 91

(1) This Convention is open for signature at the concluding meeting of the United Nations Conference on Contracts for the International Sale of Goods and will remain open for signature by all States at the Headquarters of the United Nations, New York, until 30 September 1981.

(2) This Convention is subject to ratification, acceptance or approval by the signatory States.

(3) This Convention is open for accession by all States which are not signatory States as from the date it is open for signature.

(4) Instruments of ratification, acceptance, approval and accession are to be deposited with the Secretary-General of the United Nations.

## Article 92

(1) A Contracting State may declare at the time of signature, ratification, acceptance, approval or accession that it will not be bound by Part II of this Convention or that it will not be bound by Part III of this Convention.

(2) A Contracting State which makes a declaration in accordance with the preceding paragraph in respect of Part II or Part III of this Convention is not to be considered a Contracting State within paragraph (1) of Article 1 of this Convention in respect of matters governed by the Part to which the declaration applies.

## Article 93

(1) If a Contracting State has two or more territorial units in which, according to its constitution, different systems of law are applicable in relation to the matters dealt with in this Convention, it may, at the time of signature, ratification, acceptance, approval or accession, declare that this Convention is to extend to all its territorial units or only to one or more of them, and may amend its declaration by submitting another declaration at any time.

(2) These declarations are to be notified to the depositary and are to state expressly the territorial units to which the Convention extends.

(3) If, by virtue of a declaration under this article, this Convention extends to one or more but not all of the territorial units of a Contracting State, and if the place of business of a party is located in that State, this place of business, for the purposes of this Convention, is considered not to be in a Contracting State, unless it is in a territorial unit to which the Convention extends.

(4) If a Contracting State makes no declaration under paragraph (1) of this article, the Convention is to extend to all territorial units of that State.

## Article 94

(1) Two or more Contracting States which have the same or closely related legal rules on matters governed by this Convention may at any time declare that the Convention is not to apply to contracts of sale or to their formation where the parties have their places of business in those States. Such declarations may be made jointly or by reciprocal unilateral declarations.

(2) A Contracting State which has the same or closely related legal rules on matters governed by this Convention as one or more non-Contracting States may at any time declare that the Convention is not to apply to contracts of sale or to their formation where the parties have their places of business in those States.

(3) If a State which is the object of a declaration under the preceding paragraph subsequently becomes a Contracting State, the declaration made will, as from the date on which the Convention enters into force in respect of the new Contracting State, have the effect of a declaration made under paragraph (1), provided that the new Contracting State joins in such declaration or makes a reciprocal unilateral declaration.

## Article 95

Any State may declare at the time of the deposit of its instrument of ratification, acceptance, approval or accession that it will not be bound by subparagraph (1)(b) of Article 1 of this Convention. [The United States has made such reservation.]

## Article 96

A Contracting State whose legislation requires contracts of sale to be concluded in or evidenced by writing may at any time make a declaration in accordance with Article 12 that any provision of Article 11, Article 29, or Part II of this Convention, that allows a contract of sale or its modification or termination by agreement or any offer, acceptance, or other indication of intention to be made in any form other than in writing, does not apply where any party has his place of business in that State.

## Article 97

(1) Declarations made under this Convention at the time of signature are subject to confirmation upon ratification, acceptance or approval.

(2) Declarations and confirmations of declarations are to be in writing and be formally notified to the depositary.

(3) A declaration takes effect simultaneously with the entry into force of this Convention in respect of the State concerned. However, a declaration of which the depositary receives formal notification after such entry into force takes effect on the first day of the month following the expiration of six months after the date of its receipt by the depositary. Reciprocal unilateral declarations under Article 94 take effect on the first day of the month following the expiration of six months after the receipt of the latest declaration by the depositary.

(4) Any State which makes a declaration under this Convention may withdraw it at any time by a formal notification in writing addressed to the depositary. Such withdrawal is to take effect on the first day of the

month following the expiration of six months after the date of the receipt of the notification by the depositary.

(5) A withdrawal of a declaration made under Article 94 renders inoperative, as from the date on which the withdrawal takes effect, any reciprocal declaration made by another State under that article.

**Article 98** No reservations are permitted except those expressly authorized in this Convention.

## Article 99

(1) This Convention enters into force, subject to the provisions of paragraph (6) of this article, on the first day of the month following the expiration of twelve months after the date of deposit of the tenth instrument of ratification, acceptance, approval or accession, including an instrument which contains a declaration made under Article 92.

(2) When a State ratifies, accepts, approves or accedes to this Convention after the deposit of the tenth instrument of ratification, acceptance, approval or accession, this Convention, with the exception of the Part excluded, enters into force in respect of that State, subject to the provisions of paragraph (6) of this article, on the first day of the month following the expiration of twelve months after the date of the deposit of its instrument of ratification, acceptance, approval or accession.

(3) A State which ratifies, accepts, approves or accedes to this Convention and is a party to either or both the Convention relating to a Uniform Law on the Formation of Contracts for the International Sale of Goods done at The Hague on 1 July 1964 (1964 Hague Formation Convention) and the Convention relating to a Uniform Law on the International Sale of Goods done at The Hague on 1 July 1964 (1964 Hague Sales Convention) shall at the same time denounce, as the case may be, either or both the 1964 Hague Sales Convention and the 1964 Hague Formation Convention by notifying the Government of the Netherlands to that effect.

(4) A State party to the 1964 Hague Sales Convention which ratifies, accepts, approves or accedes to the present Convention and declares or has declared under Article 92 that it will not be bound by Part II of this Convention shall at the time of ratification, acceptance, approval or accession denounce the 1964 Hague Sales Convention by notifying the Government of the Netherlands to that effect.

(5) A State party to the 1964 Hague Formation Convention which ratifies, accepts, approves or accedes to the present Convention and declares or has declared under Article 92 that it will not be bound by Part III of this Convention shall at the time of ratification, acceptance, approval or accession denounce the 1964 Hague Formation Convention by notifying the Government of the Netherlands to that effect.

(6) For the purpose of this article, ratifications, acceptances, approvals and accessions in respect of this Convention by States parties to the 1964 Hague Formation Convention or to the 1964 Hague Sales Convention shall not be effective until such denunciations as may be required on the part of those States in respect of the latter two Conventions have themselves become effective. The depositary of this Convention shall consult with the Government of the Netherlands, as the depositary of the 1964 Conventions, so as to ensure necessary co-ordination in this respect.

## Article 100

(1) This Convention applies to the formation of a contract only when the proposal for concluding the contract is made on or after the date when the Convention enters into force in respect of the Contracting States referred to in subparagraph (1)(a) or the Contracting States referred to in subparagraph (1)(b) of Article 1.

(2) This Convention applies only to contracts concluded on or after the date when the Convention enters into force in respect of the Contracting States referred to in subparagraph (1)(a) or the Contracting State referred to in subparagraph (1)(b) of Article 1.

## Article 101

(1) A Contracting State may denounce this Convention, or Part II or Part III of the Convention, by a formal notification in writing addressed to the depositary.

(2) The denunciation takes effect on the first day of the month following the expiration of twelve months after the notification is received by the depositary. Where a longer period for the denunciation to take effect is specified in the notification, the denunciation takes effect upon the expiration of such longer period after the notification is received by the depositary.

DONE at Vienna, this day of eleventh day of April, one thousand nine hundred and eighty, in a single original, of which the Arabic, Chinese, English, French, Russian and Spanish texts are equally authentic.

IN WITNESS WHEREOF the undersigned plenipotentiaries, being duly authorized by their respective Governments, have signed this Convention.

# Glossary

**abandoned** In contract law, the condition that exists when a minor has left home and given up all rights to parental support.

**abandoned property** Property that has been discarded by the owner without the intent to reclaim ownership of it. Courts require clear and convincing evidence of both the desertion by the owner and the owner's intent never to return.

**abandonment of contractual obligations** The situation that exists when a party to a contract stops performance once it has begun.

**abuse of discretion** The determination that the judge in the lower court has misused his or her authority.

**abuse of process** The use of a legal procedure for a purpose other than that for which it is legitimately intended.

**acceleration** A provision in a mortgage agreement that allows the mortgagee to demand the entire balance due when the mortgagor misses a single installment payment.

**acceptance** A promise or act on the part of an offeree indicating a willingness to be bound by the terms and conditions contained in an offer. Also, the acknowledgment of the drawee that binds the drawee to the terms of a draft.

**acceptor** A drawee of a draft who has promised to honor the draft as presented by signing it on its face.

**accommodation party** A person who signs an instrument in any capacity for the purpose of lending his or her name to another party to the instrument. That person then assumes the same liability as the marker.

**accord** The implied or expressed acceptance of less than what the creditor billed the debtor.

**accord and satisfaction** An agreement (accord) whereby a creditor accepts as full payment an amount that is less than the amount due.

**accountant** A professional who can plan, direct, and evaluate a client's financial affairs.

**accounting** A statement detailing the financial transactions of a business and the status of its assets.

**acknowledgment** The official recognition by a notary public that another's signature was made by that party's free will. The acknowledgment is accomplished when the notary has signed the document and added the official seal to it.

**active data** Data in a computer system that are actually being used at the present time.

**active fraud** A false statement made or an action actually taken by one party with the intent to deceive a second party and thus lead that second party into a deceptively based agreement.

**activist agencies** Agencies that use their regulatory powers to advance social agendas that are technically outside their legislative authority.

**actual authority rule** A rule that states a manager may be liable for exceeding his or her authority if the corporation is harmed as a result.

**actual cause** In tort law, the relationship between the unreasonable conduct and the injury to the innocent party, whether the injury was or was not foreseeable. Actual cause is also referred to as cause-in-fact.

**actual damages** A sum of money equal to the real financial loss suffered by an injured party. Also called *compensatory damages*.

**actual eviction** An eviction in which the tenant is physically deprived of the leasehold.

**actual malice** The legal test used by the courts to determine defamation against a public official or a public figure. The actual malice test requires the public official or public figure to prove not only that the statement was false, negative, and communicated to a third party, but also that it was made with the knowledge that it was false or with a reckless disregard for its truth or falsity.

**actual malice test** A defense against libel cases that states public officials must prove not only that the statement was false, negative, and communicated to a third party, but was also made with actual malice.

**add-on coverage** In insurance law, optional coverage, such as personal injury insurance, that allows a driver to receive payments without having to determine fault.

**adhesion contract** A contract drawn by one party that must be accepted on a take-it-or-leave-it basis.

**adjustable rate mortgage (ARM)** In property law, a variable or changing rate of interest in a mortgage agreement that fluctuates based on the index (the bank's prime rate or the Federal Reserve's discount rate, and so on) to which the mortgage is tied.

**administrative law** That body of law, including decrees and legal decisions, generated by administrative agencies.

**administrator (male); administratrix (female)**
A person appointed by the court to do the work of an executor if none is named in a will or if the executor either refuses to perform or is incapable of performing the duties.

**admiralty court** In the historical development of the law merchant, a local court established by a coastal city, usually in Italy, to handle commercial disputes regarding goods carried as cargo by ships docked at the city's port.

**ADR contract clause** A clause that specifies that the parties to the agreement have promised to use an alternative dispute resolution technique when a disagreement arises rather than litigating the issue.

**advance directives** Written statement in which people gives instructions for their future medical care.

**adversarial system** The system on which the American legal process is built. An orderly and aggressive way to settle disputes in which attorneys for each side attempt to persuade a judge or jury of the veracity of his or her case.

**adverse opinion** An auditor's opinion that states that deviations from generally accepted accounting principles are so serious that an unqualified opinion is impossible and a qualified opinion is not justified.

**adverse possession** Title to real property obtained by taking actual possession of the property openly, notoriously, exclusively, under a claim of right, and continuously for a period of time set by state statute.

**affirmance** See *ratification.*

**affirmative action** A policy designed to reduce the effects of past discrimination.

**affirmative defense** A set of circumstances that indicates that a defendant should not be held liable, even if the plaintiff proves all of the facts in a complaint.

**agency** A legal agreement between two persons, whereby one is designated the agent of the other.

**agency coupled with an interest** An irrevocable agency agreement in which the agent is given an interest in the subject matter of the agency. Also called *irrevocable agency.*

**agent** A person authorized to act on behalf of another and subject to the other's control in dealing with third parties.

**aggravated arson** In criminal law, using fire or explosives to create a substantial risk of harm to an individual or an occupied structure, often also including the hiring of another person to carry out the offense.

**aggravated burglary** In criminal law, gaining unlawful entry to an occupied building by using a deadly weapon, inflicting actual harm, attempting to harm, or threatening to harm, with the intent to commit a crime.

**aggravated murder** In criminal law, killing someone with premeditation or with prior calculation and design, or while committing a serious felony such as rape, robbery, or kidnapping.

**aggravated robbery** In criminal law, attempting to commit or actually committing theft using a deadly weapon or a dangerous ordnance, or doing the same by inflicting harm on the victim.

**aggregate theory** A theory in partnership law that holds that a partnership is actually a conglomeration of the partners rather than a separate legal person with its own legal identity.

**agreements in restraint of trade** Agreements that remove competition, deny to the public the services it would otherwise have, or result in higher prices and hardship.

**algorithm** A series of mathematical steps that, if followed properly, will reach a desired goal.

**alien corporation** A corporation that though incorporated in a foreign country does business in the United States.

**allonge** A strip of paper attached to a negotiable instrument for the writing of indorsements.

**alter ego** In corporate law, a subsidiary corporation set up by a parent corporation to do the bidding of the original parent corporation.

**alternative dispute resolution (ADR)** A process that occurs whenever individuals attempt to resolve a disagreement by stepping outside the usual adversarial system and applying creative settlement techniques, many of which have fact finding and the discovery of truth as their goal.

**alternative payment system** A computer based payment system such as Pay-Pal that is not card dependent.

**American Law Institute (ALI) test** A test under which a criminal defendant will be judged not guilty by reason of insanity "as a result of mental disease or defect he lacks substantial capacity either to appreciate the criminality of his conduct or to conform his conduct to the requirements of the law."

**annual percentage rate (APR)** The true rate of interest on a loan.

**annuity** A guaranteed retirement income.

**anomalous indorsement** An indorsement made by an accommodation party.

**answer** A defendant's official response to a complaint.

**antenuptial agreement** In contract law, a written agreement between two people planning marriage, who agree in writing to change the property rights they possess by law.

**anticipatory breach** A breach that occurs when a party to a contract either expresses or clearly implies an intention not to perform the contract even before being required to act. Also called *constructive breach.*

**Antitrust Procedures and Penalty Act** In federal antitrust law, a federal statute that regulates the Department of Justice's antitrust consent decrees.

**apparent authority** An accountability doctrine whereby a principal, by virtue of words or actions, leads a third party to believe that an agent has authority but no such authority was intended. Also called *ostensible authority* and *agency by estoppel.*

**appeal** The referral of a case to a higher court for review.

**appeal bond** The payment of a set sum of money into a protected account to secure the payment of that money to the plaintiff should the defendant be defeated.

**appellate jurisdiction** The power of a court to review a case for errors.

**arbitration** The process by which an outside party settles a dispute between two other parties.

**arbitrator** The third party in the arbitration procedure whose job is to settle the dispute.

**arraignment** A formal court proceeding during which the defendant, after hearing the indictment or information read, pleads either guilty or not guilty.

**arson** The willful or malicious act of causing the burning of another's property.

**Articles of Confederation** The first constitution of the United States; replaced by the U.S. Constitution in 1787.

**articles of incorporation** A written application to a state for permission to incorporate.

**articles of organization** The written application to the state for permission to form a limited liability company.

**articles of partnership** A written agreement that establishes a partnership.

**assault** An attempt to commit a battery.

**asset acquisition** The purchase of all the property of a corporation by another corporation.

**assign** To transfer property by sale, mortgage, pledge, or otherwise.

**asset-backed securities** In property law, lending money by establishing a security interest in goods such as cars, furniture, boats, and so on.

**assignee** A person to whom an assignment is made.

**assignment** The transfer of a contract right from one person to another.

**assignor** A person who assigns rights or delegates duties under an assignment.

**associative corporativism** The process of doing business as a self-governing business association, that is, as a corporation. Also known as *corporativism.*

**assume the mortgage** An agreement whereby the buyer of real property already mortgaged agrees to pay the mortgage.

**assumption of the risk** A defense against negligence that states the victim voluntarily exposed him- or herself to a known risk.

**ATM card** A card used together with a personal identification number (PIN) to gain access to an automatic teller machine (ATM).

**attachment** The act of taking a person's property and bringing it into the custody of law.

**attorney-client privilege** The guarantee that information that passes between clients and attorneys remains secret.

**auction** A sale that is open to the public, during which potential buyers compete for the right to purchase certain items by placing higher and higher bids until the highest bid is reached and the auctioneer accepts on behalf of the seller

**auction with reserve** An auction at which the auctioneer has the right to withdraw goods and not sell them if acceptable bids are not made.

**auction without reserve** An auction at which the auctioneer cannot withdraw goods unless no bid is made within a reasonable time.

**audit** An examination of the financial records of an organization to determine whether those records are a fair representation of the actual financial health of the institution.

**Auditing Standards Board** A group of experts established by the American Institute of Certified Public Accountants (AICPA) to set up auditing standards.

**auditor** The accountant who examines the financial records of an organization to determine whether those records are a fair representation of the actual financial health of the institution.

**authenticate** (*a*) to sign; or (*b*) with the intent to sign a record, otherwise to execute or adopt an electronic symbol, sound, message, or process referring to, attached to, included in, or logically associated or linked with, that record.

**automatic stay** A self-operating postponement of collection proceedings against a debtor who has filed a petition for bankruptcy.

**automatic suspension** A court order that stops a debtor's creditors from making any further moves to collect the money that the debtor owes them.

**back-up data** Data associated with a computer system that have been duplicated for safekeeping at another location.

**bailee** The person to whom personal property is transferred under a contract of bailment.

**bailment** The transfer of possession and control of personal property to another with the intent that the same property will be returned later.

**bailment by necessity** A bailment that arises when a customer must give up possession of property for the benefit of both parties; for example, when one purchases a suit or dress and is required to give up possession of one's own property while being fitted.

**bailment for the sole benefit of the bailee** A bailment in which the bailee receives all the benefits of the transaction.

**bailment for the sole benefit of the bailor** A bailment in which the bailor receives all the benefits of the transaction.

**bailor** The person who transfers personal property under a contract of bailment.

**bait-and-switch confidence game** An illegal promotional practice in which a seller attracts consumers by promoting a product (bait) that he or she does not intend to sell and then directs the consumers' attention to a higher-priced product (switch).

**balloon payment** A large final payment on a mortgage that has relatively low fixed payments during the life of the mortgage.

**balloon-payment mortgage** A mortgage that has relatively low fixed payments during the life of the mortgage followed by one large final (balloon) payment.

**bank draft** A check drawn by one bank on another bank in which it has funds on deposit in favor of a third person, the payee. Also called *teller's check.*

**bankruptcy** The legal process by which the assets of a debtor are sold to pay off creditors so that the debtor can make a fresh start financially.

**bankruptcy trustee** A person appointed by the court who is charged with the responsibility of liquidating the assets of the debtor for the benefit of all interested parties.

**bargain-and-sale deed** A deed that transfers title to real property but contains no warranties. This type of deed is not valid without consideration.

**bargained-for exchange** In reference to agreements, when a promise is made in exchange for another promise, in exchange for an act, or in exchange for a forbearance to act.

**bargaining unit** Employees joined together for the purpose of collective bargaining.

**battered spouse syndrome** A defense to criminal liability available to defendants if they can prove that they believed the only way to escape death or severe bodily injury was to use force against their tormentors.

**battery** The unlawful touching of another person.

**bearer** A person who is in possession of a negotiable instrument that is payable to the "bearer" or "cash" or that has been indorsed in blank.

**bearer paper** An instrument payable to bearer or cash that may be negotiated by delivery only.

**beneficiary** A third party receiving benefits from a contract made between two other parties. Also, the person named in an insurance policy to receive benefits paid by the insurer in event of a claim.

**bequest** Personal property left in a will. Also called *legacy.*

**best evidence rule** The legal rule that holds that the courts generally accept into evidence only the original of a writing, not a copy.

**best-price rule** Rules that prohibit suitors from offering different prices to different shareholders during a tender offer process.

**bilateral contract** A contract in which both parties make promises.

**bilateral mistake** In contract law, a mistake made by both parties to a contract. Bilateral mistake allows rescission by either party. Also called *mutual mistake.*

**bill of exchange** See *draft.*

**bill of lading** A document evidencing the receipt of goods for shipment and issued by a person engaged in the business of transporting or forwarding goods.

**bill of sale** A written statement evidencing the transfer of personal property from one person to another.

**binder** An oral or a written memorandum of an agreement for insurance intended to provide temporary insurance coverage until the policy is formally accepted.

**binding precedent** A previous case that a particular court must follow.

**blank indorsement** An indorsement made by a signature alone, with no particular indorsee, written on a negotiable instrument.

**blue laws** State statutes and local ordinances that regulate the making and performing of contracts on Sunday.

**bodily injury liability insurance** A type of automobile insurance that covers the risk of bodily injury or death to pedestrians and to the occupants of other cars arising from the negligent operation of the insured's motor vehicle.

**bond** A certificate of indebtedness that obligates a government or corporation to pay the bondholder a fixed rate of interest on the principal at regular intervals and to pay the principal on a stated maturity date. Also, a promise by the executor or administrator (and the sureties, if any) of a will to pay the amount of the bond to the probate court if the duties of the position are not faithfully performed.

**bot** A type of cyberagent that searches cyberspace for the lowest price in a contract, sifts through the net for the best accommodations, hunts cyberspace for the most economical plan, or spontaneously responds to a bidding process. Also known as *robot, shopping bot, cyberbot,* and *e-bot.*

**boycott** A concerted refusal to have dealings with someone to force the acceptance of certain conditions.

**breach of contract** The failure of one of the parties to a contract to do what was previously agreed upon.

**breaking and entering** In criminal law, using force, deceit, or cunning to trespass into an unoccupied building with the intent to commit a felony.

**bribery** The act of offering, giving, receiving, or soliciting something of value to influence official action or the discharge of a public duty.

**bright-line test** Test used by the courts that establishes violations of the best-price rule occur only during the actual tender offer.

**bulk transfer** Any transfer of a major party of the materials, supplies, merchandise, or other inventory of an enterprise that is not in the ordinary course of the transferor's business.

**burglary** The break-in of a dwelling or building for the purpose of carrying out a felony.

**business compulsion** See *economic duress.*

**business judgment rule** The rule that a corporate manager's decisions will not be interfered with by a court as long as the decision was made with due care, is in good faith, is lawful, and is in the best interest of the corporation.

**business system** Until recently, business systems were considered unpatentable because they were not a "process, machine, or composition of matter." Recently, however, some computerized business systems have been patented if they consist of some nonobvious, new, and useful feature not known or understood before the invention of this system.

**buyer in the ordinary course of business** A person who in good faith and without knowledge that the sale is in violation of ownership rights or security interests of a third party buys goods in ordinary course from a person in the business of selling goods of that kind, not including a pawnbroker.

**Buyer's Guide** A window sticker that is required by the Federal Trade Commission Act to be placed in the window of each used car offered for sale by a used car dealer. The sticker discloses the warranties that are made with the sale of the car and other consumer protection information.

**bylaws** Rules that guide a corporation's day-to-day internal affairs. Also known as regulations.

**c.f.** Cost and freight. Terms instructing a carrier to collect the cost of goods shipped and freight charges.

**c.i.f.** Cost, insurance, and freight. Terms instructing a carrier to collect the cost of goods shipped, insurance, and freight charges.

**c.o.d.** Cash on delivery. Instructs a carrier to retain goods until he or she has collected the costs of the goods.

**Can Spam Act** A federal law designed to reduce the use of unsolicited email, commonly known as spam, on the Internet.

**cancellation form** Under the Federal Trade Commission's Cooling-Off Rule, a document that can be filled out to terminate an order for consumer goods or services made at the buyer's home for consumer goods or services valued at $25 or more.

**capacity** In contract law, the legal ability to enter into a contractual relationship.

**capital** The money and property that a business needs to operate.

**capital contribution** The sum contributed by a business partner as a permanent investment in the business. It is then considered to be the property of the partnership.

**carrier** A business that undertakes to transport persons, goods, or both.

**case in chief** The collection of evidence that will prove a plaintiff's version of case to a jury.

**case trustee** A person appointed by a bankruptcy court to meet with creditors and report whether the case should proceed.

**cash dividend** Dividend paid to shareholders in the form of cash.

**cashier's check** A check drawn by a bank upon its own funds.

**cause in fact** In tort law, the relationship between the unreasonable conduct and the injury to the innocent party, whether the injury was or was not foreseeable. Cause in fact is also referred to as actual cause.

**certificate of authority** A document that grants a foreign corporation permission to do business within another state.

**certificate of deposit (CD)** An acknowledgment by a bank of the receipt of money and a promise to pay the money back on the due date, usually with interest.

**certificate of incorporation** A corporation's official authorization to do business in a state. Also called *charter* or *corporate charter*.

**certification authority (CA)** It is the job of the CA to provide businesses with digital signatures and to make certain that those signatures are kept current.

**certified check** A check that has been marked, or certified, by the bank on which it was drawn, guaranteeing payment to the holder.

**certified public accountant (CPA)** An accountant who has met certain age, character, education, experience, and testing requirements.

**chattels** Property that has substance and that can be touched.

**check** A draft drawn on a bank and payable on demand.

**Check 21 Act** A law that makes check clearing much quicker by the use of a *substitute check* in place of the original check for electronic check processing.

**chemical abuse** The use of drugs or alcohol to such an extent that a person's judgment is impaired or his or her physical body is harmed.

**chemical dependency** The state a person reaches when she or he can no longer function normally without regularly consuming drugs or alcohol.

**chose in action** Evidence of the right to property but not the property itself.

**civil litigation** The process of bringing a case to court to enforce a right.

**civilization** A group of people in a series of different nation-states that share certain common characteristics, including history, language, religion, traditions, beliefs, and sometimes blood.

**class-action lawsuit** A lawsuit that is brought by one or more plaintiffs on behalf of a class of persons.

**Clean Air Act** In environmental law, a federal statute designed to limit pollution from vehicles and from stationary sources such factories and manufacturing centers.

**Clean Water Act** In environmental law, a federal statute that sets requirements for limiting the pollution of the nation's water sources according to a schedule, based on the most effective technology currently available.

**clearly erroneous standard** The determination that the decision made in the lower court was undeniably wrong, given the facts and evidence in the case.

**click-on acceptance** A method of acceptance used in Internet contracts in which a party manifests acceptance by clicking on an icon on the computer screen that states that he or she agrees to the terms of the contract.

**close corporation** A corporation whose shares of stock and managerial control are closely held by fewer than 50 shareholders (often members of the same family) or by one person.

**close-end credit** Credit that is extended only for a specific amount of money, such as to buy a car or other expensive item.

**closed shop** A place of employment in which the employer, by agreement, hires only union members in good standing.

**code** A compilation of all the statutes of a particular state or of the federal government.

**Code of Federal Regulations (CFR)** Annual listing of finalized federal rules and regulations.

**Code of Professional Ethics** A set of rules established by the American Institute of Certified Public Accountants that outlines rules that govern the ethical conduct of accountants.

**codicil** A formal document used to supplement or change an existing will.

**coinsurance** An insurance policy provision under which the insurer and the insured share costs, after the deductible is met, according to a specific formula.

**collateral** The property that is subject to a security interest.

**collateral contract** In contract law, a contract by which one party agrees to pay the debt of another party if that party fails to meet that obligation.

**collecting bank** Any bank handling an item for collection except the payor bank.

**collective bargaining** A good faith meeting between representatives of employees and employers to discuss the terms and conditions of employment.

**collective bargaining agreement** A contract negotiated by an employer and a labor union that covers all issues related to employment.

**collision insurance** A type of automobile insurance that protects the insured against any loss arising from damage to the insured's automobile caused by accidental collision with another object or with any part of the roadbed.

**comaker** A person obligated, along with at least one other person, as a payor on a promissory note.

**commerce** Trade among the several states or between any foreign country and any state or territory.

**commerce clause** The clause in the U.S. Constitution that gives the federal government the power to regulate business among the states.

**commercial impracticability** A doctrine under which the courts may excuse the performance of one party to a contract because an unforeseen and very severe hardship has arisen that would place an enormous amount of hardship on that party.

**commercial unit** A single whole for the purpose of sale, the division of which impairs its character or value on the market, such as a set of furniture.

**commingled** Mixed together, as in goods stored at a warehouse or funds in a bank account.

**common carrier** A company that transports goods or persons for compensation and offers its facilities to the general public without discrimination. Compare *contract carrier.*

**common law** The body of recorded decisions that courts refer to and rely upon when making later legal decisions.

**common stock** The most usual type of corporate stock. It carries with it all the risks of the business and does not guarantee its holder the right to profits.

**community property** Property that is acquired by the personal effects of either spouse during marriage and which, by law, belongs to both spouses equally.

**comparative negligence** A form of contributory negligence that requires the court to assign damages according to the degree of fault of each party.

**compelling interest** The inescapable, overriding interest that the government of a nation or state has in a particular issue, such as the state or the nation's interest in the lives of its own citizens, which the government cannot ignore, and which it must pursue and protect at

the risk of losing its legitimacy as the proper governing body of that state or nation.

**compensatory damages** See *actual damages.*

**competent authority** The requirement that just war may be declared and run only by legitimately recognized nation-states.

**competitive impact statement (CIS)** In antitrust law, a decree that clarifies any potential antitrust problems inherent within a corporate expansion and the solutions to those problems.

**complaint** A legal document filed by a plaintiff to begin a lawsuit. The complaint sets forth the names of the parties, the facts in the case, the alleged legal violations by the defendant, and the relief sought by the plaintiff.

**complete performance** In contract law, the situation that exists when both parties to a contract have fully accomplished every term, condition, and promise to which they agreed.

**comprehensive coverage** A type of automobile insurance that provides protection against loss when the insured's car is damaged or destroyed by fire, lightning, flood, hail, windstorm, riot, vandalism, or theft.

**computer firmware** Computer software that is written to be used with only one type or brand of computer.

**computer hardware** The actual device known as a computer and its components, including the keyboard, screen, disk drive, and printer.

**computer information** Information in a form directly capable of being processed or used by, or obtained from or through, a computer.

**computer package** The combination of the computer hardware and the computer software when sold together.

**computer program** The instructions that tell the computer hardware what to do and when to do it.

**computer software** The card, tape, disk, or silicon chip that contains the computer program.

**concealment** In insurance, the intentional withholding of a fact that would be of material importance to the insurer's decision to issue a policy. In contract law, the intentional withholding of a material fact that the other party relies upon and which results in financial harm to the innocent party. See also *passive fraud.*

**condemnation** See *eminent domain.*

**condition concurrent** A condition in a contract that requires both parties to perform at the same time.

**condition precedent** In contract law, an act or promise that must take place or be fulfilled before the other party is obligated to perform his or her part of the agreement.

**condition subsequent** A condition in a contract in which the parties agree that the contract will be terminated depending on a prescribed event occurring or not occurring.

**conditional indorsement** An indorsement that makes the rights of the indorsee subject to the happening of a certain event or condition.

**confidential relationship** A relationship of trust and dependence between persons in a continued relationship, as between doctor and patient, between parent and child, or between a caretaker and a dependent person.

**confirmation** In bankruptcy law, the official approval of a reorganization plan.

**conforming goods** Goods that are in accordance with the obligations under the contract.

**conglomerate expansion** The joining of two companies that were not in competition with each other either because they dealt in different products or services or because they operated in different geographical areas.

**consensual** A freely given agreement to act.

**consent decree** Agreements created by the Department of Justice to help parties negotiate a legal merger.

**consent order** Under the Federal Trade Commission Act, an order under which a company agrees to stop a disputed practice without necessarily admitting that the practice violated the law.

**consequential damages** Losses that do not flow directly and immediately from an act but only from some of the consequences or results of the act.

**consideration** In contract law, the mutual promise to exchange benefits and detriments between parties.

**consignee** One to whom goods are entrusted under a *consignment contract* for the purpose of selling those goods.

**consignment contract** A type of mutual benefit bailment in which the *consignor* entrusts goods to the *consignee* for the purpose of selling them.

**consignor** One who entrusts goods under a *consignment contract* to a *consignee* for the purpose of selling them.

**consolidation** The joining of two corporations.

**conspiracy** The crime that occurs when people get together with others to talk about, plan, or agree to the commission of a crime.

**constitution** The basic law of a nation or state.

**constitutional law** That body of law that involves a constitution and its interpretation.

**construction loan** A loan for the building of a home that permits staggered payments that fall due at various stages in the building process.

**constructive discharge** Discriminatory action whereby an employee is demoted to a job with less pay, authority, or poorer working conditions than the job that person previously held or is subjected to supervisory harassment.

**constructive eviction** An eviction that occurs by the act of the landlord depriving the tenant of something of a substantial nature that was called for under the lease.

**consumer** Someone who buys or leases real estate, goods, or services for personal, family, or household purposes.

**consumer goods** Goods normally used for personal, family, or household purposes.

**consumer products** Tangible personal property normally used for personal, family, or household purposes.

**continuity of existence** A concept promoted by the Revised Uniform Partnership Act that permits a partnership to continue to operate as an entity even after individual partners are no longer associated with it.

**continuity plan** In sales law, an arrangement by which the seller of goods ships the goods to the subscriber on a regular basis without first sending an announcement of the upcoming delivery.

**contract** An agreement based on mutual promises between two or more competent parties to do or to refrain from doing some particular thing that is neither illegal nor impossible. The agreement results in an obligation or a duty that can be enforced in a court of law.

**contract carrier** A company that transports goods or persons for compensation only for those people with whom it desires to do business. Compare *common carrier*.

**contract for sale** Either a present sale of goods or a contract to sell goods at a future time.

**contract of record** A special type of formal contract usually confirmed by a court with an accompanying judgment issued in favor of one of the parties.

**contributory copyright infringement** A violation of copyright law in which one party provides a way for a second party to violate the copyright protection granted to the third party even though the first party never violates the copyright himself or herself.

**contributory negligence** A legal defense that involves the failure of an injured party to be careful enough to ensure personal safety.

**control test** In tort law and in agency law, the test within the doctrine of *respondeat superior* which asks that we determine the degree of control or right to control that the hiring person had over the hired person in order to determine liability.

**controlled company** A corporation that has more than half its voting power concentrated in one person or a small group of persons, who always vote together.

**Convention on Contracts for the International Sale of Goods (CISG)** A United Nations treaty designed to govern commercial transactions between parties whose places of business are in different countries.

**conventional mortgage** A mortgage that involves no government backing by either insurance or guarantee.

**conversion** The wrongful exercise of dominion and control over another's personal property.

**conveyance in trust** A trust in which the settlor conveys away the legal title to a trustee to hold for the benefit of either the settlor or another as beneficiary.

**Cooling-Off Rule** A Federal Trade Commission rule under which sales of consumer goods or services over $25 made away from the seller's regular place of business may be canceled within three business days after the sale occurs.

**Copenhagen Accord** An agreement made under the auspices of the UN Framework Conference on Climate Change and entered by five nations, including China, the United States, and India, to reduce greenhouse gases and to provide $30 billion annually to help developing nations balance sustainable development with environmental protection.

**copyright** A right granted to an author, composer, photographer, or artist to exclusively publish and sell an artistic or literary work for the life of the author plus 70 years.

**corporate democracy** See *shareholder democracy.*

**corporate opportunity doctrine** A principle that states corporate managers cannot take a business opportunity for themselves if they know their corporation would be interested in that opportunity.

**corporate raid** An unfriendly takeover, designed to dismantle the target corporation.

**corporate raider** An unfriendly suitor that intends to dismantle the target corporation after obtaining it.

**corporate shell** A subsidiary corporation set up as a mere instrumentality of a parent corporation.

**corporation** A legal entity (or a legal person) created by either a state or federal statute authorizing individuals to operate an enterprise.

**corporation by estoppel** The doctrine by which parties who have benefited by dealing with a business as though it were a corporation—though in law it is not—cannot deny its existence as a corporation. Similarly, individuals who have acted as if they were a corporation would not be able to deny that the corporation existed.

**corporativism** In corporate law, the process of doing business as a self-governing business association, that is, as a corporation.

**cost-benefit thinking** A system of thought that focuses on the consequences to one person or institution and then weighs the cost against the benefits of performing the action under scrutiny.

**cost of repair rule** The principle that states that an architect or contractor may have to reimburse a client for any extra money spent by the client to correct an error initially made by the architect or contractor.

**cost-plus contract** A contract in which the price is determined by the cost of labor and materials plus an agreed percentage markup.

**cotenancy** The quality or state of more than one owner of a single property.

**cotenants** Two or more persons who own real property together.

**counteroffer** A response to an offer in which the terms and conditions of the original offer are changed.

**courts** Judicial tribunals that meet in a regular place and apply the law in an attempt to settle disputes by weighing the arguments presented by advocates for each party.

**cover** Buying similar goods from someone else when a seller breaches a contract.

**creditor beneficiary** A third party to whom one or both contracting parties owe a continuing debt of obligation arising from a contract.

**crime** An offense against the public at large punishable by the official governing body of a nation or state.

**criminal simulation** In criminal law, the altering or falsifying of art objects, antiques, photos, films, recordings, manuscripts, and/or antiquities with the intent to defraud.

**cross-appeal** An appeal filed by a party that has prevailed at trial.

**cross-examination** The questioning of witnesses by an opposing attorney.

**cumulative voting** A system of voting for corporate directors that is designed to benefit minority shareholders by allowing shareholders to multiply their voting shares by the number of directors to be elected.

**cure** The correction of a defect in goods that caused the goods to be rejected by a buyer.

**current market price contract** An agreement in which the prices are determined with reference to the market price of the goods on a specified date.

**curtesy** Under common law, the right that a widower had, if children of the marriage were born alive, to a life estate in all real property owned by the wife during the marriage.

**cyber-agent (AKA electronic agent and e-agent)** A computer program that acts without human intervention to begin an activity, to answer cybermessages, to deliver or accept cybermail, or to enter cybercontracts.

**cyber-bulletin board** An electronic message board.

**cyber-commerce** Involves transacting business by any one of several types of electronic communication, from debit card purchases to buying and selling goods on the Internet.

**cyber-consumer** Someone who buys something on the Internet.

**cyber-contract** A contract involving the sale or licensing of information in a digital format.

**cybercrime** Any criminal act that includes a computer.

**cyber-defamation** The communication of false and destructive information about an individual through the use of a computer or other electronic device.

**cyber-discovery** A search for evidence using a computer. Also called *cyberspace discovery*.

**cyber-disparagement** In tort law, disparagement committed using a computer system.

**cyber-evidence** Any and all types of computer-generated data.

**cyber-germ warfare** Using viruses to attack a computer system.

**cyber-invasion of privacy** The unwelcome intrusion into private matters initiated or maintained by a computer.

**cyber-jurisdiction** The authority of a court to hear a case based on Internet-related transactions.

**cyber-pirate** Someone who registers a trademark or trademarks as a domain name with little or no intention of actually using the domain name in the hope that the actual holders of the trademark will buy the domain name for enormous sums.

**cyber-principal** A principal who places authority in the hands of a cyberagent.

**cyber-signature** An electronic sound or process attached to or logically associated with a record and executed or adopted by a person with the intent to sign a record.

**cyber-spoiler** See *cyber-pirate*.

**cyber-spoofing** Falsely adopting the identity of another computer user or creating a false identity on a computer Web site to commit fraud.

**cyber-spyware (AKA cyber-snoopware)** A program which, once it is installed in a computer, can keep a record of the keyboarding patterns established by the computer user.

**cybers-stalking** Targeting an individual for exploitation using that person's computer connections.

**cyber-terrorism** Using a computer to disrupt or destroy one of the critical elements of the nation's electronic infrastructure.

**cybertort** The invasion, distortion, theft, falsification, misuse, destruction, or financial exploitation of information stored in a computer.

**cyber-trespass** Gaining access to a computer with the intent to commit a crime.

**cyber-vandalism** Attacking a computer system so that a Web site is completely destroyed or paralyzed.

**damage cap** A limit on the amount of money that juries can award in certain types of tort law cases.

**damages** Money recovered by a party in a court action to compensate that party for injury or loss.

**database** The compilation of information in a form that can be understood and used by a computer.

*de facto* **corporation** A corporation defectively incorporated in good faith that exists in fact though not in law.

*de jure* **corporation** A corporation whose existence is the result of incorporators having fully or substantially complied with the relevant corporation statutes.

**debit card** A card used to electronically subtract money from a bank account to pay for goods or services.

**debtor in possession** A debtor who continues to operate his or her business after filing for bankruptcy.

**declaration of trust** A trust in which the settlor holds the legal title to the property as trustee for the benefit of some other person (the beneficiary) to whom the settlor now conveys the equitable title.

**deductible** An amount of any loss that is to be paid by the insured.

**deed of trust** A formal written instrument that transfers legal ownership of real property to a third party while the mortgagor remains on the property. The third party holds certain rights to that property as security for the mortgagor's creditors.

**defamation** The intentional tort that occurs when a false statement is communicated to others that harms a person's good name or reputation.

**defective agreement** An apparent contract in which mutual assent has been destroyed, thus rendering the alleged contract void.

**defective condition** A condition that makes a product unreasonably dangerous to the consumer, user, or property. See *product liability*.

**defendant** The person against whom a lawsuit is brought and from whom recovery is sought.

**defense of others** A defense to criminal liability to defendants if they can show they used force to rescue another person who was the victim of an apparent attack. The rescuer must have good reason to believe the victim was in danger of severe bodily injury or death.

***del credere* agent** (del·KREH·de·reh) A factor who guarantees the credit of a third party to a principal and guarantees the solvency of the purchaser and the performance of the contract.

**delegation** The transfer of a contractual duty.

**demand note** A promissory note that is payable whenever the payee demands payment.

**demurrage charge** A fee charged by a carrier for the storage of goods still remaining in its possession beyond the time allowed for unloading by the cosignee.

**demurrer** A motion for dismissal of a case on the grounds that a plaintiff has failed to state a claim for which relief can be granted.

**depositary bank** The first bank to which an item is transferred for collection; the depositary bank may also be the payor bank.

**deposition** An oral question-and-answer session conducted under oath during which an attorney questions parties or witnesses from the opposition in a lawsuit.

**dereliction of duty** In criminal law, an activity that involves a law enforcement officer's failure to carry out his or her lawful duties.

**derivative suit** A lawsuit brought by shareholders on behalf of the corporation.

**descriptive theory** A system of ethical thought that describes the values at work within a social system.

**descriptive threshold** In insurance law, a guideline that determines when a victim can bring a lawsuit for injuries that result from an auto accident.

**destination contract** A contract under which the seller is required to deliver goods to a place of destination. The title and risk of loss remain with the seller until the goods reach the place of destination.

**devise** Real property that is left in a will. In states that have adopted the Uniform Probate Code, the term refers to both real and personal property.

**devisee** One who receives the real property under a will. In states that have adopted the Uniform Probate Code, the term refers to a person who receives a gift of either real or personal property under a will.

**devolution** When courts redefine a right and transfer the power and the obligation to enforce that right from a higher legal authority to a lower one.

**digital information contract** A contract involving the sale or licensing of information in a digital format.

**Digital Millennium Copyright Act (DMCA)** A law that makes it illegal to use technological means to bypass or override programs designed to prevent access to a copyrighted work.

**digital signature** An encoded message that appears at the end of a contract created online.

**direct examination** The questioning of witnesses by the lawyer who has called them.

**direct suit** A suit brought by shareholders who have been deprived of a right that belongs to them as shareholders.

**disability** Any physical or mental impairment that substantially limits one or more of the major life activities.

**disaffirm** In contract law, to indicate by a statement or act an intent not to live up to the terms of the contract.

**disclaimer** In employment law, a statement that regardless of provisions or policies in an employment handbook and regardless of oral promises to the contrary, an employment-at-will situation still exists between an employer and its employees. In the accounting profession, a statement declaring that an auditor has decided not to give any opinion on a firm's financial records.

**disclaimer of general partner status** A document filed with the appropriate state office when a limited partner has been incorrectly named as a general partner.

**disclosed principal** The person known by a third party to be the principal of an agent.

**discounting** System by which a bank will buy an instrument at a price below its face amount with the aim of ultimately collecting the face amount.

**discovery** The process by which parties to a civil suit search for information relevant to the case.

**dishonor** To refuse to accept or pay a negotiable instrument when it is presented.

**disparagement** In tort law, any false statement made to others that questions the legal ownership or raises doubts as to the quality of merchandise.

**disparate impact** A type of discrimination in an employer's policy that seems neutral on the surface but has an unequal or unfair impact on members of one or more of the protected classes.

**disparate treatment** Intentional discrimination against an individual or group belonging to a protected class. The protected classes are sex, race, color, religion, and national origin.

**disposable income** The amount of money left from a person's income, after subtracting certain allowable deductions.

**Dispute Settlement Board (DSB)** See *Dispute Settlement Understanding*.

**Dispute Settlement Understanding (DSU)** A series of measures administered by an international Dispute Settlement Board that are designed to improve the way trading quarrels are handled.

**disputed amount** Consideration on which parties to a contract never agree.

**dissociation** A process authorized under the Revised Uniform Partnership Act that takes place whenever a partner is no longer associated with the running of the partnership firm.

**dissolution** A change in the relation of partners caused by any partner ceasing to be associated in the carrying on of the business.

**diversity cases** Federal lawsuits that are between persons from different states, between citizens of the United States and a foreign government, or between citizens of the United States and citizens of a foreign nation. Diversity cases must involve an amount over $75,000.

**dividends** Net profits, or surplus, set aside for shareholders.

**Division for Science and Technology** A United Nations agency created to coordinate activities regarding international cooperation in the sharing of science and technology for economic development.

**document of title** A paper that serves as evidence that the person holding the paper has title to the goods mentioned in the document.

**Dodd-Frank Wall Street and Consumer Protection Act** An act passed by Congress to deal with the 21st century financial crisis.

**domain name** The Internet address of a business, institution, or individual.

**domain name dispute** A disagreement that arises when an individual or organization has registered a domain name that is actually the protected trademark of a business or institution.

**domestic bill of exchange** A draft that is drawn and payable in the United States.

**domestic corporation** A corporation created by or organized under the laws of the state where it is operating.

**domestic violence statute** State laws that outlaw physical violence directed at any family member.

**dominant tenement** The property to which the right or privilege of an easement attaches.

**donee** One to whom a gift is given.

**donee beneficiary** A third party who provides no consideration for the benefits received and who owes the contracting parties no legal duty.

**donor** One who gives a gift.

**double indemnity** An optional provision in life insurance policies that provides that the insurer will pay double the amount due to a beneficiary if the insured dies from accidental causes.

**double jeopardy** In criminal procedure, the possibility of being tried twice for the same crime.

**dower** By common law, the vested rights of the wife to a one-third lifetime interest in the real property owned by her spouse. Compare *curtesy*.

**draft** A written order by which the party creating it orders another party to pay money to a third party. Also called *bill of exchange*.

**drawee** The party named in a draft who is ordered to pay the money to the payee.

**drawer** The party who draws a draft, that is, the party who orders that the money be paid.

**drug trafficking** The unauthorized manufacture or distribution of any controlled substance or the possession of such a substance with the intention of manufacturing or distributing it illegally.

**dummy corporation** A corporation that is set up as a mere instrumentality of a parent corporation. Also called *corporate shell* and *empty shell*.

**dunning letter** A letter representing payment for goods.

**durable power of attorney** A document that authorizes an agent to act on another's behalf, with the power either surviving incapacity or becoming effective upon incapacity.

**duress** An action by one party that forces another party to do what need not be done otherwise.

**duty** An obligation placed on individuals because of the law.

**duty of due diligence** A duty that says that corporate managers when acting on behalf of the corporation must act (1) in good faith; (2) using the same level of care that an ordinarily prudent person would use in a comparable situation, and (3) in the reasonable belief that the best interests of the corporation are being met.

**duty of loyalty** A duty that states managers must place the corporation's interests above their own.

**duty of obedience** Managers' duty to ensure their exercise of authority is not excessive and does not harm the corporation.

**e-911 location identifier system** An electronic chip located in a mobile phone that sends out a signal that is designed to ensure that EMS personnel can locate people who are unable or unwilling to reveal their location when making an emergency call.

**early neutral evaluation (ENE)** A process similar to that of a settlement hearing, which may result in a final decision or be used to help shape the final decision.

**easement** The right to use the land of another for a particular purpose.

**easement by prescription** An easement that is obtained by passing over another's property without permission openly and continuously for a period of time set by state statute (20 years in many states).

**e-check** (sometimes called *electronic check conversion*) A system in which funds are electronically transferred from a customer's checking account, eliminating the need to process a paper check.

**e-commerce** Involves transacting business by any one of several types of electronic communication, from debit card purchases to buying and selling goods on the Internet.

**economic compensatory damages** Damages that are directly quantifiable, including damages awarded for lost wages, medical expenses, and expenses incurred in the repair or replacement of property.

**economic duress** Threats of a business nature that force another party without real consent to enter a commercial agreement. Also called *business compulsion*.

**Economic Espionage Act** Legislation that outlines criminal sanctions for the theft of trade secrets and the use of fraud to obtain trade secrets.

**economic reality test** In agency law, a test used by the court in vicarious liability to determine whether a worker is a servant or an independent contractor.

**Economic Security Council (ESC)** A single, unified international agency under the management of the United Nations that would monitor the economic activities of member nations.

**e-consumer** Someone who buys something on the Internet.

**ejectment** The common law name given to the lawsuit brought by a landlord to have a tenant evicted from the premises.

**elective share** See *forced share*.

**electronic contracts** Contracts made using computers, either via e-mail or the Internet, or that involve computer-related products, such as databases and software.

**electronic data interchange (EDI)** An electronic process used to negotiate contracts.

**electronic fund transfer (EFT)** A method of banking that uses computers and electronic technology as a substitute for checks and other banking methods.

**electronic or jurisdiction** The authority of a court to hear a case based on Internet-related transactions.

**electronically stored information (ESI)** Computerized evidence.

**emancipated** In contract law, the condition that exists when minors are no longer under the control of their parents and are responsible for their contracts.

**embezzlement** The act of wrongfully taking property entrusted into one's care.

**eminent domain** The right of federal, state, and local governments, or other public bodies, to take private lands, with compensation to their owners, for public use. Also called *condemnation*.

**emotional duress** Acts or threats that create emotional distress and lead a person into a contract against his or her will.

**employment-at-will** A doctrine followed by most jurisdictions in the United States that says an employer can dismiss an employee at any time for any reason.

**employment contacts**  In employment law, an enforceable agreement between the hiring party (the employer) and the hired party (the employee).

**end user**  A purchaser who is not involved in the production or assembly of the product.

**endowment insurance**  Insurance protection that combines life insurance and investment so that if the insured outlives the time period of the policy, the face value is paid to the beneficiary.

**entity theory**  A theory in partnership law that holds that a partnership is actually a separate legal person with its own legal identity.

**entrapment**  A defense to criminal liability that claims that a previously law-abiding citizen was induced to commit a crime by a law enforcement officer.

**equal dignities rule**  The legal rule that provides that when a party appoints an agent to negotiate an agreement that must be in writing, the appointment of the agent must also be in writing.

**equipment**  Goods that are used or bought for use primarily in business.

**equitable estoppel**  See *part performance*.

**equitable remedy**  The requirement that a party do something or refrain from doing something, beyond the payment of money.

**equity financing**  The issuing and selling of shares of stock to raise capital.

**equity of redemption**  A mortgagor's right to pay off the mortgage in full, including interest.

**espionage**  The gathering or transmitting of information pertaining to the national defense of a nation for the political or military use of any foreign nation.

**estate in fee simple**  An estate in which the owner owns the land for life with the right to use it or dispose of it freely.

**estoppel**  A legal bar to denying acts, statements, or promises.

**ethic of responsibility**  The ethical principle that says that the first duty of governmental leaders is to protect their own people and their own nation-states.

**ethic of ultimate ends**  The ethical principle that holds that, since people can never know the final consequences of their actions, they must always act to promote benevolence, that is, to do good and to avoid evil.

**ethical relativism**  A system of ethical thought that says there is no objective or absolute standard of right and wrong.

**ethics**  Rules of conduct that transcend legal rules, telling people how to act when the law does not.

**EU Data Protection Directive**  A decree issued by the European Union (EU) that prevents European companies from sharing ESI with countries that do not provide the same level of protection for the ESI as the EU.

**EU E-Privacy Directive**  A decree issued by the European Union (EU) that guarantees EU citizens a high level of privacy for electronically stored information.

**euro**  The European Union's common currency.

**European Central Bank (ECB)**  The bank was established by provisions within the Maastricht Treaty and is the central hub of the European System of Central Banks.

**European System of Central Banks (ESCB)**  A system of banks including the European Central Bank and the National Central Banks.

**European Union (EU)**  A group of countries in Europe that have joined together to formulate a common European economic policy, minimize trade barriers, and introduce a common currency with the goal of making the EU a major global competitor.

**eviction**  An act of the landlord that deprives the tenant of the enjoyment of the premises.

**exculpatory agreement**  A clause that says one of the parties to a contract, generally the one who wrote the contract, is not liable for any economic loss or physical injury, even if that party caused the loss or injury.

**exculpatory clause**  A clause in a contract that releases a party from liability for his or her wrongful acts. These clauses are not favored by law.

**executed contract**  A contract whose terms have been completely and satisfactorily carried out by both parties.

**executor (male); executrix (female)**  The party named in a will to carry out the terms of the will.

**executory contract**  A contract that has not yet been fully performed by the parties.

**exempt property**  Property of a decedent that passes to the surviving spouse or children and is beyond the reach of creditors.

**express authority**  An agent's authority that the principal voluntarily and specifically sets forth as oral or written instructions in an agency agreement.

**express contract** A contract in which both parties accept mutual obligations through either oral discussion or written communication.

**express warranty** An oral or written statement, promise, or other representation about the quality of a product.

**extant data** Data that are difficult to retrieve because they are hidden within a computer system.

**extortion** The act of taking another's property with consent when such consent is coerced by threat to injure a victim's person, property, or reputation.

**f.a.s vessel** Free alongside vessel. Indicates that the seller must deliver goods, at the seller's own risk, alongside the vessel or at a dock designated by the buyer.

**f.o.b.** Free on board.

**f.o.b. the place of destination** Terms indicating that goods will be delivered free to the place of destination.

**f.o.b. the place of shipment** Terms indicating that goods will be delivered free to the place of shipment.

**factor** A special agent who is employed to sell merchandise consigned for that purpose.

**failure of consideration** A personal defense that may be used by a maker or drawer of a negotiable instrument when the party with whom the maker dealt breaches the contract by not furnishing the agreed consideration.

**fair court** Historically in the Middle Ages in Europe, a court set up at a festival (a fair) to handle disputes between merchants at that festival (fair).

**fairness rule** The rule that requires managers to be fair to the corporation when they personally benefit from their business decisions.

**false imprisonment** An intentional tort involving the unjustified confinement or detention of a person.

**family allowance** An amount of money taken from a decedent's estate and given to the family to meet its immediate needs while the estate is being probated.

**family farmer** Under Chapter 12 of the Bankruptcy Code, a farmer who receives more than half the total income from the farm. In addition, to qualify as a family farmer, 80 percent of the farmer's debt must result from farm expenses.

**farm products** Crops, livestock, or supplies used or produced in farming operations.

**fault-based insurance** An automobile insurance policy that will measure liability in an automobile accident by the degree of fault that can be assigned to each driver using negligence principles.

**featherbedding** Requiring an employer, usually by a union, to keep unneeded employees, to pay employees for not working, or to assign more employees to a given job than are needed.

**federal question** A matter that involves the U.S. Constitution, a federal statute or statutes, or a treaty; handled by federal district courts.

**Federal Register** Publication that produces a daily compilation of new regulations issued by federal administrative agencies.

**felony** A crime punishable by death or by imprisonment in a federal or state prison for a term exceeding one year.

**fiduciary** A person who acts in a position of trust or confidence.

**fiduciary relationship** A relationship based on trust such as exists between an attorney and a client, an agent and a principal, a guardian and a ward, a trustee and a beneficiary, or a director and a corporation.

**field warehousing** The practice of using goods that are stored in a warehouse as security for a loan.

**finance charge** The actual cost of a loan in dollars and cents.

**firm offer** A rule that no consideration is necessary when a merchant agrees in writing to hold an offer open for the sale of goods.

**first degree murder** In criminal law, killing someone with premeditation or with prior calculation and design, or while committing a serious felony such as rape, robbery, or kidnapping.

**fixture** An article of personal property physically attached to real property in such a way that an interest arises in it under real estate law.

**flexible-rate mortgage** A mortgage that has a rate of interest that changes according to fluctuations in the index to which it is tied. Also called *variable-rate mortgage*.

**floater policy** A policy that insures property that cannot be covered by specific insurance because the property is constantly changing in either value or location.

**floating lien** A provision, placed by the creditor, in a security agreement that a security interest of the creditor also applies to goods the debtor acquires at a later time.

**forbearance**  The act of refraining from doing (or promising not to do) something that a person has a legal right to do.

**forced share**  The portion of a decedent's estate assured to the family by state statute.

**foreclosure**  The right of a mortgagee to apply to a court to have property sold when the mortgagor defaults or fails to perform some agreement in the mortgage.

**foreign corporation**  A corporation created by or organized under the laws of a state other than the one in which it is operating.

**foreign draft**  See *international bill of exchange*.

**forgery**  The false making or alteration of a writing with the intent to defraud.

**formal contract**  Under common law, a contract that is written; signed, witnessed, and placed under the seal of the parties; and delivered.

**formalist theory**  A theory of legal interpretation under which the court will look to see if certain elements (offer, acceptance, mutual assent, consideration, capacity, and legality) exist before concluding whether or not the parties in a lawsuit have actually entered a legally binding contract.

**forum shopping**  The process of locating a jurisdiction that has a friendly track record for the type of lawsuit that is about to be filed.

**fraud**  A wrongful statement, action, or concealment pertinent to the subject matter of a contract knowingly made to damage the other party.

**fraud in the inception**  Fraud that occurs when one party tricks another into a contract by lying to the innocent party about the actual nature of the contract.

**fraud in the inducement**  Fraud that occurs when one party tricks another into a contract by lying about the terms of the agreement to get the innocent party to enter the contract under false pretenses.

**fraudulent conveyance**  A transfer of property with the intent to defraud creditors.

**fraudulent misrepresentation**  A wrongful statement, action, or concealment, pertinent to the subject matter of a contract, that is knowingly made to damage the other party.

**friendly suitor**  See *white knight*.

**frustration-of-purpose doctrine**  In contract law, the doctrine that releases a party from a contractual obligation when performing the obligations would be thoroughly impractical and senseless.

**full warranty**  A warranty under which a defective product will be repaired or replaced without charge within a reasonable time after a complaint has been made about it.

**fungible goods**  Goods of which any unit is, by nature or usage of trade, the equivalent of any like unit; wheat, flour, sugar, and liquids of various kinds are examples.

**future goods**  Goods that are not yet in existence or under the control of people; they include fish in the sea, minerals in the ground, goods not yet manufactured, and commodities futures.

**general agent**  A person who is given broad authority to act on behalf of the principal in conducting the bulk of the principal's business activities on a daily basis.

**General Agreement on Tariffs and Trade (GATT)**  A nonstatic agreement among the principal trading countries to reduce or eliminate tariffs and to promote free trade on a global basis.

**General Assembly**  The member nations of the United Nations.

**general consent**  Consent that arises automatically when a patient enters a hospital for routine tests and procedures needed for diagnosis and treatment.

**general jurisdiction**  The power of a court to hear any type of case.

**general partner**  A partner who takes an active part in running a partnership and has unlimited liability for the firm's debts.

**general release**  A document expressing the intent of a creditor to release a debtor from obligations to an existing and valid debt.

**general warranty deed**  A deed that contains express warranties under which a grantor guarantees property to be free of encumbrances created by the grantor or by others who had title previously. Also called *full convenant* and *warranty deed*.

**general welfare clause**  Article I, Section 8, Clause 1 of the U.S. Constitution which reads in part that Congress is empowered to "lay and collect taxes, Duties, Imposts, and Excises, to pay the Debts and provide for the common defense and general welfare of the United States."

**generally accepted accounting principles (GAAP)**  Rules established by the Financial Accounting Standards Board (FASB) that outline the procedures that accountants use in accumulating financial data and in preparing financial statements.

**generally accepted auditing standards (GAAS)**  Standards set up by the Auditing Standards Board of the American Institute of Certified Public Accountants (AICPA) that measure the quality of the performance of the auditing procedures.

**Genetic Information Nondiscrimination Act (GINA)** A law passed by Congress that makes it unlawful for employers or insurance companies to make decisions based on genetic information acquired by genetic testing.

**Geneva Conventions** International meetings that attempted to deal with many of the contemporary complications brought on by the nature of warfare in the twentieth century.

**gift *in causa mortis*** (in·KAWS·ah·MORE·tes) A gift given during one's lifetime in contemplation of death from a known cause.

**gift *inter vivos*** (IN·ter·VY·vose) A gift between the living. For an exchange to be valid, the donor must intend to make a gift, the gift must be delivered to the donee, and the donee must accept it.

**good faith** Honesty in fact and observance of reasonable commercial standards of fair dealings in the trade.

**goods** All things (other than money, stocks, and bonds) that are movable.

**goodwill** The expected continuance of public patronage of a business.

**governmental control** A theory of corporate control based on the belief that because corporate decision making impacts upon more individuals and groups than just shareholders and managers, those decisions should be made by a group of corporate outsiders, usually government officials. Also called *state control*.

**graduated-payment mortgage** A mortgage that has a fixed interest rate during the life of the mortgage; however, the monthly payments made by the mortgagor increase over the term of the loan.

**grantee** A person to whom title to real property is transferred in a deed.

**grantor** A person who transfers title to real property in a deed.

**gratuitous agency** An agency relationship that emerges from an agreement that is not a contract.

**gratuitous agent** An agent who is not under contract and, thus, performs his or her duties without payment.

**gratuitous bailment** A bailment for the sole benefit of either the bailor or the bailee, in which the other party receives no consideration for benefits bestowed.

**greenmail** A strategy used to shake off a bidder's hostile suit by offering to buy, at significantly higher cost, the portion of stock already owned by the bidder who is trying to take over the company.

**grievance procedure** A procedure that allows employees to appeal any decision an employer makes that employees feel violates just cause.

**gross negligence** Very great negligence.

**guaranteed insurability** An optional provision in an insurance contract that allows the insured to pay an extra premium initially in exchange for a guaranteed option to buy more insurance at certain specified times later on with no questions asked and no medical examination required.

**guarantor** The promisor.

**guaranty contract** In contract law, a contract by which one party agrees to pay the debt of another party if that party fails to meet that obligation.

**guaranty of payment** A promise to pay another's bills or to settle wrongful acts if that party does not settle them personally.

**health care proxy** A written statement authorizing an agent to make health care decisions for another in the event of incapacity.

**Health Insurance Portability and Accountability Act (HIPAA)** Legislation that guarantees patients the right to see their medical records and those of their underage children.

**heir** One who inherits property either under a will or through someone's dying without a will.

**holder** A person who is in possession of a negotiable instrument that is issued or indorsed to that person's order or to bearer.

**holder in due course** A holder who has taken a negotiable instrument for value, in good faith, without notice that it is overdue or has been dishonored and without notice of any defenses against it or claim to it.

**holder in due course rule** A rule adopted by the FTC that states that holders of consumer credit contracts who are holders in due course are subject to all claims and defenses that the buyer could use against the seller, including personal defenses.

**Home Affordable Modification Program (HAMP)** A program set up by the Department of the Treasury to support the efforts of homeowners who, though in default, wish to continue to make payments on their mortgages

**home equity loan** A line of credit made available to home-owners based on the value of the property over and above any existing mortgages.

**homeowner's policy** A type of insurance that gives protection for all types of losses and liabilities related to home ownership. Items covered include losses from fire, windstorm, burglary, vandalism, and injuries suffered by others while on the property.

**homestead exemption** A provision in the Bankruptcy Code that allows debtors to exclude a statutory amount of equity in the debtor's place of residence and in property used as a burial ground when filing for bankruptcy.

**homicide** The killing of one human being by another.

**horizontal expansion** The joining of companies involved in the same business.

**hostile bidder** See *unfriendly suitor*.

**hot-cargo contract** An agreement whereby an employer voluntarily agrees with a union not to handle, use, or deal in nonunion-produced goods for another employer.

**identified goods** Specific goods that are selected as the subject matter of a contract.

**identity theft** Using a computer to steal confidential information to clean out a person's bank account, to run up credit card debt, to divert cash transfers, and to disrupt the financial and personal life of the victim.

**illegal agreement** In contract law, a void agreement to do something that violates the law.

**illusory promise** A promise that does not obligate the promisor to anything.

**implied authority** The authority of an agent to perform acts that are necessary or customary to carry out expressly authorized duties.

**impaired classes** Creditors who receive less than the full value of their claims in bankruptcy proceedings.

**implied contract** A contract created by the actions or gestures of the parties involved in the transaction.

**implied covenant** An implied promise in any employment relationship that the employer and the employee will be fair with each other.

**implied warranty** A warranty that is imposed by law rather than by statements, descriptions, or samples given by the seller.

**implied-in-fact contract** A contract implied by direct or indirect acts of the parties.

**implied-in-law contract** A remedy imposed by a court in a situation in which the parties did not create a written, oral, or implied-in-fact agreement but one party has unfairly benefited at the innocent expense of another. Also called *quasi-contract*.

**in pari delicto** (in pah·ree de·LIK·toh) In equal fault. A contract relationship when both parties to an illegal agreement are equally wrong, in the knowledge of the operation and effect of their contract.

**inactive data** Data in a computer system that are not being used at the present time but that can be easily retrieved.

**incidental beneficiary** A third party for whose benefit a contract was not made but who would substantially benefit if the agreement were performed according to its terms and conditions.

**incidental damages** Damages awarded for losses indirectly, but closely, attributed to a breach to cover any expenses paid out by an innocent party to prevent further loss.

**incorporators** The people who actually sign the articles of incorporation to start a corporation.

**indemnification** Payment for loss or damage suffered.

**indemnify** To compensate for loss or damage or insure against future loss or damage.

**independent contractor** One who contracts to do a job and who retains complete control over the methods employed to obtain completion.

**independent directors** Directors who have no family members employed by the corporation, who are not themselves employed by the corporation, or, if they were once employed by the corporation, have not been on staff for at least three years.

**independent director control** A theory of corporate control that states that the best way to make certain that corporate decisions are made in the best interests of the corporation is to make sure that the decision makers themselves are not affected by the decisions.

**indictment** A set of formal charges against a defendant issued by a grand jury.

**individual justice** Justice that is meted out to the people on a case-by-case basis.

**indorsee** A person to whom a draft, note, or other negotiable instrument is transferred by indorsement.

**indorsement in full** See *special indorsement*.

**indorser** A person who indorses a negotiable instrument.

**infliction of emotional distress** The intentional tort that allows those injured emotionally by the wrongful acts of others to recover damages even without the accompanying physical injury.

**informal contract** An oral or written contract that is not under a seal or is not a contract of record. Also called *simple contract*.

**information** A set of formal charges against a defendant drawn up and issued by the prosecutor or district attorney.

**informed consent** Written consent given by patients for diagnostic tests or treatments that will involve danger or pain after being told about the procedure and the risks involved.

**in-house attorney** A member of the officer corps of a business who is instructed in his or her duties by a supervisor.

**injunction** A court order preventing someone from performing a particular act.

**inland marine insurance** An insurance contract that covers goods that are moved by land carriers such as rail, truck, and airplane.

**innkeeper** An operator of a hotel, motel, or inn that holds itself out to the public as being ready to accommodate travelers, strangers, and transient guests.

**inside information** Material, nonpublic, factual data that can be used to buy or sell securities at a profit.

**insider trading** Using inside information to either cheat the corporation or take unfair advantage of corporate outsiders.

**insider trading rule** A rule of corporate governance that states that when managers possess important inside information, they are obligated to reveal that information before trading on it themselves.

**insolvent** Inability of a business entity to pay its debts as they become due in the usual course of business.

**installment note** A promissory note in which the principal together with interest on the unpaid balance is payable in installments at specified times.

**insurable interest** The financial interest that a policyholder has in the person or property that is insured.

**insurance** A contract whereby one party pays premiums to another party who undertakes to pay compensation for losses resulting from risks or perils specified in the contract.

**insured** A party that is protected by an insurer against losses caused by the risks specified in an insurance policy.

**insurer** A party that accepts the risk of loss in return for a premium (payment of money) and agrees to compensate the insured against a specified loss.

**integral-part test** A finding that any type of price enhancement violates the best-price rule.

**intended beneficiary** A third party in whose favor a contract is made.

**intentional or reckless infliction of emotional distress** A tort involving someone who intentionally or recklessly causes another to undergo emotional or mental suffering.

**interest-only mortgage** In property law, a mortgage in which the borrower pays only the interest for a period of time, usually one to three years, as set by the agreement.

**interference with a contract** The international tort that results when a person, out of ill will, entices a contractual party into breaking the contract.

**interlocking directorates** In antitrust law, a situation that occurs when individuals serve as two corporations that are competitors.

**intermediary bank** Any bank to which an item is transferred in the course of collection except the depositary or payor bank.

**international arbitration agreement** A pledge to use arbitration if parties find themselves in disagreement about enforcement rights under an original contract.

**international bill of exchange** A draft that is drawn in one country but is payable in another. Also called *foreign draft*.

**International Court of Justice (ICJ)** One of the principal vehicles for the establishment of international law and justice.

**International Criminal Court (ICC)** International court that presides over trials involving genocide, war crimes, and other human rights violations.

**International Law Commission** A thirty-four-member panel of judges who seek to codify international law in as objective a manner as possible.

**International Monetary Fund (IMF)** A nongovernmental organization that is designed to help financially strapped nations to secure loans that will help them engage in programs of sustainable economic growth and development.

**international terrorism** Acts transcending national boundaries that violate a state's criminal laws and are intended to intimidate that country's civilians or influence the policy or conduct of the government.

**interrogatories** Written questions to be answered in writing under oath by the opposite party in a lawsuit.

**interstate commerce** Business activities that touch more than one state.

**interstate shipment** A shipment that goes beyond the borders of the state in which it originated.

**intestacy** The quality or state of one who dies without having prepared a valid will.

**intestate** Having died without leaving a valid will. Compare *testate*.

**intestate succession** The process by which property passes to others when people die without a will.

**intimidation** In criminal law, threats of harm to the person or the property of a public servant, a party official, or a witness, with the intent to coerce that person into violating his or her duty under the law.

**intrastate commerce** Business activities that have no out-of-state connections.

**intrastate shipment** A shipment that is entirely within a single state.

**invasion of privacy** The intentional tort that occurs when one person unreasonably denies another person the right to be left alone.

**inventory** Goods held for sale or lease, or raw materials used or consumed in a business.

**invitation to trade** An announcement published for the purpose of creating interest and attracting a response by many people.

**involuntary bailment** A bailment arising from the leaving of personal property in the possession of a bailee through an act of God, accident, or other uncontrolled phenomenon.

**involuntary manslaughter** In criminal law, the unlawful killing of another human being caused by negligence.

**irresistible impulse test** Under this rule, criminal defendants are judged not guilty by reason of insanity if, at the time of the action in question, they suffered from a mental disease that either prevented them from knowing right from wrong or compelled them to commit the criminal act.

**irrevocable offer** A rule that no consideration is necessary when a merchant agrees in writing to hold an offer open for the sale of goods. Also called *firm offer*.

**issue** Descendants (children, grandchildren, great-grandchildren).

**issuer** Either a maker or a drawer of an instrument.

**joint tenants** Two or more persons who own property where the right of any deceased owner is automatically transferred to other surviving owners.

**joint tenants with the right of survivorship** See *joint tenants*.

**judicial review** The process by which a court determines the constitutionality of various legislative statutes, administrative regulations, and executive actions.

**judicial–economic system** The interaction of the legal system and the economic system so as to become, in effect, a single system.

**junior mortgage** A mortgage subject to a prior mortgage.

**junk bonds** Bonds with high risk but also a high rate of return.

**junk science** The distorted, exaggerated, misapplied, or misrepresented use of scientific evidence.

**jurisdiction** The authority of a court to hear and decide cases.

**juriscience** In the development of the law, the point at which science, technology, and the law intersect.

**just cause** A criterion under the just war theory, which states that to be morally permissible, a war must be waged only for honorable motives.

**just war theory** A theory for determining when a war can be considered legally and morally correct.

**kidnapping** The unlawful abduction of an individual against that individual's will.

**knowledge** In criminal law, the awareness that a particular result will probably occur.

**labor union** An organization that acts on behalf of all employees in negotiations with the employer regarding terms of their employment.

**laches** The equitable doctrine that a delay or failure to assert a right or claim at the proper time, which causes a disadvantage to the adverse party, is a bar to recovery.

**lack of consideration** A personal defense that may be used by a maker or drawer of a negotiable instrument when no consideration existed in the underlying contract for which the instrument was issued.

**landlord** A person who owns real property and who rents or leases it to someone else. Also called *lessor*.

**larceny** The act of taking and carrying away the personal property of another without the right to do so.

**larceny by false pretenses** The taking of someone's money or property by intentionally deceiving that person.

**last resort** A criterion under the just war theory that states that a war must be waged only as a final course of action.

**last will and testament** A formal document that governs the transfer of property at death.

**law** A set of rules created by the governing body of a society to maintain harmony, stability, and justice in that society.

**law merchant** In England, the commercial law developed by merchants who needed a set of rules to govern their business transactions.

**leading objective test** In contract law, a test applied by the court to determine the real purpose of a guaranty contract.

**lease** A contract granting the use of certain real property to another for a specified period in return for the payment of rent.

**lease option** A contract that permits a party to lease real property while holding an option to purchase that property.

**leasehold estate** The creation of an ownership interest in the tenant. An interest in real estate that is held under a lease. Also called *tenancy*.

**legal detriment** In contract law, doing (or promising to do) something that one has a legal right not to do, giving up (or promising to give up) something that one has a legal right to keep, or refraining from doing (or promising not to do) something that one has a legal right to do.

**legal imperialism** American insistence that all disputes be resolved under American law.

**legal tender** Money that may be offered legally in satisfaction of a debt and that must be accepted by a creditor when offered.

**legatee** One who receives personal property in a will.

**lessee** See *tenant*.

**lessor** See *landlord*.

**leveraged buyout** The purchase of a controlling portion of the stock in a corporation by a group of shareholders, usually officers and directors of the company.

**lex mercatoria** In England, the commercial law developed by merchants who needed a set of rules to govern their business transactions.

**liability** The legal responsibility of an individual for his or her actions.

**liable** Legally responsible.

**libel** Any false statement that harms another person's good name or reputation made in a permanent form, such as movies, writing, and videotape, and communicated to others.

**license** A grant of permission to do a particular thing, to exercise a certain privilege, to carry on a particular business, or to pursue a certain occupation; an agreement that gives no property right or interest in land but merely allows the licensee to do certain acts that would otherwise be a trespass; a privilege granted by a state or city upon payment of a fee, which is not a contract and may be revoked for cause, conferring authority to perform a designated task, such as operating a motor vehicle.

**licensing agreement** An agreement in which one party is given permission from another party to do a particular thing in exchange for consideration.

**lien** A claim that one has against the property of another.

**life estate** An estate in which the owner owns real property for his or her life or for the life of another.

**life insurance** An insurance contract that provides monetary compensation for losses suffered by another's death.

**limited defense** See *personal defense*.

**limited liability** Status that specifies that an individual's liability will not go beyond his or her original investment.

**limited liability company (LLC)** A business organization that borrows elements from a partnership and a corporation. LLCs may come into existence only through following the steps laid out in the state code.

**limited partner** A partner who does not take part in the management of a firm and whose liability does not extend beyond his or her investment.

**limited partnership** A partnership formed by two or more persons having one or more general partners and one or more limited partners.

**limited-payment life insurance** Insurance that provides that the payment will stop after a stated length of time—usually 10, 20, or 30 years.

**limited warranty** A warranty that does not meet all of the requirements of a full warranty.

**lingering apparent authority** Apparent authority that stays with an agent if the principal has terminated the agent but has failed to give proper notice to third parties entitled to such notice.

**liquidated damages** Damages agreed to by the parties to a contract in the event of a breach.

**liquidation** The conversion of property into cash.

**litigant** A person involved in litigation.

**living trust** A trust that comes into existence while the person who establishes it is alive. Also called *inter vivos trust*.

**living will** A document in which individuals can indicate their desire not to be kept alive by artificial means if there is no hope for recovery.

**local option** The practice in a state of eliminating uniform statewide laws regulating Sunday activities and allowing the local counties, cities, towns, and villages to adopt their own special Sunday ordinances.

**locality rule** A means to judge a health care provider's actions on the basis of how other health care professionals in the same community would have acted in the same situation.

**lockup agreement** A contract between a target corporation and a white knight, giving the knight an option to buy valuable property should a hostile bidder gain control of the target corporation.

**locus sigilli** The place of the seal. The abbreviation L.S. is often used in place of the seal itself on formal written contracts.

**lodger** A person who has the use of property without actual or exclusive possession of it.

**M'Naughten Rule** The oldest test for insanity whereby a criminal defendant is declared not guilty by reason of insanity if, at the time of the criminal act, he or she suffered from a mental disease that prevented him or her from understanding the nature of the act and that the act was wrong.

**Maastricht Treaty** The outcome of a conference held in Maastricht, the Netherlands. The objectives of the treaty were to create a general European economic policy as well as a foreign policy acceptable to all member states.

**Mail Order and Telephone Order Rule** The Federal Trade Commission rule that states that sellers must ship orders within the time promised in their advertisements.

**main purpose test** In contract law, a test applied by the court to determine the real purpose of a guaranty contract.

**majority** A term used to describe persons who have reached the legal age of adulthood.

**maker** A person obligated as the payor on a promissory note. See also *comaker*.

**malicious prosecution** Bringing false criminal charges against an innocent victim.

**malpractice** Occurs when a professional accountant, health care professional, or attorney—fails to meet his or her duty of care.

**managerial control** A theory of corporate management that favors insulating managers from shareholders by limiting the shareholders' power to vote and by making it difficult for the shareholder to sue managers.

**master** An outdated term signifying an individual who has the right to control the physical conduct of a servant or employee.

**material fact** An essential or important fact; a fact of substance.

**means test** Three steps used to qualify someone for Chapter 7 bankruptcy.

**med-arb** A form of ADR that combines the best aspects of both mediation and arbitration. The parties first submit to a mediation session. If the matter cannot be settled, it moves to an arbitration hearing.

**mediation** The process by which an outside party attempts to help two other parties settle their differences.

**mediator** The third party in mediation whose job is to convince the contending parties to adjust or settle their dispute.

**Medicaid** A healthcare plan for low-income people that is administered by state governments but funded by both state and federal funds.

**medical payments insurance** A type of automobile insurance that pays for medical (and sometimes funeral) expenses resulting from bodily injuries to anyone occupying the policyholder's car at the time of an accident.

**Medicare** A federally funded health insurance program for people 65 years and over who are eligible for Social Security.

**memorandum** A written agreement containing the terms of an agreement, an identification of the subject matter of the agreement, the consideration promised, the names and identities of the parties to the agreement, and the signature of the party charged to the agreement.

**mercantile law** In England, the commercial law developed by merchants who needed a set of rules to govern their business transactions.

**merchant** A person who deals in goods of the kind sold in the ordinary course of business or who otherwise claims to have knowledge or skills peculiar to those goods.

**merger** The acquisition of one corporation by another.

**metadata** In computer jargon, data that is used to record information about other computer data.

**midnight deadline** The deadline by which banks must settle or return checks or be responsible for paying them. If the payor bank is not the depository bank, it must settle for an item by midnight of the banking day of receipt. If the payor bank is also the depository bank, the deadline is midnight of the next banking day following the banking day on which it receives the relevant item.

**military caregiver leave** A provision under the Family Medical Leave Act (FMLA) which states that an employer must give an employee up to 26 weeks of leave time in a 12-month period to care for a family member who has sustained a serious illness or injury which occurred because of military service.

**minimum contacts** The doctrine of minimum contacts identifies the fewest number of contacts that will permit a court to exercise personal jurisdiction over an out-of-state defendant.

**minority** A term used to describe persons who have not reached the legal age of adulthood.

**mirror image rule** In contract law, the rule that an acceptance must duplicate the terms in the offer.

**misdemeanor** A crime less serious than a felony that is generally punishable by a prison sentence of not more than one year.

**misrepresentation** In contract law, a false statement innocently made by one party to a contract with no intent to deceive. Also, in insurance, giving false answers to questions in an insurance application that materially affect the risk undertaken by the insurer.

**misuse of legal procedure** Bringing legal action without probable cause and with malice.

**mitigation** A principle that states an innocent party cannot take advantage by deliberately raising the level of damages that the other party will have to pay as a consequence of a breach.

**monetary threshold** In insurance law, a guideline to determine when a victim can bring a lawsuit for injuries that result from an auto accident.

**money order** A type of draft that may be purchased from banks, post offices, telegraph companies, and express companies as a substitute for a check.

**monopoly** The exclusive control of a market by a business enterprise.

**morals** Values that govern society's attitude toward right and wrong.

**mortgage** A transfer of an interest in property for the purpose of creating a security for a debt.

**mortgagee** The party who lends money and takes back a mortgage as security for the loan.

**mortgagor** The party who borrows money and gives a mortgage to the lender or mortgagee as security for the loan.

**most favored nation principle** A principle that states that the World Trade Organization nations must apply the same privileges, advantages, and benefits to all other member nations in relation to similar imports.

**mutual assent** In contract law, the state of mind that exists between an offeror and an offeree once a valid offer has been accepted and once the parties know what the terms are and have agreed to be bound by them. Also known as "a meeting of the minds."

**mutual-benefit bailment** A bailment in which both the bailor and the bailee receive some benefit.

**mutual mistake** See *bilaterial mistake.*

**mutual recession** A condition in which both parties to a contract agree to rescind the contract and return to the other any consideration already received or pay for any services or materials already rendered.

*mutuum* (MYOO·choo·um) A loan of goods with the intention that the goods may be used and later replaced with an equal amount of different goods.

**National Central Banks (NCB)** Part of the European System of Central Banks, the NCBs are located within the member nations of the EU.

**national rule** A rule that allows a court to judge a health care provider's degree of care by determining how the same procedure is performed on a national basis.

**national standard** A rule that allows a court to judge a health care provider's degree of care by determining how the same procedure is performed on a national basis.

**national treatment principle** A principle that states that the World Trade Organization nations must apply the same standards to imports that they apply to domestic goods.

**nation-states** Sovereign divisions that govern a recognized area of land on a map, may raise money within their borders, and have a responsibility to provide for their citizens.

**natural law theory** A system of ethical thought that sees an unbreakable link joining the law and morality.

**navigable airspace** The space above 1,000 feet over populated areas and above 500 feet over water and unpopulated areas.

**necessaries** Goods and services that are essential to a minor's health and welfare.

**necessary and proper clause** In constitutional law, Article I, Section 8, Clause 18, of the U.S. Constitution, which says that Congress has the power "(T)o make all Laws which shall be necessary and proper for carrying into Execution the foregoing Powers, and all other Powers vested by this Constitution in the Government of the United States, or any Department or Officer thereof."

**negative rights theory** In ethics, the theory that says that rights are human inventions created to escape moral law.

**negligence** The failure to use that amount of care that a reasonably prudent person would have used under the same circumstances and conditions.

**negligent credentialing** Occurs if a hospital has retained a physician that the governing body of the hospital knew or should have known was incompetent.

**negligent hiring** The proprietor's liability for the hiring of an incompetent contractor who consequently harms an innocent third party while performing the hired-for work.

**negligent retention** The failure of a proprietor to dismiss an incompetent contractor after the proprietor has learned of the contractor's incompetence.

**negotiable instrument** A written document that is signed by the maker or drawer and that contains an unconditional promise or order to pay a certain sum of money on delivery or at a definite time to the bearer or to order.

**negotiated rule making** Occurs when an agency that is about to create a new rule or revise existing rules enters into a cooperative process by which all parties affected by the rule have a chance to shape the final form that the rule will take.

**negotiation** The transfer of a negotiable instrument in such form that the transferee becomes a holder.

**new world order** A set of initial conditions that describes how nation-states relate to one another on a global scale.

**next of kin** Those who are most nearly related by blood.

**NINJA loan** A loan that has been negotiated by a borrower with "no income, no job, and no assets."

**No Electronic Theft Act (NET Act)** A federal law that grants limited immunity to persons who duplicate copyrighted works on the Internet, as long as those users do not profit from the copying process.

**no-fault insurance** A type of automobile insurance that allows drivers to collect damages and medical expenses from their own insurance carriers regardless of who is at fault in an accident.

**nominal damages** Token damages awarded to parties who have experienced an injury to their legal rights but no actual loss.

**nonconforming goods** Goods that are not the same as those called for under a contract or that are in some way defective.

**nonconforming uses** Uses of land permitted to continue even though newly enacted zoning laws no longer permit similar uses.

**nondelegable duty** A duty that the proprietor cannot delegate, or pass off, to another party.

**nondisclosure** See *passive fraud*.

**nondisclosure agreement** An agreement that requires employees to promise that, should they leave their employment with their present employer, they will not reveal any confidential trade secrets that they may learn at their current job.

**noneconomic compensatory damages** Damages that result from injuries that are intangible and, therefore, not directly quantifiable. Examples include damages resulting from pain and suffering, mental anguish, and loss of companionship.

**non-governmental organization (NGO)** An organization that functions beyond the boundaries of any one governmental body.

**North American Free Trade Agreement (NAFTA)** A trading coalition that includes the United States, Canada, and Mexico

**note** A written promise by one party to pay money to another party. Also called *promissory note*.

**novation** The substitution, by mutual agreement, of another party for one of the original parties to a contract.

**object code** A computer program after it has been translated by the computer into a language that only the computer can comprehend.

**obligee** In contract law, the party to whom another party owes an obligation.

**obligor** In contract law, the party who is obligated to deliver on a promise or to undertake some act.

**obstruction of justice** In criminal law, an activity designed to prevent the discovery, apprehension, arrest, prosecution, conviction, or punishment of a criminal defendant.

**obvious-to-try standard** A patent challenge that asserts anyone of ordinary skill could see the invention was obvious to try, which makes the invention not be patentable.

**ocean marine insurance** A type of insurance that covers ships at sea.

**offer** In contract law, a proposal made by one party to another indicating a willingness to enter into a contract.

**offeree** In contract law, the person to whom an offer is made.

**offeror** In contract law, the person who makes the offer.

**Office of Investor Advocate** Subtitle A of Title XI of the Dodd-Frank Act creates a new agency, referred to as the Office of Investor Advocate (OIA), the purpose of which is to help make the work of broker-dealers and investment advisors (IAs) more transparent.

**Oil Pollution Act** A federal law designed to encourage companies that ship, drill for, and store oil to develop and use the most up-to-date equipment and the most effective safety measures possible.

**open-end credit** Credit that can be increased by the debtor, up to a limit set by the creditor, by continuing to purchase goods on credit.

**open-price terms** A contract for the sale of goods that is established even though the price is not settled.

**operating agreement** An agreement containing various rights, provisions, and powers that aid in establishing the bylaws of an LLC.

**option** In contract law, the giving of consideration to support an offeror's promise to hold an offer open for a stated or reasonable length of time. Also called *option contract*.

**order bill of lading** A negotiable bill of lading.

**order for relief** In bankruptcy law, a court's command that the liquidation begin.

**order paper** A negotiable instrument that is payable to someone's order.

**ordinary life insurance** See *straight life insurance*.

**ordinary negligence** Failure to use that amount of care that a reasonable person would use under the same circumstance.

**original jurisdiction** The authority of a court to hear a case when it is first brought to court.

**ostensible authority** Occurs when a hospital leads a patient to believe that a physician with staff privileges is an employee of the hospital.

**output contract** An agreement in which a seller agrees to sell "all the goods we manufacture" or "all the crops we produce" to a particular buyer. See also *requirements contract*.

**outside party** See *third party*.

**overdraft** A payment by a bank on behalf of a customer for more than the customer has on deposit.

**paper data** Data in a computer system that have been printed out in a hard copy for storage or filing in a conventional way.

**par value** The value that is placed on the shares of stock at incorporation.

**parol evidence rule** The rule that states that evidence of oral statements made before signing a written agreement is usually not admissible in court to change or to contradict the terms of a written agreement.

**part performance** An exception to the rule that contracts for the sale of land must be in writing. It applies when a person relies on an owner's oral promise to sell real estate and then makes improvements on the property or changes his or her position in an important way. Also called *equitable estoppel*.

**partially disclosed principal** A person, in a transaction conducted by an agent, whose existence is known to the third party but whose specific identify is unknown.

**participation loan** A loan in which the borrower will transfer certain ownership or equity rights to the lender in exchange for a lower interest rate or a lower down payment.

**partnering** A process that establishes supportive relationships among the parties to a contract to head off disputes before they occur.

**partnership** An association of two or more persons to carry on a business for profit.

**partnership at will** A partnership in which any partner may leave without liability.

**partnership by estoppel** A partnership that occurs when someone says or does something that leads a third party to reasonably believe that a partnership exists.

**passenger** A person who enters the premises of a carrier with the intention of buying a ticket for a trip. One continues to be a passenger as long as the trip continues.

**passing bad checks** In criminal law, issuing or transferring a check or other negotiable instrument knowing it will be dishonored and with the intent to defraud.

**passive fraud** A failure to reveal some material fact about the subject matter of a contract that one party is obligated to reveal to the other party and that intentionally deceives that second party, leading him or her into a damaging contract. Also called *concealment* and *nondisclosure*.

**past consideration** A promise to give another something of value in return for goods or services rendered and delivered in the past.

**patent** A grant from the government that gives an inventor the exclusive right to make, use, and sell an invention for a period set by Congress.

**pawn** See *pledge*.

**payee** The party named in a note or draft to whom payment is to be made.

**payor bank** A bank by which an item is payable as drawn or accepted. It includes a drawee bank.

**per se violation** In antitrust law, a restraint of trade practice so serious that it is prohibited whether or not it actually harms anyone.

**perfected** The state of a security interest when the secured party has done everything that the law requires to give the secured party greater rights to the goods than others have.

**performance** In contract law, the situation that exists when the parties to a contract have done what they had agreed to do.

**periodic tenancy** A leasehold estate, or tenancy, that continues for successive periods until one of the parties terminates it by giving notice to the other party.

**perjury** In criminal law, making false statements under oath.

**personal defense** In negotiable-instruments law, a defense that can be used against a holder but not against a holder in due course of a negotiable instrument. Also called *limited defense*.

**personal injury protection (PIP)** Automobile insurance which places limitations on the insured's ability to sue other drivers but allows drivers to collect damages and medical expenses from their own insurance carriers, regardless of who is at fault in an accident.

**personal jurisdiction** A court's authority over the parties to a lawsuit.

**personal property** Everything that can be owned other than real estate.

**personal representative** Executors and administrators of wills in states that have adopted the Uniform Probate Code.

**persuasive precedent** A previous case that a court is free to follow or to ignore.

**phishing** A cyberspoofing method that involves sending out phony e-mails that solicit buyers and, in the process, obtaining credit card information, account numbers, passwords, and the like.

**physical duress** Violence or the threat of violence against an individual or that person's family, household, or property that is so serious that it forces a person into a contract against his or her will.

**picketing** The placement of persons for observation, patrol, and demonstration at the site of employment as part of employee pressure on an employer to meet a demand.

**pie powder court** Historically in the Middle Ages in Europe, a court set up at a festival to handle disputes between merchants at that festival.

**pierce the corporate veil** The doctrine holding shareholders of a corporation personally liable when they have used the corporation as a facade to defraud or commit some other misdeed.

**plaintiff** The person who begins a lawsuit by filing a complaint in the appropriate trial court of general jurisdiction.

**pledge** The giving up of personal property as security for performance of an act or repayment of a debt.

**pledgee** A person to whom property is given as security for a loan.

**pledgor** A person who gives property to another as security for a loan.

**plenary review** The process by which appellate courts determine if lower courts have made errors of law.

**police power** A state's authority to restrict private rights to promote and maintain public health, safety, welfare, and morals.

**policy** The contract of insurance.

**pooling agreement** An agreement made by shareholders whereby they promise to vote the same way on a particular issue. Also called *shareholder agreements* and *voting agreements*.

**Population Commission (PC)** A group that was created under the auspices of the UN Economic and Social Council to investigate demographic concerns and to consult with the ECOSOC on a variety of population issues.

**positive law theory** In ethics, the theory that says that laws originate from an outside source that emerges within society.

**post-appellate procedures** The process of taking a case that has been rejected or dismissed by a domestic court to an international organization, such as the Inter-American Commission on Human Rights of the Organization of American States.

**precedent** A model case that a court can follow when facing a similar situation.

**preemption** The process by which the courts decide that a federal statute must take precedence over a state statute.

**preemptive right** A shareholder's right to purchase a proportionate share of every new offering of stock by the corporation.

**preemptive war** A conflict waged when one nation attacks a sovereign nation to stop that nation from engaging in activities that the attacking nation has decided are against its national interests.

**preexisting duty** An obligation that a party is already bound to by law or by some other agreement. The party may not use this as consideration in a new contract.

**preferred stock** A class of stock that carries with it the right to receive payment of dividends and/or the distribution of assets on the dissolution of the corporation before other classes of stock receive their payments.

**preliminary hearing** A court procedure during which the judge decides whether probable cause exists to continue holding a defendant for a crime.

**premarriage agreement** In contract law, an agreement between two people planning marriage and who agree in writing to change the property rights they possess by law.

**premeditated murder** In criminal law, killing someone with prior calculation and design, or while committing a serious felony such as rape, robbery or kidnapping.

**premium** The consideration paid by the insured to the insurer for insurance protection.

**prenuptial agreement** An agreement between two people who are planning marriage and who agree to change the property rights they possess by law in a marriage.

**prescriptive theory** A system of ethical thought that describes how to come up with the values at work within a social system.

**presenting bank** Any bank presenting an item except a payor bank.

**presentment** A demand for acceptance or payment of a negotiable instrument made upon the maker, acceptor, or drawee by or on behalf of the holder of the instrument.

**preventative war** A war waged to prevent another nation-state from reaching a point that it would be capable of attacking the first nation.

*prima facie* **evidence** (PRY·mah FAY·shee) Evidence that is legally sufficient to prove a fact in the absence of evidence to the contrary.

**primary committee** In bankruptcy law, a committee of creditors set up to work with a debtor in drawing up a reorganization plan.

**principal** A person who authorizes an agent to act on her or his behalf and subject to her or his control.

**principal objective** The main goal that the parties to a contract hoped to meet by entering the contract in the first place.

**primary objective test** A rule that states a writing is not needed for enforcement if the promise to pay another party's debt is made to obtain a gain for the guarantor.

**principle of honorable surrender** A criterion under a modern version of the just war theory that requires a victor to accept the surrender of the enemy and to treat the defeated combatants with dignity and respect.

**principle of repentance** A criterion under a modern version of the just war theory that calls for a genuine expression of remorse for the death and destruction caused by war.

**principle of restoration** A criterion under a modern version of the just war theory that requires a victor in a conflict to act responsibly in rebuilding the defeated nation's physical environment, economy, and governmental structure.

**prior art** All relevant technical knowledge about the field to which the invention belongs.

**private carriers** Companies, not in the transportation business, that operate their own trucks and other vehicles to transport their own goods.

**private civil trial** Trials run according to the same rules of procedure and evidence as trials run under the official auspices of the court. In a private trial, the parties can hold the trial when and where they choose, and they can choose the judge. Lengthy civil cases are well-suited to this approach.

**private corporation** A corporation formed by private persons to accomplish a task best undertaken by an entity that can raise large amounts of capital quickly or that can grant the protection of limited liability.

**private information** Reports on personal matters, family matters, sexual habits, employment records, medical data, and financial records. Also called *private-private* information.

**private warehouser** A warehouser whose warehouse is not for general public use.

**privity** In contract law, the relationship that exists between two parties to a contract giving each a recognized interest in the subject matter of the contract so that they are bound to that contract.

**probability of success** A criterion under the just war theory that states a war must be waged only when there is a reasonable chance of success.

**probate** To settle the estate of a decedent under the supervision of a court.

**product liability** A law that imposes liability on the manufacturer and the seller of a product produced and sold in a defective condition.

**professional** An individual who can perform a highly specialized task because of special abilities, education, experience, and knowledge.

**promissory estoppel** The legal doctrine that restricts an offeror from revoking an offer under certain conditions, even though consideration has not been promised to bind the agreement. To be effective, promissory estoppel requires that the offeror know, or be presumed to know, that the offeree might otherwise make a definite and decided change of position in contemplation of promises contained in the offer.

**promoters** The people who do the day-to-day work involved in creating a corporation.

**property damage liability insurance** A type of automobile insurance that provides protection when other people bring claims or lawsuits against the insured for damaging property such as a car, a fence, or a tree.

**proportionality** A criterion under the just war theory that states that the good advanced by the war must exceed the negative consequences of entering the conflict.

**proprietor** An owner, as of a business. The party for which an independent contractor works.

**prosecutor** An attorney that represents the government in a criminal procedure.

**prospectus** A document published by a corporation explaining, in simplified fashion for potential investors, the details of a stock issuance and the business making the offer.

**protective war** A war aimed at providing aid and assistance to innocent civilians who are being victimized by the military of their own nation-state.

**protest** A certificate of dishonor that states that a draft was presented for acceptance or payment and was dishonored.

**provisional** Not final.

**proximate cause** In tort law, the connection between the unreasonable conduct and the resulting harm. Proximate cause is determined by asking whether the harm that resulted from the conduct was foreseeable at the time of the original negligent act.

**proxy** The authority given to one shareholder to cast another shareholder's votes.

**proxy contest** A struggle between two factions in a corporation, usually management and a group of dissident shareholders, to obtain the votes of the other shareholders.

**proxy solicitation** The process by which one shareholder asks another for his or her voting right.

**proxy statement** A document that communicates information about the identity of a solicitor, the reason for a solicitation, and all other crucial information that shareholders need to make an informed decision about a proxy.

**public accountant (PA)** An accountant who works for a variety of clients but who is not certified.

**Public Company Accounting Oversight Board** A regulatory agency that is charged with the task of making certain that correct, unbiased, and comprehensive data finds their way to potential investors, so that they can make informed decisions about investment opportunities.

**public corporation** A corporation created by the federal, state, or local government for governmental purposes. Also, a large private corporation that generally sells its stock to the public at large.

**public interest** The idea that certain activities affect the entire social structure and must, therefore, be regulated by the government.

**public offer** An offer made through the public media but intended for only one person whose identity or address is unknown to the offeror.

**public policy** The general legal principle that says no one should be allowed to do anything that tends to injure the public at large.

**public warehouser** A warehouser who owns a warehouse where any member of the public who is willing to pay the regular charge may store goods.

**pump and dump scheme** A scheme designed to lure unsuspecting investors into the trap of investing in what is essentially an empty shell, that is, a poorly financed corporation that appears to be more valuable than it really is.

**punitive damages** Damages in excess of actual losses suffered by the plaintiff awarded as a measure of punishment for the defendant's wrongful acts. Also called *exemplary damages.*

**purchase money security interest** A security interest that arises when someone lends money to a consumer and then takes a security interest in the goods that the consumer buys.

**purpose** In criminal law, the intent to cause the result that does, in fact, occur.

**qualified indorsement** An indorsement in which words, such as "without recourse," have been added to the signature to limit the liability of the indorser.

**qualified opinion** An opinion issued by an auditor saying that, as of a given date, the books of a firm represent its financial health; however, the auditor may qualify the opinion either because the firm is facing some uncertainty that might affect the company in the future or because the firm has deviated from generally accepted accounting principles (GAAP) in some minor way.

**qualifying exigency leave** Leave time that is granted to employees permitting them to use as much as 20 weeks to take care of certain nonmedical emergencies during the time that a spouse, child, or parent is on active duty in the military

**quasi-contract** See *implied-in-law contract*.

**quasi-public corporation** A corporation that is privately organized for profit but also provides a service upon which the public is dependent.

**quasi-RPM arrangement** An agreement that occurs when a manufacturer lets retailers know the price that it expects to see on an item and declines to sell that item to any retailer that does not list the item at that price.

**quid pro quo sexual harassment** A supervisor's unwelcome advancement or suggestion to a subordinate to trade sexual favors for preferential treatment.

**quiet enjoyment** The right of a tenant to the undisturbed possession of the property that he or she is renting.

**quitclaim deed** A deed that transfers to the buyer only the interest that the seller may have in a property and that contains no warranties.

**racial profiling** The act of targeting a person for criminal investigation primarily because of racial or ethnic characteristics.

**ratification** The principal's approval of an unauthorized act performed by an agent or by one who has no authority to act as an agent. Also, an approval of a contract made by a minor after reaching maturity.

**rational ethics** A system of ethical thought that uses reason as the basis for making ethical judgments.

**real defense** In negotiable-instruments law, any defense that can be used against everyone, including holders in due course. Also called *absolute defense* and *universal defense*.

**real estate** The ground and everything permanently attached to it including land, buildings, and growing trees and shrubs; the air space above the land is also included.

**real property** The ground and everything permanently attached to it including land, buildings, and growing trees and shrubs; the air space above the land is also included.

**reasonable accommodation** The quality of accommodation that allows a disabled worker to accomplish essential functions in the workplace without imposing undue hardship on the employer.

**reasonable care** The degree of care that a reasonably prudent person would have used under the same circumstances and conditions.

**reasonable time** In contract law, the time that may fairly, properly, and conveniently be required to do the task that is to be done, with regard to attending circumstances.

**rebuttable presumption** A disputable presumption that a defending party has the right to attack.

**rebuttal** The presentation of evidence to discredit the evidence by the opposition and to reestablish the credibility of his or her own evidence.

**recklessness** In criminal law, a perverse disregard for a known risk of a negative result.

**registered limited liability partnership (RLLP or LLP)** A general partnership in which partners are not jointly or severally liable for partnership liabilities caused by the act or omission of another partner or employee unless the partner had supervision over the other partner or employee.

**registration statement** A statement required by the Securities and Exchange Commission to indicate details about a business selling securities.

**reg-neg** See *negotiated rule making*.

**regulations** Rules made by the regulatory agencies of the federal and/or state governments.

**regulatory justice** A fair and balanced interpretation of the law that evolves from and is consistent with previous law.

**rehabilitate** In contract law, the process of compensating an innocent party for losses that result from a breach of contract.

**rejection** The express or implied refusal by an offeree to accept an offer.

**release** In contract law, a promise made by one party agreeing not to sue a second party.

**remainder estate** A future interest in property when title is to pass to someone other than the grantor or grantor's heirs at the expiration of a life estate.

**remitting bank** Any payor or intermediary bank remitting for an item.

**removal** A request to a U.S. District Court to accept a case that was first filed in a state court.

**renter's insurance** An insurance policy that protects tenants against loss of personal property, against liability for a visitor's personal injury, and against liability for negligent destruction of the rented premises.

**renunciation** A legal act by which a person abandons a right acquired, but without transferring it to another.

**reorganization** In bankruptcy law, a plan created by a qualified debtor that alters his or her repayment schedule and allows the debtor to stay in business.

**request for admission** A request made to secure a statement from a party that a particular fact is true or that a document or set of documents is genuine.

**request for physical or mental examination** A request for a party to undergo a physical or a mental examination.

**request for real evidence** A discovery device that asks the opposing party in a lawsuit to produce papers, records, accounts, correspondence, photographs, or other tangible evidence including ESI.

**requirements contract** An agreement in which one party agrees to purchase all of his or her requirements of a particular product from another party. See also *output contract*.

**rescission** A remedy in contract law that returns both parties to a contract back to their original positions before the contract was entered into.

**reserve funds** Earnings from a business that are held in reserve.

**resisting arrest** In criminal law, interfering with the lawful arrest of a criminal defendant.

*respondeat superior* (re·SPOND·ee·yat se·PEER·ee·or) The legal doctrine that imposes liability on employers and makes them pay for torts committed by their employees within the scope of the employer's business. Literally translated, it means "Let the master respond."

**restraint of trade** A limitation on the full exercise of doing business with others.

**restrictive covenant** A promise by an employee in an employment contract not to work for anyone else in the same field of employment for a specified time period within a particular geographical area.

**restrictive employment covenant** A promise by an employee in an employment contract not to work for anyone else in the same field of employment for a specified time period within a particular geographical area.

**restrictive indorsement** An indorsement in which words have been added to the signature of the indorser that specify the purpose of the indorsement or the use to be made of the commercial paper, such as "for deposit only."

**reverse discrimination** A practice designed to eliminate discrimination against a protected class but that has the opposite effect on members of another protected class.

**reverse mortgage** A type of loan that allows home owners, over the age of 62, to convert some of the equity in their home into cash while retaining ownership of their home.

**reversion estate** A future interest in property when title is to return to the grantor or grantor's heirs upon expiration of a life estate.

**Revised Uniform Partnership Act (RUPA)** The latest partnership statute written by the National Conference of Commissioners on Uniform State Laws.

**revocation** The calling back of an offer by the offeror.

**revolving charge account** A charge account with an outstanding balance at all times.

**right intention** A criterion under the just war theory that states that a war must be waged only if the combatant has the correct objective.

**right of way** See *easement*.

**right-to-work laws** State laws that prohibit labor-management agreements requiring union membership as a condition of getting or keeping a job.

**riparian owners** People who own land along the bank of a river or stream. They have certain rights and duties with respect to the water that flows over, under, and beside their land.

**robbery** The act of taking personal property from the possession of another against that person's will and under threat to do great bodily harm or damage.

**royalty** In intellectual property law, the consideration paid to an author or an inventor for permission to use the intellectual property of that author or inventor.

**RPM agreement** The agreement between a retailer and a manufacturer that the retailer will sell certain products at a price set by the manufacturer.

**rule of contemporary ownership** The rule that holds that shareholders must own stock at the time of the injury and at the time of the lawsuit if they wish to begin a derivative suit.

**rule-of-reason standard** In antitrust law, a doctrine that holds that a court should stop certain practices only if they are an unreasonable restriction of competition.

**S corporation** A corporation in which shareholders have agreed to have the profits (or losses) of the corporation taxed directly to them rather than to the corporation.

**Safe Harbor Principles** Principles of electronically stored information (ESI) protection established by the Department of Commerce that, if followed by American companies, will qualify them for commerce with the EU.

**sale** A contract in which ownership of goods is transferred by the seller to the buyer for a price.

**sale on approval** A conditional sale that becomes absolute only if the buyer approves or is satisfied with the article being sold.

**sale or return** A sale in which the buyer takes title to goods with the right to revest title in the seller after a specified period or reasonable time.

**sales puffery** Persuasive words or exaggerated arguments made by salespeople to induce customers to buy their product. As long as such comments are reserved to opinion and do not misstate facts, they are not actionable as fraud, even if they turn out to be grossly in error. Also called *puffery*.

**salvage** A reward given to persons who voluntarily assist a sinking ship to recover its cargo from peril or loss.

**salvor** A person who salvages. The law of salvage gives the salvor the right to compensation for assisting a foundering vessel.

**same state locality rule** A means to judge a health care provider's actions on the basis of the standard of care used in the same state in which that provider practices.

**Sarbanes-Oxley Act** Legislation that places an affirmative duty on the directors of publicly traded corporations to monitor whether they are conforming to all legal requirements.

**satisfaction** The agreed-to settlement as contained in an accord.

**satisfactory performance** In contract law, the situation that exists when either personal taste or objective standards determine the contracting parties have performed their contractual duties according to the agreement.

**science court** A proposed court that would act as a forum for disputes involving scientific and technological controversies.

**scope of authority** The range of acts done while performing agency duties. Also called *scope of employment*.

**scope of employment** See *scope of authority*.

**screen display** The audiovisual configuration that appears on the screen of the computer monitor.

**seal** A mark or impression placed on a written contract indicating that the instrument was executed and accepted in a formal manner.

**second degree murder** In criminal law, the purposeful killing of another human being without premeditation.

**second mortgage** See *junior mortgage*.

**secondary boycott** Conspiracy in which a union places pressure on a neutral customer or supplier with whom the union has no dispute in order to cause the neutral entity to cease doing business with the employer with whom the union has a dispute.

**second-level domain (SLD) name** Indicates the actual name, trade name, or other identifying mark of the institution, organization, or business using the domain name.

**secret partner** A partner whose identity and existence are not known outside of the firm but who can participate in the management of the firm.

**Secretariat** The administrative bureaucracy of the United Nations.

**Secretary-General of the United Nations** The chief administrator of the United Nations.

**secured loan** A loan in which creditors have something of value, usually called collateral, from which they can be paid if the debtor does not pay.

**secured party** A lender or seller who holds a security interest.

**securitization** The process of bundling securities and then selling them to big investors.

**security** In secured transactions, the assurance that a creditor will be paid back for any money loaned or credit extended to a debtor. In corporate law, a money investment that expects a return solely because of another person's efforts.

**security agreement** A written agreement that creates a security interest.

**security-based swaps** According to the SEC, these are "swaps based on (1) a single security, (2) a loan, (3) a narrow-based group or index of securities, or (4) events relating to a single issuer or issuers of securities in a narrow-based security index."

**Security Council** The United Nations body that deals with international crises.

**security interest** A creditor's right to use collateral to recover a debt.

**self-defense** A defense to criminal liability available to defendants if they can demonstrate (1) that they did not start the altercation, (2) that they had good reason to believe they were in danger of death or severe bodily injury, and (3) that they used only enough force to repel the attack.

**servant** An outdated term signifying a person employed to perform services in the affairs of another and who, with respect to the physical conduct in the performance of the service, is subject to the other's right to control.

**service of process**  The act of giving the summons and the complaint to a defendant.

**servient tenement**  The property through which an easement is created or through which it extends.

**settlement week**  An ADR technique in which the court clears its docket of all business except settlement hearings.

**severalty**  The quality or state of sole ownership of a single property.

**sexual harassment**  A type of sexual discrimination.

**shares**  Portions of a corporation that may be owned by the various shareholders.

**shareholder democracy**  A theory of corporate management that favors making management more responsive to shareholders by giving shareholders greater voting power and by making it easier for shareholders to sue managers.

**shareholder of record**  A person to whom stock has been transferred and whose name has been entered on the corporate books as the owner of that stock. Shareholders of record are entitled to vote, receive dividends, and enjoy all other privileges of being a shareholder.

**shareholder proposal**  A suggestion submitted by a shareholder about a broad company policy or procedure.

**shareholder resolution**  In corporate law, a suggestion about a broad company policy or procedure submitted by a shareholder.

**shareholders**  Persons who own units of ownership interest called shares of stock in a corporation. Also called *stockholders*.

**shelter provision**  A provision whereby a holder who receives an instrument from a holder in due course acquires the rights of the holder in due course even though he or she does not qualify as a holder in due course.

**shipment contract**  A contract under which a seller turns goods over to a carrier for delivery to a buyer. Both the title and risk of loss pass to the buyer when the goods are given to the carrier.

**shoplifting**  The act of stealing goods from a store.

**sight draft**  A draft that is payable as soon as it is presented to the drawee for payment.

**silent partner**  A partner who does not participate in the day-to-day business of the firm.

**similar locality rule**  The rule that allows a court to judge a health care provider's degree of care by determining how the same procedure is performed at another hospital located in a similar locality.

**similar practitioner rule**  A means to judge a health care provider's actions according to whether that provider is a general practitioner or a specialist.

**situational ethics**  A system of ethical thought that argues that each of us can judge a person's ethical decisions only by initially placing ourselves in that person's position.

**slamming**  The illegal practice of changing a consumer's telephone service without permission.

**slander**  Any false statement that harms a person's good name or reputation made in a temporary form, such as speech, and communicated to others.

**slight negligence**  The failure to use that degree of care that persons of extraordinary prudence and foresight are accustomed to use.

**social contract theory**  In ethics, a theory that says that right and wrong are measured by the obligations imposed on each individual by an implied agreement among individuals within a given social system.

**social media policy (SMP)**  In employment law, a set of rules written by an employer telling employees what they can and cannot do when using electronic communication devices, formats, Web sites, and other electronic messaging techniques, such as blogs, text messages, tweets, skype transmissions, and e-mails.

**software contract**  A contract involving the sale or licensing of information in a digital format.

**sole proprietorship**  A business formed by the sole proprietor. It is the easiest business organization to form.

**source code**  A set of instructions that tells the computer what to do or how to perform a particular task.

**source code escrow agreement**  An agreement in which the computer source code is deposited with a third party. Once the agreement is made, the code can be released only by following precisely outlined procedures and usually only if both the buyer and seller agree to the release.

**sovereign immunity**  The somewhat discredited doctrine preventing a lawsuit against government authority without the government's consent.

**spam**  Unsolicited e-mail.

**special agent**  A person who is authorized to conduct only a particular transaction or to perform only a specified act for a principal.

**special indorsement**  An indorsement made by first writing on the back of a negotiable instrument an order to pay a specified person and then signing the instrument. Also called *indorsement in full*.

**special interest group control** A corporate control theory that is based on the fact that because corporate decision making impacts special interest groups, those groups should participate in that decision-making process.

**special jurisdiction** The power of a court to hear only certain kinds of cases.

**special warranty deed** A deed containing express warranties under which the grantor guarantees that no defects arose in the title during the time that he or she owned the property.

**specific performance** A decree from a court ordering a contracting party to carry out the promises made in a contract.

**speculative damages** Damage computed on losses that have not actually been suffered and that cannot be proved; they are based entirely on an expectation of losses that might be suffered from a breach; the courts do not allow speculative damages.

**staff privileges** When a hospital grants physicians, who are not employed by the hospital, the privilege to treat their patients at that hospital.

**stale check** A check that is presented for payment more than six months after its date.

**standard construction rule** A theory of legal interpretation under which the court will determine the principal objective of the parties in the making of the contract.

**staple court** Historically in Europe in the Middle Ages, courts charged with the responsibility for cases involving a set type of goods or a set commodity (a staple).

**state control** A theory of corporate management that is based on the belief that because corporate decision making impacts upon more individuals and groups than just the shareholders and the managers, those corporate decisions should be made by an impartial group of corporate outsiders, usually government officials.

**statute** A law passed by a legislature.

**Statute of Frauds** A law requiring certain contracts to be in writing to be enforceable.

**statute of repose** An absolute time limit for bringing a cause of action regardless of when the cause of action accrues, such as a certain number of years after a defective product has been sold to an injured customer.

**statutes of limitations** State laws that restrict the time within which a party is allowed to bring legal action against another.

**statutory agent** An individual who is designated to receive service of process when a lawsuit is filed against a corporation or an LLC.

**statutory interpretation** The process by which courts analyze aspects of a statute that are unclear or ambiguous or that were not anticipated at the time the legislature passed the statute.

**stock acquisition** The purchase of enough of the voting stock of a corporation to allow the buyer to control the corporation. Also called *takeover.*

**stock certificate** Written evidence of ownership of a unit of interest in a corporation.

**stock dividends** Dividends paid to shareholders in the form of shares of capital stock.

**stoppage in transit** A right of the seller, upon learning that the buyer is insolvent, to have the delivery of goods stopped before they reach their destination.

**straight bill of lading** A bill of lading that does not contain words of negotiability.

**straight life insurance** Insurance that requires the payment of premiums throughout the life of the insured and pays the beneficiary the face value of the policy upon the insured's death.

**strict liability** The doctrine under which people may be liable for injuries to others whether or not they have been negligent or committed an international tort. Also called *absolute liability.*

**strike** A stoppage of work by employees as a means of enforcing a demand made on their employers.

**subjective ethics** An ethical theory that holds that there are no objective or absolute standards of right and wrong.

**subject matter jurisdiction** The power of a court to hear a particular type of case.

**subject to the mortgage** An agreement whereby the seller of real property that is already mortgaged agrees to continue paying the mortgage payments.

**sublease** A lease given by a lessee to a third person conveying the same interest for a shorter term than the period for which the lessee is holding it. Also called *underlease.*

**subordinate** To place in a lower order.

**subordinated mortgage** A mortgage that is reduced in priority to a person holding a second mortgage.

**subordination agreement** An agreement made by holders of first mortgages to allow their mortgage to be reduced in priority to a person holding a second mortgage.

**subrogation** The right of one party to substitute itself for another party.

**substantial performance** In contract law, the situation that results when a party to a contract, in good faith, executes all the promised terms and conditions of the contract with the exception of minor details that do not affect the real intent of their agreement.

**substantial similarity test** A test to determine whether a work has violated a copyrighted work's integrity by determining whether the two are so like one another that an ordinary reasonable observer would have no recourse other than to conclude that the second was copied from the first.

**substitute check** A paper reproduction of both sides of an original check that can be processed electronically.

**substitute transportation insurance** Insurance that reimburses the insured up to specific limits for transportation costs while a car is undergoing covered repairs.

*sui generis* A law unto itself. An area of the law that has developed its own independent self-contained rules.

**suitor** A corporation or individual who offers to purchase the voting stock of a corporation with the objective of taking over the corporation.

**summary judgment motion** A motion that asks a court for an immediate judgment for the party filing the motion because both parties agree on the facts in the case and because under law the party who introduced the motion is entitled to a favorable judgment.

**summary jury trial** A shortened version of a trial conducted in less than a day before a jury. The jury's verdict is advisory only.

**surety** One who stands behind executors or administrators and becomes responsible for their wrongdoing.

**surplus** Funds that remain after a partnership has been dissolved and all other debts and prior obligations have been settled.

**surrebuttal** A reply to the defendant's rebuttal.

**survival statute** A state law that allows a lawsuit to be brought even if both the plaintiff and the defendant are deceased.

**takeover bid** In corporate law, the offer to buy the voting stock of a corporation.

**tampering with evidence** In criminal law, altering, destroying, or removing any piece of evidence with the intent to somehow lessen the probative value of that evidence.

**target** In corporate law, a corporation that is the object of a takeover bid.

**target corporation** The object of a tender offer.

**targeted shareholder agreement** An agreement by which a suitor negotiates a deal with certain shareholders to provide them with employment-related deals that supplement the price they will receive for selling their stock.

**tariff-based principle** A principle that states that the only way that World Trade Organization nations can regulate the imports of other nations is through tariffs.

**TARP** A federal program (Troubled Asset Relief Program) that is designed to allow the government to buy troubled assets that resulted from the securitization epidemic.

**taxable costs** In procedural law, litigation costs that are charged to the losing party.

**taxable expenses** Legal expenses, such as those involved in filing a case and issuing subpoenas.

**teaching, suggestion, or motivation test, or TSM standard** A traditional test that requires patent challengers to demonstrate that the innovation would have been obvious to any one exposed to the same teaching session, the same off-hand suggestion, or the same motivation as the inventor had been exposed to.

**teller's check** See *bank draft.*

**temporary public figures** People who are placed against their will into the public view by some event beyond their control.

**tenancy** An interest in real estate that is held under a lease. Also called *leasehold estate.*

**tenancy at sufferance** A leasehold estate, or tenancy, that arises when a tenant wrongfully remains in possession of the premise after his or her tenancy has expired.

**tenancy at will** A leasehold estate, or tenancy, that continues for as long as both parties desire.

**tenancy by entirety** Ownership by husband and wife, considered by the law as one, with full ownership surviving to the living spouse on the death of the other.

**tenancy for years** A leasehold estate, or tenancy, for a fixed period of time.

**tenancy from year to year** See *periodic tenancy.*

**tenancy in partnership** Ownership in which each person has an interest in partnership property and is co-owner of such property.

**tenant** A person to whom real property is rented or leased. Also called *lessee.*

**tenants in common** Owners of an undivided interest in property, with each owner's rights going to his or her heirs upon death rather than to the surviving cotenants.

**tender** To offer to turn goods over to a buyer.

**tender of delivery** An offer by the seller of goods to turn the goods over to the buyer.

**tender of payment** An offer by the buyer of goods to turn the money over to the seller.

**tender of performance** An offer to do what one has agreed to do under the terms of a contract.

**tender offer** A public offer by a suitor to buy voting stock.

**term insurance** Insurance that is issued for a particular period, usually five or ten years.

**term partnership** A partnership that is set up to run for a set time period or in order to accomplish a task of some sort.

**termination by waiver** The situation that exists when a party to a contract with the right to complain of the other party's unsatisfactory performance or nonperformance fails to complain.

**testamentary trust** A trust that is created by a will.

**testate** Having made a valid will. Compare *intestate*.

**testator (male); testatrix (female)** A person who makes a will.

**theft** In criminal law, knowingly taking or obtaining control over the property of another without consent, using deceit, threats, or coercion.

**theft in office** In criminal law, an offense that involves the use of a governmental official's governmental or party power to obtain unlawful control over governmental or party property or services.

**third party** In contract law, a person who may, in some way, be affected by a contract but who is not one of the contracting parties. Also called *outside party*.

**third-party beneficiary** In contract law, a party who is not involved in an original contract but who, nevertheless, benefits from that contract.

**time-based threshold** In insurance law, a threshold ascertained by measuring the time that the victim has been incapacitated.

**time draft** A draft that is not payable until the lapse of a particular time period stated on the draft.

**threshold guidelines** In insurance law, guidelines that determine when victims can bring a lawsuit for injuries that result from an auto accident.

**tippees** People who receive inside information about corporate stock without being involved in any business need to obtain that information.

**title** The right of ownership to goods. Also, a subdivision of a code containing all the statutes that deal with a particular area of law.

**top-level domain (TLD) name** The portion of the domain name that identifies the addressee's zone, for example, .com, .org, or .edu.

**tort** A private wrong that injures another person's physical well-being, property, or reputation.

**tortfeasor** A person who commits a tort.

**tortious bailee** Any party unlawfully in possession of another's personal property.

**towing and labor insurance** Insurance that reimburses up to specified limits for towing and labor charges whenever a car breaks down, whether or not an accident is involved.

**trade acceptance** A draft used by a seller of goods to receive payment and also to extend credit. It is often used in combination with a bill of lading.

**trade fixtures** Items of personal property brought upon the land by a tenant that are necessary to carry on the trade or business to which the premises will be devoted. Contrary to the general rule, trade fixtures remain the personal property of the tenant and are removable at the expiration of the terms of occupancy.

**trade secrets** A plan, process, or device that is used in a business and is known only to employees who need to know the secret to carry out their jobs.

**trademark** Any word, name, symbol, or device adopted and used by a manufacturer or merchant to identify goods and distinguish them from those manufactured or sold by others.

**transactions in computer information** A contract whose subject matter entails the acquisition, development, or distribution of computer information.

**transient** A person who accepts the service of a hotel or other public accommodation without any obligation to remain a specified length of time.

**transnational organizations or transnats** Nongovernmental organizations that have neither earned status nor demonstrated the ability, or even willingness, to be accountable for their actions on the world stage.

**traveler's check** A draft purchased from a bank or express company and signed by the purchaser at the time of cashing as a precaution against forgery.

**treason** The levying of war against the United States, or the giving of aid and comfort to the nation's enemies.

**true locality rule** A means to judge a health care provider's actions on the basis of the standard of care used in the exact same locality or community.

**trust** A legal device by which property is held by one person for the benefit of another.

**trustee** A person who is entrusted with the management and control of another's property or the rights associated with that property.

**Tunney or Antitrust Procedures and Penalties Act** The federal statute that regulates the Justice Department's antitrust consent decrees.

**tying agreement** In antitrust law, an illegal practice that occurs when one party refuses to sell a given product unless the buyer also purchases another product tied to the first product.

**UN Commission on International Trade Law (UNCITRAL)** The UN organization charged with the task of organizing and integrating international law in relation to international trade.

**UN Convention on Contracts for the International Sale of Goods (CISG)** International agreement governing sales of goods between businesses located in different countries.

**unconscionable contract** A contract that is so one-sided that it is oppressive and gives unfair advantage to one of the parties.

**unconscionable** Ridiculously inadequate.

**underinsured-motorist insurance** Insurance that provides protection against the risk of being injured by an underinsured motorist.

**underlease** See *sublease.*

**undisclosed principal** A person, in a transaction conducted by an agent, whose existence and identity are unknown to the third party.

**undisputed amount** An amount upon which the parties to a contract have mutually agreed.

**undue hardship** The amount of inconvenience beyond that which is required of an employer who seeks to provide reasonable accommodation for a disabled worker.

**undue influence** The use of excessive pressure by the dominant member of a confidential relationship to convince the weaker party to enter a contract that greatly benefits the dominant party.

**unenforceable contract** A contract that cannot be upheld by a court because of some rule of law.

**unfair labor practices** Improper employment practices by either an employer or a union.

**unfriendly buyer** A buyer of a corporation who intends to change management and shake up the corporation after its takeover.

**unfriendly suitor** A suitor of a corporation who intends to change management and shake up the corporation after its takeover.

**Uniform Commercial Code (UCC)** A unified set of statutes designated to govern almost all commercial transactions.

**Uniform Computer Information Transactions Act** A statute that establishes standards for digital information contracts.

**Uniform Durable Power of Attorney Act (UDPA)** Legislation that states a person may appoint an "attorney in fact" by signing a written durable power of attorney.

**Uniform Electronic Transactions Act (UETA)** A model code that declares that if the parties to a contract have voluntarily agreed to transact business electronically, then the cyber-contract that results will be just as legally acceptable as a paper contract.

**Uniform Facsimile Signatures of Public Officials Act** A law that allows use of facsimile signatures of public officials when certain requirements are followed.

**Uniform Partnership Act (UPA)** The original partnership statute written by the National Conference of Commissioners on Uniform State Laws.

**Uniform Power of Attorney Act** A unified set of statutes designed to govern all aspects of the durable power of attorney agency relationship.

**Uniform Trade Secrets Act** Legislation written by the NCCUSL to define a trade secret, describe transgressions, and provide for both damages and injunctive relief when there has been a trade secret infringement.

**unilateral contract** An agreement in which one party makes a promise to do something in return for an act of some sort.

**unilateral mistake** In contract law, a mistake made by only one of the contracting parties. Unilateral mistake does not offer sufficient grounds for recession or renegotiation.

**unimpaired class** In bankruptcy law, a group of creditors whose collection rights are not impaired by a reorganization plan.

**uninsured-motorist insurance** A type of automobile insurance that provides protection against the risk of being injured by a motorist who does not have insurance.

**union shop** A place of employment where nonunion workers may be employed for a trial period of not more than 30 days, after which the nonunion workers must join the union or be discharged.

**United Nations Commission on International Trade (UNCITRAL)** A fraternity of 36 countries that seeks to cultivate the organization and integration of international law in relation to international trade.

**United States Antitrust Modernization Committee** A congressional think tank designed to examine antitrust law and report recommendations on how to modernize the law.

**United States Code (USC)** A compilation of all the statutes passed by Congress.

**United States Sentencing Commission** The commission that issues rules regarding federal courts' discretion in issuing punishments for crimes.

**universal defense** See *real defense.*

**universal life insurance** A form of straight life insurance that allows the policy owner flexibility in choosing and changing terms of the policy.

**unlawful detainer** A legal proceeding that provides landlords with a quick method of evicting a tenant. Also called *summary process, summary ejectment, forcible entry and detainer,* and *dispossessory warrant proceedings.*

**unqualified opinion** An opinion issued by an auditor that indicates that the financial records of a firm are an accurate reflection of the firm's financial status.

**unsecured loan** A loan in which creditors have nothing of value that they can repossess and sell in order to recover the money owed to them by the debtor.

**Uruguay Round Agreements (URA)** The eighth round of GATT talks, lasting from 1986 to 1993, out of which the World Trade Organization and the Dispute Settlement Understanding were created.

**usage of trade** Any method of dealing that is commonly used in the particular field.

**Used Car Rule** A rule established by the Federal Trade Commission requiring used car dealers to place a sticker, called a *Buyer's Guide,* in the window of each used car they offer for sale. The sticker provides consumer protection information.

**usury** The practice of charging more than the amount of interest allowed by law.

**utilitarianism** A system of ethical thought that focuses on the consequences of an action.

**utility thinking** A system of thought that focuses the consequences to one person or institution and then weighs the cost against the benefits of performing the action under scrutiny.

**uttering** The crime of offering a forged instrument to another person, knowing it to be forged.

**valid contract** A contract that is legally binding and fully enforceable by the court.

**values** A standard for determining what things hold central importance.

**vandalism** The act of willfully or maliciously causing damage to property.

**variable-rate mortgage** See *flexible-rate mortgage.*

**variance** An exemption that permits a use that differs from those allowed under the existing zoning law.

**verdict** A finding of fact by the jury in a court case; the jury's decision.

**vertical expansion** The joining of two companies that were in a customer–supplier relationship.

**vicarious liability** The concept of laying responsibility or blame upon one person for the actions of another.

**victim's rights** In criminal law, a series of rights created by the legislature for innocent people who have been victimized by crime.

**video conference** A conference that uses a televised connection to permit any number of people at widely diverse locations to discuss the details of a case.

**void contract** A contract that has no legal effect whatsoever.

**void title** No title at all.

**voidable contract** A contract that may be voided or canceled by one of the parties.

**voidable title** Title that may be voided if one of the parties elects to do so.

**voluntary manslaughter** In criminal law, a killing that results when a criminal defendant is in a state of extreme fright, terror, anger, or blind rage.

**voting trust** An agreement among shareholders to transfer their voting rights to a trustee.

**waiver** The voluntary surrender of some right, claim, or privilege.

**waiver of premium** An optional provision in an insurance contract that excuses the insured from paying premiums if the insured becomes disabled.

**warehouse** A building or structure in which any goods, but particularly wares or merchandise, are stored.

**warehouser** A person engaged in the business of storing goods for hire.

**warehouse receipt** A receipt issued by a person engaged in the business of storing goods for hire.

**warehouser's lien** The right of a warehouser to retain possession of goods stored in the warehouse until the satisfaction of the charges imposed on them.

**warranty** A promise, statement, or other representation that an item has certain qualities; also, an insured's promise to abide by restrictions, especially those written into an insurance policy. Also, an obligation imposed by law that an item will have certain qualities. Warranties made by means of a statement or other affirmation of fact are called *express warranties*; those imposed by law are *implied warranties*.

**warranty of fitness for a particular purpose** An implied warranty that goods will be fit for a particular purpose. This warranty is given by the seller to the buyer of goods whenever the seller has reason to know of any particular purpose for which the goods are needed and the buyer relies on the seller's skill and judgment to select the goods.

**warranty of habitability** The landlord warrants that the premises are fit for human habitation.

**warranty of merchantability** An implied warranty that goods are fit for the ordinary purpose for which such goods are used. Unless excluded, this warranty is always given by a merchant who sells goods in the ordinary course of business.

**warranty of title** A warranty given by a seller to a buyer of goods that states that the title being conveyed is good and that the transfer is rightful.

**waste** Substantial damage to premises that significantly decreases the value of the property.

**Web conference** A conference that is carried out online via the Internet using personal computers to permit any number of people at widely diverse locations to discuss the details of a case.

**Westphalia system** As outlined in the Treaty of Westphalia, a theory that describes nation-states as the primary international actors.

**white knight** A post-offer technique where a target company invites another suitor to outbid a hostile bidder. The second suitor agrees that it will retain the existing management.

**whole life insurance** See *straight life insurance*.

**widow's allowance** See *family allowance*.

**will** A legal document, not valid until the testator's death, expressing the testator's intent in distribution of all real and personal property.

**work product privilege** The guarantee that all notes, recordings, research documents, Q&As, voice mails, faxes, e-mails, computer records, memos, letters, flash drives, disks, DVDs, CDs, and so on that are prepared in anticipation of litigation remain confidential.

**workers' compensation** Worker protection provided for by state statutes that compensates covered workers or their dependents for injury, disease, or death that occurs on the job or as a result of it.

**workplace harassment** In employment law, misconduct in the workplace that results from quid pro quo sexual harassment or the creation of a hostile work environment

**World Bank** A nongovernmental organization that works exclusively with the poorest nations in the international community to help them secure loans.

**World Intellectual Property Organization (WIPO)** A division of the United Nations that supported the development of two international treaties designed to deal with electronic copyright problems.

**World Intellectual Property Organization Copyright Treaty** A treaty that guarantees copyright holders can use the Internet to post their works with full copyright protection.

**World Intellectual Property Organization Phonograms Treaty** A treaty that gives copyright holders the right to copy, publish, and distribute their works in any way.

**World Trade Organization (WTO)** A corporate nucleus for the management of international trade relationships.

**worldwide organization** Any international institution that transcends and unites nation-states in a common purpose on a global basis. Established worldwide organizations include diplomatic institutions such as the United Nations, legal organizations such as the International Criminal Court, and economic institutions such as the World Bank.

**writ of certiorari** An order from the U.S. Supreme Court to a lower court to deliver the records of a case to the Supreme Court for review.

**writ of execution** A court order directing the sheriff of a county to sell the property of a losing defendant to satisfy the judgment against that defendant.

**writ of replevin** A court order requiring a defendant to turn goods over to a plaintiff because the plaintiff has the right to immediate possession of the goods.

**wrongful civil proceedings** Filing a false civil lawsuit.

**wrongful death statute**  A law that allows third parties affected by a death to bring a lawsuit only if the death is caused by the negligence or intentional conduct of the defendant.

**wrongful discharge**  Exceptions to employment-at-will that give employees legal ground for lawsuits against employers who have dismissed them unfairly.

**yellow-dog contract**  An agreement whereby an employer requires, as a condition of employment, that an employee promises not to join a union.

**zoning law**  A local regulation or ordinance that restricts certain areas to specific uses; for example, areas zoned for residential, commercial, agricultural, industrial, or other uses.

# Photo Credits

# Case Index

# Subject Index